Vauxhall/Opel Omega

Service and Repair Manual

Mark Coombs and Spencer Drayton

Models covered *(3510 - 352 - 10AG1)*

Vauxhall Omega Saloon and Estate models with petrol engines, including special/limited editions
1998 cc, 2498 cc & 2969 cc petrol engines

Does not cover diesel engine or bi-fuel (LPG) models

A book in the **Haynes Service and Repair Manual Series**

ISBN **978 1 78521 518 6**

British Library Cataloguing in Publication Data
A catalogue record for this book is available from the British Library.

Haynes Group Limited
Haynes North America, Inc

www.haynes.com

Disclaimer

There are risks associated with automotive repairs. The ability to make repairs depends on the individual's skill, experience and proper tools. Individuals should act with due care and acknowledge and assume the risk of performing automotive repairs.

The purpose of this manual is to provide comprehensive, useful and accessible automotive repair information, to help you get the best value from your vehicle. However, this manual is not a substitute for a professional certified technician or mechanic.

This repair manual is produced by a third party and is not associated with an individual vehicle manufacturer. If there is any doubt or discrepancy between this manual and the owner's manual or the factory service manual, please refer to the factory service manual or seek assistance from a professional certified technician or mechanic.

Even though we have prepared this manual with extreme care and every attempt is made to ensure that the information in this manual is correct, neither the publisher nor the author can accept responsibility for loss, damage or injury caused by any errors in, or omissions from, the information given.

Contents

LIVING WITH YOUR VAUXHALL OMEGA

Roadside Repairs

Weekly Checks

MAINTENANCE

Routine Maintenance and Servicing

Contents

REPAIRS & OVERHAUL

Engine and Associated Systems

Transmission

Brakes and Suspension

Body equipment

REFERENCE

The Vauxhall Omega was introduced into the UK in April of 1994 as a replacement for the Vauxhall Carlton and Senator. At its launch, the Omega was available in both Saloon and Estate body styles with a choice of either 2.0 litre (1998 cc) or a 2.5 litre (2498 cc) petrol engine both available with either a 5-speed manual transmission unit or a 4-speed automatic transmission unit. Shortly afterwards a 3.0 (2968 cc) litre petrol engine was also introduced. A 2.5 litre Diesel engine (not covered in this manual) was also available. The petrol engines are all well-proven units which are used in many other Vauxhall vehicles; the engine is mounted at the front of vehicle with the transmission mounted on its rear.

Two versions of the four-cylinder 2.0 litre engine were used; low specification vehicles were fitted with a single overhead camshaft (SOHC) 8-valve engine were as all other vehicles were fitted with the double overhead camshaft (DOHC) 16-valve engine often referred to as the ECOTEC engine. The 2.5 and 3.0 litre engines are both V6, double overhead camshaft (DOHC) units which are also often referred as ECOTEC engines.

All models have fully-independent front and rear suspension and are equipped with front and rear disc brakes.

A wide range of standard and optional equipment is available within the range to suit most tastes, including central locking, electric windows and an electric sunroof. An air conditioning system was available as an option on certain models.

Provided that regular servicing is carried out in accordance with the manufacturer's recommendations, the vehicle should prove reliable and very economical. The engine compartment is well-designed, and most of the items requiring frequent attention are easily accessible.

Vauxhall Omega 2.0 16V Select

Vauxhall Omega Estate CD

The Vauxhall Omega Team

Haynes manuals are produced by dedicated and enthusiastic people working in close co-operation. The team responsible for the creation of this book included:

Authors	**Marc Coombs Spencer Drayton**
Sub-editor	**Ian Barnes**
Editor & Page Make-up	**Steve Churchill**
Workshop manager	**Paul Buckland**
Photo Scans	**Steve Tanswell John Martin**
Cover illustration & Line Art	**Roger Healing**
Wiring diagrams	**Matthew Marke**

We hope the book will help you to get the maximum enjoyment from your car. By carrying out routine maintenance as described you will ensure your car's reliability and preserve its resale value.

Your Vauxhall Omega manual

The aim of this manual is to help you get the best value from your vehicle. It can do so in several ways. It can help you decide what work must be done (even should you choose to get it done by a garage). It will also provide information on routine maintenance and servicing, and give a logical course of action and diagnosis when random faults occur. However, it is hoped that you will use the manual by tackling the work yourself. On simpler jobs it may even be quicker than booking the car into a garage and going there twice, to leave and collect it. Perhaps most important, a lot of money can be saved by avoiding the costs a garage must charge to cover its labour and overheads.

The manual has drawings and descriptions to show the function of the various components so that their layout can be understood. Tasks are described and photographed in a clear step-by-step sequence.

References to the 'left' and 'right' are in the sense of a person in the driver's seat, facing forwards.

Acknowledgements

Certain illustrations are the copyright of Vauxhall Motors Limited, and are used with their permission. Thanks are also due to Draper Tools Limited, who provided some of the workshop tools, and to all those people at Sparkford who helped in the production of this manual.

We take great pride in the accuracy of information given in this manual, but vehicle manufacturers make alterations and design changes during the production run of a particular vehicle of which they do not inform us. No liability can be accepted by the authors or publishers for loss, damage or injury caused by any errors in, or omissions from, the information given.

Working on your car can be dangerous. This page shows just some of the potential risks and hazards, with the aim of creating a safety-conscious attitude.

General hazards

Scalding

• Don't remove the radiator or expansion tank cap while the engine is hot.
• Engine oil, automatic transmission fluid or power steering fluid may also be dangerously hot if the engine has recently been running.

Burning

• Beware of burns from the exhaust system and from any part of the engine. Brake discs and drums can also be extremely hot immediately after use.

Crushing

• When working under or near a raised vehicle, always supplement the jack with axle stands, or use drive-on ramps. ***Never venture under a car which is only supported by a jack.***
• Take care if loosening or tightening high-torque nuts when the vehicle is on stands. Initial loosening and final tightening should be done with the wheels on the ground.

Fire

• Fuel is highly flammable; fuel vapour is explosive.
• Don't let fuel spill onto a hot engine.
• Do not smoke or allow naked lights (including pilot lights) anywhere near a vehicle being worked on. Also beware of creating sparks (electrically or by use of tools).
• Fuel vapour is heavier than air, so don't work on the fuel system with the vehicle over an inspection pit.
• Another cause of fire is an electrical overload or short-circuit. Take care when repairing or modifying the vehicle wiring.
• Keep a fire extinguisher handy, of a type suitable for use on fuel and electrical fires.

Electric shock

• Ignition HT voltage can be dangerous, especially to people with heart problems or a pacemaker. Don't work on or near the ignition system with the engine running or the ignition switched on.
• Mains voltage is also dangerous. Make sure that any mains-operated equipment is correctly earthed. Mains power points should be protected by a residual current device (RCD) circuit breaker.

Fume or gas intoxication

• Exhaust fumes are poisonous; they often contain carbon monoxide, which is rapidly fatal if inhaled. Never run the engine in a confined space such as a garage with the doors shut.
• Fuel vapour is also poisonous, as are the vapours from some cleaning solvents and paint thinners.

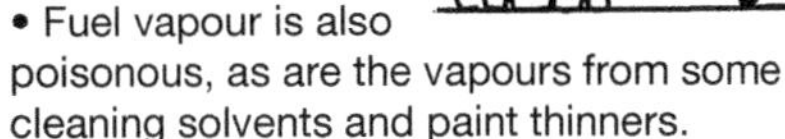

Poisonous or irritant substances

• Avoid skin contact with battery acid and with any fuel, fluid or lubricant, especially antifreeze, brake hydraulic fluid and Diesel fuel. Don't syphon them by mouth. If such a substance is swallowed or gets into the eyes, seek medical advice.
• Prolonged contact with used engine oil can cause skin cancer. Wear gloves or use a barrier cream if necessary. Change out of oil-soaked clothes and do not keep oily rags in your pocket.
• Air conditioning refrigerant forms a poisonous gas if exposed to a naked flame (including a cigarette). It can also cause skin burns on contact.

Asbestos

• Asbestos dust can cause cancer if inhaled or swallowed. Asbestos may be found in gaskets and in brake and clutch linings. When dealing with such components it is safest to assume that they contain asbestos.

Special hazards

Hydrofluoric acid

• This extremely corrosive acid is formed when certain types of synthetic rubber, found in some O-rings, oil seals, fuel hoses etc, are exposed to temperatures above 400°C. The rubber changes into a charred or sticky substance containing the acid. *Once formed, the acid remains dangerous for years. If it gets onto the skin, it may be necessary to amputate the limb concerned.*
• When dealing with a vehicle which has suffered a fire, or with components salvaged from such a vehicle, wear protective gloves and discard them after use.

The battery

• Batteries contain sulphuric acid, which attacks clothing, eyes and skin. Take care when topping-up or carrying the battery.
• The hydrogen gas given off by the battery is highly explosive. Never cause a spark or allow a naked light nearby. Be careful when connecting and disconnecting battery chargers or jump leads.

Air bags

• Air bags can cause injury if they go off accidentally. Take care when removing the steering wheel and/or facia. Special storage instructions may apply.

Diesel injection equipment

• Diesel injection pumps supply fuel at very high pressure. Take care when working on the fuel injectors and fuel pipes.

Warning: Never expose the hands, face or any other part of the body to injector spray; the fuel can penetrate the skin with potentially fatal results.

Remember...

DO

• Do use eye protection when using power tools, and when working under the vehicle.

• Do wear gloves or use barrier cream to protect your hands when necessary.

• Do get someone to check periodically that all is well when working alone on the vehicle.

• Do keep loose clothing and long hair well out of the way of moving mechanical parts.

• Do remove rings, wristwatch etc, before working on the vehicle – especially the electrical system.

• Do ensure that any lifting or jacking equipment has a safe working load rating adequate for the job.

DON'T

• Don't attempt to lift a heavy component which may be beyond your capability – get assistance.

• Don't rush to finish a job, or take unverified short cuts.

• Don't use ill-fitting tools which may slip and cause injury.

• Don't leave tools or parts lying around where someone can trip over them. Mop up oil and fuel spills at once.

• Don't allow children or pets to play in or near a vehicle being worked on.

The following pages are intended to help in dealing with common roadside emergencies and breakdowns. You will find more detailed fault finding information at the back of the manual, and repair information in the main chapters.

If your car won't start and the starter motor doesn't turn

- ☐ If it's a model with automatic transmission, make sure the selector is in 'P' or 'N'.
- ☐ Open the bonnet and make sure that the battery terminals are clean and tight.
- ☐ Switch on the headlights and try to start the engine. If the headlights go very dim when you're trying to start, the battery is probably flat. Get out of trouble by jump starting (see next page) using a friend's car.

If your car won't start even though the starter motor turns as normal

- ☐ Is there fuel in the tank?
- ☐ Is there moisture on electrical components under the bonnet? Switch off the ignition, then wipe off any obvious dampness with a dry cloth. Spray a water-repellent aerosol product (WD-40 or equivalent) on ignition and fuel system electrical connectors like those shown in the photos. Pay special attention to the ignition coil wiring connector and HT leads.

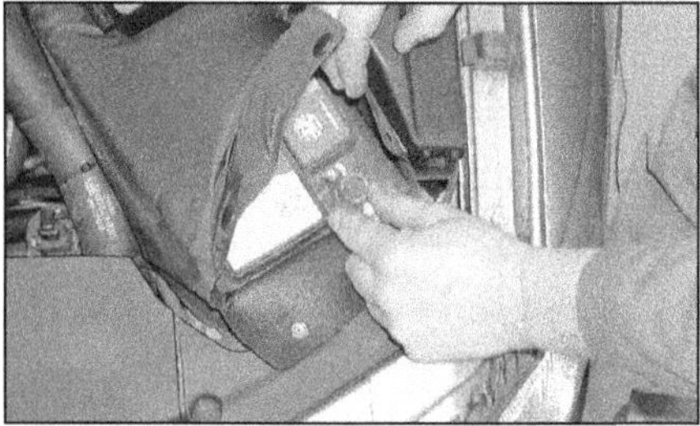

A Check the condition and security of the battery connections

B Check that the spark plug HT leads are securely connected by pushing them onto the plugs (where accessible)

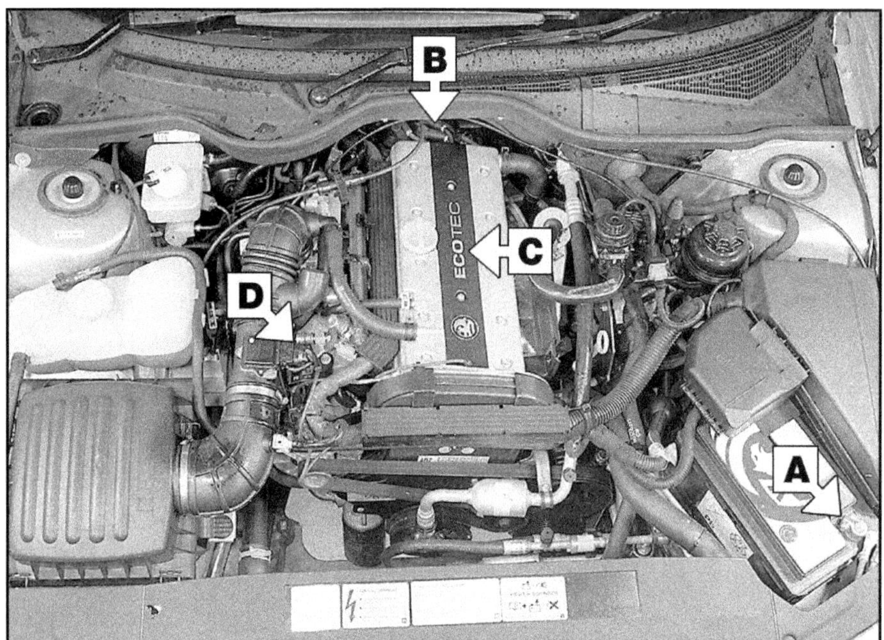

Check that electrical connections are secure (with the ignition switched off) and spray them with a water dispersant spray like WD40 if you suspect a problem due to damp

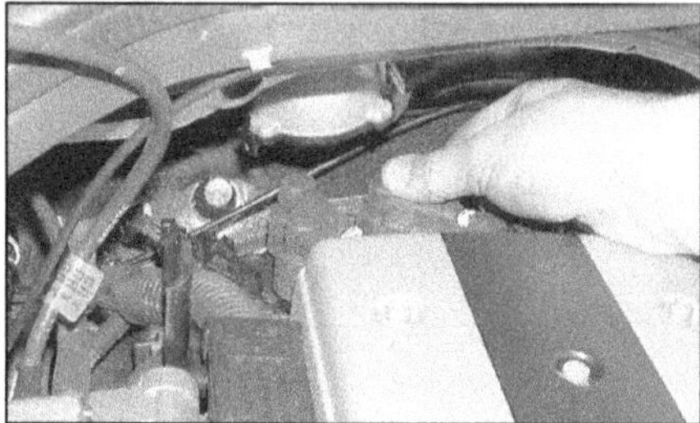

C Check that the spark plug HT leads are securely connected by pushing them onto the DIS module (where accessible)

D Check that the engine management system wiring connectors are securely connected

HAYNES HiNT *Jump starting will get you out of trouble, but you must correct whatever made the battery go flat in the first place. There are three possibilities:*

***1** The battery has been drained by repeated attempts to start, or by leaving the lights on.*

***2** The charging system is not working properly (alternator drivebelt slack or broken, alternator wiring fault or alternator itself faulty).*

***3** The battery itself is at fault (electrolyte low, or battery worn out).*

Jump starting

When jump-starting a car using a booster battery, observe the following precautions:

- ✔ Before connecting the booster battery, make sure that the ignition is switched off.
- ✔ Ensure that all electrical equipment (lights, heater, wipers, etc) is switched off.
- ✔ Take note of any special precautions printed on the battery case.
- ✔ Make sure that the booster battery is the same voltage as the discharged one in the vehicle.
- ✔ If the battery is being jump-started from the battery in another vehicle, the two vehicles MUST NOT TOUCH each other.
- ✔ Make sure that the transmission is in neutral (or PARK, in the case of automatic transmission).

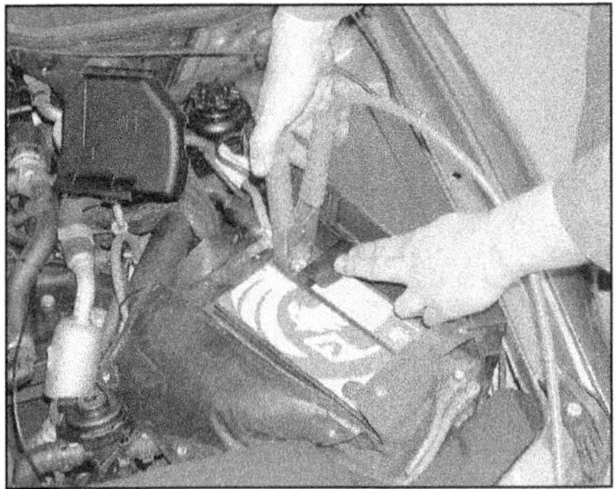

1 Connect one end of the red jump lead to the positive (+) terminal of the flat battery

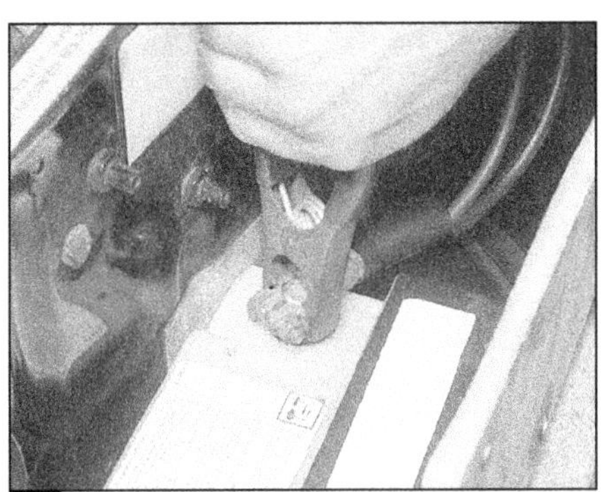

2 Connect the other end of the red lead to the positive (+) terminal of the booster battery.

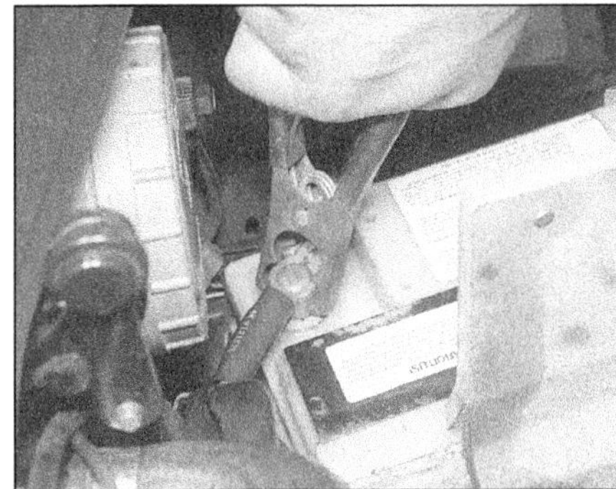

3 Connect one end of the black jump lead to the negative (-) terminal of the booster battery

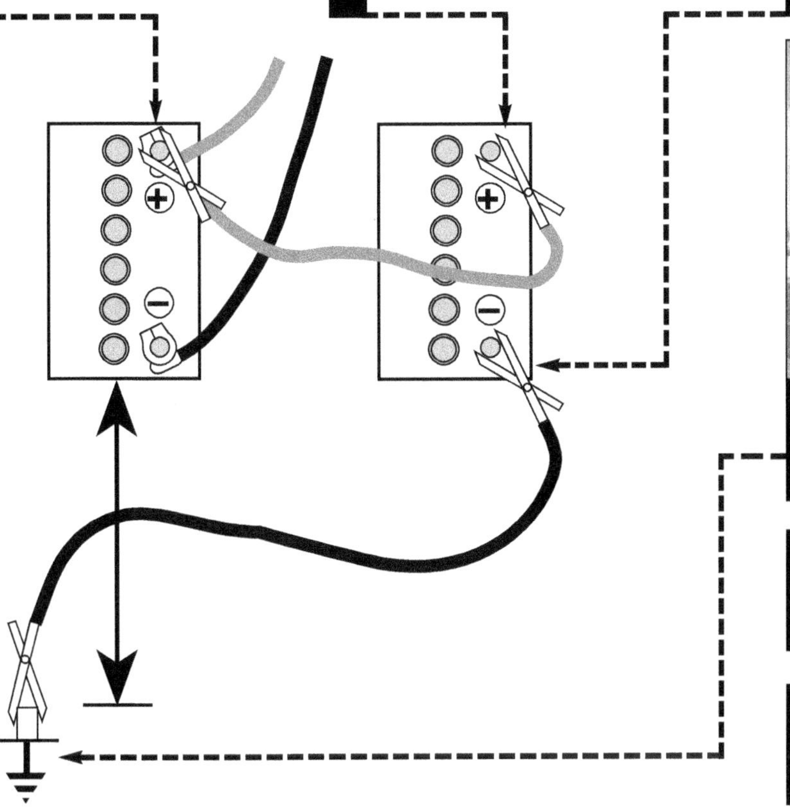

4 Connect the other end of the black jump lead to a bolt or bracket on the engine block, well away from the battery, on the vehicle to be started.

5 Make sure that the jump leads will not come into contact with the fan, drive-belts or other moving parts of the engine.

6 Start the engine using the booster battery and run it at idle speed. Switch on the lights, rear window demister and heater blower motor, then disconnect the jump leads in the reverse order of connection. Turn off the lights etc.

Wheel changing

Some of the details shown here will vary according to model.

Warning: Do not change a wheel in a situation where you risk being hit by another vehicle. On busy roads, try to stop in a lay-by or a gateway. Be wary of passing traffic while changing the wheel - it is easy to become distracted by the job in hand.

Preparation

- ☐ When a puncture occurs, stop as soon as it is safe to do so.
- ☐ Park on firm level ground, if possible, and well out of the way of other traffic.
- ☐ Use hazard warning lights if necessary.
- ☐ If you have one, use a warning triangle to alert other drivers of your presence.
- ☐ Apply the handbrake and engage first or reverse gear (or Park on models with automatic transmission.
- ☐ Chock the wheel diagonally opposite the one being removed – a couple of large stones will do for this.
- ☐ If the ground is soft, use a flat piece of wood to spread the load under the jack.

Changing the wheel

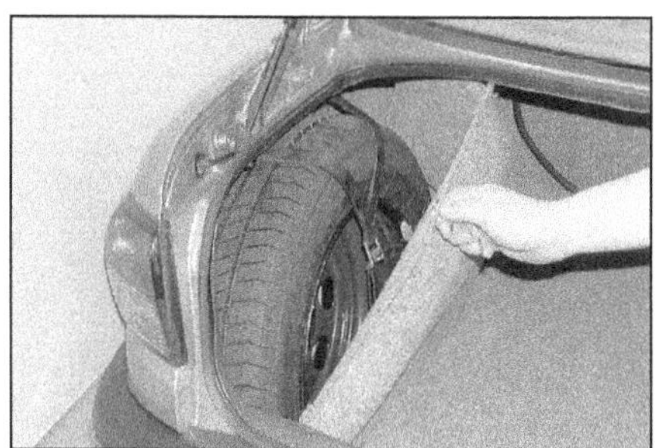

1 On Saloon models unclip the luggage compartment left-hand trim panel then release the retaining strap and remove the spare wheel . . .

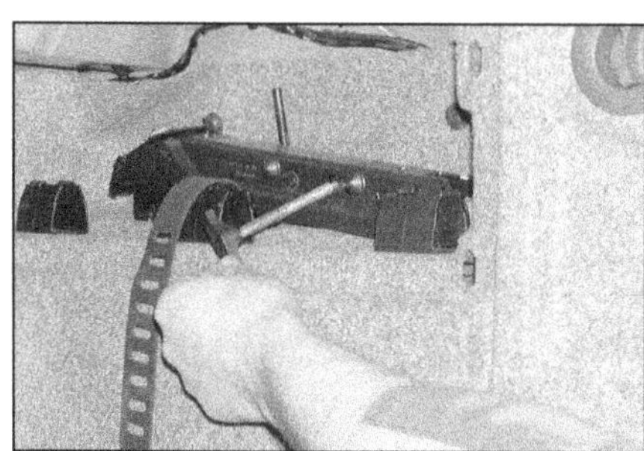

2 . . . The tools and jack are stored in the smaller compartment on the right-hand side of the luggage compartment. Remove the cover (where fitted) then unscrew the bolt and remove the jack and wheelbrace.

3 On Estate models lift up the luggage compartment floor panel and remove the tools from the centre of the spare wheel. Undo the retaining nut and remove the spare wheel . . .

4 . . . then unscrew the retaining bolt and remove the jack from behind the wheel.

5 On models with steel wheels, use the removal tool supplied to pull off the wheel trim and on models with alloy wheels, use the tool supplied to unscrew the anti-theft bolt and remove the hub cap. Slacken each wheel bolt by half a turn.

6 Unclip the access cover from the sill trim panel then make sure the jack is located on firm ground and engage the jack head correctly with the lifting point on the sill. Make sure that the lug on the jack head is correctly located in the sill seam cutout and the base of the jack is directly underneath the sill seam.

7 Raise the jack until the wheel is raised clear of the ground. Unscrew the wheel bolts and remove the wheel. Fit the spare wheel and screw on the bolts. Lightly tighten the bolts with the wheelbrace then lower the vehicle to the ground.

8 Securely tighten the wheel bolts in a diagonal sequence then refit the hub cap/wheel trim (as applicable). Note that the wheel bolts should be slackened and retightened to the specified torque at the earliest possible opportunity.

Finally...

- ☐ Remove the wheel chocks.
- ☐ Stow the punctured wheel, jack and tools in the correct locations in the car.
- ☐ Check the tyre pressure on the wheel just fitted. If it is low, or if you don't have a pressure gauge with you, drive slowly to the nearest garage and inflate the tyre to the right pressure.
- ☐ Have the damaged tyre or wheel repaired as soon as possible.

Identifying leaks

Puddles on the garage floor or drive, or obvious wetness under the bonnet or underneath the car, suggest a leak that needs investigating. It can sometimes be difficult to decide where the leak is coming from, especially if the engine bay is very dirty already. Leaking oil or fluid can also be blown rearwards by the passage of air under the car, giving a false impression of where the problem lies.

Warning: Most automotive oils and fluids are poisonous. Wash them off skin, and change out of contaminated clothing, without delay.

The smell of a fluid leaking from the car may provide a clue to what's leaking. Some fluids are distictively coloured. It may help to clean the car carefully and to park it over some clean paper overnight as an aid to locating the source of the leak. Remember that some leaks may only occur while the engine is running.

Sump oil

Engine oil may leak from the drain plug...

Oil from filter

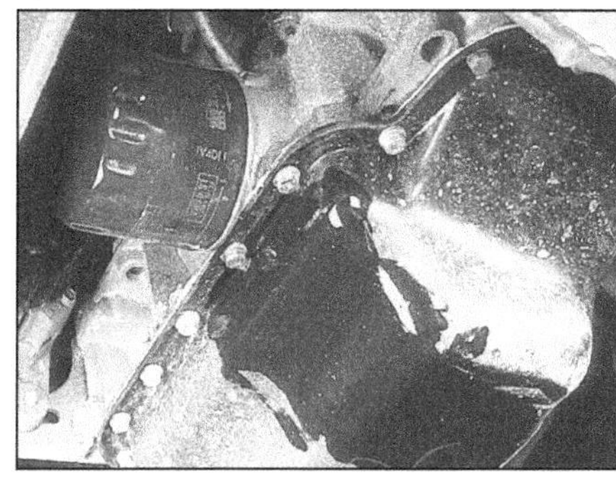

...or from the base of the oil filter.

Gearbox oil

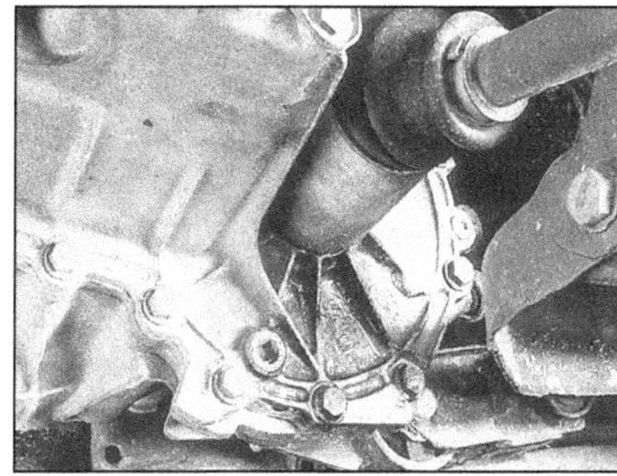

Gearbox oil can leak from the seals at the inboard ends of the driveshafts.

Antifreeze

Leaking antifreeze often leaves a crystalline deposit like this.

Brake fluid

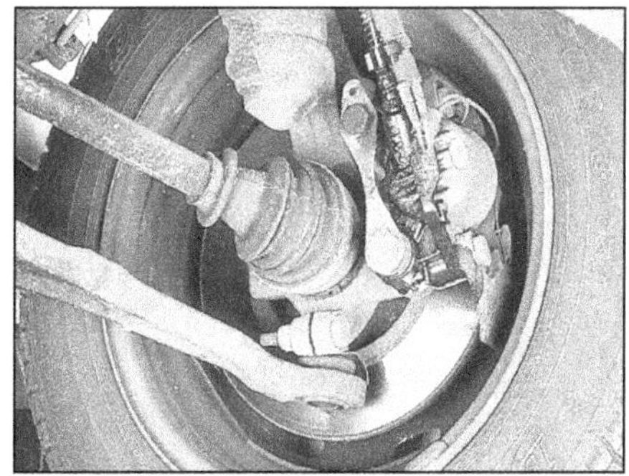

A leak occurring at a wheel is almost certainly brake fluid.

Power steering fluid

Power steering fluid may leak from the pipe connectors on the steering rack.

Towing

When all else fails, you may find yourself having to get a tow home – or of course you may be helping somebody else. Long-distance recovery should only be done by a garage or breakdown service. For shorter distances, DIY towing using another car is easy enough, but observe the following points:

☐ Use a proper tow-rope – they are not expensive. The vehicle being towed must display an 'ON TOW' sign in its rear window.

☐ Always turn the ignition key to the 'on' position when the vehicle is being towed, so that the steering lock is released, and that the direction indicator and brake lights will work.

☐ Both front and rear towing eyes are provided. They are located behind the access covers on the front and rear bumper.

☐ Before being towed, release the handbrake and select neutral on the transmission.

☐ Note that greater-than-usual pedal pressure will be required to operate the brakes, since the vacuum servo unit is only operational with the engine running.

☐ On models with power steering, greater-than-usual steering effort will also be required.

☐ The driver of the car being towed must keep the tow-rope taut at all times to avoid snatching.

☐ Make sure that both drivers know the route before setting off.

☐ Only drive at moderate speeds and keep the distance towed to a minimum. Drive smoothly and allow plenty of time for slowing down at junctions.

☐ On models with automatic transmission, special precautions apply. If in doubt, do not tow, or transmission damage may result.

Introduction

There are some very simple checks which need only take a few minutes to carry out, but which could save you a lot of inconvenience and expense.

These "Weekly checks" require no great skill or special tools, and the small amount of time they take to perform could prove to be very well spent, for example;

☐ Keeping an eye on tyre condition and pressures, will not only help to stop them wearing out prematurely, but could also save your life.

☐ Many breakdowns are caused by electrical problems. Battery-related faults are particularly common, and a quick check on a regular basis will often prevent the majority of these.

☐ If your car develops a brake fluid leak, the first time you might know about it is when your brakes don't work properly. Checking the level regularly will give advance warning of this kind of problem.

☐ If the oil or coolant levels run low, the cost of repairing any engine damage will be far greater than fixing the leak, for example.

Underbonnet check points

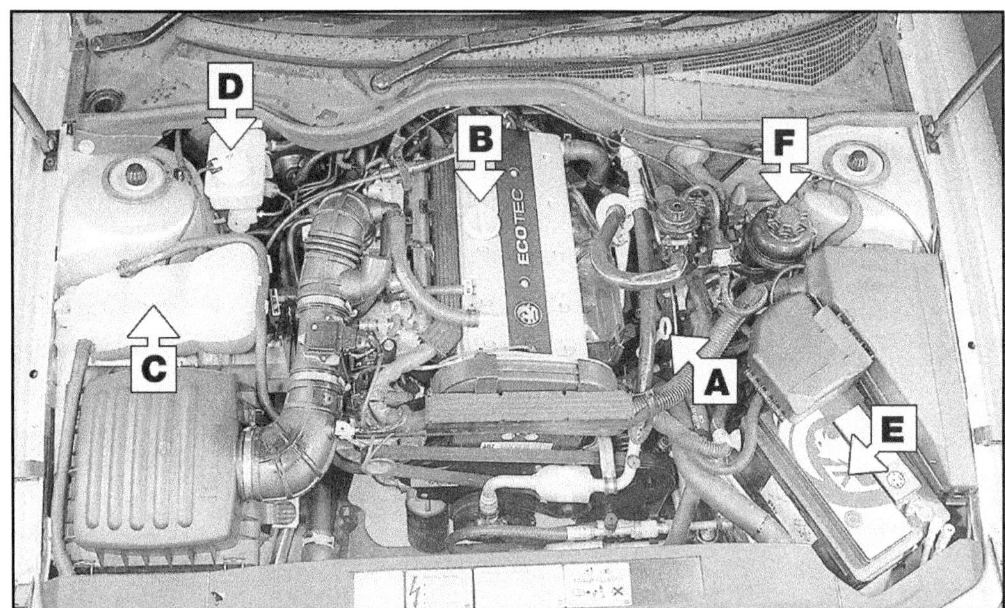

◀ **2.0 litre DOHC engine**

A *Engine oil level dipstick*
B *Engine oil filler cap*
C *Coolant expansion tank*
D *Brake (and clutch) fluid reservoir*
E *Battery*
F *Power steering fluid reservoir*

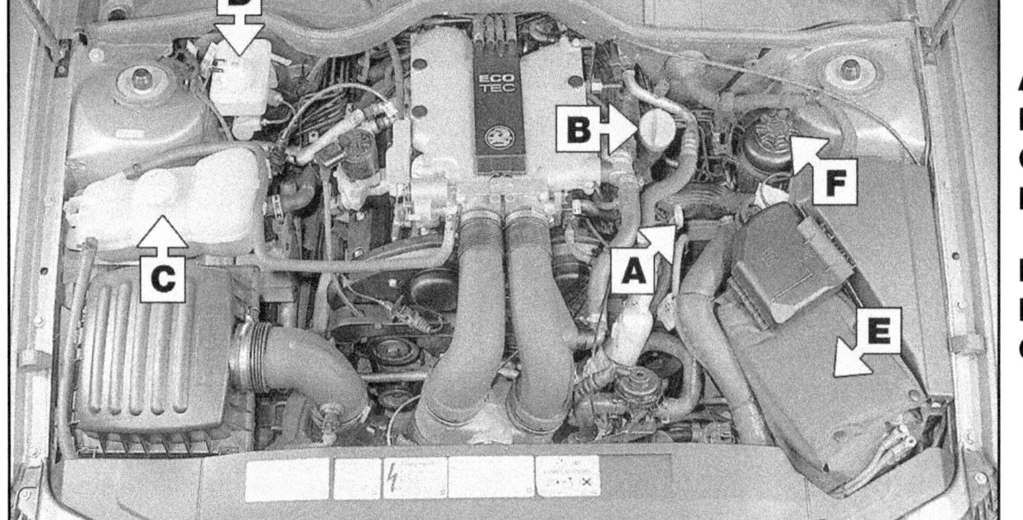

◀ **2.5 and 3.0 litre engine**

A *Engine oil level dipstick*
B *Engine oil filler cap*
C *Coolant expansion tank*
D *Brake (and clutch) fluid reservoir*
E *Battery*
F *Power steering fluid reservoir*
G *Screen washer fluid reservoir*

Engine oil level

Before you start

✔ Make sure that your car is on level ground.
✔ Check the oil level before the car is driven, or at least 5 minutes after the engine has been switched off.

If the oil is checked immediately after driving the vehicle, some of the oil will remain in the upper engine components, resulting in an inaccurate reading on the dipstick!

The correct oil

Modern engines place great demands on their oil. It is very important that the correct oil for your car is used (See "Lubricants and fluids" on page 0•16).

Car Care

● If you have to add oil frequently, you should check whether you have any oil leaks. Place some clean paper under the car overnight, and check for stains in the morning. If there are no leaks, the engine may be burning oil.

● Always maintain the level between the upper and lower dipstick marks (see photo 3). If the level is too low severe engine damage may occur. Oil seal failure may result if the engine is overfilled by adding too much oil.

1 The dipstick is located on the left-hand side of the engine (see Underbonnet check points on page 0•10 for exact location). Withdraw the dipstick.

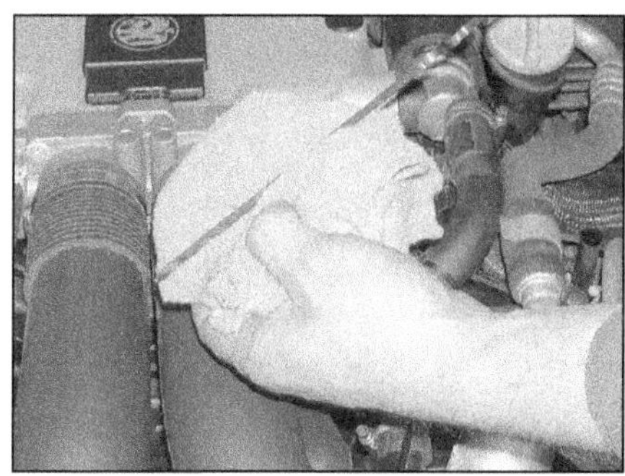

2 Using a clean rag or paper towel remove all oil from the dipstick. Insert the clean dipstick into the tube as far as it will go, then withdraw it again.

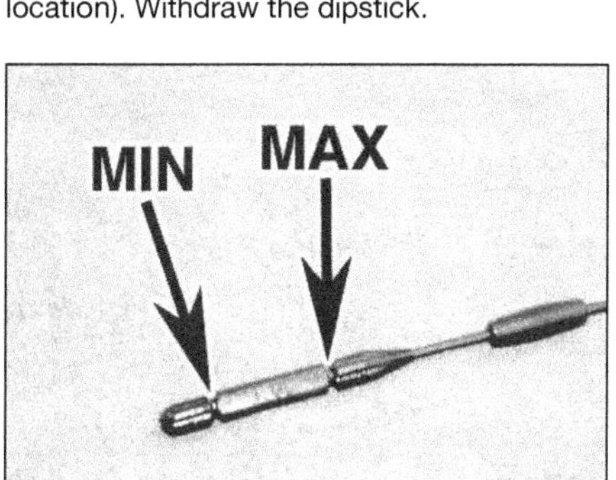

3 Note the oil level on the end of the dipstick, which should be between the upper (MAX) mark and lower (MIN) mark. Approximately 1.0 litre of oil will raise the level from the lower mark to the upper mark.

4 Oil is added through the filler cap. Rotate the cap through a quarter-turn anti-clockwise and withdraw it. Top-up the level. A funnel may help to reduce spillage. Add the oil slowly, checking the level on the dipstick often. Do not overfill.

Coolant level

Warning: DO NOT attempt to remove the expansion tank pressure cap when the engine is hot, as there is a very great risk of scalding. Do not leave open containers of coolant about, as it is poisonous.

Car Care

● With a sealed-type cooling system, adding coolant should not be necessary on a regular basis. If frequent topping-up is required, it is likely there is a leak. Check the radiator, all hoses and joint faces for signs of staining or wetness, and rectify as necessary.

● It is important that antifreeze is used in the cooling system all year round, not just during the winter months. Don't top-up with water alone, as the antifreeze will become too diluted.

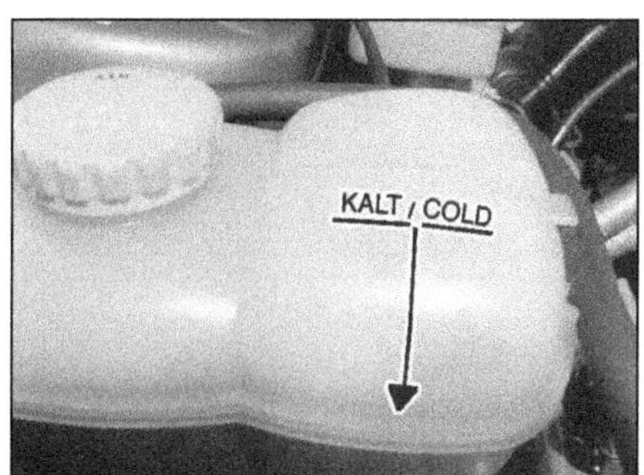

1 The coolant level varies with the temperature of the engine. When the engine is cold, the coolant level should be slightly above the KALT/COLD mark on the side of the tank. When the engine is hot, the level will rise.

2 If topping up is necessary, **wait until the engine is cold**. Slowly unscrew the expansion tank cap, to release any pressure present in the cooling system, and remove it.

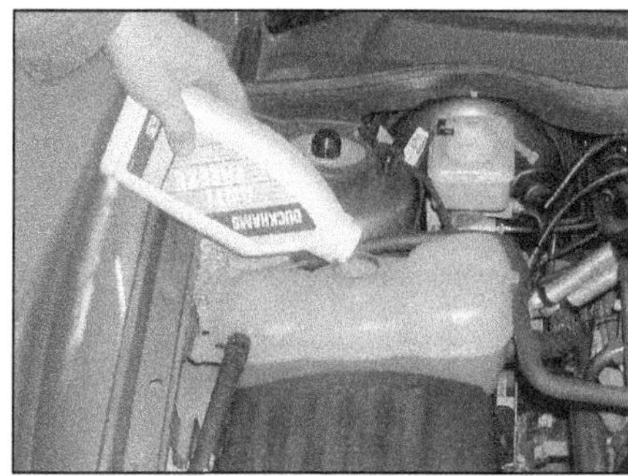

3 Add a mixture of water and antifreeze to the expansion tank until the coolant level is slightly above the KALT/COLD mark then securely refit the expansion tank cap.

Brake and clutch* fluid level

**On manual transmission models the brake fluid reservoir also supplies fluid to the clutch master cylinder.*

Warning:
- ***Brake fluid can harm your eyes and damage painted surfaces, so use extreme caution when handling and pouring it.***
- ***Do not use fluid that has been standing open for some time, as it absorbs moisture from the air, which can cause a dangerous loss of braking effectiveness.***

• Make sure that your car is on level ground.
• The fluid level in the reservoir will drop slightly as the brake pads wear down, but the fluid level must never be allowed to drop below the "MIN" mark.

Safety First!

- If the reservoir requires repeated topping-up this is an indication of a fluid leak somewhere in the system, which should be investigated immediately.

- If a leak is suspected, the car should not be driven until the braking system has been checked. Never take any risks where brakes are concerned.

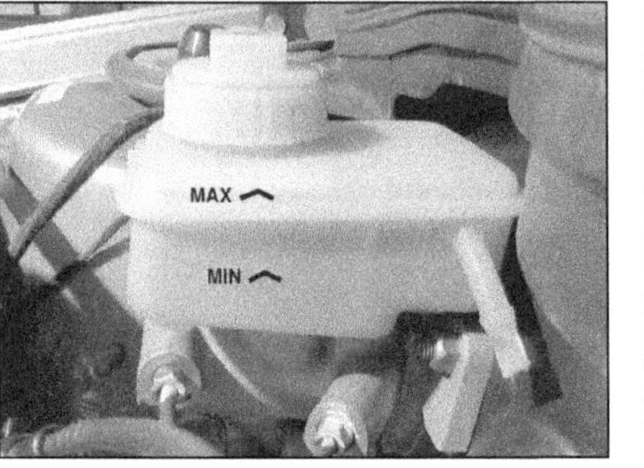

1 The upper (MAX) and lower (MIN) fluid level markings are on the side of the reservoir, which is located in the right-hand rear corner of the engine compartment. The fluid level must always be kept in between these two marks.

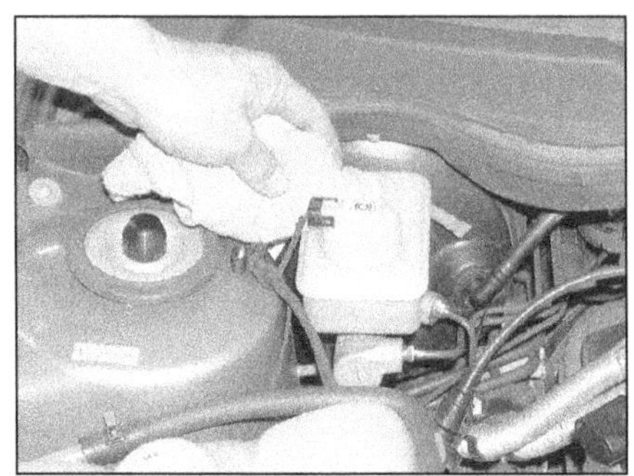

2 If topping-up is necessary, first wipe clean the area around the filler cap to prevent dirt entering the hydraulic system.

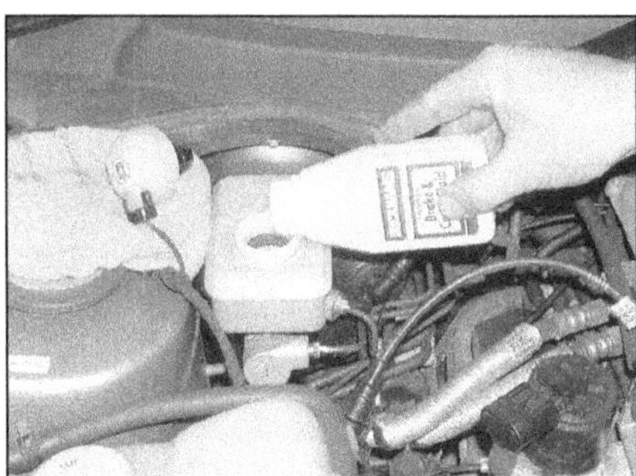

3 Carefully add fluid, taking care not to spill it onto the surrounding components. Use only the specified fluid; mixing different types can cause damage to the system. After topping-up to the correct level, securely refit the cap and wipe off any spilt fluid.

Power steering fluid level

Before you start:

✔ Park the vehicle on level ground.
✔ Set the steering wheel straight-ahead.
✔ The engine should be turned off.

For the check to be accurate, the steering must not be turned once the engine has been stopped.

Safety First!

- The need for frequent topping-up indicates a leak, which should be investigated immediately.

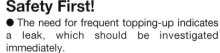

1 The power steering fluid reservoir is located on the left-hand side of the engine compartment. Wipe clean the reservoir before unscrewing and removing the cap.

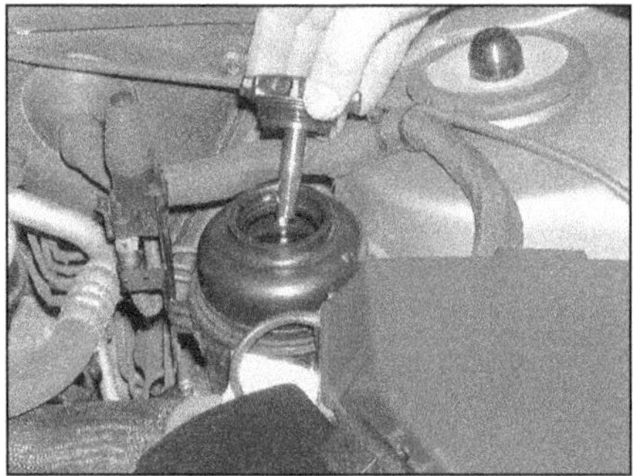

2 Wipe clean the filler cap dipstick then refit the filler cap and remove it again. Note the fluid level on the dipstick.

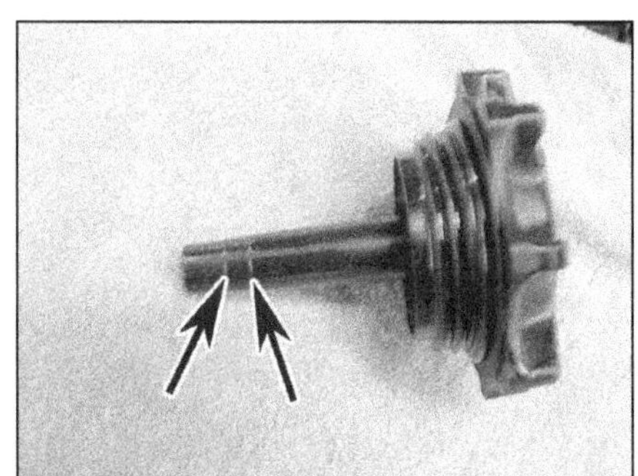

3 When the engine is cold the fluid level should be up to the lower mark up the dipstick and when the engine is at operating temperature it should be at the upper mark. Top up the fluid level using the specified type of fluid (do not overfill) then securely refit the filler cap.

Battery

Caution: *Before carrying out any work on the vehicle battery, read the precautions given in "Safety first" at the start of this manual.*

✔ Make sure that the battery tray is in good condition, and that the clamp is tight. Corrosion on the tray, retaining clamp and the battery itself can be removed with a solution of water and baking soda. Thoroughly rinse all cleaned areas with water. Any metal parts damaged by corrosion should be covered with a zinc-based primer, then painted.

✔ Periodically (approximately every three months), check the charge condition of the battery as described in Chapter 5A.

✔ If the battery is flat, and you need to jump start your vehicle, see **Roadside Repairs**.

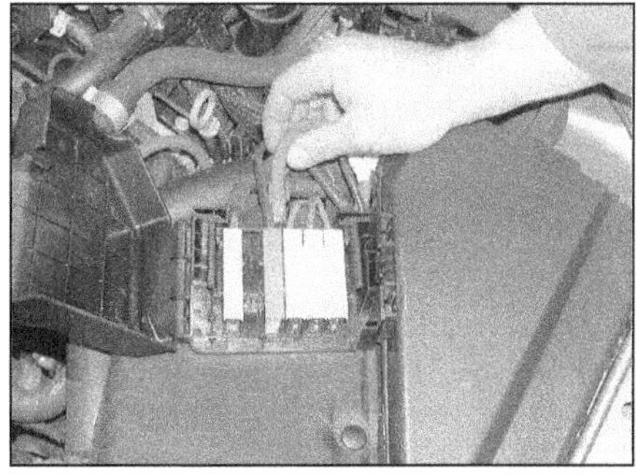

1 The battery is located at the front left-hand corner of the engine compartment. If necessary, unclip the fusible link housing (where fitted) from side of the relay box then open up the insulating cover to gain access to the battery.

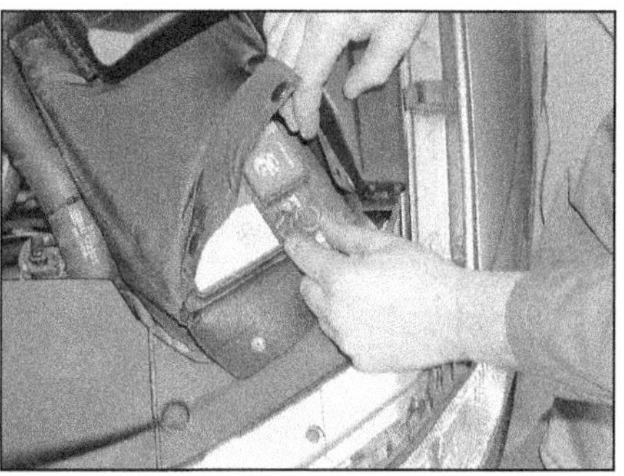

2 The exterior of the battery should be inspected periodically for damage such as a cracked case or cover. Check the battery lead clamps for tightness to ensure good electrical connections and check the leads for signs of damage.

HAYNES HiNT

Battery corrosion can be kept to a minimum by applying a layer of petroleum jelly to the clamps and terminals after they are reconnected.

3 If corrosion (white, fluffy deposits) is evident, remove the cables from the battery terminals, clean them with a small wire brush, then refit them. Automotive stores sell a tool for cleaning the battery post . . .

4 . . . as well as the battery cable clamps

Electrical systems

✔ Check all external lights and the horn. Refer to the appropriate Sections of Chapter 12 for details if any of the circuits are found to be inoperative.

✔ Visually check all accessible wiring connectors, harnesses and retaining clips for security, and for signs of chafing or damage.

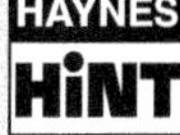

If you need to check your brake lights and indicators unaided, back up to a wall or garage door and operate the lights. The reflected light should show if they are working properly.

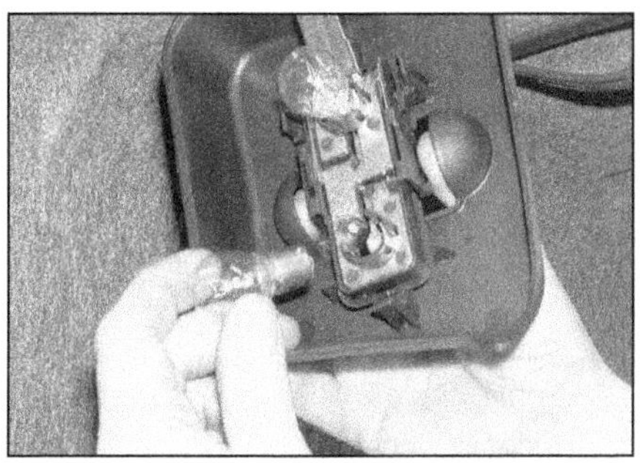

1 If a single indicator light, stop-light or headlight has failed, it is likely that a bulb has blown and will need to be replaced. Refer to Chapter 12 for details. If both stop lights have failed, it is possible that the switch has failed (see Chapter 12, Section 4).

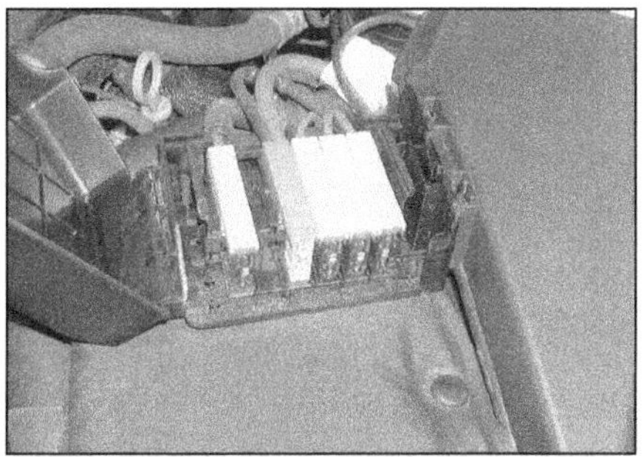

2 If more than one indicator light or tail light has failed it is likely that either a fuse has blown or that there is a fault in the circuit (see Chapter 12). Most fuses are located behind in the fusebox, behind the cover on the driver's side of the facia; depress the locking button and remove the cover to gain access. Additional fuses can be found in the engine compartment relay box and fusible link housing.

3 To replace a blown fuse, remove it, where applicable, using the plastic tool provided. Fit a new fuse of the same rating, available from car accessory shops. It is important that you find the reason that the fuse blew (see *Electrical fault finding* in Chapter 12).

Tyre condition and pressure

It is very important that tyres are in good condition, and at the correct pressure - having a tyre failure at any speed is highly dangerous. Tyre wear is influenced by driving style - harsh braking and acceleration, or fast cornering, will all produce more rapid tyre wear. As a general rule, the front tyres wear out faster than the rears. Interchanging the tyres from front to rear ("rotating" the tyres) may result in more even wear. However, if this is completely effective, you may have the expense of replacing all four tyres at once!

Remove any nails or stones embedded in the tread before they penetrate the tyre to cause deflation. If removal of a nail does reveal that the tyre has been punctured, refit the nail so that its point of penetration is marked. Then immediately change the wheel, and have the tyre repaired by a tyre dealer.

Regularly check the tyres for damage in the form of cuts or bulges, especially in the sidewalls. Periodically remove the wheels, and clean any dirt or mud from the inside and outside surfaces. Examine the wheel rims for signs of rusting, corrosion or other damage. Light alloy wheels are easily damaged by "kerbing" whilst parking; steel wheels may also become dented or buckled. A new wheel is very often the only way to overcome severe damage.

New tyres should be balanced when they are fitted, but it may become necessary to re-balance them as they wear, or if the balance weights fitted to the wheel rim should fall off. Unbalanced tyres will wear more quickly, as will the steering and suspension components. Wheel imbalance is normally signified by vibration, particularly at a certain speed (typically around 50 mph). If this vibration is felt only through the steering, then it is likely that just the front wheels need balancing. If, however, the vibration is felt through the whole car, the rear wheels could be out of balance. Wheel balancing should be carried out by a tyre dealer or garage.

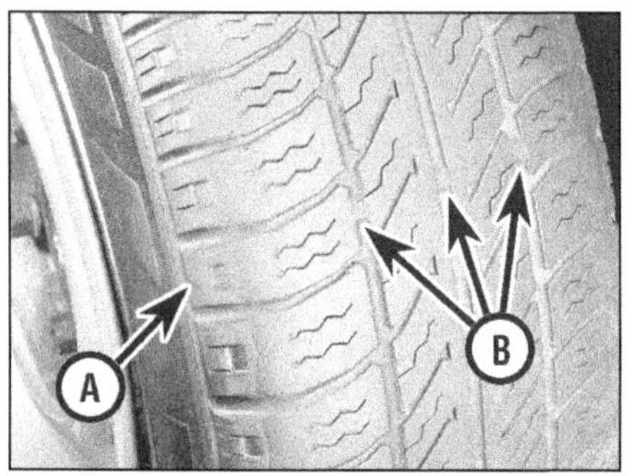

1 ***Tread Depth - visual check***
The original tyres have tread wear safety bands (B), which will appear when the tread depth reaches approximately 1.6 mm. The band positions are indicated by a triangular mark on the tyre sidewall (A).

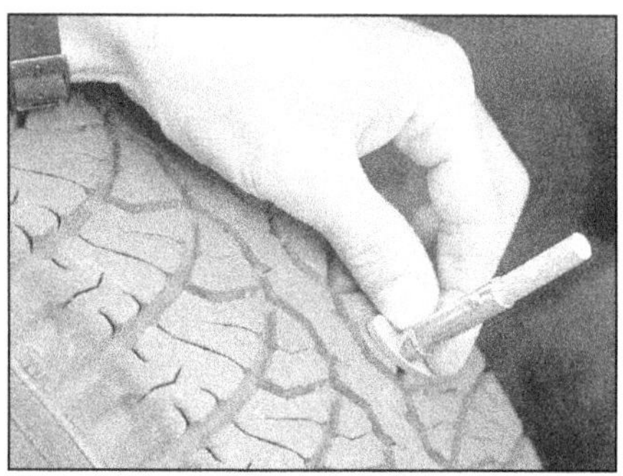

2 ***Tread Depth - manual check***
Alternatively, tread wear can be monitored with a simple, inexpensive device known as a tread depth indicator gauge.

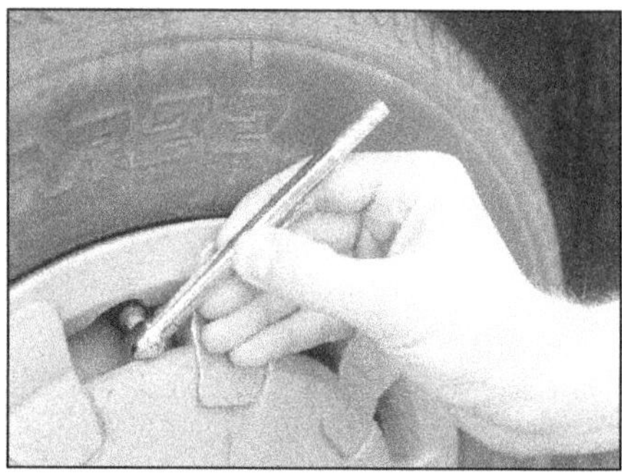

3 ***Tyre Pressure Check***
Check the tyre pressures regularly with the tyres cold. Do not adjust the tyre pressures immediately after the vehicle has been used, or an inaccurate setting will result. Tyre pressures are shown on page 0•17.

Tyre tread wear patterns

Shoulder Wear

Underinflation (wear on both sides)
Under-inflation will cause overheating of the tyre, because the tyre will flex too much, and the tread will not sit correctly on the road surface. This will cause a loss of grip and excessive wear, not to mention the danger of sudden tyre failure due to heat build-up.
Check and adjust pressures

Incorrect wheel camber (wear on one side)
Repair or renew suspension parts

Hard cornering
Reduce speed!

Centre Wear

Overinflation
Over-inflation will cause rapid wear of the centre part of the tyre tread, coupled with reduced grip, harsher ride, and the danger of shock damage occurring in the tyre casing.
Check and adjust pressures

If you sometimes have to inflate your car's tyres to the higher pressures specified for maximum load or sustained high speed, don't forget to reduce the pressures to normal afterwards.

Uneven Wear

Front tyres may wear unevenly as a result of wheel misalignment. Most tyre dealers and garages can check and adjust the wheel alignment (or "tracking") for a modest charge.

Incorrect camber or castor
Repair or renew suspension parts

Malfunctioning suspension
Repair or renew suspension parts

Unbalanced wheel
Balance tyres

Incorrect toe setting
Adjust front wheel alignment

Note: *The feathered edge of the tread which typifies toe wear is best checked by feel.*

Washer fluid level

Screenwash additives not only keep the winscreen clean during foul weather, they also prevent the washer system freezing in cold weather - which is when you are likely to need it most. Don't top up using plain water as the screenwash will become too diluted, and will freeze during cold weather. ***On no account use coolant antifreeze in the washer system - this could discolour or damage paintwork.***

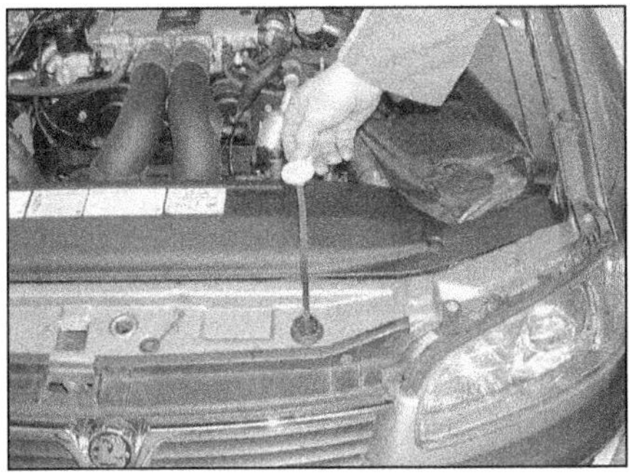

1 The reservoir for the windscreen/ tailgate/headlamps (as applicable) is located at the front of vehicle. The fluid level in the reservoir can be checked using the dipstick attached to the filler cap.

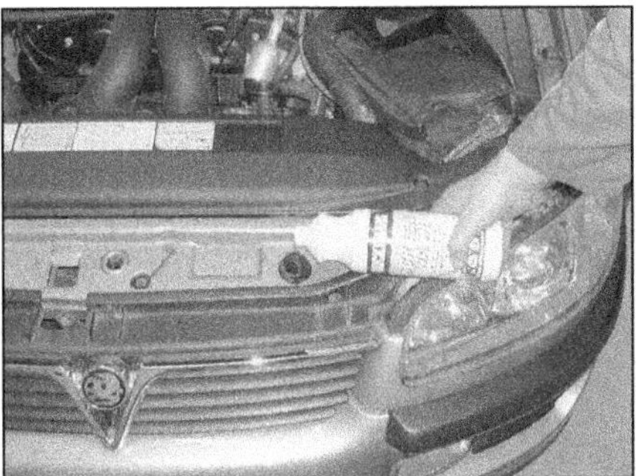

2 When topping-up the reservoir, a screenwash additive should be added in the quantities recommended on the bottle.

Wiper blades

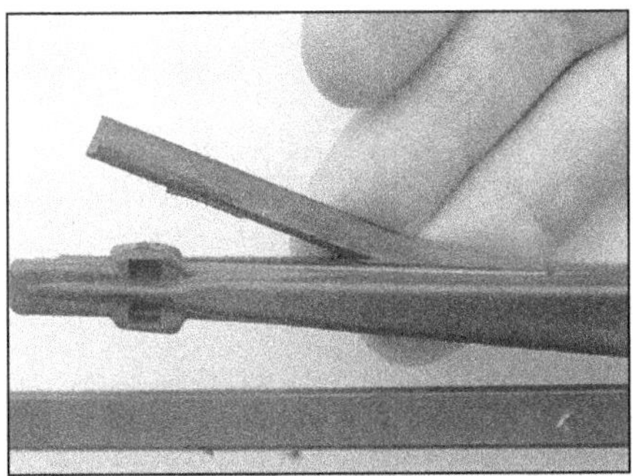

1 Check the condition of the wiper blades; if they are cracked or show any signs of deterioration, or if the glass swept area is smeared, renew them. Wiper blades should be renewed annually.

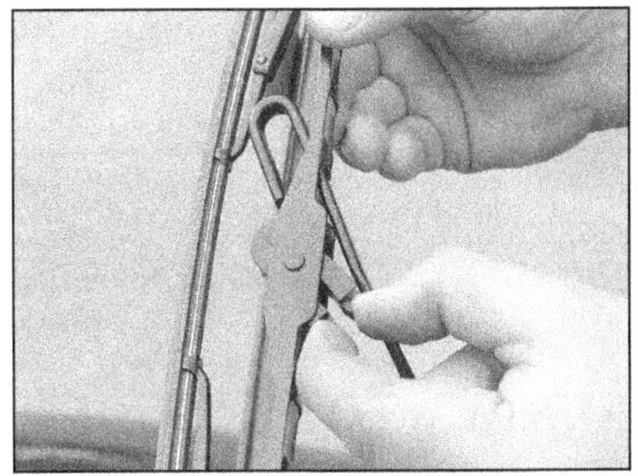

2 To remove a windscreen wiper blade, pull the arm fully away from the screen until it locks. Swivel the blade through 90°, press the locking tab with your fingers and slide the blade out of the arm's hooked end.

Lubricants and fluids

Engine	Multigrade engine oil, viscosity SAE 10W/40 to 15W/50 to API SG/CD or SH/CD
Cooling system	Ethylene glycol based antifreeze
Manual transmission:	
Early (pre 1999) vehicles:	
Up to number JP3097A01361659*	Vauxhall transmission oil 19 40 704
From number JP3097A01361659*	Vauxhall transmission oil 19 40 764
Later (1999 onwards) vehicles	Vauxhall transmission oil 19 40 768
Automatic transmission	Vauxhall transmission fluid 19 40 763
Final drive unit	See Chapter 8 specifications
Braking and clutch system	Hydraulic fluid DOT 4
Power steering	Vauxhall transmission fluid 19 40 700

The identification number is stamped on the transmission housing.* **Note: *There have been three different types of oil used in the transmission by Vauxhall. The different types of oil should never be mixed, and it is essential that the transmission is refilled either with the same type of oil as that drained, or the latest oil used in production from 1999 model year. If it is not known what type of oil has been drained, the transmission unit should be flushed before filling with the latest specification oil. To do this, refer to Chapter 7A, Section 2.*

Choosing your engine oil

Engines need oil, not only to lubricate moving parts and minimise wear, but also to maximise power output and to improve fuel economy.

HOW ENGINE OIL WORKS

• *Beating friction*

Without oil, the moving surfaces inside your engine will rub together, heat up and melt, quickly causing the engine to seize. Engine oil creates a film which separates these moving parts, preventing wear and heat build-up.

• *Cooling hot-spots*

Temperatures inside the engine can exceed 1000° C. The engine oil circulates and acts as a coolant, transferring heat from the hot-spots to the sump.

• *Cleaning the engine internally*

Good quality engine oils clean the inside of your engine, collecting and dispersing combustion deposits and controlling them until they are trapped by the oil filter or flushed out at oil change.

OIL CARE - FOLLOW THE CODE

To handle and dispose of used engine oil safely, always:

• Avoid skin contact with used engine oil. Repeated or prolonged contact can be harmful.

• Dispose of used oil and empty packs in a responsible manner in an authorised disposal site. Call 0800 663366 to find the one nearest to you. Never tip oil down drains or onto the ground.

Tyre pressures

Note: *Pressures apply to original-equipment tyres only and may vary if any other make or type of tyre is fitted; check with the tyre manufacturer or supplier for correct pressures if necessary.*
Note: *Tyre pressures must always be checked with the tyres cold to ensure accuracy.*

Saloon models

2.0 litre engine	**Front**	**Rear**
Up to 3 passengers (including driver)	28.5 psi (2.0 bar)	28.5 psi (2.0 bar)
Fully loaded	36 psi (2.5 bar)	42 psi (2.9 bar)
2.5 and 3.0 litre engine		
Up to 3 passengers (including driver)	31.5 psi (2.2 bar)	31.5 psi (2.2 bar)
Fully loaded	36 psi (2.5 bar)	42 psi (2.9 bar)

Estate models

2.0 litre engine		
Up to 3 passengers (including driver)	28.5 psi (2.0 bar)	31.5 psi (2.2 bar)
4 or 5 passengers (including driver) and 60 kg of luggage	33.0 psi (2.3 bar)	45.0 psi (3.1 bar)
Fully loaded	38.0 psi (2.6 bar)	45.0 psi (3.1 bar)
2.5 and 3.0 litre engine		
195/65 R 15 tyres:		
Up to 3 passengers (including driver)	31.5 psi (2.2 bar)	34.0 psi (2.3 bar)
4 or 5 passengers (including driver) and 60 kg of luggage	34.0 psi (2.3 bar)	46.0 psi (3.2 bar)
Fully loaded	39.0 psi (2.7 bar)	46.0 psi (3.2 bar)
205/65 R 15 and 225/55 R 15 tyres:		
Up to 3 passengers (including driver)	28.5 psi (2.0 bar)	31.5 psi (2.2 bar)
4 or 5 passengers (including driver) and 60 kg of luggage	33.0 psi (2.3 bar)	45.0 psi (3.1 bar)
Fully loaded	38.0 psi (2.6 bar)	45.0 psi (3.1 bar)

Advanced driving

Many people see the words 'advanced driving' and believe that it won't interest them or that it is a style of driving beyond their own abilities. Nothing could be further from the truth. Advanced driving is straightforward safe, sensible driving - the sort of driving we should all do every time we get behind the wheel.

An average of 10 people are killed every day on UK roads and 870 more are injured, some seriously. Lives are ruined daily, usually because somebody did something stupid. Something like 95% of all accidents are due to human error, mostly driver failure. Sometimes we make genuine mistakes - everyone does. Sometimes we have lapses of concentration. Sometimes we deliberately take risks.

For many people, the process of 'learning to drive' doesn't go much further than learning how to pass the driving test because of a common belief that good drivers are made by 'experience'.

Learning to drive by 'experience' teaches three driving skills:

- ☐ Quick reactions. (Whoops, that was close!)
- ☐ Good handling skills. (Horn, swerve, brake, horn).
- ☐ Reliance on vehicle technology. (Great stuff this ABS, stop in no distance even in the wet...)

Drivers whose skills are 'experience based' generally have a lot of near misses and the odd accident. The results can be seen every day in our courts and our hospital casualty departments.

Advanced drivers have learnt to control the risks by controlling the position and speed of their vehicle. They avoid accidents and near misses, even if the drivers around them make mistakes.

The key skills of advanced driving are **concentration,** effective all-round **observation, anticipation** and **planning.** When **good vehicle handling** is added to these skills, all driving situations can be approached and negotiated in a safe, methodical way, leaving nothing to chance.

Concentration means applying your mind to safe driving, completely excluding anything that's not relevant. Driving is usually the most dangerous activity that most of us undertake in our daily routines. It deserves our full attention.

Observation means not just looking, but seeing and seeking out the information found in the driving environment.

Anticipation means asking yourself what is happening, what you can reasonably expect to happen and what could happen unexpectedly. (One of the commonest words used in compiling accident reports is 'suddenly'.)

Planning is the link between seeing something and taking the appropriate action. For many drivers, planning is the missing link.

If you want to become a safer and more skilful driver and you want to enjoy your driving more, contact the Institute of Advanced Motorists at www.iam.org.uk, phone 0208 996 9600, or write to IAM House, 510 Chiswick High Road, London W4 5RG for an information pack.

Chapter 1
Routine maintenance and servicing

Contents

Degrees of difficulty

Easy, suitable for novice with little experience 

Fairly easy, suitable for beginner with some experience 

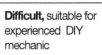

Fairly difficult, suitable for competent DIY mechanic 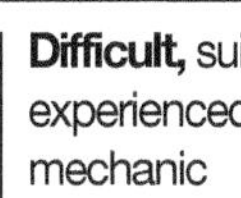

Difficult, suitable for experienced DIY mechanic

Very difficult, suitable for expert DIY or professional 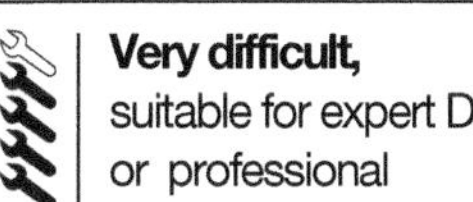

Lubricants and fluids .... Refer to end of *Weekly checks* on page 0•16

Capacities

Engine oil		
2.0 litre engine:		
SOHC engine	4.5 litres	
DOHC engine:		
Engines with a one-piece sump	4.5 litres	
Engines with a two-piece sump	5.0 litres	
2.5 and 3.0 litre engine	5.75 litres	
Difference between MIN and MAX on dipstick (all engines)	1.0 litre	
Cooling system	**Manual transmission**	**Automatic transmission**
2.0 litre engine:		
SOHC engine	9.0 litres	8.8 litres
DOHC engine	8.8 litres	8.6 litres
2.5 and 3.0 litre engine	9.7 litres	9.5 litres
Transmission		
Manual transmission (approximate)	1.2 litres	
Automatic transmission (approximate):		
From dry	8.4 litres	
After removing main sump	4.4 litres	
Final drive	1.0 litre*	

**On models with limited-slip differential, observe the notes in Chapter 8 regarding the correct mixture of oil and additive to be used when refilling the final drive unit.*

Washer fluid reservoir	
Without headlight washers	3.0 litres
With headlight washers	6.4 litres
Fuel tank	
All models	75 litres

Cooling system

Antifreeze mixture:	
50% antifreeze	Protection down to -37°C
55% antifreeze	Protection down to -45°C

Note: *Refer to antifreeze manufacturer for latest recommendations.*

Ignition system

Spark plugs:	Type	Electrode gap
All engines	Bosch FLR 8 LD+U	1.0 mm

Brakes

Friction material minimum thickness:	
Front brake pads	8.0 mm including backing plate
Rear brake pads	6.0 mm including backing plate
Handbrake shoes	1.0 mm excluding backing plate

Torque wrench settings

	Nm	lbf ft
Automatic transmission fluid level plug	33	24
Oil filter	15	11
Roadwheel bolts	110	81
Spark plugs	25	18
Sump drain plug:		
2.0 litre SOHC engine	55	41
2.0 litre DOHC engine:		
Hex-head bolt	45	33
Torx-head bolt	10	7
2.5 and 3.0 litre engine:		
Hex-head bolt	55	41
Torx-head bolt	10	7

The maintenance intervals in this manual are provided with the assumption that you, not the dealer, will be carrying out the work. These are the minimum maintenance intervals recommended by us for vehicles driven daily. If you wish to keep your vehicle in peak condition at all times, you may wish to perform some of these procedures more often. We encourage frequent maintenance, because it enhances the efficiency, performance and resale value of your vehicle.

If the vehicle is driven in dusty areas, used to tow a trailer, or driven frequently at slow speeds (idling in traffic) or on short journeys, more frequent maintenance intervals are recommended.

When the vehicle is new, and/or still within its warranty period, it should be serviced by a factory-authorised dealer service department, in order to preserve the factory warranty.

Every 5000 miles (7500 km) or 6 months, whichever comes first

☐ Engine oil and filter - renewal (Section 3)

Note: *Vauxhall recommend that the engine oil and filter are changed every 10 000 miles or 12 months. However, oil and filter changes are good for the engine and we recommend that the oil and filter are renewed more frequently, especially if the vehicle is used on a lot of short journeys.*

Every 10 000 miles (15 000 km) or 12 months, whichever comes first

☐ Monitoring, lighting and signalling equipment - check (Section 4)
☐ Front and rear brakes - pad and disc wear check (Section 5)
☐ Auxiliary drivebelt condition and tension - check and adjust (Section 6)*
☐ Underbonnet/underbody hose and fluid leak - check (Section 7)*
☐ Bodywork/underbody corrosion protection - check (Section 8)*
☐ Handbrake operation - check and adjustment (Section 9)*
☐ Suspension and steering condition and operation - check (Section 10)*
☐ Wheel bolt torque - check and adjustment (Section 11)
☐ Headlight and auxiliary driving light beam alignment - check (Section 12)*
☐ Road test (Section 13)
☐ Wheel alignment - check (Section 14)
☐ Exhaust system - check (Section 15)*

* **Note:** *On vehicles covering a high mileage (more than 20 000 miles/30 000 km annually) carry out the items marked with an asterisk at the 12 month interval; carry out the items not marked with an asterisk every 10 000 miles/15 000 km, regardless of elapsed time.*

Every 20 000 miles (30 000 km) or 2 years, whichever comes first

Carry out all the operations listed for the 15,000 km/12 month interval, plus the following additional operations:

☐ Air filter element - renewal (Section 16)
☐ Pollen filter - renewal (Section 17)
☐ Lock and hinge lubrication (Section 18)
☐ Automatic transmission fluid level check (Section 19)
☐ Handbrake - shoe condition check (Section 20)
☐ Driveshaft gaiter condition - check (Section 21)

Every 40 000 miles (60 000 km) or 4 years, whichever comes first

Carry out all the operations listed for the 15,000 km/12 month and the 30,000 km/2 year intervals, plus the following additional operations:

☐ Spark plugs - renewal (Section 22)*
☐ Fuel filter - renewal (Section 23)
☐ Timing belt - renewal (Section 24)**

* **Note:** *On pre-1999 model year vehicles, renew the spark plugs every 40 000 miles (60 000 km) regardless of the time elapsed.*

****Note:** *Since the introduction of the Omega in 1994, Vauxhall have gradually increased the specified interval for timing belt renewal as follows:*

1994 model year vehicle,
36 000 miles or 4 years, whichever comes first.
1995 and 1996 model year vehicles,
40 000 miles or 4 years, whichever comes first.
1997 model year vehicles onwards,
80 000 miles or 8 years, whichever comes first.

However, if the vehicle is used mainly for short journeys or a lot of stop-start driving, or if the vehicle's history is unknown, it is recommended that the earlier (1994 model year) recommendation is adhered to. The actual belt renewal interval is very much up to the individual owner but, bearing in mind that severe engine damage will result if the belt breaks in use, we recommend you err on the side of caution.

Every 70 000 miles (105 000 km) or 7 years whichever comes first

☐ Automatic transmission fluid - renewal (Section 25)*

Note: *This operation applies only to vehicles covering a high mileage (more than 20 000 miles/30 000 km annually)*

Every 2 years, regardless of mileage

☐ Brake fluid - renewal (Section 26)
☐ Remote control keyfob battery - renewal (Section 27)
☐ Coolant - renewal (Section 28)

Underbonnet view of a 2.0 litre DOHC engine model

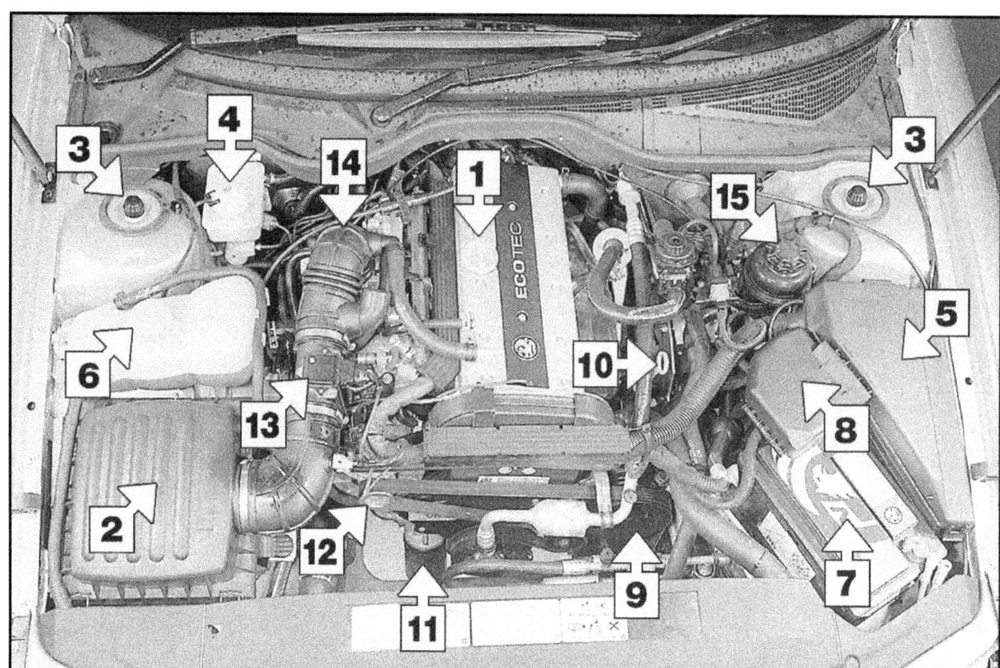

1 *Engine oil filler cap*
2 *Air cleaner*
3 *Front suspension strut upper mounting*
4 *Brake (and clutch) fluid reservoir*
5 *Relay box*
6 *Cooling system expansion tank*
7 *Battery*
8 *Fusible link housing*
9 *Power steering pump*
10 *Engine oil level dipstick*
11 *Oil filter*
12 *Alternator*
13 *Airflow meter*
14 *Throttle housing*
15 *Power steering fluid reservoir*

Underbonnet view of a 2.5 litre engine model (3.0 litre engine similar)

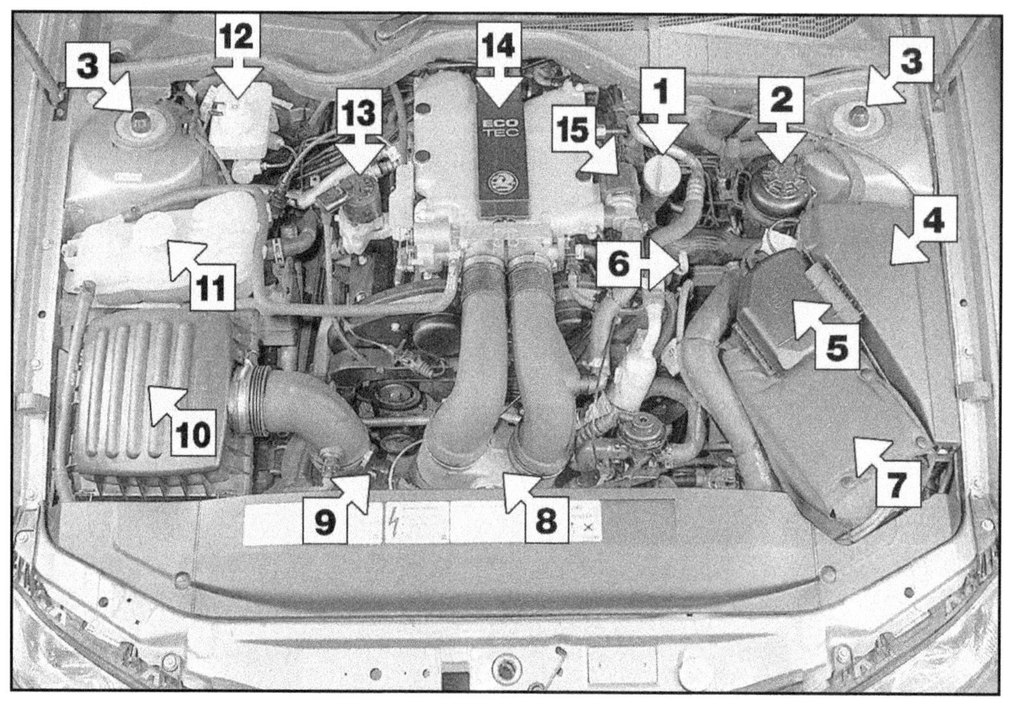

1 *Engine oil filler cap*
2 *Power steering fluid reservoir*
3 *Front suspension strut upper mounting*
4 *Relay box*
5 *Fusible link housing*
6 *Engine oil level dipstick*
7 *Battery*
8 *Multi-ram air intake system pre-volume chamber*
9 *Airflow meter*
10 *Air cleaner*
11 *Cooling system expansion tank*
12 *Brake (and clutch) fluid reservoir*
13 *Exhaust gas recirculation (EGR) valve*
14 *Inlet manifold*
15 *Idle speed adjuster valve*

Front underbody view (2.0 litre DOHC engine shown - others similar)

1 *Exhaust front downpipe*
2 *Oil filter*
3 *Engine oil drain plug*
4 *Air conditioning system compressor*
5 *Front suspension lower arm*
6 *Steering outer tie rod*
7 *Steering drop arm*
8 *Steering centre tie rod*
9 *Steering idler*
10 *Steering outer tie rod*
11 *Manual transmission*
12 *Oxygen sensor*
13 *Transmission unit rear mounting crossmember*

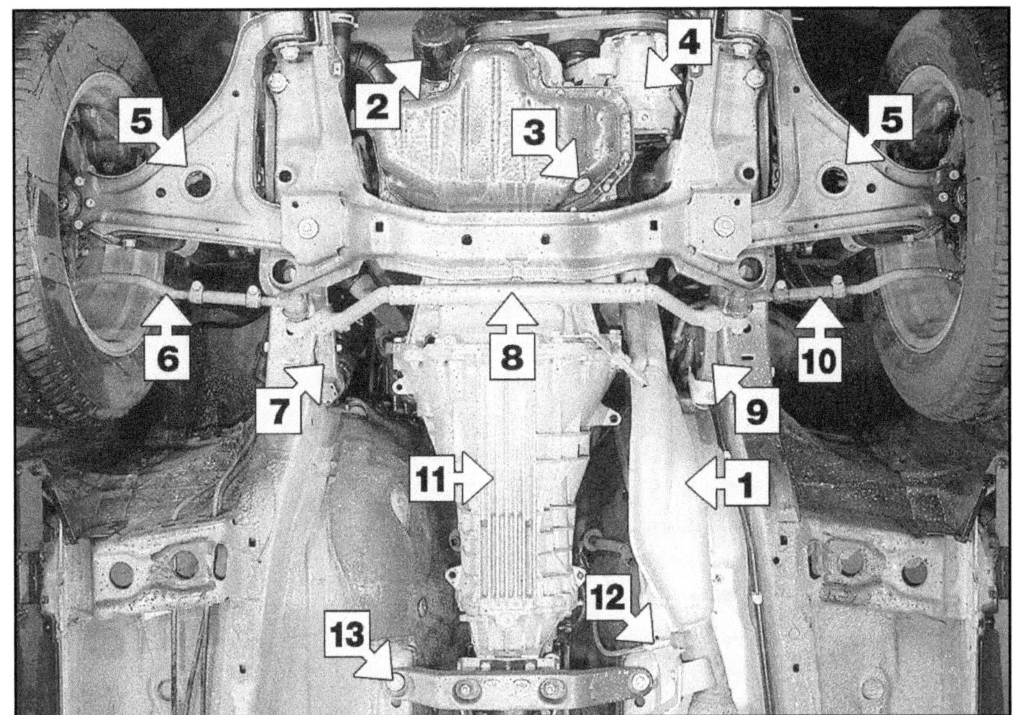

Rear underbody view (2.0 litre DOHC engine shown - others similar)

1 *Exhaust tailpipe*
2 *Fuel tank*
3 *Final drive unit*
4 *Fuel filter*
5 *Rear shock absorber*
6 *Driveshaft*
7 *Rear suspension tie rod*
8 *Rear suspension lower arm*
9 *Propeller shaft*
10 *Handbrake cable*

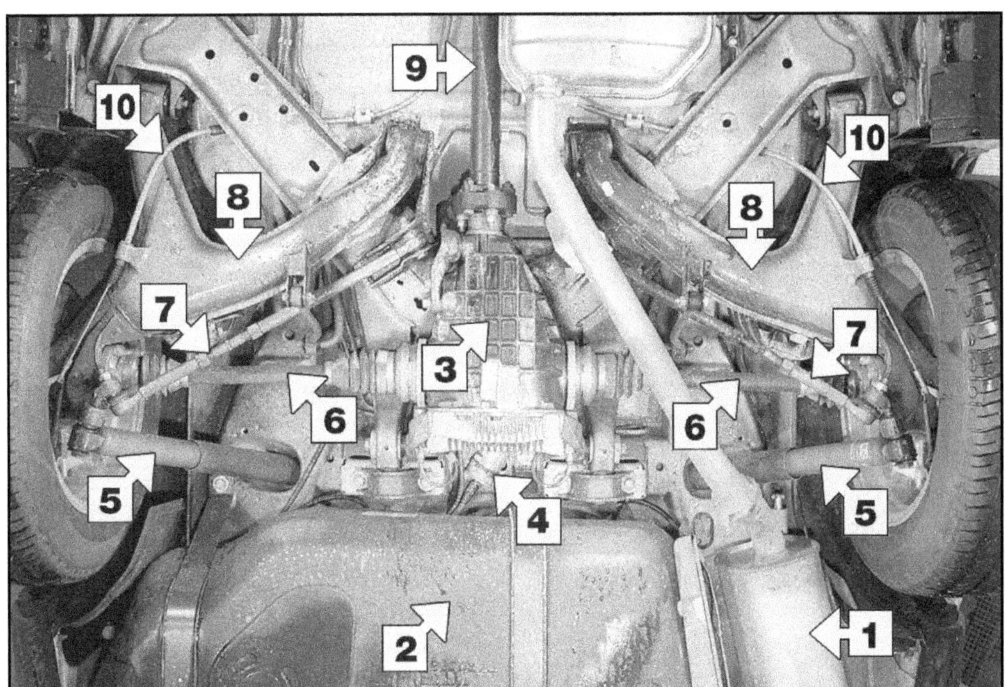

1 General information

1 This Chapter is designed to help the home mechanic maintain his/her vehicle for safety, economy, long life and peak performance.
2 The Chapter contains a master maintenance schedule, followed by Sections dealing specifically with each task in the schedule. Visual checks, adjustments, component renewal and other helpful items are included. Refer to the accompanying illustrations of the engine compartment and the underside of the vehicle for the locations of the various components.
3 Servicing your vehicle in accordance with the mileage/time maintenance schedule and the following Sections will provide a planned maintenance programme, which should result in a long and reliable service life. This is a comprehensive plan, so maintaining some items but not others at the specified service intervals, will not produce the same results.
4 As you service your vehicle, you will discover that many of the procedures can - and should - be grouped together, because of the particular procedure being performed, or because of the proximity of two otherwise-unrelated components to one another. For example, if the vehicle is raised for any reason, the exhaust can be inspected at the same time as the suspension and steering components.
5 The first step in this maintenance programme is to prepare yourself before the actual work begins. Read through all the Sections relevant to the work to be carried out, then make a list and gather all the parts and tools required. If a problem is encountered, seek advice from a parts specialist, or a dealer service department.

2 Regular maintenance

1 If, from the time the vehicle is new, the routine maintenance schedule is followed closely, and frequent checks are made of fluid levels and high-wear items, as suggested throughout this manual, the engine will be kept in relatively good running condition, and the need for additional work will be minimised.
2 It is possible that there will be times when the engine is running poorly due to the lack of regular maintenance. This is even more likely if a used vehicle, which has not received regular and frequent maintenance checks, is purchased. In such cases, additional work may need to be carried out, outside of the regular maintenance intervals.
3 If engine wear is suspected, a compression test (refer to Chapter 2A, 2B or 2C, as applicable) will provide valuable information regarding the overall performance of the main internal components. Such a test can be used as a basis to decide on the extent of the work to be carried out. If, for example, a compression test indicates serious internal engine wear, conventional maintenance as described in this Chapter will not greatly improve the performance of the engine, and may prove a waste of time and money, unless extensive overhaul work is carried out first.
4 The following series of operations are those most often required to improve the performance of a generally poor-running engine:

Primary operations

a) Clean, inspect and test the battery (refer to Weekly checks).
b) Check all the engine-related fluids (refer to Weekly checks).
c) Check the condition and tension of the auxiliary drivebelt (Section 6).
d) Renew the spark plugs (Section 22).
e) Check the condition of the air filter, and renew if necessary (Section 16).
f) Renew the fuel filter (Section 23).
g) Check the condition of all hoses, and check for fluid leak.

5 If the above operations do not prove fully effective, carry out the following secondary operations:

Secondary operations

All items listed under *Primary operations*, plus the following:

a) Check the charging system (refer to Chapter 5A).
b) Check the ignition system (refer to Chapter 5B).
c) Check the fuel system (refer to Chapter 4A).

Every 5000 miles or 6 months

3 Engine oil and filter - renewal

1 Frequent oil and filter changes are the most important preventative maintenance procedures which can be undertaken by the DIY owner. As engine oil ages, it becomes diluted and contaminated, which leads to premature engine wear.
2 Before starting this procedure, gather together all the necessary tools and materials.

3.5 Removing the sump drain plug

Also make sure that you have plenty of clean rags and newspapers handy, to mop up any spills. Ideally, the engine oil should be warm, as it will drain more easily, and more built-up sludge will be removed with it. Take care not to touch the exhaust or any other hot parts of the engine when working under the vehicle. To avoid any possibility of scalding, and to protect yourself from possible skin irritants and other harmful contaminants in used engine oils, it is advisable to wear gloves when carrying out this work.
3 Firmly apply the handbrake then jack up the front of the vehicle and support it on axle stands (see *Jacking and Vehicle Support*). Undo the retaining screws and remove the undercover from beneath the engine unit.
4 Remove the oil filler cap.
5 Using a spanner, or preferably a suitable socket and bar, slacken the drain plug about half a turn **(see illustration)**. Position the draining container under the drain plug, then remove the plug completely **(see Haynes Hint)**.
6 Allow some time for the oil to drain, noting that it may be necessary to reposition the container as the oil flow slows to a trickle.
7 After all the oil has drained, wipe the drain plug and the sealing washer with a clean rag. Examine the condition of the sealing washer, and renew it if it shows signs of scoring or other damage which may prevent an oil-tight seal. Clean the area around the drain plug opening, and refit the plug complete with the washer and tighten it to the specified torque.
8 Move the container into position under the oil filter. On 2.0 litre engines the filter is located on the front end of the engine, where

As the drain plug releases from the threads, move it quickly away so that the stream of oil running out of the sump goes into the container and not over your arm

3.8 Oil filter location - 2.0 litre engine

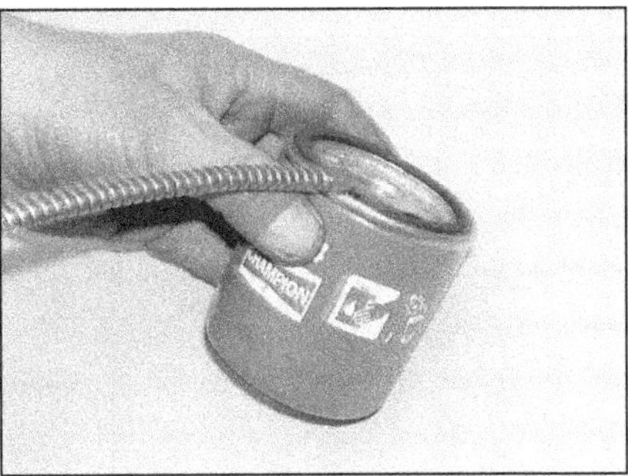

3.11a Lubricate the sealing ring of the new filter with a smear of engine oil . . .

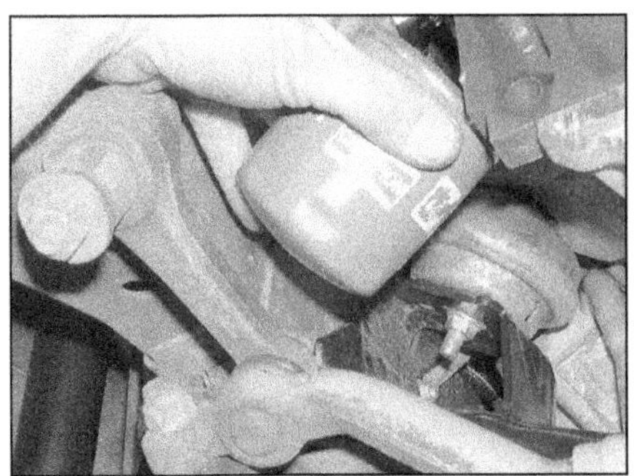

3.11b . . . then screw the filter on by hand only (2.5 litre engine shown)

it is screwed onto the oil pump housing, and on 2.5 and 3.0 litre engines it is screwed onto the left-hand side of the cylinder block **(see illustration)**.

9 Use an oil filter removal tool to slacken the filter initially, then unscrew it by hand the rest of the way. Empty the oil from the old filter into the container.

10 Use a clean rag to remove all oil, dirt and sludge from the filter sealing area on the engine.

11 Apply a light coating of clean engine oil to the sealing ring on the new filter, then screw the filter into position on the engine. Tighten the filter firmly by hand only - **do not** use any tools **(see illustrations)**. If a genuine filter is being fitted and the special oil filter tool (Tool no. KM-726A - a socket which fits over the end of the filter) is available, tighten the filter to the specified torque.

12 Refit the undercover, tightening its retaining screws securely, then remove the old oil and all tools from under the vehicle before lowering the vehicle to the ground.

13 Fill the engine through the filler hole, using the correct grade and type of oil (refer to *Weekly Checks* for details of topping-up). Pour in half the specified quantity of oil first, then wait a few minutes for the oil to drain into the sump. Continue to add oil, a small quantity at a time, until the level is up to the lower mark on the dipstick. Adding approximately a further 1.0 litre will bring the level up to the upper mark on the dipstick.

14 Start the engine and run it for a few minutes, while checking for leaks around the oil filter seal and the sump drain plug. Note that there may be a delay of a few seconds before the low oil pressure warning light goes out when the engine is first started, as the oil circulates through the new oil filter and the engine oil galleries before the pressure builds up.

15 Stop the engine, and wait a few minutes for the oil to settle in the sump once more. With the new oil circulated and the filter now completely full, recheck the level on the dipstick, and add more oil as necessary.

16 Dispose of the used engine oil safely with reference to *General repair procedures*.

Every 10 000 miles or 12 months

4 Monitoring, lighting and signalling equipment - check

1 Turn the ignition switch to the second position and check that the instrument panel CHECK lamp lights up and then extinguishes after 4 approximately seconds. If the lamp fails to extinguish, observe the fault description message(s) displayed and rectify the cause.

2 Start the engine and check that all tell-tale system operation/fault lamps extinguish. Note that some lamps (such as the automatic transmission sport programme, or traction control system lamps) may remain lit, depending on the driving mode selected; consult your drivers handbook for the exact meaning of each lamp.

3 Release handbrake, depress the brake pedal and check that the brake lights fault display extinguishes.

4 Switch on all interior and exterior lights in turn and check their operation. Pay particular attention to the tail lamps, fog lamps, brake lamps, main and dipped beam headlamps, position lamps and front and rear direction indicators. Renew any blown bulbs with reference to Chapter 12.

5 Finally, check the operation of the horn.

5 Front and rear brakes - pad and disc wear check

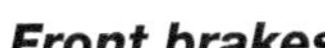

Front brakes

1 Firmly apply the handbrake, select first gear or P, then jack up the front of the vehicle and support it securely on axle stands (see *Jacking and Vehicle Support*). Remove the front roadwheels.

2 For a quick check, the pad thickness can be carried out via the inspection hole on the front surface of each caliper **(see illustration)**. Using a steel rule, measure the thickness of each pad lining, including the backing plate. This must not be less than that indicated in the Specifications.

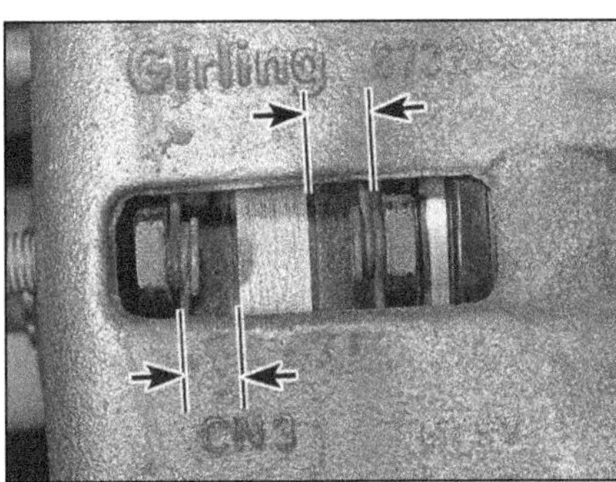

5.2 The brake pad wear can be assessed by observing the thickness of the friction material, visible through the inspection aperture at the front of the brake caliper

3 The view through the caliper inspection hole gives only a rough indication of the state of the brake pads. For a comprehensive check, the brake pads should be removed and cleaned. The operation of the caliper can then also be checked, and the condition of the brake disc itself can be fully examined on both sides. Chapter 9 contains a detailed description of how the brake discs should be checked for wear and/or damage.

4 If any pad's friction material is worn to the specified thickness or less, all four pads must be renewed as an axle set; for example - if the pads in the left hand caliper are found to be worn, those in the right hand caliper must also be renewed, regardless of their condition. Refer to Chapter 9 for details.

5 On completion, refit the roadwheels and lower the vehicle to the ground.

Rear brakes

6 Chock the front wheels, then jack up the rear of the vehicle and support it securely on axle stands (see *Jacking and Vehicle Support*). Remove the rear roadwheels.

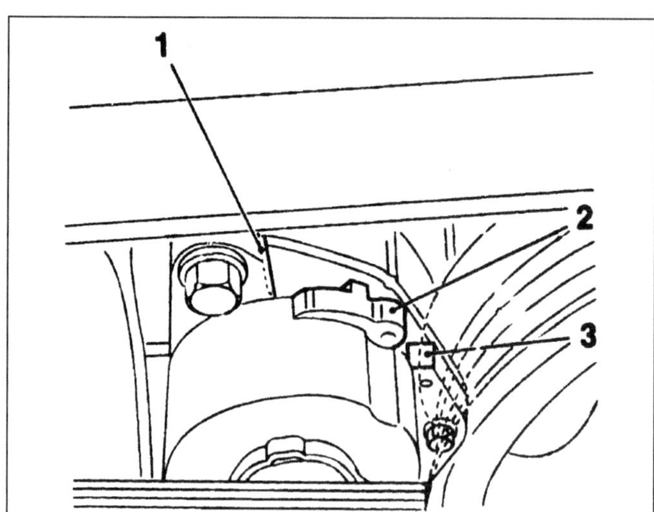

6.3a On 2.0 litre engines check that the drivebelt tensioner arm indicator (2) is correctly positioned between the stops (1 and 3) on the backplate

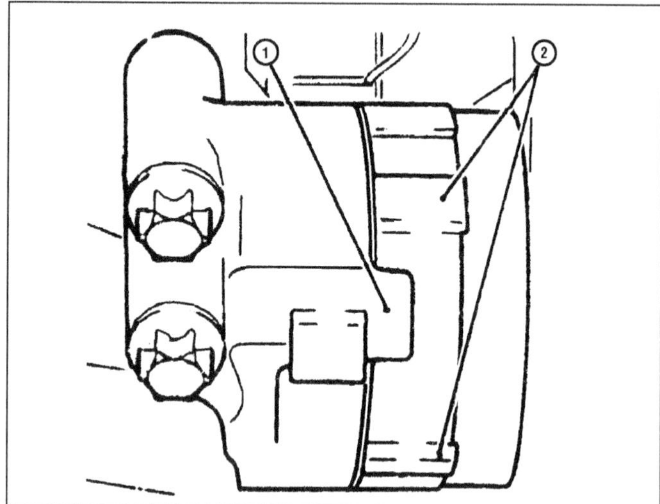

6.3b On 2.5 and 3.0 litre engines ensure the stop (1) on the drivebelt tensioner mounting plate is in between the lugs (2) on the arm

7 Proceed as described in paragraphs 2 to 4 inclusive, noting that the inspection aperture is at the rear of the caliper.
8 On completion, refit the rear roadwheels and lower the vehicle to the ground.

6 Auxiliary drivebelt - check and renewal

Check

1 Although the drivebelt tension is automatically adjusted by the spring-loaded tensioner, the belt itself should still be regularly checked for damage or deterioration.
2 With the engine stopped, inspect the full length of the drivebelt for cracks and separation of the belt plies. It will be necessary to turn the engine (using a spanner or socket and bar on the crankshaft pulley bolt) in order to move the belt from the pulleys so that the belt can be inspected thoroughly. Twist the belt between the pulleys so that both sides can be viewed. Also check for fraying, and glazing which gives the belt a shiny appearance. Check the pulleys for nicks, cracks, distortion and corrosion.

6.12 Lever the tensioner away from the belt then slip the belt off from its pulleys (2.5 litre engine shown)

3 Check the position of the drivebelt tensioner assembly arm in relation to the backplate. On 2.0 litre engines the arm indicator should be in between the stops on the backplate and should be free to move. On 2.5 and 3.0 litre engines the stop on the tensioner mounting plate should be positioned between the lugs on the arm and the arm should be free to move **(see illustrations)**.
4 If the belt shows signs of wear or damage, or the tensioner arm is against the stop, the belt must be renewed.

Renewal

2.0 litre engine

5 Prior to removal make a note of the correct routing of the belt around the various pulleys. If the belt is to be reused, also mark the direction of rotation on the belt to ensure the belt is refitted the same way around.
6 Using a suitable spanner or socket fitted to the tensioner pulley centre bolt, lever the tensioner away from the belt until there is sufficient slack to enable the belt to be slipped off from the pulleys. Carefully release the tensioner pulley until it is against its stop then remove the belt from the vehicle. If necessary, the tensioner can be locked in the released position by aligning the arm hole with the hole in the backplate and inserting a suitable tool/pin.
7 Manoeuvre the belt into position, routing it correctly around the pulleys; if the original belt is being fitted use the marks made prior to removal to ensure it is fitted the correct way around.
8 Lever the tensioner roller back against is spring, and seat the belt on the pulleys. Ensure the belt is centrally located on all pulleys then slowly release the tensioner pulley until the belt is correctly tensioned. **Do not** allow the tensioner to spring back and stress the belt.
9 Check the tensioner arm is correctly positioned in relation to the backplate (see paragraph 3).

2.5 and 3.0 litre engine

10 Remove the multi-ram air intake system pre-volume chamber and the secondary air injection system front connecting pipe as described in the relevant Parts of Chapter 4.
11 Prior to removal make a note of the correct routing of the belt around the various pulleys. If the belt is to be reused, also mark the direction of rotation on the belt to ensure the belt is refitted the same way around.
12 Using a suitable spanner or socket fitted to the tensioner pulley centre bolt, lever the tensioner away from the belt until there is sufficient slack to enable the belt to be slipped off from the pulleys **(see illustration)**. Carefully release the tensioner pulley until it is against its stop then remove the belt from the vehicle.
13 Manoeuvre the belt into position, routing it correctly around the pulleys; if the original belt is being fitted use the marks made prior to removal to ensure it is fitted the correct way around.
14 Lever the tensioner roller back against is spring, and seat the belt on the pulleys. Ensure the belt is centrally located on all pulleys then slowly release the tensioner pulley until the belt is correctly tensioned. **Do not** allow the tensioner to spring back and stress the belt.
15 Check the tensioner arm is correctly positioned in relation to the backplate (see paragraph 3) then refit the secondary air injection system connecting pipe and the multi-ram air intake system pre-volume chamber as described in the relevant part of Chapter 4.

7 Underbonnet/underbody hose and fluid leak - check

Cooling system

Warning: Refer to the safety information given in Safety First and Chapter 3 before disturbing any of the cooling system components.

1 Carefully check the radiator and heater coolant hoses along their entire length. Renew any hose which is cracked, swollen or which shows signs of deterioration. Cracks will show up better if the hose is squeezed. Pay close attention to the clips that secure the hoses to the cooling system components. Hose clips that have been over-tightened can pinch and puncture hoses, resulting in cooling system leaks **(see illustration)**.

2 Inspect all the cooling system components (hoses, joint faces, etc) for leaks. Where any problems of this nature are found on system components, renew the component or gasket with reference to Chapter 3.

HAYNES HiNT *A leak in the cooling system will usually manifest itself as white or rust-coloured, crusty deposits on the area adjacent to the leak*

Fuel system

Warning: Refer to the safety information given in Safety First and Chapter 4A before disturbing any of the fuel system components.

3 Petrol leaks can be difficult to pinpoint, unless the leakage is significant and hence easily visible. Fuel tends to evaporate quickly once it comes into contact with air, especially in a hot engine bay. Small drips can disappear before you get a chance to identify the point of leakage. If you suspect that there is a fuel leak from the area of the engine bay, leave the vehicle overnight then start the engine from cold, with the bonnet open. Metal components tend to shrink when they are cold, and rubber seals and hoses tend to harden, so any leaks will be more apparent whilst the engine is warming up from a cold start.

4 Check all fuel lines at their connections to the fuel rail, fuel pressure regulator and fuel filter (petrol models), Examine each rubber fuel hose along its length for splits or cracks. Check for leakage from the crimped joints between rubber and metal fuel lines. Examine the unions between the metal fuel lines and the fuel filter housing. Also check the area around the fuel injectors for signs of O-ring leakage.

5 To identify fuel leaks between the fuel tank and the engine bay, the vehicle should raised and securely supported on axle stands. Inspect the petrol tank and filler neck for punctures, cracks and other damage. The connection between the filler neck and tank is especially critical. Sometimes a rubber filler neck or connecting hose will leak due to loose retaining clamps or deteriorated rubber.

6 Carefully check all rubber hoses and metal fuel lines leading away from the petrol tank. Check for loose connections, deteriorated hoses, kinked lines, and other damage. Pay particular attention to the vent pipes and hoses, which often loop up around the filler neck and can become blocked or kinked, making tank filling difficult. Follow the fuel supply and return lines to the front of the vehicle, carefully inspecting them all the way for signs of damage or corrosion. Renew damaged sections as necessary.

Engine oil

7 Inspect the area around the camshaft cover, cylinder head, oil filter and sump joint faces. Bear in mind that, over a period of time, some very slight seepage from these areas is to be expected - what you are really looking for is any indication of a serious leak caused by gasket failure. Engine oil seeping from the base of the timing belt cover or the transmission bellhousing may be an indication of crankshaft or transmission input shaft oil seal failure. Should a leak be found, renew the failed gasket or oil seal by referring to the appropriate Chapters in this manual.

Automatic transmission fluid

8 Check the hoses leading to the transmission fluid cooler for leakage. Look for deterioration caused by corrosion and damage from grounding, or debris thrown up from the road surface. Automatic transmission fluid is a thin oil and is usually red in colour. Check the area around the propeller shaft seal at the rear of the transmission for signs of fluid leakage. Should a leak be found, check the fluid level as described in Section 19 then rectify the cause of leakage as soon as possible.

Power assisted steering (PAS) fluid

9 Examine the hose running between the fluid reservoir and the power steering pump, and the return hose running from the steering rack to the fluid reservoir. Also examine the high pressure supply hose between the pump and the steering rack.

10 Check the condition of each hose carefully. Look for deterioration caused by corrosion and damage from grounding, or debris thrown up from the road surface.

11 Pay particular attention to crimped unions, and the area surrounding the hoses that are secured with adjustable worm drive clips. Like automatic transmission fluid, PAS fluid is a thin oil, and is usually red or light brown in colour.

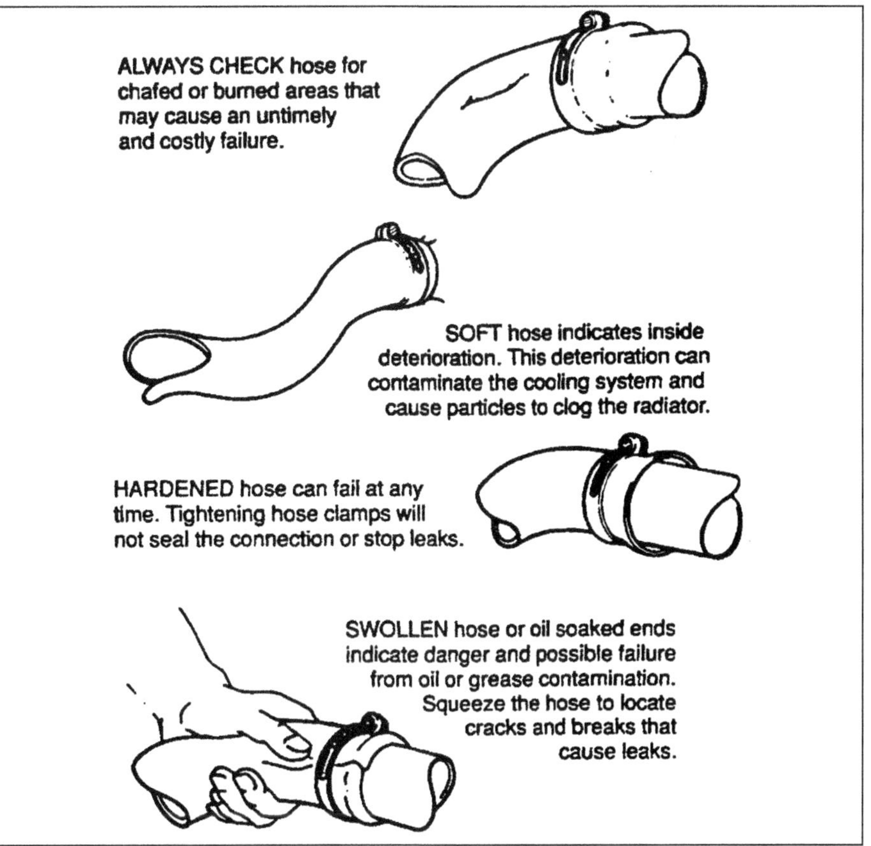

ALWAYS CHECK hose for chafed or burned areas that may cause an untimely and costly failure.
SOFT hose indicates inside deterioration. This deterioration can contaminate the cooling system and cause particles to clog the radiator.
HARDENED hose can fail at any time. Tightening hose clamps will not seal the connection or stop leaks.
SWOLLEN hose or oil soaked ends indicate danger and possible failure from oil or grease contamination. Squeeze the hose to locate cracks and breaks that cause leaks.

7.1 Possible causes of coolant hose failure

Air conditioning refrigerant

Warning: Refer to the safety information given in Safety First and Chapter 3, regarding the dangers of disturbing any of the air conditioning system components.

12 The air conditioning system is filled with a liquid refrigerant, which is retained under high pressure. If the air conditioning system is opened and depressurised without the aid of specialised equipment, the refrigerant will immediately turn into gas and escape into the atmosphere. If the liquid comes into contact with your skin, it can cause severe frostbite. In addition, the refrigerant contains substances which are environmentally damaging; for this reason, it should not be allowed to escape into the atmosphere in an uncontrolled fashion.

13 Any suspected air conditioning system leaks should be immediately referred to a Vauxhall dealer or air conditioning specialist. Leakage will be shown up as a steady drop in the level of refrigerant in the system.

14 Note that water may drip from the condenser drain pipe, underneath the car, immediately after the air conditioning system has been in use. This is normal, and should not be cause for concern.

Brake fluid

Warning: Refer to the safety information given in Safety First and Chapter 9, regarding the dangers of handling brake fluid.

15 Examine the area surrounding the brake pipe unions at the master cylinder for signs of leakage. Check the area around the base of fluid reservoir, for signs of leakage caused by seal failure. Also examine the brake pipe unions at the ABS hydraulic unit.

16 If fluid loss is evident, but the leak cannot be pinpointed in the engine bay, the brake calipers and underbody brake lines should be carefully checked with the vehicle raised and supported on axle stands **(see illustration)**. Leakage of fluid from the braking system is a serious fault that must be rectified immediately.

17 Brake/clutch hydraulic fluid is a toxic substance with a watery consistency. New fluid is almost colourless, but it becomes darker with age and use.

Manual transmission fluid

18 Check the area around the propeller shaft seal at the rear of the transmission for signs of fluid leakage. Should a leak be found, check the transmission fluid level as described in Chapter 7A then rectify the cause of leakage as soon as possible.

Final drive unit differential fluid

19 Check the area around the driveshaft and propeller shaft seals, and the flange seal on the rear of the final drive unit for signs of fluid leakage. Should a leak be found, check the differential fluid level as described in Chapter 8 then rectify the cause of leakage as soon as possible.

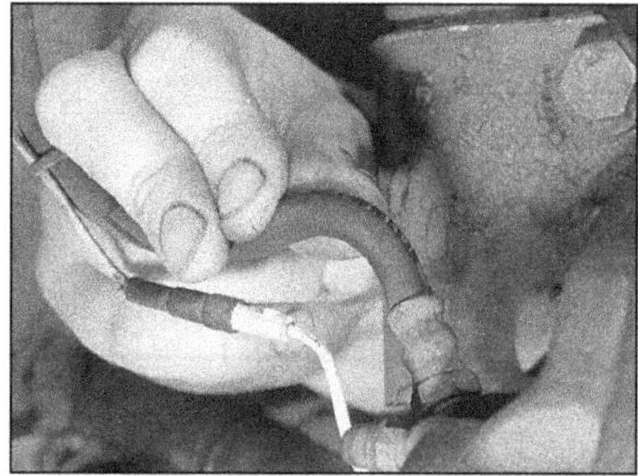

7.16 Inspecting the flexible hose connection to a front brake caliper

Unidentified fluid leaks

20 If there are signs that a fluid of some description is leaking from the vehicle, but you cannot identify the type of fluid or its exact origin, park the vehicle overnight and slide a large piece of card underneath it. Providing that the card is positioned in roughly the right location, even the smallest leak will show up on the card. Not only will this help you to pinpoint the exact location of the leak, it should be easier to identify the fluid from its colour. Bear in mind, though, that the leak may only be occurring when the engine is running!

Vacuum hoses

21 Although the braking system is hydraulically-operated, the brake servo unit amplifies the effort applied at the brake pedal, by making use of the vacuum in the inlet manifold, generated by the engine. Vacuum is ported to the servo by means of a large-bore hose. Any leaks that develop in this hose will reduce the effectiveness of the braking system, and may affect the running of the engine.

22 In addition, a number of the underbonnet components, particularly the emission control components, are driven by vacuum supplied from the inlet manifold via narrow-bore rubber and plastic hoses. A leak in a vacuum hose means that air is being drawn into the hose (rather than escaping from it) and this makes leakage very difficult to detect. One method is to use an old length of vacuum hose as a kind of stethoscope - hold one end close to (but not in!) your ear and use the other end to probe the area around the suspected leak. When the end of the hose is directly over a vacuum leak, a hissing sound will be heard clearly through the hose. Care must be taken to avoid contacting hot or moving components, as the engine must be running, when testing in this manner. Renew any vacuum hoses that are found to be defective.

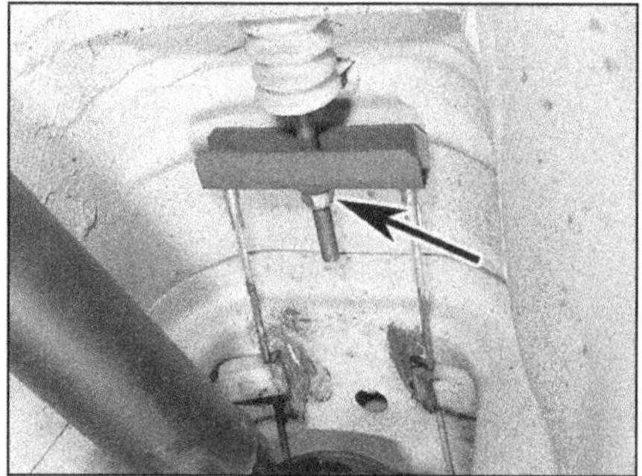

9.5 Handbrake cable adjustment nut (arrowed)

8 Bodywork/underbody corrosion protection - check

1 This work should be carried out by a Vauxhall/Opel dealer in order to validate the vehicle warranty. The work includes a thorough inspection of the vehicle paintwork and underbody for damage and corrosion

9 Handbrake operation - check and adjustment

1 Chock the front wheels, then jack up the rear of the vehicle and support it securely on axle stands (see *Jacking and Vehicle Support*). Remove the rear roadwheels.

2 Fully release the handbrake lever, then apply it to the third notch. Check that both rear wheels can still rotate by attempting to turn them by hand (ensure that the transmission is in neutral). Release the handbrake lever.

3 Fully apply the handbrake lever, so that the rear wheels are locked, counting how many notches the lever passes through. If the handbrake lever passes through more than seven notches before the rear wheels lock, adjustment is required.

4 If adjustment is necessary, first fully release the handbrake, then pull it up to the third notch.

5 Working underneath the vehicle, unbolt the exhaust system heat shields from the floorpan. Locate the handbrake cable adjustment nut, at the cable compensation bar, above the propeller shaft. Fully slacken the adjustment nut so that there is a small amount of clearance between it and the compensation bar **(see illustration)**.

6 Working on one brake disc at a time, position the hole in the disc over the serrated adjustment nut on the adjuster at the top of the backplate. Using a screwdriver inserted through the hole, turn the nut until the brake disc locks, then turn the nut in opposite direction until the disc is just free **(see illustration)**. Repeat the adjustment on the remaining rear brake.

7 Check that the handbrake lever is still positioned on the third notch, then working underneath the vehicle, tighten the handbrake cable adjustment nut against the compensation bar, until the handbrake shoes just start to take effect - test for this by turning the brake discs by hand.

8 Refit the rear wheels, then carry out a final check of the handbrake adjustment; the rear wheels should turn freely with the lever applied to the third notch and should be fully locked before passing through the seventh notch. Tighten the wheel bolts to the specified torque then lower the car the ground. Check the operation of the handbrake before using the vehicle on the road.

9 After fitting new handbrake shoes, the shoes should be bedded-in by driving a short distance (approximately 300 metres) at low speed with the handbrake lever lightly applied. Check, and if necessary adjust the handbrake again after completing the bedding-in.

10 Suspension and steering condition and operation - check

Front suspension and steering check

1 Raise the front of the vehicle, and securely support it on axle stands (see *Jacking and Vehicle Support*).

2 Visually inspect the balljoint dust covers and the steering rack-and-pinion gaiters for splits, chafing or deterioration. Any wear of these components will cause loss of lubricant, together with dirt and water entry, resulting in rapid deterioration of the balljoints or steering gear.

3 Check the power steering fluid hoses for chafing or deterioration, and the pipe and hose unions for fluid leaks. Also check for signs of fluid leakage under pressure from the steering gear rubber gaiters, which would indicate failed fluid seals within the steering gear.

4 Grasp the roadwheel at the 12 o'clock and 6 o'clock positions, and try to rock it **(see illustration)**. Very slight free play may be felt, but if the movement is appreciable, further investigation is necessary to determine the source. Continue rocking the wheel while an assistant depresses the footbrake. If the movement is now eliminated or significantly reduced, it is likely that the hub bearings are at fault. If the free play is still evident with the footbrake depressed, then there is wear in the suspension joints or mountings.

5 Now grasp the wheel at the 9 o'clock and 3 o'clock positions, and try to rock it as before. Any movement felt now may again be caused by wear in the hub bearings or the steering track-rod balljoints. If the outer balljoint is worn, the visual movement will be obvious. If the inner joint is suspect, it can be felt by

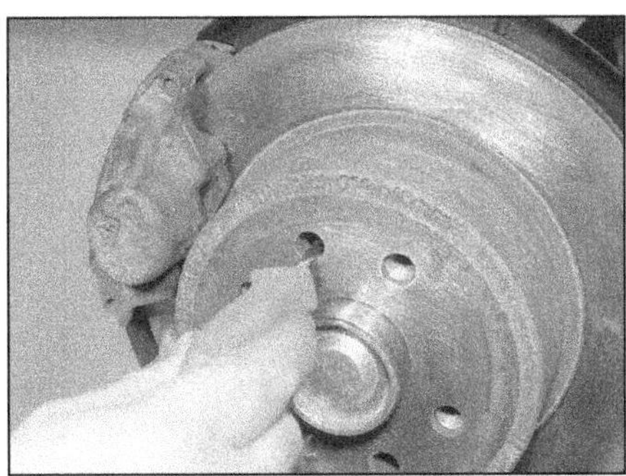

9.6 Adjusting the handbrake screws using a screwdriver through the hole in the disc/hub flange

placing a hand over the rack-and-pinion rubber gaiter and gripping the track-rod. If the wheel is now rocked, movement will be felt at the inner joint if wear has taken place.

6 Using a large screwdriver or flat bar, check for wear in the suspension mounting bushes by levering between the relevant suspension component and its attachment point. Some movement is to be expected, as the mountings are made of rubber, but excessive wear should be obvious. Also check the condition of any visible rubber bushes, looking for splits, cracks or contamination of the rubber.

7 With the car standing on its wheels, have an assistant turn the steering wheel back-and-forth, about an eighth of a turn each way. There should be very little, if any, lost movement between the steering wheel and roadwheels. If this is not the case, closely observe the joints and mountings previously described. In addition, check the steering column universal joints for wear, and also check the rack-and-pinion steering gear itself.

Rear suspension check

8 Chock the front wheels, then jack up the rear of the vehicle and support securely on axle stands (see *Jacking and Vehicle Support*).

9 Working as described previously for the front suspension, check the rear hub bearings, the suspension bushes and the strut or shock absorber mountings (as applicable) for wear.

10.4 To check for play in the wheel bearing, grasp the roadwheel at the 12 o'clock and 6 o'clock positions, and try to rock it

Shock absorber check

10 Check for any signs of fluid leakage around the shock absorber body, or from the rubber gaiter around the piston rod. Should any fluid be noticed, the shock absorber is defective internally, and should be renewed. **Note:** *Shock absorbers should always be renewed in pairs on the same axle.*

11 The efficiency of the shock absorber may be checked by bouncing the vehicle at each corner. Generally speaking, the body will return to its normal position and stop after being depressed. If it rises and returns on a rebound, the shock absorber is probably suspect. Also examine the shock absorber upper and lower mountings for any signs of wear.

11 Wheel bolt torque - check and adjustment

Note: As well as being potentially damaging to the vehicle's roadwheels, over-tightened wheel bolts may cause problems if you have to change a wheel by the side of the road. By ensuring that the wheel bolts are tightened to the correct torque, you could save yourself a lot of time and trouble in an emergency situation.

1 Slacken the front wheel securing bolts slightly, then apply the handbrake firmly, raise the front of the vehicle, and securely support it on axle stands (see *Jacking and Vehicle Support*).

2 Fully slacken the each of the wheel bolts in turn and clear any dirt of debris from the threads. Re-insert the wheel bolts and tighten them to the specified torque setting using a good quality torque wrench.

3 Repeat the operation at the opposite wheel, then lower the car the ground.

4 Chock the front wheels, then jack up the rear of the vehicle and support securely on axle stands (see *Jacking and Vehicle Support*). Repeat the operations described in paragraphs 2 and 3.

12 Headlight and auxiliary driving light beam alignment - check

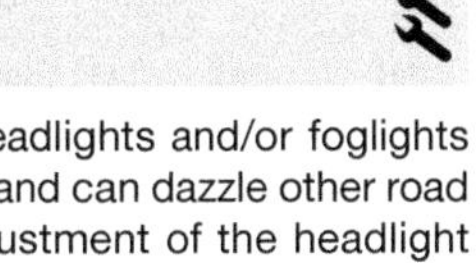

1 Badly adjusted headlights and/or foglights cause poor visibility and can dazzle other road users. Accurate adjustment of the headlight and auxiliary driving light beams is only possible using optical beam-setting equipment, and this work should therefore be carried out by a Vauxhall/Opel dealer or suitably-equipped workshop.

2 For reference, the headlights can be adjusted using the adjuster assemblies fitted to the front upper outer mounting and to the rear inner mounting. The inner screw is for horizontal adjustment and the outer one for

vertical adjustment. When adjusting the headlight aim, ensure that the facia -mounted range adjustment switch is set to position 0 (see paragraph 3).

3 All models have an electric headlight beam adjustment range system, controlled via a rotary switch in the facia*. The recommended settings are as follows.

0 Front seat(s) occupied
1 All seats occupied
2 All seats occupied, and load in luggage compartment
3 Driver's seat occupied and load in the luggage compartment

**On models built from 1998 onwards with Xenon headlights, an automatic headlamp range adjustment system is fitted, to which no manual adjustment can be made; see Chapter 12 for details.*

13 Road test

Instruments and electrical equipment

1 Check the operation of all instruments and electrical equipment.

2 Make sure that all instruments read correctly, and switch on all electrical equipment in turn, to check that it functions properly.

Steering and suspension

3 Check for any abnormalities in the steering, suspension, handling or road feel.

4 Drive the vehicle, and check that there are no unusual vibrations or noises.

5 Check that the steering feels positive, with no excessive sloppiness, or roughness, and check for any suspension noises when cornering and driving over bumps.

Drivetrain

6 Check the performance of the engine, clutch, transmission and driveshafts.

7 Listen for any unusual noises from the engine, clutch and transmission.

8 Make sure that the engine runs smoothly when idling, and that there is no hesitation when accelerating.

9 Check that, where applicable, the clutch action is smooth and progressive, that the drive is taken up smoothly, and that the pedal travel is not excessive. Also listen for any noises when the clutch pedal is depressed.

10 Check that all gears can be engaged smoothly without noise, and that the gear lever action is not abnormally vague or notchy.

11 On automatic transmission models, make sure that all gearchanges occur smoothly, without snatching, and without an increase in engine speed between changes. Check that all of the gear positions can be selected with the vehicle at rest. If any problems are found, they should be referred to a Vauxhall/Opel dealer.

Check the operation and performance of the braking system

12 Make sure that the vehicle does not pull to one side when braking, and that the wheels do not lock prematurely when braking hard.

13 Check that there is no vibration through the steering when braking.

14 Check that the handbrake operates correctly, without excessive movement of the lever, and that it holds the vehicle stationary on a slope.

15 Test the operation of the brake servo unit as follows. Depress the footbrake four or five times to exhaust the vacuum, then start the engine. As the engine starts, there should be a noticeable give in the brake pedal as vacuum builds up. Allow the engine to run for at least two minutes, and then switch it off. If the brake pedal is now depressed again, it should be possible to detect a hiss from the servo as the pedal is depressed. After about four or five applications, no further hissing should be heard, and the pedal should feel considerably harder.

14 Wheel alignment - check

1 Accurate wheel alignment is essential for positive, accurate steering, stable road holding and to prevent abnormal tyre wear. Wheel alignment checking is carried out with the car loaded to its kerbside weight, and with the tyre pressures correctly adjusted.

2 The front toe setting, front camber angle, rear toe setting and rear camber angle are all adjustable, but can only be checked using specialised equipment; work of this nature should therefore be entrusted to a garage or suitably-equipped tyre specialist.

15 Exhaust system - check

1 Park the vehicle on a level surface and switch off the engine. Chock the front wheels, then raise the rear of the vehicle and support it securely on axle stands - refer to *Jacking and vehicle support* in *Reference*.

2 With the engine cold (wait at least an hour after switching off the engine), check the complete exhaust system from the engine to the end of the tailpipe.

3 Check the exhaust pipes and connections for evidence of leaks, severe corrosion and damage. Make sure that all brackets and mountings are in good condition, and that all relevant nuts and bolts are tight. Leakage at any of the joints or in other parts of the system will usually show up as a black, sooty stain in the vicinity of the leak.

4 Rattles and vibrations can often be traced to the exhaust system. Tap the silencer units with a soft mallet and listen for noises caused by corroded or displaced baffle material. **Do not** strike the catalytic converter, as this may damage the ceramic block inside.

5 Carefully rock the pipes and silencers from side to side on their mountings. If the components are able to come into contact with the body or suspension parts, look for broken or worn rubber mountings.

Every 20 000 miles or 2 years

16 Air filter element - renewal

1 The air cleaner is located in the front right-hand corner of the engine compartment.

2 Release the retaining clip and disconnect the intake duct from the air cleaner housing.

3 Release the retaining clips then lift the air cleaner cover and filter element out of position.

4 Wipe out the casing and the cover.

5 Fit the new filter, noting that the rubber locating flange should be uppermost, and secure the cover with the clips.

6 Reconnect the intake duct to the air cleaner housing and secure it in position with the retaining clip.

17 Pollen filter - renewal

1 Open the bonnet and support it in the upright position.

2 Carefully peel the rubber beading away from the bulkhead seam, at the rear of the engine compartment, on the drivers side of the car **(see illustration)**.

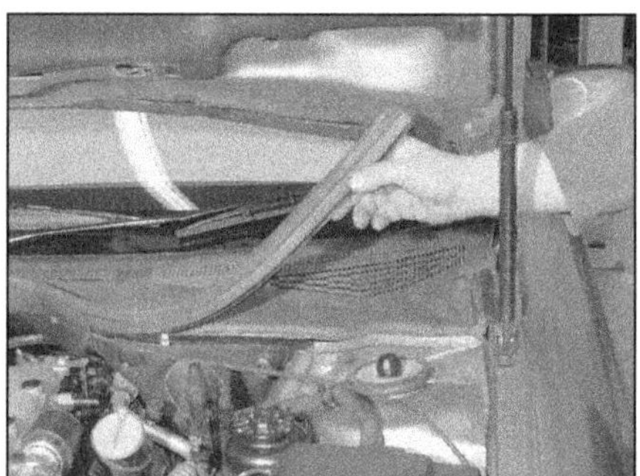

17.2 Carefully peel the rubber beading away from the bulkhead seam

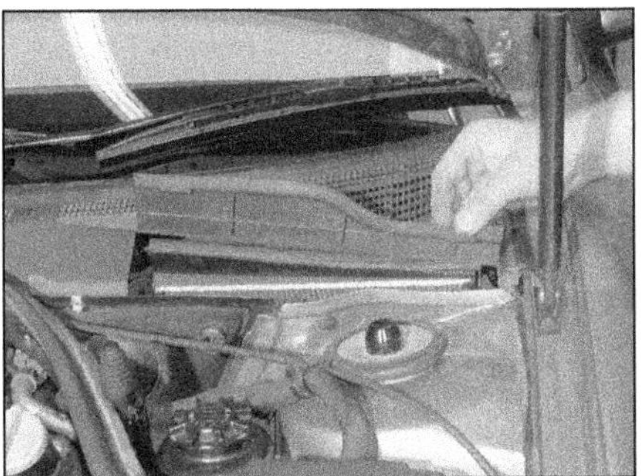
17.3 Hinge the grille panel upwards

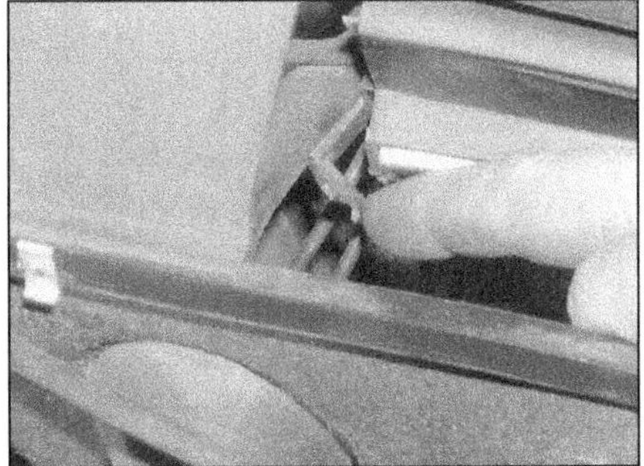
17.4a Release the clips . . .

17.4b . . . then withdraw the pollen filter element

3 Hinge the grille panel upwards to expose the pollen filter housing **(see illustration)**.
4 Release the clips at either side of the housing, then withdraw the pollen filter element **(see illustrations)**.
5 Slide the new filter element into the housing and secure it in position with the clips.
6 Hinge the grille panel down over the housing and press the rubber beading into position on the bulkhead seam.

18 Lock and hinge lubrication

1 Work around the vehicle and lubricate the hinges of the bonnet, doors and tailgate/boot lid with a light machine oil.

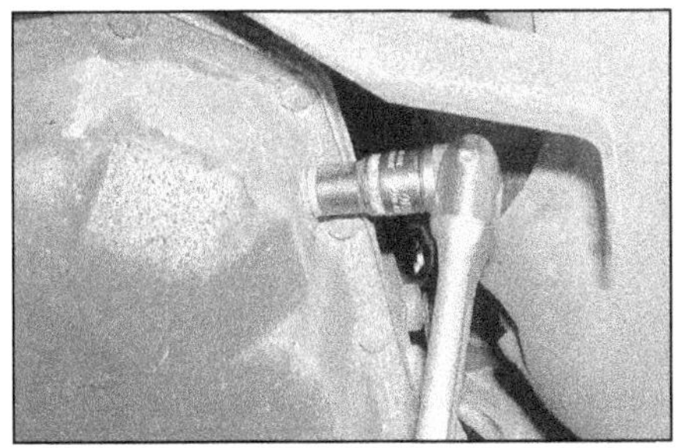
19.3 Removing the automatic transmission unit fluid level plug

2 Lightly lubricate the bonnet release mechanism and exposed section of inner cable with a smear of grease.
3 Check the security and operation of all hinges, latches and locks, adjusting them where required. Check the operation of the central locking system.
4 Check the condition and operation of the tailgate/boot lid struts, renewing them both if either is leaking or no longer able to support the tailgate/boot lid securely when raised.

19 Automatic transmission fluid level - check

1 The transmission fluid level must be checked with the engine warm. For the check to be accurate, Vauxhall state that the transmission fluid temperature should ideally be 60°C but can be anywhere in the range of 45 to 85°C (113 to 185°F).
2 Take the vehicle on a short run to warm the engine and transmission unit up to operating temperature. On your return position the vehicle over an inspection pit, on vehicle ramps, or jack it up, but make sure that it is level.
3 Start the engine and allow it to idle. Wipe clean the area around the level plug which is fitted to the right-hand side of the transmission main sump **(see illustration)**. Unscrew the plug and clean it.
4 The oil level should reach the lower edge of the level plug hole. If topping up is necessary, add the specified type of oil through the level plug hole until oil begins to trickle out.
5 Allow the excess oil to drain out then fit a new sealing washer to the level plug and refit it to the sump, tightening it to the specified torque.

20 Handbrake - shoe condition check

1 Refer to the information given in Chapter 9 for details.

21 Driveshaft gaiter condition - check

1 Chock the front wheels, then jack up the rear of the vehicle and support it on axle stands.
2 With the handbrake released turn each wheel separately and check the driveshaft rubber gaiters for splits and damage. Check that the securing clips are in good condition and shows no signs of damage or corrosion. Driveshaft grease sprayed in a line along the underside of the car, above the joint is a sign that the gaiter has failed and requires renewal.

Every 40 000 miles or 4 years

22 Spark plugs - renewal

1 The correct functioning of the spark plugs is vital for the correct running and efficiency of the engine. It is essential that the plugs fitted are appropriate for the engine; suitable types are specified at the beginning of this Chapter, or in the vehicle's Owner's Handbook. If the correct type is used and the engine is in good condition, the spark plugs should not need attention between scheduled replacement intervals. Spark plug cleaning is rarely necessary, and should not be attempted unless specialised equipment is available, as damage can easily be caused to the firing ends.
2 On 2.0 litre DOHC engines, undo the retaining screws and lift off the spark plug cover from the top of the camshaft cover **(see illustration)**.
3 On 2.5 and 3.0 litre engines, carry out the following operations referring to Chapter 4A for further information.

a) Remove the idle speed control valve.
b) On models with air conditioning, undo the retaining bolt and remove the air conditioning pipe retaining clip from the left-hand cylinder head.

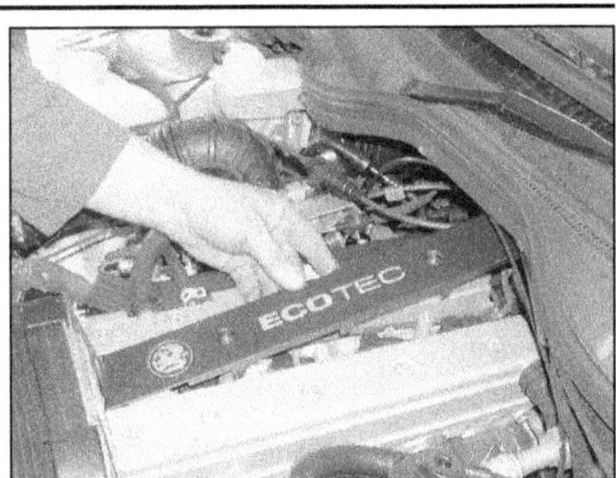

22.2 On 2.0 litre DOHC engine remove the spark plug cover to gain access to the plugs

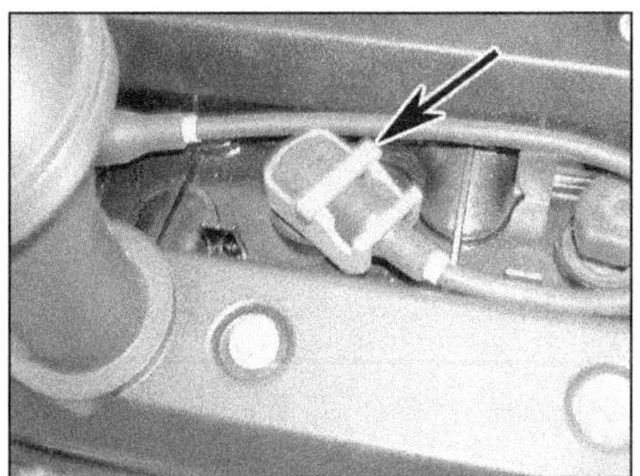
22.4a Unclip the tool (arrowed) . . .

22.4b . . . and use it to pull the HT leads off from the plugs (2.5 litre engine shown)

22.10 The multi-electrode plugs fitted as standard should not be adjusted

c) Undo the bolts securing the wiring harness cover to the inlet manifold and position the harness clear of the left-hand cylinder head spark plugs.

d) Unscrew the union nut and disconnect the braking system servo unit vacuum hose from the manifold.

e) To improve access to the plugs on the right-hand cylinder head, unclip the accelerator cable from its mounting bracket then unbolt and remove the mounting bracket from the inlet manifold.

4 On all engines, if the marks on the original-equipment spark plug (HT) leads cannot be seen, mark the leads to correspond to the cylinder the lead serves. Pull the leads from the plugs by gripping the end fitting, not the lead, otherwise the lead connection may be fractured. On 2.0 litre DOHC engines and all 2.5 and 3.0 litre engines use the tool clipped to one of the plug leads to pull the HT leads from the plugs **(see illustrations)**.

5 It is advisable to remove the dirt from the spark plug recesses using a clean brush, vacuum cleaner or compressed air before removing the plugs, to prevent dirt dropping into the cylinders.

6 Unscrew the plugs from the cylinder head using a spark plug spanner, suitable box spanner or a deep socket and extension bar. Keep the socket aligned with the spark plug - if it is forcibly moved to one side, the ceramic insulator may be broken off. As each plug is removed, examine it as follows.

7 Examination of the spark plugs will give a good indication of the condition of the engine. If the insulator nose of the spark plug is clean and white, with no deposits, this is indicative of a weak mixture or too hot a plug (a hot plug transfers heat away from the electrode slowly, a cold plug transfers heat away quickly).

8 If the tip and insulator nose are covered with hard black-looking deposits, then this is indicative that the mixture is too rich. Should the plug be black and oily, then it is likely that the engine is fairly worn, as well as the mixture being too rich.

9 If the insulator nose is covered with light tan to greyish-brown deposits, then the mixture is correct and it is likely that the engine is in good condition.

10 All engines are fitted with multi-electrode plugs as standard by Vauxhall **(see illustration)**. On these plugs, the electrode gaps are all preset and no attempt should be made to bend the electrodes.

11 If non-standard single electrode plugs are to be installed, the spark plug electrode gap is of considerable importance. If the gap is too large or too small, the size of the spark and its efficiency will be seriously impaired and it will not perform correctly under all engine speed and load conditions. The gap should be set to the value specified by the manufacturer.

12 To set the gap on a single electrode plug, measure it with a feeler blade or spark plug gap gauge and then carefully bend the outer plug electrode until the correct gap is achieved. The centre electrode should never be bent, as this may crack the insulator and cause plug failure, if nothing worse. If using feeler blades, the gap is correct when the appropriate-size blade is a firm sliding fit **(see illustrations)**.

13 Special spark plug electrode gap adjusting tools are available from most motor accessory shops, or from some spark plug manufacturers **(see illustration).**

14 Before fitting the spark plugs, check that the threaded connector sleeves are tight, and that the plug exterior surfaces and threads are clean.

HAYNES HiNT

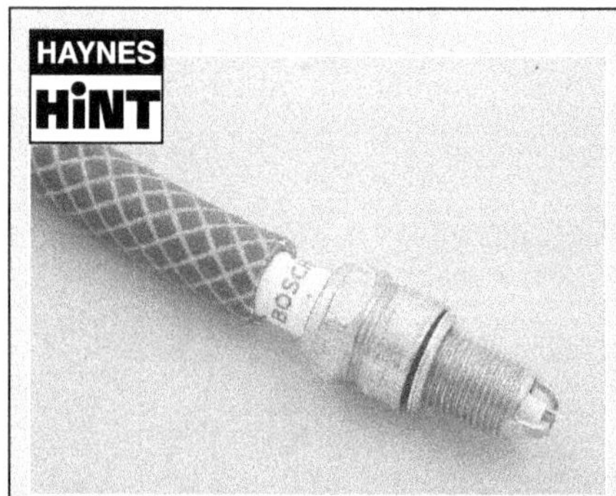

It is very often difficult to insert spark plugs into their holes without cross-threading them. To avoid this possibility, fit a short length of 5/16 inch internal diameter rubber hose over the end of the spark plug. The flexible hose acts as a universal joint to help align the plug with the plug hole. Should the plug begin to cross-thread, the hose will slip on the spark plug, preventing thread damage to the aluminium cylinder head

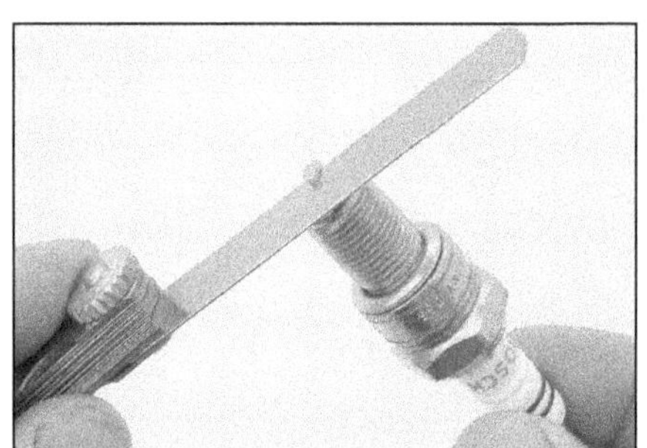
22.12a If single electrode plugs are being fitted, check the electrode gap using a feeler gauge . . .

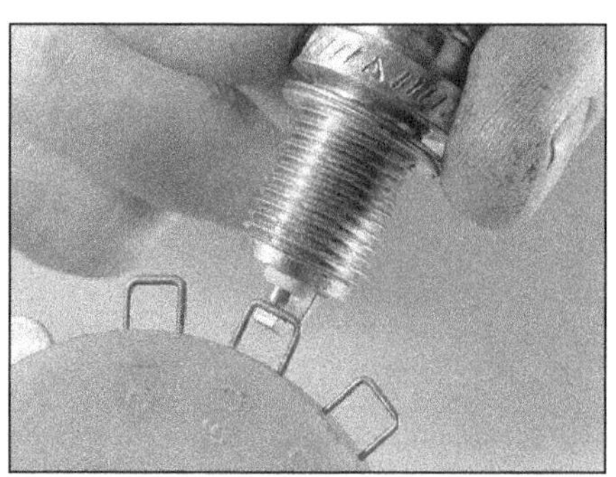
22.12b . . . or a wire gauge . . .

22.13 . . . and if necessary adjust the gap by bending the electrode

22.17 On 2.0 litre DOHC engines refit the spark plug cover and securely tighten its retaining screws

15 Remove the rubber hose (if used), and tighten the plug to the specified torque using the spark plug socket and a torque wrench. Refit the remaining spark plugs in the same manner.

16 Securely reconnect the HT leads in their correct order.

17 On 2.0 litre DOHC engines refit the spark plug cover and securely tighten its retaining screws **(see illustration)**.

18 On 2.5 and 3.0 litre engines carry out the following operations, referring to Chapter 4A for further information.

a) Refit the accelerator cable bracket to the manifold and adjust the accelerator cable.

b) Reconnect the servo unit vacuum hose to the manifold and tighten to the specified torque.

c) Refit the wiring cover bolts and (where necessary) the air conditioning pipe bracket.

d) Refit the idle speed control valve.

23 Fuel filter - renewal

1 The fuel filter is located under the rear of the vehicle, just in front of the fuel tank.

2 Depressurise the fuel system as described in Chapter 4A.

3 Chock the front wheels, then jack up the rear of the vehicle and support on axle stands (see *Jacking and Vehicle Support*).

4 Release the retaining clip holding the filter to the underbody. Before removing the filter, note the orientation of the fuel flow direction arrow **(see illustration)**.

5 Position a suitable container below the fuel filter, to catch spilt fuel.

6 Release the connectors and disconnect the fuel hoses from the fuel filter, noting their locations to ensure correct refitting **(see illustration)**. A Vauxhall/Opel special tool is available to disconnect the hose connectors, but provided care it taken, the connections can be released using a pair of pliers or a screwdriver. Be prepared for fuel spillage, and take adequate fire precautions.

7 Withdraw the filter from under the vehicle.

8 Fit the quick-release fitting clips to the new filter offer up the filter making sure the flow direction arrow on the filter body pointing in the direction of fuel flow **(see illustration)**.

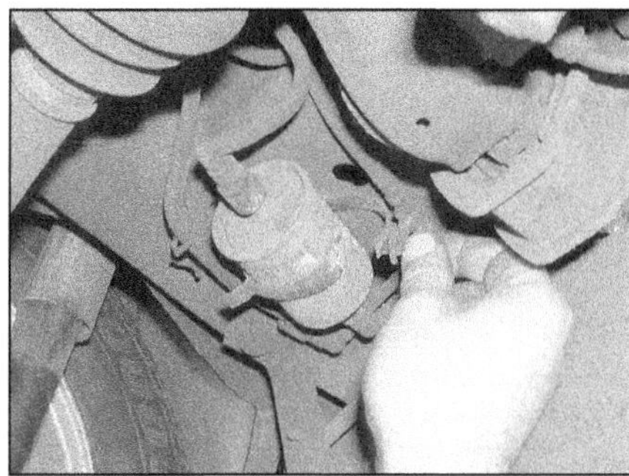
23.4 Release the retaining clip and free the fuel filter from the body

9 Securely clip both hoses onto the filter then secure the filter in position with the retaining clip.

10 Start the engine and check the filter hose unions for signs of leaks. If leakage is evident, stop the engine immediately and rectify the problem without delay.

11 If all is well, stop the engine and lower the vehicle to the ground.

24 Timing belt - renewal

1 Refer to the information given in Chapter 2A, 2B or 2C (as applicable).

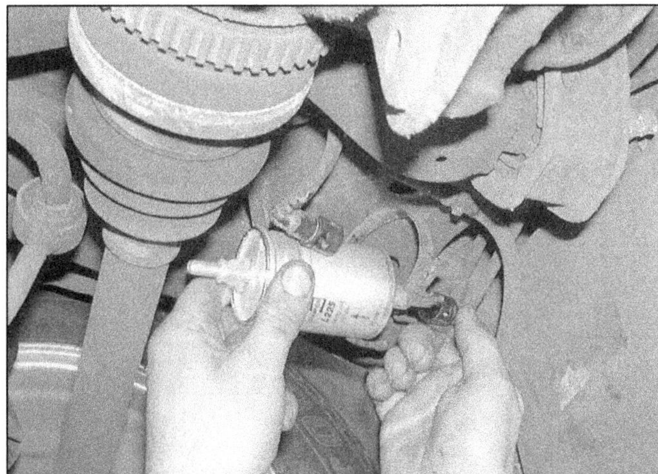
23.6 Depress the quick-release fitting tabs and detach the hoses from the fuel filter

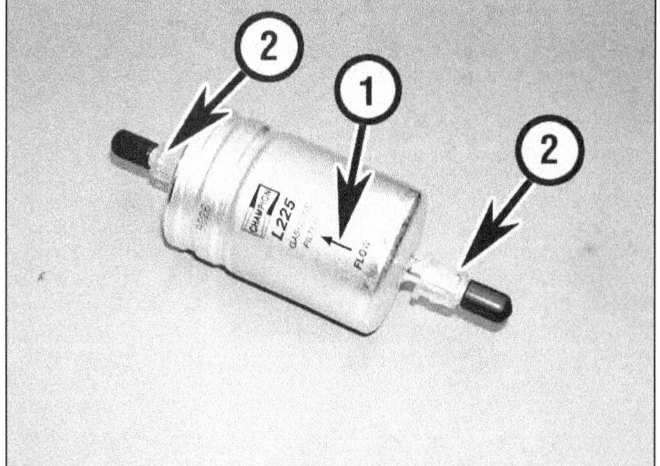

23.8 On refitting ensure the arrow (1) on the filter is pointing in the direction of fuel flow and the quick-release fitting clips (2) are correctly fitted

Every 70 000 miles or 7 years

25 Automatic transmission fluid - renewal

1 Renew the transmission fluid and filter assembly as described in Section 2 of Chapter 7B.

Every 2 years, regardless of mileage

26 Brake fluid - renewal

Warning: Brake hydraulic fluid can harm your eyes and damage painted surfaces, so use extreme caution when handling and pouring it. Do not use fluid that has been standing open for some time, as it absorbs moisture from the air. Excess moisture can cause a dangerous loss of braking effectiveness.

1 The procedure is similar to that for the bleeding of the hydraulic system as described in Chapter 9.

2 Working as described in Chapter 9, open the first bleed screw in the sequence, and pump the brake pedal gently until nearly all the old fluid has been emptied from the master cylinder reservoir. Top-up to the MAX level with new fluid, and continue pumping until only the new fluid remains in the reservoir, and new fluid can be seen emerging from the bleed screw. Tighten the screw, and top the reservoir level up to the MAX level line.

> HAYNES HiNT ***Old hydraulic fluid is invariably much darker in colour than the new, making it easy to distinguish the two.***

3 Work through all the remaining bleed screws in the sequence until new fluid can be seen at all of them. Be careful to keep the master cylinder reservoir topped-up to above the MIN level at all times, or air may enter the system and greatly increase the length of the task.

4 When the operation is complete, check that all bleed screws are securely tightened, and that their dust caps are refitted. Wash off all traces of spilt fluid, and recheck the master cylinder reservoir fluid level.

5 Check the operation of the brakes before taking the car on the road.

28.3 Open the drain plug at the base of the radiator (arrowed)

27 Remote control keyfob battery - renewal

Caution: The following procedure must be completed within 3 minutes, otherwise the remote control unit will have to be re-programmed.

1 Using a small flat-bladed screwdriver, prise the battery cover from the remote control unit.

2 Note how the battery is fitted, then carefully remove it from the contacts.

3 Fit the new battery and refit the cover making sure that it clips fully onto the base.

28 Coolant - renewal

Cooling system draining

Warning: Wait until the engine is cold before starting this procedure. Do not allow antifreeze to come in contact with your skin, or with the painted surfaces of the vehicle. Rinse off spills immediately with plenty of water. Never leave antifreeze lying around in an open container, or in a puddle in the driveway or on the garage floor. Children and pets are attracted by its sweet smell, but antifreeze can be fatal if ingested.

1 With the engine completely cold, remove the expansion tank filler cap. Turn the cap anti-clockwise, wait until any pressure remaining in the system is released, then unscrew it and lift it off.

2 Where applicable, remove the engine undershield, then position a suitable container beneath the left hand side of the radiator.

3 Open the drain plug at the base of the radiator, and allow the coolant to drain into the container **(see illustration)**.

4 When the flow of coolant stops, close the drain plug securely.

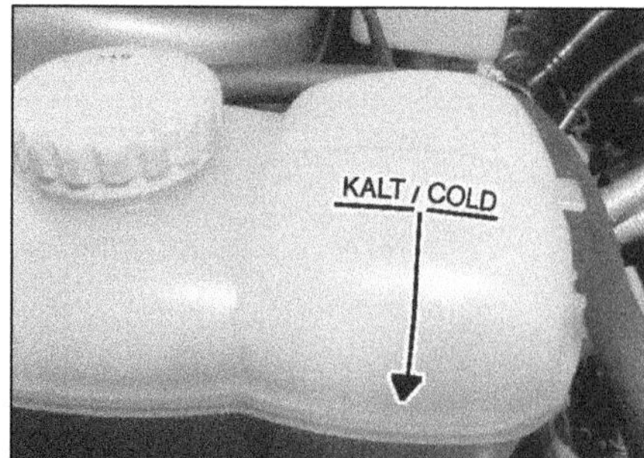

28.18 Slowly fill the system via the expansion tank filler neck, until the coolant level again reaches the KALT/COLD mark on the side of the expansion tank

5 If the coolant has been drained for a reason other than renewal, then provided it is clean and less than two years old, it can be re-used, though this is not recommended.

Cooling system flushing

6 If coolant renewal has been neglected, or if the antifreeze mixture has become diluted, then in time, the cooling system may gradually lose efficiency, as the coolant passages become restricted due to rust, scale deposits, and other sediment. The cooling system efficiency can be restored by flushing the system clean.

7 The radiator should be flushed independently of the engine, to avoid unnecessary contamination.

Radiator flushing

8 Disconnect the top and bottom hoses and any other relevant hoses from the radiator, with reference to Chapter 3.

9 Insert a garden hose into the radiator top inlet. Direct a flow of clean water through the radiator, and continue flushing until clean water emerges from the radiator bottom outlet.

10 If after a reasonable period, the water still does not run clear, the radiator can be flushed with a good proprietary cleaning agent. It is important that the manufacturer's instructions are followed carefully. If the contamination is particularly bad, remove the radiator, insert the hose in the radiator bottom outlet, and reverse-flush the radiator.

Engine flushing

11 Remove the thermostat as described in Chapter 3 then, if the radiator top hose has been disconnected from the engine, temporarily reconnect the hose.

12 With the top and bottom hoses disconnected from the radiator, insert a garden hose into the radiator top hose. Direct a clean flow of water through the engine, and continue flushing until clean water emerges from the radiator bottom hose.

13 On completion of flushing, refit the thermostat and reconnect the hoses with reference to Chapter 3.

Cooling system filling

14 Before attempting to fill the cooling system, make sure that all hoses and clips are in good condition, and that the clips are tight. Note that an antifreeze mixture must be used all year round, to prevent corrosion of the engine components.

15 Remove the expansion tank filler cap, and top the level up to the KALT/COLD mark.

6-cylinder engine models

16 Disconnect the heater supply (upper) hose from the bulkhead connection (see Chapter 3).

17 Pour coolant into the disconnected heater hose with the aid of a funnel, until no more coolant will flow in, then reconnect the heater hose to the bulkhead connection and tighten the clip securely.

18 Slowly fill the system via the expansion tank filler neck, until the coolant level again reaches the KALT/COLD mark on the side of the expansion tank **(see illustration)**.

All models

19 Refit and tighten the expansion tank filler cap.
20 Start the engine, and allow it to run until it reaches normal operating temperature (until the cooling fan cuts in and out). The cooling system will bleed automatically as the engine warms up.
21 Stop the engine, and allow it to cool, then re-check the coolant level with reference to *Weekly checks*. Top-up the level if necessary and refit the expansion tank filler cap. Where applicable, refit the engine undershield.

Antifreeze mixture

22 The antifreeze should always be renewed at the specified intervals. This is necessary not only to maintain the antifreeze properties, but also to prevent corrosion which would otherwise occur as the corrosion inhibitors become progressively less effective.
23 Always use an ethylene-glycol based antifreeze which is suitable for use in mixed-metal cooling systems. The quantity of antifreeze and levels of protection are given in the Specifications.
24 Before adding antifreeze, the cooling system should be completely drained, preferably flushed, and all hoses checked for condition and security.
25 After filling with antifreeze, a label should be attached to the expansion tank, stating the type and concentration of antifreeze used, and the date installed. Any subsequent topping-up should be made with the same type and concentration of antifreeze.
26 Do not use engine antifreeze in the windscreen/tailgate washer system, as it will cause damage to the vehicle paintwork. A screenwash additive should be added to the washer system in the quantities stated on the bottle.

Chapter 2 Part A:
2.0 litre SOHC engine in-car repair procedures

Contents

Degrees of difficulty

Easy, suitable for novice with little experience 	**Fairly easy,** suitable for beginner with some experience 	**Fairly difficult,** suitable for competent DIY mechanic	**Difficult,** suitable for experienced DIY mechanic	**Very difficult,** suitable for expert DIY or professional

Specifications

General

Engine type	Four-cylinder, in-line, water-cooled. Single overhead camshaft, belt-driven, acting on hydraulic tappets
Manufacturer's engine code:	
Models with a catalytic converter	X20SE
Models not fitted with a catalytic converter*	20SE
Bore	86 mm
Stroke	86 mm
Capacity	1998 cc
Firing order	1-3-4-2 (No 1 cylinder at timing belt end)
Direction of crankshaft rotation	Clockwise (viewed from timing belt end of engine)
Compression ratio	10:1
Maximum power	85 kW at 5400 rpm
Maximum torque	178 Nm at 2800 rpm

**This model was never available in the UK*

Compression pressures

Standard	12 to 15 bar (174 to 218 psi)
Maximum difference between any two cylinders	1 bar (15 psi)

Camshaft

Endfloat	0.09 to 0.21 mm
Maximum permissible radial run-out	0.04 mm

Lubrication system

Oil pump type	Gear type, driven directly from crankshaft
Minimum permissible oil pressure at idle speed, with engine at operating temperature (oil temperature of at least 80°C)	1.5 bar (22 psi)
Oil pump clearances:	
Gear teeth clearance	0.08 to 0.15 mm
Gear endfloat	0.03 to 0.10 mm

Torque wrench settings

	Nm	lbf ft
Camshaft cover bolts	8	6
Camshaft sprocket bolt	45	33
Camshaft thrustplate bolts	8	6
Camshaft housing end cover bolts	8	6
Connecting rod big-end bearing cap bolt:		
Stage 1	35	26
Stage 2	Angle-tighten a further 45°	
Stage 3	Angle-tighten a further 15°	
Coolant pump bolts	25	18
Crankcase breather tube bolts	25	18
Crankshaft pulley bolts	20	15
Crankshaft sensor rotor bolts	13	10
Crankshaft sprocket bolt:		
Stage 1	130	96
Stage 2	Angle-tighten a further 40 to 50°	
Cylinder head bolts:		
Stage 1	25	18
Stage 2	Angle-tighten a further 90°	
Stage 3	Angle-tighten a further 90°	
Stage 4	Angle-tighten a further 90°	
Driveplate bolts:		
Stage 1	55	41
Stage 2	Angle-tighten a further 30°	
Stage 3	Angle-tighten a further 15°	
Engine/transmission mountings:		
Left- and right-hand mountings:		
Mounting-to-subframe nut	55	41
Mounting-to-mounting bracket nut	40	30
Mounting bracket-to-cylinder block bolts	60	44
Rear mounting:		
Mounting-to-transmission bolts	40	30
Mounting-to-crossmember nuts	20	15
Crossmember-to-body bolts	45	33
Engine to transmission support bracket bolts:		
Bracket-to-engine bolt	40	30
Bracket-to-transmission bolts	22	16
Engine-to-transmission unit bolts	60	44
Flywheel bolts:		
Stage 1	65	48
Stage 2	Angle-tighten a further 30°	
Stage 3	Angle-tighten a further 15°	
Main bearing cap bolts:		
Stage 1	50	37
Stage 2	Angle-tighten a further 45°	
Stage 3	Angle-tighten a further 15°	
Oil filter	15	11
Oil pump:		
Retaining bolts	8	6
Pump cover screws	6	4
Oil pressure relief valve bolt	50	37
Oil pump pick-up/strainer bolts	8	6
Spark plug heatshields	25	18
Sump bolts:		
Retaining bolts	8	6
Drain plug	55	41
Timing belt cover bolts:		
Outer cover	4	3
Rear cover	6	4
Timing belt tensioner bolt	20	15

1 General information

How to use this Chapter

1 This Part of Chapter 2 is devoted to in-car repair procedures for the engine. All procedures concerning engine removal and refitting, and engine block/cylinder head overhaul can be found in Chapter 2D.

2 Most of the operations included in this Part are based on the assumption that the engine is still installed in the car. Therefore, if this information is being used during a complete engine overhaul, with the engine already removed, many of the steps included here will not apply.

Engine description

3 The engine is a single overhead camshaft, four-cylinder, in-line unit, mounted at the front of the car with the clutch/transmission (as applicable) on its rear.

4 The cylinder block is of the dry-liner type. The crankshaft is supported within the cylinder block on five shell-type main bearings. Thrustwashers are fitted to number 3 main bearing, to control crankshaft endfloat.

5 The connecting rods are attached to the crankshaft by horizontally split shell-type big-end bearings, and to the pistons by interference-fit gudgeon pins. The aluminium alloy pistons are of the slipper type, and are fitted with three piston rings, comprising two compression rings and a scraper-type oil control ring.

6 The camshaft runs directly in the camshaft housing, which is mounted on top of the cylinder head, and driven by the crankshaft via a toothed rubber timing belt (which also drives the coolant pump). The camshaft operates each valve via a follower. Each follower pivots on a hydraulic self-adjusting valve lifter (tappet) which automatically adjusts the valve clearance.

7 Lubrication is by pressure-feed from a gear-type oil pump, which is mounted on the front end of the crankshaft. It draws oil through a strainer located in the sump, and then forces it through an externally mounted full-flow cartridge-type filter. The oil flows into galleries in the main bearing cap bridge arrangement and cylinder block/crankcase, from where it is distributed to the crankshaft (main bearings) and camshaft. The big-end bearings are supplied with oil via internal drillings in the crankshaft, while the camshaft bearings also receive a pressurised supply. The camshaft lobes and valves are lubricated by splash, as are all other engine components.

8 A semi-closed crankcase ventilation system is employed; crankcase fumes are drawn from cylinder head cover, and passed via a hose to the inlet manifold.

Repair operations possible with the engine in the car

9 The following operations can be carried out without having to remove the engine from the vehicle:

a) Removal and refitting of the cylinder head.
b) Removal and refitting of the timing belt and sprockets.
c) Renewal of the camshaft oil seal.
d) Removal and refitting of the camshaft housing and camshaft.
e) Removal and refitting of the sump.
f) Removal and refitting of the connecting rods and pistons.*
g) Removal and refitting of the oil pump.
h) Renewal of the crankshaft oil seals.
i) Renewal of the engine mountings.
j) Removal and refitting of the flywheel/driveplate.

** Although the operation marked with an asterisk can be carried out with the engine in the car after removal of the sump, it is better for the engine to be removed, in the interests of cleanliness and improved access. For this reason, the procedure is described in Chapter 2D.*

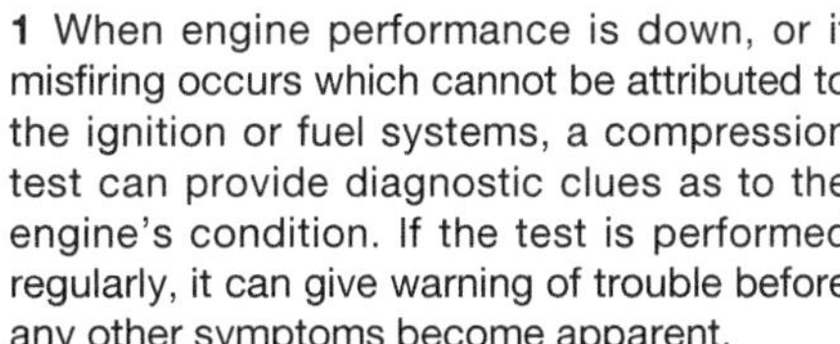

2 Compression test - description and interpretation

1 When engine performance is down, or if misfiring occurs which cannot be attributed to the ignition or fuel systems, a compression test can provide diagnostic clues as to the engine's condition. If the test is performed regularly, it can give warning of trouble before any other symptoms become apparent.

2 The engine must be fully warmed-up to normal operating temperature, the battery must be fully charged, and the spark plugs must be removed (see Chapter 1). The aid of an assistant will also be required.

3 Ensure the ignition is switched off then disable the ignition system by disconnecting the wiring connector from the DIS module (see Chapter 5B) and the fuel system by removing the fuel pump relay from the engine compartment relay box (see Chapter 4A, Section 13).

4 Fit a compression tester to the number 1 cylinder spark plug hole the type of tester which screws into the plug thread is to be preferred.

5 Have the assistant hold the throttle wide open and crank the engine on the starter motor; after one or two revolutions, the compression pressure should build up to a maximum figure, and then stabilise. Record the highest reading obtained.

6 Repeat the test on the remaining cylinders, recording the pressure in each.

7 All cylinders should produce very similar pressures; any difference greater than that specified indicates the existence of a fault. Note that the compression should build up quickly in a healthy engine; low compression on the first stroke, followed by gradually-increasing pressure on successive strokes, indicates worn piston rings. A low compression reading on the first stroke, which does not build up during successive strokes, indicates leaking valves or a blown head gasket (a cracked head could also be the cause). Deposits on the undersides of the valve heads can also cause low compression.

8 If the pressure in any cylinder is reduced to the specified minimum or less, carry out the following test to isolate the cause. Introduce a teaspoonful of clean oil into that cylinder through its spark plug hole, and repeat the test.

9 If the addition of oil temporarily improves the compression pressure, this indicates that bore or piston wear is responsible for the pressure loss. No improvement suggests that leaking or burnt valves, or a blown head gasket, may be to blame.

10 A low reading from two adjacent cylinders is almost certainly due to the head gasket having blown between them; the presence of coolant in the engine oil will confirm this.

11 If one cylinder is about 20 per cent lower than the others, and the engine has a slightly rough idle, a worn camshaft lobe could be the cause.

12 If the compression reading is unusually high, the combustion chambers are probably coated with carbon deposits. If this is the case, the cylinder head should be removed and decarbonised.

13 On completion of the test, refit the spark plugs (see Chapter 1), refit the fuel pump relay and reconnect the wiring connector to the DIS module.

3 Top dead centre (TDC) for No 1 piston - locating

1 In its travel up and down its cylinder bore, Top Dead Centre (TDC) is the highest point that each piston reaches as the crankshaft rotates. While each piston reaches TDC both at the top of the compression stroke and again at the top of the exhaust stroke, for the purpose of timing the engine, TDC refers to the piston position (usually number 1) at the top of its compression stroke.

2 Number 1 piston (and cylinder) is at the front (timing belt) end of the engine, and its TDC position is located as follows. Note that the crankshaft rotates clockwise when viewed from the front of the vehicle.

3 Disconnect the battery negative terminal. If necessary, remove all the spark plugs as described in Chapter 1 to enable the engine to be easily turned over.

4 To gain access to the camshaft sprocket timing mark, remove the timing belt outer cover as described in Section 6.

5 Using a socket and extension bar on the crankshaft sprocket bolt, turn the crankshaft whilst keeping an eye on the camshaft sprocket. Rotate the crankshaft until the timing mark on the camshaft sprocket is correctly aligned with the cutout on the top of the timing belt rear cover and the mark on the crankshaft sprocket rim is correctly aligned with the cutout on the oil pump housing **(see illustration)**.

6 With the crankshaft pulley and camshaft sprocket timing marks positioned as described, the engine is positioned with No1 piston at TDC on its compression stroke.

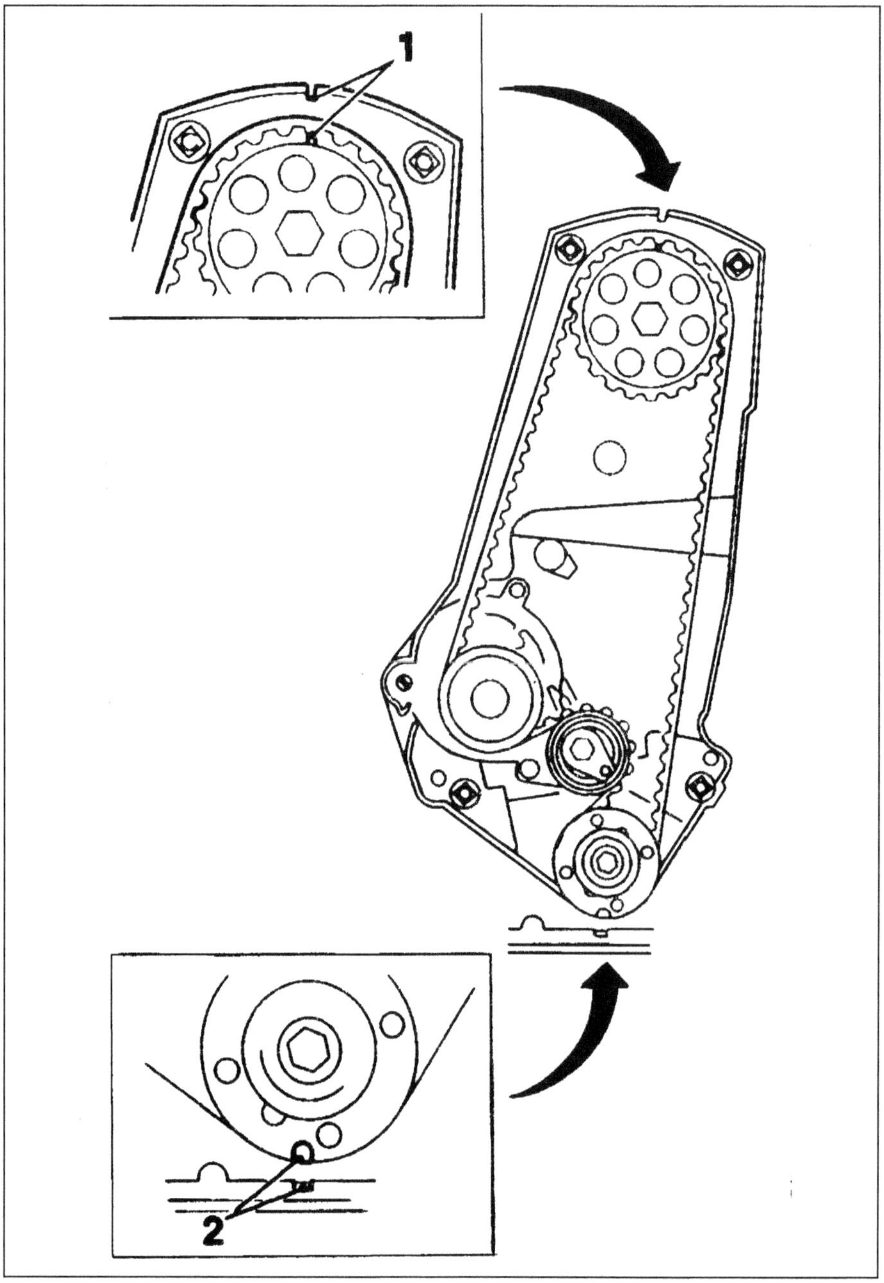

3.5 Align the camshaft sprocket timing mark with the cutout on the timing belt cover (1) and align the crankshaft sprocket mark with the cutout on the oil pump housing (2) to position No1 piston at TDC on its compression stroke

4 Camshaft cover - removal and refitting

Removal

1 Release the retaining clip and disconnect the breather hose from the camshaft cover.

2 Slacken and remove the retaining bolts, noting the correct fitted location of any clips or brackets retained by the bolts (as applicable) then lift the camshaft cover from the camshaft housing. If the cover is stuck, do not lever between the cover and camshaft housing mating surfaces - if necessary, gently tap the cover sideways to free it. Recover the gasket; if it shows signs of damage or deterioration it must be renewed.

Refitting

3 Prior to refitting, examine the inside of the cover for a build-up of oil sludge or any other contamination, and if necessary clean the cover with paraffin, or a water-soluble solvent. Examine the condition of the crankcase ventilation filter inside the camshaft cover, and clean as described for the inside of the cover if clogging is evident (if desired, the filter can be removed from the cover, after removing the securing bolts). Dry the cover thoroughly before refitting.

4 Ensure the cover is clean and dry and seat the gasket in the cover recess then refit the cover to the camshaft housing, ensuring the gasket remains correctly seated.

5 Refit the retaining bolts, ensuring all relevant clips/brackets are correctly positioned, and tighten them to the specified torque working in a diagonal sequence.

6 Reconnect the breather hose securely to the cover.

5 Crankshaft pulley - removal and refitting

Removal

1 Remove the auxiliary drivebelt as described in Chapter 1. Prior to removal, mark the direction of rotation on the belt to ensure the belt is refitted the same way around.

2 Slacken and remove the small retaining bolts securing the pulley to the crankshaft sprocket and remove the pulley from the engine. If necessary, prevent crankshaft rotation by holding the sprocket retaining bolt with a suitable socket.

Refitting

3 Seat the crankshaft pulley on the sprocket and tighten its retaining bolts to the specified torque.

4 Refit the auxiliary drivebelt as described in Chapter 1 using the mark made prior to removal to ensure the belt is fitted the correct way around.

6 Timing belt covers - removal and refitting

Outer cover

Removal

1 Remove the crankshaft pulley as described in Section 5.

2 Undo the retaining bolt and free the wiring harness guide from the top of the timing belt cover.

7.3 Slacken the timing belt tensioner bolt (1) and rotate the tensioner clockwise using an Allen key in the arm cutout (2)

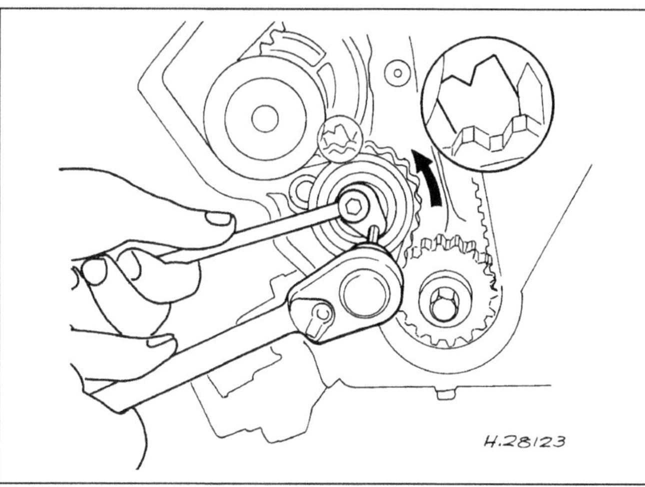

7.8 Tension the belt by rotating the tensioner arm fully anti-clockwise until the pointer is positioned as shown

3 Undo the remaining retaining bolts then unclip the timing belt outer cover and remove it from the engine.

Refitting

4 Refitting is the reverse of removal, ensuring the auxiliary drivebelt is fitted the same way around as it was prior removal.

Rear cover

Removal

5 Remove the camshaft and crankshaft timing belt sprockets and the timing belt tensioner as described in Section 8.

6 Free the crankshaft sensor wiring from the base of the timing belt rear cover, noting its correct routing.

7 Slacken and remove the bolts securing the rear cover to the camshaft housing and oil pump housing and remove the cover from the engine.

Refitting

8 Refitting is the reverse of removal, tightening the cover retaining bolts to the specified torque. Ensure the crankshaft sensor wiring is correctly routed before refitting the timing belt components.

7 Timing belt - removal and refitting

***Note**: The timing belt must be removed and refitted with the engine cold.*

Removal

1 Disconnect the battery negative terminal then remove the timing belt outer cover as described in Section 6. **Note:** *On models with a Vauxhall anti-theft warning system (ATWS), the battery negative terminal must be disconnected within 15 seconds of the ignition being switched off to prevent the alarm system being triggered.*

2 Position No 1 cylinder at TDC on its compression stroke as described in Section 3.

3 Slacken the timing belt tensioner bolt. Using an Allen key, rotate the tensioner arm clockwise to its stop, to relieve the tension in the timing belt, and hold it in position by securely tighten the retaining bolt **(see illustration)**.

4 Slide the timing belt off from its sprockets and remove it from the engine. If the belt is to be re-used, use white paint or similar to mark the direction of rotation on the belt. **Do not** rotate the crankshaft or camshaft until the timing belt has been refitted.

5 Check the timing belt carefully for any signs of uneven wear, splitting or oil contamination, and renew it if there is the slightest doubt about its condition. If the engine is undergoing an overhaul and has covered 40 000 miles or it was more than 4 years since the original belt was fitted, renew the belt as a matter of course, regardless of its apparent condition (from 1997 onwards the belt renewal interval was increased to 80 000 miles or 8 years). If signs of oil contamination are found, trace the source of the oil leak and rectify it, then wash down the engine timing belt area and all related components to remove all traces of oil.

Refitting

6 On reassembly, thoroughly clean the timing belt sprockets then check that the camshaft sprocket timing mark is still correctly aligned with the rear cover cutout and the crankshaft sprocket mark is still aligned with the mark on the oil pump housing.

7 Fit the timing belt over the crankshaft and camshaft sprockets, ensuring that the belt left-hand run is taut (ie, all slack is on the tensioner pulley side of the belt), then fit the belt over the coolant pump sprocket and tensioner pulley. Do not twist the belt sharply while refitting it. Ensure that the belt teeth are correctly seated centrally in the sprockets, and that the timing marks remain in alignment. If a used belt is being refitted, ensure that the arrow mark made on removal points in the normal direction of rotation, as before.

8 Slacken the timing belt tensioner bolt to release the tensioner spring. Rotate the tensioner arm anti-clockwise until the tensioner pointer is fully over against its stop, without exerting any excess strain on the belt **(see illustration)**. Hold the tensioner in position and securely tighten its retaining bolt.

9 Check the sprocket timing marks are still correctly aligned. If adjustment is necessary, release the tensioner again then disengage the belt from the sprockets and make any necessary adjustments.

10 Using a socket on the crankshaft sprocket bolt, rotate the crankshaft smoothly through two complete turns (720°) in the normal direction of rotation to settle the timing belt in position.

11 Check that both the camshaft and crankshaft sprocket timing marks are correctly realigned then slacken the tensioner bolt again.

12 If a new timing belt is being fitted, adjust the tensioner so that the pointer is aligned with either the cutout or NEW marking (depending on type of tensioner fitted) on the backplate **(see illustration)**. Hold the tensioner in the correct position and tighten its retaining bolt to the specified torque. Rotate the crankshaft smoothly through another two complete turns in the normal direction of rotation, to bring the sprocket timing marks back into alignment. Check that the tensioner pointer is still aligned with the backplate cutout/marking (as applicable).

13 If the original belt is being refitted, adjust the tensioner so that the pointer is either positioned 4 mm to the left of the cutout or is aligned with the USED marking (depending on the type of tensioner fitted) on the backplate **(see illustration 7.12)**. Hold the tensioner in the correct position and tighten its retaining bolt to the specified torque. Rotate the crankshaft smoothly through another two complete turns in the normal direction of

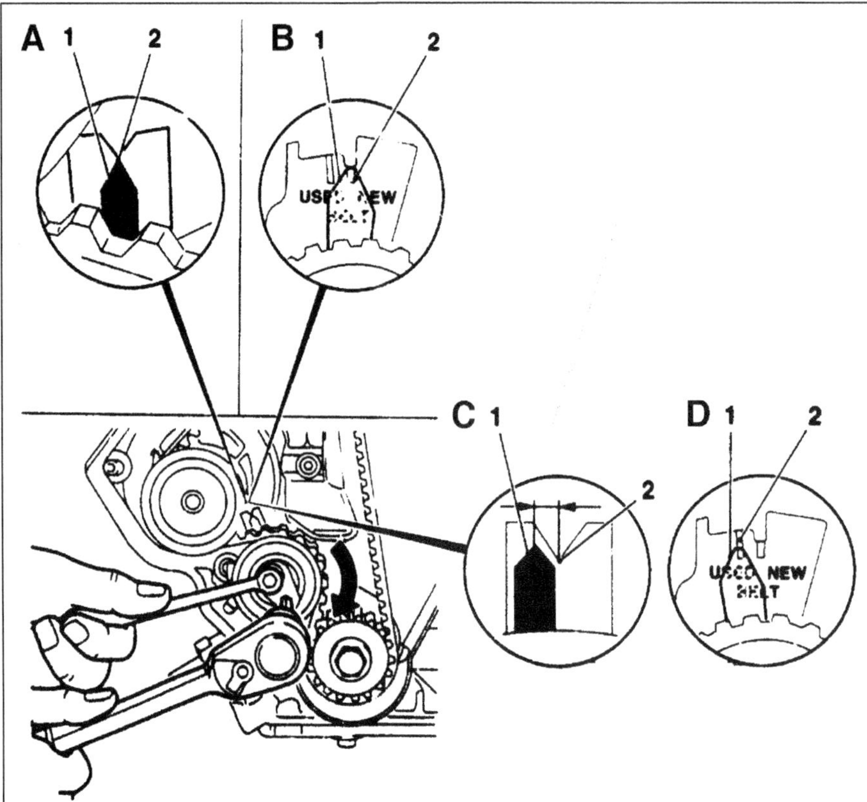

7.12 Ensure the timing belt tensioner arm (1) is correctly positioned in relation to the backplate cutout/marking (2) as described in text

A Correct position for new belt - engines with an unmarked tensioner
B Correct position for new belt - engines with a marked tensioner
C Correct position for used belt - engines with an unmarked tensioner
D Correct position for used belt - engines with a marked tensioner

rotation, to bring the sprocket timing marks back into alignment. Check that the tensioner pointer is still correctly positioned in relation to the backplate cutout/marking (as applicable).

14 If the tensioner pointer is not correctly positioned in relation to the backplate, repeat the procedure in paragraph 12 (new belt) or 13 (original belt) (as applicable).

15 Once the tensioner arm and backplate remain correctly aligned, refit the timing belt cover and crankshaft pulley as described in Sections 5 and 6.

8 Timing belt tensioner and sprockets - removal and refitting

Camshaft sprocket

Removal

1 Remove the timing belt as described in Section 7.

2 The camshaft must be prevented from turning as the sprocket bolt is unscrewed, and this can be achieved in one of two ways as follows.

a) Make up a sprocket-holding tool using two lengths of steel strip (one long, the other short), and three nuts and bolts; one nut and bolt forms the pivot of a forked tool, with the remaining two nuts and bolts at the tips of the 'forks' to engage with the sprocket spokes as shown ***(see illustration)****.*

b) Remove the camshaft cover as described in Section 4 and hold the camshaft with an open-ended spanner on the flats provided.

3 Unscrew the retaining bolt and washer and remove the sprocket from the end of the camshaft.

Refitting

4 Prior to refitting check the oil seal for signs of damage or leakage, if necessary, renewing it as described in Section 9.

5 Refit the sprocket to the end of the camshaft, aligning its cutout with the camshaft locating pin, then refit the retaining bolt and washer **(see illustration)**.

6 Tighten the sprocket retaining bolt to the specified torque whilst prevent rotation using the method employed on removal.

7 Refit the timing belt as described in Section 7 then (where necessary) refit the camshaft cover as described in Section 4.

8.2 Using a home-made sprocket holding tool to retain the camshaft sprocket whilst the bolt is slackened

8.5 Refit the camshaft sprocket making sure the locating pin (1) engages with the sprocket hole (2)

Crankshaft sprocket

Note: *A new crankshaft sprocket retaining bolt will be required on refitting.*

Removal

8 Remove the timing belt as described in Section 7.

9 The crankshaft must be prevented from turning as the sprocket bolt is unscrewed (the bolt is very tight), and this can be achieved in anyone of the following ways.

a) Use the holding tool described in paragraph 2 securing the tool to the sprocket with two bolts screwed into opposite pulley retaining bolt holes.

b) On manual transmission models have an assistant select top gear and apply the brakes firmly.

c) If the engine is removed from the vehicle or the transmission unit has been removed the flywheel/driveplate can be locked as described in Section 15.

10 Unscrew the retaining bolt and washer and remove the crankshaft sprocket from the end of the crankshaft. Discard the bolt; a new one must be used on refitting. If necessary, remove the sprocket Woodruff key from the crankshaft end and slide off the spacer.

Refitting

11 Slide the spacer (where removed) onto the crankshaft then refit the Woodruff key to the crankshaft slot.

12 Align the sprocket with the key and slide it into position, ensuring the sprocket flange is facing outwards. Fit the washer and new retaining bolt.

13 Lock the crankshaft by the method used on removal, and tighten the sprocket retaining bolt to the specified stage 1 torque setting then angle-tighten the bolt through the specified stage 2 angle, using a socket and extension bar. It is recommended that an angle-measuring gauge is used during the final stages of the tightening, to ensure accuracy. If a gauge is not available, use white paint to make alignment marks between the bolt head and sprocket prior to tightening; the marks can then be used to check that the bolt has been rotated through the correct angle.
14 Refit the timing belt as described in Section 7.

Tensioner assembly

Removal

15 Remove the timing belt as described in Section 7.
16 Slacken and remove the retaining bolt and remove the tensioner assembly from the engine.

Refitting

17 Fit the tensioner to the engine, making sure that the lug on the backplate is correctly located in the oil pump housing hole. Ensure the tensioner is correctly seated then refit the retaining bolt. Using an Allen key, rotate the tensioner arm clockwise to its stop then securely tighten the retaining bolt.
18 Refit the timing belt as described in Section 7.

9 Camshaft oil seal - renewal

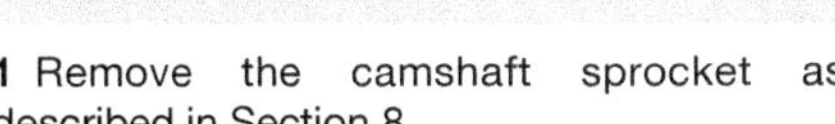

1 Remove the camshaft sprocket as described in Section 8.
2 Carefully punch or drill two small holes opposite each other in the oil seal. Screw a self-tapping screw into each, and pull on the screws with pliers to extract the seal **(see illustration)**.
3 Clean the seal housing, and polish off any burrs or raised edges which may have caused the seal to fail in the first place.
4 Lubricate the lips of the new seal with clean engine oil, and press it into position using a suitable tubular drift (such as a socket) which bears only on the hard outer edge of the seal **(see illustration)**. Take care not to damage the seal lips during fitting; note that the seal lips should face inwards.
5 Refit the camshaft sprocket as described in Section 8.

9.2 Removing the camshaft oil seal

9.4 Fitting a new camshaft oil seal

10 Camshaft housing and camshaft - removal, inspection and refitting

Removal

1 The camshaft can only be removed once the camshaft housing has been removed from the engine. Since the camshaft housing is secured in position by the cylinder head bolts, it is not possible to remove the camshaft without removing the cylinder head (see Section 12). **Note:** *In theory it is possible to remove the camshaft housing once the cylinder head bolts have been removed, and leave the head in position. However, this procedure carries a high risk of disturbing the head gasket, resulting in the head gasket blowing once the camshaft and housing are refitted. If you wish to attempt this, proceed as described in Section 12, noting that it will not be necessary to remove the manifolds, etc. Be warned though that after refitting, you may find the head gasket will need renewing, meaning that the cylinder head will have to be removed after all. The decision is yours as to whether this is a chance worth taking.*
2 With the camshaft housing removed, undo the retaining bolts and remove the end cover and gasket from the rear of the housing. Discard the gasket, a new one should be used on refitting.
3 Measure the camshaft endfloat by inserting feeler gauges between the thrustplate and the camshaft; if the endfloat is not within the limits given in the Specifications then the thrustplate will need to be renewed. Unscrew the two retaining bolts then slide out the camshaft thrustplate, noting which way round it is fitted **(see illustrations)**.
4 Carefully withdraw the camshaft from the rear of the housing, taking care not to damage the bearing journals **(see illustration)**.

Inspection

5 With the camshaft removed, examine the bearings in the camshaft housing for signs of obvious wear or pitting. If evident, a new camshaft housing will probably be required. Also check that the oil supply holes in the camshaft housing are free from obstructions.
6 The camshaft itself should show no marks or scoring on the journal or cam lobe surfaces. If evident, renew the camshaft. If the camshaft lobes show signs of wear also examine the followers (see Section 11). Check the camshaft thrustplate for signs of wear or grooves, and renew if necessary.

Refitting

7 Carefully prise the old seal out of from the camshaft housing, using a suitable

10.3a Undo the retaining bolts (arrowed) . . .

10.3b . . . then remove the thrustplate . . .

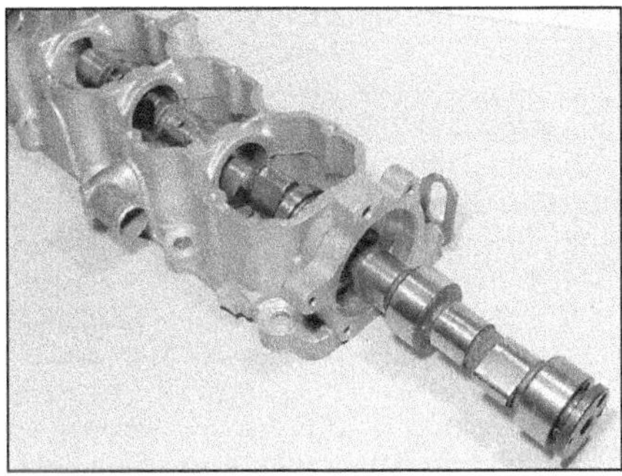

10.4 . . . and slide the camshaft out from the housing

11.8a Remove each follower . . .

11.8b . . . thrust pad . . .

11.8c . . . and hydraulic tappet from the cylinder head

screwdriver. Ensure the housing is clean then press the in new seal, ensuring its sealing lip is facing inwards, until it is flush with the housing.

8 Liberally lubricate the camshaft and housing bearings and the oil seal lip with fresh engine oil.

9 Carefully insert the camshaft into the housing, taking care not to mark the bearing surfaces or damage the oil seal lip.

10 Slide the thrustplate into position, engaging it with the camshaft slot, and tighten its retaining bolts to the specified torque. Check the camshaft endfloat (see paragraph 3).

11 Ensure the mating surfaces are clean and dry and fit a new gasket to the rear of the housing. Refit the cover and tighten its retaining bolts to the specified torque.

12 Refit the camshaft housing as described in Section 12.

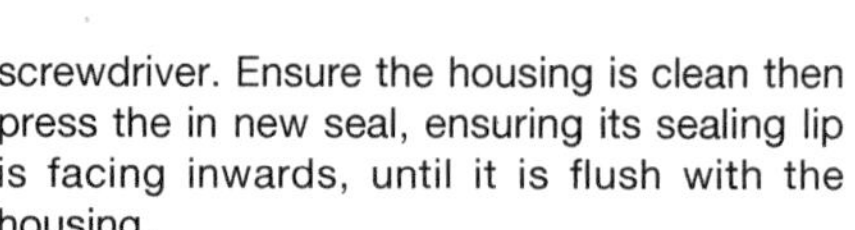

11 Camshaft followers and hydraulic tappets - removal, inspection and refitting

Using Vauxhall service tool (tool no. KM-565)

1 If access to the special tool (KM-565) or a suitable equivalent can be gained, the cam followers and tappets can be removed as follows, without disturbing the camshaft.

2 Remove the camshaft cover as described in Section 4.

3 Using a socket and extension bar, rotate the crankshaft in the normal direction of rotation until the camshaft lobe of the first follower/ tappet to be removed is pointing straight upwards. Remove the spark plug from the corresponding cylinder (see Chapter 1).

4 Fit the service tool to the top of the camshaft housing, making sure the tool end is correctly engaged with the top of the valve. Screw the tool stud into one of the housing bolt holes until the valve is sufficiently depressed to allow the follower to be slid out from underneath the camshaft. The hydraulic tappet can then also be removed as can the thrust pad from the top of the valve. Inspect the components (see paragraphs 10 and 11) and renew if worn or damaged.

5 Lubricate the tappet and follower with fresh engine oil then slide the tappet into its bore in the cylinder head. Manoeuvre the follower into position, ensuring it is correctly engaged with the tappet and valve stem, then carefully remove the service tool.

6 Repeat the operation on the remaining followers and tappets then refit the spark plug(s) (see Chapter 1).

Without special tool

Removal

7 Without the use of the special tool, it will be necessary to remove the camshaft housing to allow the followers and tappets to be removed (see Section 10, paragraph 1).

8 With the housing removed, obtain eight small, clean plastic containers, and number them 1 to 8; alternatively, divide a larger container into eight compartments. Lift out each follower, thrust pad and hydraulic tappet in turn, and place them in their respective container **(see illustrations)**. Do not interchange the cam followers, or the rate of wear will be much-increased.

Inspection

9 Examine the cam follower bearing surfaces which contact the camshaft lobes for wear ridges and scoring. Renew any follower on which these conditions are apparent. If a follower bearing surface is badly scored, also examine the corresponding lobe on the camshaft for wear, as it is likely that both will be worn. Also check the thrust pad for signs of wear or damage. Renew worn components as necessary.

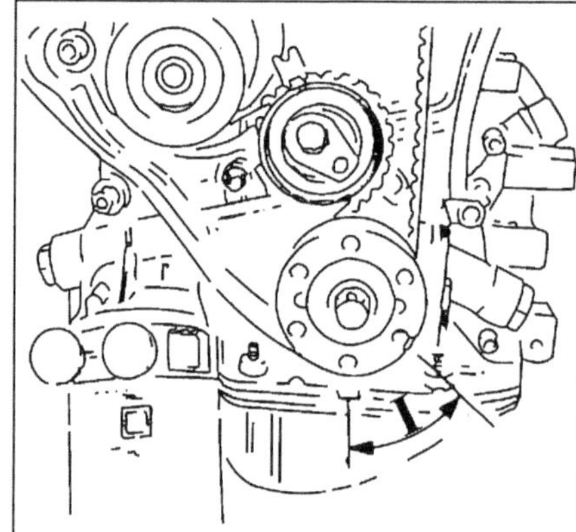

12.3 Prior to removing the timing belt, rotate the crankshaft 60° backwards to ensure the camshaft and pistons are safely positioned

10 If the hydraulic tappets are thought to be faulty they should be renewed; testing of the tappets is not possible.

Refitting

11 Lubricate the hydraulic tappets and their cylinder head bores with clean engine oil. Refit the tappets to the cylinder head, making sure they are fitted in their original locations.

12 Fit each thrust pad to the top of its respective valve.

13 Lubricate the followers with clean engine oil. Fit each follower, making sure it is correctly located with both the tappet and thrust pad, then refit the camshaft housing (see Section 10).

12 Cylinder head - removal and refitting

Removal

Note: *The engine must be cold when removing the cylinder head. New cylinder head bolts must be used on refitting.*

1 Disconnect the battery negative lead. **Note:** *On models with a Vauxhall anti-theft warning system (ATWS), the battery negative terminal must be disconnected within 15 seconds of the ignition being switched off to prevent the alarm system being triggered.*

2 Drain the cooling system and remove the spark plugs and auxiliary drivebelt as described in Chapter 1.

3 Remove the timing belt as described in Section 7. Prior to releasing the timing belt tension and removing the belt, rotate the crankshaft **backwards** by approximately 60° (4 teeth of movement); this will position the camshaft so that the valve spring pressure is evenly exerted along its the complete length, preventing the shaft turning and reducing the risk of the valves contacting the pistons **(see illustration)**.

4 Remove the inlet and exhaust manifolds as described in Chapter 4A. If no work is to be carried out on the cylinder head, the head can be removed complete with manifolds once the following operations have been carried out (see Chapters 4A and 4B).

a) Remove the duct linking the air cleaner to the throttle housing.

b) Disconnect the wiring connectors from the throttle potentiometer, idle speed adjuster, injectors, EGR valve, purge valve and oxygen sensor. Unbolt the earth connection from the fuel rail and release all wiring from the inlet manifold.

c) Depressurise the fuel system then disconnect the fuel hoses from the fuel rail.

d) Disconnect the various vacuum and coolant hoses from the inlet manifold/throttle housing.

e) Unbolt the inlet manifold support bracket and the alternator upper bracket.

f) Disconnect the accelerator cable.

g) Unbolt the exhaust front pipe from the manifold and its mounting bracket.

5 Remove the camshaft cover as described in Section 4.

6 Remove the camshaft sprocket as described in Section 8.

7 Undo the retaining bolts securing the timing belt rear cover to the camshaft housing.

8 Disconnect the wiring connectors from the DIS module, the coolant temperature sensor, the knock sensor and the crankshaft sensor. Undo the bolt(s) securing the earth lead(s) to the front of the cylinder head then position the wiring cover assembly clear of the cylinder head.

9 Slacken the retaining clips and disconnect the coolant hoses from the thermostat housing on the front end of the cylinder head. Also disconnect the wiring connector from the coolant temperature gauge sender unit on the left-hand side of the thermostat housing.

10 Make a final check to ensure that all relevant hoses, pipes and wires, etc, have been disconnected.

11 Working in the **reverse** of the tightening sequence **(see illustration 12.29)**, progressively slacken the cylinder head bolts by a quarter of a turn at a time until all bolts can be unscrewed by hand. Remove each bolt in turn, along with its washer.

12 Lift the camshaft housing from the cylinder head. If necessary, tap the housing gently with a soft-faced mallet to free it from the cylinder head, but **do not** lever at the mating faces. Note the fitted positions of the two locating dowels, and remove them for safe keeping if they are loose.

13 Lift the cylinder head from the cylinder block, taking care not to dislodge the cam followers or thrust pads. If necessary, tap the cylinder head gently with a soft-faced mallet to free it from the block, but **do not** lever at the mating faces. Note the fitted positions of the two locating dowels, and remove them for safe keeping if they are loose.

12.21 Fit the new gasket to the cylinder block, engaging it with the locating dowels (arrowed) . . .

14 Recover the cylinder head gasket, and discard it.

Preparation for refitting

15 The mating faces of the cylinder head and block must be perfectly clean before refitting the head. Use a scraper to remove all traces of gasket and carbon, and also clean the tops of the pistons. Take particular care with the aluminium surfaces, as the soft metal is damaged easily. Also, make sure that debris is not allowed to enter the oil and water channels - this is particularly important for the oil circuit, as carbon could block the oil supply to the camshaft or crankshaft bearings. Using adhesive tape and paper, seal the water, oil and bolt holes in the cylinder block. To prevent carbon entering the gap between the pistons and bores, smear a little grease in the gap. After cleaning the piston, rotate the crankshaft so that the piston moves down the bore, then wipe out the grease and carbon with a cloth rag. Clean the piston crowns in the same way.

16 Check the block and head for nicks, deep scratches and other damage. If slight, they may be removed carefully with a file. More serious damage may be repaired by machining, but this is a specialist job.

17 If warpage of the cylinder head is suspected, use a straight-edge to check it for distortion. Refer to Chapter 2D if necessary.

18 Ensure that the cylinder head bolt holes in the crankcase are clean and free of oil. Syringe or soak up any oil left in the bolt holes. This is most important in order that the correct bolt tightening torque can be applied and to prevent the possibility of the block being cracked by hydraulic pressure when the bolts are tightened.

19 Renew the cylinder head bolts regardless of their apparent condition.

Refitting

20 Ensure the crankshaft is till positioned approximately 60° BTDC and wipe clean the mating faces of the head and block.

21 Ensure that the two locating dowels are in position at each end of the cylinder block/crankcase surface **(see illustration)**.

22 Fit the new cylinder head gasket to the block, making sure it is fitted with the correct way up with its OBEN or TOP mark uppermost and at the front end of the engine **(see illustration)**.

12.22 . . . making sure its OBEN/TOP marking is uppermost

23 Carefully refit the cylinder head, locating it on the dowels.

24 Ensure the mating surfaces of the cylinder head and camshaft housing are clean and dry and that all the camshaft followers are correctly located with the tappets and thrust pad.

25 Apply a bead of suitable sealant (Vauxhall recommend the use of sealant 15 03 170 - available from your Vauxhall dealer) to the cylinder head mating surface **(see illustration)**.

26 Ensure the two locating dowels are in position then lubricate the camshaft followers with clean engine oil.

27 Carefully lower the camshaft housing assembly into position, locating it on the dowels.

28 Fit the washers to the new cylinder head bolts then carefully insert them into position (**do not drop**), tightening them finger-tight only at this stage.

29 Working progressively and in the sequence shown, first tighten all the cylinder head bolts to the stage 1 torque setting **(see illustration)**.

30 Once all bolts have been tightened to the stage 1 torque, again working in the sequence shown, tighten each bolt through its specified stage 2 angle, using a socket and extension bar.

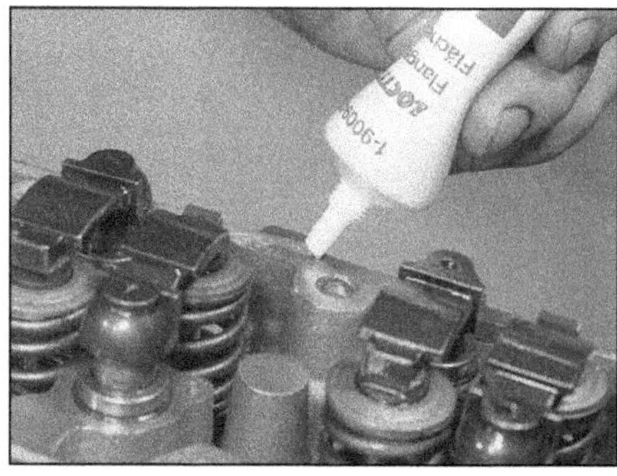

12.25 Apply sealant to the cylinder head upper mating surface then refit the camshaft housing

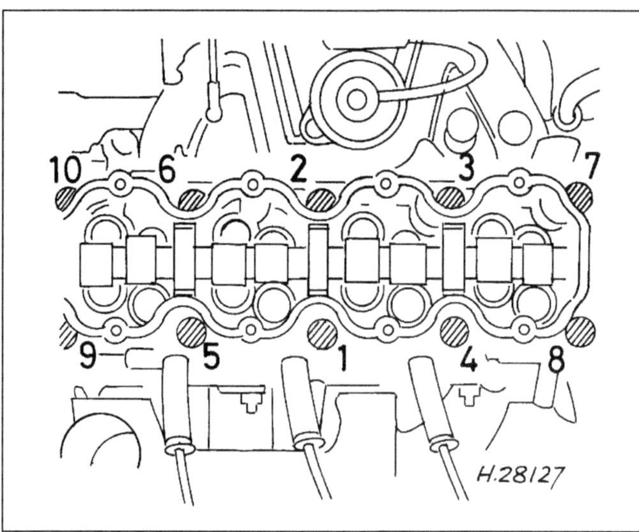

12.29 Cylinder head bolt tightening sequence

12.30 Working in the specified sequence, tighten the cylinder head bolts to the specified stage 1 torque setting and then through the various specified angles (see text)

It is recommended that an angle-measuring gauge is used during this stage of the tightening, to ensure accuracy **(see illustration)**.

31 Working in the specified sequence, go around again and tighten all bolts through the specified stage 3 angle.

32 Finally go around in the specified sequence again and tighten all bolts through the specified stage 4 angle.

33 Refit the bolts securing the timing belt rear cover to the camshaft housing and tighten them to the specified torque.

34 Refit the camshaft sprocket as described in Section 8.

35 Align all the sprocket timing marks to bring the camshaft and crankshaft back to TDC (see Section 3) then refit the timing belt as described in Section 7.

36 Reconnect the wiring connectors to the cylinder head components, ensuring all wiring is correctly routed, and secure it in position with the necessary clips.

37 Reconnect the coolant hoses to the thermostat housings and securely tighten the retaining clips.

38 Refit/reconnect the manifolds as described in Chapter 4A.

39 Refit the undercover then lower the vehicle to the floor.

40 Ensure all pipes and hoses are securely reconnected then refill the cooling system and refit the spark plugs as described in Chapter 1.

41 Reconnect the battery then start the engine and check for signs of leaks.

13 Sump - removal and refitting

Removal

Note: *A new baffle plate will be required on refitting (the sump gasket is an integral part of the plate).*

1 Disconnect the battery negative terminal. **Note:** *On models with a Vauxhall anti-theft warning system (ATWS), the battery negative terminal must be disconnected within 15 seconds of the ignition being switched off to prevent the alarm system being triggered.*

2 Firmly apply the handbrake then jack up the front of the car and support it on axle stands. Undo the retaining screws and remove the undercover from beneath the engine.

3 Drain the engine oil as described in Chapter 1, then fit a new sealing washer and refit the drain plug, tightening it to the specified torque.

4 Where necessary, disconnect the wiring connector from the oil level sender unit on the sump.

5 Slacken and remove the bolts securing the support brackets to the transmission housing and sides of the cylinder block. Remove both brackets from the engine then remove the flywheel lower cover plate from the base of the transmission housing.

6 Slacken and remove the nuts securing the left- and right-hand engine mounting brackets to the top of the rubber mountings. Unbolt the right-hand mounting bracket and remove it from the cylinder block.

7 Attach an engine hoist to the cylinder head lifting brackets then raise the hoist until it is supporting the weight of the engine.

8 Progressively slacken and remove the bolts securing the sump to the base of the cylinder block/oil pump. Break the sump joint by striking the sump with the palm of the hand, then lower the sump away from the engine and withdraw it. Raise the engine unit slightly to gain the necessary clearance required for sump removal, taking care not to place any excess strain on the engine wiring/hoses or exhaust system.

9 Undo the retaining bolts and remove the oil pump pick-up/strainer from the base of the oil pump housing, noting the sealing ring, then remove the baffle plate assembly.

10 Check the oil pump pick-up/strainer for signs of clogging or splitting and renew/clean as necessary. **Note:** *If the sump is to be removed for any length of time, refit the mounting bracket to the cylinder block and lower the engine back down onto its mounting rubbers.*

Refitting

11 Remove all traces of dirt and oil from the mating surfaces of the sump, cylinder block and oil pump housing. Also remove all traces of locking compound from the threads of the oil pump pick-up/strainer bolts and the sump retaining bolts.

12 Apply a smear of suitable sealant (Vauxhall recommend the use of sealant 15 03 295 - available from your Vauxhall dealer) to the areas of the cylinder block mating surface around the areas of the oil pump housing and rear main bearing cap joints.

13 Fit a new sealing ring to the oil pump pick-up/strainer and apply a few drops of locking compound (Vauxhall recommend the use of locking compound 15 10 181 - available from your Vauxhall dealer) to the threads of the strainer retaining bolts.

14 Offer up the new baffle plate, making sure it is correctly located, then refit the oil pump strainer tightening its retaining bolts to the specified torque.

15 Apply a drop of locking compound to each of the sump retaining bolts then offer up the sump to the cylinder block. Refit the retaining bolts and progressively tighten them to the specified torque, working out from the centre in a diagonal sequence.

16 Refit the mounting bracket to the cylinder block and tighten its retaining bolts to the specified torque. Lower the engine back down onto its mountings making sure the brackets and mounting rubbers are correctly aligned. Remove the hoist from the engine then refit the mounting nuts, tightening them to the specified torque setting.

14.8 Undo the retaining screws and remove the oil pump cover

17 Refit the flywheel lower cover plate to the transmission housing then refit the support brackets. Screw in the bolts securing the brackets to the cylinder block and transmission housing and tighten them to their specified torque settings.

18 Reconnect the oil level sender wiring connector (where fitted).

19 Refit the undercover then lower the vehicle to the ground then fill the engine with fresh oil, with reference to Chapter 1.

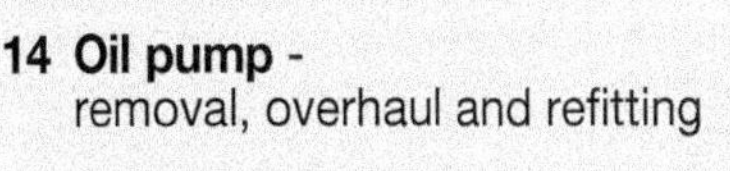

14 Oil pump - removal, overhaul and refitting

Removal

1 Drain the engine oil as described in Chapter 1, then fit a new sealing washer and refit the drain plug, tightening it to the specified torque. Remove the oil filter and discard it.

2 Remove the timing belt as described in Section 7.

3 Remove the camshaft and crankshaft timing belt sprockets and the tensioner as described in Section 8.

4 Unbolt the timing belt rear cover from the camshaft housing and oil pump and remove it from the engine.

5 Remove the sump and oil pump pick-up/strainer as described in Section 13.

6 Disconnect the wiring connector from the oil pressure switch.

7 Slacken and remove the retaining bolts then slide the oil pump housing assembly off of the end of the crankshaft, taking great care not to lose the locating dowels. Remove the housing gasket and discard it.

14.10 Lift the inner and outer gears (arrowed) out from the pump housing

Overhaul

8 Undo the retaining screws and lift off the pump cover from the rear of the housing **(see illustration)**.

9 Using a suitable marker pen, mark the surface of both the pump inner and outer gears; the marks can then be used to ensure the rotors are refitted the correct way around.

10 Lift out the inner and outer gears from the pump housing **(see illustration)**.

11 Unscrew the oil pressure relief valve bolt from the side of the housing and withdraw the spring and plunger from the housing, noting which way around the plunger is fitted **(see illustration)**. Remove the sealing washer from the valve bolt. **Note:** *The pressure relief valve can be removed with pump in position on the engine unit.*

12 Clean the components, and carefully examine the gears, pump body and relief valve plunger for any signs of scoring or wear. Renew any component which shows signs of wear or damage; if the gears or pump housing are marked then the complete pump assembly should be renewed.

13 If the components appear serviceable, measure the clearance between the inner gear to outer gear clearance using feeler blades. Also measure the gear endfloat, and check the flatness of the end cover **(see illustrations)**. If the clearances exceed the specified tolerances, the pump must be renewed.

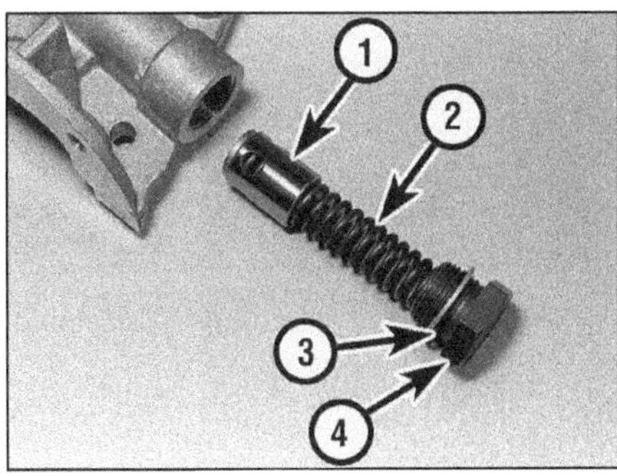

14.11 Oil pressure relief valve components

1 Plunger   *3 Sealing washer*
2 Spring   *4 Valve bolt*

14 If the pump is satisfactory, reassemble the components in the reverse order of removal, noting the following.

a) *Ensure both gears are fitted the correct way around.*
b) *Fit a new sealing washer to the pressure relief valve bolt and tighten the bolt to the specified torque.*
c) *Remove all traces of locking compound from the cover screws. Apply a drop of fresh locking compound to each screw and tighten the screws to the specified torque.*
d) *On completion prime the oil pump by filling it with clean engine oil whilst rotating the inner gear.*

Refitting

15 Prior to refitting, carefully lever out the crankshaft oil seal using a flat-bladed screwdriver. Fit the new oil seal, ensuring its sealing lip is facing inwards, and press it squarely into the housing using a tubular drift which bears only on the hard outer edge of the seal **(see illustration)**. Press the seal into position so that it is flush with the housing and lubricate the oil seal lip with clean engine oil.

16 Ensure the mating surfaces of the oil pump and cylinder block are clean and dry and the locating dowels are in position.

17 Fit a new gasket to the cylinder block.

18 Carefully manoeuvre the oil pump into position and engage the inner gear with the crankshaft end. Locate the pump on the dowels, taking great care not to damage the oil seal lip.

14.13a Using a feeler blade to check gear clearance

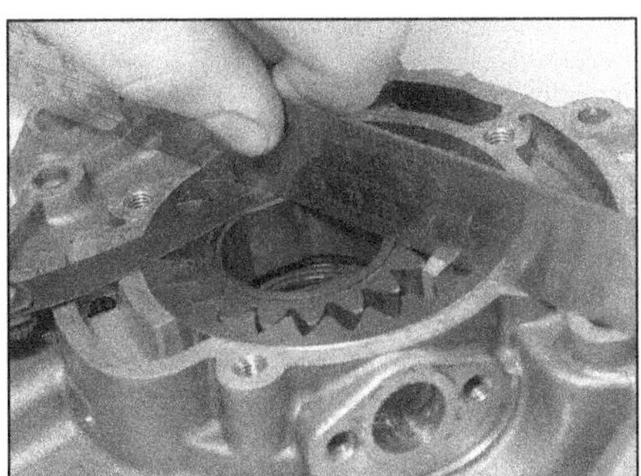

14.13b Using a straight edge and feeler blade to measure gear endfloat

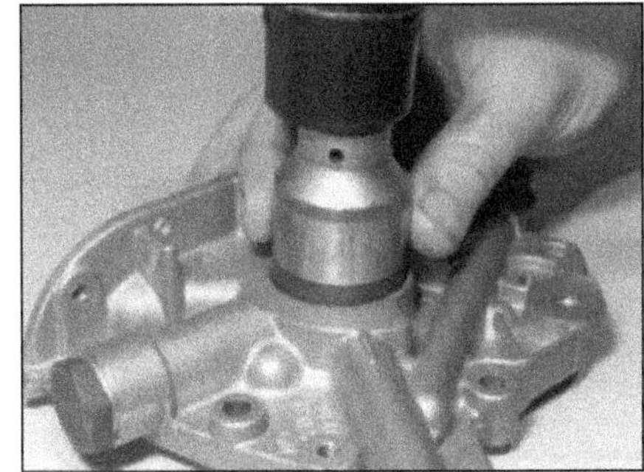

14.15 Fitting a new crankshaft oil seal to the oil pump housing

15.2 Lock the flywheel/driveplate ring gear with a tool similar to that shown

15.12a On manual transmission models, tighten the flywheel bolts to the specified stage 1 torque setting . . .

15.12b . . . then tighten them through the specified stage 2 and 3 angles

19 Refit the pump housing retaining bolts in their original locations and tighten them to the specified torque.

20 Reconnect the oil pressure sensor wiring connector.

21 Refit the oil pump pick-up/strainer and sump as described in Section 13.

22 Refit the rear timing belt cover to the engine, tightening its retaining bolts to the specified torque.

23 Refit the timing belt sprockets and tensioner then refit the belt as described in Sections 7 and 8.

24 On completion fit a new oil filter and fill the engine with clean oil as described in Chapter 1.

15 Flywheel/driveplate - removal, inspection and refitting

Note: *New flywheel/driveplate retaining bolts will be required on refitting.*

Removal

Manual transmission models

1 Remove the transmission as described in Chapter 7A then remove the clutch assembly as described in Chapter 6.

2 Prevent the flywheel from turning by locking the ring gear teeth with a similar arrangement to that shown **(see illustration)**. Alternatively, bolt a strap between the flywheel and the cylinder block/crankcase. Make alignment marks between the flywheel and crankshaft using paint or a suitable marker pen.

3 Slacken and remove the retaining bolts and remove the flywheel. Do not drop it, as it is very heavy.

Automatic transmission models

4 Remove the transmission as described in Chapter 7B.

5 Lock the driveplate as described in paragraph 2 then slacken the driveplate retaining bolts.

6 Unscrew the retaining bolts and remove the retaining plate, centering ring and driveplate from the end of the crankshaft, noting each components correct fitted location.

Inspection

7 On manual transmission models, examine the flywheel for scoring of the clutch face. If the clutch face is scored, the flywheel may be surface-ground, but renewal is preferable. Check for wear or chipping of the ring gear teeth. Renewal of the ring gear is possible on models with a normal flywheel but is not a task for the home mechanic; renewal requires the new ring gear to be heated (up to 180° to 230°C) to allow it to be fitted. On dual-mass flywheels ring gear renewal is not possible.

8 On automatic transmission models closely examine the driveplate for ring gear teeth for signs of wear or damage and check the driveplate surface for any signs of cracks.

9 If there is any doubt about the condition of the flywheel/driveplate, seek the advice of a Vauxhall dealer or engine reconditioning specialist. They will be able to advise if it is possible to recondition it or whether renewal is necessary.

Refitting

Manual transmission models

10 Clean the mating surfaces of the flywheel and crankshaft and remove all traces of locking compound from the flywheel retaining bolt threads in the crankshaft.

11 Offer up the flywheel and fit the new retaining bolts. If the original is being refitted align the marks made prior to removal.

12 Lock the flywheel by the method used on removal, and tighten the retaining bolts to the specified stage 1 torque setting then angle-tighten the bolts through the specified stage 2 angle, using a socket and extension bar, and finally through the specified stage 3 angle. It is recommended that an angle-measuring gauge is used during the final stages of the tightening, to ensure accuracy **(see illustrations)**. If a gauge is not available, use white paint to make alignment marks between the bolt head and flywheel prior to tightening; the marks can then be used to check that the bolt has been rotated through the correct angle.

13 Refit the clutch as described in Chapter 6 then remove the locking tool, and refit the transmission as described in Chapter 7A.

Automatic transmission models

14 Clean the mating surfaces of the driveplate and crankshaft and remove all traces of locking compound from the driveplate retaining bolt threads in the crankshaft.

15 Offer up the driveplate complete with the centering ring and retaining plate, making sure all components are fitted the correct way around, then screw in the new retaining bolts.

16 Tighten the retaining bolts through the specified torque and angles as described in paragraph 12 then remove the locking tool and refit the transmission as described in Chapter 7B.

16 Crankshaft oil seals - renewal

Front (timing belt end) oil seal

1 Remove the crankshaft sprocket as described in Section 8.

2 Carefully punch or drill two small holes opposite each other in the oil seal. Screw a self-tapping screw into each and pull on the screws with pliers to extract the seal **(see illustration)**. Alternatively carefully lever the seal out of position.

Caution: Great care must be taken to avoid damage to the oil pump

3 Clean the seal housing and polish off any burrs or raised edges which may have caused the seal to fail in the first place.

16.2 Removing the crankshaft front oil seal

16.4 Fitting a new crankshaft front oil seal

4 Lubricate the lips of the new seal with clean engine oil and ease it into position on the end of the shaft. Press the seal squarely into position until it is flush with the housing. If necessary, a suitable tubular drift, such as a socket, which bears only on the hard outer edge of the seal can be used to tap the seal into position **(see illustration)**. Take great care not to damage the seal lips during fitting and ensure that the seal lips face inwards.
5 Wash off any traces of oil, then refit the crankshaft sprocket as described in Section 8.

Rear (flywheel/driveplate end) oil seal

6 Remove the flywheel/driveplate as described in Section 15.
7 Renew the seal as described in paragraphs 2 to 4.
8 Refit the flywheel/driveplate as described in Section 15.

17 Engine/transmission mountings - inspection and renewal

Inspection

1 If improved access is required, raise the front of the car and support it securely on axle stands. Undo the retaining bolts and remove the undercover from beneath the engine unit.
2 Check the mounting rubber to see if it is cracked, hardened or separated from the metal at any point; renew the mounting if any such damage or deterioration is evident.
3 Check that all the mounting's fasteners are securely tightened; use a torque wrench to check if possible.
4 Using a large screwdriver or a pry bar, check for wear in the mounting by carefully levering against it to check for free play; where this is not possible, enlist the aid of an assistant to move the engine/transmission unit back and forth, or from side to side, while you watch the mounting. While some free play is to be expected even from new components, excessive wear should be obvious. If excessive free play is found, check first that the fasteners are correctly secured, then renew any worn components as described below.

Renewal

Left- and right-hand engine mountings

Note: *It is recommended that the engine mountings are replaced as a matched pair.*
5 Firmly apply the handbrake then jack up the front of the vehicle and support it on axle stands. Undo the retaining screws and remove the undercover from beneath the engine.
6 Support the weight of the engine/transmission using a trolley jack with a block of wood placed on its head. Alternatively attach an engine hoist to the lifting brackets on the cylinder head and use the hoist to support the engine.
7 Unscrew the upper and lower nuts securing the relevant engine mounting to the cylinder block bracket and subframe then raise the engine unit slightly and manoeuvre the mounting out of position. If necessary the mounting bracket can be unbolted and removed from the cylinder block. **Note:** *Take great care not to place any excess stress on any engine wiring/hoses or the exhaust system or when raising the engine.*
8 Check all components for signs of wear or damage, and renew as necessary.
9 On refitting, refit the mounting to the subframe aligning its locating lug with the subframe slot then refit the lower nut and tighten to the specified torque.
10 Refit the mounting bracket (where removed) to the cylinder block and tighten its retaining bolts to the specified torque.
11 Lower the engine unit back down onto the mounting, making sure it is correctly located, then remove the jack/hoist (as applicable). Fit the upper retaining nut to the mounting and tighten it to the specified torque.
12 Refit the undercover then lower the vehicle to the ground.

Transmission unit rear mounting

13 Firmly apply the handbrake then jack up the front of the vehicle and support it on axle stands.
14 Place a jack with a block of wood beneath the transmission, and raise the jack to take the weight of the transmission.
15 With the transmission securely supported, slacken and remove the bolts securing the transmission unit rear mounting crossmember to the vehicle body. Unscrew the nuts securing the crossmember to the mounting and remove it from the vehicle.
16 Slacken and remove the bolts and remove the mounting from the base of the transmission unit.
17 Check all components for signs of wear or damage, and renew as necessary. Remove all traces of locking compound from the crossmember to body bolt threads.
18 Fit the mounting to the transmission unit and tighten its retaining bolts to the specified torque.
19 Refit the crossmember to the mounting and lightly tighten its retaining nuts.
20 Apply a few drops of thread locking compound (Vauxhall recommend the use of locking compound 15 10 181 - available from your Vauxhall dealer) to the threads of each crossmember to body bolt then refit both bolts and tighten them to the specified torque.
21 Remove the jack from underneath the transmission unit then tighten the mounting to crossmember nuts to the specified torque before lowering the vehicle to the ground.

Chapter 2 Part B:
2.0 litre DOHC engine in-car repair procedures

Contents

Degrees of difficulty

Easy, suitable for novice with little experience 	**Fairly easy,** suitable for beginner with some experience 	**Fairly difficult,** suitable for competent DIY mechanic	**Difficult,** suitable for experienced DIY mechanic	**Very difficult,** suitable for expert DIY or professional

Specifications

General

Engine type	Four-cylinder, in-line, water-cooled. Double overhead camshaft, belt-driven
Manufacturer's engine code	X20XEV
Bore	86.0 mm
Stroke	86.0 mm
Capacity	1998 cc
Firing order	1-3-4-2 (No 1 cylinder at timing belt end)
Direction of crankshaft rotation	Clockwise (viewed from timing belt end of engine)
Compression ratio	10.8:1
Maximum power	100 kW at 5600 rpm
Maximum torque	185 Nm at 4000 rpm

Compression pressures

Standard	12 to 15 bar (174 to 218 psi)
Maximum difference between any two cylinders	1 bar (15 psi)

Camshaft

Cam lift	9.2 mm

Lubrication system

Oil pump type	Gear-type, driven directly from crankshaft
Minimum permissible oil pressure at idle speed, with engine at operating temperature (oil temperature of at least 80°C)	1.5 bar (22 psi)
Oil pump clearances:	
Gear teeth clearance	0.08 to 0.15 mm
Gear endfloat	0.03 to 0.10 mm

Torque wrench settings

	Nm	lbf ft
Camshaft bearing cap bolts	8	6
Camshaft cover bolts	8	6
Camshaft sprocket bolt:		
Stage 1	50	37
Stage 2	Angle-tighten a further 60°	
Stage 3	Angle-tighten a further 15°	
Coolant pump bolts	25	18
Connecting rod big-end bearing cap bolt:		
Stage 1	35	26
Stage 2	Angle-tighten a further 45°	
Stage 3	Angle-tighten a further 15°	
Crankcase breather tube bolts	25	18
Crankshaft balancer unit bolts - 1998-on engines:		
Stage 1	20	15
Stage 2	Angle-tighten a further 45°	
Crankshaft pulley bolts	20	15
Crankshaft sensor rotor bolts	13	10
Crankshaft sprocket bolt:		
Stage 1	130	96
Stage 2	Angle-tighten a further 40 to 50°	
Cylinder head bolts:		
Stage 1	25	18
Stage 2	Angle-tighten a further 90°	
Stage 3	Angle-tighten a further 90°	
Stage 4	Angle-tighten a further 90°	
Stage 5	Angle-tighten a further 15°	
Driveplate bolts:		
Stage 1	55	41
Stage 2	Angle-tighten a further 30°	
Stage 3	Angle-tighten a further 15°	
Engine/transmission mounting bolts:		
Left- and right-hand mountings:		
Mounting-to-subframe nut	55	41
Mounting-to-mounting bracket nut	40	30
Mounting bracket-to-cylinder block bolts	60	44
Rear mounting:		
Mounting-to-transmission bolts	40	30
Mounting-to-crossmember nuts	20	15
Crossmember-to-body bolts	45	33
Engine-to-transmission unit bolts:		
Transmission-to-cylinder block bolts	60	44
Transmission-to-sump flange bolts (engines with a two-piece sump)	40	30
Engine-to-transmission support bracket bolts - engines with one-piece sump:		
Bracket-to-engine bolt	40	30
Bracket-to-transmission bolts	22	16
Flywheel bolts:		
Stage 1	65	48
Stage 2	Angle-tighten a further 30°	
Stage 3	Angle-tighten a further 15°	
Main bearing cap bolts:		
Stage 1	50	37
Stage 2	Angle-tighten a further 45°	
Stage 3	Angle-tighten a further 15°	
Main bearing cap bridge casting/baffle plate bolts - engines with two piece sump:		
Stage 1	20	15
Stage 2	Angle-tighten a further 45°	
Oil filter	15	11
Oil pump:		
Retaining bolts	8	6
Pump cover screws	6	4
Oil pressure relief valve bolt	50	37
Oil pump pick-up/strainer bolts:		
Engines with one-piece sump	8	6

Torque wrench settings (continued)	**Nm**	**lbf ft**
Oil pump pick-up/strainer bolts (continued):		
Engines with two piece sump:		
Pick-up-to-oil pump housing bolts	8	6
Pick-up-to-casting/balancer unit bolts:		
M6 bolts	10	7
M8 bolts	20	15
Sump bolts:		
One-piece sump	15	11
Two-piece sump:		
Sump pan bolts:		
Stage 1	8	6
Stage 2	Angle-tighten a further 30°	
Main casting bolts:		
Casting-to-cylinder block/oil pump bolts	20	15
Casting flange-to-transmission bolts	40	30
Sump drain plug:		
Hex-head bolt	45	33
Torx-head bolt	10	7
Timing belt cover bolts:		
Outer cover	6	4
Rear cover	8	6
Timing belt idler pulley:		
Pulley bolt	25	18
Mounting bracket bolts	25	18
Timing belt tensioner bolt	20	15

1 General information

How to use this Chapter

1 This Part of Chapter 2 is devoted to in-car repair procedures for the engine. All procedures concerning engine removal and refitting, and engine block/cylinder head overhaul can be found in Chapter 2D.

2 Most of the operations included in this Part are based on the assumption that the engine is still installed in the car. Therefore, if this information is being used during a complete engine overhaul, with the engine already removed, many of the steps included here will not apply.

Engine description

3 The engine is a double overhead camshaft, four-cylinder, in-line unit, mounted at the front of the car with the transmission on its rear. This engine is often referred to as the 2.0 litre ECOTEC engine (Emission Consumption Optimized TEChnology).

4 The cylinder block is of the dry-liner type. The crankshaft is supported within the cylinder block on five shell-type main bearings. Thrustwashers are fitted to number 3 main bearing, to control crankshaft endfloat.

5 The connecting rods are attached to the crankshaft by horizontally split shell-type big-end bearings, and to the pistons by interference-fit gudgeon pins. The aluminium alloy pistons are of the slipper type, and are fitted with three piston rings, comprising two compression rings and a scraper-type oil control ring.

6 The camshafts run directly in the cylinder head, and are driven by the crankshaft via a toothed rubber timing belt (which also drives the coolant pump). The camshafts operate each valve via a follower. Each follower incorporates a hydraulic self-adjusting valve which automatically adjust the valve clearances.

7 Lubrication is by pressure-feed from a gear-type oil pump, which is mounted on the front end of the crankshaft. It draws oil through a strainer located in the sump, and then forces it through an externally mounted full-flow cartridge-type filter. The oil flows into galleries in the main bearing cap bridge arrangement and cylinder block/crankcase, from where it is distributed to the crankshaft (main bearings) and camshafts. The big-end bearings are supplied with oil via internal drillings in the crankshaft, while the camshaft bearings also receive a pressurised supply. The camshaft lobes and valves are lubricated by splash, as are all other engine components.

8 On later (1998 model year onwards) engines, a crankshaft balancer unit is fitted to the engine to smooth out the forces which occur during normal crankshaft/piston movement. The balancer unit houses two balance shafts and is bolted onto the base of the cylinder block, directly beneath number 2 cylinder. The balancer shaft gears are meshed together and the gear of the first shaft is driven by the crankshaft via a gear which forms the third web of the crankshaft. The crankshaft gear has twice as many teeth as the balance shaft gears and so drives the balance shaft at twice the speed of the crankshaft, the first balance shaft rotates in the opposite direction to the crankshaft and the second in the same direction.

9 A semi-closed crankcase ventilation system is employed; crankcase fumes are drawn from cylinder head cover, and passed via a hose to the inlet manifold.

Repair operations possible with the engine in the car

10 The following operations can be carried out without having to remove the engine from the vehicle.

a) Removal and refitting of the cylinder head.
b) Removal and refitting of the timing belt and sprockets.
c) Renewal of the camshaft oil seals.
d) Removal and refitting of the camshafts and followers.
e) Removal and refitting of the sump.
f) Removal and refitting of the connecting rods and pistons.*
g) Removal and refitting of the oil pump.
h) Renewal of the crankshaft balancer unit - 1998 on engines.
i) Renewal of the crankshaft oil seals.
j) Renewal of the engine mountings.
k) Removal and refitting of the flywheel/driveplate.

** Although the operation marked with an asterisk can be carried out with the engine in the car after removal of the sump, it is better for the engine to be removed, in the interests of cleanliness and improved access. For this reason, the procedure is described in Chapter 2D.*

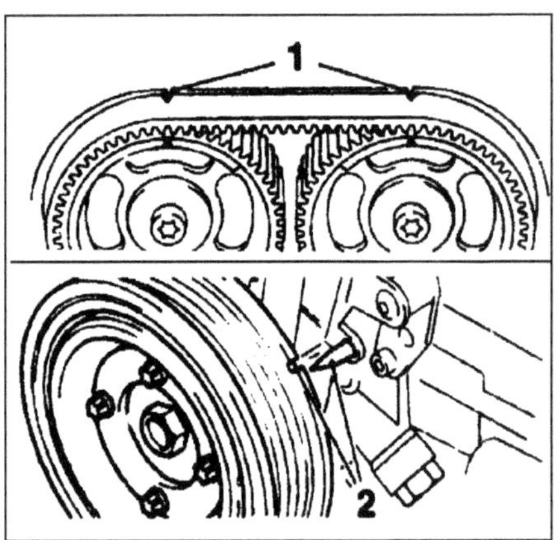

3.5 Align the camshaft sprocket timing marks with the cutout on the camshaft cover (1) and align the crankshaft pulley notch with the pointer (2) to position No 1 piston at TDC on its compression stroke

2 Compression test - description and interpretation

Refer to Chapter 2A, Section 2.

3 Top dead centre (TDC) for No 1 piston - locating

1 In its travel up and down its cylinder bore, Top Dead Centre (TDC) is the highest point that each piston reaches as the crankshaft rotates. While each piston reaches TDC both at the top of the compression stroke and again at the top of the exhaust stroke, for the purpose of timing the engine, TDC refers to the piston position (usually number 1) at the top of its compression stroke.

2 Number 1 piston (and cylinder) is at the front (timing belt) end of the engine, and its TDC position is located as follows. Note that the crankshaft rotates clockwise when viewed from the front of the vehicle.

3 Disconnect the battery negative terminal. If necessary, remove all the spark plugs as described in Chapter 1 to enable the engine to be easily turned over.

4 To gain access to the camshaft sprocket timing marks, remove the timing belt outer cover as described in Section 6.

5 Using a socket and extension bar on the crankshaft sprocket bolt, rotate the crankshaft until the timing marks on the camshaft sprockets are both at the top and are correctly aligned with the marks on the camshaft cover. With the camshaft sprocket marks correctly positioned, align the notch on the crankshaft pulley rim with the pointer **(see illustration)**. The engine is now positioned with No1 piston at TDC on its compression stroke. **Note:** *If the crankshaft pulley has been removed, use the mark on the crankshaft sprocket rim. The mark should be aligned with the cutout on the oil pump housing (see Section 7).*

4 Camshaft cover - removal and refitting

Removal

1 Slacken the retaining clips and disconnect the breather hoses from the camshaft cover **(see illustration)**.

2 Undo the retaining screws and remove the spark plug cover. Disconnect the plug caps from the plugs then unclip the HT leads and position them clear of the cover **(see illustrations)**.

3 Slacken the nut securing the engine wiring harness tray to the timing belt cover upper fixing then free the tray from the front of the cover and position it clear

4 Disconnect the camshaft sensor wiring connector and unclip the wiring from the camshaft cover.

5 Evenly and progressively slacken and remove the camshaft cover retaining bolts.

6 Lift the camshaft cover away from the cylinder head and recover the cover seal and the sealing rings which are fitted to each of the retaining bolt holes. Examine the seal and sealing rings for signs of wear or damage and renew if necessary.

Refitting

7 Ensure the cover and cylinder head surfaces are clean and dry then fit the camshaft seals securely to the cover grooves. Fit the sealing rings to the recesses around each retaining bolt hole, holding them in position with a smear of grease.

8 Apply a smear of suitable sealant (Vauxhall recommend the use of sealant 15 03 295 - available from your Vauxhall dealer) to the areas of the cylinder head surface around the front inlet and exhaust camshaft bearing caps and also to the semi-circular cutouts on the rear of the head.

9 Carefully manoeuvre the camshaft cover into position, taking great care to ensure all the sealing rings remain correctly seated. Refit the cover retaining bolts and tighten the retaining bolts to the specified torque, working in a spiral pattern from the centre outwards.

10 Reconnect the breather hoses, securing them in position with the retaining clips, and securely reconnect the plug caps to the spark plugs.

11 Reconnect the camshaft sensor wiring connector then refit the spark plug cover and securely tighten its retaining screws. Clip the wiring tray back into position and securely tighten its retaining nut.

5 Crankshaft pulley - removal and refitting

Removal

1 Remove the auxiliary drivebelt as described in Chapter 1. Prior to removal, mark the direction of rotation on the belt to ensure the belt is refitted the same way around.

2 Using a socket and extension bar on the crankshaft sprocket bolt, turn the crankshaft until the notch on the pulley rim is correctly aligned with the pointer on the cover **(see illustration)**.

3 Slacken and remove the small retaining bolts securing the pulley to the crankshaft sprocket and remove the pulley from the engine. If necessary, prevent crankshaft rotation by holding the sprocket retaining bolt with a suitable socket.

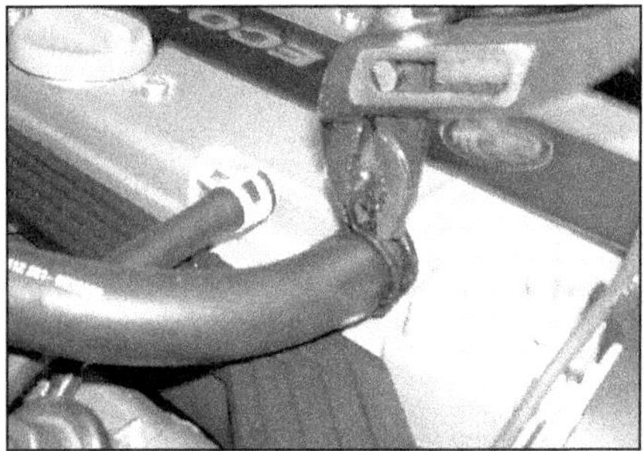

4.1 Release the retaining clips and disconnect the breather hoses from the camshaft cover

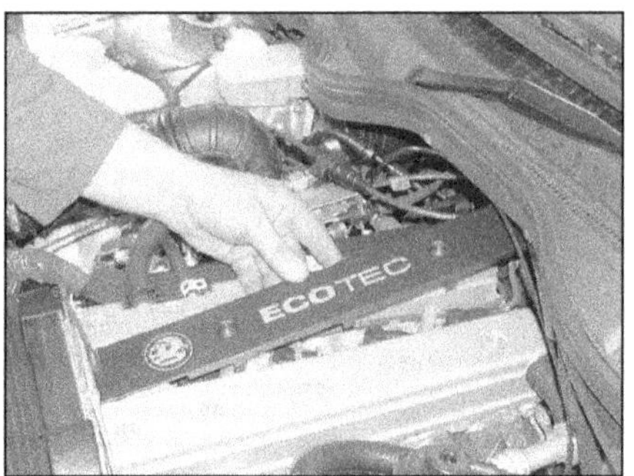

4.2a Remove the spark plug cover . . .

4.2b . . . and disconnect the plug caps from the spark plugs

5.2 Align the crankshaft pulley notch with the pointer on the cover (arrowed - shown with timing belt outer cover removed)

Refitting

4 Check that the crankshaft sprocket mark is still aligned with the mark on the oil pump housing then manoeuvre the crankshaft pulley into position. Align the notch on the pulley rim with the pointer then seat the pulley on the sprocket and tighten its retaining bolts to the specified torque.

5 Refit the auxiliary drivebelt as described in Chapter 1 using the mark made prior to removal to ensure the belt is fitted the correct way around.

6.2a Undo the retaining nut and free the wiring tray from the outer cover . . .

6 Timing belt covers - removal and refitting

Outer cover

Removal

1 Remove the auxiliary drivebelt as described in Chapter 1. Prior to removal, mark the direction of rotation on the belt to ensure the belt is refitted the same way around.

2 Slacken and remove the nut securing the engine wiring harness tray to the outer cover upper mounting and free the tray assembly from the timing belt cover. Unclip the cover from the tray then free the wiring harness and coolant hose and remove the tray from the engine compartment **(see illustrations)**.

3 Slacken and remove the retaining bolts, along with their washers and outer rubber spacers, then remove the outer cover from the engine unit along with its seal. Once the cover has been removed, recover inner rubber spacers from the mountings **(see illustrations)**.

Refitting

4 Ensure the inner rubber spacers are correctly fitted to each of the mountings then manoeuvre the cover into position **(see illustration)**.

5 Fit the washers and outer rubber spacers to the mounting bolts then refit the bolts in their original locations and tighten them to the specified torque **(see illustration)**.

6 Seat the wiring harness correctly in the tray then refit the tray cover. Clip the tray securely onto the timing belt cover and securely tighten its retaining nut.

7 Refit the auxiliary drivebelt as described in Chapter 1 using the mark made prior to removal to ensure the belt is fitted the correct way around.

Rear cover

Removal

8 Remove the timing belt as described in Section 7.

9 Remove the camshaft sprockets, crankshaft sprocket, the timing belt tensioner and the idler pulley assembly as described in Section 8.

10 Unbolt the camshaft sensor from the cylinder head.

11 Undo the retaining bolts, noting their correct fitted locations, and remove the rear cover from the engine unit.

Refitting

12 Refitting is the reverse of removal, tightening all bolts to the specified torque.

6.2b . . . then unclip the cover . . .

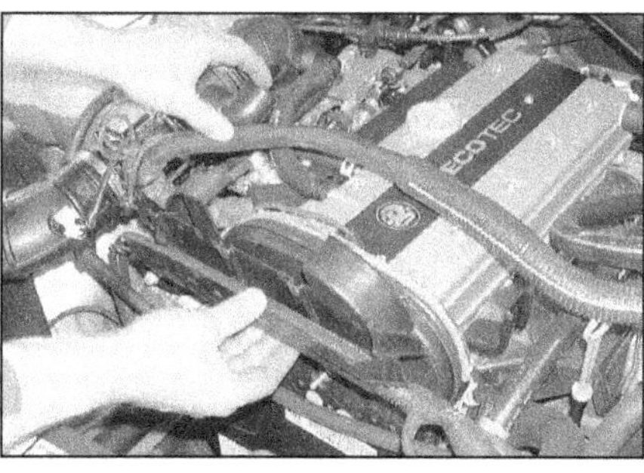

6.2c . . . and free the wiring and coolant hose and remove the tray from the engine compartment

6.3a Slacken and remove the cover retaining bolts (upper bolt shown) and recover the outer rubber spacers . . .

6.3b . . . then remove the outer cover from the engine

6.4 Ensure the inner rubber spacers are correctly fitted to the mountings before installing the outer cover . . .

6.5 . . . and ensure the outer spacers are correctly positioned before refitting the retaining bolts

7 Timing belt - removal and refitting

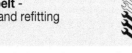

Note: The timing belt must be removed and refitted with the engine cold.

Removal

1 Disconnect the battery negative terminal then position No1 cylinder at TDC on its compression stroke as described in Section 3. **Note:** *On models with a Vauxhall anti-theft warning system (ATWS), the battery negative terminal must be disconnected within 15 seconds of the ignition being switched off to prevent the alarm system being triggered.*

2 Remove the crankshaft pulley as described in Section 5.

3 Check the camshaft sprocket timing marks are correctly aligned with the camshaft cover marks and the crankshaft sprocket timing mark is aligned with the cutout on the oil pump housing.

4 Slacken the timing belt tensioner bolt **(see illustration)**. Using an Allen key, rotate the tensioner arm clockwise to its stop, to relieve the tension in the timing belt, and hold it in position by and securely tighten the retaining bolt.

5 Slide the timing belt off from its sprockets and remove it from the engine. If the belt is to be re-used, use white paint or similar to mark the direction of rotation on the belt. **Do not** rotate the crankshaft or camshafts until the timing belt has been refitted.

6 Check the timing belt carefully for any signs of uneven wear, splitting or oil contamination, and renew it if there is the slightest doubt about its condition. If the engine is undergoing an overhaul and has covered 40 000 miles or it was more than 4 years since the original belt was fitted, renew the belt as a matter of course, regardless of its apparent condition (from 1997 onwards the belt renewal interval was increased to 80 000 miles or 8 years). If signs of oil contamination are found, trace the source of the oil leak and rectify it, then wash down the engine timing belt area and all related components to remove all traces of oil.

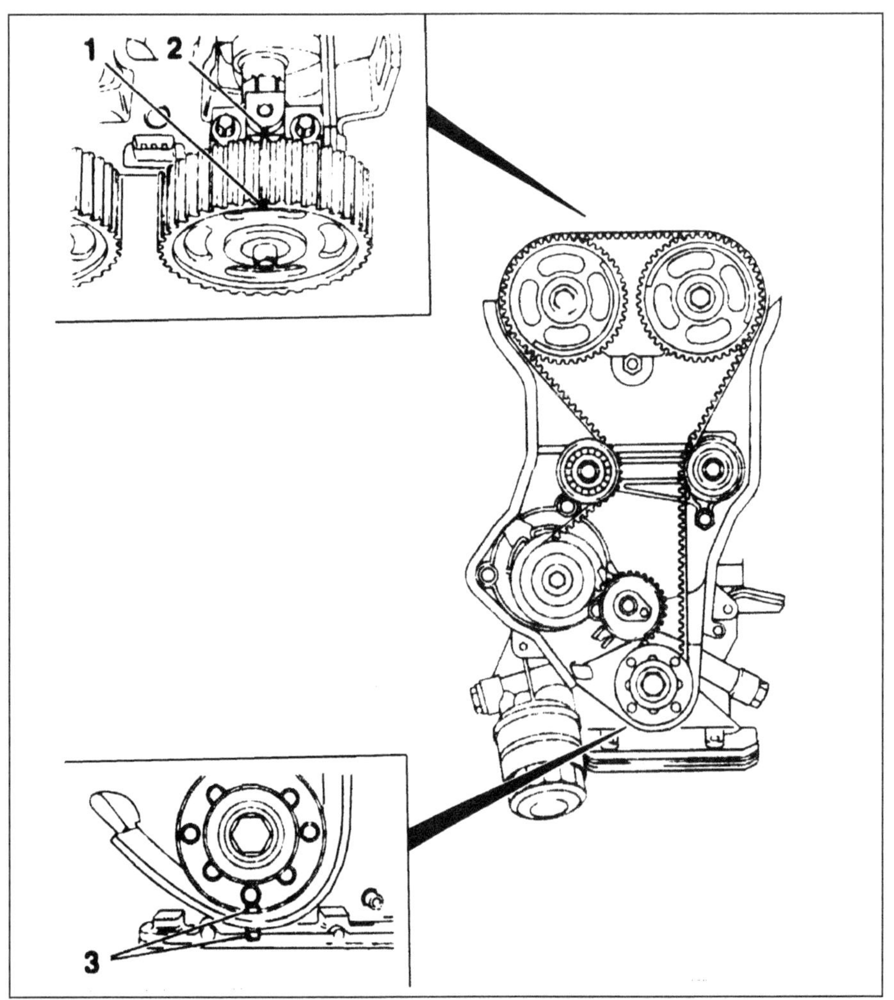

7.8 Align the camshaft sprocket marks (1) with the marks on the bearing caps (2) or cover and ensure the crankshaft sprocket timing mark is correctly aligned with the oil pump cutout (3)

7.4 Slacken the timing belt tensioner bolt (1) and rotate the tensioner clockwise using an Allen key in the arm cutout (2)

Refitting

7 On reassembly, thoroughly clean the timing belt sprockets and tensioner/idler pulleys.

8 Check that the crankshaft sprocket timing mark is still aligned with the cutout on the oil pump housing and the camshaft sprocket marks are aligned with the marks on the camshaft cover. If the camshaft cover has been removed, align the sprocket marks with the lugs on the top of the camshaft front bearing caps **(see illustration)**.

9 Fit the timing belt over the crankshaft and camshaft sprockets and around the idler pulleys, ensuring that the belt left-hand run is taut (ie, all slack is on the tensioner side of the belt), then fit the belt over the coolant pump sprocket and tensioner pulley. Do not twist the belt sharply while refitting it. Ensure that the belt teeth are correctly seated centrally in the sprockets, and that the timing marks remain in alignment. If a used belt is being refitted, ensure that the arrow mark made on removal points in the normal direction of rotation, as before.

10 Slacken the timing belt tensioner bolt to release the tensioner spring. Rotate the tensioner arm anti-clockwise until the tensioner pointer is fully over against its stop, without exerting any excess strain on the belt **(see illustration)**. Hold the tensioner in position and securely tighten its retaining bolt.

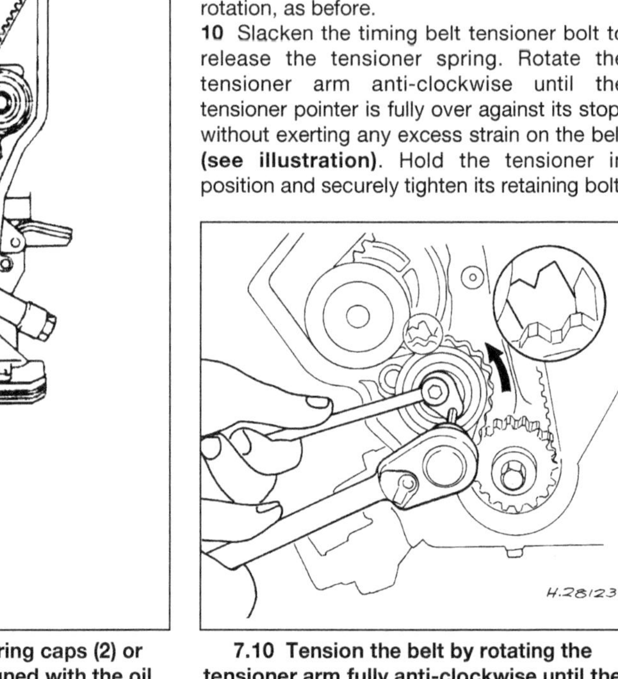

7.10 Tension the belt by rotating the tensioner arm fully anti-clockwise until the pointer is positioned as shown

11 Check the sprocket timing marks are still correctly aligned. If adjustment is necessary, release the tensioner again then disengage the belt from the sprockets and make any necessary adjustments.
12 Using a socket on the crankshaft sprocket bolt, rotate the crankshaft smoothly through two complete turns (720°) in the normal direction of rotation to settle the timing belt in position.
13 Check that both the camshaft and crankshaft sprocket timing marks are correctly realigned then slacken the tensioner bolt again.
14 If a new timing belt is being fitted, adjust the tensioner so that the pointer is aligned with either the cutout or NEW marking (depending on type of tensioner fitted) on the backplate **(see illustration)**. Hold the tensioner in the correct position and tighten its retaining bolt to the specified torque. Rotate the crankshaft smoothly through another two complete turns in the normal direction of rotation, to bring the sprocket timing marks back into alignment. Check that the tensioner pointer is still aligned with the backplate cutout/marking (as applicable).
15 If the original belt is being refitted, adjust the tensioner so that the pointer is either positioned 4 mm to the left of the cutout or is aligned with the USED marking (depending on the type of tensioner fitted) on the backplate (see illustration 7.14). Hold the tensioner in the correct position and tighten its retaining bolt to the specified torque. Rotate the crankshaft smoothly through another two complete turns in the normal direction of rotation, to bring the sprocket timing marks back into alignment. Check that the tensioner pointer is still correctly positioned in relation to the backplate cutout/marking (as applicable).
16 If the tensioner pointer is not correctly positioned in relation to the backplate, repeat the procedure in paragraph 14 (new belt) or 15 (original belt) (as applicable).
17 Once the tensioner pointer and backplate remain correctly aligned, refit the timing belt cover and crankshaft pulley as described in Sections 5 and 6.

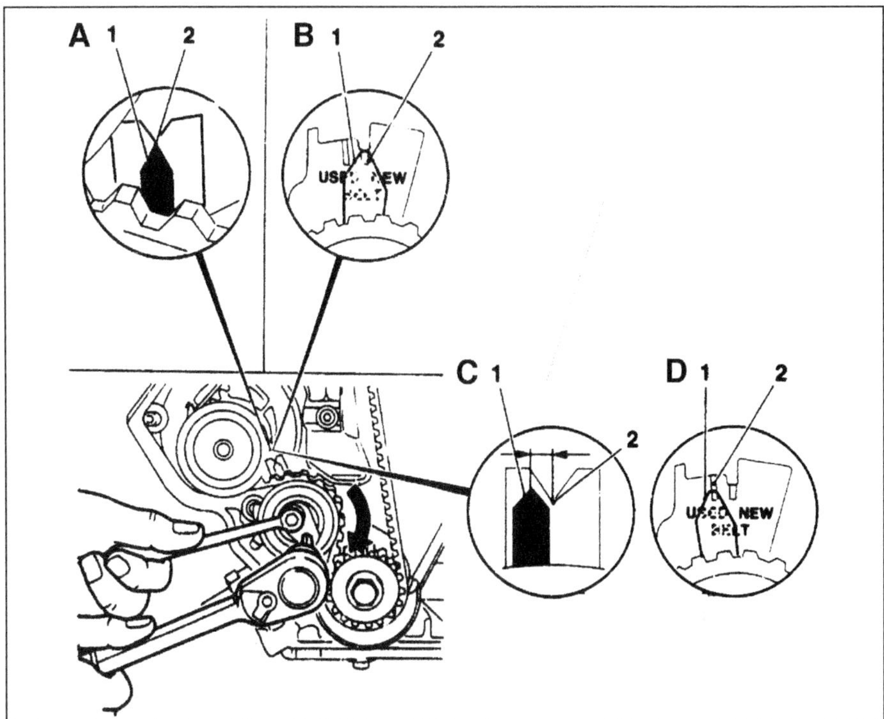

7.14 Ensure the timing belt tensioner arm (1) is correctly position in relation to the backplate cutout/marking (2) as described in text

A Correct position for new belt - engines with an unmarked tensioner
B Correct position for new belt - engines with a marked tensioner
C Correct position for used belt - engines with an unmarked tensioner
D Correct position for used belt - engines with a marked tensioner

8 Timing belt sprockets, tensioner and idler pulleys - removal and refitting

Camshaft sprockets

Note: *New sprocket retaining bolt(s) will be required on refitting.*

Removal

1 Remove the timing belt as described in Section 7.
2 The camshaft must be prevented from turning as the sprocket bolt is unscrewed, and this can be achieved in one of two ways.

a) Make up a sprocket-holding tool using two lengths of steel strip (one long, the other short), and three nuts and bolts; one nut and bolt forms the pivot of a forked tool, with the remaining two nuts and bolts at the tips of the 'forks' to engage with the sprocket spokes (see illustration 8.2 in Chapter 2A).
b) Remove the camshaft cover as described in Section 4 and hold the camshaft with an open-ended spanner on the flats provided **(see illustration)**.

3 Unscrew the retaining bolt and washer and remove the sprocket from the end of the camshaft. If the sprocket locating pin is a loose fit in the camshaft end, remove it and store it with the sprocket for safe-keeping.
4 If necessary, remove the remaining sprocket using the same method.

Refitting

5 Prior to refitting check the oil seal(s) for signs of damage or leakage. If necessary, renew as described in Section 9.
6 Ensure the locating pin is in position in the camshaft end.
7 Note that both inlet and exhaust camshaft sprockets are the same but each one is equipped with two locating pin cutouts. If the sprocket is being fitted to the inlet camshaft engage the locating pin in the IN cutout, and if the sprocket is being fitted to the exhaust camshaft engage the locating pin in the EX **(see illustration)**.
8 Ensure the camshaft locating pin is

8.2 Using an open-ended spanner to retain the camshaft sprocket whilst the sprocket bolt is slackened

8.7 Ensure the locating pin is engaged in the correct sprocket hole on refitting (see text)

engaged in the correct sprocket cutout then fit the washer and new retaining bolt.

9 Retain the sprocket by the method used on removal, and tighten the sprocket retaining bolt to the specified stage 1 torque setting then angle-tighten the bolt through the specified stage 2 angle, using a socket and extension bar, and finally through the specified stage 3 angle. It is recommended that an angle-measuring gauge is used during the final stages of the tightening, to ensure accuracy. If a gauge is not available, use white paint to make alignment marks between the bolt head and sprocket prior to tightening; the marks can then be used to check that the bolt has been rotated through the correct angle.

10 Refit the timing belt as described in Section 7 then (where necessary) refit the camshaft cover as described in Section 4.

Crankshaft sprocket

Note: *A new crankshaft sprocket retaining bolt will be required on refitting.*

Removal

11 Remove the timing belt as described in Section 7.

12 The crankshaft must be prevented from turning as the sprocket bolt is unscrewed (the bolt is very tight), and this can be achieved in anyone of the following ways.

a) Use the holding tool described in paragraph 2 securing the tool to the sprocket with two bolts screwed into opposite pulley retaining bolt holes.

b) On manual transmission models have an assistant select top gear and apply the brakes firmly.

c) If the engine is removed from the vehicle or the transmission unit has been removed the flywheel/driveplate can be locked (see Chapter 2A, Section 15).

13 Unscrew the retaining bolt and washer and remove the crankshaft sprocket from the end of the crankshaft. Discard the bolt; a new one must be used on refitting. If necessary, remove the sprocket Woodruff key from the crankshaft end and slide off the spacer.

Refitting

14 Slide the spacer (where removed) onto the crankshaft then refit the Woodruff key to the crankshaft slot.

15 Align the sprocket with the key and slide it into position, ensuring the sprocket flange is facing outwards. Fit the washer and new retaining bolt.

16 Lock the crankshaft by the method used on removal, and tighten the sprocket retaining bolt to the specified stage 1 torque setting then angle-tighten the bolt through the specified stage 2 angle, using a socket and extension bar. It is recommended that an angle-measuring gauge is used during the final stages of the tightening, to ensure accuracy. If a gauge is not available, use white paint to make alignment marks between the bolt head and sprocket prior to tightening; the marks can then be used to check that the bolt has been rotated through the correct angle.

17 Refit the timing belt as described in Section 7.

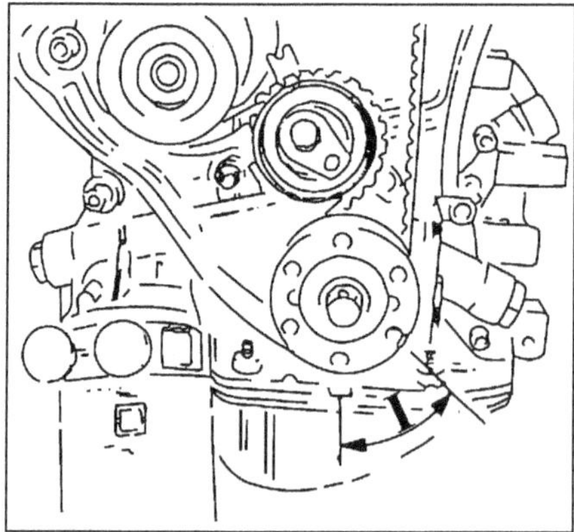

10.1 Prior to removing the timing belt, rotate the crankshaft 60° backwards to ensure the camshaft and pistons are safely positioned

Tensioner assembly

Removal

18 Remove the timing belt as described in Section 7.

19 Slacken and remove the retaining bolt and remove the tensioner assembly from the engine.

Refitting

20 Fit the tensioner to the engine, making sure that the lug on the backplate is correctly located in the oil pump housing hole. Ensure the tensioner is correctly seated then refit the retaining bolt. Using an Allen key, rotate the tensioner arm clockwise to its stop then securely tighten the retaining bolt.

21 Refit the timing belt as described in Section 7.

Idler pulleys

Removal

22 Remove the timing belt as described in Section 7.

23 Slacken and remove the retaining bolt(s) and remove the idler pulley(s) from the engine. If necessary, unbolt the pulley mounting bracket and remove it from the cylinder block.

10.3 Removing a camshaft bearing cap

Refitting

24 Refit the pulley mounting bracket (where removed) to the cylinder block and tighten its retaining bolts to the specified torque.

25 Refit the idler pulley(s) and tighten the retaining bolt(s) to the specified torque.

26 Refit the timing belt as described in Section 7.

9 Camshaft oil seals - renewal

1 Remove the relevant camshaft sprocket as described in Section 8.

2 Carefully punch or drill two small holes opposite each other in the oil seal. Screw a self-tapping screw into each, and pull on the screws with pliers to extract the seal. Alternatively carefully lever the oil seal out of position.

3 Clean the seal housing, and polish off any burrs or raised edges which may have caused the seal to fail in the first place.

4 Lubricate the lips of the new seal with clean engine oil, and press it into position using a suitable tubular drift (such as a socket) which bears only on the hard outer edge of the seal. Take care not to damage the seal lips during fitting; note that the seal lips should face inwards.

5 Refit the camshaft sprocket as described in Section 8.

10 Camshafts and followers - removal, inspection and refitting

Removal

1 Remove the timing belt as described in Section 7. Prior to releasing the timing belt tension and removing the belt, rotate the crankshaft **backwards** by approximately 60° (4 teeth of movement); this will position the camshafts so that the valve spring pressure is evenly exerted along the complete length of the shaft, reducing the risk of the bearing caps being damaged on removal/refitting **(see illustration)**.

2 Remove the camshaft sprockets as described in Section 8.

3 Starting on the inlet camshaft, working in a spiral pattern from the outside inwards, slacken the camshaft bearing cap retaining bolts by half-a-turn at a time, to relieve the pressure of the valve springs on the bearing caps gradually and evenly. Once the valve spring pressure has been relieved, the bolts can be fully unscrewed and removed along with the caps; the bearing caps and the cylinder head locations are numbered to ensure the caps are correctly positioned on refitting **(see illustration)**. Take care not to loose the locating dowels (where fitted).

10.6 Using a rubber sucker to remove a camshaft follower

Caution: If the bearing cap bolts are carelessly slackened, the bearing caps might break. If any bearing cap breaks then the complete cylinder head assembly must be renewed; the bearing caps are matched to the head and are not available separately.

4 Lift the camshaft out of the cylinder head and slide off the oil seal.

5 Repeat the operations described in paragraphs 3 and 4 and remove the exhaust camshaft.

6 Obtain sixteen small, clean plastic containers, and label them for identification. Alternatively, divide a larger container into compartments. Lift the followers out from the top of the cylinder head and store each one in its respective fitted position **(see illustration)**. **Note:** *Store all the followers the correct way up to prevent the oil draining from the hydraulic valve adjustment mechanisms.*

Inspection

7 Examine the camshaft bearing surfaces and cam lobes for signs of wear ridges and scoring. Renew the camshaft if any of these conditions are apparent. Examine the condition of the bearing surfaces both on the camshaft journals and in the cylinder head. If the head bearing surfaces are worn excessively, the cylinder head will need to be renewed.

8 Examine the follower bearing surfaces which contact the camshaft lobes for wear ridges and scoring. Check the followers and their bores in the cylinder head for signs of wear or damage. If any follower is thought to be faulty or is visibly worn it should be renewed.

Refitting

9 Where removed, lubricate the followers with clean engine oil and carefully insert each one into its original location in the cylinder head.

10 Lubricate the camshaft followers with clean engine oil then lay the camshafts in position. Ensure the crankshaft is still positioned approximately 60° BTDC and position each camshaft so that the lobes of No1 cylinder are pointing upwards. Temporarily refit the sprockets to the camshafts and position each one so that its sprocket timing mark is approximately 4 teeth before its TDC alignment position.

11 Ensure the mating surfaces of the bearing caps and cylinder head are clean and dry and lubricate the camshaft journals and lobes with clean engine oil.

12 Apply a smear of sealant (Vauxhall recommend the use of sealant 15 03 170 - available from your Vauxhall dealer) to the areas of the cylinder head mating surface around the sides of the inlet and exhaust camshaft front bearing cap oil seal apertures **(see illustration)**.

13 Ensure the locating dowels (where fitted) are in position then refit the camshaft bearing caps and the retaining bolts in their original locations on the cylinder head. The caps are numbered from front to rear and the corresponding numbers are marked on the cylinder head upper surface.

14 Working on the inlet camshaft, tighten the bearing cap bolts by hand only then, working in a spiral pattern from the centre outwards, tighten the bolts by half-a-turn at a time to gradually impose the pressure of the valve springs on the bearing caps **(see illustration)**. Repeat this sequence until all bearing caps are in contact with the cylinder head then go around and tighten the camshaft retaining bolts to the specified torque.

Caution: If the bearing cap bolts are carelessly tightened, the bearing caps might break. If any bearing cap breaks then the complete cylinder head assembly must be renewed; the bearing caps are matched to the head and are not available separately.

15 Tighten the exhaust camshaft bearing cap bolts as described in paragraph 14.

16 Fit new camshaft oil seals as described in Section 9.

17 Refit the camshaft sprockets as described in Section 8.

18 Align all the sprocket timing marks to bring the camshafts and crankshaft back to TDC then refit the timing belt as described in Section 7.

19 Refit the camshaft cover and timing belt cover as described in Sections 4 and 6.

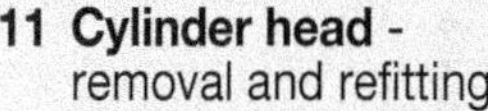

11 Cylinder head - removal and refitting

Removal

Note: *The engine must be cold when removing the cylinder head. New cylinder head bolts must be used on refitting.*

1 Disconnect the battery negative lead. **Note:** *On models with a Vauxhall anti-theft warning system (ATWS), the battery negative terminal must be disconnected within 15 seconds of the ignition being switched off to prevent the alarm system being triggered.*

2 Drain the cooling system and remove the spark plugs as described in Chapter 1.

3 Remove the inlet and exhaust manifolds as described in Chapter 4A. If no work is to be carried out on the cylinder head, the head can be removed complete with manifolds once the following operations have been carried out (see Chapter 4A).

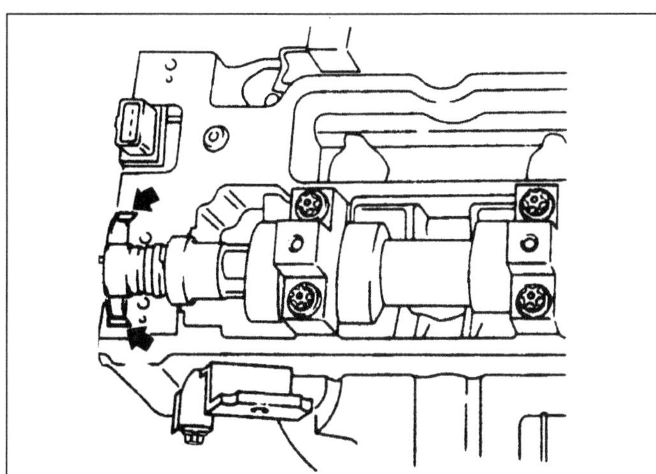

10.12 Apply sealant to the shaded areas (arrowed) on each side of the inlet and exhaust camshaft oil seal apertures

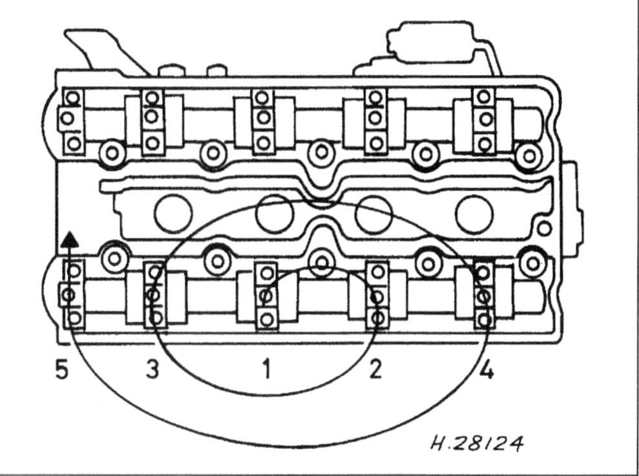

10.14 Camshaft bearing cap tightening sequence (exhaust camshaft shown - inlet the same)

11.19 Fit the new gasket to the cylinder block, engaging it with the locating dowels (arrowed) . . .

11.20 . . . making sure its OBEN/TOP marking is uppermost

a) *Remove the intake duct connecting the air cleaner to the throttle housing.*
b) *Disconnect the wiring connectors from the throttle potentiometer, idle speed adjuster, EGR valve, purge valve, coolant temperature sensor, oxygen sensor and DIS module. Unbolt the earth connection from the fuel rail and release the wiring harness from its retaining clips. Lift the wiring cover squarely off of the injectors then disconnect the knock sensor and crankshaft sensor wiring connectors before positioning the wiring cover/harness clear of the cylinder head.*
c) *Depressurise the fuel system then disconnect the fuel hoses from the fuel rail.*
d) *Disconnect the various vacuum and coolant hoses from the inlet manifold/throttle housing.*
e) *Unbolt the inlet manifold support bracket and the alternator upper brackets.*
f) *Disconnect the accelerator cable.*
g) *Remove the exhaust system front pipe.*
h) *Disconnect the air hose from the secondary air injection system non-return valve on the exhaust manifold.*

4 Remove the timing belt as described in Section 7. Prior to releasing the timing belt tension and removing the belt, rotate the crankshaft backwards by approximately 60° (4 teeth of movement); this will position the camshafts so that the valve spring pressure is evenly exerted along the complete length of the shafts, preventing the shafts turning and reducing the risk of the valves contacting the pistons (see illustration 10.1).

5 Remove the camshafts as described in Section 10.

6 Undo the retaining bolts securing the timing belt rear cover to the cylinder head.

7 Release the retaining clips and disconnect the various coolant hoses from the cylinder head/thermostat housing, noting each ones correct fitted location.

8 Unbolt the crankcase breather tube and remove it from the left-hand side of the cylinder block. Discard the gasket, a new one should be used on refitting.

9 Make a final check to ensure that all relevant hoses, pipes and wires, etc, have been disconnected.

10 Working in the reverse of the tightening sequence (see illustration 11.23), progressively slacken the cylinder head bolts by a quarter of a turn at a time until all bolts can be unscrewed by hand. Remove each bolt in turn, along with its washer.

11 Lift the cylinder head from the cylinder block. If necessary, tap the cylinder head gently with a soft-faced mallet to free it from the block, but **do not** lever at the mating faces. Note the fitted positions of the two locating dowels, and remove them for safe keeping if they are loose.

12 Recover the cylinder head gasket, and discard it.

Preparation for refitting

13 The mating faces of the cylinder head and block must be perfectly clean before refitting the head. Use a scraper to remove all traces of gasket and carbon, and also clean the tops of the pistons. Take particular care with the aluminium surfaces, as the soft metal is damaged easily. Also, make sure that debris is not allowed to enter the oil and water channels - this is particularly important for the oil circuit, as carbon could block the oil supply to the camshaft or crankshaft bearings. Using adhesive tape and paper, seal the water, oil and bolt holes in the cylinder block. To prevent carbon entering the gap between the pistons and bores, smear a little grease in the gap. After cleaning the piston, rotate the crankshaft so that the piston moves down the bore, then wipe out the grease and carbon with a cloth rag. Clean the piston crowns in the same way.

14 Check the block and head for nicks, deep scratches and other damage. If slight, they may be removed carefully with a file. More serious damage may be repaired by machining, but this is a specialist job.

15 If warpage of the cylinder head is suspected, use a straight-edge to check it for distortion. Refer to Chapter 2D if necessary.

16 Ensure that the cylinder head bolt holes in the crankcase are clean and free of oil. Syringe or soak up any oil left in the bolt holes. This is most important in order that the correct bolt tightening torque can be applied and to prevent the possibility of the block being cracked by hydraulic pressure when the bolts are tightened.

17 Renew the cylinder head bolts regardless of their apparent condition.

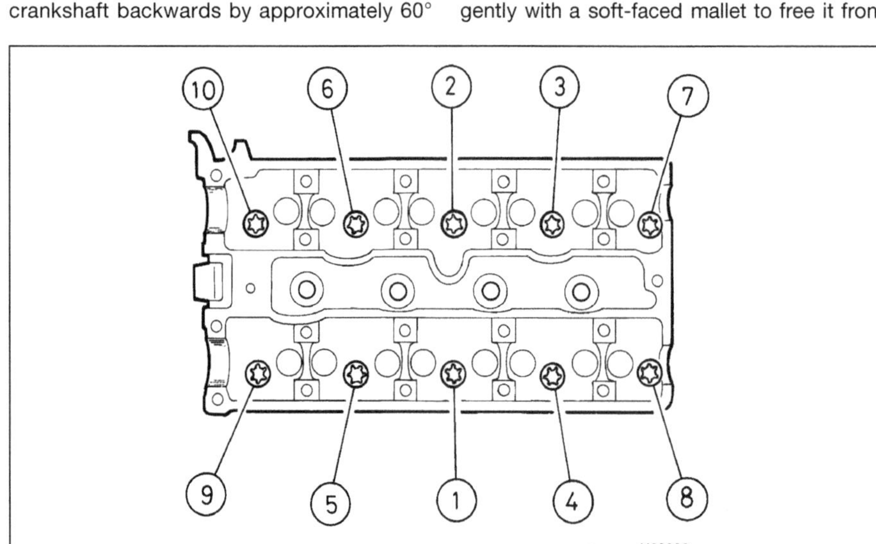

11.23 Cylinder head bolt tightening sequence

Refitting

18 Ensure the crankshaft is till positioned approximately 60° BTDC and wipe clean the mating faces of the head and block.

19 Ensure that the two locating dowels are in position at each end of the cylinder block/crankcase surface **(see illustration)**.

20 Fit the new cylinder head gasket to the block, making sure it is fitted with the correct way up with its OBEN or TOP mark uppermost and at the front end of the engine **(see illustration)**.

21 Carefully refit the cylinder head, locating it on the dowels.

22 Fit the washers to the new cylinder head bolts then carefully insert them into position (**do not drop**), tightening them finger-tight only at this stage.

23 Working progressively and in the sequence shown, first tighten all the cylinder head bolts to the stage 1 torque setting **(see illustration)**.

24 Once all bolts have been tightened to the stage 1 torque, again working in the sequence shown, tighten each bolt through its specified stage 2 angle, using a socket and extension bar. It is recommended that an angle-measuring gauge is used during this stage of the tightening, to ensure accuracy.
25 Working in the specified sequence, go around again and tighten all bolts through the specified stage 3 angle.
26 Working again in the specified sequence, go around and tighten all bolts through the specified stage 4 angle.
27 Finally go around in the specified sequence again and tighten all bolts through the specified stage 5 angle.
28 Ensure the mating surfaces are clean and dry then refit the breather tube to the cylinder block and tighten its retaining bolts to the specified torque.
29 Reconnect the coolant hoses, securing them in position with the retaining clips.
30 Refit the timing belt rear cover retaining bolts and tighten them to the specified torque.
31 Refit the camshafts as described in Section 10.
32 Align all the sprocket timing marks to bring the camshafts and crankshaft back to TDC then refit the timing belt as described in Section 7.
33 Refit the camshaft cover and timing belt cover(s) as described in Sections 4 and 5.
34 Refit/reconnect the inlet and exhaust manifolds (see Chapter 4A).
35 Ensure all pipes and hoses are securely reconnected then refill the cooling system and refit the spark plugs as described in Chapter 1.
36 Reconnect the battery then start the engine and check for signs of leaks.

12 Sump - removal and refitting

Note: *There are two possible types of sump fitted to these engines; early models had a one-piece sump made of pressed steel and later models had a two-piece sump arrangement with a small pressed steel sump pan being fitted to the base of the main sump casting which is made of aluminium alloy. Proceed as described under the relevant heading*

One-piece sump

Note: *A new baffle plate will be required on refitting (the sump gasket is an integral part of the plate).*

Removal

1 Disconnect the battery negative terminal. **Note:** *On models with a Vauxhall anti-theft warning system (ATWS), the battery negative terminal must be disconnected within 15 seconds of the ignition being switched off to prevent the alarm system being triggered.*
2 Firmly apply the handbrake then jack up the front of the car and support it on axle stands. Undo the retaining screws and remove the undercover from beneath the engine.
3 Drain the engine oil as described in Chapter 1, then fit a new sealing washer and refit the drain plug, tightening it to the specified torque.
4 Where necessary, disconnect the wiring connector from the oil level sender unit on the sump.
5 Slacken and remove the bolts securing the support brackets to the transmission housing and sides of the cylinder block. Remove both brackets from the engine then remove the flywheel lower cover plate from the base of the transmission housing.
6 Slacken and remove the nuts securing the left- and right-hand engine mounting brackets to the top of the rubber mountings. Unbolt the right-hand mounting bracket and remove it from the cylinder block.
7 Attach an engine hoist to the cylinder head lifting brackets then raise the hoist until it is supporting the weight of the engine.
8 Progressively slacken and remove the bolts securing the sump to the base of the cylinder block/oil pump. Break the sump joint by striking the sump with the palm of the hand, then lower the sump away from the engine and withdraw it. Raise the engine unit slightly to gain the necessary clearance required for sump removal, taking care not to place any excess strain on the engine wiring/hoses or exhaust system.
9 Undo the retaining bolts and remove the oil pump pick-up/strainer from the base of the oil pump housing, noting the sealing ring, then remove the baffle plate assembly.
10 Check the oil pump pick-up/strainer for signs of clogging or splitting and renew/clean as necessary. **Note:** *If the sump is to be removed for any length of time, refit the mounting bracket to the cylinder block and lower the engine back down onto its mounting rubbers.*

Refitting

11 Remove all traces of dirt and oil from the mating surfaces of the sump, cylinder block and oil pump housing. Also remove all traces of locking compound from the threads of the oil pump pick-up/strainer bolts and the sump retaining bolts.
12 Apply a smear of suitable sealant (Vauxhall recommend the use of sealant 15 03 295 - available from your Vauxhall dealer) to the areas of the cylinder block mating surface around the areas of the oil pump housing and rear main bearing cap joints.
13 Fit a new sealing ring to the oil pump pick-up/strainer and apply a few drops of locking compound (Vauxhall recommend the use of locking compound 15 10 181 - available from your Vauxhall dealer) to the threads of the strainer retaining bolts.
14 Offer up the new baffle plate, making sure it is correctly located, then refit the oil pump strainer tightening its retaining bolts to the specified torque.
15 Apply a drop of the locking compound to each of the sump retaining bolts then offer up the sump to the cylinder block. Refit the retaining bolts and progressively tighten them to the specified torque, working out from the centre in a diagonal sequence.
16 Refit the mounting bracket to the cylinder block and tighten its retaining bolts to the specified torque. Lower the engine back down onto its mountings making sure the brackets and mounting rubbers are correctly aligned. Remove the hoist from the engine then refit the mounting nuts, tightening them to the specified torque setting.
17 Refit the flywheel lower cover plate to the transmission housing then refit the support brackets. Screw in the bolts securing the brackets to the cylinder block and transmission housing and tighten them to their specified torque settings.
18 Reconnect the oil level sender wiring connector (where fitted).
19 Refit the undercover then lower the vehicle to the ground then fill the engine with fresh oil, with reference to Chapter 1.

Two-piece sump

Note: *New sump pan retaining bolts and front suspension subframe mounting bolts will be required on refitting. New retaining nuts for the centre tie rod will also be required.*

Removal

20 Carry out the operations described in paragraphs 1 to 3.
21 Referring to Chapter 12, on models with Xenon headlights, disconnect the wiring connector from the headlight system front vehicle level control sensor then unclip the link rod from the sensor arm balljoint.
22 Remove the steering linkage centre tie rod as described in Chapter 10, Section 25.
23 Slacken and remove the nuts securing the engine left- and right-hand mountings to the subframe.
24 Attach an engine hoist to the cylinder head lifting brackets then raise the hoist until it is supporting the weight of the engine. Alternatively use an engine support bar to take the weight of the engine.
25 Referring to Chapter 10, unscrew the front suspension subframe front mounting bolts by approximately 4 turns. Support the rear of the subframe with a jack then slacken and remove the rear mounting bolts. Lower the rear of the subframe approximately 10 cm to gain access to the sump pan.
26 If an oil level sensor is fitted, disconnect the wiring connector from the sensor connector on the left-hand side of the main casting then slide off the retaining clip and push the connector into the sump.
27 Slacken and remove the bolts securing the sump pan to the main casting then free the pan and remove it along with its gasket. On models with an oil level sensor, take care not to damage the sensor wiring as the pan is removed.

13.7 Undo the retaining screws and remove the oil pump cover

28 To remove the main casting from the engine, disconnect the wiring connector from the oil temperature sensor (where fitted) then slacken and remove the bolts securing the exhaust front pipe mounting bracket in position.

29 Unscrew the bolts securing the main casting flange to the transmission housing then progressively slacken and remove the bolts securing the casting to the base of the cylinder block/oil pump. Break the joint by striking the casting with the palm of the hand, then lower it away from the engine and withdraw it. Remove the gasket and discard it. **Note:** *If the sump pan/main casting are to be removed for any length of time, raise the subframe back up into position and refit its mounting bolts then lower the engine back down onto the subframe.*

30 While the sump is removed, take the opportunity to check the oil pump pick-up/strainer for signs of clogging or splitting. If necessary, unbolt the pick-up/strainer and remove it from the base of the oil pump housing along with its sealing ring. The strainer can then be cleaned easily in solvent or renewed.

Refitting

31 Remove all traces of dirt and oil from the mating surfaces of the sump pan, main casting and cylinder block and (if necessary) the pick-up/strainer and oil pump housing. Also remove all traces of locking compound from the main casting bolts and (where removed) the pick-up/strainer bolts.

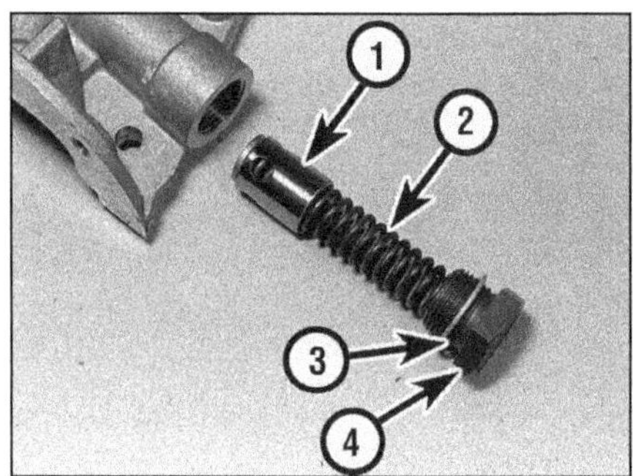

13.10 Oil pressure relief valve components

1 *Plunger*
2 *Spring*
3 *Sealing washer*
4 *Valve bolt*

13.9 Lift the inner and outer gears (arrowed) out from the pump housing

32 Where necessary, position a new sealing ring on top of the oil pump pick-up/strainer and fit the strainer. Apply locking compound (Vauxhall recommend the use of locking compound 15 10 181 - available from your Vauxhall dealer) to the threads of the retaining bolts then fit the bolts and tighten to the specified torque.

33 Apply a smear of suitable sealant (Vauxhall recommend the use of sealant 15 03 295 - available from your Vauxhall dealer) to the areas of the cylinder block mating surface around the areas of the oil pump housing and rear main bearing cap joints.

34 Fit a new gasket to the main casting then apply a drop of locking compound to the threads of the casting to cylinder block/oil pump bolts. Manoeuvre the casting into position, ensuring the gasket is correctly positioned, then loosely refit all the retaining bolts and the exhaust front pipe mounting bracket.

35 Working out from the centre in a diagonal sequence, progressively tighten the bolts securing the main casting to the cylinder block/oil pump to their specified torque setting.

36 Tighten the bolts securing the main casting flange to the transmission housing to their specified torque settings then securely tighten the exhaust bracket bolts. Where necessary, reconnect the oil temperature sensor.

37 Ensure the sump pan and main casting surfaces are clean and dry, place a new gasket on the top of the pan and offer it up to the main casting. On models with an oil level sensor, fit a new sealing ring to the wiring connector and seat the wiring connector in the main casting, securing it in position with the retaining clip, prior to seating the sump pan on the main casting.

38 Fit the new sump pan retaining bolts then go around in a diagonal sequence and tighten them to the specified stage 1 torque setting. Once all bolts have been tightened go around again and angle-tighten them through the specified stage 2 angle. It is recommended that an angle-measuring gauge is used during this stage of the tightening, to ensure accuracy.

39 Reconnect the oil level sender wiring connector (where necessary).

40 Raise the subframe back up into position making sure the engine mounting lugs engage correctly with the subframe cutouts. Fit the four new rear retaining bolts then remove the subframe front retaining bolts and fit the new ones. Tighten the subframe mounting bolts to their specified torque setting and then through the specified angles as described in Chapter 10.

41 Remove the hoist from the engine then refit the nuts securing the engine mountings to the subframe, tightening them to the specified torque.

42 Refit the steering linkage centre tie rod as described in Chapter 10

43 On models with Xenon headlights clip the link rod balljoint back onto the vehicle level control sensor and reconnect the wiring connector (see Chapter 12).

44 Refit the undercover then lower the vehicle to the ground then fill the engine with fresh oil, with reference to Chapter 1.

13 Oil pump - removal, overhaul and refitting

Removal

1 Drain the engine oil as described in Chapter 1, then fit a new sealing washer and refit the drain plug, tightening it to the specified torque. Remove the oil filter and discard it.

2 Remove the timing belt as described in Section 7.

3 Remove the rear timing belt cover as described in Section 6.

4 Remove the sump and oil pump pick-up/strainer as described in Section 12.

5 Disconnect the wiring connector from the oil pressure switch.

6 Slacken and remove the retaining bolts then slide the oil pump housing assembly off of the end of the crankshaft, taking great care not to lose the locating dowels. Remove the housing gasket and discard it.

Overhaul

7 Undo the retaining screws and lift off the pump cover from the rear of the housing **(see illustration)**.

8 Using a suitable marker pen, mark the surface of both the pump inner and outer gears; the marks can then be used to ensure the gears are refitted the correct way around.

9 Lift out the inner and outer gears from the pump housing **(see illustration)**.

10 Unscrew the oil pressure relief valve bolt from the front of the housing and withdraw the spring and plunger from the housing, noting which way around the plunger is fitted **(see illustration)**. Remove the sealing washer from the valve bolt. **Note:** *The pressure relief valve can be removed with pump in position on the engine unit. On models with air conditioning it will be necessary to unbolt the compressor mounting bracket assembly from the block to allow the valve to be removed.*

13.12a Using a feeler blade to check gear clearance

13.12b Using a straight edge and feeler blade to measure gear endfloat

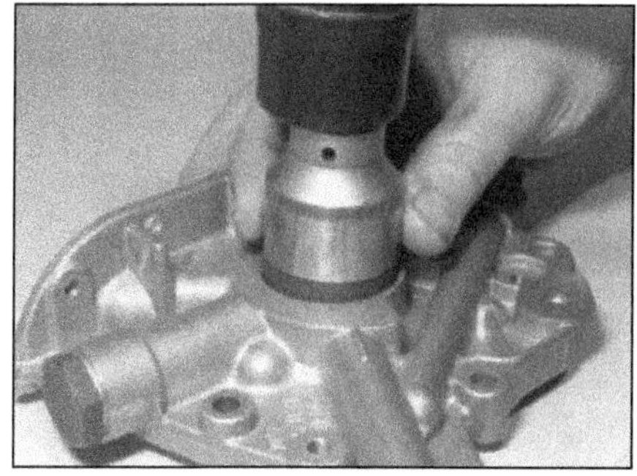

13.14 Fitting a new crankshaft oil seal to the oil pump housing

11 Clean the components, and carefully examine the gears, pump body and relief valve plunger for any signs of scoring or wear. Renew any component which shows signs of wear or damage; if the gears or pump housing are marked then the complete pump assembly should be renewed.

12 If the components appear serviceable, measure the clearance between the inner and outer gears using feeler blades. Also measure the gear endfloat, and check the flatness of the end cover **(see illustrations)**. If the clearances exceed the specified tolerances, the pump must be renewed.

13 If the pump is satisfactory, reassemble the components in the reverse order of removal, noting the following.

a) Ensure both gears are fitted the correct way around.

b) Fit a new sealing ring to the pressure relief valve bolt and tighten the bolt to the specified torque.

c) Tighten the pump cover screws to the specified torque.

d) On completion prime the oil pump by filling it with clean engine oil whilst rotating the inner gear.

Refitting

14 Prior to refitting, carefully lever out the crankshaft oil seal using a flat-bladed screwdriver. Fit the new oil seal, ensuring its sealing lip is facing inwards, and press it squarely into the housing using a tubular drift which bears only on the hard outer edge of the seal **(see illustration)**. Press the seal into position so that it is flush with the housing and lubricate the oil seal lip with clean engine oil.

15 Ensure the mating surfaces of the oil pump and cylinder block are clean and dry and the locating dowels are in position.

16 Fit a new gasket to the cylinder block.

17 Carefully manoeuvre the oil pump into position and engage the inner gear with the crankshaft end. Locate the pump on the dowels, taking great care not damage the oil seal lip.

18 Refit the pump housing retaining bolts in their original locations and tighten them to the specified torque.

19 Reconnect the oil pressure sensor wiring connector.

20 Refit the oil pump pick-up/strainer and sump as described in Section 12.

21 Refit the rear timing belt cover to the engine, tightening its retaining bolts to the specified torque.

22 Refit the timing belt sprockets, idler pulleys and tensioner then refit the belt as described in Sections 7 and 8.

23 On completion, fit a new oil filter and fill the engine with clean oil as described in Chapter 1.

14 Crankshaft balancer unit (1998 model year onwards) - removal, refitting and adjustment

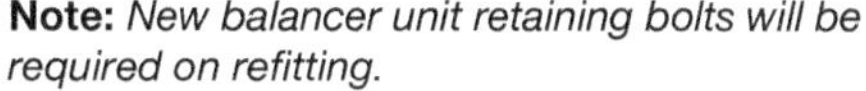

Note: *New balancer unit retaining bolts will be required on refitting.*

Removal

1 Remove the sump and oil pump pick-up/strainer pipe as described in Section 12.

2 Using a socket on the crankshaft sprocket bolt, rotate the crankshaft in the normal direction of rotation until the notch on the pulley rim is correctly aligned with the pointer on the timing belt cover. This positions number 1 cylinder at TDC. With number 1 piston at TDC the flats on the end of each balancer shaft should be correctly aligned (see paragraph 5).

3 Evenly and progressively slacken and remove the retaining bolts then remove the balancer unit from the base of the cylinder block along with the spacer plate which is fitted between the unit and block. The spacer plate is used to adjust the balancer unit gear teeth backlash (see paragraph 10).

Refitting

4 If any work has been carried out on the crankshaft or a new balancer is being installed, it will be necessary to adjust the gear teeth backlash prior to refitting. If the original balancer unit is to be refitted and no work has being carried out on the crankshaft it is permissible to refit the unit with the original spacer plate without checking the gear backlash.

5 Ensure the crankshaft pulley notch is still correctly aligned with the pointer on the rear cover then rotate the balancer unit gears until the flats on the gear shaft ends are facing downwards and are in line with each other **(see illustration)**.

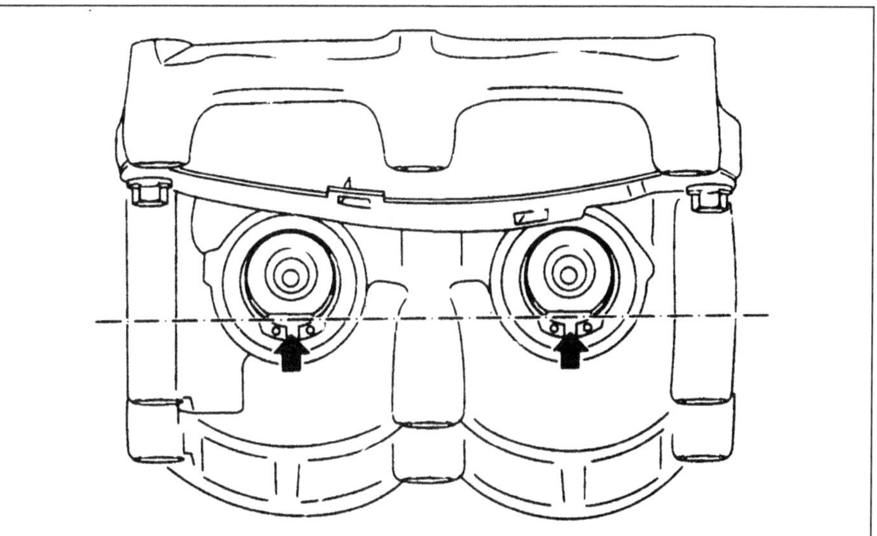

14.5 With number 1 cylinder at TDC the balancer unit gear shaft flats should be correctly aligned as shown

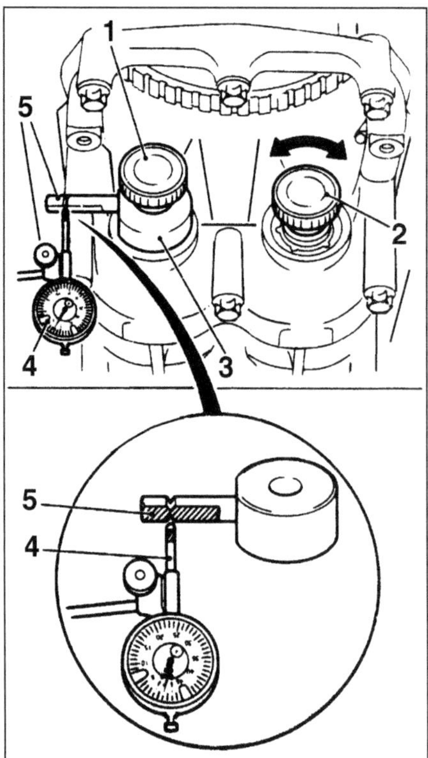

14.12 Using service tool KM-949 to check the balancer unit gear teeth backlash. Ensure the dial gauge is positioned at a right-angle to the arm and is correctly seated in the arm groove

1 Right-hand thumbwheel
2 Left-hand thumbwheel
3 Measuring arm base
4 Dial gauge
5 Measuring arm

6 Fit the spacer plate to the top of the balancer unit then refit the balancer unit to the cylinder block. Ensure the shaft gear is correctly engaged with the crankshaft gear, and screw in the new retaining bolts.

7 Tighten all the bolts by hand then check that the crankshaft pulley mark and balance shaft flats are still correctly aligned. If not, remove the balancer unit and make any necessary adjustments before refitting it to the cylinder block.

8 Once the balancer unit is correctly timed with the crankshaft, go around in a diagonal sequence and tighten the retaining bolts to the specified stage 1 torque setting. Once all bolts have been tightened go around again and angle-tighten them through the specified stage 2 angle. It is recommended that an angle-measuring gauge is used during this stage of the tightening, to ensure accuracy.

9 Refit the oil pump pick-up/strainer and sump as described in Section 12.

Adjustment

Note: *The following procedure can only be accurately carried out using Vauxhall service tool KM-949 and a dial gauge.*

10 If work has been carried out on the crankshaft or a new balancer unit is being fitted, it is necessary to check the balancer unit gear teeth backlash. The backlash is controlled by the thickness of the spacer plate which is fitted in between the balancer unit and the cylinder block. The spacer is available in the following thicknesses; the thickness can be determined by direct measurement or by the identification marking on the stamped on it.

Plate thickness	Identification marking
0.535 to 0.565 mm	55
0.565 to 0.595 mm	58
0.595 to 0.625 mm	61
0.625 to 0.655 mm	64
0.655 to 0.685 mm	67
0.685 to 0.715 mm	70
0.715 to 0.745 mm	73
0.745 to 0.775 mm	76
0.775 to 0.805 mm	79
0.805 to 0.835 mm	82
0.835 to 0.865 mm	85

11 The backlash is measured with the balancer unit correctly installed on the cylinder block. If a new balancer unit is being fitted, obtain the thickest spacer plate available (identification marking 85) and fit the balancer unit to the cylinder block using the original retaining bolts (see paragraphs 5 to 8).

12 Position number 1 cylinder at TDC (see paragraph 2) and fit the service tool KM-949. Fit the measuring arm to the right-hand (inlet manifold side) shaft, ensuring the arm is horizontal, then screw both knurled thumbwheels into the balancer shafts and tighten securely. Position the dial gauge so that it is at a right-angle to the measuring arm and its pointer is seated correctly in the arm groove **(see illustration)**.

13 Using the knurled thumbwheel, rotate the left hand (exhaust manifold side) balancer shaft fully clockwise then zero the dial gauge. Rotate the shaft fully anti-clockwise and measure the movement of the arm on the gauge, noting this figure down on paper.

14 Position the dial gauge clear of the measuring arm then rotate the crankshaft through 45° (the balance shafts will rotate 90°). Slacken the right-hand thumbwheel and return the measurement arm to the horizontal position before tightening it securely then take the backlash measurement again.

15 Repeat this procedure twice more until a total of four backlash measurements have been obtained.

16 All four backlash measurements should be within the range of 0.02 to 0.06 mm. If any one of the four measurements is outside this range then adjustment is necessary.

17 If adjustment is necessary, remove the balancer unit from the cylinder block and recover the spacer plate. Identify the thickness of the spacer plate (see paragraph 10). The backlash measurements are decreased by fitting a thinner spacer plate and increased by fitting a thicker plate. Calculate the correct thickness of spacer plate required noting that each plate thickness increases/decreases (as applicable) the backlash measurement by approximately 0.02 mm. For example, if a backlash measurement of 0.07 mm was obtained and a spacer plate with the identification marking 67 was installed, fitting a spacer plate with the identification marking 64 will decrease the measurement by approximately 0.02 mm and bring the backlash to within the specified limit.

18 Select the correct thickness of spacer plate required then refit the balancer unit as described in paragraphs 5 to 9.

15 Flywheel/driveplate - removal, inspection and refitting

Refer to Chapter 2A, Section 15.

16 Crankshaft oil seals - renewal

Front (timing belt end) oil seal

1 Remove the crankshaft sprocket as described in Section 8.

2 Carefully punch or drill two small holes opposite each other in the oil seal. Screw a self-tapping screw into each and pull on the screws with pliers to extract the seal. Alternatively carefully lever the seal out of position.

Caution: Great care must be taken to avoid damage to the oil pump

3 Clean the seal housing and polish off any burrs or raised edges which may have caused the seal to fail in the first place.

4 Lubricate the lips of the new seal with clean engine oil and ease it into position on the end of the shaft. Press the seal squarely into position until it is flush with the housing. If necessary, a suitable tubular drift, such as a socket, which bears only on the hard outer edge of the seal can be used to tap the seal into position. Take great care not to damage the seal lips during fitting and ensure that the seal lips face inwards.

5 Wash off any traces of oil, then refit the crankshaft sprocket as described in Section 8.

Rear (flywheel/driveplate end) oil seal

6 Remove the flywheel/driveplate as described in Chapter 2A, Section 15.

7 Renew the seal as described in paragraphs 2 to 4.

8 Refit the flywheel/driveplate as described in Chapter 2A, Section 15.

17 Engine/transmission mountings - inspection and renewal

Refer to Chapter 2A, Section 17.

Chapter 2 Part C:
2.5 and 3.0 litre engine in-car repair procedures

Contents

Degrees of difficulty

Easy, suitable for novice with little experience 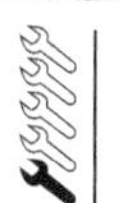	**Fairly easy,** suitable for beginner with some experience 	**Fairly difficult,** suitable for competent DIY mechanic	**Difficult,** suitable for experienced DIY mechanic	**Very difficult,** suitable for expert DIY or professional

Specifications

General

Engine type	V6 water-cooled. Double overhead camshaft, belt-driven	
	2.5 litre engine	**3.0 litre engine**
Manufacturer's engine code	X25XE	X30XE
Bore	81.6 mm	86.0 mm
Stroke	79.6 mm	85.0 mm
Capacity	2498 cc	2969 cc
Maximum power	125 kW at 6000 rpm	155 kW at 6200 rpm
Maximum torque	227 Nm at 3200 rpm	270 Nm at 3600 rpm
Firing order	1-2-3-4-5-6 (No 1 cylinder at timing belt end of right-hand cylinder bank)	
Direction of crankshaft rotation	Clockwise (viewed from timing belt end of engine)	
Compression ratio	10.8:1	

Compression pressures

Standard	12 to 15 bar (174 to 218 psi)
Maximum difference between any two cylinders	1 bar (15 psi)

Camshaft

Cam lift:	
2.5 litre engine	9.2 mm
3.0 litre engine	10.0 mm

Lubrication system

Oil pump type	Rotor-type, driven directly from crankshaft
Minimum permissible oil pressure at idle speed, with engine at operating temperature (oil temperature of at least 80°C)	1.5 bar (22 psi)
Oil pump rotor endfloat:	
Inner rotor	Less than 0.08 mm
Outer rotor	Less than 0.10 mm

Torque wrench settings

	Nm	lbf ft
Auxiliary drivebelt tensioner bolts	35	26
Baffle plate bolts	8	6
Camshaft bearing cap bolts	8	6
Camshaft cover bolts	8	6
Camshaft sensor bolt	8	6
Camshaft sprocket bolt:		
Stage 1	50	37
Stage 2	Angle-tighten a further 60°	
Stage 3	Angle-tighten a further 15°	
Connecting rod big-end bearing cap bolt:		
Stage 1	35	26
Stage 2	Angle-tighten a further 45°	
Stage 3	Angle-tighten a further 15°	
Coolant pipe (right-hand)-to-cylinder block bolts	20	15
Coolant pipe/dipstick tube/engine lifting bracket bolt	25	18
Coolant pump bolts	25	18
Coolant pump pulley bolts:		
Stage 1	8	6
Stage 2	Angle-tighten a further 30°	
Stage 3	Angle-tighten a further 30°	
Crankcase breather housing bolts	8	6
Crankshaft pulley bolts	20	15
Crankshaft sensor rotor bolts	15	11
Crankshaft sprocket bolt:		
Stage 1	250	185
Stage 2	Angle-tighten a further 45°	
Stage 3	Angle-tighten a further 15°	
Cylinder head bolts:		
Stage 1	25	18
Stage 2	Angle-tighten a further 90°	
Stage 3	Angle-tighten a further 90°	
Stage 4	Angle-tighten a further 90°	
Stage 5	Angle-tighten a further 15°	
Cylinder head coolant outlet bolts	30	22
Driveplate bolts:		
Stage 1	65	48
Stage 2	Angle-tighten a further 30°	
Stage 3	Angle-tighten a further 15°	
Engine/transmission mounting bolts:		
Left- and right-hand mountings:		
Mounting-to-subframe nut	55	41
Mounting-to-mounting bracket nut	40	30
Mounting bracket-to-cylinder block bolts	60	44
Vibration damper bolts	40	30
Rear mounting:		
Mounting-to-transmission bolts	40	30
Mounting-to-crossmember nuts	20	15
Crossmember-to-body bolts	45	33
Engine-to-transmission unit bolts:		
Transmission-to-cylinder block bolts	60	44
Transmission-to-sump flange bolts	40	30
Flywheel bolts:		
Stage 1	65	48
Stage 2	Angle-tighten a further 30°	
Stage 3	Angle-tighten a further 15°	
Main bearing cap/bridge casting:		
Main bearing cap bolts:		
Stage 1	50	37
Stage 2	Angle-tighten a further 60°	
Stage 3	Angle-tighten a further 15°	
Casting threaded sleeves	8	6
Casting-to-cylinder block (M8) bolts	20	15
Oil cooler:		
Cover bolts	20	15
Cover nuts	30	22
Oil cooler pipe union nuts and bolts	30	22

Torque wrench settings (continued)	Nm	lbf ft
Oil filter	15	11
Oil pump cover screws	8	6
Oil pump retaining bolts - see text for details:		
M6 bolts with original timing belt rear cover:		
Initial torque	8	6
Final torque	10	7
M6 bolts with modified timing belt rear cover	10	7
M8 bolts:		
Stage 1	12	9
Stage 2	20	15
Oil pump pick-up/strainer bolts	8	6
Power steering pump pulley bolts:		
Stage 1	20	15
Stage 2	Angle-tighten a further 30°	
Stage 3	Angle-tighten a further 15°	
Sump bolts:		
Sump pan bolts:		
Stage 1	8	6
Stage 2	Angle-tighten a further 30°	
Main casting bolts:		
Casting-to-cylinder block/oil pump bolts	15	11
Casting flange-to-transmission bolts	40	30
Sump drain plug:		
Hex-head bolt	55	41
Torx-head bolt	10	7
Timing belt cover bolts:		
Outer cover	8	6
Rear cover:		
M6 bolts	8	6
M8 threaded stud	10	7
Timing belt lower guide pulley bolt	40	30
Timing belt tensioner pulley/upper guide pulley assembly:		
Backplate-to-cylinder head bolts	40	30
Tensioner pulley nut	20	15
Guide pulley bolt	40	30

1 General information

How to use this Chapter

1 This Part of Chapter 2 is devoted to in-car repair procedures for the engine. All procedures concerning engine removal and refitting, and engine block/cylinder head overhaul can be found in Chapter 2D.

2 Most of the operations included in this Part are based on the assumption that the engine is still installed in the car. Therefore, if this information is being used during a complete engine overhaul, with the engine already removed, many of the steps included here will not apply.

Engine description

3 The engine is a double overhead camshaft, V6 unit, mounted at the front of the car with the transmission on its rear. The cylinder banks are arranged at a 54° angle to keep the engine as compact as possible. This engine is often referred to as the V6 ECOTEC engine (Emission Consumption Optimized TEChnology).

4 The cylinder block is of the dry-liner type. The crankshaft is supported within the cylinder block on four shell-type main bearings. Thrust-washers are fitted to number 4 (flywheel/driveplate end) main bearing, to control crank-shaft endfloat.

5 The aluminium alloy pistons are of the slipper type, and are fitted with three piston rings, comprising two compression rings and a scraper-type oil control ring. The pistons are joined to the connecting rods by gudgeon pins; on 2.5 litre engines the pins are an interference-fit and on 3.0 litre engines the pins are secured in position with circlips. On all engines, the connecting rods are attached to the crankshaft by horizontally split shell-type big-end bearings.

6 The camshafts run directly in the cylinder heads, and are driven by the crankshaft via a toothed rubber timing belt. The camshafts operate each valve via a follower. Each follower incorporates a hydraulic self-adjusting valve which automatically adjust the valve clearances.

7 Lubrication is by pressure-feed from a rotor-type oil pump, which is mounted on the front end of the crankshaft. It draws oil through a strainer located in the sump, and then forces it through an externally mounted full-flow cartridge-type filter. The oil flows into galleries in the main bearing cap bridge arrangement and cylinder block/crankcase, from where it is distributed to the crankshaft (main bearings) and camshafts. The big-end bearings are supplied with oil via internal drillings in the crankshaft, while the camshaft bearings also receive a pressurised supply. The camshaft lobes and valves are lubricated by splash, as are all other engine components. An oil cooler is fitted to help keep the oil temperature stable under arduous operating temperatures; the cooler is fitted to the top of the cylinder block where it is located in between the cylinder banks.

8 A semi-closed crankcase ventilation system is employed; crankcase fumes are drawn from cylinder head cover, and passed via a hose to the inlet manifold.

Repair operations possible with the engine in the car

9 The following operations can be carried out without having to remove the engine from the vehicle.

a) Removal and refitting of the cylinder heads.
b) Removal and refitting of the timing belt and sprockets.

3.5a Align the relevant camshaft sprockets timing marks with the cutouts on the timing belt rear cover (arrowed) on both the right-hand . . .

3.5b . . . and left-hand cylinder heads (arrowed) . . .

c) Renewal of the camshaft oil seals.
d) Removal and refitting of the camshafts and followers.
e) Removal and refitting of the sump.
f) Removal and refitting of the connecting rods and pistons.*
g) Removal and refitting of the oil pump.
h) Renewal of the crankshaft oil seals.
i) Renewal of the engine mountings.
j) Removal and refitting of the flywheel/driveplate.

* Although the operation marked with an asterisk can be carried out with the engine in the car after removal of the sump, it is better for the engine to be removed, in the interests of cleanliness and improved access. For this reason, the procedure is described in Chapter 2D.

2 Compression test - description and interpretation

Refer to Chapter 2A, Section 2.

3 Top dead centre (TDC) for No 1 piston - locating

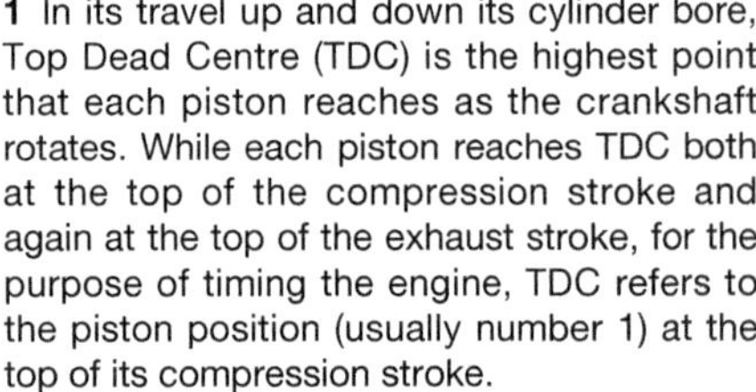

1 In its travel up and down its cylinder bore, Top Dead Centre (TDC) is the highest point that each piston reaches as the crankshaft rotates. While each piston reaches TDC both at the top of the compression stroke and again at the top of the exhaust stroke, for the purpose of timing the engine, TDC refers to the piston position (usually number 1) at the top of its compression stroke.

2 Number 1 piston (and cylinder) is at the front (timing belt) end of the right-hand cylinder bank, and its TDC position is located as follows. Note that the crankshaft rotates clockwise when viewed from the front of the vehicle.

3 Disconnect the battery negative terminal. If necessary, remove all the spark plugs as described in Chapter 1 to enable the engine to be easily turned over.

4 Remove the timing belt outer cover to gain access to the camshaft sprocket timing marks (see Section 6).

5 Using a socket and extension bar on the crankshaft sprocket bolt, rotate the crankshaft until the relevant timing marks on the camshaft sprockets are all at the top and are correctly aligned with the marks on the timing belt rear cover. Each sprocket has two timing marks the correct mark to use is as follows **(see illustrations)**.

Camshaft	Timing mark to be used
Right-hand cylinder head exhaust	1
Right-hand cylinder head inlet	2
Left-hand cylinder head inlet	3
Left-hand cylinder head exhaust	4

6 With the camshaft sprocket marks correctly positioned, align the notch on the crankshaft pulley rim with the pointer on the oil pump housing **(see illustration)**. The engine is now positioned with No1 piston at TDC on its compression stroke. **Note:** *If the crankshaft pulley has been removed, use the mark on the crankshaft sprocket rim. The mark should be aligned with the cutout on the base of the oil pump housing (see Section 7).*

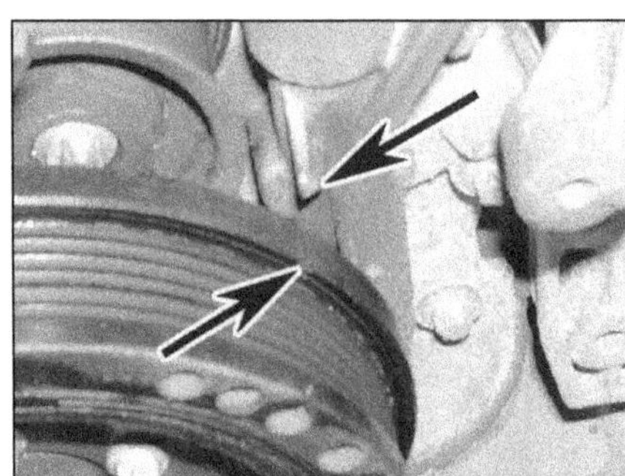

3.6 . . . and the crankshaft pulley notch with the pointer on the oil pump housing (arrowed) to position No1 piston at TDC on its compression stroke

4 Camshaft covers - removal and refitting

Removal

1 Remove the inlet manifold as described in Chapter 4A.

Right-hand cover

2 Disconnect the plug caps from the plugs then unclip the HT leads and position them clear of the cover.

3 Evenly and progressively slacken and remove the camshaft cover retaining bolts.

4 Lift the camshaft cover away from the cylinder head and recover the cover seals and the sealing rings which are fitted to each of the retaining bolt holes. Examine the seal and sealing rings for signs of wear or damage and renew if necessary.

Left-hand cover

5 To improve access, remove the windscreen wiper arms and the water deflector panel (see Chapter 12, Sections 15 and 16). Access can be further improved by disconnecting the engine wiring harness as described in paragraphs 14 to 16 of Section 11 and positioning it clear of the cover.

6 On models with air conditioning, unbolt the air conditioning pipe/hose bracket from the front of the cylinder head and position the hose/pipe to one side.

7 Lift the oil filler neck retaining tab then twist the neck anti-clockwise and remove it from the top of the cover **(see illustrations)**. Recover the neck sealing ring and discard it; a new one should be used on refitting.

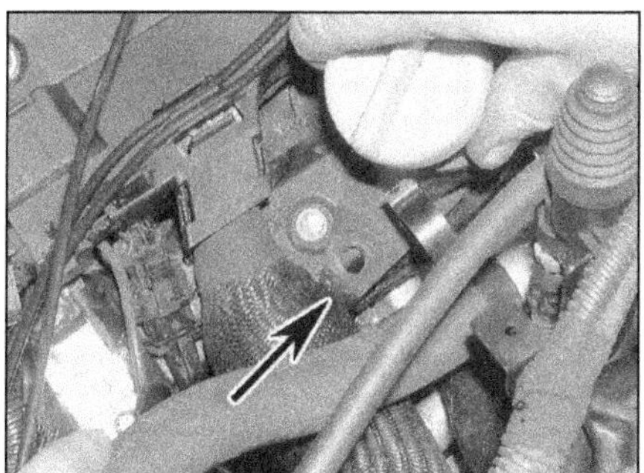
4.7a Lift the retaining tab (arrowed) . . .

4.7b . . . and rotate the oil filler neck anti-clockwise to free it from the left-hand camshaft cover

4.8 Removing the left-hand camshaft cover

8 Remove the cover as described in paragraphs 3 and 4 **(see illustration)**.

Refitting

Right-hand cover

9 Ensure the cover and cylinder head surfaces are clean and dry then fit the seals securely to the cover grooves. Fit the sealing rings to the recesses around each retaining bolt hole, holding them in position with a smear of grease **(see illustrations)**.

10 Apply a smear of suitable sealant (Vauxhall recommend the use of sealant 15 03 295 - available from your Vauxhall dealer) to the areas of the cylinder head surface around the front inlet and exhaust camshaft bearing caps and also to the semi-circular cutouts on the rear of the head **(see illustrations)**.

11 Carefully manoeuvre the camshaft cover into position, taking great care to ensure all the sealing rings remain correctly seated.

12 Refit the cover retaining bolts and tighten the retaining bolts to the specified torque, working in a spiral pattern from the centre outwards.

13 Securely reconnect the plug caps to the spark plugs making sure the HT leads are clipped securely in position.

14 Refit the inlet manifold as described in Chapter 4A.

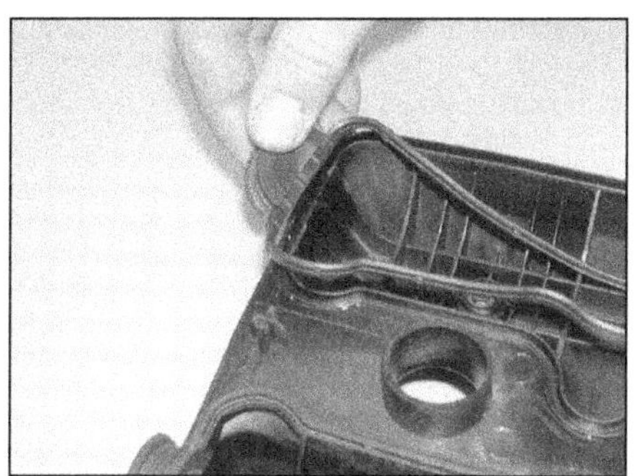
4.9a Fit the new seals securely to the cover grooves . . .

4.9b . . . and install the sealing rings in the bolt hole grooves

Left-hand cover

15 Refit the cover as described in paragraphs 9 to 12.

16 Fit a new sealing ring to the filler neck then refit the neck to the cover making sure its retaining tab is correctly engaged with the cover retaining bolt.

17 Where necessary, refit the air conditioning pipe/hose retaining clip and securely tighten its retaining bolt.

18 Refit the windscreen wiper motor cover panel and wiper arms as described in Chapter 12. Where necessary, reconnect the engine wiring harness making sure the wiring is correctly routed and all connectors are securely connected.

5 Crankshaft pulley - removal and refitting

Removal

1 Remove the auxiliary drivebelt as described in Chapter 1. Prior to removal, mark the direction of rotation on the belt to ensure the belt is refitted the same way around.

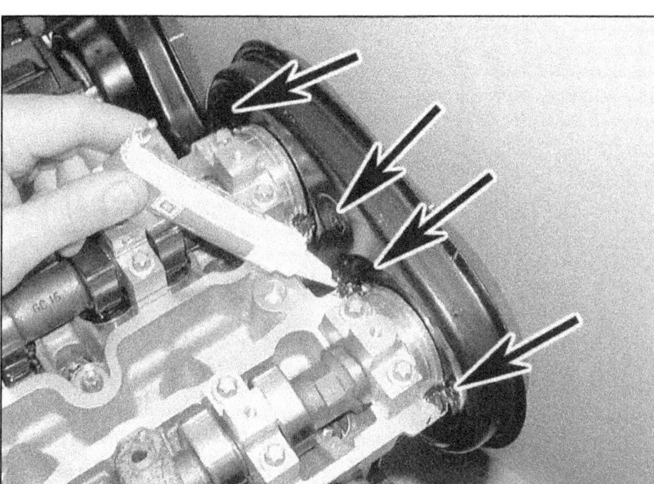
4.10a Apply sealant to the areas at the sides of the camshaft front bearing caps (arrowed) . . .

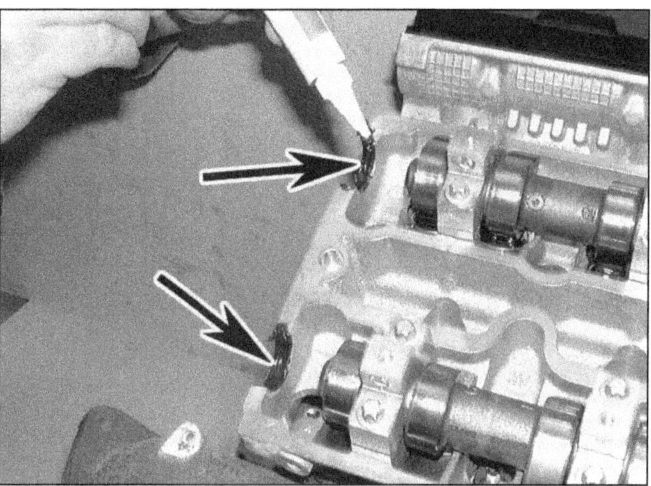
4.10b . . . and also to the semi-circular cut-outs (arrowed) on the rear of the cylinder head

6.4a Retain the coolant pump shaft with an open-ended spanner then undo the retaining bolts . . .

2 Using a socket and extension bar on the crankshaft sprocket bolt, turn the crankshaft until the notch on the pulley rim is correctly aligned with the pointer on the cover.

3 Slacken and remove the small retaining bolts securing the pulley to the crankshaft sprocket and remove the pulley from the engine. If necessary, prevent crankshaft rotation by holding the sprocket retaining bolt with a suitable socket.

Refitting

4 Check that the crankshaft sprocket mark is still aligned with the mark on the oil pump housing then manoeuvre the crankshaft pulley into position. Align the notch on the pulley rim with the pointer then seat the pulley on the sprocket and tighten its retaining bolts to the specified torque.

6.4b . . . and remove the pulley from the engine

5 Refit the auxiliary drivebelt as described in Chapter 1 using the mark made prior to removal to ensure the belt is fitted the correct way around.

6 Timing belt covers - removal and refitting

Outer cover

Note: *New coolant pump and power steering pump pulley bolts will be required on refitting.*

Removal

1 Remove the multi-ram air intake system pre-volume chamber assembly as described in Chapter 4A.

2 Remove the secondary air injection system front connecting pipe as described in Chapter 4B.

3 Remove the auxiliary drivebelt as described in Chapter 1. Prior to removal, mark the direction of rotation on the belt to ensure the belt is refitted the same way around.

4 Slacken and remove the coolant pump drivebelt pulley retaining bolts whilst retaining the pump shaft with an open-ended spanner. Remove the pulley and discard the bolts; new ones must be used on refitting **(see illustrations)**.

5 Insert a socket and extension bar in through the one of the power steering pump pulley holes and locate it on a pump mounting bolt to prevent rotation. Slacken and remove the pulley retaining bolts and remove the pulley, noting which way around it is fitted **(see illustrations)**. Discard the bolts; new ones must be used on refitting.

6 Disconnect the right-hand cylinder bank knock sensor wiring connector and unclip it from the front of the timing belt cover.

7 Unclip the covers from the front and right-hand end of the wiring harness tray which runs across the front of the timing belt cover. Disconnect the wiring connector from the EGR valve and position the wiring harness clear of the timing belt cover then undo the retaining bolts and remove the tray from the belt cover **(see illustrations)**.

8 Slacken and remove the retaining bolts and remove the auxiliary drivebelt tensioner assembly from the right-hand cylinder head **(see illustration)**.

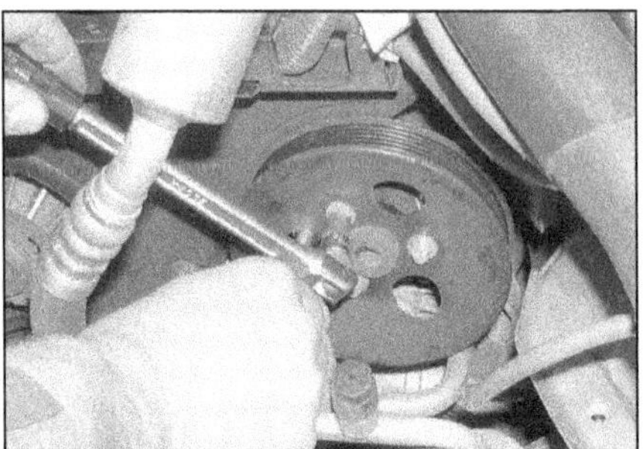

6.5a Insert a socket and extension bar through the power steering pump pulley then undo the retaining bolts . . .

6.5b . . . and remove the pulley from the pump

6.7a Unclip the front . . .

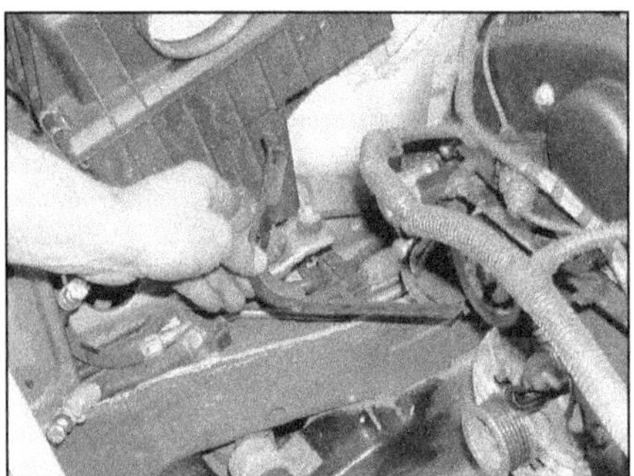

6.7b . . . and right-hand covers and position the wiring harness clear of the tray

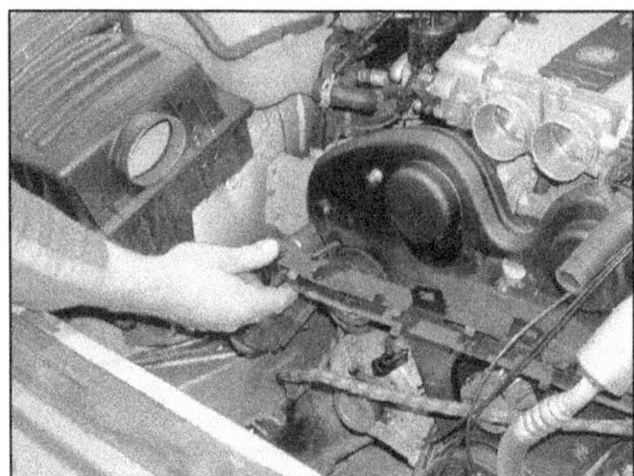

6.7c Undo the retaining bolts and remove the tray from the timing belt cover

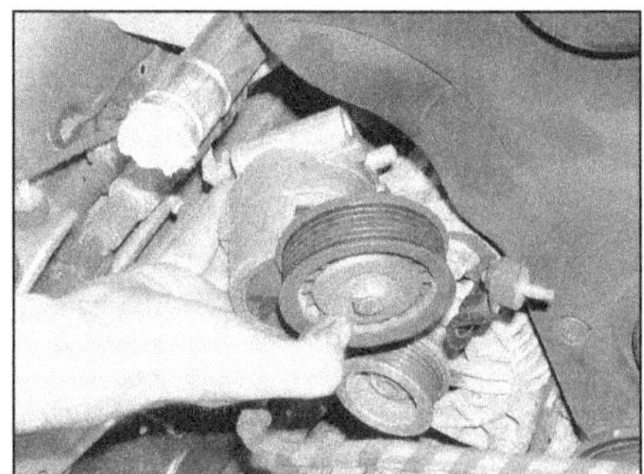

6.8 Undo the retaining bolts and remove the auxiliary drivebelt tensioner

9 Slacken and remove the retaining bolts then remove the outer cover from the engine unit along with its seal **(see illustration)**.

Refitting

10 Ensure the seal is firmly fixed to the cover prior to refitting. If necessary, glue it in position with a suitable adhesive (Vauxhall recommend the use of adhesive 08 983 341). Refit the cover to the engine and tighten its retaining bolts to the specified torque.

11 Refit the auxiliary drivebelt tensioner and tighten its retaining bolts to the specified torque.

12 Refit the wiring harness tray onto the cover and securely tighten its retaining bolts. Seat the wiring correctly in the tray then clip on the front and right-hand covers.

13 Refit the drivebelt pulleys to the coolant and power steering pump then fit the new retaining bolts. Tighten the pulley bolts to the specified stage 1 torque then angle-tighten through the specified stage 2 and 3 angles. It is recommended that an angle-measuring gauge is used during the final stages of the tightening, to ensure accuracy.

14 Refit the auxiliary drivebelt as described in Chapter 1 using the mark made prior to removal to ensure the belt is fitted the correct way around.

15 Refit the air injection system pipe and the pre-volume chamber as described in Chapter 4A and 4B.

Rear cover

Removal

16 Remove the timing belt as described in Section 7.

17 Remove the camshaft sprockets, the timing belt tensioner pulley/upper guide pulley assembly and the lower guide pulley as described in Section 8.

18 Drain the cooling system and remove the coolant pump (see Chapters 1 and 3).

19 Undo the retaining bolts, noting the correct fitted location of the threaded stud, and remove the rear cover from the engine unit **(see illustration)**.

Refitting

20 Refit the rear cover to the engine and tighten its retaining bolts and the threaded stud to their specified torque settings.

21 Refit the coolant pump as described in Chapter 3.

22 Refit the guide pulley, tensioner assembly, camshaft sprockets and crankshaft sprocket as described in Section 8 then refit the timing belt as described in Section 7.

23 On completion, refill the cooling system as described in Chapter 1.

7 Timing belt - removal and refitting

***Note:** Accurate adjustment of the timing belt requires the use of the following Vauxhall service tools; camshaft sprocket locking tools (KM-800-1 and KM-800-2), crankshaft sprocket locking tool (KM-800-10), timing belt locating wedge (KM-800-30) and a camshaft sprocket timing gauge (KM-800-20)* **(see illustration)**. *If the belt is to be refitted without the use of the service tools, it is recommended that the belt adjustment is checked at the earliest possible opportunity by a Vauxhall dealer.*

***Note**: The timing belt must be removed and refitted with the engine cold.*

Removal

1 Disconnect the battery negative lead then position No1 cylinder at TDC on its compression stroke as described in Section 3. **Note:** *On models with a Vauxhall anti-theft warning system (ATWS), the battery negative terminal must be disconnected within 15 seconds of the ignition being switched off to prevent the alarm system being triggered.*

6.9 Removing the timing belt outer cover

2 Remove the crankshaft pulley as described in Section 5.

3 Check the camshaft sprocket timing marks are all correctly aligned with the rear cover marks and the crankshaft sprocket timing mark is aligned with the cutout on the oil pump housing.

4 If the Vauxhall service tools are available, fix the service tool (KM-800-10) to the crankshaft sprocket and lock the crankshaft in position by clamping the tool locking arm firmly around the coolant pump flange. Lock the camshafts in position by inserting the service tools making sure the TOP marking on each tool is uppermost; the sprockets on the right-hand cylinder head must be locked with KM-800-1 (tool is stamped with numbers 1 and 2 and handle is coloured red) and the left-hand cylinder head sprockets with KM-800-2 (tool is stamped with numbers 3 and 4 and handle is coloured green) **(see illustrations)**.

6.19 Ensure the threaded stud is correctly positioned when refitting the timing belt rear cover

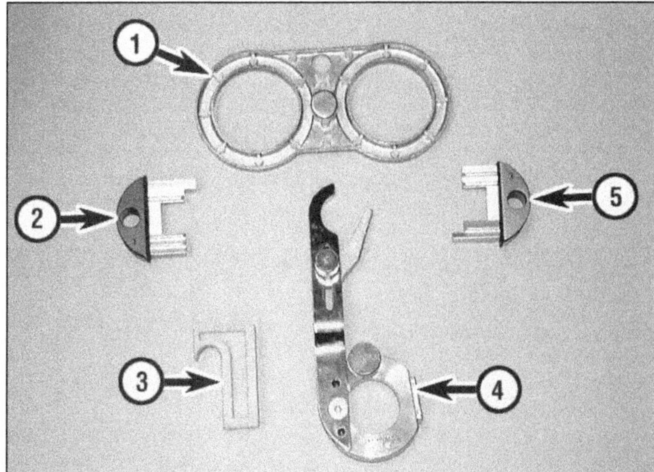

7.0 Vauxhall timing belt service tools

1 Timing gauge (KM-800-20)
2 Sprocket locking tool (KM-800-1)
3 Timing belt wedge (KM-800-30)
4 Crankshaft locking tool (KM-800-10)
5 Sprocket locking tool (KM-800-2)

7.4a If the service tools are available, firmly attach the crankshaft locking tool to the sprocket . . .

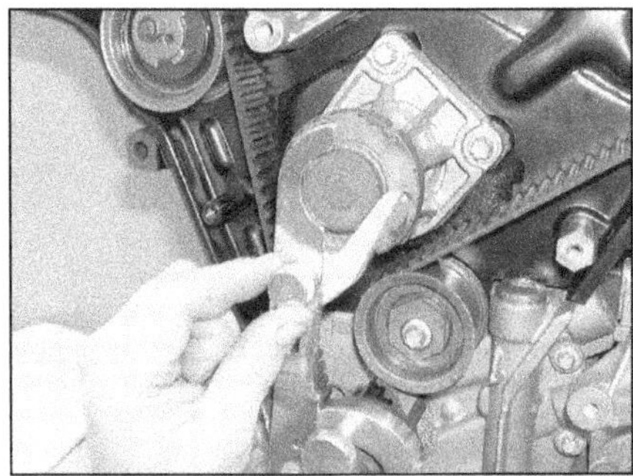

7.4b . . . and clamp its locking arm firmly around the coolant pump flange

7.4c Insert the locking tools correctly in between the sprockets . . .

7.4d . . . making sure their TOP markings are uppermost

7.5a Slacken the tensioner pulley retaining nut . . .

7.5b . . . then rotate the pulley clockwise, positioning it just before its stop, and secure it by retightening the nut

5 Slacken the timing belt tensioner pulley nut. Using an Allen key fitted to the hexagonal cutout, rotate the tensioner pulley clockwise so it is positioned just before its stop and hold it in position by securely tighten the retaining nut **(see illustrations)**.

6 Slacken the retaining bolts for the timing belt upper and lower guide pulleys **(see illustrations)**.

7 Slide the timing belt off from its sprockets and remove it from the engine. If the new belt is not being fitted straight away and the service tools are not being used, rotate the crankshaft **backwards** by approximately 60°; this will position the pistons approximately halfway up the bores reducing the risk of the valves contacting the pistons should the camshafts move.

7.6a Slacken the retaining bolts securing the upper guide pulley . . .

8 Check the timing belt carefully for any signs of uneven wear, splitting or oil contamination, and renew it if there is the slightest doubt about its condition. If the fitting markings on the outside of the original belt are no longer visible the belt must be renewed regardless of its apparent condition (see paragraph 12). If the engine is undergoing an overhaul and has covered 40 000 miles or it was more than 4 years since the original belt was fitted, renew the belt as a matter of course, regardless of its apparent condition (from 1997 onwards the belt renewal interval was increased to 80 000 miles or 8 years). If signs of oil contamination are found, trace the source of the oil leak and rectify it, then wash down the engine timing belt area and all related components to remove all traces of oil.

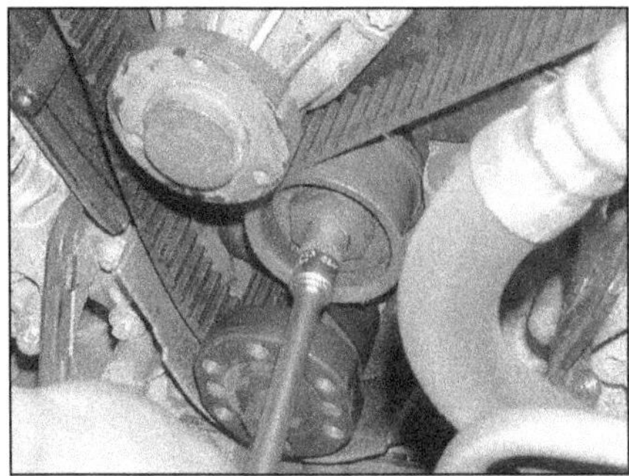

7.6b . . . and lower guide pulley in position then slide the belt off the sprockets

Refitting

Note: *There are two different types of timing belt and tensioner assembly available for this engine and it is essential that the timing belt is of the correct type for the tensioner. A modified tensioner assembly and timing belt were fitted as standard to later (1997 on model year) engines, enabling the belt renewal interval on these engines to be extended to 80 000 miles or 8 years. The modified tensioner assembly can be identified by checking the letter stamped on the tensioner pulley/upper guide roller backplate; the original tensioner is marked with D and the modified assembly marking has an E in it (EA or EB) (see illustration 7.15). It is most important to check the tensioner backplate marking before ordering a timing belt since the modified tensioner and belt can also be installed on early (pre 1997 model year) engines to enable the timing belt renewal interval to be extended. See your Vauxhall dealer for further details.*

9 On reassembly, thoroughly clean the timing belt sprockets and tensioner/guide pulleys.

10 Check that the crankshaft sprocket timing mark is still aligned with the cutout on the oil pump housing and the camshaft sprocket marks are aligned with the marks on the rear cover (see Section 3) **(see illustrations)**. If the crankshaft was moved back 60°, rotate it back to TDC to bring the marks into alignment.

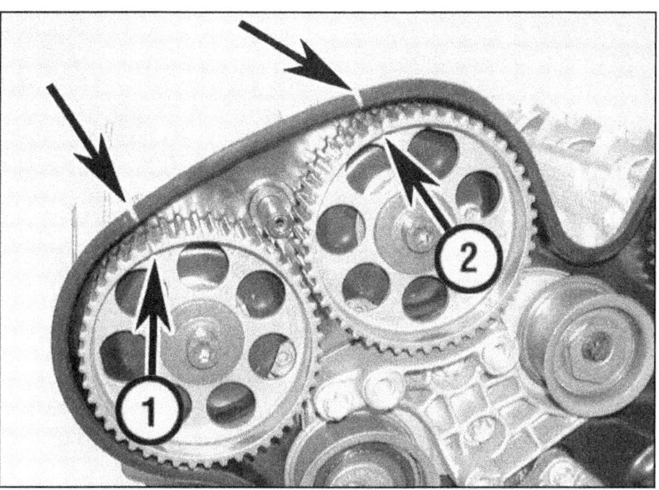

7.10a Ensure the right-hand cylinder head camshaft sprocket markings (1 and 2) . . .

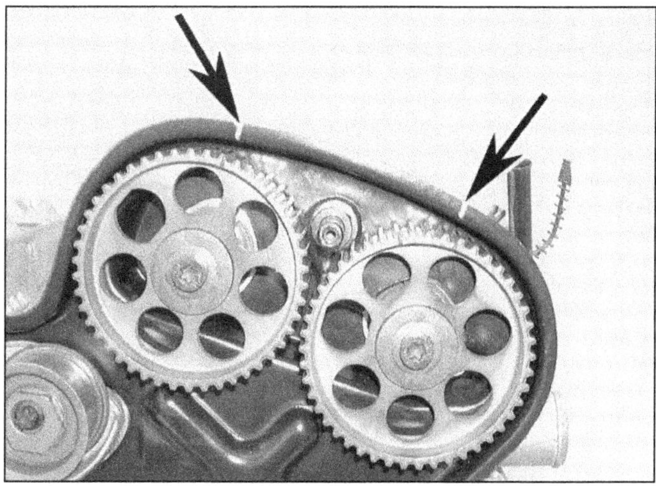

7.10b . . . and the left-hand cylinder head camshaft markings (3 and 4) are all correctly aligned with the rear cover cutouts (arrowed) . . .

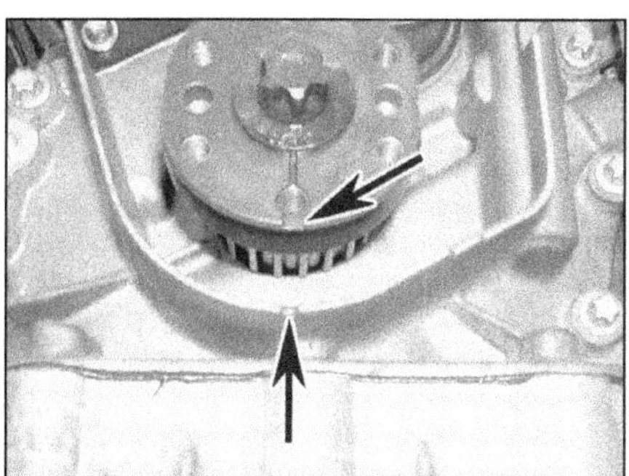

7.10c . . . and the crankshaft sprocket timing mark is correctly aligned with the oil pump housing cutout (arrowed)

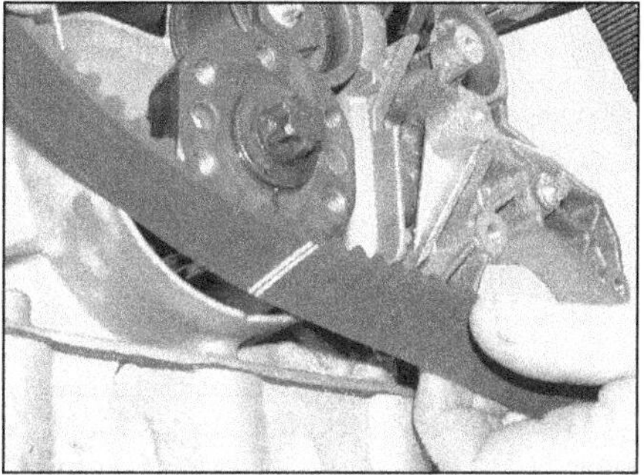

7.13a Align the double line on the timing belt with the crankshaft sprocket timing mark

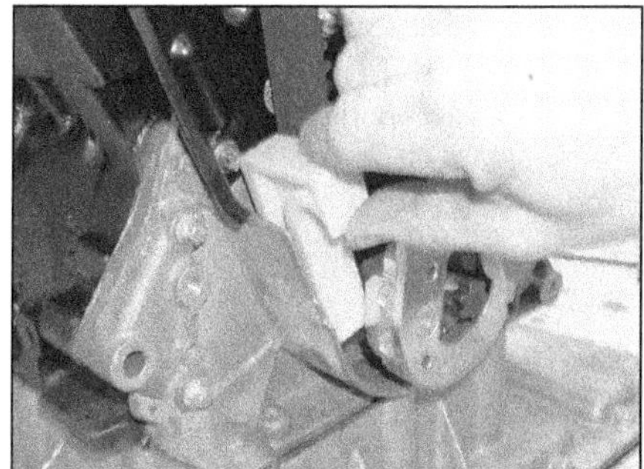

7.13b If the service tool is available secure the belt in position with the wedge

11 If the special tools are available lock the camshaft sprockets and crankshaft sprocket in position as described in paragraph 4.

12 Examine the fitting marks on the outer face of the timing belt. The arrows on the belt must point in the direction of rotation and the double line on the belt should be aligned with the crankshaft sprocket mark. The four single lines on the belt will then align with the camshaft sprocket timing marks if the belt is correctly installed.

13 Ensure the arrows on the belt are pointing in the correct direction of rotation then align the double line on the belt with the crankshaft sprocket timing mark and engage the belt with the sprocket. If the locating wedge (KM-800-30) is available secure the belt in position by inserting the wedge in between the right-hand side of the belt and the rear cover **(see illustrations).**

14 Check the identification marking stamped onto the tensioner pulley/upper guide pulley backplate (see Note at the start of the refitting procedure).

15 On early engines with the original tensioner (marked with a D - **see illustration**), fit the timing belt over the lower guide pulley then around the left-hand cylinder head camshaft sprockets making sure the belt fitting marks are correctly aligned with the sprocket marks. Fit the belt around the upper guide pulley then over the right-hand cylinder camshaft, again making sure the fitting marks are correctly aligned and tensioner pulley. Do not twist the belt sharply while refitting it.

16 On all engines fitted with the modified tensioner (marked with an E - see illustration 7.15), fit the belt behind the tensioner pulley and then over the right-hand cylinder head camshaft sprockets ensuring that the fitting marks are both correctly aligned with the sprocket marks. Fit the belt around the upper guide pulley then over the left-hand cylinder camshaft sprockets, again making sure the fitting marks are correctly aligned, and finally over the lower guide pulley **(see illustrations)**. Do not twist the belt sharply while refitting it.

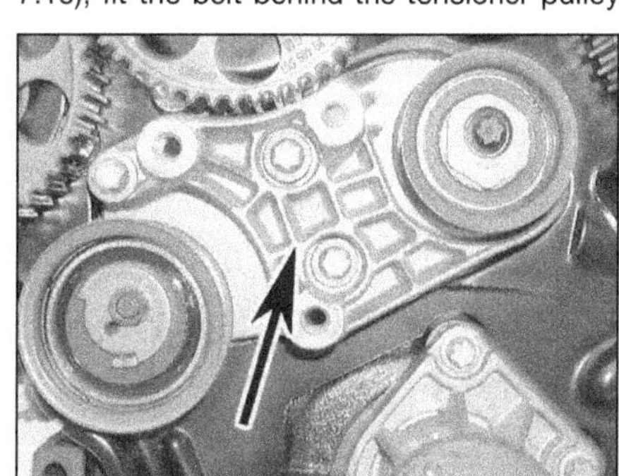

7.15 Checking the marking (location arrowed) on the tensioner/upper guide pulley backplate to identify which type of tensioner assembly is fitted to your engine - see text

7.16a On engines with a modified tensioner, work around in a clockwise direction and engage the belt first with the right-hand cylinder head sprockets . . .

7.16b . . . and then the left-hand head sprockets (directional fitting arrows arrowed), making sure the fitting lines are all correctly aligned with the sprockets . . .

7.16c . . . and finally over the lower guide pulley

17 On all engines, ensure that the belt teeth are correctly seated centrally in the sprockets and the sprocket timing marks/belt fitting marks are correctly aligned. If adjustment is necessary, disengage the belt from the sprockets and make any necessary adjustments.

7.18a Remove all slack from the left-hand run of the belt by rotating the lower guide pulley whilst making sure the sprocket timing marks remain in alignment (timing gauge shown) . . .

18 Slacken the lower guide pulley retaining bolt. Rotate the pulley anti-clockwise to remove all slack from the left-hand run of the belt without placing any excess strain on the belt. Ensure that all the sprocket timing marks remain in alignment as the pulley is moved; if the service tools are available, remove the locking tools and use the timing gauge (KM-800-20) to check the sprocket mark positions. Once the pulley is correctly positioned, hold it stationary and tighten its retaining bolt to the specified torque **(see illustrations)**.

19 Slacken the upper guide pulley retaining bolt. Rotate the pulley anti-clockwise to remove all slack from the top run of the belt without placing any excess strain on the belt. Ensure that all the sprocket timing marks remain in alignment as the pulley is moved. Once the pulley is correctly positioned, hold it stationary and tighten its retaining bolt to the specified torque **(see illustration)**.

20 Slacken the timing belt tensioner pulley nut then, using an Allen key, rotate the tensioner arm anti-clockwise until the gap between the tensioner plate and its stop is 0.5 to 1.5 mm **(see illustration)**. Hold the tensioner pulley in this position and securely tighten its retaining nut.

21 Remove all the service tools (where fitted) then using a socket on the crankshaft sprocket bolt, rotate the crankshaft smoothly through two complete turns (720°) in the normal direction of rotation to settle the timing belt in position.

22 Check that all the camshaft and crankshaft sprocket timing marks are correctly realigned then slacken the tensioner nut again. **Note:** *The belt fitting lines will not be realigned with the sprocket marks; they serve no purpose once the belt has been installed.*

23 Using an Allen key, position the tensioner pulley so that the index mark on the tensioner plate is positioned 3 to 4 mm above the mark on the backplate stop **(see illustration)**. Hold the tensioner correctly in position and tighten its retaining nut to the specified torque.

24 Rotate the crankshaft smoothly through

7.18b . . . then hold the pulley stationary and tighten its retaining bolt to the specified torque

7.19 Remove all slack from the top run of the belt then hold the upper pulley stationary and tighten its retaining bolt to the specified torque

7.20 Rotate the tensioner pulley anti-clockwise until the gap (arrowed) is 0.5 to 1.5 mm then securely tighten its retaining nut

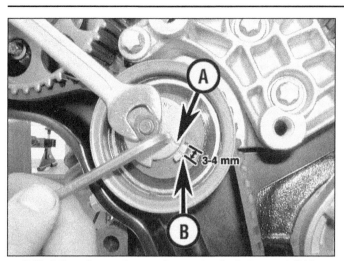

7.23 Adjust the tensioner pulley so that its index mark (A) is positioned 3 to 4 mm above backplate mark (B) then tighten its retaining nut to the specified torque

8.2a Using a home-made tool to prevent rotation as the camshaft sprocket bolt is slackened

another two complete turns (720°) in the normal direction of rotation to bring the sprocket timing marks back into alignment.

25 If the service tools are available, lock the crankshaft in position (KM-800-10) and check the camshaft sprocket timing marks are correctly positioned using the timing gauge (KM-800-20).

26 If the service tools are not available, ensure the crankshaft sprocket timing mark is correctly aligned with the cutout on the oil pump housing and all the camshaft sprocket timing marks are exactly aligned with the cutouts on the rear cover.

27 If adjustment is necessary repeat the operations described in paragraphs 18 to 26.

28 Once the timing marks are all correctly aligned, refit the timing belt cover and crankshaft pulley as described in Sections 5 and 6. **Note:** *If refitting has been carried out without the use of the service tools, it is advisable to have the belt adjustment checked by a Vauxhall dealer at the earliest possible opportunity.*

8 Timing belt sprockets, tensioner and guide pulleys - removal and refitting

Camshaft sprockets

Note: *New sprocket retaining bolt(s) will be required on refitting.*

Removal

1 Remove the timing belt as described in Section 7. Once the belt has been removed, rotate the crankshaft **backwards** by approximately 60°; this will position the pistons approximately halfway up the bores reducing the risk of the valves contacting the pistons.

2 The camshaft must be prevented from turning as the sprocket bolt is unscrewed, and this can be achieved in one of two ways.

a) *Make up a sprocket-holding tool using two lengths of steel strip (one long, the other short), and three nuts and bolts; one nut and bolt forms the pivot of a forked tool, with the remaining two nuts and bolts at the tips of the 'forks' to engage with the sprocket spokes* **(see illustration)**.

b) *Remove the camshaft cover as described in Section 4 and hold the camshaft with an open-ended spanner on the flats provided* **(see illustration)**.

3 Unscrew the retaining bolt and washer and remove the sprocket from the end of the camshaft **(see illustrations)**. If the sprocket locating pin is a loose fit in the camshaft end, remove it and store it with the sprocket for safe-keeping.

4 If necessary, remove the remaining sprocket(s) using the same method.

Refitting

5 Prior to refitting check the oil seal(s) for signs of damage or leakage. If necessary, renew as described in Section 9.

6 Ensure the locating pin is in position in the camshaft end.

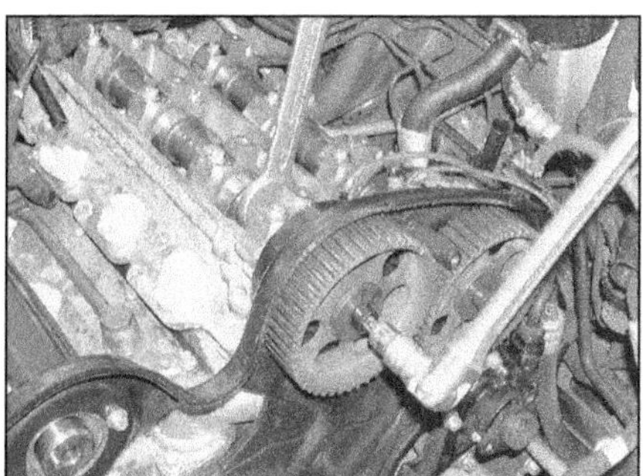

8.2b If the camshaft cover has been removed, the camshaft can be held with an open-ended spanner on the flats provided

8.3a Unscrew the retaining bolt and washer . . .

8.3b . . . and remove the sprocket from the camshaft

8.7a Right-hand cylinder head camshaft sprocket. Ensure timing mark and slot 1 are used on the exhaust camshaft and 2 on the inlet camshaft

8.7b Left-hand cylinder head camshaft sprocket. Ensure timing mark and slot 3 are used on the inlet camshaft and 4 on the exhaust camshaft

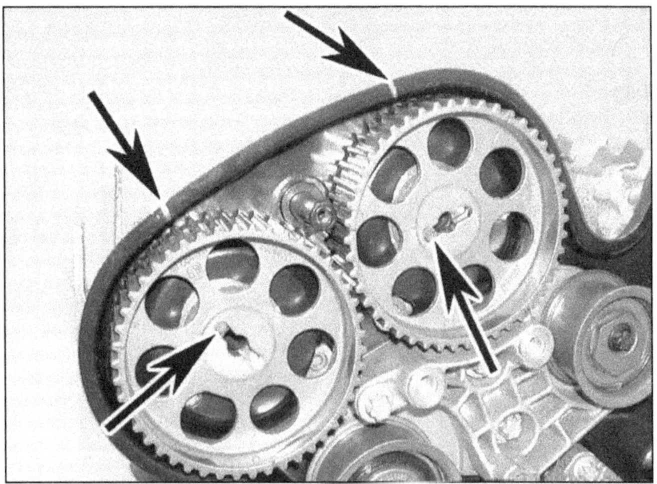

8.8a Ensure the locating pins are engaged in the correct sprocket slots (arrowed) . . .

8.8b . . . and the relevant sprocket timing marks are correctly aligned with the rear cover cutouts (arrowed)

7 Note that there are two pairs of camshaft sprockets, one for the right-hand cylinder head and the other for the left-hand cylinder head; the right-hand cylinder head sprockets carry the identification marks 1 and 2 and the left-hand cylinder head sprockets the marks 3 and 4. The inlet and exhaust camshaft sprockets on each head are the same but each one is equipped with two locating pin cutouts and two timing marks. On refitting is vital that the sprocket locating pin is engaged in the correct sprocket slot as follows and the correct timing mark is used **(see illustrations)**.

Camshaft	Sprocket slot/timing mark number to be used
Right-hand cylinder head exhaust	1
Right-hand cylinder head inlet	2
Left-hand cylinder head inlet	3
Left-hand cylinder head exhaust	4

8.9a Retaining the sprocket/camshaft then tighten the retaining bolt first to the stage 1 torque . . .

8.9b . . . and then through the specified stage 2 and 3 angles

8 Ensure the camshaft locating pin is engaged in the correct sprocket cutout then fit the washer and new retaining bolt **(see illustrations)**.

9 Retain the sprocket by the method used on removal, and tighten the sprocket retaining bolt to the specified stage 1 torque setting then angle-tighten the bolt through the specified stage 2 angle, using a socket and extension bar, and finally through the specified stage 3 angle **(see illustrations)**. It is recommended that an angle-measuring gauge is used during the final stages of the tightening, to ensure accuracy. If a gauge is not available, use white paint to make alignment marks between the bolt head and sprocket prior to tightening; the marks can then be used to check that the bolt has been rotated through the correct angle.

8.13 Home-made tool for preventing crankshaft rotation as the sprocket bolt is slackened

8.14a Unscrew the retaining bolt . . .

8.14b . . . then slide off the crankshaft sprocket . . .

10 Ensure the relevant camshaft sprocket timing marks are all correctly aligned with the cutouts on the rear cover then carefully rotate the crankshaft in the normal direction of rotation until the sprocket mark is correctly realigned with the notch on the oil pump housing.

11 Refit the timing belt as described in Section 7 then (where necessary) refit the camshaft cover as described in Section 4.

Crankshaft sprocket

Note: *A new crankshaft sprocket retaining bolt will be required on refitting.*

Removal

12 Remove the timing belt as described in Section 7.

13 The crankshaft must be prevented from turning as the sprocket bolt is unscrewed (the bolt is very tight), and this can be achieved in anyone of the following ways.

- a) *Use the holding tool described in paragraph 2 securing the tool to the sprocket with two bolts screwed into opposite pulley retaining bolt holes* **(see illustration)**.
- b) *On manual transmission models have an assistant select top gear and apply the brakes firmly.*
- c) *If the engine is removed from the vehicle or the transmission unit has been removed the flywheel/driveplate can be locked (see Section 15).*

14 Unscrew the retaining bolt and remove the crankshaft sprocket from the end of the crankshaft. Discard the bolt; a new one must be used on refitting. If necessary, slide the spacer out from the oil seal and remove it from the crankshaft; if the outer surface of the spacer is damaged it should be renewed **(see illustrations)**.

Refitting

15 Prior to refitting, examine the oil seal for signs of damage or deterioration and renew if necessary (see Section 16).

16 Slide the spacer (where removed) onto the crankshaft and into position taking care not to damage the oil seal lip.

17 Align the sprocket with the crankshaft slot and slide it into position, ensuring the sprocket flange is facing outwards. Fit the new retaining bolt.

18 Lock the crankshaft by the method used on removal, and tighten the sprocket retaining bolt to the specified stage 1 torque setting then angle-tighten the bolt through the specified stage 2 angle, using a socket and extension bar, and finally through the specified stage 3 angle. It is recommended that an angle-measuring gauge is used during the final stages of the tightening, to ensure accuracy **(see illustrations)**. If a gauge is not available, use white paint to make alignment marks between the bolt head and sprocket prior to tightening; the marks can then be used to check that the bolt has been rotated through the correct angle.

19 Refit the timing belt as described in Section 7.

8.14c . . . and, if necessary, withdraw the spacer from the oil seal

Tensioner pulley/ upper guide pulley assembly

Note: *The tensioner pulley/upper guide pulley assembly must be renewed as a complete unit. It is not possible to renew the individual components of the assembly separately.*

Removal

20 Remove the timing belt as described in Section 7.

21 Slacken and remove the retaining bolts securing the backplate to the cylinder head and remove the assembly from the engine **(see illustrations)**.

Refitting

22 Fit the tensioner pulley/upper guide pulley assembly to the cylinder head and tighten its retaining bolts to the specified torque.

8.18a Tighten the crankshaft sprocket bolt to the specified stage 1 torque setting . . .

8.18b . . . then tighten it through the specified stage 2 and 3 angles

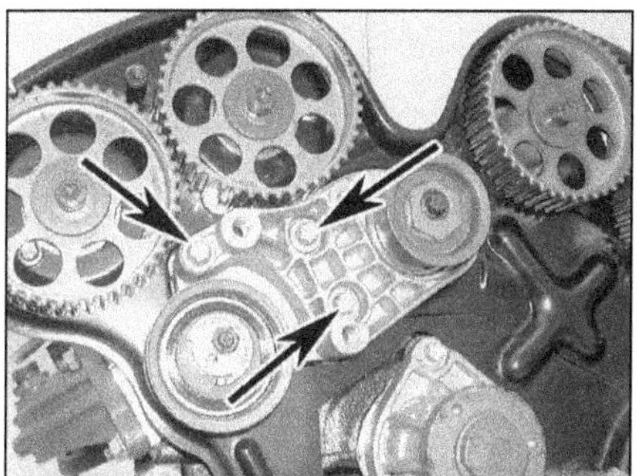
8.21a Undo the retaining bolts (arrowed) . . .

8.21b . . . and remove the tensioner pulley/upper guide pulley assembly from the cylinder head

23 Refit the timing belt as described in Section 7. If a new tensioner assembly has been fitted, fit a new timing belt ensuring it is of the correct type for the tensioner.

Lower guide pulley

Removal

24 Remove the timing belt as described in Section 7.

25 Slacken and remove the retaining bolt and remove the lower guide pulley and its spacer from the engine **(see illustration)**.

Refitting

26 Position the spacer behind the guide pulley then refit the pulley retaining bolt, tightening it lightly only at this stage.

27 Refit the timing belt as described in Section 7.

9.2a Carefully drill/punch holes in the oil seal . . .

8.25 Unscrew the retaining bolt and remove the lower guide pulley and its spacer (arrowed) from the engine

9 Camshaft oil seals - renewal

1 Remove the relevant camshaft sprocket as described in Section 8.

2 Carefully punch or drill two small holes opposite each other in the oil seal. Screw a self-tapping screw into each, and pull on the screws with pliers to extract the seal **(see illustrations)**. Alternatively carefully lever the oil seal out of position.

3 Clean the seal housing, and polish off any burrs or raised edges which may have caused the seal to fail in the first place.

4 Lubricate the lips of the new seal with clean engine oil, and press it into position using a suitable tubular drift (such as a socket) which bears only on the hard outer edge of the seal **(see illustration)**. Take care not to damage the seal lips during fitting; note that the seal lips should face inwards.

5 Refit the camshaft sprocket as described in Section 8.

10 Camshafts and followers - removal, inspection and refitting

Removal

1 Remove the camshaft cover as described in Section 4.

2 Remove the camshaft sprockets as described in Section 8. If the right-hand cylinder head camshafts are to be removed, rotate both the inlet and exhaust camshaft **backwards** approximately 60°; this will minimise the valve spring pressure being exerted on the bearing caps and so lessen the risk of damage as the caps are removed. The left-hand cylinder head camshafts are best left positioned at TDC.

3 Starting on the inlet camshaft, working in a spiral pattern from the outside inwards, slacken the camshaft bearing cap retaining bolts by half-a-turn at a time, to relieve the pressure of the valve springs on the bearing caps gradually and evenly. Once the valve spring pressure has been relieved, the bolts can be fully unscrewed and removed along with the caps. The bearing caps and the cylinder head locations are numbered to ensure the caps are correctly positioned on refitting; an identification letter is also stamped on each cap **(see illustration)**.

Caution: If the bearing cap bolts are carelessly slackened, the bearing caps might break. If any bearing cap breaks then the complete cylinder head assembly must be renewed; the bearing caps are matched to the head and are not available separately.

4 Lift the camshaft out of the cylinder head and slide off the oil seal. Using a dab of paint or a suitable marker pen, make an identification mark on the inlet camshaft to avoid getting the camshafts mixed up on refitting; the inlet and exhaust camshafts are the same but it is important they are not interchanged as this will increase the rate of wear.

5 Repeat the operations described in paragraphs 3 and 4 and remove the exhaust camshaft. If the work is being carried out on the left-hand cylinder head, prior to removing the bearing caps, unbolt the camshaft sensor (see Chapter 4A, Section 14) and position it clear of the front bearing cap and free the knock sensor wiring.

6 Obtain twelve small, clean plastic containers, and label them for identification. Alternatively, divide a larger container into compartments. Lift the followers out from the

9.2b . . . then screw in a self-tapping screw and pull out the oil seal with pliers/grips

9.4 Tap the new seal into position using a socket which bears only on the seal outer edge as a drift

10.3 Prior to removal note the identification markings on the camshaft caps and cylinder head (arrowed)

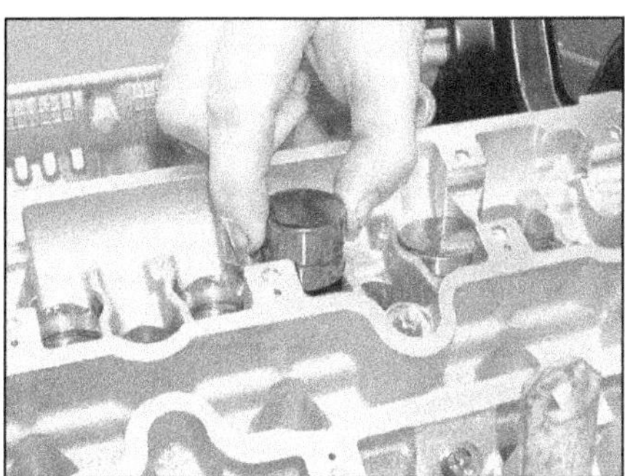
10.6 Removing a camshaft follower

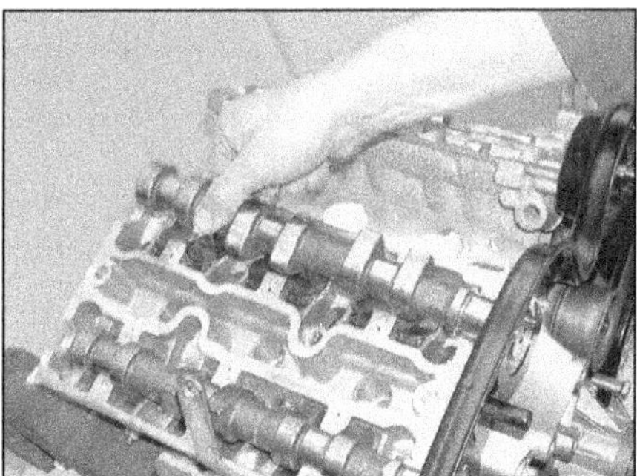
10.11a Lay the camshafts in position . . .

10.11b . . . then temporarily refit the sprockets to position the shafts correctly (see text)

top of the cylinder head and store each one in its respective fitted position **(see illustration)**. **Note:** *Store all the followers the correct way up to prevent the oil draining from the hydraulic valve adjustment mechanisms.*

7 If necessary, repeat the operations described in paragraphs 1 to 6 and remove the camshafts and followers from the other cylinder head. If all the camshafts are to be removed at the same time, make identification marks on the shafts to ensure they are refitted in their original locations, and note the camshaft bearing caps identification letter locations to ensure the caps are refitted to the correct cylinder head.

Inspection

8 Examine the camshaft bearing surfaces and cam lobes for signs of wear ridges and scoring. Renew the camshaft if any of these conditions are apparent. Examine the condition of the bearing surfaces both on the camshaft journals and in the cylinder head. If the head bearing surfaces are worn excessively, the cylinder head will need to be renewed.

9 Examine the follower bearing surfaces which contact the camshaft lobes for wear ridges and scoring. Check the followers and their bores in the cylinder head for signs of wear or damage. If any follower is thought to be faulty or is visibly worn it should be renewed.

Refitting

10 Where removed, lubricate the followers with clean engine oil and carefully insert each one into its original location in the cylinder head.

11 Lubricate the camshaft followers with clean engine oil then lay the camshafts in position. Ensure the crankshaft is still positioned approximately 60° BTDC then temporarily refit the sprockets (see Section 8 for details) to the camshafts **(see illustrations)**. On the left-hand cylinder head position each shaft so that its sprocket timing mark is aligned with cutouts on the rear cover and on the right-hand cylinder head position each shaft so that its sprocket timing mark is approximately 60∞ before the rear cover cutouts. This will position each camshaft so that the valve spring pressure will be equally exerted along its length as the bearing caps are tightened.

12 Ensure the mating surfaces of the bearing caps and cylinder head are clean and dry and lubricate the camshaft journals and lobes with clean engine oil.

13 Apply a smear of sealant (Vauxhall recommend the use of sealant 15 03 170 - available from your Vauxhall dealer) to cylinder mating surfaces on each side of the camshaft oil seal apertures **(see illustration)**.

14 Refit the camshaft bearing caps and the retaining bolts in their original locations on the cylinder head. The exhaust camshaft caps are numbered 1 to 4 from front to rear and the inlet camshaft caps 5 to 8 from front to rear with the corresponding numbers being marked on the cylinder head upper surface **(see illustration)**.

15 Working on the exhaust camshaft, tighten the bearing cap bolts by hand only then, working in a spiral pattern from the centre outwards, tighten the bolts by half-a-turn at a time to gradually impose the pressure of the valve springs on the bearing caps. Repeat this sequence until all bearing caps are in contact with the cylinder head then go around and tighten the camshaft retaining bolts to the specified torque **(see illustration)**.

Caution: If the bearing cap bolts are carelessly tightened, the bearing caps might break. If any bearing cap breaks then the complete cylinder head assembly must be renewed; the bearing caps are matched to the head and are not available separately.

16 Tighten the inlet camshaft bearing cap bolts as described in paragraph 15.

17 If necessary, repeat the operations in paragraphs 10 to 15 and refit the camshafts to the opposite cylinder head.

18 Fit new camshaft oil seals as described in Section 9.

19 Refit the camshaft sprockets as described in Section 8.

20 Ensure the camshaft sprocket timing marks are all correctly aligned with the cutouts on the rear cover then carefully rotate the crankshaft in the normal direction of rotation until the sprocket mark is correctly realigned with the notch on the oil pump housing.

21 Refit the timing belt as described in Section 7.

22 Refit the camshaft cover(s) and timing belt cover as described in Sections 4 and 6.

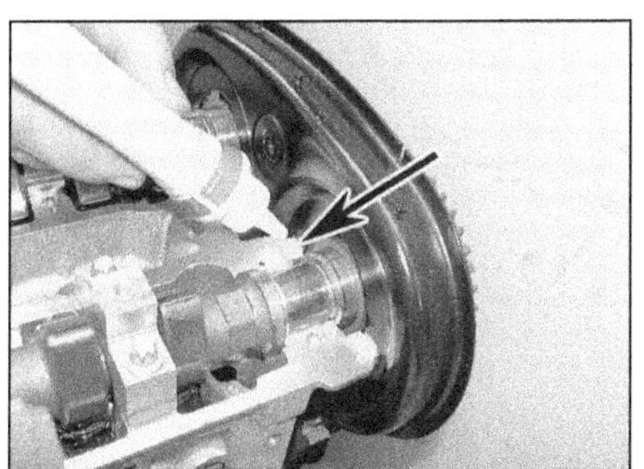
10.13 Apply sealant to the cylinder head surface on each side of the camshaft oil seal apertures (arrowed)

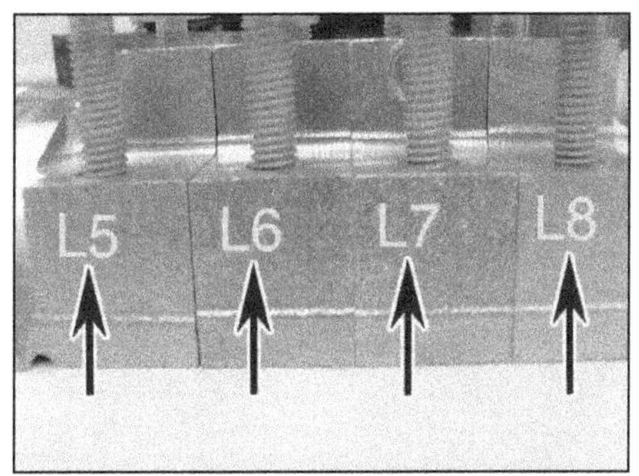

10.14 Use the identification markings (arrowed) to ensure that the bearing caps are refitted in their original locations

10.15 Carefully tighten the camshaft bearing cap bolts as described in text

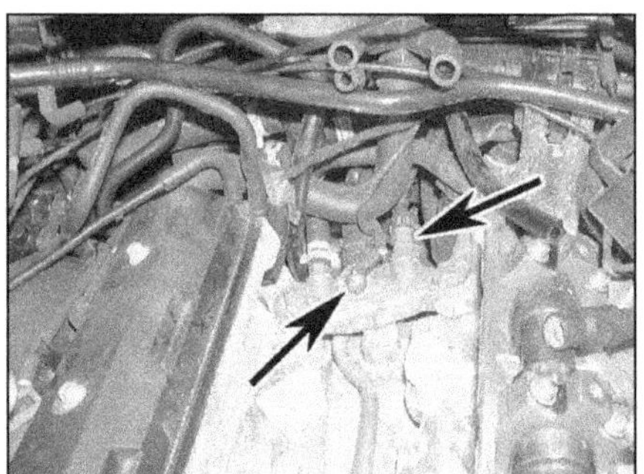
11.5 Disconnect the wiring connectors (arrowed) from the coolant temperature sender and sensor . . .

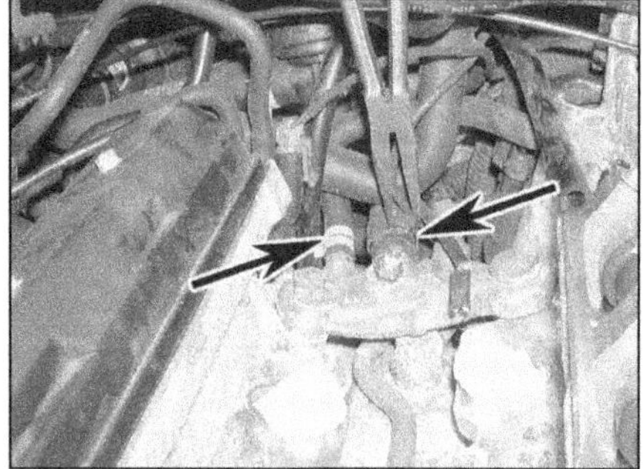
11.6 . . . then release the retaining clips and disconnect the coolant hoses from the outlet elbow

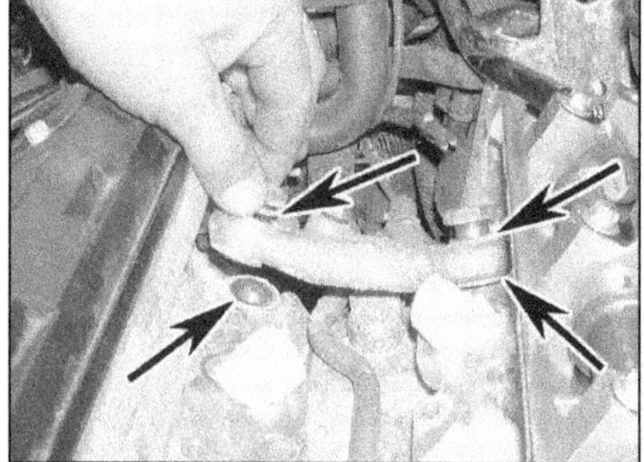
11.7 Unscrew the retaining bolts then remove the coolant outlet elbow from between the cylinder heads and recover the sealing washers (arrowed)

11 Cylinder head - removal and refitting

Removal

Note: *The engine must be cold when removing the cylinder head. New cylinder head bolts must be used on refitting.*

1 Remove the battery as described in Chapter 5A. **Note:** *On models with a Vauxhall anti-theft warning system (ATWS), the battery negative terminal must be disconnected within 15 seconds of the ignition being switched off to prevent the alarm system being triggered.*

2 Remove the windscreen wiper arms and the water deflector panel (see Chapter 12, Sections 15 and 16).

11.14 Disconnecting the wiring connector from the engine management ECU

3 Remove the complete inlet manifold assembly, including the manifold flange, as described in Chapter 4A.

4 Drain the cooling system and remove the spark plugs as described in Chapter 1.

5 Disconnect the wiring connectors from the coolant temperature gauge sender and the engine management system coolant temperature sensor which are screwed into the coolant outlet which links the rear of the cylinder heads **(see illustration)**.

6 Slacken the retaining clips and disconnect the coolant hoses from the cylinder head outlet **(see illustration)**.

7 Unscrew the retaining bolts and remove the coolant outlet from the cylinder heads. Recover the sealing rings and discard them; new ones must be used on refitting **(see illustration)**.

8 Remove the timing belt as described in Section 7.

9 Remove the camshaft sprockets, the timing belt tensioner pulley/upper guide pulley assembly and the lower guide pulley as described in Section 8.

10 Remove the coolant pump as described in Chapter 3.

11 Undo the retaining bolts and remove the timing belt rear cover from the engine unit (see Section 6). Proceed as described under the relevant sub-heading.

Left-hand cylinder head

12 Remove the camshaft cover as described in Section 4.

13 Disconnect the wiring connector and the right-hand cylinder head plug leads from the DIS module so the module is free to be removed with the head. Also unbolt the earth connections from the rear of the left-hand cylinder head.

14 Remove the cover from the relay box in the left-hand corner of the engine compartment. Lift out the engine management electronic control unit (ECU) then release the retaining clip and disconnect its wiring connector (see Chapter 4A, Section 14) **(see illustration)**. The ECU can be left in position in the box.

15 Trace the engine wiring harness back from the left-hand cylinder head to the engine compartment relay box. Unclip the injection system relay connectors from the box then disconnect the harness connector and free the sealing grommet from the relay box **(see illustrations)**.

16 Disconnect the harness connectors which are located at the rear of the battery then disconnect the camshaft sensor and left-hand cylinder bank knock sensor wiring connectors. Free the engine wiring harness auxiliary connections from the battery positive terminal and position the harness clear of the cylinder head. On some models the harness is connected to the fusible link housing instead of the battery terminal; where this is the case, remove the fusible link and unclip the connector from the housing **(see illustrations)**.

17 Remove the exhaust system left-hand front pipe as described in Chapter 4A.

11.15a Unclip the injection system relays . . .

11.15b . . . then disconnect the wiring connector . . .

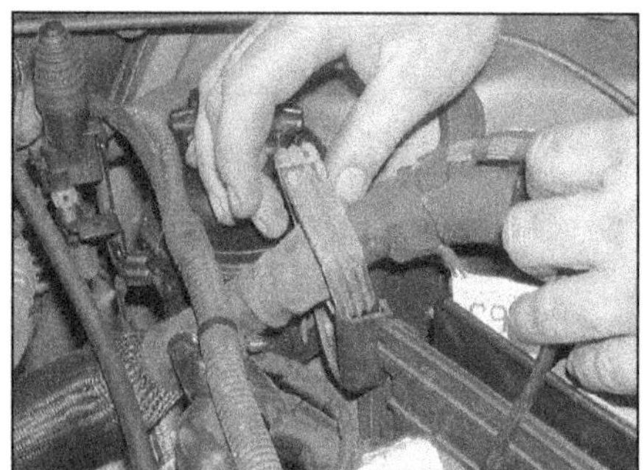
11.15c . . . and free the wiring harness from the relay box

11.16a Disconnect the harness connectors located at the rear of the battery

18 Remove the power steering pump as described in Chapter 10.

19 Slacken the retaining clip and disconnect the radiator upper coolant hose from the pipe at the front of the left-hand cylinder head.

20 Unscrew the bolt and spacer securing the coolant pipe and engine lifting bracket to the cylinder head and remove the lifting bracket. Move the coolant pipe to the left to free it from the thermostat housing then manoeuvre it out of position **(see illustrations)**. Remove the sealing rings from the inner end of the pipe and discard them; new ones must be used on refitting.

21 Remove the dipstick then free the dipstick tube from the cylinder block and remove it from the engine. Discard the tube sealing rings; new ones should be used on refitting.

22 Remove the exhaust camshaft as described in Section 10.

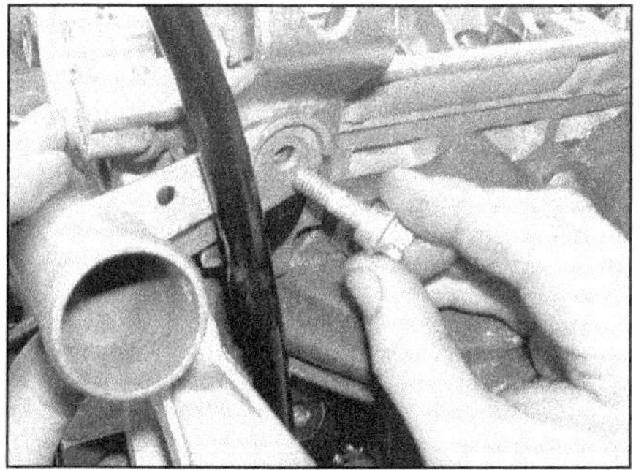

11.20a Slacken and remove the retaining bolt and spacer . . .

11.23 Evenly and progressively slacken and remove the cylinder head bolts . . .

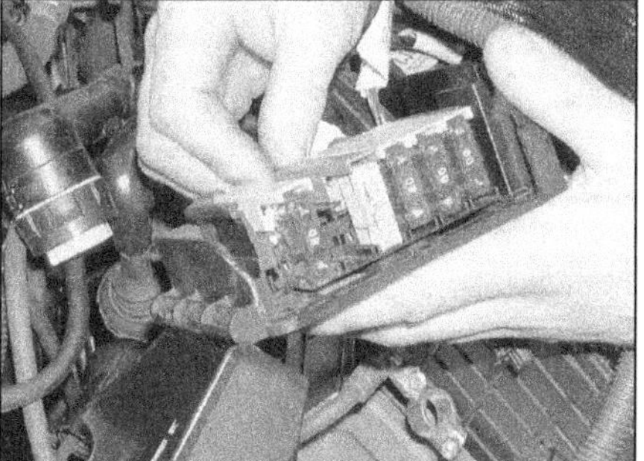

11.16b Where the engine harness is connected to the fusible link housing, remove the fusible link . . .

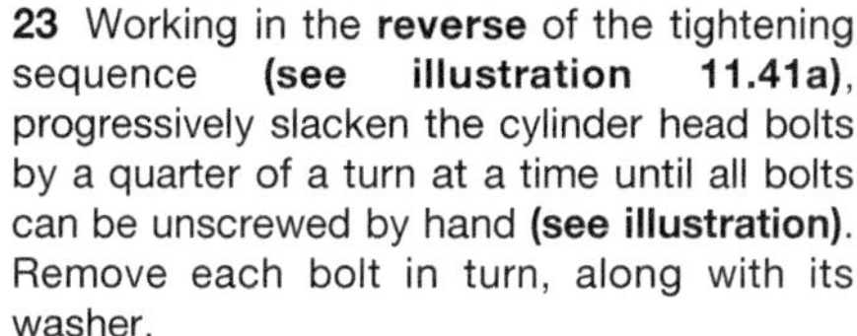

23 Working in the **reverse** of the tightening sequence **(see illustration 11.41a)**, progressively slacken the cylinder head bolts by a quarter of a turn at a time until all bolts can be unscrewed by hand **(see illustration)**. Remove each bolt in turn, along with its washer.

24 Lift the cylinder head from the cylinder block **(see illustration)**. If necessary, tap the cylinder head gently with a soft-faced mallet to free it from the block, but **do not** lever at the mating faces. Note the fitted positions of the two locating dowels, and remove them for safe keeping if they are loose.

25 Recover the cylinder head gasket, and discard it.

Right-hand cylinder head

26 Position a suitable container beneath the oil filter. Unscrew the filter using an oil filter removal tool if necessary, and drain the oil into the container. If the oil filter is damaged or distorted during removal, it must be renewed. Given the low cost of a new oil filter relative to the cost of repairing the damage which could result if a re-used filter springs a leak, it is probably a good idea to renew the filter in any case.

11.20b . . . then remove the coolant pipe from the thermostat housing (shown with engine removed)

11.24 . . . then lift the cylinder head off the block

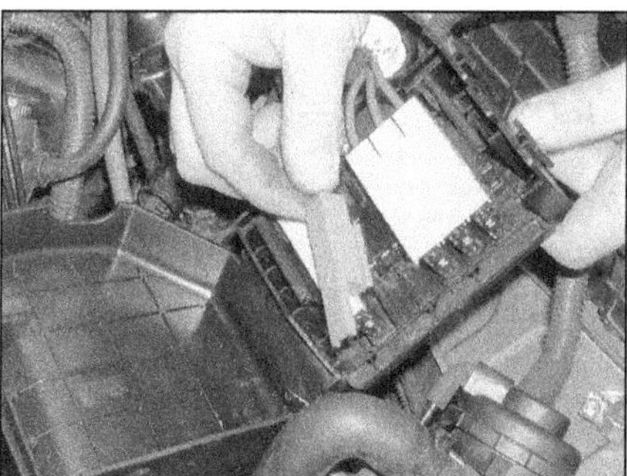

11.16c . . . then unclip the connector from the housing

11.16d Once all the wiring has been disconnected, position the harness clear of the cylinder head

27 Unscrew the union nuts securing the oil cooler pipes to the cylinder block then unscrew the union bolts securing the pipes to the cooler. Recover the sealing washers from each side of the oil cooler unions and move the pipes to the rear **(see illustrations)**.

28 Release the retaining clips and disconnect the radiator bottom hose, expansion tank hose and heater hose from the coolant pipe which runs along the right-hand side of the engine. Slacken and remove the retaining bolts then remove the pipe from the engine.

11.27a Unscrew the union nuts (arrowed) securing the oil pipes to the cylinder block . . .

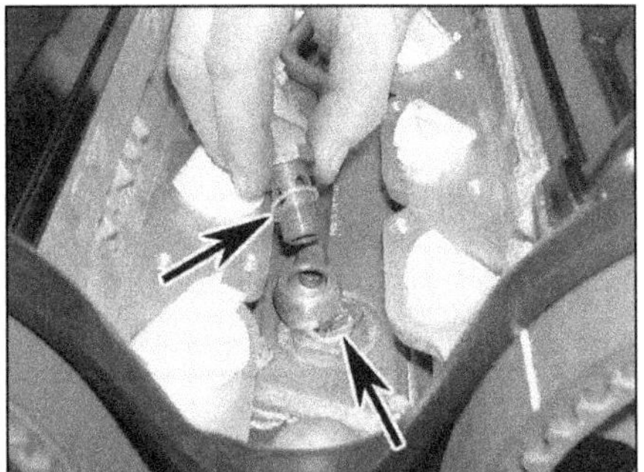

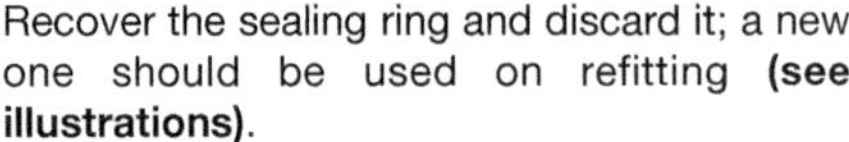

11.27b . . . then remove the union bolts and sealing washers (arrowed) and free the pipes from the oil cooler

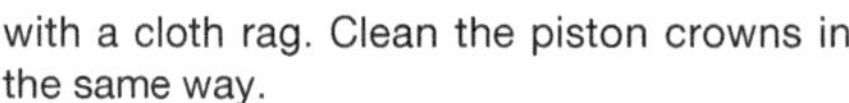

11.28a Disconnect the expansion tank hose . . .

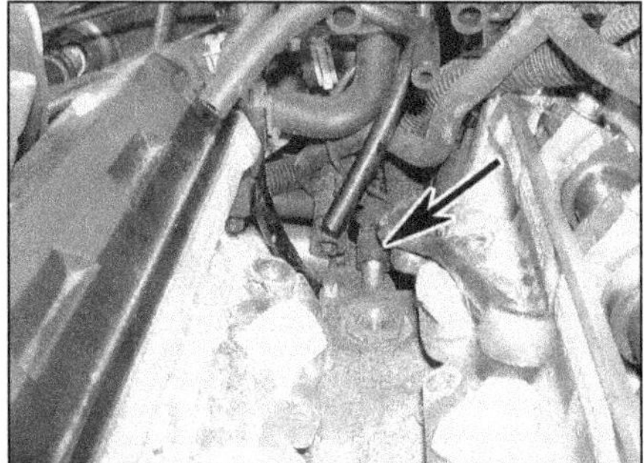

11.28b . . . and heater hose (arrowed) from the coolant pipe . . .

Recover the sealing ring and discard it; a new one should be used on refitting **(see illustrations)**.

29 Remove the exhaust system right-hand front pipe as described in Chapter 4A.

30 Remove the exhaust camshaft as described in Section 10.

31 Remove the cylinder head as described in paragraphs 23 to 25 **(see illustration)**.

Preparation for refitting

32 The mating faces of the cylinder head and block must be perfectly clean before refitting the head. Use a scraper to remove all traces of gasket and carbon, and also clean the tops of the pistons. Take particular care with the aluminium surfaces, as the soft metal is damaged easily. Also, make sure that debris is not allowed to enter the oil and water channels - this is particularly important for the oil circuit, as carbon could block the oil supply to the camshaft or crankshaft bearings. Using adhesive tape and paper, seal the water, oil and bolt holes in the cylinder block. To prevent carbon entering the gap between the pistons and bores, smear a little grease in the gap. After cleaning the piston, rotate the crankshaft so that the piston moves down the bore, then wipe out the grease and carbon with a cloth rag. Clean the piston crowns in the same way.

33 Check the block and head for nicks, deep scratches and other damage. If slight, they may be removed carefully with a file. More serious damage may be repaired by machining, but this is a specialist job.

34 If warpage of the cylinder head is suspected, use a straight-edge to check it for distortion. Refer to Chapter 2D if necessary.

35 Ensure that the cylinder head bolt holes in the crankcase are clean and free of oil. Syringe or soak up any oil left in the bolt holes. This is most important in order that the correct bolt tightening torque can be applied and to prevent the possibility of the block being cracked by hydraulic pressure when the bolts are tightened. Renew the cylinder head bolts regardless of their apparent condition.

Refitting

Left-hand cylinder head

36 Ensure the crankshaft is till positioned approximately 60° BTDC and wipe clean the mating faces of the head and block.

37 Ensure that the two locating dowels are in position at each end of the cylinder block/crankcase surface.

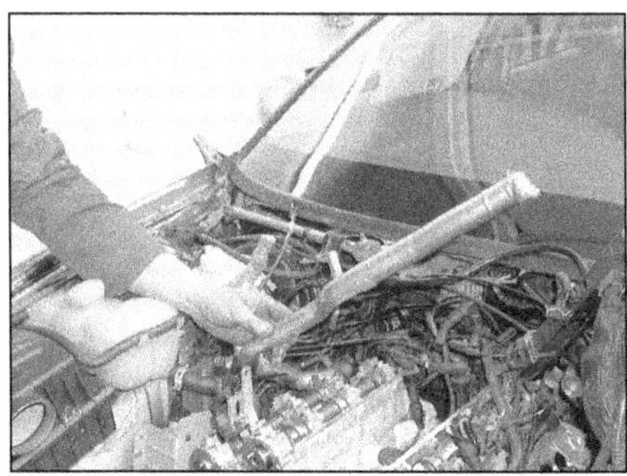

11.28c . . . then undo the retaining bolts and remove the pipe from the engine

38 Fit the new cylinder head gasket to the block, making sure it is fitted with the correct way up with its OBEN or TOP mark uppermost and at the front end of the engine **(see illustration)**.

39 Carefully refit the cylinder head (complete with exhaust manifold), locating it on the dowels.

40 Lightly lubricate the threads and heads of the new cylinder head bolts with engine oil then carefully insert them into position (**do not drop**), tightening them finger-tight only at this stage.

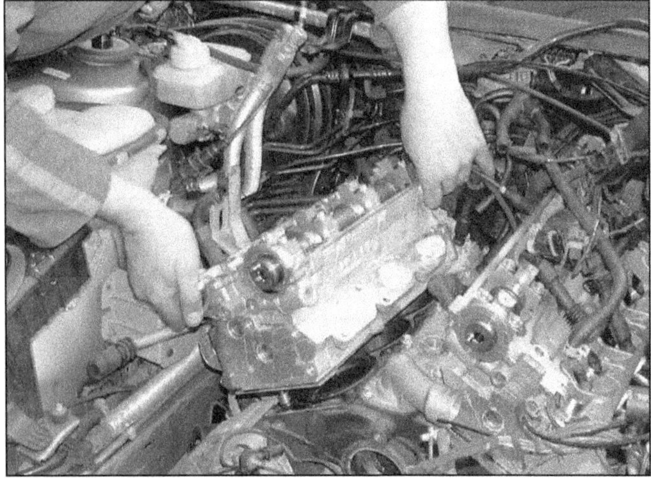

11.31 Removing the right-hand cylinder head assembly

11.38 Ensure the locating dowels (arrowed) are in position then fit the new head gasket

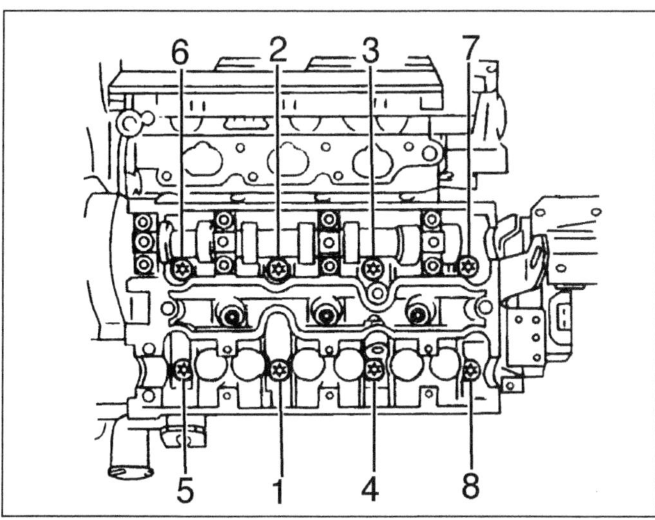

11.41a Cylinder head bolt tightening sequence (left-hand head shown)

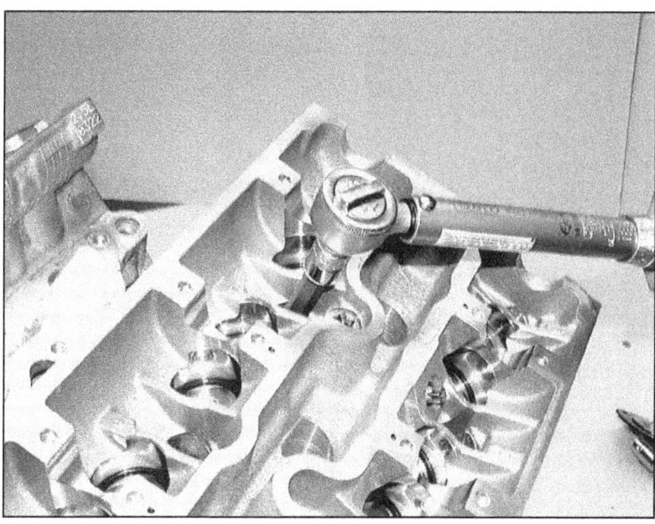

11.41b Working in the specified sequence, tighten the cylinder head bolts to the specified stage 1 torque . . .

41 Working progressively and in the sequence shown, first tighten all the cylinder head bolts to the stage 1 torque setting **(see illustrations)**.

42 Once all bolts have been tightened to the stage 1 torque, again working in the sequence shown, tighten each bolt through its specified stage 2 angle, using a socket and extension bar. It is recommended that an angle-measuring gauge is used during this stage of the tightening, to ensure accuracy **(see illustration)**.

43 Working in the specified sequence, go around again and tighten all bolts through the specified stage 3 angle.

44 Working again in the specified sequence, go around and tighten all bolts through the specified stage 4 angle.

45 Finally go around in the specified sequence again and tighten all bolts through the specified stage 5 angle.

46 The remainder of the refitting procedure is the reverse of removal noting the following points

- *a) If the right-hand cylinder head has also been removed, refit this to the block before connecting any ancillaries.*
- *b) Fit new sealing rings to the dipstick tube and thermostat housing coolant pipe. Ensure the coolant pipe, dipstick tube and lifting bracket are correctly positioned before refitting the retaining bolt and spacer and tightening to the specified torque.*
- *c) Ensure the engine wiring harness is correctly routed and securely reconnect all the wiring connectors. Also make sure the earth lead retaining bolts are securely tightened.*
- *d) Refit the camshaft, timing belt and associated components as described in Sections 6 to 10.*
- *e) Use new sealing rings when refitting the coolant outlet to the cylinder heads and tighten the retaining bolts to the specified torque.*
- *f) Ensure all coolant hoses are correctly reconnected and securely retained by their clips.*
- *g) Refit the exhaust front pipe and inlet manifold as described in Chapter 4A.*
- *h) On completion refill the cooling system and power steering fluid reservoir (see Chapter 1 and Weekly checks).*

Right-hand cylinder head

47 Refit the cylinder head as described in paragraphs 36 to 45 noting that the cylinder head gasket OBEN or TOP mark must be uppermost and at the rear end of the engine.

48 The remainder of the refitting procedure is the reverse of removal noting the following points

- *a) If the left-hand cylinder head has also been removed, refit this to the block before connecting any ancillaries.*
- *b) Fit a new sealing ring to coolant pipe and securely tighten the pipe retaining bolts.*
- *c) Fit new sealing washers to each side of the oil cooler pipe unions and tighten the pipe union nuts and bolts to the specified torque.*
- *d) Refit the camshaft, timing belt and associated components as described in Sections 6 to 10.*
- *e) Use new sealing rings when refitting the coolant outlet to the cylinder heads and tighten the retaining bolts to the specified torque.*
- *f) Ensure all coolant hoses are correctly reconnected and securely retained by their clips.*
- *g) Refit the exhaust front pipe and inlet manifold as described in Chapter 4A.*
- *h) Fit a new oil filter and refill the cooling system as described in Chapter 1.*
- *i) On completion, check the engine oil level as described in Weekly checks.*

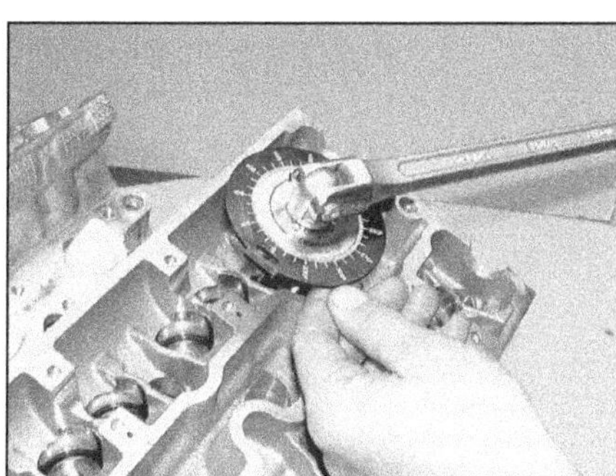

11.42 . . . and then through the specified stage 2 to 5 angles using an angle measuring gauge for accuracy

12 Sump - removal and refitting

Removal

Sump pan

Note: *New sump pan retaining bolts will be required on refitting.*

1 Disconnect the battery negative terminal. **Note:** *On models with a Vauxhall anti-theft warning system (ATWS), the battery negative terminal must be disconnected within 15 seconds of the ignition being switched off to prevent the alarm system being triggered.*

2 Firmly apply the handbrake then jack up the front of the car and support it on axle stands. Undo the retaining screws and remove the undercover from beneath the engine.

3 Drain the engine oil as described in Chapter 1, then fit a new sealing washer and refit the drain plug, tightening it to the specified torque.

4 Disconnect the wiring connector from the oil level sensor connector on the right-hand

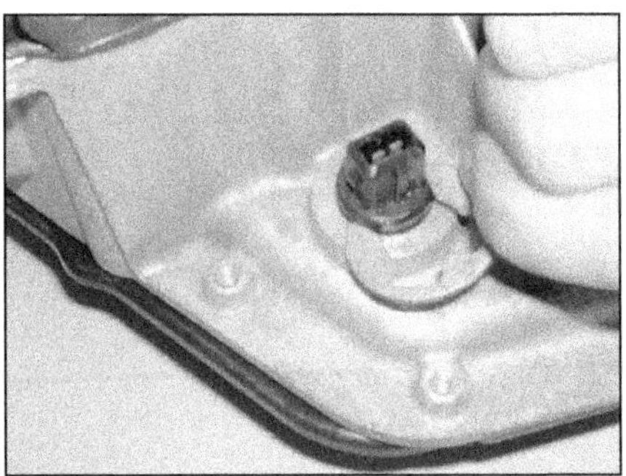
12.4 Slide off the retaining clip and push the oil level sensor wiring connector into the sump

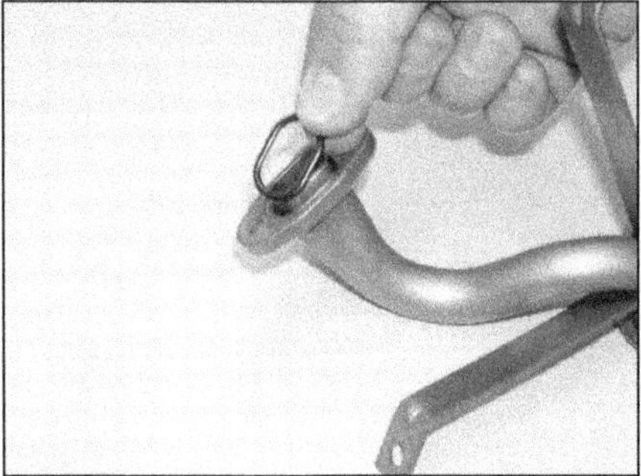
12.16 Fit a new sealing ring to the oil pump pick-up/strainer before refitting

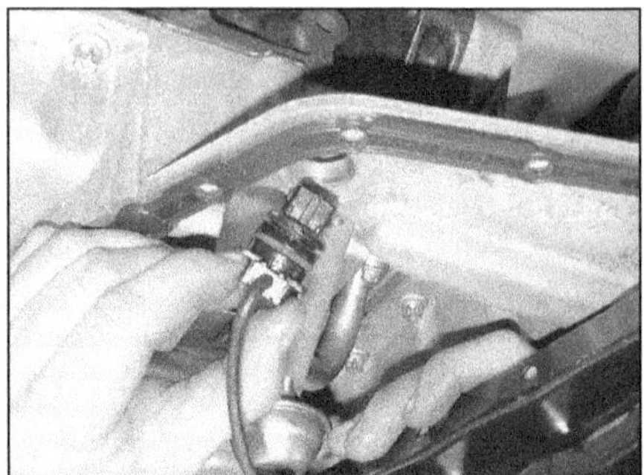
12.18 On refitting, locate the oil level sensor wiring connector in the main casting before bolting the sump pan in position

side of the main casting then slide off the retaining clip and push the connector into the sump **(see illustration)**.

5 Slacken and remove the sump pan retaining bolts then free it from the main casting and remove it along with its gasket. Take care not to damage the oil level sensor wiring as the pan is removed.

6 If necessary, undo the retaining bolts (one is tricky to reach) and remove the oil pump pick-up/strainer from the base of the oil pump housing along with its sealing ring. Check the oil pump pick-up/strainer for signs of clogging or splitting and renew/clean as necessary.

Main casting

Note: *New front suspension subframe mounting bolts will be required on refitting. New retaining nuts for the centre tie rod will also be required.*

7 Remove the sump pan and oil pick-up/strainer as described in paragraphs 1 to 6.

8 Referring to Chapter 12, on models with Xenon headlights, disconnect the wiring connector from the headlight system front vehicle level control sensor then unclip the link rod from the sensor arm balljoint.

9 Remove the steering linkage centre tie rod as described in Chapter 10, Section 25.

10 Slacken and remove the mounting bolts and remove the vibration dampers from the left- and right-hand engine mountings

11 Slacken and remove the nuts securing the engine left- and right-hand mountings to the subframe.

12 Attach an engine hoist to the engine lifting brackets then raise the hoist until it is supporting the weight of the engine. Alternatively use an engine support bar to take the weight of the engine.

13 Referring to Chapter 10, unscrew the front suspension subframe front mounting bolts by approximately 4 turns. Support the rear of the subframe with a jack then slacken and remove the rear mounting bolts. Lower the rear of the subframe approximately 10 cm to gain access to the main casting.

14 Unscrew the bolts securing the main casting flange to the transmission housing then progressively slacken and remove the bolts securing the main casting to the base of the cylinder block/oil pump. Break the joint by striking the casting with the palm of the hand, then lower it away from the engine and withdraw it. Remove the seal and discard it. **Note:** *If the main casting is to be removed for any length of time, raise the subframe back up into position and refit its mounting bolts then lower the engine back down onto the subframe.*

Refitting

Sump pan

15 Remove all traces of dirt and oil from the mating surfaces of the sump pan, main casting and (if necessary) the pick-up/strainer and oil pump housing.

16 Where necessary, position a new sealing ring on top of the oil pump pick-up/strainer then refit the strainer, tightening its retaining bolts to the specified torque **(see illustration)**.

17 Ensure the sump pan and main casting surfaces are clean and dry and fit a new sealing ring to the oil level sensor wiring connector.

18 Place a new gasket on the top of the pan and offer it up to the main casting. Seat the oil level sensor wiring connector in the main casting, securing it in position with the retaining clip, then seat the sump pan on the main casting **(see illustration)**.

19 Fit the new sump pan retaining bolts then go around in a diagonal sequence and tighten them to the specified stage 1 torque setting. Once all bolts have been tightened go around again and angle-tighten them through the specified stage 2 angle. It is recommended that an angle-measuring gauge is used during this stage of the tightening, to ensure accuracy.

20 Reconnect the oil level sender wiring connector then refit the undercover.

21 Lower the vehicle to the ground then fill the engine with fresh oil, with reference to Chapter 1.

Main casting

22 Remove all traces of dirt and oil from the mating surfaces of the main casting and cylinder block.

23 Ensure the main casting seal groove is completely dry then apply a bead of sealant (Vauxhall recommend the use of sealant 15 03 298 - available from your Vauxhall dealer) to the areas of the groove shown **(see illustration)**. **Note:** *If the Vauxhall sealant is being used, the main casting must be bolted in position on the cylinder block within ten minutes of applying the sealant.*

24 Locate the new seal correctly in its groove then apply a bead of the sealant, approximately 3mm in diameter, to the main casting surface as shown **(see illustrations)**. The sealant should go around the outside of the seal around the front of the casting and the inside at the rear, making sure the sealant overlaps at the points shown.

25 Apply a smear of suitable sealant (Vauxhall recommend the use of sealant 15 03 295 - available from your Vauxhall dealer) to the areas of the cylinder block mating surface

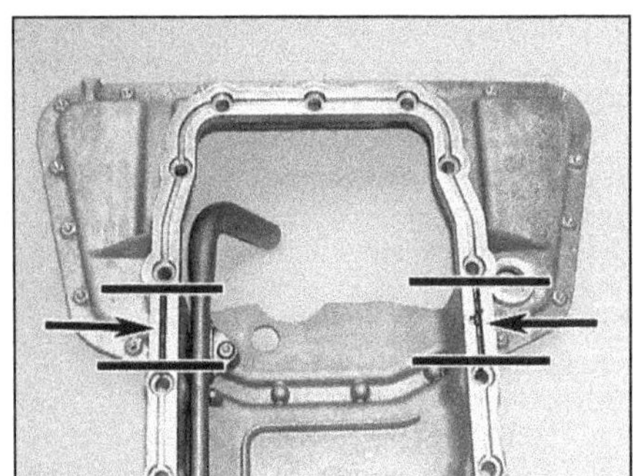
12.23 Apply a bead of sealant (arrowed) to the main casting seal groove in between the lines shown . . .

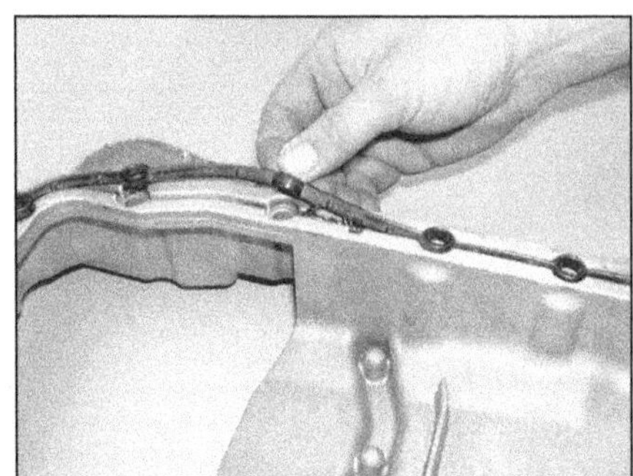
12.24a . . . then locate the new seal in the casting groove

around the areas of the oil pump housing and rear main bearing cap joints **(see illustrations)**.

26 Manoeuvre the casting into position and loosely refit all its retaining bolts.

27 Working out from the centre in a diagonal sequence, progressively tighten the bolts securing the main casting to the cylinder block/oil pump to their specified torque setting.

28 Tighten the bolts securing the casting flange to the transmission housing to their specified torque settings.

29 Raise the subframe back up into position making sure the engine mounting lugs engage correctly with the subframe cutouts. Fit the four new rear retaining bolts then remove the subframe front retaining bolts and fit the new ones. Tighten the subframe mounting bolts to their specified torque setting and then through the specified angles as described in Chapter 10.

30 Remove the hoist/support bar from the engine then refit the nuts securing the engine mountings to the subframe, tightening them to the specified torque. Refit the vibration dampers to the mountings and tighten their mounting bolts to the specified torque.

31 Refit the steering linkage centre tie rod as described in Chapter 10

32 On models with Xenon headlights clip the link rod balljoint back onto the vehicle level control sensor and reconnect the wiring connector (see Chapter 12).

33 Refit the sump pan as described in paragraphs 15 to 21.

13 Oil pump - removal, overhaul and refitting

Removal

1 Remove the timing belt as described in Section 7.

2 Remove all the camshaft sprockets, the crankshaft sprocket, the belt tensioner pulley/upper guide pulley assembly and the lower guide pulley as described in Section 8.

3 Undo the retaining bolts and remove the rear timing belt cover from the front of the engine (see Section 6).

4 Remove the sump pan, oil pump pick-up/strainer and main casting as described in Section 12.

5 Slacken and remove the alternator lower mounting bolt then slacken the upper bolt and pivot the alternator clear of the oil pump housing.

6 Disconnect the wiring connector from the oil pressure switch then unscrew the bolt securing the wiring guide to the front of the pump housing.

7 Slacken and remove the retaining bolts then slide the oil pump housing assembly off of the end of the crankshaft, taking great care not to lose the locating dowels. Remove the housing gasket and discard it.

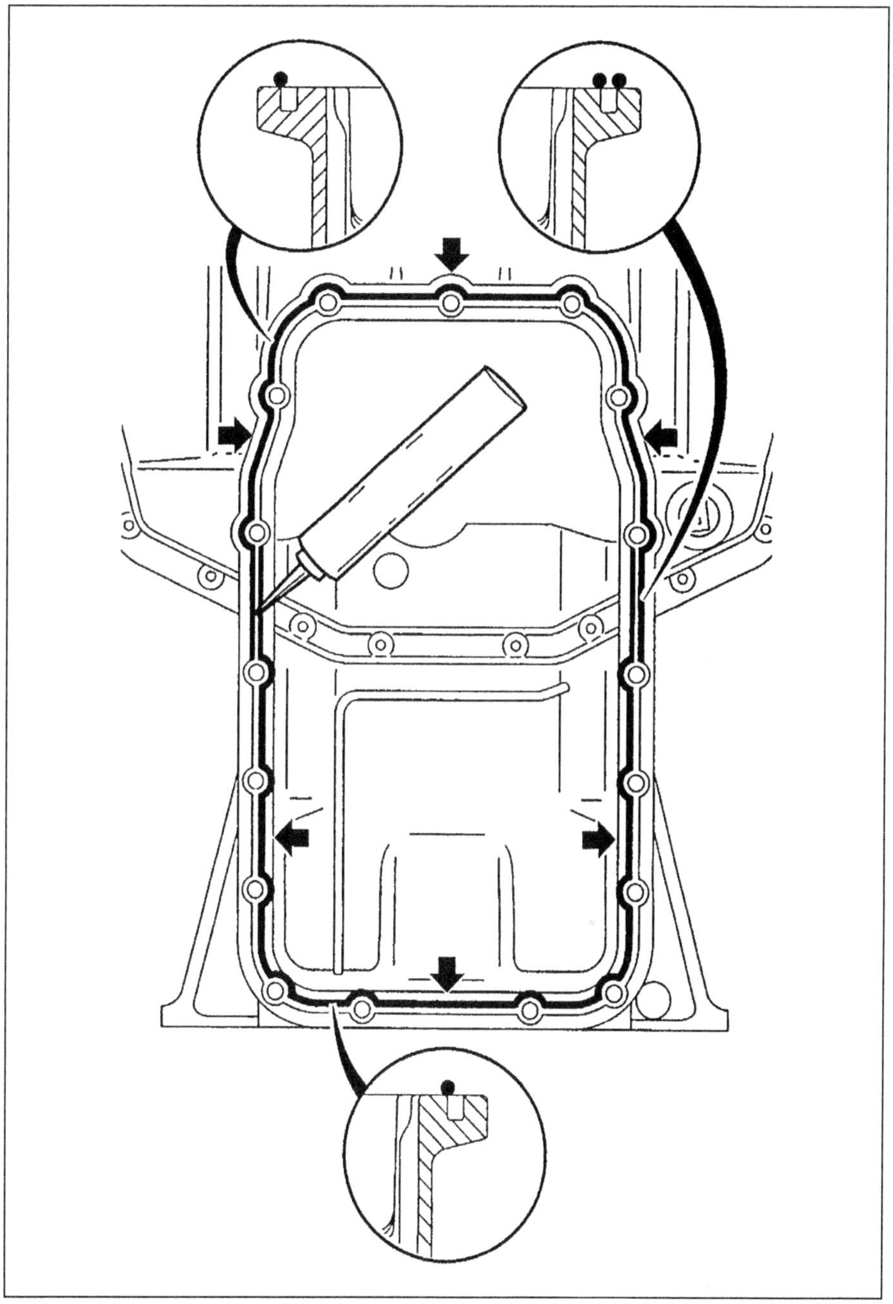

12.24b Apply beads of sealant to the main casting mating surface as shown

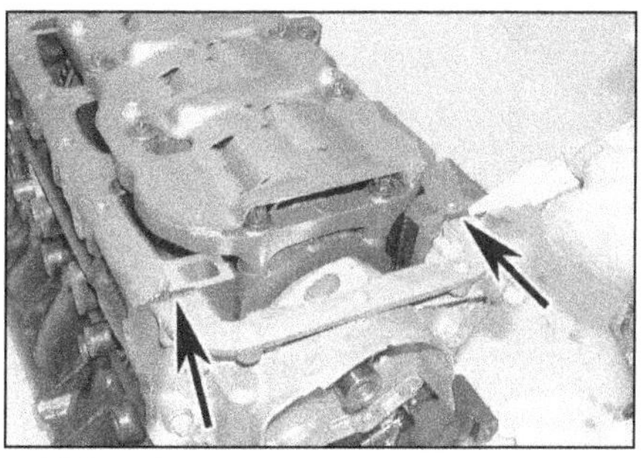

12.25a Apply a smear of sealant to the joints between the oil pump housing and cylinder block . . .

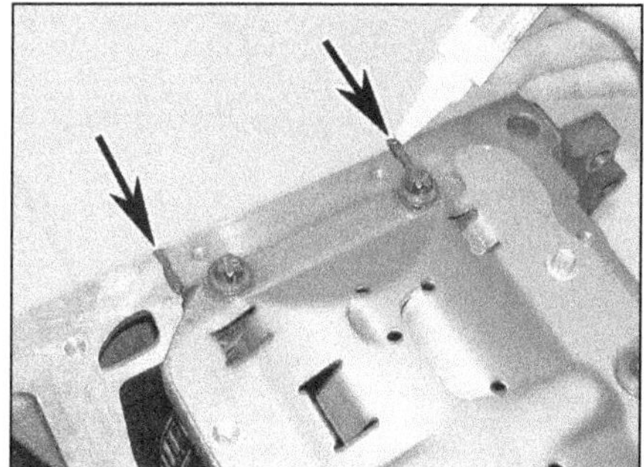

12.25b . . . and the rear main bearing cap and block

13.8 Undo the retaining screws and remove the cover from the oil pump

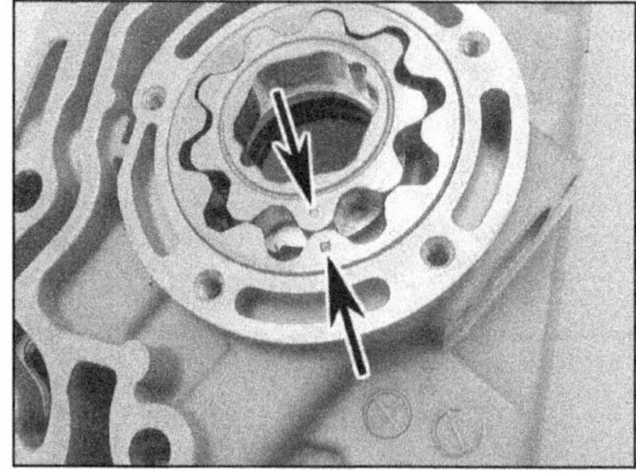
13.9 Note the identification markings (where present) on the pump rotors . . .

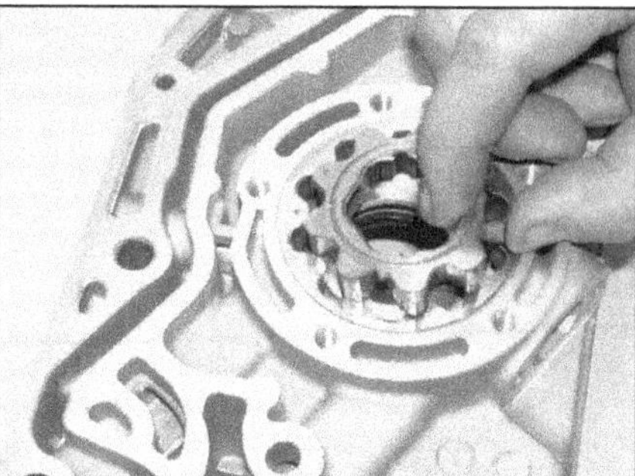
13.10 . . . then lift both rotors out of the housing

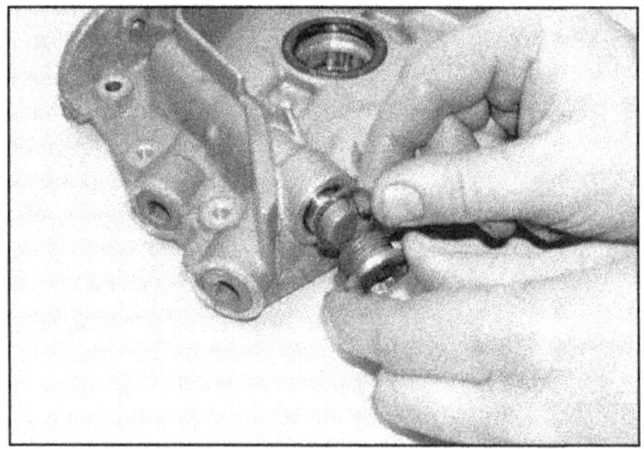
13.11a Slacken and remove the oil pressure relief valve bolt and sealing washer . . .

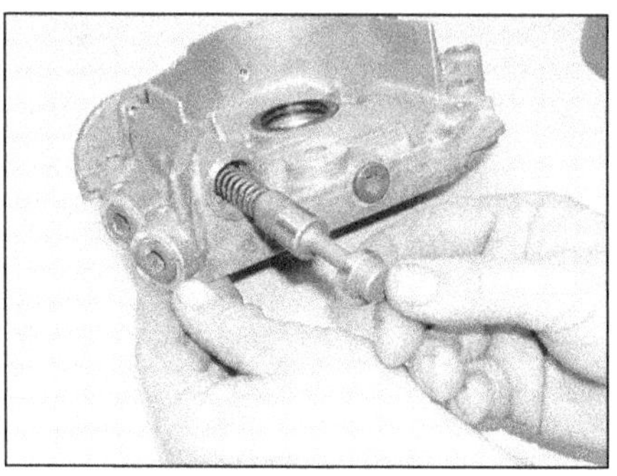
13.11b . . . then remove the valve plunger and spring from the pump

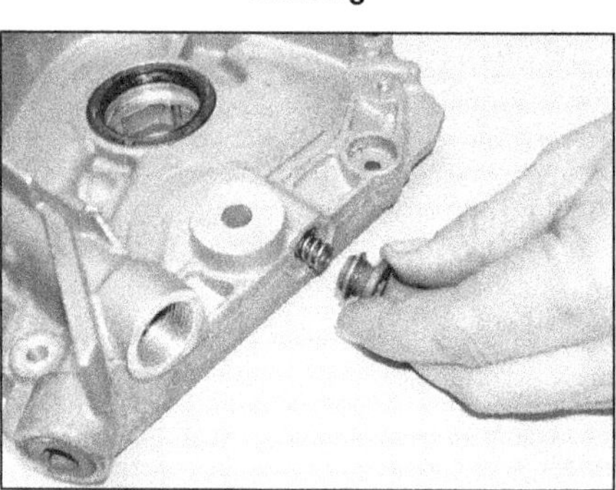
13.11c Slacken and remove the safety valve bolt and sealing washer . . .

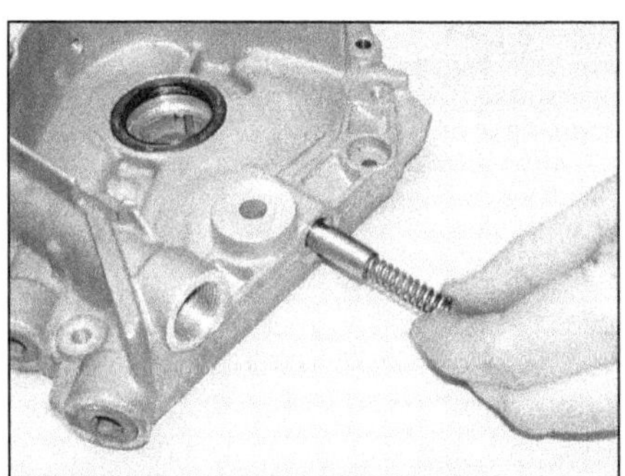
13.11d . . . and withdraw the spring and plunger from the pump

Overhaul

8 Undo the retaining screws and lift off the pump cover from the rear of the housing **(see illustration)**.

9 Using a suitable marker pen, mark the surface of both the pump inner and outer rotors; the marks can then be used to ensure the rotors are refitted the correct way around. On some pump identification marks may already exist on the rotors **(see illustration)**.

10 Lift out the inner and outer rotors from the pump housing **(see illustration)**.

11 Unscrew the oil pressure relief valve and the safety valve bolts from the top of the housing and withdraw the valve springs and plungers from the housing, noting which way around the plungers are fitted. Remove the sealing washers from the valve bolts **(see illustrations)**. **Note:** *The pressure relief valve can be removed with pump in position on the engine unit once the timing belt front cover has been removed.*

12 Clean the components, and carefully examine the rotors, pump body and valve plungers for any signs of scoring or wear. Renew any component which shows signs of wear or damage; if the rotors or pump housing are marked then the complete pump assembly should be renewed.

13 If the components appear serviceable, measure the rotor endfloat, and check the flatness of the end cover. If the clearances exceed the specified tolerances, the pump must be renewed.

14 If the pump is satisfactory, reassemble the components in the reverse order of removal, noting the following.

a) Ensure both rotors are fitted the correct way around.

b) Tighten the pump cover screws to the specified torque.

c) Fit new sealing rings to the valve bolts and ensure the plungers and springs are fitted the correct way around **(see illustrations)**.

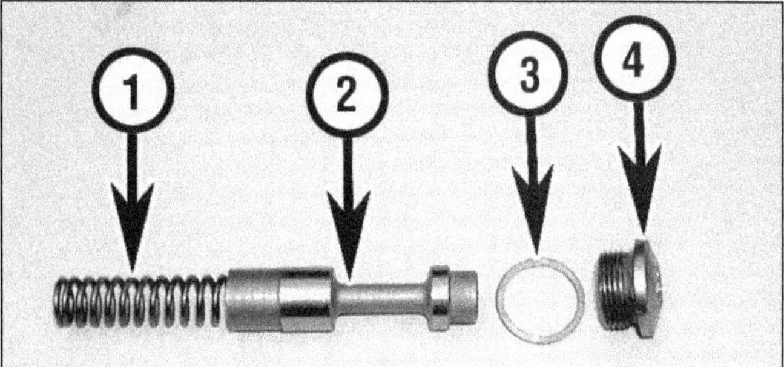

13.14a Oil pressure relief valve components

1 Spring
2 Plunger
3 Sealing washer
4 Valve bolt

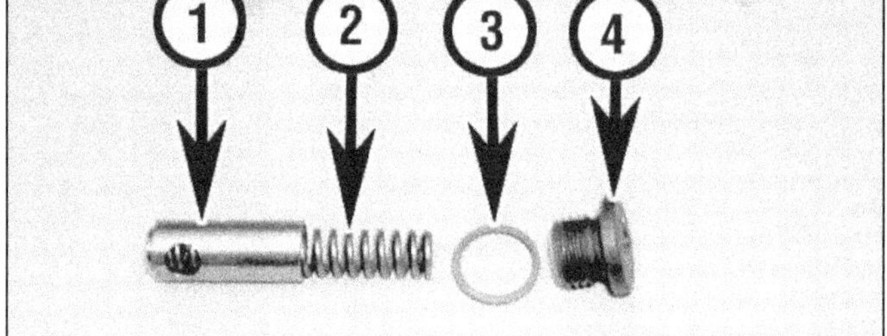

13.14b Safety valve components

1 Plunger
2 Spring
3 Sealing washer
4 Valve bolt

d) On completion prime the oil pump by filling it with clean engine oil whilst rotating the inner rotor.

Refitting

15 Prior to refitting it is necessary to determine which of the three possible types of oil pump assembly is fitted to your engine. The first step is to check the diameter of the oil pump retaining bolts; during the 1999 model year the pump retaining bolt diameter was increased from M6 to M8. If M6 retaining bolts are used, it will then be necessary to determine whether the engine is fitted with an original oil pump and timing belt rear cover arrangement or the modified arrangement **(see illustration)**. The modified cover has an additional hole through which the oil pump upper bolt (number 6 in the tightening sequence) can be reached and this affects the refitting procedure. Proceed as described under the relevant sub-heading.

Oil pump with M6 retaining bolts and the original timing belt rear cover

16 Prior to refitting, carefully lever out the crankshaft oil seal using a flat-bladed screwdriver. Fit the new oil seal, ensuring its sealing lip is facing inwards, and press it squarely into the housing using a tubular drift which bears only on the hard outer edge of the seal **(see illustrations)**. Press the seal into position so that it is flush with the housing and lubricate the oil seal lip with clean engine oil.

17 Ensure the mating surfaces of the oil pump and cylinder block are clean and dry and the locating dowels are in position.

18 Apply a thin coat of sealant (Vauxhall recommend the use of sealant 15 03 170 - available from your Vauxhall dealer), approximately 0.2 mm thick, to the shaded areas of the oil pump side of the new pump gasket as shown **(see illustration)**.

19 Fit the gasket to the cylinder block then carefully manoeuvre the oil pump into position and engage the inner rotor with the crankshaft end. Locate the pump on the dowels, taking great care not damage the oil seal lip **(see illustrations)**.

20 Refit the pump housing retaining bolts in their original locations and tighten them to the initial specified torque in the order shown **(see illustration)**.

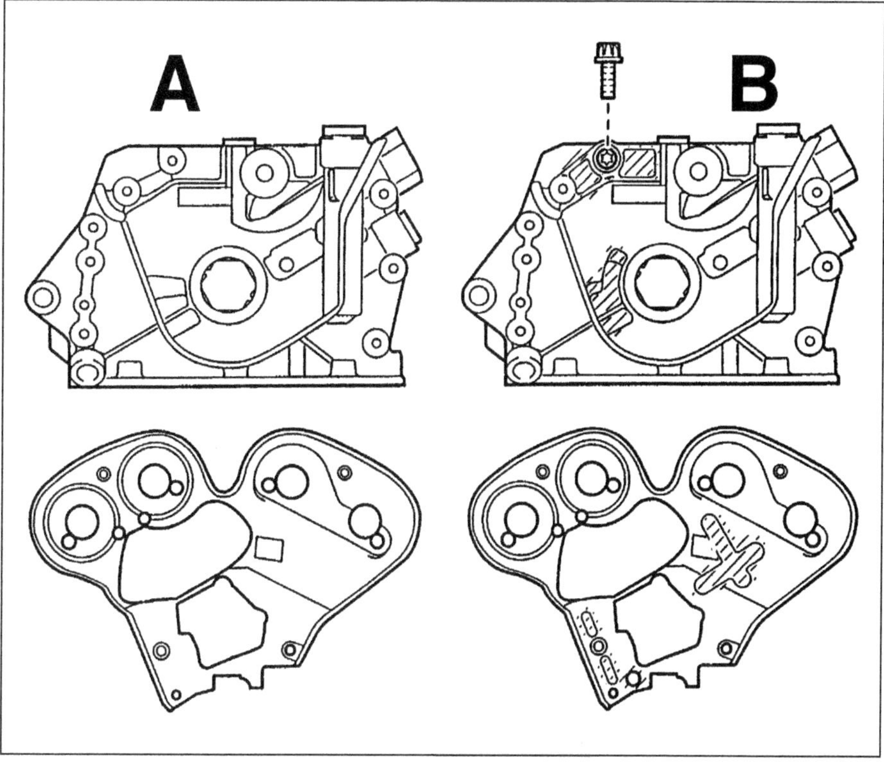

13.15 Oil pump and timing belt rear cover identification details (pump retained by M6 bolts)

A Original pump and timing belt cover
B Modified pump and timing belt cover (shaded areas show differences) which allow access to the bolt shown with the cover in position

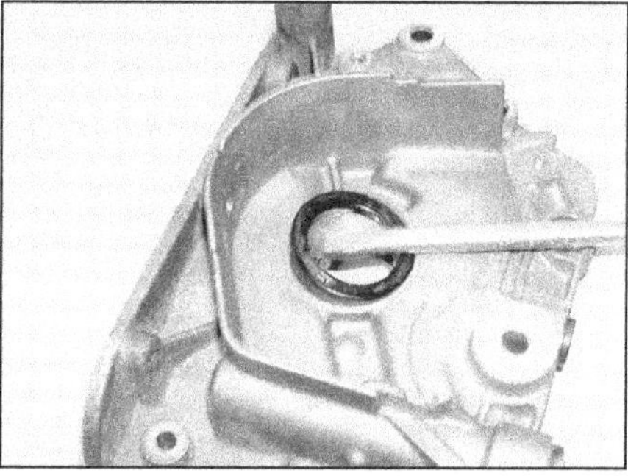

13.16a Lever out the oil seal out from the pump with a large flat-bladed screwdriver . . .

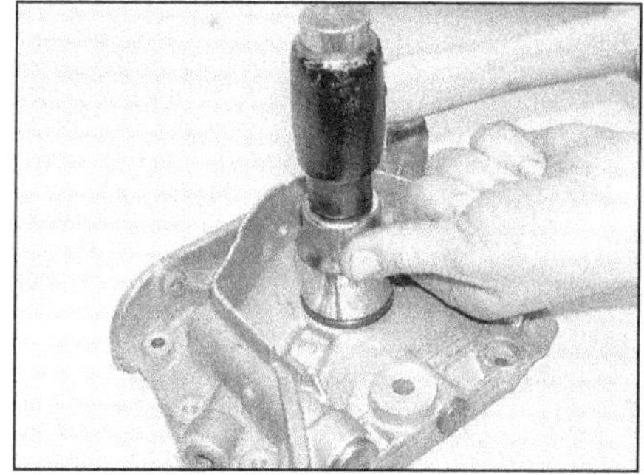

13.16b . . . and tap the new seal squarely into position, using a socket which bears only on the seal outer edge

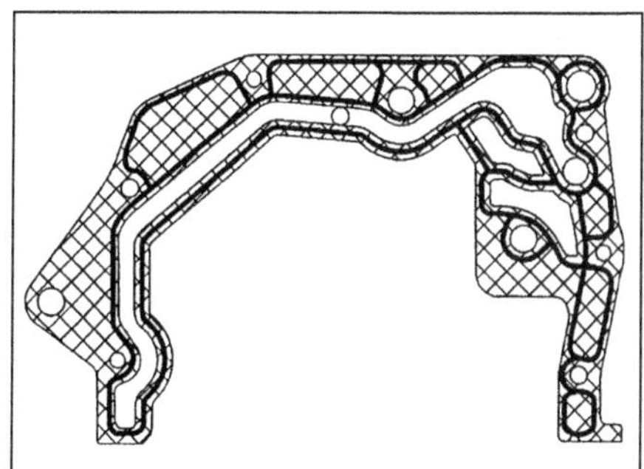

13.18 Apply sealant (see text) to the shaded areas of the oil pump side of the new gasket

13.19a Locate the pump gasket on the dowels . . .

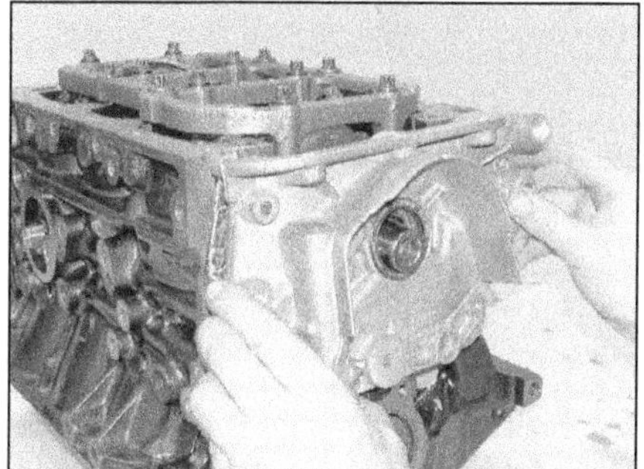

13.19b . . . then refit the oil pump assembly

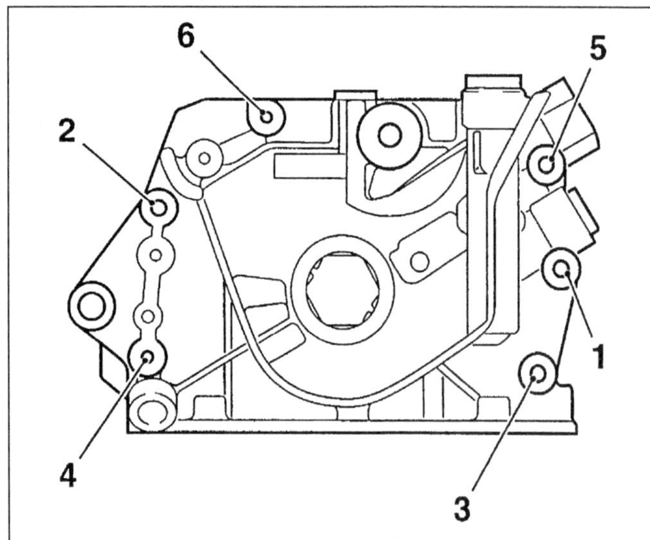

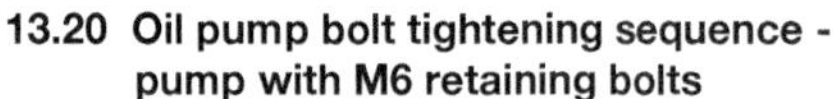
13.20 Oil pump bolt tightening sequence - pump with M6 retaining bolts

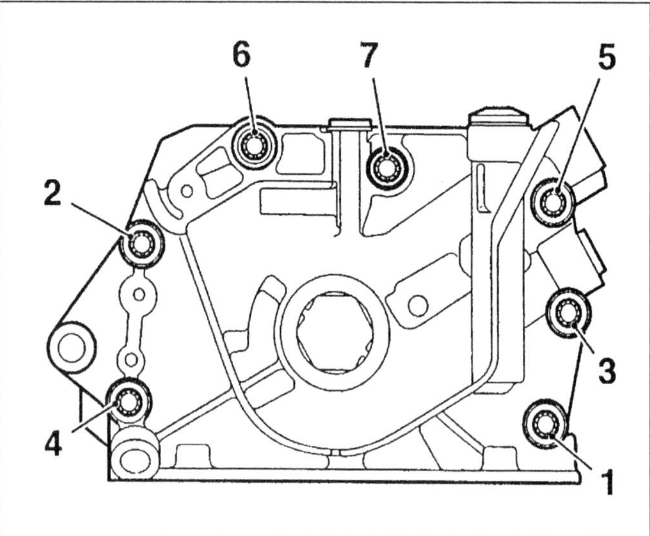

13.40 Oil pump bolt tightening sequence - pump with M8 retaining bolts

21 Fit the timing belt lower guide pulley to the pump and tighten its retaining bolt to the specified torque.
22 Refit the alternator lower mounting bolt and tighten to the specified torque (see Chapter 5A).
23 Wait approximately 10 minutes to allow the sealant on the pump gasket to cure then go around again in the specified sequence and tighten them to the final specified torque setting.
24 Remove the lower guide pulley from the oil pump and refit the timing belt rear cover (see Section 6), tightening its retaining bolts to the specified torque.
25 Reconnect the oil pressure sensor wiring connector and secure the wiring guide in position with the bolt.
26 Refit the sump main casting, oil pump pick-up/strainer and sump pan as described in Section 12.
27 Refit the timing belt sprockets, guide pulleys and tensioner then refit the belt as described in Sections 7 and 8.
28 On completion, fit a new oil filter and fill the engine with clean oil as described in Chapter 1.

Oil pump with M6 retaining bolts and the modified timing belt rear cover

29 Carry out the operations described in paragraphs 16 to 19.
30 Refit the pump housing retaining bolts in their original locations and tighten them to the specified torque in the order shown **(see illustration 13.20)**.
31 Refit the alternator lower mounting bolt and tighten to the specified torque (see Chapter 5A).
32 Refit the timing belt rear cover (see Section 6) and tighten its retaining bolts to the specified torque.
33 Reconnect the oil pressure sensor wiring connector and secure the wiring guide in position with the retaining bolt.
34 Refit the sump main casting, oil pump pick-up/strainer and sump pan as described in Section 12.
35 Refit the timing belt sprockets, guide pulleys and tensioner then refit the belt as described in Sections 7 and 8. Prior to refitting the timing belt outer cover, go around in the specified sequence **(see illustration 13.20)** and retighten all the oil pump retaining bolts to the specified torque.
36 On completion, fit a new oil filter and fill the engine with clean oil as described in Chapter 1.

Oil pump with M8 retaining bolts

37 Remove all traces of locking compound from the oil pump retaining bolt threads.
38 Carry out the operations described in paragraphs 16 to 19.
39 Apply a drop of locking compound (Vauxhall recommend the use of locking compound 15 10 181 - available from your Vauxhall dealer) to the thread of each pump retaining bolt then refit the bolts in their original locations, tightening them by hand only.

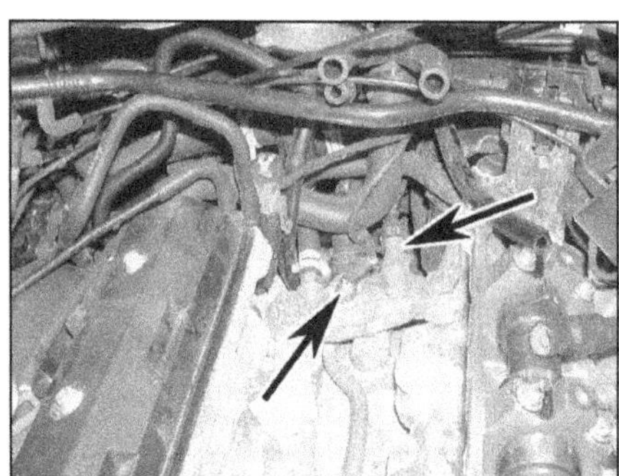
14.3 Disconnect the wiring connectors (arrowed) from the coolant temperature sender and sensor . . .

40 Go around in the specified sequence and tighten all the pump retaining bolts to the specified stage 1 torque setting **(see illustration)**.
41 Refit the alternator lower mounting bolt and tighten to the specified torque (see Chapter 5A).
42 Go around again in the specified sequence and tighten all the pump retaining bolts to the specified stage 2 torque setting.
43 Reconnect the oil pressure sensor wiring connector and secure the wiring guide in position with the retaining bolt.
44 Refit the timing belt rear cover (see Section 6) and tighten its retaining bolts to the specified torque.
45 Refit the sump main casting, oil pump pick-up/strainer and sump pan as described in Section 12.
46 Refit the timing belt sprockets, guide pulleys and tensioner then refit the belt as described in Sections 7 and 8.
47 On completion, fit a new oil filter and fill the engine with clean oil as described in Chapter 1.

14 Oil cooler - removal and refitting

Removal

1 Drain the cooling system as described in Chapter 1.
2 Remove the complete inlet manifold, including the manifold flange, as described in Chapter 4A.
3 Disconnect the wiring connectors from the coolant temperature gauge sender and the engine management system coolant temperature sensor which are screwed into the coolant outlet which links the rear of the cylinder heads **(see illustration)**.

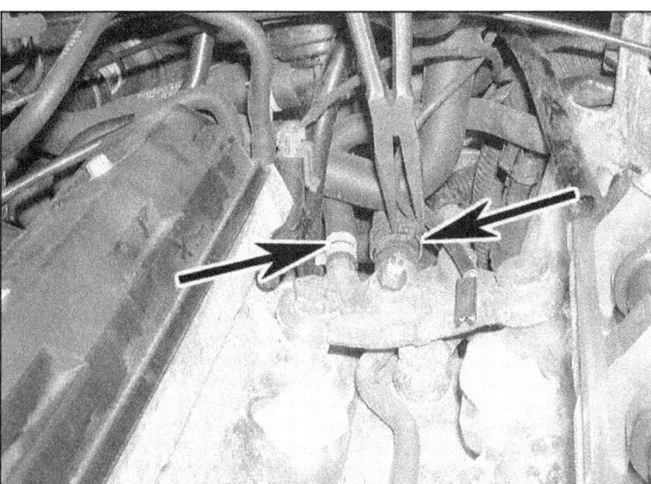

14.4 . . . then release the retaining clips and disconnect the coolant hoses from the outlet elbow

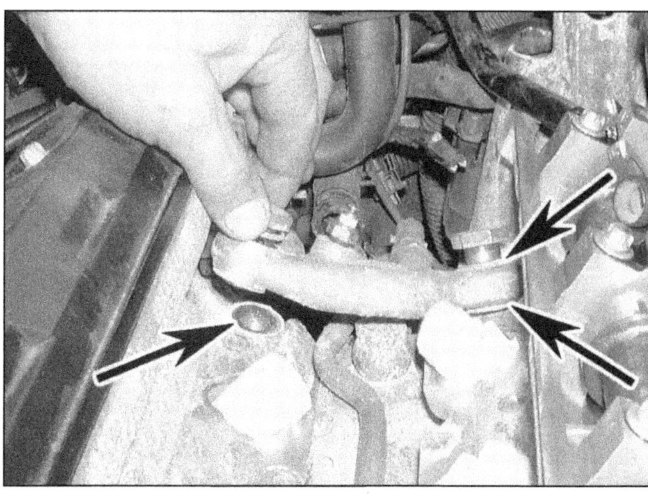

14.5 Unscrew the retaining bolts then remove the coolant outlet elbow from between the cylinder heads and recover the sealing washers (arrowed)

4 Slacken the retaining clips and disconnect the coolant hoses from the cylinder head outlet **(see illustration)**.

5 Unscrew the retaining bolts and remove the coolant outlet from the cylinder heads. Recover the sealing rings and discard them; new ones must be used on refitting **(see illustration)**.

6 Undo the retaining bolts and remove the upper heatshield from the left-hand cylinder bank exhaust manifold. If necessary, to improve access to the rear bolt remove the exhaust system front pipe as described in Chapter 4A.

7 Position a suitable container beneath the oil filter. Unscrew the filter using an oil filter removal tool if necessary, and drain the oil into the container. If the oil filter is damaged or distorted during removal, it must be renewed. Given the low cost of a new oil filter relative to the cost of repairing the damage which could result if a re-used filter springs a leak, it is probably a good idea to renew the filter in any case.

8 Unscrew the union nuts securing the oil cooler pipes to the cylinder block then unscrew the union bolts securing the pipes to the cooler. Recover the sealing washers from each side of the oil cooler unions and position the pipes clear of the oil cooler **(see illustrations)**.

9 Unscrew the large nuts securing the oil cooler unions to the cover then undo the retaining bolts and remove the cover from the top of the cylinder block **(see illustrations)**. Recover the gasket (where fitted) and discard it; sealant will be needed to replace the gasket on refitting.

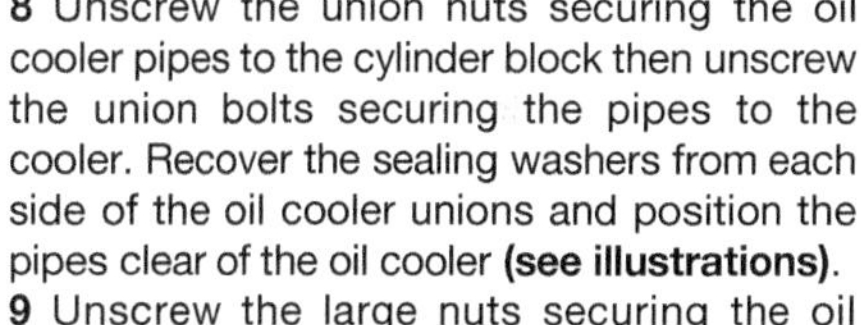

10 Lift out the oil cooler and remove it from the engine, keeping it upright to prevent oil spillage **(see illustration)**. Recover the sealing rings from the cooler unions and discard them; new ones must be used on refitting.

11 If the oil cooler shows signs of damage it must be renewed.

Refitting

12 Ensure the mating surfaces of the oil cooler, cover and cylinder block are clean and dry.

13 Fit new sealing rings to the oil cooler unions then refit the cover and screw on the large nuts, tightening them by hand only at this stage.

14.8a Slacken the union nuts (arrowed) securing the oil pipes to the block . . .

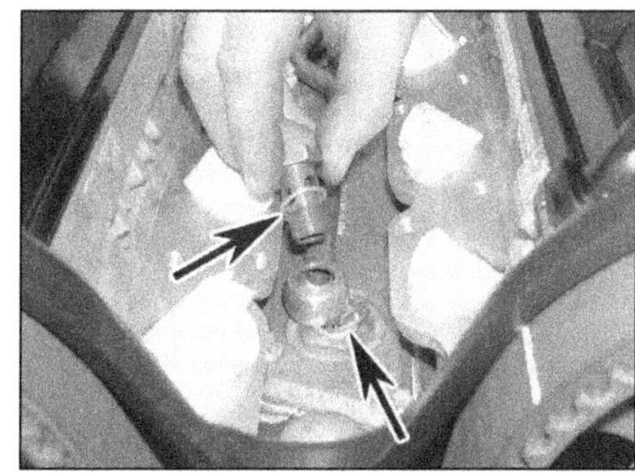

14.8b . . . then remove the union bolts and sealing washers (arrowed) and free the pipes from the oil cooler

14.9a Unscrew the large nuts from the cooler unions . . .

14.9b . . . then undo the retaining bolts and lift off the oil cooler cover

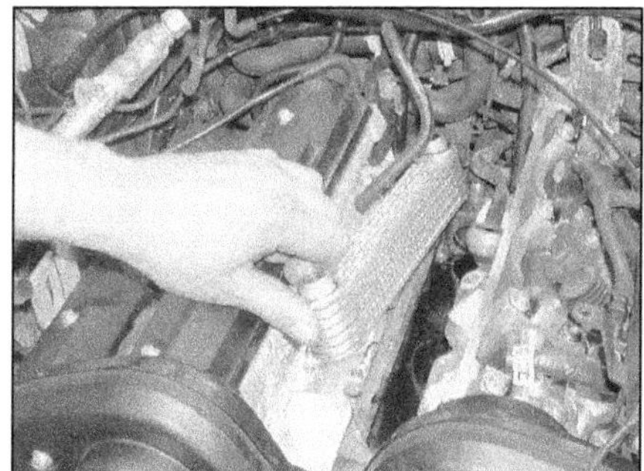

14.10 Removing the oil cooler from the cylinder block

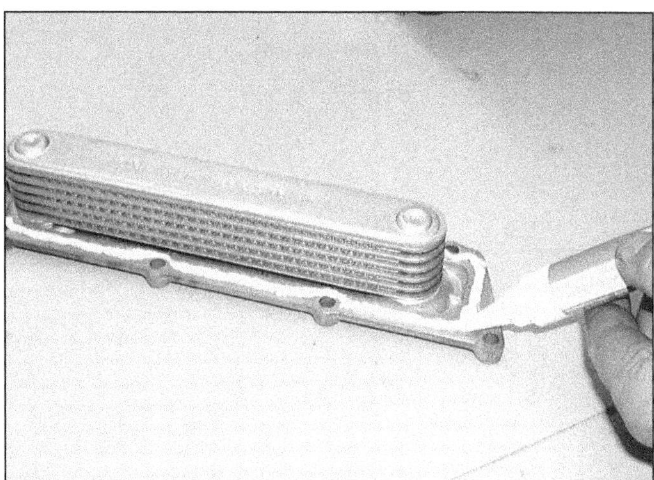
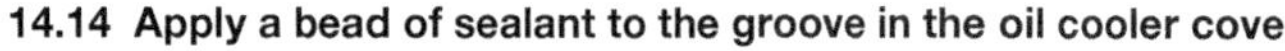
14.14 Apply a bead of sealant to the groove in the oil cooler cover

14.15 Tighten the cover retaining bolts to the specified torque then tighten the cooler nuts to their specified torque

14 Apply a bead of suitable sealant (Vauxhall recommend the use of sealant 15 03 296 - available from your Vauxhall dealer), approximately 2 mm in diameter, to the groove on the oil cooler cover **(see illustration)**.

15 Refit the cooler assembly to the cylinder block and refit the cover retaining bolts, tightening them evenly and progressively to their specified torque. Once the cover bolts are correctly tightened, tighten the cooler nuts to their specified torque **(see illustration)**.

16 Manoeuvre the oil cooler pipes into position and screw their union nuts into the cylinder block by a few turns each. Position a new sealing washer on each side of the pipe unions then refit the union bolts. Tighten the union bolts to the specified torque then tighten the pipe union nuts to the specified torque.

17 Fit new sealing rings to each side of the coolant outlet then refit it to the cylinder heads, tightening its retaining bolts to the specified torque. Reconnect the hoses to the outlet, securing them in position with the retaining clips, and the temperature sensor wiring connectors.

18 Refit the inlet manifold as described in Chapter 4A and install the exhaust manifold heatshield and (where necessary) front pipe.

15.2 Lock the flywheel/driveplate ring gear with a tool similar to that shown

19 Fit a new oil filter and refill the cooling system as described in Chapter 1.

20 On completion, check the engine oil level as described in Weekly checks.

15 Flywheel/driveplate - removal, inspection and refitting

Note: *New flywheel/driveplate retaining bolts will be required on refitting.*

Removal

Manual transmission models

1 Remove the transmission as described in Chapter 7A then remove the clutch assembly as described in Chapter 6.

2 Prevent the flywheel from turning by locking the ring gear teeth with a similar arrangement to that shown **(see illustration)**. Alternatively, bolt a strap between the flywheel and the cylinder block/crankcase. Make alignment marks between the flywheel and crankshaft using paint or a suitable marker pen.

3 Slacken and remove the retaining bolts and remove the flywheel. Do not drop it, as it is very heavy.

Automatic transmission models

4 Remove the transmission as described in Chapter 7B.

5 Lock the driveplate as described in paragraph 2 then slacken the driveplate retaining bolts.

6 Unscrew the retaining bolts and remove the retaining plate, centering ring and driveplate from the end of the crankshaft, noting each components correct fitted location.

Inspection

7 On manual transmission models, examine the flywheel for scoring of the clutch face. If the clutch face is scored, the flywheel may be surface-ground, but renewal is preferable. Check for wear or chipping of the ring gear teeth, if the teeth are damaged the flywheel must be renewed (ring gear renewal is not possible).

8 On automatic transmission models closely examine the driveplate for ring gear teeth for signs of wear or damage and check the driveplate surface for any signs of cracks.

9 If there is any doubt about the condition of the flywheel/driveplate, seek the advice of a Vauxhall dealer or engine reconditioning specialist. They will be able to advise if it is possible to recondition it or whether renewal is necessary.

Refitting

Manual transmission models

10 Clean the mating surfaces of the flywheel and crankshaft and remove all traces of locking compound from the flywheel retaining bolt threads in the crankshaft.

11 Offer up the flywheel and fit the new retaining bolts. If the original is being refitted align the marks made prior to removal.

12 Lock the flywheel by the method used on removal, and tighten the retaining bolts to the specified stage 1 torque setting then angle-tighten the bolts through the specified stage 2 angle, using a socket and extension bar, and finally through the specified stage 3 angle. It is recommended that an angle-measuring gauge is used during the final stages of the tightening, to ensure accuracy. If a gauge is not available, use white paint to make alignment marks between the bolt head and flywheel prior to tightening; the marks can then be used to check that the bolt has been rotated through the correct angle.

13 Refit the clutch as described in Chapter 6 then remove the locking tool, and refit the transmission as described in Chapter 7A.

Automatic transmission models

14 Clean the mating surfaces of the driveplate and crankshaft and remove all traces of locking compound from the driveplate retaining bolt threads in the crankshaft.

15 Offer up the driveplate complete with the centering ring and retaining plate, making sure all components are fitted the correct way around, then screw in the new retaining bolts.

16 Tighten the retaining bolts through the specified torque and angles as described in paragraph 12 then remove the locking tool and refit the transmission as described in Chapter 7B.

16 Crankshaft oil seals - renewal

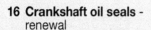

Front (timing belt end) oil seal

1 Remove the crankshaft sprocket and spacer as described in Section 8.

2 Carefully punch or drill two small holes opposite each other in the oil seal. Screw a self-tapping screw into each and pull on the screws with pliers to extract the seal. Alternatively carefully lever the seal out of position.

Caution: Great care must be taken to avoid damage to the oil pump

3 Clean the seal housing and polish off any burrs or raised edges which may have caused the seal to fail in the first place.

4 Lubricate the lips of the new seal with clean engine oil and ease it into position on the end of the shaft. Press the seal squarely into position until it is flush with the housing. If necessary, a suitable tubular drift, such as a socket, which bears only on the hard outer edge of the seal can be used to tap the seal into position. Take great care not to damage the seal lips during fitting and ensure that the seal lips face inwards.

5 Wash off any traces of oil, then refit the spacer and crankshaft sprocket as described in Section 8.

16.7 Fitting a new crankshaft rear oil seal

Rear (flywheel/driveplate end) oil seal

6 Remove the flywheel/driveplate as described in Section 15.

7 Renew the seal as described in paragraphs 2 to 4 **(see illustration)**.

8 Refit the flywheel/driveplate as described in Section 15.

17 Engine/transmission mountings - inspection and renewal

Inspection

1 If improved access is required, raise the front of the car and support it securely on axle stands. Undo the retaining bolts and remove the undercover from beneath the engine unit.

2 Check the mounting rubber to see if it is cracked, hardened or separated from the metal at any point; renew the mounting if any such damage or deterioration is evident.

3 Check that all the mounting's fasteners are securely tightened; use a torque wrench to check if possible.

4 Using a large screwdriver or a pry bar, check for wear in the mounting by carefully levering against it to check for free play; where this is not possible, enlist the aid of an assistant to move the engine/transmission unit back and forth, or from side to side, while you watch the mounting. While some free play is to be expected even from new components, excessive wear should be obvious. If excessive free play is found, check first that the fasteners are correctly secured, then renew any worn components as described below.

Renewal

Left- and right-hand engine mountings

Note: *It is recommended that the engine mountings are replaced as a matched pair.*

5 Firmly apply the handbrake then jack up the front of the vehicle and support it on axle stands. If necessary, to improve access undo the retaining screws and remove the undercover from beneath the engine unit.

6 Support the weight of the engine/transmission using a trolley jack with a block of wood placed on its head. Alternatively attach an engine hoist/support bar to the lifting brackets on the cylinder head and use this to support the engine.

7 Slacken and remove the mounting bolts and remove the vibration damper (where fitted) from the mounting assembly.

8 Unscrew the upper and lower nuts securing the relevant engine mounting to the cylinder block bracket and subframe then raise the engine unit slightly and manoeuvre the mounting out of position **(see illustrations)**. If necessary the mounting bracket can be unbolted and removed from the cylinder block. **Note:** *Take great care not to place any excess stress on any engine wiring/hoses or the exhaust system or when raising the engine.*

9 Check all components for signs of wear or damage, and renew as necessary.

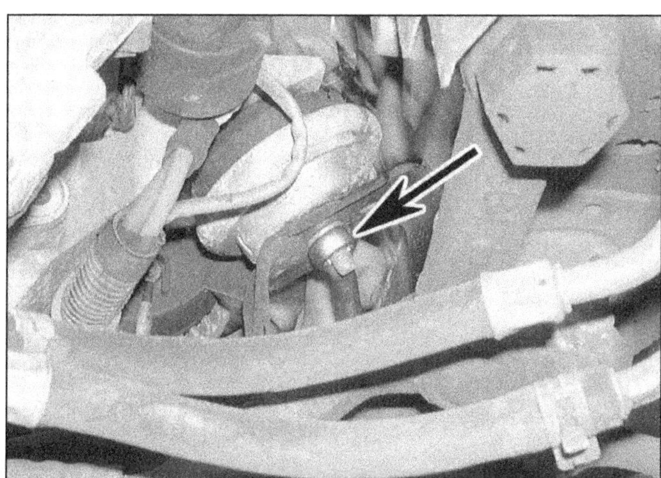

17.8a Slacken and remove the upper and lower nuts . . .

17.8b . . . then lift the engine slightly until there is sufficient clearance to manoeuvre the mounting out of position

10 On refitting, refit the mounting to the subframe aligning its locating lug with the subframe slot then refit the lower nut and tighten to the specified torque.

11 Refit the mounting bracket (where removed) to the cylinder block and tighten its retaining bolts to the specified torque.

12 Lower the engine unit back down onto the mounting then refit the upper retaining nut to the mounting, tightening it to the specified torque.

13 Where necessary, refit the vibration damper to the mounting bracket and subframe and tighten its mounting bolts to the specified torque.

14 Refit the undercover (where removed) then lower the vehicle to the ground.

Transmission unit rear mounting

15 Firmly apply the handbrake then jack up the front of the vehicle and support it on axle stands.

16 Place a jack with a block of wood beneath the transmission, and raise the jack to take the weight of the transmission.

17 With the transmission securely supported, slacken and remove the bolts securing the transmission unit rear mounting crossmember to the vehicle body. Unscrew the nuts securing the crossmember to the mounting and remove it from the vehicle.

18 Slacken and remove the bolts and remove the mounting from the base of the transmission unit.

19 Check all components for signs of wear or damage, and renew as necessary. Remove all traces of locking compound from the crossmember to body bolt threads.

20 Fit the mounting to the transmission unit and tighten its retaining bolts to the specified torque.

21 Refit the crossmember to the mounting and lightly tighten its retaining nuts.

22 Apply a few drops of thread locking compound (Vauxhall recommend the use of locking compound 15 10 181 - available from your Vauxhall dealer) to the threads of each crossmember to body bolt then refit both bolts and tighten them to the specified torque.

23 Remove the jack from underneath the transmission unit then tighten the mounting to crossmember nuts to the specified torque before lowering the vehicle to the ground.

Chapter 2 Part D:
General engine overhaul procedures

Contents

Degrees of difficulty

Easy, suitable for novice with little experience 	**Fairly easy,** suitable for beginner with some experience 	**Fairly difficult,** suitable for competent DIY mechanic	**Difficult,** suitable for experienced DIY mechanic	**Very difficult,** suitable for expert DIY or professional

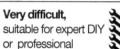

Specifications

Cylinder head

2.0 litre engine

Maximum gasket face distortion	0.05 mm
Cylinder head height:	
SOHC engine	95.75 to 96.25 mm
DOHC engine	134 mm
Valve seat width:	
SOHC engine:	
Inlet	1.0 to 1.5 mm
Exhaust	1.7 to 2.2 mm
DOHC engine:	
Inlet	1.0 to 1.4 mm
Exhaust	1.4 to 1.8 mm
Valve guide height in cylinder head:	
SOHC engine	83.25 to 84.05 mm
DOHC engine	13.70 to 14.00 mm

2.5 and 3.0 litre engine

Maximum gasket face distortion	0.05 mm
Cylinder head height	134 mm
Valve seat width:	
Inlet	1.0 to 1.4 mm
Exhaust	1.4 to 1.8 mm
Valve guide height in cylinder head	13.7 to 14.0 mm

Valves and guides

2.0 litre engine

Valve stem diameter*:	
SOHC engine:	
Inlet:	
Standard (GM)	6.998 to 7.012 mm
1st oversize (0.075 mm - GM K1)	7.073 to 7.087 mm
2nd oversize (0.150 mm - GM K2)	7.148 to 7.162 mm
3rd oversize (0.250 mm - A)	7.248 to 7.262 mm
Exhaust:	
Standard (GM)	6.978 to 6.992 mm
1st oversize (0.075 mm - GM K1)	7.053 to 7.067 mm
2nd oversize (0.150 mm - GM K2)	7.128 to 7.142 mm
3rd oversize (0.250 mm - A)	7.228 to 7.262 mm
DOHC engine:	
Inlet:	
Standard (GM)	5.955 to 5.970 mm
1st oversize (0.075 mm - GM K1)	6.030 to 6.045 mm
2nd oversize (0.150 mm - GM K2)	6.105 to 6.120 mm
Exhaust:	
Standard (GM)	5.945 to 5.960 mm
1st oversize (0.075 mm - GM K1)	6.020 to 6.035 mm
2nd oversize (0.0150 mm - GM K2)	6.095 to 6.110 mm
Valve stem runout	Less than 0.03 mm
Valve guide bore diameter:	
SOHC engine:	
Standard	7.030 to 7.050 mm
1st oversize (0.075 mm)	7.105 to 7.125 mm
2nd oversize (0.150 mm)	7.180 to 7.200 mm
3rd oversize (0.250 mm)	7.280 to 7.300 mm
DOHC engine:	
Standard	6.000 to 6.012 mm
1st oversize (0.075 mm)	6.075 to 6.090 mm
2nd oversize (0.150 mm)	6.150 to 6.165 mm
Stem-to-guide clearance:	
SOHC engine:	
Inlet	0.018 to 0.052 mm
Exhaust	0.038 to 0.072 mm
DOHC engine:	
Inlet	0.030 to 0.057 mm
Exhaust	0.040 to 0.067 mm
Valve length:	
SOHC engine:	
Inlet:	
Standard valve	104.0 to 104.4 mm
Oversize valve	103.6 to 104.0 mm
Exhaust:	
Standard valve	103.75 to 104.25 mm
Oversize valve	103.35 to 103.85 mm
DOHC engine:	
Inlet:	
Standard valve	101.9 to 102.3 mm
Oversize valve	101.5 to 101.9 mm
Exhaust:	
Standard valve	92.05 to 92.45 mm
Oversize valve	91.65 to 92.05 mm
Valve stem fitted height:	
SOHC engine	17.85 to 18.25 mm
DOHC engine:	
Standard valve	39.6 to 40.2 mm
Oversize valve	39.2 to 39.8 mm
Valve head diameter:	
SOHC engine:	
Inlet	41.8 mm
Exhaust	36.5 mm
DOHC engine:	
Inlet	31.9 to 32.1 mm
Exhaust	28.9 to 29.1 mm

Valves and guides (continued)

2.5 and 3.0 litre engine

Valve stem diameter*:	
Inlet:	
Standard (GM)	5.955 to 5.970 mm
1st oversize (0.075 mm - GM K1)	6.030 to 6.045 mm
2nd oversize (0.150 mm - GM K2)	6.105 to 6.120 mm
Exhaust:	
Standard (GM)	5.945 to 5.960 mm
1st oversize (0.075 mm - GM K1)	6.020 to 6.035 mm
2nd oversize (0.0150 mm - GM K2)	6.095 to 6.110 mm
Valve stem runout	Less than 0.03 mm
Valve guide bore diameter:	
Standard	6.000 to 6.012 mm
1st oversize (0.075 mm)	6.075 to 6.090 mm
2nd oversize (0.150 mm)	6.150 to 6.165 mm
Stem-to-guide clearance:	
Inlet	0.030 to 0.057 mm
Exhaust	0.040 to 0.067 mm
Valve length:	
Inlet:	
Standard valve	101.9 to 102.3 mm
Oversize valve	101.5 to 101.9 mm
Exhaust:	
Standard valve	92.05 to 92.45 mm
Oversize valve	91.65 to 92.05 mm
Valve head diameter:	
Inlet	31.9 to 32.1 mm
Exhaust	28.9 to 29.1 mm

**Identification marking in brackets*

Cylinder block

2.0 litre engine

Maximum gasket face distortion	0.05 mm
Cylinder bore diameter:	
Standard:	
Size group 8	85.975 to 85.985 mm
Size group 99	85.985 to 85.995 mm
Size group 00	85.995 to 86.005 mm
Size group 01	86.005 to 86.015 mm
Size group 02	86.015 to 86.025 mm
Oversize (0.5 mm)	86.465 to 86.475 mm
Maximum cylinder bore ovality	0.013 mm
Maximum cylinder bore taper	0.013 mm

2.5 and 3.0 litre engine

Maximum gasket face distortion	0.05 mm
Cylinder bore diameter:	
2.5 litre engine:	
Standard:	
Size group 8	81.575 to 81.585 mm
Size group 99	81.585 to 81.595 mm
Size group 00	81.595 to 81.605 mm
Size group 01	81.605 to 81.615 mm
Size group 02	81.615 to 81.625 mm
Oversize (0.5 mm)	82.065 to 82.075 mm
3.0 litre engine:	
Standard:	
Size group 8	85.975 to 85.985 mm
Size group 99	85.985 to 85.995 mm
Size group 00	85.995 to 86.005 mm
Size group 01	86.005 to 86.015 mm
Size group 02	86.015 to 86.025 mm
Oversize (0.5 mm)	86.465 to 86.475 mm
Maximum cylinder bore ovality	0.013 mm
Maximum cylinder bore taper	0.013 mm

Pistons and rings

2.0 litre engine

Piston diameter:	
Standard:	
Size group 8	85.945 to 85.955 mm
Size group 99	85.955 to 85.965 mm
Size group 00	85.965 to 85.975 mm
Size group 01	85.975 to 85.985 mm
Size group 02	85.985 to 85.995 mm
Oversize (0.5 mm) - size group 7 + 0.5	86.435 to 86.445 mm
Piston-to-bore clearance	0.02 to 0.04 mm
Piston ring end gaps (fitted in bore):	
Top and second compression rings	0.3 to 0.5 mm
Oil control ring	0.4 to 1.4 mm
Piston ring thickness:	
Top and second compression ring	1.5 mm
Oil control ring	3.0 mm
Piston ring-to-groove clearance:	
Top and second compression ring	0.02 to 0.04 mm
Oil control ring	0.01 to 0.03 mm

2.5 and 3.0 litre engine

Piston diameter:	
2.5 litre engine:	
Standard:	
Size group 8	81.540 to 81.550 mm
Size group 99	81.550 to 81.560 mm
Size group 00	81.560 to 81.570 mm
Size group 01	81.570 to 81.580 mm
Size group 02	81.580 to 81.590 mm
Oversize (0.5 mm)	82.030 to 82.040 mm
3.0 litre engine:	
Standard:	
Size group 8	85.940 to 85.950 mm
Size group 99	85.950 to 85.960 mm
Size group 00	85.960 to 85.970 mm
Size group 01	85.970 to 85.980 mm
Size group 02	85.980 to 85.990 mm
Oversize (0.5 mm)	86.430 to 86.440 mm
Piston-to-bore clearance	0.025 to 0.045 mm
Piston ring end gaps (fitted in bore):	
Top and second compression rings	0.3 to 0.5 mm
Oil control ring	0.4 to 1.4 mm
Piston ring thickness:	
Top and second compression ring	1.5 mm
Oil control ring	3.0 mm
Piston ring-to-groove clearance:	
Top and second compression ring	0.02 to 0.04 mm
Oil control ring	0.01 to 0.03 mm

Gudgeon pins

2.0 litre engine

Diameter	20.990 to 21.000 mm
Length	61.2 to 61.8 mm
Gudgeon pin-to-piston clearance	0.011 to 0.014 mm

2.5 and 3.0 litre engine

Diameter	20.990 to 21.000 mm
Length:	
2.5 litre engine	55.7 to 56.0 mm
3.0 litre engine	57.7 to 58.0 mm
Gudgeon pin-to-piston clearance:	
2.5 litre engine	0.011 to 0.014 mm
3.0 litre engine	0.001 to 0.015 mm
Gudgeon pin-to-connecting rod clearance:	
2.5 litre engine	Interference-fit
3.0 litre engine	0.014 to 0.030 mm

Crankshaft

2.0 litre engine

Endfloat	0.05 to 0.15 mm
Main bearing journal diameter:	
Standard:	
1st size group (white)	57.974 to 57.981 mm
2nd size group (green)	57.981 to 57.988 mm
3rd size group (brown)	57.988 to 57.995 mm
1st (0.25 mm) undersize	57.732 to 57.745 mm
2nd (0.50 mm) undersize	57.482 to 57.495 mm
Big-end bearing journal (crankpin) diameter:	
Standard	48.970 to 48.988 mm
1st (0.25 mm) undersize	48.720 to 48.738 mm
2nd (0.50 mm) undersize	48.470 to 48.488 mm
Journal out-of round	0.04 mm
Journal taper	0.04 mm
Crankshaft runout	Less than 0.03 mm
Main bearing running clearance	0.015 to 0.043 mm
Big-end bearing (crankpin) running clearance	0.006 to 0.031 mm

2.5 and 3.0 litre engine

Endfloat	0.01 to 0.76 mm
Main bearing journal diameter:	
Standard	67.980 to 67.996 mm
1st (0.25 mm) undersize	67.730 to 67.746 mm
2nd (0.50 mm) undersize	67.480 to 67.496 mm
Big-end bearing journal (crankpin) diameter:	
2.5 litre engine:	
Standard	48.971 to 48.990 mm
1st (0.25 mm) undersize	48.721 to 48.740 mm
2nd (0.50 mm) undersize	48.471 to 48.490 mm
3.0 litre engine:	
Standard	53.971 to 53.990 mm
1st (0.25 mm) undersize	53.721 to 53.740 mm
2nd (0.50 mm) undersize	53.471 to 53.490 mm
Journal out-of round	0.04 mm
Journal taper	0.04 mm
Crankshaft runout	Less than 0.03 mm
Main bearing running clearance	0.014 to 0.043 mm
Big-end bearing (crankpin) running clearance	0.010 to 0.061 mm

Torque wrench settings

2.0 litre engine

SOHC engine - Refer to Chapter 2A Specifications
DOHC engine - Refer to Chapter 2B Specifications

2.5 and 3.0 litre engine

Refer to Chapter 2C Specifications

1 General information

1 Included in this Part of Chapter 2 are details of removing the engine from the vehicle and general overhaul procedures for the cylinder head, cylinder block and all other engine internal components.

2 The information given ranges from advice concerning preparation for an overhaul and the purchase of replacement parts, to detailed step-by-step procedures covering removal, inspection, renovation and refitting of engine internal components.

3 After Section 5, all instructions are based on the assumption that the engine has been removed from the car. For information concerning in-car engine repair, as well as the removal and refitting of those external components necessary for full overhaul, refer to the relevant in-car repair procedure section (Chapter 2A to 2C) of this Chapter and to Section 7. Ignore any preliminary dismantling operations described in the relevant in-car repair sections that are no longer relevant once the engine has been removed from the car.

4 Apart from torque wrench settings, which are given at the beginning of the relevant in-car repair procedure Chapter (2A to 2C), all specifications relating to engine overhaul are at the beginning of this Part of Chapter 2.

2 Engine overhaul - general information

1 It is not always easy to determine when, or if, an engine should be completely overhauled, as a number of factors must be considered.

2 High mileage is not necessarily an indication that an overhaul is needed, while low mileage does not preclude the need for an overhaul. Frequency of servicing is probably the most important consideration. An engine which has had regular and frequent oil and filter changes, as well as other required maintenance, should give many thousands of miles of reliable service. Conversely, a neglected engine may require an overhaul very early in its life.

3 Excessive oil consumption is an indication that piston rings, valve seals and/or valve guides are in need of attention. Make sure that oil leaks are not responsible before deciding that the rings and/or guides are worn. Perform a compression test, as described in Part A of this Chapter, to determine the likely cause of the problem.

4 Check the oil pressure with a gauge fitted in place of the oil pressure switch, and compare it with that specified. If it is extremely low, the main and big-end bearings, and/or the oil pump, are probably worn out.

5 Loss of power, rough running, knocking or metallic engine noises, excessive valve gear noise, and high fuel consumption may also point to the need for an overhaul, especially if they are all present at the same time. If a complete service does not remedy the situation, major mechanical work is the only solution.

6 An engine overhaul involves restoring all internal parts to the specification of a new engine. During an overhaul, the pistons and the piston rings are renewed. New main and big-end bearings are generally fitted; if necessary, the crankshaft may be reground/renewed, to restore the journals. The valves are also serviced as well, since they are usually in less-than-perfect condition at this point. While the engine is being overhauled, other components, such as the starter and alternator, can be overhauled as well. The end result should be an as-new engine that will give many trouble-free miles. **Note:** *Critical cooling system components such as the hoses, thermostat and coolant pump should be renewed when an engine is overhauled. The radiator should be checked carefully, to ensure that it is not clogged or leaking. Also, it is a good idea to renew the oil pump whenever the engine is overhauled.*

7 Before beginning the engine overhaul, read through the entire procedure, to familiarise yourself with the scope and requirements of the job. Overhauling an engine is not difficult if you follow carefully all of the instructions, have the necessary tools and equipment, and pay close attention to all specifications. It can, however, be time-consuming. Plan on the car being off the road for a minimum of two weeks, especially if parts must be taken to an engineering works for repair or reconditioning. Check on the availability of parts and make sure that any necessary special tools and equipment are obtained in advance. Most work can be done with typical hand tools, although a number of precision measuring tools are required for inspecting parts to determine if they must be renewed. Often the engineering works will handle the inspection of parts and offer advice concerning reconditioning and renewal. **Note:** *Always wait until the engine has been completely dismantled, and until all components (especially the cylinder block and the crankshaft) have been inspected, before deciding what service and repair operations must be performed by an engineering works. The condition of these components will be the major factor to consider when determining whether to overhaul the original engine, or to buy a reconditioned unit. Do not, therefore, purchase parts or have overhaul work done on other components until they have been thoroughly inspected.* As a general rule, time is the primary cost of an overhaul, so it does not pay to fit worn or sub-standard parts.

8 As a final note, to ensure maximum life and minimum trouble from a reconditioned engine, everything must be assembled with care, in a spotlessly-clean environment.

3 Engine removal - methods and precautions

1 If you have decided that the engine must be removed for overhaul or major repair work, several preliminary steps should be taken.

2 Locating a suitable place to work is extremely important. Adequate work space, along with storage space for the car, will be needed. If a workshop or garage is not available, at the very least, a flat, level, clean work surface is required.

3 Cleaning the engine compartment and engine/transmission before beginning the removal procedure will help keep tools clean and organised.

4 An engine hoist or A-frame will also be necessary. Make sure the equipment is rated in excess of the weight of the engine. Safety is of primary importance, considering the potential hazards involved in lifting the engine out of the car.

5 If this is the first time you have removed an engine, an assistant should ideally be available. Advice and aid from someone more experienced would also be helpful. There are many instances when one person cannot simultaneously perform all of the operations required when lifting the engine out of the vehicle.

6 Plan the operation ahead of time. Before starting work, arrange for the hire of or obtain all of the tools and equipment you will need. Some of the equipment necessary to perform engine removal and installation safely and with relative ease (in addition to an engine hoist) is as follows: a heavy duty trolley jack, complete sets of spanners and sockets as described in the front of this manual, wooden blocks, and plenty of rags and cleaning solvent for mopping up spilled oil, coolant and fuel. If the hoist must be hired, make sure that you arrange for it in advance, and perform all of the operations possible without it beforehand. This will save you money and time.

7 Plan for the car to be out of use for quite a while. An engineering works will be required to perform some of the work which the do-it-yourselfer cannot accomplish without special equipment. These places often have a busy schedule, so it would be a good idea to consult them before removing the engine, in order to accurately estimate the amount of time required to rebuild or repair components that may need work.

8 Always be extremely careful when removing and refitting the engine. Serious injury can result from careless actions. Plan ahead and take your time, and a job of this nature, although major, can be accomplished successfully.

4 Engine - removal and refitting

Note: *On 2.5 and 3.0 litre engine models with air conditioning, it will be necessary to disconnect the refrigerant lines in order to remove the engine unit from the vehicle (see Warnings in Chapter 3). Have the refrigerant discharged by an air conditioning specialist before starting work and have ready some caps/plugs to plug the hose/pipe end fittings whilst the engine is removed. On completion it will be necessary to have the system recharged by an air conditioning specialist.* ***Do not*** *operate the air conditioning system whilst it is discharged.*

Removal

1 Park the vehicle on firm, level ground then remove the bonnet as described in Chapter 11.

2 Remove the battery as described in Chapter 5A.

3 Chock the rear wheels, then firmly apply the handbrake. Apply the handbrake, then jack up the front of the vehicle. Securely support it on axle stands then undo the retaining screws and remove the undercover from beneath the engine unit.

4 Drain the cooling system as described in Chapter 1. If the engine is to be dismantled, also drain the engine oil and remove the oil filter.

5 Working as described in Chapter 4A, depressurise the fuel system then remove the engine management electronic control unit (ECU).

6 Remove the lid from the engine compartment relay box and trace the engine wiring harness into the box. Unclip the injection system relay connectors from the box then disconnect the harness connector(s) **(see illustrations)**. Free the sealing grommet and position the harness clear of the relay box.

7 Disconnect the engine wiring harness connectors which are located at the rear of the battery **(see illustration)**.

4.6a Unclip the injection system relays . . .

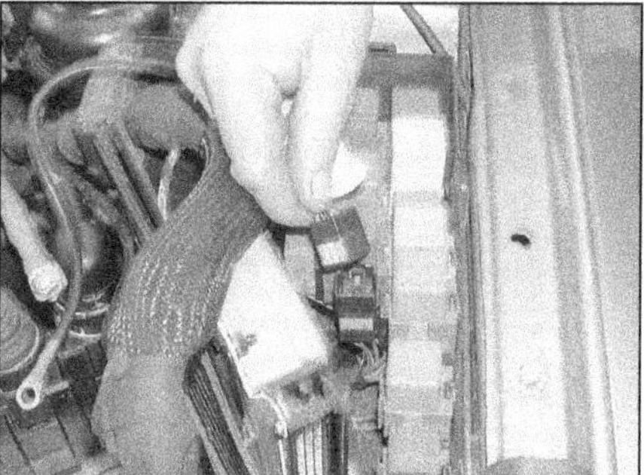
4.6b . . . and disconnect the engine wiring harness connector from the relay box

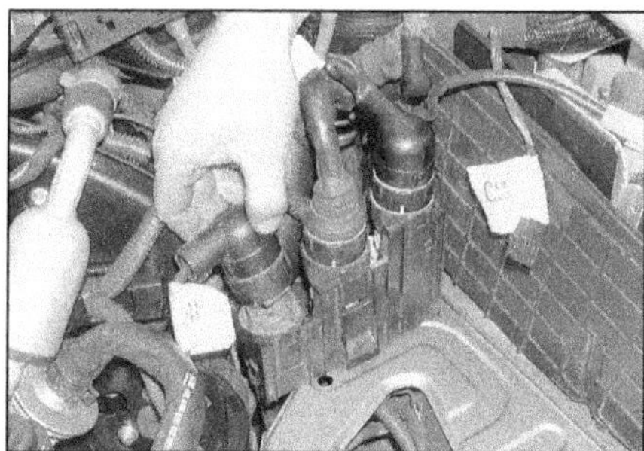
4.7 Disconnect the engine wiring harness connectors which are located at the rear of the battery

8 Free the engine wiring harness auxiliary connections connector from the battery positive terminal so the harness is free to be removed with the engine and (where necessary) unbolt the earth lead from the front of the engine. On some models the harness is connected to the fusible link housing instead of the battery terminal; where this is the case, remove the fusible link and unclip the connector from the housing **(see illustrations)**. Proceed as described under the relevant sub-heading.

2.0 litre SOHC engine

9 Referring to Chapter 4A, carry out the following procedures.

a) Remove the air cleaner housing and intake ducts.
b) Remove the exhaust front pipe.
c) Disconnect the fuel feed and return hoses from the fuel rail.
d) Disconnect the accelerator cable and (where necessary) cruise control cable from the throttle linkage then unbolt the cable mounting bracket and position it clear of the engine.
e) Disconnect the brake servo hose and various vacuum hoses and from the inlet manifold, noting each hoses correct fitted location. Also disconnect the coolant hose from the throttle housing.

10 Remove the DIS module as described in Chapter 5B. Once the module has been removed, refit the lifting bracket to the cylinder head and securely tighten the retaining bolt.

11 Disconnect the engine coolant hose from the rear of the coolant pipe on the right-hand side of the engine compartment. Also disconnect the radiator top hose from the cylinder head.

12 Remove the cooling fan from the rear of the radiator as described in Chapter 3.

13 Referring to Chapter 10, unbolt the power steering pump and position it clear of the engine unit with its hoses still attached.

14 On models with air conditioning, unbolt the compressor and position it clear of the engine with its pipes/hoses still attached. **Do not** open the refrigerant system (see Chapter 3).

15 Attach the hoist to the engine lifting brackets then remove the transmission unit as described in Chapter 7A or 7B, as applicable.

16 Make a final check that any components which would prevent the removal of the engine from the car have been removed or disconnected. Ensure all wiring/hoses are secured so that they cannot be damaged on removal.

17 Slacken and remove the nuts securing the left- and right-hand engine mounting brackets to the top of the mountings

18 With the aid of assistant, lift the engine until the brackets are clear of the mountings then carefully move the engine forwards sufficiently to allow it to be lifted cleanly out of position and clear of the vehicle. Great care must be taken to ensure that no components are trapped and damaged during the removal procedure.

19 Lower the engine onto a suitable work area and detach the hoist.

2.0 litre DOHC engine

20 Referring to Chapter 4A, carry out the following procedures.

a) Remove the air cleaner housing and intake ducts.
b) Remove the throttle housing.
c) Remove the exhaust front pipe.
d) Disconnect the fuel feed and return hoses from the fuel rail.
e) Disconnect the brake servo hose and various vacuum hoses and from the inlet manifold, noting each hoses correct fitted location. Also disconnect the hose from the secondary air injection valve on the exhaust manifold.

21 Disconnect the engine coolant hose from the rear of the coolant pipe on the right-hand side of the engine compartment. Also disconnect the radiator top hose from the cylinder head and the hose from the DIS module mounting bracket on the rear of the cylinder head.

22 Remove the engine as described in paragraphs 12 to 19.

2.5 and 3.0 litre engine

23 Remove the windscreen wiper motor as described in Chapter 12.

24 Remove the radiator as described in Chapter 3.

25 Slacken the retaining clip and disconnect the radiator top hose from the coolant pipe on the left-hand cylinder head.

26 Wipe clean the area around the hose/pipe unions on the power steering pump **(see illustration)**. Slacken the retaining clip then disconnect the fluid supply hose from the pump and drain the reservoir contents into a suitable container. Unscrew the union nut and

4.8a Where necessary, remove the fusible link . . .

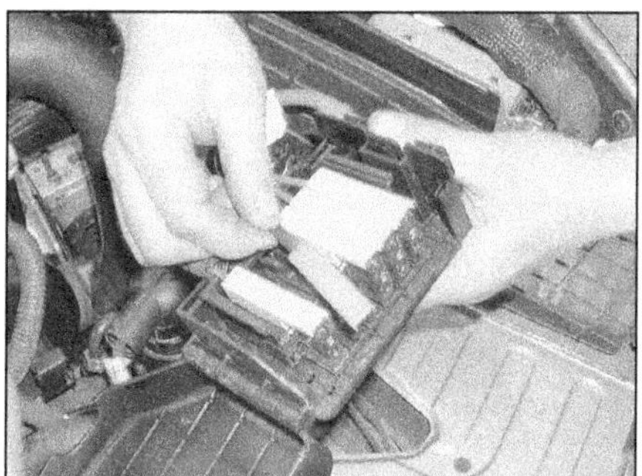
4.8b . . . and unclip the engine harness connector from the fusible link housing

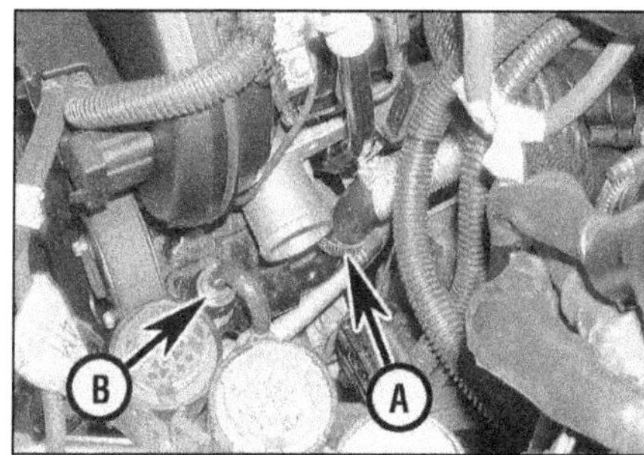

4.26 On 2.5 and 3.0 litre engines, disconnect the fluid supply hose (A) and the feed pipe (B) from the power steering pump

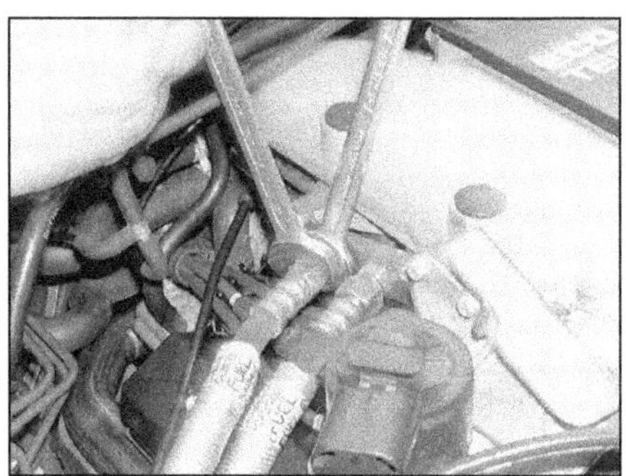
4.27a Slacken the union nuts and disconnect the fuel hoses from the fuel rail

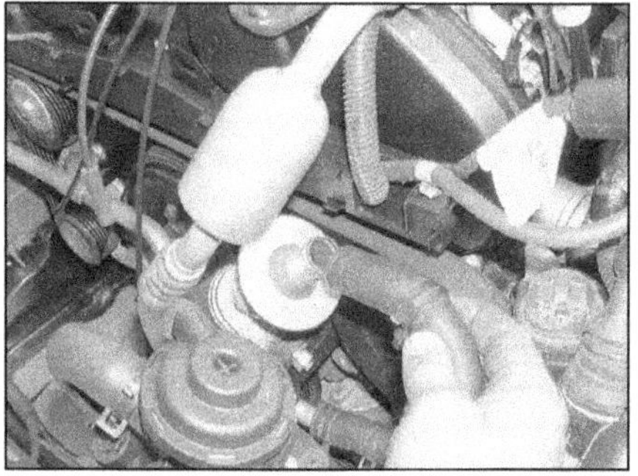
4.27b Disconnecting the hose from the secondary air injection non-return valve

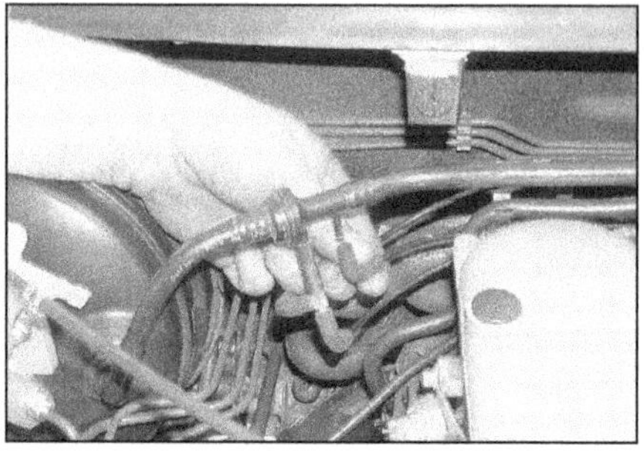
4.27c Disconnect the multi-ram intake system vacuum hoses from the servo unit pipe

disconnect the feed pipe from the pump then plug the hose and pump unions to minimise fluid loss and prevent the entry of dirt into the system.

27 Referring to Chapter 4A, carry out the following procedures.

a) *Remove the air cleaner housing and intake ducts.*
b) *Disconnect the accelerator cable and (where necessary) cruise control cable from the throttle linkage and free them from the mounting bracket.*
c) *Remove the exhaust front pipes.*
d) *Disconnect the fuel feed and return hoses from the fuel rail* **(see illustration).**
e) *Disconnect the brake servo hose from the inlet manifold then disconnect the breather hoses from the rear of the manifold and position the servo hose clear of the engine.*
f) *Disconnect the air hose from the secondary air injection non-return valve at the front of the engine* **(see illustration).**
g) *Disconnect the carbon canister hose from the purge valve and multi-ram intake system vacuum hoses from the servo unit vacuum pipe* **(see illustration).**

28 Release the retaining clips and disconnect the engine coolant hoses from the expansion tank. Remove the retaining clip and slide the tank out of the engine compartment, disconnecting the wiring connector from the level sender as it becomes accessible **(see illustrations).**

29 Locate the heater matrix coolant hose unions on the bulkhead. Pull back on the quick-release fitting collars and detach both hoses from their unions. Disconnect the vacuum hose from the heater cut-off valve **(see illustrations).**

30 On models with air conditioning, disconnect the wiring connector from the compressor. Referring to Chapter 3, having had the refrigerant discharged by a specialist, disconnect the compressor refrigerant pipes at their unions on the receiver/drier damper and directly above the left-hand cylinder head. On models with quick-release fittings, separate the unions by sliding back the dust seal and releasing the locking collar tabs by inserting a collar (special tools KM-917-1 and KM-917-2 are designed for this task) into the fitting and on models with screw-type fittings, unscrew the union nuts then disconnect the pipes and recover the union sealing rings. Immediately fit the closure cap/plugs to the pipe/union ends to keep moisture out of the system. Unscrew the mounting clamp bolts and position the damper clear of the engine unit **(see illustrations).**

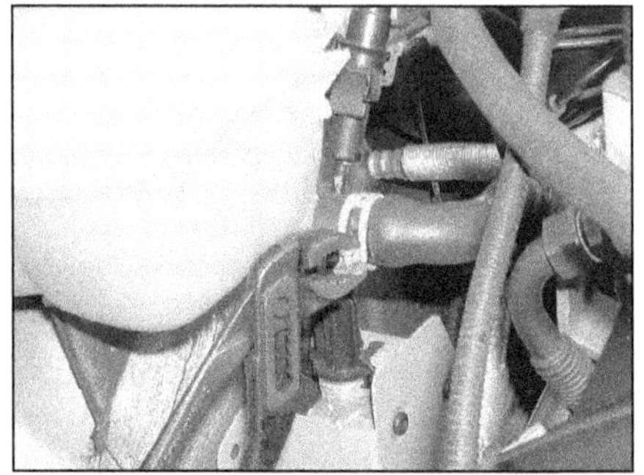
4.28a Disconnect the engine coolant hoses from the expansion tank . . .

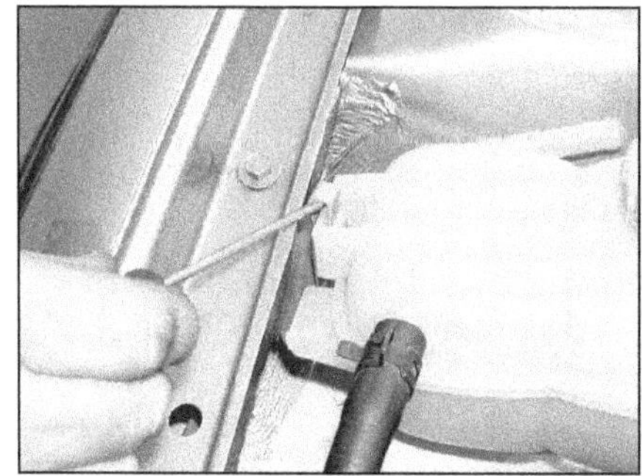
4.28b . . . and remove the tank retaining clip

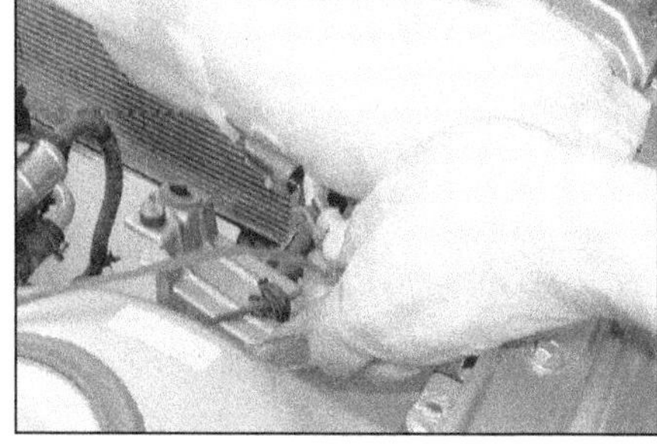
4.28c Free the expansion tank from its mountings and remove it, disconnecting the wiring connector from the level sender

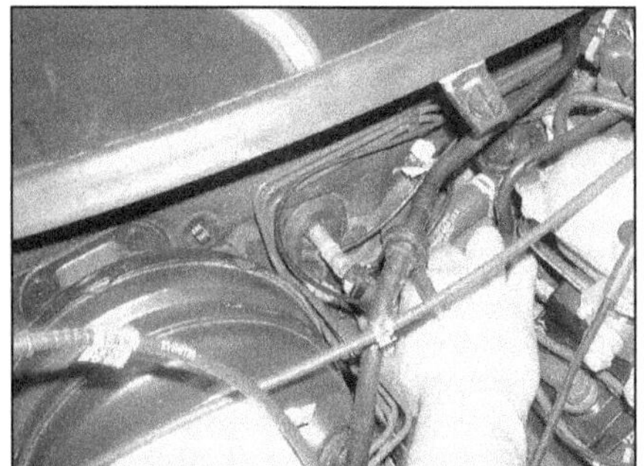
4.29a Pull back on the locking collars and detach the heater matrix coolant hoses from their unions on the bulkhead . . .

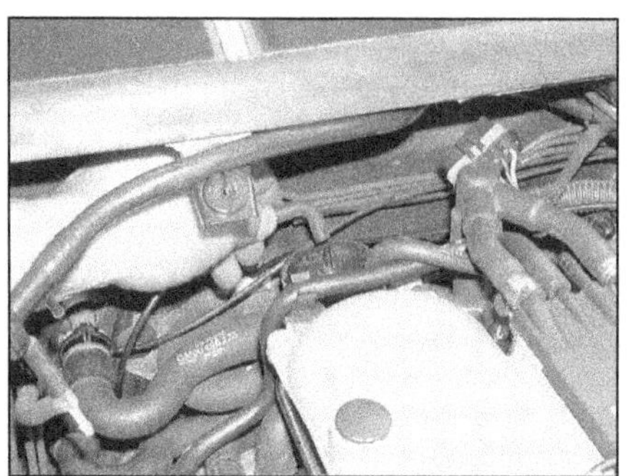
4.29b . . . then disconnect the vacuum hose from the heater cut-off valve

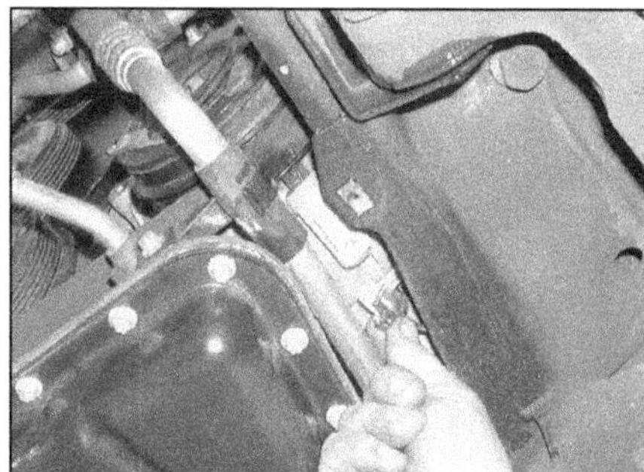
4.30a On models with air conditioning disconnect the wiring connector from the compressor . . .

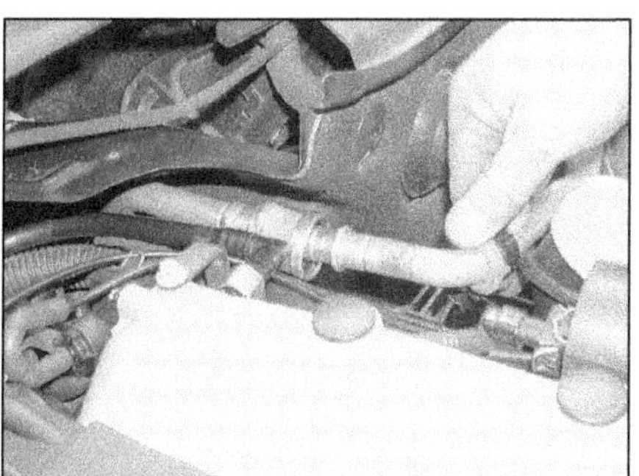

4.30b . . . and separate the air refrigerant pipes at the unions above the left-hand cylinder head . . .

4.30c . . . and at the front of the engine (quick-release fitting pipes shown)

4.30d Release the receiver/drier damper mounting bracket and position the damper clear of the engine

31 Attach the hoist to the engine lifting brackets then remove the transmission unit as described in Chapter 7A or 7B, as applicable **(see illustration)**.

32 Make a final check that any components which would prevent the removal of the engine from the car have been removed or disconnected. Ensure all wiring/hoses are secured so that they cannot be damaged on removal.

33 Unscrew the mounting bolts and remove the vibration dampers (where fitted) from the left- and right-hand engine mountings.

34 Slacken and remove the nuts securing the left- and right-hand engine mountings to the subframe and engine brackets.

35 With the aid of assistant, lift the engine until the brackets are clear of the mountings then remove both mountings from the vehicle. Carefully move the engine forwards sufficiently to allow it to be lifted cleanly out of position and clear of the vehicle **(see illustration)**. Great care must be taken to ensure that no components are trapped and damaged during the removal procedure.

36 Lower the engine onto a suitable work area and detach the hoist.

Refitting

37 Reconnect the hoist to the engine lifting brackets and, with the aid of an assistant, carefully lift the assembly into position the engine compartment taking great care not to trap any components.

38 Align the engine mounting brackets with the left- and right-hand mountings and lower the engine onto its mounting rubbers. Ensure the brackets are correctly engaged with the mountings then refit the mounting nuts and tighten to the specified torque setting.

39 The remainder of the refitting procedure is a direct reversal of removal, noting the following.

a) Refit the transmission unit as described in Chapter 7A or 7B, as applicable.
b) On 2.5 and 3.0 litre models with air conditioning, fit new sealing rings to the compressor pipe unions and securely tighten the union nuts (screw-type fittings) or ensure the pipes are pushed securely together until an audible click is emitted (quick-release fittings). On completion have the refrigerant system recharged by an air conditioning specialist before using the vehicle.
c) Ensure that all wiring is correctly routed and retained by all the relevant retaining clips and that all connectors are correctly and securely reconnected.
d) Ensure that all disturbed hoses are correctly reconnected, and securely retained by their retaining clips. Ensure all the cooling system quick-release fittings are securely retained by their collars.
e) Adjust the accelerator cable as described in the Chapter 4A.
f) Fit a new oil filter (where necessary) and refill the engine with fresh oil as described in Chapter 1.
g) Refill the cooling system as described in Chapter 1.

4.31 Remove the covers from the engine lifting brackets and attach the hoist

4.35 Lifting the engine unit out of position

5 Engine overhaul - dismantling sequence

1 It is much easier to dismantle and work on the engine if it is mounted on a portable engine stand. These stands can often be hired from a tool hire shop. Before the engine is mounted on a stand, the flywheel/driveplate should be removed, so that the stand bolts can be tightened into the end of the cylinder block.

2 If a stand is not available, it is possible to dismantle the engine with it blocked up on a sturdy workbench, or on the floor. Be extra-careful not to tip or drop the engine when working without a stand.

3 If you are going to obtain a reconditioned engine, all the external components must be removed first, to be transferred to the replacement engine (just as they will if you are doing a complete engine overhaul yourself). These components include the following:

a) Inlet and exhaust manifolds (Chapter 4A).
b) Alternator/power steering pump/air conditioning compressor bracket(s) (as applicable).
c) Coolant pump (Chapter 3).
d) Fuel system components (Chapter 4A).
e) Wiring harness and all electrical switches and sensors.
f) Oil filter (Chapter 1).
g) Flywheel/driveplate (relevant part of this Chapter).

Note: *When removing the external components from the engine, pay close attention to details that may be helpful or important during refitting. Note the fitted position of gaskets, seals, spacers, pins, washers, bolts, and other small items.*

4 If you are obtaining a 'short' engine (which consists of the engine cylinder block, crankshaft, pistons and connecting rods all assembled), then the cylinder head(s), sump, oil pump, and timing belt will have to be removed also.

5 If you are planning a complete overhaul, the engine can be dismantled, and the internal components removed, in the order given below, referring to the relevant part of this Chapter unless otherwise stated.

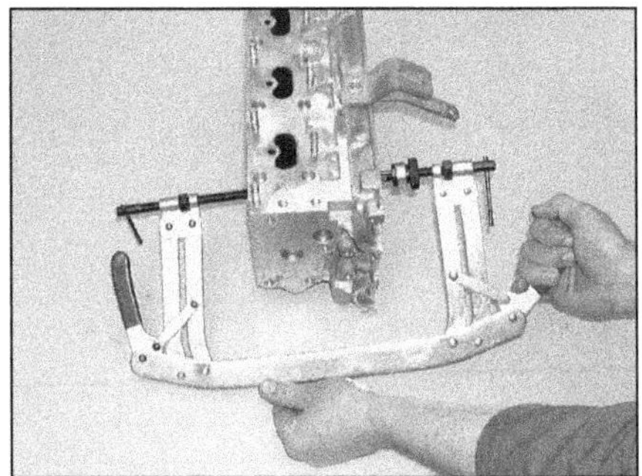

6.4a Using a valve spring compressor

6.4b Pull off the valve stem seals using a pair of pliers

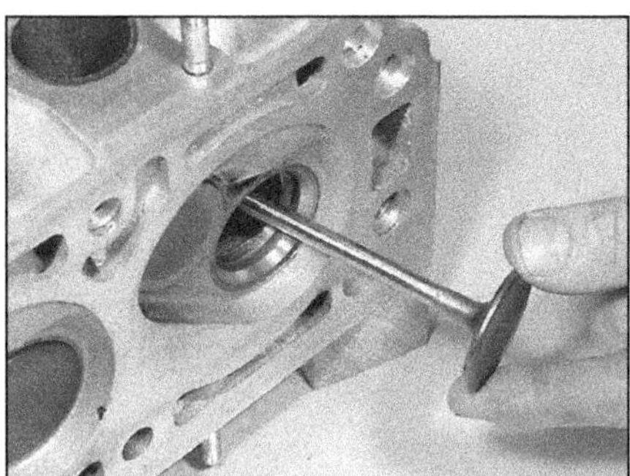

6.6 Removing a valve

a) Inlet and exhaust manifolds (Chapter 4A).
b) Timing belt, sprockets and tensioner.
c) Cylinder head(s).
d) Flywheel/driveplate.
e) Sump.
f) Oil pump.
g) Piston/connecting rod assemblies.
h) Crankshaft.

6 Before beginning the dismantling and overhaul procedures, make sure that you have all of the correct tools necessary. Refer to the *Tools and working facilities* Section of this manual for further information.

6 Cylinder head - dismantling

Note: *New and reconditioned cylinder heads are available from the manufacturer, and from engine overhaul specialists. Be aware that some specialist tools are required for the dismantling and inspection procedures, and new components may not be readily available. It may therefore be more practical and economical for the home mechanic to purchase a reconditioned head, rather than dismantle, inspect and recondition the original head.*

HAYNES HiNT

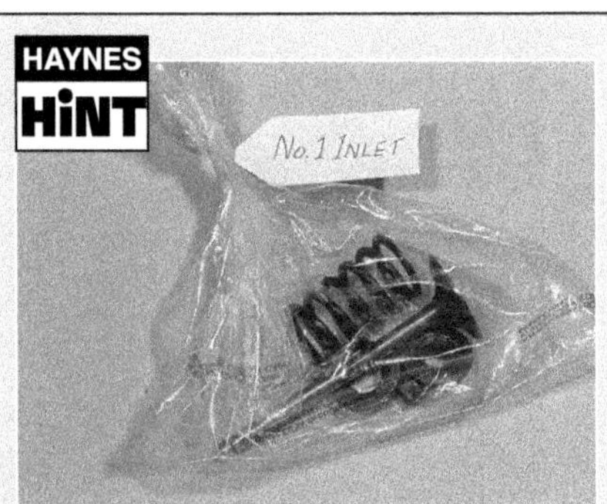

If the components are to be refitted, place each valve and its associated components in a labelled polythene bag or similar small container. Mark the bag/container with the relevant valve number to ensure that it is refitted in its original location

1 On 2.0 litre SOHC engines, referring to Part A of this Chapter, remove the cylinder head from the engine then lift the camshaft followers, thrust pads and hydraulic tappets out from the cylinder head.

2 On 2.0 litre DOHC engines remove the camshafts and followers as described in Part B of this Chapter then remove the cylinder head from the engine.

3 On 2.5 and 3.0 litre engines remove the camshafts and followers as described in Part C of this Chapter then remove the cylinder head(s) from the engine.

4 On all models, using a valve spring compressor, compress each valve spring in turn until the split collets can be removed. Release the compressor, and lift off the spring retainer and spring. Using a pair of pliers, carefully extract the valve stem seal from the top of the guide then slide off the spring seat **(see illustrations)**.

5 If, when the valve spring compressor is screwed down, the spring retainer refuses to free and expose the split collets, gently tap the top of the tool, directly over the retainer, with a light hammer. This will free the retainer.

6 Withdraw the valve through the combustion chamber **(see illustration)**. It is essential that each valve is stored together with its collets, retainer, spring, and spring seat. The valves should also be kept in their correct sequence, unless they are so badly worn that they are to be renewed (see **Haynes hint**).

7 Cylinder head and valves - cleaning and inspection

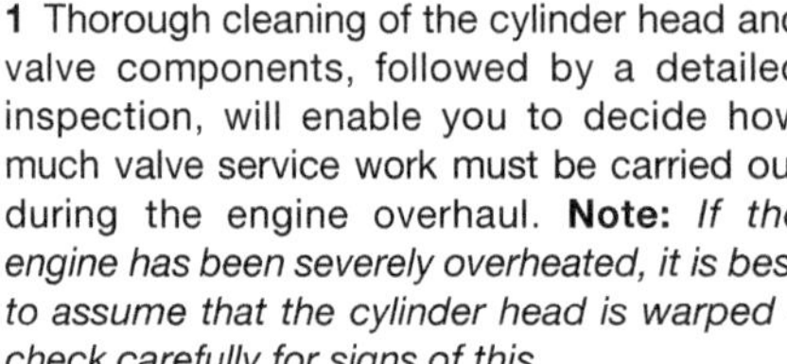

1 Thorough cleaning of the cylinder head and valve components, followed by a detailed inspection, will enable you to decide how much valve service work must be carried out during the engine overhaul. **Note:** *If the engine has been severely overheated, it is best to assume that the cylinder head is warped - check carefully for signs of this.*

Cleaning

2 Scrape away all traces of old gasket material from the cylinder head.

3 Scrape away the carbon from the combustion chambers and ports, then wash the cylinder head thoroughly with paraffin or a suitable solvent. Scrape off any heavy carbon deposits that may have formed on the valves, then use a power-operated wire brush to remove deposits from the valve heads and stems.

4 Ensure the cylinder head oilways are clean and free of obstructions. If you have access to compressed air, use it to blow out the oilways and galleries. To ensure a thorough job is done, remove all oil gallery plugs prior to cleaning. Once the galleries are clean, apply suitable sealant to the oil gallery plugs and refit them to the cylinder head, tightening them securely.

Warning: Wear eye protection when using compressed air!

Inspection

Note: *Be sure to perform all the following inspection procedures before concluding that the services of a machine shop or engine overhaul specialist are required. Make a list of all items that require attention.*

Cylinder head

5 Inspect the head very carefully for cracks, evidence of coolant leakage, and other damage. If cracks are found, a new cylinder head should be obtained.

6 Use a straight-edge and feeler blade to check that the cylinder head surface is not distorted **(see illustration)**. If it is, it may be possible to resurface it, provided that the cylinder head is not reduced to less than the minimum specified height.

7.6 Checking the cylinder head surface for distortion

7 Examine the valve seats in each of the combustion chambers. If they are severely pitted, cracked or burned, then they will need to be renewed (if possible) or recut by an engine overhaul specialist. If they are only slightly pitted, this can be removed by grinding-in the valve heads and seats with fine valve-grinding compound, as described below.
8 If the valve guides are worn (indicated by a side-to-side motion of the valve, and accompanied by excessive blue smoke in the exhaust when running) new guides must be fitted. Measure the diameter of the existing valve stems (see below) and the bore of the guides, then calculate the clearance and compare the result with the specified value. If the clearance is not within the specified limits, renew the valves and/or guides as necessary.
9 The renewal of valve guides is best carried out by an engine overhaul specialist. If the work is to be carried out at home, however, use a stepped, double-diameter drift to drive out the worn guide towards the combustion chamber. On fitting the new guide, place it first in a deep-freeze for one hour, then drive it into its cylinder head bore from the camshaft side until it projects the specified amount above the cylinder head surface.
10 If the valve seats are to be re-cut this must be done only after the guides have been renewed.

Valves

Caution: On 3.0 litre engines, the exhaust valves are filled with sodium and must therefore be disposed of carefully. Wearing protective goggles, gloves and some overalls, cut the exhaust valves in half then immerse them in water noting that the sodium will react violently as soon as it contacts the water. When the reaction between the sodium and water has finished, the valves can then be disposed of normally. Dispose of the water bearing in mind that it will contain sodium hydroxide (caustic soda) which is highly corrosive.

11 Examine the head of each valve for pitting, burning, cracks and general wear, and check the valve stem for scoring and wear ridges. Rotate the valve, and check for any obvious indication that it is bent. Look for pitting and excessive wear on the tip of each valve stem. Renew any valve that shows any such signs of wear or damage.
12 If the valve appears satisfactory at this stage, measure the valve stem diameter at several points using a micrometer **(see illustration)**. Any significant difference in the readings obtained indicates wear of the valve stem. Should any of these conditions be apparent, the valve(s) must be renewed.
13 If the valves are in satisfactory condition, they should be ground (lapped) into their respective seats, to ensure a smooth gas-tight seal. If the seat is only lightly pitted, or if it has been re-cut, fine grinding compound **only** should be used to produce the required finish. Coarse valve-grinding compound should **not** be used unless a seat is badly burned or deeply pitted; if this is the case, the cylinder head and valves should be inspected by an expert to decide whether seat re-cutting, or even the renewal of the valve or seat insert, is required.
14 Valve grinding is carried out as follows. Place the cylinder head upside-down on a bench.
15 Smear a trace of the appropriate grade of valve-grinding compound on the seat face, and press a suction grinding tool onto the valve head. With a semi-rotary action, grind the valve head to its seat, lifting the valve occasionally to redistribute the grinding compound **(see illustration)**. A light spring placed under the valve head will greatly ease this operation.
16 If coarse grinding compound is being used, work only until a dull, matt even surface is produced on both the valve seat and the valve, then wipe off the used compound and repeat the process with fine compound. When a smooth unbroken ring of light grey matt finish is produced on both the valve and seat, the grinding operation is complete. **Do not** grind in the valves any further than absolutely necessary, or the seat will be prematurely sunk into the cylinder head.
17 When all the valves have been ground-in, carefully wash off all traces of grinding compound using paraffin or a suitable solvent before reassembly of the cylinder head.

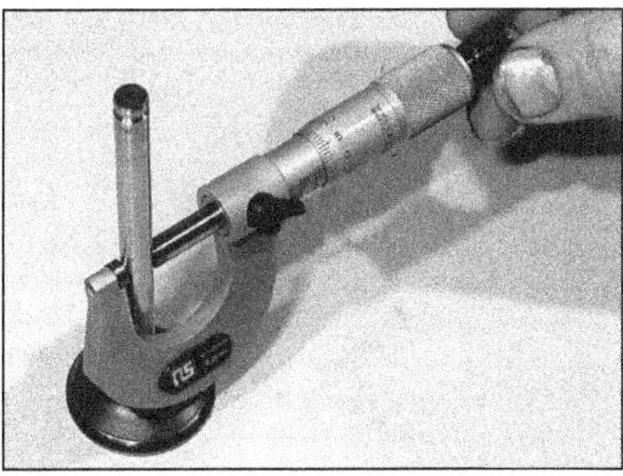

7.12 Using a micrometer to measure valve stem diameter

7.15 Grinding in a valve

Valve components

18 Examine the valve springs for signs of damage and discoloration; if possible; also compare the existing spring free length with new components.
19 Stand each spring on a flat surface, and check it for squareness. If any of the springs are damaged, distorted or have lost their tension, obtain a complete new set of springs.

8 Cylinder head - reassembly

1 Lubricate the stems of the valves, and insert them into their original locations **(see illustration)**. If new valves are being fitted, insert them into the locations to which they have been ground.
2 Working on the first valve, refit the spring seat. Dip the new valve stem seal in fresh engine oil, then carefully locate it over the valve and onto the guide. Take care not to damage the seal as it is passed over the valve stem. Use a suitable socket or metal tube to press the seal firmly onto the guide **(see illustrations)**. **Note:** *If genuine seals are being fitted there maybe an oil seal protector supplied with the seals; the protector fits over the valve stem and prevents the oil seal lip being damaged on the valve.*
3 Locate the spring on the seat and fit the spring retainer **(see illustration)**.

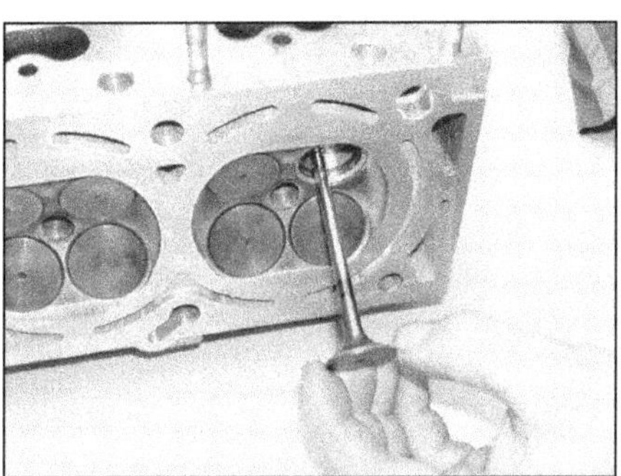

8.1 Lubricate the valve stem with engine oil and insert it into the correct guide

8.2a Fit the spring seat . . .

8.2b . . . then fit the seal protector (where provided) . . .

8.2c . . . and install the valve stem oil seal

8.2d Press the oil seal fully onto the guide with a suitable socket

8.3 Fit the valve spring and spring retainer

4 Compress the valve spring, and locate the split collets in the recess in the valve stem **(see illustration)**. Release the compressor, then repeat the procedure on the remaining valves.

HAYNES HiNT

Use a little dab of grease to hold the collets in position on the valve stem while the spring compressor is released

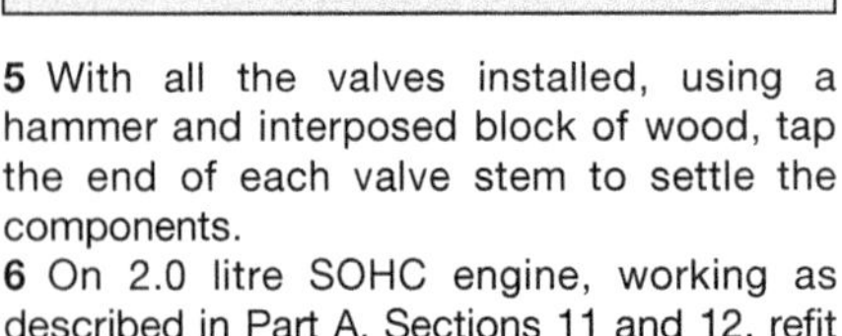

5 With all the valves installed, using a hammer and interposed block of wood, tap the end of each valve stem to settle the components.

6 On 2.0 litre SOHC engine, working as described in Part A, Sections 11 and 12, refit the hydraulic tappets, thrust pads and followers to the head then refit the cylinder head.

7 On 2.0 litre DOHC engine, working as described in Part B, refit the cylinder head to the engine and install the followers and camshafts.

8.4 Compress the valve and locate the collets in the recess on the valve stem

8 On 2.5 and 3.0 litre engines, working as described in Part C, refit the cylinder head to the engine and install the followers and camshafts.

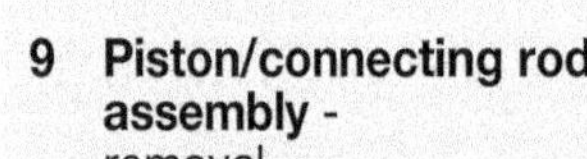

9 Piston/connecting rod assembly - removal

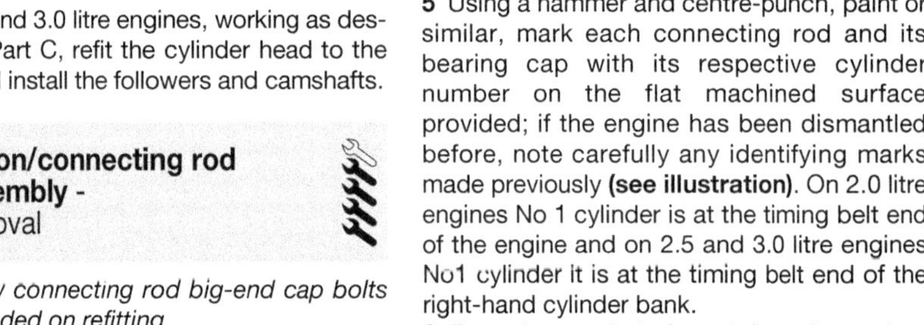

Note: *New connecting rod big-end cap bolts will be needed on refitting*

1 On 2.0 litre SOHC engines, working as described in Part A of this Chapter, remove the cylinder head and sump then unbolt the pick-up/strainer and remove the baffle plate.

2 On 2.0 litre DOHC engines, referring to Part B of this Chapter, remove the cylinder head, sump and oil pick-up/strainer. On later (1998 model year onwards) engines, remove the crankshaft balancer unit. On early (pre 1998 model year) engines with a two-piece sump, unscrew the retaining bolts and remove the baffle plate from the base of the cylinder block; discard the retaining bolts new ones should be used on refitting.

9.3 Removing the baffle plate - 2.5 and 3.0 litre engine

3 On 2.5 and 3.0 litre engines remove the cylinder heads and sump as described in Part C of this Chapter. Unbolt the baffle plate and remove it from the base of the main bearing bridge casting **(see illustration)**.

4 On all models, if there is a pronounced wear ridge at the top of any bore, it may be necessary to remove it with a scraper or ridge reamer, to avoid piston damage during removal. Such a ridge indicates excessive wear of the cylinder bore.

5 Using a hammer and centre-punch, paint or similar, mark each connecting rod and its bearing cap with its respective cylinder number on the flat machined surface provided; if the engine has been dismantled before, note carefully any identifying marks made previously **(see illustration)**. On 2.0 litre engines No 1 cylinder is at the timing belt end of the engine and on 2.5 and 3.0 litre engines No1 cylinder it is at the timing belt end of the right-hand cylinder bank.

6 Turn the crankshaft to bring piston 1 to BDC (bottom dead centre).

7 Unscrew the bolts from No 1 piston big-end bearing cap. Take off the cap and recover the bottom half bearing shell. If the bearing shells are to be re-used, tape the cap and the shell together.

9.5 Make identification markings on the connecting rods and bearing caps (circled). Note that the lug on the bearing cap faces towards the flywheel/driveplate end of the engine

Caution: On some engines, the connecting rod/bearing cap mating surfaces are not machined flat; the big-end bearing caps are 'cracked' off from the rod during production and left untouched to ensure the cap and rod mate perfectly. Where this type of connecting rod is fitted, great care must be taken to ensure the mating surfaces of the cap and rod are not marked or damaged in anyway. Any damage to the mating surfaces will adversely affect the strength of the connecting rod and could lead to premature failure.

8 Using a hammer handle, push the piston up through the bore, and remove it from the top of the cylinder block. Recover the bearing shell, and tape it to the connecting rod for safe-keeping.

9 Loosely refit the big-end cap to the connecting rod, and secure with the bolts - this will help to keep the components in their correct order.

10 On 2.0 litre engines, remove No 4 piston assembly in the same way then turn the crankshaft through 180° to bring pistons 2 and 3 to BDC (bottom dead centre), and remove them in the same way.

11 On 2.5 and 3.0 litre engines, remove the remaining five piston assemblies in the same way, positioning the crankshaft as necessary to gain access to the bearing cap bolts.

10 Crankshaft - removal

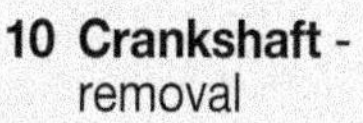

2.0 litre engine

Note: *New main bearing cap bolts will be required on refitting.*

1 Remove the oil pump and flywheel/driveplate. Refer to Part A for information on SOHC engine and Part B for information on the DOHC engine.

2 Remove the piston and connecting rod assemblies as described in Section 9. If no work is to be done on the pistons and connecting rods, unbolt the caps and push the pistons far enough up the bores that the connecting rods are positioned clear of the crankshaft journals.

3 On earlier DOHC engines with a two-piece sump, evenly and progressively slacken the remaining bolts and remove the main bearing ladder casting from the base of the block. Discard the retaining bolts; new ones must be used on refitting.

4 Check the crankshaft endfloat as described in Section 13, then proceed as follows.

5 The main bearing caps should be numbered 1 to 5 from the timing belt end of the engine **(see illustration)**. **Note:** *On some engines the flywheel/driveplate end (number 5) bearing cap may not be numbered but is easily identified anyway.* If the bearing caps are not marked, using a hammer and punch or a suitable marker pen, number the caps from 1 to 5 from the timing belt end of the engine and mark each cap to indicate its correct fitted direction to avoid confusion on refitting.

10.5 The main bearing caps should be numbered (No 1 cap shown)

6 Working in a diagonal sequence, evenly and progressively slacken the ten main bearing cap retaining bolts by half a turn at a time until all bolts are loose. Remove all bolts.

7 Carefully remove each cap from the cylinder block, ensuring that the lower main bearing shell remains in position in the cap **(see illustration)**.

8 Carefully lift out the crankshaft, taking care not to displace the upper main bearing shells **(see illustration)**. Remove the flywheel/driveplate end oil seal and discard it.

9 Recover the upper bearing shells from the cylinder block, and tape them to their respective caps for safe-keeping **(see illustration)**.

2.5 and 3.0 litre engines

Note: *New main bearing cap/bridge bolts will be required on refitting.*

10 Remove the oil pump and flywheel/driveplate as described in Part C of this Chapter.

11 Remove the piston and connecting rod assemblies as described in Section 9. If no work is to be done on the pistons and connecting rods, unbolt the caps and push the pistons far enough up the bores that the connecting rods are positioned clear of the crankshaft journals.

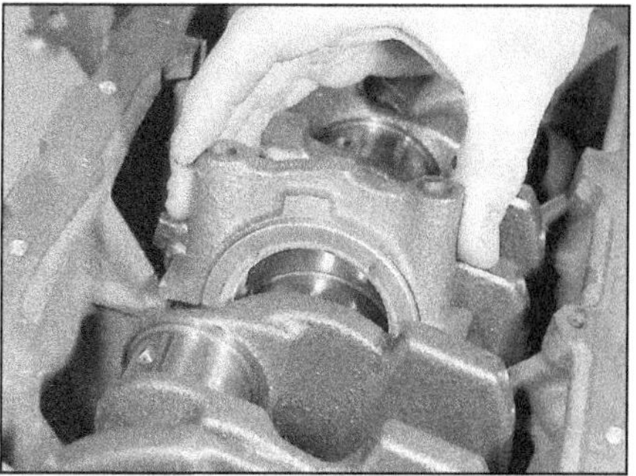

10.7 Removing the centre (No 3) main bearing cap. Note the thrust flanges incorporated into the bearing shell

12 Check the crankshaft endfloat as described in Section 13, then proceed as follows.

13 Prior to removal, check the main bearing bridge casting fitting mark is clearly visible. There should be an arrow on the casting which points towards the timing belt end of the engine.

14 With the cylinder block upside down, slacken and remove the four bolts securing the main bearing bridge casting to the cylinder block.

15 Working in a diagonal sequence, evenly and progressively slacken the eight main bearing cap/bridge retaining bolts by half a turn at a time until all bolts are loose. Remove the bolts then lift off the bridge casting from the cylinder block.

16 The main bearing caps should be numbered 1 to 3 from the timing belt end of the engine; the flywheel/driveplate end bearing cap is not numbered but is easily identified anyway. If the bearing caps are not marked, using a hammer and punch or a suitable marker pen, number the caps from 1 to 3 from the timing belt end of the engine and mark each cap to indicate its correct fitted direction to avoid confusion on refitting.

17 Carefully remove each cap from the cylinder block, ensuring that the lower main bearing shell remains in position in the cap. If the rear cap is a tight-fit, screw two M8 bolts into the threaded holes and use the bolts to pull the cap out **(see illustration)**.

18 Carefully lift out the crankshaft, taking care not to displace the upper main bearing

10.8 Remove the crankshaft . . .

10.9 . . . and lift out the upper main bearing shells from the cylinder block

10.17 If the rear cap is tight, screw two M8 bolts into the cap and use them to work the cap free

10.18 Removing the crankshaft - 2.5 and 3.0 litre engine

shells **(see illustration)**. Remove the flywheel/driveplate end oil seal and discard it.

19 Recover the upper bearing shells from the cylinder block, and tape them to their respective caps for safe-keeping.

11 Cylinder block - cleaning and inspection

Cleaning

1 Remove all external components and electrical switches/sensors from the block. For complete cleaning, the core plugs should ideally be removed. On 2.0 litre engines the core plugs are a press-fit; to remove a plug, drill a small hole then insert a self-tapping screw into the hole and pull out the plug either with a pair of grips or a slide hammer. On 2.5 and 3.0 litre engines the core plugs are screwed in position.

2 Scrape all traces of gasket from the cylinder block taking care not to damage the gasket/sealing surfaces.

3 Remove all oil gallery plugs (where fitted). The plugs are usually very tight - they may have to be drilled out, and the holes re-tapped. Use new plugs when the engine is reassembled. On 2.5 and 3.0 litre engines, it is recommended that the oil bypass valve is also removed; the valve is located behind the oil filter (a new one will be needed on refitting). To remove the bypass valve, cut a thread into the centre of the valve bore with an M10 tap; use the finishing (blunt-ended) tap to ensure the valve is threaded right up to the ball. Draw the valve out from the block using an M10 bolt and washers and a socket as a spacer **(see illustrations)**.

4 If any of the castings are extremely dirty, all should be steam-cleaned.

5 After the castings are returned, clean all oil holes and oil galleries one more time. Flush all internal passages with warm water until the water runs clear. Dry thoroughly, and apply a light film of oil to all mating surfaces, to prevent rusting. Also oil the cylinder bores. If you have access to compressed air, use it to speed up the drying process, and to blow out all the oil holes and galleries **(see illustration)**.

Warning: Wear eye protection when using compressed air!

6 If the castings are not very dirty, you can do an adequate cleaning job with hot (as hot as you can stand!), soapy water and a stiff brush. Take plenty of time, and do a thorough job. Regardless of the cleaning method used, be sure to clean all oil holes and galleries very thoroughly, and to dry all components well. Protect the cylinder bores as described above, to prevent rusting.

7 All threaded holes must be clean, to ensure accurate torque readings during reassembly. To clean the threads, run the correct-size tap into each of the holes to remove rust, corrosion, thread sealant or sludge, and to restore damaged threads. If possible, use compressed air to clear the holes of debris produced by this operation. A good alternative is to inject aerosol-applied water-dispersant lubricant into each hole, using the long spout usually supplied.

Warning: Wear eye protection when cleaning out these holes in this way!

8 Apply suitable sealant to the new oil gallery plugs, and insert them into the holes in the block. Tighten them securely.

9 If the engine is not going to be reassembled right away, cover it with a large plastic bag to keep it clean; protect all mating surfaces and the cylinder bores as described above, to prevent rusting.

Inspection

10 Visually check the castings for cracks and corrosion. Look for stripped threads in the threaded holes. If there has been any history of internal water leakage, it may be worthwhile having an engine overhaul specialist check the cylinder block/crankcase with special equipment. If defects are found, have them repaired if possible, or renew the assembly.

11 Check the bore of each cylinder for scuffing and scoring.

12 Measure the diameter of each cylinder bore at the top (just below the wear ridge), centre and bottom of the bore, both parallel to the crankshaft axis and at right angles to it, so that a total of six measurements are taken. Note that there are various size groups of standard bore diameter to allow for manufacturing tolerances; the size group markings are stamped on the cylinder block upper surface.

13 Compare the results with the Specifications at the beginning of this

11.3a On 2.5 and 3.0 litre engines cut an M10 thread into the oil bypass valve . . .

11.3b . . . then use an M10 bolt and washer and a suitable socket . . .

11.3c . . . to draw the valve assembly out from the cylinder block

11.5 Use compressed air to blow out all the cylinder block internal drillings and oilways

Chapter; if any measurement exceeds the service limit specified, the cylinder block must be rebored if possible, or renewed and new piston assemblies fitted.

14 If the cylinder bores are badly scuffed or scored, or if they are excessively worn, out-of-round or tapered, or if the piston-to-bore clearances is excessive (see Section 12), the cylinder block must be rebored (if possible) or renewed and new pistons fitted. Oversize (0.5 mm) pistons are available for all engines.

15 If the bores are in reasonably good condition and not worn to the specified limits, then the piston rings should be renewed. If this is the case, the bores should be honed to allow the new rings to bed in correctly and provide the best possible seal. The conventional type of hone has spring-loaded stones, and is used with a power drill. You will also need some paraffin (or honing oil) and rags. The hone should be moved up and down the bore to produce a crosshatch pattern, and plenty of honing oil should be used. Ideally, the crosshatch lines should intersect at approximately a 60° angle. Do not take off more material than is necessary to produce the required finish. If new pistons are being fitted, the piston manufacturers may specify a finish with a different angle, so their instructions should be followed. Do not withdraw the hone from the bore while it is still being turned – stop it first. After honing a bore, wipe out all traces of the honing oil. If equipment of this type is not available, or if you are not sure whether you are competent to undertake the task yourself, an engine overhaul specialist will carry out the work at moderate cost.

16 On 2.5 and 3.0 litre engines, on completion fit a new oil bypass valve to the cylinder block and tap it fully into position using a hammer and tubular drift (a 15 mm socket is ideal) **(see illustrations)**.

11.16a On 2.5 and 3.0 litre engines, insert the new bypass valve into the cylinder block . . .

11.16b . . . and tap it fully into position using a hammer and socket

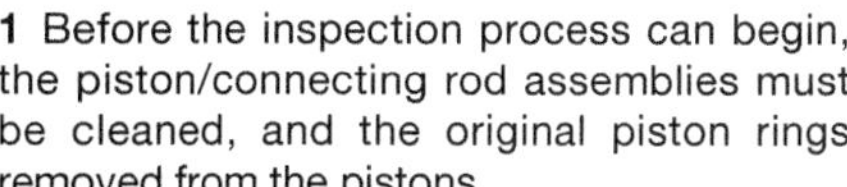

12 Piston/connecting rod assembly - inspection

1 Before the inspection process can begin, the piston/connecting rod assemblies must be cleaned, and the original piston rings removed from the pistons.

2 Carefully expand the old rings over the top of the pistons **(see illustration)**. The use of two or three old feeler blades will be helpful in preventing the rings dropping into empty grooves. Be careful not to scratch the piston with the ends of the ring. The rings are brittle, and will snap if they are spread too far. They're also very sharp - protect your hands and fingers. Note that the third (oil control) ring consists of a spacer and two side rails. Always remove the rings from the top of the piston. Keep each set of rings with its piston if the old rings are to be re-used.

3 Scrape away all traces of carbon from the top of the piston. A hand-held wire brush (or a piece of fine emery cloth) can be used, once the majority of the deposits have been scraped away. The piston identification markings should now be visible.

4 Remove the carbon from the ring grooves in the piston, using an old ring. Break the ring in half to do this (be careful not to cut your fingers - piston rings are sharp). Be careful to remove only the carbon deposits - do not remove any metal, and do not nick or scratch the sides of the ring grooves.

5 Once the deposits have been removed, clean the piston/connecting rod assembly with paraffin or a suitable solvent, and dry thoroughly. Make sure that the oil return holes in the ring grooves are clear.

6 If the cylinder bores are not damaged or worn excessively, and if the cylinder block does not need to be rebored (see Section 11), check the pistons as follows.

7 Carefully inspect each piston for cracks around the skirt, around the gudgeon pin holes, and at the piston ring 'lands' (between the ring grooves).

8 Look for scoring and scuffing on the piston skirt, holes in the piston crown, and burned areas at the edge of the crown. If the skirt is scored or scuffed, the engine may have been suffering from overheating, and/or abnormal combustion which caused excessively high operating temperatures. The cooling and lubrication systems should be checked thoroughly. Scorch marks on the sides of the pistons show that blow-by has occurred. A hole in the piston crown, or burned areas at the edge of the piston crown, indicates that abnormal combustion (pre-ignition, knocking, or detonation) has been occurring. If any of the above problems exist, the causes must be investigated and corrected, or the damage will occur again. The causes may include incorrect ignition timing or a faulty injector.

9 Corrosion of the piston, in the form of pitting, indicates that coolant has been leaking into the combustion chamber and/or the crankcase. Again, the cause must be corrected, or the problem may persist in the rebuilt engine.

10 Measure the piston diameter at right angles to the gudgeon pin axis; compare the results with the Specifications at the beginning of this Chapter. Note that there are various size groups of standard piston diameter to allow for manufacturing tolerances; the size group markings are stamped on the piston crown.

11 To measure the piston-to-bore clearance, either measure the bore (see Section 11) and piston skirt as described and subtract the skirt diameter from the bore measurement, or insert each piston into its original bore, then select a feeler gauge blade and slip it into the bore along with the piston. The piston must be aligned exactly in its normal attitude, and the feeler gauge blade must be between the piston and bore, on one of the thrust faces, just up from the bottom of the bore. If the clearance is excessive, a new piston will be required. If the piston binds at the lower end of the bore and is loose towards the top, the bore is tapered. If tight spots are encountered as the piston/feeler gauge blade is rotated in the bore, the bore is out-of-round.

12 Repeat this procedure for the remaining pistons and cylinder bores. Any piston which is worn beyond the specified limits must be renewed.

13 Examine each connecting rod carefully for signs of damage, such as cracks around the big-end and small-end bearings. Check that the rod is not bent or distorted. Damage is highly unlikely, unless the engine has been seized or badly overheated. Detailed checking of the connecting rod assembly can only be carried out by a Vauxhall dealer or engine repair specialist with the necessary equipment.

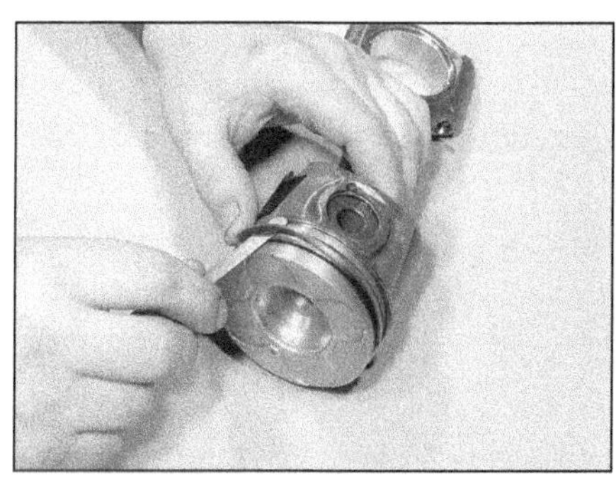

12.2 Using a feeler blade to remove a piston ring

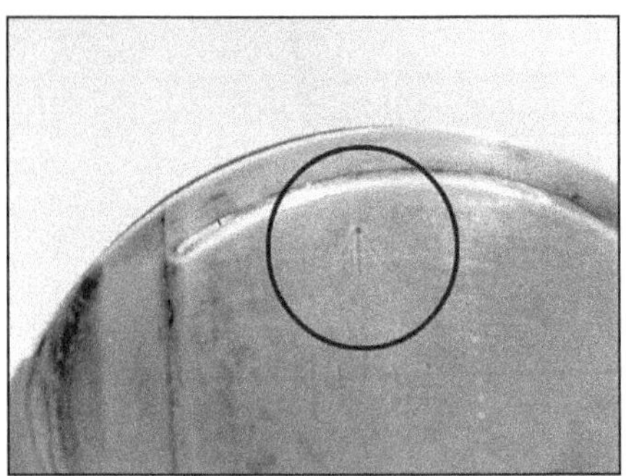

12.20a Ensure the piston and connecting rod are assembled so the arrow on the piston crown (circled) is pointing away from . . .

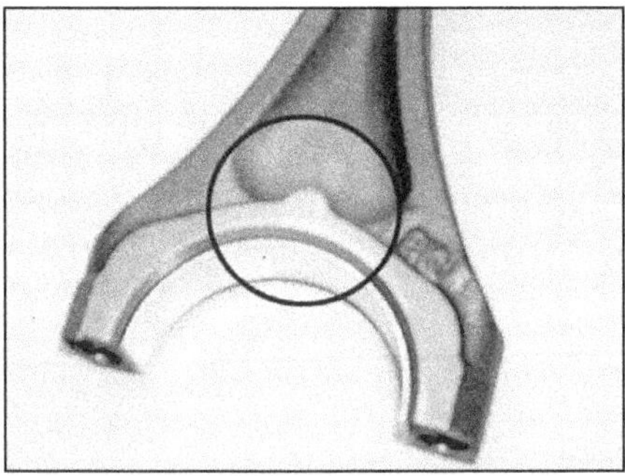

12.20b . . . the assembly mark (circled) on the side of the connecting rod

14 On 2.0 and 2.5 litre engines, the gudgeon pins are an interference fit in the connecting rod small-end bearing. Therefore, piston and/or connecting rod renewal should be entrusted to a Vauxhall dealer or engine repair specialist, who will have the necessary tooling to remove and install the gudgeon pins. If new pistons are to be fitted, ensure that the correct size group pistons are fitted to each bore (see Section 12). **Note:** *Vauxhall state that the piston/connecting rod assemblies should not be disassembled. If any components requires renewal, then the complete assembly must be renewed. Do not fit a new piston to an old connecting rod or vice versa.*

15 On 3.0 litre engines, the gudgeon pins are of the floating type, secured in position by two circlips. On these engines, the pistons and connecting rods can be separated as follows.

16 Using a small flat-bladed screwdriver, prise out the circlips, and push out the gudgeon pin. Hand pressure should be sufficient to remove the pin. Identify the piston and rod to ensure correct reassembly. Discard the circlips - new ones *must* be used on refitting.

17 Examine the gudgeon pin and connecting rod small-end bearing for signs of wear or damage. Wear will require the renewal of both the pin and connecting rod.

18 The connecting rods themselves should not be in need of renewal, unless seizure or some other major mechanical failure has occurred. Check the alignment of the connecting rods visually, and if the rods are not straight, take them to an engine overhaul specialist for a more detailed check.

19 Examine all components, and obtain any new parts from your Vauxhall dealer. If new pistons are purchased, they will be supplied complete with gudgeon pins and circlips. Circlips can also be purchased individually.

20 Assemble the piston and connecting rod so that the arrow on the piston crown is pointing away from the assembly mark which is cast onto one side of the connecting rod, on the top of the big-end bore **(see illustrations)**.

21 Apply a smear of clean engine oil to the gudgeon pin. Slide it into the piston and through the connecting rod small-end. Check that the piston pivots freely on the rod, then secure the gudgeon pin in position with two new circlips, ensuring that each circlip is correctly located in its groove in the piston.

13 Crankshaft - inspection

Checking crankshaft endfloat

1 If the crankshaft endfloat is to be checked, this must be done when the crankshaft is still installed in the cylinder block, but is free to move (see Section 10).

2 Check the endfloat using a dial gauge in contact with the end of the crankshaft **(see illustration)**. Push the crankshaft fully one way, and then zero the gauge. Push the crankshaft fully the other way, and check the endfloat. The result can be compared with the specified amount, and will give an indication as to whether new main bearing shells are required.

3 If a dial gauge is not available, feeler gauges can be used **(see illustration)**. First push the crankshaft fully towards the flywheel/driveplate end of the engine, then use feeler gauges to measure the gap between the web of the crankpin and the side of thrustwasher which is incorporated into number 3 main bearing shells on 2.0 litre engines and number 4 shell on 2.5 and 3.0 litre engines.

Inspection

4 Clean the crankshaft using paraffin or a suitable solvent, and dry it, preferably with compressed air if available. Be sure to clean the oil holes with a pipe cleaner or similar probe, to ensure that they are not obstructed.

Warning: Wear eye protection when using compressed air.

5 Check the main and big-end bearing journals for uneven wear, scoring, pitting and cracking.

6 Big-end bearing wear is accompanied by distinct metallic knocking when the engine is running (particularly noticeable when the engine is pulling from low speed) and some loss of oil pressure.

7 Main bearing wear is accompanied by severe engine vibration and rumble - getting progressively worse as engine speed increases - and again by loss of oil pressure.

8 Check the bearing journal for roughness by running a finger lightly over the bearing surface. Any roughness (which will be accompanied by obvious bearing wear) indicates that the crankshaft requires regrinding (where possible) or renewal.

9 Check for burrs around the crankshaft oil holes (the holes are usually chamfered, so burrs should not be a problem unless regrinding has been carried out carelessly). Remove any burrs with a fine file or scraper, and thoroughly clean the oil holes as described previously.

10 Using a micrometer, measure the diameter of the main and big-end bearing journals, and compare the results with the Specifications **(see illustration)**. By measuring the diameter

13.2 Checking crankshaft endfloat with a dial gauge

13.3 Using a feeler blade to measure crankshaft endfloat (2.0 litre engine shown)

13.10 Using a micrometer to measure a main bearing journal

at a number of points around each journal's circumference, you will be able to determine whether or not the journal is out-of-round. Take the measurement at each end of the journal, near the webs, to determine if the journal is tapered. Compare the results obtained with those given in the Specifications. If the crankshaft paint markings are still visible, the bearing journal size can be determined from these.

11 Check the oil seal contact surfaces at each end of the crankshaft for wear and damage. If the seal has worn a deep groove in the surface of the crankshaft, consult an engine overhaul specialist; repair may be possible, but otherwise a new crankshaft will be required.

12 Set the crankshaft up in V-blocks, and position a dial gauge on the top of the crankshaft number 1 main bearing journal. Zero the dial gauge, then slowly rotate the crankshaft through two complete revolutions, noting the journal run-out. Repeat the procedure on the remaining main bearing journals, so that a run-out measurement is available for all main bearing journals. If the difference between the run-out of any two journals exceeds the service limit given in the Specifications, the crankshaft must be renewed.

13 Undersize big-end and main bearing shells are produced by Vauxhall for all engines. If the crankshaft journals have not already been reground, it may be possible to have the crankshaft reconditioned, and to fit undersize shells. Main bearing shells are available in 0.25 and 0.50 mm undersizes and the big-end bearing shells are available in 0.25 and 0.50 mm undersizes for the 2.5 and 3.0 litre engines and 0.25 mm undersize for 2.0 litre engine.

14 Main and big-end bearings - inspection

1 Even though the main and big-end bearings should be renewed during the engine overhaul, the old bearings should be retained for close examination, as they may reveal valuable information about the condition of the engine. The identification number stamped on the rear of the bearing shells can be used by a Vauxhall dealer to identify the size group of the bearing **(see illustration)**.

2 Bearing failure can occur due to lack of lubrication, the presence of dirt or other foreign particles, overloading the engine, or corrosion **(see illustration)**. Regardless of the cause of bearing failure, the cause must be corrected (where applicable) before the engine is reassembled, to prevent it from happening again.

3 When examining the bearing shells, remove them from the cylinder block, the main bearing caps, the connecting rods and the connecting rod big-end bearing caps. Lay them out on a clean surface in the same

14.1 Typical main bearing shell identification marking

general position as their location in the engine. This will enable you to match any bearing problems with the corresponding crankshaft journal.

4 Dirt and other foreign matter gets into the engine in a variety of ways. It may be left in the engine during assembly, or it may pass through filters or the crankcase ventilation system. It may get into the oil, and from there into the bearings. Metal chips from machining operations and normal engine wear are often present. Abrasives are sometimes left in engine components after reconditioning, especially when parts are not thoroughly cleaned using the proper cleaning methods. Whatever the source, these foreign objects often end up embedded in the soft bearing material, and are easily recognised. Large particles will not embed in the bearing, and will score or gouge the bearing and journal. The best prevention for this cause of bearing failure is to clean all parts thoroughly, and keep everything spotlessly-clean during engine assembly. Frequent and regular engine oil and filter changes are also recommended.

5 Lack of lubrication (or lubrication

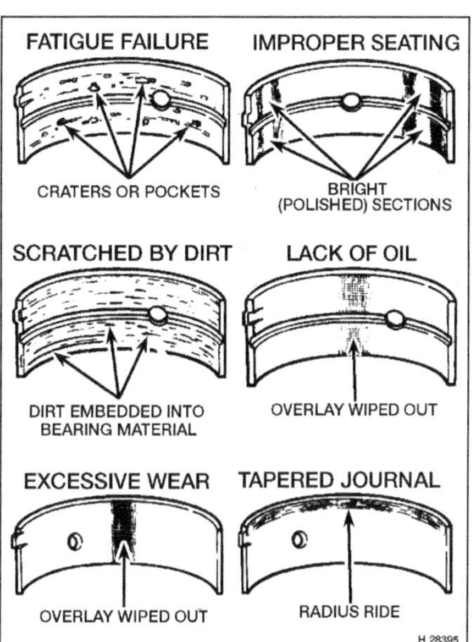

14.2 Typical bearing failures

breakdown) has a number of interrelated causes. Excessive heat (which thins the oil), overloading (which squeezes the oil from the bearing face) and oil leakage (from excessive bearing clearances, worn oil pump or high engine speeds) all contribute to lubrication breakdown. Blocked oil passages, which usually are the result of misaligned oil holes in a bearing shell, will also oil-starve a bearing, and destroy it. When lack of lubrication is the cause of bearing failure, the bearing material is wiped or extruded from the steel backing of the bearing. Temperatures may increase to the point where the steel backing turns blue from overheating.

6 Driving habits can have a definite effect on bearing life. Full-throttle, low-speed operation (labouring the engine) puts very high loads on bearings, tending to squeeze out the oil film. These loads cause the bearings to flex, which produces fine cracks in the bearing face (fatigue failure). Eventually, the bearing material will loosen in pieces, and tear away from the steel backing.

7 Short-distance driving leads to corrosion of bearings, because insufficient engine heat is produced to drive off the condensed water and corrosive gases. These products collect in the engine oil, forming acid and sludge. As the oil is carried to the engine bearings, the acid attacks and corrodes the bearing material.

8 Incorrect bearing installation during engine assembly will lead to bearing failure as well. Tight-fitting bearings leave insufficient bearing running clearance, and will result in oil starvation. Dirt or foreign particles trapped behind a bearing shell result in high spots on the bearing, which lead to failure.

9 As mentioned at the beginning of this Section, the bearing shells should be renewed as a matter of course during engine overhaul; to do otherwise is false economy.

15 Engine overhaul - reassembly sequence

1 Before reassembly begins, ensure that all new parts have been obtained, and that all necessary tools are available. Read through the entire procedure to familiarise yourself with the work involved, and to ensure that all items necessary for reassembly of the engine are at hand. In addition to all normal tools and materials, thread-locking compound will be needed. A good quality tube of liquid sealant will also be required for the joint faces that are fitted without gaskets (the numbers of the Vauxhall recommended sealants are given in the text).

2 In order to save time and avoid problems, engine reassembly can be carried out in the following order:

a) Crankshaft.
b) Piston/connecting rod assemblies.
c) Oil pump.

16.4 Measuring a piston ring end gap using a feeler gauge

d) Sump.
e) Flywheel/driveplate.
f) Cylinder head(s).
g) Timing belt tensioner and sprockets, and belts.
h) Inlet and exhaust manifolds (Chapter 4A).
i) Engine external components.

3 At this stage, all engine components should be absolutely clean and dry, with all faults repaired. The components should be laid out (or in individual containers) on a completely clean work surface.

16 Piston rings - refitting

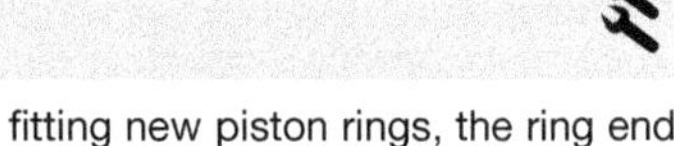

1 Before fitting new piston rings, the ring end gaps must be checked as follows.

2 Lay out the piston/connecting rod assemblies and the new piston ring sets, so that the ring sets will be matched with the same piston and cylinder during the end gap measurement and subsequent engine reassembly.

3 Insert the top ring into the first cylinder, and push it down the bore using the top of the piston. This will ensure that the ring remains square with the cylinder walls. Push the ring down into the bore until it is positioned 15 to 20 mm down from the top edge of the bore, then withdraw the piston.

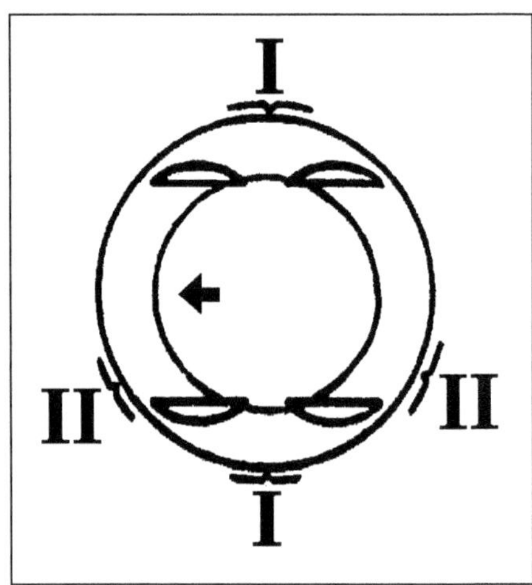

16.11b Piston ring end gap positions

I Top and second compression rings
II Oil control ring side rails

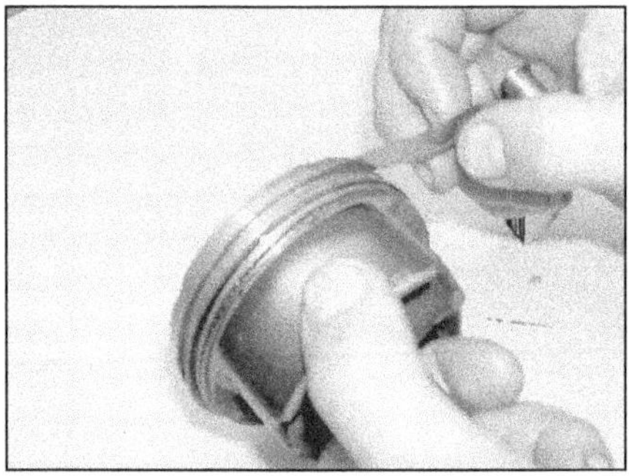

16.11a Checking the piston ring-to-groove clearance using a feeler gauge

4 Measure the end gap using feeler gauges, and compare the measurements with the figures given in the Specifications **(see illustration)**.

5 If the gap is too small (unlikely if genuine Vauxhall parts are used), it must be enlarged, or the ring ends may contact each other during engine operation, causing serious damage. Ideally, new piston rings providing the correct end gap should be fitted. As a last resort, the end gap can be increased by filing the ring ends very carefully with a fine file. Mount the file in a vice with soft jaws, slip the ring over the file with the ends contacting the file face, and slowly move the ring to remove material from the ends. Take care, as piston rings are sharp, and are easily broken.

6 With new piston rings, it is unlikely that the end gap will be too large. If the gaps are too large, check that you have the correct rings for your engine and for the particular cylinder bore size.

7 Repeat the checking procedure for each ring in the first cylinder, and then for the rings in the remaining cylinders. Remember to keep rings, pistons and cylinders matched up.

8 Once the ring end gaps have been checked and if necessary corrected, the rings can be fitted to the pistons.

9 Fit the piston rings using the same technique as for removal. Fit the bottom (oil control) spacer first then install both the side rails, noting that both the spacer and side rails can be installed either way up.

10 The second and top compression rings are different and can be identified by their cross-sections; the top ring is square whilst the second ring is tapered. Fit the second and top compression rings ensuring that each ring is fitted the correct way up with its identification (TOP) mark uppermost. **Note:** *Always follow any instructions supplied with the new piston ring sets - different manufacturers may specify different procedures. Do not mix up the top and second compression rings. On some engines the top ring will not have an identification marking and can be fitted either way up.*

11 With the piston rings correctly installed, check that each ring is free to rotate easily in its groove. Check the ring-to-groove clearance of each ring using feeler gauges and check that the clearance is within the specified range then position the ring end gaps as shown **(see illustrations)**.

17 Crankshaft - refitting and main bearing running clearance check

Note: *It is recommended that new main bearing shells are fitted regardless of the condition of the original ones.*

Selection of bearing shells

1 Although the original bearing shells fitted at the factory maybe of various grades, all replacement bearing shells sold are of the same grade. Vauxhall supply both standard size bearing shells and undersize shells for use when the crankshaft has been reground. The required size of shell required can be determined by measuring the crankshaft journals (see Section 13).

Main bearing running clearance check

2 Clean the backs of the bearing shells and the bearing locations in both the cylinder block and the main bearing caps.

3 Press the bearing shells into their locations, ensuring that the tab on each shell engages in the notch in the cylinder block or main bearing cap **(see illustration)**. If the original bearing shells are being used for the check ensure they are refitted in their original locations. When fitting new shells on 2.5 and 3.0 litre engines, note that No1 bearing is wider than No2 and 3 and that the grooved shell of No2 and 3 bearing should be fitted in the upper location. The clearance can be checked in either of two ways.

4 One method (which will be difficult to achieve without a range of internal micrometers or internal/external expanding calipers) is to refit the main bearing caps to the cylinder block, with bearing shells in place. With the cap retaining bolts correctly tightened (use the original bolts for the check, not the new ones), measure the internal diameter of each assembled pair of bearing

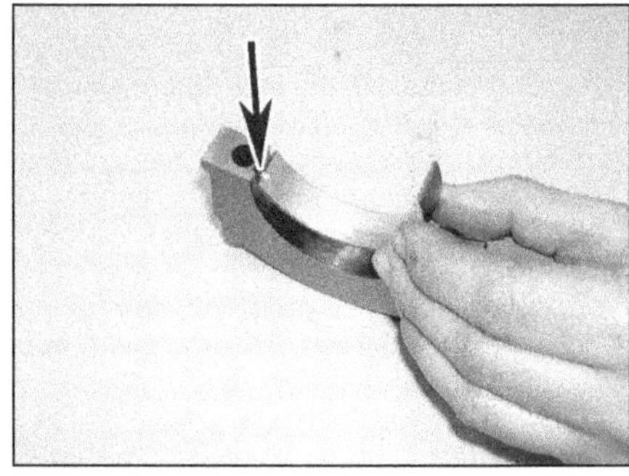

17.3 Fit each main bearing shell making sure its tab is correctly seated in the notch (arrowed)

17.7 Plastigauge in place on a crankshaft journal

17.10 Measure the width of the crushed Plastigauge using the scale on the card provided

shells. If the diameter of each corresponding crankshaft journal is measured and then subtracted from the bearing internal diameter, the result will be the main bearing running clearance.

5 The second (and more accurate) method is to use a product known as Plastigauge. This consists of a fine thread of perfectly round plastic which is compressed between the bearing shell and the journal. When the shell is removed, the plastic is deformed and can be measured with a special card gauge supplied with the kit. The running clearance is determined from this gauge. Plastigauge is sometimes difficult to obtain but enquiries at one of the larger specialist quality motor factors should produce the name of a stockist in your area. The procedure for using Plastigauge is as follows.

6 With the main bearing upper shells in place, carefully lay the crankshaft in position. Do not use any lubricant; the crankshaft journals and bearing shells must be perfectly clean and dry.

7 Cut several lengths of the appropriate size Plastigauge (they should be slightly shorter than the width of the main bearings) and place one length on each crankshaft journal axis **(see illustration)**.

8 With the main bearing lower shells in position, refit the main bearing caps, using the identification marks to ensure each one is correctly positioned. On 2.5 and 3.0 litre engines also refit the main bearing bridge casting ensuring the arrow cast on it is pointing towards the timing belt end of the engine.

9 Refit the original main bearing retaining bolts and tighten them to the specified stage 1 torque and then through the stage 2 and 3 angles (see paragraphs 22 and 23). Take care not to disturb the Plastigauge and **do not** rotate the crankshaft at any time during this operation. Evenly and progressively slacken and remove the main bearing cap bolts then lift off the caps again taking great care not to disturb the Plastigauge or rotate the crankshaft.

10 Compare the width of the crushed Plastigauge on each journal to the scale printed on the Plastigauge envelope to obtain the main bearing running clearance **(see illustration)**. Compare the clearance measured with that given in the Specifications at the start of this Chapter.

11 If the clearance is significantly different from that expected, the bearing shells may be the wrong size (or excessively worn if the original shells are being re-used). Before deciding that the crankshaft is worn, make sure that no dirt or oil was trapped between the bearing shells and the caps or block when the clearance was measured. If the Plastigauge was wider at one end than at the other, the crankshaft journal may be tapered.

12 Before condemning the components concerned, seek the advice of your Vauxhall dealer or suitable engine repair specialist. They will also be able to inform as to the best course of action or whether renewal will be necessary.

13 Where necessary, obtain the correct size of bearing shell and repeat the running clearance checking procedure as described above.

14 On completion, carefully scrape away all traces of the Plastigauge material from the crankshaft and bearing shells using a fingernail or other object which is unlikely to score the bearing surfaces.

Final crankshaft refitting

2.0 litre engine

15 Carefully lift the crankshaft out of the cylinder block once more. If a new crankshaft is being fitted, do not forget to transfer the crankshaft sensor rotor over from the original crankshaft to the new one. Secure the rotor in position with new retaining bolts, tightening them to the specified torque **(see illustration)**.

16 Place the bearing shells in their locations as described above in paragraphs 2 and 3 **(see illustration)**. If new shells are being fitted, ensure that all traces of the protective grease are cleaned off using paraffin. Wipe dry the shells and caps with a lint-free cloth.

17.15 Crankshaft sensor rotor is secured to the crankshaft by four bolts (three arrowed)

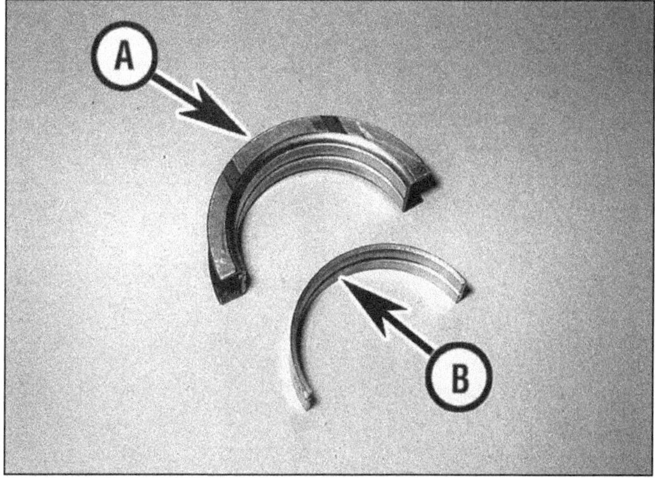

17.16 The bearing shells which incorporate the thrust flanges (A) must be fitted to the centre (No 3) bearing on 2.0 litre engines and the rear (No 4) bearing on 2.5 and 3.0 litre engine. All other shells have no flanges (B)

17.17 Lubricate the upper bearing shells with clean engine oil then lower the crankshaft into position

17.19 Refit the bearing caps number 1 to 4 ensuring each one is refitted in its original location

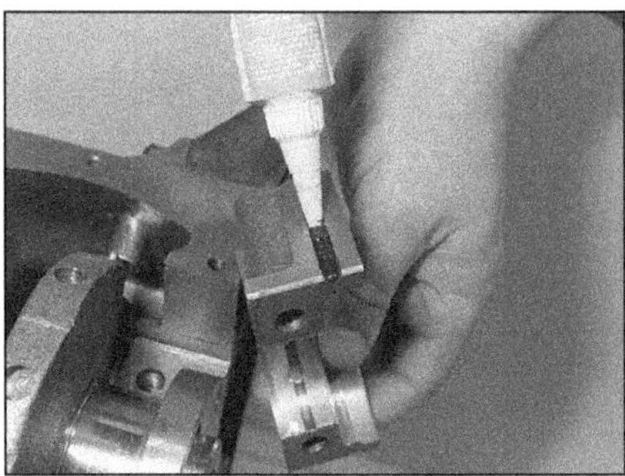
17.20 Fill the side grooves of the rear (number 5) bearing cap with sealant prior to refitting it to the engine

17 Lubricate the upper shells with clean engine oil then lower the crankshaft into position **(see illustration)**.

18 Ensure the crankshaft is correctly seated then check the endfloat as described in Section 13.

19 Ensure the bearing shells are correctly located in the caps and refit the caps number 1 to 4 to the cylinder block **(see illustration)**. Ensure the caps are fitted in their correct locations, with number 1 cap at the timing belt end.

20 Ensure the rear (number 5) bearing cap is clean and dry then fill the groove on each side of the cap with sealing compound (Vauxhall recommend the use of sealant 15 03 295 - available from your Vauxhall dealer) **(see illustration)**. Fit the bearing cap to the engine, ensuring it is fitted the correct way around.

17.21 Lubricate the threads of the new main bearing cap bolts . . .

21 Apply a smear of clean engine to oil to the threads and underneath the heads of the new main bearing cap bolts. Fit the bolts tightening them all by hand **(see illustration)**.

22 Working in a diagonal sequence from the centre outwards, tighten the main bearing cap bolts to the specified Stage 1 torque setting **(see illustration)**.

23 Once all bolts are tightened to the specified Stage 1 torque, go around again and tighten all bolts through the specified Stage 2 angle then go around for once more and tighten all bolts through the specified Stage 3 angle. It is recommended that an angle-measuring gauge is used during the final stages of the tightening, to ensure accuracy **(see illustration)**. If a gauge is not available, use white paint to make alignment marks between the bolt head and cap prior to tightening; the marks can then be used to check that the bolt has been rotated through the correct angle.

24 Once all the bolts have been tightened, inject more sealant down the grooves in the rear main bearing cap until sealant is seen to be escaping through the joints. Once you are sure the cap grooves are full of sealant, wipe off all excess sealant using a clean cloth.

25 Check that the crankshaft is free to rotate smoothly; if excessive pressure is required to turn the crankshaft, investigate the cause before proceeding further.

26 On earlier DOHC engines with a two-piece sump, ensure the mating surfaces are clean and dry then refit the main bearing ladder casting to the block. Fit the new retaining bolts to the casting centre retaining holes (the outer bolts are fitted later with the baffle plate) and tighten them first to the specified stage 1 torque setting then tighten them through the specified stage 2 angle.

27 On all engines refit/reconnect the piston connecting rod assemblies to the crankshaft as described in Section 18.

28 Referring to Part A (SOHC engine) or Part B (DOHC engine), fit a new crankshaft oil seal then refit the flywheel/driveplate, oil pump, cylinder head, timing belt sprocket(s) and fit a new timing belt.

2.5 and 3.0 litre petrol engines

29 Refit the crankshaft as described in paragraphs 15 to 18.

30 Ensure the bearing shells are correctly located in the caps and refit the caps number 1 to 3 to the cylinder block **(see illustration)**. Ensure the caps are fitted in their correct locations, with number 1 cap at the timing belt end.

31 Ensure the rear bearing cap is clean and dry then fill the groove on each side of the cap with sealing compound (Vauxhall recommend the use of sealant 15 03 295 - available from your Vauxhall dealer). Fit the bearing cap to the engine, ensuring it is fitted the correct way around **(see illustrations)**.

32 Back off the threaded sleeves until they no longer protrude from the main bearing bridge casting then refit the casting, making sure the arrow is pointing towards the timing belt end of the engine **(see illustration)**.

17.22 . . . then tighten the bolts to the specified stage 1 torque setting . . .

17.23 . . . and then through the specified stage 2 and 3 angles

17.30 Refit the bearing caps number 1 to 3 ensuring each one is refitted in its original location

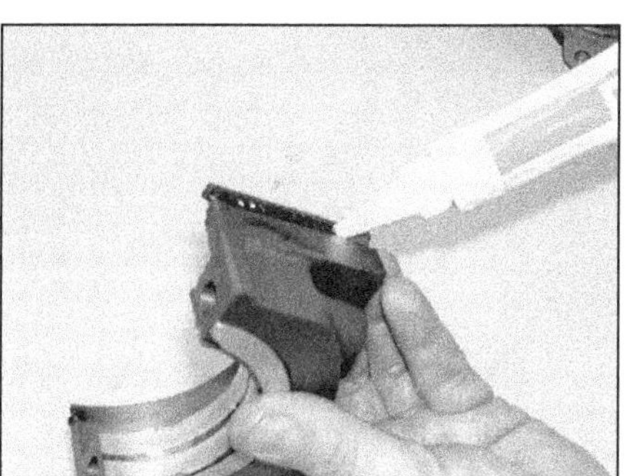
17.31a Fill the side grooves of the rear (number 4) bearing cap with sealant . . .

17.31b . . . then refitting it to the cylinder block

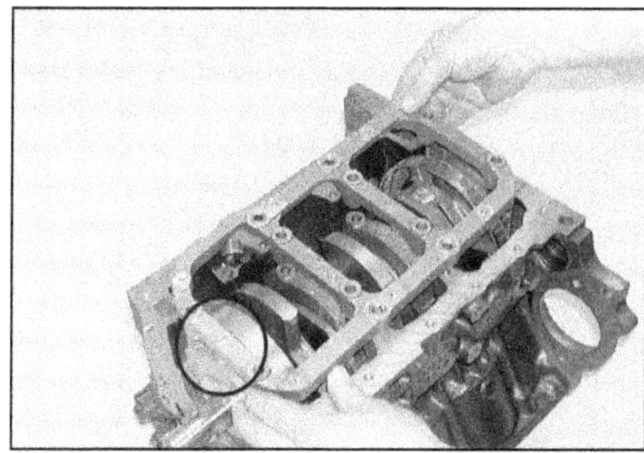
17.32 Refit the main bearing bridge casting making sure the arrow (circled) is pointing towards the timing belt end of the engine

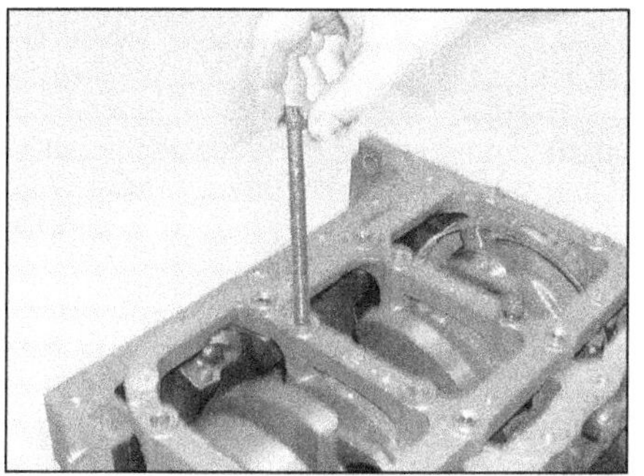
17.33 Lubricate the threads of the new main bearing cap bolts . . .

17.34 . . . then tighten the bolts to the specified stage 1 torque setting . . .

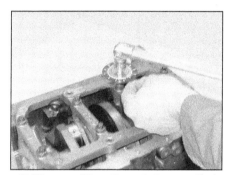

17.35 . . . and then through the specified stage 2 and 3 angles

33 Apply a smear of clean engine to oil to the threads and underneath the heads of the new main bearing cap bolts **(see illustration)**. Fit the bolts tightening them all by hand.

34 Working in a diagonal sequence from the centre outwards, evenly and progressively tighten the main bearing cap bolts to the specified Stage 1 torque setting **(see illustration)**.

17.36 Inject sealant down each of the rear main bearing cap grooves until it is seen to be escaping through the joints (arrowed)

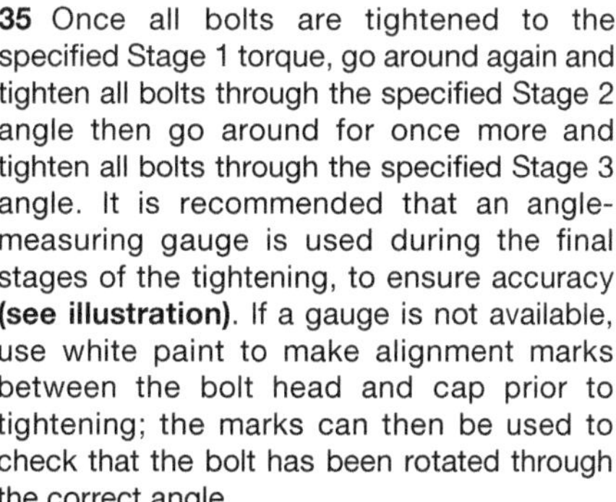

35 Once all bolts are tightened to the specified Stage 1 torque, go around again and tighten all bolts through the specified Stage 2 angle then go around for once more and tighten all bolts through the specified Stage 3 angle. It is recommended that an angle-measuring gauge is used during the final stages of the tightening, to ensure accuracy **(see illustration)**. If a gauge is not available, use white paint to make alignment marks between the bolt head and cap prior to tightening; the marks can then be used to check that the bolt has been rotated through the correct angle.

36 Once all the bolts have been tightened, inject more sealant down the grooves in the rear main bearing cap until sealant is seen to be escaping through the joints **(see illustration)**. Once you are sure the cap grooves are full of sealant, wipe off all excess sealant using a clean cloth.

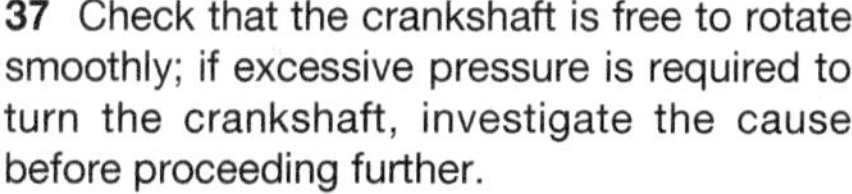

37 Check that the crankshaft is free to rotate smoothly; if excessive pressure is required to turn the crankshaft, investigate the cause before proceeding further.

38 Tighten the threaded sleeves to the main bearing bridge casting and tighten them to the specified torque. Once the sleeves are tight, refit the bolts securing the casting to the cylinder block and tighten them to the specified torque **(see illustrations)**.

39 Refit/reconnect the piston connecting rod assemblies to the crankshaft as described in Section 18.

40 Referring to Part C, fit a new crankshaft oil seal then refit the flywheel/driveplate, oil pump, cylinder heads, timing belt sprockets and fit a new timing belt.

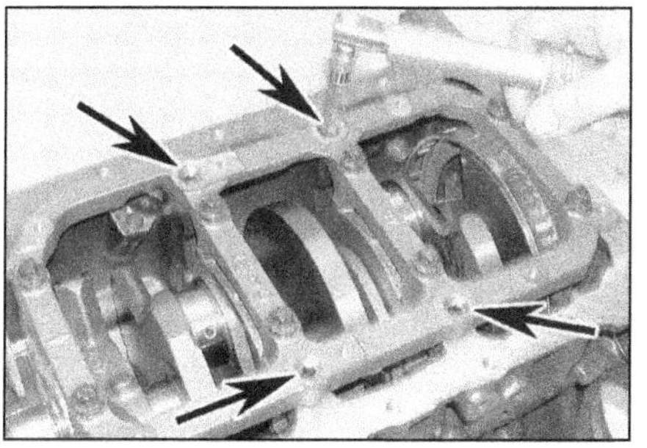
17.38a Tighten the main bearing bridge casting threaded sleeves (arrowed) to the specified torque . . .

17.38b . . . then refit the bolts securing the casting to the cylinder block . . .

17.38c . . . and tighten them (arrowed) to their specified torque setting

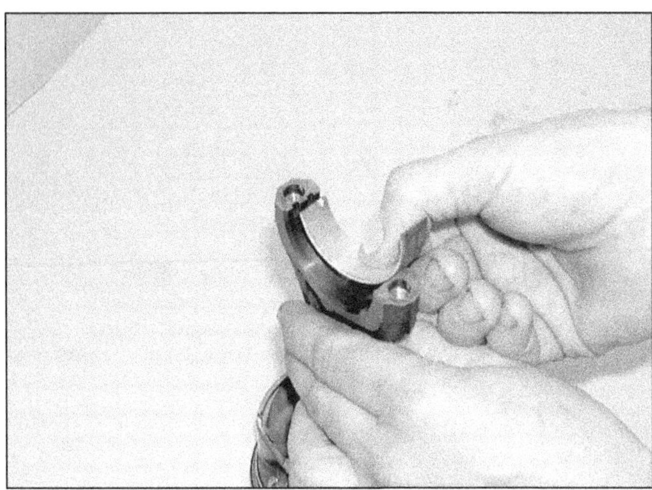

18.3 Fit the bearing shells to the connecting rod and cap making sure their tabs are correctly seated in the cutouts

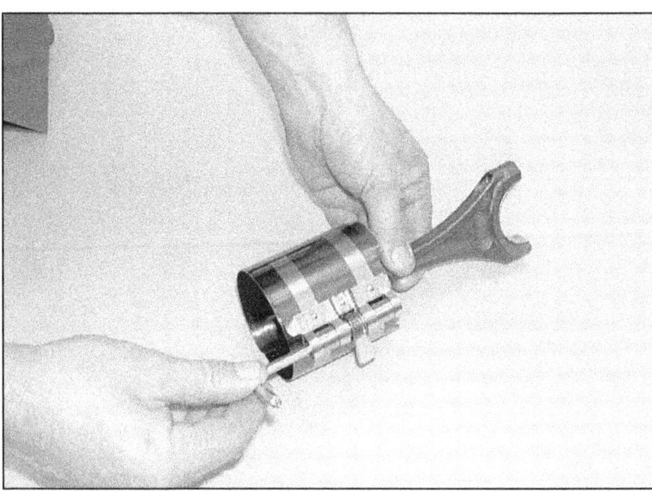

18.8 Ensure the piston ring end gaps are correctly positioned then clamp them in position with a ring compressor

18 Piston/connecting rod assembly - refitting and big-end running clearance check

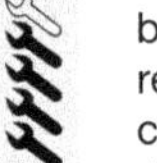

Note: *It is recommended that new piston rings and big-end bearing shells are fitted regardless of the condition of the original ones.*

Selection of bearing shells

1 Although the original bearing shells fitted at the factory maybe of various grades, all replacement bearing shells sold are of the same grade. Vauxhall supply both standard size bearing shells and undersize shells for use when the crankshaft has been reground. The required size of shell required can be determined by measuring the crankshaft journals (see Section 13).

Big-end bearing running clearance check

2 Clean the backs of the bearing shells and the bearing locations in both the connecting rod and bearing cap.

3 Press the bearing shells into their locations, ensuring that the tab on each shell engages in the notch in the connecting rod and cap **(see illustration)**. If the original bearing shells are being used for the check ensure they are refitted in their original locations. The clearance can be checked in either of two ways.

4 One method is to refit the big-end bearing cap to the connecting rod, with bearing shells in place. With the cap retaining bolts (use the original bolts for the check) correctly tightened, use an internal micrometer or vernier caliper to measure the internal diameter of each assembled pair of bearing shells. If the diameter of each corresponding crankshaft journal is measured and then subtracted from the bearing internal diameter, the result will be the big-end bearing running clearance.

5 The second method is to use Plastigauge as described in Section 17, paragraphs 5 to 14. Place a strand of Plastigauge on each (cleaned) crankpin journal and refit the (clean) piston/connecting rod assemblies, shells and big-end bearing caps. Tighten the bolts (see paragraphs 13 - use the original bolts for the check) correctly taking care not to disturb the Plastigauge. Dismantle the assemblies without rotating the crankshaft and use the scale printed on the Plastigauge envelope to obtain the big-end bearing running clearance. On completion of the measurement, carefully scrape off all traces of Plastigauge from the journal and shells using a fingernail or other object which will not score the components.

Final piston/connecting rod assembly refitting

6 Ensure the bearing shells are correctly refitted as described above in paragraphs 2 and 3. If new shells are being fitted, ensure that all traces of the protective grease are cleaned off using paraffin. Wipe dry the shells and connecting rods with a lint-free cloth.

7 Lubricate the bores, the pistons and piston rings then lay out each piston/connecting rod assembly in its respective position.

8 Starting with assembly number 1, make sure that the piston rings are still spaced as described in Section 16, then clamp them in position with a piston ring compressor **(see illustration)**.

9 Insert the piston/connecting rod assembly into the top of cylinder No 1, ensuring that the arrow marking on the piston crown is pointing towards the timing belt end of the engine. Using a block of wood or hammer handle against the piston crown, tap the assembly gently (do not force it) into the cylinder until the piston crown is flush with the top of the cylinder **(see illustration)**. As the piston is fitted make sure the connecting rod lower end remains correctly aligned with the crankshaft to avoid damage.

10 Taking care not to mark the cylinder bore, liberally lubricate the crankpin and both bearing shells, then pull the piston/connecting rod assembly down the bore and onto the crankpin.

11 Ensure the connecting rod and bearing cap mating surfaces are completely clean and dry; this is most important on engines where the bearing caps are 'cracked' off of the rod.

12 Refit the big-end bearing cap, using the markings to ensure it is fitted the correct way around (the lug on the bearing cap base should be facing the flywheel/driveplate end of the engine), then screw in the new retaining bolts **(see illustrations)**.

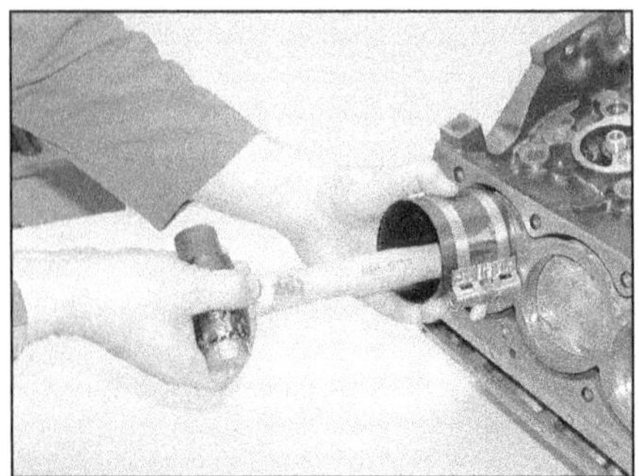

18.9 Insert the piston into the correct bore, tapping it gently into position with the handle of a hammer

18.12a Refit the bearing cap making sure the lug is facing towards the flywheel/driveplate end of the engine . . .

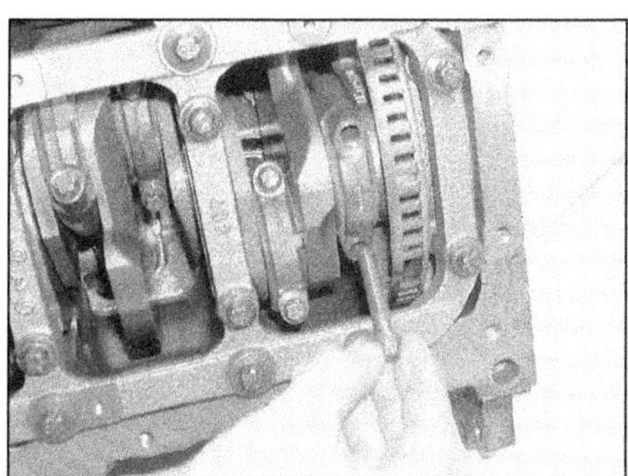
18.12b . . . and screw in the new retaining bolts

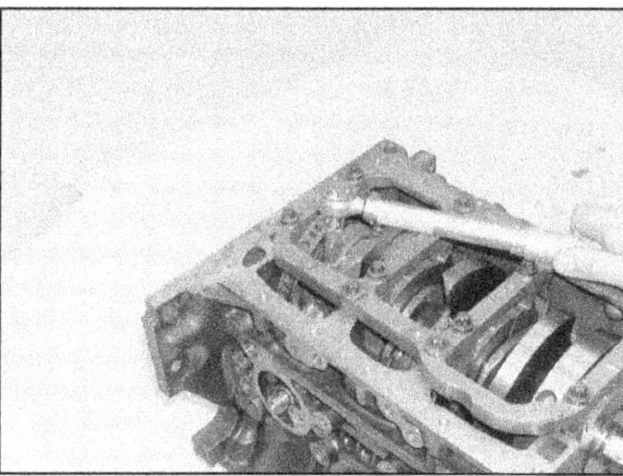
18.13a Tighten both bolts to the specified stage 1 torque setting . . .

18.13b . . . then tighten them through the specified stage 2 and 3 angles

13 Tighten both bearing cap bolts to the specified Stage 1 torque setting then tighten them through the specified Stage 2 angle, and finally through the specified Stage 3 angle. It is recommended that an angle-measuring gauge is used during the final stages of the tightening, to ensure accuracy **(see illustrations)**. If a gauge is not available, use white paint to make alignment marks between the bolt head and cap prior to tightening; the marks can then be used to check that the bolt has been rotated through the correct angle.

14 Refit the remaining piston and connecting rod assemblies in the same way.

15 Rotate the crankshaft, and check that it turns freely, with no signs of binding or tight spots.

16 On 2.0 litre SOHC engines, working as described in Part A of this Chapter, fit the baffle plate, oil pump pick-up/strainer and sump to the cylinder block then refit the cylinder head.

17 On 2.0 litre DOHC engines carry out the following:

a) *On early (pre 1998 model year) engines with a two-piece sump, refit the baffle plate to the main bearing ladder casting and screw in the new retaining bolts. Working in a diagonal sequence from the centre outwards, tighten the bolts first to the specified stage 1 torque and then tighten them through the specified stage 2 angle.*

b) *On later engines refit the crankshaft balancer unit as described in Part B.*

c) *On all engines refit the oil pump pick-up/strainer and sump then refit the cylinder head as described in Part B.*

18 On 2.5 and 3.0 litre engines refit the baffle plate to the base of the main bearing bridge casting and tighten its retaining bolts to the specified torque **(see illustration)**. Working as described in Part C of this Chapter, refit the sump then install the cylinder heads.

19 Engine - initial start up after overhaul

1 With the engine refitted in the vehicle, double-check the engine oil and coolant levels. Make a final check that everything has been reconnected, and that there are no tools or rags left in the engine compartment.

2 Ensure the ignition is switched off then disable the ignition system by disconnecting the wiring connector from the DIS module (see Chapter 5A) and the fuel system by removing the fuel pump relay from the engine compartment relay box (see Chapter 4A, Section 13).

3 Turn the engine on the starter until the oil pressure warning light goes out then stop. Ensure the ignition is switched off then securely refit the relay and reconnect the wiring connector.

4 Start the engine as normal noting that this may take a little longer than usual, due to the fuel system components having been disturbed.

18.18 On 2.5 and 3.0 litre engines, refit the baffle plate and tighten its retaining bolts to the specified torque

5 While the engine is idling, check for fuel, water and oil leaks. Don't be alarmed if there are some odd smells and smoke from parts getting hot and burning off oil deposits.

6 Assuming all is well, keep the engine idling until hot water is felt circulating through the top hose, then switch off the engine.

7 Allow the engine to cool then recheck the oil and coolant levels as described in *Weekly checks*, and top-up as necessary.

8 If new pistons, rings or crankshaft bearings have been fitted, the engine must be treated as new, and run-in for the first 500 miles (800 km). *Do not* operate the engine at full-throttle, or allow it to labour at low engine speeds in any gear. It is recommended that the oil and filter be changed at the end of this period.

Chapter 3
Cooling, heating and ventilation systems

Contents

Degrees of difficulty

Easy, suitable for novice with little experience 	**Fairly easy,** suitable for beginner with some experience 	**Fairly difficult,** suitable for competent DIY mechanic 	**Difficult,** suitable for experienced DIY mechanic 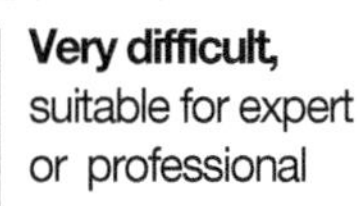	**Very difficult,** suitable for expert DIY or professional

Specifications

System type

All models	Pressurised, with cross-flow radiator, centrifugal water pump driven by timing belt, bypass thermostat, and remote expansion tank. Thermostatically controlled electric main cooling fan, with one or two auxiliary electric cooling fans, depending on specification.

Thermostat

Opening commences	92°C (198°F)
Fully open	107°C (225°F)

Coolant

Type	Refer to *Weekly checks*
Capacity	Refer to Chapter 1

Torque wrench settings

	Nm	lbf ft
All models		
Air conditioning compressor:		
Front mounting bracket bolts	35	26
Rear mounting bracket bolts	20	15
Air conditioning refrigerant lines unions:		
To bulkhead flange	20	15
To compressor (M10)	40	30
To condenser	20	15
To expansion valve	9	7
To pulsation damper	27	20
To receiver/dryer	20	15
Air conditioning tri-switch	7	5
Coolant pump	25	28
Steering column bracing strut:		
To steering column	22	16
To floorpan	22	16
4-cylinder models		
Coolant pipe to thermostat cover	8	6
Temperature gauge sender unit	11	8
Thermostat housing cover	15	11
6-cylinder models		
Coolant bridge to cylinder head	30	22
Coolant intake pipe to cylinder block	20	15
Coolant intake pipe to exhaust manifold	6	4
Coolant pipe to cylinder head	25	18
Temperature gauge sender unit	18	13
Thermostat housing cover	20	15

1 General description

1 The cooling system comprises a radiator, timing belt driven coolant pump (depending on engine), a waxstat-type bypass thermostat, and a remotely-mounted plastic expansion tank. A thermostatically-controlled electric cooling fan is fitted to all models, between the front of the engine and the radiator. An auxiliary cooling fan is also fitted, in front of the radiator. Models with air conditioning also have a second electric auxiliary cooling fan, to cope with the extra demand of cooling the refrigerant condenser.

2 Cold water from the coolant pump is forced around the cylinder block, cylinder head and heater matrix during the warm up cycle. When the engine reaches a predetermined temperature, the thermostat starts to open and the coolant then circulates through the radiator via a transfer pipe, to provide extra cooling. The main cooling fan is controlled by the temperature of air behind the radiator.

2 Radiator - removal and refitting

Removal

Models with 6-cylinder engines

1 Ensure that the engine has cooled completely before starting work. Drain the cooling system as described in Chapter 1.

2 Remove the screws and lift out the radiator upper cover panel **(see illustration)**.

3 Disconnect the negative and positive cables from the battery terminals, then remove the battery as described in Chapter 5A.

4 Refer to Chapter 4A and remove multi-ram air intake pre-volume chamber.

5 Disconnect the wiring from cooling fan thermo-switches, secondary air-cut-off valve, and auxiliary coolant pump (as applicable) **(see illustrations)**. Label each connector carefully, to aid correct refitting.

6 Disconnect all coolant hoses from the radiator; these include the expansion tank hose, the radiator top and bottom hoses, and the auxiliary coolant pump hose (where applicable) **(see illustrations)**.

7 Release the securing clips and disconnect the air hoses from secondary air cut-off valve.

8 On models with air conditioning, unscrew the securing bolts and disconnect the refrigerant condenser from radiator **(see illustration)**.

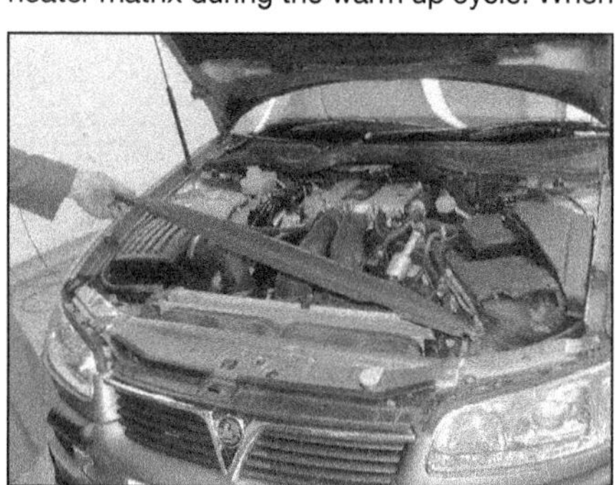

2.2 Lift out the radiator upper cover panel

2.5a Disconnect the wiring from cooling fan thermo-switches . . .

2.5b . . . secondary air-cut-off valve . . .

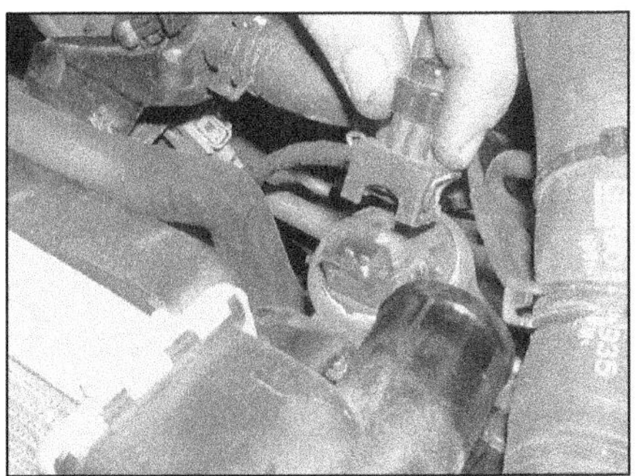

2.5c . . . and auxiliary coolant pump

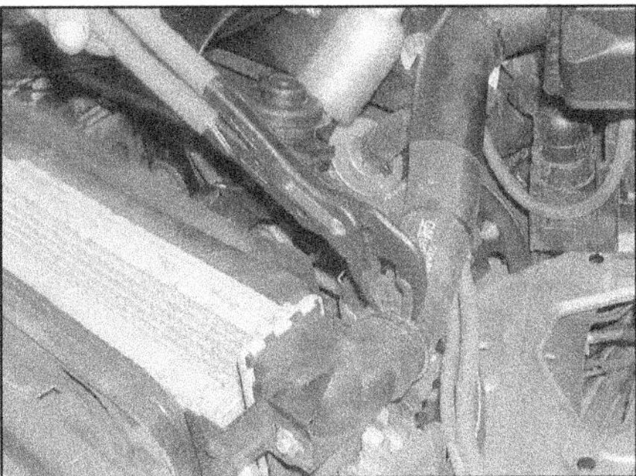

2.6a Disconnect the top hose from the radiator

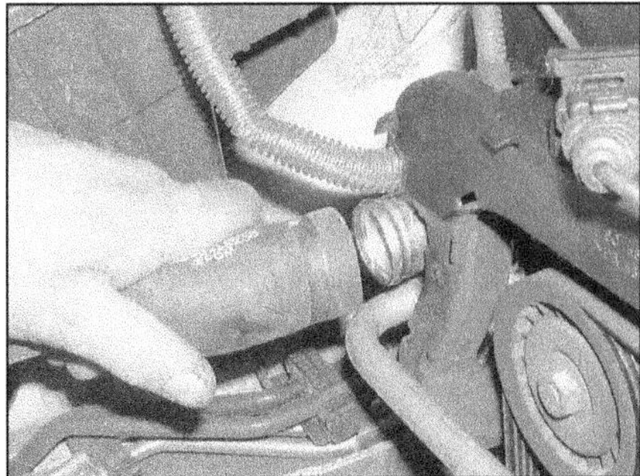

2.6b Disconnect the bottom hose from the engine coolant transfer pipe

2.6c Disconnect the coolant expansion tank hose from the radiator

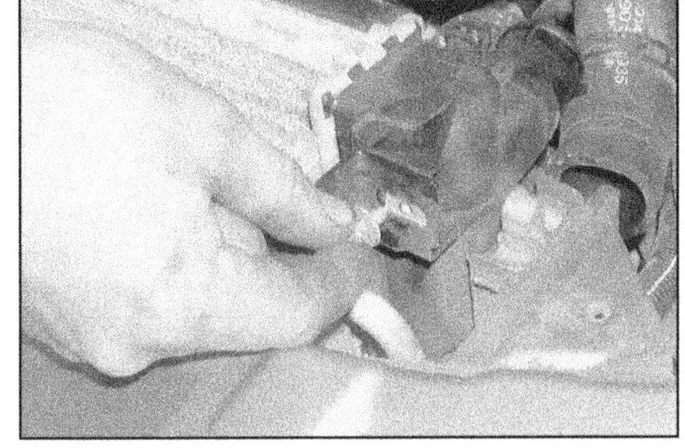

2.8 Unscrew the securing bolts and disconnect the air conditioning refrigerant condenser from radiator

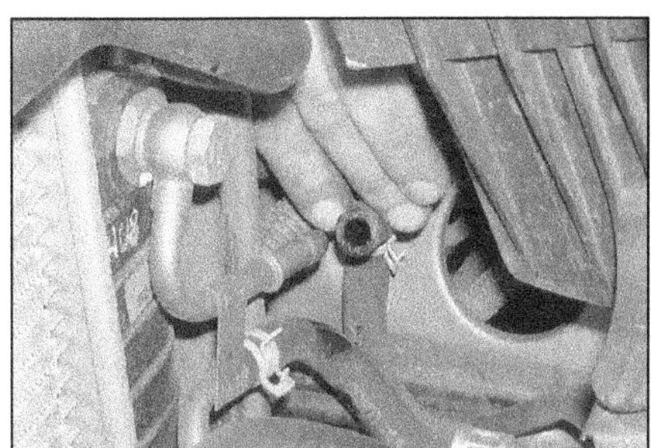

2.9 Disconnect the narrow bore transmission fluid cooler hoses from the radiator

9 On models with automatic transmission, release the hose clips and disconnect the narrow bore hoses from the transmission fluid cooler **(see illustration)**. Plug the pipes to prevent excessive fluid loss and the ingress of debris.

10 Release the spring clips at the top of the radiator, then withdraw radiator complete with the cooling fan from engine compartment **(see illustrations).**

Models with 4-cylinder engines

11 Ensure that the engine has cooled completely before starting work. Drain the cooling system as described in Chapter 1.

12 Disconnect the negative cable from the battery and position it away from the terminal.

13 Disconnect the wiring from main cooling fans and is associated thermo-switch. Label the connector(s), to aid correct refitting.

14 Disconnect all coolant hoses from the radiator, including the expansion tank hose, and the radiator top and bottom hoses.

15 On models with air conditioning, undo the screws and disconnect the refrigerant heat exchanger from radiator**.**

16 On models with automatic transmission, release the hose clips and disconnect the narrow bore pipes from the transmission fluid cooler. Plug the pipes to prevent excessive fluid loss and the ingress of debris.

17 Release the spring clips at the top of the radiator, then withdraw radiator complete with the cooling fan from engine compartment.

Refitting

18 Refitting is a reversal of the removal procedure, noting the following points:.

a) Ensure that all coolant hose clips are securely tightened.

b) On models with automatic transmission, use new union seals when reconnecting the automatic transmission fluid cooler pipes.

c) On models with air conditioning, secure the heat exchanger to the base of the radiator and tighten the retaining bolts securely.

d) Refill the cooling system as described in Chapter 1.

e) Where applicable, top up the level of automatic transmission fluid as described in Chapter 1.

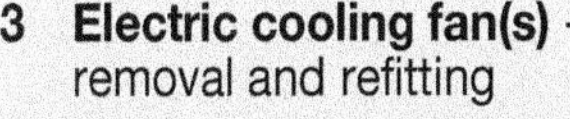

3 Electric cooling fan(s) - removal and refitting

Main cooling fan

Removal - Models with 4-cylinder engines

1 Disconnect the battery negative cable and position it away from the terminal.

2 Unplug the wiring from the rear of the fan motor, at the connector.

3 Remove the two screws that secure the fan/cowling assembly to the rear of the radiator.

4 Disengage the fan housing from its lower mounting, then lift the fan and housing from of the engine bay, taking care not to damage the cooling fins of the radiator (and air-conditioning heat exchanger, where fitted).

5 The fan motor can be separated from the

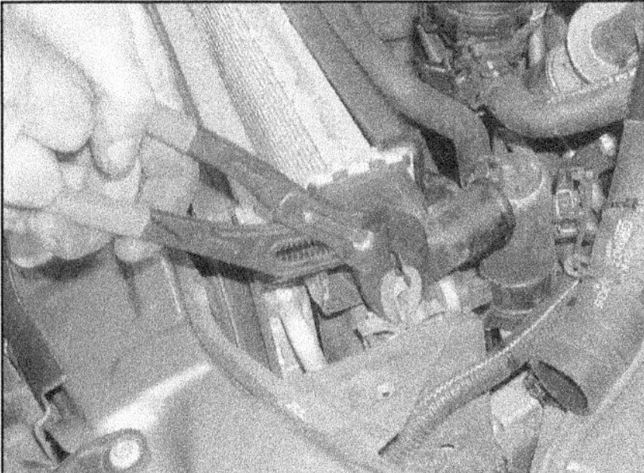

2.10a Release the spring clips at the top of the radiator . . .

2.10b . . . then withdraw radiator complete with the cooling fan from engine compartment

3.12 Slacken and remove the securing screws . . .

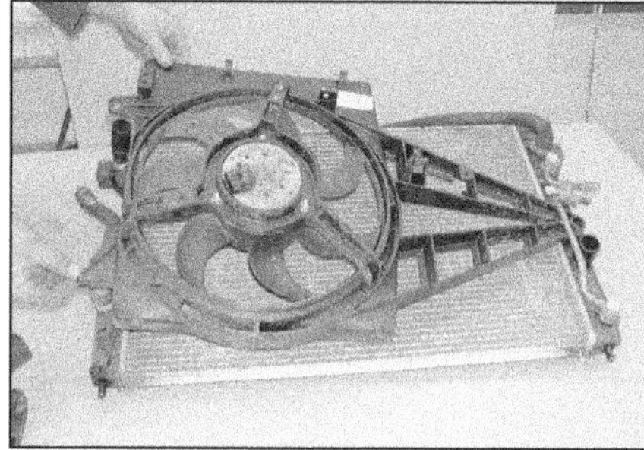

3.13 . . . and remove the cooling fan together with its housing from the radiator (shown with radiator removed for clarity)

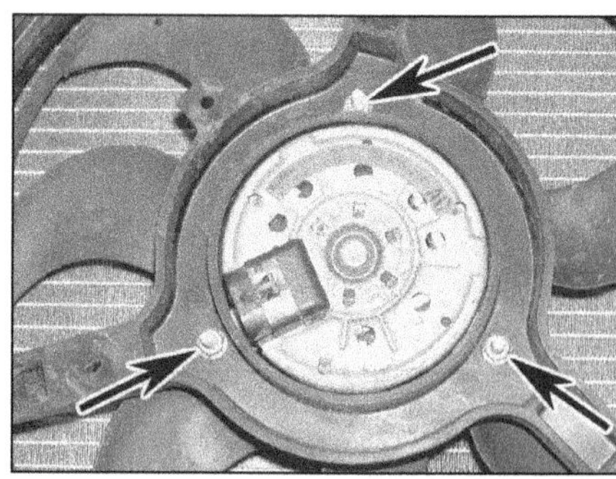

3.14 Fan motor securing nuts (arrowed)

housing by slackening and removing the three securing nuts.

Removal - Models with 6-cylinder engines

6 Disconnect the negative and positive cables from the battery terminals, then remove the battery as described in Chapter 5A.

7 Release the mounting bracket and detach secondary air cut-off valve from the fan housing.

8 Remove the screws and lift off the radiator upper cover panel.

9 Refer to Chapter 4A and remove multi-ram air intake pre-volume chamber.

10 Disconnect the wiring from the rear of the fan motor. Label each connector carefully, to aid correct refitting.

11 Release the mounting bracket and detach the auxiliary coolant pump from the side of the fan housing (where applicable).

12 Remove the three screws that secure the fan/cowling assembly to the rear of the radiator **(see illustration)**.

13 Disengage the fan housing from its lower mounting, then lift the fan and housing from of the engine bay, taking care not to damage the cooling fins of the radiator (and air-conditioning heat exchanger, where fitted) **(see illustration)**.

14 The fan motor can be separated from the housing by slackening and removing the three securing nuts **(see illustration)**.

Refitting (all models)

15 Refit the cooling fan by following the removal procedure in reverse.

Auxiliary cooling fan(s)

Refitting

16 Disconnect the battery negative cable and position it away from the terminal.

17 With reference to Chapter 11, remove the radiator grille, then unbolt and remove the cross-member from the front of the engine compartment.

18 Undo the securing screws and detach the air intake duct from the crossmember **(see illustration)**.

19 Unclip the cover panel then unplug the wiring harness from the auxiliary fan at the multi-way connector. Release the harness from the cable ties **(see illustrations)**.

20 To improve access, unclip the wiring harness conduit from the bodywork **(see illustration)**.

21 Slacken and remove the securing screws then withdraw the fan and motor from its housing **(see illustrations)**.

Refitting

22 Refitting is a reversal of removal.

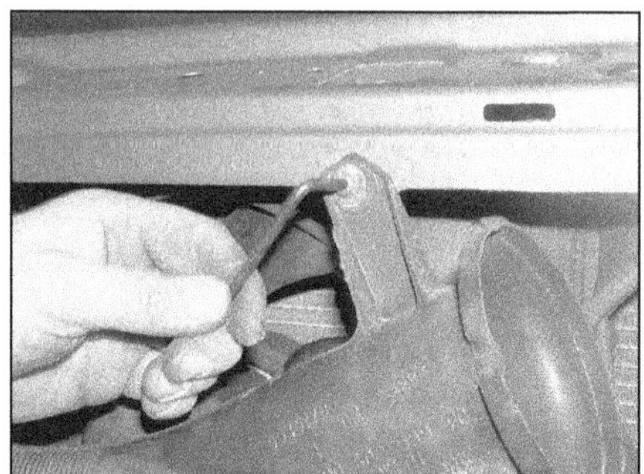

3.18 Undo the securing screws and detach the air intake duct from the crossmember

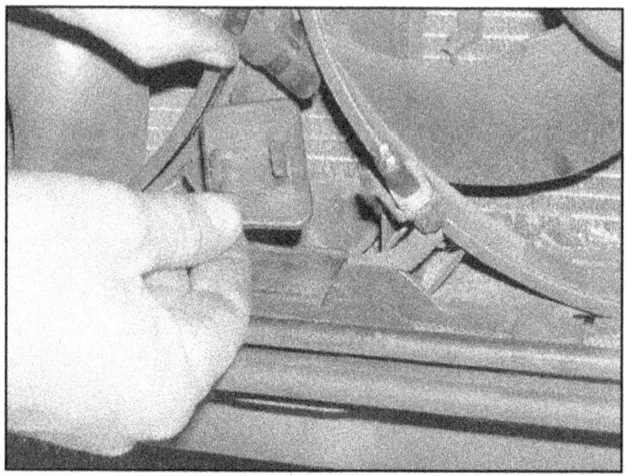

3.19a Unclip the cover panel . . .

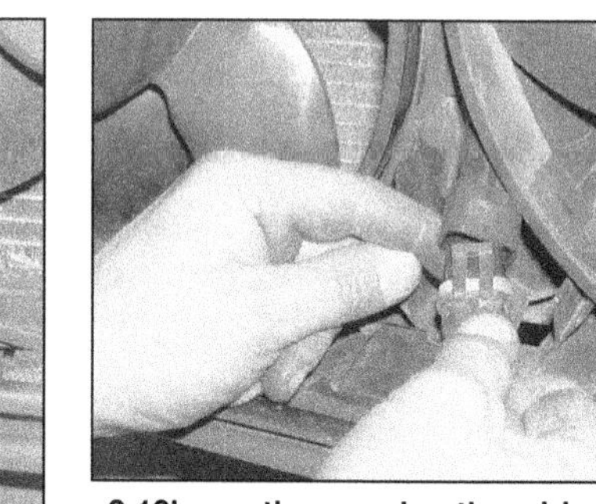

3.19b . . . then unplug the wiring harness from the auxiliary fan at the multi-way connector

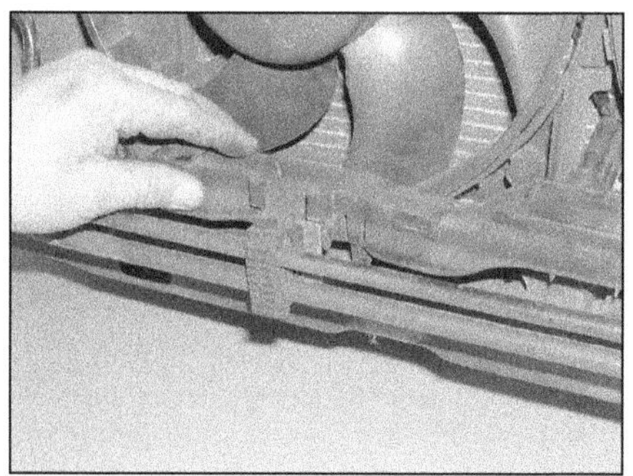

3.20 Unclip the wiring harness conduit from the bodywork

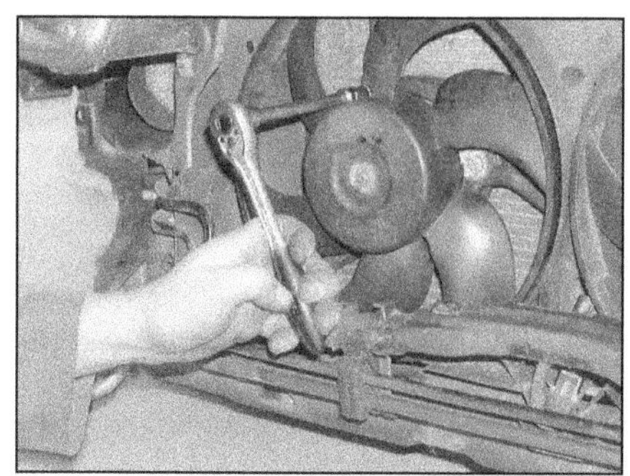

3.21a Slacken and remove the securing screws . . .

3.21b . . . then withdraw the fan and motor from its housing

4 Thermostat - removal, testing and refitting

Models with 4-cylinder engines

Removal

1 Drain the cooling system as described in Chapter 1.
2 Loosen the clip and disconnect the coolant hose from the thermostat housing cover.
3 Unscrew the bolts and remove the cover. Note that the thermostat is integral with the cover.
4 Carefully clean the mating surface of the thermostat housing.

Refitting

5 Refitting is a reversal of the removal procedure. Use a new thermostat housing cover sealing ring and ensure that the securing screws are tightened to the specified torque. On completion, refill the cooling system as described in Chapter 1.

Models with 6-cylinder engines

Removal

6 Drain the cooling system as described in Chapter 1.
7 Release the clip and disconnect the radiator top hose from the engine coolant transfer pipe.
8 Slacken and remove the bolt securing the coolant transfer pipe to the cylinder head. Note that this bolt also secures one of the engine lifting eyelets and the dipstick tube.
9 Carefully pull the coolant transfer pipe from the thermostat housing, using just enough effort to disengage the O-ring seals **(see illustrations)**.
10 Remove the upper half of the inlet manifold, with reference to Chapter 4A.
11 Unscrew the bolts and remove the cover. Note that the thermostat is integral with the cover **(see illustration)**.

Refitting

12 Refitting is a reversal of the removal procedure, noting the following points **(see illustration)**:.

a) Fit a new sealing ring to the thermostat cover.
b) Ensure that the thermostat cover securing screws are tightened to the specified torque.
c) Use new O-ring seals when refitting the coolant transfer pipe to the thermostat housing.
d) On completion, refill the cooling system as described in Chapter 1.

Thermostat testing

13 A rough test of the thermostat may be made by suspending it on the end of a piece of string in a saucepan full of water. Bring the water to the boil and check that the thermostat begins to open. If a suitably graduated thermometer is available, the temperature at which the thermostat begins to open may be determined and then compared with the figure given in the Specifications. Note that as tap water begins to boil as its temperature approaches 100°, it will not be possible to test the thermostat in its fully open position. Using additives to raise the boiling point of the water may adversely affect the operation of thermostat, hence this is not recommended.
14 A thermostat which fails to close as the water cools must also be considered faulty and should be renewed.

4.9a Carefully pull the coolant transfer pipe from the thermostat housing . . .

4.9b . . . using just enough effort to disengage the O-ring seals

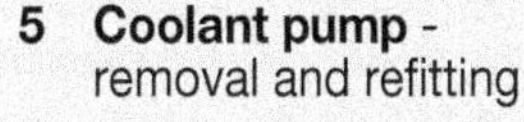

5 Coolant pump - removal and refitting

Models with 4-cylinder engines

Removal

1 Drain the cooling system as described in Chapter 1.
2 Remove the camshaft timing belt tensioner pulley, as described in Chapter 2A/B.
3 Release the crankshaft sensor wiring from the timing belt cover, noting its routing ensure correct refitting.
4 Progressively slacken and remove the water pump retaining bolts. Note that the bolts are of different lengths; make a note of the fitted position of each bolt to ensure correct refitting.
5 Lift the coolant pump away from the engine and recover the seal.

Refitting

6 Refit the coolant pump by following the removal procedure in reverse, noting these points:.

a) Use a new coolant pump sealing ring.
b) Coat the new sealing ring and the pump mating surface with silicon grease before fitting.
c) The lug on the side of the coolant pump flange must be aligned with the corresponding recess in the cylinder block.
d) Tighten the coolant pump securing bolts to the specified torque.
e) Refit the timing belt tensioner pulley, according to the information given in Chapter 2A/B (as applicable).
f) On completion, refill the cooling system with the specified quantity of correctly-mixed coolant.

Models with 6-cylinder engines

Removal

7 Drain the cooling system as described in Chapter 1.
8 Remove the camshaft timing belt front cover, as described in Chapter 2C. Note that this entails the removal of the auxiliary drivebelt (see Chapter 1) and the coolant pump pulley.

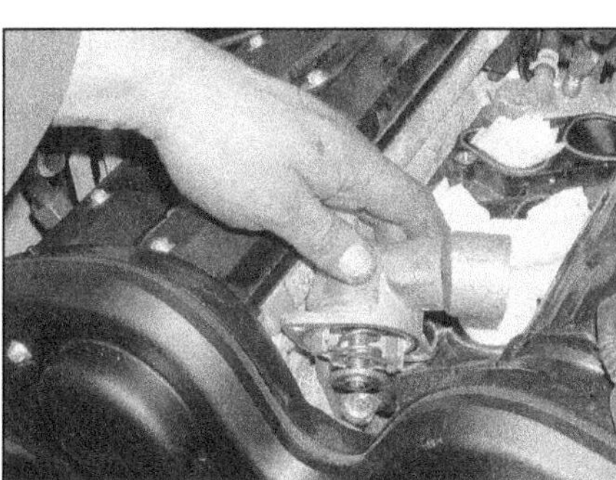

4.11 Unscrew the bolts, then remove the cover and integral thermostat

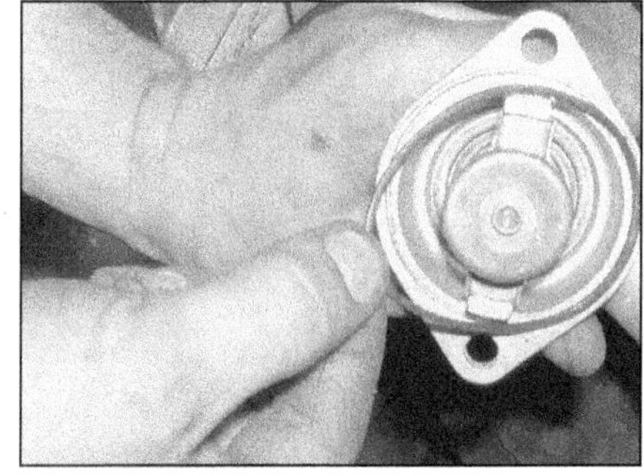

4.12 Fit a new sealing ring to the thermostat cover

5.9 Progressively slacken and remove the water pump retaining bolts

9 Progressively slacken and remove the water pump retaining bolts **(see illustration)**. Note that the bolts are of different lengths; make a note of the fitted position of each bolt to ensure correct refitting.

10 Lift the coolant pump away from the engine and recover the seal **(see illustrations)**.

Refitting

11 Refit the coolant pump by following the removal procedure in reverse, noting these points:.

- *a) Use a new coolant pump sealing ring..*
- *b) Coat the new sealing ring and the pump mating surface with silicon grease before fitting.*
- *c) Tighten the coolant pump securing bolts to the specified torque.*
- *d) Refit the timing belt cover, coolant pump pulley and auxiliary drive belt, according to the information given in Chapter 2C and Chapter 1 (as applicable).*
- *e) On completion, refill the cooling system with the specified quantity of correctly-mixed coolant.*

6 Expansion tank - removal and refitting

Removal

1 Drain the cooling system as described in Chapter 1.

2 Remove the filler cap.

3 Where applicable, loosen the clip and disconnect the radiator vent hose.

4 Unclip the expansion tank from the front suspension turret.

5 Loosen the clips and disconnect the coolant supply and return hoses.

6 Withdraw the expansion tank from the engine compartment.

Refitting

7 Refitting is a reversal of the removal procedure. On completion, refill the cooling system with reference to Chapter 1 .

7 Temperature gauge sender unit - removal and refitting

Removal

Warning: If the engine is hot, allow it to cool before attempting to remove the unit.

1 On all models, the temperature gauge sender unit is located on the rear of the cylinder block between the cylinder heads. Note that the gauge sender has a single electrical terminal; do not confuse it with the engine management coolant temperature sensor which has a two-way electrical connector. To gain access, refer to Chapter 4A and remove the upper section of the inlet manifold.

2 Remove the filler cap from the radiator or expansion tank to release any remaining pressure, then refit the cap - the vacuum will help to reduce the loss of coolant.

3 Disconnect the wiring from the terminal on the sender unit.

4 Unscrew and remove the sender unit, recovering the sealing ring (where fitted). Temporarily plug the aperture with a suitable bung. **Note:** *Be prepared for an amount of coolant loss - position a container under the thermostat housing and pad the area with absorbent rags .*

Refitting

5 Refitting is a reversal of the removal procedure. Use a new sealing ring and tighten the sender to the specified torque. On completion, top up the cooling system as detailed in *Weekly checks*.

5.10a Lift the coolant pump away from the engine . . .

5.10b . . . and recover the seal

8 Heater/ventilation system components - removal and refitting

Note: *For models equipped with Electronic Climate Control, refer to the information given in Section 13.*

Heater control panel switches

Removal

1 Disconnect the battery negative cable and position it away from the terminal.

2 The number and types of switches fitted will vary with model specification, but the removal method for each switch is identical.

3 Obtain two small flat bladed screwdrivers. Pad the ends of the blades with insulating tape.

4 Insert the screwdrivers into the recesses at either side of the switch to be removed. Carefully depress the locking tabs and lever the switch button away from the switch body.

5 Squeeze the locking tabs at either side of the switch body together, then slide the switch body from the heater control panel.

Refitting

6 Refitting is a reversal of the removal procedure.

Heater control panel

Removal

7 Remove the switches from the heater control panel as described in the previous sub-Section.

8 Pull the rotary knobs from the four heat and air distribution control shafts.

9 Remove radio unit from the facia as described in Chapter 12.

10 Unclip and remove the storage compartment adjacent to the radio aperture.

11 Slacken and remove the five heater control panel securing screws; one at the rear of the radio aperture, one at the rear of the storage compartment aperture, and one below each heat/air distribution control shaft.

12 Withdraw the heater control panel from heater control unit.

13 At the rear of the control panel, slide the locking bars to one side and unplug the electrical connectors from the panel. Also unplug the wiring for the panel illumination bulbs and the cigarette lighter.

Refitting

14 Refitting is a reversal of the removal procedure.

Heater control unit

15 Remove the heater control panel as described in the previous sub-Section.

16 Remove the screws and detach the heater control unit from the facia.

17 Prise open the retaining brackets and release both air temperature control cables from the control shafts.

18 Unplug the wiring connector from the rear of the fan control switch.
19 Disconnect the vacuum control hose manifold from the rear of the control panel.
20 Remove the control panel from the vehicle.

Refitting

21 Refitting is a reversal of the removal procedure.

Air distribution unit

Note: *On models with air conditioning, this procedure involves having the refrigerant circuit discharged by a Vauxhall dealer or an air conditioning specialist.*

Removal

22 Drain the coolant as described in Chapter 1.
23 Remove the facia as described in Chapter 11.
24 On models with air conditioning, the refrigerant circuit must be now be discharged by an air conditioning specialist or a Vauxhall dealer, to allow the air conditioning lines to be disconnected from the engine compartment bulkhead. Refer to the precautions given in Section 11 before proceeding.
25 Unclip and remove the duct for the face level air vent on the drivers side of the vehicle.
26 With reference to Chapter 10, unbolt and remove the steering column bracing strut, from the steering column and the floorpan.
27 Undo the bolt and release the earth cable from the bulkhead.
28 Unplug the wiring connector from the blower motor resistor pack, at the connector.
29 Place a suitable container beneath the point where the heater matrix coolant pipes enter the air distribution unit.
30 Unscrew the bolt to release the pipe retaining plate, then disconnect the coolant pipes from the heater matrix, at the right hand side of the air distribution unit. Allow the escaping coolant to drain into the container. Press the coolant pipes back towards the engine compartment, clear of the air distribution unit.
31 On models with air conditioning, disconnect the black vacuum hose from the coolant cut-off valve.
32 Unplug the wiring connector from the recirculation valve solenoid.
33 On models without electronic climate control, disconnect the yellow vacuum hose from the air distribution unit.
34 Undo the securing screws and detach the rear passenger compartment footwell ducts from the distribution unit.
35 Disconnect the blue vacuum hose from the recirculation valve vacuum unit.
36 On models with automatic transmission, release the cable ties and separate the selector cable from the recirculation valve solenoid.
37 Working in the engine compartment, slacken and withdraw the two distribution unit securing bolts, located near the upper edge of the bulkhead.
38 Working inside the car, unscrew and remove the last distribution unit securing bolt.
39 Pull the unit up and away from the facia, the lift it over the facia wiring harness and remove it from the vehicle.

Refitting

40 Refitting is a reversal of the removal procedure, noting the following points:.

a) Use new O-ring seals when reconnecting the heater matrix coolant pipes.
b) Use new O-ring seals when reconnecting the air conditioning refrigerant pipes to the bulkhead.
c) Observe the correct tightening torques when reconnecting the steering column bracing strut (see Chapter 10).
d) On model with air conditioning, have the refrigerant circuit evacuated and recharged by an air conditioning specialist or a Vauxhall dealer.
e) Ensure that all vacuum and electrical connections are securely re-made
f) On completion, refill the cooling system as described in Chapter 1.

Heater matrix

41 See Section 9.

Blower motor and fan

42 See Section 10.

Heater control cable - driver's side

Removal

43 Release the facia from the bulkhead, with reference to Chapter 11. Pull it away from the bulkhead just far enough to gain access to the rear of the air distribution unit.
44 Prise open the retaining clip and then disconnect the cable inner from the operating lever on the air distributor unit.
45 Remove the heater control panel as described earlier in this Section.
46 Prise open the retaining clip and then disconnect the cable inner from the quadrant at the end of the control shaft.
47 Remove the cable from the vehicle.

Refitting

48 Refitting is a reversal of the removal procedure. Set the operating lever on the air distributor unit in the vertical position before reconnecting the control cable inner.

Heater control cable - passenger side

49 Proceed as described for the driver's side control cable, in the previous sub-Section, noting that the air duct for the passenger footwell vent must be removed to gain access to the cable.

Recirculation air valve solenoid

Removal

50 Disconnect the battery negative cable and position it away from the terminal.
51 On right hand drive models, remove the glove compartment from the facia, as described in Chapter 11, then unclip and remove the air duct for the passenger footwell vent.
52 On left hand drive models, remove the lower trim panel from the drivers side of the facia, then unclip and remove the air duct for the drivers footwell vent.
53 The solenoid is mounted on the left hand side of the air distributor unit. Note the connection order of each of the vacuum hoses, then disconnect them from the solenoid valve ports.
54 Unplug the wiring connector from the solenoid valve.
55 Slacken and withdraw the securing screw then remove the solenoid valve from the vehicle.

Refitting

56 Refitting is a reversal of the removal procedure. Ensure that the valve sits squarely in its guide slots, and that the vacuum hoses are correctly reconnected according to the notes made during removal.

Recirculation air valve vacuum unit

Removal

57 Remove the glove compartment from the facia, as described in Chapter 11.
58 Release the cable ties, then depress the locking tabs and disengage the wiring harness support from the facia. Unclip and remove the air ducting.
59 The recirculation air valve vacuum unit is located on the left hand side of the blower motor housing, and is distinguished by the blue vacuum hose leading to it.
60 Disconnect the vacuum hose from the side of the vacuum unit.
61 Lever the unit from its mounting boss. Disconnect the actuator arm from the lever at the base of the vacuum unit, then remove the vacuum unit from the vehicle.

Refitting

62 Refitting is a reversal of the removal procedure.

Defroster valve vacuum unit

63 Proceed as described for the recirculation valve vacuum unit, in the previous sub-Section. The defroster valve vacuum unit is located on the right hand side of the air distributor unit and is distinguished by the brown vacuum hose leading to it.

Footwell valve vacuum unit

64 Proceed as described for the recirculation valve vacuum unit, in the previous sub-Section. The footwell valve vacuum unit is located on the right hand side of the air distributor unit and is distinguished by the green vacuum hose leading to it.

Vacuum control circuit

General information

65 The heating and ventilation system is controlled by a series of valves which direct air through the required air ducts, according to the position of the control knobs on the heater control panel. The valves are actuated by vacuum supplied engine inlet manifold. The following diagram is provided to show the order of vacuum hose and vacuum unit connection **(see illustration).**

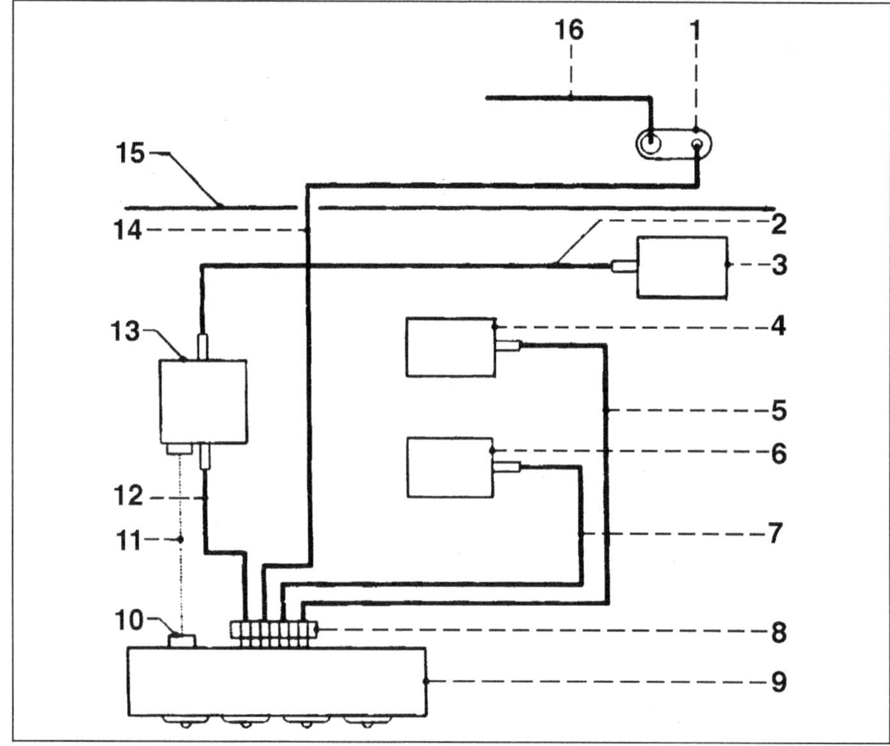

8.65 Heating/ventilation system vacuum control circuit

1 *Vacuum reservoir*
2 *Blue vacuum hose*
3 *Vacuum unit, recirculating air valve*
4 *Vacuum unit, defroster valve*
5 *Brown vacuum hose*
6 *Vacuum unit, footwell valve*
7 *Green vacuum hose*
8 *Connector, vacuum hoses*
9 *Heater controls*
10 *Recirculating air switch*
11 *Solenoid valve wiring, recirculating air valve*
12 *Blue vacuum hose*
13 *Solenoid valve, recirculating air valve*
14 *Yellow vacuum hose*
15 *Bulkhead*
16 *Vacuum supply hose*

9 Heater matrix - removal and refitting

Removal

1 Disconnect the battery negative cable and position it away from the terminal.
2 Drain the coolant as described in Chapter 1.
3 Refer to Chapter 11 and remove the facia.
4 With reference to Chapter 10, unbolt the lower end of the steering column bracing strut and pivot it upwards away from the floorpan.
5 Remove the securing screw and unclip the air duct for the drivers footwell vent from the side of the air distributor unit.
6 Detach the drivers side control cable from the air distributor unit, as described in the previous Section.
7 Place a suitable container beneath the point where the heater matrix coolant pipes enter the air distribution unit.
8 Unscrew the bolt to release the pipe retaining plate, then disconnect the coolant pipes from the heater matrix, at the right hand side of the air distribution unit, and recover the O-ring seals. Allow the escaping coolant to drain into the container. Press the coolant pipes back towards the engine compartment, clear of the air distribution unit.
9 Slacken and remove the securing screws then withdraw the heater matrix from the side of the air distribution unit, recover the rubber seal **(see illustration)**. If a new heater matrix is to be fitted, extract the captive nut (for the coolant pipe retaining plate) from the plastic casing of the old matrix and transfer it to the new one.

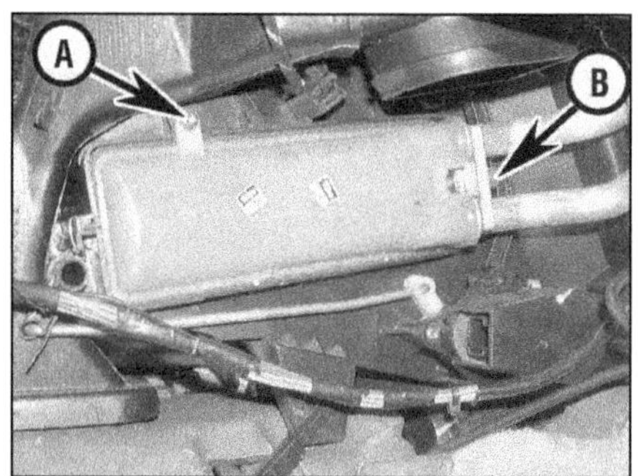

9.9 Heater matrix securing screw (A) and coolant pipe retaining plate bolt (B)

Refitting

10 Refitting is a reversal of the removal procedure, noting the following points:.

a) *Use new O-ring seals when reconnecting the heater matrix coolant pipes.*
b) *Observe the correct tightening torques when reconnecting the steering column bracing strut (see Chapter 10).*
c) *On completion, refill the cooling system as described in Chapter 1.*

10 Blower motor and series resistor - removal and refitting

Blower motor

Removal

1 Disconnect the battery negative cable and position it away from the terminal.
2 Remove the glove compartment from the facia as described in Chapter 11.
3 Release the cable ties, then depress the locking tabs and disengage the wiring harness support from the facia. Unclip and remove the air ducting.
4 Disconnect the vacuum hose from the side of the air recirculation valve vacuum unit then remove the unit from its mounting bracket (see Section 8).
5 Unplug the wiring harness leading to the blower motor series resistor.
6 Slacken and remove the securing screws, then withdraw the blower motor and fan assembly from its housing **(see illustrations)**.

Refitting

7 Refitting is a reversal of the removal procedure.

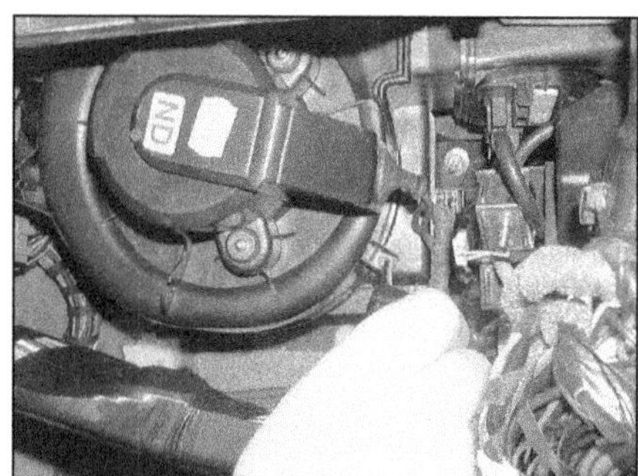

10.6a Slacken and remove the securing screws . . .

Series resistor

Removal

8 Proceed as described in paragraphs 1 to 3 inclusive in the previous sub-Section.

9 Unplug the wiring harness from the blower motor series resistor at the connector **(see illustration)**.

10 Depress the retaining tabs and withdraw the resistor from the fan/motor housing **(see illustration)**.

Refitting

11 Refitting is a reversal of removal.

11 Air conditioning system - description and precautions

General information

1 An air conditioning system is available on certain models. When activated, the air conditioning system allows air entering the passenger to be cooled giving greater control over the temperature inside the car and leading to increased comfort. The cooled air is also dehumidified, enabling faster windscreen demisting.

2 The cooling side of the system works in the same way as a domestic refrigerator. Refrigerant gas, contained in a sealed network of alloy pipes, is drawn into a belt-driven compressor, and is forced through a condenser mounted on the front of the radiator. On entering the condenser, the refrigerant changes state from gas to liquid and releases heat, which is absorbed by the air flowing into the engine compartment through the condenser. The liquid refrigerant passes through an expansion valve to an evaporator, where it changes from liquid under high pressure to gas under low pressure. This change in state is accompanied by a drop in temperature, which cools the evaporator. Air passing through the evaporator is cooled before flowing into the air distribution unit. The refrigerant then returns to the compressor, and the cycle begins again.

3 Cool air passes to the air distribution unit, where it is mixed with hot air blown through the heater matrix, to achieve the desired

10.6b . . . then withdraw the blower motor and fan assembly from its housing

temperature in the passenger compartment. On models with Electronic Climate control, the cabin temperature is regulated automatically by a system of air valves controlled by servo motors.

4 The heating side of the system works in the same way as on models without air conditioning (see Section 8).

5 The operation of the system is controlled by an electronic control unit, which controls the electric cooling fan, the compressor, and the facia-mounted warning light. Any problems with the system should be referred to a Vauxhall dealer.

Precautions

6 When an air conditioning system is fitted, it is necessary to observe special precautions whenever dealing with any part of the system, or its associated components. If for any reason the system must be disconnected, you must entrust this task to a Vauxhall dealer or an air conditioning specialist. Similarly, the system can only be evacuated and recharged by a dealer or air conditioning specialist.

Warning: The air conditioning system contains a pressurised liquid refrigerant. If the system is discharged in an uncontrolled manner without the aid of specialist equipment, the refrigerant will boil as soon as it is exposed to the atmosphere, causing severe frostbite if it comes into contact with unprotected skin. In addition, certain refrigerants, in the presence of a naked flame (including a lit cigarette), will burn to form a highly poisonous gas. It is therefore extremely dangerous to disconnect any part of the air conditioning system without specialised knowledge and equipment.

7 Uncontrolled discharging of the refrigerant can also be damaging to the environment, as certain refrigerants contain CFCs.

8 Do not operate the air conditioning system if it is known to be short of refrigerant, as this will damage the compressor.

12 Air conditioning system components - removal and refitting

Warning: Do not attempt to discharge the refrigerant circuit yourself - refer to the precautions given in Section 11. Have the air conditioning system discharged by a qualified engineer. On completion, have the refrigerant engineer fit new O-rings to the line connections and evacuate and re-charge the system.

Auxiliary coolant pump

Removal

1 Drain the coolant as described in Chapter 1.

2 Remove the battery as described in Chapter 5A.

3 Remove the screws and lift the upper cover from the top of the radiator.

4 Unplug the wiring from the auxiliary coolant pump at the connector.

5 Release the securing clips and detach the auxiliary coolant pump from the radiator.

Refitting

6 Refitting is a reversal of removal. On completion, top up the cooling system as described in *Weekly checks*.

Compressor

Removal - Models with 4-cylinder engines

7 Have the air conditioning system discharged by a qualified engineer.

8 Remove the battery as described in Chapter 5A.

9 Remove the auxiliary drivebelt as described in Chapter 1.

10 Unbolt the refrigerant lines from the compressor.

11 Unplug the wiring connector from the clutch unit at the underside of the compressor.

12 Unscrew the three securing bolts from the front of the compressor.

13 Unscrew the three securing bolts from the rear of the compressor, then remove the compressor from its mounting bracket.

Refitting - Models with 4-cylinder engines

14 Refitting is a reversal of the removal procedure; ensure that all fixings are tightened to the specified torque, where given. On

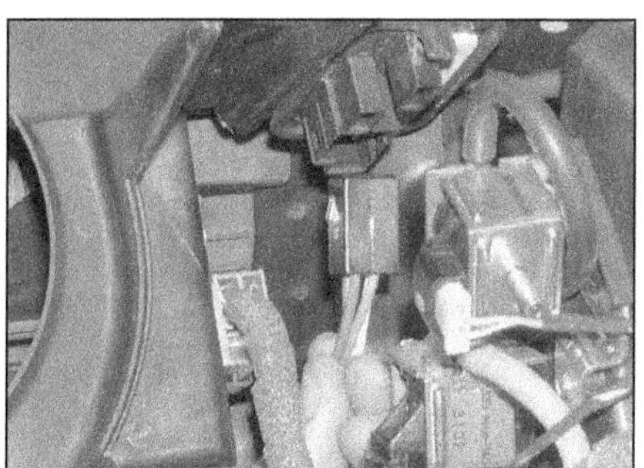

10.9 Unplug the wiring harness from the blower motor series resistor at the connector

10.10 Withdraw the resistor from the fan/motor housing

completion, have the refrigerant engineer fit new O-rings to the line connections and evacuate and re-charge the refrigerant circuit.

Removal - Models with 6-cylinder engines

15 Have the air conditioning system discharged by a qualified engineer.
16 Remove the battery as described in Chapter 5A.
17 Remove the auxiliary drivebelt as described in Chapter 1.
18 Uncouple the low pressure refrigerant pipe at the service union. Work along the length of the pipe that remains connected to the compressor and release it from any retaining brackets.
19 Uncouple the high pressure refrigerant pipe at the pulsation damper unit. Work along the length of the pipe that remains connected to the compressor and release it from any retaining brackets.
20 Unplug the wiring connector from the clutch unit at the underside of the compressor.
21 Unscrew the three securing bolts from the front of the compressor.
22 Unscrew the two securing bolts from the rear of the compressor.
23 Rotate the compressor so that the fluid filler bolt faces towards the engine sump, then remove the compressor from its mounting bracket.

Refitting - Models with 6-cylinder engines

24 Refitting is a reversal of the removal procedure; ensure that all fixings are tightened to the specified torque, where given. On completion, have the refrigerant engineer fill the compressor with lubricant, fit new O-rings to the line connections and then evacuate and re-charge the refrigerant circuit.

Expansion valve

25 Have the air conditioning system discharged by a qualified engineer.
26 Disconnect the battery negative cable and position it away from the terminal.
27 Refer to Chapter 11 and remove the glove compartment.
28 Refer to Section 10 and remove the blower motor.
29 Disconnect the refrigerant lines at the engine compartment bulkhead.
30 Unbolt the solenoid valves from the evaporator housing and position them to one side.
31 Remove the six securing screws and lift the evaporator cover from the air distributor unit.
32 Unbolt the retainer plate, disconnect the refrigerant lines, then unbolt the expansion valve from the evaporator.

Refitting

33 Refitting is a reversal of removal. Ensure that all fixings are tightened to the specified torque, where given. On completion, have the refrigerant engineer fit new O-rings to the line connections and then evacuate and re-charge the refrigerant circuit.

Evaporator

Removal

34 Remove the expansion valve as described in previous sub-Section, then withdraw the evaporator from the air distributor unit.

Refitting

35 Refitting is a reversal of removal.

Condenser

Removal - Models with 4 cylinder engines

36 Have the air conditioning system discharged by a qualified engineer.
37 Disconnect the battery negative cable and position it away from the terminal.
38 Remove the radiator as described in Section 2.
39 Slacken and separate the unions, then disconnect the refrigerant lines from the condenser and tape over or plug them.
40 Carefully lift the condenser from its rubber guide and withdraw it from the vehicle.

Refitting

41 Refitting is a reversal of removal. Have a refrigerant engineer fit new O-rings to the line connections and then evacuate and re-charge the refrigerant circuit. On completion, refill the cooling system with reference to Chapter 1.

Removal - Models with 6 cylinder engines

42 Have the air conditioning system discharged by a qualified engineer.
43 Disconnect the battery negative cable and position it away from the terminal.
44 Remove the radiator as described in Section 2.
45 Slacken and separate the unions, then disconnect the refrigerant lines from the condenser and tape over or plug them.
46 Carefully lift the condenser from its rubber guide and tilt it backwards towards the engine.
47 Slacken and separate the unions, then disconnect the refrigerant lines from the receiver/dryer unit and tape over or plug them.
48 Undo the screws and detach the receiver/dryer unit mounting bracket from the condenser.
49 Carefully lift the condenser from its rubber guide and withdraw it from the vehicle, together with the receiver/dryer unit.

Refitting - Models with 6 cylinder engines

50 Refitting is a reversal of removal. Have a refrigerant engineer fit new O-rings to the line connections and then evacuate and re-charge the refrigerant circuit. On completion, refill the cooling system with reference to Chapter 1.

Receiver/dryer

Removal

51 Have the air conditioning system discharged by a qualified engineer.
52 Disconnect the battery negative cable and position it away from the terminal.
53 Refer to Chapter 11 and remove the radiator grille.
54 Detach the filler neck from the top of the windscreen washer fluid reservoir. On models with 6-cylinder engines, unbolt and remove the crossmember from the front of the engine compartment.
55 Punch out the pre-stressed holes in the cooling fan casing to gain access to the refrigerant line unions, at the top of the receiver/dryer unit.
56 Slacken and separate the unions, then disconnect the refrigerant lines from the receiver/dryer unit and tape over or plug them.
57 Undo the screws and detach the receiver/dryer unit mounting bracket from the front of the vehicle. Remove the unit from the engine compartment, together with its mounting bracket.

Refitting

58 Refitting is a reversal of removal. On completion, have a refrigerant engineer fit new O-rings to the line connections and then evacuate and re-charge the refrigerant circuit.

Tri-switch

Removal

59 The tri-switch is located beneath receiver/dryer unit at the front left hand corner of the engine compartment. Have the air conditioning system discharged by a qualified engineer.
60 Disconnect the battery negative cable and position it away from the terminal.
61 Unplug the wiring from the tri-switch at the multi-way connector.
62 Counterhold the refrigerant line union and unscrew the tri-switch.

Refitting

63 Refitting is a reversal of removal. On completion, have a refrigerant engineer fit new O-rings to the line connections and then evacuate and re-charge the refrigerant circuit.

Cooling fan thermo-switches

Main radiator fan

64 The main radiator fan thermo-switch is located at the lower edge of the radiator.
65 Drain the cooling system as described in Chapter 1.
66 Disconnect the battery negative cable and position it away from the terminal.
67 Unplug the wiring from the switch at the multi-way connector.
68 Unscrew the switch from the radiator.
69 Refitting is a reversal of removal, but use a new switch sealing ring. On completion refill the cooling system as described in Chapter 1.

Auxiliary fan

70 The auxiliary radiator fan thermo-switch is located at the left hand side of the radiator.
71 Drain the cooling system as described in Chapter 1.

13.4 Slacken and remove the securing screws from the lower edge of the ECC panel

72 Disconnect the battery negative cable and position it away from the terminal.
73 Unplug the wiring from the switch at the multi-way connector.
74 Unscrew the switch from the radiator.
75 Refitting is a reversal of removal, but use a new switch sealing ring. On completion refill the cooling system as described in Chapter 1.

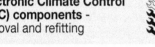

13 Electronic Climate Control (ECC) components - removal and refitting

ECC control panel and switches

Removal

1 Disconnect the battery negative cable and position it away from the terminal.
2 Remove ashtray from the facia as described in Chapter 11.
3 Remove radio unit from the facia as described in Chapter 12, then remove the radio mounting frame.
4 Slacken and remove the securing screws from the lower edge of the control panel **(see illustration)**.
5 Reach through the radio aperture and pull down on the aluminium locking bar at the rear of the upper edge of the control panel **(see illustrations)**.
6 Remove the panel from the facia. At the rear of the control panel, slide the locking bars to one side and unplug the electrical connectors from the panel. Also unplug the wiring for the control panel and ashtray illumination bulbs **(see illustrations)**.
7 If required, the ECC switch controls can be detached from the control panel by removing the relevant securing screws.

Refitting

8 Refitting is a reversal of removal, noting the following points:.

a) Ensure that locking bar at the rear upper edge of the control panel is correctly engaged.
b) On completion, synchronise the air valve servo motors as follows: Switch the ignition to the On position, then depress and hold the Auto and Off keys on the ECC control panel for more than 5 seconds.

13.5a Reach through the radio aperture . . .

Defroster air valve servo motor

Removal

9 Disconnect the battery negative cable and position it away from the terminal. Remove the lower trim panel from the drivers side of the facia, then unclip and remove the air duct for the drivers footwell vent.
10 The servo motor is mounted on the right hand side of the air distributor unit **(see illustration)**.
11 Unplug the wiring harness from the servo motor at the multiway connector.
12 Undo the securing screws and withdraw the servo motor from the air distributor unit.
13 Disengage the motor spindle arm from the actuator rod.

Refitting

14 Refitting is a reversal of removal. On completion, synchronise the air valve servo

13.5b . . . and pull down on the aluminium locking bar at the rear of the upper edge of the control panel (shown with panel removed for clarity)

motors as follows: turn the ignition switch to the On position, then depress and hold the Auto and Off keys on the ECC control panel for more than 5 seconds.

Footwell air valve servo motor

Removal

15 Refer to the previous sub-Section and remove the defroster air valve servo motor.
16 The servo motor is mounted on the right hand side of the air distributor unit, in front of the defroster air valve servo motor **(see illustration)**.
17 Unplug the wiring harness from the servo motor at the multiway connector.
18 Undo the securing screws and withdraw the servo motor from the air distributor unit.

13.6a Unplug the wiring harness connectors . . .

13.6b . . . and remove the ECC panel from the facia

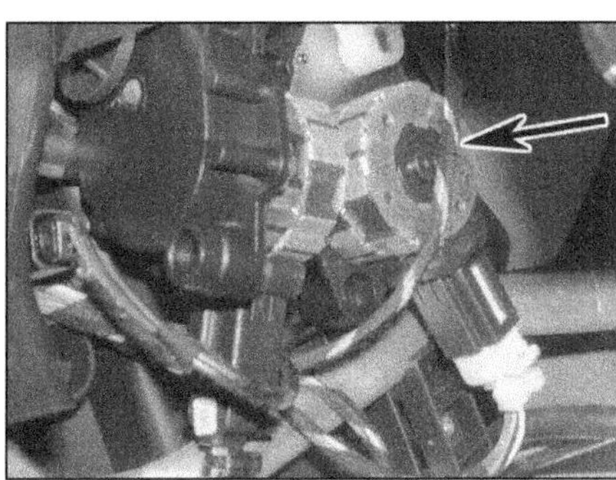

13.10 Location of the ECC defroster air valve servo

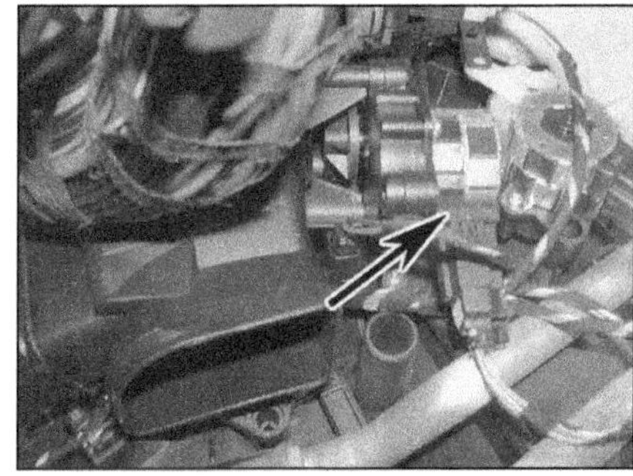

13.16 Location of the ECC footwell air valve servo

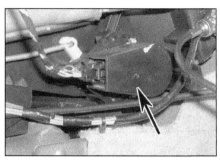

13.32 Unclip the cover panel to expose the right hand vent servo motor

Refitting

19 Turn the servo motor spindle gear fully clockwise to the end of its stop. Similarly, turn the spindle gear air distributor housing fully clockwise to the end of its stop.

20 Refit the motor and tighten its securing screws. Reconnect the wiring harness.

21 Refit the defroster air valve servo motor as described in the previous sub-Section. Refit all components removed for access.

22 On completion, synchronise the air valve servo motors as follows: turn the ignition switch to the On position, then depress and hold the Auto and Off keys on the ECC control panel for more than 5 seconds.

Centre vent servo motor

Removal

23 Disconnect the battery negative cable and position it away from the terminal.

24 Remove the lower trim panel from the drivers side of the facia, then unclip and remove the air duct for the drivers footwell vent.

25 The servo motor is mounted on the right hand side of the air distributor unit, above the defroster air valve servo motor.

26 Unplug the wiring harness from the servo motor at the multiway connector.

27 Undo the securing screws and withdraw the servo motor from the air distributor unit.

28 Disengage the motor spindle arm from the actuator rod.

Refitting

29 Refitting is a reversal of removal. On completion, synchronise the air valve servo motors as follows: turn the ignition switch to the On position, then depress and hold the Auto and Off keys on the ECC control panel for more than 5 seconds.

Right hand vent servo motor

Removal

30 Disconnect the battery negative cable and position it away from the terminal.

31 Remove the lower trim panel from the drivers side of the facia, then unclip and remove the air duct for the drivers footwell vent.

32 Unclip the cover panel to expose the servo motor **(see illustration)**.

33 Unplug the wiring harness from the servo motor at the multiway connector.

34 Undo the securing screws and withdraw the servo motor from the air distributor unit.

35 Disengage the motor spindle arm from the actuator rod and actuator lever.

Refitting

36 Refitting is a reversal of removal. On completion, synchronise the air valve servo motors as follows: turn the ignition switch to the On position, then depress and hold the Auto and Off keys on the ECC control panel for more than 5 seconds.

Left hand vent servo motor

Removal

37 Disconnect the battery negative cable and position it away from the terminal. Remove the glove compartment from the facia, as described in Chapter 11.

38 Release the cable ties, then depress the locking tabs and disengage the wiring harness support from the facia. Unclip and remove the air ducting.

39 Unclip the cover panel to expose the servo motor.

40 Unplug the wiring harness from the servo motor at the multiway connector.

41 Undo the securing screws and withdraw the servo motor from the air distributor unit.

42 Disengage the motor spindle arm from the actuator rod and actuator lever.

Refitting

43 Refitting is a reversal of removal. On completion, synchronise the air valve servo motors as follows: turn the ignition switch to the On position, then depress and hold the Auto and Off keys on the ECC control panel for more than 5 seconds.

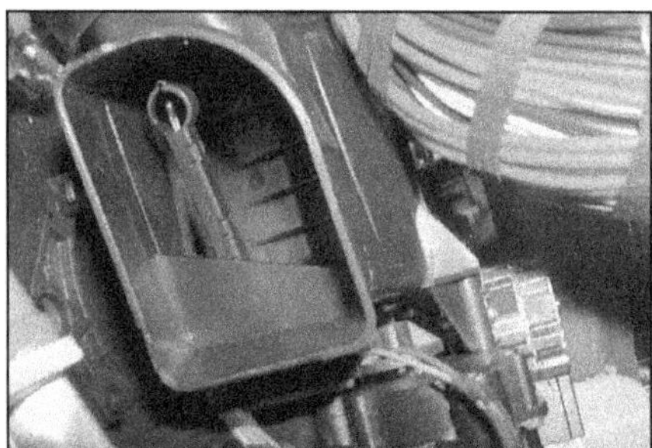

13.46 Location of the ECC right hand vent temperature sensor

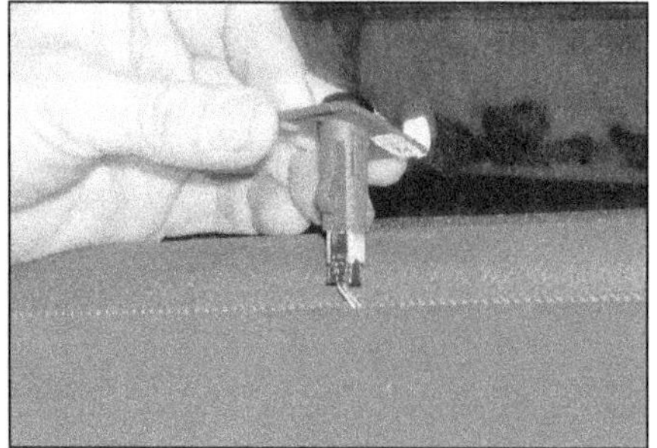

13.56 Carefully lever the sun sensor from the upper surface of the facia

Right hand vent temperature sensor

Removal

44 Remove the footwell air valve servo motor as described earlier in this Section.

45 Unplug the wiring from the sensor at the connector.

46 Carefully prise the sensor body away from its mounting clip and withdraw the probe from the air ducting **(see illustration)**.

Refitting

47 Refitting is a reversal of removal. On completion, refit the footwell air valve servo motor, then synchronise the air valve servo motors as follows: turn the ignition switch to the On position, then depress and hold the Auto and Off keys on the ECC control panel for more than 5 seconds.

Left hand vent temperature sensor

Removal

48 Disconnect the battery negative cable and position it away from the terminal. Remove the glove compartment from the facia, as described in Chapter 11.

49 Release the cable ties, then depress the locking tabs and disengage the wiring harness support from the facia. Unclip and remove the air ducting.

50 Note the direction that the wiring connector is facing, then pull the sensor to release it from the air distributor unit, then rotate it clockwise through half a turn and unplug the wiring connector.

51 Tilt the sensor to the left and withdraw it from its aperture.

Refitting

52 Refitting is a reversal of removal. Ensure that when the sensor is refitted, the wiring connector faces the right hand side of the vehicle, as noted during removal.

Blower motor regulator

Removal

53 Disconnect the battery negative cable and position it away from the terminal. Remove the glove compartment from the facia, as described in Chapter 11.

54 Depress the retaining lugs and withdraw the regulator from the fan housing. Unplug the wiring from the regulator at the connector.

Refitting

55 Refitting is a reversal of removal.

Sun sensor

Removal

56 Carefully lever the sensor from the facia using blunt soft bladed instrument **(see illustration)**.

57 Secure a cable tie around the wiring harness to prevent it from falling back into the facia, then disconnect it from the sensor.

Refitting

58 Refitting is a reversal of removal.

Chapter 4 Part A:
Fuel and exhaust systems

Contents

Degrees of difficulty

Easy, suitable for novice with little experience 	**Fairly easy,** suitable for beginner with some experience 	**Fairly difficult,** suitable for competent DIY mechanic 	**Difficult,** suitable for experienced DIY mechanic 	**Very difficult,** suitable for expert DIY or professional

Specifications

System type

2.0 litre SOHC engine	Bosch Motronic M1.5.4*
2.0 litre DOHC engine	Simtec 56.1 or 56.5*
2.5 and 3.0 litre engine	Bosch Motronic M2.8.1 or M2.8.3*

**See Section 6 for further information*

Fuel system data

Fuel pump type	Electric, immersed in tank
Fuel pump regulated pressure (approximate)	3.0 bar
Specified idle speed	Not adjustable - controlled by ECU
Idle mixture CO content	Not adjustable - controlled by ECU

Recommended fuel

Minimum octane rating	95 RON* unleaded (UK unleaded premium). Leaded fuel must not be used

**91 RON unleaded fuel can be used but a slight power loss maybe noticeable.*

Torque wrench settings

	Nm	lbf ft
Auxiliary drivebelt tensioner mounting bolts - 2.5 and 3.0 litre engines	35	26
Braking system vacuum hose union nut	20	15
Camshaft sensor bolt:		
2.0 litre DOHC engine	6	4
2.5 and 3.0 litre engines	8	6
Crankshaft sensor bolt	8	6
EGR pipe union nuts - 2.5 and 3.0 litre engine	25	18
Exhaust manifold heatshield bolts	8	6
Exhaust manifold nuts:		
2.0 litre engine	22	16
2.5 and 3.0 litre engine	20	15
Exhaust system fasteners:		
Front pipe to manifold bolts:		
2.0 litre engine	25	18
2.5 and 3.0 litre engine	30	22
Front pipe to mounting bracket bolt	20	15
Front pipe to intermediate pipe bolts	18	13
Intermediate pipe to tailpipe clamp	17	13
Fuel hose union nuts/bolts	15	11
Fuel pressure regulator clamp screw		
Fuel rail bolts	8	6
Fuel tank retaining strap bolts	30	22
Inlet manifold nuts and bolts:		
2.0 litre engine	22	16
2.5 and 3.0 litre engines:		
Flange to cylinder head bolts	20	15
Lower section:		
Retaining bolts	20	15
Fuel pipe adaptor mounting bolts	8	6
Upper section retaining bolts	8	6
Knock sensor bolt	20	15
Oil cooler pipe union nuts and bolts - 2.5 and 3.0 litre engines	30	22
Spark plug heatshields - 2.0 litre SOHC engine	25	18
Throttle housing nuts/bolts:		
2.0 litre engine	9	7
2.5 and 3.0 litre engine	8	6

1 General information and precautions

1 The fuel system consists of a fuel tank (which is mounted under the rear of the car, with an electric fuel pump immersed in it), a fuel filter and the fuel feed and return lines. The fuel pump supplies fuel to the fuel rail, which acts as a reservoir for the fuel injectors (one for each cylinder) which inject fuel into the inlet tracts. In addition, there is an Electronic Control Unit (ECU) and various sensors, electrical components and related wiring.

2 Refer to Section 6 for further information on the operation of each fuel injection system, and to Section 18 for information on the exhaust system.

Warning: Many of the procedures in this Chapter require the removal of fuel lines and connections, which may result in some fuel spillage. Before carrying out any operation on the fuel system, refer to the precautions given in Safety first! at the beginning of this manual, and follow them implicitly. Petrol is a highly-dangerous and volatile liquid, and the precautions necessary when handling it cannot be overstressed.

Note: *Residual pressure will remain in the fuel lines long after the vehicle was last used. Before disconnecting any fuel line, first depressurise the fuel system as described in Section 7.*

2 Air cleaner assembly and intake ducts - removal and refitting

Removal

Note: *On 2.5 and 3.0 litre engines, refer to Section 17 for information on the multi-ram air intake system.*

1 To remove the air cleaner housing slacken the retaining clip and disconnect the duct from the outlet then unclip the housing from its mounting rubbers. Free the housing from the intake duct and remove it from the engine compartment.

2 The various ducts can be disconnected and removed once the retaining clips have been slackened. In some cases it will be necessary to disconnect breather hoses and wiring connectors to allow the duct to be removed; some duct sections are also bolted to a support bracket.

Refitting

3 Refitting is the reverse of removal, noting the following.

a) *Examine the housing mounting rubbers for signs of damage or deterioration and renew if necessary.*
b) *On refitting, remove the mounting rubbers from the body and fit them to the housing pins. Ease installation by lubricating the mounting rubbers with a spray-based silicone lubricant.*
c) *Ensure all ducts are securely joined and retained by the necessary clips and screws.*

3 Accelerator cable - removal and refitting

Removal

1 Working in the engine compartment, unclip the inner cable retaining clip then slide the clip out of the end fitting and release the cable from the throttle cam **(see illustration)**.

2 Free the accelerator outer cable from its mounting bracket, taking care not to lose the adjusting clip **(see illustration)**. Work back along the length of the cable, free it from any retaining clips or ties, noting its correct routing. On models with automatic transmission it will be necessary to disconnect the wiring from the kickdown switch which is built into the cable.

3 To improve access, remove the windscreen wiper arms and the water deflector panel from the base of the windscreen (see Chapter 12, Sections 15 and 16).

4 From inside the vehicle, release the retaining clips (rotate them through 90°) then remove the undercover panel from the drivers' side of the facia. Remove the fastener (prise out the centre pin then pull out the fastener outer section) then unclip and remove the heater/ventilation duct to improve access to the accelerator pedal **(see illustrations)**.

5 Reaching up behind the facia, unclip the accelerator inner cable from the top of the accelerator pedal **(see illustration)**.

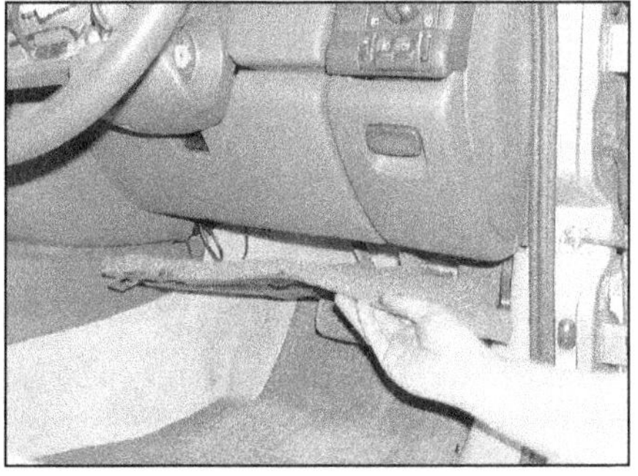

3.4a Release the retaining clips and remove the undercover panel from the driver's side of the facia

3.1 Remove the retaining clip and detach the inner cable from the throttle cam . . .

6 Return to the engine compartment then free the cable sealing grommet from the bulkhead and remove the cable and grommet from the vehicle.

7 Examine the cable for signs of wear or damage and renew if necessary.

Refitting

8 Feed the cable into position from the engine compartment and seat the outer cable grommet in the bulkhead.

9 From inside the vehicle, clip the inner cable end fitting into position in the pedal end and check to make sure the grommet is correctly located in the bulkhead. Check that the cable is securely retained, then refit the heater/ventilation duct and undercover to the facia.

10 From within the engine compartment, ensure the outer cable is correctly seated in the bulkhead, then work along the cable, securing it in position with the retaining clips and ties, and ensuring that the cable is correctly routed. On models with automatic transmission, reconnect the kickdown switch wiring connector making sure the wiring is correctly routed.

11 Refit the water deflector panel and install both wiper arms (see Chapter 12).

12 Connect the inner cable to the throttle cam and secure it in position with the retaining clip. Clip the outer cable into its mounting bracket and adjust the cable as described below.

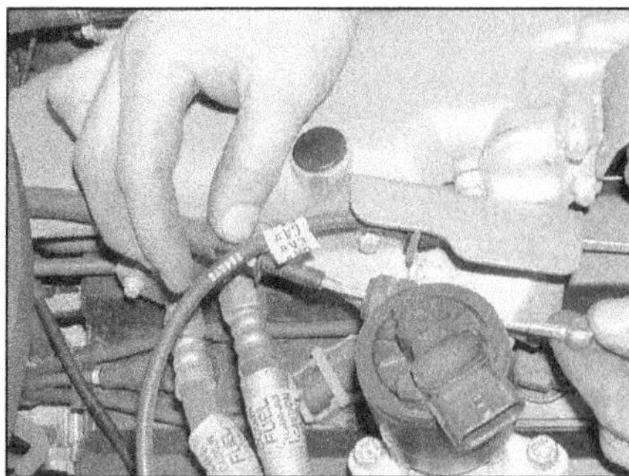

3.2 . . . then free the outer cable from the mounting bracket

Adjustment

13 Working in the engine compartment, slide off the adjustment clip from accelerator outer cable.

14 With the clip removed, ensure that the throttle cam is fully against its stop. Gently pull the cable out of its grommet until all free play is removed from the inner cable.

15 With the cable held in this position, refit the spring clip to the last exposed outer cable groove in front of the rubber grommet. When the clip is refitted and the outer cable is released, there should be only a small amount of free play in the inner cable.

16 Have an assistant depress the accelerator pedal, and check that the throttle cam opens fully and returns smoothly to its stop.

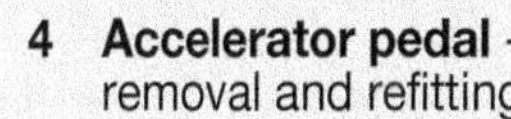

4 Accelerator pedal - removal and refitting

Removal

1 From inside the vehicle, release the retaining clips (rotate them through 90°) then remove the undercover panel from the drivers' side of the facia. Remove the fastener (prise out the centre pin then pull out the fastener outer section) then unclip and remove the heater/ventilation duct to improve access to the accelerator pedal (see illustrations 3.4a to 3.4c).

3.4b Prise out the centre pin then remove the fastener outer section . . .

3.4c . . . and unclip the heater/ventilation duct

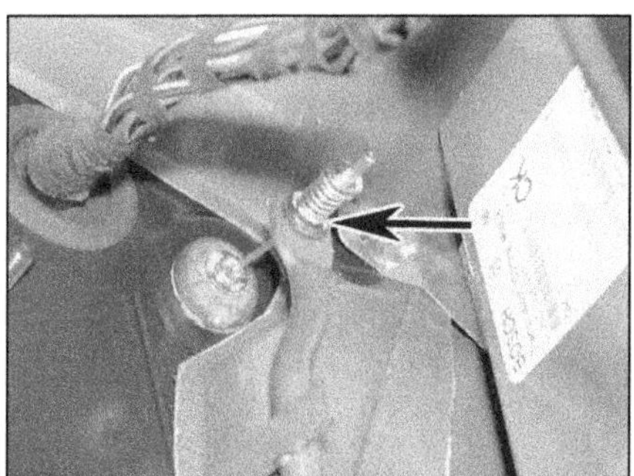

3.5 Unhook the accelerator cable (arrowed) from the upper end of the pedal

4.3 Undo the retaining nuts (arrowed) and remove the accelerator pedal from the vehicle

2 Reaching up behind the facia, unclip the accelerator inner cable end fitting from the top of the accelerator pedal (see illustration 3.5).

3 Unscrew the retaining nuts and remove the pedal assembly from the bulkhead **(see illustration)**.

4 Inspect the pedal assembly for signs of wear, paying particular attention to the pedal bushes, and renew as necessary. To dismantle the assembly, unhook the return spring then slide off the retaining clip and separate the pedal, mounting bracket, return spring and pivot bushes.

Refitting

5 If the assembly has been dismantled, apply a smear of multi-purpose grease to the pedal pivot shaft and bushes. Fit the bushes and return spring to the mounting bracket and insert the pedal, making sure it passes through the return spring bore. Secure the pedal in position with the retaining clip and hook the return spring back behind the pedal.

6 Refit the pedal assembly and securely tighten its retaining nuts.

7 Clip the accelerator cable end fitting into the pedal then refit the heater/ventilation duct and undercover to the facia.

8 On completion, adjust the accelerator cable as described in Section 3.

5 Unleaded petrol - general information and usage

Note: *The information given in this Chapter is correct at the time of writing. If updated information is thought to be required, check with a Vauxhall dealer. If travelling abroad, consult one of the motoring organisations (or a similar authority) for advice on the fuel available.*

1 The fuel recommended by Vauxhall is given in the Specifications Section of this Chapter, followed by the equivalent petrol currently on sale in the UK.

2 All petrol models are designed to run on fuel with a minimum octane rating of 95 (RON). Lower octane fuel, down to minimum of rating 91 (RON), can be safely used since the engine management system automatically adjusts the ignition timing to suit (using the information supplied by the knock sensor). However, a slight power loss is likely if fuel with a octane rating of less than 95 (RON) is used. Vauxhall state that if 91 octane fuel is to be used, as a precautionary measure, it is wise to avoid placing the engine under severe loads for any length of time (eg. towing or full throttle driving).

3 All UK models have a catalytic converter, and so must be run on unleaded fuel only. Under no circumstances should leaded fuel (UK 4-star) be used, as this may damage the converter.

4 Super unleaded petrol (98 octane) can also be used in all models if wished, though there is no advantage in doing so.

6 Fuel injection systems - general information

2.0 litre SOHC engine models - Bosch Motronic M1.5.4 system

1 All 2.0 litre SOHC engine models are equipped with a Bosch Motronic engine management (fuel injection/ignition) system **(see illustration)**. On UK models the system incorporates a closed-loop catalytic converter, an evaporative emission control system and an exhaust gas recirculation (EGR) system and complies with the latest emission control standards. The fuel injection side of the system operates as follows; refer to Chapter 5B for information on the ignition system.

2 The fuel pump, immersed in the fuel tank, pumps fuel from the fuel tank to the fuel rail, via a filter mounted underneath the rear of the vehicle. Fuel supply pressure is controlled by the pressure regulator which allows excess fuel to be returned to the tank.

3 The electrical control system consists of the ECU, along with the following sensors.

a) Throttle potentiometer - informs the ECU of the throttle position, and the rate of throttle opening or closing.

b) Coolant temperature sensor - informs the ECU of engine temperature.

c) Airflow meter - informs the ECU of the amount of air entering the inlet manifold.

d) Intake air temperature sensor - informs the ECU of the temperature of the air entering the manifold.

e) Crankshaft sensor - informs the ECU of engine speed and crankshaft position.

f) Knock sensor - informs the ECU when pre-ignition (pinking) is occurring.

g) Oxygen sensor (UK models) - informs the ECU of the oxygen content of the exhaust gases (explained in greater detail in Part B of this Chapter).

h) ABS control unit - informs the ECU of the vehicle speed.

i) Air conditioning system compressor switch (where fitted) - informs ECU when the air conditioning system is switched on.

4 All the above information is analysed by the ECU and, based on this, the ECU determines the appropriate ignition and fuelling requirements for the engine. The ECU controls the fuel injector by varying its pulse width - the length of time the injector is held open - to provide a richer or weaker mixture, as appropriate. The mixture is constantly varied by the ECU, to provide the best setting for cranking, starting (with either a hot or cold engine), warm-up, idle, cruising, and acceleration.

5 The ECU also has full control over the engine idle speed, via the idle speed adjuster which is fitted to the throttle housing. The adjuster controls the opening of an air passage which bypasses the throttle valve. When the throttle valve is closed (accelerator pedal released), the ECU uses the adjuster to vary the amount of air entering the engine and so controls the idle speed.

6 The ECU also controls the exhaust and evaporative emission control systems, which are described in detail in Part B of this Chapter.

7 If there is an abnormality in any of the readings obtained from any sensor, the ECU enters its back-up mode. In this event, the ECU ignores the abnormal sensor signal, and assumes a pre-programmed value which will allow the engine to continue running (albeit at reduced efficiency). If the ECU enters this back-up mode, the warning light on the instrument panel will come on, and the relevant fault code will be stored in the ECU memory.

8 If the warning light comes on, the vehicle should be taken to a Vauxhall dealer at the earliest opportunity. A complete test of the engine management system can then be carried out, using a special electronic diagnostic test unit which is simply plugged into the system's diagnostic connector. The connector is located behind the fusebox cover panel on the drivers' side of the facia.

2.0 litre DOHC engine models - Simtec 56.1 or 56.5 system

9 All 2.0 litre DOHC engine models are equipped with a Simtec engine management (fuel injection/ignition) system **(see illustration overleaf)**. The system is almost identical in operation to the Motronic system fitted to SOHC engines (see paragraphs 1 to 8). The only major change to the system is that a camshaft sensor is also incorporated into the system. The camshaft sensor informs the ECU of the speed and position of the exhaust camshaft.

10 In order to reduce exhaust emissions even further, a secondary air system is also incorporated. This is explained in greater detail in Part B of this Chapter.

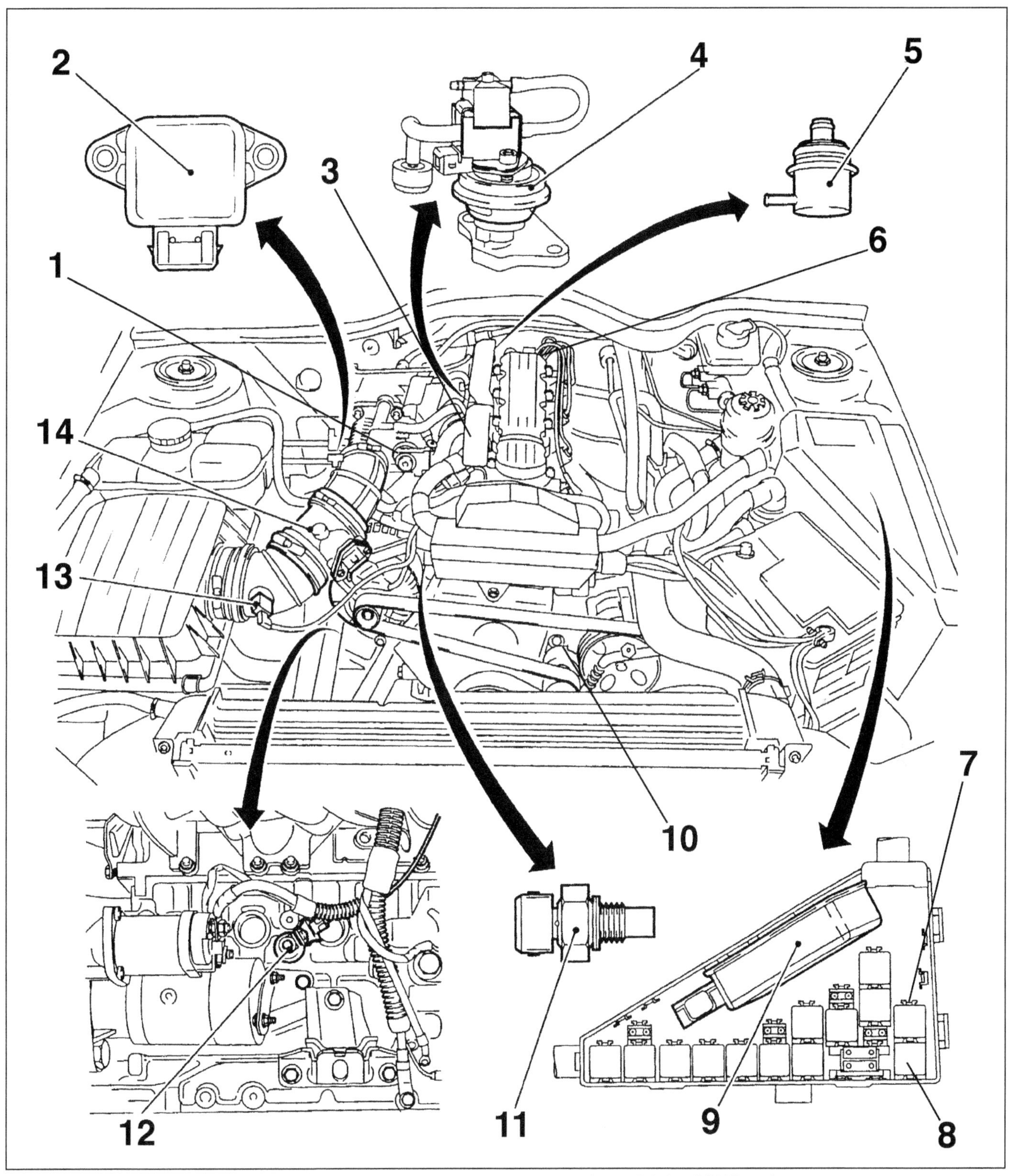

6.1 Engine management system component locations - 2.0 litre SOHC engine

1 Idle speed adjuster valve
2 Throttle potentiometer
3 Evaporative emission system purge valve
4 Exhaust gas recirculation (EGR) valve
5 Fuel pressure regulator
6 DIS module
7 Fuel pump relay
8 Injection system relay
9 Electronic control unit (ECU)
10 Crankshaft sensor
11 Coolant temperature sensor
12 Knock sensor
13 Intake air temperature sensor
14 Airflow meter

2.5 and 3.0 litre engines - Bosch Motronic M2.8.1 or 2.8.3 system

11 All 2.5 and 3.0 litre engine models are equipped with a Bosch Motronic engine management (fuel injection/ignition) system **(see illustration)**. The system is almost identical in operation to the Motronic system fitted to 2.0 litre SOHC engine (see paragraphs 1 to 8). The only major change to the system is that a camshaft sensor is also incorporated into the system. The camshaft sensor is fitted to the left-hand cylinder bank informs the ECU of the speed and position of the exhaust camshaft. Due to the V6 layout of the engine there are two knock sensors and two oxygen sensors, one for each bank of cylinders.

12 In order to reduce exhaust emissions even

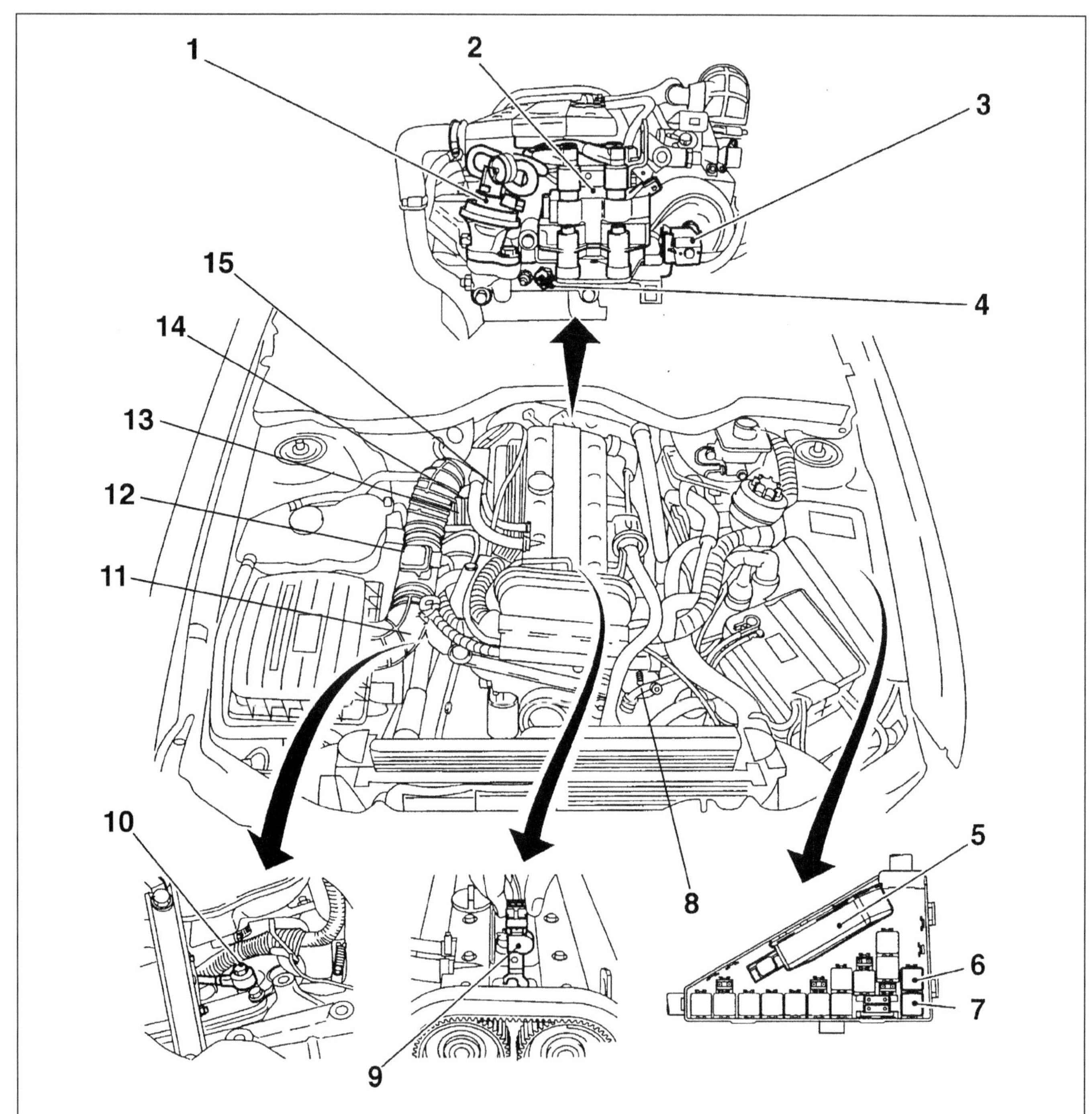

6.9 Engine management system component locations - 2.0 litre DOHC engine

1 Exhaust gas recirculation (EGR) valve
2 DIS module
3 Evaporative emission system purge valve
4 Coolant temperature sensor
5 Electronic control unit (ECU)
6 Fuel pump relay
7 Injection system relay
8 Crankshaft sensor
9 Camshaft sensor
10 Knock sensor
11 Intake air temperature sensor
12 Airflow meter
13 Idle speed adjuster valve
14 Throttle potentiometer
15 Fuel pressure regulator

further, a secondary air system is also incorporated. This is explained in greater detail in Part B of this Chapter.

13 The ECU also has full control over the multi-ram air intake system described in Section 17.

14 On some later models the original M2.8.1 system was replaced with the later M2.8.3 system. The M2.8.3 system is identical in operation to the earlier system but incorporates an additional power steering system sensor which informs the ECU when load is being placed on the steering pump. Modifications to the injection/ignition settings within the ECU also result in more efficient engine operation.

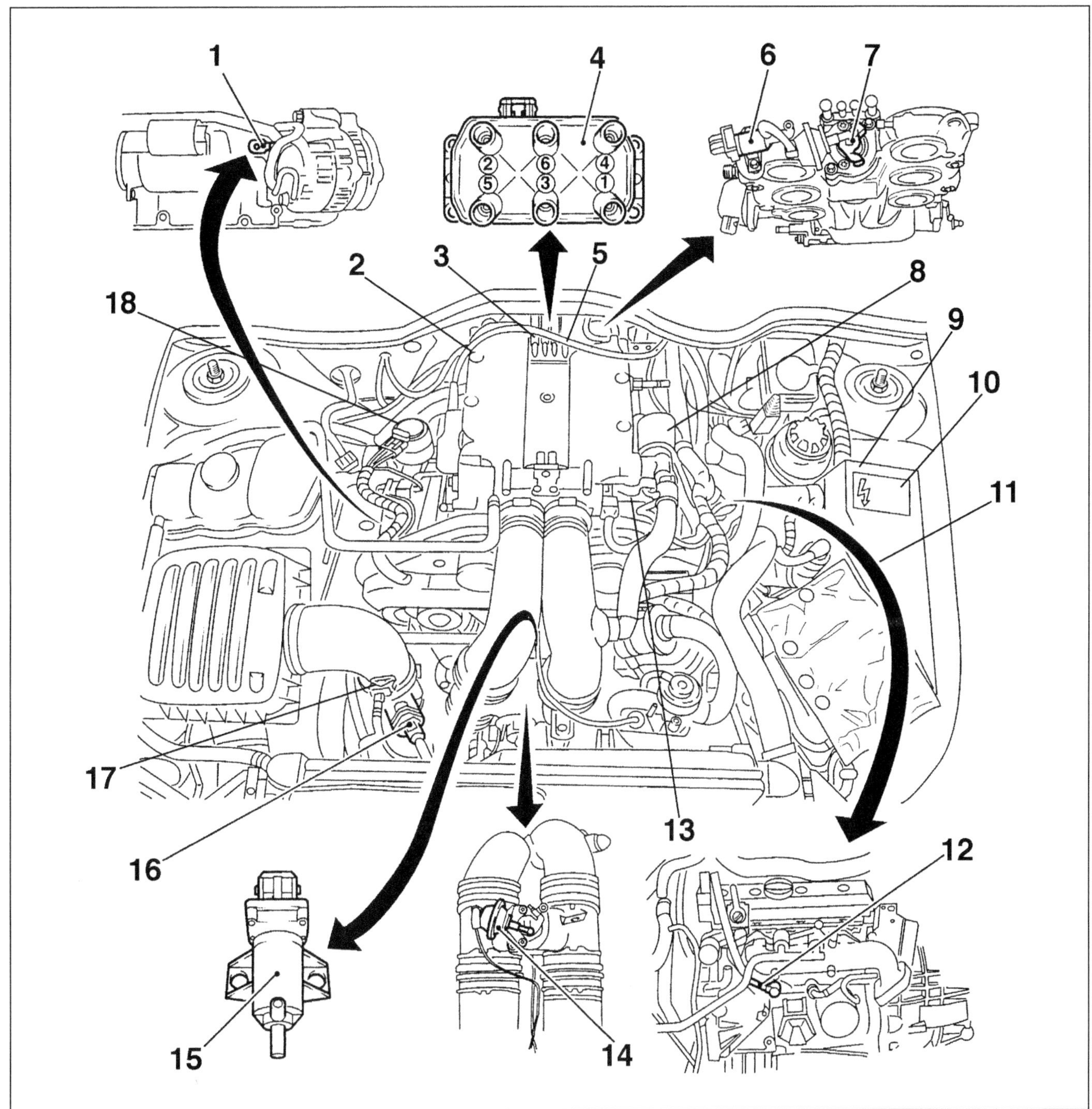

6.11 Engine management system component locations - 2.5 and 3.0 litre engine

1 Right-hand cylinder bank knock sensor
2 Evaporative emission system purge valve
3 Coolant temperature sensor
4 DIS module
5 Fuel pressure regulator
6 Inlet manifold switchover valve solenoid valve
7 Inlet manifold switchover valve
8 Idle speed adjuster valve
9 Fuel pump relay
10 Injection system relay
11 Electronic control unit (ECU)
12 Left-hand cylinder bank knock sensor
13 Camshaft sensor
14 Intake duct switchover valve
15 Intake duct switchover valve solenoid valve
16 Airflow meter
17 Intake air temperature sensor
18 Exhaust gas recirculation (EGR) valve

7.2a On 2.0 litre DOHC engines the fuel valve is located on the top of the fuel rail

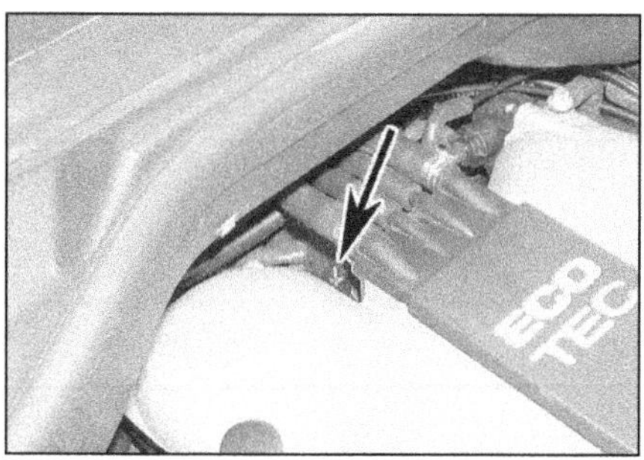

7.2b On 2.5 and 3.0 litre engines the fuel valve (arrowed) is located at the rear of the inlet manifold

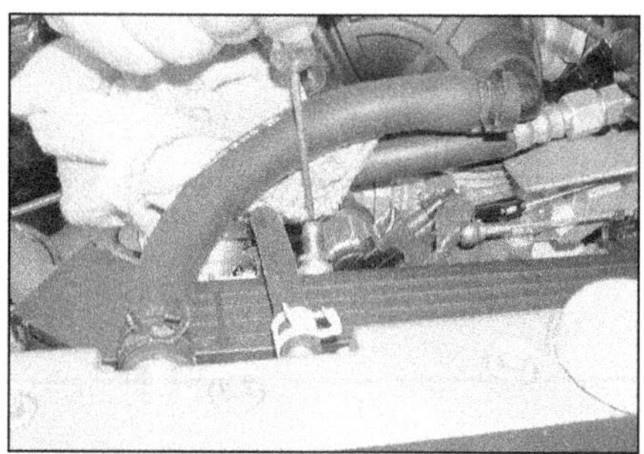

7.3 Place a wad of rag around the valve and depress the valve with a screwdriver to relieve the pressure in the fuel system

7 Fuel injection system - depressurisation

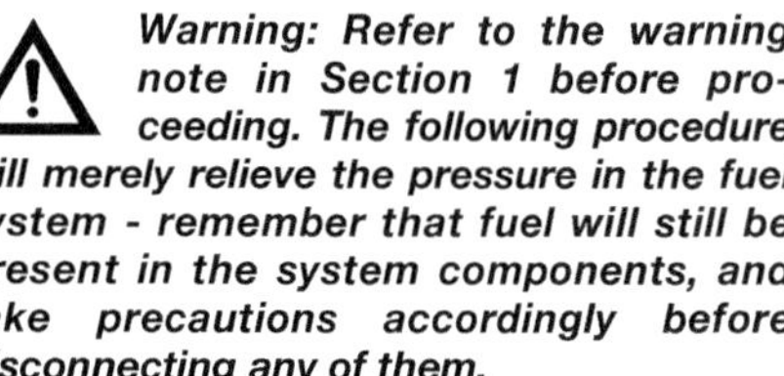

Warning: Refer to the warning note in Section 1 before proceeding. The following procedure will merely relieve the pressure in the fuel system - remember that fuel will still be present in the system components, and take precautions accordingly before disconnecting any of them.

1 The fuel system referred to in this Section is defined as the tank-mounted fuel pump, the fuel filter, the fuel injectors and the pressure regulator, and the metal pipes and flexible hoses of the fuel lines between these components. All these contain fuel which will be under pressure while the engine is running, and/or while the ignition is switched on. The pressure will remain for some time after the ignition has been switched off, and it must be relieved in a controlled fashion when any of these components are disturbed for servicing work.

2 Locate the valve assembly which is fitted to the fuel rail on the inlet manifold. On 2.0 litre engines it can be found on the top of the rail and on 2.5 and 3.0 litre engines it is located at the rear of the fuel rail, directly below the breather hose connections on the rear of the inlet manifold upper section **(see illustrations)**.

3 Unscrew the cap from the valve and position a container beneath the valve. Hold a wad of rag over the valve and relieve the pressure in the fuel system by depressing the valve core with a suitable screwdriver **(see illustration)**. Be prepared for the squirt of fuel as the valve core is depressed and catch it with the rag. Hold the valve core down until no more fuel is expelled from the valve.

4 Once all pressure is relieved, securely refit the valve cap.

8 Fuel pump - removal and refitting

Warning: Refer to the warning note in Section 1 before proceeding.

Note: *A new fuel pump cover sealing ring will be required on refitting.*

Removal

1 Depressurise the fuel system as described in Section 7 then disconnect the battery negative lead. **Note:** *On models with a Vauxhall anti-theft warning system (ATWS), the battery negative terminal must be disconnected within 15 seconds of the ignition being switched off to prevent the alarm system being triggered.*

2 On Saloon models lift up the luggage compartment carpet/floor to reveal the fuel pump access cover.

3 On Estate models lift up the luggage compartment floor then undo the fasteners and lift up the right-hand side section of the carpet to gain access to the fuel pump cover. If necessary, remove the CD autochanger as described in Chapter 12, Section 19.

4 Undo the retaining screws and remove the access cover from the floor to expose the fuel pump **(see illustration)**. Recover the cover gasket; it should be renewed if it is damaged.

5 Disconnect the wiring connector from the fuel pump cover and tape the connector to the vehicle body to prevent it disappearing behind the tank **(see illustration)**.

6 Mark the fuel hoses for identification purposes. Release the retaining clips and disconnect both hoses from the pump cover then plug the hose ends to minimise fuel loss **(see illustration)**. Where the hoses are fitted with quick-release fittings, compress the clips located on each side of the fitting and ease the fitting off of its union.

7 Unscrew the locking ring and remove it from the tank **(see illustration)**. This is best accomplished by using a screwdriver on the raised ribs of the locking ring. Tap the screwdriver to turn the ring anti-clockwise until it can be unscrewed by hand.

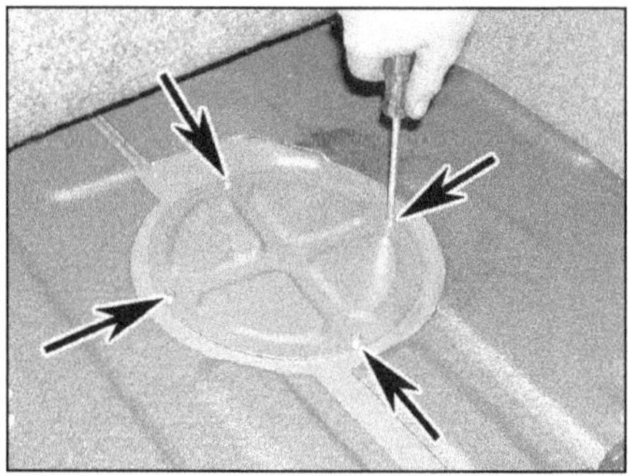

8.4 Undo the retaining screws (arrowed) and remove the access cover . . .

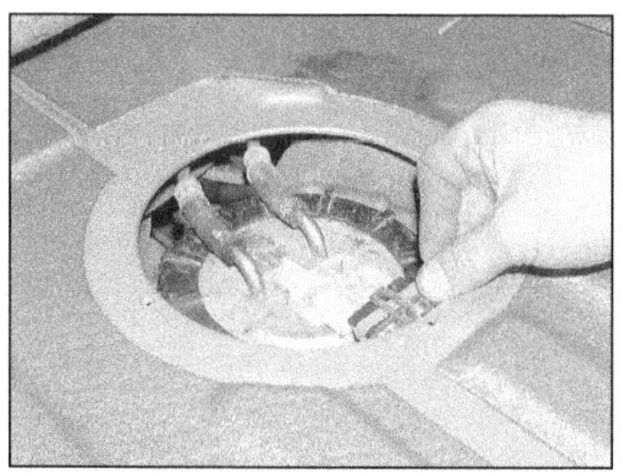

8.5 . . . then disconnect the wiring connector from the fuel pump cover

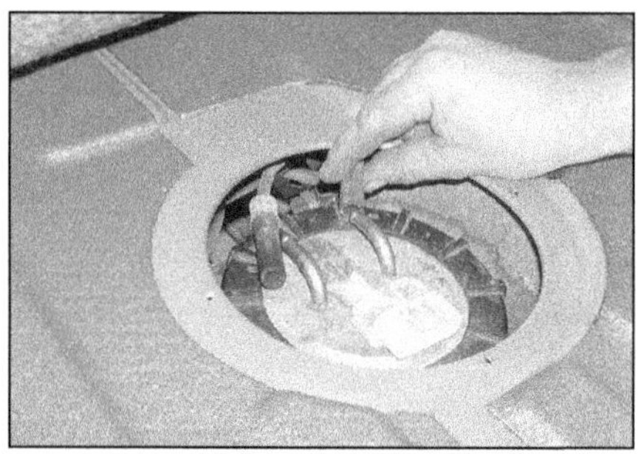

8.6 Release the retaining clips and disconnect the fuel hoses from the pump cover

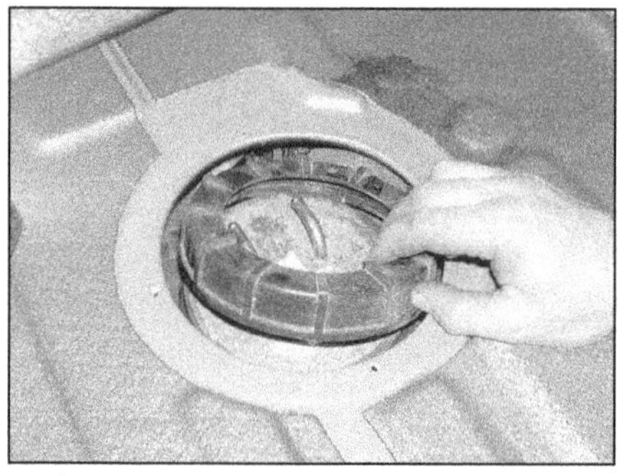

8.7 Unscrew and remove the locking ring . . .

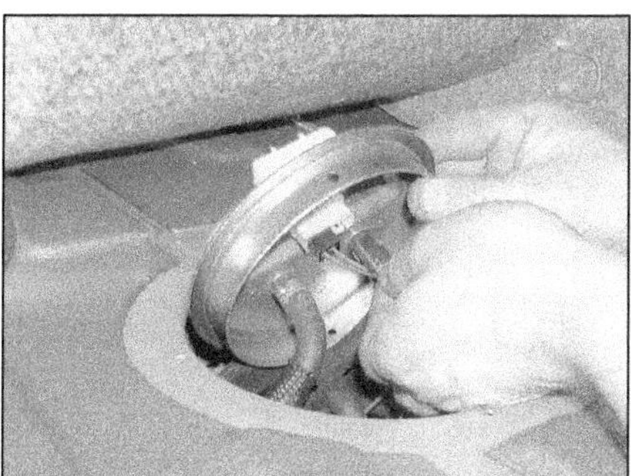

8.8a . . . then lift up pump cover and disconnect the wiring connector . . .

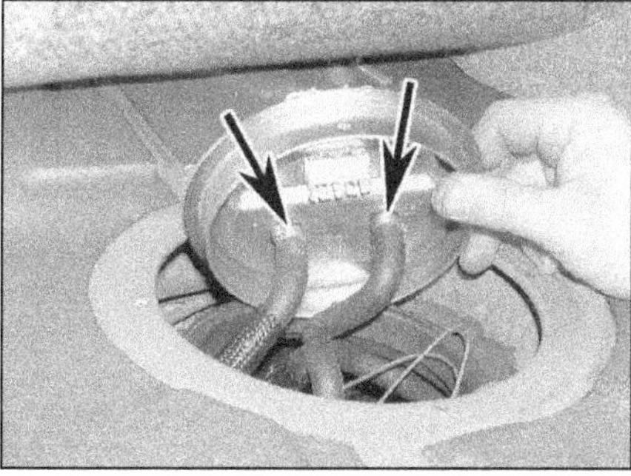

8.8b . . . and fuel hoses and remove the cover from the vehicle

8.9a Release the retaining clips and withdraw the pump housing assembly from the tank with a piece of welding rod

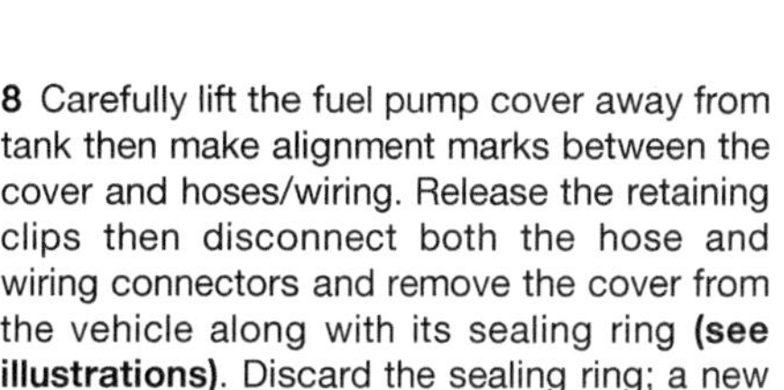

8 Carefully lift the fuel pump cover away from tank then make alignment marks between the cover and hoses/wiring. Release the retaining clips then disconnect both the hose and wiring connectors and remove the cover from the vehicle along with its sealing ring **(see illustrations)**. Discard the sealing ring; a new one must be used on refitting.

9 Release the three retaining clips by pressing them inwards then lift the fuel pump housing assembly out of the fuel tank using a piece of hooked welding rod engaged with the hole if the housing lug. As the pump is removed take great care not to displace the fuel filter which is fitted to the pump base and also try not to spill fuel onto the interior of the vehicle **(see illustrations)**.

10 Inspect the fuel filter for signs of damage or deterioration and renew if necessary.

11 If necessary the pump housing assembly can be dismantled and the pump removed, noting the wiring connectors correct locations.

Refitting

12 Where necessary, reassembly the pump and housing components ensuring the wiring connectors are correctly and securely reconnected.

13 Ensure the filter is securely fitted to the base of the pump then carefully manoeuvre the pump assembly into position, making sure it clips securely into position.

14 Fit a new sealing ring to the tank.

15 Reconnect the fuel hoses and wiring connectors to the pump cover, using the marks made on removal to ensure they are correctly reconnected. Secure the hoses in position with the retaining clips then seat the pump cover on the tank.

16 Refit the locking ring to the fuel tank and tighten it securely.

17 Reconnect the fuel hoses to the pump cover, ensuring each fitting clicks securely into position, and reconnect the wiring connector.

18 Reconnect the battery then start the engine and check for fuel leaks. If all is well, refit the access cover and gasket then lay the luggage compartment carpet/floor back in position.

9 Fuel gauge sender unit - removal and refitting

Warning: Refer to the warning note in Section 1 before proceeding.

Note: *A new fuel pump cover sealing ring will be required on refitting.*

Removal

1 Carry out the operations described in paragraphs 1 to 8 of Section 8 to remove the fuel pump cover.

2 The fuel gauge sender unit is clipped to the side of the fuel pump mounting reservoir. Carefully release the retaining clip then slide the sender unit upwards to release it from its mounting.

3 Manoeuvre the sender unit through the fuel tank aperture, taking great care not damage the float arm **(see illustration)**.

Refitting

4 Manoeuvre the sender unit carefully in through the tank aperture and slide it into position on the side of the fuel pump reservoir.

5 Ensure the sender unit is clipped securely in position then refit the fuel pump cover as described in paragraphs 14 to 18 of Section 8.

10 Fuel tank - removal and refitting

Warning: Refer to the warning note in Section 1 before proceeding.

Removal

1 Depressurise the fuel system as described in Section 7 then disconnect the battery negative terminal. **Note:** *On models with a Vauxhall anti-theft warning system (ATWS), the battery negative terminal must be disconnected within 15 seconds of the ignition being switched off to prevent the alarm system being triggered.*

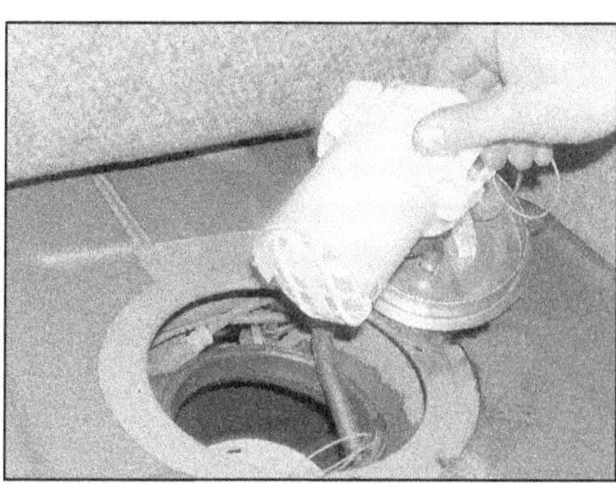

8.9b Ensure the pump filter is clean and undamaged

2 Before removing the fuel tank, all fuel must be drained from the tank. Since a fuel tank drain plug is not provided, it is therefore preferable to carry out the removal operation when the tank is nearly empty. The remaining fuel can then be siphoned or hand-pumped from the tank.

3 Open up the fuel filler flap and remove the rubber cover from around the filler neck aperture.

4 Chock the front wheels then jack up the rear of the vehicle and support it on axle stands. Remove the right-hand rear roadwheel.

5 Remove the retaining screws and fasteners and remove the wheelarch liner from the rear, right-hand arch then proceed as described under the relevant sub-heading.

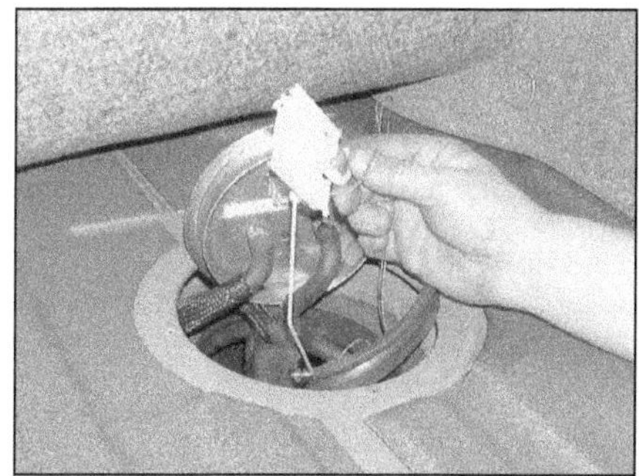

9.3 Removing the fuel gauge sender unit

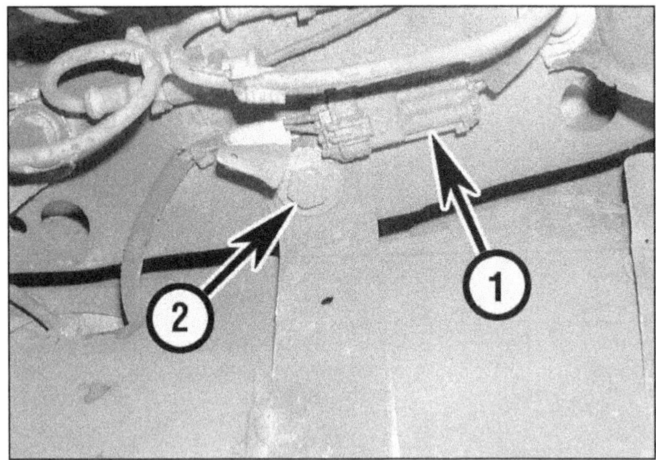

10.6 On Saloon models disconnect the pump/gauge sender unit wiring connector (1) which is located at the front of the fuel tank (2 is tank mounting bolt)

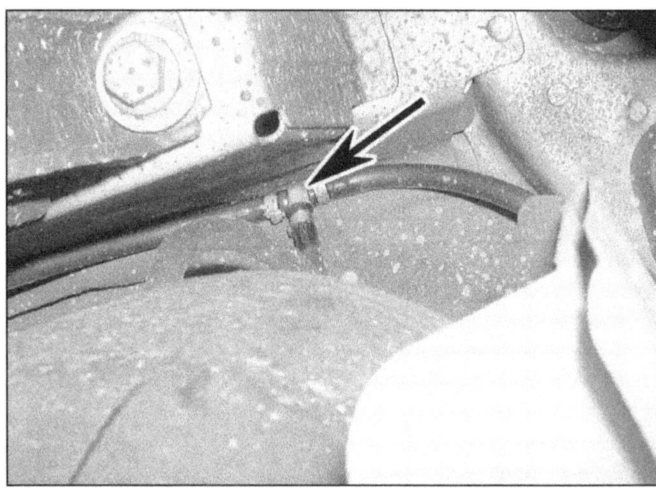

10.16 On Estate models locate the vent hose T-piece (arrowed) and disconnect the tank hoses

Saloon models

6 Locate the fuel pump/gauge sender unit wiring connector at the front of the fuel tank and disconnect the connector **(see illustration)**.

7 Trace the filler neck vent hose back to its connection on the right-hand side of the tank. Slacken the retaining clip and disconnect the hose so that it is free to be removed with the tank.

8 Trace the fuel feed and return hoses from the tank to their unions in front of the tank then mark the fuel hoses for identification purposes. The hoses are equipped with quick-release fittings to ease removal. To disconnect each hose, compress the clips located on each side of the fitting and ease the fitting off of its union. Disconnect both hoses from the top of the pump, noting the correct fitted position of the sealing rings and plug the hose ends to minimise fuel loss.

9 Place a trolley jack with an interposed block of wood beneath the tank, then raise the jack until it is supporting the weight of the tank.

10 Slacken and remove the retaining nut and bolts and remove the two retaining straps from underneath the fuel tank.

11 Slowly lower the fuel tank out of position, disconnecting any other relevant vent pipes as they become accessible (where necessary), and remove the tank from underneath the vehicle.

12 If the tank is contaminated with sediment or water, remove the fuel pump cover (Section 8), and swill the tank out with clean fuel. The tank is injection-moulded from a synthetic material - if seriously damaged, it should be renewed. However, in certain cases, it may be possible to have small leaks or minor damage repaired. Seek the advice of a specialist before attempting to repair the fuel tank.

Estate models

13 Lift up the luggage compartment floor then remove the fasteners and lift up the right-hand side section of the carpet to gain access to the fuel pump access cover. Undo the retaining screws and remove access cover from the floor to expose the fuel pump cover. Recover the cover gasket; it should be renewed if it is damaged.

14 Disconnect the wiring connector from the fuel pump cover and tape the connector to the vehicle body to prevent it disappearing behind the tank.

15 Release the retaining clip and disconnect the vent hose from the rear of the fuel tank.

16 Locate the vent hose T-piece on the front, left-hand corner of the fuel tank. Free the T-piece from its retaining clip then slacken the clips and detach both the tank hoses **(see illustration)**.

17 Remove the fuel tank as described in paragraphs 7 to 13 **(see illustration)**.

Refitting

18 Refitting is the reverse of the removal procedure, noting the following points:

a) *When lifting the tank back into position, take care to ensure that none of the hoses become trapped between the tank and vehicle body. Refit the retaining straps and tighten the nut and bolts to the specified torque.*

b) *Ensure all pipes and hoses are correctly routed and all hoses unions are securely joined.*

c) *On completion, refill the tank with a small amount of fuel, and check for signs of leakage prior to taking the vehicle out on the road.*

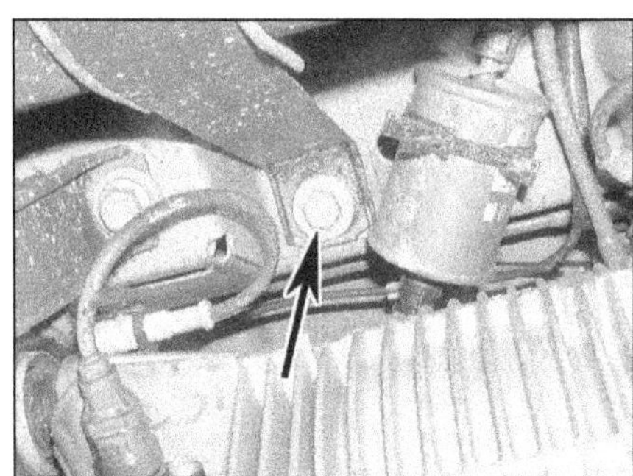

10.17 Fuel tank retaining bolt - Estate model

11 Throttle housing - removal and refitting

2.0 litre SOHC engine models

Removal

1 Disconnect the battery negative terminal. **Note:** *On models with a Vauxhall anti-theft warning system (ATWS), the battery negative terminal must be disconnected within 15 seconds of the ignition being switched off to prevent the alarm system being triggered.*

2 Disconnect the wiring connectors from the intake air temperature sensor and the airflow meter.

3 Slacken the retaining clips then disconnect the intake duct from the air cleaner and throttle housing and remove the duct assembly from the engine compartment.

4 Remove the retaining clip and detach the accelerator cable from the throttle cam balljoint and unclip the cable from its mounting bracket. On models with cruise control it will also be necessary to remove the second retaining clip and detach the cruise control cable.

5 Undo the retaining bolts and free the cable mounting bracket from the manifold noting the correct fitted location of the spring.

6 Clamp the coolant hoses which are connected to the rear of the throttle body then release the retaining clips and disconnect both hoses. Wipe away any spilt coolant.

7 Disconnect the wiring connectors from the throttle potentiometer and the idle speed adjuster.

8 Disconnect the vacuum/breather hoses from the throttle body, noting their correct

11.11 Disconnect the wiring connectors from the intake air temperature sensor and the airflow meter (arrowed)

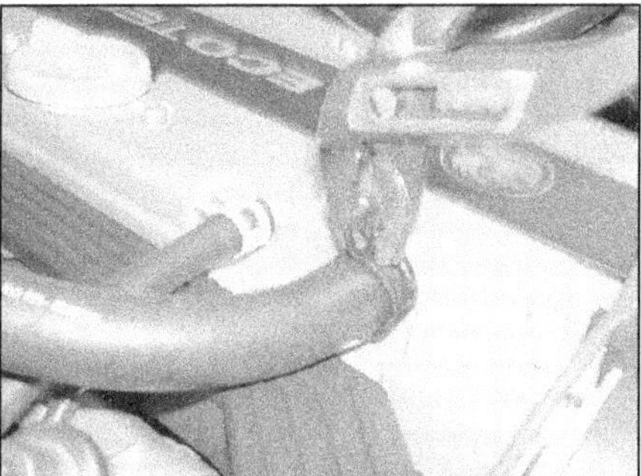
11.12a Disconnect the breather hose from the cylinder head cover . . .

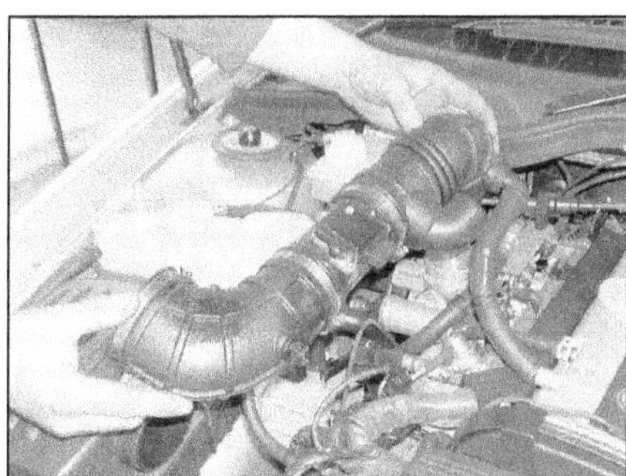
11.12b . . . then release the retaining clips and remove the intake duct assembly from the engine compartment

fitted locations, then undo the retaining nuts and remove the housing from the manifold. Remove the gasket and discard it, a new one should be used on refitting.

Refitting

9 Refitting is the reverse of removal, bearing in mind the following points.

a) Ensure the mating surfaces are clean and dry then fit a new gasket and tighten the housing nuts to the specified torque.

b) Ensure all hoses are correctly and securely reconnected.

c) On completion adjust the accelerator cable as described in Section 3.

2.0 litre DOHC engine models

Warning: Refer to the warning note in Section 1 before proceeding.

Removal

10 Disconnect the battery negative terminal then depressurise the fuel system as described in Section 7. **Note:** *On models with a Vauxhall anti-theft warning system (ATWS), the battery negative terminal must be disconnected within 15 seconds of the ignition being switched off to prevent the alarm system being triggered.*

11 Disconnect the wiring connectors from the intake air temperature sensor and the airflow meter **(see illustration)**.

12 Slacken the retaining clip and disconnect the intake duct breather hose from the cylinder head cover. Slacken the retaining clips then disconnect the intake duct from the air cleaner and throttle housing and remove the duct assembly from the engine compartment **(see illustrations)**.

13 Remove the retaining clip and detach the accelerator cable from the throttle cam balljoint and unclip the cable from its mounting bracket. On models with cruise control it will also be necessary to remove the second retaining clip and detach the cruise control cable.

14 Unscrew the nut and disconnect the fuel feed hose from its union on the rear of the fuel rail. As the union nut is slackened, retain the pipe end fitting with an open-ended spanner to prevent any excess strain being placed on the pipe. Plug the hose and pipe ends to minimise fuel loss and prevent the entry of dirt then undo the retaining bolt securing the fuel pipe to the throttle housing bracket **(see illustration)**.

15 Clamp the coolant hoses which are connected to the throttle housing then release the retaining clips and disconnect both hoses **(see illustration)**. Wipe away any spilt coolant.

16 Disconnect the wiring connectors from the throttle potentiometer and the idle speed adjuster.

17 Disconnect the vacuum hose(s) from the throttle body, noting their correct fitted locations, then undo the retaining nuts and remove the housing from the manifold. Remove the gasket and discard it, a new one should be used on refitting.

Refitting

18 Refitting is the reverse of removal, bearing in mind the following points.

a) Ensure the mating surfaces are clean and dry then fit a new gasket and tighten the housing nuts to the specified torque.

b) Ensure all hoses are correctly and securely reconnected.

c) On completion adjust the accelerator cable as described in Section 3.

2.5 and 3.0 litre engines

Removal

19 Remove the inlet manifold upper section as described in Section 15.

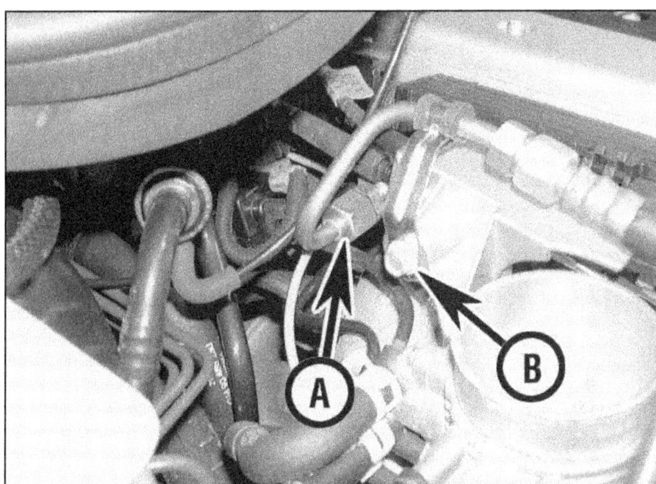

11.14 Unscrew the fuel feed pipe union nut (A) then undo the pipe retaining bolt (B)

11.15 Release the retaining clips and disconnect the coolant hoses (arrowed) from the throttle housing

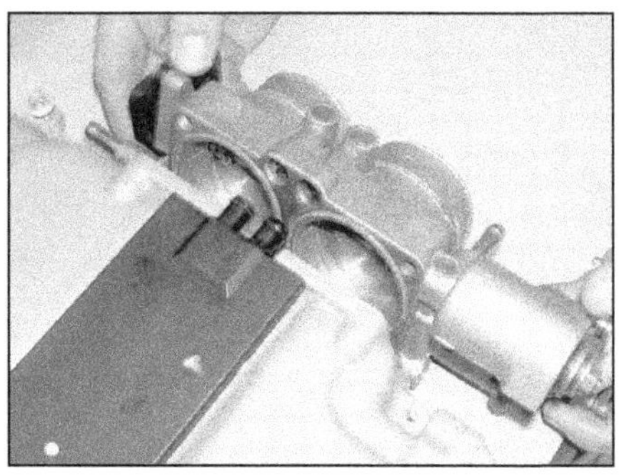

11.20 Removing the throttle housing - 2.5 and 3.0 litre engines

20 Slacken and remove the retaining bolts and separate the throttle body from the manifold **(see illustration)**. Recover the large sealing rings from the throttle body bores and the small rings from the manifold breather passages and discard them; new sealing rings should be used on refitting.

Refitting

21 Fit new sealing rings to the manifold breather passages and the throttle body bores then carefully ease the throttle housing assembly into position on the manifold upper section, ensuring all the sealing rings remain correctly seated **(see illustration)**.

22 Tighten the throttle body retaining bolts to the specified torque then refit the manifold upper section as described in Section 15.

12 Fuel injection system - testing and adjustment

Testing

1 If a fault appears in the fuel injection system, first ensure that all the system wiring connectors are securely connected and free of corrosion. Ensure that the fault is not due to poor maintenance; ie, check that the air cleaner filter element is clean, the spark plugs are in good condition and correctly gapped, the cylinder compression pressures are correct, and that the engine breather hoses are clear and undamaged, referring to Chapters 1 and 2A, 2B or 2C for further information (as applicable).

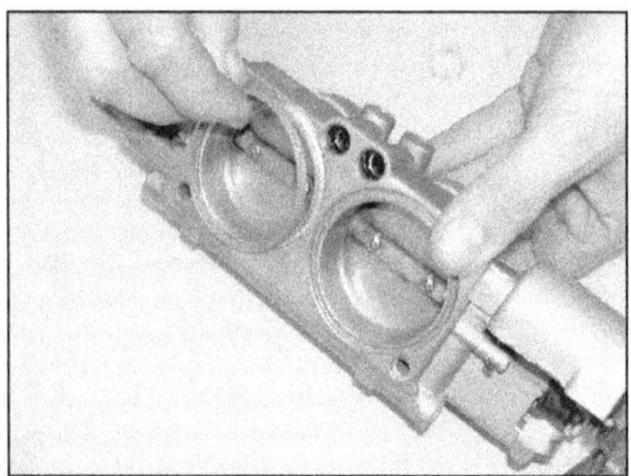

11.21 On refitting, fit new sealing rings to the throttle housing recesses

2 If these checks fail to reveal the cause of the problem, the vehicle should be taken to a suitably-equipped Vauxhall dealer for testing. A wiring block connector is incorporated in the engine management circuit, into which a special electronic diagnostic tester can be plugged (see Section 6). The tester will locate the fault quickly and simply, alleviating the need to test all the system components individually, which is a time-consuming operation that carries a risk of damaging the ECU.

Adjustment

3 Experienced home mechanics with a considerable amount of skill and equipment (including a tachometer and an accurately calibrated exhaust gas analyser) may be able to check the exhaust CO level and the idle speed. However, if these are found to be in need of adjustment, the car will have to be taken to a suitably-equipped Vauxhall dealer who has access to the necessary diagnostic equipment required to test and (where possible) adjust the settings.

13 Fuel injection system components (2.0 litre engine) - removal and refitting

Fuel injector

Warning: Refer to the warning note in Section 1 before proceeding.

Note: *If a faulty injector is suspected, before condemning the injector, it is worth trying the effect of one of the proprietary injector-cleaning treatments.*

SOHC engine

1 Depressurise the fuel system as described in Section 7 then disconnect the battery negative terminal. **Note:** *On models with a Vauxhall anti-theft warning system (ATWS), the battery negative terminal must be disconnected within 15 seconds of the ignition being switched off to prevent the alarm system being triggered.*

2 Disconnect the vacuum hoses from the inlet manifold and fuel pressure regulator and position the hose clear of the fuel rail.

3 Remove the retaining clip and detach the accelerator cable from the throttle cam balljoint and unclip the cable from its mounting bracket. On models with cruise control it will also be necessary to remove the second retaining clip and detach the cruise control cable.

4 Undo the retaining bolts and free the cable mounting bracket from the manifold noting the correct fitted location of the spring.

5 Unscrew the union bolts and disconnect the fuel feed and return hoses from the fuel rail. Recover the sealing washers from each hose union and discard; new ones should be used on refitting.

6 Release the retaining clips and disconnect the wiring connectors from the injectors.

7 Unscrew the nut and detach the earth lead from the fuel rail rear retaining bolt.

8 Slacken and remove the retaining bolts then carefully ease the fuel rail and injector assembly out of position and remove it from the manifold. Remove the lower sealing rings from the injectors and discard them; they must be renewed whenever they are disturbed.

9 Slide off the relevant retaining clip and withdraw the injector from the fuel rail. Remove the upper sealing ring from the injector and discard it; all disturbed sealing rings must be renewed.

10 Refitting is a reversal of the removal procedure, noting the following points.

a) *Renew all disturbed sealing rings and apply a smear of engine oil to them to aid installation.*

b) *Ease the injector(s) into the fuel rail, ensuring that the sealing ring(s) remain correctly seated, and secure in position with the retaining clips.*

c) *On refitting the fuel rail, take care not to damage the injectors and ensure that all sealing rings remain in position. Once the fuel rail is correctly seated, tighten its retaining bolts to the specified torque.*

d) *Fit new sealing washers to each side of the fuel feed and return hose unions then screw in the union bolts. Ensure both hose unions are correctly positioned then tighten the unions bolts to the specified torque.*

e) *On completion start the engine and check for fuel leaks. Adjust the accelerator cable as described in Section 3.*

DOHC engine

11 Depressurise the fuel system as described in Section 7 then disconnect the battery negative terminal. **Note:** *On models with a Vauxhall anti-theft warning system (ATWS), the battery negative terminal must be disconnected within 15 seconds of the ignition being switched off to prevent the alarm system being triggered.*

12 Release the retaining clips and disconnect the breather hoses from the right-hand side of the cylinder head cover. Also disconnect the vacuum hose from the fuel pressure regulator.

13 Disconnect the wiring connectors from the intake air temperature sensor and the airflow meter.

14 Slacken the retaining clips then disconnect the intake duct from the air cleaner and throttle housing and remove the duct assembly from the engine compartment, freeing it from the wiring harness.

15 Remove the retaining clip and detach the accelerator cable from the throttle cam balljoint and unclip the cable from its mounting bracket. On models with cruise control it will also be necessary to detach the cruise control cable.

16 Unscrew the nuts and disconnect the fuel feed hose from its union on the rear of the fuel rail and the return pipe from the front end of the fuel rail. As the union nuts are slackened, retain the pipe end fitting with an open-ended spanner to prevent any excess strain being placed on the pipe. Plug the hose and pipe ends to minimise fuel loss and prevent the entry of dirt then undo the retaining bolt securing the fuel feed rail pipe to the throttle housing bracket **(see illustrations)**.

17 Disconnect the wiring connector from the idle control stepper motor then undo the retaining bolts and free the cable mounting bracket from the throttle housing, noting the correct fitted location of the spring.

18 Unscrew the retaining nut and detach the earth lead from the fuel rail front retaining bolt.

19 Carefully release the retaining clips and lift off the injector wiring cover assembly squarely away from the top of the injectors; the wiring connectors are an integral part of the cover. Disconnect the crankshaft sensor and knock sensor wiring connectors (where necessary) from the underside of the injector wiring cover then position the cover assembly clear of the fuel rail.

20 Slacken and remove the retaining bolts then carefully ease the fuel rail and injector assembly out of position and remove it from the manifold. Remove the lower sealing rings from the injectors and discard them; they must be renewed whenever they are disturbed.

21 Slide off the relevant retaining clip and withdraw the injector from the fuel rail. Remove the upper sealing ring from the injector and discard it; all disturbed sealing rings must be renewed.

22 Refitting is a reversal of the removal procedure, noting the following points.

a) *Renew all disturbed sealing rings and apply a smear of engine oil to them to aid installation.*
b) *Ease the injector(s) into the fuel rail, ensuring that the sealing ring(s) remain correctly seated, and secure in position with the retaining clips. Ensure that the retaining clips are correctly positioned otherwise it will not be possible to refit the wiring cover assembly.*
c) *On refitting the fuel rail, take care not to damage the injectors and ensure that all sealing rings remain in position. Once the fuel rail is correctly seated, tighten its retaining bolts to the specified torque.*
d) *On completion, adjust the accelerator cable as described in Section 3 then start the engine and check for fuel leaks.*

Fuel pressure regulator

Warning: Refer to the warning note in Section 1 before proceeding.

23 Depressurise the fuel system as described in Section 7 then disconnect the battery negative terminal. **Note:** *On models with a Vauxhall anti-theft warning system (ATWS), the battery negative terminal must be disconnected within 15 seconds of the ignition being switched off to prevent the alarm system being triggered.*

24 Disconnect the vacuum hose from the regulator **(see illustration)**.

25 Slacken the retaining clamp then carefully ease the pressure regulator out from the top of the fuel rail. Remove the both sealing rings from the regulator and discard them; new ones must be used on refitting.

26 Refitting is the reverse of removal, using new sealing rings and lubricating them with a smear of engine oil to ease installation. Ensure the regulator is correctly positioned then tighten the retaining clamp screw to the specified torque. On completion start the engine and check for signs of fuel leakage.

Idle speed adjuster valve

27 On DOHC engines, disconnect the wiring connectors from the intake air temperature sensor and the airflow meter then slacken the retaining clips then disconnect the intake duct from the air cleaner and throttle housing. Position the duct assembly clear of the throttle housing to improve access to the adjuster valve.

28 On all engines, disconnect the wiring connector then undo the retaining screws and remove the motor assembly from the side of the throttle housing. Remove the gasket and discard it; a new one should be used on refitting.

29 Refitting is the reverse of removal using a new gasket.

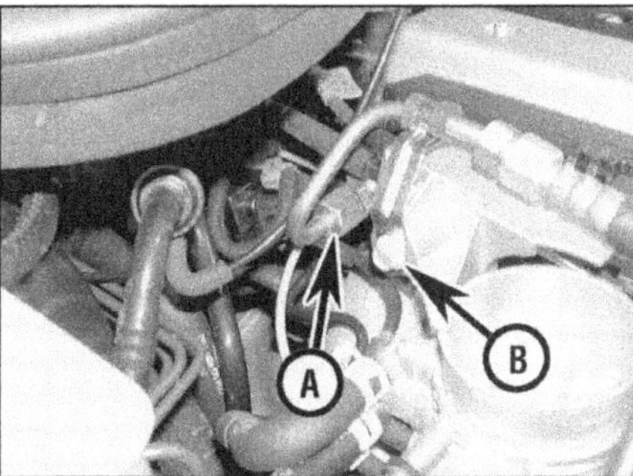

13.16a Unscrew the fuel feed pipe union nut (A) and bolt (B) . . .

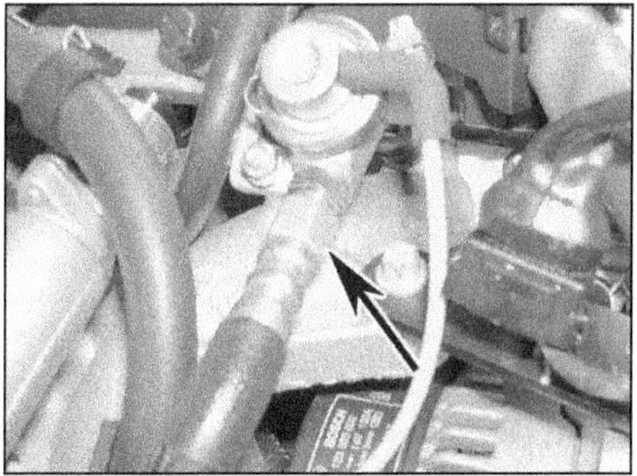

13.16b . . . and the fuel return pipe union nut

Throttle potentiometer

30 Ensure the ignition is switched off then disconnect the wiring connector from the throttle potentiometer which is fitted to the throttle housing.

31 Slacken and remove the retaining screws then remove the potentiometer from the housing **(see illustration)**.

32 Refitting is the reverse of removal making sure the potentiometer is correctly engaged with the throttle valve spindle.

Coolant temperature sensor

SOHC engine

33 The coolant temperature sensor is screwed into the front, right-hand end of the cylinder head. Refer to Chapter 3, Section 7 for removal and refitting details noting that it maybe necessary to unbolt the upper mounting brackets and pivot the alternator away from the cylinder block to gain the necessary clearance required to remove the sensor.

DOHC engine

34 The coolant temperature sensor is screwed into the rear of the cylinder head where it is located beneath the DIS module. Refer to Chapter 3, Section 7 for removal and refitting details.

Intake air temperature sensor

35 Ensure ignition is switched off then disconnect the wiring connector from the sensor.

36 Slacken the retaining clips then detach the intake duct from the airflow meter and air

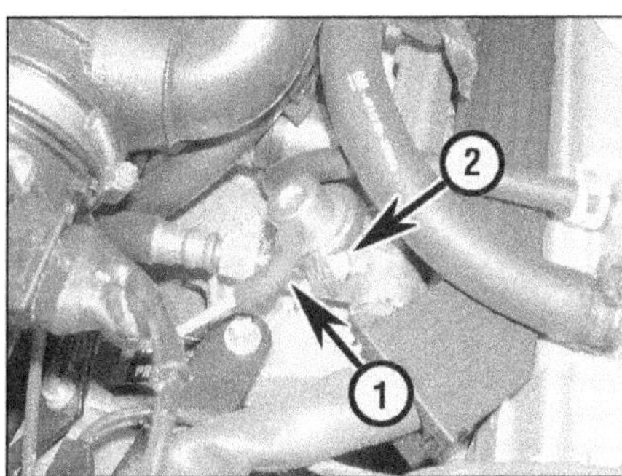

13.24 Fuel pressure regulator vacuum hose (1) and retaining clamp (2)

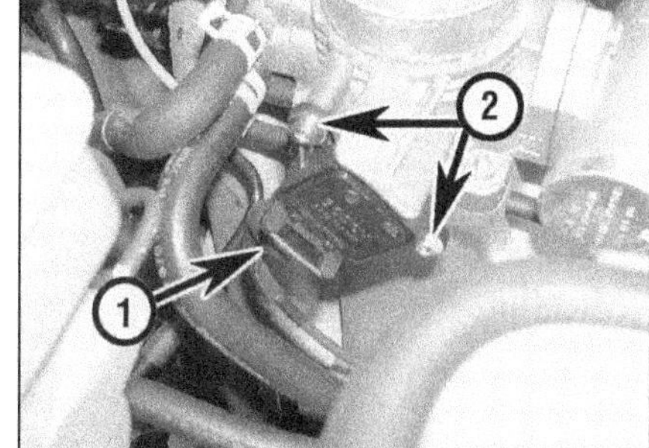

13.31 Disconnect the wiring connector (1) then undo the retaining screws (2) and remove the throttle potentiometer

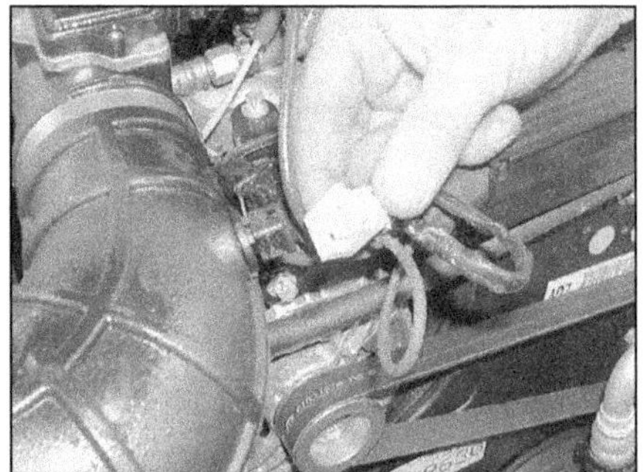
13.36a Disconnect the wiring connector from the intake air temperature sensor . . .

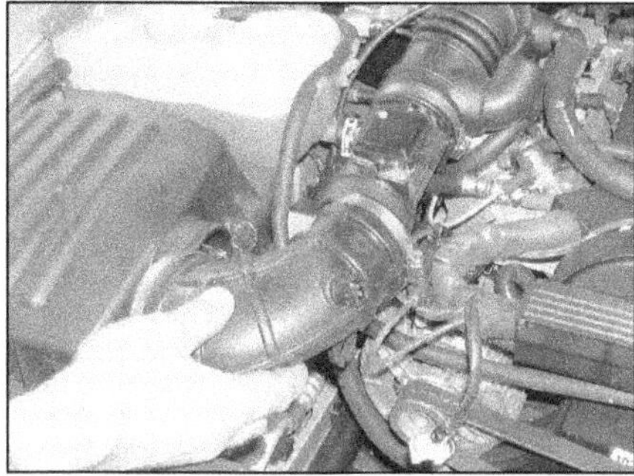
13.36b . . . then slacken the retaining clips and remove the intake duct

cleaner housing and remove it from the vehicle **(see illustrations)**.

37 Carefully ease the sensor out of position, taking great care not to damage the duct.

38 Refitting is the reverse of removal noting that the sensor must be fitted so that its flat edge aligns with the flat on the intake duct. Aid installation by lubricating the duct with a silicone-based spray.

Airflow meter

39 Ensure the ignition is switched off then disconnect the wiring connector from the airflow meter and intake air temperature sensor **(see illustration)**.

40 Slacken the retaining clips then detach the intake duct from the airflow meter and air cleaner housing and remove it from the vehicle.

41 Slacken the retaining clip then remove the airflow meter from the vehicle **(see illustration)**. Inspect the meter for signs of damage and renew if necessary.

42 Refitting is the reverse of removal ensuring the intake ducts are correctly engaged with the meter recesses.

Crankshaft sensor

SOHC engine

43 Remove the timing belt front cover as described in Chapter 2A. The sensor is mounted on the left-hand side of the cylinder block, beneath the power steering pump.

44 To improve access, firmly apply the handbrake then jack up the front of the vehicle and support it securely on axle stands. Undo the retaining screws and remove the undercover from beneath the engine.

45 On models with air conditioning, to improve access to the sensor remove the engine/transmission left-hand mounting and mounting bracket from the cylinder block (see Chapter 2A).

46 Work back along the sensor wiring and release it from all the relevant clips and ties whilst noting its correct routing. Disconnect the wiring connector so the wiring is free to be removed with the sensor.

47 Unscrew the retaining bolt and remove the sensor from the front of the cylinder block, along with its sealing ring. Discard the sealing ring, a new one should be used on refitting.

48 Refitting is the reverse of removal using a new sealing ring and tightening the sensor bolt to the specified torque. Ensure the wiring is correctly routed and retained by all the necessary clips before refitting the timing belt cover (see Chapter 2A).

DOHC engine

49 The sensor is fitted to the left-hand side of the cylinder block, beneath the power steering pump. Removal and refitting is as follows.

50 Firmly apply the handbrake then jack up the front of the vehicle and support it securely on axle stands. Undo the retaining screws and remove the undercover from beneath the engine.

51 Trace the wiring back from the sensor, over the top of the cylinder head to its wiring connector. On early models the connector is connected to the underside of the front of the injector wiring cover assembly whereas on later models it is connected to the engine harness connector on the front of the engine.

52 Release the retaining clip and disconnect the crankshaft sensor connector from the injector cover/engine harness (as applicable) **(see illustration)**. On early models if the connector proves difficult to disconnect, free the injector wiring cover from the injectors as described earlier in this section then disconnect the connector.

53 Work along the sensor wiring, releasing it from all the relevant clips and ties whilst noting its correct routing.

54 On models with air conditioning, to improve access to the sensor remove the engine/transmission left-hand mounting and mounting bracket from the cylinder block (see Chapter 2B).

55 Unscrew the retaining bolt and remove the sensor from the front of the cylinder block, along with its sealing ring. Discard the sealing ring, a new one should be used on refitting.

56 Refitting is the reverse of removal using a new sealing ring and tightening the sensor bolt to the specified torque. Ensure the wiring is correctly routed and retained by all the necessary clips and ties.

Knock sensor

SOHC engine

57 The knock sensor is mounted onto the centre of the right-hand side of the cylinder block. To improve access, firmly apply the handbrake then jack up the front of the vehicle and support it on axle stands so the sensor can also be reached from below.

58 Ensure the ignition is switched off then disconnect the wiring connector from the sensor.

59 Slacken and remove the retaining bolt and remove the sensor from the engine.

60 On refitting ensure the mating surfaces are clean and dry. Fit the sensor then tighten its retaining bolt to the specified torque and reconnect the wiring connector.

DOHC engine

61 The sensor is fitted to the centre of the right-hand side of the cylinder block. Removal and refitting is as follows.

62 Firmly apply the handbrake then jack up the front of the vehicle and support it securely on axle stands. Undo the retaining screws and remove the undercover from beneath the engine.

13.39 Disconnect the wiring connector from the airflow meter

13.41 Removing the airflow meter

13.52 On later models the crankshaft sensor wiring connector (arrowed) is easily accessible

13.75a Slide out the ECU then lift the retaining clip . . .

63 If necessary, to improve access, remove the starter motor as described in Chapter 5A.

64 Trace the wiring back from the sensor to its wiring connector. On early models the connector is connected to the underside of the injector wiring cover assembly (in between number 3 and 4 injectors) whereas on later models it is connected to the engine harness connector located on the underside of the inlet manifold.

65 Release the retaining clip and disconnect the crankshaft sensor connector from the injector cover/engine harness (as applicable). On early models if the connector proves difficult to disconnect, free the injector wiring cover from the injectors as described earlier in this section then disconnect the connector.

66 Work along the sensor wiring, releasing it from all the relevant clips and ties whilst noting its correct routing.

67 Slacken and remove the retaining bolt and remove the sensor from the engine.

68 On refitting ensure the mating surfaces are clean and dry then fit the sensor and tighten its retaining bolt to the specified torque. Ensure the wiring is correctly routed and securely reconnected.

Camshaft sensor - DOHC engine

69 Undo the retaining screws and remove the spark plug cover from the top of the cylinder head cover.

70 Ensure the ignition is switched off then disconnect the wiring connector from the camshaft sensor.

71 Remove the timing belt front cover as described in Chapter 2B.

13.75b . . . and disconnect its wiring connector

72 Unscrew the retaining bolt and remove the camshaft sensor from the top of the cylinder head.

73 Refitting is the reverse of removal tightening the sensor retaining bolt to the specified torque.

Electronic control unit (ECU)

74 Disconnect the battery negative terminal then unclip the lid from the engine compartment relay box. **Note:** *On models with a Vauxhall anti-theft warning system (ATWS), the battery negative terminal must be disconnected within 15 seconds of the ignition being switched off to prevent the alarm system being triggered.*

75 Slide the ECU out of position until access to the wiring connector retaining clip can be gained. Lift the retaining clip and carefully disconnect the wiring connector then remove the ECU from the vehicle **(see illustrations)**. If necessary, undo the retaining nuts and separate the ECU from its mounting plate.

76 Refitting is the reverse of removal making sure the wiring connector is correctly reconnected. On later DOHC engines (with Simtec 56.5 system) if a new ECU has been fitted it will be necessary to take the vehicle to a Vauxhall dealer to have the unit coded to match the performance of your engine.

Injection system relays

77 The injection system relays are located in the engine compartment relay box.

78 Unclip the lid from the relay box. The injection system relays are the two relays situated at the rear of the box; the fuel pump

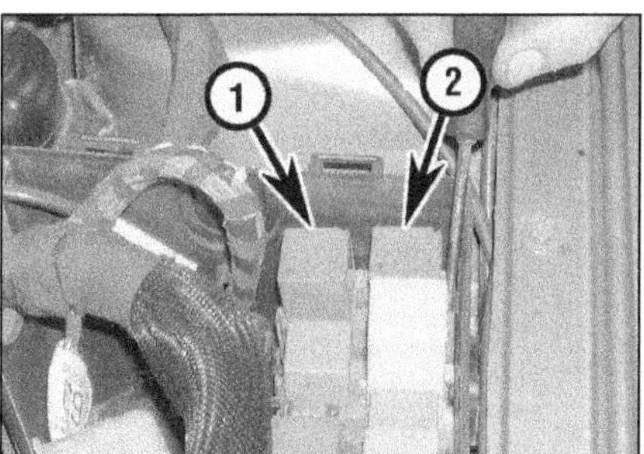

13.78 The fuel pump relay (1) and injection system relay (2) are located in the engine compartment relay box

relay is the right-hand (inner) relay of the two and the injection system/protection relay is the left-hand (outer) relay **(see illustration)**.

79 Ensure the ignition is switched off then pull the relevant relay out of its socket and remove it from the vehicle **(see illustration)**.

80 Refitting is the reverse of removal.

Air conditioning system switch

81 The air conditioning system switch is screwed into one of the refrigerant pipes and cannot be removed without first discharging the refrigerant (see Chapter 3). Renewal of the switch should therefore be entrusted to a suitably equipped garage.

14 Fuel injection system components (2.5 and 3.0 litre engines) - removal and refitting

Fuel injector

Warning: Refer to the warning note in Section 1 before proceeding.

Note: *If a faulty injector is suspected, before condemning the injector, it is worth trying the effect of one of the proprietary injector-cleaning treatments.*

1 Remove the lower section of the inlet manifold as described in Section 15.

2 Depress the retaining clips and disconnect the wiring connectors from the six injectors. Unclip the wiring harness cover from the top of the fuel rail and remove it from the manifold **(see illustrations)**.

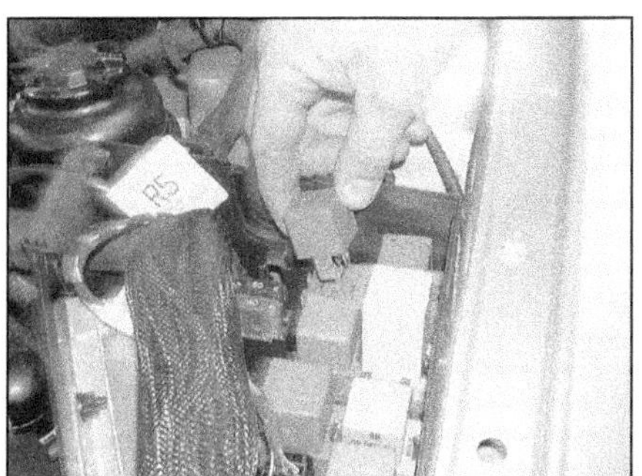

13.79 Removing the fuel pump relay

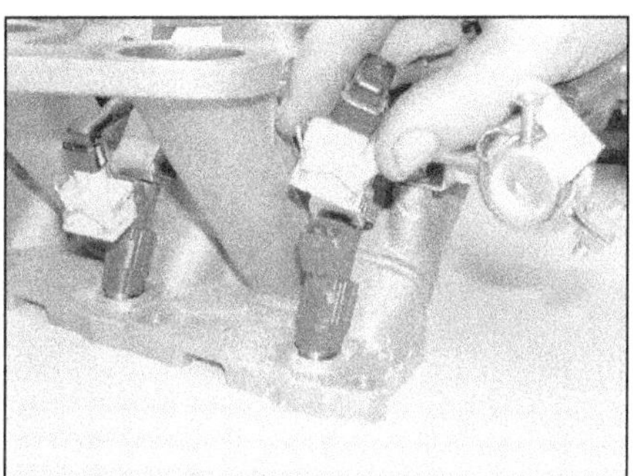

14.2a Disconnect the wiring connectors from the injectors . . .

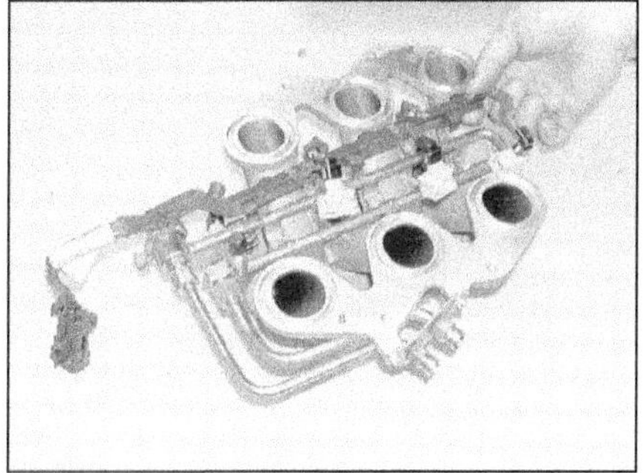

14.2b . . . then unclip the cover assembly from the fuel rail

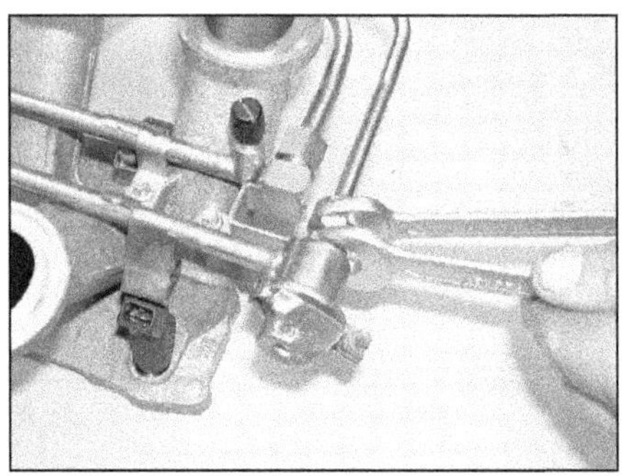
14.3a Slacken the union nuts . . .

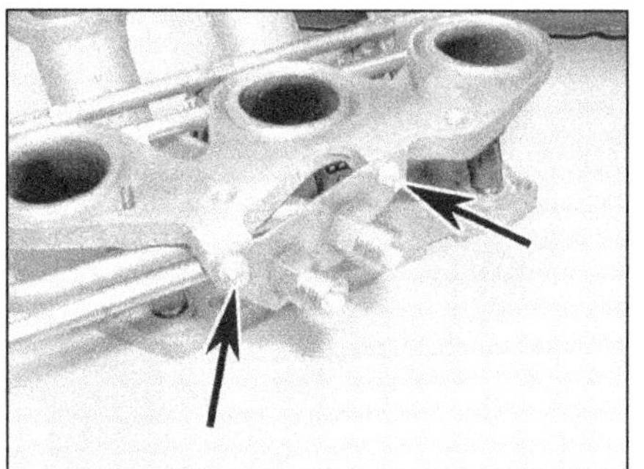
14.3b . . . then undo the retaining bolts (arrowed) . . .

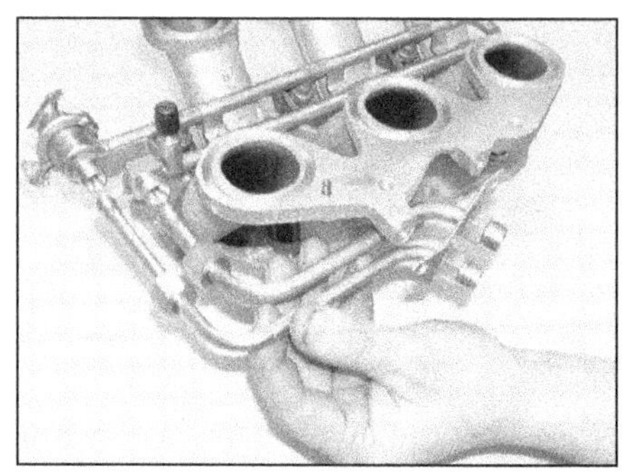
14.3c . . . and remove the fuel pipes from the manifold

3 Slacken the union nuts securing the fuel pipes to the fuel rail whilst (where possible) retaining the fuel rail with an open-ended spanner. Unscrew the retaining bolts and remove the pipe assembly from the manifold lower section **(see illustrations)**.

4 Slacken and remove the retaining bolts then carefully ease the fuel rail and injector assembly out from the manifold. Remove the lower sealing rings from the injectors and discard them. Slide off the relevant retaining clip and withdraw the injector from the fuel rail. Remove the upper sealing ring from the injector and discard it. All disturbed sealing rings must be renewed **(see illustrations)**.

5 Refitting is a reversal of the removal procedure, noting the following points.

a) Renew all disturbed sealing rings and apply a smear of engine oil to them to aid installation **(see illustration)**.

b) Ease the injector(s) into the fuel rail, ensuring that the sealing ring(s) remain correctly seated, and secure in position with the retaining clips.

c) On refitting the fuel rail, take care not to damage the injectors and ensure that all sealing rings remain in position. Once the fuel rail is correctly seated, tighten its retaining bolts to the specified torque.

d) Tighten the fuel pipe union nuts and retaining bolts to the specified torque then refit the wiring cover assembly making sure all the wiring connectors are securely reconnected.

e) Refit the manifold as described in Section 15. On completion start the engine and check for fuel leaks.

Fuel pressure regulator

Warning: Refer to the warning note in Section 1 before proceeding.

6 Depressurise the fuel system as described in Section 7 then disconnect the battery negative terminal. **Note:** *On models with a Vauxhall anti-theft warning system (ATWS), the battery negative terminal must be disconnected within 15 seconds of the ignition being switched off to prevent the alarm system being triggered.*

7 To gain access to the pressure regulator, remove the windscreen wiper arms and the water deflector panel from the base of the windscreen (see Chapter 12, Sections 15 and 16) **(see illustration)**.

8 Unclip the wiring connector holder from the lifting bracket on the rear of the cylinder head and position the wiring clear of the regulator.

9 Disconnect the vacuum hose from the fuel pressure regulator.

10 Slacken the retaining clamp then carefully ease the pressure regulator out from the fuel rail. Remove both sealing rings from the

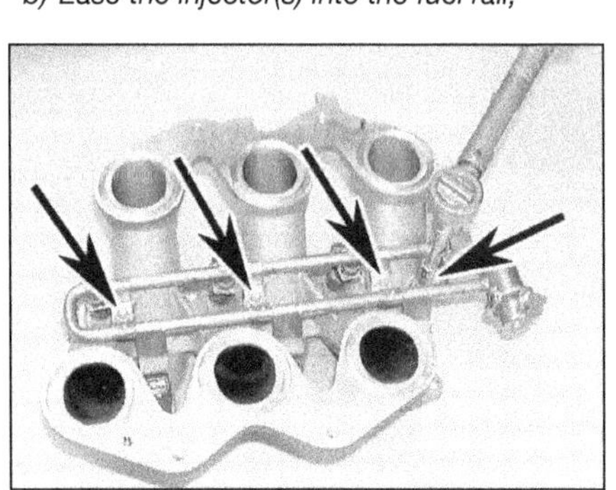
14.4a Undo the retaining bolts (arrowed) . . .

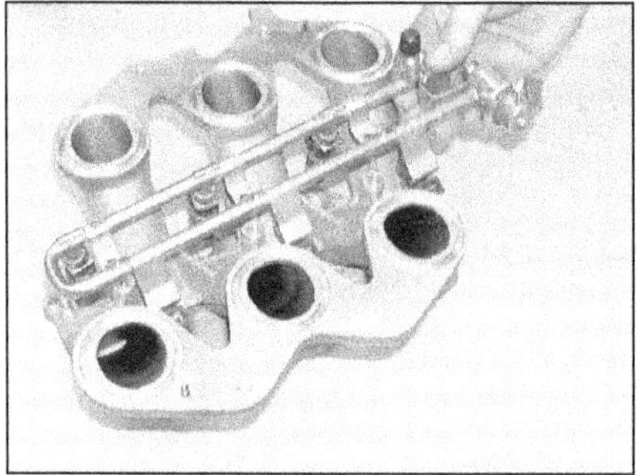
14.4b . . . and ease the fuel rail and injector assembly out of position

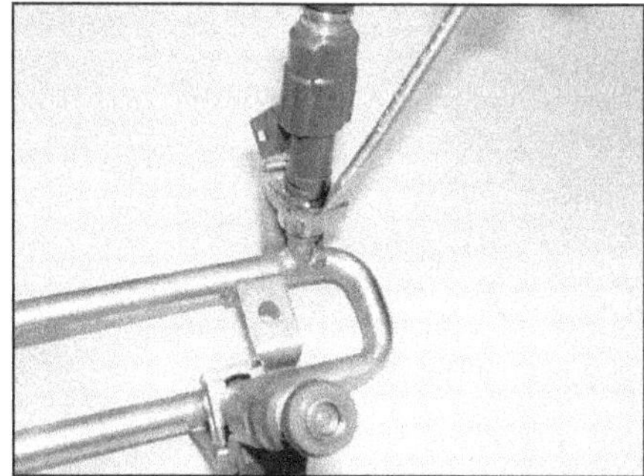
14.4c Slide off the relevant retaining clip . . .

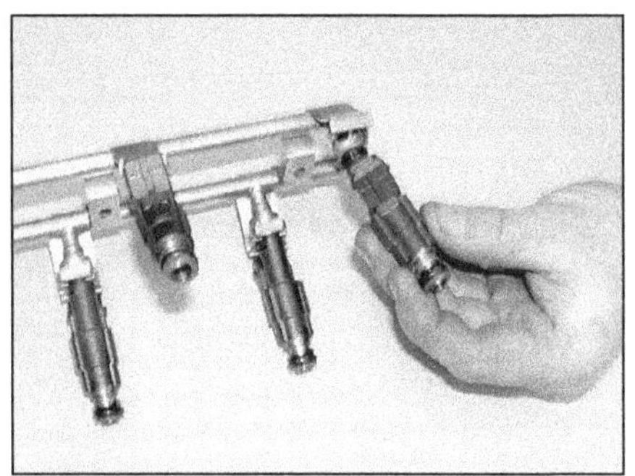
14.4d . . . then ease the injector out from the fuel rail

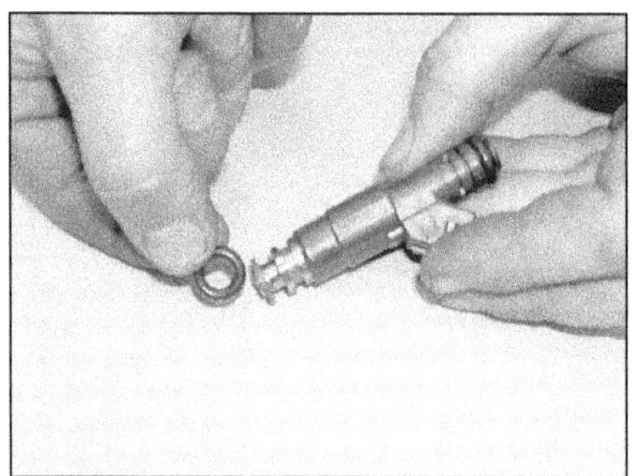
14.5 On refitting be sure to renew all injector sealing rings

14.7 The fuel pressure regulator is located at the rear of the inlet manifold (shown with engine removed)

14.12 Disconnect the wiring connector from the idle speed adjuster valve . . .

14.13 . . . then release the retaining clip and detach the air hose

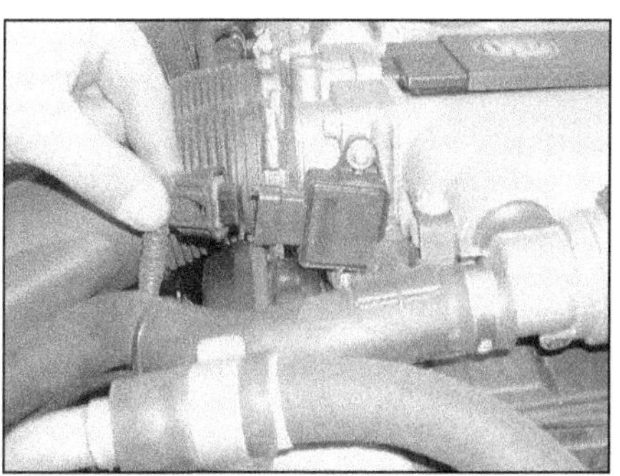

14.15 Disconnecting the throttle potentiometer wiring connector

regulator and discard them; new ones must be used on refitting.

11 Refitting is the reverse of removal, using new sealing rings and lubricating them with a smear of engine oil to ease installation. Ensure the regulator is correctly positioned then securely tighten the retaining clamp screw. On completion start the engine and check for signs of fuel leakage.

Idle speed adjuster valve

12 Ensure the ignition is switched off then disconnect the wiring connector from the valve which is fitted to the left-hand side of the inlet manifold **(see illustration)**.

13 Slacken the retaining clip and disconnect the hose from the valve then carefully ease the valve assembly out from the manifold **(see illustration)**. If necessary separate the valve and its mounting rubber. Inspect the mounting rubber for signs of damage or deterioration and renew if necessary.

14 Refitting is the reverse of removal making sure the mounting rubber grommet is correctly positioned. Aid installation by lubricating the grommet with a silicone-based spray.
On completion start the engine and check for air leaks.

Throttle potentiometer

15 Ensure the ignition is switched off then disconnect the wiring connector from the throttle potentiometer which is fitted to the left-hand side of the throttle housing **(see illustration)**.

16 Slacken and remove the retaining screws then remove the potentiometer from the housing.

17 Refitting is the reverse of removal making sure the potentiometer is correctly engaged with the throttle valve spindle.

Coolant temperature sensor

18 The coolant temperature sensor is screwed into the coolant outlet which links the rear of the cylinder heads. Refer to Chapter 3 for removal and refitting details noting that it will be necessary to remove the inlet manifold to gain access to the sensor **(see illustration)**.

Intake air temperature sensor

19 Ensure ignition is switched off then disconnect the wiring connector from the sensor.

20 Slacken the retaining clips then detach the intake duct from the airflow meter and air cleaner housing and remove it from the vehicle **(see illustration)**.

21 Carefully ease the sensor out of position and recover is sealing grommet. Inspect the grommet for signs of damage or deterioration and renew if necessary.

22 Refitting is the reverse of removal making sure the sensor and grommet are correctly seated.

Airflow meter

23 Ensure the ignition is switched off then disconnect the wiring connectors from the airflow meter and intake air temperature sensor.

24 Slacken the retaining clips then detach the intake duct from the airflow meter and air cleaner housing and remove it from the vehicle.

25 Slacken the retaining clip then remove the airflow meter from the vehicle. Inspect the meter for signs of damage and renew if necessary.

26 Refitting is the reverse of removal ensuring the intake ducts are correctly engaged with the meter recesses.

Crankshaft sensor

27 The sensor is mounted on the left-hand side of the cylinder block, directly below the oil filter, and its wiring connector is clipped onto the holder on the rear of the left hand cylinder head.

28 To gain access to the wiring connector, remove the windscreen wiper arms and the water deflector panel from the base of the windscreen (see Chapter 12, Sections 15 and 16).

29 Ensure the ignition is switched off then unclip the sensor wiring connector from its holder and disconnect it **(see illustration)**.

30 Firmly apply the handbrake then jack up the front of the vehicle and support it on axle stands.

31 Work back along the sensor wiring and release it from all the relevant clips and ties whilst noting its correct routing.

32 Unscrew the retaining bolt and remove the sensor from the cylinder block, along with

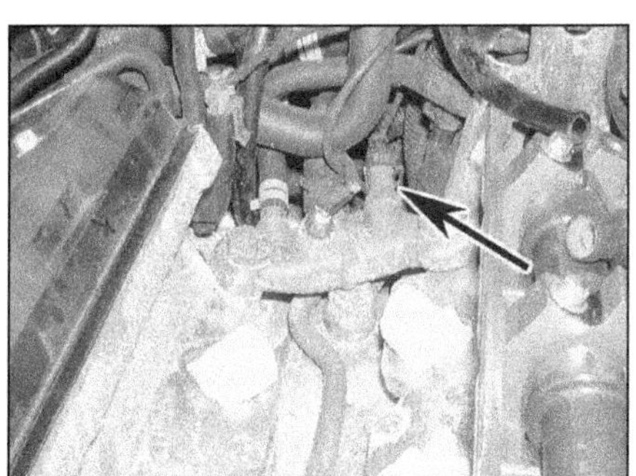

14.18 The coolant temperature sensor is screwed into the coolant outlet (shown with inlet manifold removed)

14.20 Disconnect the wiring connector from the intake air sensor then release the retaining clips (arrowed) and remove the intake duct

14.29 The crankshaft sensor wiring connector (arrowed) is clipped onto the engine rear lifting bracket (shown with engine removed)

14.32 Removing the crankshaft sensor (shown with oil filter removed)

its sealing ring. Discard the sealing ring, a new one should be used on refitting **(see illustration)**.

33 Refitting is the reverse of removal using a new sealing ring and tightening the sensor bolt to the specified torque. Ensure the wiring is correctly routed and retained by all the necessary clips so that it is in no danger of contacting the exhaust manifold.

Knock sensor - right-hand cylinder bank

34 Remove the auxiliary drivebelt as described in Chapter 1 then unbolt the drivebelt tensioner pulley assembly from the side of the cylinder head.

35 Remove the alternator upper mounting bolt then slacken the lower mounting and pivot the alternator away from the block (see Chapter 5A).

36 Trace the wiring back from the sensor to the front of the timing belt cover, releasing it from all the relevant clips and ties whilst noting its correct routing. Ensure the ignition is switched off then disconnect the sensor wiring connector.

37 Slacken and remove the retaining bolt and remove the sensor from the engine **(see illustration)**.

38 On refitting ensure the mating surfaces are clean and dry then fit the sensor and tighten its retaining bolt to the specified torque. Ensure the wiring is correctly routed and securely retained by all the necessary clips so that it is no danger of contacting the auxiliary drivebelt. Refit the alternator and drivebelt tensioner, tightening their retaining bolts to the specified torque settings (see Chapter 5A) and refit the auxiliary drivebelt (see Chapter 1).

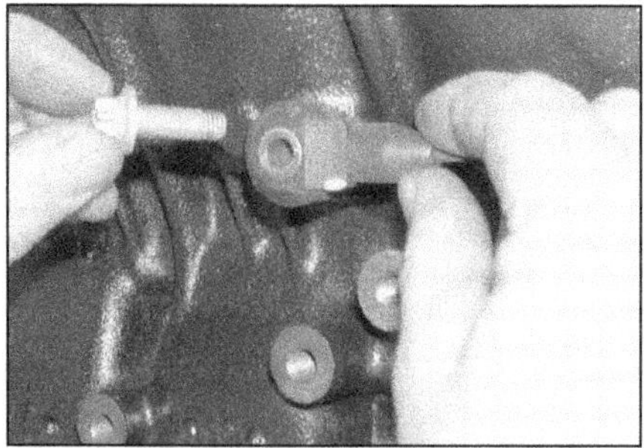

14.37 Unscrew the retaining bolt and remove the knock sensor from the right-hand side of the cylinder block

Knock sensor - left-hand cylinder bank

39 The knock sensor is situated on the left-hand side of the cylinder block, just in front of the oil filter and is wiring connector is connected to the wiring harness cover above the left-hand cylinder head. To gain access to the sensor, firmly apply the handbrake then jack up the front of the vehicle and support it on axle stands.

40 On models with air conditioning, to improve access to the sensor remove the engine/transmission left-hand mounting and mounting bracket from the cylinder block (see Chapter 2C).

41 Trace the wiring back from the sensor, releasing it from all the relevant clips and ties whilst noting its correct routing. Disconnect the wiring connector and tie a length of string to it; the string can then be used on refitting to draw the wiring connector up and into position.

42 Slacken and remove the retaining bolt and remove the sensor from the engine. Untie the string and leave in position for use on refitting.

43 On refitting then use the string to draw the wiring connector up and into position. Ensure the mating surfaces are clean and dry then fit the sensor and tighten its retaining bolt to the specified torque **(see illustration)**. Ensure the wiring is correctly routed and securely retained by all the necessary clips so that it is no danger of contacting the exhaust system or auxiliary drivebelt. On models with air conditioning refit the engine mounting bracket and mounting as described in Chapter 2C.

14.43 On refitting ensure the knock sensor is correctly positioned then tighten its retaining bolt to the specified torque

Camshaft sensor

44 The sensor is mounted onto the top of the left-hand cylinder bank exhaust camshaft where it is directly behind the timing belt cover. On models with air conditioning, to improve access to the sensor, unbolt the air conditioning pipe/hose bracket from the cylinder head and position the hose/pipe to one side.

45 Ensure the ignition is switched off then disconnect the wiring connector from the camshaft sensor

46 Unscrew the retaining bolt and remove the camshaft sensor from the camshaft bearing cap **(see illustration)**.

47 Refitting is the reverse of removal tightening the sensor retaining bolt to the specified torque.

14.46 Removing the camshaft sensor

Electronic control unit (ECU)

48 Refer to Section 13.

Injection system relays

49 Refer to Section 13.

Air conditioning system switch

50 The air conditioning system switch is screwed into one of the refrigerant pipes and cannot be removed without first discharging the refrigerant (see Chapter 3). Renewal of the switch should therefore be entrusted to a suitably equipped garage.

15 Inlet manifold - removal and refitting

Warning: Refer to the warning note in Section 1 before proceeding.

2.0 litre SOHC engine

Removal

1 Depressurise the fuel system as described in Section 7 then disconnect the battery negative terminal. **Note:** *On models with a Vauxhall anti-theft warning system (ATWS), the battery negative terminal must be disconnected within 15 seconds of the ignition being switched off to prevent the alarm system being triggered.*

2 Remove the auxiliary drivebelt and drain the cooling system as described in Chapter 1.

3 Disconnect the wiring connectors from the intake air temperature sensor and the airflow meter.

4 Slacken the retaining clips then disconnect the intake duct from the air cleaner and throttle housing and remove the duct assembly from the engine compartment.

5 Remove the retaining clip and detach the

accelerator cable from the throttle cam balljoint and unclip the cable from its mounting bracket. On models with cruise control it will also be necessary to remove the second retaining clip and detach the cruise control cable.

6 Undo the retaining bolts and free the cable mounting bracket from the manifold noting the correct fitted location of the spring.

7 Undo the retaining bolts and remove the support bracket and alternator mounting bracket from the front of the manifold.

8 Unscrew the union bolts and disconnect the fuel feed and return hoses from the fuel rail. Recover the sealing washers from each hose union and discard; new ones should be used on refitting. Plug the hose ends to minimise fuel loss and prevent the entry of dirt into the system.

9 Disconnect the wiring connectors from the throttle potentiometer, the idle speed adjuster valve, the injectors, the purge valve, the DIS module and the exhaust gas recirculation (EGR) valve.

10 Unscrew the nut/bolt and detach the earth leads from the fuel rail rear retaining bolt and camshaft housing.

11 Note the correct routing of the wiring then undo the wiring cover retaining bolts and position the cover assembly clear of the inlet manifold.

12 Disconnect the various breather/vacuum hoses from the throttle housing and manifold (as applicable) noting each ones correct fitted location.

13 Slacken the retaining clips and disconnect the coolant hose from the throttle housing.

14 Unscrew the union nut and disconnect the braking system servo unit hose from the manifold.

15 Check that all the necessary vacuum/breather hoses have been disconnected then slacken and remove the manifold retaining nuts.

16 Remove the manifold from the engine and recover the manifold gasket, noting which way around it is fitted.

Refitting

17 Refitting is the reverse of removal bearing in mind the following points.

a) *Prior to refitting, check the manifold studs and renew any that are worn or damaged.*
b) *Ensure the manifold and cylinder mating surfaces are clean and dry and fit the new gasket. Refit the manifold and tighten the retaining nuts evenly and progressively to the specified torque.*
c) *Ensure that all relevant hoses are reconnected to their original positions, and are securely held (where necessary) by their retaining clips.*
d) *Fit new sealing washers to each side of the fuel feed and return hose unions then screw in the union bolts. Ensure both hose unions are correctly positioned then tighten the unions bolts to the specified torque.*
e) *Tighten all fixings to their specified torque setting (where given).*
f) *Refit the auxiliary drivebelt and refill the cooling system as described in Chapter 1.*
g) *On completion, adjust the accelerator cable as described in Section 3.*

2.0 litre DOHC engine

Note: *New manifold retaining will be required on refitting.*

Removal

18 Remove the auxiliary drivebelt and drain the cooling system as described in Chapter 1.

19 Remove the throttle housing as described in Section 11.

20 Unscrew the nut and disconnect the fuel return pipe from the end of the fuel rail. As the union nuts are slackened, retain the pipe end fitting with an open-ended spanner to prevent any excess strain being placed on the pipe. Plug the hose and pipe end to minimise fuel loss and prevent the entry of dirt.

21 Unscrew the retaining nut and detach the earth lead from the fuel rail front retaining bolt.

22 Carefully release the retaining clips and lift off the injector wiring cover assembly squarely away from the top of the injectors; the wiring connectors are an integral part of the cover. Disconnect the crankshaft sensor and knock sensor wiring connectors (where necessary) from the injector wiring cover then position the cover assembly clear of the manifold.

23 Unscrew the union nut and disconnect the braking system servo unit hose from the manifold.

24 Disconnect all remaining vacuum/breather hoses from the manifold, noting each ones correct fitted location.

25 Undo the retaining bolts and remove the alternator mounting brackets from the front of the inlet manifold.

26 Undo the retaining bolts and remove the support bracket from the base of the manifold.

27 Slacken and remove the retaining nuts and bolts and manoeuvre the manifold assembly away from the engine. Remove the gasket and discard it also discard the manifold nuts; new ones should be used on refitting.

Refitting

28 Refitting is the reverse of removal noting the following.

a) *Prior to refitting, check the manifold studs and renew any that are worn or damaged.*
b) *Ensure the manifold and cylinder mating surfaces are clean and dry and fit the new gasket. Refit the manifold then fit the retaining bolts and new nuts tightening them evenly and progressively to the specified torque.*
c) *Ensure that all relevant hoses are reconnected to their original positions, and are securely held (where necessary) by their retaining clips.*
d) *Tighten all fixings to their specified torque setting (where given).*

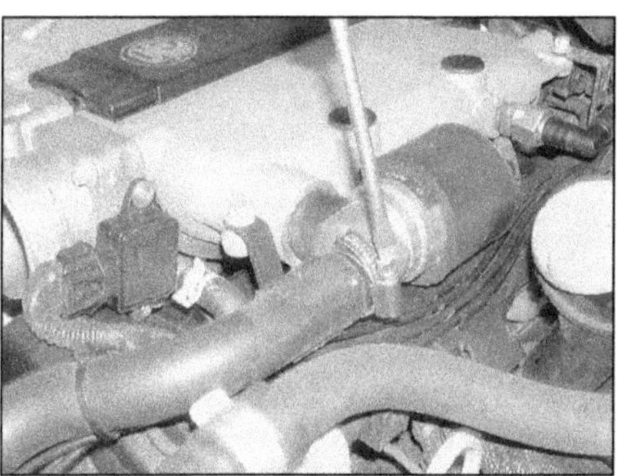

15.30 Slacken the retaining clip and detach the air hose from the idle speed adjuster valve

e) *Refit the auxiliary drivebelt and refill the cooling system as described in Chapter 1.*
f) *On completion, adjust the accelerator cable as described in Section 3.*

2.5 and 3.0 litre engines

Removal

Note: *If only the upper section is to be removed carry out the operations described in paragraphs 29 to 39.*

29 Disconnect the battery negative terminal. **Note:** *On models with a Vauxhall anti-theft warning system (ATWS), the battery negative terminal must be disconnected within 15 seconds of the ignition being switched off to prevent the alarm system being triggered.*

30 Slacken the retaining clip and disconnect the inlet hose from the idle speed adjuster **(see illustration)**.

31 Slacken the retaining clips securing the intake ducts to the throttle housing and intake pre-volume valve and remove both ducts.

32 Remove the retaining clip and detach the accelerator cable from the throttle cam balljoint then unclip the cable from its mounting bracket. On models with cruise control it will also be necessary to remove the second retaining clip and detach the cruise control cable **(see illustrations)**.

33 Clamp the coolant hoses which are connected to the throttle housing then release the retaining clips and disconnect both hoses **(see illustration)**. Wipe away any spilt coolant.

15.32a Remove the retaining clip and detach the accelerator inner cable from the throttle cam

15.32b On models with cruise control prise off the second retaining clip . . .

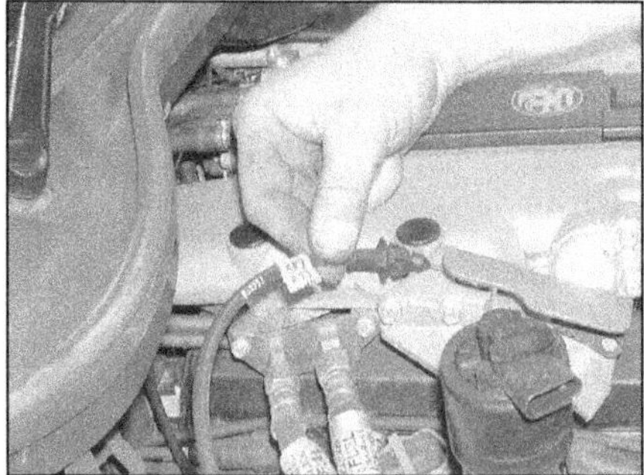

15.32c . . . and free the cruise control cable from the throttle cam and bracket

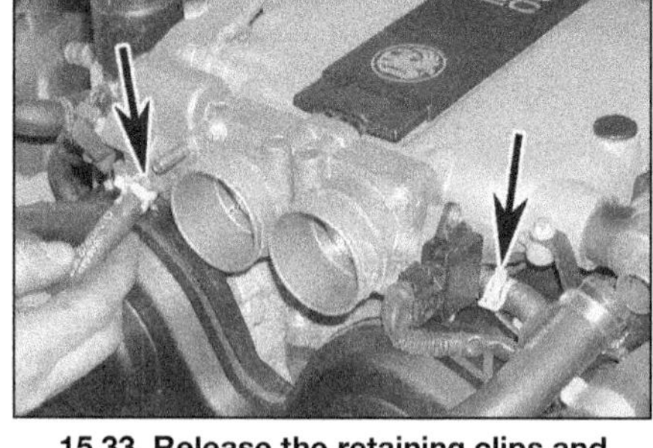

15.33 Release the retaining clips and detach the coolant hoses (arrowed) from the throttle housing

34 Disconnect the wiring connectors from the throttle valve potentiometer, the idle speed adjuster, the inlet manifold switchover valve solenoid and the exhaust gas recirculation (EGR) valve.

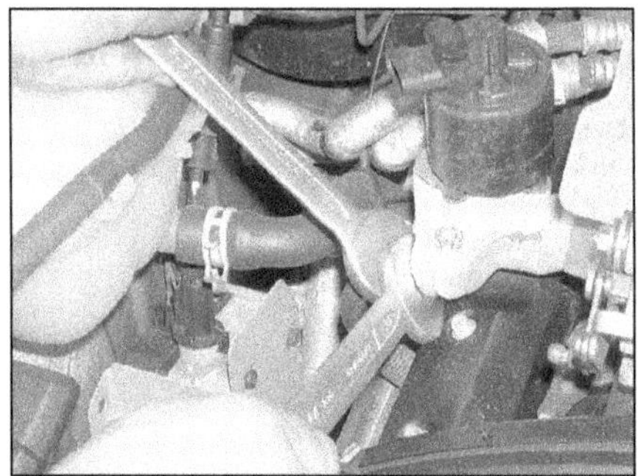

15.35a Unscrew the union nut and free the EGR pipe from the EGR valve

35 Unscrew the union nut and disconnect the pipe from the EGR valve then unscrew the retaining bolt and free the pipe bracket from the valve **(see illustrations)**. Where necessary, disconnect the connector and free the knock sensor wiring connector from the EGR valve bracket.

36 Unscrew the union nut and disconnect the braking system servo unit vacuum hose from the manifold upper section **(see illustration)**.

37 Make a note of the correct fitted locations of the vacuum/breather hoses connected to the rear of the manifold upper section then release the retaining clips (where fitted) and disconnect them **(see illustration)**.

38 Unscrew the retaining bolts and detach the hose/wiring brackets from the corners of the manifold upper section **(see illustration)**.

39 Remove the caps from the top of the manifold then slacken and remove the upper section retaining bolts. Lift off the manifold upper section, disconnecting the vacuum hoses from the manifold switchover solenoid valve as they become accessible **(see illustrations)**. Remove the sealing rings from the top of manifold lower section and discard them; new ones should be used on refitting.

Caution: Take great care not to allow any foreign object to drop down into the cylinder head intake ports.

40 Depressurise the fuel system (Section 7) then unscrew the nuts and disconnect the fuel feed and return hoses from their unions on the right-hand side of the manifold. As each union nut is slackened, retain the pipe end fitting with an open-ended spanner to prevent any excess strain being placed on the pipes **(see illustration)**. Plug the hose and pipe ends to minimise fuel loss and prevent the entry of dirt.

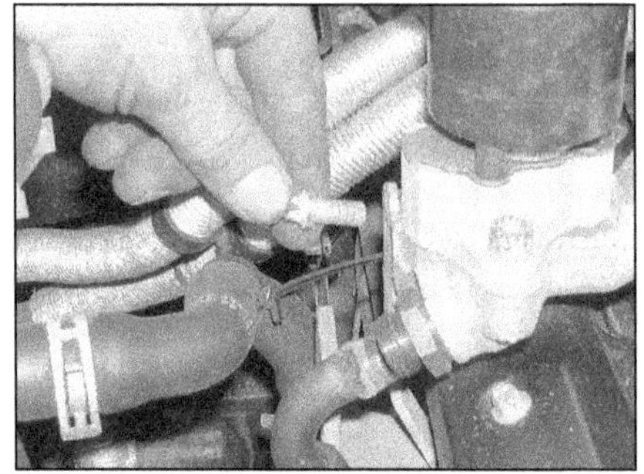

15.35b . . . then remove the bracket retaining bolt

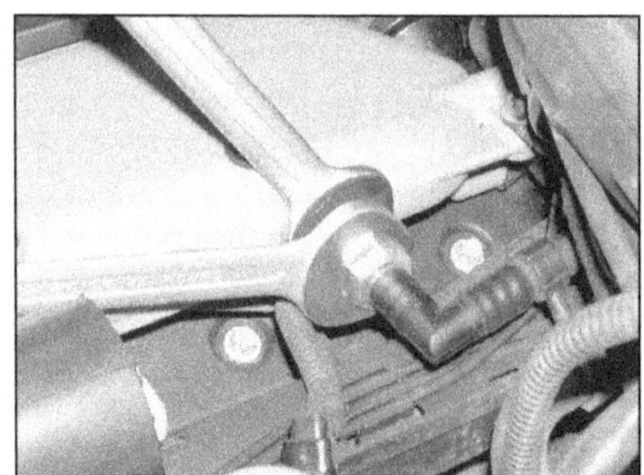

15.36 Unscrew the union nut and disconnect the braking system servo unit hose

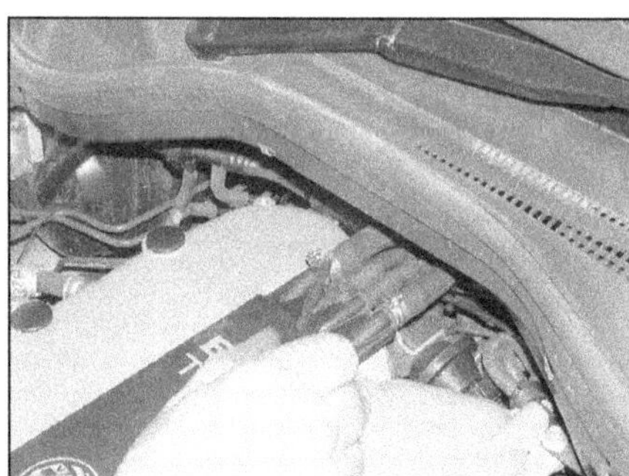

15.37 Release the retaining clips and disconnect the vacuum and breather hoses from the rear of the manifold

15.38 Undo the retaining bolts and free the hose/wiring brackets from the manifold

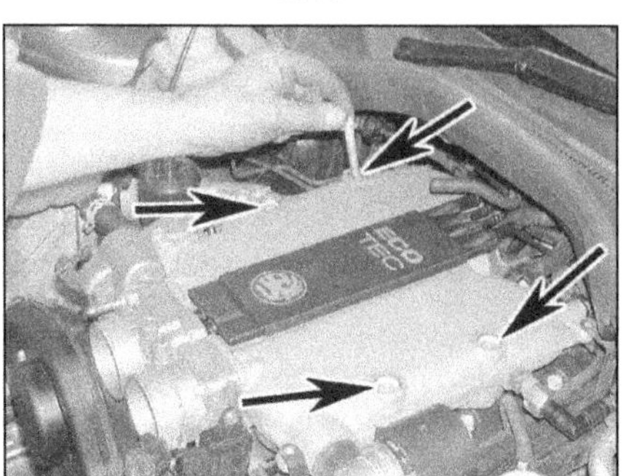

15.39a Remove the caps then unscrew the retaining bolts . . .

15.39b . . . and remove the manifold upper section

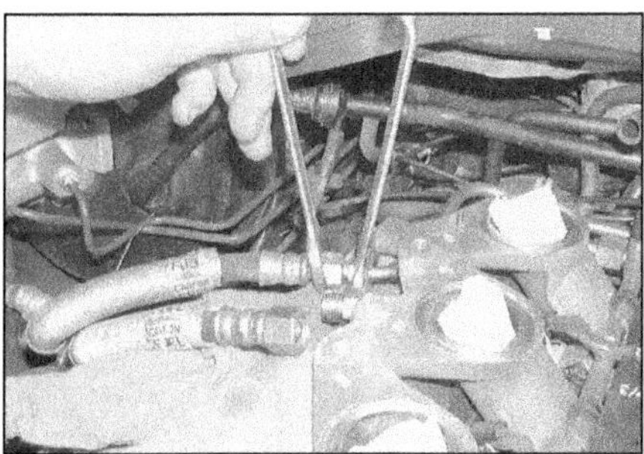

15.40 Unscrew the union nuts and disconnect the fuel feed and return hoses from the manifold

41 Disconnect the injector wiring harness connector and the vacuum hose from the fuel pressure regulator **(see illustration)**.

42 Slacken and remove the retaining bolts then lift the manifold lower section away from the cylinder head. Remove the seals from the manifold flange recesses and discard them; new ones must be used on refitting **(see illustrations)**.

43 If necessary, undo the retaining bolts and remove the intake manifold flange from the top of the cylinder head **(see illustration)**. Recover the flange seals and discard them; new ones must be used on refitting.

Refitting

44 Refitting is the reverse of removal noting the following.

a) *Ensure all the mating surfaces are clean and dry and the new seals/sealing rings are correctly seated in their recesses* **(see illustration)**. *Tighten all the manifold retaining bolts evenly and progressively to their specified torque settings.*
b) *Ensure that all relevant hoses are reconnected to their original positions, and are securely held (where necessary) by their retaining clips.*
c) *Tighten the fuel hose and vacuum servo hose union nuts to their specified torque settings.*
d) *Ensure the EGR valve and pipe mating surfaces are clean and dry and apply a smear of high-temperature grease to the threads of the union nut (Vauxhall recommend the use of assembly paste 19 48 569 - available from your Vauxhall dealer). Reconnect the pipe to the valve and tighten its union nut to the specified torque.*
e) *On completion, adjust the accelerator cable as described in Section 3.*

15.41 The injector wiring harness connector (arrowed) is clipped onto the engine rear lifting bracket (shown with engine removed)

16 Exhaust manifold - removal and refitting

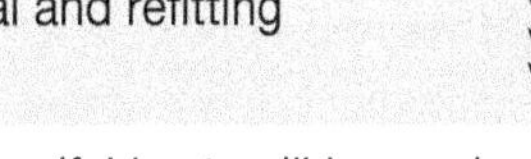

Note: *New manifold nuts will be required on refitting.*

2.0 litre SOHC engine

Removal

1 Firmly apply the handbrake then jack up the front of the vehicle and support it on axle stands. If necessary, to improve access undo the retaining bolts and remove the undercover from beneath the engine.

2 Slacken and remove the bolt(s) securing the exhaust system front pipe to its mounting bracket then unscrew the bolts securing the front pipe to the manifold. Free the pipe from the manifold taking care not to place any strain on the oxygen sensor wiring. Discard the front pipe gasket; a new one should be used on refitting.

3 Undo the retaining bolts and remove the heatshield from the exhaust manifold.

4 Remove the engine oil dipstick and pull the plug caps off from the centre (No 2 and 3) spark plugs. Unscrew the centre spark plug heatshields and remove them from the manifold (a special socket, number KM-834, is available to ease removal of the heatshields).

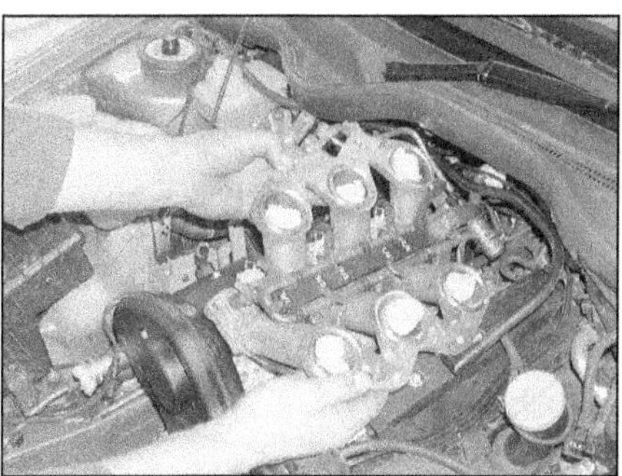

15.42a Remove the manifold lower section . . .

5 Undo the retaining nuts securing the manifold to the head. Manoeuvre the manifold out of the engine compartment, complete with the gasket. Discard both the gasket and retaining nuts; new ones should be used on refitting.

Refitting

6 Examine all the exhaust manifold studs for signs of damage and corrosion; remove all traces of corrosion, and repair or renew any damaged studs.

7 Ensure that the manifold and cylinder head sealing faces are clean and flat, and fit the new gasket.

8 Refit the manifold then fit the new retaining nuts and tighten them to the specified torque.

9 Apply a smear of high-temperature grease (Vauxhall recommend the use of assembly paste 19 48 569 - available from your Vauxhall dealer) to the threads of the spark plug heatshields then refit the shields and tighten them to the specified torque. Reconnect the plug caps and refit the dipstick.

10 Apply the high-temperature grease to the heatshield bolts then refit the heatshield to the manifold and securely tighten the bolts.

11 Fit a new gasket to the exhaust front pipe joint and lubricate the front pipe to manifold bolts with the high-temperature grease. Refit the bolts to the manifold, tightening them to the specified torque, then securely tighten the bolt(s) securing the front pipe to its mounting bracket.

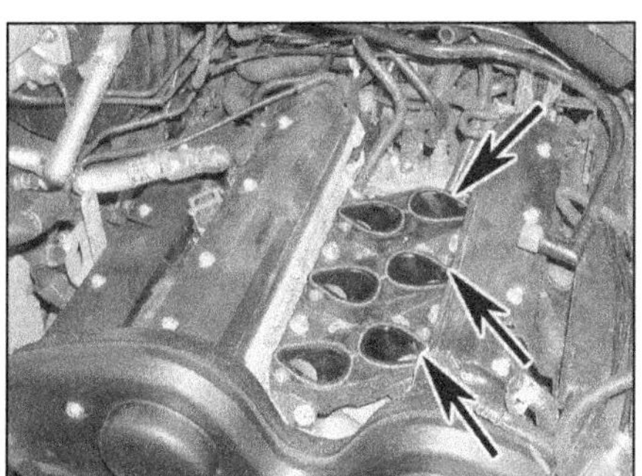

15.42b . . . and recover the seals (arrowed) from the flange

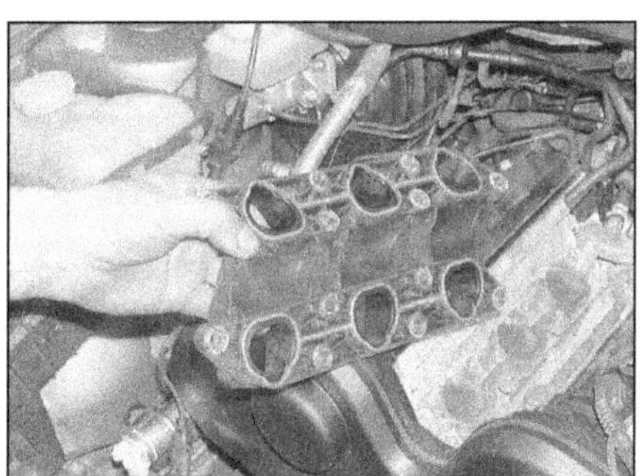

15.43 Removing the manifold flange

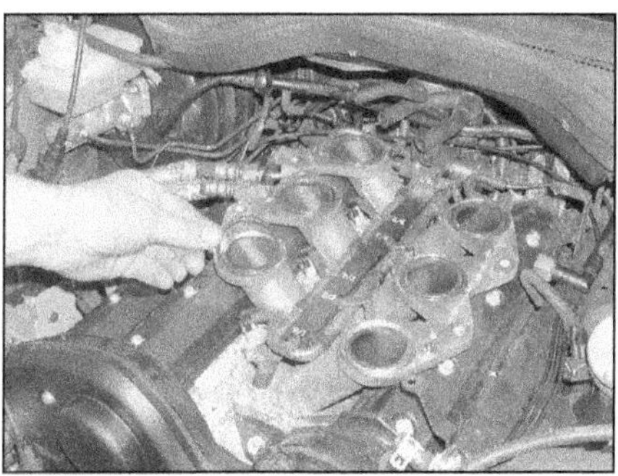

15.44 On refitting be sure to renew all manifold seals and sealing rings

16.20 Disconnect the wiring connectors from the coolant sensor and sender . . .

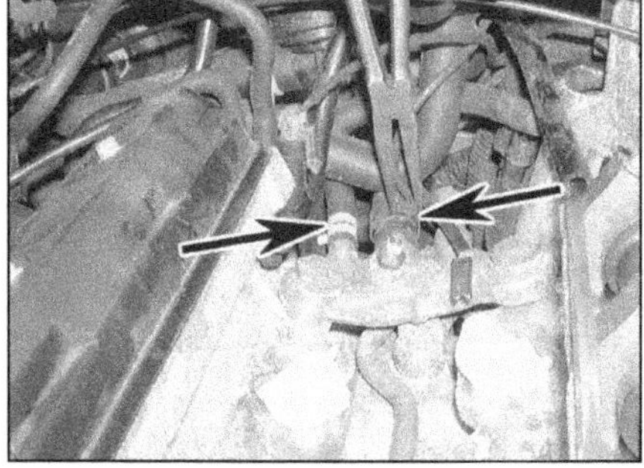

16.21 . . . then release the retaining clips and disconnect the coolant hoses

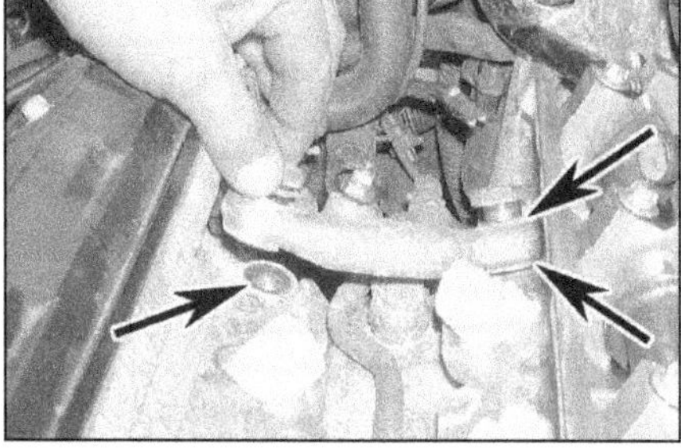

16.22 Unscrew the retaining bolts and remove the coolant outlet from the engine (sealing rings arrowed)

2.0 litre DOHC engine

Removal

12 Remove the secondary air injection system air valve and connecting pipe as described in Chapter 4B.

13 Carry out the operations described in paragraphs 1 and 2.

14 Undo the retaining nuts then remove the exhaust manifold and gasket from the cylinder head. Discard both the gasket and retaining nuts; new ones should be used on refitting.

Refitting

15 Refit the manifold as described in paragraphs 6 to 8.

16 Fit a new gasket to the exhaust front pipe joint and lubricate the front pipe to manifold bolts with high-temperature grease (Vauxhall recommend the use of assembly paste 19 48 569 - available from your Vauxhall dealer). Refit the bolts to the manifold, tightening them to the specified torque, then securely tighten the bolt(s) securing the front pipe to its mounting bracket.

17 Refit the secondary air injection system connecting pipe and air valve as described in Chapter 4B.

2.5 and 3.0 litre engine

Right-hand cylinder bank

18 Remove the inlet manifold and flange as described in Section 15.

19 Drain the cooling system as described in Chapter 1.

20 Disconnect the wiring connectors from the coolant temperature gauge sender and the engine management system coolant temperature sensor which are screwed into the coolant outlet which links the rear of the cylinder heads **(see illustration)**.

21 Slacken the retaining clips and disconnect the coolant hoses from the cylinder head outlet **(see illustration)**.

22 Unscrew the retaining bolts and remove the coolant outlet from the cylinder heads **(see illustration)**. Recover the sealing rings and discard them; new ones must be used on refitting.

23 Position a container beneath the oil filter. Unscrew the filter using an oil filter removal tool if necessary, and drain the oil into the container. If the oil filter is damaged or distorted during removal, it must be renewed. Given the low cost of a new oil filter relative to the cost of repairing the damage which could result if a re-used filter springs a leak, it is probably a good idea to renew the filter in any case.

24 Unscrew the union nuts securing the oil cooler pipes to the cylinder block then unscrew the union bolts securing the pipes to the cooler. Recover the sealing washers from each side of the oil cooler unions and move the pipes to the rear **(see illustrations)**.

25 Release the retaining clips and disconnect the radiator bottom hose, expansion tank hose and heater hose from the coolant pipe on the right-hand side of the engine. Slacken and remove the retaining bolts then remove the pipe from the engine **(see illustration)**. Recover the sealing ring and discard it; a new one should be used on refitting. Note that it maybe necessary to remove the camshaft cover from the right-hand cylinder head to gain the clearance required to remove the coolant pipe.

26 Undo the retaining bolts and remove the heatshields from the exhaust manifold **(see illustrations)**.

16.24a Unscrew the union nuts securing the oil pipes to the block . . .

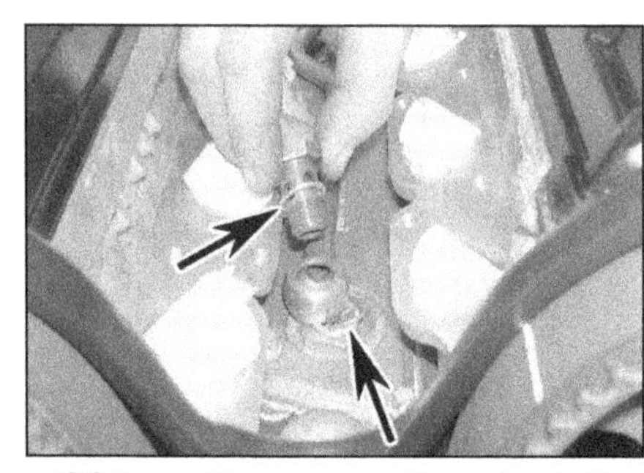

16.24b . . . then unscrew the union bolts and detach the pipes from the oil cooler (sealing washers arrowed)

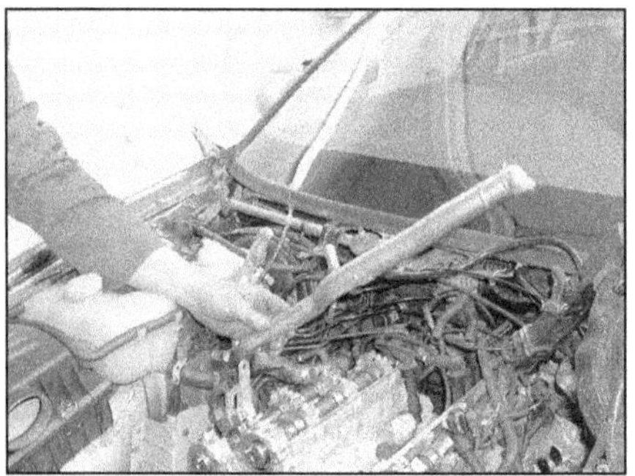

16.25 Removing the engine coolant pipe

16.26a Undo the retaining bolts and remove the lower . . .

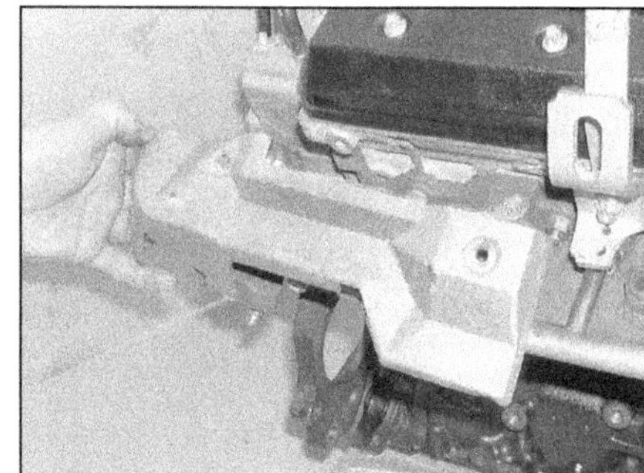

16.26b . . . and upper heatshields from the right-hand exhaust manifold

27 Slacken and remove the bolt securing the exhaust system right-hand front pipe to its mounting bracket then unscrew the bolts securing the pipe to the manifold. Free the pipe from the manifold taking care not to place any strain on the oxygen sensor wiring, and recover the gasket. Discard the front pipe gasket; a new one should be used on refitting.
28 Unscrew the union nuts and remove the pipe connecting the exhaust gas recirculation (EGR) valve to the manifold.
29 Slacken the clip securing the connecting hose to the right-hand cylinder bank secondary air injection system pipe then unscrew the bolts securing the pipe to the manifold. Remove the pipe from the vehicle and discard its gaskets **(see illustration)**.
30 Undo the retaining nuts then remove the exhaust manifold and gasket from the cylinder head. Discard both the gasket and retaining nuts; new ones should be used on refitting.
31 Refitting is the reverse of removal, noting the following points.

- a) *Prior to refitting, check the manifold studs and renew any that are worn or damaged.*
- b) *Ensure all mating surfaces are clean and dry and use new gaskets, sealing rings and washers.*
- c) *Secure the manifold in position with new retaining nuts, tightening them evenly and progressively to the specified torque.*
- d) *Prior to refitting, lubricate the threads of the secondary air injection system pipe bolts, the EGR valve pipe nuts, the front pipe to manifold bolts and the heatshield bolts with a smear of high-temperature grease (Vauxhall recommend the use of assembly paste 19 48 569 - available from your Vauxhall dealer).*
- e) *Tighten all fixings to their specified torque setting (where given).*
- f) *Ensure that all relevant hoses are reconnected to their original positions, and are securely held (where necessary) by their retaining clips.*
- g) *Fit new sealing washers to each side of the oil cooler pipe unions and tighten the pipe union nuts and bolts to the specified torque.*
- i) *Fit a new oil filter and refill the cooling system as described in Chapter 1.*
- j) *On completion, check the engine oil level as described in Weekly checks.*

Left-hand cylinder bank

32 It is not possible to remove the exhaust manifold from the left-hand cylinder bank with the engine in the vehicle. This leaves two possible options, the first is to remove the engine unit from the vehicle and the second is to remove the cylinder head assembly. Decide on the course of action which is best suited then proceed as follows.
33 Working as described in Chapter 2C, either remove the engine unit from the vehicle or alternatively remove the cylinder head assembly from the engine.
34 If the engine has been removed, unscrew

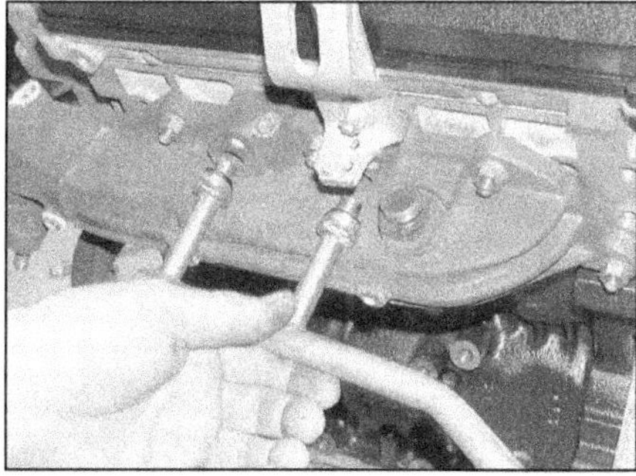

16.29 Undo the retaining bolts and remove the secondary air connecting pipe

the bolt and spacer securing the coolant pipe and engine lifting bracket to the cylinder head and remove the lifting bracket. Free the coolant pipe from the thermostat housing then manoeuvre it out of position then withdraw the dipstick and ease the dipstick tube out from the cylinder block. Discard the coolant pipe and dipstick tube sealing rings; new ones should be used on refitting.
35 Undo the retaining bolts and remove the heatshields from the exhaust manifold.
36 Unscrew the retaining bolts and remove the secondary air injection system pipe from the manifold. Recover the gaskets fitted between the pipe and manifold and discard them.
37 Undo the retaining nuts then remove the exhaust manifold and gasket from the cylinder head. Discard both the gasket and retaining nuts; new ones should be used on refitting.
38 Refitting is the reverse of removal, noting the following points.

- a) *Prior to refitting, check the manifold studs and renew any that are worn or damaged.*
- b) *Ensure the manifold and cylinder head mating surfaces are clean and dry then fit the new gasket. Refit the manifold then fit the new retaining nuts, tightening them evenly and progressively to the specified torque.*
- c) *Lubricate the threads of the secondary air injection system pipe bolts with a smear of high-temperature grease (Vauxhall recommend the use of assembly paste 19 48 569 - available from your Vauxhall dealer). Fit new gaskets to the pipe unions then refit the pipe to the cylinder head and tighten the retaining bolts to the specified torque (see Chapter 4B).*
- d) *Lubricate the manifold heatshield bolts with the high-temperature grease before installation.*
- e) *If the engine was removed, fit new sealing rings to the dipstick tube and thermostat housing coolant pipe. Ensure the coolant pipe, dipstick tube and lifting bracket are correctly positioned before refitting the retaining bolt and spacer and tightening to the specified torque.*

17.4 The intake duct switchover valve solenoid valve (arrowed) is mounted on the rear of the pre-volume chamber (shown with chamber removed)

17 Multi-ram air intake system - information and component removal and refitting

Information

1 All 2.5 and 3.0 litre engines are fitted with a multi-ram air intake system to help increase torque output at all engine speeds. The system consists of the pre-volume chamber, which splits the air cleaner intake duct into two separate ducts, and two valves, one linking the intake ducts in between the pre-volume chamber and throttle housing, and the second linking the left- and right-hand chambers of the inlet manifold upper section. Each valve is controlled the engine management ECU via a solenoid valve and vacuum diaphragm unit.
2 There are four possible combinations of valve position, each of which is suited to a particular engine speed range, they are as follows.

- a) *Idle speed - intake duct valve closed, manifold valve open*
- b) *Full load at low engine speeds - intake duct and manifold valves both closed.*
- c) *Full load at medium engine speeds - intake duct valve open, manifold valve closed.*
- d) *Full load at high engine speeds - intake valve and manifold valve both open.*

3 Testing of the system can only be carried out using the special electronic diagnostic test unit which is plugged into the system's diagnostic connector (see Section 6). The multi-ram intake system components can be removed and refitted as follows.

Component removal and refitting

Intake duct switchover valve solenoid valve

4 The intake duct switchover valve solenoid valve is mounted onto the rear of the pre-volume chamber **(see illustration)**.
5 Ensure the ignition is switched off then disconnect the wiring connector from the valve.
6 Disconnect the vacuum pipes from the valve, noting their correct fitted locations,

17.11 Undo the retaining screws (arrowed) and remove the switchover valve assembly from its housing

17.13 The manifold switchover valve solenoid valve (arrowed) is mounted onto the rear of the inlet manifold (shown with engine removed)

then undo the retaining screws and remove the valve from the engine compartment.

7 Refitting is the reverse of removal ensuring the vacuum hoses are correctly reconnected.

Intake duct switchover valve housing

8 Slacken the retaining clip and disconnect the idle speed adjuster hose from the intake duct.

9 Slacken the retaining clips securing the intake ducts to the throttle housing and valve housing and remove both ducts from the engine compartment.

10 Disconnect the vacuum hose from the switchover valve diaphragm then slacken the lower retaining clips and remove the housing from the vehicle.

11 If necessary, slacken the retaining screws and remove the valve assembly from its housing, along with its sealing ring **(see illustration)**.

12 Refitting is the reverse of removal ensuring all the intake ducts are securely reconnected.

Manifold switchover valve solenoid valve

13 The manifold switchover valve solenoid valve is mounted onto the rear of the inlet manifold upper section on the left-hand side **(see illustration)**.

14 To gain access to the valve, remove the windscreen wiper arms and the water deflector panel from the base of the windscreen (see Chapter 12, Sections 15 and 16).

15 Ensure the ignition is switched off then disconnect the wiring connector from the valve.

16 Disconnect the vacuum pipes from the valve, noting their correct fitted locations, then undo the retaining screws and remove the valve from the manifold.

17 Refitting is the reverse of removal ensuring the vacuum hoses are correctly reconnected.

Manifold switchover valve assembly

18 Remove the upper section of the inlet manifold as described in Section 15.

19 Disconnect the vacuum hose from the diaphragm unit then undo the retaining bolts and remove the valve assembly from the manifold ill **(see illustration)**. Recover the sealing ring and discard it; a new one should be used on refitting.

20 On refitting fit a new sealing ring to the valve assembly then refit the valve to the manifold. Securely tighten the valve retaining bolts then refit the manifold upper section (see Section 15).

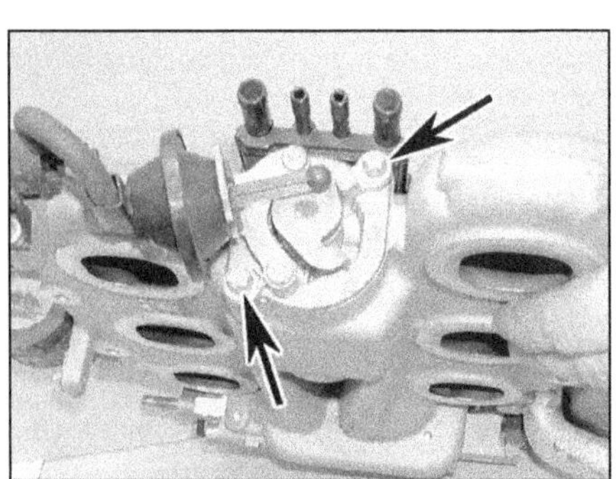
17.19 Undo the retaining bolts (arrowed) and withdraw the switchover valve assembly from the manifold upper section

17.25 Removing the pre-volume chamber assembly

Pre-volume chamber assembly

21 Remove the airflow meter as described in Section 14.

22 Slacken the retaining clip and disconnect the idle speed adjuster hose from the intake duct.

23 Slacken the retaining clips securing the intake ducts to the throttle housing and switchover valve and remove both ducts from the engine compartment.

24 Disconnect the wiring connector and vacuum hose from the intake duct switchover valve solenoid valve on the rear of the chamber.

25 Unscrew the mounting nuts then free the chamber assembly from its lower mounting rubber and manoeuvre it out of position **(see illustration)**.

26 Refitting is the reverse of removal ensuring the chamber is correctly engaged with its lower mounting rubber.

18 Exhaust system - general information, removal and refitting

General information

1 On 2.0 litre engine models, the exhaust system consists of three sections: the front pipe which incorporates the catalytic converter, the intermediate pipe and centre silencer, and the tailpipe and main silencer box.

2 On 2.5 and 3.0 litre engine models the exhaust system consists of five sections; there is a separate front pipe (incorporating a catalytic converter) and intermediate pipe (incorporating a centre silencer) for each bank of cylinders with both exhaust sections being joined to a single tailpipe and main silencer.

3 The front pipe joints are flange joints which are secured by bolts and the tailpipe is secured to the intermediate pipe by a clamping ring. The system is suspended throughout its entire length by rubber mountings.

Removal

4 Each exhaust section can be removed individually, or alternatively, the complete system can be removed as a unit. Even if only one part of the system needs attention, it is often easier to remove the whole system and separate the sections on the bench.
5 To remove the system or part of the system, first jack up the front or rear of the car and support it securely on axle stands. Alternatively, position the car over an inspection pit or on car ramps.

Front pipe

6 Trace the wiring back from the oxygen sensor, noting its correct routing, and disconnect its wiring connector **(see illustration)**. Free the wiring from any clips so the sensor is free to be removed with the front pipe.
7 Slacken and remove the bolts securing the front pipe flange joint to the manifold.
8 Unscrew the bolt(s) securing the front pipe to its mounting bracket(s) **(see illustration)**.
9 Slacken and remove the bolts securing the front pipe to the intermediate pipe and remove the front pipe from the vehicle **(see illustration)**. Recover the gasket from the front pipe to manifold joint.

Intermediate pipe

10 Slacken and remove the bolts securing the intermediate pipe to the front pipe. On 2.5 and 3.0 litre engines also remove the bolts securing the other intermediate pipe to its front pipe.
11 Slacken the clamp securing the pipe to the tailpipe then free the intermediate pipe from its mounting rubbers. Ease the intermediate pipe out from the tailpipe and remove it from underneath the vehicle.

Tailpipe

12 Slacken the clamp(s) securing the tailpipe to the intermediate pipe(s) (as applicable) **(see illustration)**.
13 Free the tailpipe from its mounting rubbers then disengage it from the intermediate pipe(s) and remove it from the underneath the vehicle.

Complete system

14 Trace the wiring back from the oxygen sensor(s), noting its correct routing, and disconnect the wiring connector(s). Free the wiring from any clips so the sensor(s) is free to be removed with the front pipe.
15 Unscrew the bolts securing the front pipe(s) to the mounting bracket.
16 Slacken and remove the bolts securing the front pipe flange joint(s) to the manifold(s) and recover the gasket(s).
17 Free the exhaust system from all its mounting rubbers and lower it from underneath the vehicle.

Heat shield(s)

18 The heat shields are secured to the underside of the body by various nuts and bolts. Each shield can be removed once the relevant exhaust section has been removed. If a shield is being removed to gain access to a component located behind it, it may prove sufficient in some cases to remove the retaining nuts and/or bolts, and simply lower the shield, without disturbing the exhaust system.

Refitting

19 Each section is refitted by reversing the removal sequence, noting the following points:

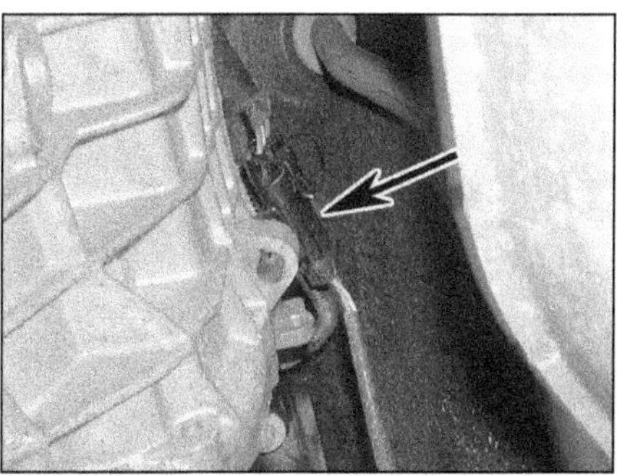

18.6 The oxygen sensor wiring connector (arrowed) is clipped to the side of the transmission unit

a) Ensure that all traces of corrosion have been removed from the flanges.
b) Inspect the rubber mountings for signs of damage or deterioration, and renew as necessary.
c) Always renew the front pipe manifold gasket whenever it is disturbed.
d) Where no gasket is fitted to a joint, apply a smear of exhaust system jointing paste to ensure a gas-tight seal.
e) Prior to refitting, lubricate the threads of the front pipe to manifold bolts with a smear of high-temperature grease (Vauxhall recommend the use of assembly paste 19 48 569 - available from your Vauxhall dealer).
f) Prior to tightening the exhaust system fasteners to the specified torque, ensure that all rubber mountings are correctly located, and that there is adequate clearance between the exhaust system and vehicle underbody.

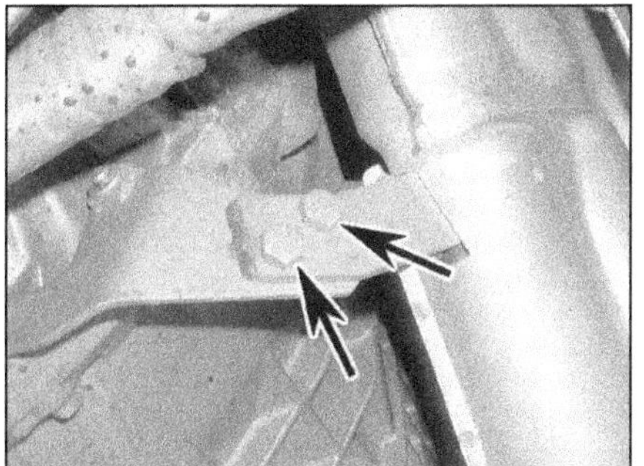

18.8 Front pipe-to-mounting bracket bolts - 2.0 litre DOHC engine

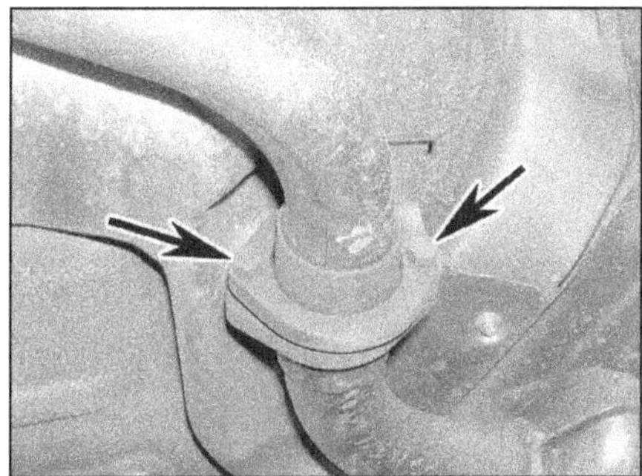

18.9 Front pipe-to-intermediate pipe bolts - 2.0 litre DOHC engine

18.12 Tailpipe-to-intermediate pipe clamp - 2.0 litre DOHC engine

Notes

Chapter 4 Part B: Emission control systems

Contents

Degrees of difficulty

Easy, suitable for novice with little experience 	**Fairly easy,** suitable for beginner with some experience 	**Fairly difficult,** suitable for competent DIY mechanic	**Difficult,** suitable for experienced DIY mechanic 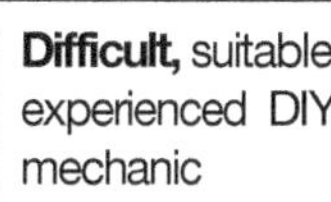	**Very difficult,** suitable for expert DIY or professional

Specifications

Torque wrench settings	**Nm**	**lbf ft**
EGR valve bolts	20	15
EGR pipe union nuts - 2.5 and 3.0 litre engine	25	18
EGR valve adaptor bolts - 2.5 and 3.0 litre engine	8	6
Exhaust manifold shroud bolts	8	6
Oxygen sensor	30	22
Roadwheel bolts	110	81
Secondary air injection system:		
Connecting pipe bolts:		
M6 bolt	8	6
M8 bolt	20	15
Non-return valve	30	22
Pump assembly:		
Pump/mounting rubber nuts/bolts	10	7
Mounting bracket-to-body nuts	20	15
Air filter retaining clamp nut	4	3

1 General information

1 All UK models use unleaded petrol and also have various other features built into the fuel system to help minimise harmful emissions. All models are equipped with a crankcase emission-control system, a catalytic converter, an exhaust gas recirculation (EGR) system and an evaporative emission control system to keep fuel vapour/exhaust gas emissions down to a minimum. All models except those with a 2.0 litre SOHC engine are also fitted with the secondary air injection system to further improve the exhaust gas emissions during engine warm-up.

Crankcase emission control

2 To reduce the emission of unburned hydrocarbons from the crankcase into the atmosphere, the engine is sealed and the blow-by gases and oil vapour are drawn from inside the crankcase, through a wire mesh oil separator, into the inlet tract to be burned by the engine during normal combustion.

3 Under conditions of high manifold depression (idling, deceleration) the gases will be sucked positively out of the crankcase. Under conditions of low manifold depression (acceleration, full-throttle running) the gases are forced out of the crankcase by the (relatively) higher crankcase pressure; if the engine is worn, the raised crankcase pressure (due to increased blow-by) will cause some of the flow to return under all manifold conditions.

Exhaust emission control

Note: *All 2.5 and 3.0 litre engines have two catalytic converters and two oxygen sensors; one for each bank of cylinders.*

4 To minimise the amount of pollutants which escape into the atmosphere, all models are fitted with a catalytic converter in the exhaust system. The system is of the closed-loop type, in which a oxygen sensor in the exhaust system provides the engine management (fuel-injection/ignition) system ECU with constant feedback, enabling the ECU to adjust the mixture to provide the best possible conditions for the converter to operate.

5 The oxygen sensor's tip is sensitive to oxygen and sends the ECU a varying voltage depending on the amount of oxygen in the exhaust gases; if the intake air/fuel mixture is too rich, the exhaust gases are low in oxygen so the sensor sends a low-voltage signal, the voltage rising as the mixture weakens and the amount of oxygen rises in the exhaust gases. Peak conversion efficiency of all major pollutants occurs if the intake air/fuel mixture is maintained at the chemically-correct ratio for the complete combustion of petrol of 14.7 parts (by weight) of air to 1 part of fuel (the stoichiometric ratio). The sensor output voltage alters in a large step at this point, the ECU using the signal change as a reference point and correcting the intake air/fuel mixture accordingly by altering the fuel injector pulse width.

Evaporative emission control

6 To minimise the escape into the atmosphere of unburned hydrocarbons, an evaporative emissions control system is also fitted to all models. The fuel tank filler cap is sealed and a charcoal canister is mounted behind the right-hand front wing. The canister collects the petrol vapours generated in the tank when the car is parked and stores them until they can be cleared from the canister (under the control of the engine management system ECU) via the purge valve into the inlet tract to be burned by the engine during normal combustion.

7 To ensure that the engine runs correctly when it is cold and/or idling and to protect the catalytic converter from the effects of an over-rich mixture, the purge control valve is not opened by the ECU until the engine has warmed up, and the engine is under load; the valve solenoid is then modulated on and off to allow the stored vapour to pass into the inlet tract.

Exhaust gas recirculation (EGR) system

8 This system is designed to recirculate small quantities of exhaust gas into the inlet tract, and therefore into the combustion process. This process reduces the level of unburnt hydrocarbons present in the exhaust gas before it reaches the catalytic converter. The system is controlled by the Engine management (fuel-injection/ignition) ECU, using the information from its various sensors, via the EGR valve.

9 On 2.0 litre engines the EGR valve assembly contains the vacuum-operated valve and the electrical solenoid valve which is used to switch the valve on and off. On SOHC engines the valve is mounted onto the top of the inlet manifold and on DOHC engines it is mounted onto the rear of the cylinder head.

10 On 2.5 and 3.0 litre engines the EGR valve is an electrically-operated valve mounted on and adaptor situated on the right-hand side of the engine.

Secondary air injection system - 2.0 litre DOHC engine and all 2.5 and 3.0 litre engines

11 The purpose of the secondary air injection system is to decrease exhaust gas emissions when the engine is cold. The system achieves this by raising the temperature of the exhaust gases which has the effect of quickly warming the catalytic converter up to its normal operating temperature. Once the catalytic converter is up to temperature the air injection system is switched off.

12 The system consists of the pump, the air cut-off valve and the solenoid valve and is controlled by the engine management (fuel-injection/ignition) ECU. When the engine is cold, the solenoid valve switches the air valve to open and the pump injects a controlled amount of air into the cylinder head exhaust ports. The air then mixes with the exhaust gases, causing any unburned particles of the fuel in the mixture to be burnt in the exhaust port/manifold which effectively raises the temperature of the exhaust gases. Once the catalytic converter is up to temperature, the solenoid valve closes the air valve and the pump is switched off. A non-return valve prevents the exhaust gases passing through the air valve.

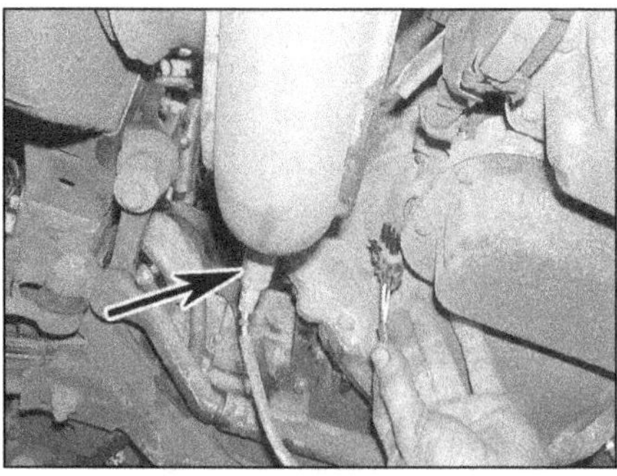

3.3 Disconnect the wiring connector then unscrew the oxygen sensor (arrowed) from the front pipe (2.5 litre engine shown)

2 Emission control system testing - general information

1 If any of the emission control systems are thought to be faulty, first ensure that all the system wiring connectors are securely connected and free of corrosion. Ensure that the fault is not due to poor maintenance; ie, check that the air cleaner filter element is clean, the spark plugs are in good condition and correctly gapped, the cylinder compression pressures are correct, and that the engine breather hoses are clear and undamaged, referring to Chapters 1 and 2A, 2B or 2C for further information (as applicable).

2 If these checks fail to reveal the cause of the problem, the vehicle should be taken to a suitably-equipped Vauxhall dealer for testing. A wiring block connector is incorporated in the engine management circuit, into which a special electronic diagnostic tester can be plugged (see Chapter 4A, Section 6). The tester will locate the fault quickly and simply, alleviating the need to test all the system components individually, which is a time-consuming operation that carries a risk of damaging the ECU.

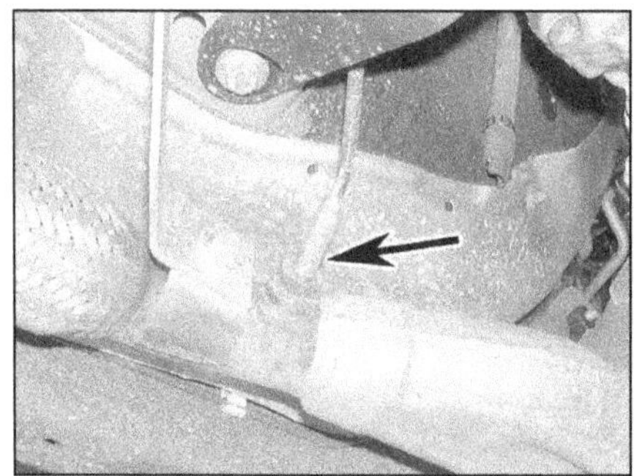

3.4 Oxygen sensor - 2.0 litre DOHC engine

3 Exhaust emission control system components - removal and refitting

Note: *All 2.5 and 3.0 litre engines have two catalytic converters and two oxygen sensors; one for each bank of cylinders.*

Catalytic converter

1 The catalytic converter is an integral part of the exhaust system front pipe. Refer to Chapter 4A for removal and refitting details.

Oxygen sensor

Note: *The oxygen sensor is delicate and will not work if it is dropped or knocked, if its power supply is disrupted, or if any cleaning materials are used on it.*

2 Firmly apply the handbrake then jack up the front of the vehicle and support it on axle stands. Disconnect the battery negative terminal.

3 Trace the wiring back from the oxygen sensor, which is screwed into the exhaust front pipe, to its connector which is clipped to the transmission unit. Disconnect the wiring connector and free the wiring from any relevant retaining clips or ties, noting its correct routing **(see illustration)**.

4 Unscrew the sensor and remove it from the exhaust system front pipe **(see illustration)**. Recover the sealing washer and discard it a new one should be used on refitting.

5 Refitting is a reverse of the removal procedure using a new sealing washer. Prior to installing the sensor apply a smear of high temperature grease to the sensor threads (Vauxhall recommend the use of special grease 19 48 602 - available from your Vauxhall dealer). Tighten the sensor to the specified torque and ensure that the wiring is correctly routed and in no danger of contacting either the exhaust system or engine.

4 Evaporative emission control system components - removal and refitting

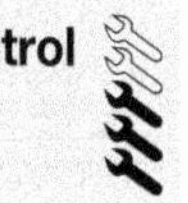

Charcoal canister

1 The charcoal canister is located behind the right-hand front wing. To gain access to the canister, firmly apply the handbrake then jack up the front of the vehicle and support it on axle stands. Remove the right-hand front roadwheel.

2 Remove the retaining nuts and fasteners and remove the wheelarch liner to gain access to the canister. The fasteners are released by pressing out their centre pins and then prising

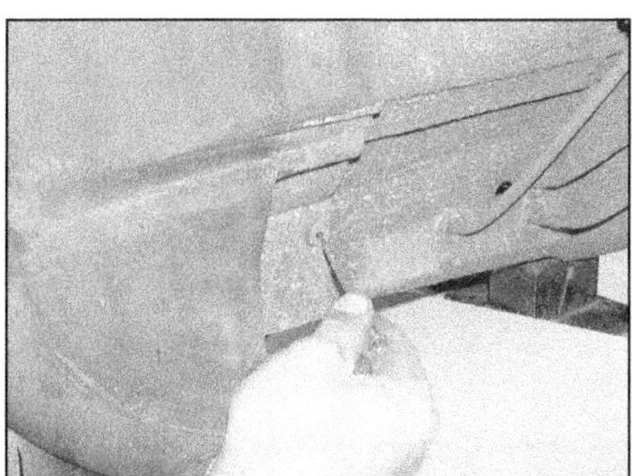
4.2a Unscrew the retaining nuts then press out the centre pins . . .

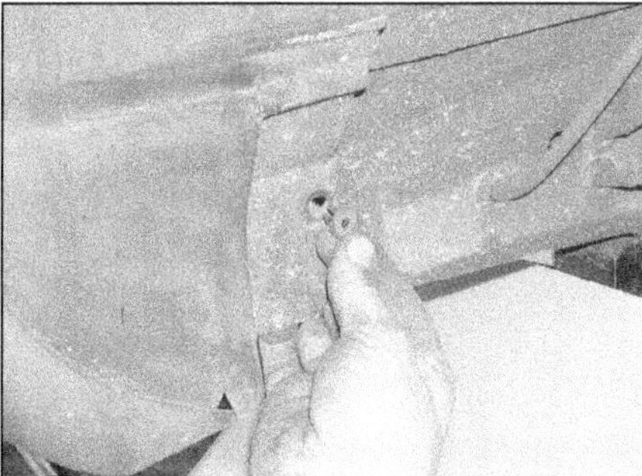
4.2b . . . and remove the fastener outer sections . . .

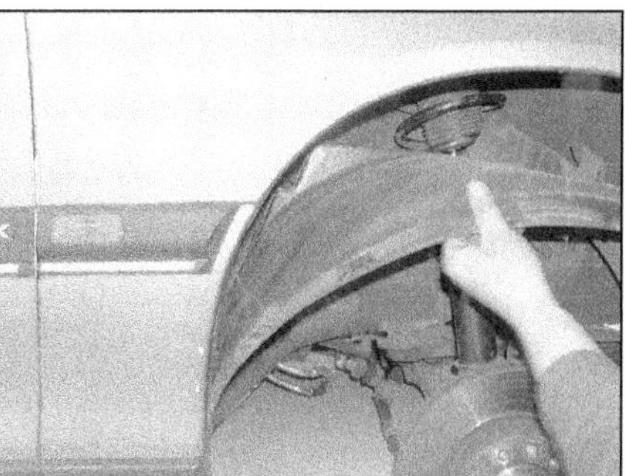
4.2c . . . and remove the right-hand front wheelarch liner

out the outer section; the centre pins must be recovered so they can be reused on refitting **(see illustrations)**.

3 Slacken and remove the retaining nut and free the canister from its mounting. Mark the hoses for identification purposes then disconnect them and remove the canister from the vehicle **(see illustrations)**.

4 Refitting is a reverse of the removal procedure ensuring the hoses are correctly and securely reconnected.

Purge valve

2.0 litre SOHC engine

5 The purge valve is mounted onto the top of the inlet manifold.

6 Undo the bolts securing the wiring cover to the camshaft housing and position the cover clear of the purge valve.

7 To improve access to the valve, release the retaining clips and disconnect the breather hoses from the camshaft housing.

8 Ensure the ignition is switched off then depress the retaining clip and disconnect the wiring connector from the valve.

9 Slacken and remove the valve bracket upper screw then loosen the lower screw and free the valve bracket from the engine. Disconnect the hoses from the valve, noting their correct fitted locations and remove the valve from the engine. The valve and bracket can then be separated.

10 Refitting is a reversal of the removal procedure ensuring the hoses are securely connected.

2.0 litre DOHC engine

11 The purge valve is mounted on the rear of the cylinder head, on the right-hand side of the DIS module.

12 Firmly apply the handbrake then jack up the front of the vehicle and support it on axle stands. Access the valve can then be gained from above and underneath.

13 Ensure the ignition is switched off then disconnect the wiring connector from the valve.

14 Release the retaining clip and free the wiring harness from the purge valve bracket then undo the retaining screws and free the purge valve bracket from the cylinder head.

15 Disconnect the vacuum hoses, noting their correct fitted locations and remove the purge valve and mounting bracket from the vehicle. The valve and bracket can then be separated.

16 Refitting is a reversal of the removal procedure ensuring the hoses are securely connected.

2.5 and 3.0 litre engines

17 The purge valve is located at the rear of the right-hand cylinder head.

18 Remove the inlet manifold upper section as described in Chapter 4A. To further improve access, remove the windscreen wiper arms and the water deflector panel from the base of the windscreen (see Chapter 12, Sections 15 and 16).

19 Slacken and remove the valve bracket retaining bolt then, ensuring the ignition is switched off, disconnect the wiring connector from the valve **(see illustration)**.

20 Disconnect the vacuum hoses, noting their correct fitted locations and remove the purge valve and mounting bracket from the engine. The valve and bracket can then be separated.

21 Refitting is a reversal of the removal procedure ensuring the hoses are securely connected.

5 Exhaust gas recirculation (EGR) system components - removal and refitting

EGR valve

2.0 litre SOHC engine

1 On 2.0 litre SOHC engines, to improve access undo the bolts securing the wiring cover to the camshaft housing and position the cover clear of the EGR valve which is mounted onto the top of the inlet manifold.

2 Ensure the ignition is switched off then disconnect the wiring connector and vacuum hose from the valve.

3 Undo the retaining screws and remove the valve and its gasket, noting which way around the valve is fitted.

4 Refitting is the reverse of removal using a new gasket. Ensure the valve is fitted the correct way around and tighten its retaining bolts to the specified torque.

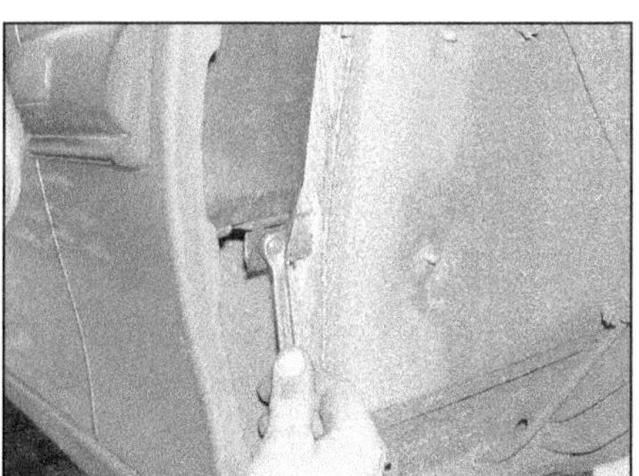
4.3a Unscrew the retaining nut . . .

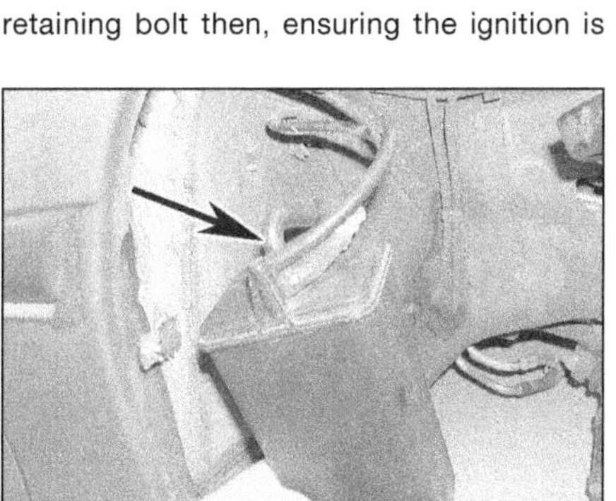
4.3b . . . then free the charcoal canister from its mounting and disconnect it from its hoses

4.19 On 2.5 and 3.0 litre engines the purge valve (arrowed) is mounted on the rear of the right-hand cylinder head (shown with engine removed)

5.7 On 2.5 and 3.0 litre engines, disconnect the wiring connector . . .

2.0 litre DOHC engine

5 The valve is mounted on the rear of the cylinder head. Removal and refitting is as described in paragraphs 2 to 4.

2.5 and 3.0 litre engine

6 The valve is mounted onto an adaptor on the right-hand cylinder head.
7 Ensure the ignition is switched off then disconnect the wiring connector from the valve **(see illustration)**.
8 Undo the retaining screws and remove the valve and its gasket, noting which way around the valve is fitted **(see illustration)**.
9 Refitting is the reverse of removal using a new gasket. Ensure the valve is fitted the correct way around and tighten its retaining bolts to the specified torque.

EGR valve pipe - 2.5 and 3.0 litre engines

10 Slacken the union nuts and remove the pipe connecting the valve adaptor to the right-hand cylinder bank exhaust manifold **(see illustrations)**.
11 On refitting, lubricate the threads of the union nuts with a smear of high-temperature grease (Vauxhall recommend the use of assembly paste 19 48 569 - available from your Vauxhall dealer) and tighten them to the specified torque.

EGR valve adaptor - 2.5 and 3.0 litre engines

12 Remove the EGR valve and pipe as described earlier in this Section.

5.8 . . . then undo the retaining bolts (arrowed) and remove the EGR valve from its adaptor

13 Unclip the accelerator cable from its mounting bracket then unbolt and remove the mounting bracket.
14 Unbolt the bracket from the end of the adaptor then slacken then remove the retaining bolts and remove the adaptor and gasket from the inlet manifold.
15 Refitting is the reverse of removal using a new gasket. Tighten the retaining bolts to the specified torque then refit the EGR valve and pipe (see paragraphs 9 and 11).

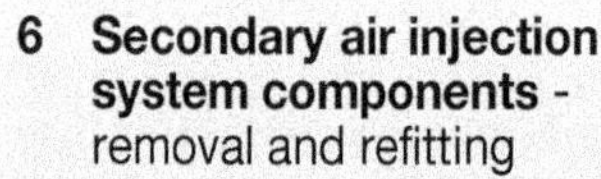

6 Secondary air injection system components - removal and refitting

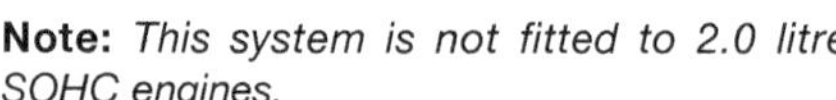

Note: *This system is not fitted to 2.0 litre SOHC engines.*

2.0 litre DOHC engine

Pump and filter assembly

Note: *The filter can be renewed without removing the pump assembly from the vehicle. Detach the hose from the filter then unscrew the nut and remove the retaining clamp and filter from the bracket.*

1 The pump and filter assembly is located behind the left-hand front wing. To gain access to the canister, firmly apply the handbrake then jack up the front of the vehicle and support it on axle stands. Remove the left-hand front roadwheel.
2 Remove the retaining nuts and fasteners

5.10a Unscrew the union nuts . . .

5.10b . . . and remove the EGR valve pipe from the engine

and remove the wheelarch liner to gain access to the canister. The fasteners are released by pressing out their centre pins and then prising out the outer section; the centre pins must be recovered so they can be reused on refitting.
3 Unbolt the horn assembly from the pump mounting bracket and position it clear.
4 Disconnect the pump wiring connector then slacken the retaining clip and disconnect the air hose from the pump **(see illustrations)**.
5 Slacken and remove the pump mounting bracket retaining nuts then manoeuvre the assembly out from underneath the vehicle **(see illustration)**.
6 To separate the pump and bracket first slacken the retaining clips and disconnect the hose connecting the pump to its air filter. If necessary, undo the nut then remove the retaining clamp and air filter from the bracket **(see illustration)**.

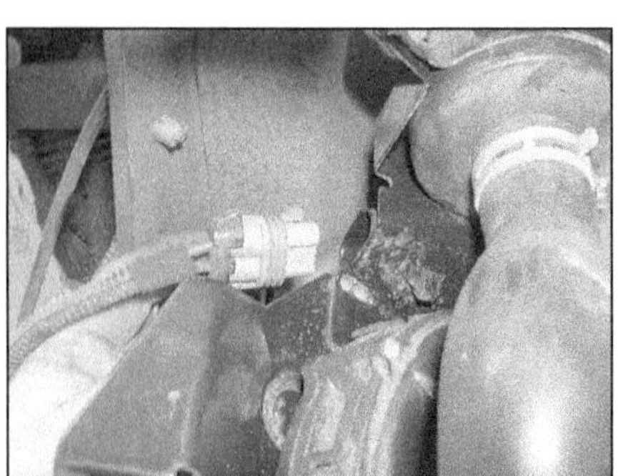

6.4a Disconnect the wiring connector . . .

6.4b . . . then release the retaining clip and disconnect the hose from the air pump

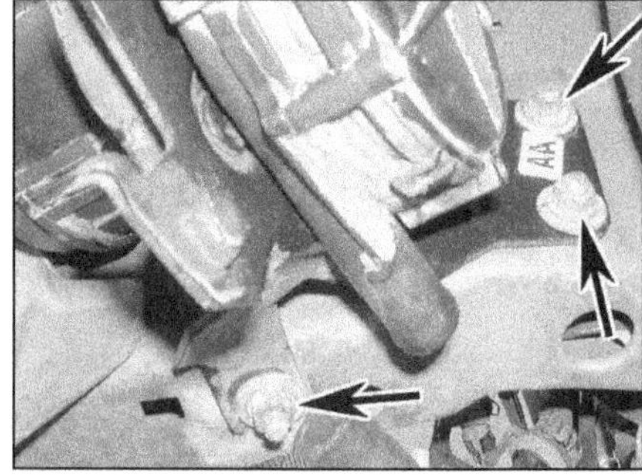

6.5 Undo the retaining nuts (arrowed) and remove the pump and filter assembly from the vehicle

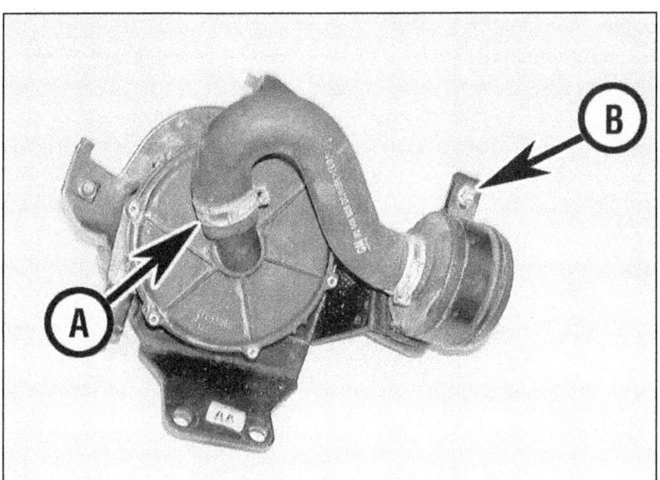

6.6 Release the retaining clip (A) and disconnect the hose then undo the retaining nut (B) and remove the clamp and filter assembly

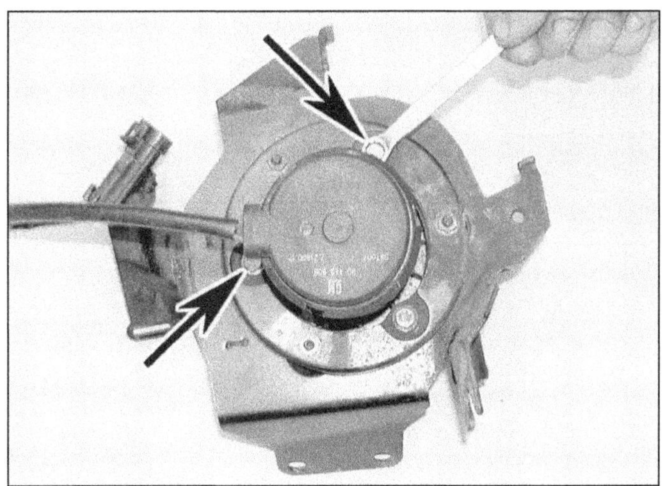
6.8a Undo the retaining bolts (arrowed) . . .

6.8b . . . and separate the pump from its mounting bracket

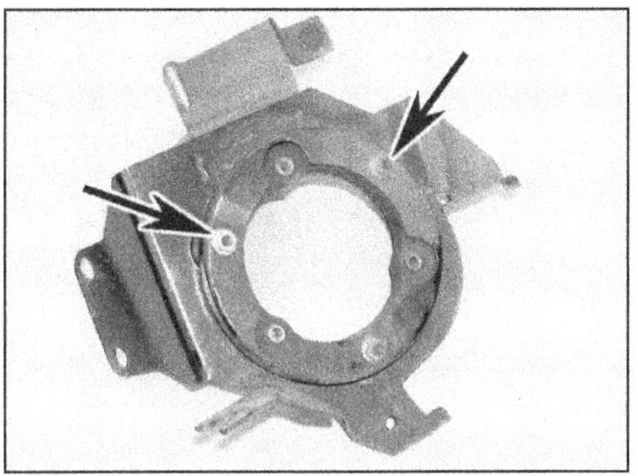
6.8c If necessary, undo the retaining nuts (arrowed) and remove the mounting plate and rubber from the bracket

7 Make alignment marks between the pump, bracket, mounting plate and rubber then free the pump wiring connector from the bracket.

8 Undo the retaining bolts and remove the pump from its mounting bracket. If necessary, unscrew the retaining nuts and remove the mounting plate and rubber from the bracket **(see illustrations)**.

9 Refitting is the reverse of removal aligning the marks made prior to removal and tighten the mounting nuts and bolts to their specified torque settings.

Cut-off valve

10 The valve is located on the left-hand side of the engine compartment. Disconnect the vacuum pipe from the valve then release the retaining clips and disconnect the air hoses **(see illustration)**.

11 Slacken and remove the retaining bolts and remove the valve from the vehicle, noting which way around it is fitted.

12 Refitting is the reverse of removal making sure the valve is fitted the correct way around; the arrow on the valve must point in the direction of air flow (towards the engine).

Cut-off valve solenoid

13 The solenoid valve is located next to the cut-off valve on the left-hand side of the engine compartment **(see illustration)**.

14 Ensure the ignition is switched off then disconnect the wiring connector from the valve and detach the vacuum hoses, noting each ones correct fitted location.

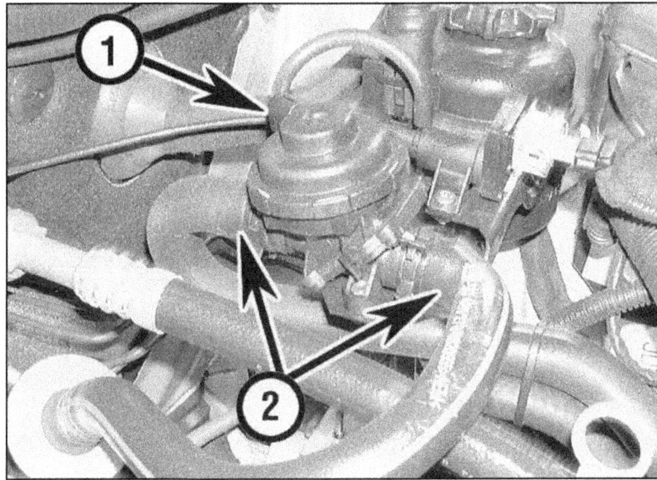

6.10 On 2.0 litre DOHC engines disconnect the vacuum hose (1) then release the retaining clips and free the air hoses (2) from the cut-off valve

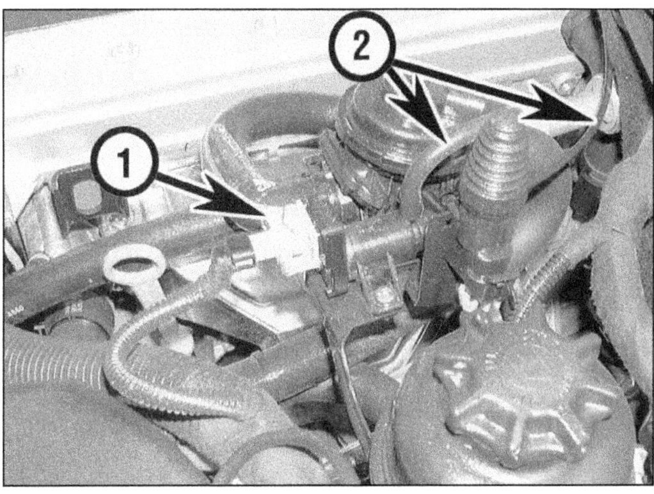

6.13 Disconnect the wiring connector (1) and vacuum hoses (2) from the cut-off valve solenoid

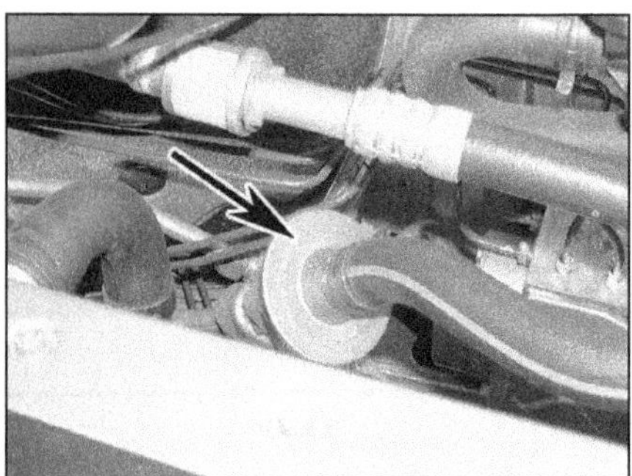
6.18 Release the retaining clip and disconnect the air hose from the non-return valve (arrowed)

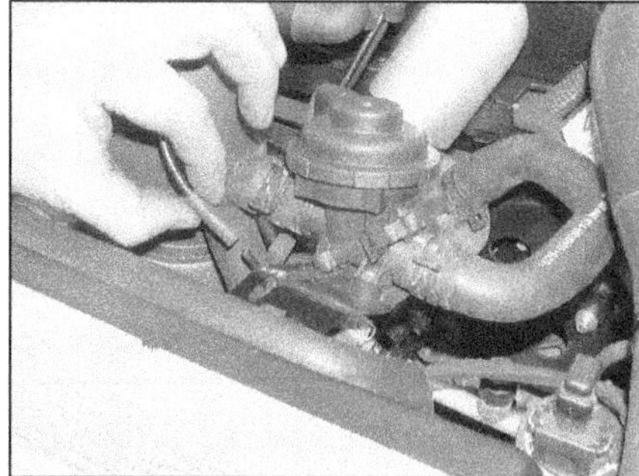
6.28a Disconnect the vacuum pipe from the solenoid valve . . .

6.28b . . . then release the retaining clips and disconnect the hoses from the cut-off valve

15 Undo the retaining screws and remove the valve from the engine compartment.

16 Refitting is the reverse of removal ensuring the vacuum hoses are correctly reconnected.

Non-return valve

17 The non-return valve is located on the top of the exhaust manifold.

18 Release the retaining clip and disconnect the air hose from the pipe then unscrew the valve and remove it from the connecting pipe **(see illustration)**.

19 On refitting, clean the valve threads and apply a smear of fresh sealing compound to them (Vauxhall recommend the use of sealing compound 15 03 295 - available from your Vauxhall dealer). Refit the valve to its pipe and tighten it to the specified torque before securely reconnecting the air hose.

Connecting pipe

20 Release the retaining clip and disconnect the air hose from the connecting pipe non-return valve.

21 Slacken and remove the retaining bolts and remove the bracket securing the connecting pipe to the exhaust manifold.

22 Undo the retaining bolts and remove the heatshield from the exhaust manifold.

23 Slacken the retaining clip and disconnect the breather hose from the left-hand side of the cylinder head cover.

24 Undo the retaining bolts and remove the connecting pipe from the cylinder head/ manifold. Recover the gaskets which are fitted between the pipe unions and cylinder head and discard them.

25 Refitting is the reverse of removal, noting the following.

a) Ensure the mating surfaces are clean and dry and use new gaskets.

b) Apply a smear of high-temperature grease (Vauxhall recommend the use of assembly paste 19 48 569 - available from your Vauxhall dealer) to the threads of the pipe retaining bolts and heatshield bolts prior to refitting.

c) Tighten all bolts to their specified torque settings (where given).

2.5 and 3.0 litre engines

Pump and filter assembly

26 Refer to paragraphs 1 to 9.

Cut-off valve and solenoid valve

27 The cut-off valve and its solenoid are mounted onto a bracket which is secured to the rear of the radiator.

28 Disconnect the vacuum pipe from the solenoid valve then release the retaining clips and disconnect the air hoses from the cut-off valve **(see illustrations)**.

29 Slacken and remove the retaining bolts securing the valve mounting bracket to the radiator and remove the bracket assembly from the vehicle, disconnecting the valve wiring connector as it becomes accessible **(see illustration)**.

30 Undo the retaining bolts and remove the cut-off valve/solenoid valve (as applicable) from the bracket, noting which way around it is fitted **(see illustration)**.

31 Refitting is the reverse of removal. If the cut-off valve has been removed, make sure it is fitted the correct way around with the arrow pointing in the direction of air flow (towards the engine).

Non-return valve

32 The non-return valve is screwed onto the left-hand end of the front connecting pipe and is located just in front of the timing belt cover **(see illustration)**. To improve access to the valve unbolt the air conditioning pipe/hose bracket from the cylinder head and position the hose/pipe to one side.

33 Release the retaining clip and disconnect the air hose from the pipe then unscrew the valve and remove it from its pipe.

6.29 Undo the retaining bolts and disconnect the wiring connector (arrowed) then remove the bracket assembly from the vehicle

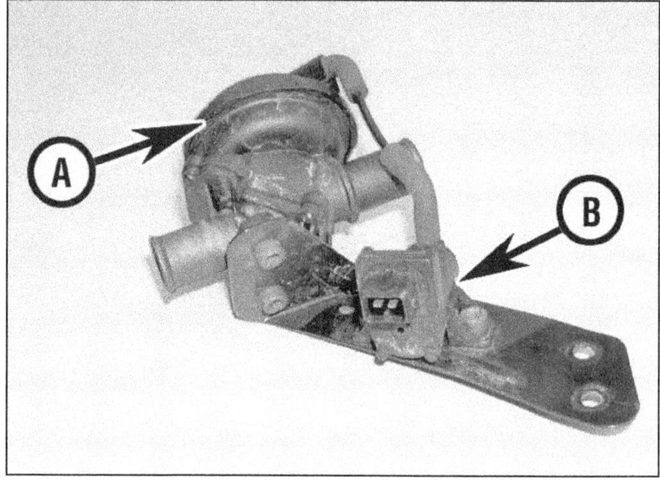

6.30 Air cut-off valve (A) and solenoid valve (B) can then be unbolted from the bracket

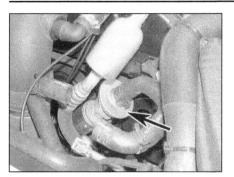

6.32 Non return valve location - 2.5 and 3.0 litre engines

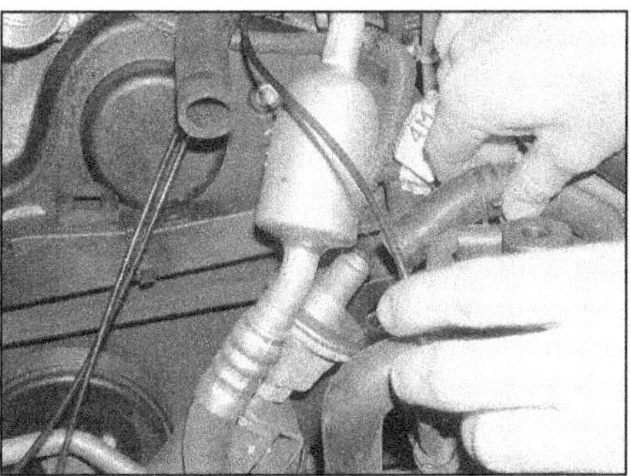

6.36 Disconnect the air hose from the non-return valve on the front connecting pipe

6.37a Slacken and remove the left-hand . . .

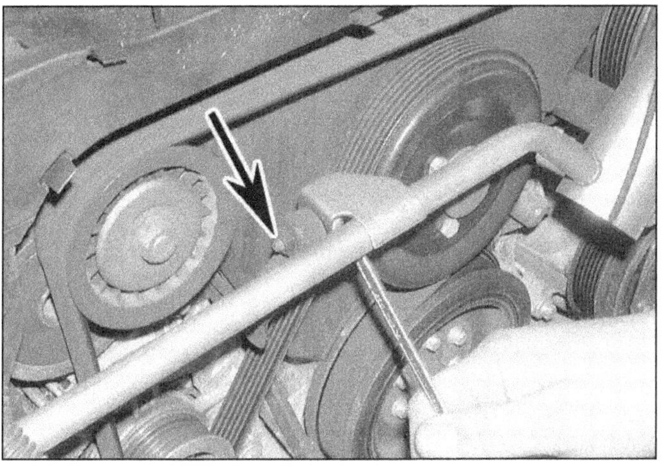

6.37b . . . and right-hand retaining nuts then (if necessary) slacken the alternator mounting nut and pivot the bracket (arrowed) clear of the pipe . . .

6.37c . . . to allow the front connecting pipe to be removed from the engine

34 On refitting, clean the valve threads and apply a smear of fresh sealing compound to them (Vauxhall recommend the use of sealing compound 15 03 295 - available from your Vauxhall dealer). Refit the valve to its pipe and tighten it to the specified torque before securely reconnecting the air hose.

Front connecting pipe

35 Remove the multi-ram air intake system pre-volume chamber as described in Chapter 4A.

36 Release the retaining clip and disconnect the air hose from the front connecting pipe non-return valve **(see illustration)**.

37 Unscrew the pipe retaining nuts then release the retaining clips securing the pipe ends to the hoses and remove the assembly from the engine compartment. If necessary, slacken the alternator upper mounting nut and pivot the pipe bracket out of position to gain the necessary clearance required for removal **(see illustrations)**.

38 Refitting is the reverse of removal ensuring the hose are correctly and securely reconnected.

Left-hand cylinder head connecting pipe

39 Remove the exhaust system left-hand front pipe as described in Chapter 4A.

40 On models with air conditioning, remove the auxiliary drivebelt then unbolt the compressor and position it clear of its mounting bracket (see Chapters 1 and 3).

Warning: Do not disconnect any of the refrigerant pipes/hoses

41 Slacken and remove the bolts securing the upper and lower heatshields to the left-hand exhaust manifold. Remove the lower heatshield and position the upper one clear of the manifold so access can be gained to the connecting pipe bolts.

42 Slacken and remove the retaining bolts and free the connecting pipe from the manifold **(see illustration)**. Release the retaining clip securing the rubber hose to the front of the connecting pipe then disconnect the pipe and manoeuvre it out from underneath the vehicle. Recover the gaskets which are fitted between the pipe and manifold and discard them.

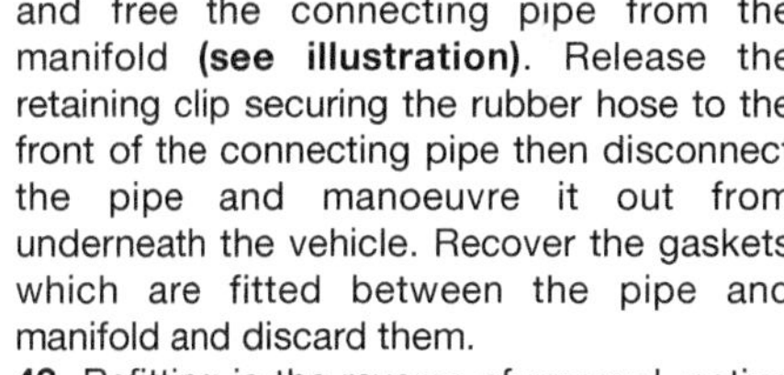

43 Refitting is the reverse of removal, noting the following points.

a) *Ensure the mating surfaces are clean and dry and use new gaskets* **(see illustration)**.

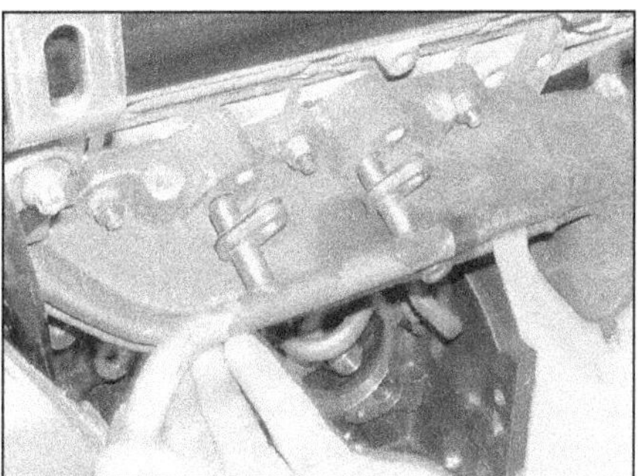

6.42 Removing the left-hand connecting pipe from the manifold (shown with engine removed)

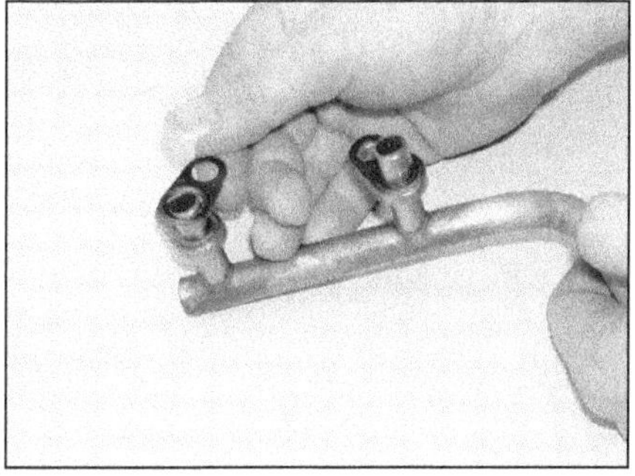

6.43 On refitting, ensure the mating surfaces are clean and dry and fit new gaskets to the connecting pipe

6.45a Undo the retaining bolts and remove the lower . . .

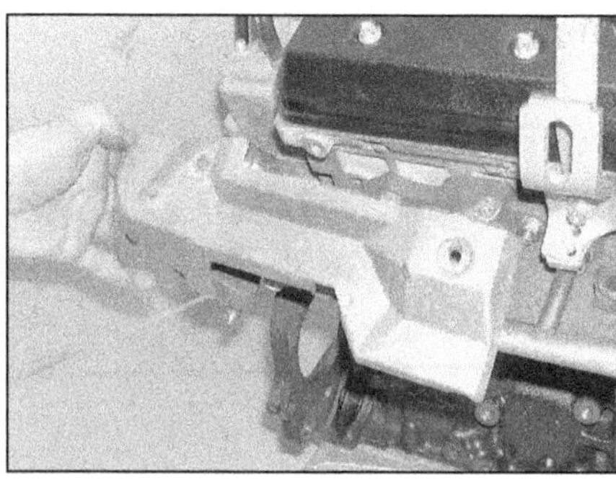
6.45b . . . and upper heatshields from the right-hand exhaust manifold (shown with engine removed)

6.47 Removing the right-hand connecting pipe from the manifold

b) Apply a smear of high-temperature grease (Vauxhall recommend the use of assembly paste 19 48 569 - available from your Vauxhall dealer) to the threads of the pipe retaining bolts and the heatshield bolts prior to refitting.

c) Tighten all bolts to their specified torque settings (where given).

Right-hand cylinder head connecting pipe

44 Slacken and remove the bolt securing the coolant pipe bracket to the right-hand cylinder head.

45 Slacken and remove the retaining bolts then remove the lower and upper heatshields from the exhaust manifold **(see illustrations)**.

46 Taking care not to place excess strain on the coolant pipe, slacken and remove the retaining bolts securing the connecting pipe to the manifold.

47 Free the connecting pipe from the manifold then release the retaining clip securing the rubber hose to the front of the connecting pipe then disconnect the pipe and manoeuvre it out of position **(see illustration)**. Recover the gaskets which are fitted between the pipe and manifold and discard them.

48 Refitting is the reverse of removal, noting the following points.

a) Ensure the mating surfaces are clean and dry and use new gaskets.

b) Apply a smear of high-temperature grease (Vauxhall recommend the use of assembly paste 19 48 569 - available from your Vauxhall dealer) to the threads of the pipe retaining bolts and heatshield bolts prior to refitting.

c) Tighten all bolts to their specified torque settings (where given).

7 Catalytic converter - general information and precautions

1 The catalytic converter is a reliable and simple device which needs no maintenance in itself, but there are some facts of which an owner should be aware if the converter is to function properly for its full service life.

a) DO NOT use leaded petrol in a car equipped with a catalytic converter - the lead will coat the precious metals, reducing their converting efficiency and will eventually destroy the converter.

b) Always keep the ignition and fuel systems well-maintained in accordance with the manufacturer's schedule.

c) If the engine develops a misfire, do not drive the car at all (or at least as little as possible) until the fault is cured.

d) DO NOT push- or tow-start the car - this will soak the catalytic converter in unburned fuel, causing it to overheat when the engine does start.

e) DO NOT switch off the ignition at high engine speeds.

f) DO NOT use fuel or engine oil additives - these may contain substances harmful to the catalytic converter.

g) DO NOT continue to use the car if the engine burns oil to the extent of leaving a visible trail of blue smoke.

h) Remember that the catalytic converter operates at very high temperatures. DO NOT, therefore, park the car in dry undergrowth, over long grass or piles of dead leaves after a long run.

i) Remember that the catalytic converter is FRAGILE - do not strike it with tools during servicing work.

j) In some cases a sulphurous smell (like that of rotten eggs) may be noticed from the exhaust. This is common to many catalytic converter-equipped cars and once the car has covered a few thousand miles the problem should disappear.

k) The catalytic converter, used on a well-maintained and well-driven car, should last indefinitely - if the converter is no longer effective it must be renewed.

Chapter 5 Part A:
Starting and charging systems

Contents

Degrees of difficulty

Easy, suitable for novice with little experience 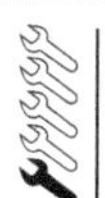	**Fairly easy,** suitable for beginner with some experience 	**Fairly difficult,** suitable for competent DIY mechanic	**Difficult,** suitable for experienced DIY mechanic 	**Very difficult,** suitable for expert DIY or professional

Specifications

System type	12-volt, negative earth	
Battery		
Charge condition:		
Poor	12.5 volts	
Normal	12.6 volts	
Good	12.7 volts	

Torque wrench settings	**Nm**	**lbf ft**
Alternator mounting bolts:		
2.0 litre engine:		
Lower bolt	35	26
Upper bracket bolts:		
SOHC engine	18	13
DOHC engine	20	15
2.5 and 3.0 litre engine	35	26
Oil level sensor bolts	8	6
Oil pressure switch	40	30
Starter motor bolts:		
2.0 litre engine:		
Lower bolt	45	33
Rear mounting bracket to block bolt	25	18
Upper bolt	60	44
2.5 and 3.0 litre engine	40	30

1 General information and precautions

General information

1 The engine electrical system consists mainly of the charging and starting systems. Because of their engine-related functions, these components are covered separately from the body electrical devices such as the lights, instruments, etc (which are covered in Chapter 12). Refer to Part B for information on the ignition system.

2 The electrical system is of the 12-volt negative earth type.

3 The battery is of the low maintenance or maintenance-free (sealed for life) type and is charged by the alternator, which is belt-driven from the crankshaft pulley.

4 The starter motor is of the pre-engaged type incorporating an integral solenoid. On starting, the solenoid moves the drive pinion into engagement with the flywheel ring gear before the starter motor is energised. Once the engine has started, a one-way clutch prevents the motor armature being driven by the engine until the pinion disengages from the flywheel.

Precautions

5 Further details of the various systems are given in the relevant Sections of this Chapter. While some repair procedures are given, the usual course of action is to renew the component concerned. The owner whose interest extends beyond mere component renewal should obtain a copy of the *Automobile Electrical & Electronic Systems Manual*, available from the publishers of this manual.

6 It is necessary to take extra care when working on the electrical system to avoid damage to semi-conductor devices (diodes and transistors), and to avoid the risk of personal injury. In addition to the precautions given in *Safety first!* at the beginning of this manual, observe the following when working on the system:

7 *Always remove rings, watches, etc before working on the electrical system.* Even with the battery disconnected, capacitive discharge could occur if a component's live terminal is earthed through a metal object. This could cause a shock or nasty burn.

8 *Do not reverse the battery connections.* Components such as the alternator, electronic control units, or any other components having semi-conductor circuitry could be irreparably damaged.

9 If the engine is being started using jump leads and a slave battery, connect the batteries *positive-to-positive* and *negative-to-negative* (see *Jump starting*). This also applies when connecting a battery charger.

10 Never disconnect the battery terminals, the alternator, any electrical wiring or any test instruments when the engine is running.

11 Do not allow the engine to turn the alternator when the alternator is not connected.

12 Never test for alternator output by flashing the output lead to earth.

13 Never use an ohmmeter of the type incorporating a hand-cranked generator for circuit or continuity testing.

14 Always ensure that the battery negative lead is disconnected before carrying out any serious work on the electrical system. **Note:** *On models with a Vauxhall anti-theft warning system (ATWS), the battery negative terminal must be disconnected within 15 seconds of the ignition being switched off to prevent the alarm system being triggered.*

15 Before using electric-arc welding equipment on the car, disconnect the battery, alternator and components such as the engine management electronic control unit to protect them from the risk of damage.

16 The radio/cassette unit fitted as standard equipment by Vauxhall is equipped with a built-in security code to deter thieves. If the power source to the unit is cut, the anti-theft system will activate. Even if the power source is immediately reconnected, the radio/ cassette unit will not function until the correct security code has been entered. Therefore, if you do not know the correct security code for the radio/ cassette unit **do not** disconnect the battery negative terminal of the battery or remove the radio/cassette unit from the vehicle. Refer to *Radio/cassette unit anti-theft system precaution* Section for further information.

2 Electrical fault finding - general information

Refer to Chapter 12.

3 Battery - testing and charging

Standard and low maintenance battery - testing

1 If the vehicle covers a small annual mileage, it is worthwhile checking the specific gravity of the electrolyte every three months to determine the state of charge of the battery. Use a hydrometer to make the check and compare the results with the following table. Note that the specific gravity readings assume an electrolyte temperature of 15°C (60°F); for every 10°C (18°F) below 15°C (60°F) subtract 0.007. For every 10°C (18°F) above 15°C (60°F) add 0.007.

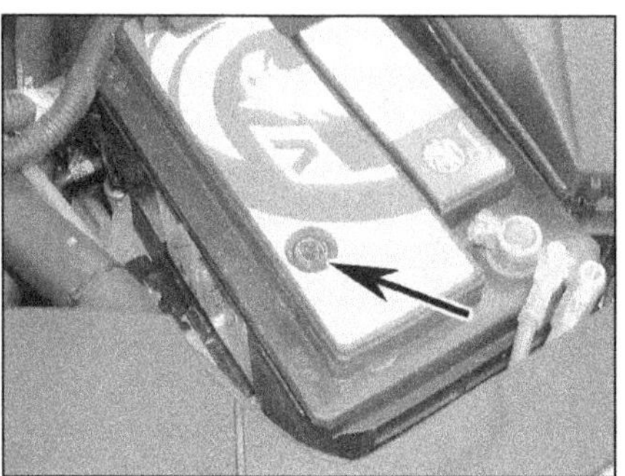

3.5 Standard Vauxhall battery with built-in charge indicator (arrowed)

Ambient temperature - 25°C (77°F)

	Above	Below
Charged	*1.210 to 1.230*	*1.270 to 1.290*
70% charged	*1.170 to 1.190*	*1.230 to 1.250*
Discharged	*1.050 to 1.070*	*1.110 to 1.130*

2 If the battery condition is suspect, first check the specific gravity of electrolyte in each cell. A variation of 0.040 or more between any cells indicates loss of electrolyte or deterioration of the internal plates.

3 If the specific gravity variation is 0.040 or more, the battery should be renewed. If the cell variation is satisfactory but the battery is discharged, it should be charged as described later in this Section.

Maintenance-free battery - testing

4 In cases where a sealed for life maintenance-free battery is fitted, topping-up and testing of the electrolyte in each cell is not possible. The condition of the battery can therefore only be tested using a battery condition indicator or a voltmeter.

5 Certain models may be fitted with a Delco or Vauxhall type maintenance-free battery, with a built-in charge condition indicator **(see illustration)**. The indicator is located in the top of the battery casing, and indicates the condition of the battery from its colour. If the indicator shows green, then the battery is in a good state of charge. If the indicator turns darker, eventually to black, then the battery requires charging, as described later in this Section. If the indicator shows clear/yellow, then the electrolyte level in the battery is too low to allow further use, and the battery should be renewed. **Do not** attempt to charge, load or jump start a battery when the indicator shows clear/yellow.

6 If testing the battery using a voltmeter, connect the voltmeter across the battery and compare the result with those given in the Specifications under charge condition. The test is only accurate if the battery has not been subjected to any kind of charge for the previous six hours. If this is not the case, switch on the headlights for 30 seconds, then wait four to five minutes before testing the battery after switching off the headlights. All other electrical circuits must be switched off, so check that the doors and tailgate are fully shut when making the test.

7 If the voltage reading is less than 12.2 volts, then the battery is discharged, whilst a reading of 12.2 to 12.4 volts indicates a partially discharged condition.

8 If the battery is to be charged, remove it from the vehicle (Section 4) and charge it as described later in this Section.

Standard and low maintenance battery - charging

Note: *The following is intended as a guide only. Always refer to the manufacturer's recommendations (often printed on a label attached to the battery) before charging a battery.*

9 Charge the battery at a rate of 3.5 to 4 amps and continue to charge the battery at this rate until no further rise in specific gravity is noted over a four hour period.

10 Alternatively, a trickle charger charging at the rate of 1.5 amps can safely be used overnight.

11 Specially rapid boost charges which are claimed to restore the power of the battery in 1 to 2 hours are not recommended, as they can cause serious damage to the battery plates through overheating.

12 While charging the battery, note that the temperature of the electrolyte should never exceed 37.8°C (100°F).

Maintenance-free battery - charging

Note: *The following is intended as a guide only. Always refer to the manufacturer's recommendations (often printed on a label attached to the battery) before charging a battery.*

13 This battery type takes considerably longer to fully recharge than the standard type, the time taken being dependent on the extent of discharge, but it can take anything up to three days.

14 A constant voltage type charger is required, to be set, when connected, to 13.9 to 14.9 volts with a charger current below 25 amps. Using this method, the battery should be usable within three hours, giving a voltage reading of 12.5 volts, but this is for a partially discharged battery and, as mentioned, full charging can take considerably longer.

15 If the battery is to be charged from a fully discharged state (condition reading less than 12.2 volts), have it recharged by your Vauxhall dealer or local automotive electrician, as the charge rate is higher and constant supervision during charging is necessary.

4 Battery - removal and refitting

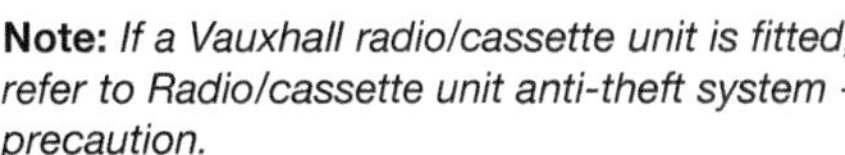

Note: *If a Vauxhall radio/cassette unit is fitted, refer to Radio/cassette unit anti-theft system - precaution.*

Removal

1 The battery is located on the left-hand side of the engine compartment. On some models the battery will be housed in a protective casing.

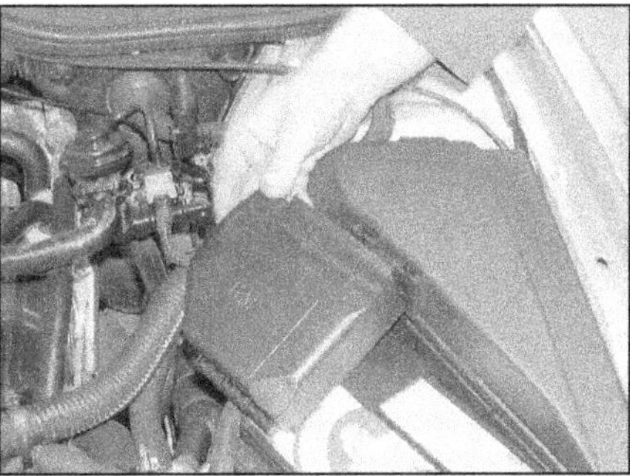

4.3 Where necessary, unclip the fusible link housing from the relay box and position it clear of the battery

2 Unclip the cover (where fitted) then slacken the clamp nut and disconnect the clamp from the battery negative (earth) terminal. **Note:** *On models with a Vauxhall anti-theft warning system (ATWS), the battery negative terminal must be disconnected within 15 seconds of the ignition being switched off to prevent the alarm system being triggered.*

3 On models where a fusible link housing is clipped onto the engine compartment relay box, unclip the housing and position it clear of the battery **(see illustration)**.

4 Lift the insulation cover and disconnect the positive terminal lead in the same way.

5 Unscrew the bolt and remove the battery retaining clamp and lift the battery out of the engine compartment.

Refitting

6 Refitting is a reversal of removal, but smear petroleum jelly on the terminals when reconnecting the leads, and always reconnect the positive lead first, and the negative lead last.

5 Charging system - testing

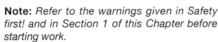

Note: *Refer to the warnings given in Safety first! and in Section 1 of this Chapter before starting work.*

1 If the ignition warning light fails to illuminate when the ignition is switched on, first check the alternator wiring connections for security. If satisfactory, check that the warning light bulb has not blown, and that the bulbholder is secure in its location in the instrument panel. If the light still fails to illuminate, check the continuity of the warning light feed wire from the alternator to the bulbholder. If all is satisfactory, the alternator is at fault and should be renewed or taken to an auto-electrician for testing and repair.

2 If the ignition warning light illuminates when the engine is running, stop the engine and check that the drivebelt is correctly tensioned (see Section 6) and that the alternator connections are secure. If all is so far satisfactory, have the alternator checked by an auto-electrician for testing and repair.

3 If the alternator output is suspect even though the warning light functions correctly, the regulated voltage may be checked as follows.

4 Connect a voltmeter across the battery terminals and start the engine.

5 Increase the engine speed until the voltmeter reading remains steady; the reading should be approximately 12 to 13 volts, and no more than 14 volts.

6 Switch on as many electrical accessories (eg, the headlights, heated rear window and heater blower) as possible, and check that the alternator maintains the regulated voltage at around 13 to 14 volts.

7 If the regulated voltage is not as stated, the fault may be due to worn brushes, weak brush springs, a faulty voltage regulator, a faulty diode, a severed phase winding or worn or damaged slip rings. The alternator should be renewed or taken to an auto-electrician for testing and repair.

7.2 On 2.0 litre DOHC engines, disconnect the wiring connector from the intake air temperature sensor and airflow meter . . .

6 Alternator drivebelt - removal, refitting and tensioning

1 Refer to the procedure given for the auxiliary drivebelt in Chapter 1.

7 Alternator - removal and refitting

Removal

1 Disconnect the battery negative lead and proceed as described under the relevant sub-heading. **Note:** *On models with a Vauxhall anti-theft warning system (ATWS), the battery negative terminal must be disconnected within 15 seconds of the ignition being switched off to prevent the alarm system being triggered.*

2.0 litre engine

2 Disconnect the wiring connectors from the intake air temperature sensor and the airflow meter **(see illustration)**.

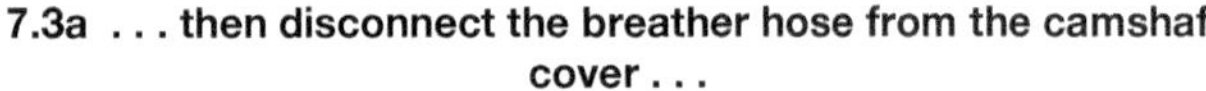

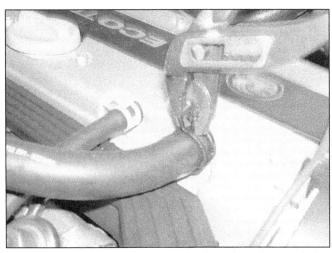

7.3a . . . then disconnect the breather hose from the camshaft cover . . .

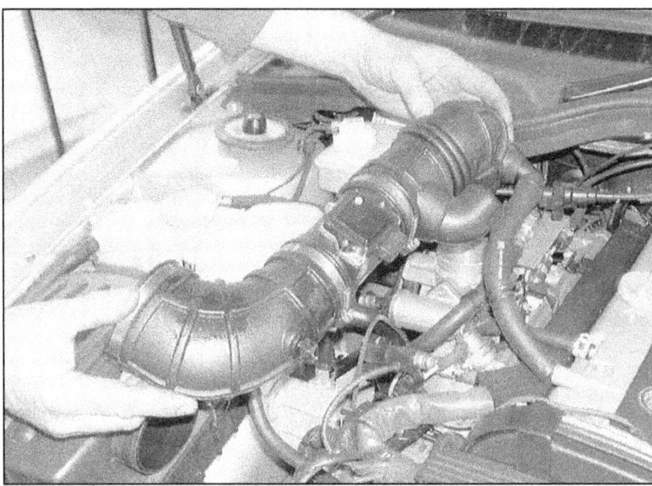

7.3b . . . before slackening the retaining clips and removing the intake duct assembly

3 Slacken the retaining clips then disconnect the intake duct from the air cleaner and throttle housing and remove the duct assembly from the engine compartment. On DOHC engines it will be necessary to disconnect the breather hose in order to allow the duct to be removed **(see illustrations)**.

4 Release the auxiliary drivebelt as described in Chapter 1 and disengage it from the alternator pulley.

5 Undo the bolts and remove the support brackets securing the alternator to the inlet manifold and cylinder head. Slacken the lower mounting bolt and pivot the alternator away from the block to improve access to the wiring connections.

6 Remove the rubber covers (where fitted) from the alternator terminals, then unscrew the retaining nuts and disconnect the wiring from the rear of the alternator.

7 Unscrew the nut from the lower mounting bolt then withdraw the bolt and manoeuvre the alternator out of position.

2.5 and 3.0 litre engines

8 Firmly apply the handbrake then jack up the front of the vehicle and support it on axle stands. Undo the retaining screws and remove the undercover from beneath the engine so access to the alternator can be gained from below.

9 Release the auxiliary drivebelt as described in Chapter 1 and disengage it from the alternator pulley.

10 Remove the rubber covers (where fitted) from the alternator terminals, then unscrew the retaining nuts and disconnect the wiring from the rear of the alternator **(see illustration)**.

11 Slacken and remove the upper and lower mounting nut and bolt then manoeuvre the alternator out of position.

Refitting

12 Refitting is the reverse of removal tightening all mounting bolts to their specified torque settings (where given). Ensure the drivebelt is correctly refitted and tensioned as described in Chapter 1.

8 Alternator - testing and overhaul

1 If the alternator is thought to be suspect, it should be removed from the vehicle and taken to an auto-electrician for testing. Most auto-electricians will be able to supply and fit brushes at a reasonable cost. However, check on the cost of repairs before proceeding as it may prove more economical to obtain a new or exchange alternator.

9 Starting system - testing

Note: *Refer to the precautions given in Safety first! and in Section 1 of this Chapter before starting work.*

1 If the starter motor fails to operate when the ignition key is turned to the appropriate position, the following possible causes may be to blame.

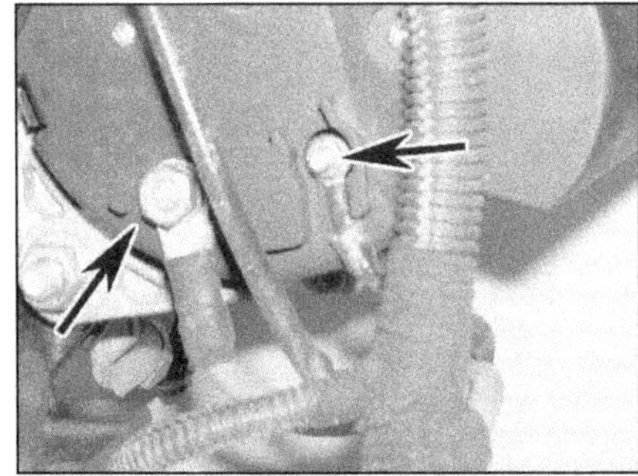

7.10 Slacken the retaining nuts (arrowed) and disconnect the wiring from the rear of the alternator (shown with engine removed)

a) The battery is faulty.
b) The electrical connections between the switch, solenoid, battery and starter motor are somewhere failing to pass the necessary current from the battery through the starter to earth.
c) The solenoid is faulty.
d) The starter motor is mechanically or electrically defective.

2 To check the battery, switch on the headlights. If they dim after a few seconds, this indicates that the battery is discharged - recharge (see Section 3) or renew the battery. If the headlights glow brightly, operate the ignition switch and observe the lights. If they dim, then this indicates that current is reaching the starter motor, therefore the fault must lie in the starter motor. If the lights continue to glow brightly (and no clicking sound can be heard from the starter motor solenoid), this indicates that there is a fault in the circuit or solenoid - see following paragraphs. If the starter motor turns slowly when operated, but the battery is in good condition, then this indicates that either the starter motor is faulty, or there is considerable resistance somewhere in the circuit.

3 If a fault in the circuit is suspected, disconnect the battery leads (including the earth connection to the body), the starter/solenoid wiring and the engine/transmission earth strap. Thoroughly clean the connections, and reconnect the leads and wiring, then use a voltmeter or test lamp to check that full battery voltage is available at the battery positive lead connection to the solenoid, and that the earth is sound. Smear petroleum jelly around the battery terminals to prevent corrosion - corroded connections are amongst the most frequent causes of electrical system faults.

4 If the battery and all connections are in good condition, check the circuit by disconnecting the wire from the solenoid blade terminal. Connect a voltmeter or test lamp between the wire end and a good earth (such as the battery negative terminal), and check that the wire is live when the ignition switch is turned to the start position. If it is, then the circuit is sound - if not the circuit wiring can be checked as described in Chapter 12, Section 2.

5 The solenoid contacts can be checked by connecting a voltmeter or test lamp between the battery positive feed connection on the starter side of the solenoid, and earth. When the ignition switch is turned to the start position, there should be a reading or lighted bulb, as applicable. If there is no reading or lighted bulb, the solenoid is faulty and should be renewed.

6 If the circuit and solenoid are proved sound, the fault must lie in the starter motor. In this event, it may be possible to have the starter motor overhauled by a specialist, but check on the cost of spares before proceeding, as it may prove more economical to obtain a new or exchange motor.

10 Starter motor - removal and refitting

Removal

1 Disconnect the battery negative lead then firmly apply the handbrake then jack up the front of the vehicle and support it on axle stands. Undo the retaining screws and remove the undercover from beneath the engine then proceed as described under the relevant sub-heading. **Note:** *On models with a Vauxhall anti-theft warning system (ATWS), the battery negative terminal must be disconnected within 15 seconds of the ignition being switched off to prevent the alarm system being triggered.*

2.0 litre engine

2 Slacken and remove the two retaining nuts and disconnect the wiring from the starter motor solenoid. Recover the washers under the nuts. On DOHC engine models, to improve access to the motor, undo the retaining bolts and remove the inlet manifold support bracket.

3 Unscrew the retaining bolt securing the starter motor rear bracket to the cylinder block.

4 Slacken and remove the upper and lower retaining bolts, noting the bolts are different lengths, and remove the starter motor from the vehicle. The upper bolt comes through from behind and secures the transmission unit to the cylinder block.

2.5 and 3.0 litre engine

5 Remove the right-hand engine mounting and bracket as described in Chapter 2C.

6 Slacken and remove the two retaining nuts and disconnect the wiring from the starter motor solenoid. Recover the washers under the nuts.

7 Slacken and remove the upper and lower retaining bolts and remove the starter motor from the vehicle.

Refitting

8 Refitting is a reversal of removal tightening the retaining bolts to the specified torque. Ensure all wiring is correctly routed and its retaining nuts are securely tightened.

11 Starter motor - testing and overhaul

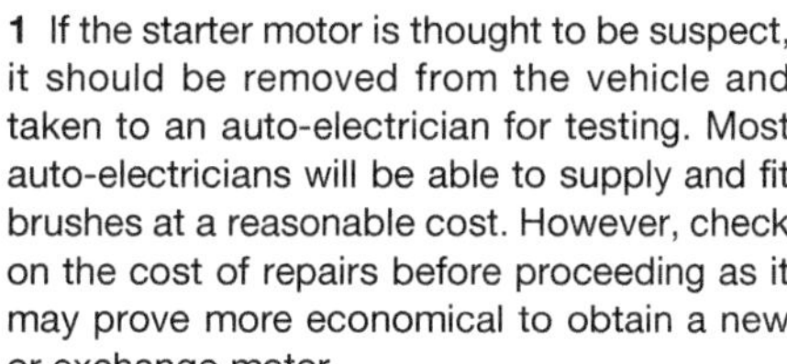

1 If the starter motor is thought to be suspect, it should be removed from the vehicle and taken to an auto-electrician for testing. Most auto-electricians will be able to supply and fit brushes at a reasonable cost. However, check on the cost of repairs before proceeding as it may prove more economical to obtain a new or exchange motor.

12 Ignition switch - removal and refitting

1 The ignition switch is integral with the steering column lock, and can be removed as described in Chapter 10.

13 Oil pressure warning light switch - removal and refitting

Removal

1 The switch is screwed into the oil pump housing which is located on the front of the engine, on the end of the crankshaft. On 2.0 litre engines the switched is screwed into the rear of the housing and on 2.5 and 3.0 litre engines it is screwed into the front of the housing.

2 To improve access to the switch, firmly apply the handbrake then jacked up the front of the vehicle and support it on axle stands. Undo the retaining bolts and remove the undercover from beneath the engine unit.

3 Disconnect the wiring connector then unscrew the switch and recover the sealing washer. Be prepared for oil spillage, and if the switch is to be left removed from the engine for any length of time, plug the switch aperture.

Refitting

4 Examine the sealing washer for signs of damage or deterioration and if necessary renew.

5 Refit the switch and washer, tightening it to the specified torque, and reconnect the wiring connector.

6 Refit the undercover then lower the vehicle to the ground. Check and, if necessary, top up the engine oil as described in *Weekly checks*.

14 Oil level sensor - removal and refitting

2.0 litre SOHC engine

Removal

1 The oil level sensor (where fitted) is located on the right-hand face of the engine sump.

2 To gain access to the sensor, firmly apply the handbrake then jack up the front of the vehicle and support it on axle stands. Where necessary, undo the retaining screws and remove the undercover from beneath the engine unit.

3 Drain the engine oil into a clean container then refit the drain plug and tighten it to the specified torque setting (see Chapter 1).

4 Disconnect the wiring connector from the sensor.

5 Unscrew the retaining bolts then ease the sensor out from the sump and remove it along with its sealing ring. Discard the sealing ring, a new one should be used on refitting.

Refitting

6 Refitting is the reverse of removal using a new sealing ring. On completion refill the engine with oil (see Chapter 1).

2.0 litre DOHC engine

Engines with a one-piece sump

7 Remove and refit the sensor as described in paragraphs 1 to 6.

Engines with a two-piece sump

8 Remove and refit the sensor as described in paragraphs 9 to 11.

2.5 and 3.0 litre engine

Removal

9 Remove the sump pan as described in Chapter 2C.

10 Unscrew the retaining bolts and remove the sensor from the sump pan, noting which way around it is fitted **(see illustration)**.

Refitting

11 Ensure the sensor is correctly positioned then tighten its retaining bolts to the specified torque. Refit the sump pan as described in Chapter 2C.

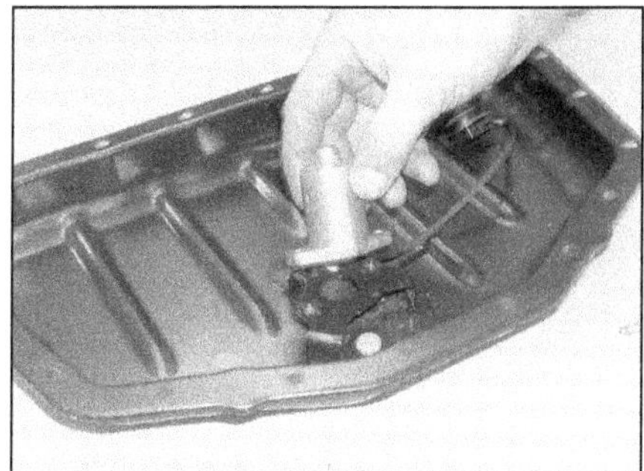

14.10 Removing the oil level sensor (2.5 litre engine shown)

Chapter 5 Part B: Ignition system

Contents

Degrees of difficulty

Easy, suitable for novice with little experience 	**Fairly easy,** suitable for beginner with some experience 	**Fairly difficult,** suitable for competent DIY mechanic 	**Difficult,** suitable for experienced DIY mechanic 	**Very difficult,** suitable for expert DIY or professional

Specifications

System type

System type	Distributorless ignition system controlled by engine management ECU

Firing order

2.0 litre engine	1-3-4-2 (No 1 cylinder at timing belt end)
2.5 and 3.0 litre engine	1-2-3-4-5-6 (No1 cylinder at timing belt end of right-hand cylinder bank)

Torque wrench settings

Torque wrench settings	Nm	lbf ft
DIS module bolts	8	6
DIS module bracket bolts - 2.0 litre SOHC engine	15	11

1 Ignition system - general information

Warning: Voltages produced by an electronic ignition system are considerably higher than those produced by conventional ignition systems. Extreme care must be taken when working on the system with the ignition switched on. Persons with surgically-implanted cardiac pacemaker devices should keep well clear of the ignition circuits, components and test equipment.

2.0 litre engine

1 The ignition system is integrated with the fuel injection system to form a combined engine management system under the control of one ECU (See Chapter 4A, Section 13 for further information). The ignition side of the system is of the distributorless type, and consists of the DIS (distributorless ignition system) module and the knock sensor.

2 The DIS module is actually a four output ignition coil. The module actually consists of two separate HT coils which supply two cylinders each (one coil supplies cylinders 1 and 4, and the other cylinders 2 and 3). Under the control of the ECU, the module operates on the wasted spark principle, ie. each spark plug sparks twice for every cycle of the engine, once on the compression stroke and once on the exhaust stroke. The ECU uses its inputs from the various sensors to calculate the required ignition advance setting and coil charging time.

3 The knock sensor is mounted onto the cylinder block and informs the ECU when the engine is pinking under load. The sensor is sensitive to vibration and detects the knocking which occurs when the engine starts to pink (pre-ignite). The knock sensor sends an electrical signal to the ECU which in turn retards the ignition advance setting until the pinking ceases.

2.5 and 3.0 litre engine

4 Refer to the information given in paragraphs 1 to 3 noting that there are two knock sensors (one for the left-hand bank of cylinders and one for the right-hand bank) and the DIS module is a six output coil consisting of three separate HT coils which supply two cylinders each.

2 Ignition system - testing

1 If a fault appears in the engine management (fuel injection/ignition) system first ensure that the fault is not due to a poor electrical connection or poor maintenance; ie, check that the air cleaner filter element is clean, the spark plugs are in good condition and correctly gapped, that the engine breather hoses are clear and undamaged, referring to Chapter 1 for further information. Also check that the accelerator cable is correctly adjusted as described in Chapter 4A. If the engine is running very roughly, check the compression pressures as described in Chapter 2A. Whilst checking the spark plugs, also check the HT leads as follows.

2 Check inside the HT lead end fitting for signs of corrosion, which will look like a white crusty powder. Push the end fitting back onto the spark plug, ensuring that it is a tight fit on the plug. If not, remove the lead again and use pliers to carefully crimp the metal connector inside the end fitting until it fits securely on the end of the spark plug.

3 Using a clean rag, wipe the entire length of the lead to remove any built-up dirt and grease. Once the lead is clean, check for burns, cracks and other damage. Do not bend the lead excessively, nor pull the lead lengthwise - the conductor inside might break.

4 Disconnect the other end of the lead from the DIS module (see Section 3) and check for corrosion and a tight fit in the same manner as the spark plug end. Ensure that the leads are numbered before removing them, to avoid confusion when refitting. Pull the leads from the plugs by gripping the end fitting, not the lead, otherwise the lead connection may be fractured. Refit the lead securely on completion.

5 Check the remaining leads one at a time, in the same way. If new spark plug (HT) leads are required, purchase a set for your specific car and engine.

3.6 **DIS module wiring connector (1) and HT leads (2) from the DIS module - 2.0 litre DOHC engine**

3.8 **On 2.5 and 3.0 litre engines the DIS module is mounted on the rear of the left-hand cylinder head (later model shown with engine removed)**

6 If these checks fail to reveal the cause of the problem the vehicle should be taken to a suitably equipped Vauxhall dealer for testing. A wiring block connector is incorporated in the engine management circuit into which a special electronic diagnostic tester can be plugged (see Chapter 4A, Section 6). The tester will locate the fault quickly and simply alleviating the need to test all the system components individually which is a time consuming operation that carries a high risk of damaging the ECU. If necessary, the system wiring and wiring connectors can be checked, ensuring that the ECU wiring connector has first been disconnected.

3 DIS module - removal and refitting

Removal

2.0 litre SOHC engine

1 The DIS module is mounted onto the rear of the cylinder head. Firmly apply the handbrake then jack up the front of the vehicle and support it on axle stands; access can then be gained both from above and below.

2 Ensure the ignition is switched off then disconnect the wiring connector from the DIS module.

3 Slacken and remove the bolts securing the DIS module mounting bracket to the cylinder head noting the correct fitted location of the engine lifting bracket. Free the wiring from the bracket then manoeuvre the module and bracket assembly out from behind the cylinder head.

4 Disconnect the HT leads from the DIS module and remove the module from the vehicle. The module HT lead terminals are numbered (the leads should also be numbered) with their respective cylinder number to avoid confusion on refitting. If necessary, undo the bolts and separate the module and bracket.

2.0 litre DOHC engine

5 Undo the retaining screws and remove the spark plug cover from the cylinder head cover.

6 Ensure the ignition is switches off then disconnect the wiring connector and HT leads from the DIS module **(see illustration)**. The module HT lead terminals are numbered (the leads should also be numbered) with their respective cylinder number to avoid confusion on refitting.

7 Slacken and remove the retaining bolts and remove the DIS module from the rear of the cylinder head.

2.5 and 3.0 litre engine

8 The DIS module is mounted onto the rear of the left-hand cylinder head **(see illustration)**. To gain access to the module remove the wiper motor as described in Chapter 12. The module is very awkward to remove; access can by further improved by unclip the wiring connector holder from the lifting bracket on the rear of the cylinder head and disconnecting the pipes/hoses which pass over the module.

9 Slacken and remove the retaining bolts and free the module from cylinder head. On early models the module is bolted directly onto the head (as opposed to being mounted on a bracket on later models), access to the lower bolts may be easier from below once the vehicle has been raised and supported.

10 Disconnect the wiring connector and HT leads from the DIS module and remove the module from the vehicle. The module HT lead terminals are numbered (the leads should also be numbered) with their respective cylinder number to avoid confusion on refitting.

Refitting

11 Refitting is the reverse of removal, ensuring each HT lead is securely reconnected to its corresponding terminal on the DIS module using the numbers on the leads and module. Tighten the retaining bolts to the specified torque and securely reconnect the wiring connector.

4 Ignition timing - checking and adjustment

1 There are no timing marks on the flywheel or crankshaft pulley. The timing is constantly being monitored and adjusted by the engine management ECU, and nominal values cannot be given. Therefore, it is not possible for the home mechanic to check the ignition timing.

2 The only way in which the ignition timing can be checked and (where possible) adjusted is by using special electronic test equipment, connected to the engine management system diagnostic connector (refer to Chapter 4A, Section 6 for further information). Refer to your Vauxhall dealer for further information.

Chapter 6
Clutch

Contents

Degrees of difficulty

Easy, suitable for novice with little experience 	**Fairly easy,** suitable for beginner with some experience 	**Fairly difficult,** suitable for competent DIY mechanic 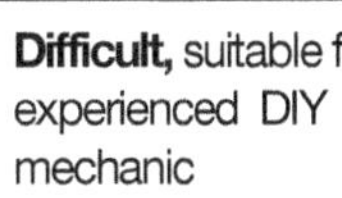	**Difficult,** suitable for experienced DIY mechanic	**Very difficult,** suitable for expert DIY or professional

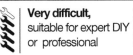

Specifications

Type	Single dry plate with diaphragm spring, hydraulically operated	
Friction plate		
Diameter:		
2.0 litre engine models	216 mm	
2.5 litre engine models	228 mm	
3.0 litre engine models	240 mm	
Torque wrench settings	**Nm**	**lbf ft**
Bleed screw	9	7
Hydraulic pipe union nut	14	10
Master cylinder retaining nuts	20	15
Pedal:		
Mounting bracket bolt	18	13
Pivot bolt nut	18	13
Pressure plate retaining bolts:		
M7 bolts	15	11
M8 bolts	28	21
Release cylinder mounting bolts	22	16

1 General information

1 The clutch consists of a friction plate, a pressure plate assembly, and the hydraulic release cylinder and bearing; all of these components are contained in the large cast-aluminium alloy bellhousing, sandwiched between the engine and the transmission.

2 The friction plate is fitted between the engine flywheel and the clutch pressure plate, and is allowed to slide on the transmission input shaft splines.

3 The pressure plate assembly is bolted to the engine flywheel. When the engine is running, drive is transmitted from the crankshaft, via the flywheel, to the friction plate (these components being clamped securely together by the pressure plate assembly) and from the friction plate to the transmission input shaft.

4 To interrupt the drive, the spring pressure must be relaxed. This is achieved using a hydraulic release mechanism which consists of the master cylinder, the release cylinder and the pipe/hose linking the two components. Depressing the pedal pushes on the master cylinder pushrod which hydraulically forces the release cylinder bearing against the pressure plate spring fingers. This causes the springs to deform and releases the clamping force on the friction plate.

5 The clutch is self-adjusting and requires no manual adjustment.

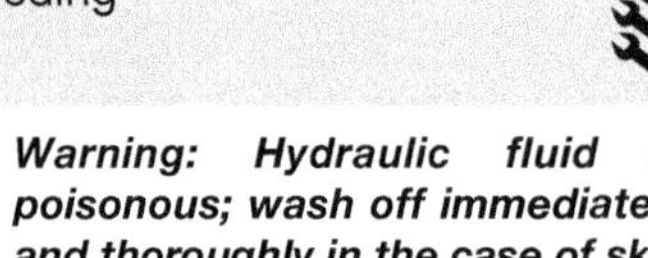

2 Clutch hydraulic system - bleeding

Warning: Hydraulic fluid is poisonous; wash off immediately and thoroughly in the case of skin contact, and seek immediate medical advice if any fluid is swallowed or gets into the eyes. Certain types of hydraulic fluid are flammable, and may ignite when allowed into contact with hot components; when servicing any hydraulic system, it is safest to assume that the fluid is flammable, and to take precautions against the risk of fire as though it is petrol that is being handled. Hydraulic fluid is also an effective paint stripper, and will attack plastics; if any is spilt, it should be washed off immediately, using copious quantities of fresh water. Finally, it is hygroscopic (it absorbs moisture from the air) - old fluid may be contaminated and unfit for further use. When topping-up or renewing the fluid, always use the recommended type, and ensure that it comes from a freshly opened sealed container.

1 The correct operation of any hydraulic system is only possible after removing all air from the components and circuit; this is achieved by bleeding the system.

2 During the bleeding procedure, add only clean, unused hydraulic fluid of the recommended type; never re-use fluid that has already been bled from the system. Ensure that sufficient fluid is available before starting work.

3 If there is any possibility of incorrect fluid being already in the system, the hydraulic circuit must be flushed completely with uncontaminated, correct fluid.

4 If hydraulic fluid has been lost from the system, or air has entered because of a leak, ensure that the fault is cured before continuing further.

5 The bleed screw is located on the right-hand side of the transmission bellhousing **(see illustration)**. To gain access, firmly apply the handbrake then jack up the front of the vehicle and support it on axle stands so that the screw can be reached from below.

6 Check that all pipes and hoses are secure, unions tight and the bleed screw is closed. Clean any dirt from around the bleed screw.

7 Unscrew the master cylinder fluid reservoir cap (the clutch shares the same fluid reservoir as the braking system), and top the master cylinder reservoir up to the upper (MAX) level line. Refit the cap loosely, and remember to maintain the fluid level at least above the lower (MIN) level line throughout the procedure, or there is a risk of further air entering the system.

8 There are a number of one-man, do-it-yourself bleeding kits currently available from motor accessory shops. It is recommended that one of these kits is used whenever possible, as they greatly simplify the bleeding operation, and reduce the risk of expelled air and fluid being drawn back into the system. If such a kit is not available, the basic (two-man) method must be used, which is described in detail below.

9 If a kit is to be used, prepare the vehicle as described previously, and follow the kit manufacturer's instructions, as the procedure may vary slightly according to the type being used; generally, they are as outlined below in the relevant sub-section.

Bleeding - basic (two-man) method

10 Collect a clean glass jar, a suitable length of plastic or rubber tubing which is a tight fit over the bleed screw, and a ring spanner to fit the screw. The help of an assistant will also be required.

11 Remove the dust cap from the bleed screw. Fit the spanner and tube to the screw, place the other end of the tube in the jar, and pour in sufficient fluid to cover the end of the tube.

12 Ensure that the fluid level is maintained at least above the lower level line in the reservoir throughout the procedure.

13 Have the assistant fully depress the clutch pedal several times to build up pressure, then maintain it on the final downstroke.

14 While pedal pressure is maintained, unscrew the bleed screw (approximately one turn) and allow the compressed fluid and air to flow into the jar. The assistant should maintain pedal pressure and should not release it until instructed to do so. When the flow stops, tighten the bleed screw again, have the assistant release the pedal slowly, and recheck the reservoir fluid level.

15 Repeat the steps given in paragraphs 13 and 14 until the fluid emerging from the bleed screw is free from air bubbles. If the master cylinder has been drained and refilled allow approximately five seconds between cycles for the master cylinder passages to refill.

16 When no more air bubbles appear, tighten the bleed screw to the specified torque, remove the tube and spanner, and refit the dust cap. Do not overtighten the bleed screw.

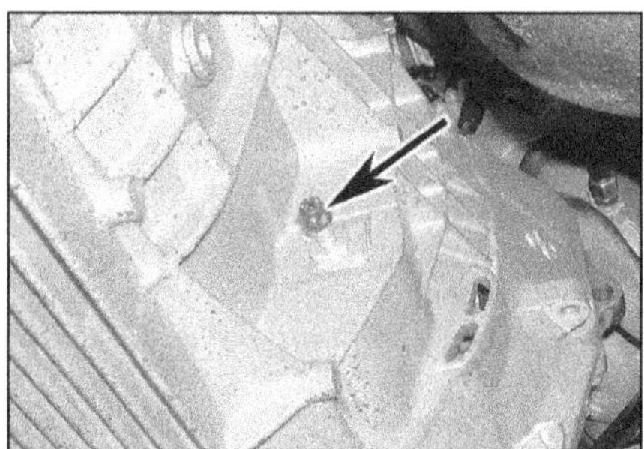

2.5 Clutch bleed screw location (arrowed)

Bleeding - using a one-way valve kit

17 As their name implies, these kits consist of a length of tubing with a one-way valve fitted, to prevent expelled air and fluid being drawn back into the system; some kits include a translucent container, which can be positioned so that the air bubbles can be more easily seen flowing from the end of the tube.

18 The kit is connected to the bleed screw, which is then opened. The user returns to the driver's seat, depresses the clutch pedal with a smooth, steady stroke, and slowly releases it; this is repeated until the expelled fluid is clear of air bubbles.

19 Note that these kits simplify work so much that it is easy to forget the clutch fluid reservoir level; ensure that this is maintained at least above the lower level line at all times.

Bleeding - using a pressure-bleeding kit

20 These kits are usually operated by the reservoir of pressurised air contained in the spare tyre. However, note that it will probably be necessary to reduce the pressure to a lower level than normal; refer to the instructions supplied with the kit.

21 By connecting a pressurised, fluid-filled container to the clutch fluid reservoir, bleeding can be carried out simply by opening the bleed screw and allowing the fluid to flow out until no more air bubbles can be seen in the expelled fluid.

22 This method has the advantage that the large reservoir of fluid provides an additional safeguard against air being drawn into the system during bleeding.

All methods

23 When bleeding is complete, and correct pedal feel is restored, tighten the bleed screw to the specified torque and wash off any spilt fluid. Refit the dust cap to the bleed screw.

24 Check the hydraulic fluid level in the master cylinder reservoir, and top-up if necessary (see *Weekly checks*).

25 Discard any hydraulic fluid that has been bled from the system; it will not be fit for re-use.

26 Check the operation of the clutch pedal. If the clutch is still not operating correctly, air must still be present in the system, and further bleeding is required. Failure to bleed satisfactorily after a reasonable repetition of the bleeding procedure may be due to worn master cylinder/release cylinder seals.

3 Master cylinder - removal and refitting

Removal

1 On 2.5 and 3.0 litre right-hand drive models and all left-hand drive models, to improve access to the master cylinder remove the windscreen wiper arms and the water deflector panel from the base of the windscreen (see Chapter 12, Sections 15 and 16).

2 On all models, remove all traces of dirt from the outside of the master cylinder and position some cloth beneath the cylinder to catch any spilt fluid.

3 Slacken the retaining clip then disconnect the master cylinder hose from the reservoir outlet. Plug the reservoir outlet to minimise fluid loss then wash off any spilt fluid immediately.

4 Slide out the retaining clip and free the hydraulic pipe from the front of the master cylinder. Plug pipe end and master cylinder port to minimise fluid loss and prevent the entry of dirt. Refit the retaining clip to the master cylinder groove, ensuring its is correctly located.

5 From inside the vehicle, release the retaining clips (rotate them through 90°) then remove the undercover panel from the drivers' side of the facia. Remove the fastener (prise out the centre pin then pull out the fastener outer section) then unclip and remove the heater/ventilation duct to improve access to the pedal.

6 Slide off the retaining clip and remove the clevis pin securing the master cylinder pushrod to the pedal then slacken and remove the cylinder retaining nuts.

7 Return to the engine compartment and remove the master cylinder from the vehicle noting that it maybe necessary to unclip the brake pipes from the bulkhead to gain the necessary clearance required. If the master cylinder is faulty it must be renewed; overhaul of the unit is not possible.

Refitting

8 Ensure the cylinder and bulkhead mating surfaces then manoeuvre the master cylinder into position.

9 From inside the vehicle, ensure the pushrod clevis is correctly engaged with the pedal then refit the master cylinder retaining nuts, tightening them to the specified torque.

10 Apply a smear of multi-purpose grease to the clevis pin then align the clevis and pedal and insert the pin. Secure the clevis pin in position with the retaining clip, making sure it is correctly located in the pin groove, then refit the heater/ventilation duct and facia undercover.

11 Working in the engine compartment, ensure that the retaining clip is correctly located in the master cylinder groove and the clutch pipe sealing ring is in good condition. Ease the pipe union into position until the retaining clip is heard to click then check that the pipe is securely retained.

12 Reconnect the master cylinder pipe to the fluid reservoir outlet and securely tighten its retaining clip.

13 Where necessary, refit the water deflector panel and bulkhead sealing strip then refit both windscreen wiper arms (see Chapter 12).

14 Top up the fluid reservoir and bleed the clutch hydraulic system (see Section 2).

4 Release cylinder - removal and refitting

Removal

Note: *Refer to the warning concerning the dangers of asbestos dust at the beginning of Section 6.*

1 Remove the transmission unit as described in Chapter 7A.

2 Remove the release bearing from the cylinder noting which way around it is fitted.

3 Wipe clean the outside of the release cylinder then slacken the union nut securing the feed pipe to the cylinder. Free the rubber grommet from the transmission housing and remove the pipe assembly.

4 Slacken the union nut and free the bleed screw pipe from the release cylinder. If necessary, slide off the retaining clip and remove the bleed screw assembly from the transmission housing.

5 Unscrew the three retaining bolts and slide the release the cylinder off from the transmission input shaft. Remove the sealing ring which is fitted to the rear of the release cylinder and discard it; a new one must be used on refitting. Whilst the cylinder is removed, take care not to allow any debris to enter the transmission unit.

6 The release cylinder is a sealed unit and must be renewed if faulty. The only component which can be replaced is the input shaft seal which is fitted to the rear of the cylinder (see Chapter 7A, Section 5).

7 Also check the release bearing noting that it is often considered worthwhile to renew it as a matter of course. Check that the contact surface rotates smoothly and easily, with no sign of noise or roughness, and that the surface itself is smooth and unworn, with no signs of cracks, pitting or scoring. If there is any doubt about its condition, the bearing must be renewed.

Refitting

8 If the original cylinder is being refitted it is recommended that the input shaft oil seal is renewed, regardless of its apparent condition (see Chapter 7A, Section 5).

9 Ensure the release cylinder and transmission mating surfaces are clean and dry and fit the new sealing ring to the recess on the rear of the release cylinder.

10 Lubricate the release cylinder seal with a smear of transmission oil then carefully ease the cylinder along the input shaft and into position. Ensure the sealing ring is still correctly seated in its groove then refit the release cylinder retaining bolts and tighten them to the specified torque.

11 Reconnect the bleed screw pipe to the release cylinder and tighten its union nut to the specified torque. Where necessary secure the bleed screw assembly in position with the retaining clip.

12 Reconnect the feed pipe to the release cylinder and seat the sealing grommet in the transmission housing. Make sure the pipe is centrally position in the housing aperture then tighten the union nut to the specified torque.

13 Lubricate the inner bore of the release bearing with a smear of high temperature grease (Vauxhall recommend the use of lubricating paste 19 42 530 - available from your Vauxhall dealer); do apply too much or there is risk of the clutch friction plate becoming contaminated. Fit the release bearing to the cylinder making sure it is the correct way around.

14 Refit the transmission unit as described in Chapter 7A.

5 Clutch pedal - removal and refitting

Removal

1 From inside the vehicle, release the retaining clips (rotate them through 90°) then remove the undercover panel from the drivers' side of the facia. Remove the fastener (prise out the centre pin then pull out the fastener outer section) then unclip and remove the heater/ventilation duct to improve access to the pedals.

2 Slide off the retaining clip and remove the clevis pin securing the master cylinder pushrod to the pedal.

3 Where necessary, disconnect the wiring connector from the clutch pedal switch.

4 Slacken and remove the master cylinder retaining nuts and free the cylinder pushrod from the pedal.

5 Fully depress the clutch pedal then slacken and remove the pedal mounting bracket upper retaining bolt and manoeuvre the pedal assembly out from underneath the facia.

6 If necessary, clamp the pedal bracket firmly in a vice and disassemble as follows.

7 On 2.0 litre engine models unhook the return spring, noting its correct fitted position. Remove the retaining clip from the pivot bolt nut then slacken and remove the nut and washer. Remove the pivot bolt and separate the pedal and return spring from the mounting bracket.

8 On 2.5 and 3.0 litre engine models carefully unhook the return spring lower end fitting from the pedal and remove the spring assembly noting which way around the end fittings are positioned. Remove the retaining clip from the pivot bolt nut then slacken and remove the nut and washer. Remove the pivot bolt and separate the pedal from the mounting bracket noting the correct fitted location of the thrustwasher.

9 On all models check the pedal components for signs of damage. If any components is worn or damage it should be renewed.

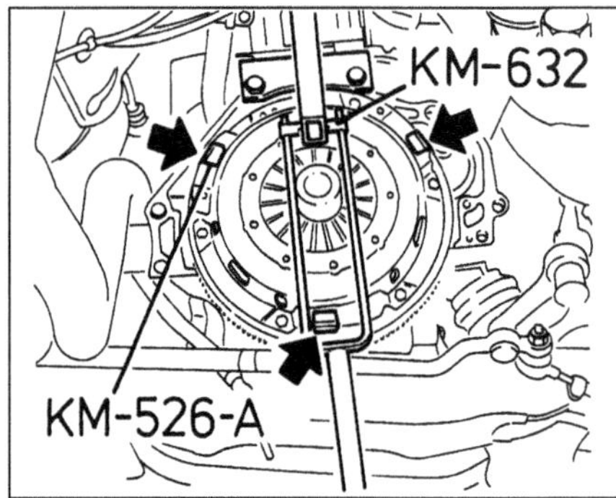

6.3 Vauxhall service tool for depressing the diaphragm spring on engines with a normal flywheel

Arrows indicate where pressure plate retaining clips are fitted

Refitting

10 If the pedal and bracket assembly has been dismantled, apply a smear of multi-purpose grease to the pedal pivot bolt and bushes prior to reassembly.

11 On 2.0 litre engine models, fit the return spring to the pedal then refit the assembly to the mounting bracket. Insert the pivot bolt then refit the washer and nut, tightening it to the specified torque. Secure the pivot bolt nut in position with the retaining clip then hook the return spring back into position.

12 On 2.5 and 3.0 litre engine models refit the pedal to the mounting bracket then, making sure the thrustwasher is correctly positioned, insert the pivot bolt. Refit the washer and nut to the pivot bolt then tighten it to the specified torque and secure in position with the retaining clip. Ensure the end fittings are correctly seated on the return spring then refit the assembly to the pedal and bracket making sure the smaller end fitting is positioned at the pedal end.

13 On all models, manoeuvre the pedal and bracket assembly into position and refit the upper retaining bolt. Engage the master cylinder pushrod with the pedal then refit the master cylinder retaining nuts. Tighten both the master cylinder nuts and the pedal bracket bolt to their specified torque settings.

14 Apply a smear of multi-purpose grease to the clevis pin then align the clevis and pedal and insert the pin. Secure the clevis pin in 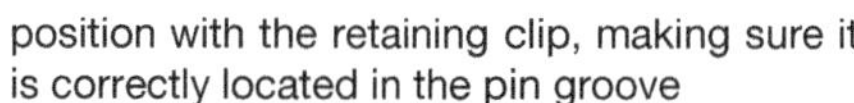position with the retaining clip, making sure it is correctly located in the pin groove

15 Reconnect the wiring connector to the clutch pedal switch (where fitted) then refit the heater/ventilation duct and facia undercover.

6 Clutch assembly - removal, inspection and refitting

Warning: Dust created by clutch wear and deposited on the clutch components may contain asbestos, which is a health hazard. DO NOT blow it out with compressed air, or inhale any of it. DO NOT use petrol or petroleum-based solvents to clean off the dust. Brake system cleaner or methylated spirit should be used to flush the dust into a suitable receptacle. After the clutch components are wiped clean with rags, dispose of the contaminated rags and cleaner in a sealed, marked container.

Note: *Although some friction materials may no longer contain asbestos, it is safest to assume that they do, and to take precautions accordingly.*

Removal

1 Remove the transmission as described in Chapter 7A.

2 Before disturbing the clutch, use chalk or a marker pen to mark the relationship of the pressure plate assembly to the flywheel.

3 Working in a diagonal sequence, evenly and progressively slacken the pressure plate bolts by half a turn at a time, until spring pressure is released and the bolts can be unscrewed by hand.

Caution: To avoid the risk of distorting the pressure plate diaphragm spring it is most important that the pressure plate bolts are evenly slackened. To avoid this, on models with a normal flywheel (it is not possible if a dual-mass flywheel is fitted) Vauxhall dealers use a special tool to depress the diaphragm spring and then hold the spring in its compressed state by fitting special clips to the pressure plate assembly (see illustration). Removal of the clips and fitting to a new pressure plate will then require the use of a press. However, provided adequate care is taken to unscrew the pressure plate bolts evenly no distortion should occur.

4 Remove the pressure plate assembly and collect the friction plate, noting which way round the friction plate is fitted.

Inspection

Note: *Due to the amount of work necessary to remove and refit clutch components, it is usually considered good practice to renew the clutch friction plate, pressure plate assembly and release bearing as a matched set, even if only one of these is actually worn enough to require renewal. It is also worth considering the renewal of the clutch components on a preventive basis if the engine and/or transmission have been removed for some other reason.*

5 Remove the clutch assembly.

6 When cleaning clutch components, read first the warning at the beginning of this Section; remove dust using a clean, dry cloth, and working in a well-ventilated atmosphere.

7 Check the friction plate facings for signs of wear, damage or oil contamination. If the friction material is cracked, burnt, scored or damaged, or if it is contaminated with oil or grease (shown by shiny black patches), the friction plate must be renewed.

8 If the friction material is still serviceable, check that the centre boss splines are unworn, that the torsion springs are in good condition and securely fastened, and that all the rivets are tight. If any wear or damage is found, the friction plate must be renewed.

9 If the friction material is fouled with oil, this must be due to an oil leak from the crankshaft oil seal, from the sump-to-cylinder block joint, or from the release cylinder assembly (either the input shaft seal or the sealing ring). Renew the crankshaft oil seal or repair the sump joint as described in the relevant part of Chapter 2, before installing the new friction plate. The clutch release cylinder is covered in Section 4.

10 Check the pressure plate assembly for obvious signs of wear or damage; shake it to check for loose rivets or worn or damaged fulcrum rings, and check that the drive straps securing the pressure plate to the cover do not show signs (such as a deep yellow or blue discoloration) of overheating. If the diaphragm spring is worn or damaged, or if its pressure is in any way suspect, the pressure plate assembly should be renewed.

11 Examine the machined bearing surfaces of the pressure plate and of the flywheel; they should be clean, completely flat, and free from scratches or scoring. If either is discoloured from excessive heat, or shows signs of cracks, it should be renewed - although minor damage of this nature can sometimes be polished away using emery paper.

12 Also check that the release cylinder bearing rotates smoothly and easily, with no sign of noise or roughness. Also check that the surface itself is smooth and unworn, with

6.14 Refit the friction plate making sure its spring hub assembly faces away from the flywheel

6.17 Centralising the friction plate with an aligning tool

no signs of cracks, pitting or scoring. If there is any doubt about its condition, the bearing should be renewed (see Section 4).

Refitting

13 On reassembly, ensure that the bearing surfaces of the flywheel and pressure plate are completely clean, smooth, and free from oil or grease. Use solvent to remove any protective grease from new components.

14 Fit the friction plate so that its spring hub assembly faces away from the flywheel; there may also be a marking showing which way round the plate is to be refitted **(see illustration)**.

15 Refit the pressure plate assembly, aligning the marks made on dismantling (if the original pressure plate is re-used). Fit the pressure plate bolts, but tighten them only finger-tight, so that the friction plate can still be moved.

16 The friction plate must now be centralised, so that when the transmission is refitted, its input shaft will pass through the splines at the centre of the friction plate.

17 Centralisation can be achieved by passing a screwdriver or other long bar through the friction plate and into the hole in the crankshaft; the friction plate can then be moved around until it is centred on the crankshaft hole. Alternatively, a clutch-aligning -tool can be used to eliminate the guesswork; these can be obtained from most accessory shops **(see illustration)**. A home-made aligning tool can be fabricated from a length of metal rod or wooden dowel which fits closely inside the crankshaft hole, and has insulating tape wound around it to match the diameter of the friction plate splined hole.

18 When the friction plate is centralised, tighten the pressure plate bolts evenly and in a diagonal sequence to the specified torque setting. Once all the bolts have been tightened remove the alignment tool. Where necessary, use the service tool to remove the retaining clips from the pressure plate.

Caution: To avoid the risk of distorting the pressure plate diaphragm spring it is most important that the pressure plate bolts are evenly and progressively tightened.

19 Refit the transmission as described in Chapter 7A.

Chapter 7 Part A:
Manual transmission

Contents

Degrees of difficulty

Easy, suitable for novice with little experience 	**Fairly easy,** suitable for beginner with some experience 	**Fairly difficult,** suitable for competent DIY mechanic 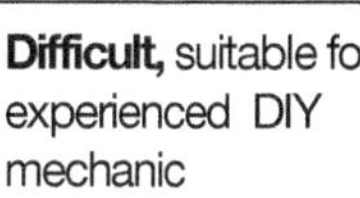	**Difficult,** suitable for experienced DIY mechanic	**Very difficult,** suitable for expert DIY or professional 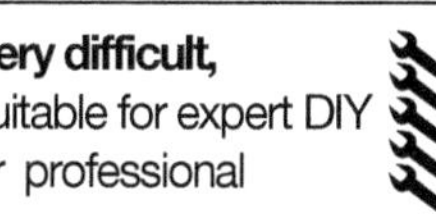

Specifications

General

Type	Manual, five forward speeds and reverse. Synchromesh on all forward speeds
Identification code:	
2.0 and 2.5 litre engines	R25
3.0 litre engines	R28

Torque wrench settings

	Nm	lbf ft
Drain plug	30	22
Engine to transmission support bracket bolts - 2.0 litre engines with one-piece sump:		
Bracket-to-engine bolt	40	30
Bracket-to-transmission bolts	22	16
Filler plug	30	22
Gearchange lever retaining bolts	10	7
Gearchange linkage rod clamp bolt:		
Stage 1	14	10
Stage 2	Angle-tighten a further 135 to 180°	
Propeller shaft flange nut	150	110
Reversing light switch	20	15
Transmission unit mounting bolts:		
Transmission-to-cylinder block bolts	60	44
Transmission-to-sump flange bolts (engines with a two-piece sump)	40	30
Rear upper mounting bracket bolts	22	16
Rear mounting crossmember-to-body bolts	45	33

1 General information

1 The transmission is contained in a cast-aluminium alloy casing bolted to the rear of the engine. Drive is transmitted from the crankshaft via the clutch to the transmission input shaft, which has a splined extension to accept the clutch friction plate. The transmission input shaft transfers drive to the auxiliary shaft which is positioned directly below the main shaft, both shafts being parallel to the crankshaft and propeller shaft.

2 Gear selection is via a floor-mounted lever and selector linkage mechanism. The selector linkage cause the appropriate selector fork to move its respective synchro-sleeve along the shaft, to lock the gear pinion to the synchro-hub. Since the synchro-hubs are splined to the main shaft, this locks the pinion to the shaft, so that drive can be transmitted. To ensure that gear-changing can be made quickly and quietly, a synchro-mesh system is fitted to all forward gears, consisting of baulk rings and spring-loaded fingers, as well as the gear pinions and synchro-hubs. The synchro-mesh cones are formed on the mating faces of the baulk rings and gear pinions.

2 Transmission oil - draining, refilling and checking

Note: *There have been three different types of oil used in the manual transmission unit by Vauxhall (see Lubricants and fluids in Weekly checks). Bearing in mind that the different types of oil should never be mixed, it is essential that the transmission unit is refilled either with the same type of oil as that which has been drained or the very latest specification oil (used in production from 1999 model year onwards). If it is not known what type of oil has been drained,*

2.4 Removing the transmission drain plug

the transmission unit should be flushed before filling with the latest specification oil. To do this, using the latest type of oil (part number 19 40 768), refill the transmission unit so that the oil level is right up to the base of the filler plug aperture then refit the plug. Take the vehicle on a journey of approximately 15 miles (20 km) then, on your return, drain the oil out again and refill the transmission as normal with the latest type of oil. If the flushing process has already been carried out an early (pre 1999 model year) vehicle, the drain plug will be marked with a dot of green paint.

Draining

1 This operation is much quicker and more efficient if the car is first taken on a journey of sufficient length to warm the engine/transmission up to normal operating temperature.

2 Park the car on level ground, switch off the ignition and apply the handbrake firmly. For improved access, jack up the front of the car and support it securely on axle stands. Note that the car must be lowered to the ground and level, to ensure accuracy, when refilling and checking the oil level.

3 Remove all traces of dirt then unscrew the filler plug from the right-hand side of the transmission housing.

4 Position a suitable container under the drain plug situated on the base of the transmission housing then unscrew the drain plug and allow the oil to drain completely into the container **(see illustration)**. Clean both the filler and the drain plugs, being especially careful to wipe any metallic particles off the magnetic inserts.

Warning: If the oil is hot, take precautions against scalding.

5 When the oil has finished draining, clean the drain plug threads and those of the transmission casing then refit the drain plug and tighten to the specified torque.

Refilling

6 Refilling the transmission is an extremely awkward operation. Above all, allow plenty of time for the oil level to settle properly before checking it. Note that the car must be parked on flat level ground when checking the oil level.

7 Refill the transmission with the exact amount of the specified type of oil then check the oil level as described in paragraphs 12 and 13. When the level is correct, refit the filler plug and tighten it to the specified torque.

8 Take the vehicle on a short journey so that the new oil is distributed fully around the transmission components.

9 On your return, park the vehicle on level ground and recheck the transmission oil level again to ensure the level is correct.

Checking

Note: *It is essential that the transmission unit is topped up with the same type of oil as that with which it is filled; there are three different types of oil available and they must never be mixed. If it is not known which type of oil the transmission is filled with, it is recommended that the unit is drained, flushed and then refilled with the latest type of oil (see Note at the start of the Section).*

10 Position the vehicle over an inspection pit, on vehicle ramps, or jack it up, but make sure that it is level. The oil level must be checked before the car is driven, or at least 5 minutes after the engine has been switched off. If the oil is checked immediately after driving the car, some of the oil will remain distributed around the transmission components, resulting in an inaccurate level reading.

11 Wipe clean the area around the filler plug which is located on the right-hand side of the transmission housing. Unscrew the plug and clean it.

12 To check the oil level, it will be necessary to fabricate a dipstick. This can be made out of a piece of welding rod with a right-angled bend in it. Insert the rod into the filler hole and check the oil level; the oil level should be approximately 9 mm below the lower edge of the filler plug aperture.

Caution: When checking the oil level, take great care not to drop the dipstick into the transmission unit.

13 If topping up is necessary, add the correct type of oil through the filler hole until the oil level is correct. **Note:** *Do not overfill the transmission as this will adversely affect the gearchange action. Any excess oil must be either be siphoned or drained from the transmission unit before the vehicle is used.*

14 Once the transmission oil level is correct, refit the filler plug and tighten it to the specified torque.

3 Gearchange linkage - adjustment

Note: *Vauxhall service tool KM-631A will be required to carry out this procedure.*

1 Adjustment of the gearchange linkage is not a routine operation and should only be needed if the mechanism has been removed. If the gearchange action is stiff or imprecise, check that it is correctly adjusted as follows.

2 Position the gearchange lever in the neutral position, firmly apply the handbrake then jack up the front of the vehicle and support it on axle stands.

3 Remove the retaining clips securing the protective cover to the vehicle underbody then fold the cover forwards to gain access to the clamp bolt on the rear end of the gearchange linkage rod. Slacken the clamp bolt so that the end fitting is free to move easily in the rod **(see illustrations)**.

4 From inside the vehicle, unclip the gearchange lever gaiter from the centre console and fold it back over the lever. Free the rubber gaiter from the mounting plate and fold it back to gain access to the base of the gearchange lever.

5 Lock the gearchange lever in position by fitting the service tool (KM-631A) into the gearchange lever housing whilst holding the lever over to the right.

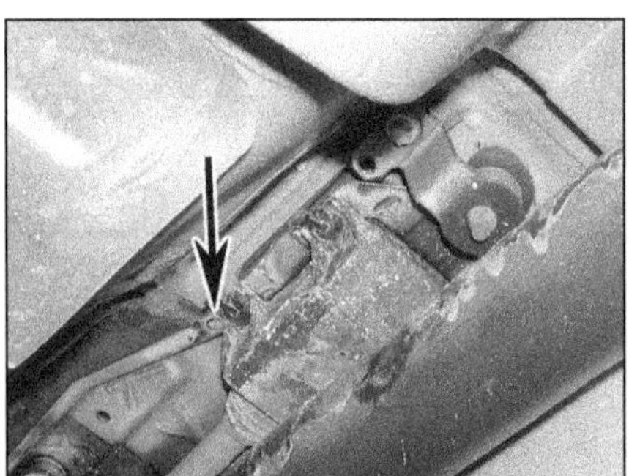

3.3a Release the retaining clips (arrowed) . . .

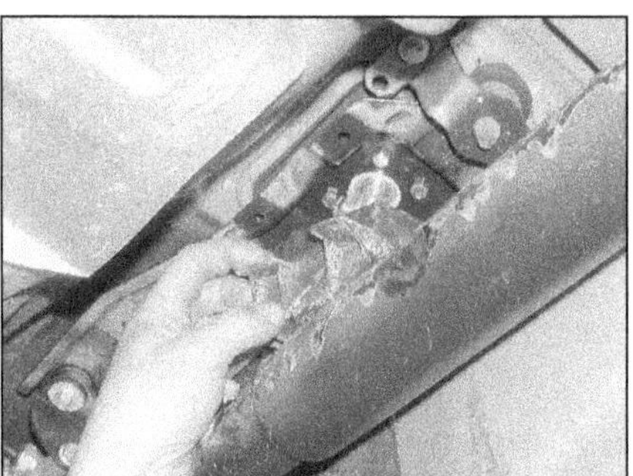

3.3b . . . and peel back the protective cover . . .

3.3c . . . to gain access to the gearchange linkage clamp bolt (arrowed)

6 From underneath the vehicle, using an open-ended spanner on the flats provided, turn the gearchange linkage rod fully clockwise (as viewed from the rear of the vehicle). Hold the rod in this position then tighten the rod clamp bolt first to the specified stage 1 torque and then through the specified stage 2 angle.
7 Remove the service tool and check the operation of the gearchange lever before seating the rubber gaiter onto its mounting and clipping the gaiter back into the centre console.
8 Ensure the protective cover is correctly seated on the base of the gearchange lever, securing it in position with the retaining clips, then lower the vehicle to the ground.

4 Gearchange linkage - removal and refitting

Removal

Gearchange lever

1 Firmly apply the handbrake then jack up the front of the vehicle and support it on axle stands.
2 Remove the retaining clips securing the protective cover to the vehicle underbody then fold the cover forwards to gain access to the base of the gearchange lever (see illustrations 3.3a and 3.3b).
3 Slide off the retaining clip and withdraw the pivot pin from the lever end of the linkage rod **(see illustration)**. Free the rod from the base of the gearchange lever taking care not to lose the pivot bushes.
4 Slacken and remove the four bolts securing the lever assembly to the floor.
5 From inside the vehicle, unclip the gearchange lever gaiter from the centre console and fold it back over the lever.
6 Free the rubber gaiter from the mounting plate and remove the lever assembly from the vehicle, taking care not to lose the threaded retaining plates. Recover the sealing washer which is fitted between the lever mounting and floor.
7 Check the lever assembly for signs of wear or damage and renew damaged components as necessary.

Linkage rod

8 Carry out the operations described in paragraphs 1 to 3.
9 Slacken and remove the nut and bolt securing the front end of the linkage rod to the transmission selector rod joint and remove the rod from underneath the vehicle **(see illustration)**. Recover the spacer from the joint and inspect the joint pivot bushes for signs of wear.

Refitting

Gearchange lever

10 Lubricate the lever pivot ball and bushes

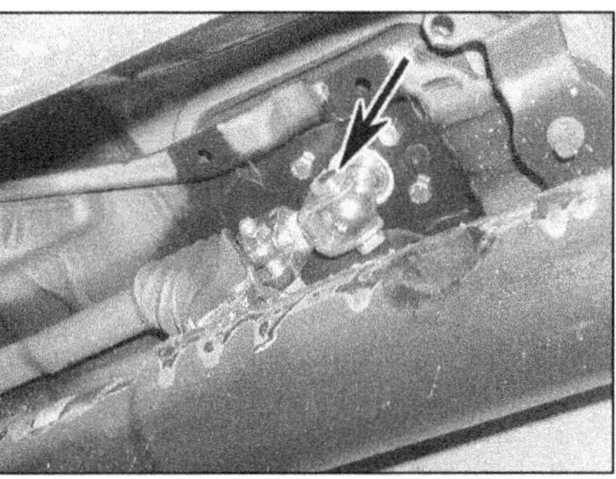

4.3 Slide off the retaining clip (arrowed) then withdraw the pivot pin securing the linkage rod to the gearchange lever

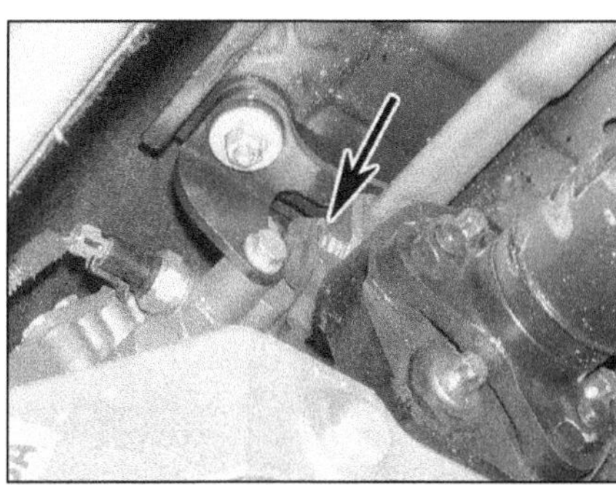

4.9 Slacken and remove the nut and pivot bolt (arrowed) securing the linkage rod to the transmission unit

and the threaded retaining plates with multi-purpose grease (Vauxhall recommend the use of grease 19 48 606 or 19 48 608 - available from your Vauxhall dealer) and stick the sealing washer to the base of the mounting.
11 Ensure the retaining plates are correctly positioned then refit the lever assembly to the vehicle. Make sure the lever mounting lugs are correctly seated (the larger lug should be at the rear) then refit the retaining bolts and tighten them to the specified torque.
12 Align the linkage rod with the lever then insert the pivot pin and secure it in position with the retaining clip. Ensure the protective cover is correctly seated on the base of the gearchange lever and secure it in position with the retaining clips.
13 Seat the gearchange lever rubber gaiter onto its mounting and clipping the gaiter back into the centre console.

Linkage rod

14 Refitting is the reverse of removal lubricating the pivots with multi-purpose grease.

5 Oil seals - renewal

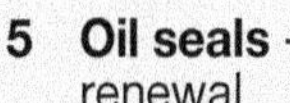

Propeller shaft flange oil seal

1 Working as described in Chapter 8, free the front end of the propeller shaft from the transmission flange and remove the vibration damper (where fitted). If necessary, to improve access to the flange remove the shaft completely.
2 To prevent the rotation as the shaft nut is slackened bolt a length of bar with two holes drilled in it to the flange. Alternatively, a tool can be fabricated from two lengths of steel strip (one long, one short) and a nut and bolt; the nut and bolt forming the pivot of a forked tool **(see illustration)**.
3 Hold the flange then slacken and remove the retaining nut from the end of the transmission main shaft. Remove the holding tool and slide off the flange **(see illustration)**.
4 Note the correct fitted depth of the seal in the transmission housing then carefully prise it out of position using a large flat-bladed screwdriver.
5 Check the propeller flange sealing surface for signs of wear or damage. If there is visible signs of damage, renew the flange.
6 Clean all traces of dirt from the area around the oil seal aperture and remove all traces of thread locking compound from the main shaft and flange nut threads.
7 Apply a smear of grease to the outer lip of the new oil seal then, making sure its sealing lip is facing inwards, slide it over the main shaft end. Tap the seal squarely into position, using a suitable tubular drift (such as a socket) which bears only on the hard outer edge of the seal, until it is positioned at the same depth in the housing that the original was.
8 Lubricate the seal with a smear of

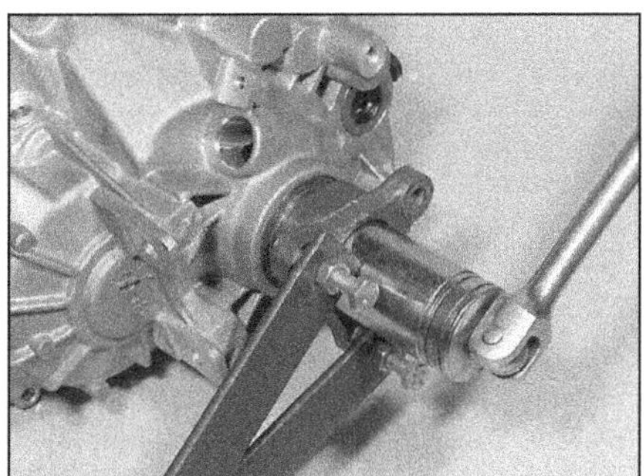

5.2 Slacken and remove the retaining nut whilst retaining the propeller shaft flange with a home-made tool . . .

5.3 . . . then remove the flange from the output shaft (shown with transmission removed)

transmission oil then carefully slide the propeller flange into position, taking care not to damage the seal lip.

9 Apply a few drops of thread locking compound (Vauxhall recommend the use of locking compound 15 10 181 - available from your Vauxhall dealer) to the threads of the flange retaining nut. Refit the nut and tighten it to the specified torque using the method employed on removal to prevent rotation.

10 Reconnect/refit the propeller shaft as described in Chapter 8 then check the transmission oil level as described in Section 2.

Input shaft oil seal

Note: *A leak around the transmission input shaft can come either from the input shaft seal or from the clutch release cylinder sealing ring. Whilst the cylinder is removed renew both items regardless of their apparent condition.*

11 Remove the clutch release cylinder as described in Chapter 6.

12 Note the correct fitted depth of the seal in the release cylinder then carefully prise it out of position using a large flat-bladed screwdriver.

13 Clean all traces of dirt from the area around the oil seal aperture and apply a smear of grease to the outer lip of the new oil seal. Making sure its sealing lip is facing outward (towards the transmission unit when the cylinder is fitted), seat the seal in the rear of the cylinder and press it squarely into position until it is positioned at the same depth in the housing that the original was. If necessary, tap the seal into position, using a suitable tubular drift (such as a socket) which bears only on the hard outer edge of the seal.

14 Fit a new sealing ring and refit the release cylinder as described in Chapter 6.

6 Reversing light switch - testing, removal and refitting

Testing

1 The reversing light circuit is controlled by a plunger-type switch that is screwed into the rear of the transmission, above and to the left of the propeller shaft. If a fault develops in the circuit, first ensure that the circuit fuse has not blown.

2 To test the switch, disconnect the wiring connector. Use a multimeter (set to the resistance function) or a battery-and-bulb test circuit to check that there is continuity between the switch terminals only when reverse gear is selected. If this is not the case, and there are no obvious breaks or other damage to the wires, the switch is faulty, and must be renewed.

Removal

3 Firmly apply the handbrake then jack up the front of the vehicle and support it on axle stands.

4 Disconnect the wiring connector, then unscrew the switch and remove it from the transmission casing along with its sealing washer.

Refitting

5 Fit a new sealing washer to the switch, then screw it back into position in the top of the transmission housing and tighten it to the specified torque. Reconnect the wiring connector and test the operation of the circuit then lower the vehicle to the ground.

7 Transmission - removal and refitting

Removal

1 Disconnect the battery negative terminal. **Note:** *On models with a Vauxhall anti-theft warning system (ATWS), the battery negative terminal must be disconnected within 15 seconds of the ignition being switched off to prevent the alarm system being triggered.*

2 Chock the rear wheels, then firmly apply the handbrake. Jack up the front of the vehicle, and securely support it on axle stands. Undo the retaining bolts and remove the undercover from beneath the engine/transmission unit.

3 Trace the clutch hydraulic hose/pipe back from the transmission unit to connector on the engine compartment bulkhead. Minimise fluid loss by clamping the fluid supply hose linking the fluid reservoir to the clutch master cylinder then release the connector from the bulkhead. Slide out the retaining clip and separate the two halves of the pipe, plugging the pipe ends to minimise fluid loss and prevent the entry of dirt. Refit the retaining clip to the connector groove, ensuring its is correctly located, then check the lower end of the pipe is free to removed with the transmission unit.

Caution: Do no depress the clutch pedal whilst the hose is disconnected.

4 Disconnect the wiring connector from the reversing light switch, which is located at the rear of the transmission unit.

5 Working as described in Chapter 8, unbolt the front end of the propeller shaft from the transmission flange and remove the vibration damper (where fitted). Position the propeller shaft to the right of the transmission unit and tie it to the vehicle underbody.

6 Remove the gearchange linkage rod as described in Section 4 and proceed as described under the relevant sub-heading.

2.0 litre engines

7 On SOHC engines, disconnect the wiring connector from the DIS module. Slacken and remove the module mounting bracket retaining bolts, noting the correct fitted location of the engine lifting bracket, then free the wiring harness and remove the DIS module and bracket from the rear of the cylinder head. Free the HT leads from their retaining clips and position the assembly clear of the transmission unit.

8 On all models unclip the oxygen sensor wiring connector from transmission unit and disconnect it.

9 Slacken and remove the exhaust system front pipe mounting bracket retaining bolts and remove the bracket. Also remove the bolts securing the front pipe to the intermediate pipe and separate the two exhaust sections.

10 On models with a one-piece engine sump, slacken and remove the bolts securing the support brackets to the transmission housing and sides of the cylinder block. Remove both brackets from the engine then remove the flywheel lower cover plate from the base of the transmission housing.

11 On all models slacken and remove the two bolts securing the rear of the transmission unit to the upper mounting bracket.

12 Place a jack with a block of wood beneath the transmission, and raise the jack to take the weight of the transmission.

13 With the transmission securely supported, slacken and remove the bolts securing the transmission unit rear mounting crossmember to the vehicle body.

14 Lower the transmission unit slightly then slacken and remove all the bolts securing the transmission housing to the engine unit. Note the correct fitted positions of each bolt, and the necessary brackets, as they are removed, to use as a reference on refitting. Make a final check that all components have been disconnected, and are positioned clear of the transmission so that they will not hinder the removal procedure.

15 With the bolts removed, move the trolley jack and transmission to the rear, to free it from its locating dowels. Once the transmission is free, lower the jack and manoeuvre the unit out from under the vehicle. Remove the locating dowels from the transmission or engine if they are loose, and keep them in a safe place.

16 With the transmission removed from the vehicle, slide off the clutch release bearing from the release cylinder and check it for wear. The bearing contact surface should rotate smoothly and easily, with no sign of noise or roughness, and that the surface itself is smooth and unworn, with no signs of cracks, pitting or scoring. If there is any doubt about its condition, the bearing should be renewed.

2.5 and 3.0 litre engines

17 Remove both exhaust system front pipes as described in Chapter 4A.

18 Remove the transmission unit as described in paragraphs 11 to 16.

Refitting

19 The transmission is refitted by a reversal of the removal procedure, bearing in mind the following points.

a) Remove all traces of dirt and grease from the input shaft splines and the contact surfaces of the clutch release bearing and release cylinder. Lubricate the inner bore of the release bearing with a smear of high temperature grease (Vauxhall recommend the use of lubricating paste 19 42 530 - available from your Vauxhall dealer) and apply a thin smear of grease to the input shaft splines; do apply too much or there is risk of the clutch friction plate becoming contaminated. Fit the release bearing to the cylinder making sure it is the correct way around.

b) Ensure the locating dowels are correctly positioned prior to refitting the transmission to the engine. As the transmission unit is fitted, take great care not to allow the weight of the unit to hang on the input shaft.

c) Remove all traces of locking compound from the transmission unit rear mounting crossmember to body bolt threads. Apply a few drops of thread locking compound (Vauxhall recommend the use of locking compound 15 10 181 - available from your Vauxhall dealer) to the threads of each bolt prior to refitting and tighten both bolts to the specified torque.

d) Tighten all nuts and bolts to the specified torque (where given).

e) Ensure the clutch hydraulic pipe connector sealing ring is in good condition before clipping the hose/pipe end fitting into position. Ensure the end fitting is securely retained by its clip then remove the clamp from the master cylinder hose and bleed the hydraulic system as described in Chapter 6.

f) On completion check and, if necessary, top up the transmission oil level as described in Section 2. If necessary, also adjust the gearchange linkage as described in Section 3.

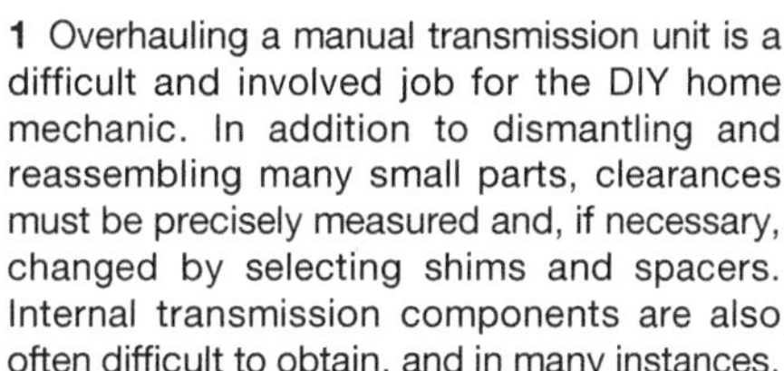

8 Transmission overhaul - general information

1 Overhauling a manual transmission unit is a difficult and involved job for the DIY home mechanic. In addition to dismantling and reassembling many small parts, clearances must be precisely measured and, if necessary, changed by selecting shims and spacers. Internal transmission components are also often difficult to obtain, and in many instances, extremely expensive. Because of this, if the transmission develops a fault or becomes noisy, the best course of action is to have the unit overhauled by a specialist repairer, or to obtain an exchange reconditioned unit.

2 Nevertheless, it is not impossible for the more experienced mechanic to overhaul the transmission, provided the special tools are available, and the job is done in a deliberate step-by-step manner, so that nothing is overlooked.

3 The tools necessary for an overhaul include internal and external circlip pliers, bearing pullers, a slide hammer, a set of pin punches, a dial test indicator, and possibly a hydraulic press. In addition, a large, sturdy workbench and a vice will be required.

4 During dismantling of the transmission, make careful notes of how each component is fitted, to make reassembly easier and more accurate.

5 Before dismantling the transmission, it will help if you have some idea what area is malfunctioning. Certain problems can be closely related to specific areas in the transmission, which can make component examination and replacement easier. Refer to the *Fault finding* Section of this manual for more information.

Chapter 7 Part B: Automatic transmission

Contents

Degrees of difficulty

Easy, suitable for novice with little experience 

Fairly easy, suitable for beginner with some experience 

Fairly difficult, suitable for competent DIY mechanic

Difficult, suitable for experienced DIY mechanic

Very difficult, suitable for expert DIY or professional 

Specifications

General

Type	Four-speed electronically-controlled automatic with three (normal, sport and winter) driving modes
Identification code*:	
2.0 and 2.5 litre models	AR25
3.0 litre models	AR35

**The code is marked on the identification plate which is attached to the left-hand side of the transmission unit, behind the selector lever.*

Torque wrench settings

Torque wrench settings	Nm	lbf ft
Engine-to-transmission support bracket bolts - 2.0 litre engines with one-piece sump:		
Bracket-to-engine bolt	40	30
Bracket-to-transmission bolts	22	16
Fluid cooler pipe unions:		
Union bolts	25	18
Union nut	30	22
Fluid filter retaining bolts	20	15
Fluid level plug	33	24
Output speed sensor bolt	12	9
Propeller shaft centre bearing bracket bolts	20	15
Propeller shaft flange nut	100	74
Rear mounting crossmember-to-body bolts	45	33
Selector lever position switch bolts	13	10
Selector linkage fixings:		
Linkage rod clamp bolt	8	6
Lever pivot shaft nut	28	21
Lever to transmission selector shaft nut	20	15
Sump retaining bolts	12	9
Torque converter-to-driveplate bolts	30	22
Transmission unit mounting bolts:		
Transmission-to-cylinder block bolts	60	44
Transmission-to-sump flange bolts (engines with a two-piece sump)	40	30

1 General information

Note: *On later models, if the battery is disconnected with the selector lever in the P position, the lever will be locked in position. To manually release the lever, carefully unclip the selector lever gaiter from the top of the centre console then, depress the yellow release lever on the left-hand side of the selector lever with a pen or screwdriver* **(see illustrations)**. *The selector lever can then be moved as normal.*

1 Most models covered in this manual were offered with the option of a four-speed, electronically-controlled automatic transmission, consisting of a torque converter, an epicyclic geartrain, and hydraulically-operated clutches and brakes. The unit is controlled by the electronic control unit (ECU) via electrically-operated solenoid valves. The transmission unit has three driving modes; normal (economy), sport and winter modes.

1.0a On later models, to release the selector lever from the P position with the battery disconnected, unclip the selector lever gaiter . . .

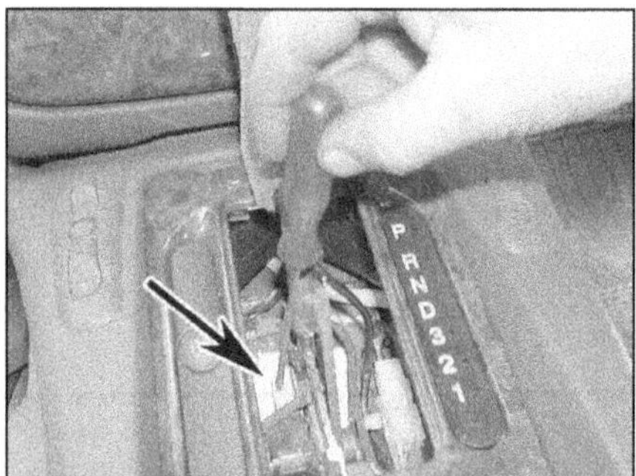
1.0b . . . then depress the yellow release lever (arrowed) on the selector lever mounting

2 The normal (economy) mode is the standard mode for driving in which the transmission shifts up at relatively low engine speeds to combine reasonable performance with economy. If the transmission unit is switched into sport mode, using the button on the selector lever, the transmission shifts up only at high engine speeds, giving improved acceleration and overtaking performance. When the transmission is in sport mode, the indicator light in the instrument panel is illuminated. If the transmission is switched into winter mode, using the button on the centre console, the transmission will be select third gear as the vehicle pulls away from a standing start; this helps to maintain traction on very slippery surfaces.

3 The torque converter provides a fluid coupling between engine and transmission, which acts as an automatic clutch, and also provides a degree of torque multiplication when accelerating.

4 The epicyclic geartrain provides either of the four forward or one reverse gear ratios, according to which of its component parts are held stationary or allowed to turn. The components of the geartrain are held or released by brakes and clutches which are activated by the control unit. A fluid pump within the transmission provides the necessary hydraulic pressure to operate the brakes and clutches.

5 Driver control of the transmission is by a seven-position selector lever. The drive D position, allows automatic changing throughout the range of all four gear ratios. An automatic kickdown facility shifts the transmission down a gear if the accelerator pedal is fully depressed. The transmission also has three hold positions, 1 means only the first gear ratio can be selected, 2 allows both the first and second gear ratios position to be automatically selected and 3 allows automatic changing between the first three gear ratios. These hold positions are useful for providing engine braking when travelling down steep gradients. Note, however, that the transmission should *never* be shifted down a position at high engine speeds.

6 If the ECU senses a fault in the transmission operation it will illuminate the warning light on the instrument panel and the relevant fault code will be stored in the ECU memory. If the warning light comes on, the vehicle should be taken to a Vauxhall dealer at the earliest opportunity. A complete test of the transmission unit can then be carried out, using a special electronic diagnostic test unit which is simply plugged into the system's diagnostic connector. The connector is located behind the fusebox cover panel on the drivers' side of the facia.

7 Due to the complexity of the automatic transmission, any repair or overhaul work must be left to a Vauxhall dealer. The contents of the following Sections are therefore confined to supplying general information, and any service information and instructions that can be used by the owner.

2 Transmission fluid - draining and refilling

Note: *A new main sump gasket will be required for this operation. If the intermediate sump is also to be removed, obtain a new gasket for that as well.*

1 Since the transmission fluid is not renewed as part of the manufacturers maintenance schedule, no drain plug is fitted to the transmission. If for any reason the transmission needs to be drained, the only way of doing so is to remove the main sump and, if necessary, the intermediate sump.

2 Park the vehicle on level ground, switch off the ignition, and apply the handbrake firmly. For improved access, jack up the front of the car and support it securely on axle stands but note that the vehicle must be level when the transmission is refilled.

3 Position a container under the fluid level plug on the right-hand side of the transmission main sump. Unscrew the plug and remove it along with its sealing washer **(see illustration)**.

4 Allow the fluid to drain out into the container then refit the level plug **(see illustration)**.

5 Bearing in mind that the sump will still be full of oil, position a large container underneath the main sump. Evenly and progressively slacken and remove the sump retaining bolts, noting the correct location of the cooler pipe retaining clip(s) **(see illustration)**. Carefully remove the sump and empty its contents into the container. Remove the gasket and discard it; a new one should be used on refitting.

6 To drain the transmission unit completely, slacken and remove the retaining bolts, then remove the intermediate sump from the transmission unit and empty its contents into the container. Remove the gasket and discard it; a new one should be used on refitting.

7 Whilst the main sump is removed, take the opportunity to check the transmission fluid filter. Undo the three retaining bolts, then remove the filter from the underside of the transmission **(see illustrations)**. Clean the filter element in a bath of solvent, then examine the element for signs of clogging or damage. If the filter element is split or blocked

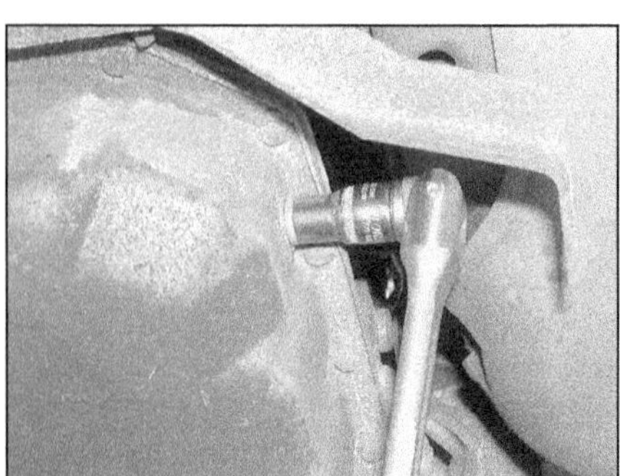
2.3 Slacken and remove the fluid level plug from the main sump . . .

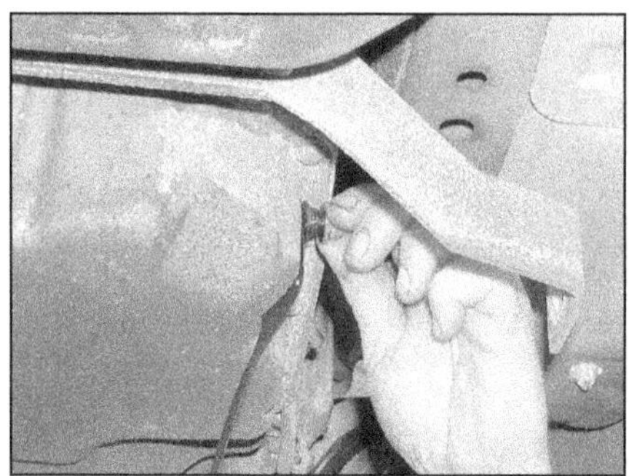
2.4 . . . and allow the transmission fluid to drain into a suitable container

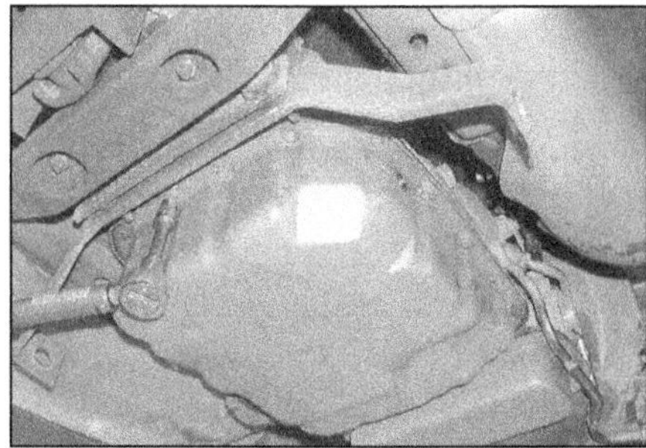
2.5 Unscrew the retaining bolts and remove the main sump from the transmission unit

2.7a Undo the retaining bolts (arrowed) . . .

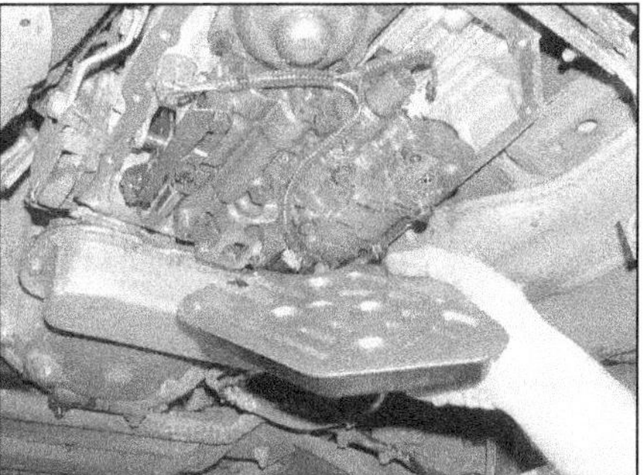

2.7b . . . and remove the fluid filter from the transmission unit

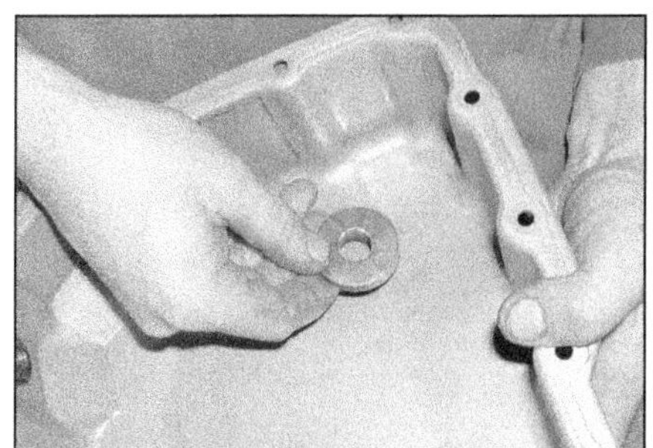

2.8 Clean all traces of metal fillings from magnet which is fitted inside the main sump

or its seal is damaged, then the filter must be renewed (the seal is not available separately).

8 Remove all traces of dirt and fluid from the sump and transmission mating surfaces and wipe clean the inside of the sump(s). Remove the magnet from inside the main sump and clean all traces of metal filings from it; the filings should be very fine - any sizeable chips of metal indicate a worn component in the transmission **(see illustration)**. Also remove all traces of locking compound from the threads of the sump retaining bolts.

9 Ensure that the filter element and transmission mating surfaces are clean and dry. Offer up the filter to the transmission then refit the retaining bolts and tighten them to the specified torque.

10 Where necessary, ensure the mating surfaces are clean and dry then refit the intermediate sump to the transmission unit, complete with a new gasket **(see illustration)**. Apply a drop of thread locking compound (Vauxhall recommend the use of locking compound 15 10 181 - available from your Vauxhall dealer) to the each of the retaining bolts then refit the bolts, tightening them evenly and progressively to the specified torque setting.

11 Ensure the mating surfaces of the main sump and transmission unit are clean and dry. Fit a new gasket to the sump and apply a drop of thread locking compound (Vauxhall recommend the use of locking compound 15 10 181 - available from your Vauxhall dealer) to the each of the retaining bolts. Offer up the sump and gasket then refit the bolts, tightening them evenly and progressively to the specified torque setting **(see illustration)**.

12 Refilling the transmission is an awkward operation, adding the specified type and amount of fluid to the transmission a little at a time via the level plug hole in the main sump. Ensure that the vehicle is level then fill the transmission with new fluid of the specified type allowing plenty of time for the fluid level to settle properly. Once the fluid level is up to the base of the level plug aperture with the engine stopped, it will be necessary to start the engine and add the rest of the fluid with the engine running.

13 Start the engine and allow it to idle then carefully add the rest of the fluid. Once the fluid level is up to the base of the level plug aperture, refit the level plug and sealing washer and tighten to the specified torque.

14 Take the car on a short run to fully distribute the new fluid around the transmission, then recheck the fluid level as described in Chapter 1 with the transmission at normal operating temperature. Once the fluid level is correct fit a new sealing washer to the level plug then refit the plug and tighten it to the specified torque.

3 Selector linkage - adjustment

1 Operate the selector lever throughout its entire range and check that the transmission engages the correct gear indicated on the selector lever position indicator. If adjustment is necessary, continue as follows.

2 Position the selector lever in the P (park) position. Firmly apply the handbrake then jack up the front of the vehicle and support it on axle stands.

3 Locate the selector lever on the left-hand side of the transmission unit and slacken the clamp bolt at the transmission end of the linkage rod **(see illustration)**. Pull the transmission selector lever fully backwards to ensure it is located in the P (Park) position then tighten the linkage rod clamp bolt to the specified torque.

4 Check the operation of the selector lever and the position indicator switch. If necessary, adjust the switch as described in Section 8 then lower the vehicle to the ground.

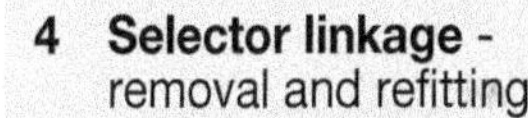

4 Selector linkage - removal and refitting

Removal

1 Firmly apply the handbrake then jack up the front of the vehicle and support it on axle stands.

2 Slide off the retaining clips then free the linkage rod from the transmission and selector lever and manoeuvre it out from underneath the vehicle **(see illustration)**. Recover the bushes which are fitted to the lever pivot pins and renew them if they show signs of wear or damage.

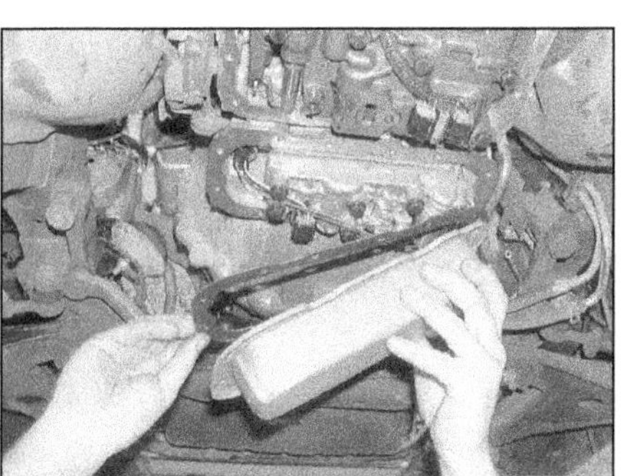

2.10 Refit the intermediate sump using a new gasket

2.11 Ensure the mating surfaces are clean and dry then refit the main sump complete with a new gasket

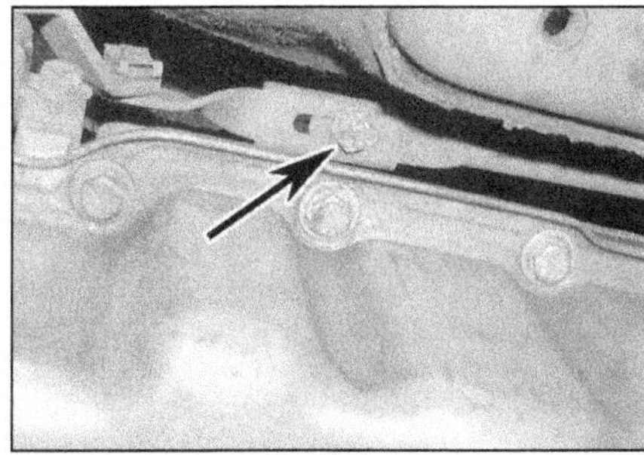

3.3 Slacken the clamp bolt (arrowed) and adjust the selector linkage as described in text

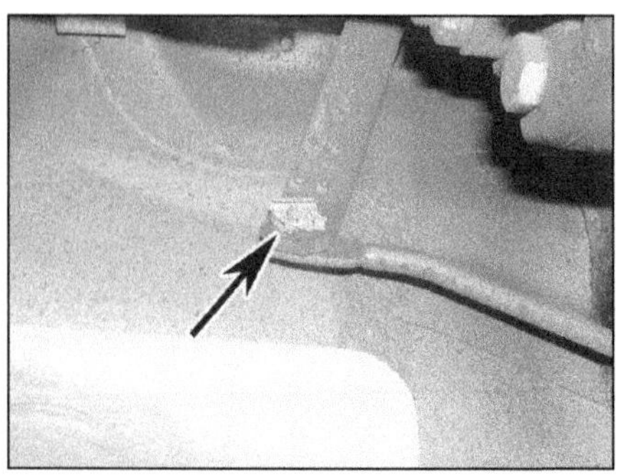

4.2 Slide off the retaining clip (arrowed) and detach the selector linkage rod from the selector lever

Refitting

3 Apply a smear of multi-purpose grease to the linkage rod pivot pins. Ensure the bushes are in position then refit the rod to the transmission and selector lever and secure it in position with the retaining clips.

4 Check the operation of the selector linkage and, if necessary, adjust as described in Section 3 before lower the vehicle to the ground.

5 Selector lever assembly - removal and refitting

Note: *Renewal of the lever switches is covered in Section 8*

Removal

Note: *A pop rivet gun and new rivets will be required on refitting.*

1 Remove the centre console as described in Chapter 11 then position the selector lever in the P (park) position.

2 Firmly apply the handbrake then jack up the front of the vehicle and support it on axle stands.

3 Slide off the retaining clip and detach the selector linkage rod from the base of the lever. Take care not to lose the lever pivot bush.

4 Slacken and remove the retaining nuts and bolt then remove the front and rear support brackets from the rear heater/ventilation duct. Unclip the duct and remove it from the around the selector lever.

5 Disconnect the wiring connector from the selector lever mode switch and unclip the wiring so that it is free to be removed with the lever. On later models were the lever is fitted with a selector lever pawl, remove the pawl switch and the ignition key release switch as described in Section 8.

6 Carefully drill off the heads from the rivets securing the lever mounting plate to the floor then ease the selector lever out of position. Recover seal (where fitted) which is fitted between the housing and floor.

7 Inspect the selector lever mechanism for signs of wear or damage and renew worn components as necessary

Refitting

8 Ensure the mating surfaces of the lever mounting plate and body are clean and dry. Where a seal was fitted between the mounting plate and body ensure the seal is in good condition then position it on the body. Where no seal was fitted apply and thin film of sealant to the mating surface of the mounting plate to ensure a water-tight seal.

9 Manoeuvre the lever assembly into position and seat it on the body. Locate all the new pop rivets in the mounting plate holes to ensure the lever is correct positioned then secure all the rivets in position with a pop rivet gun.

10 Ensure the lever mode switch wiring is correctly routed then reconnect its connector. Where necessary, refit the pawl switch and the ignition key release switch as described in Section 8.

11 Clip the rear heater/ventilation duct back into position then refit the support brackets, tightening their retaining bolt/nuts securely.

12 Refit the centre console as described in Chapter 11.

13 Ensure the pivot bush is correctly positioned then reconnect the linkage rod to the transmission selector lever and secure it in position with the retaining clip.

14 Check the operation of the selector linkage and, if necessary, adjust as described in Section 3 before lower the vehicle to the ground.

6 Oil seals - renewal

Propeller shaft flange oil seal

Note: *A new flange sealing ring and retaining nut will be required.*

1 Working as described in Chapter 8, free the front end of the propeller shaft from the transmission flange and remove the vibration damper (where fitted). If necessary, to improve access to the flange remove the shaft completely.

2 To prevent the rotation as the shaft nut is slackened bolt a length of bar with two holes drilled in it to the flange. Alternatively, a tool can be fabricated from two lengths of steel strip (one long, one short) and a nut and bolt; the nut and bolt forming the pivot of a forked tool.

3 Hold the flange then slacken and remove the retaining nut from the end of the transmission main shaft. Remove the holding tool and slide off the flange complete with its sealing ring. Discard the nut and sealing ring; new ones should be used on refitting.

4 Note the correct fitted depth of the seal in the transmission housing then carefully prise it out of position using a large flat-bladed screwdriver.

5 Check the propeller flange sealing surface for signs of wear or damage. If there is visible signs of damage, renew the flange.

6 Clean all traces of dirt from the area around the oil seal aperture then apply a smear of grease to the outer lip of the new oil seal.

7 Making sure its sealing lip is facing inwards, slide the new seal over the main shaft end and tap it squarely into position, using a suitable tubular drift (such as a socket) which bears only on the hard outer edge of the seal. Ensure the seal is positioned at the same depth in the housing that the original was.

8 Fit the new sealing ring to the flange then lubricate the seal with a smear of transmission oil. Carefully slide the propeller flange into position, taking care not to damage the seal lip. Fit the new nut and tighten it to the specified torque using the method employed on removal to prevent rotation.

9 Reconnect/refit the propeller shaft as described in Chapter 8.

10 Take the vehicle on a short run then check the transmission fluid level as described in Chapter 1.

Selector shaft oil seal

11 Remove the selector lever position switch as described in Section 8.

12 Using a small flat-bladed screwdriver, carefully lever the oil seal out from the housing then slide it off of the shaft.

13 Clean all traces of dirt from the area around the oil seal aperture then apply a smear of grease to the outer edge and lip of the new oil seal.

14 Making sure its sealing lip is facing inwards, slide the new seal along the selector shaft and tap it squarely into position, using a suitable tubular drift (such as a socket) which bears only on the hard outer edge of the seal.

15 Refit the selector lever position switch as described in Section 8.

7 Fluid cooler - general information

1 The transmission fluid cooler is an integral part of the radiator assembly. Refer to Chapter 3 for removal and refitting details, if the cooler is damaged the complete radiator assembly must be renewed.

8 Transmission control system electrical components - removal and refitting

Selector lever position switch

1 The switch is a multi-function switch, performing the reversing light and starter inhibitor switch functions as well as operating the selector lever position indicator panel. If at any time the indicator panel or reversing light operation becomes faulty, or it is noted that the engine can be started with the selector lever in any position other than P (park) or N (neutral), then it is likely that the switch is faulty. If adjustment fails to correct the fault then the switch assembly must be renewed.

Removal

2 Position the selector lever in the N (neutral) position. Firmly apply the handbrake then jack up the rear of the vehicle and support it on axle stands.

3 Referring to Chapter 4A, slacken and remove the bolts securing the front pipe/ catalytic converter to the intermediate pipe and separate the flange joint; on 2.5 and 3.0 litre models disconnect both left- and right-hand sides. Unbolt the heatshield(s) from the vehicle underbody to gain access to the propeller shaft centre bearing.

4 Slacken and remove the two bolts securing the propeller shaft centre bearing bracket to the vehicle body (see Chapter 8). Recover any washers (where fitted) which are positioned between the bracket and vehicle body.

5 Trace the wiring back from the switch and disconnect it at the wiring connector. Unclip the wiring connector from the side of the transmission housing so that it is free to be removed with the switch. If the connector retaining clip is broken on removal, obtain a new one for refitting.

6 Unclip the protective cover from the switch then unscrew the retaining nut and free the selector lever from the end of the transmission shaft **(see illustrations)**.

7 Place a jack with a block of wood beneath the transmission, and raise the jack to take the weight of the transmission.

8 With the transmission securely supported, slacken and remove the bolts securing the transmission unit rear mounting crossmember to the vehicle body.

9 Lower the transmission slightly until access can be gained to the switch retaining bolts. As the transmission is lowered, take great care to ensure excess strain is not placed on the propeller shaft or any of the engine components and enlist the help of an assistant to make sure nothing becomes trapped between the rear of the engine and bulkhead. **Note:** *On 2.0 litre SOHC engines it maybe necessary to remove the DIS module assembly to gain the necessary clearance required (see Chapter 5B).*

10 Slacken and remove the retaining bolts and slide the switch off of the selector shaft. Whilst the switch is removed check the shaft oil seal for signs of leakage and renew if necessary (see Section 6).

Refitting

11 Prior to refitting, first make sure that the transmission selector shaft is still in the N (neutral) position. If there is any doubt, engage the selector lever with the transmission shaft and move the lever fully backwards (to the P position) then move it two notches forwards.

12 If a new switch is being fitted, locate the switch on the shaft then refit the retaining bolts, tightening them to the specified torque. Note that it is not necessary to adjust the switch since it is set at the factory and sealed in position; the seal will be broken the first time the selector lever is moved.

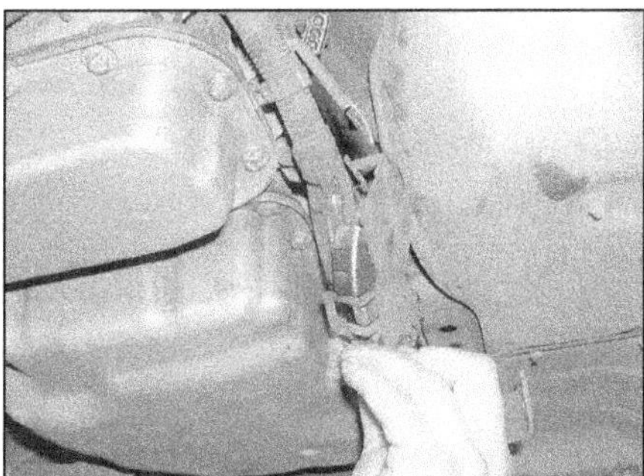

8.6a Unclip the protective cover from the position switch . . .

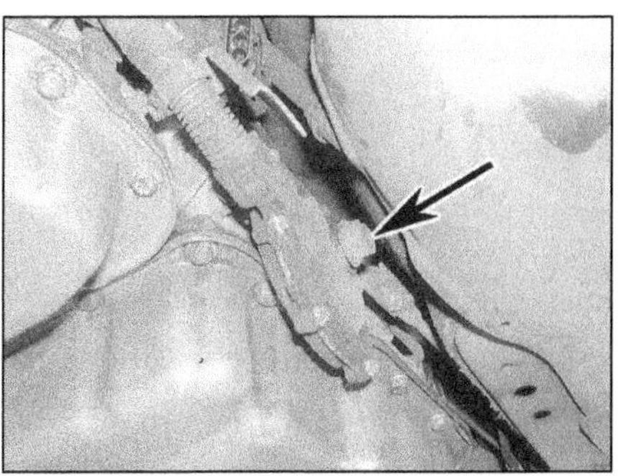

8.6b . . . then slacken and remove the retaining nut (arrowed) and free the selector lever from the shaft

13 If the original switch is being refitting, locate the switch on the transmission shaft then refit the retaining bolts. Adjust the switch as described in paragraph 21 before tightening the retaining bolts to the specified torque.

14 Reconnect the selector lever to the transmission shaft then refit the retaining nut. Tighten the nut to the specified torque setting then clip the protective cover back onto the switch.

15 Securely reconnect the wiring connector then clip the switch connector back onto the transmission unit and raise the transmission unit back up into position.

16 Remove all traces of locking compound from the transmission unit rear mounting crossmember to body bolt threads. Apply a few drops of thread locking compound (Vauxhall recommend the use of locking compound 15 10 181 - available from your Vauxhall dealer) to the threads of each bolt then refit the bolts and tighten to the specified torque.

17 Align the propeller shaft centre bearing bracket with the body making sure any necessary washers (where fitted) are positioned between the bracket and body. Refit the bracket retaining bolts and tighten to the specified torque.

18 Referring to Chapter 4A, refit the heat-shields and reconnect the exhaust system flange joint(s) then lower the vehicle to the ground.

Adjustment

Note: *Before adjusting the switch first ensure the selector linkage is correctly adjusted (see Section 3). A short length of welding rod with a diameter of 2.0 to 2.3 mm will be required for adjustment.*

19 Position the selector lever in the N (neutral) position. Firmly apply the handbrake then jack up the rear of the vehicle and support it on axle stands.

20 Unclip the protective cover from the switch then unscrew the retaining nut and free the selector lever from the end of the transmission shaft.

21 With the transmission in neutral, the slot on the switch body should be correctly aligned with the slot on the switch inner ring. Check this by inserting the welding rod **(see illustration)**. If adjustment is necessary, slacken the switch retaining bolts and rotate the switch assembly as necessary before retightening the bolts to the specified torque setting.

22 Refit the selector lever to the shaft and tighten its retaining nut to the specified torque.

23 Clip the protective cover back onto the switch then lower the vehicle to the ground.

Sport mode switch

Note: *A soldering iron and solder will be required to renew the switch.*

Removal

24 Unclip the selector lever gaiter from the centre console.

25 Push the switch out of the top of the selector lever by inserting a length of welding rod up through the selector lever bore.

26 Make identification marks between the switch and wires then carefully unsolder the wires from the switch terminals and remove the switch.

Refitting

27 Solder the wires to the terminals of the switch, using the marks made prior to removal to ensure they are correctly connected.

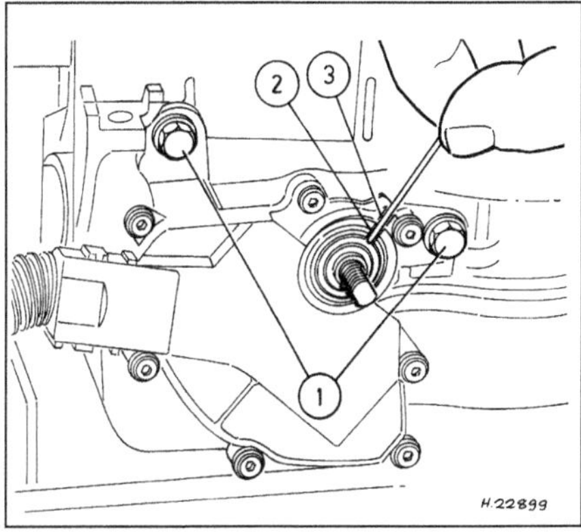

8.21 Adjusting the selector lever position switch

1 Switch retaining bolts *2 Switch grooves* *3 Welding rod*

8.30 **Removing the winter mode switch panel from the centre console**

28 Push the switch securely into position then clip the selector lever gaiter back onto the console.

Winter mode switch

Removal

29 Unclip the selector lever gaiter from the centre console.

30 Reach in behind the console and push the switch panel out of position, disconnecting its wiring connector as it becomes accessible **(see illustration)**. The switch and panel can then be separated.

Refitting

31 Refitting is the reverse of removal ensuring the wiring is correctly routed.

Kickdown switch

32 The kickdown switch is an integral part of the accelerator cable and cannot be renewed separately. Refer to Chapter 4A for details of accelerator cable removal and refitting.

Selector lever pawl contact switch - later models

Note: *New switch retaining clips should be used on refitting.*

Removal

33 Remove the centre console as described in Chapter 11 then position the selector lever in the P (park) position.

34 Slacken and remove the retaining nuts and bolt then remove the front and rear support brackets from the rear heater/ventilation duct. Unclip the duct and remove it from the around the selector lever.

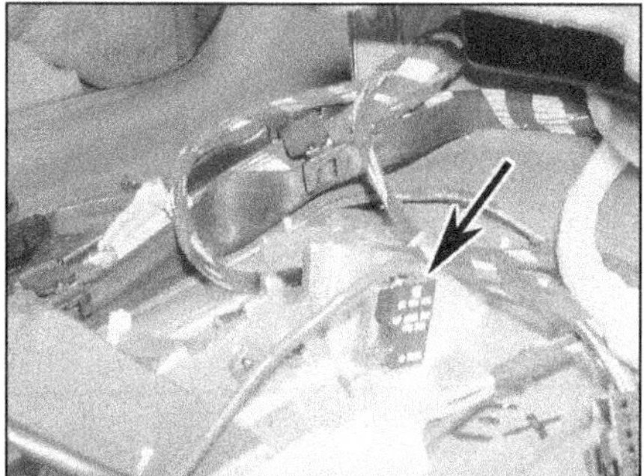

8.35 Selector lever pawl switch - later models

35 Disconnect the wiring connectors then prise off the retaining clips and remove the switch from the selector lever mounting plate **(see illustration)**.

Refitting

36 Refitting is the reverse of removal ensuring the switch is securely retained by the new clips.

Selector lever pawl starter solenoid - later models

Removal

37 Remove the selector lever as described in Section 5 **(see illustration)**.

38 Disconnect the solenoid earth lead from the lever mounting plate and carefully free the solenoid wiring from the main wiring connector.

39 Undo the retaining screws and remove the solenoid from the lever mounting plate.

Refitting

40 Refitting is the reverse of removal making sure the solenoid is correctly engaged with the pawl.

Ignition key release contact switch - later models

Note: *New switch retaining clips should be used on refitting.*

Removal

41 Carry out the operations described in paragraphs 33 and 34.

42 Disconnect the selector lever main wiring connector then carefully free the ignition key switch wiring from the rear of the connector. Disconnect the switch earth lead from the lever mounting plate.

43 Prise off the retaining clips and remove the switch from the vehicle **(see illustration)**.

Refitting

44 Refitting is the reverse of removal using new retaining clips.

Electronic control unit (ECU)

Removal

45 The ECU is located behind the right-hand side of the facia. Prior to removal, disconnect the battery negative terminal.

46 On right-hand drive models, release the retaining clips (rotate them through 90°) then remove the undercover panel from the drivers' side of the facia. Remove the fastener (prise out the centre pin then pull out the fastener outer section) then unclip and remove the heater/ventilation duct.

47 On left-hand drive models remove the glovebox (see Chapter 11).

48 On all models, unscrew the retaining nuts securing the ECU to the pillar then carefully lower the ECU out of position. Release the retaining clip and disconnect the wiring connector then remove the ECU from the vehicle.

Refitting

49 Refitting is the reverse of removal ensuring that the wiring is securely reconnected. If a brand new ECU has been fitted it will be necessary to take the vehicle to a Vauxhall dealer to have the unit coded to match the performance of the relevant engine fitted to your vehicle.

Transmission output shaft speed sensor

Removal

50 The output shaft speed sensor is fitted to the rear of the transmission unit where it is located above and to the left off the propeller shaft flange **(see illustration)**.

51 To gain access to the sensor, firmly apply the handbrake then jack up the front of the vehicle and support it on axle stands.

52 Disconnect the wiring connector and wipe

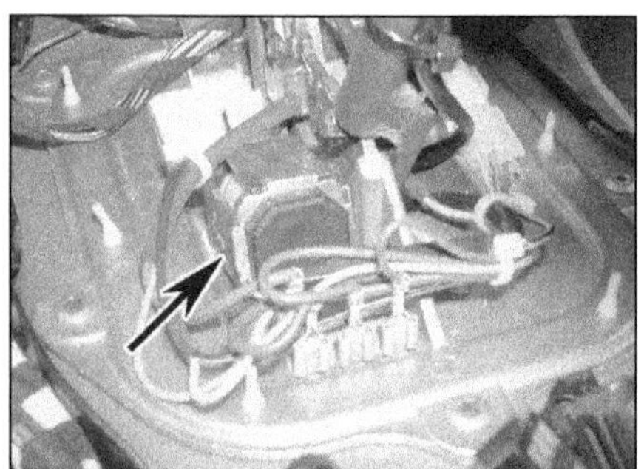

8.37 Selector lever pawl starter solenoid - later models

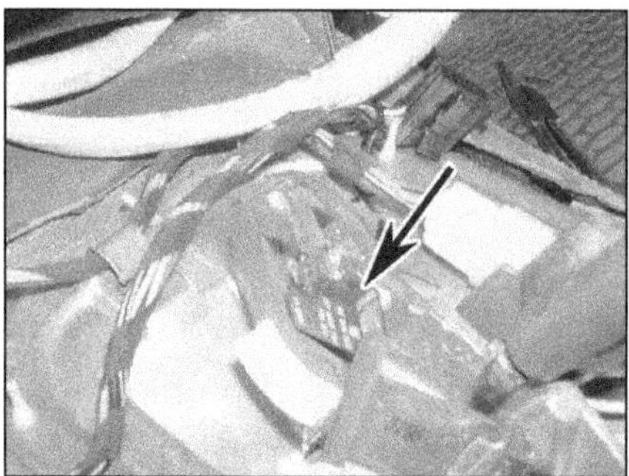

8.43 Ignition key release contact switch - later models

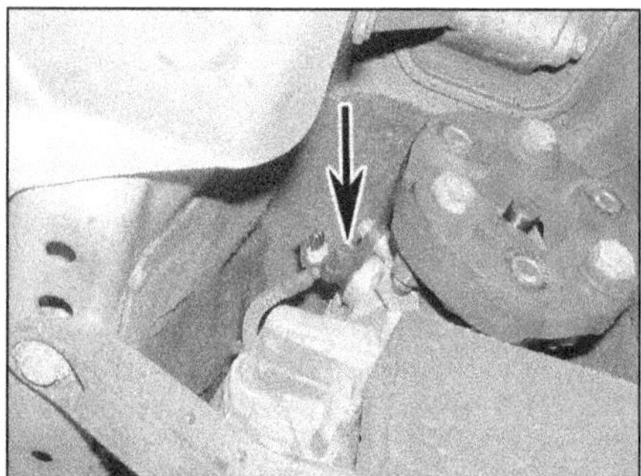

8.50 Transmission output shaft speed sensor location

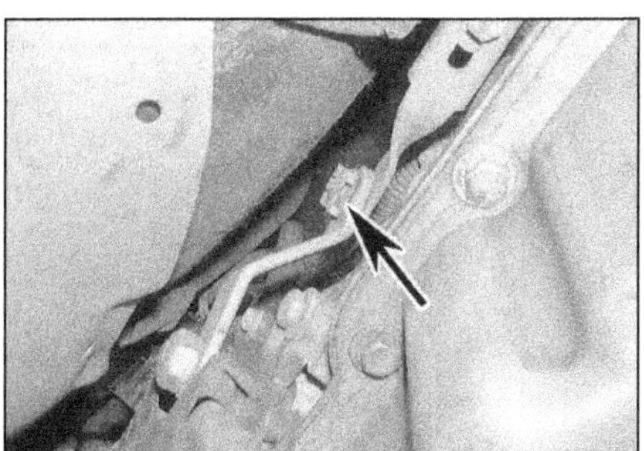
9.3 Slide off the retaining clip and detach the selector linkage rod from the transmission

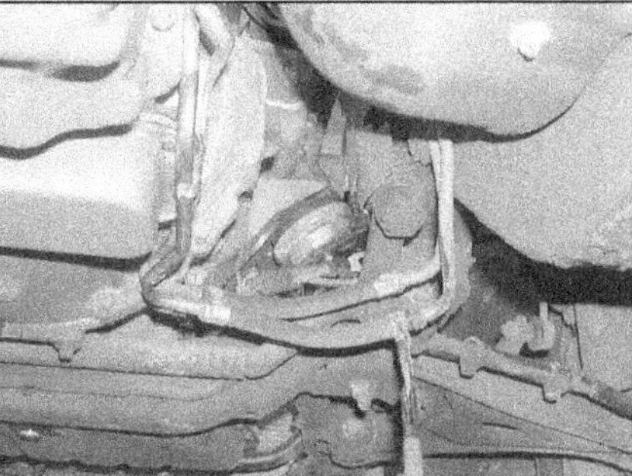
9.4a Release the retaining clips and disconnect the oil cooler pipes . . .

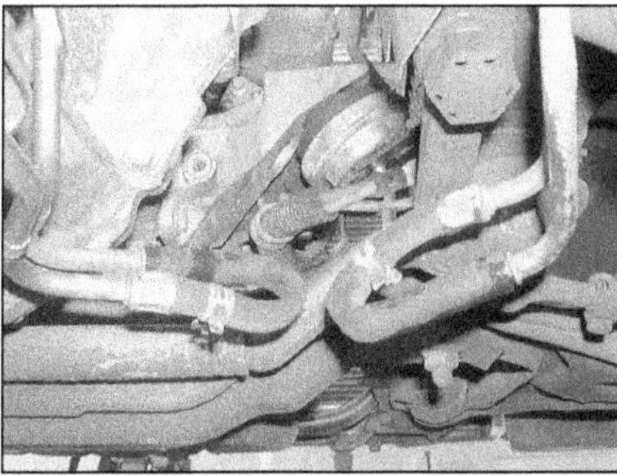
9.4b . . . then fold them back and connect them as shown to minimise fluid loss

clean the area around the sensor.

53 Undo the retaining bolt and remove the sensor from the transmission. Remove the sealing ring from the sensor and discard it, a new one should be used on refitting.

Refitting

54 Fit the new sealing ring to the sensor groove and lubricate it with a smear of transmission fluid.

55 Ease the sensor into position then refit the retaining bolt and tighten it to the specified torque setting. Reconnect the wiring connector then lower the vehicle to the ground.

Transmission solenoid valves

56 Removal and refitting of the various solenoid valves should be entrusted to a Vauxhall dealer.

9 Automatic transmission - removal and refitting

Removal

1 Chock the rear wheels, apply the handbrake, and place the selector lever in the N (neutral) position. Jack up the front of the vehicle, and securely support it on axle stands. Undo the retaining screws and remove the undercover from beneath the engine unit. Disconnect the battery negative terminal. **Note:** *On models with a Vauxhall anti-theft warning system (ATWS), the battery negative terminal must be disconnected within 15 seconds of the ignition being switched off to prevent the alarm system being triggered.*

2 Working as described in Chapter 8, unbolt the front end of the propeller shaft from the transmission flange and remove the vibration damper (where fitted). Position the propeller shaft to the right of the transmission unit and tie it to the vehicle underbody.

3 Slide off the retaining clips and detach the selector linkage rod from the transmission unit and selector lever and remove it from the vehicle **(see illustration)**. Take care not to lose the lever pivot bushes.

4 Trace the fluid cooler pipes back from the transmission unit to their flexible hoses. Remove all traces of dirt then slacken the retaining clips and disconnect both hoses. Minimise fluid loss by folding each hose back on itself and securely connecting it to its adjacent pipe **(see illustrations)**.

5 Disconnect the wiring connector from the output shaft speed sensor (see illustration 8.50), which is located at the rear of the transmission unit, and free the wiring from the transmission unit.

2.0 litre engines

6 On SOHC engines, disconnect the wiring connector from the DIS module (see Chapter 5B). Slacken and remove the module mounting bracket retaining bolts, noting the correct fitted location of the engine lifting bracket, then free the wiring harness and remove the module and bracket from the rear of the cylinder head. Free the HT leads from their retaining clips and position the assembly clear of the transmission unit.

7 On all models unclip the oxygen sensor wiring connector from transmission unit and disconnect it.

8 Slacken and remove the exhaust system front pipe mounting bracket bolt then remove the bolts securing the front pipe to the intermediate pipe and separate the two exhaust sections.

9 On models with a one-piece engine sump, slacken and remove the bolts securing the support brackets to the transmission housing and sides of the cylinder block. Remove both brackets from the engine then remove the torque converter lower cover plate from the base of the transmission housing.

10 On models with a two-piece engine sump, remove the cover from the sump flange to gain access to the torque converter to driveplate bolts.

11 Slacken and remove the visible bolt(s) then, using a socket and extension bar to rotate the crankshaft pulley, undo the remaining bolts securing the torque converter to the driveplate as they become accessible; there are six bolts in total. If necessary, to prevent rotation as the bolts are slackened, remove the cover from the base of the torque converter housing and retain the driveplate by inserting a large screwdriver in through the hole.

12 Place a jack with a block of wood beneath the transmission, and raise the jack to take the weight of the transmission **(see illustration)**.

13 With the transmission securely supported, slacken and remove the bolts securing the transmission unit rear mounting crossmember to the vehicle body **(see illustration)**.

14 Lower the transmission unit slightly and disconnect the vent hose from the top of the transmission housing.

15 Trace the wiring back from the selector lever position switch and disconnect it at the wiring connector. Unclip the wiring connector and position it clear of the transmission housing; if the connector retaining clip is broken on removal, obtain a new one for refitting.

16 Release the retaining clips and disconnect the wiring connectors from the side of the transmission main and intermediate housings **(see illustration)**. Release all the wiring from its retaining clips, noting its correct routing, and position it clear of the transmission unit.

9.12 Securely support the transmission unit with a suitable jack . . .

9.13 . . . then slacken and remove the bolts securing the transmission unit crossmember to the body

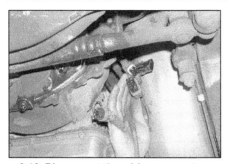

9.16 **Disconnect the wiring connectors from the transmission unit and free the wiring from its retaining clips**

17 Slacken and remove all the bolts securing the transmission housing to the engine. Note the correct fitted positions of each bolt, and the necessary brackets, as they are removed, to use as a reference on refitting. Make a final check that all components have been disconnected, and are positioned clear of the transmission so that they will not hinder the removal procedure.

18 To ensure that the torque converter does not fall out as the transmission is removed, slide the converter along the shaft and fully into the transmission housing.

19 Move the trolley jack and transmission to the rear, to free it from its locating dowels. Once the transmission is free, carefully lower the jack and manoeuvre the unit out from under the vehicle. Remove the locating dowels from the transmission or engine if they are loose, and keep them in a safe place.

2.5 and 3.0 litre models

20 Remove both the exhaust system front pipes as described in Chapter 4A.

21 Remove the cover from the sump flange to gain access to the torque converter retaining bolts. Slacken and remove the visible bolt then, using a socket and extension bar to rotate the crankshaft pulley, undo the remaining bolts securing the torque converter to the driveplate as they become accessible; there are six bolts in total. If necessary, to prevent rotation as the bolts are slackened, remove the cover from the base of the torque converter housing and retain the driveplate by inserting a large screwdriver in through the hole **(see illustrations)**.

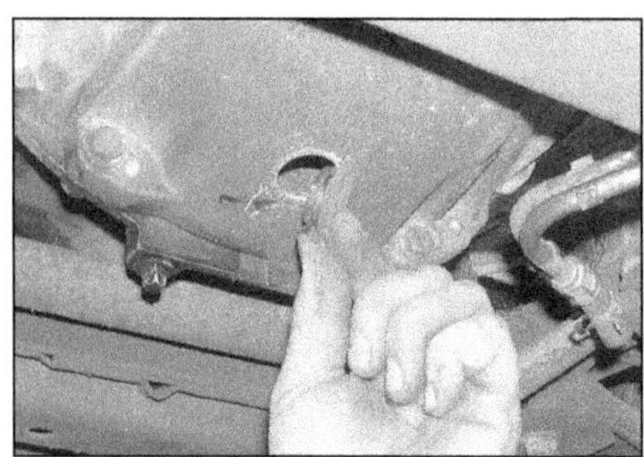

9.21c If necessary, the driveplate can be retained by removing the cover and inserting a large screwdriver in through the hole

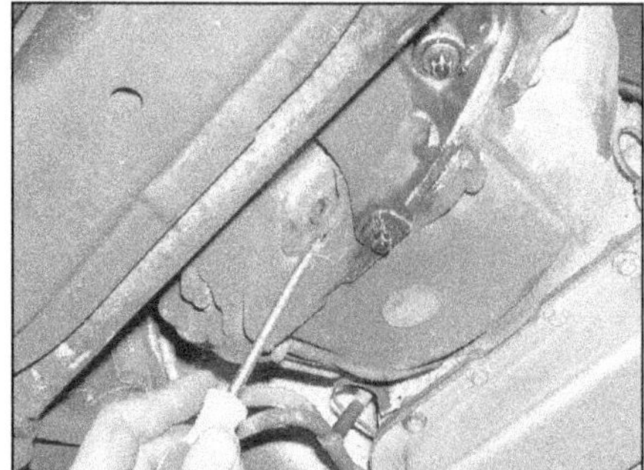

9.21a Prise out the cover from the sump flange . . .

22 Remove the transmission as described in paragraphs 12 to 19.

Refitting

23 The transmission is refitted by a reversal of the removal procedure, bearing in mind the following points.

a) If a new transmission unit is being installed, drain the fluid cooler and blow out the cooler lines using low-pressure compressed air.

b) Check the torque converter centering pin and the crankshaft bush for signs of wear or damage. Remove all traces of dirt and rust then lubricate the bush a pin with a thin smear of molybdenum disulphide grease (Vauxhall recommend the use of lubricating grease 19 48 568 - available from your Vauxhall dealer).

c) Prior to refitting, ensure that the torque converter is correctly engaged with the transmission by measuring the distance from the converter driveplate bolt lugs to the transmission mating surface. This should be 15 mm ***(see illustration)****.*

d) Ensure the locating dowels are correctly positioned and take great care not to allow the weight of the unit to hang on the torque converter as it is installed. Once the transmission and engine are correctly joined, refit the securing bolts, tightening them to the specified torque setting.

e) Align the torque converter with the driveplate then refit the retaining bolts tightening them lightly only to start then go around and tighten them to the specified torque setting in a diagonal sequence.

f) Ensure that the transmission wiring/hoses are correctly routed and retained by all the necessary clips.

g) Remove all traces of locking compound from the transmission unit rear mounting crossmember to body bolt threads. Apply a few drops of thread locking compound (Vauxhall recommend the use of locking compound 15 10 181 - available from your Vauxhall dealer) to the threads of each bolt prior to refitting and tighten both bolts to the specified torque.

h) Tighten all nuts and bolts to the specified torque (where given).

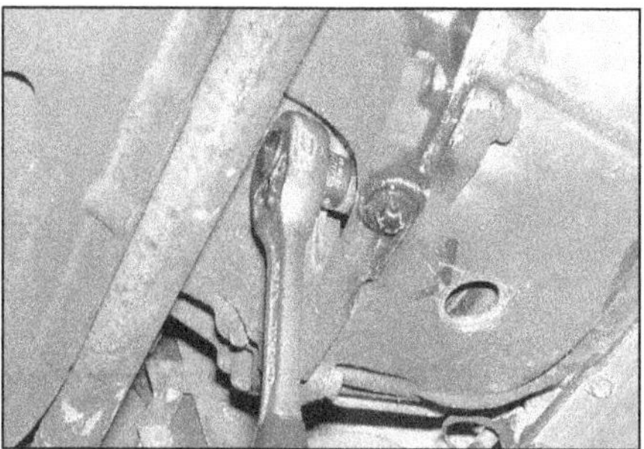

9.21b . . . then slacken and remove the torque converter to driveplate bolts as described in text

i) On completion, refill the transmission with the specified type and quantity of fluid as described in Section 2 and adjust the selector linkage as described in Section 3.

10 Automatic transmission overhaul - general information

1 Overhaul of an automatic transmission unit is beyond the scope of the home mechanic and should be entrusted to a transmission specialist.

2 In the event of a fault occurring with the transmission, the vehicle should be taken to a suitably-equipped Vauxhall dealer for testing. A wiring block connector is incorporated in the electronic control circuit, into which a special electronic diagnostic tester can be plugged (see Section 1) and this should locate the fault.

3 Do not remove the transmission from the car for possible repair before professional fault diagnosis has been carried out, since most tests require the transmission to be in the vehicle.

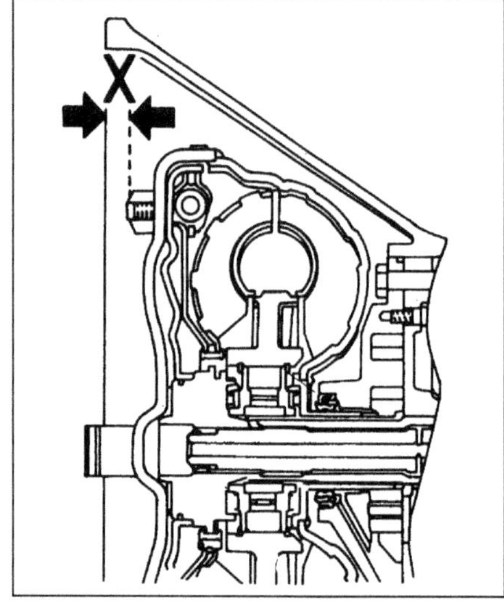

9.23 Check the torque converter is fully engaged by measuring the distance (X) from the converter bolt lugs to the transmission surface. This should be 15 mm

Chapter 8
Final drive, driveshafts and propeller shaft

Contents

Degrees of difficulty

Easy, suitable for novice with little experience 	**Fairly easy,** suitable for beginner with some experience 	**Fairly difficult,** suitable for competent DIY mechanic	**Difficult,** suitable for experienced DIY mechanic 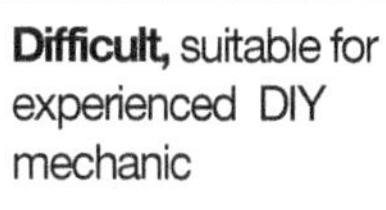	**Very difficult,** suitable for expert DIY or professional

Specifications

Final drive

Type	Unsprung, attached to rear suspension crossmember and underbody. Limited slip differential optional.
Final drive ratio:	
Up to 1998 model year:	
All 2.0 litre 4-cylinder models	3.90 : 1
2.5 litre 6-cylinder models:	
Manual transmission	3.70 : 1
Automatic transmission	3.90 : 1
3.0 litre 6-cylinder models:	
Manual transmission	3.70 : 1
Automatic transmission	3.70 : 1
From 1998 model year:	
All 2.0 litre 4-cylinder models	3.90 : 1
2.5 litre 6-cylinder models:	
Manual transmission	3.90 : 1
Automatic transmission	4.22 : 1
3.0 litre 6-cylinder models:	
Manual transmission	3.70 : 1
Automatic transmission	3.90 : 1
Limited slip differential lock-up value:	
Typical	45 %
Minimum	25 %

Driveshaft

Type	Maintenance-free double constant velocity joint

Propeller shaft

Type	Two-piece tubular shaft with centre bearing, centre universal joint, and flexible disc joint connections to transmission and differential

Lubrication

Final drive lubricant capacity	1.0 litre
Final drive lubricant type/specification:	
Excluding limited-slip differential:	
Renewal	GM special lubricant 19 42 382 (9 293 688)
Top-up	Hypoid gear oil, viscosity SAE 90
Limited-slip differential:	
Renewal:	
First 0.25 litres	GM special fluid additive 19 70 452 (90 004 033)
Remaining 0.75 litres	GM special lubricant 19 42 382 (9 293 688)
Top-up	GM special lubricant 19 42 382 (9 293 688)
Driveshaft CV joint grease type	GM special grease 19 41 522 (90 007 999)

Torque wrench settings

Torque wrench settings	Nm	lbf ft
Damping bracket to final drive unit*:		
Stage 1	90	66
Stage 2	Tighten a further 45°	
Stage 3	Tighten a further 15°	
Disc joint to propeller shaft transmission or differential:		
Hexagon bolt	95	70
Torx bolt*:		
Stage 1	50	37
Stage 2	Tighten a further 75°	
Stage 3	Tighten a further 15°	
Driveshaft to hub:		
Stage 1	50	37
Stage 2	Tighten a further 60°	
Stage 3	Tighten a further 15°	
Final drive oil level check plug:		
Stage 1	22	16
Stage 2	Tighten a further 90°	
Stage 3	Tighten a further 180°	
Final drive unit damping bracket bush to rear crossmember*:		
Stage 1	100	74
Stage 2	Tighten a further 75°	
Stage 3	Tighten a further 15°	
Final drive unit rear cover	60	44
Final drive unit to crossmember*:		
Stage 1	90	66
Stage 2	Tighten a further 30°	
Stage 3	Tighten a further 15°	
Propeller shaft centre bearing bracket to underbody	20	15
Propeller shaft centre bearing to bracket	22	16
Propeller shaft to flexible joint:		
Hexagon bolt	95	70
Torx bolt*:		
Stage 1	50	37
Stage 2	Tighten a further 45°	
Stage 3	Tighten a further 15°	
Speed sensor to bracket (with ABS)	4	3

**Indicates that a new bolt/nut must be used.*

1 General description

1 The final drive unit houses the differential gears and is bolted directly to the rear suspension crossmember. The unit has a cast aluminium casing which incorporates external ribs to improve structural rigidity and fluid cooling. A bracket with an integral rubber damping block bolted between the final drive casing and the suspension crossmember controls the movement of the final drive during operation.

2 A limited-slip differential may be fitted as an option; this incorporates a clutch mechanism which controls the difference in speed between the left and right hand driveshafts. Under normal conditions, the clutch slips allowing the driveshafts to rotate at different speeds, such as during cornering. When the speed differential increases beyond a preset limit, such as during wheelspin caused by rapid acceleration or poor road surfaces, the clutch locks thus preventing the differential from supplying all available drive to the spinning wheel, and ensuring equal distribution of drive to both rear wheels.

3 Two driveshafts, incorporating Rzeppa-type constant velocity joints, transmit drive from the final drive differential to the rear wheels. The inner joints incorporates the Anti-lock Braking System (ABS) rear wheel sensor reluctor discs - see Chapter 9 for details. Flexible rubber gaiters filled with grease encapsulate each joint, keeping the joint lubricated and preventing the ingress of dirt and debris.

4 A two-piece, tubular propeller shaft transmits drive from the transmission from to the final drive unit. It incorporates a centre bearing supported in a rubber insulator. The rear section of the shaft has a universal joint at its front end, and the front section has a slider joint at its rear end. The propeller shaft is secured to the transmission and differential by flexible disc joints.

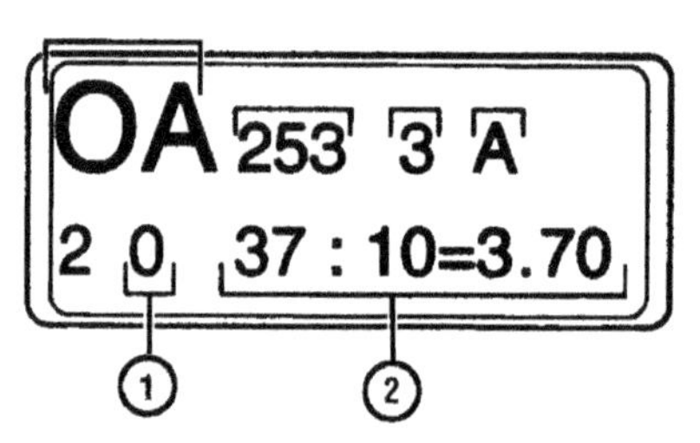

1.5 Final drive unit identification plate

1 Limited slip differential (S = yes, 0 = no)
2 Final drive ratio

Final drive identification

5 The type of final drive unit fitted can be determined by examining the identification plate affixed to the underside of the final drive unit **(see illustration).**

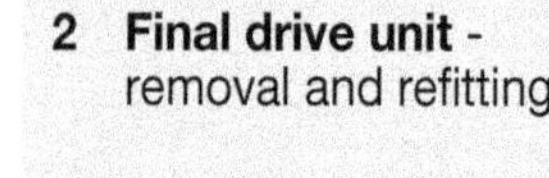

2 Final drive unit - removal and refitting

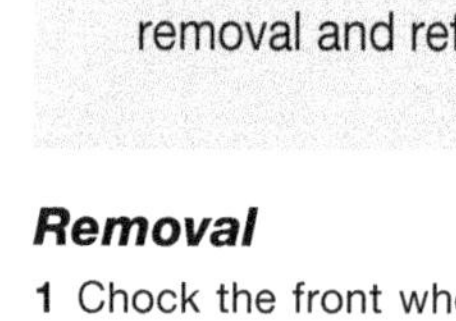

Removal

1 Chock the front wheels securely. Jack up the rear of the vehicle, support it on axle stands and remove both rear wheels.

2 Remove both driveshafts with reference to Section 8.

3 Unhook the exhaust system mounting rubbers and lower the rear of the system approximately 300 mm (12.0 in). Support or tie the system in this position.

4 Unbolt the propeller shaft rear flange from the flexible drive joint and lever the propeller shaft from the joint. Support the propeller shaft on an axle stand - do not let it hang by the universal joint.
5 Position a trolley jack underneath the final drive unit, and raise it until it just comes into contact with the underside of the casing.
6 Unplug the wiring from both ABS wheel sensors at the connectors.
7 Unscrew the bolt securing the damping bracket at the front of the final drive casing to the suspension crossmember.
8 Unscrew and withdraw the bolt securing the rear of the final drive casing to the suspension crossmember.
9 Lower the trolley jack and remove the final drive from the underside of the vehicle.

Refitting

10 Refitting is a reversal of removal, noting the following points:.

a) *Check that the distance between the two final drive bushes on the suspension crossmember is between 300 and 302 mm. If necessary, adjust this dimension by altering the position of the bushes in the crossmember, using a universal puller or similar tool.*
b) *Ensure that the wiring for the ABS wheel sensors is securely reconnected.*
c) *Use new bolts/nuts where indicated (see Specifications) and tighten all fixings to the specified torque.*
d) *Refit the driveshafts with reference to Section 8.*
e) *On completion, check the oil level in the final drive unit as described in Section 3.*

3 Final drive unit - oil level check

Level check

1 Jack up the front and rear of the vehicle and support it on axle stands so that the vehicle is level.
2 Using a hexagon key, unscrew the filler plug from the right-hand side of the final drive unit. On models with a limited slip differential, it will be necessary to prise the bung from the centre of the plug first **(see illustration)**.
3 Check that the oil level is up to the lower edge of the filler plug aperture using a (clean) piece of bent wire as a dipstick.
4 If necessary, top-up with the correct type of oil as given in the Specifications.
5 Refit and tighten the filler plug to the specified torque, and wipe clean. Refit the plastic bung to the centre of the plug on models with a limited slip differential.
6 Check the pinion final drive unit oil seal and differential bearing oil seals for leaks. If evident, renew them.
7 Lower the car to the ground.

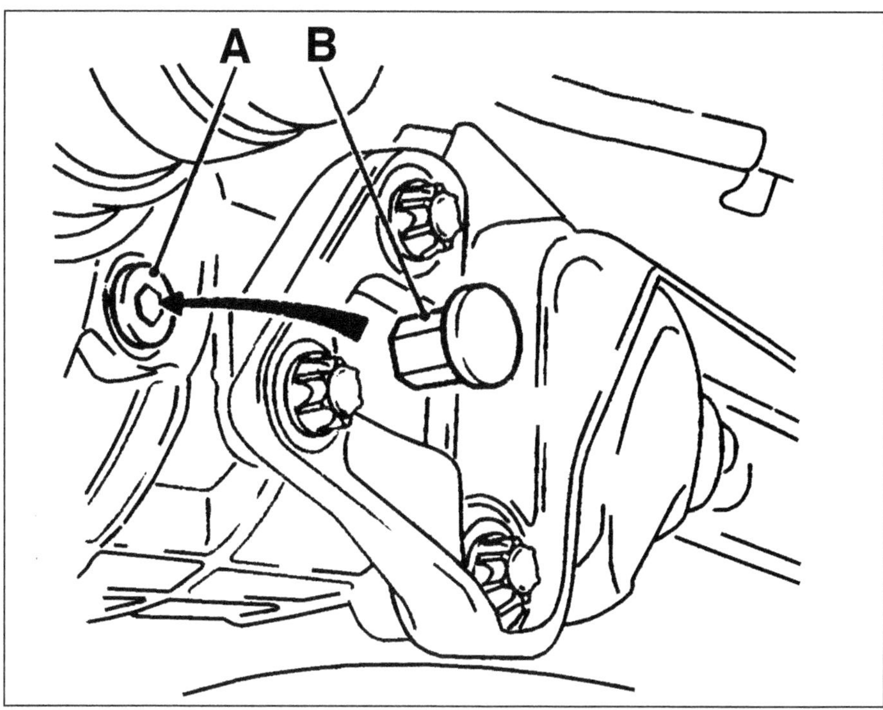

3.2 Final drive unit oil filler/level plug (A) and plastic bung (B)

Complete refill

8 Proceed as described for *Level check* noting the following points:.

a) *On models* ***without*** *a limited slip differential, GM special differential oil must be used if the final drive is being refilled from empty, rather than just topped-up (see Specifications).*
b) *On models with a limited slip differential, if the final drive is being refilled from empty, rather than just topped-up, the procedure must be carried out in two stages:*
   1) *Pour 0.25 litres of GM special differential oil additive into the final drive*
   2) *Pour approximately 0.75 litres of GM special differential oil into the final drive, until the level reaches the lower edge of the filler plug aperture (see Specifications).*

4 Final drive unit damping bushes - renewal

Front bush

1 Chock the front wheels. Jack up the rear of the vehicle and support it on axle stands.
2 Support the final drive unit on a trolley jack.
3 Unplug the wiring from both ABS wheel sensors at the connectors.
4 Slacken and withdraw the bolts securing the rear of the final drive unit to the suspension crossmember.
5 Fully unscrew the bolt securing the damping bush bracket to the front of the suspension crossmember. Lower the final drive unit slightly, using the trolley jack.
6 Slacken and withdraw the three bolts securing the damping bracket to the final drive unit casing. Be prepared for some oil leakage - position a drip tray underneath the final drive casing to catch the oil.
7 Detach the damping bush bracket from the final drive casing and remove it from the vehicle. Withdraw the securing bolt from the damper bush.
8 Press the old bush from the bracket using a hydraulic press, or drive it out using a suitable drift. Drive or press the new bush into position, ensuring that the recessed section of the bush is correctly aligned with the bracket boss **(see illustration)**.
9 Commence refitting by inserting the securing bolt through the centre of the damper bush.

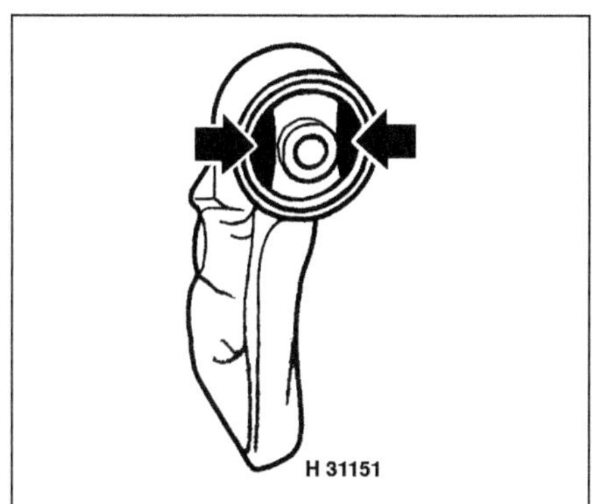

4.8 Ensuring that the recessed section of the bush is aligned with the bracket boss as shown

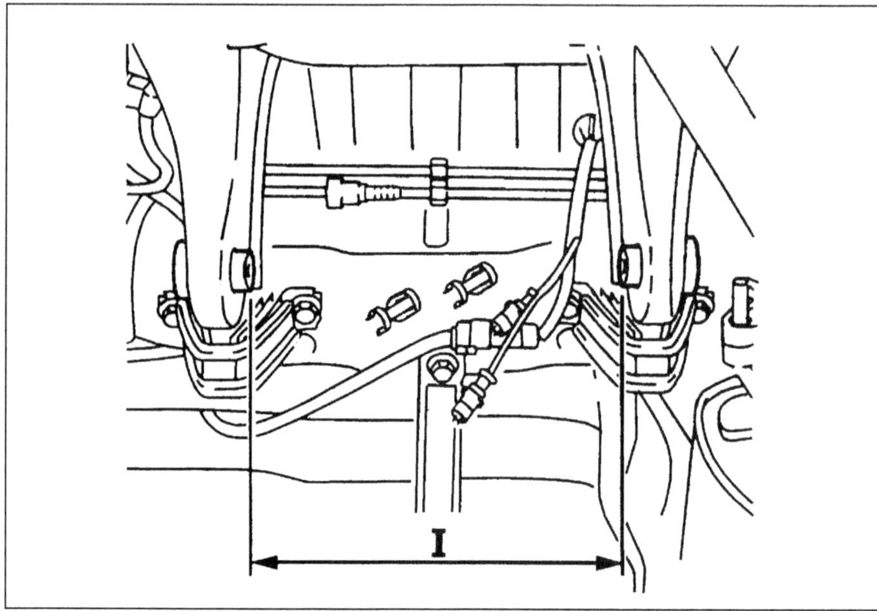

4.19 Press the new bushes into the crossmember, ensuring that the distance measured between their inner edges (I) is between 300 and 302 mm

10 Offer the bracket, bush and securing bolt up to the final drive casing. Insert the three bracket securing bolts and tighten them to the specified torque.
11 Raise the final drive casing up into position using the trolley jack, then tighten the damper bush-to-suspension crossmember bolt and tighten it to the specified torque.
12 Refit the two rear final drive casing-to-suspension crossmember bolts and tighten them to the specified torque.
13 Reconnect the wiring for the ABS wheel sensors.
14 On completion, top-up the differential oil with reference to Section 3, then lower the vehicle to the ground.

Rear bushes

15 Remove the final drive unit as described in Section 2.
16 Unbolt the fuel filter from its mountings and move to one side, with reference to Chapter 1. There should be no need to disconnect the fuel lines from it.
17 With reference to Chapter 4A, unhook the exhaust system intermediate silencer from its mountings and support it on axle stand.
18 Extract the bushes from the suspension crossmember using a universal puller or similar tool. The bushes are removed from the outside of the crossmember.
19 Press the new bushes into the crossmember, ensuring that the distance measured between their inner edges is between 300 and 302 mm **(see illustration)**.
20 Refit the final drive unit as described in Section 2.
21 Refit the fuel filter and exhaust system silencer as described in Chapters 1 and 4A respectively.

5 Final drive unit rear cover gasket - renewal

1 Remove the final drive unit as described in Section 2.
2 Place the final drive unit in a suitable drip tray, then unbolt and remove the rear cover from the casing. Remove the gasket and allow the oil to drain.
3 Thoroughly clean the joint faces of the final drive casing and cover.
4 Apply a coat of the recommended sealant to the mating surface of the final drive casing.
5 Refit the cover, then insert and tighten the bolts progressively to the specified torque. It is recommended that new bolts are used.
6 Refit the final drive unit to the vehicle as described in Section 2.
7 Lower the vehicle to the ground. On completion, refill the final drive unit with the specified quantity and grade(s) of oil, as described in Section 3.

6 Final drive unit pinion oil seal - renewal

Caution: The pinion bearing pre-load will be affected by the renewal of the pinion oil seal and must be reset accurately following repair work. The following procedure describes how to reset the bearing pre-load approximately, using rudimentary tools, but we recommend that the pre-load is set accurately by a Vauxhall dealer, or an engineering workshop.

1 Remove the final drive unit as described in Section 2.
2 Mount the unit in a vice.
3 Measure the pinion bearing pre-load as follows: fit a socket on the pinion nut, and using an adjustable low-torque wrench, measure the torque which must be applied to cause pinion to just start to rotate - the figure should be approximately 90 to 120 Ncm. Record this figure for later reference.
4 Mark the drive flange nut in relation to the drive flange and pinion.
5 Hold the drive flange stationary by bolting a length of metal bar to it, then unscrew the nut noting the exact number of turns necessary to remove it.
6 Using a suitable puller, draw the drive flange from the pinion.
7 Lever the oil seal from the final drive casing with a screwdriver. Wipe clean the oil seal seating.
8 Smear a little differential oil (see *Specifications*) on the sealing lip of the new oil seal, then drive it squarely into the casing until flush with the outer face. Ideally use metal tubing to fit the oil seal, but alternatively a block of wood may be used on each side of the pinion.
9 Locate the drive flange on the pinion in its original position, then refit the nut to its original position, using the markings and notes made during removal.
10 The pinion drive bearing pre-load must now be reset to its original value. Measure the torque required to turn the pinion, as described in paragraph 3. Adjust the position of the pinion nut until the measured value is the same as that recorded earlier.
11 Refit the final drive unit with reference to Section 2.

7 Final drive unit differential bearing oil seal - renewal

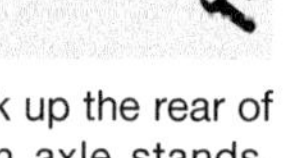

1 Chock the front wheels. Jack up the rear of the vehicle and support it on axle stands. Remove the appropriate rear wheel.
2 Remove the appropriate driveshaft with reference to Section 8.
3 Note the fitted depth of the oil seal in the final drive casing.
4 Using a screwdriver or hooked instrument, lever out the oil seal **(see illustration)**, taking

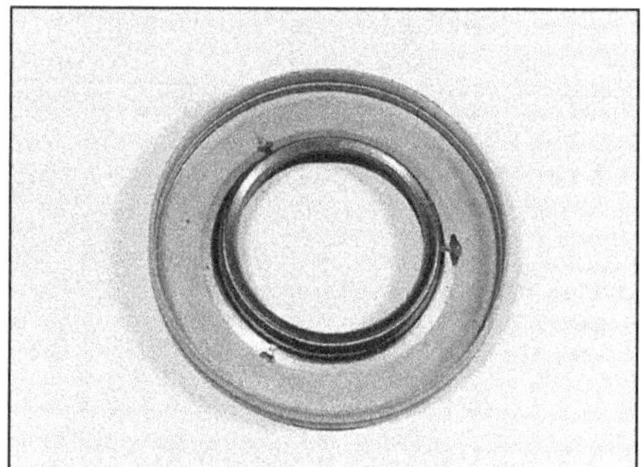

7.4 Differential bearing oil seal

great care avoid damaging the surface of the seal housing. Wipe the oil from the oil seal housing.
5 Smear a little oil on the sealing lip of the new oil seal. Using suitable metal tubing drive the oil seal squarely into the casing to the previously noted position.
6 Refit the driveshaft with reference to Section 8.
7 Refit the wheel and lower the vehicle to the ground.

8 Driveshaft - removal and refitting

Removal

1 Chock the front wheels, then jack up the rear of the vehicle and support it on axle stands.
2 Unscrew the socket-head bolts securing the driveshaft to the rear hub while holding the rear wheel stationary. Recover the lock-washers.
3 Lever the driveshaft from the rear hub and support it above the disc brake assembly.
4 Remove the rear wheel.
5 Position a container under the final drive unit to catch any spilled oil.
6 Carefully lever the driveshaft from the final drive unit differential. On models with anti-lock braking take care not to damage the wheel speed sensor and reluctor wheel.
7 Withdraw the driveshaft from the side of the vehicle.
8 Check the circlip on the inner end of the driveshaft and if necessary renew it.

Refitting

9 Refitting is a reversal of removal, but make sure that the driveshaft is fully entered in the differential side gear with the circlip engaged in its groove. Tighten the mounting bolts in three stages, as detailed in the Specifications **(see illustrations)**. Check and if necessary top up the oil level in the final drive unit, as described in Section 3.

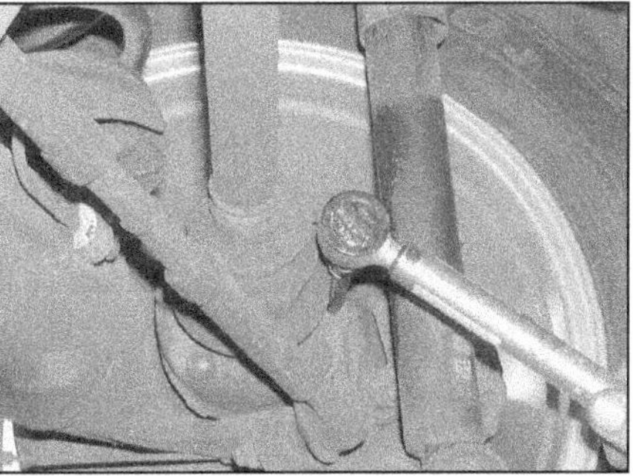

8.9a Tighten the driveshaft mounting bolts to the specified first stage torque . . .

9 Driveshaft rubber gaiters and outer constant velocity joint - renewal

1 Remove the driveshaft as described in Section 8 and mount it in a vice.
2 Using a small drift, tap the metal cover from the outer joint.
3 Loosen and remove both clips from the rubber bellows.
4 Using a sharp knife slice through the rubber bellows and remove them from the driveshaft.
5 Scoop out the grease from the joint and wipe the driveshaft clean.
6 Using circlip pliers, extract the circlip from the outer end of the driveshaft.
7 Support the outer joint on a vice, then tap the driveshaft down through it.
8 Fill the inner joint with the specified type of grease using a wooden spatula.
9 Fit the new inner bellows, check that it is not twisted then fit and tighten the clips.
10 Locate the outer bellows on the drive-shaft.
11 Fit the outer joint, using a tubular metal drift, with the driveshaft mounted in a vice. Make sure that the joint abuts the shoulder.
12 Fit the circlip making sure that it fully enters the groove.
13 Using the wooden spatula fill the outer joint with grease.
14 Locate the outer bellows on the plate, check that it is not twisted then fit and tighten the clips.

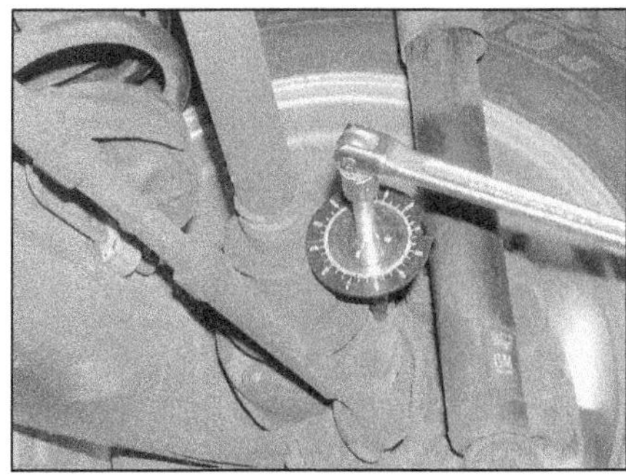

8.9b . . . then angle tighten to the specified second and third stages

15 Locate the cover on the joint using two driveshaft bolts to ensure correct alignment. Tap the cover on the joint with a soft-faced mallet.
16 Extract the retaining circlip from the inner end of the driveshaft and fit a new one.
17 Refit the driveshaft with reference to Section 8.

10 Propeller shaft - removal and refitting

Removal

1 Chock the front wheels. Jack up the rear of the vehicle and support it on axle stands.
2 On models equipped with a catalytic converter, from underneath the vehicle, undo the retaining bolts and remove both the large and small catalytic converter heatshields from the vehicle underbody **(see illustration)**.
3 At the sliding joint, mark the relationship between the front and rear sections of the propeller shaft. If the two halves of the shaft become separated during removal, reconnect them using the alignment markings, to preserve the balance characteristics.
4 Using a conventional, or Torx, socket as applicable, unscrew the bolts securing the front flexible disc joint to the transmission output flange **(see illustration)**.
5 At the rear of the propeller shaft, unscrew the bolts securing the rear disc joint to the differential flange **(see illustration)**.

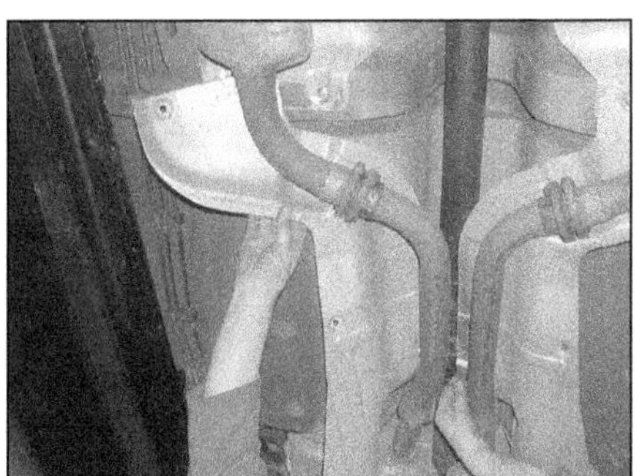

10.2 Remove the exhaust heat shields from the vehicle underbody

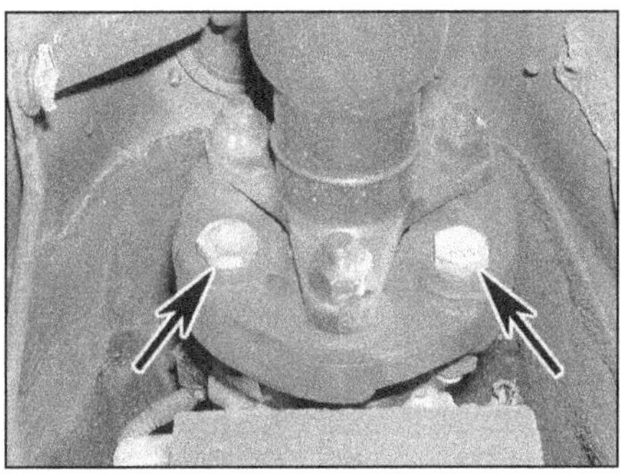

10.4 Unscrew the bolts (arrowed) securing the front flexible disc joint to the transmission output flange

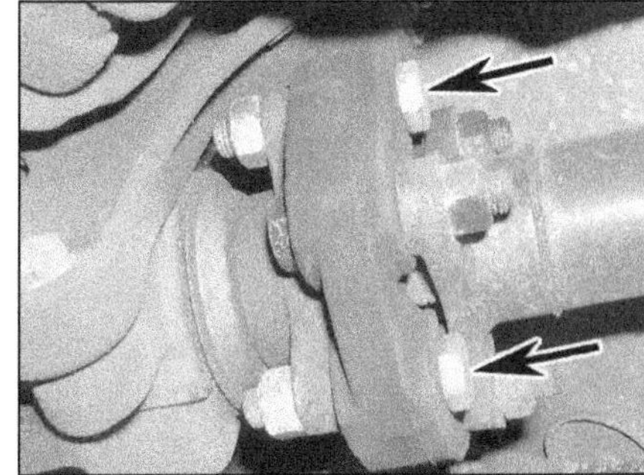

10.5 Unscrew the bolts (arrowed) securing the rear disc joint to the differential flange

10.6 Centre bearing support bracket bolts (arrowed)

6 Support the centre of the propeller shaft on an axle stand, then unbolt the centre bearing support bracket from the underbody, noting the location of any alignment shims **(see illustration)**.

7 Push the front section rearwards along the slider joint splines until clear of the transmission output flange.

8 Withdraw the propeller shaft forwards, making sure that the front section remains on the slider joint splines (see paragraph 3).

9 Unbolt the centre support bracket from the centre bearing, noting the location of any alignment shims.

10 Unbolt the front and rear disc joints from the propeller shaft. Note that on some models a vibration damper is fitted at the front of the propeller shaft.

Refitting

11 Refitting is a reversal of removal, noting the following points:.

a) Coat the inboard splines of the driveshaft with differential oil before inserting them into the final drive.

b) Tighten all nuts and bolts to the specified torque.

11 Propeller shaft centre bearing - renewal

1 Remove the propeller shaft as described in Section 10.

2 Mount the rear propeller shaft section in a vice, using shaped blocks of wood to prevent damage.

3 Mark the front and rear sections in relation to each other, then pull the front section from the splines.

4 Slide off the rubber sleeve, then using circlip pliers, extract the circlip from the groove in front of the centre bearing **(see illustration)**. Extract the dust seal washer.

5 Unbolt the centre bearing from its mounting bracket.

6 Support the centre bearing on a vice, and press or drive the rear propeller shaft section down through the bearing. Recover the dust seal washer.

7 Similarly, press or drive the ball bearing from the centre bearing housing, and remove the dust cover.

8 Clean the removed components and the end of the propeller shaft. Lightly grease the splines.

9 Press or drive the new ball bearing into the housing, and align the dust washer.

10 Support the rear section universal joint on a vice, and press or drive the centre bearing over the splines using a metal tube on the inner track. Make sure that the bearing makes contact with its seating shoulder.

11 Bolt the mounting bracket to the centre bearing and tighten the bolts to the specified torque.

12 Mount the rear section in a vice, and fit the front dust washer and the circlip, making sure that it is correctly located in the groove.

13 Locate the rubber sleeve over the splines.

14 Fit the front section on the rear section splines, making sure that the previously-made marks are aligned, to preserve the balance characteristics. Note that a master spline is provided to ensure correct assembly **(see illustration)**.

15 Refit the propeller shaft as described in Section 10.

12 Propeller shaft disc joints - renewal

1 Chock the front wheels. Jack up the rear of the vehicle and support it on axle stands.

2 Apply the handbrake, then where applicable, unbolt and remove the heatshields from the vehicle underbody to gain access to the disc joints.

3 If removing the rear disc joint, unbolt the propeller shaft centre bearing mounting bracket from the underside of the vehicle and support the propeller shaft on an axle stand.

4 Unbolt the propeller shaft flange(s) from the flexible disc joint(s).

5 Unbolt the flexible disc joint from the transmission and/or differential drive flange(s).

6 Push the appropriate propeller shaft section towards the centre bearing and remove the disc joint(s). If necessary, use a lever to prise the propeller shaft clear of the drive flange(s).

7 Fit the new flexible disc joint(s) using a reversal of the removal procedure, noting the following points:.

a) Bolt the disc joint to the propeller first, then to the transmission/final drive flange.

b) Tighten all nuts and bolts to the specified torque (see Specifications).

c) Where applicable, refit the propeller shaft centre bearing mounting bracket to the underside of the vehicle as described in Section 11.

d) Securely refit all heatshield panels removed for access.

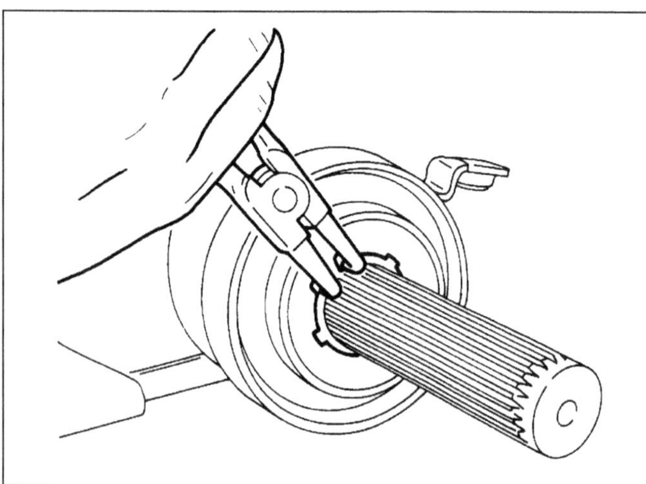

11.4 Extract the circlip from the groove in front of the centre bearing

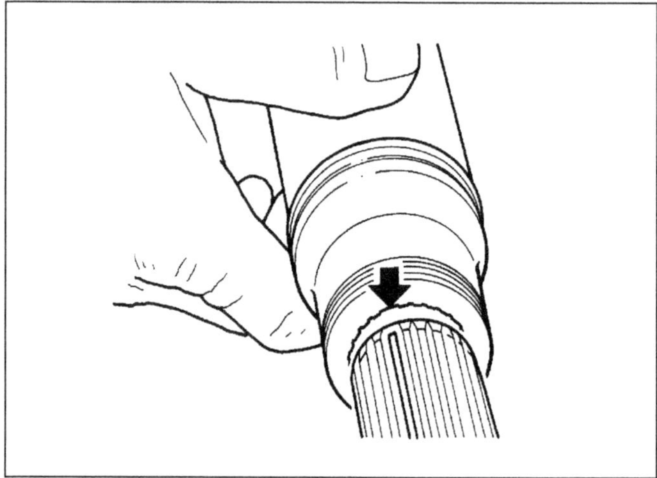

11.14 Note that a master spline (arrowed) is provided to ensure correct assembly

Chapter 9
Braking system

Contents

Degrees of difficulty

Easy, suitable for novice with little experience 	**Fairly easy,** suitable for beginner with some experience 	**Fairly difficult,** suitable for competent DIY mechanic 	**Difficult,** suitable for experienced DIY mechanic	**Very difficult,** suitable for expert DIY or professional

Specifications

General

System type	Front and rear discs, floating front caliper, fixed rear caliper, tandem master cylinder with hydraulic system split front/rear, vacuum servo unit, rear brake proportioning valve on certain models. Electronic anti-lock braking system (ABS) on all models. Cable-operated handbrake to shoes bearing on drums incorporated into rear discs.
Servo diameter	200/225 mm
Servo piston rod, adjustment length	106 + 0.5 mm
Brake fluid capacity	0.5 litre (approx.)
Brake pedal travel to illuminate brake lights	15 ± 5 mm
Master cylinder, nominal diameter:	
Up to 1998 model year:	
4 cylinder engine models	23.81/20.64 mm
6 cylinder engine models	25.40/20.64 mm
From 1998 model year:	
All models	25.40 mm

Front brakes

Disc diameter:	
Up to 1998 model year:	
4 cylinder engine models	286 mm
6 cylinder engine models	296 mm
From 1998 model year:	
All models	296 mm
Disc thickness (new):	
Up to 1998 model year:	
4 cylinder engine models	24 mm
6 cylinder engine models	28 mm
From 1998 model year:	
All models	28 mm
Disc thickness (minimum, after machining*):	
Up to 1998 model year:	
4 cylinder engine models	22.5 mm
6 cylinder engine models	26.5 mm
From 1998 model year:	
All models	26.5 mm

Front brakes (continued)

Disc thickness (minimum, wear limit):	
Up to 1998 model year:	
4 cylinder engine models	21 mm
6 cylinder engine models	25 mm
From 1998 model year:	
All models	25 mm
Disc maximum thickness variation	0.01 mm
Disc maximum run-out	0.12 mm
Disc maximum score depth	0.4 mm
Brake pad thickness (including backplate):	
New	17.5 ± 0.6 mm
Minimum	8.0 mm
Caliper piston diameter:	
Up to 1998 model year:	
4 cylinder engine models	54 mm
6 cylinder engine models	54 mm
From 1998 model year:	
All models	57 mm

**After machining the disc surface, new brake pads must be fitted. Once these are worn, no more new pads may be used with the same discs - new discs must then be fitted.*

Rear brakes

Discs diameter (new)	286 mm
Disc thickness:	
New	12.0 mm
Minimum (after machining*)	11.0 mm
Minimum (wear limit)	10.0 mm
Variation (maximum)	0.01 mm
Run-out (maximum)	0.12 mm
Caliper piston diameter	40.0 mm
Brake pad thickness (including backplate):	
New	17.0 mm
Minimum	6.0 mm
Handbrake shoe minimum thickness (lining only)	1.0 mm
Handbrake drum diameter:	
New	160.0 mm
Maximum (wear limit**)	161.0 mm

**After machining the disc surface, new brake pads must be fitted. Once these are worn, no more new pads may be used with the same discs - new discs must then be fitted.*
***After machining the drum surface, new brake shoes must be fitted. Once these are worn, no more new shoes may be used with the same drums - new drums must then be fitted.*

Torque wrench settings

	Nm	lbf ft
ABS control unit bracket to modulator	8	6
ABS modulator to bodywork	10	7
ABS modulator-to-bracket nuts	8	6
ABS wheel sensor securing screws	8	6
Brake disc locking screw	4	3
Brake line union nuts/bolts	16	12
Brake pedal bracket to bulkhead	20	15
Brake pedal shaft to bracket	18	13
Caliper bleed screw	9	7
Caliper brake hose union bolt	40	30
Caliper guide bolt	30	22
Front caliper mounting bracket-to-steering knuckle bolts (all calipers)*:		
Stage 1	95	70
Stage 2	Angle-tighten through 30° to 45°	
Handbrake lever	20	15
Master cylinder front mounting	22	16
Master cylinder to vacuum servo	22	16
Rear caliper mounting bolts	80	59
Road wheel bolts	110	81
Vacuum servo	21	15

**Use new bolts.*

Note: *The threads of all fasteners secured with locking compound must be thoroughly cleaned and, if necessary, re-cut to remove all traces of the old locking compound. Fresh locking compound should then be reapplied at reassembly.*

1 General description

1 The braking system is of dual hydraulic circuit type with front and rear discs. The front and rear hydraulic circuits are operated independently, so that in the event of a failure in one circuit the remaining circuit still functions. The floor-mounted handbrake lever operates brake shoes by means of a cable. The handbrake shoes are mounted inside the rear brake discs; the inner surface of each rear brake disc incorporates a brake drum. The disc brakes are self-adjusting in use, however the handbrake is adjusted manually.

2 An Anti-lock Braking System (ABS) is fitted as standard equipment on all models. Pre-1998 models have 3-channnel ABS, with independent hydraulic circuits for each front brake, and a shared hydraulic circuit for the rear brakes. Later models have 4-channel ABS, with independent circuits for all four brakes.

3 During braking, the ABS system adjusts the braking system hydraulic pressure, to prevent the road wheels from locking, thereby reducing the likelihood of skidding in slippery conditions and/or during heavy braking. The system incorporates an electronic control unit which is supplied with signals from the wheel speed sensors. The signals are compared with each other and, if one wheel is found to be decelerating more rapidly than the others, the hydraulic pressure to that wheel is reduced until its speed matches the other wheels. The ABS unit is fitted in the hydraulic lines leading from the master cylinder to the brakes, the vacuum servo unit and master cylinder being of similar type for both non-ABS and ABS models. The ABS control system also manages the operation of the Traction Control (TC) system fitted to models with 6-cylinder engines. For more details of the ABS/TC systems, refer to Sections 17 and 18.

4 Should the ABS develop a fault, it is recommended that a complete system check is carried out by a GM dealer or ABS specialist, who will have access to the specialist equipment necessary to make an accurate diagnosis of the problem.

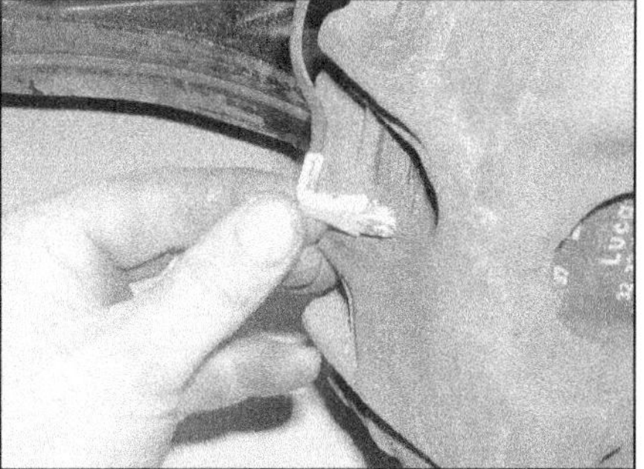

2.5 Unclip the pad wear sensor from the caliper aperture

2 Front brake pads - inspection, removal and refitting

Warning: Renew both sets of front brake pads at the same time - never renew the pads on only one wheel, as uneven braking may result. Note that the dust created by wear of the pads may contain asbestos, which is a health hazard. Never blow it out with compressed air, and don't inhale any of it. An approved filtering mask should be worn when working on the brakes. DO NOT use petroleum-based solvents to clean brake parts - use brake cleaner or methylated spirit only.

Removal

1 Apply the handbrake. Jack up the front of the vehicle and support it on axle stands. Remove the front wheels.

2 Turn the steering to full right-hand lock and check the wear of the linings on the right-hand brake pads through the inspection aperture at the front of the caliper body. Check that the thickness of the lining including the backing plate is as shown in the Specifications using a steel rule or vernier calipers.

3 Turn the steering to full left-hand lock and check the left-hand brake pads in the same way.

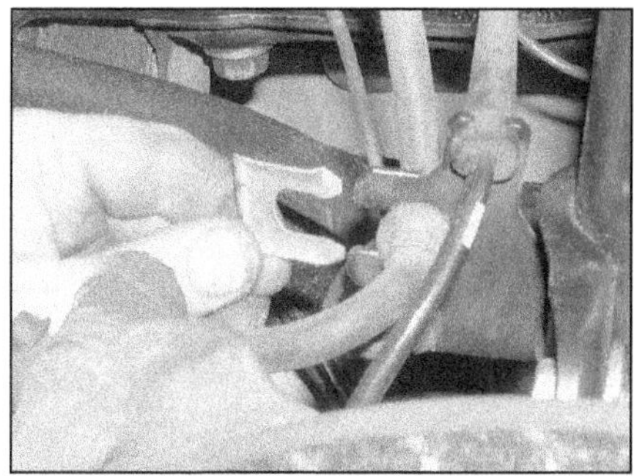

2.6 Slide out the metal retaining clip and release the brake hose from the suspension strut

4 If any brake pad is worn below the minimum thickness, renew all the front pads as a set together with new anti-rattle springs, as described in the following paragraphs.

5 Using a small flat bladed screwdriver, unclip the pad wear sensor from the caliper aperture, and position it clear of the work area **(see illustration)**.

6 Slide out the metal retaining clip and release the brake hose from its support bracket at the side of the suspension strut **(see illustration)**.

4-cylinder engined models up to 1998

7 Remove the large spring clip from the side of the brake caliper **(see illustration)**. The clip is under relatively high tension and may fly off with some force when released; to prevent injury, cover the spring with a large rag before prising it from the caliper with a stout screwdriver.

8 Remove the dust caps from the caliper guide pin bolt holes, then slacken and remove the two guide pin bolts **(see illustrations)**, and withdraw them from the caliper.

9 Withdraw the caliper from its mounting bracket, then tie the caliper to the suspension strut, using a suitable piece of wire **(see illustration)**.

Warning: Take great care to avoid kinking or placing any strain on the flexible brake hose.

10 Remove the outer pad from the caliper mounting bracket.

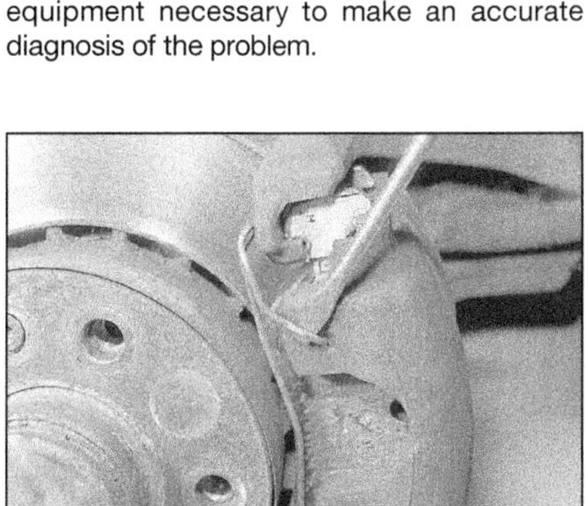

2.7 Remove the large spring clip from the side of the brake caliper

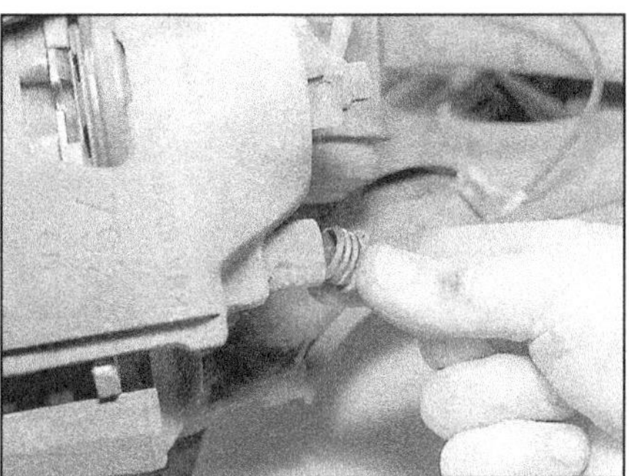

2.8a Remove the dust caps . . .

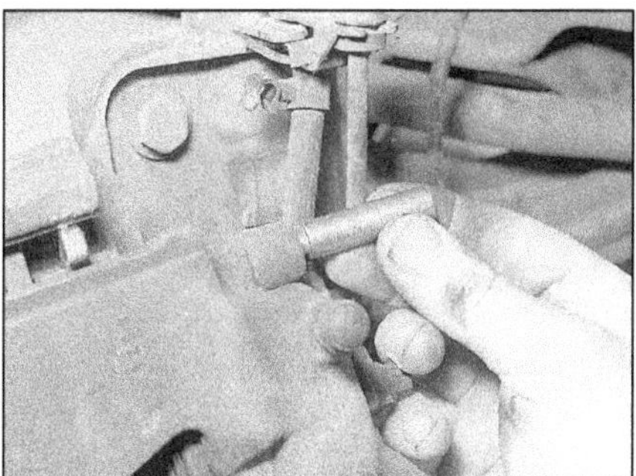

2.8b . . . then slacken and remove the two guide pin bolts

2.9 Remove the caliper from its mounting brackets

11 Carefully prise the inner pad from the caliper piston, which is retained by metal spring clip attached to the rear of the pad backing plate **(see illustration)**.

4-cylinder engined models from 1998 and all 6-cylinder engined models

12 Remove the dust caps from the caliper lower guide pin bolt hole, then slacken the lower guide pin bolt, and withdraw it from the caliper. Counterhold the guide pin with a second spanner **(see illustrations)**.

13 Pivot the caliper upwards **(see illustration)**, to expose the brake disc and pads. Suspend the caliper in the vertical position, using a suitable piece of wire.

Warning: Take great care to avoid kinking or placing any strain on the flexible brake hose.

14 Remove both brake pads from the caliper bracket **(see illustrations)**.

2.11 Carefully prise the inner pad from the caliper piston

Inspection

15 First measure the thickness of each brake pad (friction material and backing plate) **(see illustration)**. If either pad is worn at any point to the specified minimum thickness (see Specifications), *all four front brake pads must be renewed*, so that even braking balance is maintained. The pads should also be renewed if any are fouled with oil or grease; there is no satisfactory way of degreasing friction material, once it is contaminated. If any of the brake pads are worn unevenly or fouled with oil or grease, trace and rectify the cause before reassembly. If the pad wear sensor has been in contact with the brake disc (causing the brake pad warning light to illuminate), that must also be renewed.

16 Inspect the brake disc with reference to the information given in Section 6.

17 If the brake pads are still serviceable, carefully clean them using a clean, fine wire brush or similar, paying particular attention to the sides and back of the metal backing. Clean out the grooves in the friction material (where applicable), and pick out any large embedded particles of dirt or debris. Carefully clean the pad locations in the caliper body and mounting bracket. Check that the guide pins are free to slide easily in the caliper mounting bushes. Brush the dust and dirt from the caliper and piston, but **do not** inhale it, as it is injurious to health. Inspect the dust seal around the piston for damage, and the piston for evidence of fluid leaks, corrosion or damage. If attention to any of these components is necessary, refer to the information given in the following sub-section.

18 If new brake pads are being fitted, the caliper piston must be pushed back into the cylinder to make room for the greater depth of friction material. Either use a G-clamp or similar tool, or use suitable pieces of wood as levers **(see illustration)**. Provided that the master cylinder reservoir has not been overfilled with hydraulic fluid, there should be no spillage, but keep a careful watch on the fluid level while retracting the piston. If the fluid level rises above the maximum level mark, the surplus should be siphoned off using a syringe, or ejected via a plastic tube connected to the bleed screw, to avoid overflow, before retracting the piston any further.

19 Prior to fitting the pads, check that the guide bolts are a snug fit in the caliper bushes. Remove any remaining dust and dirt

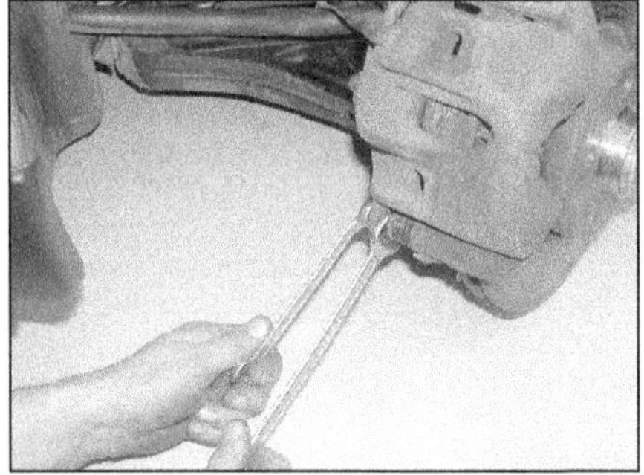

2.12a Slacken the lower guide pin bolt, counterholding the guide pin with a second spanner . . .

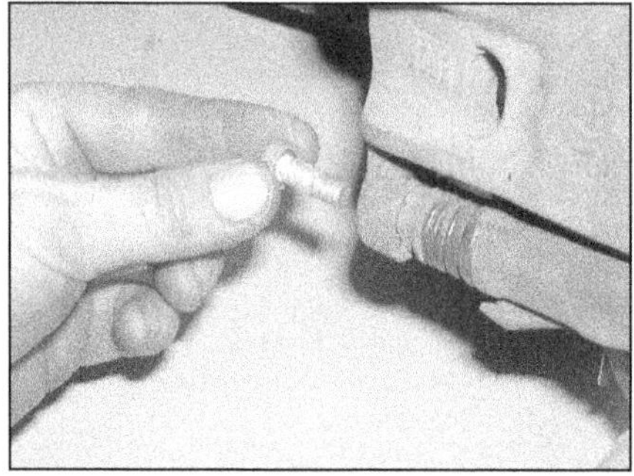

2.12b . . . and withdraw the guide pin bolt from the caliper

2.13 Pivot the caliper upwards to expose the brake pads

2.14a Remove the outer . . .

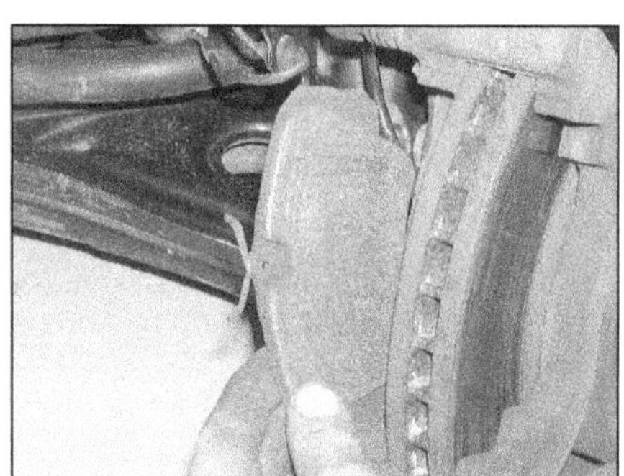

2.14b . . . and inner brake pads from the caliper bracket

2.15 Measuring the thickness of a brake pad

2.18 Using a retraction tool to push the piston back into the brake caliper

2.19a Apply a little high-melting-point copper brake grease to the brake pad backing plates . . .

2.19b . . . and the brake pad contact points on the caliper mounting bracket

from the caliper, piston and caliper mounting bracket using a stiff brush and proprietary brake component cleaning fluid - the use of other solvents or cleaning agents may cause damage to the caliper rubber seals. Apply a little high-melting-point copper brake grease to the areas on the pad backing plates and caliper mounting bracket which contact the caliper and piston **(see illustrations)**.

Caution: Take great care to avoid contaminating the pad friction material and brake disc surface.

Inspect the dust seal around the piston for damage, and the piston for evidence of fluid leaks, corrosion or damage. If attention to any of these components is necessary, refer to front brake caliper overhaul information in Section 4.

Refitting

4-cylinder engined models up to 1998

20 Fit the inner brake pad to the caliper by pressing the spring clip on the pad backing plate into the piston. Check that the butterfly spring at the edge of the pad bears on the inside of the caliper and is not jammed in the caliper inspection aperture.

21 Place the outer pad in the caliper mounting bracket, with the friction material facing the disc, and check that it slides freely along its guides towards the brake disc.

22 Fit the brake caliper and outer pad over the disc, ensuring that the outer edge of the caliper bears squarely on the rear of the outer brake pad's backing plate. Check that the butterfly spring at the edge of the pad bears on the inside of the caliper and is not jammed in the caliper inspection aperture.

23 Thoroughly clean the threads of the caliper guide pin bolts, fit them to the caliper and then tighten them to the specified torque. Refit the dust covers.

24 Refit the caliper spring, ensuring that its ends are firmly pressed into the holes in the side of the caliper body **(see illustration)**.

4-cylinder engined models from 1998 and all 6-cylinder engined models

25 Fit the inner and outer brake pads to the caliper mounting bracket ensuring that the friction material is facing the surface of the brake disc. Check that the pads slide easily along their guides towards the brake disc.

26 Pivot the caliper body down over the pads, ensuring that caliper piston bears against the rear of the inner pad's backing plate and that the outer edge of the caliper bears against the rear of the outer pad's backing plate. Check that the butterfly springs at the edge of the pad bear on the inside of the caliper and are not jammed in the caliper inspection aperture.

27 Thoroughly clean the threads of the caliper lower guide pin bolt, fit it to the caliper and then tighten it to the specified torque. Refit the dust cover.

All models

28 Clip the pad wear sensor into position on the inner brake pad. If a new sensor is being installed, trace the wiring of the original sensor back to the connector, then disconnect it and remove the old sensor from the vehicle. Connect the wiring connector of the new sensor, ensuring that the wiring is correctly routed and retained by all the necessary clips.

29 Check that the caliper body slides smoothly on its guide pins, then depress the brake pedal repeatedly until the pads are pressed into firm contact with the brake disc, and normal (non-assisted) pedal pressure is restored.

30 Repeat the above procedure on the remaining front brake caliper.

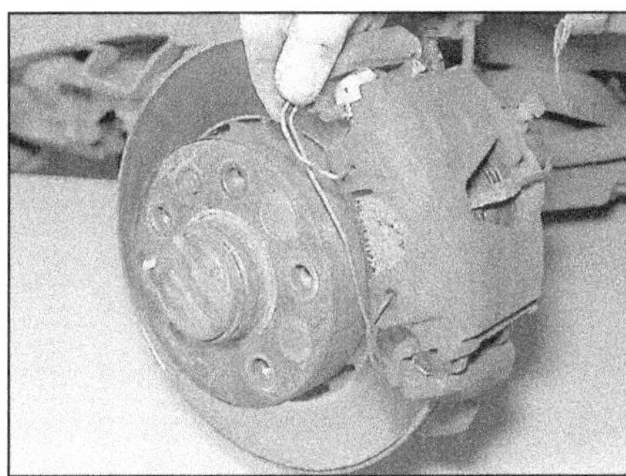
2.24 Refit the caliper spring, ensuring that its ends are firmly pressed into the holes in the side of the caliper body

31 Refit the roadwheels, then lower the car to the ground and tighten the roadwheel bolts to the specified torque setting.

32 Check the hydraulic fluid level and top up if necessary.

3 Rear brake pads - inspection and renewal

Note: *Before starting work, refer to the note at the beginning of Section 2 concerning the dangers of hydraulic fluid, and asbestos dust.*

Inspection

1 Chock the front wheels then jack up the rear of the vehicle and support it on axle stands. Release the handbrake. Remove the rear wheels.

2 Inspect the brake pad linings for wear. Using a steel rule or vernier calipers, check that the thickness of the lining including the backing plate is as shown in the Specifications.

3 If any brake pad is worn below the minimum thickness, renew all the rear pads as a set together with new anti-rattle springs.

Removal

4 Note how the anti-rattle spring is located, then drive out the upper pad securing pin using a thin punch from the outside **(see illustration)**.

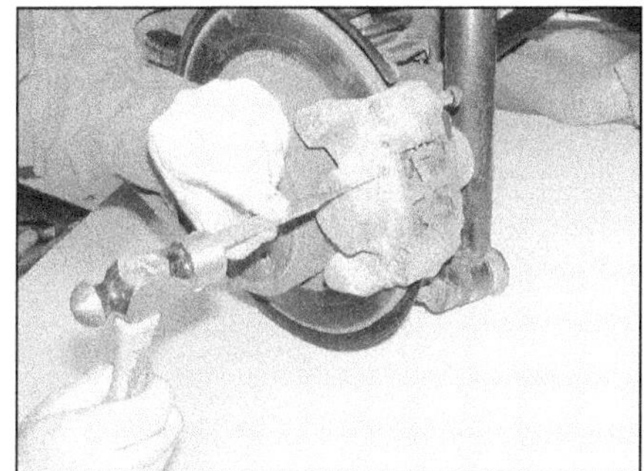
3.4 Driving out the upper rear brake pad pins using a thin punch

3.5a Remove the anti-rattle spring . . .

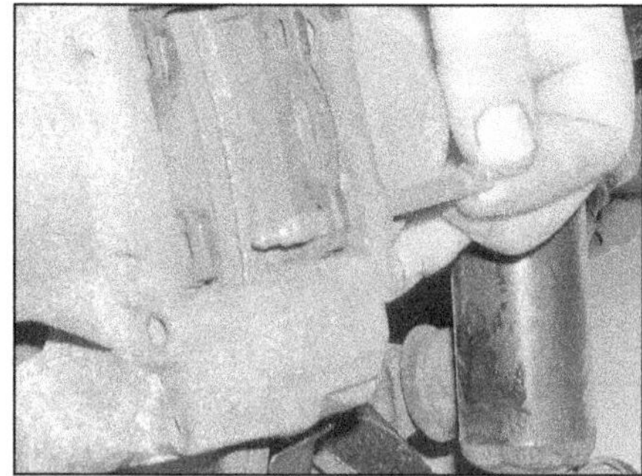

3.5b . . . then drive out the lower pad securing pin

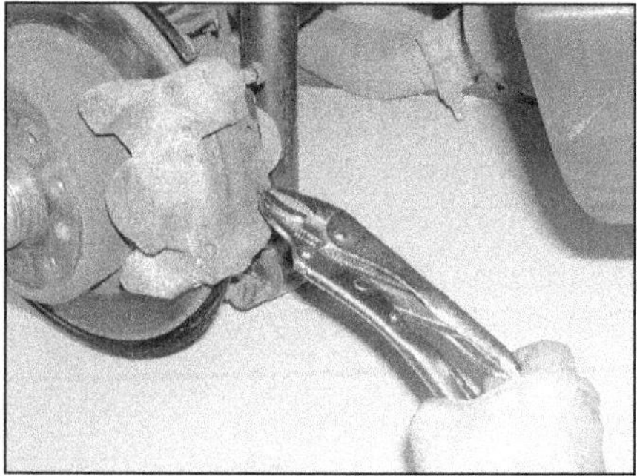

3.6a Use a pair of grips . . .

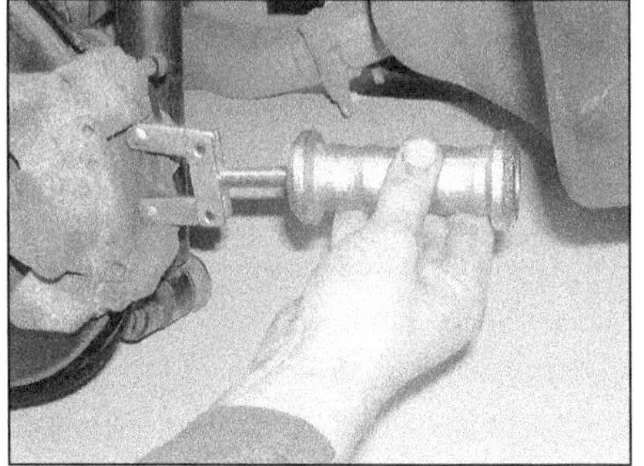

3.6b . . . or a pad extraction tool . . .

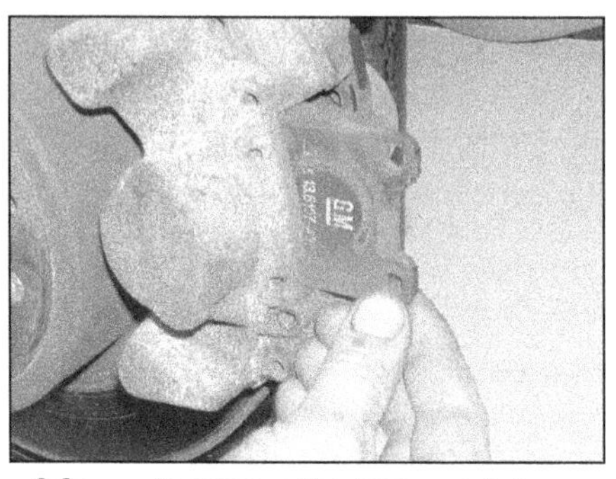

3.6c . . . to remove the brake pads from the caliper

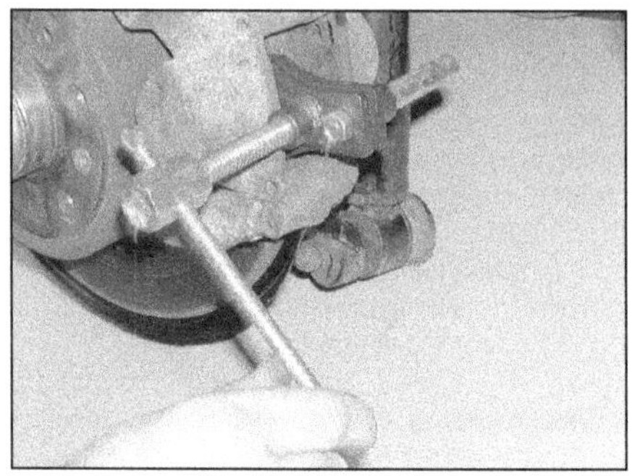

3.8 Using a retraction tool to press the pistons back into the caliper body

5 Remove the anti-rattle spring, then drive out the lower pad securing pin **(see illustrations)**.

6 Push the brake pads apart slightly to give a small amount of clearance then pull them from the caliper **(see illustrations)**. If they are tight, use pliers or a pad extraction tool to remove them.

Refitting

7 Brush the dust and dirt from the caliper and intermediate plates, but take care not inhale it. Clean any rust from the edge of the brake disc.

8 Press both pistons fully into their cylinders using a length of wood or piston retraction tool **(see illustration)**.

9 Check that the cut-away recesses on the pistons are positioned downwards at approximately 23° to the horizontal. A template made of card may be used to check the setting **(see illustration)**. If necessary, turn the pistons to their correct positions.

10 Apply a little high-melting point grease to the top and bottom edges of the backplates on the new brake pads **(see illustration)**. Take great care to avoid contaminating the brake pad friction material with grease.

11 Insert the new brake pads in the caliper and check that they are free to move.

12 Locate the anti-rattle spring on the pads, then insert the pins from the inside while depressing the spring. Tap the pins firmly into the caliper **(see illustration)**.

13 Renew the brake pads on the remaining rear wheel in the same manner.

14 Depress the footbrake pedal several times in order to reset the brake pads to their normal position.

15 Refit the rear wheels and lower the vehicle to the ground. Check the brake fluid level with reference to *Weekly checks.*

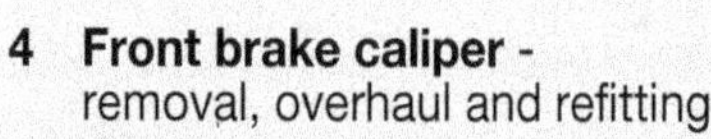

4 Front brake caliper - removal, overhaul and refitting

Removal

Note: *Before starting work, refer to the note at the beginning of Section 2 concerning the dangers of hydraulic fluid, and asbestos dust.*

1 Apply the handbrake then jack up the front of the vehicle and support it on axle stands. Remove the relevant road wheel.

2 On pre-1998 models with 4-cylinder engines, locate the large spring clip at the

3.9 Check that the cut-away recesses on the pistons are positioned downwards at approximately 23° to the horizontal

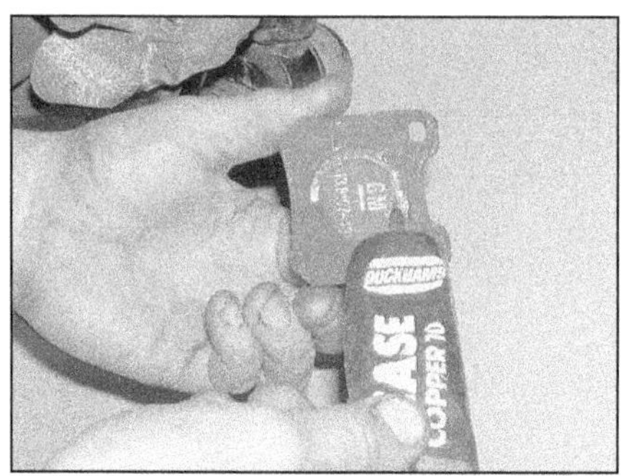

3.10 Apply a little high-melting point grease to the top and bottom edges of the backplates on the brake pads

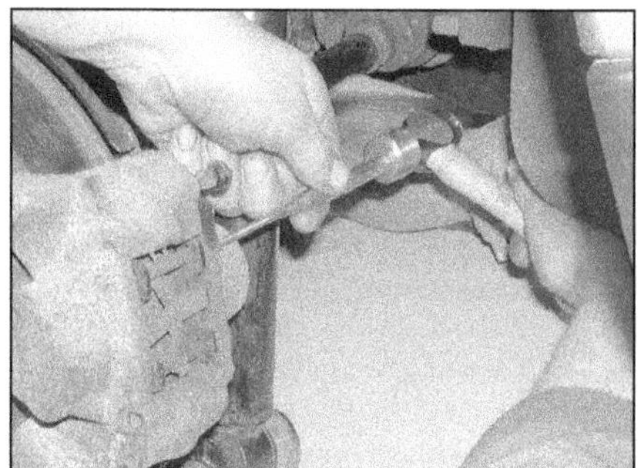

3.12 Drive the brake pad securing pins in from the inner surface of the caliper

4.3a Slacken the upper guide pin bolt, counterholding the guide pin with a second spanner . . .

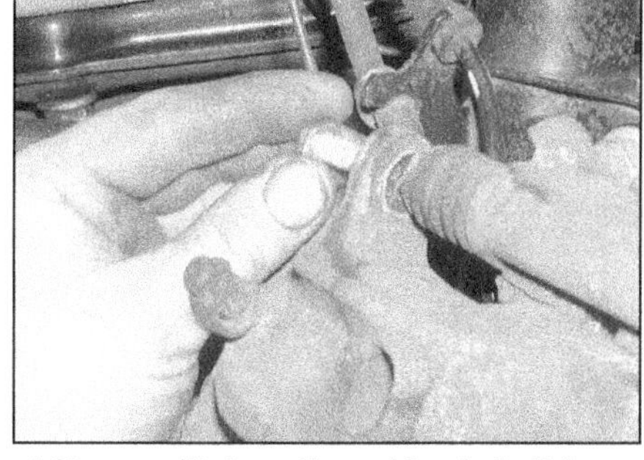
4.3b . . . withdraw the guide pin bolt from the caliper . . .

4.3c . . . and remove the caliper from its mounting bracket

side of the brake caliper. The clip is under relatively high tension and may fly off with some force when released; to prevent injury, cover the spring with a large rag before prising it from the caliper with a stout screwdriver.

3 Remove the dust caps from the caliper guide pin bolt holes, then slacken both guide pin bolts, and withdraw them from the caliper **(see illustrations)**.

4 Withdraw the caliper from its mounting bracket, then tie the caliper to the suspension strut, using a suitable piece of wire.

Warning: Take great care to avoid kinking or placing any strain on the flexible brake hose.

5 On post-1998 models with 4-cylinder engines and all models with 6-cylinder engines, remove both brake pads from the caliper mounting bracket.

6 On pre-1998 models with 4-cyliner engines, remove the outer pad from the caliper mounting bracket, then carefully prise the inner pad from the caliper piston, which is retained by metal spring attached to the rear of the pad backing plate.

7 Fit a brake hose clamp to the flexible hose leading to the brake caliper. Alternatively remove the cap from the hydraulic fluid reservoir and refit it with a piece of polythene sheeting covering the opening to help minimise the loss of brake fluid when the caliper hose is disconnected.

8 Clean the area around the union, then undo the brake hose union bolt, and disconnect the hose from the caliper - be prepared for some brake fluid leakage. Plug the end of the hose and the caliper orifice, to prevent dirt entering the hydraulic system. Discard the sealing washers; they must be renewed whenever disturbed.

9 Slacken and remove the two securing bolts, then detach the caliper mounting bracket from the hub carrier **(see illustrations)**.

Overhaul

10 With the caliper on the bench, wipe away all traces of dust and dirt using copious quantities of brake cleaning fluid.

Warning: Avoid inhaling the brake dust, as it may contain asbestos which is injurious to health.

11 On post-1998 models with 4-cylinder engines and all models with 6-cylinder engines, prise open the three tangs and remove the protective plate from the contact face of the piston.

12 Withdraw the piston from the caliper body, and remove the dust seal. The piston can be withdrawn by hand, or can if necessary be pushed out by applying compressed air to the brake pipe union bolt hole. Only low pressure should be required, such as that generated by a foot pump - place a block of hardwood between the end of the piston and the caliper body to prevent damage to the piston as it exits from the cylinder.

Warning: Use eye protection during this procedure, as droplets of brake fluid may be ejected as the piston leaves the cylinder under pressure. Keep your hands away from the end of the piston as it will leave the cylinder with considerable force.

13 Using a blunt, non-metallic instrument (such as an old plastic knife), extract the piston hydraulic seal, taking great care not to damage the caliper bore.

14 Press the rubber guide sleeves out of the caliper body using a suitable socket **(see illustration)**.

15 Thoroughly clean all components, using only clean brake fluid as a cleaning medium. Never use mineral-based solvents such as petrol or paraffin, as they will attack the hydraulic system's rubber components. Dry the components immediately, using compressed air or a clean, lint-free cloth. Use compressed air to blow clear the fluid passages.

Warning: Wear eye protection when using compressed air!

16 Check all components, and renew any that are worn or damaged. Pay particular attention to the cylinder bore and piston; these must be renewed if they are scratched, worn or corroded in any way **(see illustration)**.

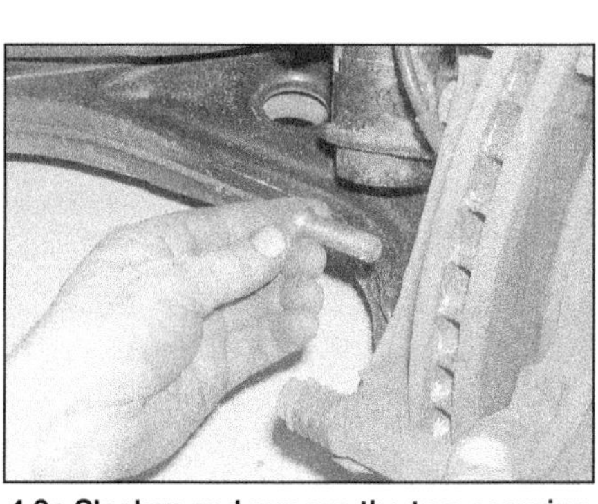
4.9a Slacken and remove the two securing bolts . . .

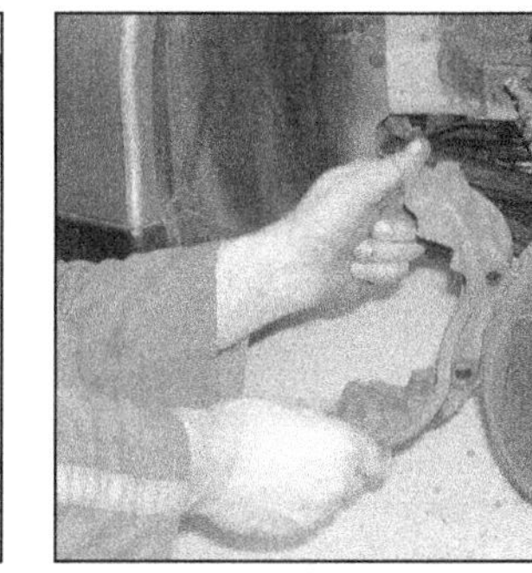
4.9b . . . then detach the caliper mounting bracket from the hub carrier

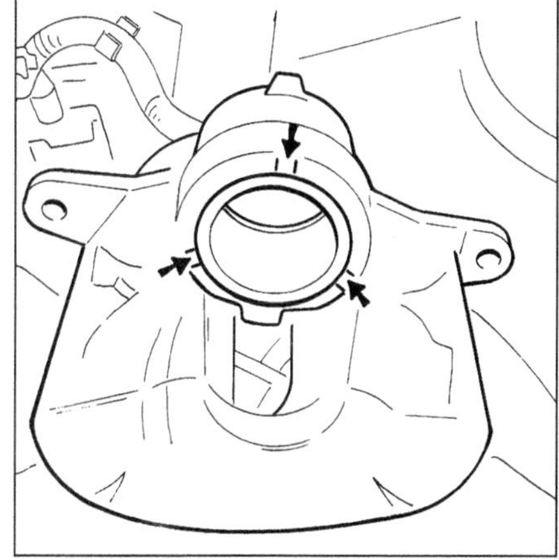
4.14 Prise open the three tangs and remove the protective plate from the contact face of the piston

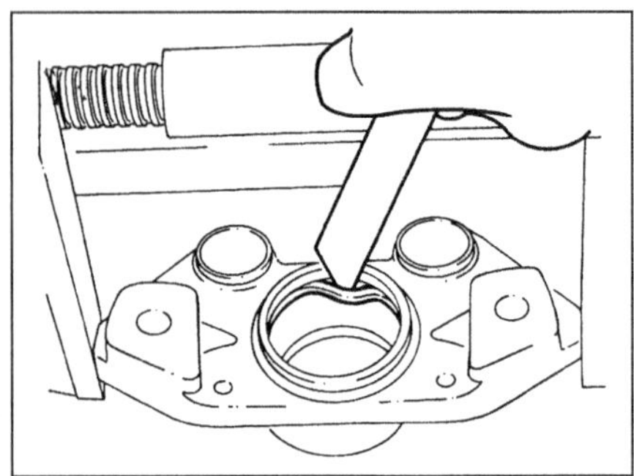

4.16 Extract the piston hydraulic seal using a blunt, non-metallic instrument

Warning: Do not use abrasives or tools to remove any material from the piston or cylinder in an attempt to effect a repair or remove corrosion - the piston and caliper body must be renewed as a complete assembly.

17 Where applicable, check the condition of the guide bolts/pins and their sleeves; both guide bolts/pins should be undamaged and (when cleaned) a reasonably-tight sliding fit in the sleeves. If there is any doubt about the condition of any component, renew it.

18 If the assembly is fit for further use, obtain new piston and dust seals, and a tube of brake cylinder paste from a Vauxhall dealer.

19 Smear a little brake cylinder paste onto the surfaces of the caliper bore, piston and piston seal.

20 Install the piston seal in the caliper bore, using only your fingers to manipulate it into its groove - do not use tools that may damage the new seal.

21 Fit the new dust seal to the caliper cylinder, ensuring that the inner edge seats correctly in the cylinder groove.

22 Offer up the piston to the cylinder and ease the lip at the outer edge of the dust seal over the end of the piston.

23 Carefully press the piston to the caliper bore, using a twisting motion, ensuring that it enters the bore squarely.

24 Press the piston fully into the bore, until the outer edge of the dust seal drops into the groove at the outer edge of the piston. On pre-1998 models with 4-cyliner engines, rotate the piston so that the raised section of the piston contact surface is positioned horizontally in relation to the caliper body **(see illustration).**

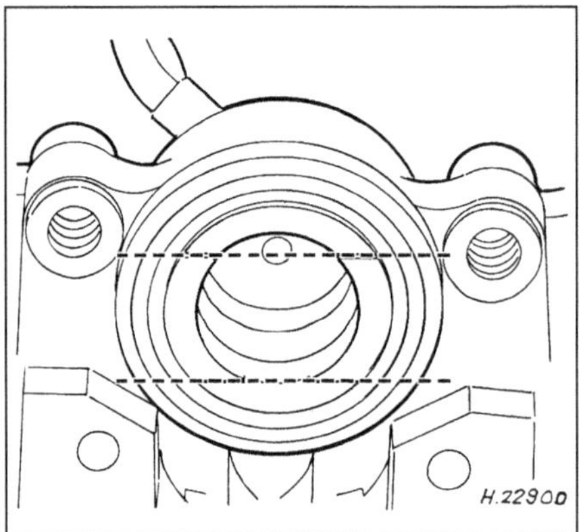

4.24 Rotate the piston so that the raised section of the piston contact surface is positioned horizontally in relation to the caliper body

25 On post-1998 models with 4-cylinder engines and all models with 6-cylinder engines, fit the protective plate in position on the piston contact surface and press the three tangs into their corresponding recesses.

26 Lubricate the rubber caliper guide sleeves with a little soapy water, then press them into position in the caliper body.

27 Finally, clean the caliper mounting bracket to remove all traces of dust and corrosion, using a wire brush if necessary. Pay particular attention to the machined surfaces which come into contact with the brake pads.

Refitting

28 Refit the caliper mounting bracket to the hub carrier, then fit new securing bolts and tighten them to the specified torque.

29 Apply a little high-melting-point brake grease to the areas on the pad backing plates and caliper mounting bracket which contact the caliper and piston.

Caution: Take great care to avoid contaminating the pad friction material and brake disc surface.

4-cylinder engined models up to 1998

30 Fit the inner brake pad to the caliper by pressing the spring clip on the pad backing plate into the piston. Check that the butterfly spring at the edge of the pad bears on the inside of the caliper and is not jammed in the caliper inspection aperture.

31 Place the outer pad in the caliper mounting bracket, with the friction material facing the disc, and check that it slides freely along its guides towards the brake disc.

32 Fit the brake caliper and outer pad over the disc, ensuring that the outer edge of the caliper bears squarely on the rear of the outer brake pad's backing plate. Check that the butterfly spring at the edge of the pad bears on the inside of the caliper and is not jammed in the caliper inspection aperture.

33 Thoroughly clean the threads of the caliper guide pin bolts, fit them to the caliper and then tighten them to the specified torque. Refit the dust covers.

34 Refit the caliper spring, ensuring that its ends are firmly pressed into the holes in the side of the caliper body.

4-cylinder engined models from 1998 and all 6-cylinder engined models

35 Fit the inner and outer brake pads to the caliper mounting bracket ensuring that the friction material is facing the surface of the brake disc. Check that the pads slide easily along their guides towards the brake disc.

36 Place the caliper body in position over the brake pads, ensuring that caliper piston bears against the rear of the inner pad's backing plate and that the outer edge of the caliper bears against the rear of the outer pad's backing plate. Check that the butterfly springs at the edge of the pad bear on the inside of the caliper and are not jammed in the caliper inspection aperture.

37 Thoroughly clean the threads of the caliper guide pin bolts, fit them to the caliper and then tighten them to the specified torque. Refit the dust covers.

All models

38 Position a new sealing washer on each side of the brake hose union, then pass the bolt through the union and thread it into the caliper. Ensure that the brake hose union is correctly positioned against the lug on the caliper, and tighten the union bolt to the specified torque setting. Remove the brake hose clamp (where applicable).

39 Clip the pad wear sensor into position on the inner brake pad. If a new sensor is being installed, trace the wiring of the original sensor back to the connector, then disconnect it and remove the old sensor from the vehicle. Connect the wiring plug of the new sensor, ensuring that the wiring is correctly routed and retained by all the necessary clips.

40 Bleed the hydraulic system as described in Section 12. Note that, providing the precautions described were taken to minimise brake fluid loss, it should only be necessary to bleed the relevant caliper.

41 Refit the roadwheel, then lower the car to the ground and tighten the roadwheel bolts to the specified torque.

42 Thoroughly check the operation of the braking system before bringing the vehicle back into service on the public highway.

5 Rear brake caliper - removal, overhaul and refitting

Removal

1 Chock the front wheels then jack up the rear of the vehicle and support it on axle stands. Remove the wheel.

2 Fit a brake hose clamp to the flexible hose leading to the brake caliper **(see illustration).**

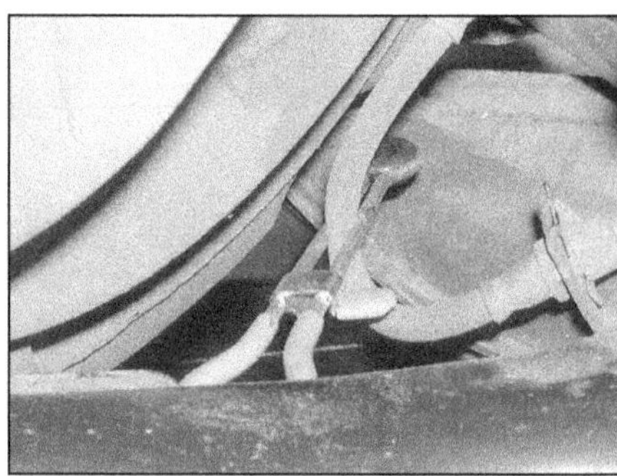

5.2 Fit a brake hose clamp to the flexible hose leading to the brake caliper

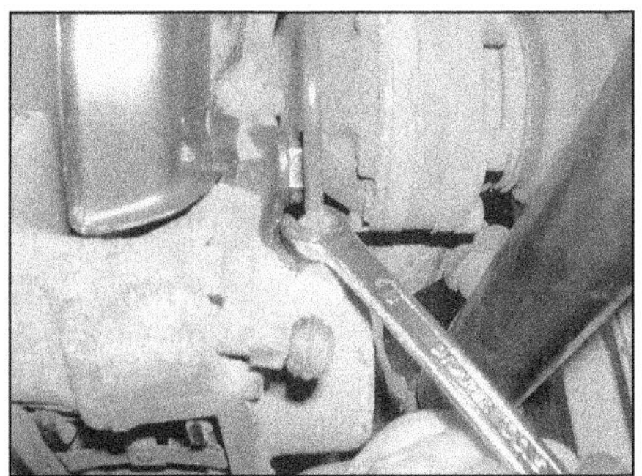
5.4a Unscrew the union nut . . .

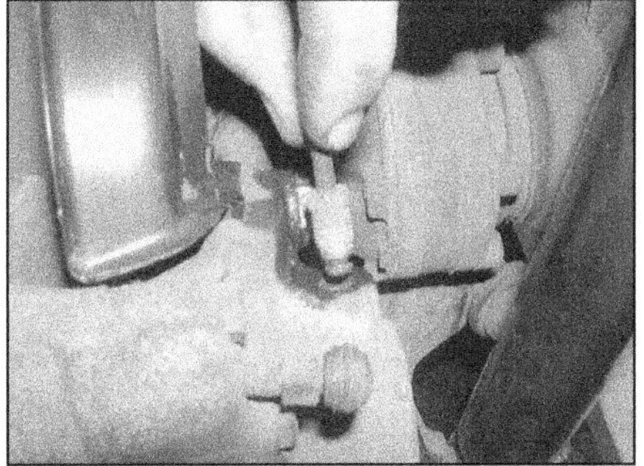
5.4b . . . and disconnect the rigid brake line from the caliper

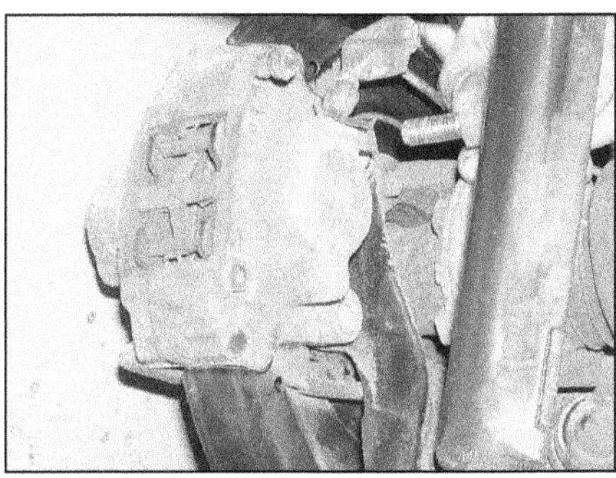
5.5a Unscrew the hexagon mounting bolts . . .

Alternatively remove the cap from the hydraulic fluid reservoir and refit it with a piece of polythene sheeting covering the opening to help prevent loss of brake fluid when the caliper hose is disconnected.

3 Remove the brake pads as described in Section 3.

4 Unscrew the union nut securing the rigid brake line to the caliper, and remove the brake line **(see illustrations)**.

5 Unscrew the hexagon mounting bolts and withdraw the caliper from the semi-trailing arm **(see illustration)**.

Overhaul

6 Clean the outer surfaces of the caliper.

7 Note that no attempt must be made to separate the two halves of the caliper.

8 Prise the rings and dust covers from each side of the caliper and pull the covers from the piston grooves **(see illustration)**.

9 Position a thin piece of wood between the pistons, then using air pressure from an air line or foot pump through the fluid inlet, carefully force the pistons from the cylinders. If one piston exits before the other, remove the piston and then seal off the open cylinder to allow the remaining piston to be ejected.

10 Prise the piston seals from the cylinders, taking care not to scratch the bore surfaces.

11 Clean the pistons and cylinders with new brake fluid and allow to dry. Examine the surfaces of the pistons and cylinder bores for wear, damage and corrosion. If evident, renew the caliper complete, however if the surfaces are good obtain a repair kit which includes piston seals and dust covers. Also obtain a tube of brake cylinder paste.

12 Apply a little brake cylinder paste to the pistons, cylinder bores and piston seals.

13 Locate the piston seals in the cylinder grooves, then insert the pistons carefully until they enter the seals. It may be necessary to rotate the pistons to prevent them jamming in the seals. Do not press the pistons fully into the cylinders at this stage as it will be difficult to fit the dust covers.

14 Ease the dust covers into the piston grooves then locate them on the caliper housing. Press the retaining rings over the dust covers.

15 Press the pistons into their cylinders, then rotate them so that the cut-away recesses are positioned downwards at an angle of approximately 23°; this ensures that only the raised section of the piston contact face bears on the rear of the pad.

Make up a card template to check the setting.

Refitting

16 To refit the caliper locate it on the semi-trailing arm, insert the mounting bolts and tighten them to the specified torque **(see illustration)**.

17 Locate the rigid brake line on the caliper and tighten the union nut to the specified torque.

18 Refit the brake pads with reference to Section 3.

19 Remove the brake hose clamp or polythene sheeting and bleed the hydraulic system as described in Section 12. Provided that there has been no loss of brake fluid, it should only be necessary to bleed the caliper which was removed, however if brake fluid has been lost, then bleed the complete system.

20 Refit the wheel and lower the vehicle to the ground. Check the operation of the braking system before using the vehicle.

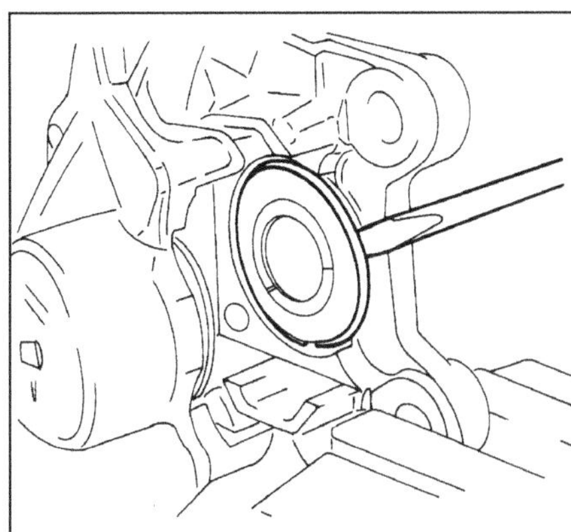
5.8 Removing the dust cover ring from the rear brake caliper

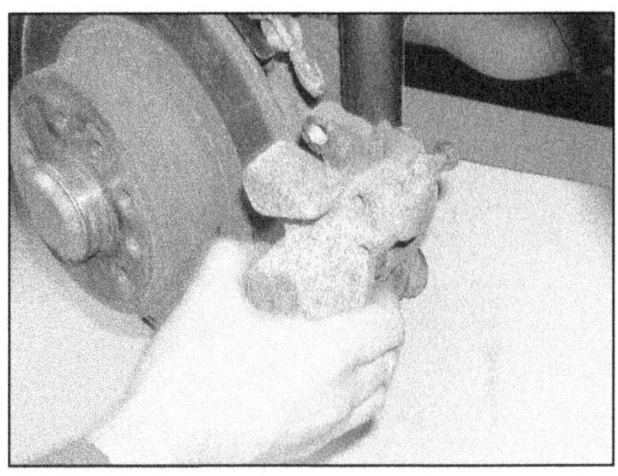
5.5b . . . and withdraw the caliper from the semi-trailing arm

6 Brake disc - inspection, removal and refitting

Inspection

1 Jack up the front or rear of the vehicle as applicable and support it on axle stands. Release the handbrake and chock the front wheels if checking a rear disc. Remove the appropriate wheel.

2 Check that the brake disc securing screw is tight, then refit and tighten a wheel bolt opposite the screw using a spacer washer approximately 10.0 mm (0.4 in) thick.

3 Rotate the brake disc and examine it for deep scoring or grooving. Light scoring is normal, but if excessive, the disc should be removed and either renewed or machined within limits by a suitable engineering works.

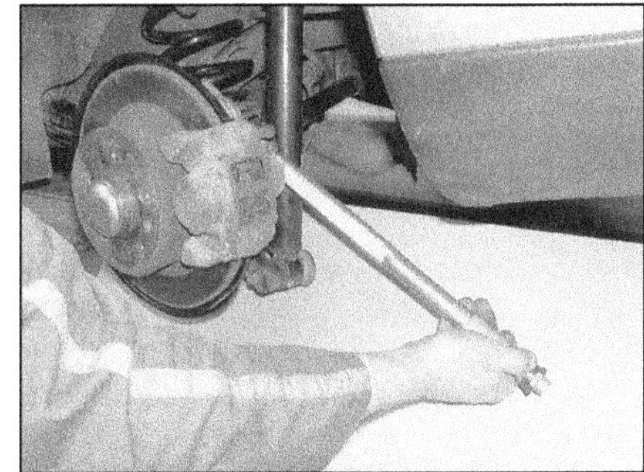
5.16 Tighten the caliper mounting bolts to the specified torque

6.4 Checking the front brake disc runout

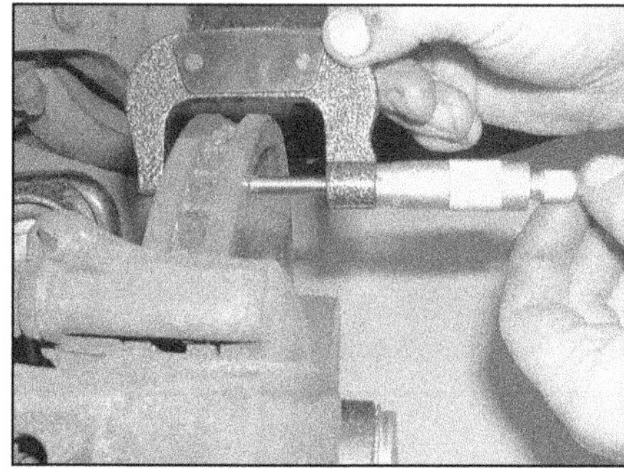

6.6 Checking the thickness of the front brake disc using a micrometer

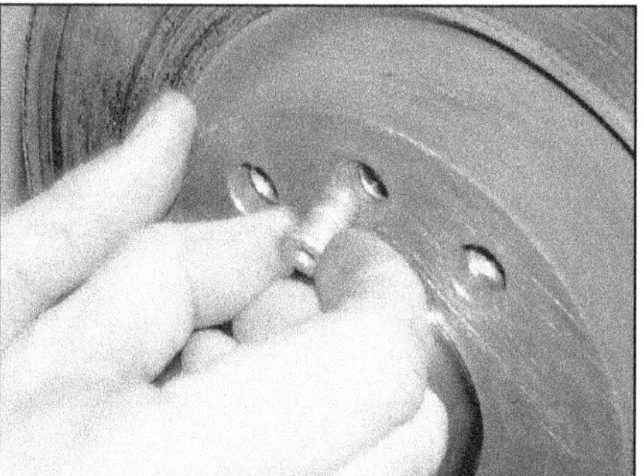

6.8a Remove the securing screw . . .

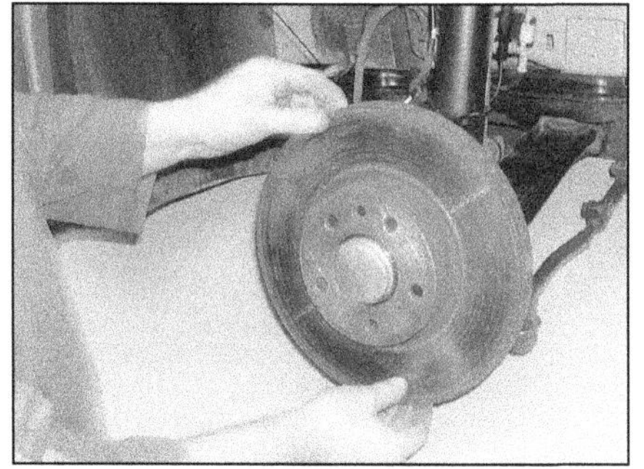

6.8b . . . then withdraw the front brake disc from the hub

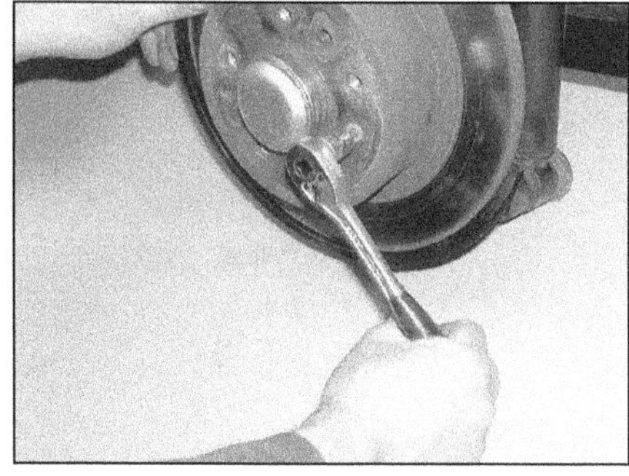

6.9a Remove the securing screw . . .

6.9b . . . and withdraw the rear brake disc from the hub

It is worth mentioning that some garages may be able to regrind the discs *in situ*, using a specially adapted electric grinder.

4 Using a dial gauge, or metal block and feeler gauges, check that the disc run-out does not exceed the amount given in Specifications, measured at a radius of approximately 10.0 mm from the outer edge of the disc **(see illustration)**. Check the run-out at several positions around the disc.

5 If the run-out is excessive, remove the disc and check that the disc-to-hub surfaces are perfectly clean. Refit the disc and check the run-out again.

6 Check the thickness of the disc using a micrometer at several points across the area swept by the brake pads **(see illustration)**. Compare your measurement with the figures listed in the Specifications. If either of the discs has worn beyond its minimum permissible thickness at any point, both discs must be renewed as pair.

Removal

7 To remove the brake disc, first remove the brake pads as described in Section 2 (front brake pads) or Section 3 (rear brake pads). On models with 6-cylinder engines and post-1998 models with 4-cylinder engines, unbolt the caliper body from its mounting bracket, as described in Section 4.

8 To remove a front disc, remove the securing screw then withdraw the disc from the hub, tilting it as necessary to clear the brake caliper **(see illustrations)**. On later models it may be necessary to unbolt the caliper mounting bracket from the hub carrier, as described in Section 4.

9 To remove a rear disc, unbolt the brake caliper from the semi-trailing arm as described in Section 5, and support it away from the disc, taking care not to damage the rigid brake line. Slacken the handbrake adjustment screw via the access hole in brake disc, as described in Chapter 1, Section 9 - this will retract the handbrake shoes from the inside of the disc. Remove the securing screw and withdraw the brake disc from the hub **(see illustrations)**.

Refitting

10 Refitting is a reversal of removal, but make sure that the mating faces of the disc and hub are perfectly clean, and before inserting the securing screw apply a little locking fluid to its threads. Refit the brake pads with reference to Section 2 or 3 (as applicable). After refitting a rear brake disc, adjust the handbrake as described in Chapter 1, Section 9.

7.6 Handbrake shoe anti-rattle spring (arrowed) - early model

7 Handbrake shoes - inspection, removal and refitting

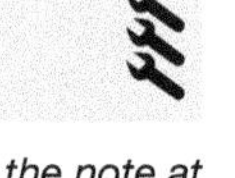

Note: *Before starting work, refer to the note at the beginning of Section 2 concerning the dangers of hydraulic fluid, and asbestos dust.*

Inspection

1 Remove the rear brake discs as described in Section 6.

2 Brush the dust and dirt from the shoes, backplate and from inside the disc drum.

3 Check the thickness of the linings on the shoes and if less than shown in the Specifications, renew the shoes *at both rear brakes* as a complete axle set.

4 Also check the surface inside the drums. These should not normally be worn unless the handbrake has been binding; check the diameter of the inner surface and compare it with the figure listed in *Specifications.*

Removal

5 Unhook the return spring from the lever on the rear of the brake backplate then unhook the handbrake cable from it.

6 Using a screwdriver through a hole in the hub flange, twist and remove the brake shoe anti-rattle springs and retaining pins **(see illustration)**.

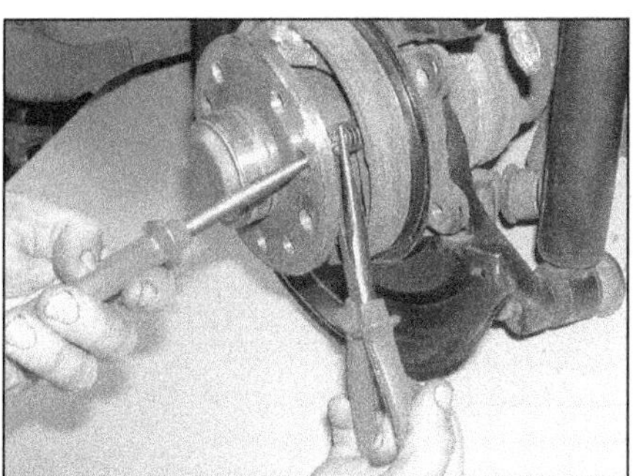

7.7 On later models, where the retaining pins are not cross-headed, depress the spring cups and turn them through 90° using two pairs of pliers

7.9a Handbrake shoe adjuster (A) and spring (B)

7.9b Handbrake shoe lower lever assembly

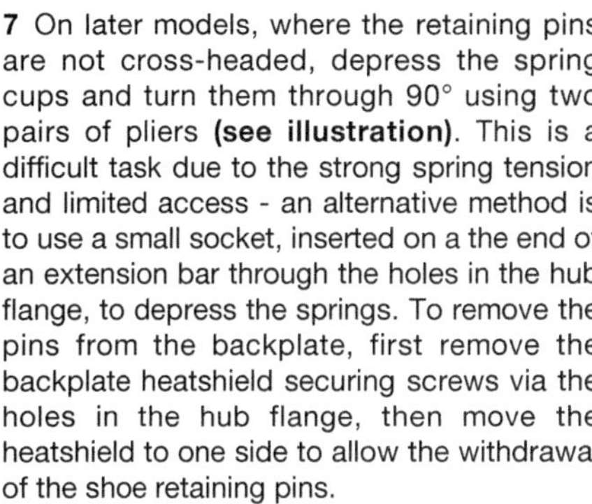

7 On later models, where the retaining pins are not cross-headed, depress the spring cups and turn them through 90° using two pairs of pliers **(see illustration)**. This is a difficult task due to the strong spring tension and limited access - an alternative method is to use a small socket, inserted on a the end of an extension bar through the holes in the hub flange, to depress the springs. To remove the pins from the backplate, first remove the backplate heatshield securing screws via the holes in the hub flange, then move the heatshield to one side to allow the withdrawal of the shoe retaining pins.

8 Mark the brake shoes for location. Also note the fitted positions of the return springs.

9 Prise the brake shoes from the adjuster and lever. Disconnect the upper and lower return springs from the brake shoes **(see illustrations)**, then remove the brake shoes from the backplate.

10 Remove the adjuster and handbrake cable shoe actuator lever.

11 Clean the backplate, springs, adjuster and lever.

12 Apply a little brake grease to the threads of the adjuster then screw it together to its minimum length.

Refitting

13 Prior to installation, clean the backplate thoroughly. The handbrake shoes can be reassembled using a reversal of the dismantling procedure, however improved access is possible by removing the rear hub assembly as described in Chapter 10 and temporarily holding the backplate in position on the trailing arm using two bolts. After reassembly the rear hub can then be refitted.

14 Reassemble the lever assembly and apply a little copper grease to the contact surfaces, then refit to the backplate and insert through the rubber grommet **(see illustrations)**.

15 Refit the handbrake cable to the shoe actuator lever, then refit the return spring **(see illustration)**.

16 Apply a thin smear of high-temperature copper-based brake grease or anti-seize compound to the shoe contact surfaces on the backplate.

17 With the pins already fitted to the backplate, refit the front (trailing) shoe and secure with the hold-down spring and cup **(see illustrations)**.

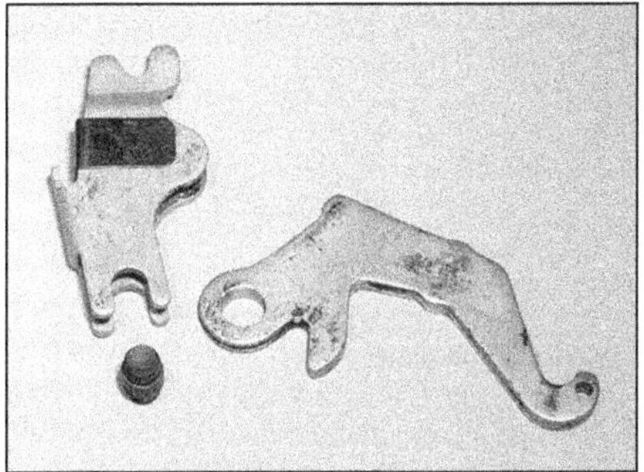

7.14a The lever assembly dismantled

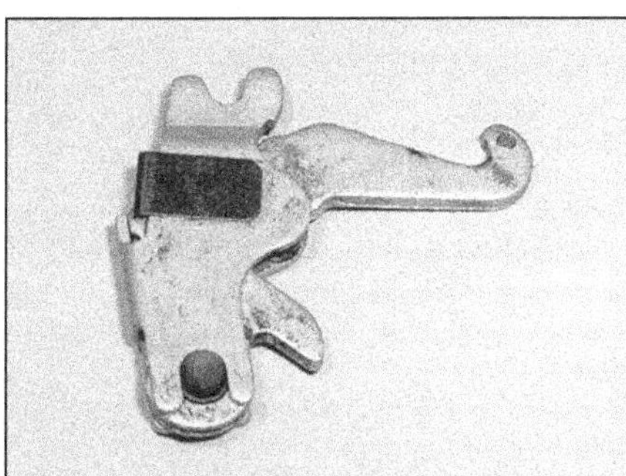

7.14b The lever assembled

7.14c Refitting the lever assembly to the backplate

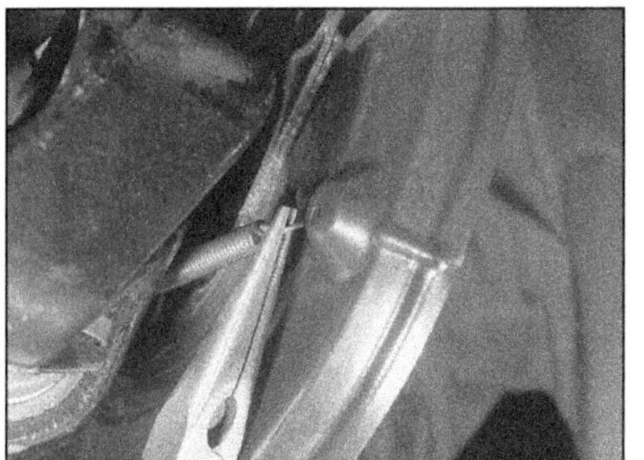

7.15 Refitting the return spring

7.17a Locate the front (trailing) shoe on the backplate . . .

7.17b . . . then refit the spring and cup . . .

7.17c . . . and use a pair of pliers to depress and turn the cup

7.18a Refit the rear (leading) shoe and the lower return spring

7.18b Engage the bottom of the shoe on the lever . . .

7.19 . . . then refit the hold-down spring and cup

7.20 Refit the adjuster between the upper ends of the shoes

7.21 Hook the upper return spring on the shoes

18 Locate the rear (leading) shoe on the lever assembly and refit the lower return spring **(see illustrations)**.

19 Refit the hold-down spring and cup to secure the leading shoe to the backplate **(see illustration)**.

20 Refit the adjuster between the upper ends of the shoes **(see illustration)**.

21 Hook the upper return spring on the shoes **(see illustration)**.

22 Where removed the rear hub can now be refitted **(see illustration)**.

23 Temporarily refit the disc over the shoes to determine the adjustment, then if necessary use a screwdriver to turn the serrated adjuster nut until it is just possible to refit the disc over the shoes without them binding **(see illustration)**.

24 Refit the brake disc with reference to Section 6.

25 Adjust the handbrake as described in Chapter 1.

26 Refit the roadwheels and lower the vehicle to the ground.

8 Handbrake cable - removal and refitting

Removal

1 Chock the front wheel, then jack up the rear of the vehicle and support it on axle stands. Remove the rear wheels and release the handbrake.

2 On models with 4-cylinder engines, unhook the rear and intermediate silencer rubber mountings from their floorpan mountings. Suspend the rear section of the exhaust system on axle stands, or using lengths of wire, so that access to the heat shields can be gained. See Chapter 4A for details.

3 On models with 6-cylinder engines, unbolt the rear section of the exhaust system at the joints downstream of both catalytic converters. Remove the tailpipe and intermediate silencers from underneath the vehicle as a complete assembly. See Chapter 4A for details.

4 Unscrew the securing bolts and lower the exhaust system heatshields away from the underside of the vehicle **(see illustration)**.

5 Unscrew and remove the propeller shaft centre bearing retaining bolts, with reference to Chapter 8, Section 11. Support the centre bearing on an axle stand.

6 Locate the compensator bar at the front end of the handbrake cable **(see illustration)**. Unscrew the adjustment nut from the threaded handbrake lever rod, counting the

7.22 The handbrake shoes assembled ready for refitting of the rear hub

7.23 Using a screwdriver through the hole in the drive flange to turn the serrated nut on the adjuster

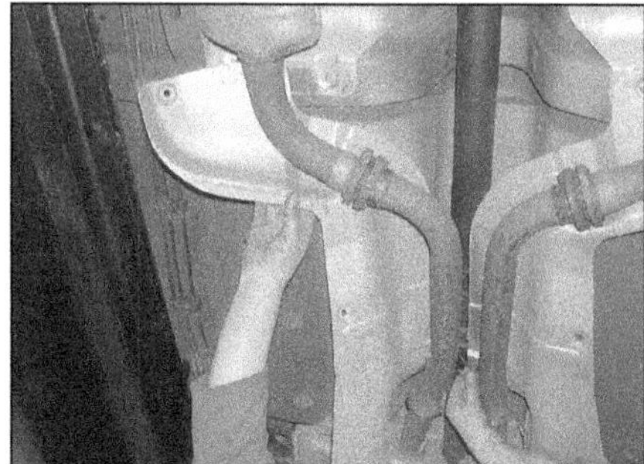

8.4 Unscrew the securing bolts and lower the exhaust system heatshields away from the underside of the vehicle

number of turns required to remove it; record the number for use later.

7 Slide the compensator bar from the threaded handbrake lever rod.

8 Working at each rear brake caliper in turn, unhook the return spring from the lever on the rear of the brake backplate, then unhook the handbrake cable.

9 Pull the rear of the outer cable from the guide on the semi-trailing arm on both sides.

10 Pull the front ends of the outer cables from the guides, and unhook the inner cables. Release the remainder of each cable from its respective retaining clips, then withdraw the cable assembly from under the vehicle.

Refitting

11 Refitting is a reversal of removal, noting the following points:.

a) Use a new compensator bar adjustment nut and screw it onto the threaded handbrake lever rod by the number of turns noted during removal.
b) Apply some molybdenum disulphide paste to the plastic guides at the front of the inner cables.
c) Refit the exhaust system with reference to Chapter 4A.
d) Refit the propeller shaft centre bearing with reference to Chapter 8.
e) Finally, adjust the handbrake as described in Chapter 1.

9 Handbrake lever - removal and refitting

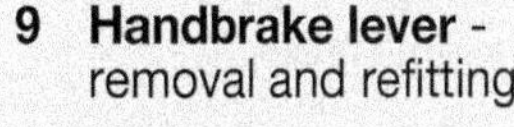

Removal

1 Chock the front wheels then jack up the rear of the vehicle and support it on axle stands.

2 Remove the screws and lower the metal heat shield away from the propeller shaft centre bearing. Unbolt and withdraw the propeller shaft centre bearing bolts as described in Chapter 8. Support the centre bearing on an axle stand.

3 At the front of the handbrake cable unscrew the adjustment nut from the threaded handbrake lever rod, and slide off the compensator bar; see Section 8 for details.

4 Prise the rubber gaiter from the underbody and remove it from the handbrake lever rod.

5 Remove the rear section of the centre console; see Chapter 11 Section 30 for details.

6 Unclip and remove the handbrake lever folding cover. Remove the securing nuts and detach the air ducting from its support bracket. Move the ducting to the left, away from the work area.

7 Unscrew the handbrake lever mountings bolts, then disconnect the wiring from the warning switch.

8 Remove the handbrake lever from the vehicle.

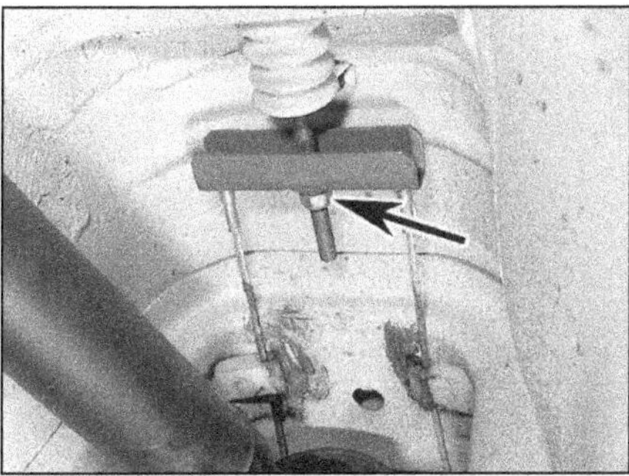

8.6 Handbrake cable compensator bar adjuster nut (arrowed)

Refitting

9 Refitting is a reversal of removal, but on completion adjust the handbrake cable as described in Chapter 1.

10 Master cylinder - removal and refitting

Removal

1 Depress the footbrake pedal several times to dissipate the vacuum in the servo unit.

2 Remove the fluid reservoir from the master cylinder, as described in Section 11.

3 Locate a container beneath the master cylinder to catch spilled brake fluid.

4 Identify the brake lines for position, then unscrew the union nuts and pull the lines from the master cylinder. Plug the open ports and brake pipes to minimise fluid leakage and prevent the ingress of foreign material.

5 Unscrew the mounting nuts and withdraw the master cylinder from the studs on the vacuum servo unit **(see illustration)**. Take care not to drop any brake fluid on the body paintwork. If accidentally spilt, wash off immediately with copious amounts of cold water.

6 Extract the O-ring seal from the master cylinder sealing surface, and the rubber grommets from the fluid reservoir ports, then discard them as new items must be fitted.

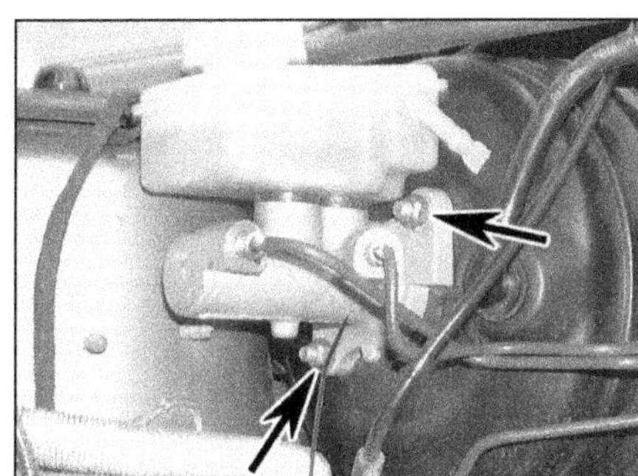

10.5 Master cylinder mounting nuts (arrowed)

Refitting

7 Fit a new O-ring seal to the master cylinder mating surface, and new rubber grommets to the fluid reservoir ports.

8 Refit the master cylinder to the brake servo, then fit and tighten the mounting nuts to the specified torque.

9 Reconnect the brake pipes to the master cylinder ports and tighten the unions to the specified torque. A crow's-foot adapter may be required to apply torque to the union nuts.

10 Refit the brake fluid reservoir as described in Section 11.

11 On completion, bleed the entire brake hydraulic system as described in Section 12.

12 Check the master cylinder unions for signs of leakage and test the operation of the braking system thoroughly before using the vehicle on the road.

11 Brake fluid reservoir and level sensor - removal and refitting

Reservoir

Removal

1 Ensure that ignition key is turn to the Off position, then unplug the wiring from the fluid reservoir level sensor at the connector.

2 Unscrew the cap from the fluid reservoir, then remove as much of the brake fluid as is possible; use an old poultry baster or similar tool - do not siphon the fluid out as it is poisonous. Discard the fluid as it will not be fit for re-use.

3 Slacken and separate the union, then disconnect the clutch master cylinder supply pipe from the side of the fluid reservoir.

4 Carefully prise the fluid reservoir from the brake master cylinder ports. Extract the rubber grommets from the brake master cylinder and discard them. Clean the ports at the base of the fluid reservoir.

Refitting

5 Fit new rubber grommets to the brake master cylinder ports.

6 Press the fluid reservoir into the brake master cylinder ensuring that the rubber grommets do not become dislodged.

7 Reconnect the clutch master cylinder supply pipe, then tighten the union securely.

8 Fill the reservoir up the MAX marking with new brake fluid of the specified grade.

9 On completion, bleed the brake hydraulic system as described in Section 12. Check the operation of the braking system before using the vehicle on the road.

Level sensor

Removal

10 The sensor is integral with the brake fluid reservoir filler cap. Ensure that ignition key is turn to the Off position, then unplug the wiring from the sensor at the connector.

11 Unscrew the cap from the reservoir and allow the excess fluid to drain off.

Refitting

12 Refitting is a reversal of removal. After reconnecting the wiring, the operation of the sensor can be tested by suspending the reservoir cap above the reservoir, so that the float slides down to the end of its travel. The facia tell-tale warning lamp should illuminate.

12 Hydraulic system - bleeding

Warning: Hydraulic fluid is poisonous; thoroughly wash off spills from bare skin without delay. Seek immediate medical advice if any fluid is swallowed or gets into the eyes. Certain types of hydraulic fluid are flammable and may ignite when brought into contact with hot components; when servicing any hydraulic system, it is safest to assume that the fluid is inflammable and to take precautions against the risk of fire as though it were petrol that was being handled. Hydraulic fluid is an effective paint stripper and will also attack many plastics. If spillage occurs onto painted bodywork or fittings, it should be washed off immediately, using copious quantities of fresh water. It is also hygroscopic i.e. it can absorb moisture from the air, which then renders it useless. Old fluid may have suffered contamination and should never be re-used. When topping-up or renewing the fluid, always use the recommended grade, and ensure that it comes from a new, sealed container.

General information

1 The correct operation of any hydraulic braking system relies on the fact that the fluid used in it is incompressible, otherwise the effort exerted at the brake pedal and master cylinder will not be fully transmitted to the brake calipers or wheel cylinders. The presence of contaminants (such as air) in the hydraulic system will result in a spongy feel to the brakes and unpredictable performance, in the form of brake fade or at worst brake failure. In addition, brake fluid deteriorates with age through oxidation and water absorption. This lowers its boiling point and may cause vaporisation under hard braking, again affecting brake performance. For this reason, old or contaminated brake fluid must be renewed regularly (see Chapter 1 for the service interval) - this is achieved by bleeding the entire system. Similarly, if you have disturbed any part of the hydraulic system during repair or servicing, the system must be bled to remove the air that will have been admitted.

2 When refilling the system, use only clean, new hydraulic fluid of the recommended type and grade; *never* re-use fluid that has already been bled from the system. Ensure that sufficient fluid is available before starting work.

3 If there is any possibility of there being incorrect fluid in the system already, the brake components and circuits must be flushed completely with new fluid of the correct type and grade and new seals should be fitted throughout the system.

4 If hydraulic fluid has been lost from the system, or air has entered because of a leak, ensure that the fault is corrected before proceeding further.

5 Park the vehicle on level ground, switch off the engine and select first or reverse gear (manual transmission) or Park (automatic transmission), then chock the wheels and release the handbrake.

6 Check that all pipes and hoses are secure, unions tight and bleed screws closed. Remove the dust caps and clean off all dirt from around the bleed screws.

7 Unscrew the master cylinder reservoir cap, and top the master cylinder reservoir up to the MAX level line; refit the cap loosely, and remember to maintain the fluid level at least above the MIN level line throughout the procedure, otherwise there is a risk of further air entering the system, as the level drops.

8 There are a number of one-man, do-it-yourself brake bleeding kits currently available from motor accessory shops. It is recommended that one of these kits is used whenever possible, as they greatly simplify the bleeding operation, and also reduce the risk of expelled air and fluid being drawn back into the system. If such a kit is not available, the basic (two-man) method must be used, which is described in detail below.

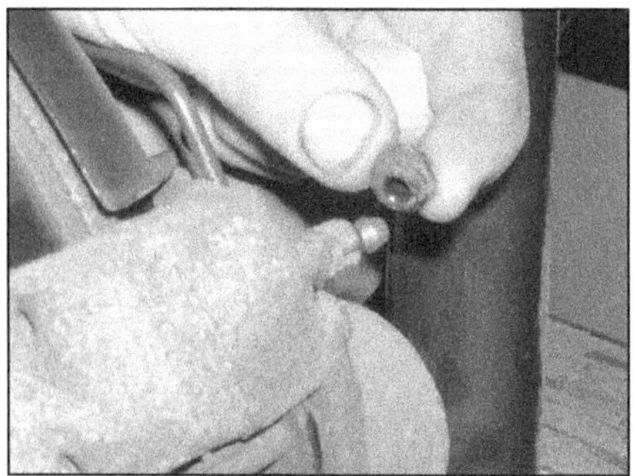

12.14a Remove the dust cap from the caliper bleed screw

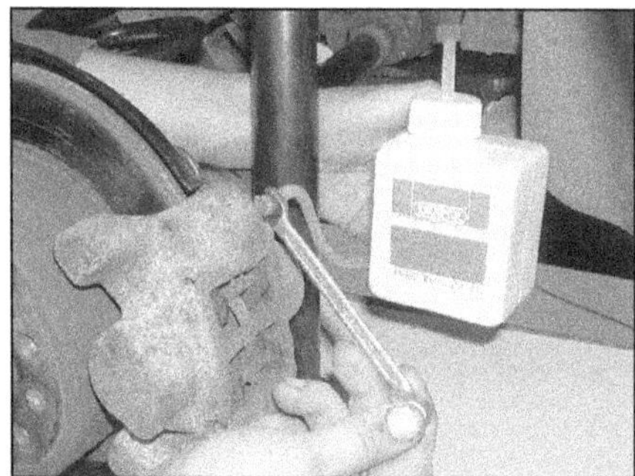

12.14b Fit the spanner over the bleed screw and push the tube onto the bleed screw nipple

9 If a kit is to be used, prepare the vehicle as described previously, and follow the kit manufacturer's instructions, as the procedure may vary slightly according to the type being used. Generally, they are as outlined below in the relevant sub-section.

10 Whichever method is used, the same sequence must be followed to ensure the removal of all air from the system.

Bleeding sequence

Note: *It is possible to partially bleed the system, i.e. just one brake line and caliper at a time. Providing fluid loss is kept to a minimum and air is not drawn into the system, it will not be necessary to bleed the other brake lines as well.*

Pre-1998 models with 3-channel ABS

11 Bleed the system in the following sequence:.

1 *Front left hand brake*
2 *Front right hand brake*
3 *Rear left hand brake*
4 *Rear right hand brake*

Post-1998 models with 4-channel ABS

12 Bleed the system in the following sequence:.

1 *Left-hand rear brake.*
2 *Right-hand front brake.*
3 *Right-hand rear brake.*
4 *Left-hand front brake.*

Bleeding - basic (two-man) method

13 Obtain a clean glass jar, a suitable length of plastic or rubber tubing which is a tight fit over the bleed screw, and a ring spanner to fit the screw. Alternatively, a proprietary brake bleeding kit can be obtained. **Note:** *The help of an assistant will also be required.*

14 Remove the dust cap from the first caliper's bleed screw. Fit the spanner over the bleed screw and push the tube onto the bleed screw nipple **(see illustrations)**. Place the other end of the tube in the jar and pour in sufficient fluid to cover the end of the tube.

15 Throughout the procedure, keep an eye on the reservoir fluid level and ensure that it is maintained above the MIN level line as the brakes are bled; top it up before starting if necessary.

16 Have the assistant fully depress the brake pedal several times to build up pressure - then on the final downstroke, keep it depressed.

17 While pedal pressure is maintained, slacken the bleed screw (approximately one turn) and allow the brake fluid to flow into the jar. Pedal pressure should be maintained throughout; follow the pedal down to the end of its travel if necessary, but do not release it. When the flow stops, tighten the bleed screw again, then have your assistant release the pedal slowly. Re-check the reservoir fluid level and top it up if necessary.

18 If air is present in the brake lines, it will appear as bubbles in the expelled fluid. Repeat the steps given in the two previous paragraphs until the fluid emerging from the bleed screw is free from air bubbles. If the master cylinder has been drained and refilled and air is being bled from the first brake line in the sequence, allow several seconds between cycles for the master cylinder passages to refill.

19 When no more air bubbles appear, tighten the bleed screw securely, remove the tube and spanner then refit the dust cap.

Caution: Do not overtighten the bleed screw.

20 Repeat the procedure on the remaining brake lines to be bled, until all air is removed from the system and the brake pedal feels firm again.

Bleeding - using a one-way valve kit

21 As their name implies, these kits consist of a length of tubing with a one-way valve fitted, to prevent expelled air and fluid being drawn back into the system; some kits include a translucent container, which can be positioned so that the air bubbles can be more easily seen flowing from the end of the tube.

22 The kit is connected to the bleed screw, which is then opened. The user returns to the driver's seat, depresses the brake pedal with a smooth, steady stroke and slowly releases it; this process is repeated until the expelled fluid is free of air bubbles .

23 Note that the use of these kits can simplify the bleed operation so much, that it is easy to forget the reservoir fluid level. Ensure that it is maintained at least above the MIN level line at all times, or air may be drawn into the system.

Bleeding - using a pressure-bleeding kit

24 These kits are usually powered by pressurised air, such as that provided by the vehicle's spare tyre. However, note that it will probably be necessary to reduce the tyre pressure to a lower level than normal before connecting to the bleeding kit; refer to the manufacturer's instructions supplied with the kit.

25 The method involves connecting a pressurised, fluid-filled container to the master cylinder reservoir. Bleeding can then be carried out simply by opening each bleed screw in turn, and allowing the fluid to flow out under moderate pressure until no more air bubbles can be seen in the expelled fluid.

26 This method has the advantage that the large reservoir of fluid provides an additional safeguard against air being drawn into the system during bleeding.

27 Pressure-bleeding is particularly effective when bleeding difficult systems, or when bleeding the complete system at the time of routine fluid renewal.

All methods

28 When bleeding is complete, and firm pedal feel is restored, wash off any spilt fluid, tighten the bleed screws securely, and refit their dust caps (where applicable).

29 Check the hydraulic fluid level in the master cylinder reservoir; top it up if necessary (see *Weekly checks*).

30 Dispose of any hydraulic fluid that has been bled from the system; it must not be re-used.

31 Check the feel of the brake pedal. If it feels at all spongy, or has greater travel than expected, it is probable that air is still present in the system; further bleeding will therefore be required. If the bleeding procedure has been repeated several times and brake feel has still not been restored, the problem may be caused by air trapped in ABS hydraulic modulator. This can be dislodged by actuating the ABS return pump during the bleeding process, but note that this operation can only be carried out by a Vauxhall dealer with the necessary ABS diagnostic equipment.

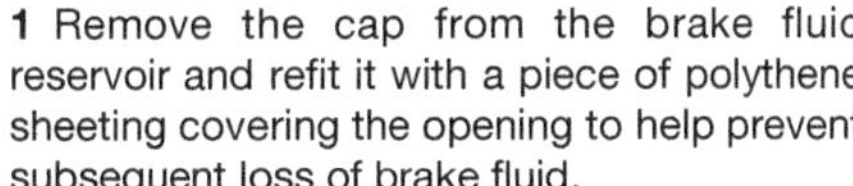

13 Hydraulic brake lines and hoses - removal and refitting

1 Remove the cap from the brake fluid reservoir and refit it with a piece of polythene sheeting covering the opening to help prevent subsequent loss of brake fluid.

2 Jack up the front or rear of the vehicle, as applicable, and support it on axle stands.

Front flexible hose

3 Remove the front wheel.

4 Turn the steering on full lock. Unscrew the bolt securing the hose to the caliper and recover the copper washers.

5 Pull the locking plates from the mountings and disconnect the hose from the retaining clips.

6 Unscrew the rigid brake line union, and remove the hose.

7 Refitting is a reversal of removal, but make sure that the hose is not twisted or kinked. Bleed the hydraulic system as described in Section 12 .

Rear flexible hose

8 Pull the locking plates from the mountings.

9 Unscrew the rigid brake line unions, and remove the hose.

10 Refitting is a reversal of removal, but make sure that the hose is not twisted or kinked. Bleed the hydraulic system as described in Section12 .

Brake lines

11 Some commonly-used brake lines can be obtained from GM parts stores already formed complete with unions, however other brake lines must be prepared from brake pipes of the required diameter. Kits for making the brake lines can be obtained from motor accessory shops.

12 To remove a brake line, unscrew the unions at each end and release it from the clips.

13 Refitting is a reversal of removal. Bleed the hydraulic system as described in Section 12.

14 Vacuum servo hose and non-return valve - renewal

1 When new, the vacuum hose is shrunk onto the non-return valve using a heat process, therefore when the valve is first renewed it is necessary to fit a conventional vacuum hose, using hose clips to secure the valve. Thereafter the hose and valve may be renewed separately.

2 Unscrew the hose union nut at the inlet manifold.

3 Pull or prise the elbow connector out of the servo. Note that some models may be equipped with a quick-release fitting. To disconnect the fitting, depress the catch at the side of the fitting and separate the two halves of the fitting.

4 Release the hose from the plastic straps. Where applicable, unplug the narrow-bore vacuum hose from the T-piece.

5 Cut the hose off the non-return valve, the elbow and the inlet manifold union.

6 Cut the new braided vacuum hoses to length (it is sold in 5.0 metre lengths) and secure to the non-return valve, elbow and union using proprietary clips. Make sure that the arrows on the valve point towards the inlet manifold end.

7 Press the elbow into the servo rubber grommet (or reconnect the quick-release union, as applicable) and tighten the union nut on the inlet manifold. Fit new plastic straps to secure the hose in position. Reconnect the narrow-bore vacuum hoses to the T-pieces.

8 Check the operation of the vacuum servo (see Section 15), then entire braking system, before using the vehicle on the road.

15 Vacuum servo unit - testing, removal and refitting

Testing

1 To establish whether or not the servo is operating, proceed as follows.

2 With the engine stopped, apply the brake pedal several times in order to dissipate the vacuum from the servo unit.

3 Hold the brake pedal depressed, then start the engine. The pedal should move a small distance towards the floor with the additional assistance of the servo unit. If not, check the vacuum hose and non-return valve. If these prove to be satisfactory, the servo unit itself is faulty and should be renewed.

Removal

4 Depress the footbrake pedal several times to dissipate the vacuum in the servo unit.
5 Disconnect the wiring for the brake fluid level warning lamp from the reservoir filler cap.
6 With reference to Chapter 12, remove both windscreen wiper arms from their respective shafts.
7 Carefully peel the rubber sealing strips from the rear edge of the engine compartment bulkhead, then remove the securing screws and withdraw the cowl panel from the lower edge of the windscreen.
8 Unscrew the master cylinder mounting nuts and pull the unit from the studs on the vacuum servo unit sufficiently to allow room for removal of the servo unit. Leave the brake lines connected to the master cylinder, but do not exert excessive force on the brake lines as this may cause them to fracture.
9 Pull or prise out the vacuum hose elbow connector, or unplug the quick-release connector, as applicable. Move the bulkhead wiring harness to one side.
10 Working inside the vehicle, in the driver's footwell, remove the screws and lower the cover panel away from the underside of the facia. Unscrew the fixings and remove the footwell air ducting.
11 Unhook the return spring from the brake pedal. Remove the brake light switch from its mounting bracket (see Chapter 12, Section 4).
12 Extract the spring clip and pull out the clevis pin, to disconnect the servo pushrod from the brake pedal.
13 Unscrew the mounting nuts, then tilt the servo unit and remove it from the bulkhead into the engine compartment. Recover the gasket. Note that the nuts double up as the brake pedal bracket mounting nuts (see Section 16).
14 Loosen the locknut and unscrew the clevis fork from the pushrod. Unscrew the locknut.
15 Unscrew the nuts and remove the support bracket and gaskets from the servo unit.

Refitting

16 Commence refitting by placing the support bracket together with a new gasket in position on the servo and tightening the securing nuts to the specified torque.
17 Screw the locknut and clevis fork onto the pushrod. With the pushrod in its rest position adjust the fork so that the distance between the servo support bracket face and the clevis pin centre line is 106.0 + 0.5 mm. Tighten the locknut to secure the fork in this position.
18 Refit the servo unit to the bulkhead using a new gasket. Fit the mounting nuts and tighten them to the specified torque.
19 Connect the pushrod to the brake pedal with the clevis pin and spring clip.
20 Reconnect the brake pedal return springs, then refit the brake light switch with reference to Chapter 12, Section 4.
21 Refit the footwell ventilation ducting and facia lower cover panelling.
22 Press the vacuum hose elbow connector in the servo rubber grommet, or reconnect the quick release fitting, as applicable.
23 If necessary, renew the O-ring seal on the master cylinder flange then locate the unit on the servo studs and tighten the mounting nuts (see Section 10 for details).
24 Press the brake pipes firmly into their retaining clips on the engine compartment bulkhead.
25 Reconnect the level sensor wiring to the brake fluid reservoir filler cap.
26 Refit the cowl panel to the lower edge of the windscreen, and secure it in position with the screws.
27 Press the rubber sealing strips into position at the rear of the engine compartment, then refit the windscreen wiper arms with reference to Chapter 12.
28 Test the operation of the vacuum servo as described at the beginning of this Section. Test the operation of the entire braking system before using the vehicle on the road.

16 Brake pedal - removal and refitting

Removal

1 Working inside the vehicle, in the driver's footwell, remove the screws and lower the cover panel away from the underside of the facia. Unscrew the fixings and remove the footwell air ducting.
2 Disconnect the wiring from the brake stop-lamp switch, then unclip the switch from the pedal bracket, noting its fitted position.
3 Unhook both the brake pedal return springs.
4 Extract the spring clip and pull out the clevis pin securing the servo pushrod to the brake pedal.
5 Slacken and withdraw the uppermost pedal bracket securing bolt.
6 Unscrew the nuts holding the pedal bracket to the bulkhead; note that these nuts double up as the servo mounting nuts (see Section 15). Pull the servo away from the bulkhead slightly, to withdraw the servo studs from pedal bracket.
7 Pivot the bracket downwards to release it from the upper servo studs then remove the bracket and pedal assembly from the vehicle.
8 Remove the spring clip, the unscrew the nut from the end of the pedal shaft, and remove the washer.
9 Remove the pedal location clips and carefully drive the shaft from the bracket, until the brake pedal can be removed. Recover the thrust washers (where fitted) and the centre spring **(see illustration)**.

Refitting

10 Refitting is a reversal of removal, but lubricate the pedal shaft with grease. Tighten all fixings to the specified torque where applicable. Refer to the information given in Chapter 12, Section 4 when refitting the brake light switch.

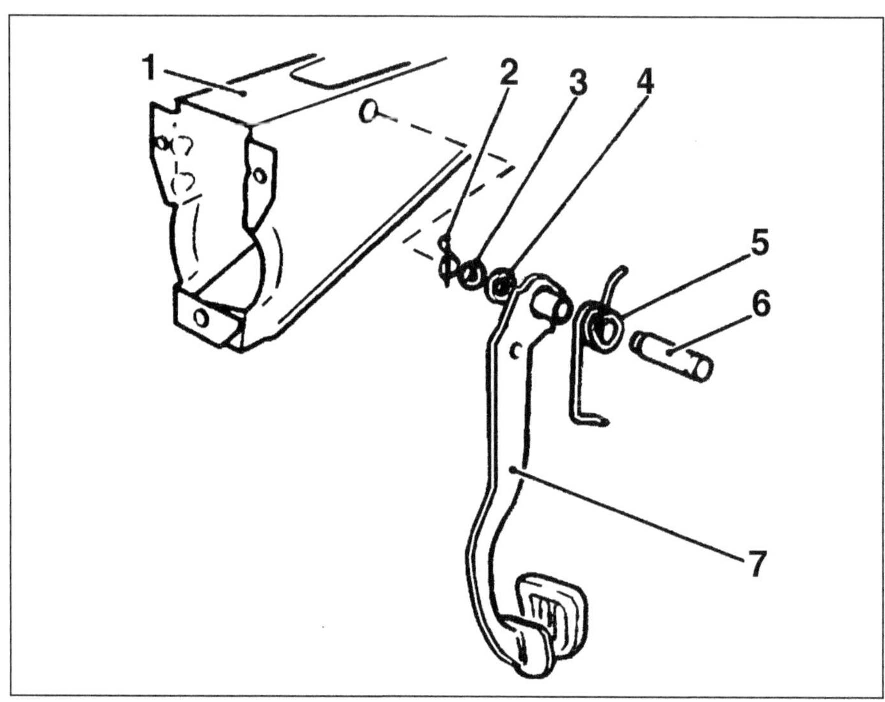

16.9 Brake pedal and associated components

1 Pedal bracket *2 Spring clip* *3 Nut* *4 Washer* *5 Return spring* *6 Pedal shaft* *7 Pedal*

17 Anti-lock Braking System/ Traction Control system (ABS/TC) - information

Information

1 ABS is fitted as standard to all models. Traction control is fitted as standard to models with 6-cylinder engines.

2 The ABS system comprises a hydraulic modulator and electronic control unit together with four roadwheel sensors. The hydraulic modulator contains the electronic control unit (ECU), the hydraulic solenoid valves and the electrically-driven return pump. The purpose of the system is to prevent the road wheel(s) locking during braking. This is achieved by automatic adjustment of the hydraulic pressure applied to the brake on the wheel(s) that is/are about to skid. During normal operation, the system functions in the same way as a non-ABS braking system. In the event of ABS failure, the braking system reverts to conventional, non-ABS operation.

3 The solenoid valves are controlled by the ECU, which receives wheel rotation speed information from each of the four wheel speed sensors. By comparing these signals, the ECU can determine the speed at which the vehicle is travelling. It can then use this speed to determine when a wheel is decelerating at an abnormal rate, compared to the speed of the vehicle, and therefore predicts when a wheel is about to lock.

4 If the ECU senses that a wheel is about to lock, it operates the relevant solenoid valve(s) in the hydraulic unit, which then isolates from the master cylinder the relevant brake(s) on the wheel(s) which is/are about to lock, effectively sealing-in the hydraulic pressure. On models built before 1998 model year, the two front brakes are modulated separately, but the two rear brakes are modulated together via a shared hydraulic circuit. On later models, the hydraulic pressure to each caliper is modulated individually.

5 If the speed of rotation of the wheel continues to decrease at an abnormal rate, the ECU operates the electrically-driven pump which pumps the hydraulic fluid back into the master cylinder, releasing the brake. Once the speed of rotation of the wheel returns to an acceptable rate, the pump stops, and the solenoid valves switch again, allowing the hydraulic master cylinder pressure to return to the caliper/wheel cylinder (as applicable), which then re-applies the brake. This cycle can be carried out many times per second.

6 The action of the solenoid valves and return pump creates pulses in the hydraulic circuit. When the ABS system is functioning, these pulses can be felt through the brake pedal and the return pump can also be heard to operate.

7 On models with 6-cylinder models, the hydraulic unit incorporates an additional set of solenoid valves which operate the Traction Control (TC) system. The system operates at speeds up to approximately 30 mph (60 km/h) using the signals supplied by the wheel sensors. If the ECU senses that a driving wheel is about to lose traction, it prevents this by momentarily applying the relevant rear brake.

8 The operation of the ABS and the traction control system is entirely dependent on electrical signals. To prevent the system responding to any inaccurate signals, a built-in safety circuit monitors all signals received by the ECU. If an inaccurate signal or low battery voltage is detected, the system is automatically shut down, and the warning light on the instrument panel is illuminated, to inform the driver that the system is not operational. Normal braking is still available, however.

Precautions

a) Do not disconnect the ABS/TC control unit multiway harness plug with the ignition switched on.

b) Do not use a battery booster to start the engine.

c) Unplug the multi-way wiring connector from the ABS/TC control unit before carrying out any electrical welding on the car.

d) Do not expose the unit to temperatures exceeding 80°C (e.g. during paint-oven work).

18 Anti-lock Braking System/ Traction Control system - component removal and refitting

Hydraulic modulator - early models with (3-channel) ABS 2-SH or 2-SH/TC

Removal

1 Disconnect the battery negative cable and position it away from the terminal.

2 Remove the cap from the brake fluid reservoir and refit it with a piece of polythene sheeting covering the opening to help prevent subsequent loss of brake fluid.

3 Unplug the wiring from the alarm system bonnet switch, then unscrew the bolt from the power steering reservoir clamp and tie the reservoir to one side.

4 Remove the ABS control unit as described later in this Section. Undo the securing screws and remove the ABS control unit mounting bracket from the modulator.

4-cylinder engined models

5 Identify all five brake lines on the modulator for location, then unscrew the union nuts and pull the brake lines just clear of the modulator. Be prepared for brake fluid leakage - place a suitable container underneath the unions before disconnection. If possible, plug the ends of the brake lines, or at least cover them to prevent excessive fluid brake fluid loss the ingress of dust and dirt. Also cover the hydraulic modulator ports.

6 Slacken and remove the securing screws, then remove the heat shield from the modulator.

6-cylinder engined models

7 Identify the three uppermost brake lines on the modulator for location, then unscrew the union nuts and pull the brake lines just clear of the modulator. Be prepared for brake fluid leakage - place a suitable container underneath the unions before disconnection. If possible, plug the ends of the brake lines, or at least cover them to prevent excessive fluid brake fluid loss the ingress of dust and dirt. Also cover the hydraulic modulator ports.

8 Apply the handbrake, raise the front of the vehicle and rest it securely on axle stands.

9 Remove the engine compartment lower cover panel to allow access to the underside of the hydraulic modulator.

10 Slacken and remove the securing screws, then remove the heat shield from the modulator.

11 Identify the two lowermost brake lines on the modulator for location, then unscrew the union nuts and pull the brake lines just clear of the modulator. Again, be prepared for brake fluid leakage.

All models

12 Unscrew the nut and disconnect the earth cable from the rear of the hydraulic modulator.

13 Unscrew the securing nuts from the hydraulic modulator guide pins, then move the brake lines carefully to one side and slide the modulator from the guide pins.

14 Remove the modulator from the engine compartment taking care to prevent brake fluid from running out of the modulator ports.

15 Check that the guide pin rubber mountings on the modulator are in good condition. No further dismantling of the hydraulic modulator is possible.

Refitting

16 Refitting is a reversal of removal but tighten all nuts and bolts to the correct torque (where specified), and finally bleed the hydraulic system as described in Section 12. Check that the ABS warning light extinguishes at the first application of the brake pedal after starting the engine. On completion take the vehicle to a GM dealer and have the system's operation verified with ABS test equipment.

Hydraulic modulator and ABS/TC control unit - later models with (4-channel) ABS 5.3 or 5.3/TC

Removal

17 Disconnect the battery negative cable and position it away from the terminal.

18 Apply the handbrake, raise the front of the vehicle and support it securely on axle stands.

19 Undo the screws and lower the cover panel away from the underside of the engine compartment.

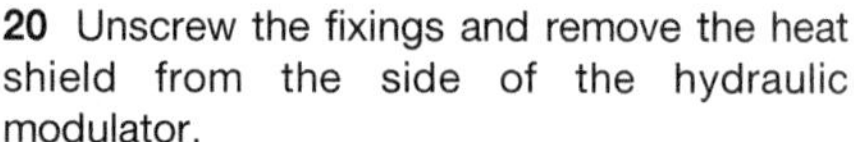

18.46a Unscrew the mounting bolt . . .

18.46b . . . and withdraw the ABS sensor

18.51 ABS rear wheel speed sensors (arrowed)

20 Unscrew the fixings and remove the heat shield from the side of the hydraulic modulator.
21 With reference to Chapter 10 Section 26 disconnect the high pressure hydraulic fluid delivery pipe from the power steering pump. Position a container underneath the disconnected union to catch escaping hydraulic fluid.
22 Unclip the cover from the engine compartment auxiliary fusebox and detach the fuseholder from the base of the fusebox.
23 Unclip the cover from the engine compartment relay box. Withdraw the engine management system electronic control unit, then unplug the multiway connector from it; refer to Chapter 4A for details.
24 Release the engine management system relay from the relay box, together with its mounting bracket.
25 Disconnect the three main wiring harness plugs located at the rear of the main engine compartment fusebox.
26 Remove as much hydraulic fluid as possible from the power steering fluid reservoir, using an old (but clean) poultry baster or similar.
27 Slacken the hose clips and disconnect the two fluid hoses from the base of the power steering fluid reservoir. Place a suitable container underneath the reservoir to catch the hydraulic fluid that will run out.
28 Remove the power steering fluid reservoir from its mounting bracket then unbolt the bracket from the bodywork and remove it.
29 Undo the securing screw and unplug the multiway wiring harness connector from the ABS/TC control unit.
30 Remove as much hydraulic fluid as possible from the brake fluid reservoir, using an old (but clean) poultry baster or similar.
31 With reference to Section 10, undo the unions and disconnect the brake pipes from the side of the master cylinder. Place a suitable container underneath the reservoir to catch the brake fluid that will run out. Plug the ends of the brake lines.
32 Carefully label all six brake lines at the hydraulic modulator (to ensure that they are reconnected in correct order later) then unscrew the union nuts and pull the brake lines just clear of the modulator. Be prepared for brake fluid leakage - place a suitable container underneath the unions before disconnection. If possible, plug the ends of the brake lines, or at least cover them to prevent excessive fluid brake fluid loss, and the ingress of dust and dirt. Also cover the hydraulic modulator ports.
33 Detach the hydraulic modulator from its mounting bracket and remove it from the engine compartment, taking care to prevent brake fluid from running out of the modulator ports.

Refitting

34 Refitting is a reversal of removal, noting the following points:.

a) Tighten all nuts and bolts to the correct torque (where specified)
b) Top up the power steering system with the correct grade of fluid as described in Weekly checks.
c) Bleed the hydraulic system as described in Section 12.
d) Check that the ABS warning light extinguishes at the first application of the brake pedal after starting the engine.
e) On completion take the vehicle to a GM dealer and have the system's operation verified with ABS test equipment.

ABS/TC control unit - early models with (3-channel) ABS 2-SH or 2-SH/TC

Removal

35 Disconnect the battery negative cable and position it away from the terminal.
36 Unscrew the securing bolt and remove the cover panel from the ABS/TC control unit.
37 Unplug the three multiway wiring harness connectors from the ABS/TC control unit.
38 Slacken and remove the securing bolts and then lift the ABS/TC control unit away from the engine compartment.
Refitting**.**
39 Refitting is a reversal of removal. On completion take the vehicle to a GM dealer and have the system's operation verified with ABS test equipment.

Traction Control switch

Removal

40 Ensure that ignition key is turned to the Off position, then carefully prise the switch from the facia panel, using a small screwdriver. Use card or cloth to prevent damage to the facia.
41 Unplug the wiring connector from the rear of the switch.

Refitting

42 Refitting is a reversal of removal.

Front wheel speed sensors

Removal

43 Disconnect the battery negative lead.
44 Apply the handbrake, then jack up the front of the vehicle and support it on axle stands (see Jacking and Vehicle Support). Remove the relevant front roadwheel.
45 Disconnect the sensor wiring and release it from the clips on the front suspension strut and wheel arch. Do not confuse it with the brake pad wear sensor wiring connector.
46 Unscrew the mounting bolt using a Torx key and withdraw the sensor from the mounting bracket **(see illustrations)**.

Refitting

47 Refitting is a reversal of removal but smear a little anti-seize grease on the sides of the sensor casing before inserting it. On completion take the vehicle to a GM dealer and have the system's operation verified with ABS test equipment.

ABS rear wheel speed sensors

Removal

48 Disconnect the battery negative lead.
49 Chock the front wheels, then jack up the rear of the vehicle and support it on axle stands (see Jacking and Vehicle Support). Remove the relevant rear roadwheel.
50 Disconnect the sensor wiring and release it from the clips on the underbody.
51 Unscrew the mounting bolt using a Torx key and withdraw the sensor from the final drive unit **(see illustration)**.

Refitting

52 Refitting is a reversal of removal but smear a little anti-seize grease on the sides of the sensor casing before inserting it into the final drive unit. On completion take the vehicle to a GM dealer and have the system's operation verified with ABS test equipment.

Chapter 10
Suspension and steering

Contents

Degrees of difficulty

Easy, suitable for novice with little experience 	**Fairly easy,** suitable for beginner with some experience 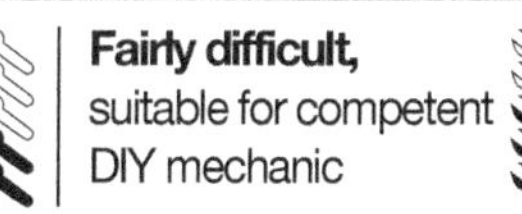	**Fairly difficult,** suitable for competent DIY mechanic	**Difficult,** suitable for experienced DIY mechanic	**Very difficult,** suitable for expert DIY or professional

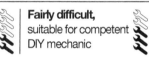

Specifications

Front suspension

Type	Independent MacPherson struts, coil springs and anti-roll bar, double-acting telescopic shock absorbers. Adjustable camber.

Rear suspension

Type	Independent, semi-trailing arms and coil springs, anti-roll bar, double-acting telescopic shock absorbers. Adjustable track control arms.

Steering

Type	Recirculating ball, worm shaft and nut with sector shaft and drop arm, adjustable track control rods. Hydraulic power-assistance on all models, Servotronic speed-sensitive power assistance on 6-cylinder models.
Overall steering ratio	14.8:1
Lubricant quantity	1.3 litres
Hydraulic fluid pressure:	
At full lock	100 to 110 bar
At rest in centre position	2 to bar

Front suspension

Coil springs (typical):	Colour code	Spring length	Compression rate
SOHC 4-cylinder engines up to 1998	Blue/Brown	368 mm	21 N/mm
DOHC 4-cylinder engines, with air conditioning from 1998	Blue/Orange	390 mm	21 N/mm
6-cylinder engines, without air conditioning, up to 1998	Yellow/Lilac	362 mm	24 N/mm
6-cylinder engines, with air conditioning, from 1998	Brown/Brown	373 mm	24 N/mm

Front wheel alignment*

Camber:	
Saloon	-1°40' ± 45'
Estate	-1°40' ± 45'
Maximum deviation, left to right wheel	1°
Castor:	
Saloon	5°40' ± 1°
Estate	5° ± 1°
Maximum deviation, left to right wheel	1°
Toe-in:	
Saloon	0°10' ± 10'
Estate	0°10' ± 10'
Variation with inner wheel turned in at 20‡	1°40' ± 45'

Rear wheel alignment*

Camber:	
Saloon	-1°50' ± 40'
Estate	-1°40' ± 40'
Maximum deviation, left to right wheel	45'
Toe-in:	
Saloon	-0°20' ± 10'
Estate	-0°20' ± 10'
Maximum deviation, left to right wheel	25'

***Note:** *Measurements taken and adjustments made with all tyres inflated to their fully laden pressures and the vehicle laden, i.e. a 70kg load in each front seat and a full tank of fuel.*

Wheels

Type	Pressed steel or alloy
Size	6 1/2 J x 15, 7J x 15 or 7J x 16, depending on model and specification.

Tyres

Sizes

Saloon and estate models with 4-cylinder engines	195/65 R 15, 205/65 R 15 or 225/55 R 16
Saloon and estate models with 6-cylinder engines	205/65 R 15 or 225/55 R 16

** Refer to vehicle handbook or Vauxhall dealer for tyre speed ratings.*

Pressures Refer to end of *Weekly checks* on page 0•17

Torque wrench settings

Front suspension	Nm	lbf ft
Anti-roll bar bearing bracket bolts:		
Stage 1	20	15
Stage 2	angle tighten through 30°	
Stage 3	angle tighten through 15°	
Anti-roll bar link rod to anti-roll bar	65	48
Anti-roll bar link rod to strut	65	48
Front subframe*:		
Front mounting bolts:		
Stage 1	65	48
Stage 2	angle tighten through 30°	
Stage 3	angle tighten through 15°	
Centre mounting bolts:		
Stage 1	150	112
Stage 2	angle tighten through 30°	
Stage 3	angle tighten through 15°	
Rear mounting bolts:		
Stage 1	130	96
Stage 2	angle tighten through 30°	
Stage 3	angle tighten through 15°	
Hub nut*	320	236
Lower balljoint to arm	35	26
Lower balljoint to knuckle	100	74
Lower suspension arm pivot bolt:*		
Front:		
Stage 1	120	89
Stage 2	angle tighten through 30°	
Stage 3	angle tighten through 15°	

Torque wrench settings (continued)	Nm	lbf ft
Front suspension (continued)		
Lower suspension arm pivot bolt (continued):*		
Rear:		
Stage 1	120	89
Stage 2	angle tighten through 30°	
Stage 3	angle tighten through 15°	
Strut damper rod nut	70	52
Strut mounting nuts	55	41
Strut to steering knuckle:*		
Stage 1	90	66
Stage 2	angle tighten through 45°	
Stage 3	angle tighten through 15°	
Rear suspension		
Anti-roll bar drop link to semi-trailing arm	20	15
Anti-roll bar to subframe	22	16
Damping blocks to body	65	48
Damping blocks to subframe:		
Stage 1	90	66
Stage 2	angle tighten through 30°	
Stage 3	angle tighten through 15°	
Driveshaft to rear hub:		
Stage 1	50	37
Stage 2	angle tighten through 60°	
Stage 3	angle tighten through 15°	
Rear hub nut*	300	221
Semi-trailing arm pivot bolt	100	74
Shock absorber lower mounting	110	81
Shock absorber upper mounting	20	15
Subframe to body	65	48
Subframe to differential damping bush	125	92
Track control arm to semi-trailing arm	45	33
Track control arm to subframe*	90	66
Steering		
Airbag unit to steering wheel	8	6
Centre tie rod to drop arm	60	44
Centre tie rod to idler	60	44
Drop arm	160	118
Fuel supply and return union nuts	28	21
Idler mounting	60	44
Outer tie-rod clamp bolt	15	11
Outer tie rods to centre tie rod	60	44
Power steering pump:		
4-cylinder engines	25	18
6-cylinder engines	20	15
Power steering pump hydraulic fluid union	28	21
Power steering pump pulley	20	15
Steering column	22	16
Steering column support bracket nut	22	16
Steering gear clamp bolt	22	16
Steering gear heat shields	15	11
Steering gear mounting	55	41
Steering pump support brackets	20	15
Steering shaft clamp bolt	22	16
Steering wheel	20	15
Tie-rod balljoint nut*	60	44
Wheels		
Wheel bolts	110	81

**Use a new nut/bolt*

Note 1: *As a general rule, any fastener which has been angle-tightened should be renewed.*

Note 2: *The threads of all fasteners secured with locking compound must be thoroughly cleaned and, if necessary, re-cut to remove all traces of the old locking compound. Fresh locking compound should then be reapplied at reassembly.*

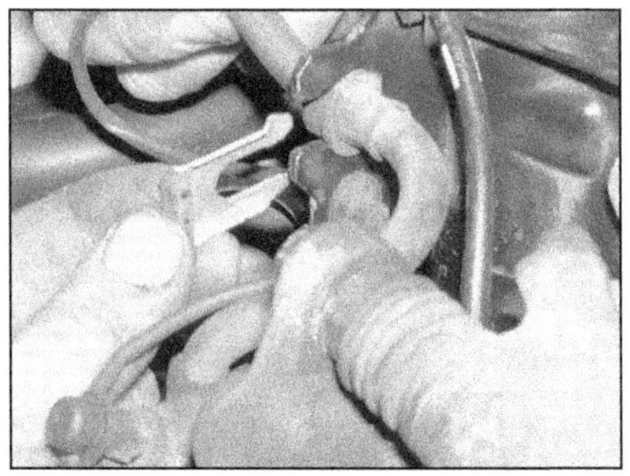

2.4a Pull out the retaining clip . . .

1 General description

1 The front suspension is of independent MacPherson strut type incorporating coil springs and double-acting telescopic shock absorbers. An anti-roll bar, connected to the suspension struts via drop links is mounted forward of the suspension arms.

2 The rear suspension is of independent type with coil springs, double-acting gas-filled telescopic shock absorbers, semi-trailing arms, anti-roll bar and adjustable track control arms. All components are mounted on a single subframe, which also houses the final drive unit (see Chapter 8 for general information relating to the final drive unit).

3 Power-assisted steering is fitted to all models, consisting of a recirculating ball and worm-type steering box with drop arm, a centre tie rod, idler arm and adjustable outer tie rods. 6-cylinder models are fitted with Servotronic speed sensitive power steering.

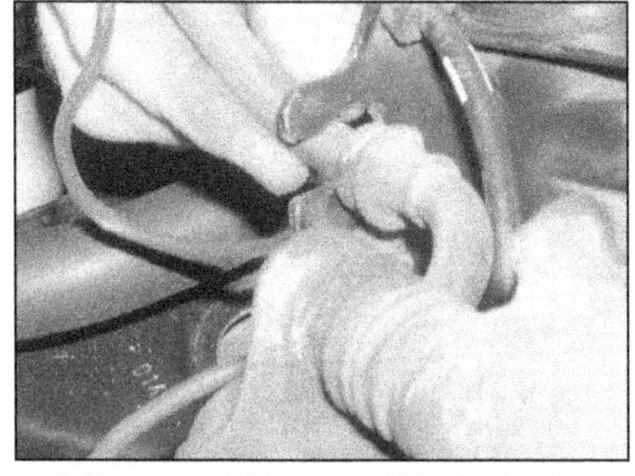

2.4b . . . and disconnect the hydraulic hose from the bracket on the strut

2 Front suspension strut - removal and refitting

Warning: If you are renewing the strut as part of the overhaul procedure, both the left and right hand struts should be renewed as a pair, to preserve the handling characteristics of the vehicle.

Removal

1 Apply the handbrake, then jack up the front of the vehicle and support it on axle stands.

2 Remove the relevant front road wheel.

3 Remove the brake caliper from the steering knuckle, as described in Chapter 9. Support the caliper to avoid straining the brake hose.

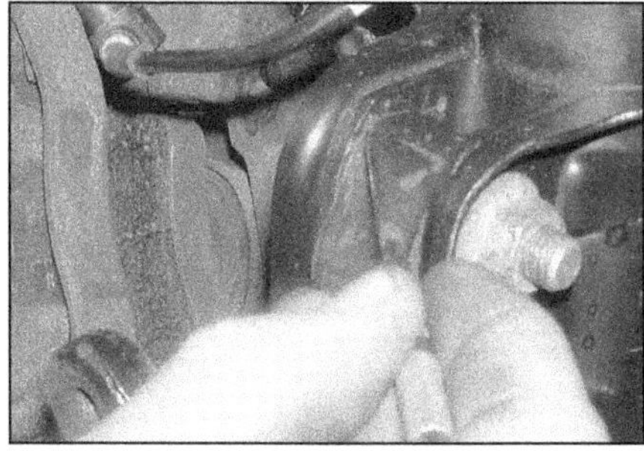

2.7a Mark the top of the steering knuckle in relation to the strut, to retain the camber setting . . .

4 Pull out the retaining clip and disconnect the hydraulic hose from the bracket on the strut **(see illustrations)**.

5 Remove the ABS wheel speed sensor from the steering knuckle and disconnect the wiring with reference to Chapter 9.

6 Unscrew the nut and separate the bottom of the anti-roll bar link from the end of the anti-roll bar (see Section 7). To prevent the ball-pin from turning, hold it stationary with a spanner on the two flats provided.

7 Mark the top of the steering knuckle in relation to the strut, to retain the camber setting then unscrew and withdraw the strut lower securing bolts **(see illustrations)**. Pull down on the lower suspension arm, to release the strut from the top of the steering knuckle.

8 Support the suspension strut by hand, then remove the cap, unscrew the upper mounting nut and remove the upper plate. Counterhold the damper rod with a second spanner to prevent it from rotating **(see illustrations)**.

2.7b . . . then unscrew . . .

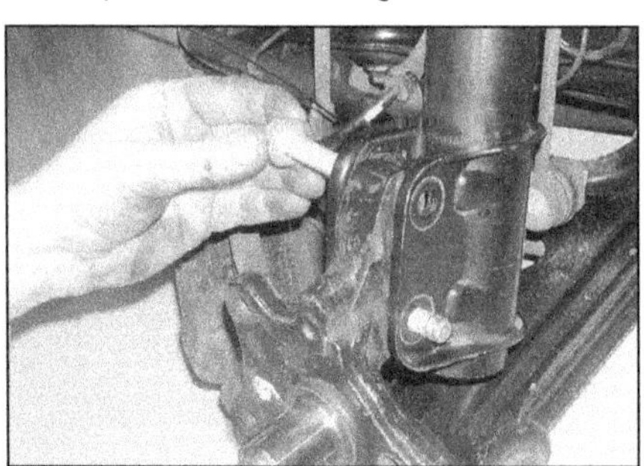

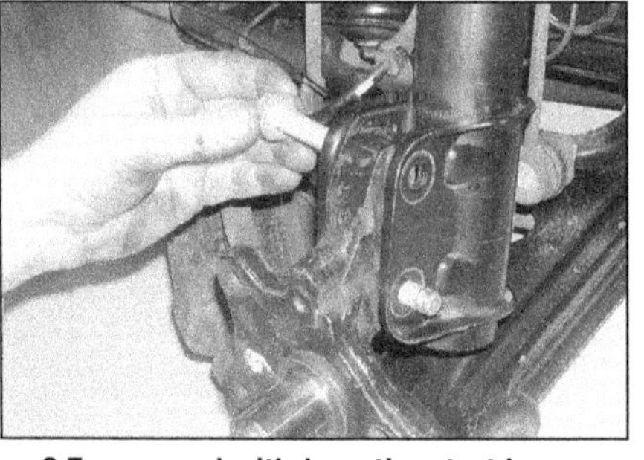

2.7c . . . and withdraw the strut lower securing bolts

2.8a Remove the cap . . .

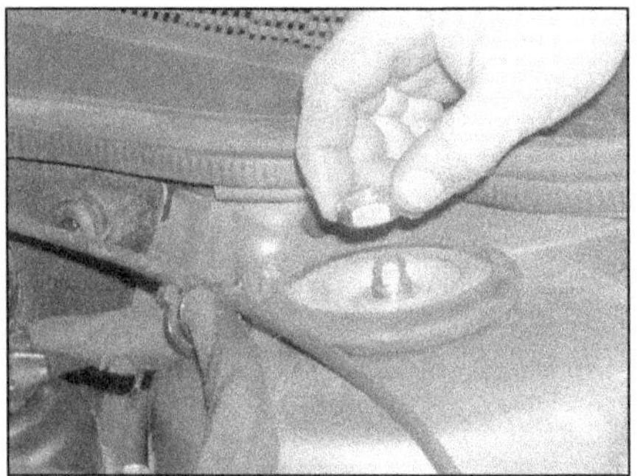

2.8b . . . unscrew the upper mounting nut . . .

2.8c . . . and remove the upper plate

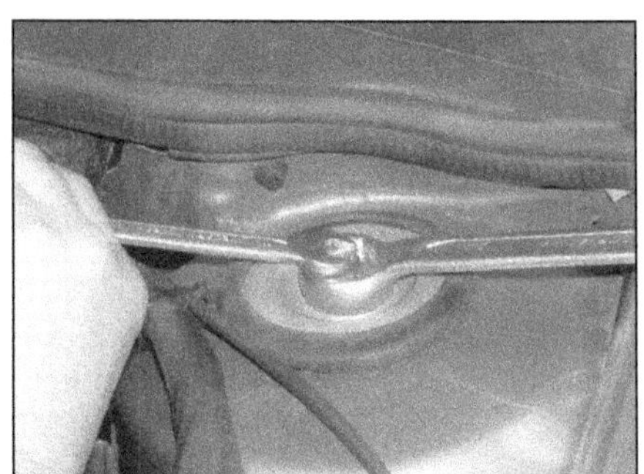

2.8d Counterhold the damper rod with a second spanner to prevent it from rotating

2.9 Withdrawing the front suspension strut from the wheel arch

2.11 Fitting the spring compressor to the strut coil spring

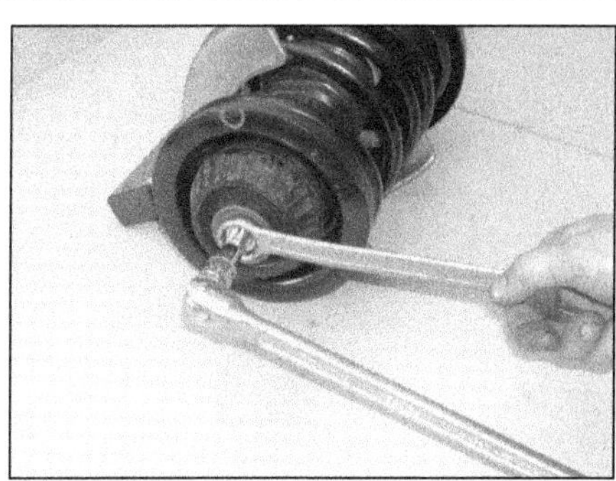

2.12a Hold the piston rod stationary with an Allen key . . .

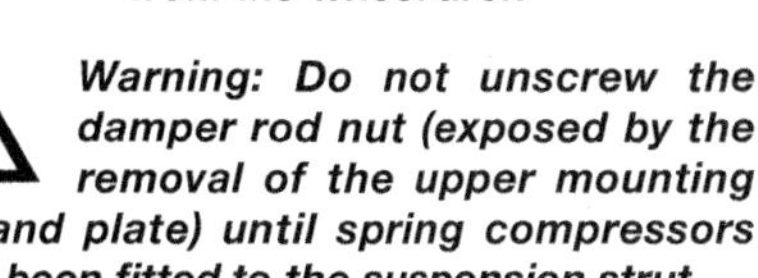

Warning: Do not unscrew the damper rod nut (exposed by the removal of the upper mounting nut and plate) until spring compressors have been fitted to the suspension strut.

9 Pivot the lower end of the strut away from the wheel arch, then lower it away from the upper mounting and withdraw it from under the vehicle **(see illustration)**.

Overhaul

Note: *A purpose-made spring compressor is essential for this work. Use of makeshift or unsuitable tools may result in injury.*

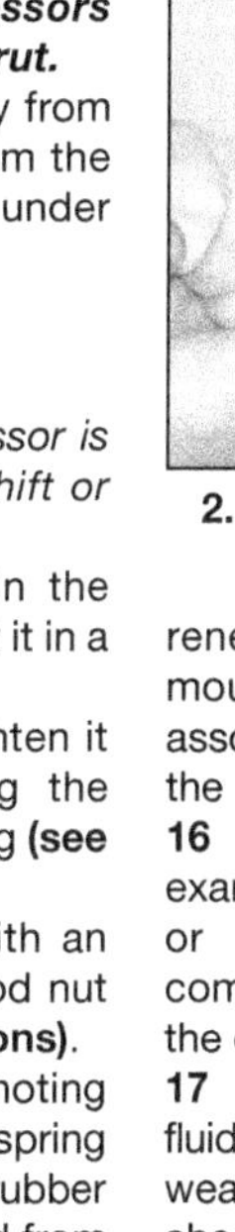

10 Remove the strut as described in the previous sub-Section. If required, mount it in a vice with padded jaws.

11 Fit the spring compressor and tighten it compress the coil spring, unloading the pressure on the upper seat and mounting **(see illustration)**.

12 Hold the piston rod stationary with an Allen key, then unscrew the damper rod nut and withdraw the washer **(see illustrations)**.

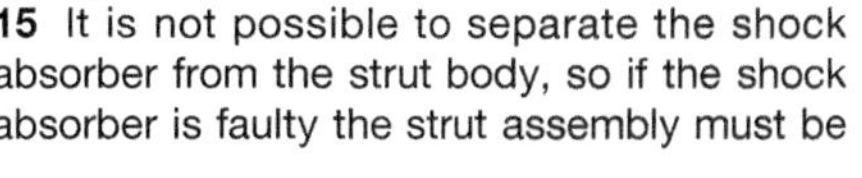

13 Remove the bearing and washer (noting its orientation), then slide off the upper spring seat, upper rubber damper, bump stop rubber and dust cover from the damper rod and from the top of the coil spring. Extract the rubber damper from the lower spring seat **(see illustrations)**.

14 Lift off the coil spring together with the spring compressors.

15 It is not possible to separate the shock absorber from the strut body, so if the shock absorber is faulty the strut assembly must be renewed (in which case, the spring, upper mounting components, bushes, and associated components can be transferred to the new strut).

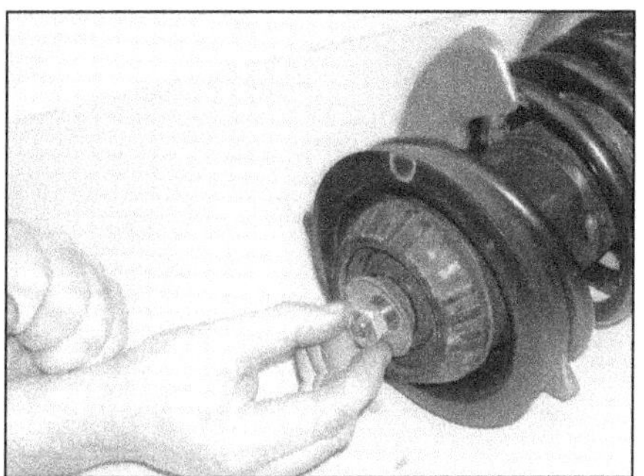

2.12b . . . then unscrew the damper rod nut . . .

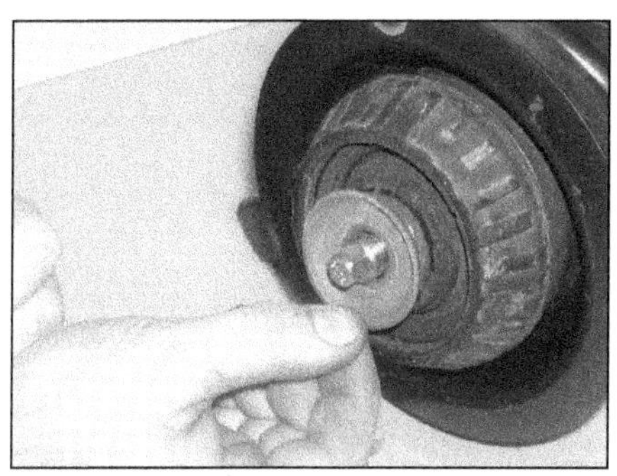

2.12c . . . and withdraw the washer

16 With the strut assembly now dismantled, examine all the components for wear, damage or deformation. Check the rubber components for deterioration. Renew any of the components as necessary.

17 Examine the shock absorber for signs of fluid leakage. Check the damper rod for signs of wear or corrosion along its entire length, and check the strut body for signs of damage or corrosion. While holding it in an upright position, test the operation of the strut by moving the damper rod through a full stroke, and then through short strokes of 50 to 100 mm. In both cases, the resistance felt should be smooth and continuous. If the resistance is jerky, or uneven, or if there is any visible sign of wear or damage to the strut, renewal is necessary.

18 If any doubt exists about the condition of the coil spring, carefully release the spring compressors, and check the spring for distortion and signs of cracking. Measure the unloaded height of the spring and compare it with the figure listed in the Specifications.

19 If a new shock absorber is being fitted, before reassembly push the damper rod fully into the shock absorber body, and then extend the rod to end of its travel. Do this three or four times to ensure that the shock absorber is fully primed.

20 Refit the rubber damper to the lower spring seat. Ensure that the coil spring is compressed sufficiently to enable the upper mounting components to be fitted, then lower the coil spring (together with the spring compressors) onto the lower spring seat, ensuring that the lower end of the coil spring abuts the stepped section of the rubber damper **(see illustrations)**.

2.13a Remove the bearing . . .

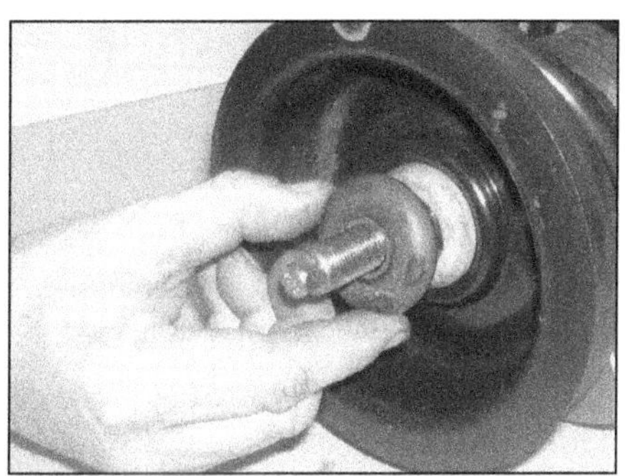

2.13b . . . and washer . . .

2.13c . . . then slide off the upper spring seat, upper rubber damper, bump stop rubber and dust cover

2.20a Refit the rubber damper to the lower spring seat

21 Locate the rubber damper in the upper spring seat, then slide the upper spring seat, bump stop rubber and dust cover over the damper rod **(see illustration)**.

22 Ensure that the upper end of the coil spring abuts the stepped section of the rubber damper.

23 Fit the washer and strut bearing to the strut damper rod and secure them in position with the washer and a new damper rod nut. Hold the damper rod stationary using an Allen key and then tighten the nut to specified torque. A crow's foot adapter may be required to allow the damper rod to be held still as the nut is tightened.

24 Slowly release the spring compressor and make sure that the coil spring locates correctly on the damping rings.

25 Refit the front suspension strut, as described in the following sub-Section.

Refitting

26 Commence refitting by inserting the strut up into the upper mounting. Refit the upper plate, then fit a new securing nut. Tighten the nut to the specified torque whilst holding the piston rod stationary with an Allen key. A crow's foot adapter may be required to allow the damper rod to be held still as the nut is tightened.

27 Fit the lower end of the strut to the steering knuckle and insert a pair of new securing bolts, noting that the bolts are inserted from the front of the strut, so that the heads face front of the car. Ensure that the lower end of the strut is positioned according

2.21 Locate the rubber damper in the upper spring seat

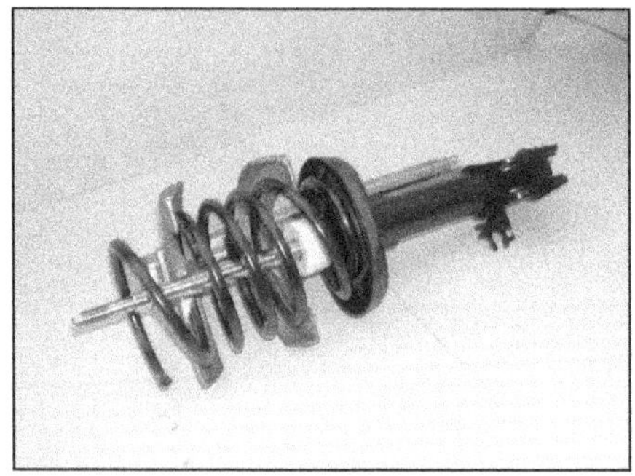

2.20b Lower the coil spring, together with the spring compressors, onto the lower spring seat

to the markings made on the steering knuckle during removal, to preserve the camber setting, then fit the new nuts, and tighten them to the specified torque.

Note: *If the original front wheel camber setting has been lost, or if new struts are being fitted, the camber setting must be checked and adjusted, using a camber gauge, before the strut lower nuts are tightened to their final torque setting; see Section 3 for details.*

28 Reconnect the drop link to the end of the anti-roll bar and tighten the nut to the specified torque; see Section 7 for details.

29 Refit the ABS wheel speed sensor and reconnect the cable, with reference to Chapter 9.

30 Press the brake hydraulic hose into the bracket on the strut and secure with the metal retaining clip. Refit the brake caliper with reference to Chapter 9.

31 Refit the front wheel, then lower the vehicle to the ground and tighten the wheel bolts to the specified torque.

32 Finally, have the front wheel toe-in adjustment checked and if necessary adjusted.

3 Front suspension camber - adjustment

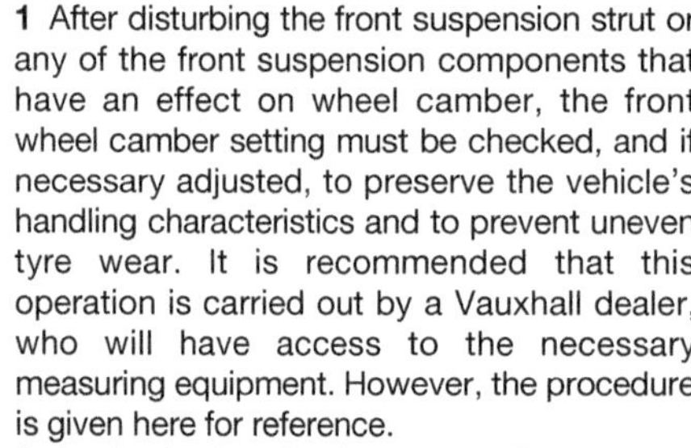

1 After disturbing the front suspension strut or any of the front suspension components that have an effect on wheel camber, the front wheel camber setting must be checked, and if necessary adjusted, to preserve the vehicle's handling characteristics and to prevent uneven tyre wear. It is recommended that this operation is carried out by a Vauxhall dealer, who will have access to the necessary measuring equipment. However, the procedure is given here for reference.

2 Apply the handbrake, select first gear or Park (as applicable) then jack up the front of the vehicle and support it on axle stands.

3 Remove both front road wheels.

4 Remove both brake calipers from the steering knuckles, as described in Chapter 9. Support the calipers to avoid straining the brake hoses.

5 Working on one side of the vehicle, slacken and withdraw the front suspension strut lower securing bolts. Fit two new securing bolts and nuts, noting that the bolts are fitted from the front of the strut so that their heads face the front of the car.

6 Set the wheel to maximum positive camber by pressing the top of the brake disc inwards, towards the engine compartment. The strut lower mountings bolts will pivot on their slotted mounting holes. Tighten the nuts to *approximately 20 Nm only,* then refit the brake caliper (see Chapter 9) and the road wheel.

7 Repeat the operations in paragraphs 5 and 6 on the opposite front wheel.

8 Carefully lower the vehicle to the ground and tighten the road wheel bolts to the specified torque.

9 Load the vehicle to its specified adjustment weight, as described in *Specifications, Front wheel alignment.*

10 Using a proprietary camber gauge, set the front wheels to the specified camber angle. Adjustments are made by grasping the top of the road wheel and pivoting the steering knuckle inwards or outwards to achieve the correct camber angle.

11 When the correct camber angles are obtained, tighten the strut lower mounting nuts progressively in two stages; first to 50 Nm, then to 90 Nm.

12 Release the handbrake and select neutral, then rock the vehicle on its road wheels to settle the suspension.

13 Recheck the camber setting; if further adjustment is required, repeat the operations described in paragraphs 2 to 12 inclusive. If no further adjustment is required, tighten the strut lower mounting nuts to their specified Stage 1 and Stage 2 torque settings.

4 Front lower suspension arm - removal and refitting

Removal

1 Apply the handbrake, then jack up the front of the vehicle and support it on axle stands.

2 Remove the relevant front road wheel.

3 Unscrew and remove the pinch-bolt, and pull down the lower suspension arm to release the balljoint from the steering knuckle.

4 Unscrew the vertical front mounting bolt and the horizontal rear mounting bolt, discard them, and withdraw the lower suspension arm from under the vehicle. Note the horizontal bolt head faces towards the rear of the car. Note also that access to the front mounting bolt is via the top of the suspension subframe and access is very limited due to the proximity of the engine mounting bracket.

5 Refer to Section 5 if renewing the suspension balljoint. Examine the rubber bushes in the arm and if necessary renew them using a hydraulic press. Note the orientation of the existing bushes in the lower arm before pressing them out, and ensure that the new bushes are fitted in the same way.

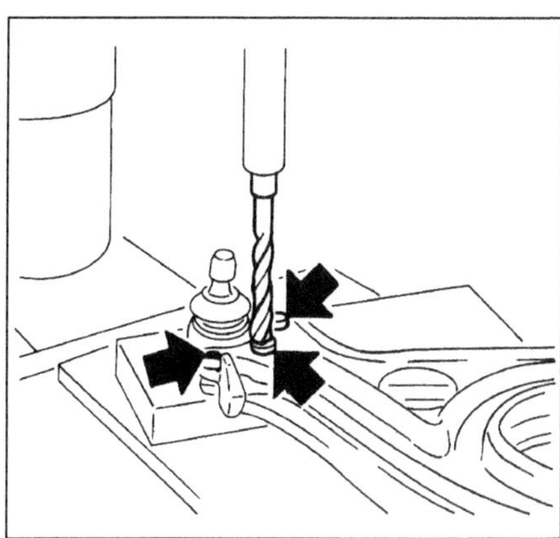
5.2 Drilling out the front suspension lower balljoint rivets

Refitting

6 Commence refitting by locating the arm on the underbody and inserting the new mounting bolts. Do not re-use the old mounting bolts. Insert the front mounting bolt from back to front, and insert the (shorter) rear mounting bolt from top to bottom.

7 Hold the arm horizontally and tighten the securing nuts and bolts to the specified torque.

8 Insert the balljoint in the steering knuckle and fit a pinch-bolt, with its head facing the rear of the vehicle. Fit a new nut and tighten to the specified torque.

9 Reconnect the links to the anti-roll bar and tighten the nuts.

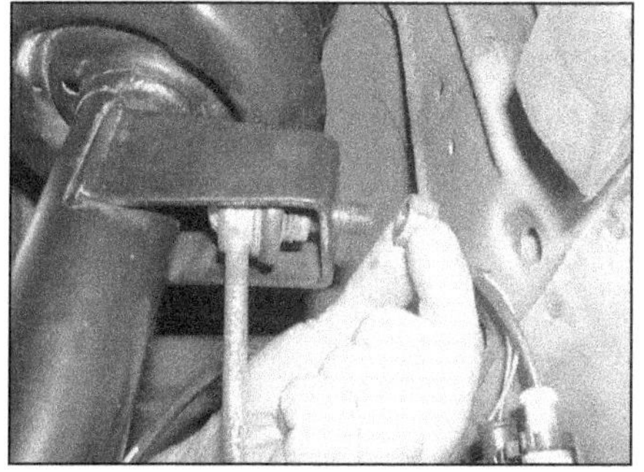
7.2a Unscrew the upper nut . . .

10 Refit the front wheel and lower the vehicle to the ground.

11 Finally, have the front wheel alignment checked and if necessary adjusted.

5 Front suspension lower balljoint - renewal

1 Remove the front lower suspension arm as described in Section 4.

2 The balljoint is riveted to the suspension arm when new, with subsequent balljoints bolted on. Where necessary drill out the rivets using a 12.0 mm drill. One side of each rivet has a centre punch to facilitate accurate drilling in order to prevent enlarging the holes in the arm **(see illustration)**.

3 Coat the newly-drilled holes with a suitable rust-preventing agent.

4 Using only the special bolts supplied the new balljoint, fit the balljoint and tighten the nuts to the specified torque. The nuts must face downwards.

5 Refit the front lower suspension arm with reference to Section 4.

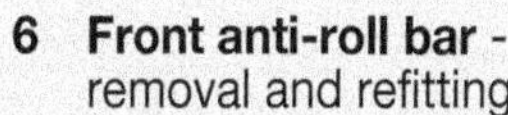

6 Front anti-roll bar - removal and refitting

Removal

1 Apply the handbrake, then jack up the front of the vehicle and support it on axle stands. Remove the front wheels.

2 Unscrew the nuts and separate the lower ends of the drop links from the ends of the anti-roll bar (see Section 7). Prevent the link ball-pins from turning by holding them with a spanner on the two flats provided.

3 Refer to Section 10 and remove the front suspension subframe.

4 From inside the engine compartment unscrew the anti-roll bar mounting clamp bolts, and unclip the clamps **(see illustration)**.

5 Withdraw the anti-roll bar from under the vehicle.

6.4 Unscrew the anti-roll bar mounting clamp bolts (arrowed)

Refitting

6 Examine the mounting rubbers for wear and deterioration and, if necessary, prise them from the bar. Coat the new rubbers with a silicone-based spray and fit them on the bar with their slits facing towards the rear of the vehicle.

7 Insert the anti-roll bar from under the front of the vehicle, and refit the clamps. Insert the bolts loosely.

8 Reconnect the drop links to the ends of the anti-roll bar; use new securing nuts and tighten them to the specified torque.

9 Tighten the anti-roll bar mounting clamp bolts to the specified torque.

10 Refit the front wheels and lower the vehicle to the ground.

7 Front anti-roll bar drop link - removal and refitting

Removal

1 Apply the handbrake, then jack up the front of the vehicle and support it on axle stands. Remove the appropriate front wheel.

2 Note which way round the link is fitted then unscrew the nuts while holding the ball-pins with a spanner on the two flats provided **(see illustrations)**.

3 Remove the link from the strut and anti-roll bar.

7.2b . . . and detach the drop link from the suspension strut

7.2c Detach the drop link from the anti-roll bar

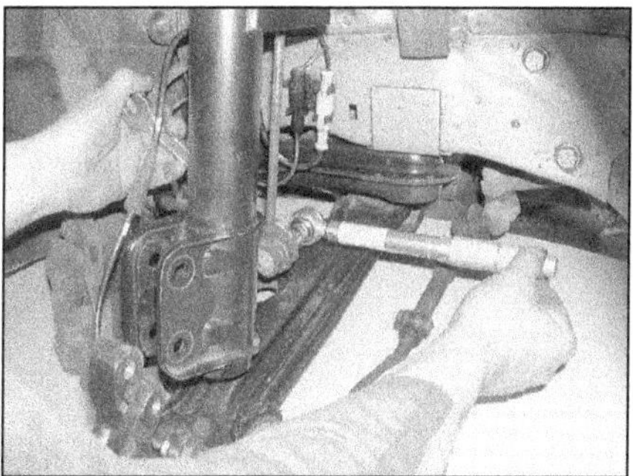
7.2d Counterhold the drop link stud using the flats provided

7.4 Tighten the anti-roll bar drop link securing nuts to the specified torque

Refitting

4 Refitting is a reversal of removal but fit new securing nuts and tighten them to the specified torque **(see illustration)**.

8 Steering knuckle - removal and refitting

Removal

1 Remove the front hub as described in Section 9.

2 Unbolt the brake disc shield from the steering knuckle.

3 With reference to Section 24, unscrew the nut from the steering tie-rod balljoint, and use a proprietary balljoint separator to release the ball joint pin from the steering knuckle lug.

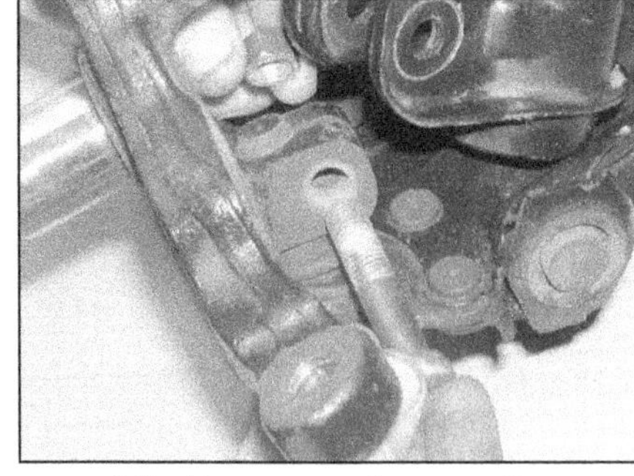

8.6a Unscrew and remove the pinch-bolt . . .

8.6b . . . and then lift the knuckle from the lower arm

4 Remove the ABS wheel speed sensor and disconnect the cable with reference to Chapter 9, Section 18.

5 Mark the top of the steering knuckle in relation to the strut in order to retain the camber setting, then unscrew and discard the bolts and separate the strut from the knuckle. Note that the bolt heads face forwards.

6 Unscrew and remove the pinch-bolt, and then lift the knuckle from the lower arm **(see illustrations)**.

Refitting

7 Refitting is a reversal of removal, but be sure to use new bolts and nuts. On no account should the old bolts be re-used. Tighten to the specified torque wrench settings and if necessary have the camber and wheel alignment checked by a Vauxhall dealer.

9 Front hub and bearings - removal and refitting

Note: *A torque wrench capable of measuring the high torque of the front hub nut should be obtained before commencing work.*

Removal

1 Apply the handbrake, then jack up the front of the vehicle and support it on axle stands. Remove the appropriate front road wheel.

2 Lever the dust cap from the hub, then refit the road wheel and lower the vehicle to the ground; with the road wheel in contact with the ground, it will be much easier to slacken the hub nut.

3 Chock the roadwheels securely, then using a socket, sturdy T-bar and a long extension bar for leverage, slacken the hub nut by about half a turn. Note that the nut is tightened to a very high torque setting, and considerable effort will be required to slacken it.

4 Jack up the front of the vehicle again and support it on axle stands. Remove the appropriate road wheel.

5 Remove the brake caliper and brake disc with reference to Chapter 9.

6 Fully unscrew and remove the hub nut, and pull the hub from the stub axle **(see illustrations)**. If the inner bearing track remains on the stub axle, remove it with a universal bearing puller and recover the oil seal which will have been pulled out of the hub.

9.6a Fully unscrew . . .

Refitting

7 The bearings cannot be renewed separately to the hub, so if the bearings are worn or the oil seal leaking the complete hub must be renewed. The new hub includes a plastic sleeve which holds the bearing inner tracks together while fitting the hub.

8 Locate the hub and plastic sleeve on the stub axle, then carefully drive the inner tracks onto the stub axle using a suitable size socket or metal tube **(see illustration)**. Remove the plastic sleeve.

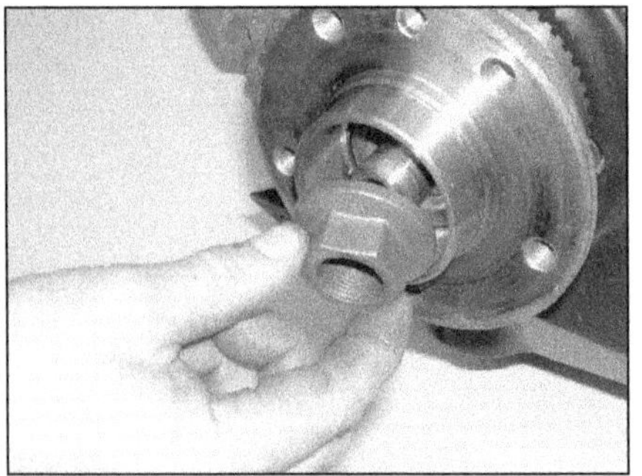

9.6b . . . and remove the hub nut . . .

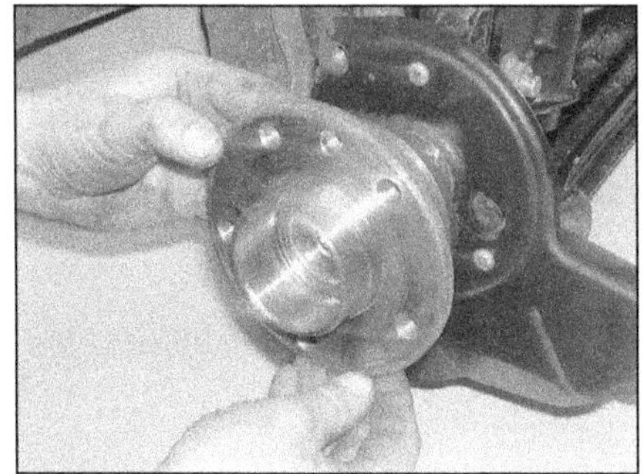

9.6c . . . and pull the hub from the stub axle

9.8 Carefully drive the hub onto the stub axle using a suitable socket

Refitting

9 Refit the components in the reverse order to removal, noting the following points **(see illustration)**:

a) Tighten all nuts and bolts to the specified torque.
b) Use a new hub nut and ensure that it tightened to the specified torque
c) Refit the brake disc and caliper as described in Chapter 9.
d) Fit a new hub dust cap.

10 Front suspension subframe - removal and refitting

Removal

1 Apply the handbrake, then jack up the front of the vehicle and support it securely on axle stands. Unscrew the fixings and lower the cover panel away from the underside of the engine compartment.

2 On models with Xenon headlamps, unplug the wiring from the front vehicle level sensor; refer to Chapter 12, Section 13 for details.

3 Unbolt both lower suspension arm balljoints from the base of each steering knuckle, as described in Section 4.

4 Unbolt the anti-roll bar drop links from the ends of the anti-roll bar, as described in Section 7.

5 Unscrew the nuts securing both engine mountings to the subframe and engine brackets, with reference to Chapter 2A. Where applicable, also unbolt the engine vibration damper strut from the subframe.

6 Position an engine hoist or lifting beam over the engine compartment. Attach the lifting jib to the engine lifting eyelets at the side of the cylinder head(s) and raise it to take the weight of the engine.

7 Mark the relationship between the subframe and underbody using a marker pen to ensure correct alignment on refitting.

8 Support the weight of the subframe using a trolley jack and a stout length of wood.

9 Identify the six subframe mounting bolts for position. Progressively slacken and remove the bolts, noting that they are of different lengths and diameters, then lower the subframe to the ground using the trolley jack.

9.9 Fitting a new hub dust cap

Refitting

10 Refitting is a reversal of removal, noting the following points:

a) Refit the subframe according to the alignment markings made during removal.
b) Fit new subframe securing bolts..
c) Tighten all nuts and bolts to the correct torque, where specified.
d) On completion have the front wheel alignment (see Section 27) and camber setting (see Section 3) checked and if necessary corrected.

11 Rear shock absorber - removal and refitting

Note: *Shock absorbers should always be renewed as a pair, to preserve the handling characteristics of the vehicle.*

Removal

1 Chock the front wheels, then jack up the rear of vehicle and support it securely on axle stands.

2 Raise the relevant semi-trailing arm using a trolley jack to relieve the load on the shock absorber.

3 On Saloon models, remove the trim panel from the side of the boot space, then prise the rubber cap from the top of the shock absorber upper mounting.

4 On Estate models, fold back the load space carpet, then remove the screws and lift off the cover to expose the shock absorber upper mountings.

5 Unscrew the upper mounting nuts and remove the washer and rubber buffers **(see illustration)**.

6 On models fitted with rear suspension level control, reach in through the rear wheel arch and release the air pressure from the valve on the side of the shock absorber body. Release the clip and disconnect the pressure line from the shock absorber.

7 Lower the semi-trailing arm using the trolley jack, then unscrew the lower mounting bolt and washer, then remove the shock absorber **(see illustrations)**.

8 With the shock absorber removed, examine it for wear, damage or deformation. Check the rubber mounting components for deterioration. Renew any of the components as necessary.

9 Examine the shock absorber for signs of fluid leakage. Check the damper rod for signs of wear or corrosion along its entire length, and check the strut body for signs of damage or corrosion. While holding it in an upright position, test the operation of the shock absorber by moving the damper rod through one or two full strokes, and then through short strokes of about 50 to 100 mm. In both cases, the resistance felt should be smooth and continuous. If the resistance is jerky, or uneven, or if there is any visible sign of wear or damage to the strut, renewal is necessary.

10 If a new shock absorber is being fitted, before reassembly push the damper rod fully into the shock absorber body, and then pull the rod out to end of its travel. Do this three or four times to ensure that the shock absorber is fully primed.

Refitting

11 Commence refitting by locating the shock absorber on the semi trailing arm and inserting the bottom mounting bolt loosely. Ensure that the bush engages with the recess in the lower mounting.

12 Raise the semi-trailing arm using a trolley jack and guide the top of the shock absorber through its upper wheel arch mountings.

11.5 Unscrew the rear shock absorber upper mounting nut

11.7a Unscrew the rear shock absorber lower mounting bolt and washer . . .

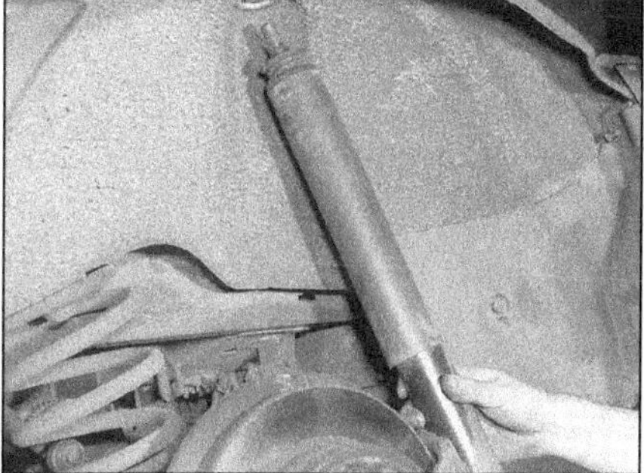

11.7b . . . then remove the shock absorber from the wheel arch

13 On models with rear suspension level control, charge the shock absorber slightly with compressed air. An exact initial pressure is not specified by the manufacturer but carefully inflate the shock absorber until it protrudes through the upper mountings. Refit the pressure line to the shock absorber valve and secure it in position with the retaining clip. Ensure that the pressure line is positioned so that it does not foul any suspension components.

14 Refit the upper mounting rubber buffers and washer. Fit a new securing nut and tighten it to the specified torque.

15 Tighten the lower shock absorber mounting bolt to the specified torque.

16 On estate models, refit the cover panel and secure it position with the screws.

17 On Saloon models, press the rubber cap onto the top of the shock absorber.

18 Refit the road wheels and lower the vehicle to the ground.

19 Carry out a check of the rear suspension level control system's operation, where applicable.

12 Rear semi-trailing arm - removal and refitting

Removal

1 Chock the front wheels, then jack up the rear of the vehicle and support on axle stands positioned under the subframe mountings.

2 With reference to Chapter 8, Section 8, unbolt the relevant driveshaft from the rear hub and support it to one side.

3 Disconnect the hydraulic brake hose from the bracket on the semi-trailing arm.

4 Remove the rear brake caliper and brake disc as described in Chapter 9.

5 Unhook the return spring and disconnect the handbrake cable from the lever on the semi-trailing arm. Disconnect the cable from the bracket.

6 On models with rear suspension level control, unplug the wiring from the rear vehicle level sensor. Mark the relationship between the level sensor actuator arm and the anti-roll bar drop link, to ensure correct alignment on refitting, then prise the link rod from the balljoint on the sensor actuator arm.

7 Using a socket through the unthreaded holes in the hub unscrew the brake anchor plate bolts and remove the locking plate.

8 Remove the rear hub with reference to Section 20, then withdraw the brake anchor plate and brake shoes as an assembly.

9 Unbolt the track control arm from the semi-trailing arm, with reference to Section 15.

10 With reference to Chapter 4A, disconnect the mounting rubbers from the exhaust system intermediate and rear silencers, then lower the exhaust system away from the floorpan by approximately 30 cm. Support the exhaust in this position with wire or nylon cable ties.

11 Unbolt the rear anti-roll bar drop link from the semi-trailing arm. Pivot the link upwards to keep it clear of the work area.

12 Raise the semi-trailing arm slightly using a trolley jack, to relieve the load on the shock absorber.

13 On models fitted with rear suspension level control, release the air pressure via the shock absorber valve by disconnecting the pressure line from the shock absorber (see Section 11).

14 Unscrew and withdraw the shock absorber lower mounting bolt with reference to Section 11.

15 Lower the semi-trailing arm using the trolley jack until the rear coil spring and damping rubbers can be removed (see Section 13).

16 Position a trolley jack underneath the final drive unit, the raise the jack head until it is just support the weight of the unit.

17 Remove the heat shield panels, then with reference to Chapter 8, unbolt the propeller shaft centre bearing support bracket from the underbody. Support the propeller shaft on an axle stand.

18 Slacken and remove the bolts securing the leading edge of the rear subframe to the floorpan. Lower the final drive unit and subframe slightly, using the trolley jack, until the semi-trailing arm bolts are accessible.

19 Slacken and withdraw the pivot bolts and remove the semi-trailing arm from the subframe.

20 If the pivot bushes are worn, they may be renewed. Cut the shoulders from the old bushes and press them from the semi-trailing arm using a hydraulic press. Fit the new bushes in a similar way, but dip them in soapy water first to assist fitting. Note that the plastic-coated bush, nearest the final drive unit, is fitted with its collar facing the final drive unit.

Refitting

21 Refitting is a reversal of removal, noting the following points.

a) Tighten all nuts and bolts to the specified torque.
b) The semi-trailing arm pivot bolt must be inserted such that their heads face away from final drive unit.
c) On vehicles with rear suspension level control, refit the level sensor connecting rod with respect to the alignment markings made during removal.
d) When reconnecting the pressure line to the shock absorber on models with rear suspension level control, ensure that the line cannot be fouled by any of the suspension components.
e) On models with Xenon headlamps, reconnect the wiring to the vehicle level sensor.

22 On completion adjust the handbrake with reference to Chapter 1, then have the rear wheel alignment checked and if necessary adjusted by a Vauxhall dealer. On models with Xenon headlamps, it is also recommended that the headlight beam alignment is checked by a Vauxhall dealer.

13 Rear coil spring - removal and refitting

Note: *Suspension coil springs should always be renewed as a matched pair, to preserve the handling characteristics of the vehicle.*

Removal

1 Chock the front wheels, then jack up the rear of the vehicle and support on axle stands. Remove the relevant rear wheel.

2 Disconnect the hydraulic brake hose from the bracket on the semi-trailing arm by pulling out the locking plate.

3 With reference to Chapter 4A, disconnect the mounting rubbers from the exhaust system intermediate and rear silencers, then lower the exhaust system away from the floorpan by approximately 30 cm. Support the exhaust in this position with wire or nylon cable ties.

4 On models with rear suspension level control, unplug the wiring from the rear vehicle level sensor. Mark the relationship between the level sensor actuator arm and the anti-roll bar drop link, to ensure correct alignment on refitting, then prise the link rod from the balljoint on the sensor actuator arm.

5 Using a trolley jack, slightly raise the semi-trailing arm to relieve the load on the shock absorber.

6 On models fitted with rear suspension level control, release the air pressure via the shock absorber valve by disconnecting the pressure line from the shock absorber (see Section 11).

7 Unbolt the lower end of the shock absorber with reference to Section 11.

8 Unclip the ABS rear wheel speed sensor cables from the underbody, then unplug the cables from the sensor at the connectors; see Chapter 9 for details.

9 Using a trolley jack, support the final drive unit then unbolt the subframe rear damping brackets from the underbody (see Section 19).

10 Lower the final drive unit, subframe and semi-trailing arm until the rear coil spring and damping rubbers can be removed. Note that the upper damping rubber incorporates a buffer.

Refitting

11 Refitting is a reversal of removal, noting the following points.

a) When refitting the coil spring, ensure that the end face of the top of the coil is facing the rear of the vehicle.
b) Tighten all nuts and bolts to the specified torques.
c) On vehicles with rear suspension level control, refit the level sensor connecting rod with respect to the alignment markings made during removal.
d) Refit the ABS wheel speed sensors with reference to Chapter 9.

14 Rear anti-roll bar - removal and refitting

Removal

1 Chock the front wheels, then jack up the rear of the vehicle and support securely on axle stands.

2 On models with rear suspension level control, mark the relationship between the level sensor actuator arm and the anti-roll bar drop link, to ensure correct alignment on refitting, then prise the link rod from the balljoint on the sensor actuator arm.

3 Disconnect the wiring from the ABS wheel speed sensors, then release the wiring from the clips on the rear subframe.

4 Unbolt the two anti-roll bar drop links from the ends semi-trailing arms, and remove the rubber mountings **(see illustration)**.

5 Support the final drive unit on a trolley jack. Unbolt the subframe rear damping brackets from the underbody, then lower the final drive unit slightly, until access to the anti-roll bar mounting clamp bolts can be gained.

6 Unscrew the clamp bolts from the top of the subframe and release the clamps from the anti-roll bar. Pass the anti-roll bar over the rear of the subframe and withdraw it together with its drop links from under the vehicle.

7 Unbolt the drop links from the anti-roll bar. If necessary, the clamp mounting rubbers may be pressed from the links and renewed, using a hydraulic press. Dip the new rubbers in soapy water to assist fitting them.

Refitting

8 Refitting is a reversal of removal, but tighten all nuts and bolts to their correct torques, where specified.

15 Rear track control arm - removal and refitting

Removal

1 Chock the front wheels, then jack up the rear of the vehicle and support securely on axle stands.

2 Unscrew the nut securing the track control arm to the semi-trailing arm **(see illustration)**. Disconnect the rod from the arm using a proprietary ball joint separator.

3 Unbolt the track control arm from the subframe **(see illustration)**, and remove the arm from the vehicle.

4 If the track control arm is to be dismantled, first measure its overall length to obtain an approximate rear wheel alignment setting after refitting.

Refitting

5 Refit the track control arm by following the removal procedure in reverse, using new

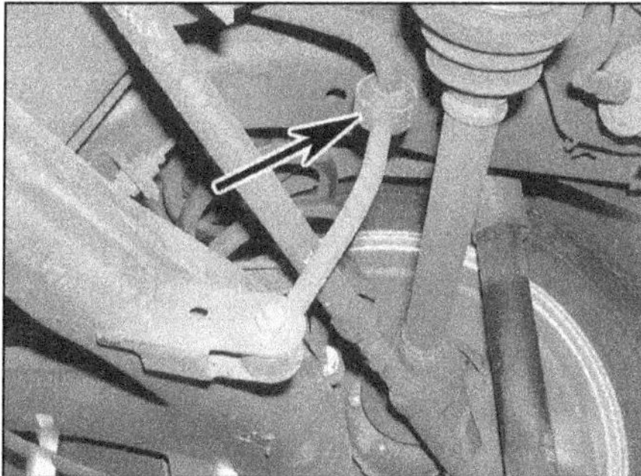

14.4 Rear anti-roll bar-to-drop link bolt

nuts/bolts where indicated in the *Specifications*. Tighten all fixings to the specified torque. On completion, have the rear wheel alignment checked and if necessary adjusted by a Vauxhall dealer.

16 Rear suspension level control system - component removal and refitting

Compressor

Removal

1 The compressor is located in the right hand front wheel arch. To gain access, raise the front of the vehicle and rest it securely on axle stands. Remove the right hand roadwheel, the unscrew the fixings and detach the liner from the right hand wheel arch.

2 Unplug the wiring connector from the compressor.

3 Disconnect the air intake hose from the cavity behind the right hand headlight unit.

4 Release the securing clip and detach the air pressure pipe from the top of the compressor.

5 Slacken and withdraw the securing screws then remove the compressor together with its mounting bracket from the bodywork.

Refitting

6 Refitting is a reversal of removal. On completion, check the operation of the level control system as described in the last sub-Section.

Pressure line

Removal

7 Disconnect the pressure line from the compressor as described in the previous sub-Section.

8 Raise the rear of the vehicle and rest it securely on axle stands.

9 Release the metal spring clip and disconnect the pressure line from the valve on the side of the first rear shock absorber. Disconnect the pressure pipe from the opposite shock absorber in a similar manner.

10 Locate the pressure T-piece which is mounted on vehicle underbody. Release the clips and disconnect the pressure pipe from the T-piece.

11 Work along the underside of the vehicle, releasing the pressure pipe from its securing clips, then remove the pipe from the vehicle.

Refitting

12 Refitting is a reversal of removal. When refitting the pressure pipes to the rear shock absorbers, ensure that they are positioned such that they cannot be fouled by the rear suspension components. On completion, check the operation of the level control system as described in the last sub-Section.

Level sensor

Removal

13 Disconnect the battery negative cable and position it away from the terminal.

14 Chock the front wheels, then raise the rear of the vehicle and support it securely on axle stands. Remove the rear road wheels.

15 Unplug the wiring from the level sensor at the multiway connector.

16 Prise the connecting rod from the balljoint on the sensor's actuator arm.

17 Undo the securing screws and remove the sensor together with its bracket from the subframe.

Refitting

18 Refitting is a reversal of removal. On completion, check the operation of the level control system as described in the next sub-Section.

System operation check

19 Park the vehicle (unloaded) on level

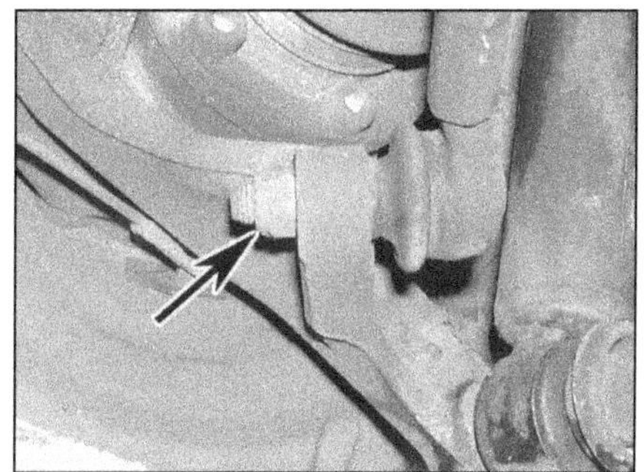

15.2 Track control arm-to-semi-trailing arm bolt

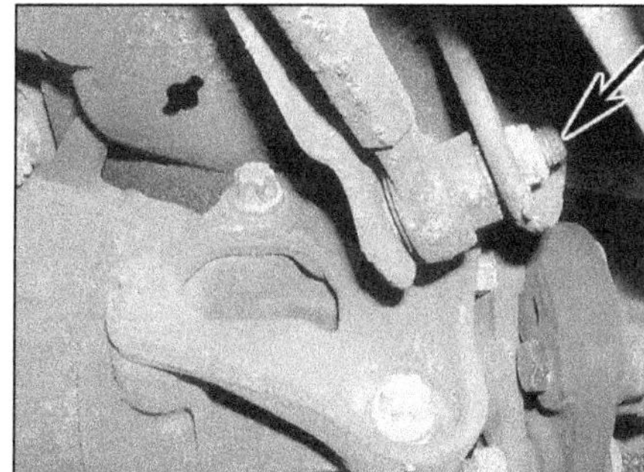

15.3 Track control arm-to-subframe bolt

ground. Release the handbrake and let the engine idle for while, to allow the rear suspension ride height to stabilise. Re-apply the handbrake.

20 Measure the vertical distance from the ground to a convenient point on the rear bumper.

21 Place a heavy load in the boot/load space. Release the handbrake and let the engine idle for while, to allow the rear suspension ride height to stabilise. Re-apply the handbrake.

22 Repeat the measure carried out in paragraph 20. If operating correctly, the rear suspension control system should control the loaded ride height to a value 3 to 5 cm less than the unloaded ride height within 20 seconds.

23 Remove the load and allow the rear ride height to stabilise again. The system should return the ride height to the original unloaded ride height within 20 seconds.

17 Rear axle (complete assembly) - removal and refitting

Removal

1 Chock the front wheels, then jack up the rear of the vehicle and support it on axle stands. Position the axle stands such access can still be gained to all the rear subframe mounting bolts. Remove both rear road wheels.

2 Remove the intermediate and rear sections of the exhaust system with reference to Chapter 4A.

3 Note the position of the adjustment nut on the handbrake rod, then unscrew it and slide off the compensator bar; see Chapter 9, Section 8.

4 With reference to Chapter 9, unbolt both rear brake calipers from the semi-trailing arms and support them away from the disc, taking care not to damage the rigid brake lines.

5 Release the handbrake cables and hydraulic brake hoses from the brackets on both semi-trailing arms.

6 On models with Xenon headlamps, unplug the wiring from the rear vehicle level sensor; see Chapter 12 Section 13.

7 Unbolt the ABS wheel speed sensors from the final drive unit, with reference to Chapter 9, Section 18.

8 At the rear of the propeller shaft unscrew the bolts securing the rear disc joint to the differential flange.

9 Position a length of wood beneath the semi-trailing arms and support in the middle with a trolley jack.

10 Unbolt the final drive unit rear damping brackets from the underbody and lower the unit onto the length of wood.

11 Unscrew the shock absorber bottom mounting bolts on each side.

12 Lower the trolley jack until both rear coil springs and damping rubbers can be removed. Note that the upper damping rubbers incorporate buffers.

13 Raise the trolley jack until the rear damping bracket touches the underbody, then unscrew the three bracket bolts and centre bolt from the subframe front mountings **(see illustration)**. As a precaution, have an assistant steady the assembly to prevent it falling from the trolley jack.

14 Lower the rear axle assembly to the ground and withdraw from under the vehicle. Be prepared to support the propeller shaft as it releases from the final drive unit.

Refitting

15 Refitting is a reversal of removal, noting the following points.

a) Tighten all nuts and bolts to the correct torque settings, where specified.

b) Adjust the handbrake with reference to Chapter 1.

c) On completion it is recommended that the rear wheel alignment is checked and if necessary corrected by a Vauxhall dealer.

18 Rear suspension subframe - removal and refitting

Removal

1 Remove the rear axle assembly as described in Section 17.

2 Unscrew the anti-roll bar clamp bolts from the top of the subframe and release the clamps.

3 Unscrew the final drive unit mounting bolts and lower the unit from the subframe.

4 Unscrew and remove the semi-trailing arm pivot bolts, noting that the bolt heads are facing each other on each arm. Remove the subframe.

5 If necessary renew the mountings with reference to Section 19.

Refitting

6 Refitting is a reversal of removal, but tighten all nuts and bolts to the specified torques. The semi-trailing arms should be positioned horizontally before tightening the pivot bolts.

19 Rear suspension subframe mountings - renewal

Removal

1 Chock the front wheels, then jack up the rear of the vehicle and support on axle stands positioned under the rear underbody channel sections. Remove both rear wheels.

2 Disconnect the exhaust rear mounting rubbers and lower the exhaust approximately 30 cm. Temporarily support the exhaust in this position with wire or nylon cable ties.

3 Disconnect the hydraulic brake hoses from the brackets on the semi-trailing arms by pulling out the locking plates.

4 Support the final drive unit on a trolley jack.

5 Unscrew the three bracket bolts and one centre bolt from the subframe mountings on each side and remove the brackets.

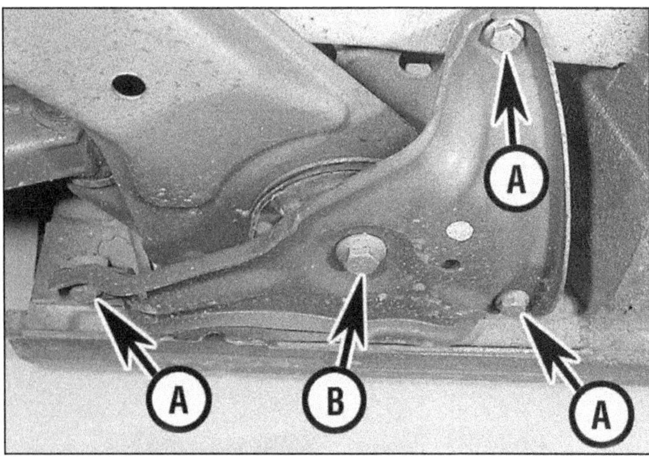

17.13 Unscrew the three bracket bolts (A) and centre bolt (B) from the subframe front mountings

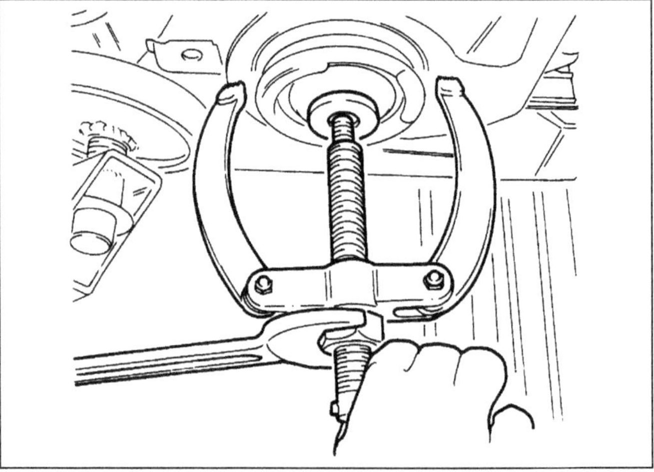

19.6 Withdrawing the subframe mountings

6 The mountings must now be pulled from the subframe. The Vauxhall tool for this task is shown in **(see illustration)**. The subframe is lowered slightly and the mounting bolt inserted from the top, then the puller is assembled as shown and the nut tightened to withdraw the mounting. If a similar arrangement using a conventional puller is not possible, use metal tubing, a long bolt, and large washers or a metal plate to remove the mounting.
7 The Vauxhall tool for inserting the mountings is shown in **(see illustration)**, and here again a similar tool may be fabricated from metal plate and a long bolt.

Refitting

8 Refitting is a reversal of removal.

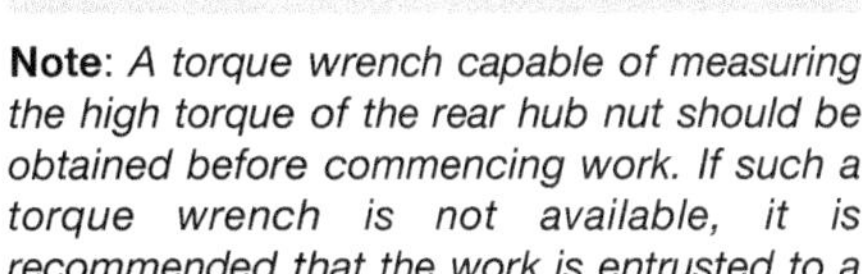

20 Rear hub and bearing - removal and refitting

Note: *A torque wrench capable of measuring the high torque of the rear hub nut should be obtained before commencing work. If such a torque wrench is not available, it is recommended that the work is entrusted to a Vauxhall dealer.*

Removal

1 Chock the front wheels, then jack up the rear of the vehicle and support it on axle stands.
2 Unscrew the socket-head bolts securing the driveshaft to the rear hub while holding the rear wheel stationary. Recover the lock-washers.
3 Lever the driveshaft from the rear hub and support it to one side.
4 Remove the rear wheel.
5 Disconnect the hydraulic brake hose from the bracket on the semi-trailing arm by pulling out the locking plate.
6 Unbolt and remove the brake caliper and support it to one side without straining the hydraulic brake hose Unscrew the retaining screw and remove the brake disc. Refer to Chapter 9 for details of both operations.
7 Refer to Chapter 10 and unbolt the shock absorber lower mounting bolt from the semi-trailing arm. Support the semi-trailing arm on the head of a trolley jack.
8 Using an Allen key through an unthreaded hole in the hub drive flange, unscrew the brake backplate mounting bolts. Note that the upper bolts are shorter and are fitted with a locking plate.
9 Insert the wheel bolts and use a long bar to hold the hub stationary, then remove the locking plate and unscrew the central hub-securing nut (exposed by the removal of driveshaft) from the rearward-facing surface of the hub **(see illustration)**.
10 Pull off the driveshaft flange using a suitable puller.
11 Press the rear hub outwards from the bearing using a suitable puller bolted to the semi-trailing arm.

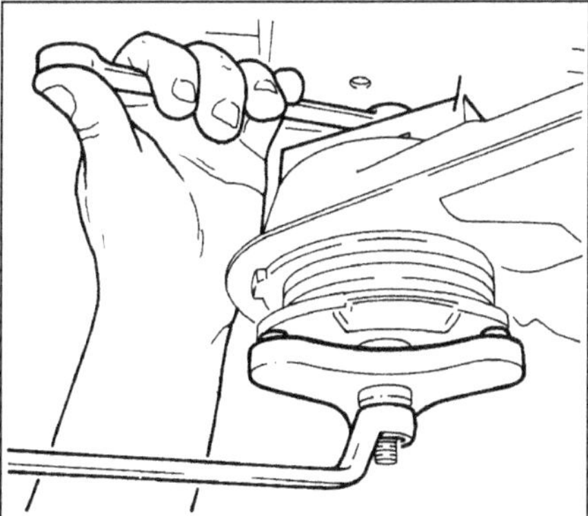

19.7 Pressing in the subframe mountings

12 Extract the circlip from the semi-trailing arm then press out the bearing, again using a bearing puller bolted to the arm.
13 If the inner bearing track has remained on the hub remove it with a bearing puller.
14 Clean all the components and examine them for wear and damage. Obtain a new bearing.

Refitting

15 Press the new bearing into the semi-trailing arm using pressure on the outer track. If necessary, a long bolt and a selection of flat washers may be used to do this.
16 Fit the bearing retaining circlip.
17 Support the wheel bearing inner track on the inside with a metal tube, then carefully drive in the rear hub from the outside.
18 Fit the driveshaft flange on the inside of the hub. If necessary, support the outside of the hub and drive the flange fully on from the inside.
19 Refit the hub nut and tighten to the specified torque while holding the hub stationary. Drive in the special locking plate to secure the nut in position.
20 The remainder of the refitting procedure is a reversal of removal, but note the following points.

a) Tighten all nuts and bolts to the specified torque wrench settings
b) Adjust the handbrake with reference to Chapter 1.

20.9 Driveshaft flange and rear hub nut

21 Steering wheel - removal and refitting

Models without driver's airbag

Removal

1 Disconnect the battery negative lead.
2 Set the front wheels in the straight-ahead position.
3 Prise the horn pad from the centre of the steering wheel and disconnect the two wires.
4 With the ignition key inserted check that the steering lock is disengaged.
5 Bend back the locktab and unscrew the retaining nut. Remove the locktab.
6 Mark the inner column and steering wheel in relation to each other then remove the steering wheel by carefully rocking it from side to side. Do not use a hammer or mallet to remove it.
7 If necessary, unclip the horn contact ring from the steering wheel, noting that the direction indicator return segment points to the left.
8 Check that the spring is located on the inner column, and lightly lubricate the horn contact finger with a copper-based grease.

Refitting

9 Refitting is a reversal of removal, but tighten the nut to the specified torque and bend up the locktab to lock the nut in position.

Models with driver's airbag

Warning: Refer to the Supplementary Restraint System (SRS) precautions given in Chapter 12 before disturbing the driver's airbag.

Removal

10 Before removing the driver's airbag, carry out the following operations: disconnect the negative cable from the battery and position it clear of the terminal. Wait at least one minute before proceeding, to allow the SRS control unit capacitor to discharge. Failure to observe these steps may result in accidental detonation of the airbag.
11 Remove the driver's airbag from the steering wheel, as described in Chapter 12, Section 24: Supplementary Restraint System (SRS) components - removal and refitting.
12 Set the steering wheel in the straight ahead position, then remove the ignition key and allow the steering column lock to engage. Ensure that the steering column remains in this position throughout the entire procedure.
13 Mark the relationship between the steering wheel and column to ensure correct alignment on refitting.
14 Unplug the horn button wiring at the multiway connector. Where applicable, also unplug the audio remote control button wiring **(see illustration)**.

21.14 Unplug the horn button/audio control wiring at the multiway connector(s)

21.15a Bend back the locktab . . .

21.15b . . . and then slacken . . .

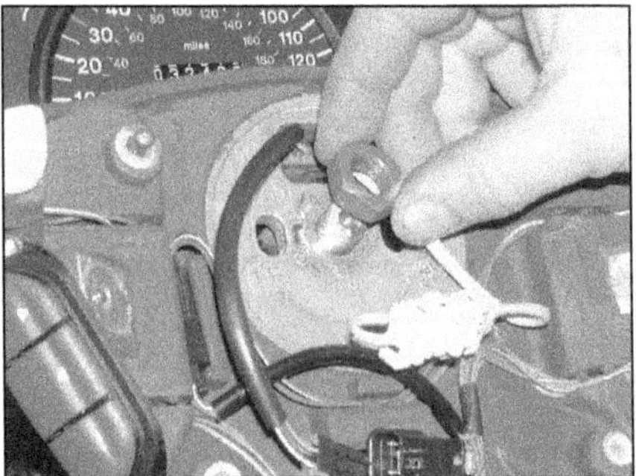

21.15c . . . and remove the steering wheel retaining nut . . .

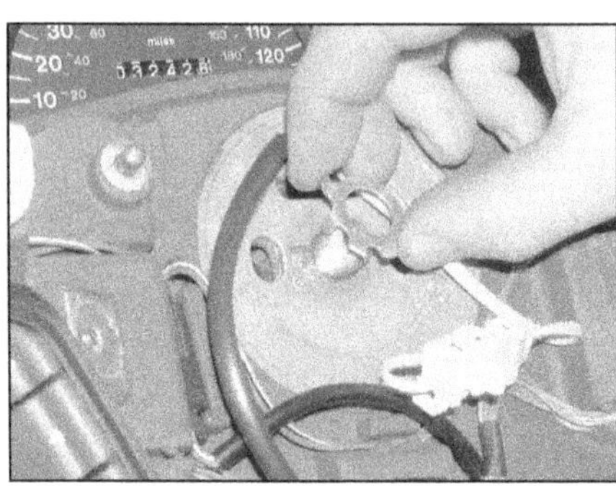

21.15d . . . and remove the locktab

21.16a Remove the steering wheel from the steering column

21.16b If necessary, use a proprietary steering wheel puller to assist removal

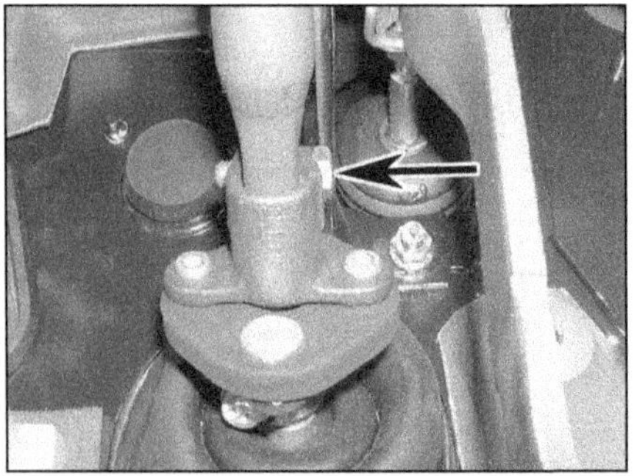

22.2 Unscrew and remove the upper clamp bolt (arrowed) to separate the inner section of the steering column from the flexible joint

15 Bend back the locktab and then unscrew the steering wheel retaining nut. Remove the locktab **(see illustrations)**.

16 Remove the steering wheel from the steering column by carefully rocking it from side to side. Do not use a hammer or mallet to remove it. Guide the horn and audio control wiring through the aperture at the centre of the steering wheel **(see illustrations)**.

Refitting

17 Refitting is a reversal of removal, but tighten the nut to the specified torque and bend up the locktab to lock the nut in position. Refit the driver's airbag with reference to Chapter 12, Section 24: Supplementary Restraint System (SRS) components - removal and refitting.

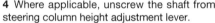

22 Steering column - removal and refitting

Removal

1 Park the vehicle on level ground with the steering wheel turned to the straight-ahead position. Disconnect the battery negative lead.

2 Working in the driver's footwell, release the clip and screws and detach the lower trim panel from underside of the facia. Mark the inner section of the steering column in relation to the flexible joint, then unscrew and remove the upper clamp bolt, to separate the end of the inner section of the steering column from the flexible joint **(see illustration)**.

3 Remove the steering wheel as described in Section 21. On models fitted with a driver's airbag, remove the airbag contact unit, with reference to Chapter 12, Section 24.

Warning: Refer to the precautions given in Chapter 12 before disturbing the any of Supplementary Restraint System (SRS) components.

4 Where applicable, unscrew the shaft from steering column height adjustment lever.

5 Remove the screws and withdraw the upper and lower shroud panels from the steering column.

6 Remove the steering column lock cylinder with reference to Section 23.

7 Remove the ignition switch contact unit with reference to Section 23.

8 Depress the locking clips and remove the stalk switch units from the steering column; refer to Chapter 12, Section 4.

9 At the lower edge of the facia, below the steering column, release the securing clip and hinge the access panel downwards away from the fuse box and relay box. Remove the screws, unhook the check strap and remove the lid from the facia.

10 Slacken and withdraw the securing screws, then release the fuse box and relay box from the facia, leaving the wiring harnesses connected.

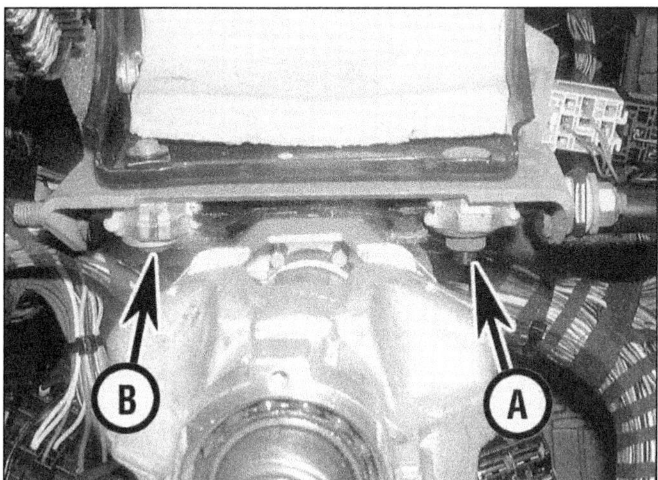

22.11 Steering column upper mounting nut (A) and shear bolt (B)

23.3 Slide the immobiliser receiver from the lock cylinder housing

11 The upper column mounting consists of a nut and a shear bolt **(see illustration)**. Ideally a bolt extractor should be used to remove the shear bolt by first drilling a 3.2 mm hole then using the extractor to unscrew the bolt. Alternatively, drill off the head and use grips to unscrew the remainder of the bolt later.

12 Unscrew the upper mounting nut and withdraw the steering column rearwards from the flexible coupling. The column should be handled carefully to avoid damage to the latticed safety outer column and special inner column.

Refitting

13 Refitting is a reversal of removal but tighten all nuts and bolts to the specified torque. Before tightening the shear bolt, check that the column is correctly aligned then tighten the bolt until the head shears off. Check that, with the front wheels in the straight-ahead position, the steering wheel spokes are centred. Before tightening the clamp bolt, check that the steering column is not stressed, then tighten the bolt to the specified torque. Make sure that the switch rubber grommets are correctly located in the upper shroud.

23 Steering column lock/ignition switch - removal and refitting

Lock cylinder

Removal

1 Remove the steering wheel as described in Section 21.

2 Slacken and withdraw the screws, then detach the upper lower sections of the shroud panelling from the steering column.

3 Unplug the wiring and slide the immobiliser receiver from the lock cylinder housing **(see illustration)**.

4 Insert the ignition key into the lock cylinder and turn it to position I.

5 Depress the recessed locking button with a suitable tool and withdraw the lock cylinder, together with the key from, from the housing **(see illustrations)**.

Refitting

6 Before inserting the lock cylinder into its housing, check that the steering lock bolt has not engaged; if this is the case, it will not be possible to fully insert the lock cylinder into the housing. Correct this condition by inserting a flat bladed screwdriver into the housing and pressing the locking button latch downwards, until the bolt disengages **(see illustration)**.

7 Slide the lock cylinder into its housing, until the locking bolt engages.

8 Where applicable, slide the immobiliser receiver into position over the lock cylinder housing and reconnect the wiring.

9 Refit the steering column shroud panelling and tighten the screws securely.

10 Reconnect the battery negative cable.

Ignition switch contact unit

Removal

11 Remove the lock cylinder as described in the previous sub-Section.

12 Unplug the multiway connector from the rear of the switch contact unit. To release the connector, depress the locking tab at the centre of the connector body using a thin flat bladed screwdriver **(see illustration)**. Carefully prise the connector from the contact unit by gently levering between them with a screwdriver - take care to avoid damaging the connector terminals.

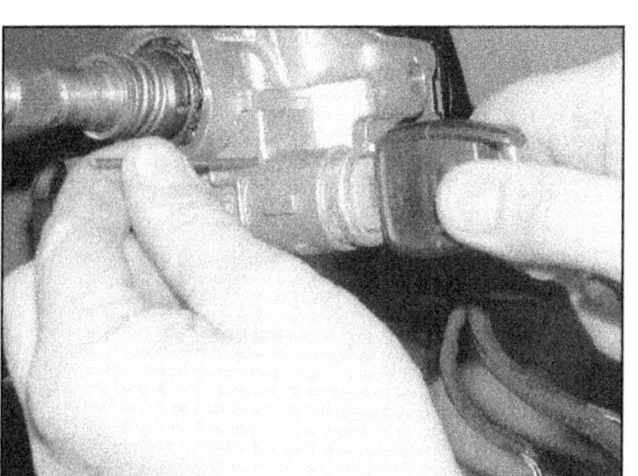
23.5a Depress the recessed locking button with a suitable tool . . .

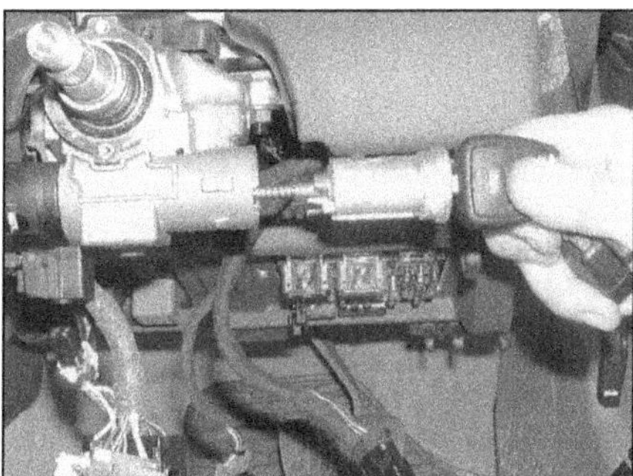
23.5b . . . and withdraw the lock cylinder, together with the key from, from the housing

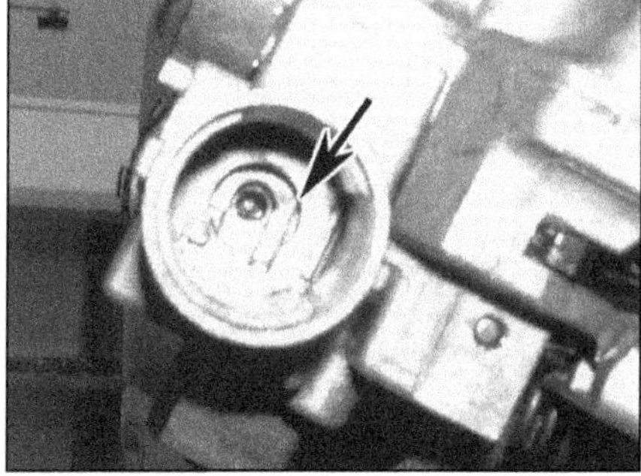
23.6 If necessary, press the locking button latch (arrowed) downwards, until the steering lock bolt disengages

23.12 Depress the connector body locking tab and unplug connector from the rear of the ignition switch contact unit

13 Depress the locking button using a suitable tool and withdraw the contact unit from the rear of the lock cylinder housing **(see illustrations)**.

Refitting

14 Refitting is a reversal of removal.

24 Steering gear - removal and refitting

Models with 4-cylinder engines

Removal

1 Park the vehicle on a level surface and set the steering wheel in the straight ahead position. On models with a driver's airbag, remove the ignition key and engage the steering column lock, to prevent rotation of the steering wheel.

2 Disconnect the battery negative cable and position it away from the terminal.

3 Apply the handbrake, select first gear (or Park, as applicable), then jack up the front of the vehicle and support it securely on axle stands.

4 Where applicable, remove the fixings and lower the undertray away from the engine bay.

5 Mark the position of the steering drop arm in relation to the steering gear arm. Unscrew the nut securing the steering drop arm to the bottom of the steering gear, then use a suitable puller to pull the arm from the splines on the sector shaft.

6 Working in the driver's footwell, remove the securing clips/screws and detach the trim panel from the lower side of the facia.

7 Unscrew and remove the upper clamp bolt from the steering column flexible coupling; refer to Section 22. Slacken and remove the lower clamp bolt, that secures the flexible joint to the top of the steering gear. Prise the flexible joint apart, to release it from the steering gear, then slide it upwards onto the steering column as far as it will go.

8 Position a container beneath the steering gear to catch any spilt hydraulic fluid.

9 Identify the pressure and return lines for location then unscrew the union nuts and pull the lines from the steering gear. Plug the line

23.13a Depress the locking button . . .

ends and steering gear ports to reduce leakage and to prevent the ingress of debris.

10 Unscrew the securing bolts and remove the metal heat shield from the steering gear casing.

11 Unscrew the mounting bolts and nuts and withdraw the steering gear via the underside of the vehicle. Recover any shims fitted and make a note of their locations to aid correct refitting.

Refitting

Note: *If you are fitting a new steering gear assembly to a pre- 1996 vehicle, it will be necessary to fit a modified steering gear-to-bulkhead rubber seal.*

12 Where applicable (see *Note* above), slide the new rubber seal over the steering gear, such that the OBEN marking is aligned with the identification plate on the steering gear.

13 With the steering wheel centralised, lift the steering gear into position and insert each of the securing bolts, together with any shims recovered during removal. Tighten the bolts progressively to the specified torque, in a clockwise sequence, starting with the upper left hand bolt, as viewed from the right hand wheel arch.

14 Ensure that the steering wheel and road wheels are still in the straight ahead position, then reconnect the steering drop arm to the steering gear sector shaft and tighten the nut to the specified torque. On models equipped with a driver's airbag, insert the ignition key to release the steering column lock and observe the alignment markings made during removal when reconnecting the drop arm to the steering gear.

15 Fit the heat shield to the steering gear casing, then insert and tighten the securing bolts to the specified torque.

16 Working inside the vehicle, slide the flexible coupling down the inner section of the steering column and engage it with the top of the steering gear. Insert the flexible coupling upper and lower clamp bolts and tighten them to the specified torque.

17 Refit the lower trim panel to the underside of the facia.

18 Fit new O-ring seals to the hydraulic pressure and return lines. Remove the plugs, then reconnect the pressure and return lines to the steering gear ports and tighten the

23.13b . . . and withdraw the contact unit from the rear of the lock cylinder housing

union nuts to the specified torque.

19 Refit the engine compartment undertray and tighten the screws securely.

20 Lower the vehicle to the ground, then reconnect the battery negative cable.

21 Check the fluid level in the power steering fluid reservoir. Top up if necessary and refit the cap.

22 With the engine idling, turn the steering from lock to lock several times in order to bleed trapped air from the system, then recheck and top-up the power steering fluid level.

Models with 6- cylinder engines

Removal

23 Park the vehicle on a level surface and set the steering wheel in the straight ahead position.

24 Disconnect the battery negative cable and position it away from the terminal.

25 Apply the handbrake, select first gear (or Park, as applicable), then jack up the front of the vehicle and support it securely on axle stands.

26 Remove the fixings and lower the undertray away from the engine bay.

27 Mark the position of the steering drop arm in relation to the steering gear arm. Unscrew the nut securing the steering drop arm to the bottom of the steering gear, then use a suitable puller to pull the arm from the splines on the sector shaft.

28 Unscrew the securing bolts and remove the metal heat shield from the steering gear casing.

29 Unplug the wiring harness from the steering gear transducer at the multiway connector.

30 Unbolt the engine movement damping strut from the right hand side of the engine, then remove the nut securing the right hand engine mounting block to the chassis bracket; see Chapter 2C, Section 17, for details.

31 On models with a driver's airbag, remove the ignition key and engage the steering column lock, to prevent rotation of the steering wheel.

32 Disconnect the vacuum hose from the brake servo, with reference to Chapter 9, Section 15.

33 Depressurise the fuel system as described in Chapter 4A, then unscrew the union nuts and disconnect the fuel supply and return lines from the manifold.

34 Unbolt the coolant reservoir from the bodywork and position it to one side, leaving the coolant hoses connected.
35 Disconnect the fuel vapour hoses from the charcoal canister ports, as described in Chapter 4B, Section 4.
36 Position a container beneath the steering gear to catch any spilt hydraulic fluid.
37 Identify the pressure and return lines for location then unscrew the union nuts and pull the lines from the steering gear **(see illustration)**. Plug the line ends and steering gear ports to reduce leakage and to prevent the ingress of debris.
38 Working in the driver's footwell, remove the securing clips/screws and detach the trim panel from the lower side of the facia. Remove the securing screws and detach the ventilation duct from the rear of the vent grille assembly and the side of the air distributor.
39 Unscrew and remove the upper clamp bolt from the steering column flexible coupling; refer to Section 22. Slacken and remove the lower clamp bolt, that secures the flexible joint to the top of the steering gear. Prise the flexible joint apart, to release it from the steering gear, then slide it upwards onto the steering column as far as it will go.
40 Attach an engine lifting hoist or beam to the engine lifting eyelets and raise the right hand side of the engine slightly - refer to the information given in Chapter 2C, Section 17. Raise the engine by about 3 cm to allow access to the steering gear.
41 Remove the starter motor as described in Chapter 5A.
42 Unscrew the mounting bolts and nuts and withdraw the steering gear via the underside of the vehicle **(see illustration)**. Recover any shims fitted and make a note of their locations to aid correct refitting.

Refitting

Note: *If you are fitting a new steering gear assembly to a pre- 1996 vehicle, it will be necessary to fit a modified steering gear-to-bulkhead rubber seal.*
43 Where applicable (see *Note* above), slide the new rubber seal over the steering gear, such that the OBEN marking is aligned with the identification plate on the steering gear.
44 With the steering wheel centralised, lift the steering gear into position and push the upper shaft as far as possible into the flexible joint. Insert each of the steering gear securing bolts, together with any shims/spacers recovered during removal. Tighten the bolts progressively to the specified torque, in a clockwise sequence, starting with the upper left hand bolt, as viewed from the right hand wheel arch.

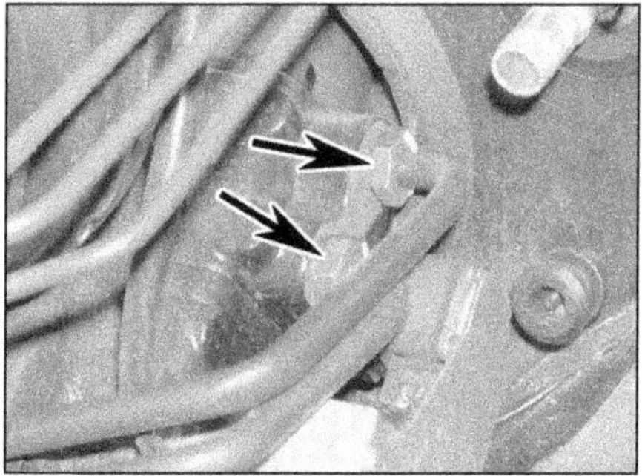
24.37 Power steering gear fluid pressure and return lines (arrowed)

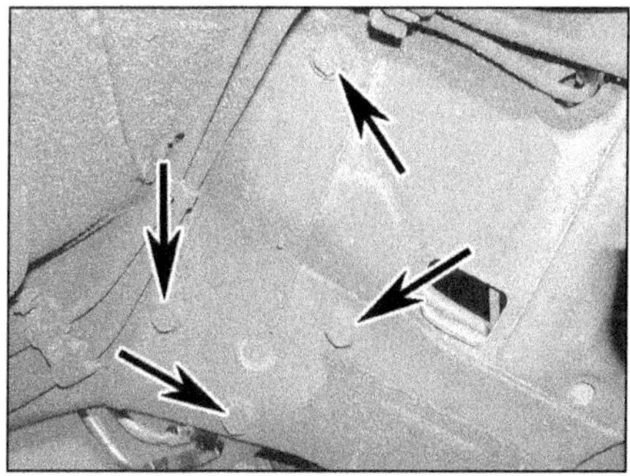
24.42 Steering gear mounting bolts viewed via right hand wheel arch

45 Reconnect the wiring to the steering gear transducer.
46 Refit the starter motor as described in Chapter 5A.
47 Working inside the vehicle, slide the flexible coupling down the inner section of the steering column and engage it with the top of the steering gear. Insert the flexible coupling upper and lower clamp bolts and tighten them to the specified torque.
48 Refit the ventilation duct, then refit the lower trim panel to the underside of the facia.
49 Lower the engine and remove the engine lifting equipment. Refit the engine mounting block securing nuts and the engine movement damper strut, as described in Chapter 2C, Section 17.
50 Reconnect the vacuum hose to the brake servo, with reference to Chapter 9, Section 15.
51 Refit the coolant reservoir to the bodywork and tighten the bolts securely.
52 Fit new O-ring seals to the hydraulic pressure and return lines. Remove the plugs, then reconnect the pressure and return lines to the steering gear ports and tighten the union nuts to the specified torque.
53 Reconnect the fuel supply and return lines to the manifold and tighten the union nuts to the specified torque.
54 Reconnect the fuel vapour hoses to the charcoal canister ports, with reference to Chapter 4B, Section 4.
55 Ensure that the steering wheel and road wheels are still in the straight ahead position, then reconnect the steering drop arm to the steering gear sector shaft and tighten the nut to the specified torque. Observe the alignment markings made during removal when reconnecting the drop arm to the steering gear.
56 Fit the heat shield to the steering gear casing, then insert and tighten the securing bolts to the specified torque.
57 Refit the engine compartment undertray and tighten the screws securely.
58 Lower the vehicle to the ground, then reconnect the battery negative cable.
59 Check the fluid level in the power steering fluid reservoir. Top up if necessary and refit the cap.
60 With the engine idling, turn the steering from lock to lock several times in order to bleed trapped air from the system, then recheck and top-up the power steering fluid level.

25 Steering tie-rods - removal and refitting

Removal

1 Apply the handbrake, jack up the front of the vehicle and support it on axle stands. Remove the front wheels.
2 To remove a side tie-rod unscrew the nuts and use a proprietary balljoint removal tool to press out the ball-pins **(see illustrations)**.

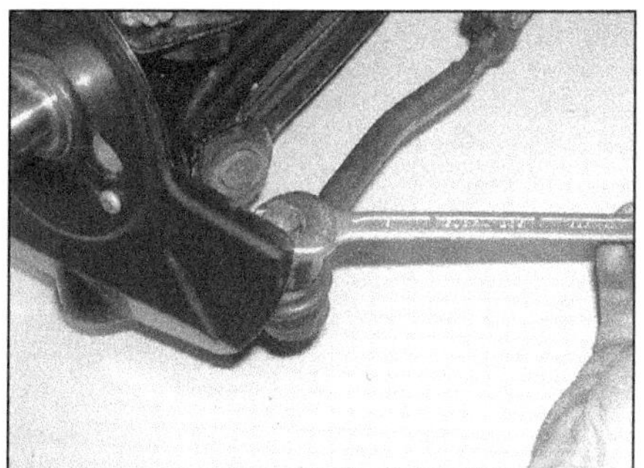
25.2a Unscrew the securing nut . . .

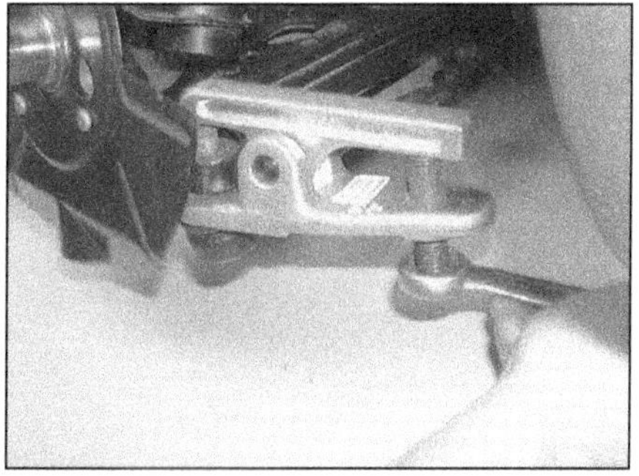
25.2b . . . and use a proprietary balljoint removal tool . . .

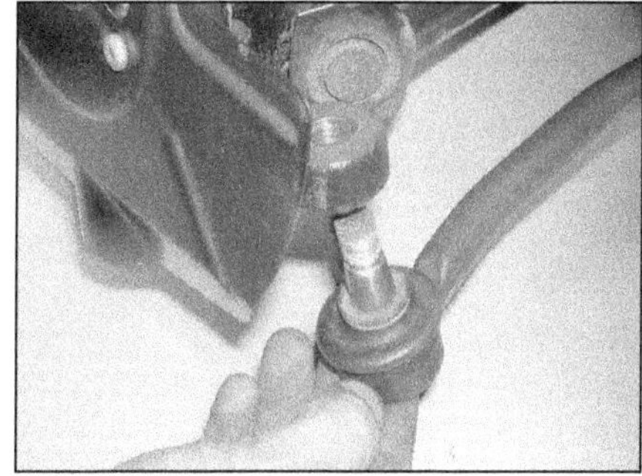
25.2c . . . to separate the tie rod from the steering knuckle

25.5a Centre tie rod - engine and transmission removed for clarity

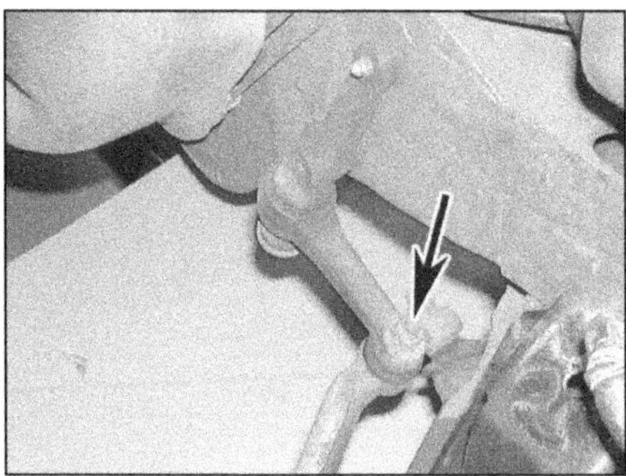

25.5b Centre tie-rod-to-idler balljoint nut (arrowed)

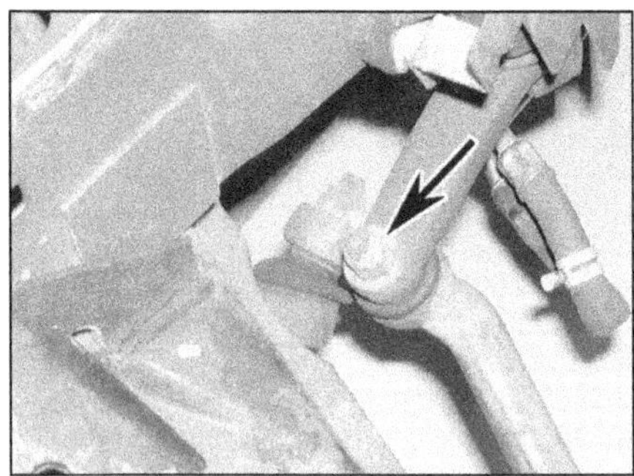

25.5c Centre tie-rod-to-steering gear drop arm balljoint nut (arrowed)

If it is required to renew just one tie-rod end, disconnect the appropriate end only.

3 Loosen the clamp bolts and unscrew the tie-rod ends from the tie-rod tube, counting the exact number of turns required to remove them.

4 To remove the centre tie-rod, the side tie-rods must first be disconnected at their inner ends as described in paragraph 2. Note the fitted position of the centre tie-rod, to ensure correct refitting: the light-coloured rubber cover is nearest the idler arm, the darker-coloured rubber cover is nearest the steering arm.

5 Unscrew the nuts and disconnect the centre tie-rod from the drop arm and idler arm using the balljoint removal tool **(see illustration)**.

Refitting

6 Refitting is a reversal of removal; screw the tie-rod ends into the tie rod tube by the same number of turns counted during removal. Use new self-locking nuts and tighten all nuts and bolts to the specified torques **(see illustration)**. On completion check and if necessary adjust the front wheel toe-in setting as described in Section 27.

26 Steering idler - removal and refitting

Removal

1 Apply the handbrake, jack up the front of the vehicle and support on axle stands. Remove the left-hand wheel.

2 Disconnect the centre tie-rod by unscrewing the nut and using a balljoint removal tool to press out the ball-pin.

3 Unscrew the nut from the bottom of the idler bracket, and remove the heat shield followed by the idler arm. It is not possible to renew the bush separately from the arm.

4 If necessary, unbolt the idler bracket from the underbody.

Refitting

5 Refitting is a reversal of removal, but use new self-locking nuts, and tighten nuts and bolts to the specified torques. When fitting the idler bracket bolts apply a little locking compound to their threads.

27 Power steering pump - removal and refitting

Models with 4-cylinder engines

Removal

1 Remove the auxiliary drive belt as described in Chapter 1.

2 Position a container beneath the power steering pump, then unscrew the union nut and disconnect the pressure pipe. Loosen the clip and disconnect the supply hose - allow the excess hydraulic fluid to drain into the container.

3 Support the pump and remove the three mounting bolts. Withdraw the pump from the engine compartment.

Refitting

4 Refit the power steering pump using a reversal of the removal procedure. Fit a new O-ring seal to the pump pressure pipe and tighten all unions, nuts and bolts to the specified torque wrench settings.

5 Refit the auxiliary drivebelt with reference to Chapter 1.

6 Pour fresh hydraulic fluid into the reservoir to the maximum level. Start the engine briefly, then switch off and top-up the fluid level. Do this several times until the level remains constant. With the engine idling, slowly turn the steering several times from lock to lock in order to purge air from the system.

7 With the engine stopped top up the fluid to the hot or cold level on the dipstick depending on the temperature of the engine (see *Weekly checks*). Refit the cap on completion.

25.6 Tighten all tie-rod nuts to the specified torques

Models with 6-cylinder engines

Removal

8 On models with air conditioning, have the refrigerant circuit discharged by a Vauxhall dealer or an air-conditioning specialist.

9 Remove the auxiliary drivebelt with reference to Chapter 1.

10 Grip the power steering pump pulley with a strap wrench, then slacken and remove the pulley securing bolts. Separate the pulley from the pump shaft.

11 Position a container beneath the power steering pump, then unscrew the union nut and disconnect the pressure pipe. Loosen the clip and disconnect the supply hose - allow the excess hydraulic fluid to drain into the container.

12 Raise the front of the vehicle and rest it securely on axle stands. Remove the securing screws and detach the cover from the underside of the engine compartment.

13 Remove the screw and disconnect the earth cable from the power steering pump support mounting bracket.

14 Unbolt and remove the exhaust gas recirculation (EGR) valve bracing bar. Remove the securing screws and detach the support bracket from the underside of the power steering pump.

15 Unbolt the air conditioning refrigerant compressor from the power steering pump mounting bracket, with reference to Chapter 3, Section 12.

16 Slacken and withdraw the three bolts and withdraw the power steering pump mounting bracket from the engine, with the pump still attached.

17 Unbolt the power steering pump from its support bracket.

Refitting

18 Refit the power steering pump using a reversal of the removal procedure. Fit a new O-ring seal to the pump pressure pipe and tighten all unions, nuts and bolts to the correct torque wrench settings, where specified.

19 Refit the auxiliary drivebelt with reference to Chapter 1.

20 Have the air conditioning system recharged by a Vauxhall dealer, or an air conditioning specialist.

21 Pour fresh hydraulic fluid into the reservoir to the maximum level. Start the engine briefly, then switch off and top-up the fluid level. Do this several times until the level remains constant. With the engine idling, slowly turn the steering several times from lock to lock in order to purge air from the system.

22 With the engine stopped top up the fluid to the hot or cold level on the dipstick depending on the temperature of the engine (see *Weekly checks*). Refit the filler cap on completion.

28 Wheel alignment - checking and adjustment

1 Accurate wheel alignment is essential for positive, accurate steering, stable road holding and to prevent abnormal tyre wear. Wheel alignment checking is carried out with the car loaded to its kerbside weight, and with the tyre pressures correctly adjusted.

2 The front toe setting, front camber angle, rear toe setting and rear camber angle are all adjustable, but can only be checked using specialised equipment; work of this nature should therefore be entrusted to a Vauxhall dealer or suitably-equipped tyre specialist.

Chapter 11
Bodywork and fittings

Contents

Degrees of difficulty

Easy, suitable for novice with little experience 

Fairly easy, suitable for beginner with some experience 

Fairly difficult, suitable for competent DIY mechanic 

Difficult, suitable for experienced DIY mechanic 

Very difficult, suitable for expert DIY or professional

Specifications

Torque wrench settings	**Nm**	**lbf ft**
Driver's airbag unit to steering wheel	8	6
Front seat to floorpan*	20	15
Passenger airbag mounting bracket*	20	15
Passenger airbag unit to mounting bracket*	8	6
Seat belt anchor bolts	35	26
Seat belt height adjustment bracket	20	15
Seat belt inertia reel	35	26
Steering wheel	20	15

* *Use a new nut/bolt/screw*

1 General information

The bodyshell is of four-door Saloon, or five-door Estate configuration, and is made of high-strength low alloy sheet metal sections. The sections are alloy-galvanized on one or both sides, depending on their position on the vehicle. Most components are welded together, but some use is made of structural adhesives. The front wings are bolted on.

The bonnet, doors and some other vulnerable panels are made of zinc-coated metal, and are further protected by being coated with an anti-chip primer prior to being sprayed. The front and rear doors incorporate safety bars as protection in the event of a side impact.

Electrically operated front windows are fitted to all models. Electrically operated rear windows fitted as standard equipment on CD, CDX and Elite models and are optional on lower specification models.

Extensive use is made of plastic materials, mainly in the interior, but also in exterior components. The front and rear bumpers and the front grille are injection-moulded from a synthetic material which is very strong, and yet light. Plastic components such as wheel arch liners are fitted to the underside of the vehicle, to improve the body's resistance to corrosion.

2 Maintenance - bodywork and underframe

The general condition of a vehicle's bodywork is the one thing that significantly affects its value. Maintenance is easy, but needs to be regular. Neglect, particularly after minor damage, can lead quickly to further deterioration and costly repair bills. It is important also to keep watch on those parts of the vehicle not immediately visible, for instance the underside, inside all the wheel arches, and the lower part of the engine compartment.

The basic maintenance routine for the bodywork is washing - preferably with a lot of water, from a hose. This will remove all the loose solids which may have stuck to the vehicle. It is important to flush these off in such a way as to prevent grit from scratching the finish. The wheel arches and underframe need washing in the same way, to remove any accumulated mud which will retain moisture and tend to encourage rust. Paradoxically enough, the best time to clean the underframe and wheel arches is in wet weather, when the mud is thoroughly wet and soft. In very wet weather, the underframe is usually cleaned of large accumulations automatically, and this is a good time for inspection.

Periodically, except on vehicles with a wax-based underbody protective coating, it is a good idea to have the whole of the underframe of the vehicle steam-cleaned, engine compartment included, so that a thorough inspection can be carried out to see what minor repairs and renovations are necessary. Steam-cleaning is available at many garages, and is necessary for the removal of the accumulation of oily grime, which sometimes is allowed to become thick in certain areas. If steam-cleaning facilities are not available, there are one or two excellent grease solvents available, which can be brush-applied; the dirt can then be simply hosed off. Note that these methods should not be used on vehicles with wax-based underbody protective coating, or the coating will be removed. Such vehicles should be inspected annually, preferably just prior to Winter, when the underbody should be washed down, and any damage to the wax coating repaired. Ideally, a completely fresh coat should be applied. It would also be worth considering the use of such wax-based protection for injection into door panels, sills, box sections, etc, as an additional safeguard against rust damage, where such protection is not provided by the vehicle manufacturer.

After washing paintwork, wipe off with a chamois leather to give an unspotted clear finish. A coat of clear protective wax polish will give added protection against chemical pollutants in the air. If the paintwork sheen has dulled or oxidised, use a cleaner/polisher combination to restore the brilliance of the shine. This requires a little effort, but such dulling is usually caused because regular washing has been neglected. Care needs to be taken with metallic paintwork, as special non-abrasive cleaner/polisher is required to avoid damage to the finish. Always check that the door and ventilator opening drain holes and pipes are completely clear, so that water can be drained out. Brightwork should be treated in the same way as paintwork. Windscreens and windows can be kept clear of the smeary film which often appears, by the use of proprietary glass cleaner. Never use any form of wax or other body or chromium polish on glass.

3 Maintenance - upholstery and carpets

Mats and carpets should be brushed or vacuum-cleaned regularly, to keep them free of grit. If they are badly stained, remove them from the vehicle for scrubbing or sponging, and make quite sure they are dry before refitting. Seats and interior trim panels can be kept clean by wiping with a damp cloth. If they do become stained (which can be more apparent on light-coloured upholstery), use a little liquid detergent and a soft nail brush to scour the grime out of the grain of the material. Do not forget to keep the headlining clean in the same way as the upholstery. When using liquid cleaners inside the vehicle, do not over-wet the surfaces being cleaned. Excessive damp could get into the seams and padded interior, causing stains, offensive odours or even rot. If the inside of the vehicle gets wet accidentally, it is worthwhile taking some trouble to dry it out properly, particularly where carpets are involved. *Do not leave oil or electric heaters inside the vehicle for this purpose.*

4 Minor body damage - repair

Repairs of minor scratches in bodywork

If the scratch is very superficial, and does not penetrate to the metal of the bodywork, repair is very simple. Lightly rub the area of the scratch with a paintwork renovator, or a very fine cutting paste, to remove loose paint from the scratch, and to clear the surrounding bodywork of wax polish. Rinse the area with clean water.

Apply touch-up paint to the scratch using a fine paint brush; continue to apply fine layers of paint until the surface of the paint in the scratch is level with the surrounding paintwork. Allow the new paint at least two weeks to harden, then blend it into the surrounding paintwork by rubbing the scratch area with a paintwork renovator or a very fine cutting paste. Finally, apply wax polish.

Where the scratch has penetrated right through to the metal of the bodywork, causing the metal to rust, a different repair technique is required. Remove any loose rust from the bottom of the scratch with a penknife, then apply rust-inhibiting paint, to prevent the formation of rust in the future. Using a rubber or nylon applicator, fill the scratch with bodystopper paste. If required, this paste can be mixed with cellulose thinners, to provide a very thin paste which is ideal for filling narrow scratches. Before the stopper-paste in the scratch hardens, wrap a piece of smooth cotton rag around the top of a finger. Dip the finger in cellulose thinners, and quickly sweep it across the surface of the stopper-paste in the scratch; this will ensure that the surface of the stopper-paste is slightly hollowed. The scratch can now be painted over as described earlier in this Section.

Repairs of dents in bodywork

When deep denting of the vehicle's bodywork has taken place, the first task is to pull the dent out, until the affected bodywork almost attains its original shape. There is little point in trying to restore the original shape completely, as the metal in the damaged area will have stretched on impact, and cannot be reshaped fully to its original contour. It is better to bring the level of the dent up to a point which is about 3 mm below the level of the surrounding bodywork. In cases where the dent is very shallow anyway, it is not worth trying to pull it out at all. If the underside of the dent is accessible, it can be hammered out gently from behind, using a mallet with a wooden or plastic head. Whilst doing this, hold a suitable block of wood firmly against the outside of the panel, to absorb the impact from the hammer blows and thus prevent a large area of the bodywork from being 'belled-out'.

Should the dent be in a section of the bodywork which has a double skin, or some other factor making it inaccessible from behind, a different technique is called for. Drill several small holes through the metal inside the area - particularly in the deeper section. Then screw long self-tapping screws into the holes, just sufficiently for them to gain a good purchase in the metal. Now the dent can be pulled out by pulling on the protruding heads of the screws with a pair of pliers.

The next stage of the repair is the removal of the paint from the damaged area, and from an inch or so of the surrounding 'sound' bodywork. This is accomplished most easily by using a wire brush or abrasive pad on a power drill, although it can be done just as effectively by hand, using sheets of abrasive paper. To complete the preparation for filling, score the surface of the bare metal with a screwdriver or the tang of a file, or alternatively, drill small holes in the affected area. This will provide a really good 'key' for the filler paste.

To complete the repair, see the Section on filling and respraying.

Repairs of rust holes or gashes in bodywork

Remove all paint from the affected area, and from an inch or so of the surrounding 'sound' bodywork, using an abrasive pad or a wire brush on a power drill. If these are not available, a few sheets of abrasive paper will do the job most effectively. With the paint removed, you will be able to judge the severity of the corrosion, and therefore decide whether to renew the whole panel (if this is possible) or to repair the affected area. New body panels are not as expensive as most people think, and it is often quicker and more satisfactory to fit a new panel than to attempt to repair large areas of corrosion.

Remove all fittings from the affected area, except those which will act as a guide to the original shape of the damaged bodywork (eg headlamp shells etc). Then, using tin snips or a hacksaw blade, remove all loose metal and any other metal badly affected by corrosion. Hammer the edges of the hole inwards, in order to create a slight depression for the filler paste.

Wire-brush the affected area to remove the powdery rust from the.
surface of the remaining metal. Paint the affected area with rust-inhibiting paint; if the back of the rusted area is accessible, treat this also.

Before filling can take place, it will be necessary to block the hole in some way. This can be achieved by the use of aluminium or plastic mesh, or aluminium tape.

Aluminium or plastic mesh, or glass-fibre matting is probably the best material to use for a large hole. Cut a piece to the approximate size and shape of the hole to be filled, then position it in the hole so that its edges are below the level of the surrounding bodywork. It can be retained in position by several blobs of filler paste around its periphery.

Aluminium tape should be used for small or very narrow holes. Pull a piece off the roll, trim it to the approximate size and shape required, then pull off the backing paper (if used) and stick the tape over the hole; it can be overlapped if the thickness of one piece is insufficient. Burnish down the edges of the tape with the handle of a screwdriver or similar, to ensure that the tape is securely attached to the metal underneath.

Bodywork repairs - filling and respraying

Before using this Section, see the Sections on dent, deep scratch, rust holes and gash repairs.

Many types of bodyfiller are available, but generally speaking, those proprietary kits which contain a tin of filler paste and a tube of resin hardener are best for this type of repair. A wide, flexible plastic or nylon applicator will be found invaluable for imparting a smooth and well-contoured finish to the surface of the filler.

Mix up a little filler on a clean piece of card or board - measure the hardener carefully (follow the maker's instructions on the pack), otherwise the filler will set too rapidly or too slowly. Using the applicator, apply the filler paste to the prepared area; draw the applicator across the surface of the filler to achieve the correct contour and to level the surface. As soon as a contour that approximates to the correct one is achieved, stop working the paste - if you carry on too long, the paste will become sticky and begin to 'pick-up' on the applicator. Continue to add thin layers of filler paste at 20-minute intervals, until the level of the filler is just proud of the surrounding bodywork.

Once the filler has hardened, the excess can be removed using a metal plane or file. From then on, progressively-finer grades of abrasive paper should be used, starting with a 40-grade production paper, and finishing with a 400-grade wet-and-dry paper. Always wrap the abrasive paper around a flat rubber, cork, or wooden block - otherwise the surface of the filler will not be completely flat. During the smoothing of the filler surface, the wet-and-dry paper should be periodically rinsed in water. This will ensure that a very smooth finish is imparted to the filler at the final stage.

At this stage, the 'dent' should be surrounded by a ring of bare metal, which in turn should be encircled by the finely 'feathered' edge of the good paintwork. Rinse the repair area with clean water, until all of the dust produced by the rubbing-down operation has gone.

Spray the whole area with a light coat of - this will show up any imperfections in the surface of the filler. Repair these imperfections with fresh filler paste or bodystopper, and once more smooth the surface with abrasive paper. If bodystopper is used, it can be mixed with cellulose thinners, to form a really thin paste which is ideal for filling small holes. Repeat this spray-and-repair procedure until you are satisfied that the surface of the filler, and the feathered edge of the paintwork, are perfect. Clean the repair area with clean water, and allow to dry fully.

The repair area is now ready for final spraying. Paint spraying must be carried out in a warm, dry, windless and dust-free atmosphere. This condition can be created artificially if you have access to a large indoor working area, but if you are forced to work in the open, you will have to pick your day very carefully. If you are working indoors, dousing the floor in the work area with water will help to settle the dust which would otherwise be in the atmosphere. If the repair area is confined to one body panel, mask off the surrounding panels; this will help to minimise the effects of a slight mis-match in paint colours. Bodywork fittings (eg chrome strips, door handles etc) will also need to be masked off. Use genuine masking tape, and several thicknesses of newspaper, for the masking operations.

Before commencing to spray, agitate the aerosol can thoroughly, then spray a test area (an old tin, or similar) until the technique is mastered. Cover the repair area with a thick coat of primer; the thickness should be built up using several thin layers of paint, rather than one thick one. Using 400 grade wet-and-dry paper, rub down the surface of the primer until it is really smooth. While doing this, the work area should be thoroughly doused with water, and the wet-and-dry paper periodically rinsed in water. Allow to dry before spraying on more paint.

Spray on the top coat, again building up the thickness by using several thin layers of paint. Start spraying in the centre of the repair area, and then, using a circular motion, work outwards until the whole repair area and about 2 inches of the surrounding original paintwork is covered. Remove all masking material 10 to 15 minutes after spraying on the final coat of paint.

Allow the new paint at least two weeks to harden, then, using a paintwork renovator or a very fine cutting paste, blend the edges of the paint into the existing paintwork. Finally, apply wax polish.

Plastic components

With the use of more and more plastic body components by the vehicle manufacturers (eg bumpers. spoilers, and in some cases major body panels), rectification of more serious damage to such items has become a matter of either entrusting repair work to a specialist in this field, or renewing complete components. Repair of such damage by the DIY owner is not really feasible, owing to the cost of the equipment and materials required for effecting such repairs. The basic technique involves making a groove along the line of the crack in the plastic, using a rotary burr in a power drill. The damaged part is then welded back together, using a hot air gun to heat up and fuse a plastic filler rod into the groove. Any excess plastic is then removed, and the area rubbed down to a smooth finish. It is important that a filler rod of the correct plastic is used, as body components can be made of a variety of different types (eg polycarbonate, ABS, polypropylene).

Damage of a less serious nature (abrasions, minor cracks etc) can be repaired by the DIY owner using a two-part epoxy filler repair. Once mixed in equal, this is used in similar fashion to the bodywork filler used on metal panels. The filler is usually cured in twenty to thirty minutes, ready for sanding and painting.

If the owner is renewing a complete component himself, or if he has repaired it with epoxy filler, he will be left with the problem of finding a suitable paint for finishing which is compatible with the type of plastic used. At one time, the use of a universal paint was not possible, owing to the complex range of plastics encountered in body component applications. Standard paints, generally speaking, will not bond to plastic or rubber satisfactorily, but suitable paints to match any plastic or rubber finish, can be obtained from dealers. However, it is now possible to obtain a plastic body parts finishing kit which consists of a pre-primer treatment, a primer and coloured top coat. Full instructions are normally supplied with a kit, but basically, the method of use is to first apply the pre-primer to the component concerned, and allow it to dry for up to 30 minutes. Then the primer is applied, and left to dry for about an hour before finally applying the special-coloured top coat. The result is a correctly-coloured component, where the paint will flex with the plastic or rubber, a property that standard paint does not normally possess.

5 Major body damage - repair

Where serious damage has occurred, or large areas need renewal due to neglect, it means that complete new panels will need welding-in, and this is best left to professionals. If the damage is due to impact, it will also be necessary to check completely the alignment of the bodyshell, and this can only be carried out accurately by a Vauxhall/Opel dealer using special jigs. If the body is left misaligned, it is primarily dangerous, as the car will not handle properly, and secondly, uneven stresses will be imposed on the steering, suspension and possibly transmission, causing abnormal wear, or complete failure, particularly to such items as the tyres.

6 Bumpers - removal and refitting

Front bumper

Removal

1 Remove the radiator grille as described in Section 7. Remove the securing screws and detach the trim panels from the lower edge of each headlamp unit **(see illustrations).**

2 Remove the screws securing the lower edge of the front wheel arch liner in position, then unscrew and remove the two mounting screws from the trailing edge of the bumper moulding **(see illustrations).**

3 Remove the plastic rivets securing the lower edge of the front bumper to the front valance. To do this, depress the centre pins using a screwdriver, then prise out the rivet body **(see illustrations)**.

4 Unscrew and remove the upper mounting bolts, located next to the headlamp units, then carefully withdraw the front bumper from the front of the vehicle **(see illustrations)**. As the wiring becomes accessible, unplug the wiring from the foglamps and ambient air temperature sensor (where applicable).

5 If required, slacken and withdraw the securing bolts and then withdraw the bumper centre member from the front of the vehicle **(see illustrations).**

6.1a Remove the securing screws . . .

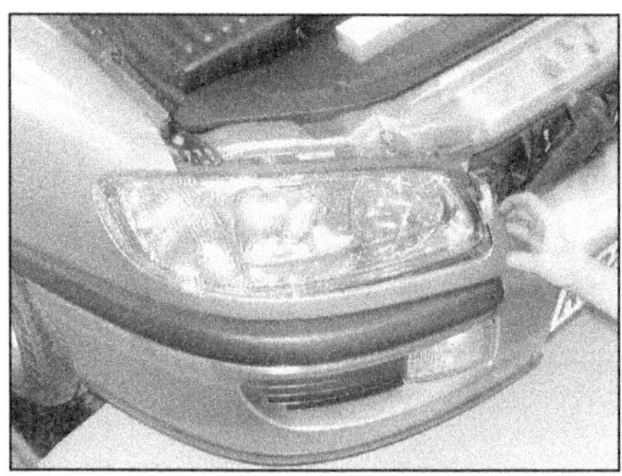

6.1b . . . and detach the trim panels from the lower edge of each headlamp unit

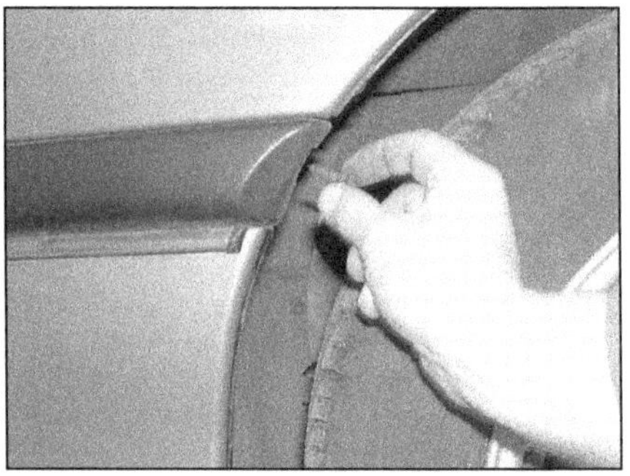

6.2a Unscrew and remove the upper . . .

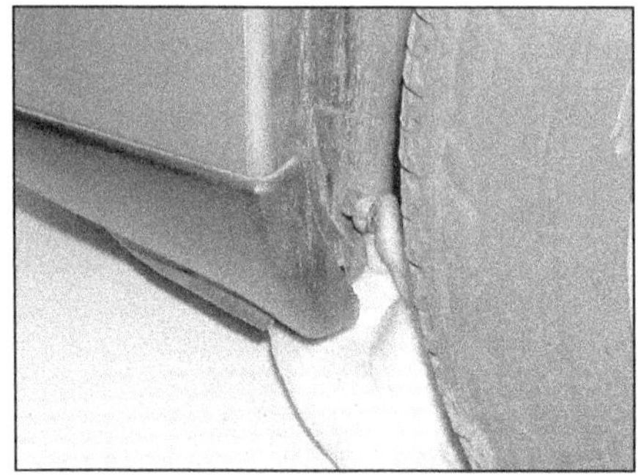

6.2b . . . and lower mounting screws from the trailing edge of the bumper moulding

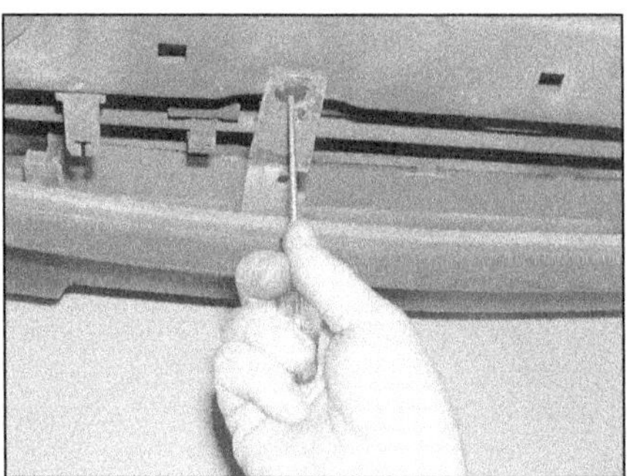

6.3a Depress the centre pins using a screwdriver . . .

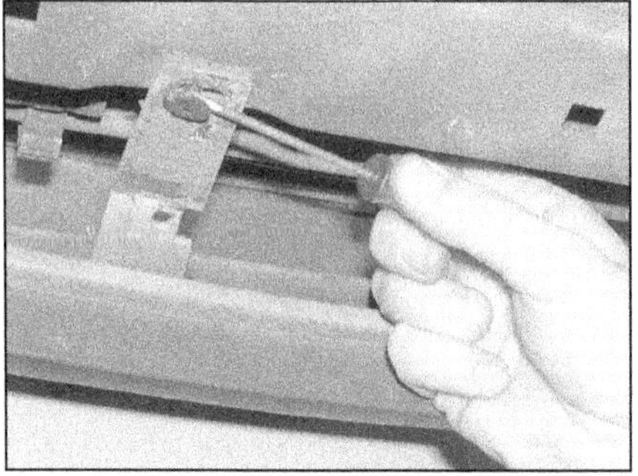

6.3b . . . then remove the plastic rivets securing the lower edge of the front bumper to the front valance

6.4a Unscrew and remove the upper mounting bolts . . .

6.4b . . . then carefully withdraw the front bumper from the front of the vehicle

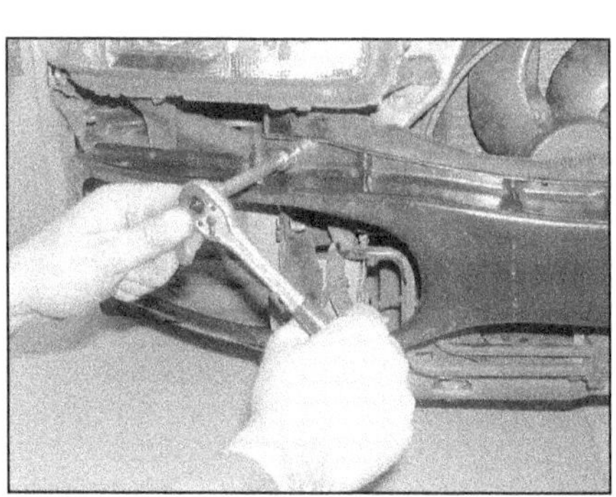

6.5a Slacken and withdraw the securing bolts . . .

6.5b . . . and then withdraw the bumper centre member from the front of the vehicle

6.7 Unscrew the bolts securing the upper and lower leading edge of the bumper moulding to the bodywork

6.8 Remove the screws and withdraw the boot striker trim panel

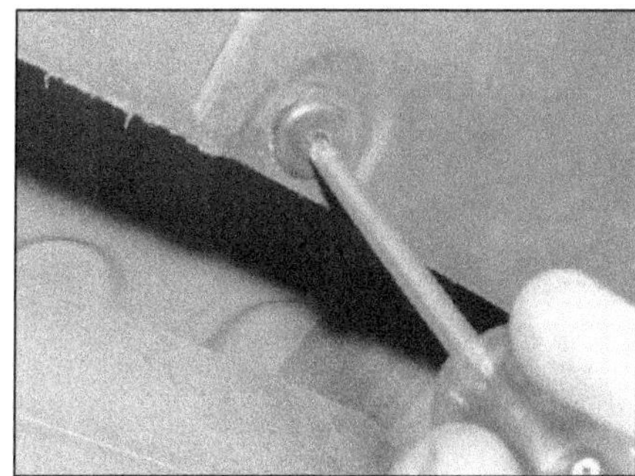

6.9a Depress the centre pins using a screwdriver . . .

Refitting

6 Refitting is a reversal of removal, noting the following points.

a) Tighten all fixings to the correct torque, where specified.

b) When refitting the headlamp trim panels, ensure that the locating lugs engage which their corresponding recesses.

c) Ensure that the ambient temperature sensor wiring is securely reconnected, where applicable.

Rear bumper - Saloon models

Removal

7 At the rear of each wheel arch, unscrew the

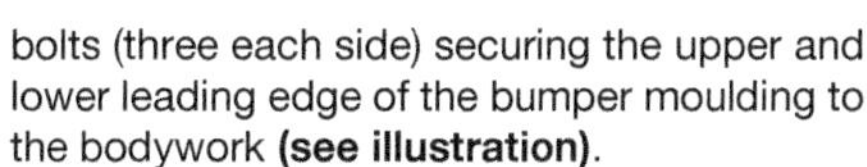

bolts (three each side) securing the upper and lower leading edge of the bumper moulding to the bodywork **(see illustration)**.

8 Open the bootlid, then remove the screws and withdraw the boot striker trim panel **(see illustration).**

9 Remove the plastic rivets securing the lower edge of the bumper to the rear valance. To do this, depress the centre pins using a screwdriver, then prise out the rivet body **(see illustrations)**.

10 Prise off the protective caps, then unscrew the four screws securing the upper edge of the bumper moulding to the bodywork **(see illustration)**.

11 Carefully withdraw the rear bumper from the rear of the vehicle, disconnecting the number plate lamp unit wiring as it becomes accessible **(see illustration)**.

12 To remove the rear bumper centre member, slacken and withdraw the securing nuts, then detach the centre member from its mounting bracket **(see illustrations)**.

Refitting

13 Refitting is a reversal of removal but tighten all fixings to the correct torque, where specified.

Rear bumper - Estate models

Removal

14 Remove the securing screws and detach the lower edges of the plastic liners from both rear wheel arches **(see illustration)**.

6.9b . . . then prise out the plastic rivets securing the lower edge of the bumper to the rear valance

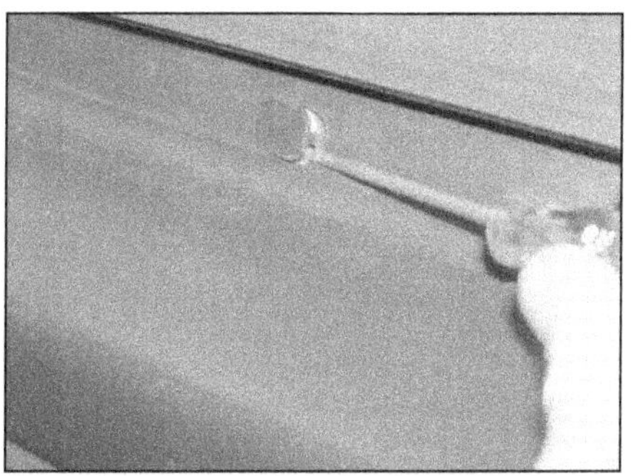

6.10 Prise off the protective caps and remove the screws securing the upper edge of the bumper moulding to the bodywork

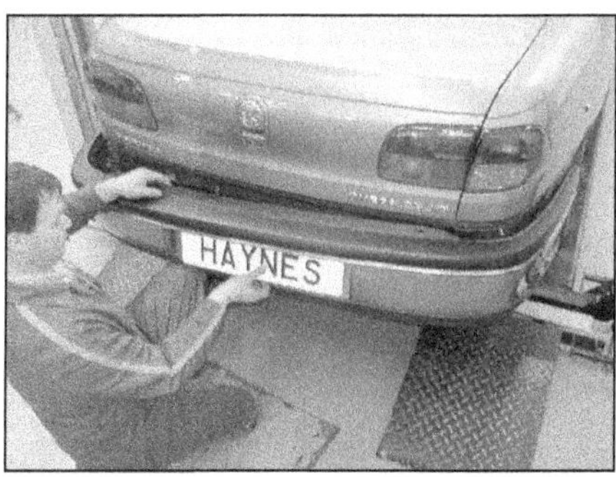

6.11 Carefully withdraw the rear bumper from the vehicle

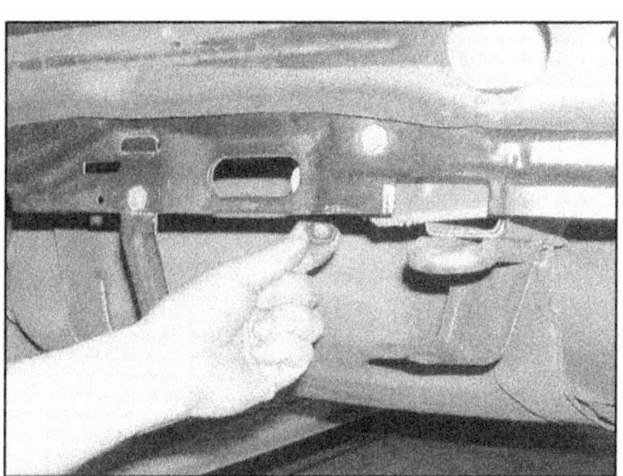

6.12a Slacken and withdraw the securing nuts . . .

6.12b . . . then detach the centre member from its mounting bracket

6.14 Remove the securing screws and detach the lower edges of the plastic liners from both rear wheel arches

6.15 Unscrew the securing bolts and remove the reflectors from the underside of each rear light unit

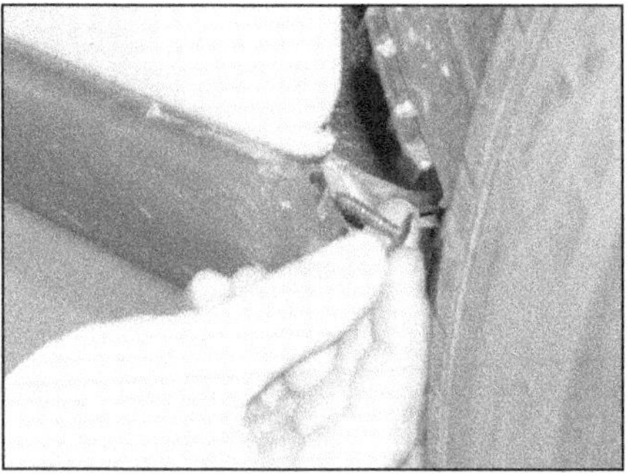
6.16 unscrew the bolts securing the leading edge of the bumper moulding to the bodywork

6.17a Depress the centre pins using a screwdriver . . .

6.17b . . . then prise out the plastic rivets securing the lower edge of the bumper to the rear valance

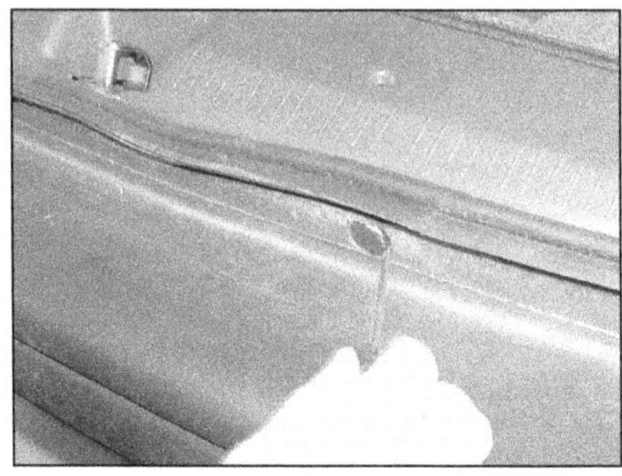
6.18a Prise off the protective caps . . .

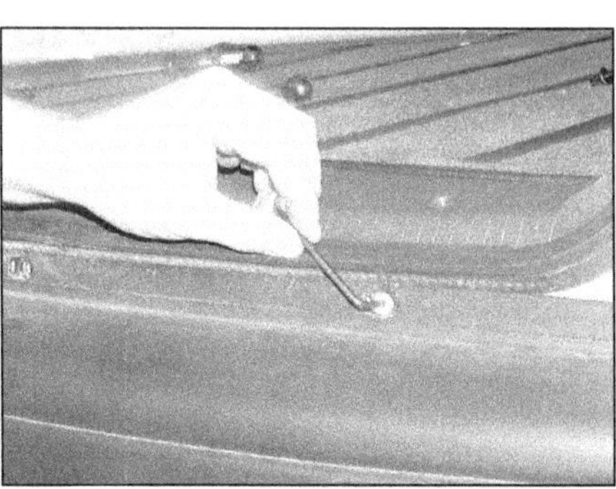
6.18b . . . then unscrew the screws securing the upper edge of the bumper moulding to the bodywork

15 Unscrew the securing bolts and remove the reflectors from the underside of each rear light unit **(see illustration)**.

6.19 Carefully withdraw the rear bumper from the rear of the vehicle

16 At the rear of each wheel arch, unscrew the bolts (one each side) securing the leading edge of the bumper moulding to the bodywork **(see illustration)**.

17 Remove the plastic rivets securing the lower edge of the bumper to the rear valance. To do this, depress the centre pins using a screwdriver, then prise out the rivet body **(see illustrations)**.

18 Prise off the protective caps, then unscrew the six screws securing the upper edge of the bumper moulding to the bodywork **(see illustrations)**.

19 Carefully withdraw the rear bumper from the rear of the vehicle **(see illustration)**. To remove the rear bumper centre member, slacken and withdraw the four securing bolts, then detach the centre member from its mounting bracket.

Refitting

20 Refitting is a reversal of removal but tighten all fixings to the correct torque, where specified.

7 Radiator grille - removal and refitting

Removal

1 Open the bonnet, then slacken and withdraw the radiator grille upper mounting screws **(see illustration)**.

2 Depress the locking catch, then lift the radiator grille from the front bumper **(see illustrations)**.

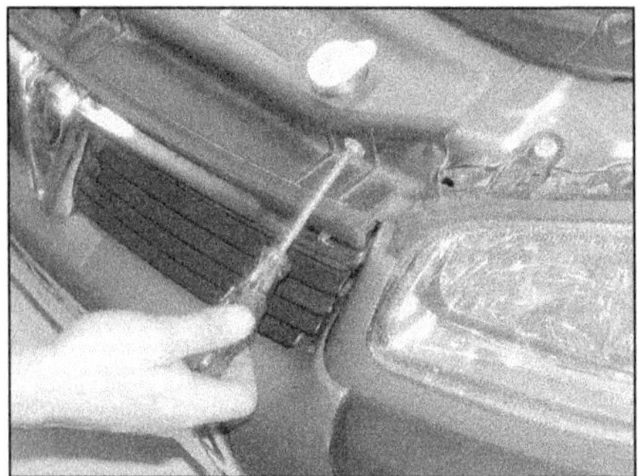
7.1 Slacken and withdraw the radiator grille upper mounting screws

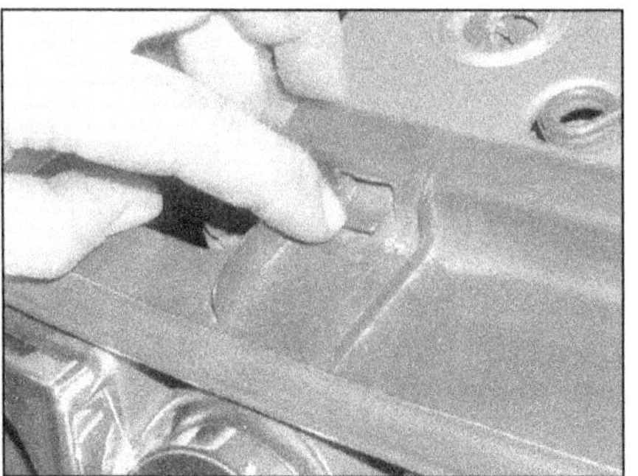
7.2a Depress the locking catch . . .

7.2b . . . then lift the radiator grille from the front bumper

Refitting

3 Refitting is a reversal of removal, ensuring that the lugs on the lower edge of the grille engage correctly with the corresponding recesses in the upper edge of the bumper.

8 Bonnet and support struts - removal, refitting and adjustment

Bonnet

Removal

1 Open the bonnet, and have an assistant support it. Disconnect the support struts from the bonnet balljoints, as described in the next sub-Section.
2 Using a marker pen or paint, mark around the hinge positions on the bonnet.
3 Disconnect the windscreen washer fluid hose at the connector and support. Unplug the wiring harness at the connector.
4 With the aid of the assistant, unscrew the bolts securing the bonnet to the hinges on both sides.
5 Lift off the bonnet taking care not to damage the vehicle paintwork.

Refitting

6 With the aid of the assistant, align the marks made on the bonnet before removal with the hinges, then refit and tighten the bonnet securing bolts.
7 Reconnect the windscreen washer fluid hose and wiring harness.
8 Refit the support struts to the bonnet as described in the next sub-Section, then check the bonnet adjustment as follows.

Adjustment

9 Lower the bonnet slowly to its closed position, ensuring that misalignment does not cause the edges of the bonnet to strike the wings. Check that there is an equal gap between the sides of the bonnet and the wing panels, and between the front of the bonnet and the upper edges of the headlamp units. Check also that the bonnet sits flush in relation to the surrounding body panels.
10 The bonnet should close smoothly and positively without excessive pressure. If this is not the case, adjustment will be required.
11 To adjust the bonnet alignment, loosen the bonnet mounting bolts, and move the bonnet on the bolts as required (the bolt holes in the hinges are elongated to allow adjustment). To adjust the bonnet front height in relation to the front wings, adjustable rubber bump stops are fitted to the front corners of the bonnet. These may be screwed in or out as necessary. After making an adjustment, the bonnet striker must be adjusted so that the lock spring holds the bonnet firmly against the rubber bump stops. Loosen the locknut and screw the striker in or out as necessary.

Support struts

Removal

12 Open the bonnet, and have an assistant support it.
13 Using a screwdriver prise out the retaining spring clips and disconnect the upper end of the strut from the balljoints on the bonnet.
14 Unscrew the securing bolts and detach the lower end of the strut from the bodywork. Note which way round the strut is fitted.

Refitting

15 Refitting is a reversal of removal.

9 Bonnet release cable - removal and refitting

Removal

1 Remove the lower trim panel from under the driver's side of the facia. Undo the screws and remove the plastic panel to the right of the drivers footwell, to expose the release cable handle mountings.
2 Open the bonnet and remove the radiator grille as described in Section 7. Release the securing clips, undo the screws and remove the cover panel from above the radiator.
3 Disconnect the front end of the release cable from the bonnet lock spring, by reaching between the radiator and the bodywork. On models with air conditioning, it will be necessary to remove the left hand auxiliary cooling fan (see Chapter 3) from the condenser to allow access to the underside of the bonnet lock.
4 Unbolt the release lever and its mounting bracket from the bodywork at the right of the driver's footwell. Note that the release handle and cable are only available as a complete assembly.
5 Release the cable from the support clips in the engine compartment, then withdraw the cable through the rubber grommet and withdraw into the engine compartment. Note that the cable runs from the bonnet lock around the left hand side of the engine compartment behind the main fusebox, then along the bulkhead to the right hand side of the engine compartment before passing through the bulkhead and entering the passenger compartment. As an aid to refitting, tie a length of string to the cable before removing it and leave the string in position ready for refitting.

Refitting

6 Refitting is a reversal of removal, but tie the string to the release lever end of the cable, and use the string to pull the cable into position. Ensure that the cable is routed as noted before removal, and make sure that the grommet is correctly seated.

10 Bonnet lock spring - removal and refitting

Removal

1 The bonnet is held in its locked position by means of a strong coil spring and a pin, which engages with the striker plate on the front edge of the bonnet. The release cable is connected to the striker plate catch, which is held in the locked position by a spring.
2 The pin and its coil spring may be removed from the bonnet by unscrewing it from the locknut, however measure its fitted length first as a guide to refitting it.
3 To remove the striker plate spring, first remove the radiator grille (see Section 7) then disconnect the bonnet release cable and unhook the spring from the front crossmember.

Refitting

4 Refitting is a reversal of removal.

11 Door - removal and refitting

Front door

Removal

1 The door hinges are welded onto the door frame and the body pillar. Where necessary, adjustment is carried out using special tools to bend the hinges.
2 Open the door to gain access to the wiring connector, which is fixed to the front inside edge of the door. Disconnect the wiring connector from the front edge of the door. To do this, unscrew the connector locking ring, then pull the connector away from the door **(see illustration)**.
3 Unscrew and remove the bolt securing the door check link to the vehicle body **(see illustration)**.

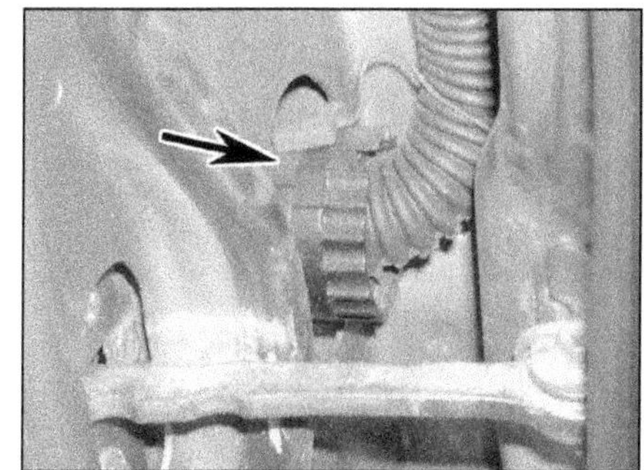

11.2 Location of the front door wiring connector (arrowed)

11.3 Unscrew and remove the bolt (arrowed) securing the door check link to the vehicle body

4 Remove the plastic covers from the door hinge pins **(see illustration)**. Have an assistant support the door, then drive both hinge pins out of position using a hammer and suitable punch. **Note:** *Vauxhall/Opel technicians use a special hinge pin removal tool which acts like a slide hammer.* Remove the door from the vehicle.

5 Inspect the hinge pins for signs of wear or damage, and renew if necessary.

Refitting

6 Refitting is a reversal of removal, but check that when shut the door is positioned centrally within the body aperture. If the hinge pins have been renewed and adjustment is still required, the hinges will have to be re-aligned using special tools. This work must be carried out by a Vauxhall/Opel dealer, however minor adjustment may be possible by physically lifting the door on its hinges. After adjustment, make sure that the door lock engages correctly with the striker on the body pillar. If necessary loosen the striker retaining screws using a Torx key, then reposition the striker and tighten the screws.

Rear door

7 The removal and refitting procedure is the same as that described for the front door, except that the wiring harness is located behind a rubber grommet at the base of the B-pillar. To gain access to it, open the front and rear door, prise the grommet from the bodywork and withdraw the connector from the B-pillar.

12 Door inner trim panel - removal and refitting

Front door

Removal

1 Disconnect the battery negative (earth) lead (see Chapter 5A).

2 On models with manually-adjustable door mirrors, carefully pull off the mirror adjustment handle, then prise off the triangular plastic cover taking care not to damage the retaining clips. Remove the foam padding. On models with electrically adjustable door mirrors, carefully prise off the triangular plastic cover panel, remove the foam padding and unplug the wiring from the tweeter unit (see Section 23 for details).

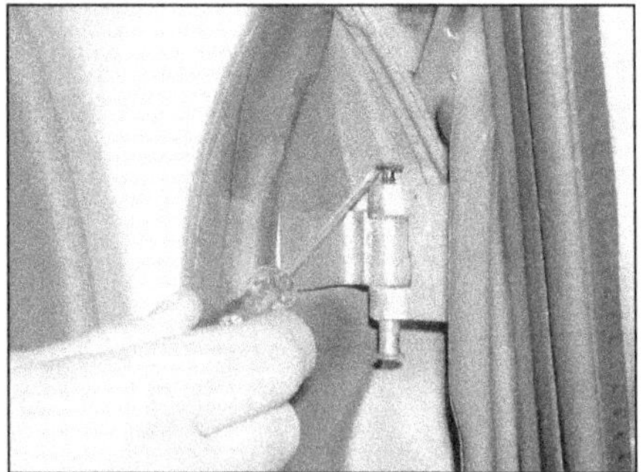

11.4 Remove the plastic covers from the door hinge pins

3 Prise the plastic cover from the inside of the interior door handle **(see illustration)**.

4 Carefully prise the grip from the underside of the door pull handle **(see illustration)**.

5 Prise off the small plastic covers to expose the heads of the door handle surround securing screws. Undo the screws and remove the door pull handle. **(see illustrations)**.

6 On base models, remove the window regulator handle by first closing the window and noting the fitted angle of the handle. Using a piece of cloth rag inserted behind the handle, release the clip then withdraw the handle from the splined shaft.

7 Prise the clip from the door locking knob, then detach the knob from the locking rod. Undo the screw and remove the locking knob trim panel **(see illustrations)**.

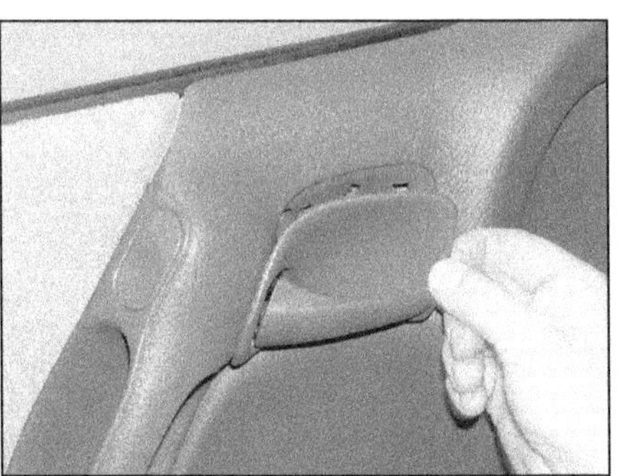

12.3 Prise the plastic cover from the inside of the interior door handle

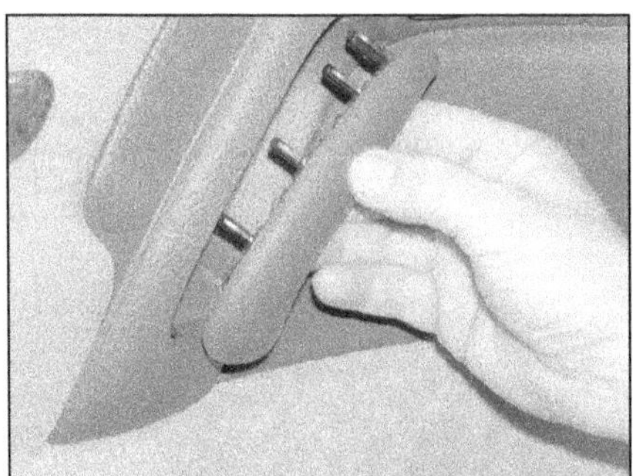

12.4 Carefully prise the grip from the underside of the door pull handle

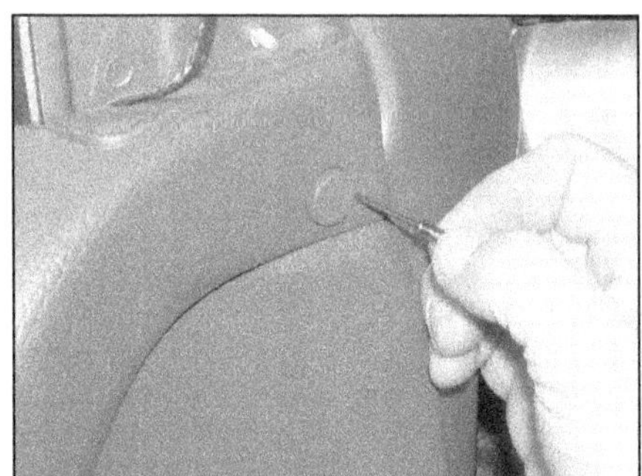

12.5a Prise off the small plastic covers . . .

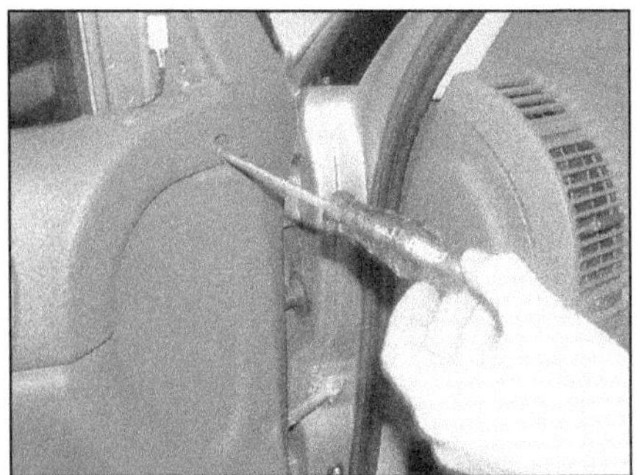

12.5b . . . undo the screws . . .

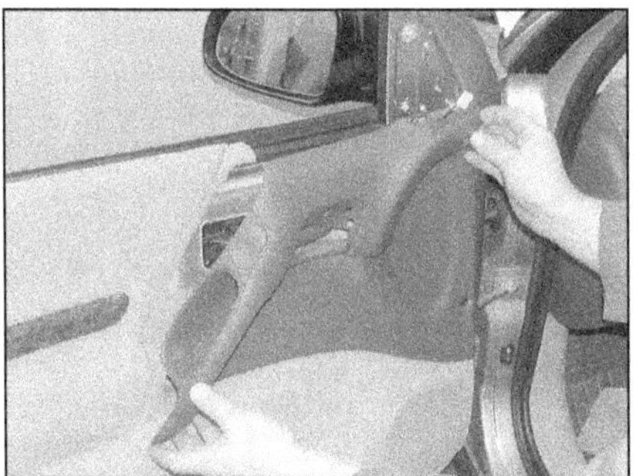

12.5c . . . and remove the door pull handle

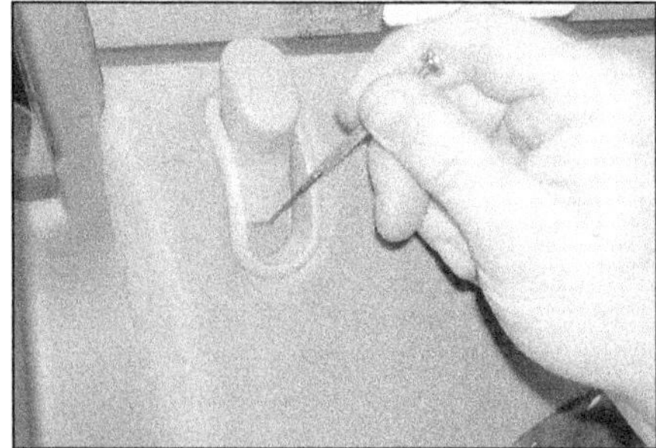

12.7a Prise the clip from the door locking knob and then detach the knob from the locking rod

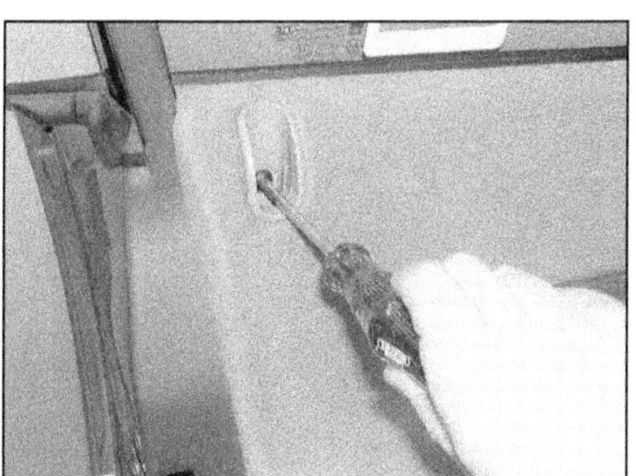

12.7b Undo the screw . . .

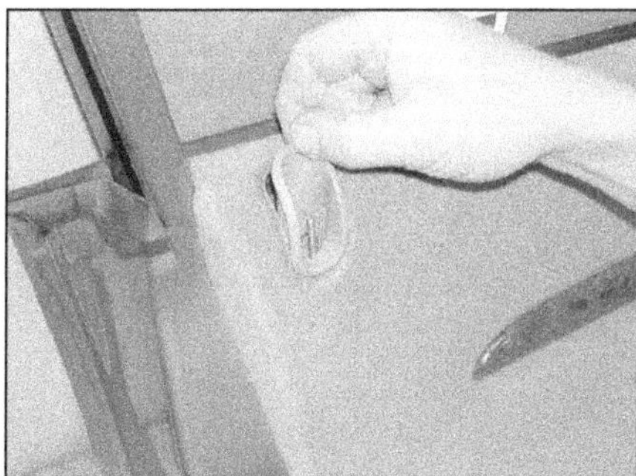

12.7c . . . and remove the locking knob trim panel

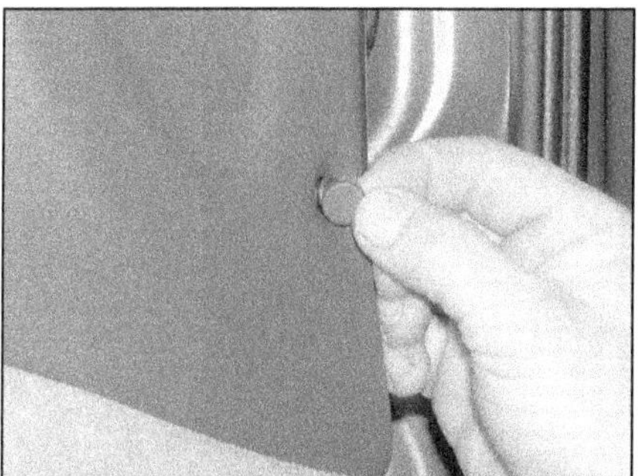

12.8a Prise off the protective caps . . .

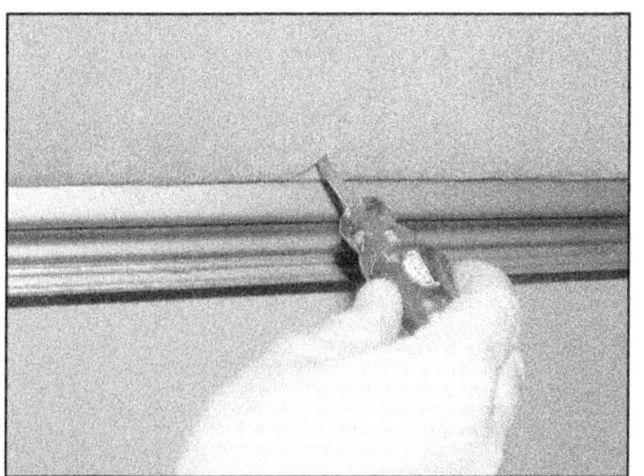

12.8b . . . then remove the screws from the lower and front edges of the trim panel

12.9 Remove the trim panel from the door

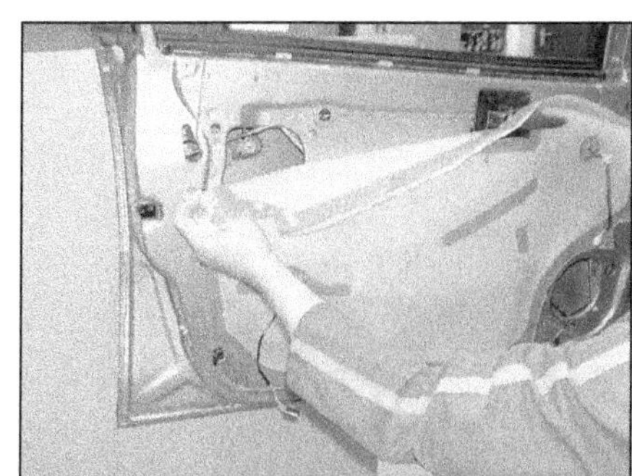

12.10 If necessary, carefully peel the protective plastic membrane from the door

8 Prise off the protective caps (where applicable) then unscrew and remove the screws from the lower and front edges of the trim panel **(see illustrations)**.

9 Use a wide-bladed screwdriver or trim removal tool to carefully prise the panel clips from the door. Unhook the top of the panel and remove it from the door **(see illustration)**.

10 If necessary, carefully peel the protective plastic membrane from the door **(see illustration)**. Note that it will necessary to cut around some of the panel securing clips to release the membrane from the door.

Warning: On later models where the Supplementary Restraint System (SRS) includes side airbags, the door side impact sensors are air pressure sensitive and will only operate correctly if the protective plastic door membrane is refitted correctly; bear this in mind when removing the membrane from the door. See Chapter 12 for more information on the Supplementary Restraint System.

Refitting

11 Refitting is a reversal of removal. On models fitted with side airbags, ensure that the plastic door membrane is securely refitted **(see illustration).** The sealing strip around the edge of the membrane must adhere to the door without gaps, to form an airtight seal. If the membrane was cut or torn during its removal, ensure that the loose edges are stuck to the door using a suitable adhesive/sealant. If you are in doubt about the integrity of the seal, it's best to renew the membrane and sealing strip entirely.

Rear door

Removal

12 Disconnect the battery negative (earth) lead (see Chapter 5A).

13 Use a small screwdriver to carefully prise off the ashtray unit from the armrest **(see illustration)**.

14 Unclip the trim panel from behind the door lock release handle **(see illustration)**.

15 Carefully prise the grip from the underside off the door pull handle **(see illustration)**.

16 Prise the clip from the door locking knob, then detach the knob from the locking rod. Undo the screw and remove the locking knob trim panel **(see illustrations)**.

17 Unscrew and remove the door pull handle retaining screws and then remove the pull handle from the door. Where applicable, unplug the window switch wiring connector as it becomes accessible **(see illustrations)**. On models with rear door window demister fans, it will be necessary to lift the door pull handle assembly upwards, to detach it from the air ducting.

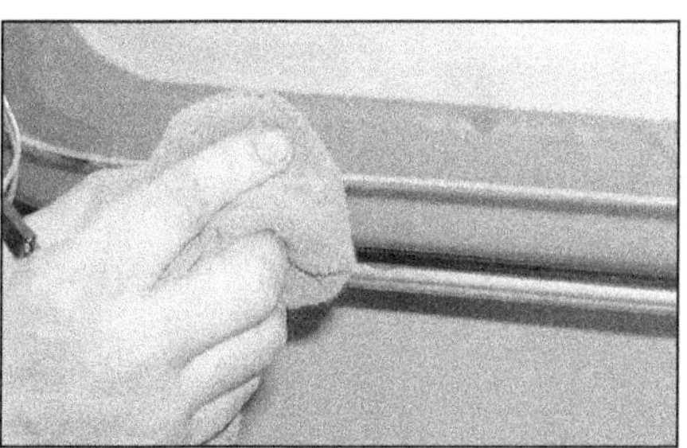

12.11 On models fitted with side airbags, it is important that the sealing strip around the edge of the membrane adheres to the door without gaps, to form an airtight seal

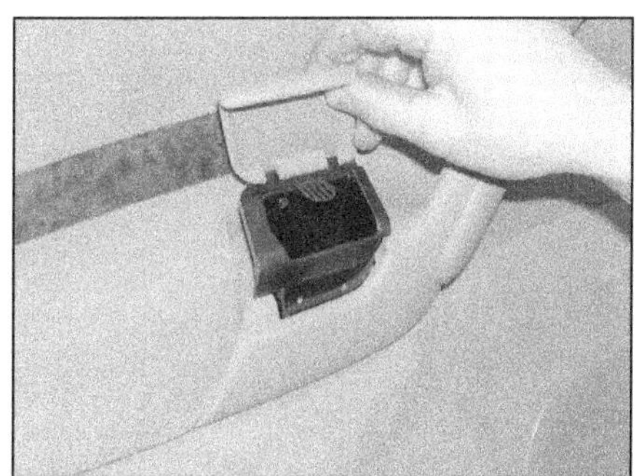

12.13 Use a small screwdriver to carefully prise off the ashtray unit from the armrest

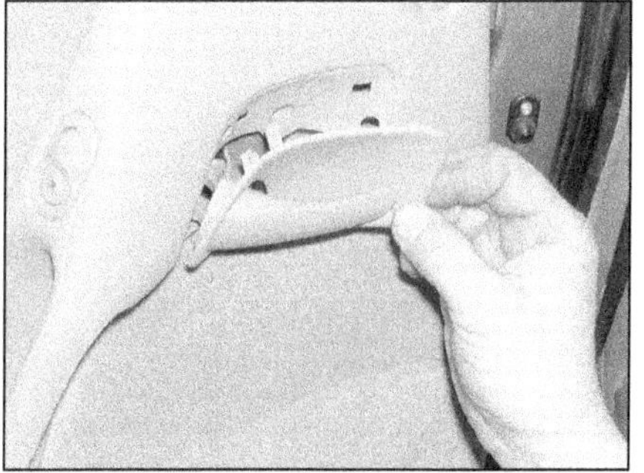

12.14 Unclip the trim panel from behind the door lock release handle

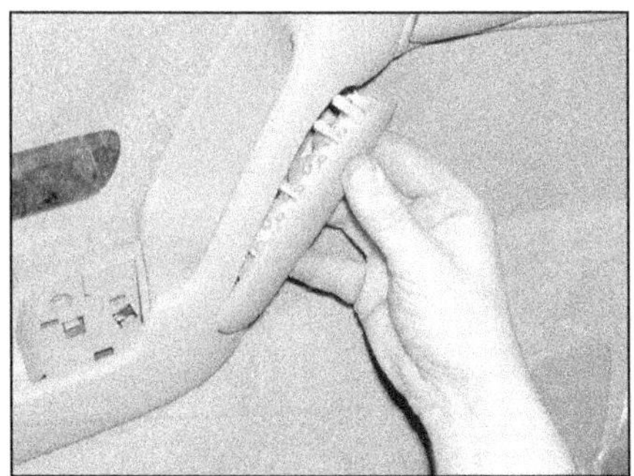
12.15 Carefully prise the grip from the underside of the door pull handle

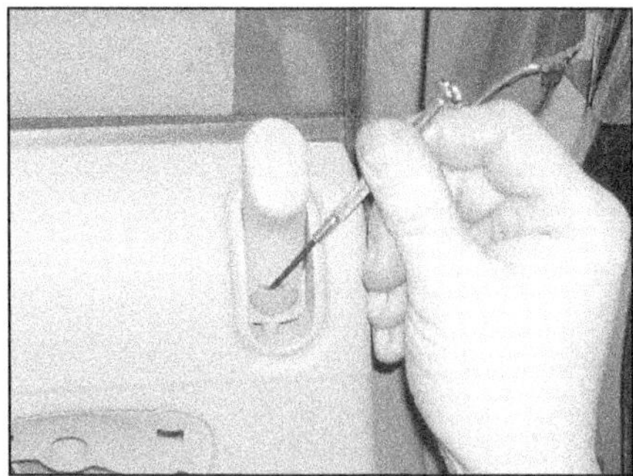
12.16a Prise the clip from the door locking knob . .

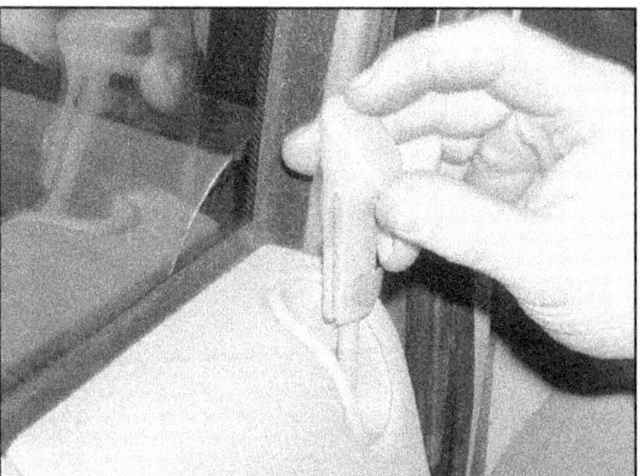
12.16b . . . then detach the knob from the locking rod

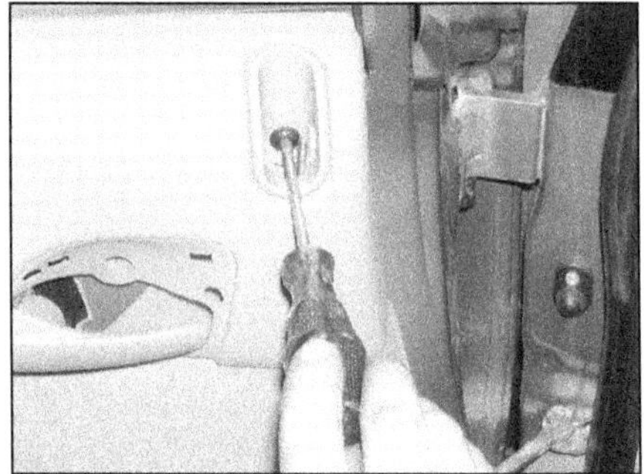
12.16c Undo the screw . . .

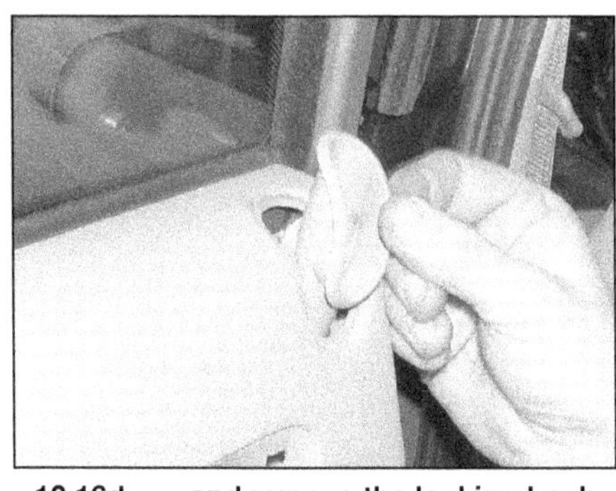
12.16d . . . and remove the locking knob trim panel

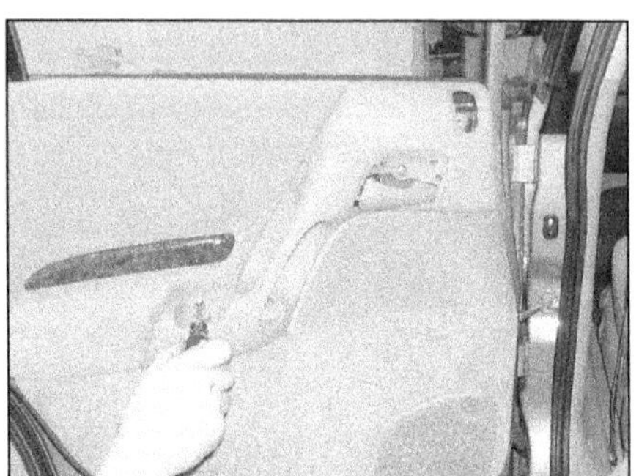
12.17a Unscrew and remove the door pull handle retaining screws . . .

18 Where a manual window regulator is fitted, fully close the window and note the position of the regulator handle. The handle must now be removed from the splined shaft. To do this, locate a cloth rag between the handle and the trim panel and pull it to one side to release the spring clip. The handle can now be removed from the splined shaft and the escutcheon removed.

19 Prise the kerb lamp unit from the door trim panel and disconnect the wiring from it (see Chapter 12, Section 6).

20 Unscrew and remove the screws from the rear and lower edges of the trim panel, then use a wide-bladed screwdriver or removal tool

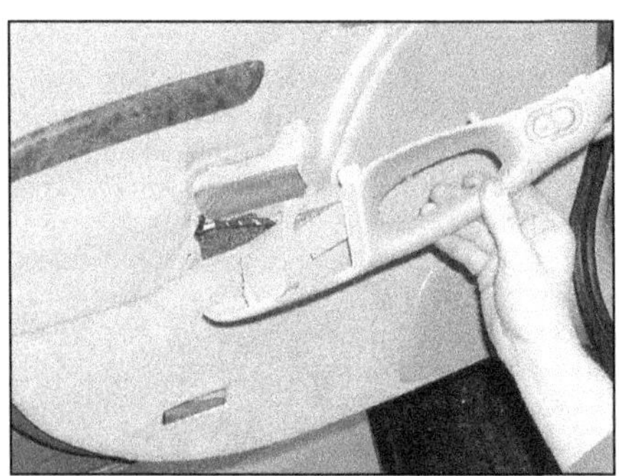
12.17b . . . and then remove the pull handle from the door

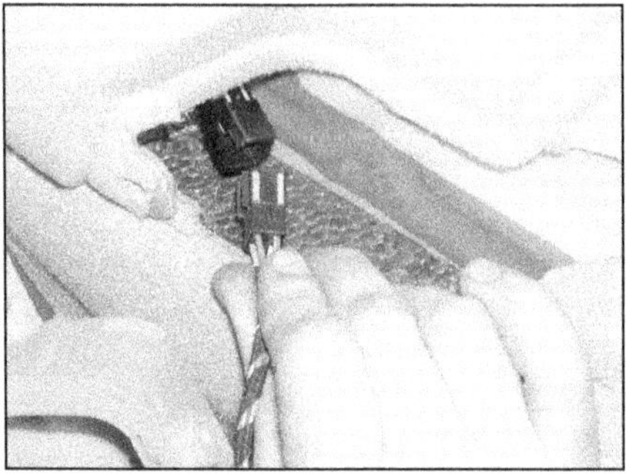
12.17c Where applicable, unplug the window switch wiring connector

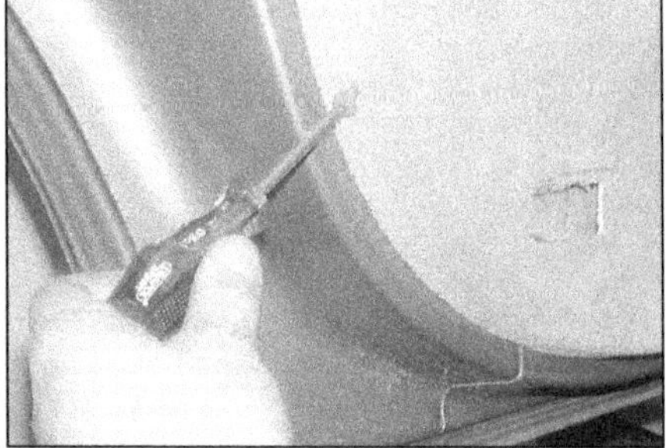
12.20a Unscrew and remove the screws from the rear and lower edges of the trim panel . . .

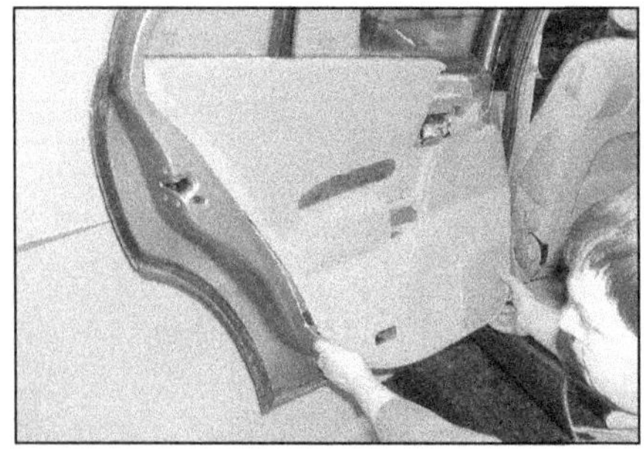
12.20b . . . lift the panel upwards to disengage it from the door, then remove it from the vehicle

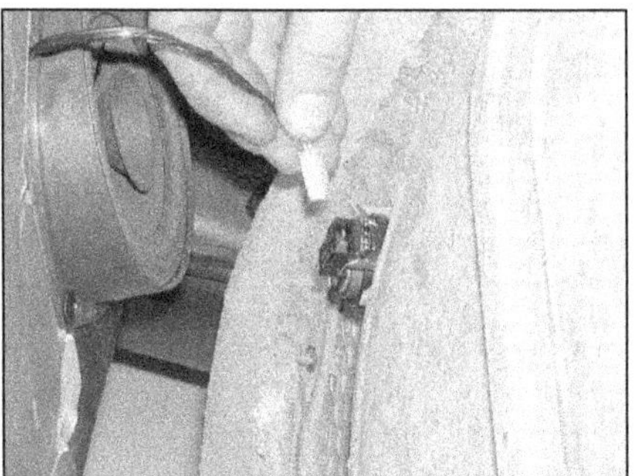
12.20c Unplug the speaker wiring as it becomes accessible

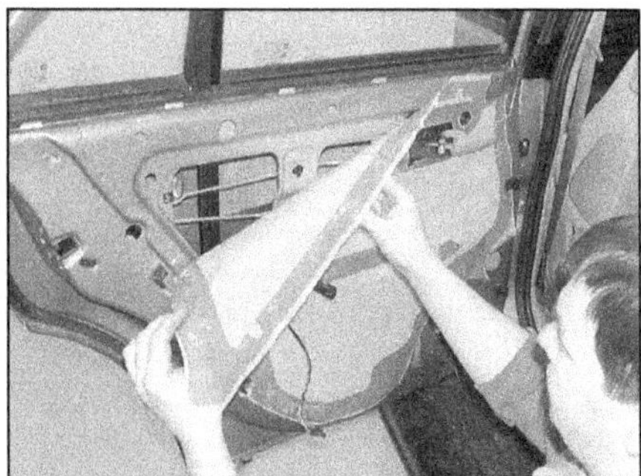
12.21 If necessary, carefully peel the protective plastic membrane from the door

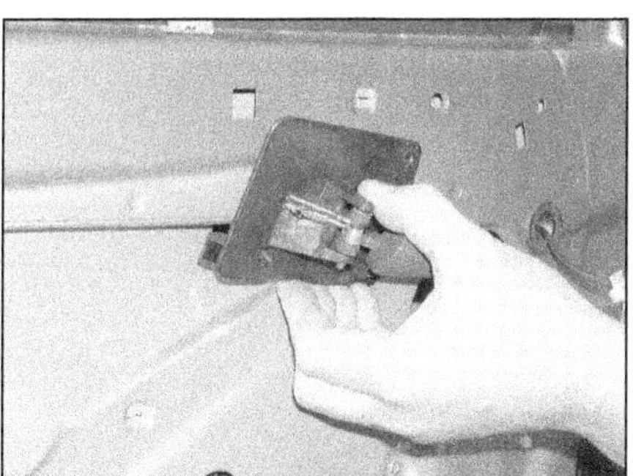
13.2 Press the interior handle forwards to release it from the elongated slots in the door panel

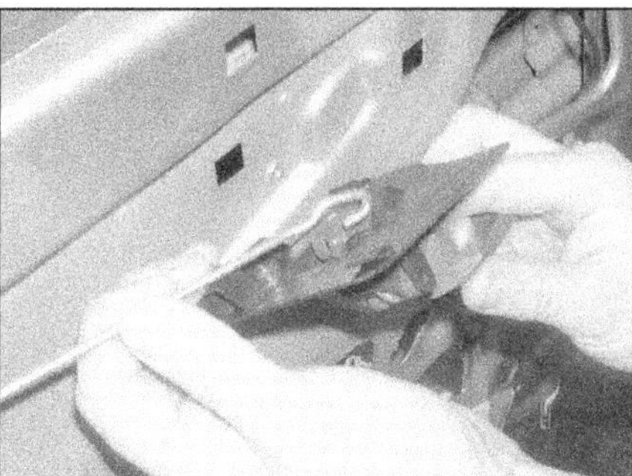
13.3 Twist the handle anticlockwise to unhook it from the link rod

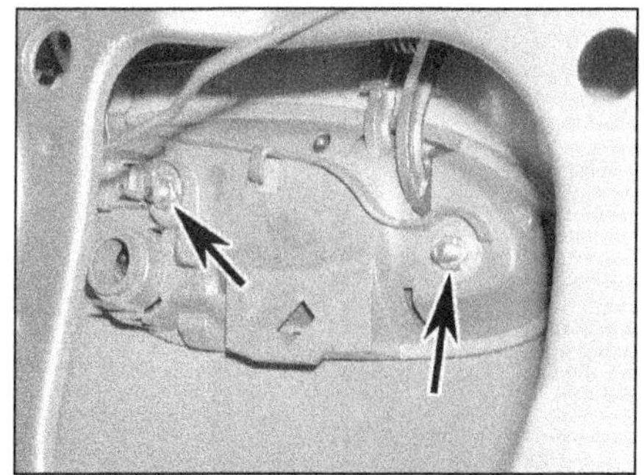
13.7 Unscrew the nuts (arrowed) from the rear of the exterior handle

to carefully prise the inner trim panel clips from the inside of the rear door. Lift the panel upwards to disengage it from the door, then unplug the speaker wiring as it becomes accessible. Remove the trim panel from the vehicle **(see illustrations).**

21 If necessary, carefully peel the protective plastic membrane from the door **(see illustration)**. Note that it will necessary to cut around some of the panel securing clips to release the membrane from the door.

Refitting

22 Refitting is a reversal of removal.

13 Door handles and lock components - removal and refitting

Door interior handle

Removal

1 Remove the door inner trim panel and peel back the protective plastic membrane as described in Section 12.

2 Press the interior handle forwards to release it from the elongated slots in the door panel **(see illustration)**.

3 Twist the handle anticlockwise to unhook it from the link rod **(see illustration)**.

Refitting

4 Refitting is a reversal of removal.

13.9a Release the plastic clip . . .

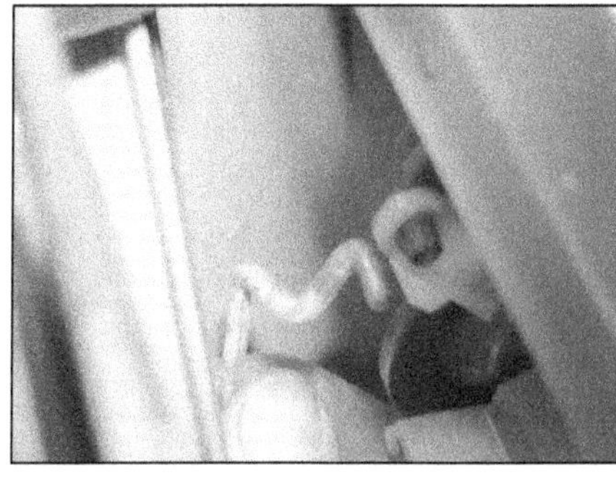
13.9b . . . detach the door lock mechanism link rod . . .

Front door exterior handle

Removal

5 Remove the door inner trim panel, and peel back the protective plastic membrane as described in Section 12.

6 On models fitted with side air bags, remove the door side impact sensor together with its mounting bracket; refer to Section 24 of Chapter 12.

7 Unscrew the nuts from the rear of the exterior handle using a socket inserted through the aperture provided **(see illustration)**.

8 Carefully withdraw the exterior handle from the door taking care not to damage the paintwork. Unplug the wiring connector, where applicable - cable tie the wire to the handle aperture, to prevent it dropping down inside the door.

9 Release the plastic clip, detach the door lock mechanism link rod and withdraw the handle from the door through handle aperture **(see illustrations)**.

Refitting

10 Refitting is a reversal of removal, but before refitting the inner trim panel, screw down the knurled nut on the handle linkage until it is free of play.

Rear door exterior handle

Removal

11 Remove the door inner trim panel, and peel back the protective plastic membrane as described in Section 12.

12 Undo the securing screw and remove the plastic security panel from the door lock mechanism **(see illustrations)**.

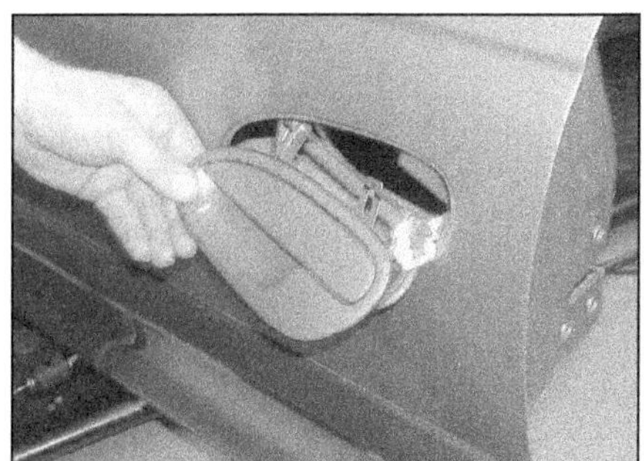
13.9c . . . and withdraw the handle from the door through handle aperture

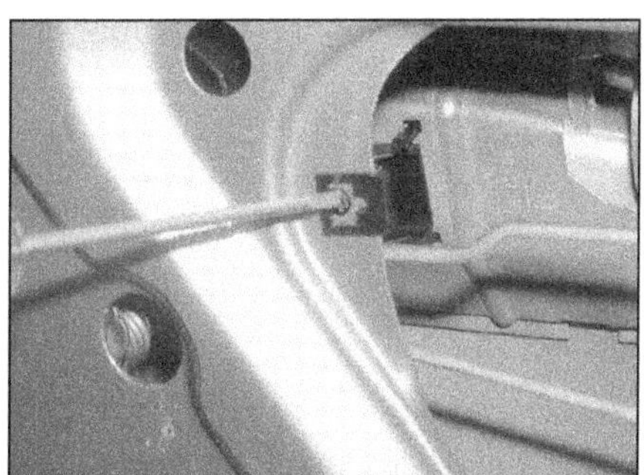
13.12a Undo the securing screw . . .

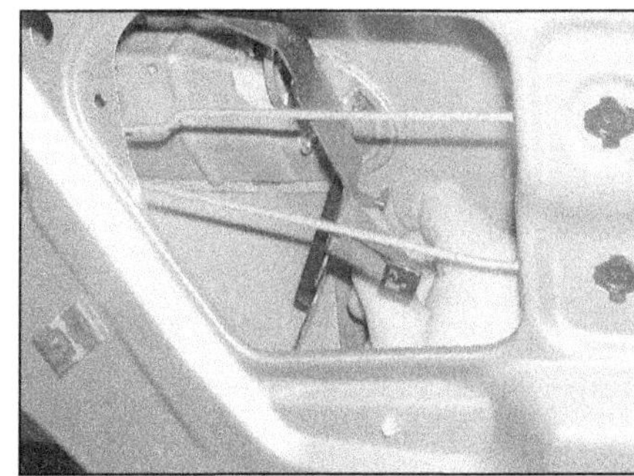
13.12b . . . and remove the plastic security panel from the door lock mechanism

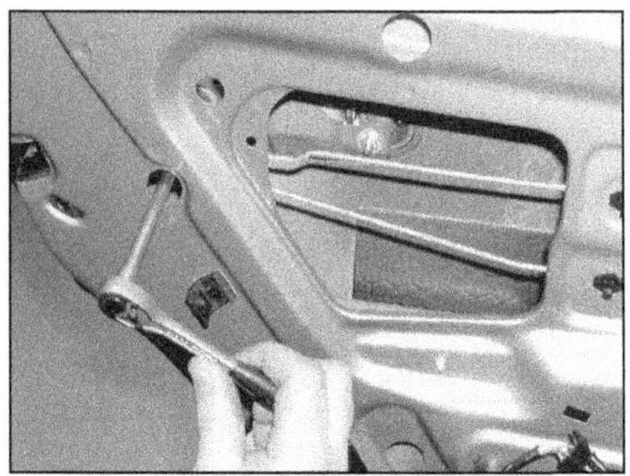
13.13a Unscrew the nuts, using a socket inserted through the aperture provided . . .

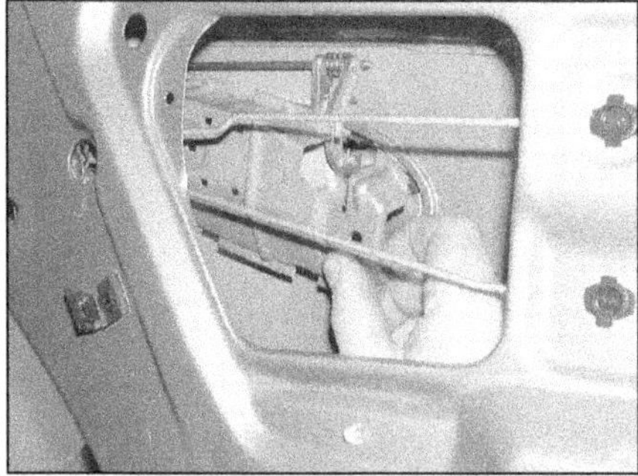
13.13b . . . and remove the mounting plate from the rear of the exterior door handle

13.14 Disconnect the link rod from the door handle by prising open the plastic clip

13 Unscrew the nuts, using a socket inserted through the aperture provided, and remove the mounting plate from the rear of the exterior door handle **(see illustrations)**.

14 Disconnect the handle link rod from the door lock by prising open the plastic clips **(see illustration)**.

15 Withdraw the handle from the door taking care not to damage the paintwork **(see illustration)**.

Refitting

16 Refitting is a reversal of removal, but before refitting the inner trim panel, screw down the knurled nut on the handle link rod until it is free of play.

Front door lock cylinder - models with conventional lock cylinder

Removal

17 Remove the exterior handle as described previously in this Section.

18 Insert the key in the lock cylinder and turn it to the right.

19 Prise off the circlip and remove the cylinder from the rear of the handle assembly.

Refitting

20 Refitting is a reversal of removal.

Front door lock cylinder - models with freewheeling lock cylinder

Removal

21 Remove the exterior handle assembly as described previously in this Section.

22 Note the orientation of the cylinder housing, then drive out the roll pin using a suitable punch, and rotate the cylinder housing to release it from the exterior handle assembly.

23 Withdraw the lock cylinder from the handle assembly.

Refitting

24 Refitting is a reversal of removal. After securing the cylinder housing in position with a new roll pin, turn the handle assembly over and splay out the end roll pin using the punch, to ensure that the pin cannot fall out **(see illustration)**.

Front door lock

Removal

25 Remove the door inner trim panel, and peel back the protective plastic membrane as described in Section 12.

26 On models fitted with side air bags, remove the door side impact sensor together

13.15 Withdraw the handle from the door

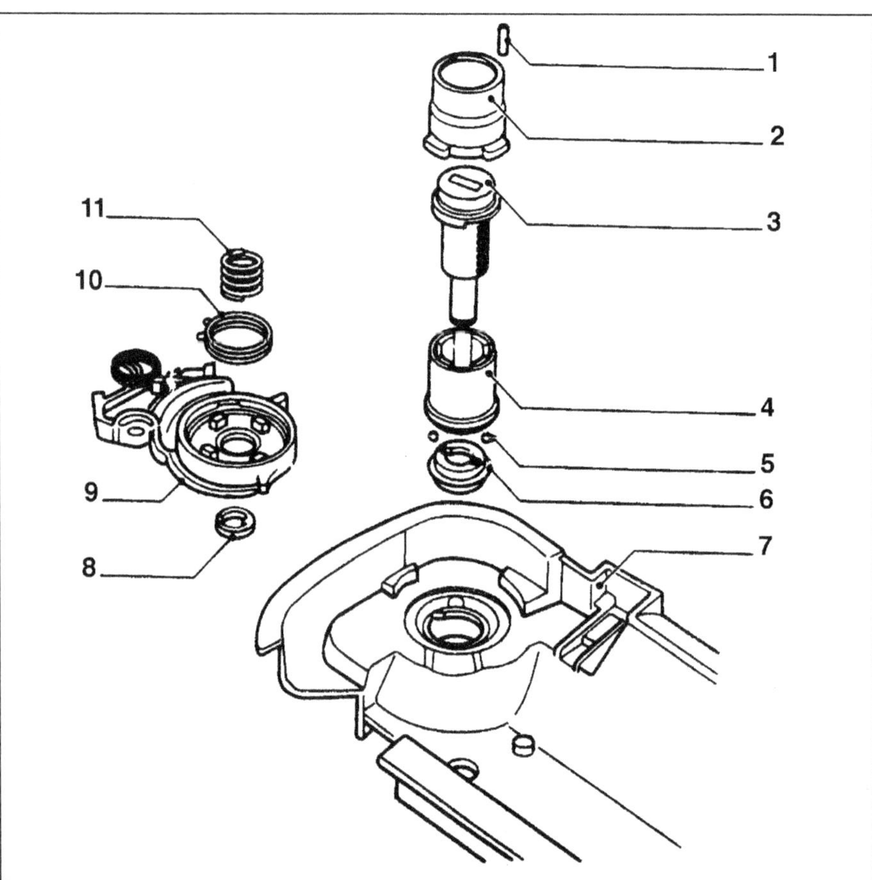

13.24 Exploded view of front door lock cylinder assembly - models with free-wheeling locks

1 Roll pin
2 Housing
3 Lock cylinder
4 Channel sleeve
5 Ball
6 Clutch
7 Bracket
8 Washer
9 Carrier and lever
10 Torsion spring
11 Pressure spring

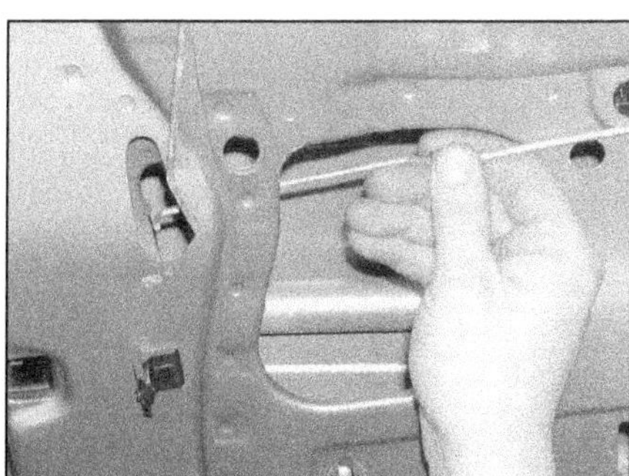

13.29 Disconnecting the inner door handle link rod

13.30 Unscrew and remove the front door lock retaining screws

13.34 Disconnect the locking knob and interior handle link rods from the lock by releasing the plastic clips

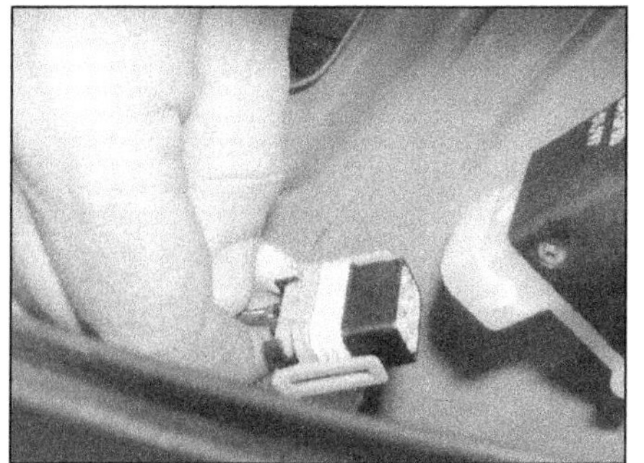

13.35 Disconnect the central locking wiring at the connector

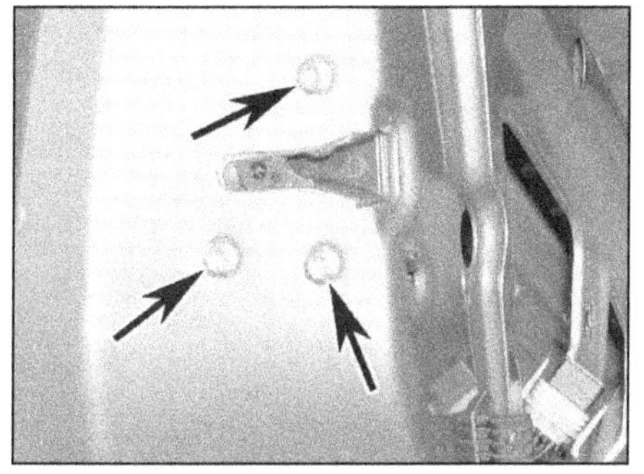

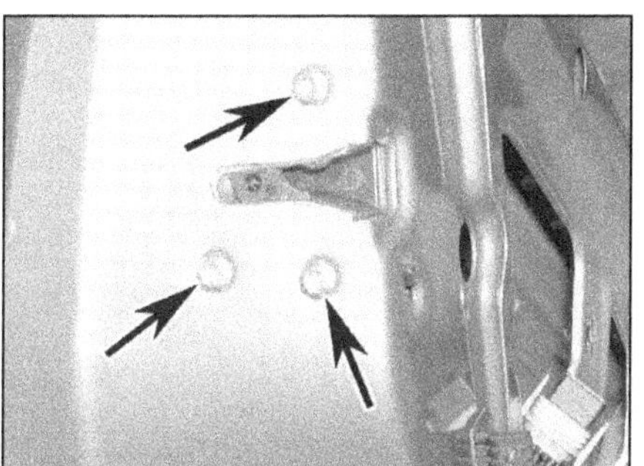

13.36a Unscrew the lock mechanism mounting screws (arrowed) . . .

13.36b . . . and withdraw the lock mechanism through the exterior handle door aperture

with its mounting bracket; refer to Section 24 of Chapter 12.

27 Remove the exterior door handle as described previously in this Section.

28 Where fitted, disconnect the central locking wiring from the lock by levering up the plastic retainer and separating the connector.

29 Disconnect the link rods arms for the outer door handle, lock cylinder (where applicable) and inner door handle from the lock **(see illustration)**.

30 At the rear edge of the door, undo the three retaining screws then withdraw the lock from inside the door while guiding the locking knob link rod through the hole provided **(see illustration)**.

Refitting

31 Refitting is a reversal of removal.

Rear door lock

Removal

32 Remove the door inner trim panel, and peel back the protective plastic membrane as described in Section 12.

33 Remove the rear door exterior handle as described previously in this Section.

34 Disconnect the locking knob and interior handle link rods from the lock by releasing the plastic clips **(see illustration)**.

35 Disconnect the central locking wiring by levering up the plastic retainer and separating the connector **(see illustration)**.

36 Unscrew the lock mechanism mounting screws and withdraw the lock mechanism through the exterior handle door aperture **(see illustrations)**.

Refitting

37 Refitting is a reversal of removal.

14 Door window regulator and glass - removal and refitting

Window regulator

Note: *New rivets will be required to secure the regulator mechanism to the door on refitting.*

Removal

1 Operate the window so that it is about three quarters open. Disconnect the battery negative cable and position it away from the terminal.

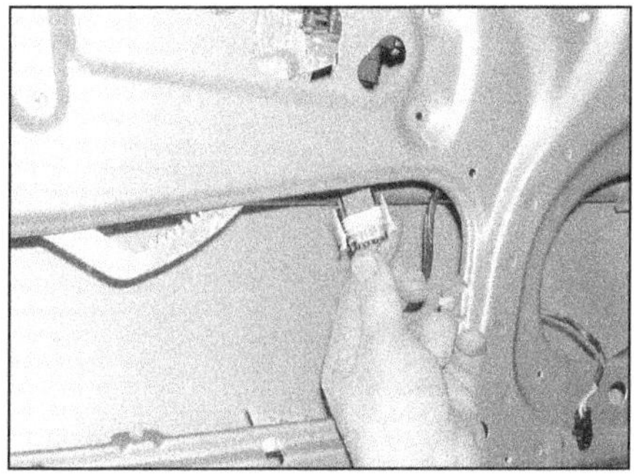

14.5 On models with electric windows, unplug the winder motor wiring at the connector

2 Remove the door inner trim panel, and peel back the protective plastic membrane as described in Section 12.

3 If working on a rear door, remove the interior door handle, as described in Section 13.

4 On models fitted with side air bags, remove the door side impact sensor together with its mounting bracket; refer to Section 24 of Chapter 12.

5 On models with electric window regulators, unplug the winder motor wiring connector, by squeezing the retaining tags **(see illustration)**.

6 Mark the position of the regulator guide rail mounting bolts in their in the elongated slots, then unscrew and remove the bolts **(see illustration)**.

7 Have an assistant hold the window glass in position, then drill out the rivets securing the

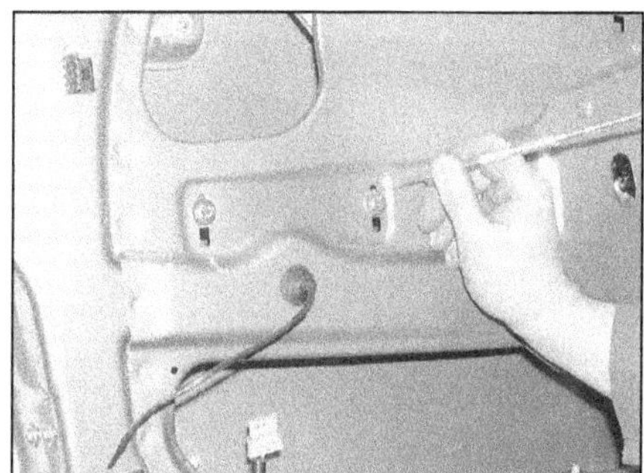

14.6 Mark the position of the regulator guide rail mounting bolts then unscrew and remove the bolts

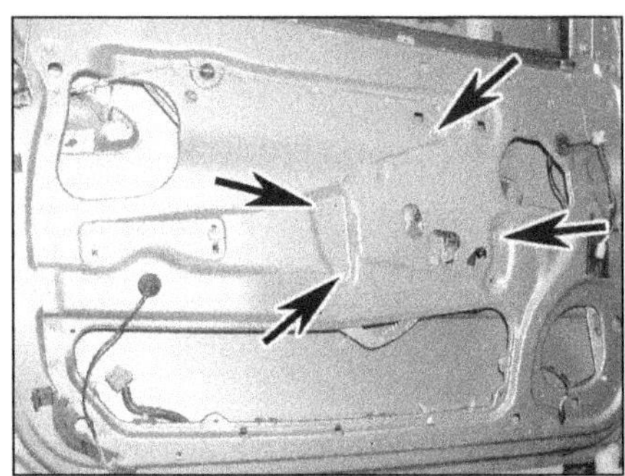

14.7a Drill out the rivets securing the regulator to the door (arrowed - front door shown)

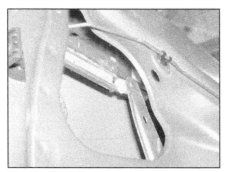

14.7b Slide the arm extensions from the channels at the bottom of the glass

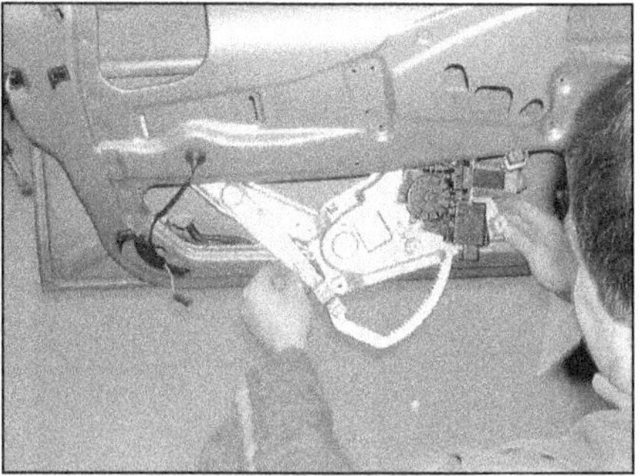

14.8 Manoeuvre the regulator mechanism out through the aperture in the door

regulator to the door; there are four rivets on the front door, six on rear doors with manual actuation and five on rear doors with electric actuation. Slide the arm extensions from the channels at the bottom of the glass **(see illustrations)**.

8 Manoeuvre the regulator mechanism out through the aperture in the door **(see illustration)**.

Refitting

9 Refitting is a reversal of removal but use a pop-rivet gun to secure the regulator with new pop rivets **(see illustration)**. Before refitting the inner trim panel and protective plastic membrane, adjust the position of the regulator by inserting the guide rail mounting bolts hand-tight, then raising and lowering the window fully. Tighten the guide rail mounting bolts and check that the window opens and closes correctly. Finally refit the plastic membrane and inner trim panel.

10 After reconnecting the battery on models with electric window regulators the winder mechanism control electronics must be reprogrammed as follows: fully close the window then keep the switch held down for a further 5 seconds.

Window glass - front door sash window

Removal

11 Remove the regulator as previously described in this Section.

12 Remove the exterior door mirror, as described in Section 23.

13 Undo the securing screws and remove the speaker from the door.

14 Remove the sealing strips from the inside and outside of the lower edge of the door window aperture **(see illustration).**

15 Peel the weather strip from the front edge of the door window aperture **(see illustration).**

16 Remove the rubber seal from the window guide channel **(see illustration).**

17 Slacken the window guide channel upper and lower securing bolts **(see illustrations).**

18 Slide the window glass to the top of the door, then tilt its upper corner forward to disengage it from the door and remove it **(see illustration).**

Refitting

19 Refitting is a reversal of removal. Ensure that the leading edge of the window glass engages with the guide channel, and that the

14.9 Use a pop-rivet gun to secure the regulator with new pop rivets

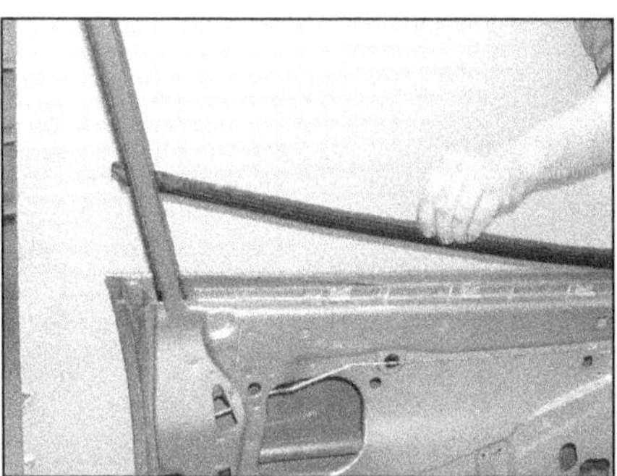

14.14 Remove the sealing strips from the inside and outside of the lower edge of the door window aperture

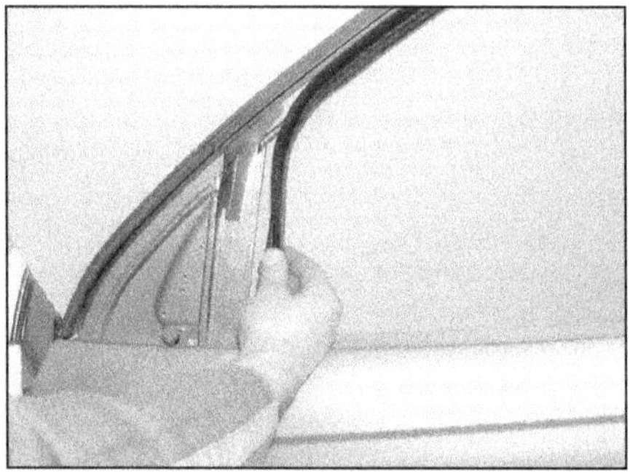

14.15 Peel the weather strip from the front edge of the door window aperture

14.16 Remove the rubber seal from the window guide channel

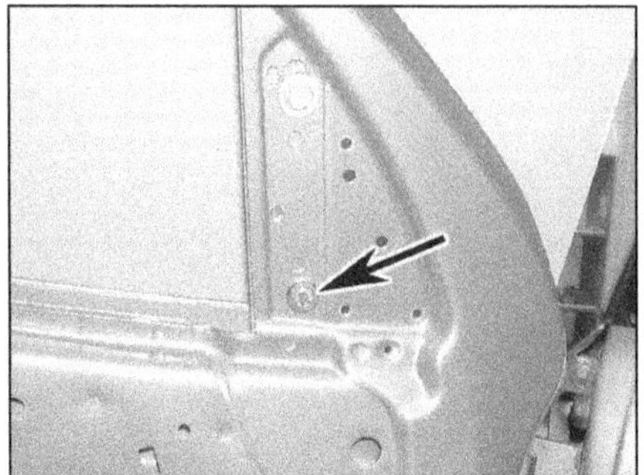

14.17a Slacken the window guide channel upper . . .

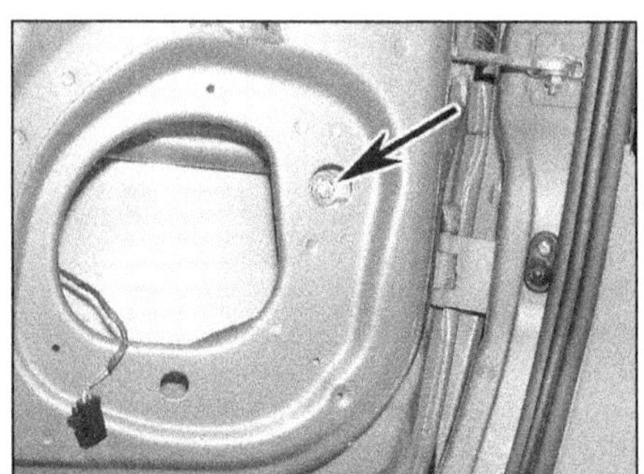

14.17b . . . and lower securing bolts

14.18 Tilt the window glass upper corner forward to disengage it, then remove it from the door

channel at the trailing edge of the glass engages with the rear edge of the door **(see illustrations).**

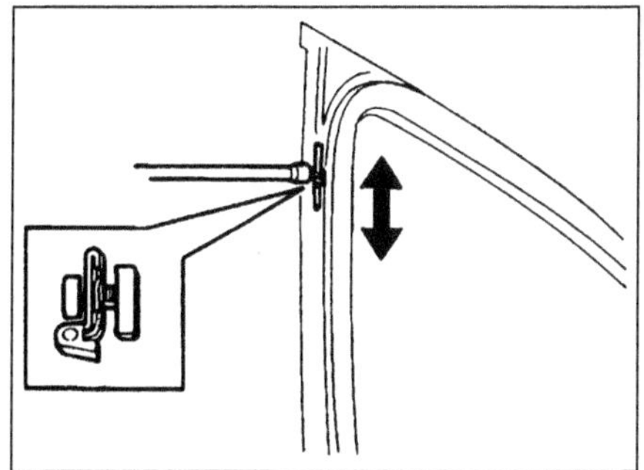

14.20 Location of front door sash window stop bolt

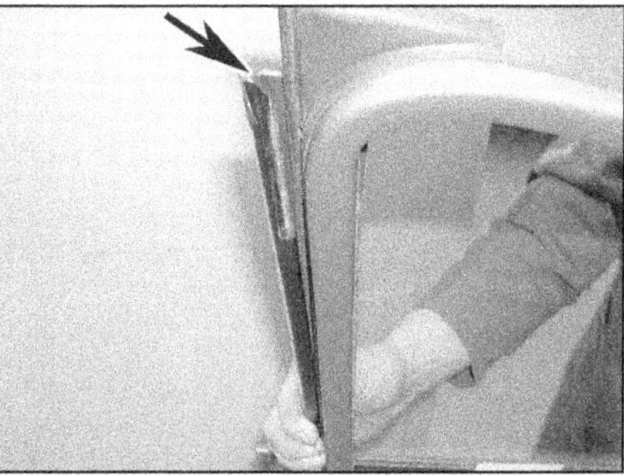

14.19a Ensure that the channel (arrowed) at the trailing edge of the glass engages with the rear edge of the door

20 To adjust the height of the window glass in the closed position, slacken the window glass stop bolt **(see illustration)** then wind the window up until its upper edge is flush with the door weather strip. Tighten the window glass stop bolt.

Window glass - rear door sash window

Removal

21 Remove the regulator as previously described in this Section.

22 Remove the sealing strips from the inside and outside of the lower edge of the door window aperture **(see illustrations).**

23 Peel the weather strip from the rear edge of the door window aperture **(see illustration).**

24 Slacken and remove the window guide channel upper, centre and lower securing

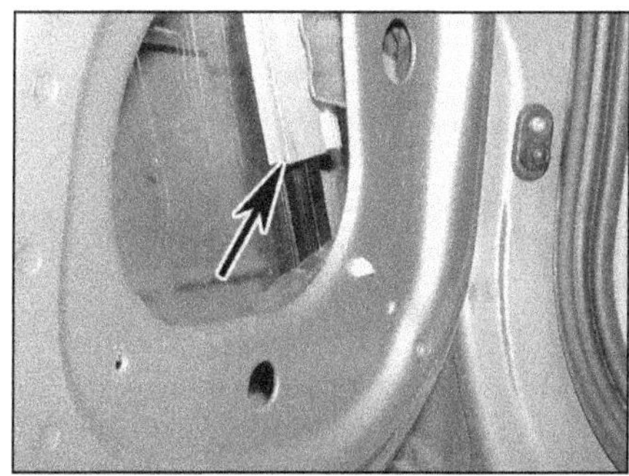

14.19b Ensure that the leading edge of the window glass engages with the guide channel (arrowed)

bolts (four bolts in total), then withdraw the guide channel from the door **(see illustration).**

25 Slide the window glass to the top of the door, then tilt its upper corner forward to disengage it from the door and remove it **(see illustration).**

Refitting

26 Refitting is a reversal of removal. Ensure that the trailing edge of the window glass engages with the guide channel, and that the channel at the leading edge of the glass engages with the front edge of the door **(see illustrations)**.

27 To adjust the height of the window glass in the closed position, slacken the window glass front and rear stop bolts then wind the window up until its upper edge is flush with the door weather strip **(see illustrations).** Tighten the window glass stop bolts.

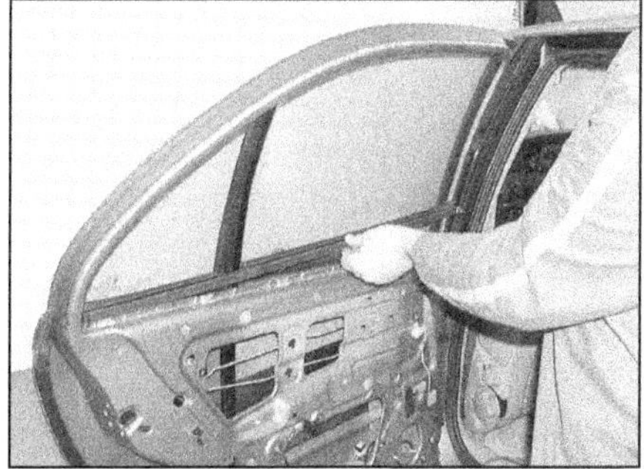

14.22a Remove the sealing strips from the inside . . .

14.22b . . . and outside of the lower edge of the door window aperture

14.23 Peel the weather strip from the rear edge of the door window aperture

14.24a Slacken and remove the window guide channel upper . . .

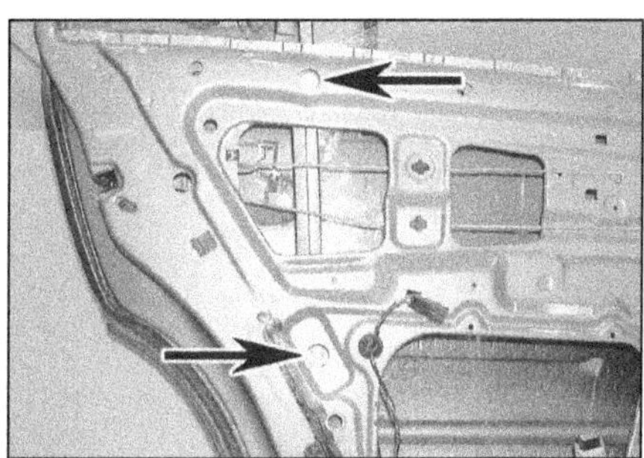

14.24b . . . centre and lower securing bolts (arrowed), then withdraw the guide channel from the door

14.25 Slide the window glass to the top of the door, then tilt its upper corner forward to disengage it from the door and remove it

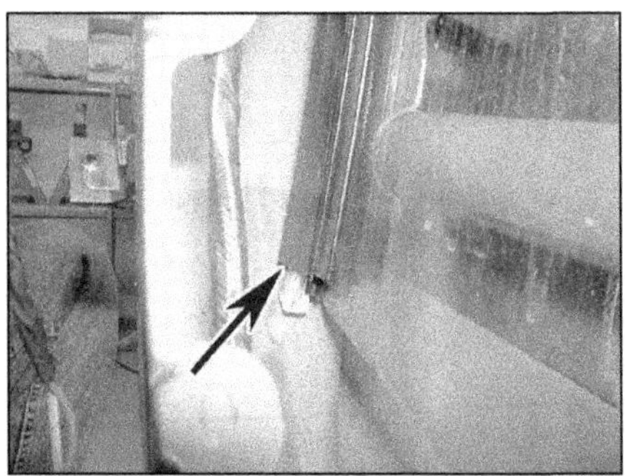

14.26a Ensure that the trailing edge of the window glass engages with the guide channel (arrowed) . . .

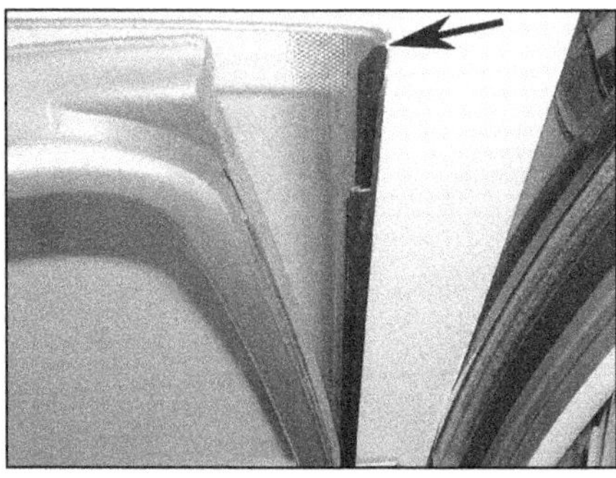

14.26b . . . and that the channel (arrowed) at the leading edge of the glass engages with the front edge of the door

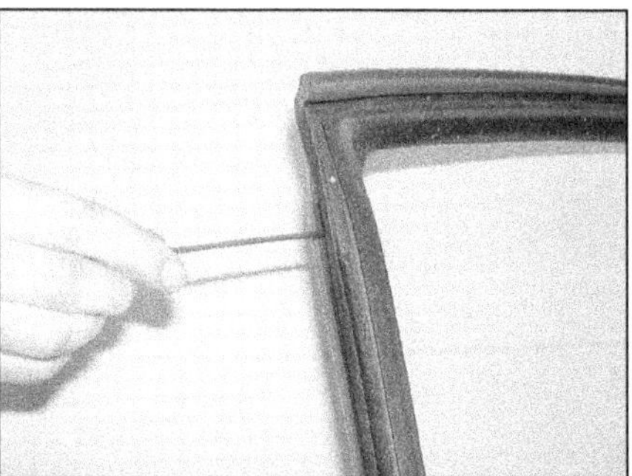

14.27a Slacken the window glass front . . .

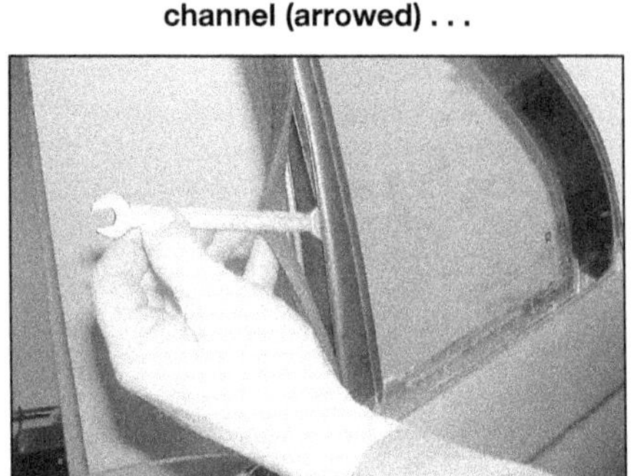

14.27b . . . and rear stop bolts

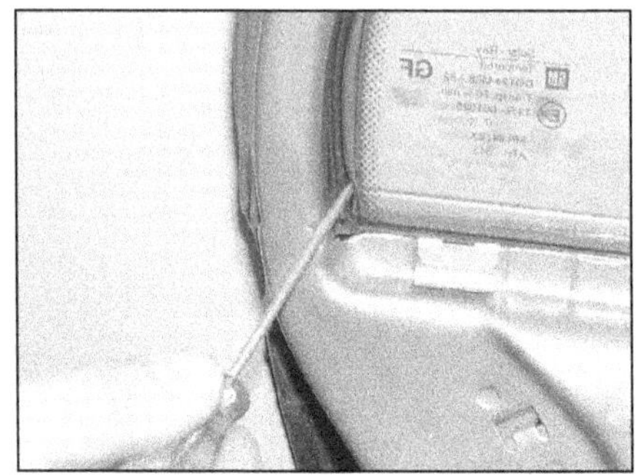

14.29a Carefully prise the rubber seal away from the window aperture . . .

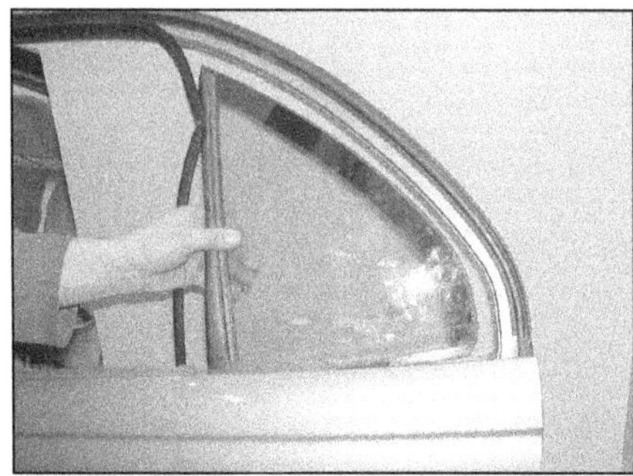

14.29b . . . then slide the glass towards the front of the door and remove it

Window glass - rear door fixed quarter window

Removal

28 Remove the rear door sash window as described previously in this Section.

29 Carefully prise the rubber seal away from the window aperture, then slide the glass towards the front of the door and remove it **(see illustrations).**

Refitting

30 Refitting is a reversal of removal. Ensure that the rubber seal is pressed firmly into the window aperture.

15 Rear quarter window glass (estate models) - removal and refitting

Removal

1 Unclip and remove the load space cover panel, then slacken and remove the screws and detach the relevant cover panel slider housing bodywork.

2 Unclip the cover panel and unbolt the rear seat belt upper anchor bracket from the C-pillar.

3 Unbolt and remove the rear passenger grab handle.

4 Prise out the plastic caps, then remove the C-pillar upper and lower trim panel securing screws. Release the clips using a blunt flat bladed tool and detach the upper and lower trim panels from the C-pillar. Remove the B- and D-pillar trim panels in a similar manner.

5 Unscrew the nuts (13 in total) and remove the window glass from the body. Where applicable, unplug the wiring from the alarm system glass break sensor.

Refitting

6 Refitting is a reversal of removal. Ensure that the rear passenger seat belt upper anchor bracket bolt is tightened to the specified torque wrench setting.

16 Fuel filler flap lock and release cable - removal and refitting

Note: *Refer to Section 21 for details of fuel filler flap locking servo removal and refitting.*

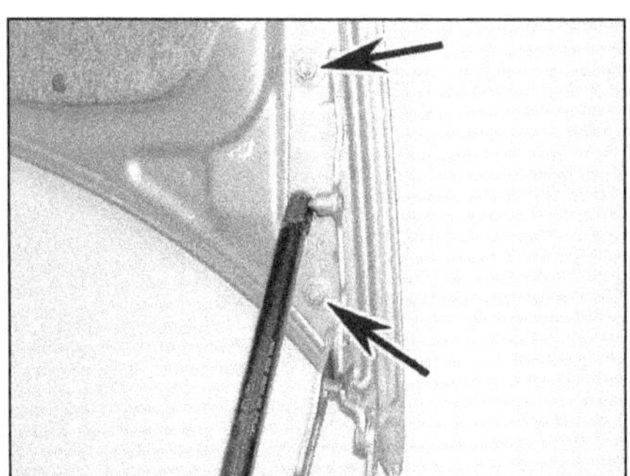

17.3 Unscrew the nuts (arrowed) that secure boot lid to the hinges

Removal

1 Open the fuel flap and remove the filler cap.

2 Undo the two screws and withdraw the fuel filler flap.

Refitting

3 Refitting is a reversal of removal but use suitable adhesive to stick the new rubber seal to the edge of the fuel filler flap. Note that a new flap must be painted with the body colour before fitting.

17 Bootlid and support struts - removal, refitting and adjustment

Bootlid

Removal

1 Open the bootlid, then disconnect the wiring harness at the connector.

2 Using a pencil or marker pen, mark around the hinges on the bootlid as a guide for refitting.

3 With the aid of an assistant, unscrew the nuts that secure boot lid to the hinges, then lift off the boot lid **(see illustration).**

4 The hinges can be removed if required by unhooking the return springs and unbolting the hinges from the body.

Refitting and adjustment

5 Refitting is a reversal of removal, but make sure that the hinges are positioned as noted on removal and tighten the mounting bolts securely. With the bootlid closed, check that it is positioned centrally within the body aperture. If adjustment is necessary, turn the adjusting bolts and rubber buffers to reposition the bootlid. Check that the striker enters the lock centrally, and if necessary adjust the striker position by loosening the mounting bolt. Tighten the bolt on completion.

Support struts

Removal

6 Open the boot lid and note which way round the struts are fitted. Have an assistant support the boot lid in its open position.
7 Using a small screwdriver, prise the spring clip from the top of the strut and disconnect it from the ball on the tailgate **(see illustration)**.
8 Unbolt the bottom of the strut from the bodywork and remove it from the vehicle.

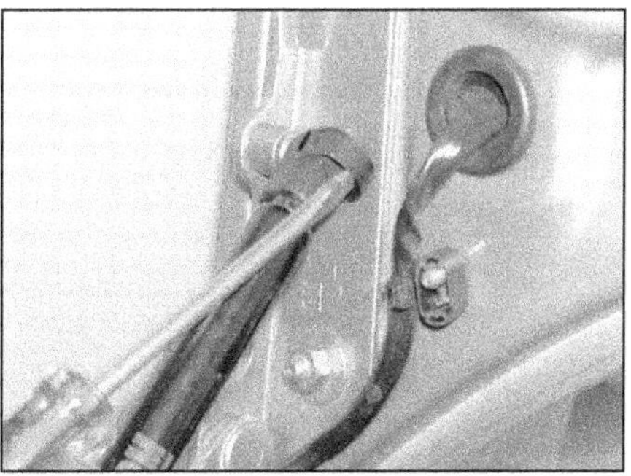
17.7 Using a small screwdriver, prise the spring clip from the top of the strut

Refitting

9 Refitting is a reversal of removal.

18 Bootlid lock components - removal and refitting

Lock cylinder and handle assembly

Removal

1 Open the bootlid and remove the trim panel by prising carefully using a forked tool to release the press-stud fixings **(see illustrations)**.
2 Disconnect the lock link rods from the rear of the lock assembly by prising up the plastic retainer **(see illustration)**.
3 Unscrew the mounting nuts, then withdraw the lock from inside the bootlid. Remove the lock handle and gasket from the outside of the bootlid **(see illustrations).**

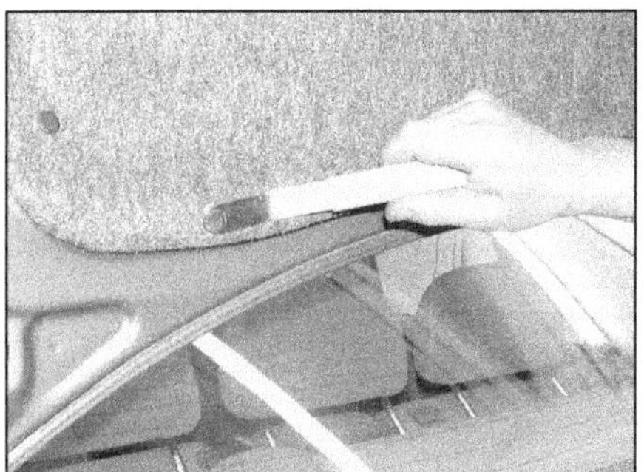
18.1a Prise carefully using a forked tool to release the press-stud fixings . . .

Refitting

4 Refitting is a reversal of removal. Check that when closed the bootlid lock engages the lock striker centrally. If necessary loosen the bolt and adjust the position of the striker, then tighten the bolt.

Lock mechanism

Removal

5 Open the bootlid and remove the trim panel, as described in the previous sub-section.
6 Disconnect the lock cylinder and handle assembly link rods by prising up their plastic retainers.
7 Unscrew the securing screws, then remove the lock mechanism from the bootlid **(see illustration).**

Refitting

8 Refitting is a reversal of removal.

19 Tailgate and support struts - removal, refitting and adjustment

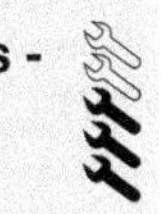

Tailgate

Removal

1 Disconnect the battery negative (earth) lead (see Chapter 5A).

18.1b . . . and remove the trim panel from the inside of the bootlid

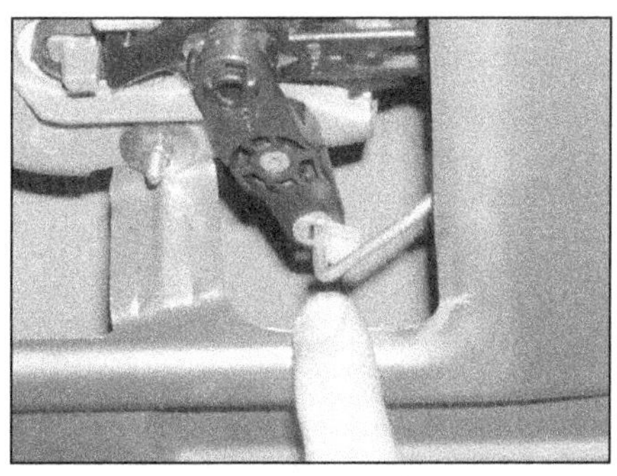
18.2 Disconnect the lock link rods from the rear of the lock assembly

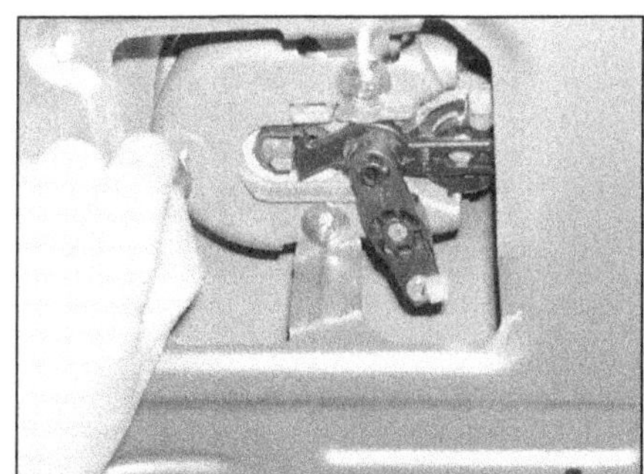
18.3a Unscrew the mounting nuts . . .

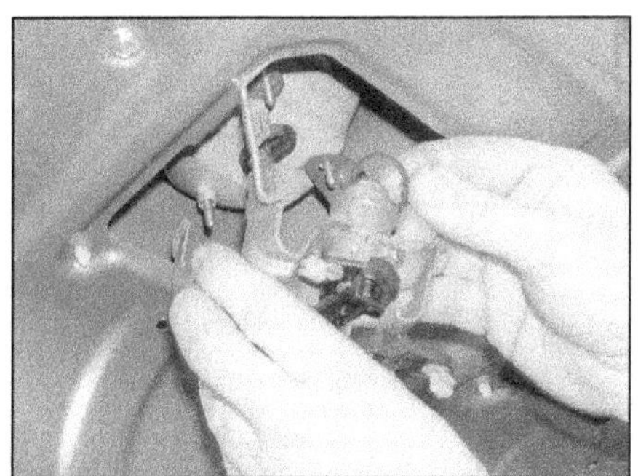
18.3b . . . then withdraw the lock from inside the bootlid

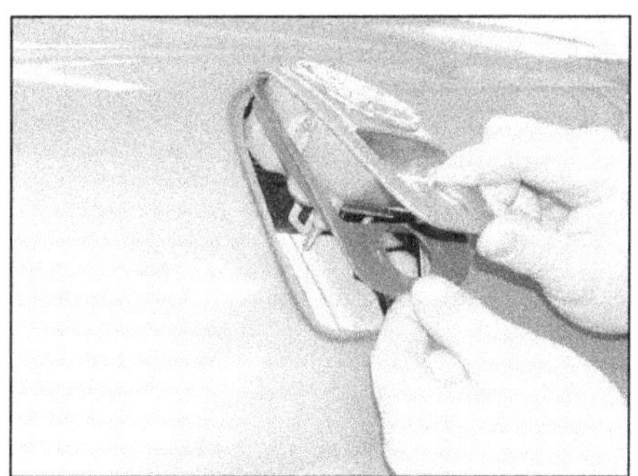
18.3c Remove the exterior handle and gasket from the outside of the bootlid

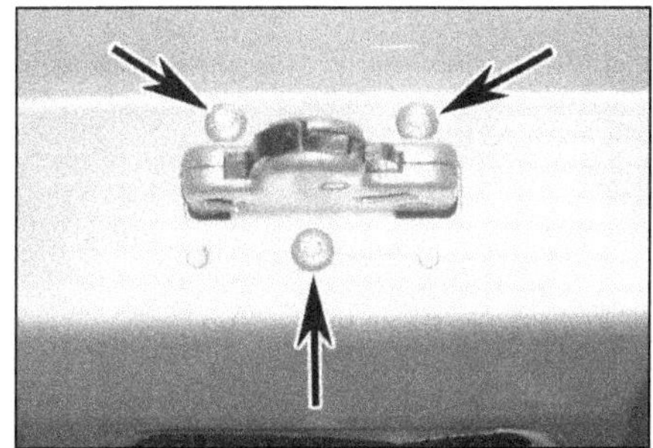
18.7 Unscrew the securing screws, then remove the lock mechanism from the bootlid

19.5 Extract the clips (arrowed) from the tailgate hinge pivot pins

2 Unplug the tailgate wiring harness connector.

3 Disconnect the tailgate washer hose.

4 Have an assistant support the tailgate, then disconnect the tops of the support struts by prising out the spring clips with a small screwdriver. Lower the struts to the body.

5 Extract the clips from the hinge pivot pins, then drive out the pins with a suitable drift while the assistant supports the tailgate. Withdraw the tailgate from the body **(see illustration)**.

Refitting

6 Refitting is a reversal of removal, but check that when closed the tailgate is positioned centrally within the body aperture and flush with the surrounding bodywork. If necessary, remove the trim from the rear of the roof headlining and loosen the hinge mounting bolts. Reposition the tailgate then tighten the bolts and refit the trim. If necessary, adjust the position of the rubber supports so that the tailgate is flush with the surrounding bodywork. After making adjustments, check that the striker enters the lock centrally and if necessary loosen the striker bolts to reposition it. Remove the rear trim panel where necessary. Tighten the bolts and refit the trim on completion.

Support struts

Removal

7 Open the tailgate and note which way round the struts are fitted. Have an assistant support the tailgate in its open position.

8 Using a small screwdriver, prise the spring clip from the top of the strut and disconnect it from the ball on the tailgate.

9 Unbolt the strut lower mounting bracket from the bodywork and remove the strut from the vehicle.

Refitting

10 Refitting is a reversal of removal.

20 Tailgate lock components - removal and refitting

Lock mechanism

Removal

1 Open the tailgate and remove the trim panel.

2 Remove the tailgate lock cylinder as described later in this Section.

3 Using a Torx key unscrew the mounting bolts then withdraw the lock from the tailgate.

Refitting

4 Refitting is a reversal of removal.

Lock cylinder assembly

Removal

5 Open the tailgate and remove the trim panel.

6 Disconnect the central locking linkage by prising up the plastic retainer.

7 Unscrew the mounting nuts, then unhook the lock cylinder assembly from the lock linkage rod and remove from the tailgate.

Refitting

8 Refitting is a reversal of removal.

21 Central locking system components - removal and refitting

Door servo motor

Removal and refitting

1 Remove the relevant door locks, as described in Section 13. Undo the screws, unhook the link rod and detach the servo motor from the lock mechanism **(see illustrations)**.

Control unit

Note: *On model built from 1996 onwards, the central locking control unit is combined with the anti-theft warning system.*

Removal

2 Remove the trim panel from the right-hand front footwell.

3 Release the catch and disconnect the wiring from the bottom of the control unit.

4 Unscrew the mounting nuts and remove the control unit from the vehicle.

Refitting

5 Refitting is a reversal of removal, but tighten the mounting nuts securely.

Bootlid servo motor

Removal

6 Undo the screws, release the clips and remove the bootlid trim panel, as described earlier in this Section.

7 Disconnect the central locking link rod from the servo motor by prising up the plastic retainer **(see illustration)**.

8 Disconnect the wiring connector(s) from the motor, then unscrew the mounting bolts and remove the servo motor from the bootlid **(see illustrations)**.

Refitting

9 Refitting is a reversal of removal, but tighten the mounting bolts securely.

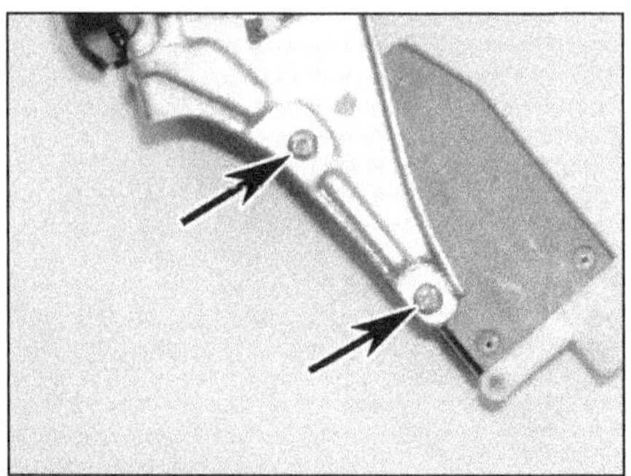

21.1a Undo the screws (arrowed) . . .

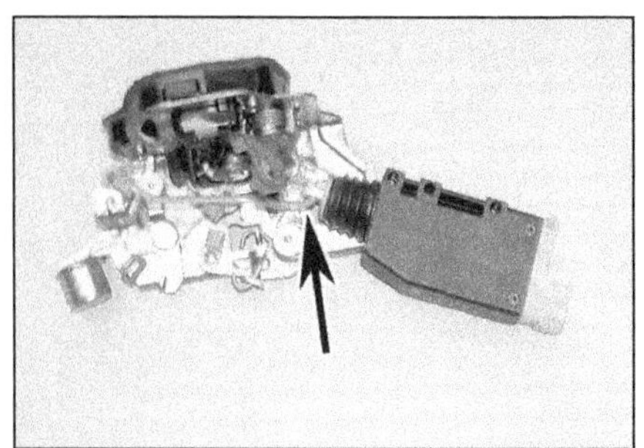

21.1b . . . then unhook the link rod (arrowed) and detach the servo motor from the lock mechanism

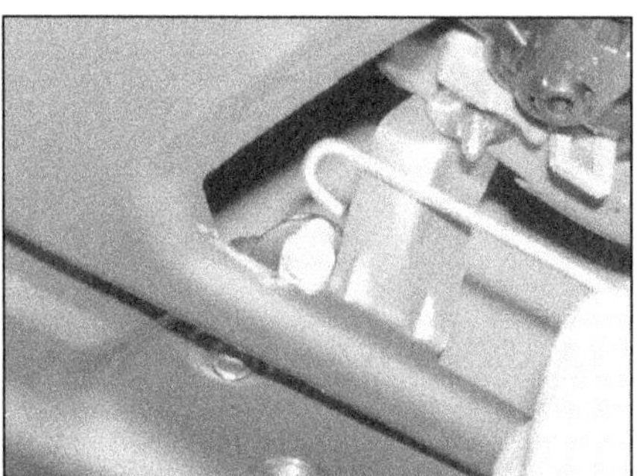

21.7 Disconnect the central locking link rod from the servo motor

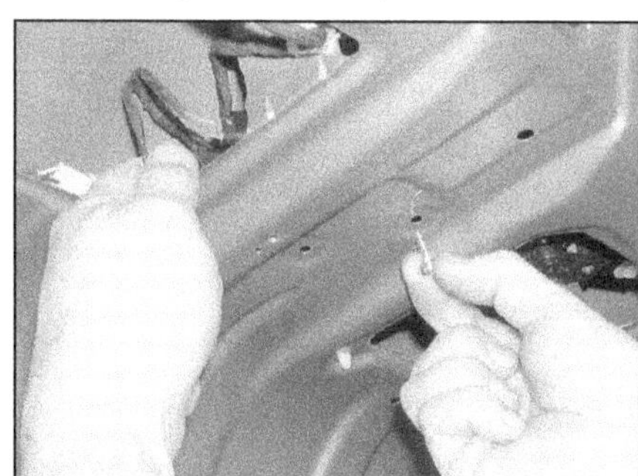

21.8a Unscrew the mounting bolts . . .

Tailgate servo motor

Removal

10 Open the tailgate and remove the trim panel.
11 Disconnect the servo motor linkage from the lock cylinder by prising up the plastic retainer.
12 Unscrew the mounting bolts.
13 Disconnect the wiring connector from the motor and remove the servo motor from the tailgate.

Refitting

14 Refitting is a reversal of removal, but tighten the mounting bolts securely.

Fuel filler flap servo motor

Removal

15 Open the right-hand side luggage compartment side trim lid. Disconnect the wiring plug from the servo motor **(see illustration)**.
16 Unscrew the two mounting bolts and remove the servo motor and bracket from the bodywork. Withdraw from inside the vehicle **(see illustrations)**.

Refitting

17 Refitting is a reversal of removal. Ensure that the servo motor locking rod passes through the grommet in the bodywork and engages with the filler flap lock plate **(see illustrations)**.

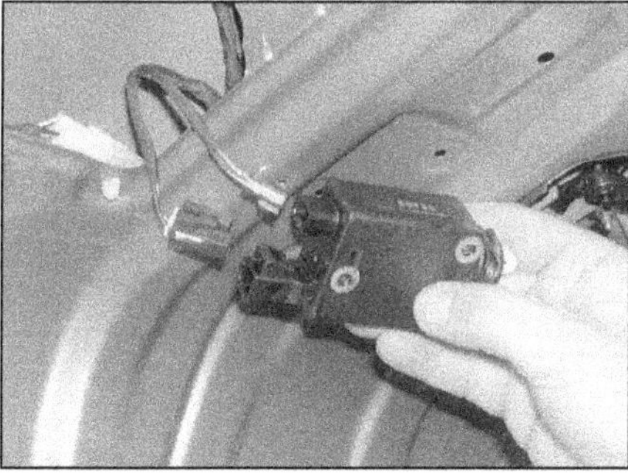

21.8b and remove the servo motor from the bootlid

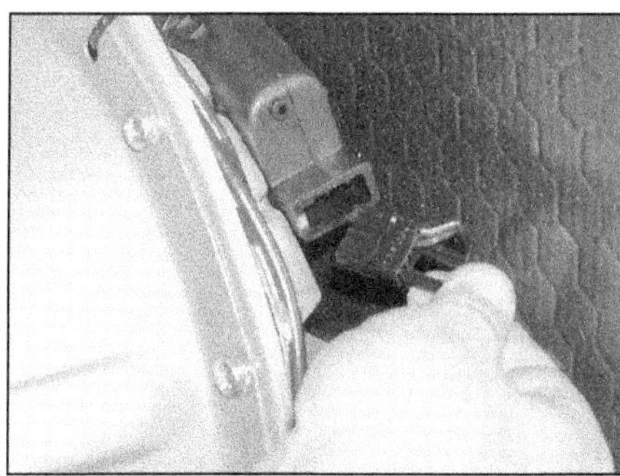

21.15 Disconnect the wiring plug from the servo motor

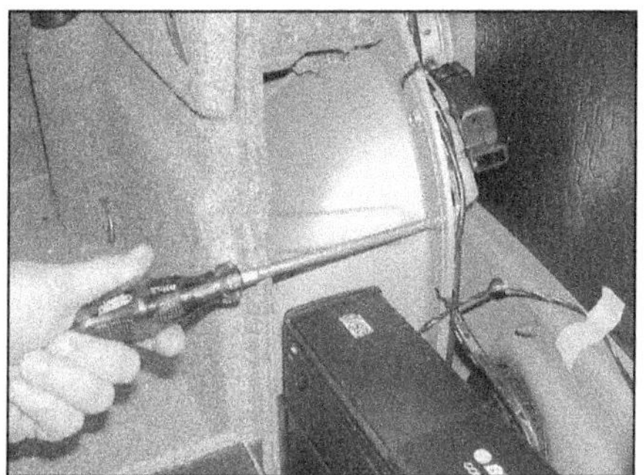

21.16a Unscrew the two mounting bolts . . .

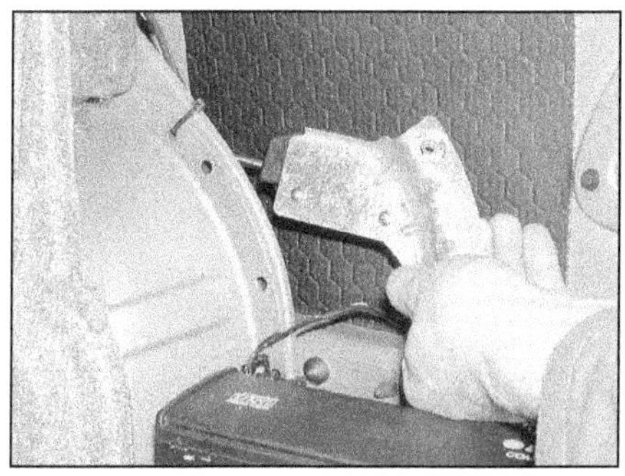

21.16b . . . and remove the servo motor and bracket from the bodywork

22 Electric window components - removal and refitting

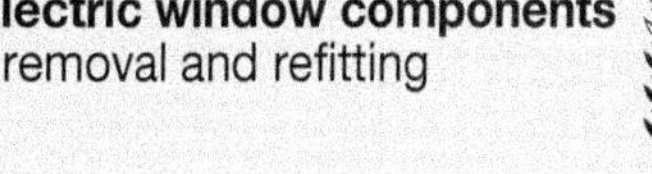

Note: *Disconnect the battery negative cable before starting work. After reconnecting the battery, renewing fuses or reconnecting the window winder wiring plugs, each window winder motor must be reprogrammed, as described at the end of this Section.*

Centre console control switch

Removal

Note: *On models with rear passenger compartment heating vents, it will be necessary to remove the centre console, as described in Chapter 11, to gain access to the switch wiring connectors.*
1 Unclip the gear lever gaiter from the centre console and fold it upwards over the gear lever knob.
2 On models with automatic transmission, carefully prise the winter driving mode switch unit and the gear position indicator unit from the centre console.
3 Undo the securing screws and remove the trim panel from the top of the console.
4 Trace the window switch wiring back to its respective connectors and unplug them.
5 Carefully lever the switch unit from the centre console moulding.

Refitting

6 Refitting is a reversal of removal.

Rear door control switch

Removal

7 Use a small screwdriver to carefully prise off the ashtray unit from the armrest.
8 Unclip the trim panel from behind the door lock release handle.
9 Carefully prise the grip from the underside off the door pull handle, unscrew and remove the door pull handle retaining screws and then remove the pull handle from the door.
10 Unplug the window switch wiring connector as it becomes accessible.
11 Unclip the switch from the door pull handle assembly.

Refitting

12 Refitting is a reversal of removal.

Window winder motor

Removal

13 Remove the window regulator as described in Section 14.
14 Unbolt the motor from the regulator.

Refitting

15 Refitting is a reversal of removal.

Programming

16 After refitting a window winder motor or reconnecting the battery, each motor must be programmed in its fully closed position.
17 With the ignition switched on, close all doors.
18 Working on each window in turn, completely close the window by pressing and holding down the rocker switch; keep the switch held the switch down for at least 5 more seconds after the window has reached the full closed position.

21.17a Ensure that the servo motor locking rod passes through the grommet in the bodywork . . .

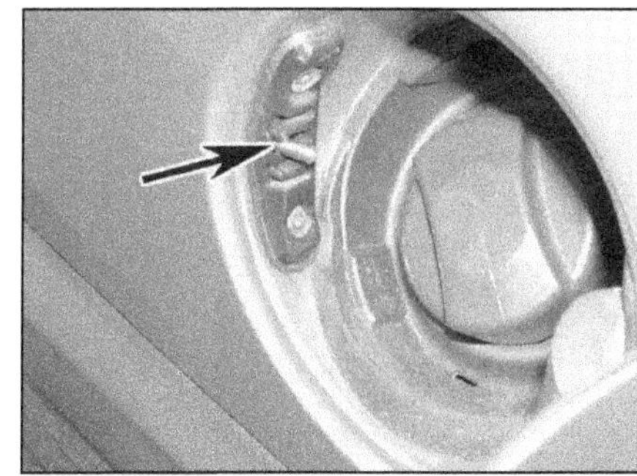

21.17b . . . and engages with the filler flap lock plate

23.1a Carefully prise off the triangular plastic cover panel at the rear of the mirror mountings . . .

23.1b . . . and remove the foam padding

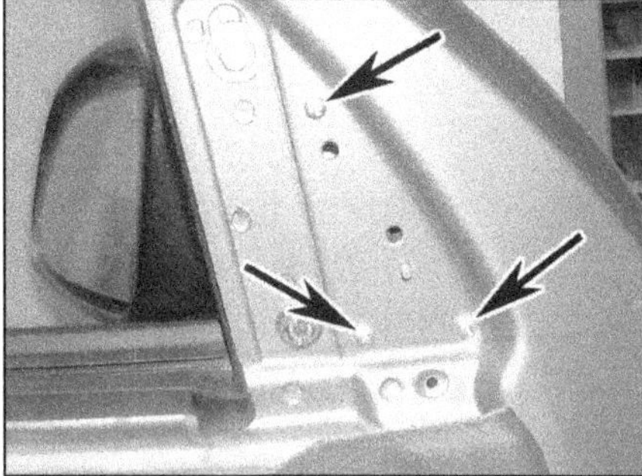
23.5a Unscrew the three mounting bolts (arrowed) . . .

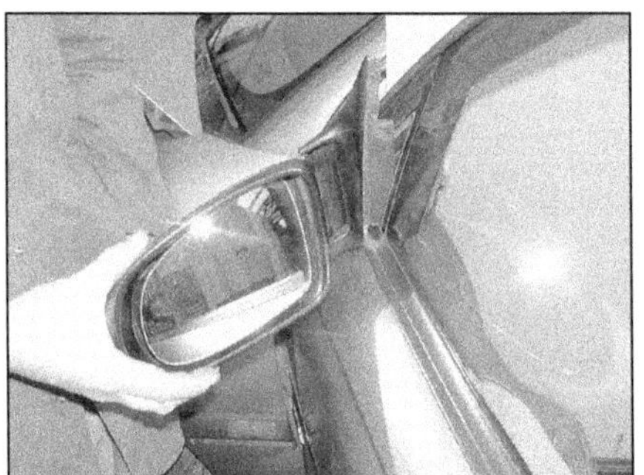
23.5b . . . and lift the mirror from the door

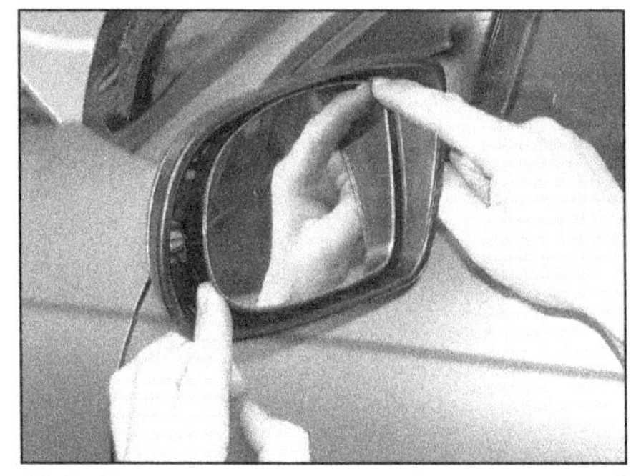
23.7 Gently press the upper inner corner of the glass inwards so that the lower outer corner protrudes from the mirror housing

23.8 Unclip the mirror glass from its mountings

23 Exterior mirrors and associated components - removal and refitting

Exterior mirror housing

Removal

1 Carefully prise off the triangular plastic cover panel at the rear of the mirror mountings, then remove the foam padding and unplug the wiring from the tweeter unit **(see illustrations)**.

2 Prise the plastic cover from the inside of the interior door handle.

3 Carefully prise the grip from the door pull handle.

4 Prise off the small plastic covers to expose the heads of the door handle surround securing screws. Undo the screws and remove the door pull handle (see Section 13). Locate the mirror wiring harness and unplug it at the connector.

5 Support the mirror then unscrew the three mounting bolts and lift the mirror from the door **(see illustrations)**.

Refitting

6 Refitting is a reversal of removal. Ensure that the door weather strip fits over the outside of the mirror casing.

Mirror glass

Removal

7 Gently press the upper inner corner of the glass inwards so that the lower outer corner protrudes from the mirror housing **(see illustration)**.

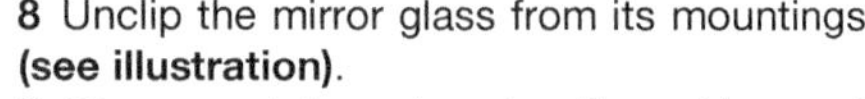

8 Unclip the mirror glass from its mountings **(see illustration)**.

9 Disconnect the mirror heating wiring and withdraw the mirror from the housing **(see illustration)**.

Refitting

10 Refitting is a reversal of removal. Carefully press the mirror into the housing until the centre retainer engages.

Servo motor

Removal

11 Remove the mirror glass as described earlier in this Section.

12 Undo the two screws and withdraw the servo motor from the mirror housing. Unplug the wiring at the connector **(see illustrations)**.

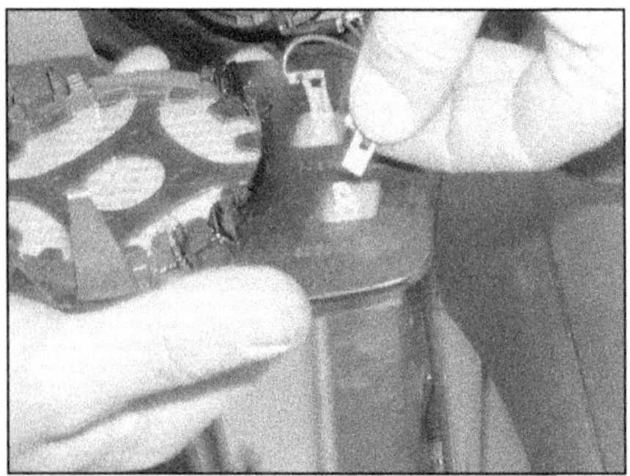
23.9 Disconnect the mirror heating wiring

23.12a Undo the two screws . . .

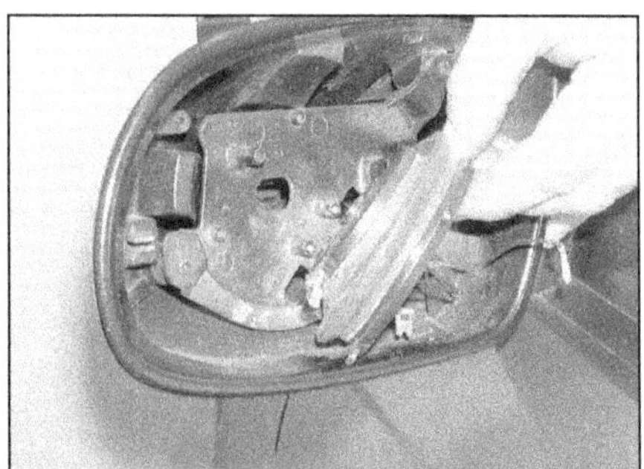
23.12b . . . and withdraw the servo motor from the mirror housing

23.12c Unplug the wiring at the connector

23.21a Undo the screws . . .

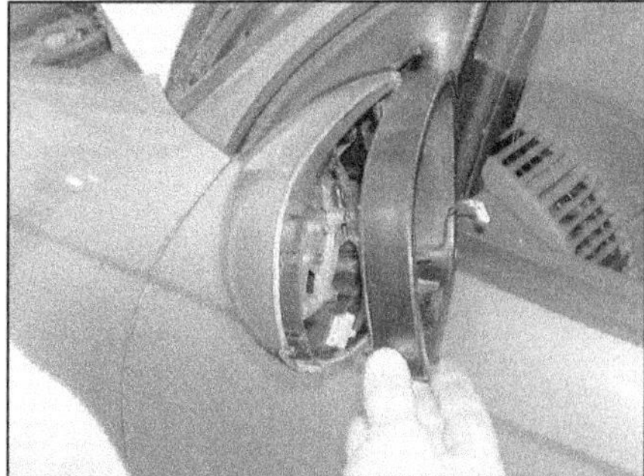

23.21b . . . and lift off the mirror housing frame

Refitting

13 Refitting is a reversal of removal.

Mirror door switch

Removal

14 Carefully prise off the triangular plastic cover panel at the rear of the mirror mountings, then remove the foam padding and unplug the wiring from the tweeter unit.
15 Prise the plastic cover from the inside of the interior door handle.
16 Carefully prise the grip from the door pull handle.
17 Prise off the small plastic covers to expose the heads of the door handle surround securing screws. Undo the screws and remove the door pull handle.
18 Disconnect the wiring from the rear of the mirror switch, then depress the locking tabs and remove the switch from the door pull handle assembly.

Refitting

19 Refitting is a reversal of removal.

Mirror cover

Removal

20 Remove the mirror glass and motor as described earlier in this Section.
21 Undo the screws and lift off the mirror housing frame **(see illustrations).**
22 Remove the screws and detach the cover from the front of the mirror housing **(see illustrations)**.

Refitting

23 Refitting is a reversal of removal.

24 Windscreen and fixed window glass - general information

The windscreen, rear/tailgate screen and rear quarter window glass (Estate models) are cemented in position with a special adhesive and require the use of specialist equipment for their removal and refitting. Renewal of such fixed glass is considered beyond the scope of the home mechanic. Owners are strongly advised to have the work carried out by a windscreen fitting specialists.

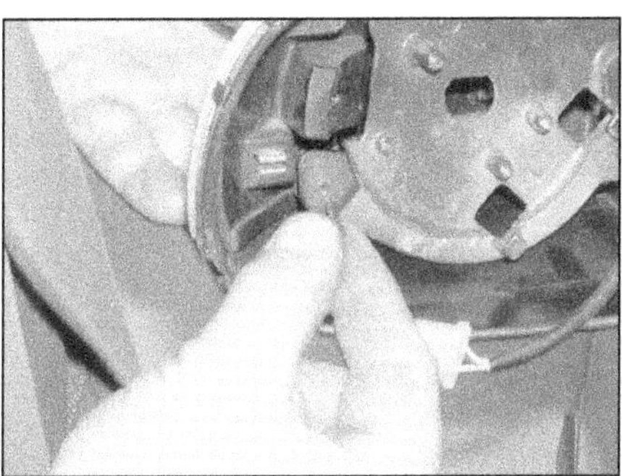

23.22a Remove the screws . . .

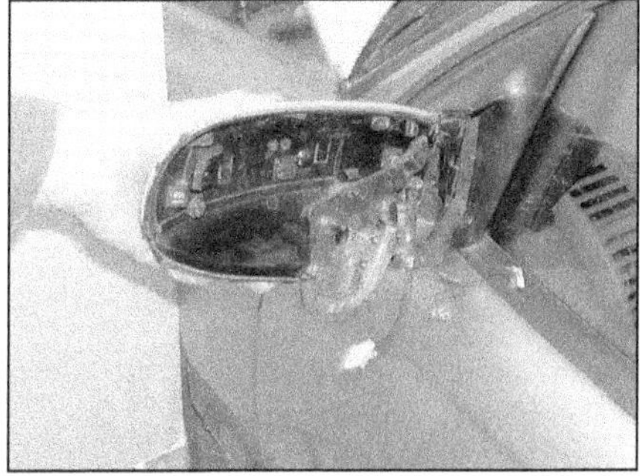

23.22b . . . and detach the cover from the front of the mirror housing

On Estate models the rear quarter window glass incorporates a breakage sensor which is linked to the anti-theft security system, and the rear screen incorporates an aerial for the radio.

25 Sunroof components - removal and refitting

Sunroof glass

Removal

1 Slide back the sun screen and half open the sunroof.
2 Undo the screws from the rear edge of the sunroof and remove the trim.
3 Close the sunroof then unclip the side trim using a screwdriver.
4 Mark the position of the side screws then unscrew them and withdraw the glass.

Refitting

5 Refitting is a reversal of removal; ensure that the safety code labelling on the glass is positioned towards the rear of the sunroof aperture. Adjust the height of the glass as follows. With the side screws loose, position the glass so that the front edge is flush with the front of the roof or a maximum of 1.0 mm below the roof and the rear edge is flush with the rear of the roof or a maximum of 1.0 mm above the roof. Tighten the screws to the specified torque with the glass in this position.

Sunroof interior screen

Removal

6 Remove the sunroof glass as described earlier in this Section.
7 Undo the screws and remove the water gutter from the front of the roof aperture.
8 Remove the front sliders, then pull the screen forwards and remove the rear sliders.
9 Withdraw the screen from the roof.

Refitting

10 Refitting is a reversal of removal.

Wind deflector

Removal

11 Half open the glass then undo the screws and detach the deflector lifter mechanism from the front of the sunroof aperture.
12 Rotate the deflector so that it is positioned vertically, then release the deflector from the lifter mechanism.

Refitting

13 Refitting is a reversal of removal.

Sunroof motor, gear housing and control switch assembly

Removal

14 Set the sunroof glass in the closed position, then disconnect the battery negative cable.
15 Unclip the cover panel from the sunroof control console **(see illustration).**

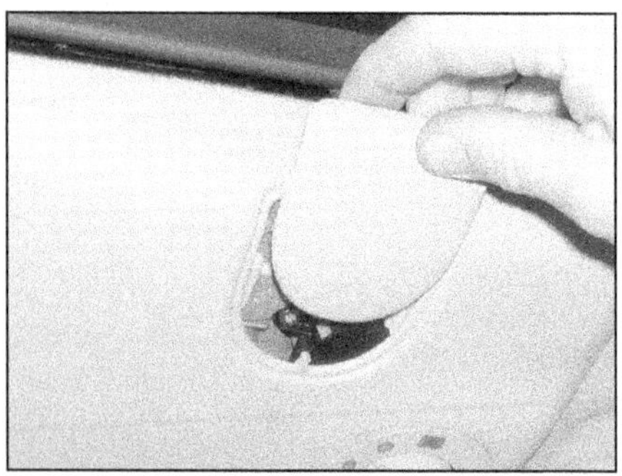
25.15 Unclip the cover panel from the sunroof control console

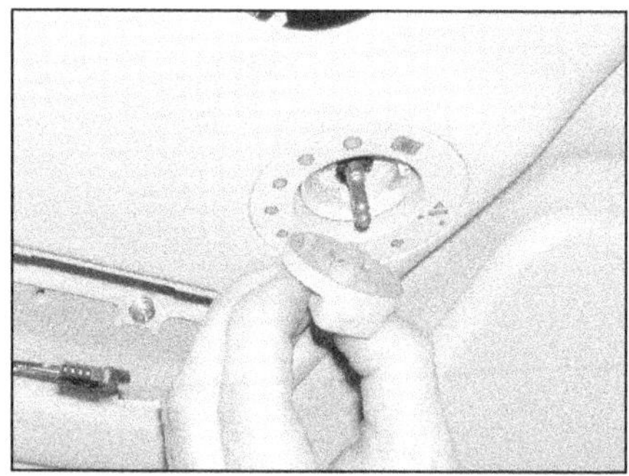
25.16 Detach the control knob from the sunroof switch

16 Detach the control knob from the sunroof switch **(see illustration).**

17 Remove the lens, then unclip the interior lamp unit from the console and disconnect the wiring **(see illustrations).**

18 Release the control switch from the panel by depressing the clips with a screwdriver **(see illustration).**

19 Release the sealing strip from the front of the console **(see illustration).**

20 Undo the securing screws located inside the interior lamp recess, then detach the console from the roof **(see illustrations).**

21 Slacken and withdraw the motor assembly securing screws, then unplug the wiring connector and remove the assembly from the roof.

Refitting

22 Refitting is a reversal of removal. If a new motor assembly is being installed, unclip the protective cap and dummy knob from the sunroof switch shaft before fitting. On completion, adjust the operation of the control switch as described in the next sub-section.

Adjustment

23 Turn the ignition switch to position II.

24 Press and hold the sunroof switch until the sunroof closes and the motor is heard to stop turning. Release the switch.

25 Turn the sunroof switch to the tilt position - the motor should set the sunroof in the tilt position.

26 Press and hold the sunroof switch until the sunroof closes and the motor is heard to stop turning. Release the switch.

27 Turn the sunroof switch to the fully open position - the motor should slide the sunroof glass back to the fully open position.

28 Turn the sunroof switch to the closed position - the motor should slide the sunroof glass forward.

29 Press and hold the sunroof switch until the sunroof closes completely and the motor is heard to stop turning. Release the switch.

30 The preceding steps should allow the sunroof motor control electronics to learn the open, closed and tilt positions of the sunroof glass. If at any time during the adjustment procedure, the sunroof glass opens unexpectedly, repeat the steps in paragraphs 25 to 30 inclusive as necessary, until operation is satisfactory.

Sunroof assembly and control cables

Removal and refitting

31 Removal and refitting of the complete sunroof assembly and control cables is considered beyond the scope of the average home mechanic as it involves the removal of the headlining. This work should therefore be carried out by a Vauxhall/Opel dealer. **Note:** *In an emergency, the sunroof glass can be operated by removing the cover panel and turning the manual drive shaft with a screwdriver* ***(see illustration).***

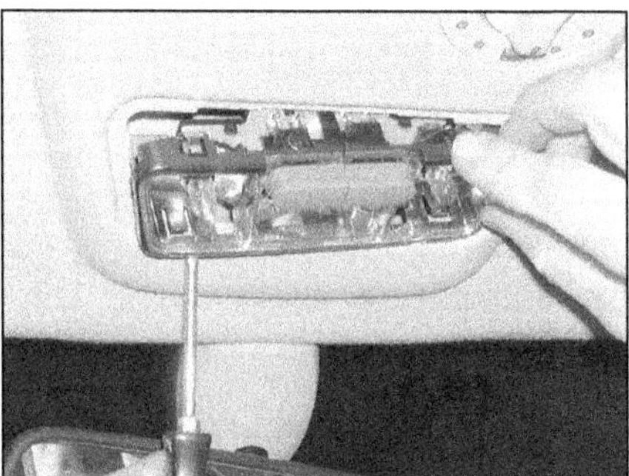
25.17a Remove the lens, then unclip the interior lamp unit from the console . . .

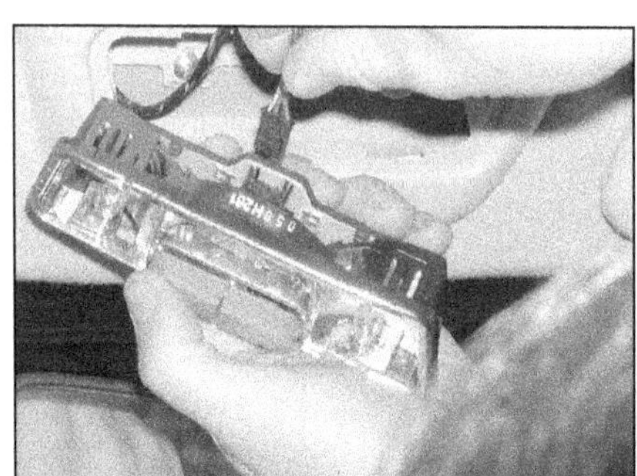
25.17b . . . and disconnect the wiring

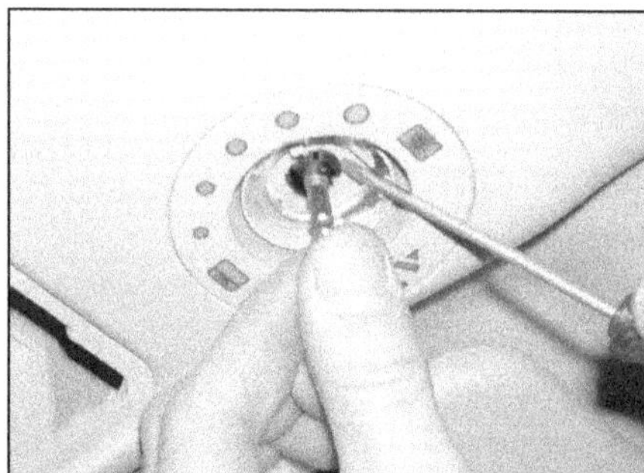
25.18 Release the control switch from the panel by depressing the clips with a screwdriver

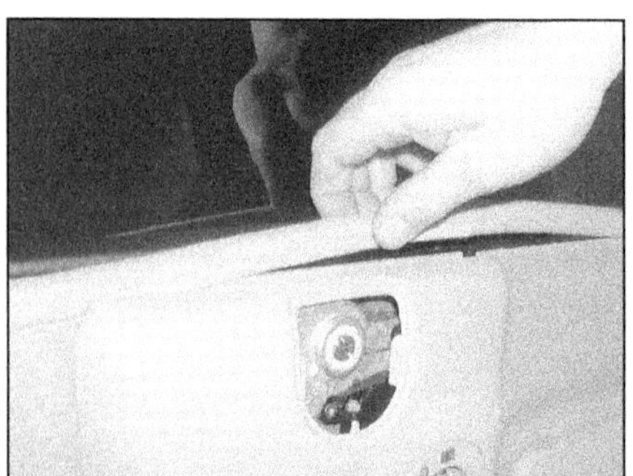
25.19 Release the sealing strip from the front of the console

25.20a Undo the securing screws located inside the interior lamp recess . . .

25.20b . . . then detach the console from the roof

25.31 In an emergency, the sunroof glass can be operated by removing the cover panel and turning the manual drive shaft with a screwdriver

26 Body exterior fittings - removal and refitting

Water deflector panel

Removal

1 Open the bonnet then remove the windscreen wiper arms as described in Chapter 12.
2 Pull the rubber weatherstrip from the front of the bulkhead.
3 Release the rubber sealing strip from the lower edge of the windscreen.
4 Prise off the plastic caps, the slacken and withdraw the panel securing screws.
5 Pull the water deflector panel from the bulkhead, noting that it is in two sections.

Refitting

6 Refitting is a reversal of removal.

Wheel arch liners

Removal and refitting

7 The wheel arch liners are secured by a combination of self-tapping screws, push-fit clips and nuts. Removal is self-evident after supporting the vehicle on axle stands and removing the roadwheel (see *Jacking and Vehicle Support*). The clips are removed by pushing the centre pins through, and are secured by inserting the centre pins and pushing them in flush.

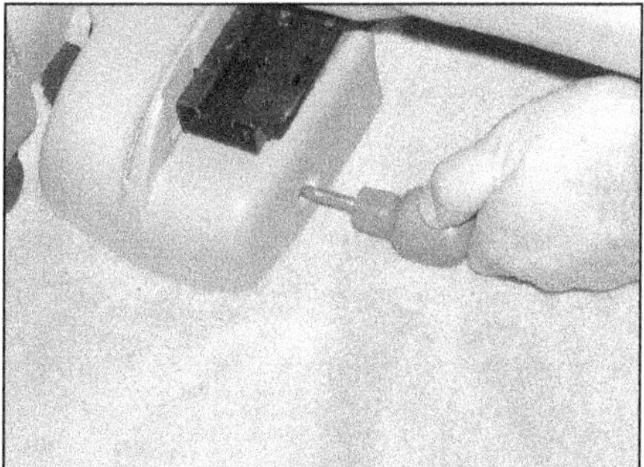
27.2a Undo the securing screw . . .

Body trim strips and badges

Removal and refitting

8 The various body trim strips and badges are held in position with a special adhesive. Removal requires the trim/badge to be heated, to soften the adhesive, and then cut away from the surface. Due to the high risk of damage to the vehicle paintwork during this operation, it is recommended that this task should be entrusted to a Vauxhall/Opel dealer.

27 Seats - removal and refitting

Front seat

Warning: The front seats are fitted with seat belt tensioners and on some models, side impact air bags. Before removing the front seats, the seat belt tensioners and side impact airbags must be disabled - refer to the Supplementary Restraint System (SRS) safety information given in Chapter 12, Section 23 before proceeding.

Removal

1 Ensure that the Supplementary Restraint System (SRS) is disabled before proceeding; refer to Chapter 12 Section 23 for details.
2 Undo the securing screw and detach the plastic end cap from the outer seat runner. Unclip the trim panel from the side of the seat runner **(see illustrations).**

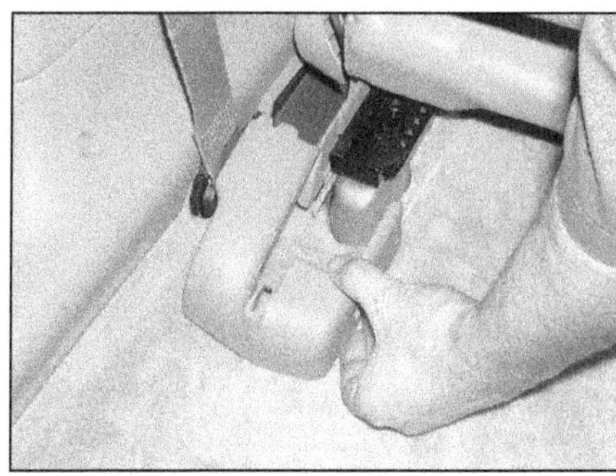
27.2b . . . and detach the plastic end cap from the outer seat runners

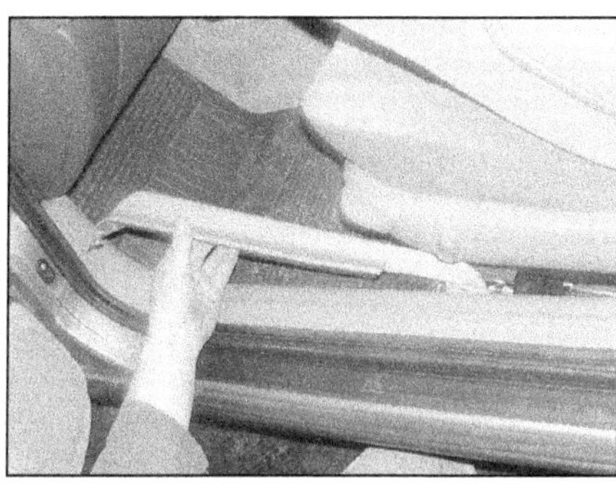
27.2c Unclip the trim panel from the side of the seat runner

3 On models with mechanical seat belt tensioners, ensure that the special locking tool is inserted to prevent the accidental triggering of the tensioner mechanism; refer to the Supplementary Restraint System (SRS) safety information given in Chapter 12, Section 23 before proceeding.
4 Adjust the seat to the fully forwards position, then unscrew the rear mounting screws **(see illustration)**.
5 Slide the seat backwards to the end of its travel, then unscrew the front mounting screws **(see illustration)**.
6 Unplug the wiring at the connector(s) and remove the front seat from inside the vehicle **(see illustrations)**.

Refitting

7 Refitting is a reversal of removal but use new mounting screws and tighten them to the

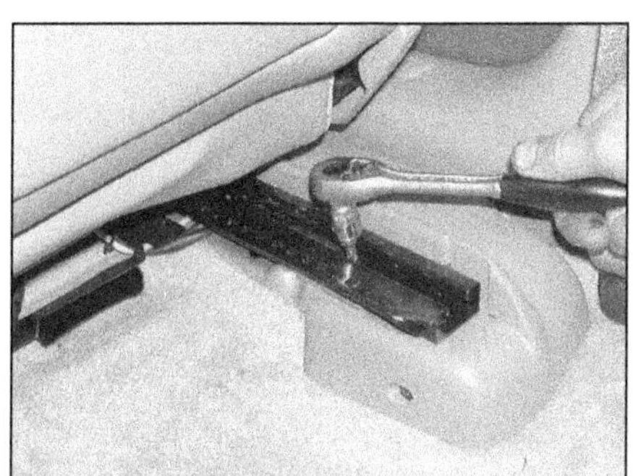
27.4 Unscrew the seat rear mounting screws

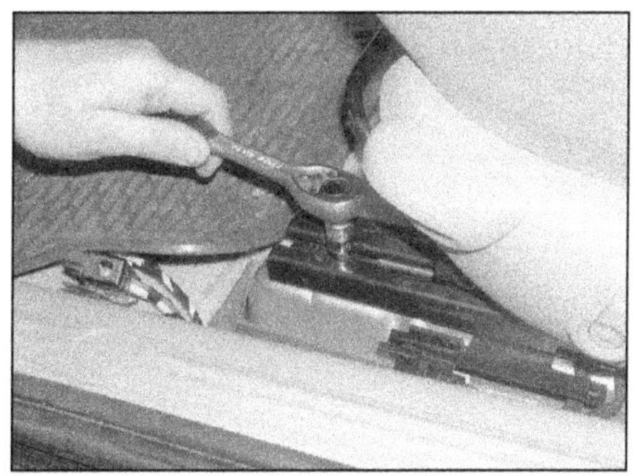
27.5 Unscrew the seat front mounting screws

27.6a Unplug the wiring at the connector(s) . . .

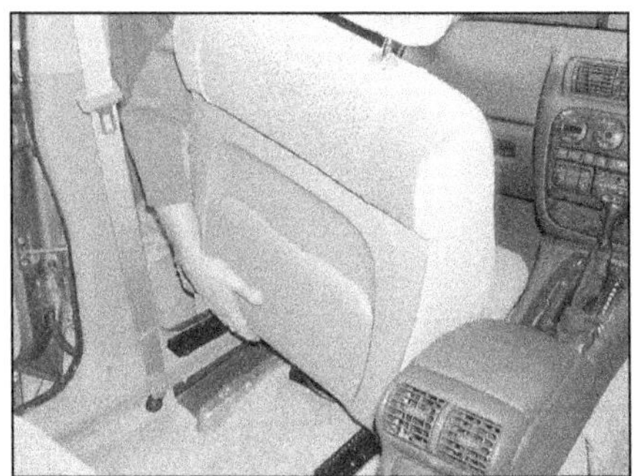

27.6b . . . and remove the front seat from inside the vehicle

specified torque in the sequence shown **(see illustration)** On models with mechanical seat belt tensioners, remove the forked locking tool before refitting the seat runner trim panels.

Rear seat cushion

Removal

8 Grasp the seat cushion lock straps, located at the front lower edge of the seat , and pull them to disengage the locks **(see illustration).**

9 Pivot the seat cushion backwards and unplug the wiring for the heating elements (where fitted).

10 Pass the seat belt buckles through the hole in the seat cushion, then remove the seat from the vehicle **(see illustration).**

Refitting

11 Refitting is a reversal of removal. Ensure that the seat belt buckles pass through the hole in the seat cushion before locking it in position.

Rear seat backrest - Saloon models

Removal

12 Remove the rear seat cushion, as described earlier in this Section.

13 Depress the locking button and detach the centre seat belt from its buckle.

14 Bend up the metal securing tabs, then pivot the side cushions upwards and remove them from the car **(see illustration).**

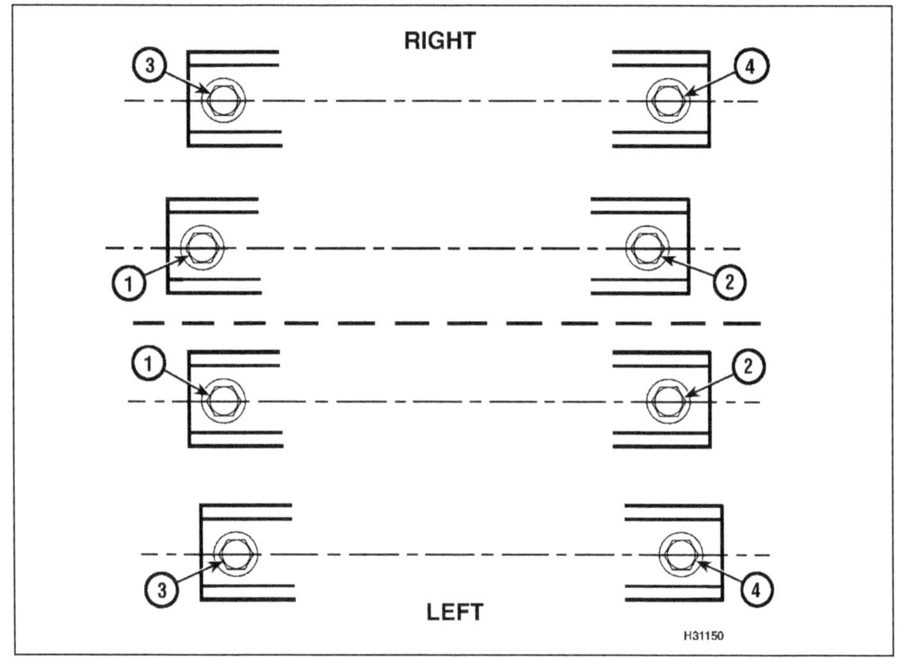

27.7 Front seat bolt tightening sequence

15 Press the release buttons and allow the seat back to pivot forwards.

16 Unclip the carpet trim from rear bulkhead, then unscrew the hinge bolts and remove the rear seat back from the car. Where applicable, unplug the seat heating element wiring at the connector.

Refitting

17 Refitting is a reversal of removal. Ensure that all fixings are tightened to the correct torque, where specified.

Rear seat back - Estate models

Removal

18 Remove the rear seat cushion, as described earlier in this Section.

19 Depress the locking button and detach the centre seat belt from its buckle (where fitted).

20 Where a single-section seat back rest is fitted, undo the pivot bolts at both ends of the back rest, recovering the washers, and remove the back rest from the vehicle.

21 Where a split rear seat back rest is fitted, undo the pivot bolts at both ends of the back rest, recovering the washers, then unbolt the centre hinges from the support bracket and remove the back rest from the vehicle.

Refitting

22 Refitting is a reversal of removal. Ensure that all fixings are tightened to the correct torque, where specified.

28 Seat belt components - removal and refitting

Front seat belt and reel

Removal

1 Prise off the cap, then slacken and withdraw the bolt and detach the seat belt

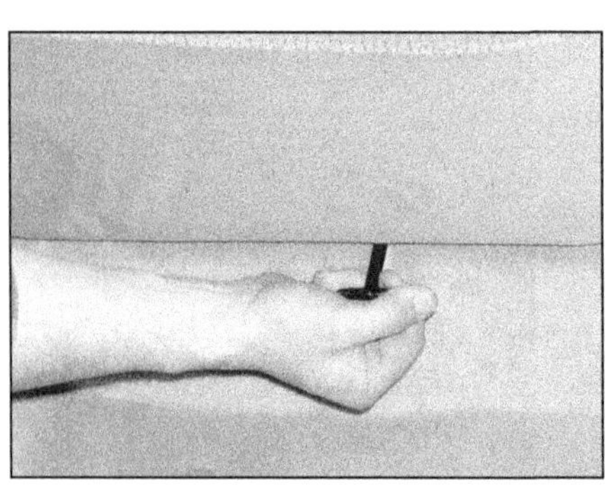

27.8 Pull the seat cushion lock straps

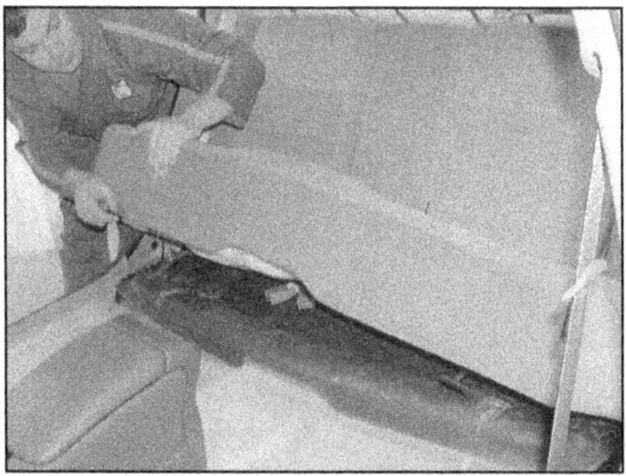

27.10 Remove the seat cushion from the vehicle

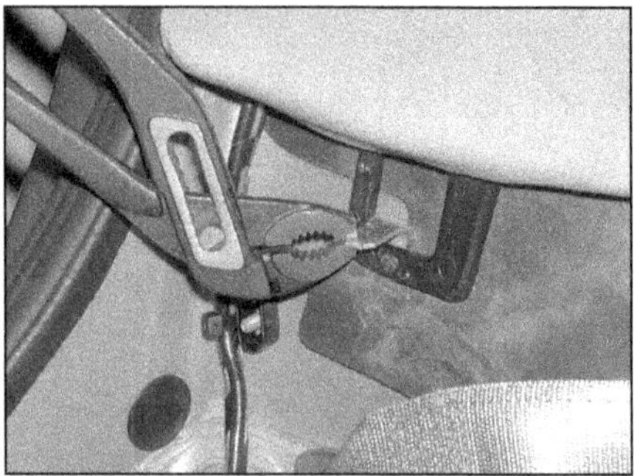

27.14 Bend up the metal securing tabs to release the seat back side cushions

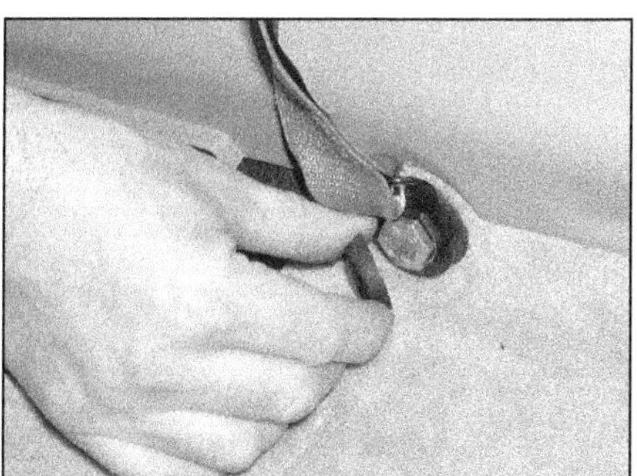
28.1a Prise off the cap . . .

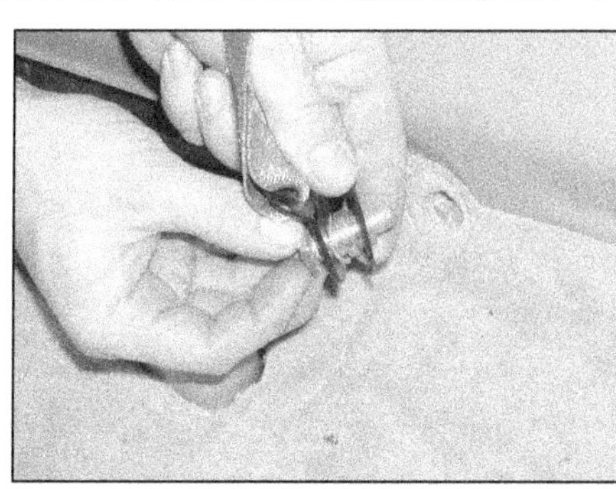
28.1b then slacken and withdraw the bolt and detach the seat belt lower anchor from the sill

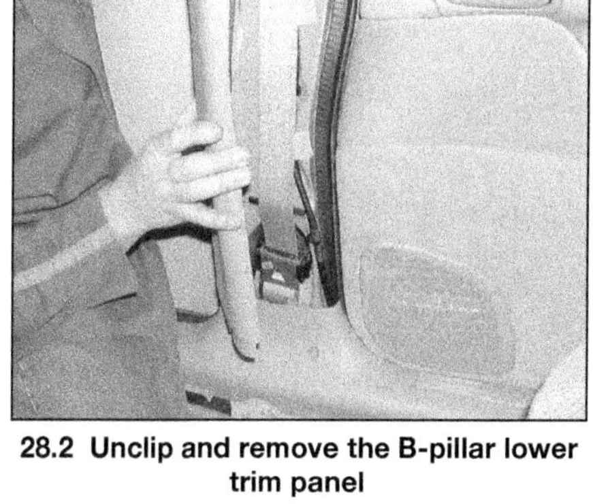
28.2 Unclip and remove the B-pillar lower trim panel

lower anchor from the sill. Recover the washers **(see illustrations)**.

2 Unclip and remove the B-pillar lower trim panel **(see illustration)**.

3 Unclip the alarm system interior sensor unit from the B-pillar upper trim panel and unplug the wiring at the connector **(see illustration)**.

4 Undo the screws and remove the B-pillar upper trim panel. Feed the seat belt clasp through the trim panel aperture **(see illustrations)**.

5 Prise the cover strip from the sill trim panel. Undo the screws and remove the panel from the sill **(see illustrations)**.

6 Slacken and withdraw the bolt and detach the seat belt upper anchor from the adjustment bar slider **(see illustration)**.

7 Unbolt the inertia reel from the base of the B-pillar and remove the seat belt assembly from the vehicle **(see illustration)**.

Refitting

8 Refitting is a reversal of removal, but tighten all mounting bolts to the correct torque, where specified.

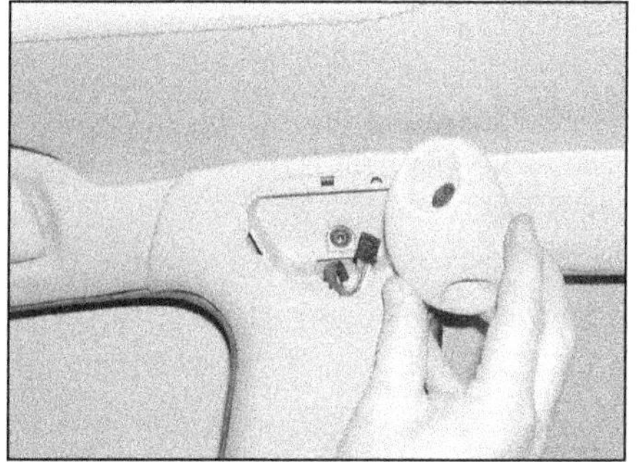
28.3 Unclip the alarm system interior sensor unit from the B-pillar upper trim panel . . .

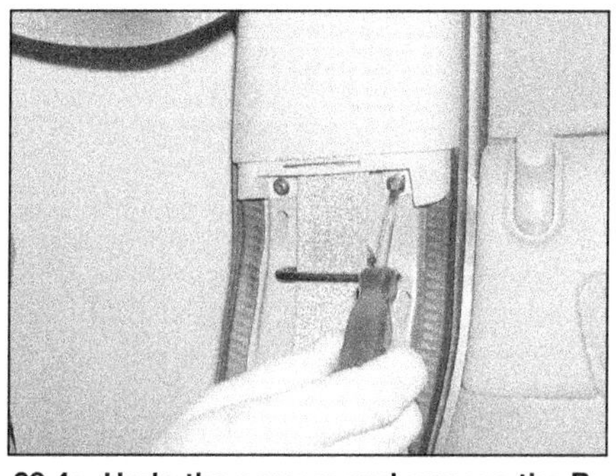
28.4a Undo the screws and remove the B-pillar upper trim panel

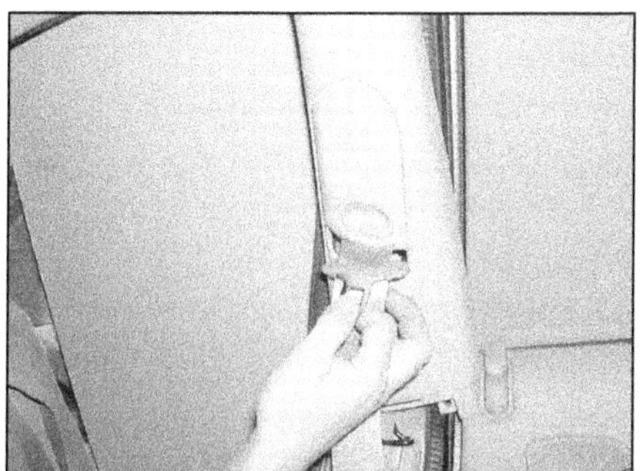
28.4b Feed the seat belt clasp through the trim panel aperture

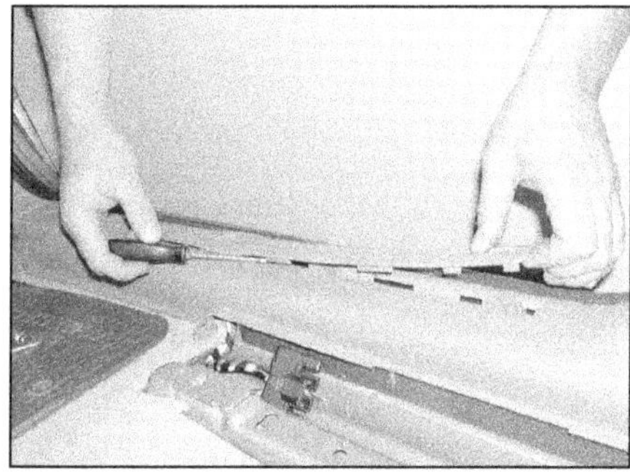
28.5a Prise the cover strip from the sill trim panel

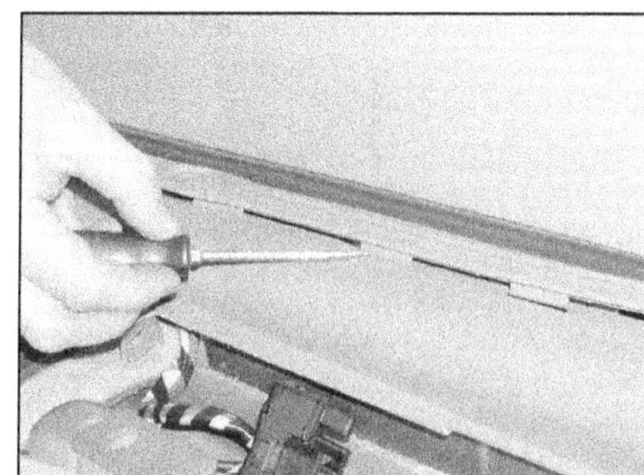
28.5b Undo the screws . . .

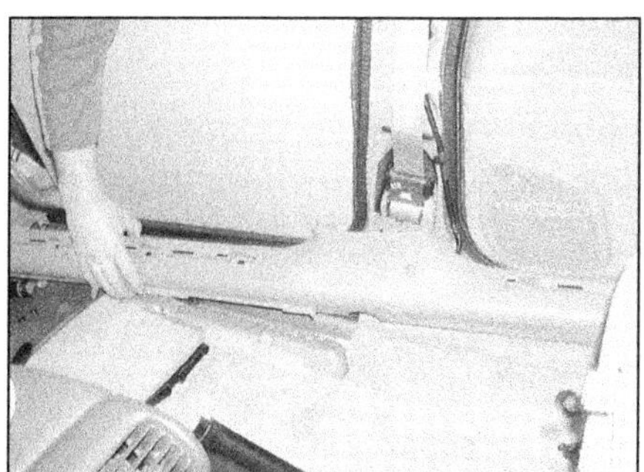
28.5c . . . and remove the panel from the sill

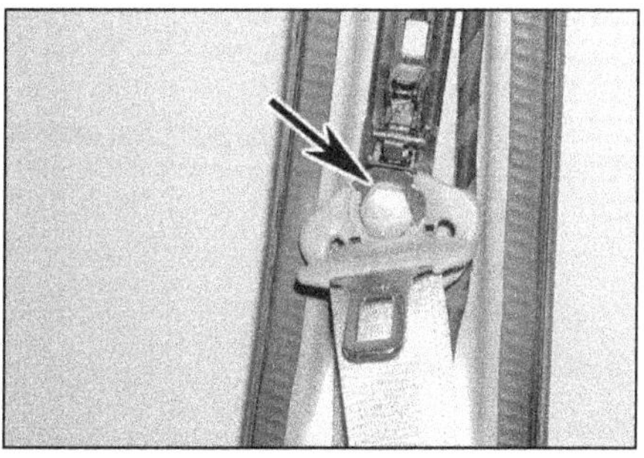
28.6 Slacken and withdraw the bolt (arrowed) and detach the seat belt upper anchor from the adjustment bar slider

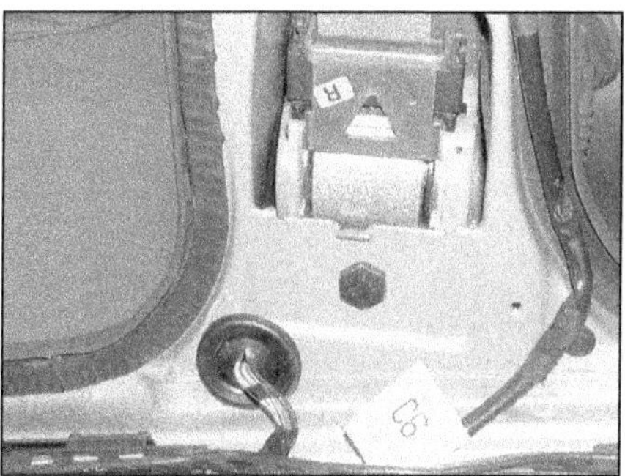
28.7 Inertia reel securing bolt

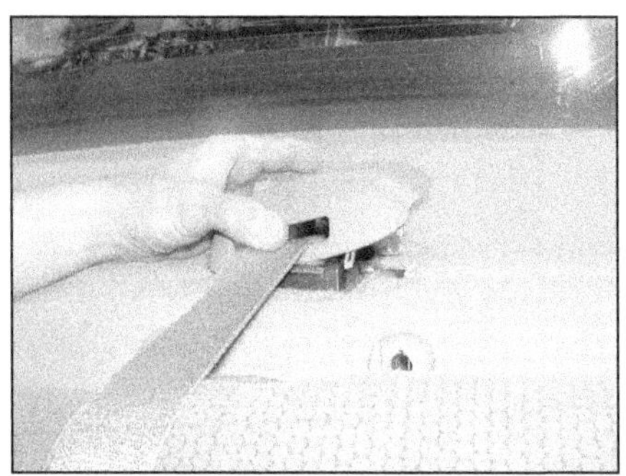

28.9a Unclip the cover from the parcel shelf . . .

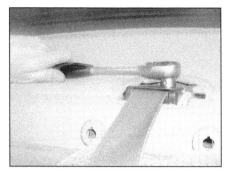

28.9b . . . unbolt the inertia reel . . .

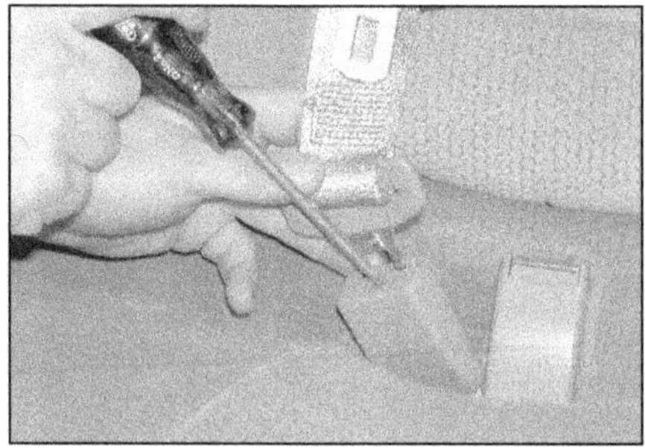

28.9c . . . and then depress the locking button to release the lower belt anchor from its buckle

Rear seat belt and reel - Saloon models

Removal

9 The centre rear seat belt can be removed by unclipping the cover from the parcel shelf, unbolting the inertia reel and then depressing the locking button to release the lower belt anchor from its buckle **(see illustrations).**

10 The outer seat belts are removed as follows. Refer to Section 27 and remove the rear seat cushion and backrests.

11 Slacken and withdraw the bolt and detach the seat belt lower anchor from the bodywork.

12 Remove the cap then slacken and withdraw the bolt and detach the seat belt upper anchor from the bodywork.

13 Unbolt the inertia reel from the C-pillar and remove the seat belt assembly from the vehicle **(see illustration).**

Refitting

14 Refitting is a reversal of removal, but tighten all mounting bolts to the correct torque, where specified.

Rear seat belt and reel - Estate models

Removal

15 To remove the centre seat belt, first remove the rear seat back as described in Section 27. Remove the upholstery from the seat back by releasing the securing clips. The inertia reel can then be unbolted, allowing the seat belt to be removed.

16 The outer seat belts are removed as follows. Refer to Section 27 and remove the rear seat cushion and backrests.

17 Slacken and withdraw the bolt and detach the seat belt lower anchor from the bodywork.

18 Remove the cap, slacken and withdraw the bolt and detach the seat belt upper anchor from the bodywork.

19 Release the securing clips and detach the lower trim panel from the C-pillar. Similarly, remove the trim panel from the side of the load space.

20 Unbolt the inertia reel from the bodywork and remove the seat belt assembly from the vehicle.

Refitting

21 Refitting is a reversal of removal, but tighten the mounting bolts to the specified torque.

28.13 Unbolting the outer rear seat belt inertia reel from the C-pillar

29 Interior trim - removal and refitting

1 The interior trim panels are secured by a combination of clips and screws. Removal and refitting is generally self-explanatory, noting that it may be necessary to remove or loosen surrounding panels to allow a particular panel to be removed. The following paragraphs describe the removal and refitting of the major panels in more detail.

Front footwell side trim panel

Removal

2 Open the front door and pull the weatherstrip away from the side trim panel. Loosen the front end of the sill trim panel, as described later in this Section.

3 Undo the screws, then pull the bonnet release handle forwards and remove the side trim panel.

Refitting

4 Refitting is a reversal of removal.

B-pillar trim panel

Removal

5 Where fitted, carefully lever off the alarm system sensor and disconnect the wiring.

6 Unbolt the front seat belt from the height adjuster mechanism with reference to Section 28.

7 Pull the door weatherstrip away from the trim.

8 Release the press-stud clips with a flat bladed instrument and prise the lower trim panel from the B-pillar.

9 Undo the screws, then remove the upper trim panel from the B-pillar, feeding the seat belt buckle through the slot.

Refitting

10 Refitting is a reversal of removal.

Sill inner trim panel

Removal

11 Remove the B-pillar lower trim panel as described earlier in this Section.

12 Prise the cover strip from the centre of the sill trim panel.

13 Undo the screws and unclip the panel from the sill.

Refitting

14 Refitting is a reversal of removal.

Luggage compartment side trim panel (Estate models)

Removal

15 Remove the rear luggage compartment cover, then remove the rear seat as described in Section 27.

16 Slacken and withdraw the securing screws and remove the C-pillar lower trim panel.

17 Undo the screws then prise out the side trim panel using a screwdriver to release the retaining clips.

Refitting

18 Refitting is a reversal of removal.

Luggage compartment side trim panel (Saloon models)

Removal

19 Open the bootlid and remove the vehicle tools.

20 Fold the rear seat backrest forwards, then prise the rubber beading from the edge of the rear bulkhead aperture.

21 Unclip the rubber cap from the top of the rear suspension strut mounting nut.

22 Lift the carpet trim from the floor of the loadspace, then unclip the cover from the spare wheel.
23 Remove the trim panel from the side of the luggage compartment.

Refitting

24 Refitting is a reversal of removal.

Carpets

Removal

25 The front and rear carpets can be removed after removing the front seats, centre console and rear footwell air distribution ducts together with side trim panels and remaining brackets.
26 On Estate models the rear luggage compartment carpet can be removed by releasing the clips located on the backrest and rear valance then removing the tools and spare wheel cover.

Refitting

27 Refitting is a reversal of removal.

Headlining

28 The headlining is secured to the roof with clips and screws, and can be withdrawn once all fittings such as the grab handles, sun visors, sunroof, front, centre and rear pillar trim panels, and associated components have been removed. The door and tailgate aperture weatherseals will also have to be prised clear.
29 Note that headlining removal requires considerable skill and experience if it is to be carried out without damage, and is therefore best entrusted to an expert.

30.2a Open the lid of the storage box to the rear of the handbrake lever, then undo the four screws . . .

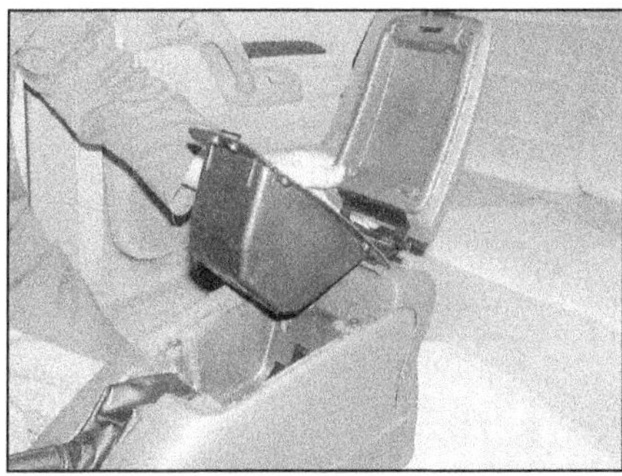

30.2b . . . and withdraw the storage box moulding from the console

30 Centre console - removal and refitting

Removal

1 Disconnect the battery negative (earth) lead (see Chapter 5A).
2 Open the lid of the storage box to the rear of the handbrake lever, then undo the four screws and withdraw the storage box moulding from the console **(see illustrations)**.
3 Where applicable, unbolt the car telephone mounting bracket, then unplug the wiring harness and remove the bracket from the console.
4 Remove the screws and detach the rear passenger air vent module (where fitted) from the rear of the console **(see illustrations)**. Unplug the wiring at the connector(s).
5 Unclip the gear lever gaiter from the console and fold it up over the gear lever knob **(see illustration)**.
6 On automatic models, prise the gear position indicator module and winter mode switch module from the console **(see illustrations)**. Unplug the wiring at the connectors.
7 Undo the securing screws and remove the gear lever trim panel from the surround **(see illustrations)**.

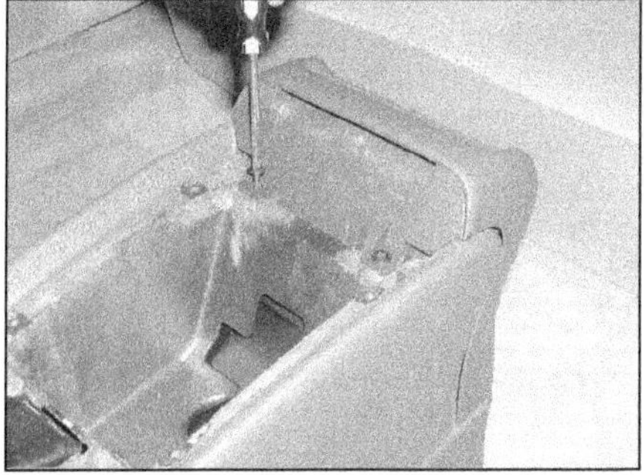

30.4a Remove the screws . . .

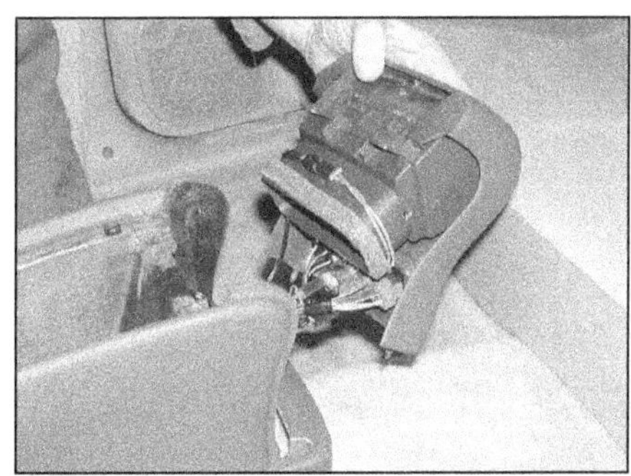

30.4b . . . and detach the rear passenger air vent module (where fitted) from the rear of the console

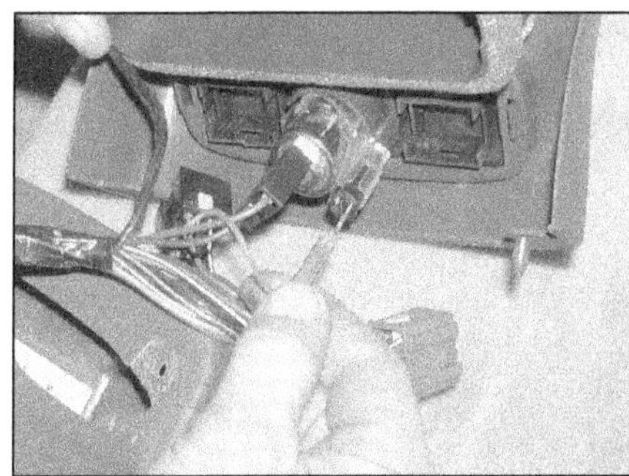

30.4c Unplug the wiring at the connector(s)

30.5 Unclip the gear lever gaiter from the console and fold it up over the gear lever knob

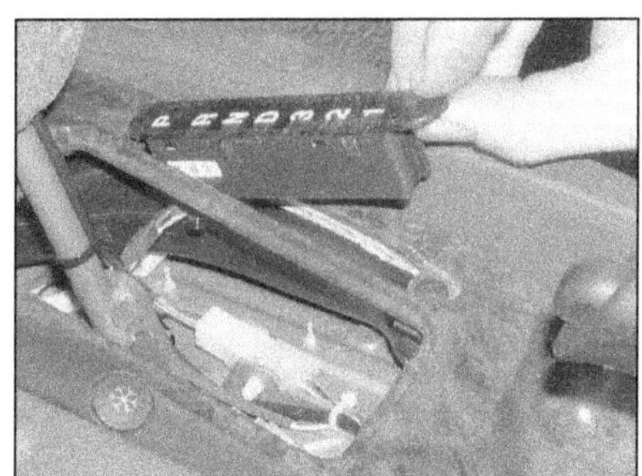

30.6a On automatic models, prise the gear position indicator module . . .

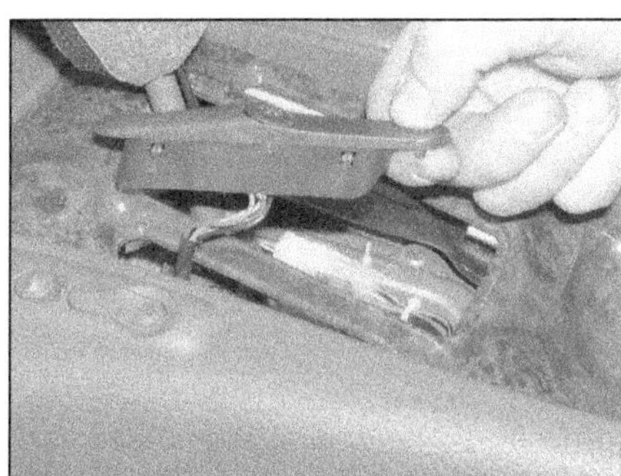

30.6b . . . and winter mode switch module from the console

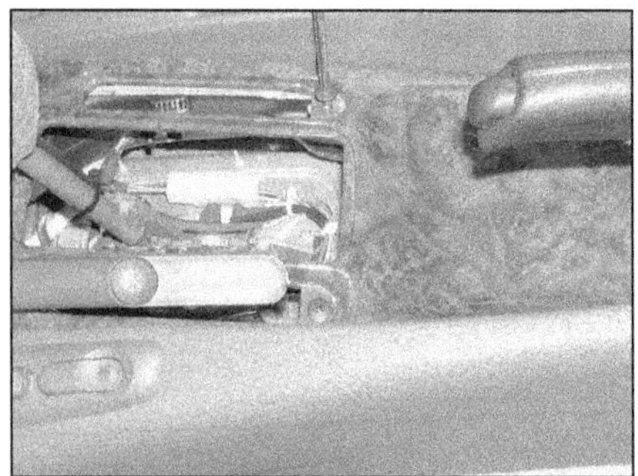
30.7a Undo the securing screws . . .

30.7b . . . and remove the gear lever trim panel from the surround

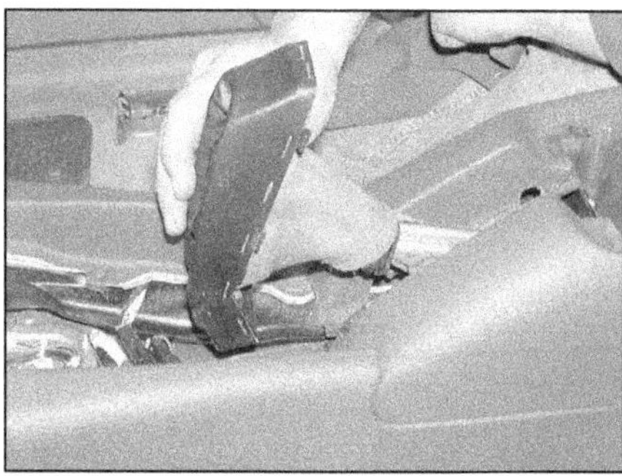
30.8 Unclip the gaiter from the handbrake lever and remove it

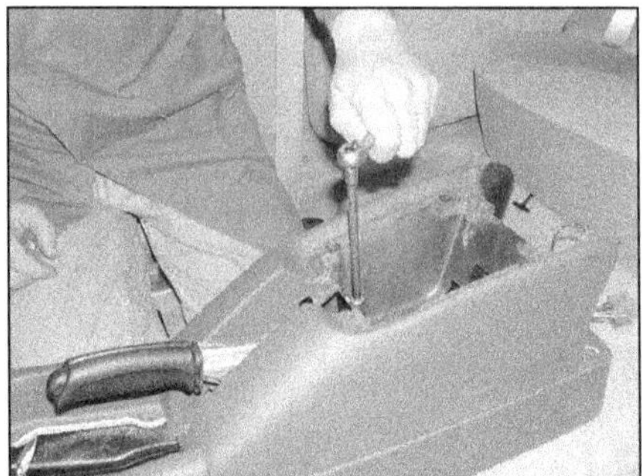
30.9a Slacken and withdraw the securing screws . . .

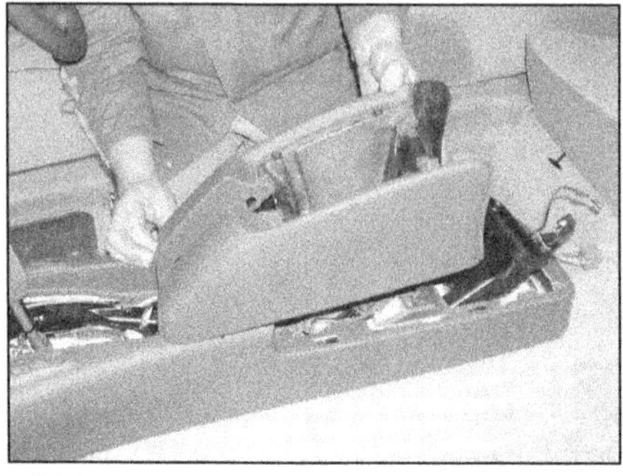
30.9b . . . and lift off the centre arm rest (where fitted)

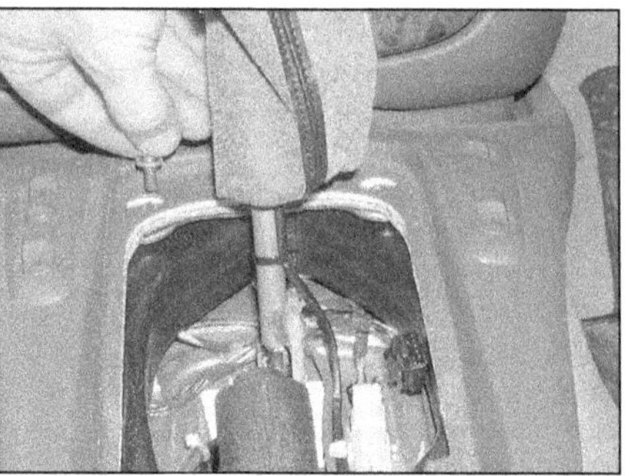
30.10a Undo the centre console securing screws . . .

30.10b . . . remove the support bracket . . .

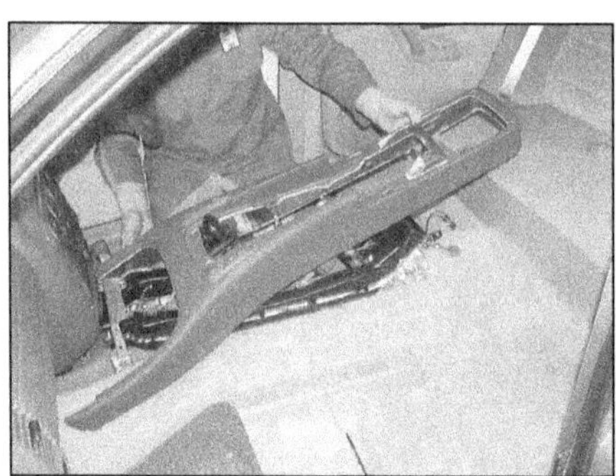
30.10c . . . then lift the console away from the floorpan

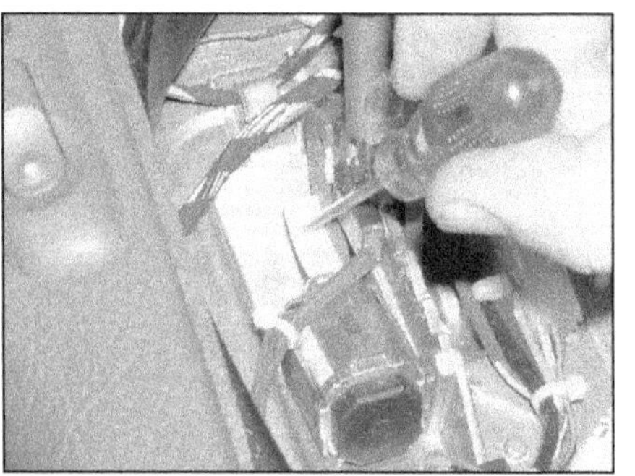
30.11 On automatic models, it may be necessary to release the gear selector from the PARK position, by depressing the yellow release lever, to allow the removal of the console from the floorpan

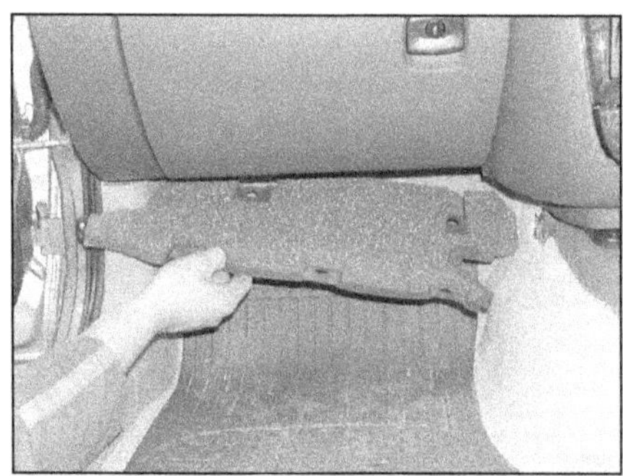
31.2 Release the press-stud clips and detach the trim panel from the underside of the facia

8 Unclip the gaiter from the handbrake lever and remove it **(see illustration)**.

9 Slacken and withdraw the securing screws and lift off the centre arm rest (where fitted) **(see illustrations)**.

10 Undo the centre console securing screws, remove the support bracket, then lift the console away from the floorpan. Unplug the electric window switch wiring at the connectors, as it becomes accessible **(see illustrations)**.

11 Remove the console from the vehicle. Note that on automatic models, it may be necessary to release the gear selector from the P position, by depressing the yellow release lever, to allow the removal of the console from the floorpan **(see illustration)**.

Refitting

12 Refitting is a reversal of removal.

31 Glovebox - removal and refitting

Removal

1 Disconnect the battery negative cable and position it away from the terminal.

2 Release the press-stud clips and detach the trim panel from the underside of the facia **(see illustration)**.

3 Slacken and withdraw the screws that secure the lower edge of the passenger airbag

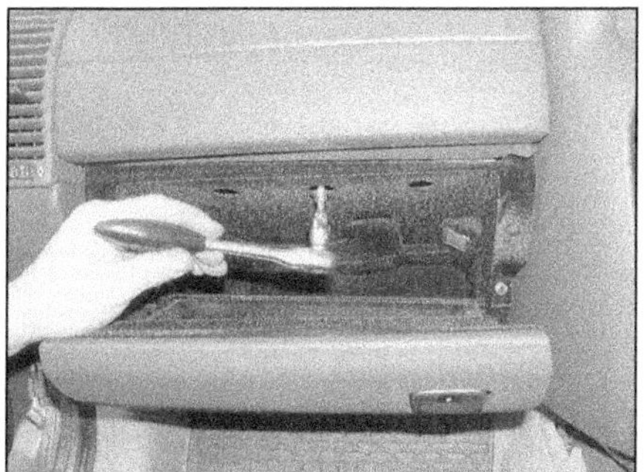

31.3 Slacken and withdraw the screws that secure the lower edge of the passenger airbag unit cover panel to the facia

unit cover panel to the facia - there is no need to remove the cover panel completely **(see illustration)**. Refer to Chapter 12 Section 24 for details of the passenger air bag unit cover.

4 Open the glovebox lid, then lift the passenger airbag unit cover panel slightly and undo the glovebox upper mounting screws, to release the top of the glovebox to the facia panel **(see illustration)**.

5 Undo the two lower screws and withdraw the glovebox from the facia panel sufficient to disconnect the wiring from the illumination lamp and its switch.

6 On models fitted with air conditioning detach the air hose from the cooling slider.

7 Withdraw the glovebox from the facia and remove it from the facia.

Refitting

8 Refitting is a reversal of removal. Ensure that the passenger airbag unit cover panel securing screws and tightened to the specified torque.

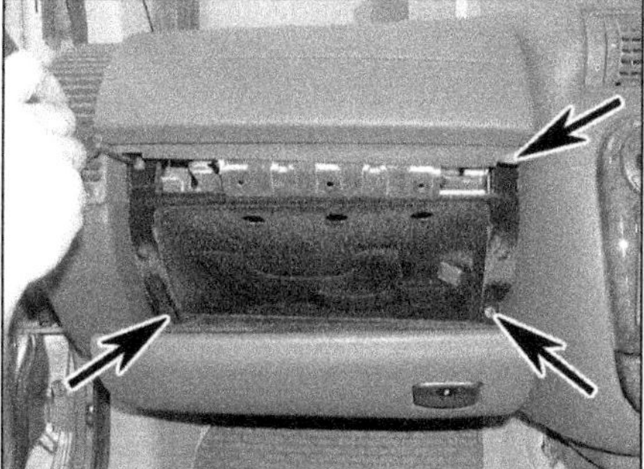

31.4 Undo the glovebox mounting screws (arrowed)

32 Facia assembly - removal and refitting

Removal

Warning: Refer to the Supplementary Restraint System (SRS) precautions given in Chapter 12 Section 23 before disturbing the driver or passenger airbag units.

1 Note that this procedure involves the removal of the driver and passenger airbag units. Before proceeding, carry out the Supplementary Restraint System (SRS) deactivation procedure, as described in Chapter 12 Section 23. Failure to carry out this procedure may result in accidental detonation of the airbag(s).

2 Remove the drivers airbag unit from the steering wheel as described in Chapter 12 Section 24.

3 Set the steering wheel in the straight ahead position, then remove the ignition key and allow the steering column lock to engage. Ensure that the steering column remains in this position throughout the entire procedure.

4 Remove the steering wheel as described in Chapter 10.

5 Undo the screws and remove the upper and lower sections of the steering column cowling.

6 Remove the wiper and indicator switches from the steering column as described in Chapter 12, Section 4. Unbolt and remove the switch plastic mounting bracket.

7 Remove the ignition switch unit from the rear of the steering column lock assembly, with reference to Chapter 10.

8 Remove the airbag contact unit as described in Chapter 12 Section 24.

9 At the underside of the steering column, unclip and remove the lower trim panel, then open the fusebox cover and unhook the check strap from it. Pull out the hinge pins and remove the fusebox cover from the facia **(see illustrations).**

10 Carefully lever the cover panel from the side of the right hand facia end section **(see illustration).**

11 Remove the headlamp switch unit, as described in Chapter 12, Section 4.

12 Unclip the headlamp switch base plate from the facia end section.

13 Unclip the bulb holder from the rear of the air vent housing and position it to one side **(see illustration)**.

14 Unclip the air vent nozzle from its housing, then undo the screws and remove the air vent/headlamp switch housing **(see illustrations).**

15 Slacken and withdraw the securing screws and remove the right hand facia end section **(see illustrations)**.

16 Remove the glovebox as described in Section 31.

32.9a Open the fusebox cover and unhook the check strap from it

32.9b Pull out the hinge pins . . .

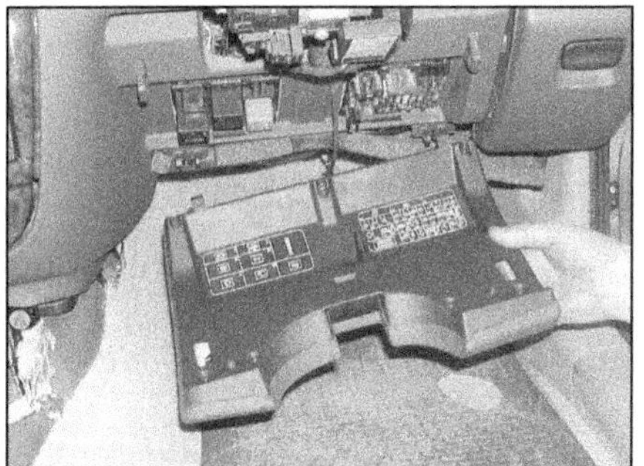

32.9c . . . and remove the fusebox cover from the facia

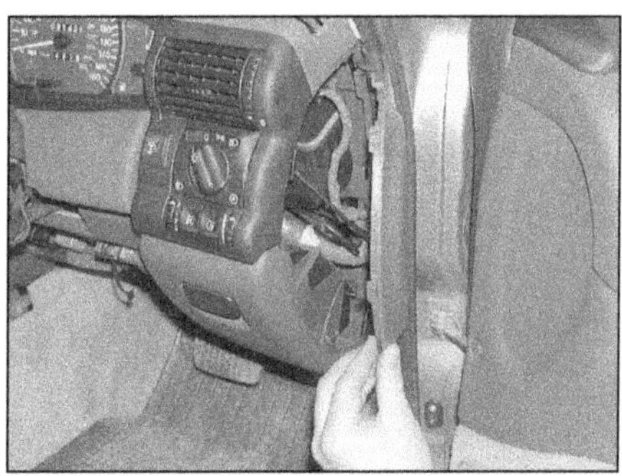

32.10 Lever the cover panel from the side of the right hand facia end section

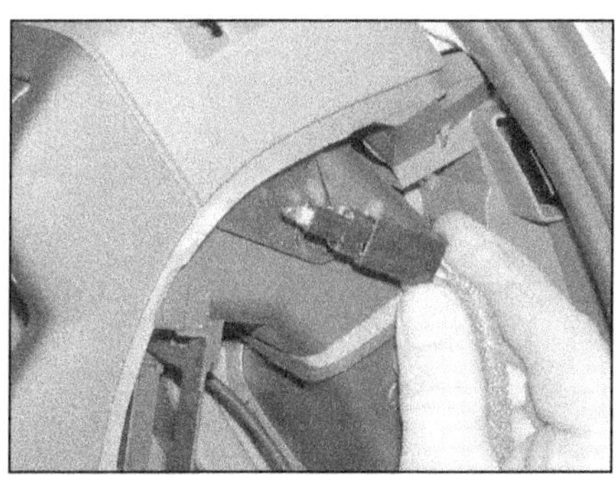

32.13 Unclip the bulb holder from the rear of the air vent housing

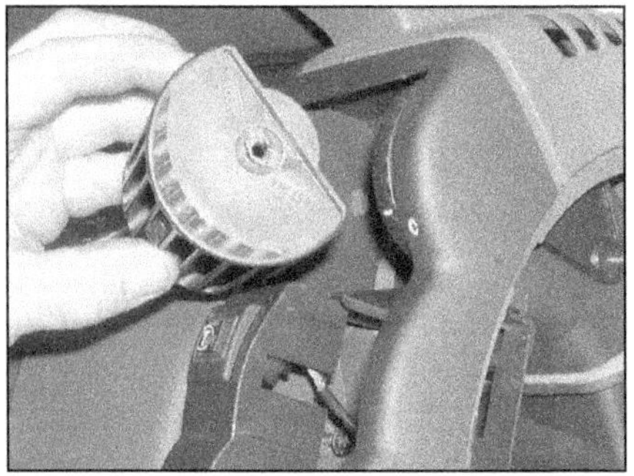

32.14a Unclip the air vent nozzle from its housing . . .

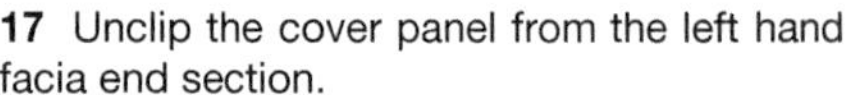

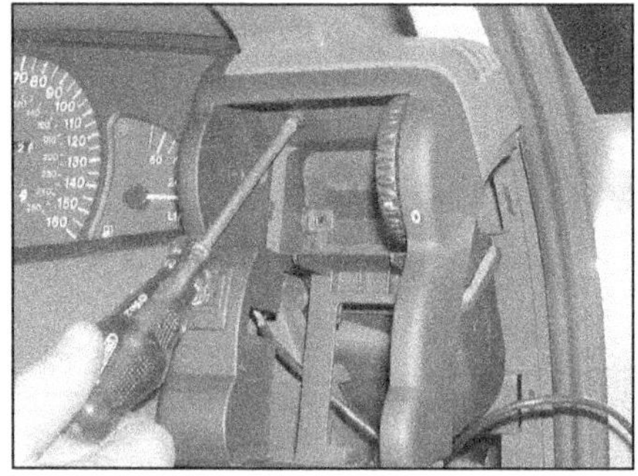

32.14b . . . then undo the screws . . .

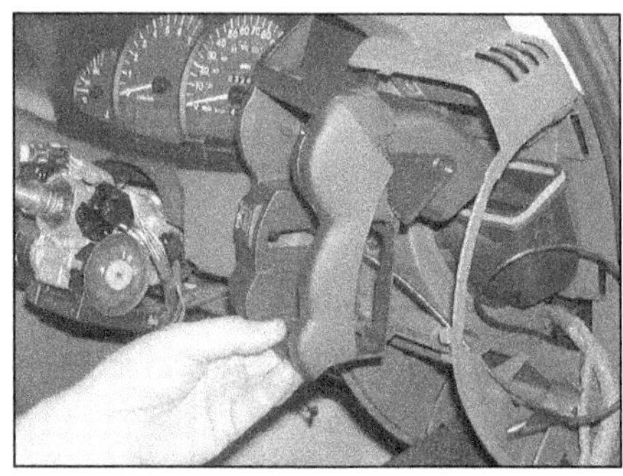

32.14c . . . and remove the air vent/headlamp switch housing

17 Unclip the cover panel from the left hand facia end section.

18 Unclip the bulb holder from the rear of the air vent housing and position it to one side.

19 Slacken and withdraw the securing screws then detach the nozzle from the left hand air vent housing **(see illustrations)**.

20 Undo the securing screws and remove the left hand end section from the facia **(see illustrations)**.

21 Remove the passenger airbag as described in Chapter 12 Section 24, then unbolt and remove the passenger airbag mounting bracket.

22 Carefully prise the two nozzles from the

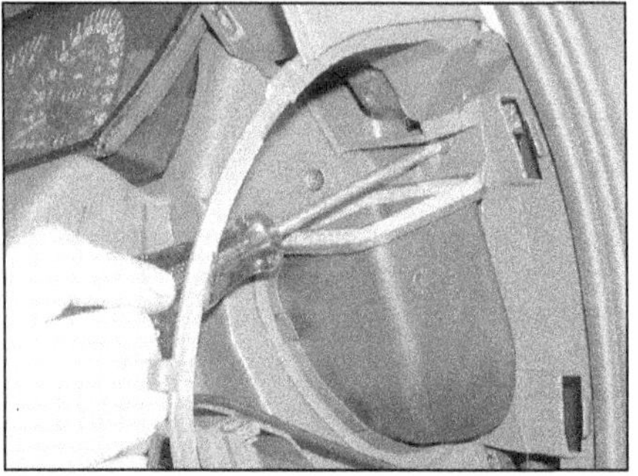

32.15a Slacken and withdraw the securing screws . . .

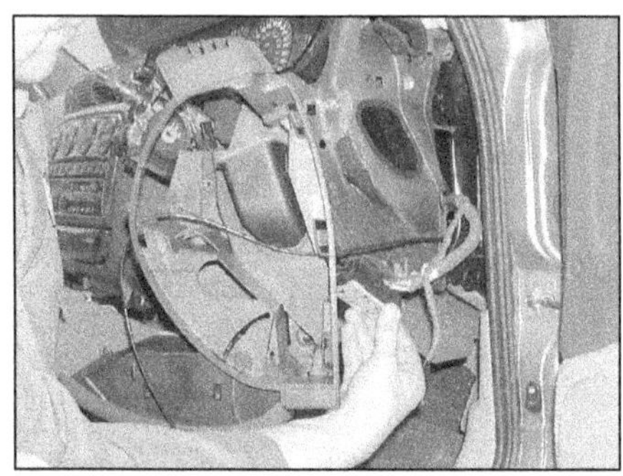

32.15b . . . and remove the right hand facia end section

32.19a Slacken and withdraw the securing screws . . .

32.19b . . . then detach the nozzle from the left hand air vent housing

32.20a Undo the securing screws . . .

32.20b . . . and remove the left hand end section from the facia

32.22a Carefully prise the two nozzles from the centre air vent housing . . .

32.22b . . . then undo the securing screws . . .

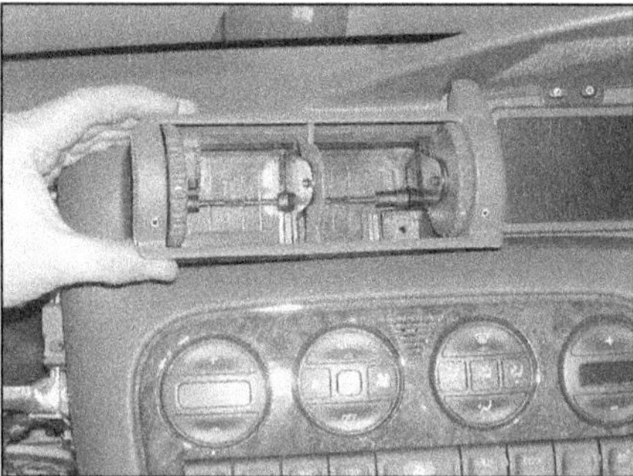

32.22c . . . and remove the vent housing from the facia

32.29a Release the main wiring harness from the mounting on the facia, behind the relay base plate, by compressing the press-stud clip with a pair of pliers . . .

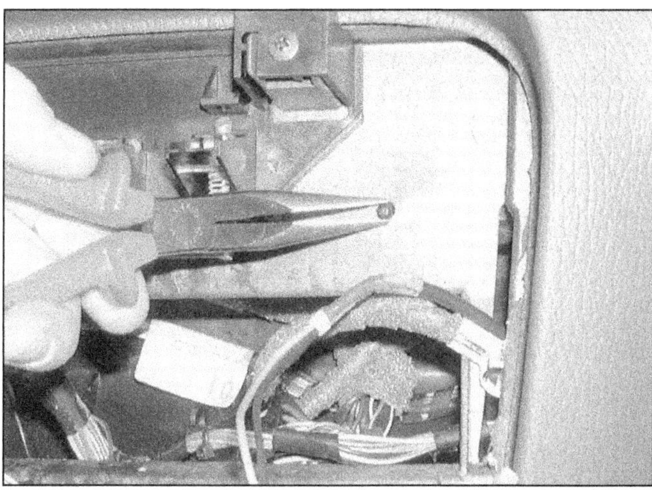

32.29b . . . release the three clips from the panel behind the heater/ECC control panel mounting aperture in a similar manner

centre air vent housing, then undo the securing screws and remove the vent housing from the facia **(see illustrations)**.

23 Remove the instrument pack as described in Chapter 12 Section 9.

24 Remove the heater control panel (or Electronic Climate Control panel, as applicable) from the facia as described in Chapter 3.

25 Remove the centre console as described in Section 30.

26 Slacken and withdraw the screws securing the fusebox panel and the relay panel to the facia. Pull the panels away from the facia slightly, leaving the wring harnesses attached.

27 Working underneath the facia on the passengers side, remove the securing screws and detach the moulded air duct that runs from the air distributor unit to the left hand end of the facia.

28 Withdraw the exit vent and disconnect the moulded air ducting that runs from the air distributor housing to the right hand end of the facia.

29 Release the main wiring harness from the mounting on the facia, behind the relay base plate, by compressing the press-stud clip with a pair of pliers and pushing it through its mounting hole. Release the three clips from the panel behind the heater/ECC control panel mounting aperture in a similar manner **(see illustrations)**.

30 Release the main wiring harness from the cable tie clips, located inside the facia, above the transmission tunnel. Access to the clips (via the radio/cassette mounting aperture) is extremely limited. Take great care to avoid damaging the wiring harness during this operation, as the air bag control unit wiring is routed through this section of the harness.

31 Remove the Electronic Climate Control (ECC) sun sensor from the top of the facia (where applicable) with reference to Chapter 3, Section 13.

32 Unbolt and remove the driver and passenger grab handles, then unclip the trim panels from both A-pillars **(see illustrations).**

33 Slacken and withdraw the facia securing bolts; there are seven bolts in total: one at the lower edge of the facia, in front of the gear lever, two each at the extreme right and left hand ends of the facia, one behind the instrument panel mounting aperture, and one adjacent to the upper right hand corner of the passenger air bag mounting bracket aperture.

34 Carefully withdraw the facia from the bulkhead, ensuring that the wiring harness has been completely released from the rear of the facia assembly **(see illustration)**. Remove the assembly from the vehicle.

Refitting

35 Refit the facia by following the reversal procedure in reverse. If a new facia assembly is to be fitted, make sure that the airbag warning stickers are transferred from the old facia.

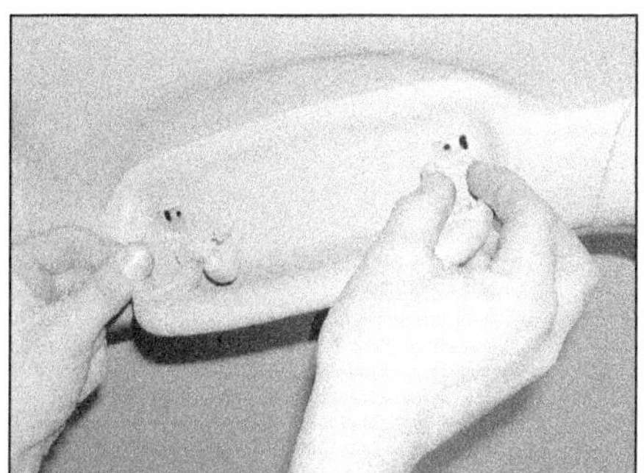

32.32a Unbolt and remove the driver and passenger grab handles . . .

32.32b . . . then unclip the trim panels from both A-pillars

32.34 Carefully withdraw the facia from the bulkhead

Chapter 12
Body electrical system

Contents

Degrees of difficulty

Easy, suitable for novice with little experience 	**Fairly easy,** suitable for beginner with some experience 	**Fairly difficult,** suitable for competent DIY mechanic 	**Difficult,** suitable for experienced DIY mechanic 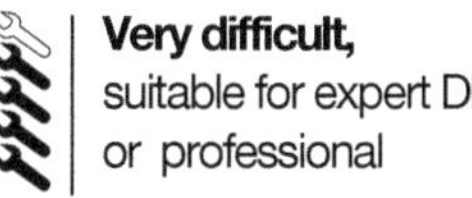	**Very difficult,** suitable for expert DIY or professional

Specifications

System type . . . 12-volt negative earth

Fuses

Main interior fusebox

Fuse	Rating	Circuits protected
F1	30	Front window motors
F2	15	Brake lights, Hazard lights
F3	30	Windscreen/rear screen wash/wipe system
F4	15	Cooling fan
F5	30	Electric seats
F6	20	Audio equipment
F7	30	Rear window motors
F8	10	Daytime driving lights
F9	10	Automatic transmission
F10		Blank
F11	10	Heated door mirrors
F12	20	Interior lights, Radio, Central locking remote receiver, Direction indicators, Hazard lights, Multi-function display
F13	10	Electric exterior door mirrors
F14	30	Power steering, Cigarette lighter, Air circulation system, Air conditioning system, Heated rear window, Heated seats
F15	20	Reversing lights, Glove compartment light, Automatic level control system, Cruise control system, Sunroof, Instrument illumination, Headlight range adjustment
F16	20	Fog lights
F17	20	Horn
F18	20	Fuel pump
F19	10	Anti-lock braking/traction control system
F20	20	Central locking, Courtesy lights

Fuses (continued)

Fuse	Rating	Circuits protected
F21	10	Main beam (left)
F22	15	Dipped beam (left), Headlight range adjustment
F23	10	Parking and tail lights
F24	20	Coolant heater
F25	20	Sunroof
F26	10	Number plate lights, Headlight washer system
F27	20	Automatic level control system
F28	20	Fog tail light
F29	20	Caravan/trailer constant current supply
F30	10	Parking/tail lights (right)
F31	15	Dipped beam (right), Headlight range adjustment
F32	10	Main beam (right)
F33	30	Blower motor

1 General information and precautions

Warning: Before carrying out any work on the electrical system, read through the precautions given in Safety first! at the beginning of this manual, and in Chapter 5A.

1 The electrical system is of 12-volt negative earth type. Power for the lights and all electrical accessories is supplied by a lead acid type battery, which is charged by the alternator.

2 This Chapter covers repair and service procedures for the various electrical components not associated with the engine. Information on the battery, alternator and starter motor can be found in Chapter 5A.

3 It should be noted that, before working on any component in the electrical system, the battery negative terminal should first be disconnected, to prevent the possibility of electrical short-circuits and/or fires.

4 At regular intervals, carefully check the routing of the wiring harness, ensuring that it is correctly secured by the clips or ties provided so that it cannot chafe against other components. If evidence is found of the harness having chafed against other components, repair the damage and ensure that the harness is secured or protected so that the problem cannot occur again.

Caution: If the audio unit fitted to the vehicle is one with an anti-theft security code, refer to the audio unit anti-theft precautions in the Reference Section of this manual before disconnecting the battery.

2 Electrical fault-finding - general information

Note: *Refer to the precautions given in Safety first! (at the beginning of this manual) and to Section 1 of this Chapter before starting work. The following tests relate to testing of the main electrical circuits, and should not be used to test sensitive electronic circuits (such as anti-lock braking systems), particularly where an electronic control module is used.*

General

1 A typical electrical circuit consists of an electrical component, any switches, relays, motors, fuses, fusible links or circuit breakers related to that component, and the wiring and connectors that link the component to both the battery and the chassis. To help to pinpoint a problem in an electrical circuit, wiring diagrams are included at the end of this chapter.

2 Before attempting to diagnose an electrical fault, first study the appropriate wiring diagram to obtain a complete understanding of the components included in the particular circuit concerned. The possible sources of a fault can be narrowed down by noting whether other components related to the circuit are operating properly. If several components or circuits fail at one time, the problem is likely to be related to a shared fuse or earth connection.

3 Electrical problems usually stem from simple causes, such as loose or corroded connections, a faulty earth connection, a blown fuse, a melted fusible link, or a faulty relay (refer to Section 3 for details of testing relays). Visually inspect the condition of all fuses, wires and connections in a problem circuit before testing the components. Use the wiring diagrams to determine which terminal connections will need to be checked, to pinpoint the trouble-spot.

4 The basic tools required for electrical fault-finding include the following.

a) A circuit tester or voltmeter (a 12-volt bulb with a set of test leads can also be used for certain tests).
b) A self-powered test light (sometimes known as a continuity tester).
c) An ohmmeter (to measure resistance).
d) A battery.
e) A set of test leads.
f) A jumper wire, preferably with a circuit breaker or fuse incorporated, which can be used to bypass suspect wires or electrical components.

Before attempting to locate a problem with test instruments, use the wiring diagram to determine where to make the connections.

5 To find the source of an intermittent wiring fault (usually due to a poor or dirty connection, or damaged wiring insulation), a 'wiggle' test can be performed on the wiring. This involves moving the wiring by hand, to see if the fault occurs as the wiring is moved. It should be possible to narrow down the source of the fault to a particular section of wiring. This method of testing can be used in conjunction with any of the tests described in the following sub-Sections.

6 Apart from problems due to poor connections, two basic types of fault can occur in an electrical circuit - open-circuit and short-circuit.

7 Open-circuit faults are caused by a break somewhere in the circuit, which prevents current from flowing. An open-circuit fault will prevent a component from working, but will not cause the relevant circuit fuse to blow.

8 Short-circuit faults are caused by a 'short' somewhere in the circuit, which allows the current flowing in the circuit to 'escape' along an alternative route, usually to earth. Short-circuit faults are normally caused by a breakdown in wiring insulation, which allows a feed wire to touch either another wire, or an earthed component such as the bodyshell. A short-circuit fault will normally cause the relevant circuit fuse to blow.

Finding an open-circuit

9 To check for an open-circuit, connect one lead of a circuit tester or voltmeter to either the negative battery terminal or a known good earth.

10 Connect the other lead to a connector in the circuit being tested, preferably nearest to the battery or fuse.

11 Switch on the circuit, remembering that some circuits are live only when the ignition switch is moved to a particular position.

12 If voltage is present (indicated either by the tester bulb lighting or a voltmeter reading, as applicable), this means that the section of

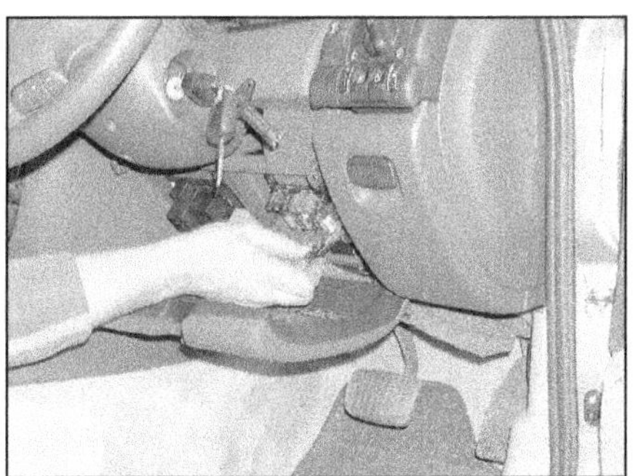

3.2 The main fuses and relays are located in a panel beneath a cover under the driver's side of the facia

3.3a Additional fuses and relays are housed in an auxiliary fusebox, located in the engine compartment

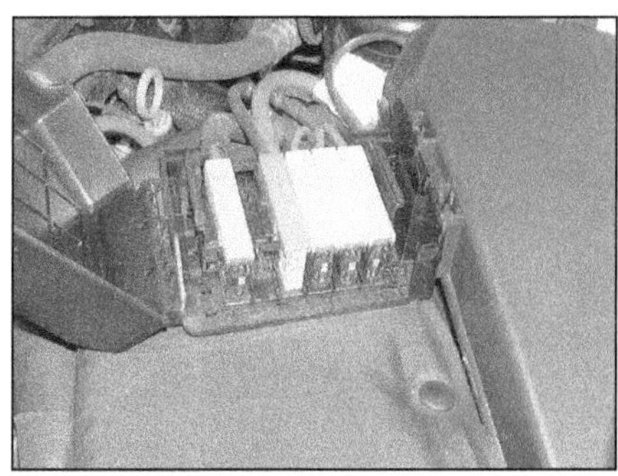

3.3b On some models, a secondary auxiliary fusebox, clipped to the top of the battery houses a number of fusible links

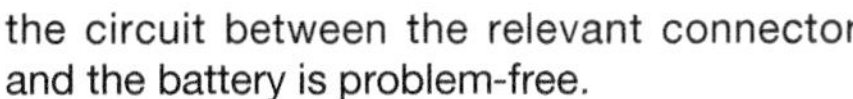

the circuit between the relevant connector and the battery is problem-free.

13 Continue to check the remainder of the circuit in the same fashion.

14 When a point is reached at which no voltage is present, the problem must lie between that point and the previous test point with voltage. Most problems can be traced to a broken, corroded or loose connection.

Finding a short-circuit

15 To check for a short-circuit, first disconnect the load(s) from the circuit (loads are the components that draw current from a circuit, such as bulbs, motors, heating elements, etc.).

16 Remove the relevant fuse from the circuit, and connect a circuit tester or voltmeter to the fuse connections.

17 Switch on the circuit, remembering that some circuits are live only when the ignition switch is moved to a particular position.

18 If voltage is present (indicated either by the tester bulb lighting or a voltmeter reading, as applicable), this means that there is a short-circuit.

19 If no voltage is present, but the fuse still blows with the load(s) connected, this indicates an internal fault in the load(s).

Finding an earth fault

20 The battery negative terminal is connected to 'earth' (the metal of the engine/transmission and the car body), and most systems are wired so that they only receive a positive feed. The current returning through the metal of the car body. This means that the component mounting and the body form part of that circuit. Loose or corroded mountings can therefore cause a range of electrical faults, ranging from total failure of a circuit, to a puzzling partial fault. In particular, lights may shine dimly (especially when another circuit sharing the same earth point is in operation). Motors (eg wiper motors or the radiator cooling fan motor) may run slowly, and the operation of one circuit may have an affect on another. Note that on many vehicles, earth straps are used between certain components, such as the engine/transmission and the body, usually where there is no metal-to-metal contact between components, due to flexible rubber mountings, etc.

21 To check whether a component is properly earthed, disconnect the battery, and connect one lead of an ohmmeter to a known good earth point. Connect the other lead to the wire or earth connection being tested. The resistance reading should be zero; if not, check the connection as follows.

22 If an earth connection is thought to be faulty, dismantle the connection, and clean back to bare metal both the bodyshell and the wire terminal or the component earth connection mating surface. Be careful to remove all traces of dirt and corrosion, then use a knife to trim away any paint, so that a clean metal-to-metal joint is made. On reassembly, tighten the joint fasteners securely; if a wire terminal is being refitted, use serrated washers between the terminal and the bodyshell, to ensure a clean and secure connection. When the connection is remade, prevent the onset of corrosion in the future by applying a coat of petroleum jelly or silicone-based grease.

3 Fuses and relays - general information

Fuses

1 Fuses are designed to break a circuit when a predetermined current is reached, to protect the components and wiring which could be damaged by excessive current flow. Any excessive current flow will be due to a fault in the circuit, usually a short-circuit (see Section 2).

2 The main fuses and relays are located in a panel beneath a cover under the driver's side of the facia **(see illustration)**. The circuits protected by the various fuses and relays are marked on the inside of the panel cover.

3 Additional fuses and relays are housed in an auxiliary fusebox, located in the engine compartment. On some models, a secondary auxiliary fusebox, clipped to the top of the battery houses a number of fusible links **(see illustrations)**.

4 A blown fuse or fusible link can be recognised from its melted or broken wire.

5 To remove a fuse, first ensure that the relevant circuit is switched off. Then open the cover and pull the relevant fuse from the panel using the tweezers supplied. If desired, the lower end of the panel can be tilted forwards, after releasing the retaining clip, to improve access.

6 Before renewing a blown fuse, trace and rectify the cause, and always use a fuse of the correct rating. Never substitute a fuse of a higher rating, or make temporary repairs using wire or metal foil, as more serious damage, or even fire, could result.

7 Spare fuses are generally provided in the blank terminal positions in the fusebox.

8 Note that the fuses are colour-coded, see Specifications. Refer to the wiring diagrams for details of the fuse ratings and the circuits protected.

Relays

9 A relay is an electrically-operated switch, which is used for the following reasons:

a) A relay can switch a heavy current remotely from the circuit in which the control current is flowing, allowing the use of lighter-gauge wiring and control switch contacts.

b) A relay can receive more than one control input, unlike a mechanical switch.

c) A relay can have a timer function.

10 If a circuit or system controlled by a relay develops a fault, and the relay is suspect, operate the system. If the relay is functioning, it should be possible to hear it click as it is energised. If this is the case, the fault lies with the components or wiring of the system. If the relay is not being energised, then either the relay is not receiving a main supply or a switching voltage, or the relay itself is faulty. Testing is by the substitution of a known good unit, but be careful - while some relays are identical in appearance and in operation, others look similar but perform different functions.

11 To remove a relay, first ensure that the relevant circuit is switched off. The relay can then simply be pulled out from the socket, and pushed back into position.

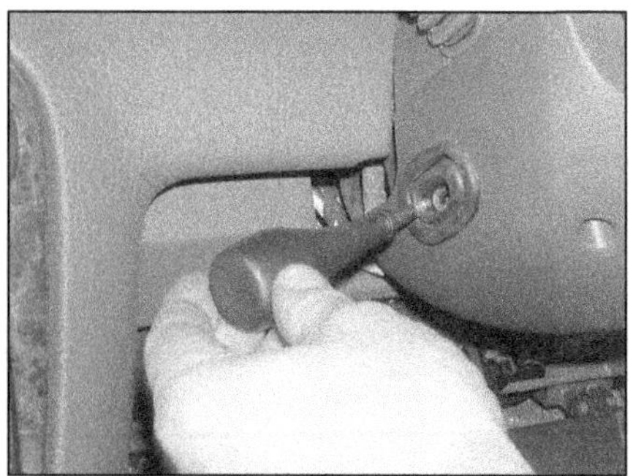
4.4a Unscrew the lever from the steering column tilt mechanism . . .

4.4b . . . then remove the screws from the end face . . .

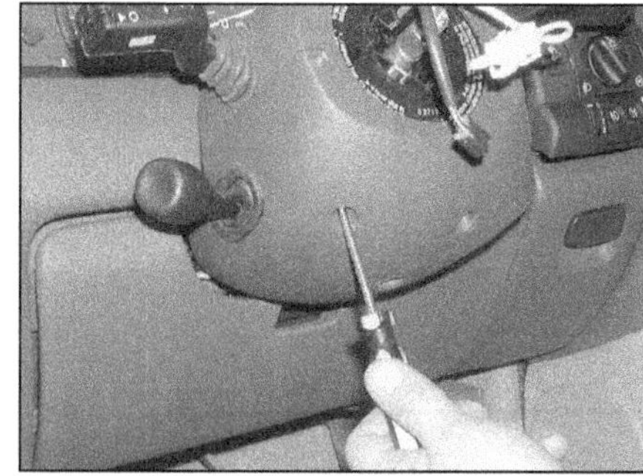
4.4c . . . and underside . . .

4 Switches - removal and refitting

Ignition switch/ steering column lock cylinder

1 Refer to the information given in Chapter 10.

Turn signal/ wiper switch assembly

2 The turn signal and wiper switch assemblies are removed identically.

3 Remove the steering wheel as described in Chapter 10.

4 Unscrew the lever from the steering column tilt mechanism, then remove the screws and detach the upper and lower sections of the shroud panels from the steering column **(see illustrations)**.

5 Depress the upper and lower locking tabs, then carefully slide the switch unit from the top of the housing. Disconnect the wiring and remove the switch from the vehicle **(see illustrations)**.

6 Refitting is a reversal of removal.

Facia-mounted push button switches (except hazard warning)

7 A small, hooked instrument or length of welding rod is required to pull the switch from the facia.

8 Carefully insert the hooked instrument between the switch and surround, then pull out the switch **(see illustration)**.

9 Disconnect the wiring from the switch.

10 Refitting is a reversal of removal.

Lighting and fog light switch

11 Carefully prise the cover panel from the end face of the drivers side of the facia moulding.

12 Using a pair of small screwdrivers or lengths of thin metal strip, depress the locking catches at the side of the switch unit, then carefully slide it from the facia **(see illustrations)**. Prevent damage to the facia by placing a wad of cloth beneath the screwdrivers/metal strips. Note that the terminals on the rear of the switch locate directly in the sockets in the switch base plate.

13 To remove the fog light switch, release the tab and slide the switch from the base of the unit.

14 Refitting is a reversal of removal.

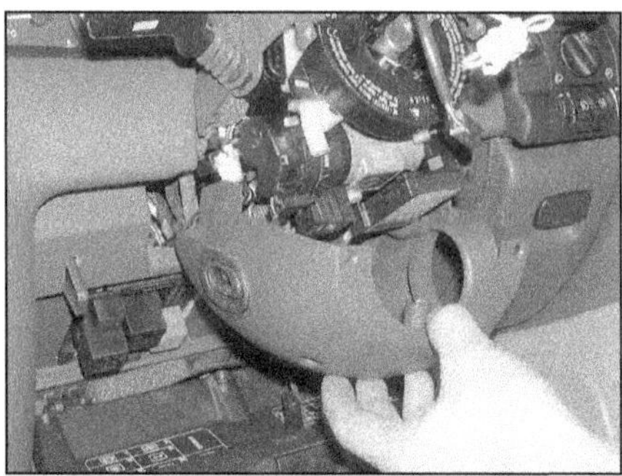
4.4d . . . then detach the lower . . .

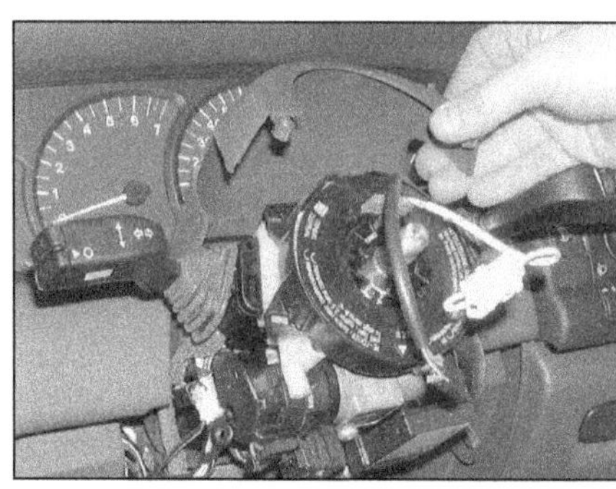
4.4e . . . and upper sections of the shroud panels from the steering column

4.5a Depress the upper and lower locking tabs, then carefully slide the switch unit from the top of the housing . . .

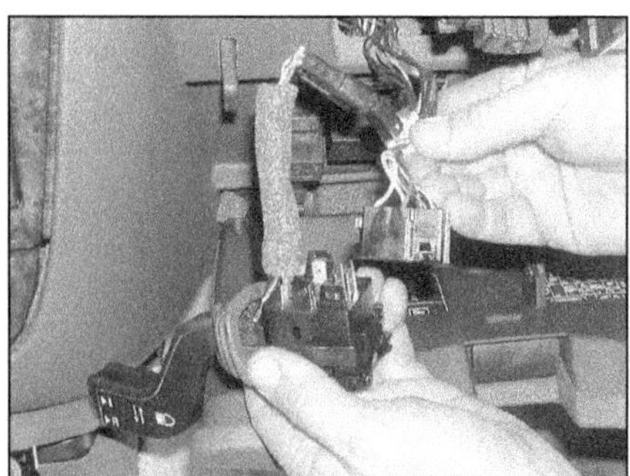
4.5b . . . and disconnect the wiring

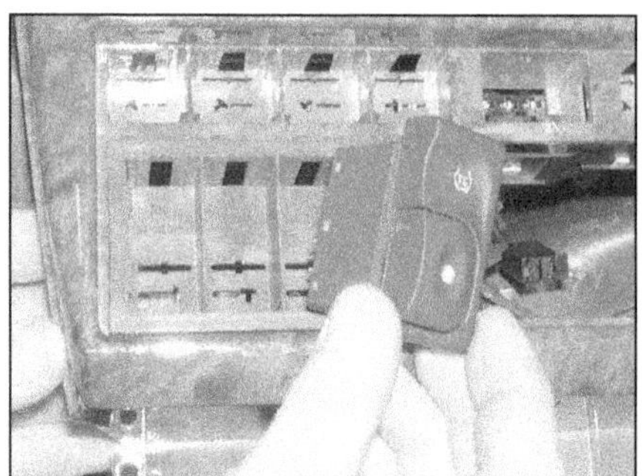
4.8 Removing a push button switch from the facia

4.12a Depress the locking catches at the side of the switch unit . . .

4.12b . . . then carefully slide the switch from the facia

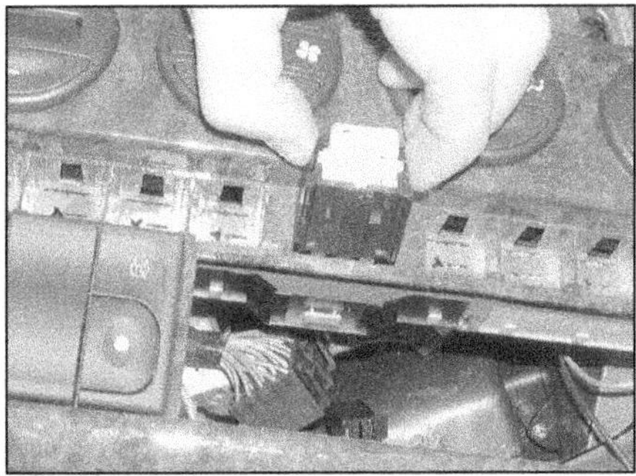
4.17 Removing the hazard warning switch body from the facia

4.27 Undo the retaining screw (arrowed) and withdraw the switch - Estate model shown

Hazard warning switch

15 It is easier to remove the hazard warning switch when in the ON position.
16 Carefully unclip the cover from the switch button.
17 Insert screwdrivers into the channel on either side of the switch and carefully prise it from the facia, or use a small, hooked instrument or length of welding rod to remove the switch **(see illustration)**.
18 Refitting is a reversal of removal.

Heater blower motor switch

19 Refer to the information given in Chapter 3 Section 8, for models with conventional heating systems or Chapter 3 Section 13, for models with Electronic Climate Control.

Stop light switch

Removal

20 The stop-light switch is located on the pedal bracket in the driver's footwell.
21 To remove the switch, first remove the lower facia trim panel (see Chapter 11, Section 32), then disconnect the heating duct for access to the switch.
22 Disconnect the wiring plug from the top of the switch, then depress the switch locking tabs and remove it from the pedal bracket.

Refitting

23 Before refitting the switch, pull the actuation pin fully out.
24 Press the switch into its support bracket.
25 Depress the brake pedal then pull the actuation pin fully out of the switch so that it contacts the pedal. Now release the pedal to set the pin.
26 Refit the heating duct and the lower facia trim panel. Check the operation of the stop-light.

Courtesy light switch and rear luggage compartment switch

27 Undo the retaining screw and withdraw the switch **(see illustration)**.
28 Disconnect the wiring and tape it to the panel to prevent it dropping out of reach.
29 Make sure that the retaining screw makes good contact with the body and switch. If necessary clean the contact points.
30 Refitting is a reversal of removal.

Electrically-operated window switch

Front window switches

31 Refer to the information given in Chapter 11, Section 22.

Reversing light switch

Manual transmission

32 Refer to the information given in Chapter 7A.

Automatic transmission

33 Refer to the information given in Chapter 7B, Section 8.

5 Bulbs (exterior lights) - renewal

1 Whenever a bulb is renewed, note the following points.

a) *Remember that, if the light has just been in use, the bulb may be extremely hot.*
b) *Do not touch the bulb glass with the fingers, as this can result in early failure or a dull reflector.*
c) *Always check the bulb contacts and holder, ensuring that there is clean metal-to-metal contact between the bulb and its live(s) and earth. Clean off any corrosion or dirt before fitting a new bulb.*
d) *Ensure that the new bulb is of the correct rating.*

Headlight - dipped beam

Models with conventional headlights

2 With the bonnet open, release fastening screws and detach the cover panel from above the headlight unit. Remove the cover from the rear of the relevant headlight **(see illustrations)**. Note that the outer headlight is for dipped beam and the inner headlight is for the main beam.
3 Disconnect the wiring plug from the bulb **(see illustration)**.

5.2a Detach the cover panel from above the headlight unit

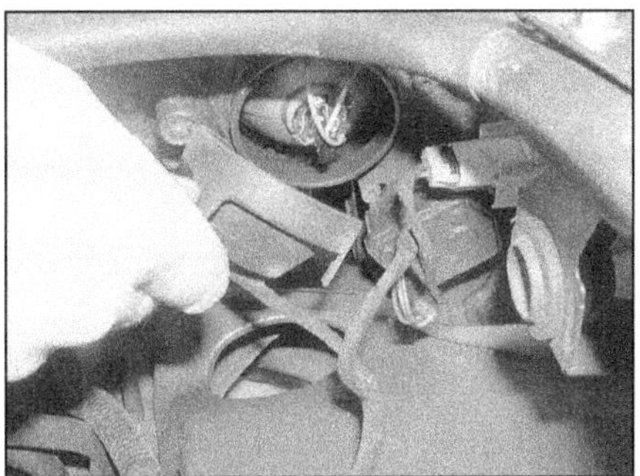
5.2b Remove the cover from the rear of the relevant headlight

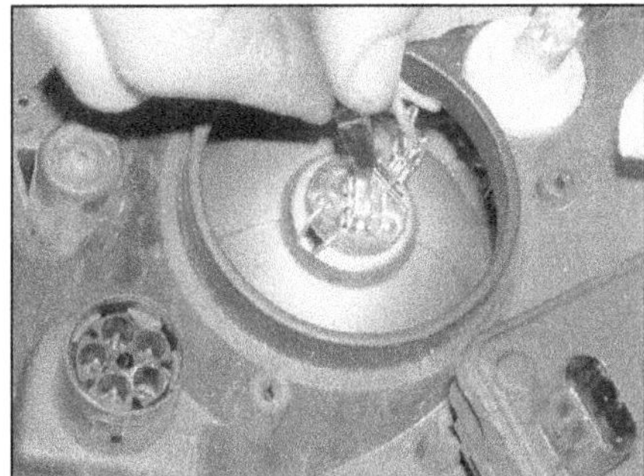
5.3 Disconnect the wiring plug from the bulb

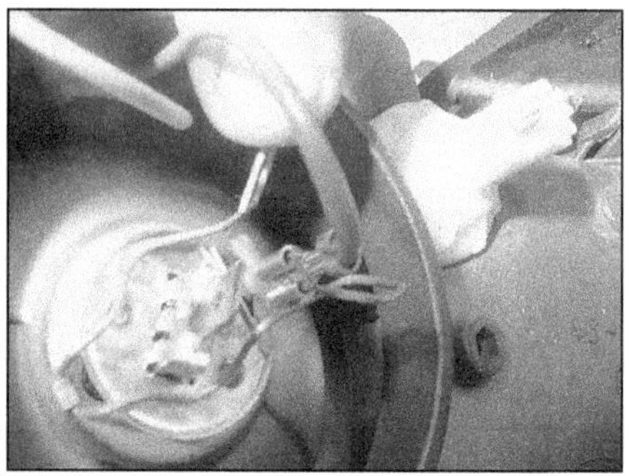
5.4a Depress and unhook the retaining clip . . .

5.4b . . . then withdraw the bulb from the headlight

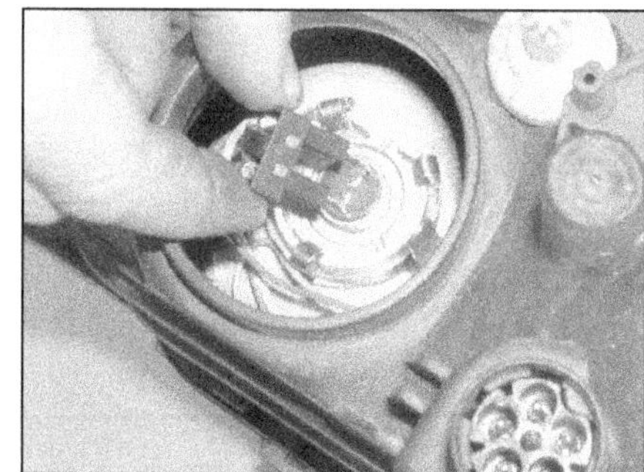
5.14 Unplug the wiring connector from the rear of the bulb

4 Depress and unhook the retaining clip, then withdraw the bulb from the headlight **(see illustrations)**.

5 When handling the new bulb, use a tissue or clean cloth, to avoid touching the glass with the fingers; moisture and grease from the skin can cause blackening and rapid failure of this type of bulb. If the glass is accidentally touched, wipe it clean using a small quantity of methylated spirit.

6 Fit the new bulb using a reversal of the removal procedure, making sure that the bulb is seated correctly in the cut-outs in the headlight and that it is held is position with the spring clip.

Models with Xenon discharge headlights

Warning: The Xenon discharge bulbs operate at very high voltage; before starting work, disconnect the battery negative cable and remove the dipped beam fuses from the interior fusebox.

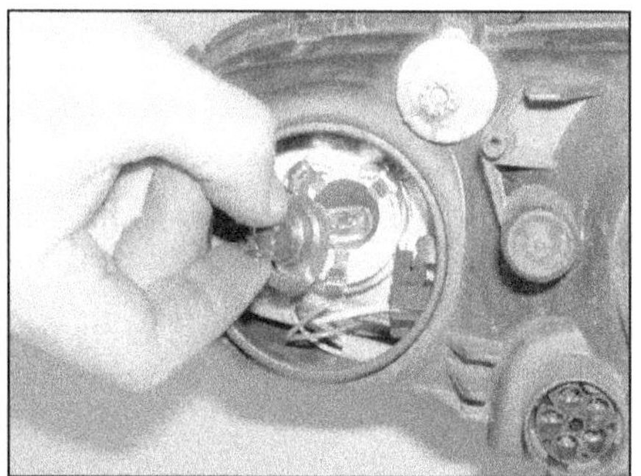
5.16 Press the bulb squarely into its housing until it is felt to engage with its retaining clips

7 With the bonnet open, release fastening screw and detach the cover panel from above the headlight unit. If working on the left hand headlight, first remove the battery with reference to Chapter 5A. If working on the right hand headlight, first remove the air cleaner housing with reference to Chapter 4A.

8 At the rear of the headlight unit, undo the three Torx screws and remove the protective cap from the rear of the bulb connector.

9 Turn the bulb connector to the left to disconnect it.

10 Rotate the retaining ring to the left then remove it from the rear of the bulb housing.

11 Withdraw the bulb from its housing.

12 Refitting is a reversal of removal. Ensure that the headlight beam alignment is checked by a Vauxhall dealer as soon as possible.

Headlight - main beam

13 With the bonnet open, release fastening screws and detach the cover panel from above the headlight unit. Remove the cover from the rear of the relevant headlight (refer to illustration 5.2b). Note that the outer headlight is for dipped beam and the inner headlight is for the main beam.

14 Unplug the wiring connector from the rear of the bulb **(see illustration)**.

15 Carefully press down on the rear of the bulb, until it releases from its retaining clips.

16 Refitting is a reversal of removal. Press the bulb squarely into its housing until it is felt to engage with its retaining clips **(see illustration)**.

Models with Xenon discharge headlights

Warning: The Xenon discharge bulbs operate at very high voltage; before starting work, disconnect the battery negative cable and remove the main beam fuses from the interior fusebox.

17 The renewal procedure is similar to that described for the dipped beam bulb.

Front sidelight

18 The front sidelight bulb is located at the side of the main beam headlight reflector. First remove the cover the rear of the main beam headlight (refer to illustration 5.2b).

19 Withdraw the sidelight bulbholder from the rear of the headlight **(see illustration)**.

20 Remove the bulb from the holder **(see illustration)**.

21 Fit the new bulb using a reversal of the removal procedure.

Front direction indicator light

22 With the bonnet open, release the fastening screw and detach cover panel from above the relevant headlight unit (refer to illustration 5.2a).

23 Grasp the direction indicator bulbholder and rotate it anticlockwise to release it from the rear of the light unit **(see illustration).**

5.19 Withdraw the sidelight bulbholder from the rear of the headlight

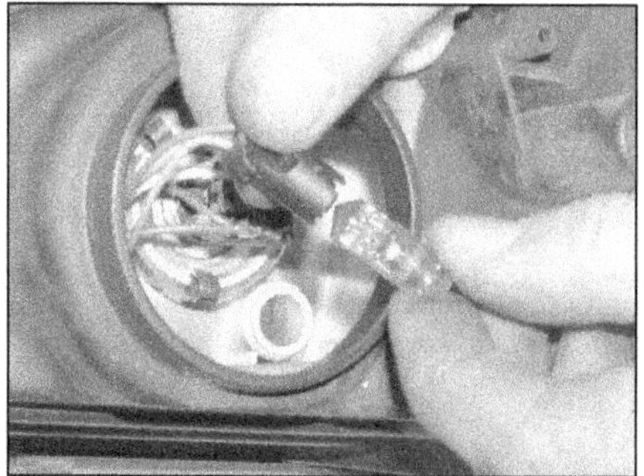
5.20 Remove the bulb from the holder

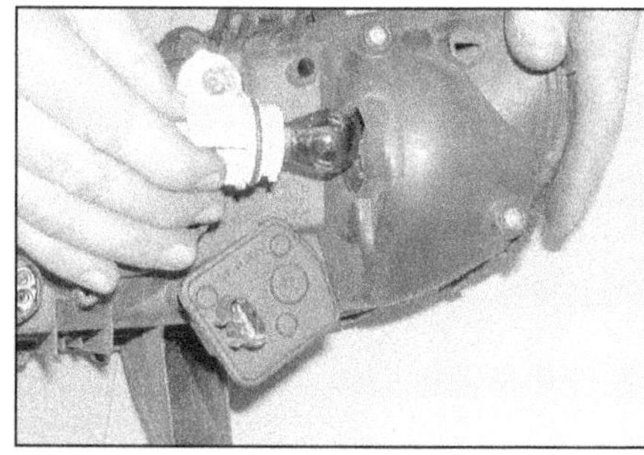
5.23 Rotate the indicator bulbholder anticlockwise to release it from the rear of the light unit

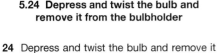

5.24 Depress and twist the bulb and remove it from the bulbholder

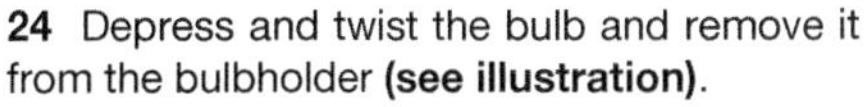

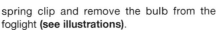

5.26 Remove the screws and detach the grille adjacent to the relevant fog light

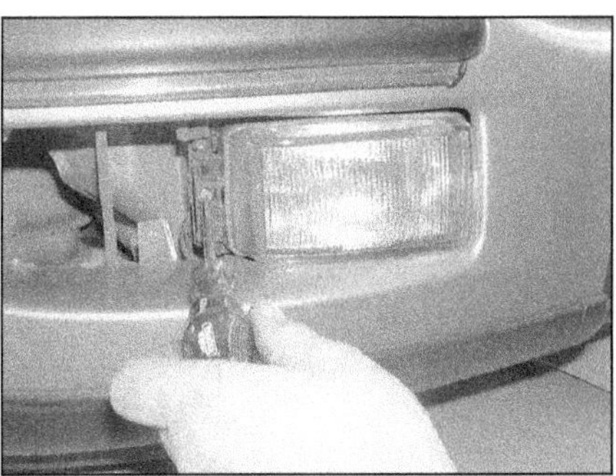

5.27 Undo the securing screws and pivot the fog light lens forwards

24 Depress and twist the bulb and remove it from the bulbholder **(see illustration)**.

25 Fit the new bulb using a reversal of the removal procedure.

Front foglight

26 Remove the screws and detach the grille adjacent to the relevant fog light, located in the front bumper valence **(see illustration)**.

27 Undo the securing screws and pivot the fog light lens forwards **(see illustration)**.

28 Rotate the protective cap and remove it from the rear of the foglight **(see illustration)**.

29 Disconnect the wiring, then release the spring clip and remove the bulb from the foglight **(see illustrations)**.

30 Fit the new bulb using a reversal of the removal procedure. When refitting the light ensure that the lug at the inner edge engages correctly with the recess in the front bumper valence **(see illustration)**.

Front direction indicator side repeater light

31 Using a small screwdriver, carefully lever the side repeater light from the front wing moulding **(see illustration)**.

32 Hold the bulbholder, then twist the lens to remove it **(see illustration)**.

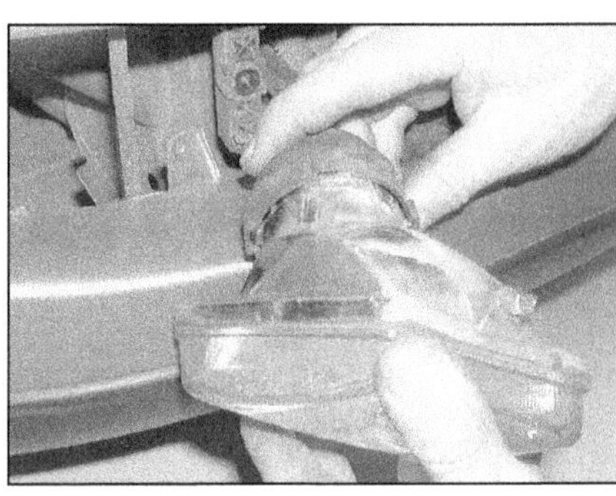

5.28 Rotate the protective cap and remove it from the rear of the foglight

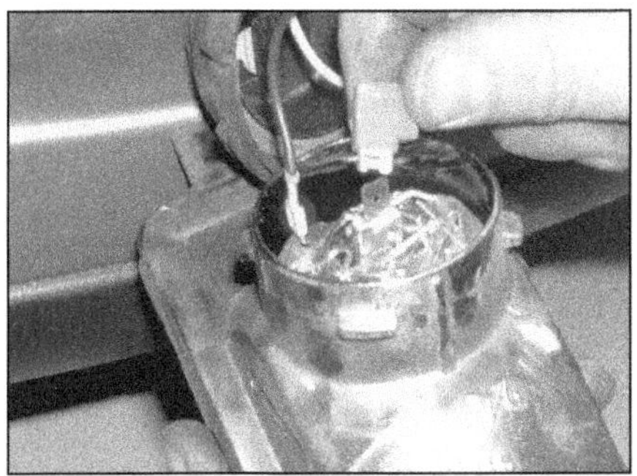

5.29a Disconnect the wiring . . .

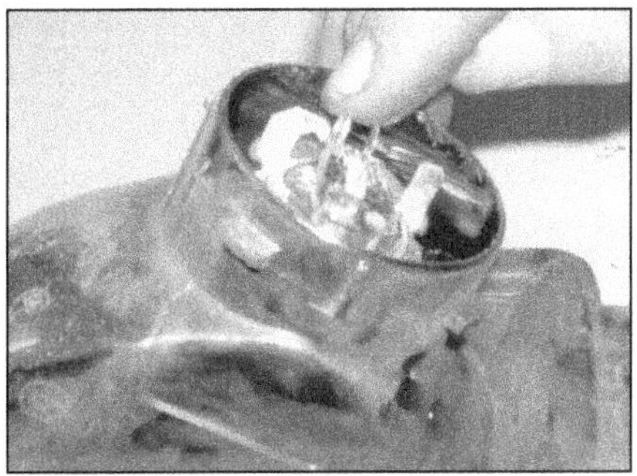

5.29b . . . then release the spring clip . . .

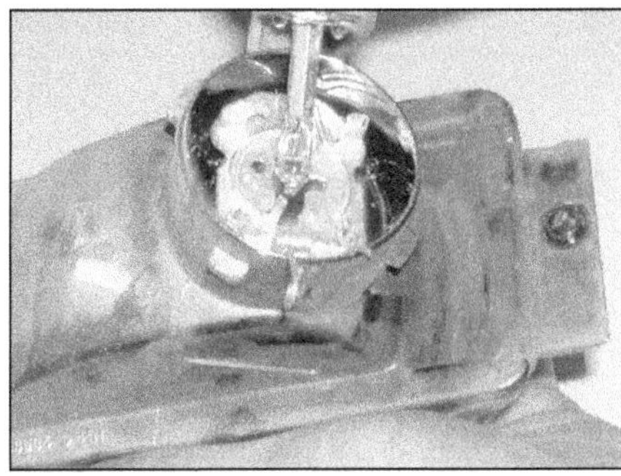

5.29c . . . and remove the bulb from the foglight

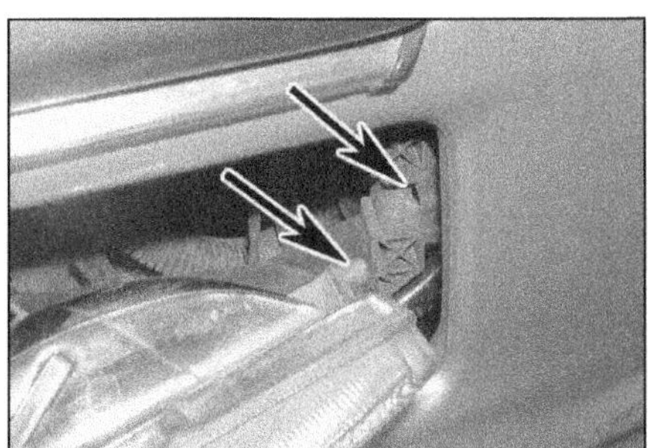

5.30 When refitting the light ensure that the lug (arrowed) at the inner edge engages correctly with the recess in the front bumper valence

5.31 Carefully lever the side repeater light from the front wing moulding

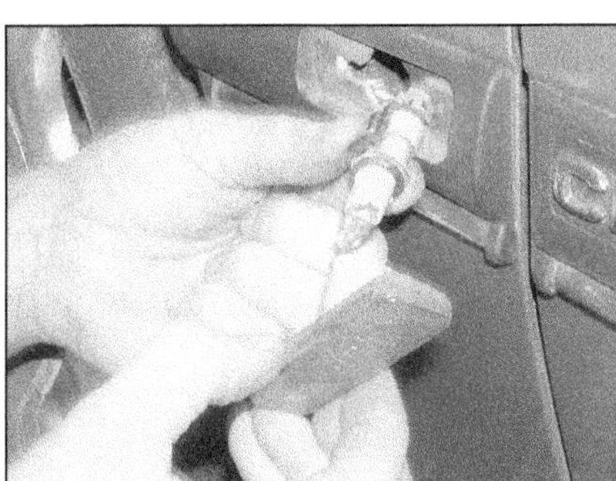

5.32 Hold the bulbholder, then twist the lens to remove it

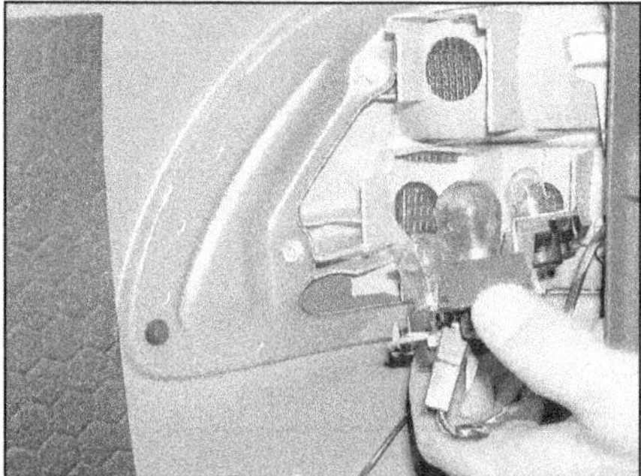

5.33 Pull the wedge-type bulb from the bulbholder

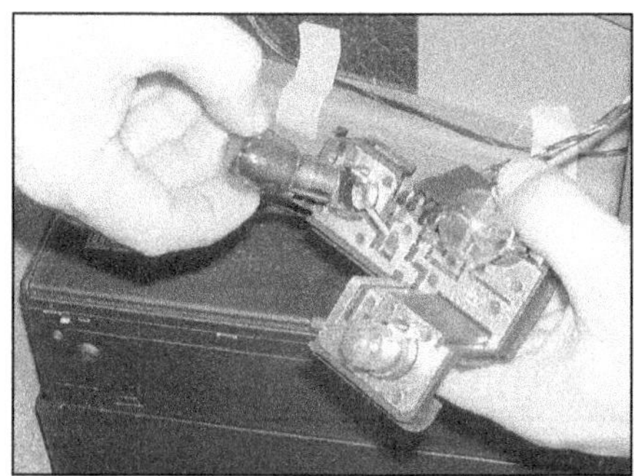

5.36 Withdraw the bulbholder from the rear light

5.37 Depress and twist the relevant bulb to remove it

33 Pull the wedge-type bulb from the bulbholder **(see illustration)**.

34 Fit the new bulb using a reversal of the removal procedure.

Rear light cluster - rear wing

35 In the luggage compartment, remove the side trim cover. If working on the right-hand side, remove the first aid kit and warning triangle. If working on the left hand side, first remove the spare wheel. On Estate models, the left-hand cover is removed by twisting the fastener.

36 Depress the retaining lug in the middle of the rear light cluster, and withdraw the bulbholder from the rear light **(see illustration)**.

37 Depress and twist the relevant bulb to remove it **(see illustration)**.

38 Fit the new bulb using a reversal of the removal procedure.

Rear light cluster - boot lid

39 Open the boot lid.

40 Depress the retaining lugs at either side of the bulbholder, then withdraw the bulbholder from the rear of the light unit **(see illustration)**.

41 Depress and twist the relevant bulb to remove it **(see illustration)**.

42 Fit the new bulb using a reversal of the removal procedure.

Rear number plate light - Saloon models

43 Open the bootlid, then depress the clip and remove the light unit from the bumper **(see illustration)**.

44 Unclip the lens from the light unit then depress and twist the bulb from its contacts **(see illustrations)**.

45 Fit the new bulb using a reversal of the removal procedure.

Rear number plate light - Estate models

46 Open the tailgate halfway, then undo the screws from the relevant light and withdraw the light unit from under the handle moulding.

47 Release the festoon type bulb from the spring contacts.

48 Fit the new bulb using a reversal of the removal procedure. Make sure that the bulb is held firmly between the spring contacts, and if necessary pretension the contacts before fitting the bulb.

High level stop light - Saloon models

49 Unclip the cover from the high level stop light **(see illustration).**

50 Unplug the wiring at the connector **(see illustration).**

51 Unclip the bulbholder from the cover **(see illustration).**

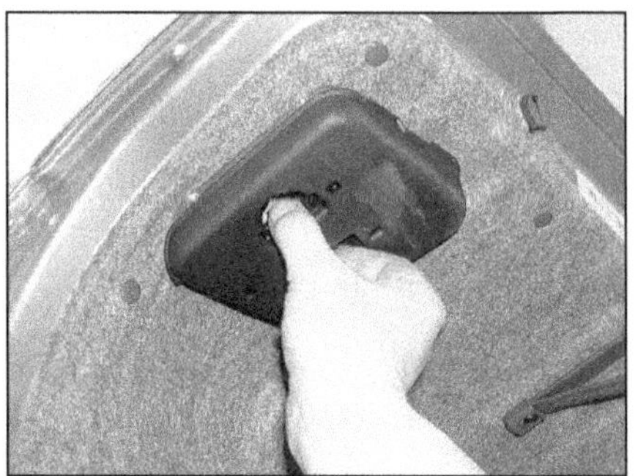

5.40 Withdraw the bulbholder from the rear of the light unit

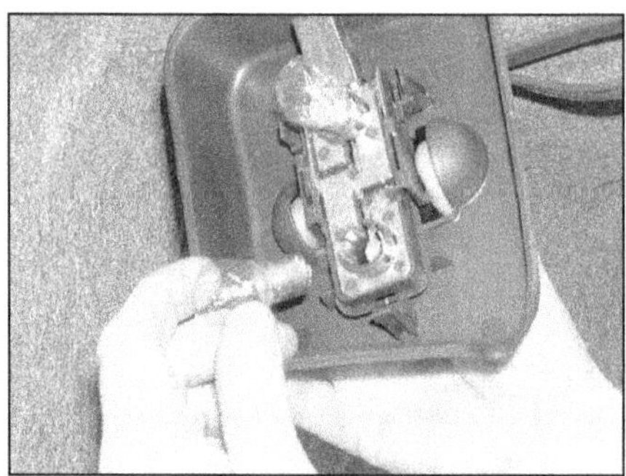

5.41 Depress and twist the relevant bulb to remove it

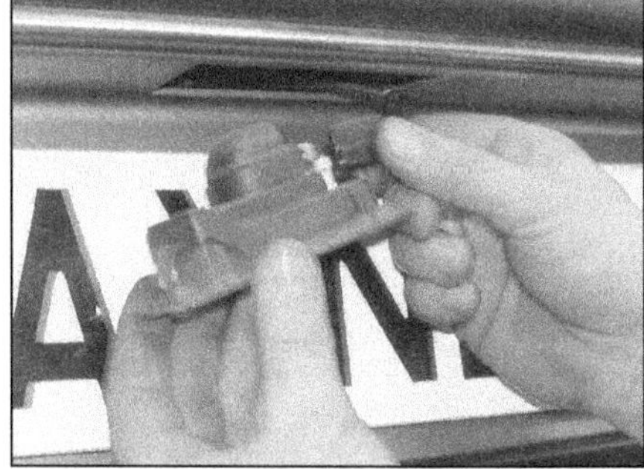

5.43 Depress the clip and remove the light unit from the bumper

5.44a Unclip the lens from the light unit . . .

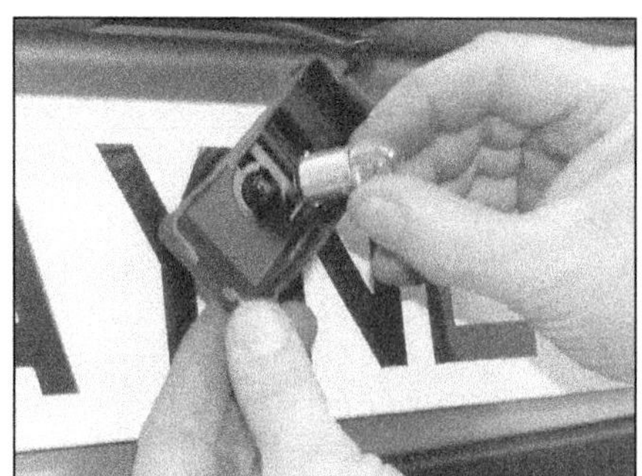

5.44b . . . then depress and twist the bulb from its contacts

5.49 Unclip the cover from the high level stop light

52 Remove the bulb(s) as necessary.
53 Fit the new bulb using a reversal of the removal procedure.

High level stop light - Estate models

54 With the tailgate open, unclip the centre section of the tailgate upper trim panelling.
55 Rotate the relevant bulbholder to remove it from its bayonet contacts.
56 Fit the new bulb using a reversal of the removal procedure.

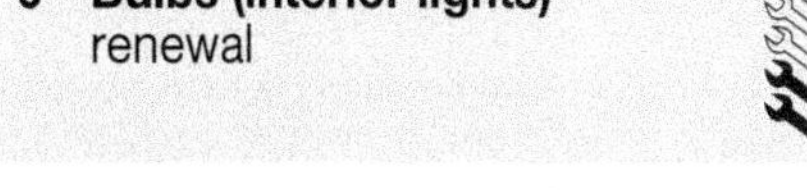

6 Bulbs (interior lights) - renewal

1 Whenever a bulb is renewed, note the following points.

a) Remember that, if the light has just been in use, the bulb may be extremely hot.
b) Do not touch the bulb glass with the fingers, as this can result in early failure or a dull reflector.
c) Always check the bulb contacts and holder, ensuring that there is clean metal-to-metal contact between the bulb and its live(s) and earth. Clean off any corrosion or dirt before fitting a new bulb.
d) Ensure that the new bulb is of the correct rating.

Front interior light

2 Ensure that the bulb contacts are not live, by closing all doors and ensuring that the light switch is off. Carefully prise the lens from the interior light using a screwdriver **(see illustration)**.
3 Remove the relevant bulb from its contacts **(see illustration)**. The main light is a festoon style bulb which can be prised from its spring loaded contacts, while the map reading light bulbs can be pulling them from their contacts.
4 Fit the new bulb using a reversal of the removal procedure.

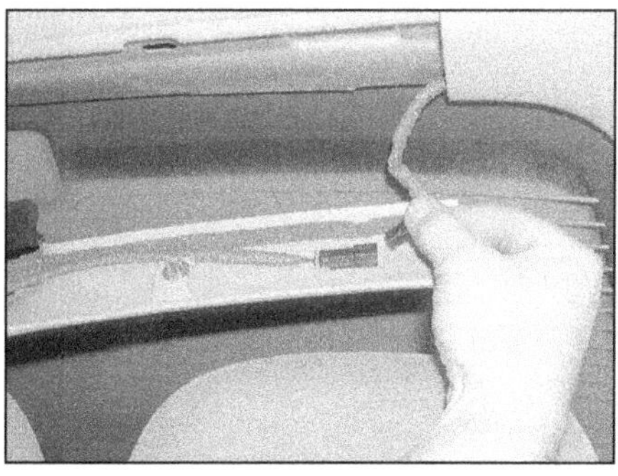

5.50 Unplug the wiring at the connector

Rear interior light

5 Carefully prise the interior light from the door upper trim panel **(see illustration).**
6 Remove the bulb from its contacts **(see illustration)**.
7 Fit the new bulb using a reversal of the removal procedure. Make sure that the bulb is held firmly between the spring contacts.

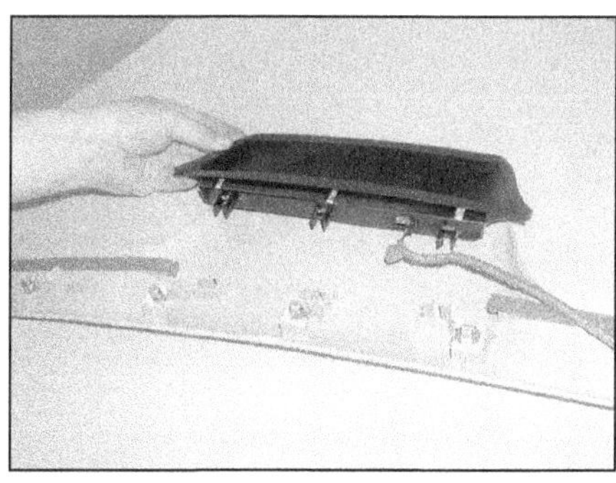

5.51 Unclip the bulbholder from the cover

Luggage compartment interior light

8 Carefully prise the light from the side trim **(see illustration)**.
9 Remove the bulb from its contacts **(see illustration)**.
10 Fit the new bulb using a reversal of the removal procedure. Make sure that the bulb is held firmly between the spring contacts.

Glovebox light

11 With the glovebox open, carefully prise out the light unit.
12 Remove the festoon type bulb from the spring contacts.
13 Fit the new bulb using a reversal of the removal procedure. Make sure that the bulb is held firmly between the spring contacts.

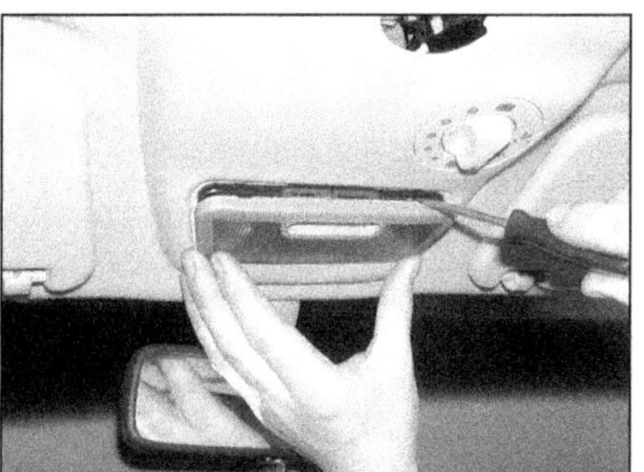

6.2 Carefully prise the lens from the front interior light using a screwdriver

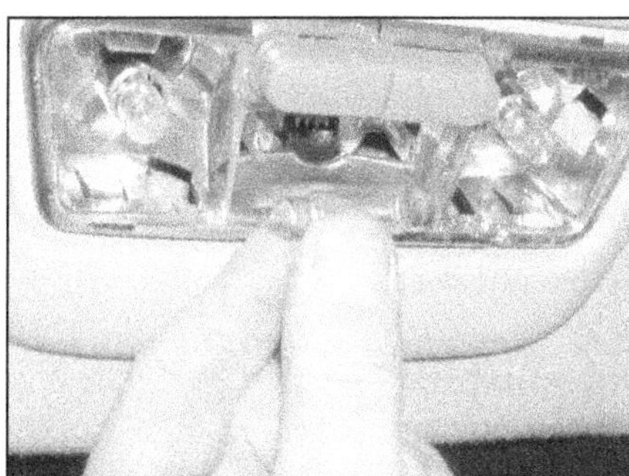

6.3 Remove the relevant bulb from its contacts

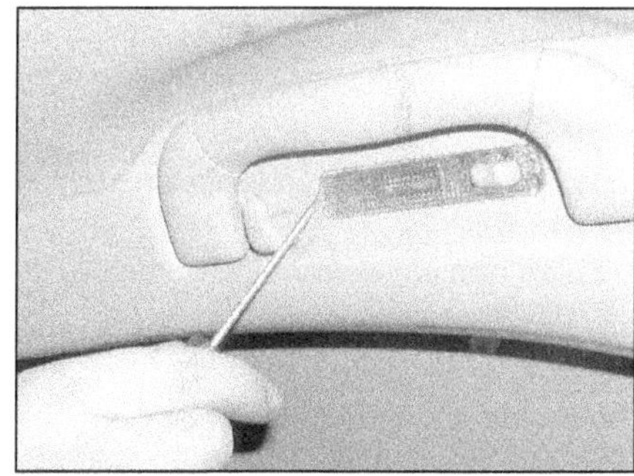

6.5 Carefully prise the rear interior light from the door upper trim panel

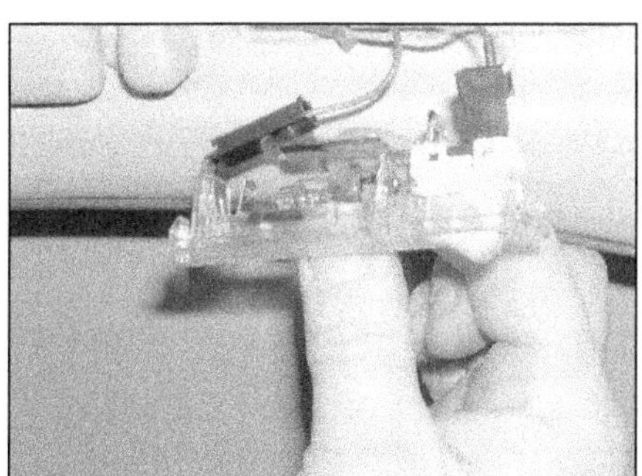

6.6 Remove the bulb from its contacts

6.8 Carefully prise the light from the luggage compartment side trim

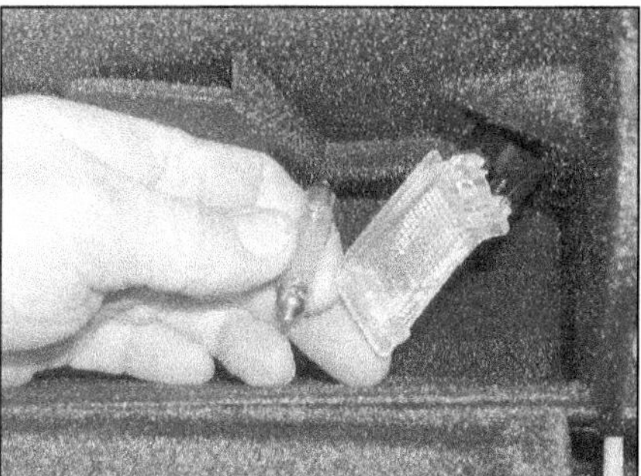

6.9 Remove the bulb from its contacts

6.14 Carefully lever the light unit from the door trim panel

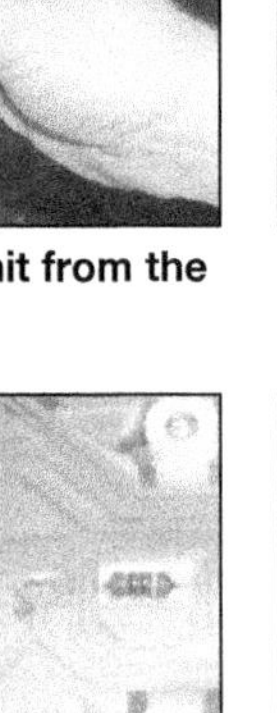

6.19 Removing instrument pack illumination bulb

Door mounted interior light

14 Carefully lever the light from the door trim panel **(see illustration).**

15 Remove the heat shield, then remove the festoon type bulb from the spring contacts **(see illustrations)**.

16 Fit the new bulb using a reversal of the removal procedure. Make sure that the bulb is held firmly between the spring contacts.

Instrument panel illumination and warning light bulbs

17 Remove the instrument panel as described in Section 9.

18 The central bulbholders are for the instrument illumination and the lower bulbholders on the circuit board are the warning tell-tale lights.

19 To remove the bulbs twist and turn the bulbholder and remove from the instrument panel, then, where applicable, remove the bulb from the bulbholder. Note that some bulbs cannot be removed from their bulbholders **(see illustration)**.

7.2 Remove the trim panel from underneath the headlight unit

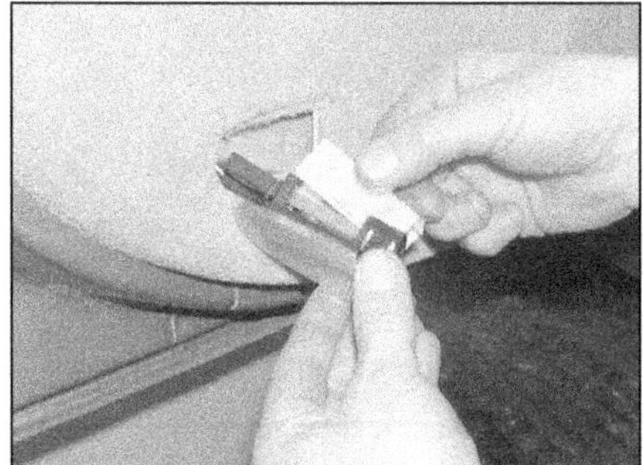

6.15a Remove the heat shield . . .

6.25 Removing a clock/multi-function display unit illumination bulb

20 Fit the new bulb using a reversal of the removal procedure.

Light switch illumination

21 Remove the light switch as described in Section 4.

22 Using a screwdriver, twist the bulbholder from the rear of the switch.

23 Fit the new bulb using a reversal of the removal procedure.

Clock/multi-function display unit illumination

24 Remove the instrument panel as described in Section 9. The clock/multi-function display unit is located on the rear of the instrument panel.

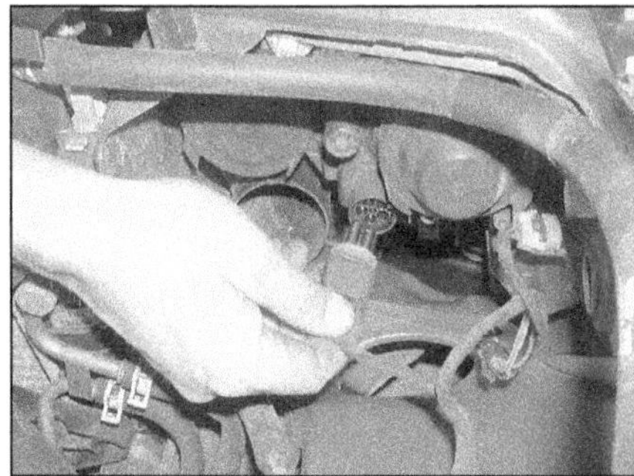

7.3 Disconnect the wiring plugs from the rear of the headlight

6.15b . . . then remove the bulb from the spring contacts

25 Using a screwdriver if necessary, twist the relevant bulbholder from the rear of the display unit **(see illustration)**.

26 Fit the new bulb using a reversal of the removal procedure.

Heater control illumination

27 Remove the heater control panel/Electronic Climate Control panel as described in Chapter 3.

28 Remove the relevant bulb from the rear of the panel.

29 Fit the new bulb using a reversal of the removal procedure.

7 Exterior light units - removal and refitting

Headlight

Warning: The discharge bulbs fitted to models with Xenon headlights operate at very high voltage; before starting work, disconnect the battery negative cable and remove fuses F22 and F31 from the interior fusebox.

Removal

1 Remove the radiator grille as described in Chapter 11. Release the fastening screws and remove the cover panel from the above the headlight unit.

2 Undo the securing screw and remove the trim panel from underneath the headlight unit **(see illustration).** Where applicable, disconnect the nozzle from the headlight washer hose.

3 Disconnect the wiring plugs from the rear of the headlight **(see illustration)**. On models with Xenon headlights, disconnect the wiring connectors from the rear of the bulbs as described for bulb renewal in Section 5.

4 Unscrew the three headlight mounting bolts located above and below the unit, and withdraw the headlight from the front of the vehicle **(see illustrations)**.

5 If necessary, the headlight range control servo may be removed by twisting it anti-clockwise **(see illustration)**.

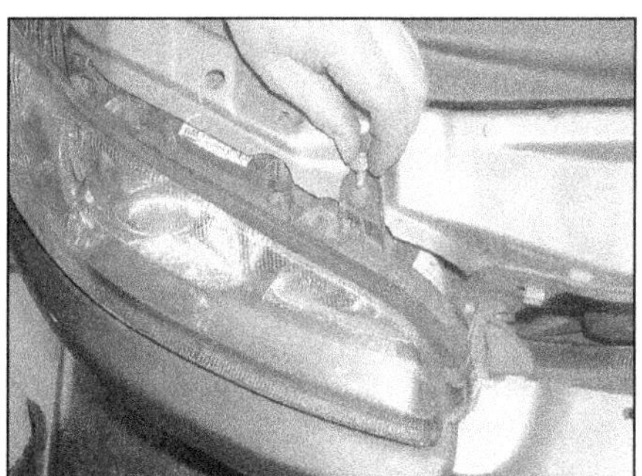
7.4a Unscrew the headlight mounting bolts located above . . .

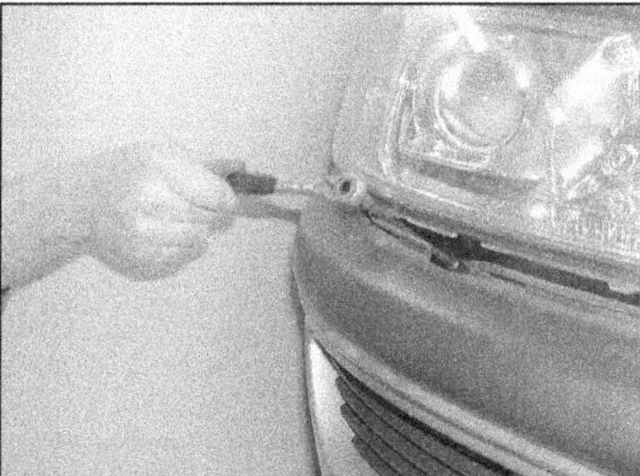
7.4b . . . and below the unit . . .

7.4c . . . and withdraw the headlight from the front of the vehicle

Refitting

6 Refitting is a reversal of removal, but make sure that the locating lug on the headlight engages with the corresponding hole in the front valance and, on completion, have the headlight beam alignment checked at the earliest opportunity.

Front direction indicator light

7 The direction indicator is integral with the headlight unit.

Front foglight

Removal

8 Remove the front bumper as described in Chapter 11.

9 Unscrew the three mounting bolts and remove the foglight from the bumper, then disconnect the wiring **(see illustration).**

Refitting

10 Refitting is a reversal of removal.

Front direction indicator side repeater light

11 The procedure is as described in Section 5 for bulb renewal. The wiring connector can be unplugged from the rear of the bulbholder to allow removal of the light unit and the bulbholder as a complete assembly.

Rear light cluster

Bootlid cluster

12 Open the bootlid and unclip the bulbholder from the rear of the light unit (see Section 5).

13 Unplug the wiring connector from the bulbholder **(see illustration)**.

14 Remove the nuts/screws and detach the light cluster from the bootlid **(see illustrations)**.

15 Refitting is a reversal of removal.

Rear wing cluster

16 In the luggage compartment, remove the side trim cover. If working on the right-hand side, remove the first aid kit and warning triangle. If working on the left hand side, remove the spare wheel. On Estate models, the left-hand cover is removed by twisting the fastener.

17 Depress the retaining lug in the middle of the rear light cluster, and withdraw the bulbholder from the rear light (see Section 5). Unplug the wiring connector from the edge of the bulbholder.

18 Slacken and withdraw the securing screws/nuts and withdraw the light cluster from the rear of the vehicle **(see illustrations)**.

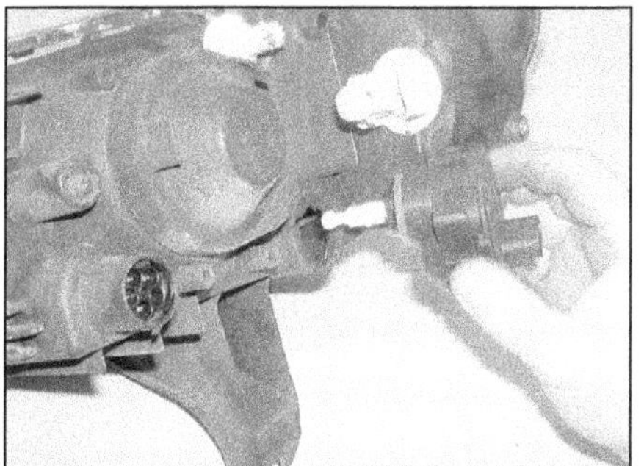
7.5 The headlight range control servo may be removed by twisting it anti-clockwise

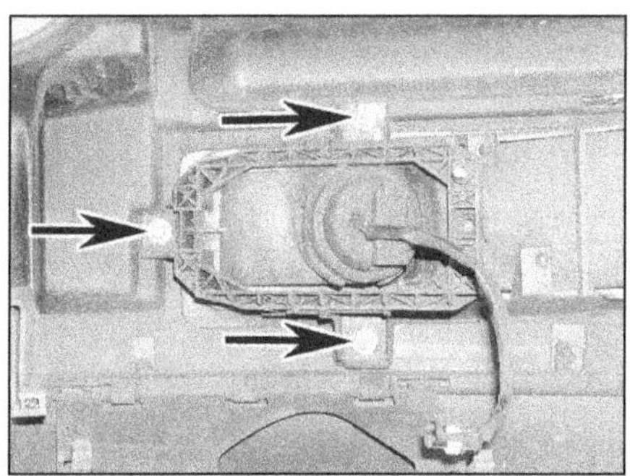
7.9 Unscrew the three mounting bolts (arrowed) and remove the foglight from the bumper

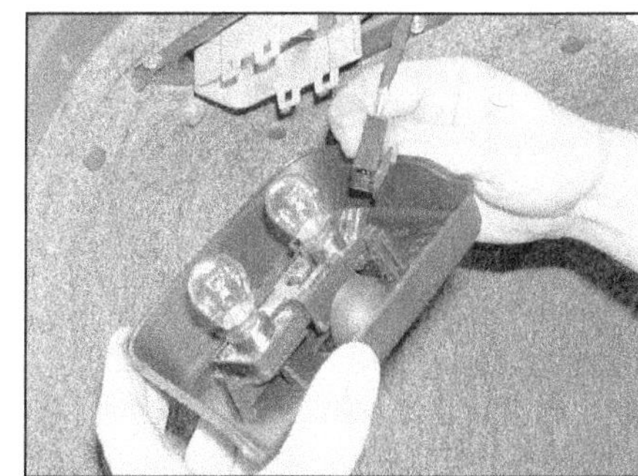
7.13 Unplug the wiring connector from the bulbholder

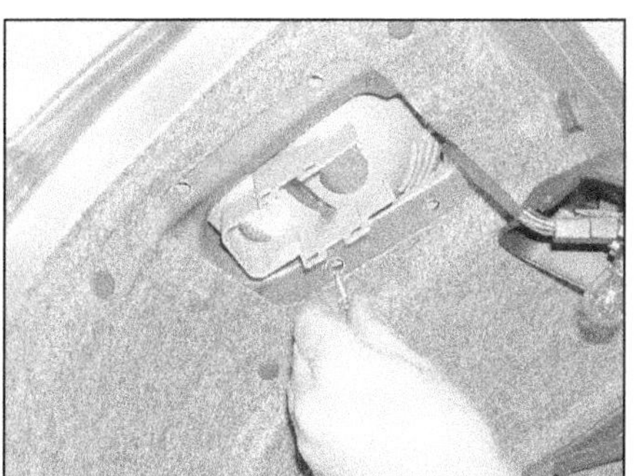
7.14a Remove the nuts/screws . . .

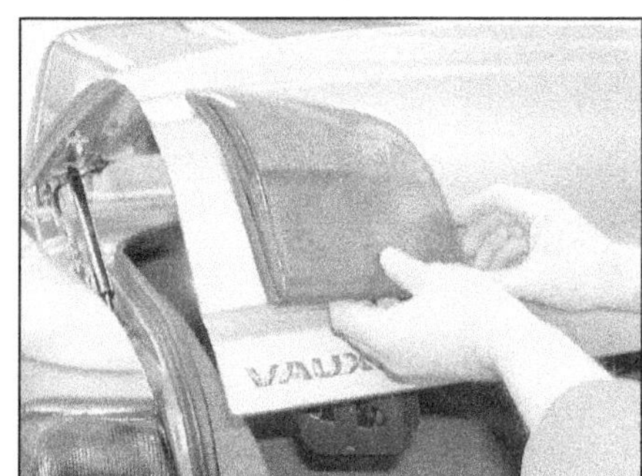
7.14b . . . and detach the light cluster from the bootlid

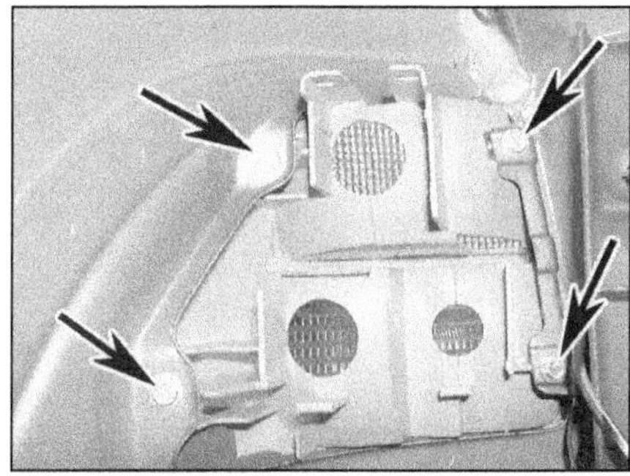
7.18a Slacken and withdraw the securing screws/nuts (saloon models) . . .

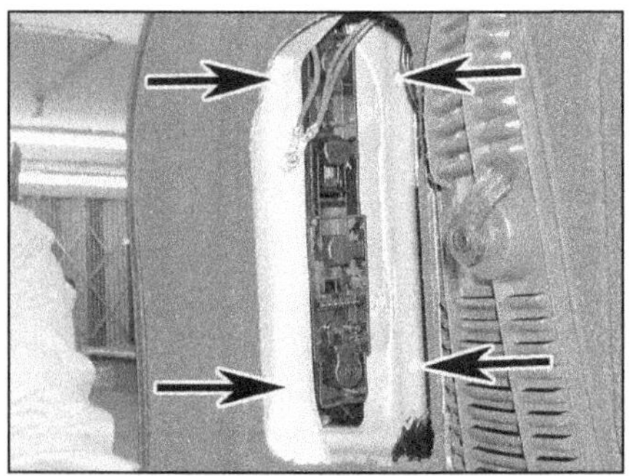
7.18b Slacken and withdraw the securing screws/nuts (estate models) . . .

Take care not to damage the vehicle paintwork.

19 Refitting is a reversal of removal.

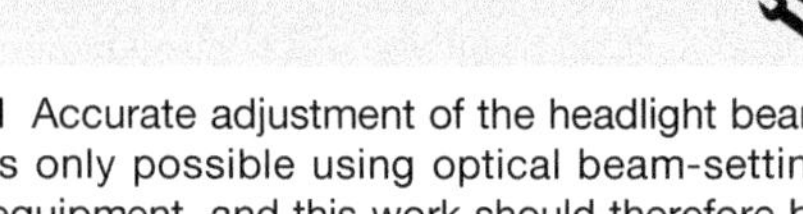

8 Headlight beam alignment - general information

1 Accurate adjustment of the headlight beam is only possible using optical beam-setting equipment, and this work should therefore be carried out by a Vauxhall/Opel dealer or suitably-equipped workshop.

2 For reference, the headlights can be adjusted using the adjuster assemblies fitted to the front upper outer mounting and to the rear inner mounting. The inner screw is for horizontal adjustment and the outer one for vertical adjustment.

3 All models have an electrically-operated headlight beam adjustment range system,

9.5a Undo the left hand . . .

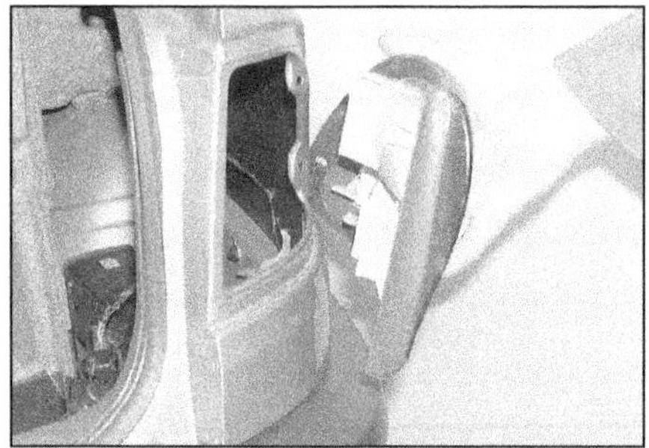
7.18c . . . and withdraw the light cluster from the rear of the vehicle (saloon models) . . .

controlled via a switch in the facia. The recommended settings are as follows.

0 *Front seat(s) occupied*
1 *All seats occupied*
2 *All seats occupied, and load in luggage compartment*
3 *Driver's seat occupied and load in the luggage compartment*

Note: *When adjusting the headlight aim, ensure that the switch is set to position 0.*

4 On Estate models with automatic self-levelling control, the headlight range adjustment should be reduced by one setting after completing approximately 3 km (1.8 miles).

Models with Xenon headlights

5 Due to the intensity of the light emitted by Xenon discharge headlight bulbs, it is vitally important that the operation of the automatic beam level control system is checked by a Vauxhall dealer, using dedicated electronic test equipment. Failure to do so could result in other road uses being severely dazzled by your headlights. This applies equally to the main and dipped beam headlights.

9 Instrument panel - removal and refitting

Removal

1 Disconnect the battery negative cable and position it away from the terminal.

2 Remove the steering wheel as described in Chapter 10, then remove the securing screws

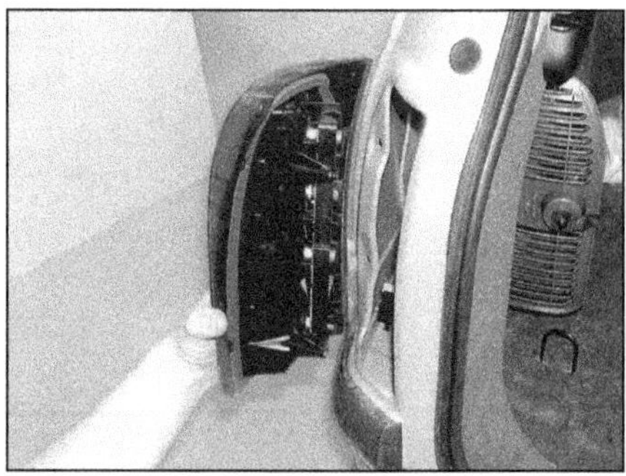
7.18d . . . and withdraw the light cluster from the rear of the vehicle (estate models)

and detach the upper and lower shroud panels from the steering column.

3 Carefully prise the centre and driver's side air vents from the facia, using a small screwdriver or alternatively feeler blades to depress the side clips. Place a wad of cloth beneath the screwdriver to prevent damage. Remove the screws and withdraw the air vent housing from the facia (refer to the illustrations in Chapter 11, Section 32.

5 Undo the two mounting screws, detach the mounting bracket and withdraw the instrument panel from the facia **(see illustrations)**.

6 Carefully pivot the instrument panel towards the passenger side of the car, until the fixed multiway wiring connector is felt to disengage.

7 Disconnect the wiring from the rear of the multi-function display unit and then withdraw the instrument panel from the facia **(see illustration)**.

Refitting

8 Refitting is a reversal of removal, but check the operation of all the warning and illumination bulbs on completion.

10 Instrument panel components - removal and refitting

Removal

1 With the instrument panel removed as described in Section 9, remove the warning and illumination bulbs as described in Section 6.

9.5b . . . and lower mounting bracket screws . . .

9.5c . . . and withdraw the instrument panel from the facia

9.7 Disconnect the wiring from the rear of the multi-function display unit

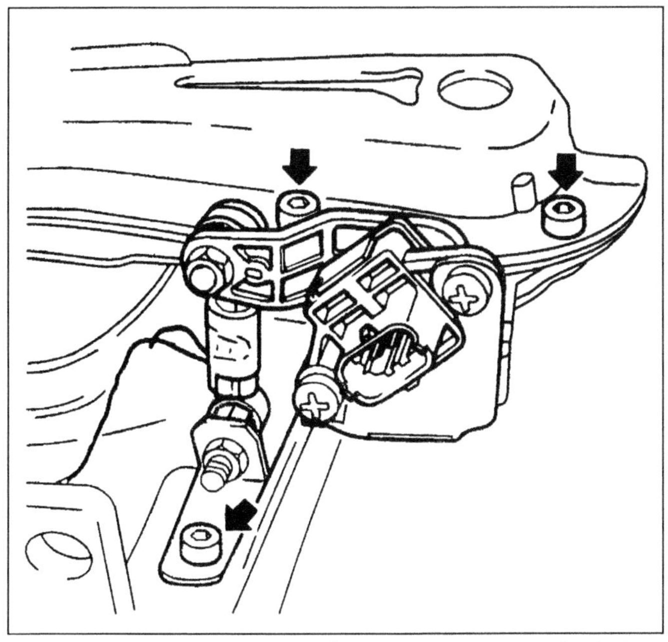

13.7 Xenon headlight front vehicle level sensor mounting bolts (arrowed)

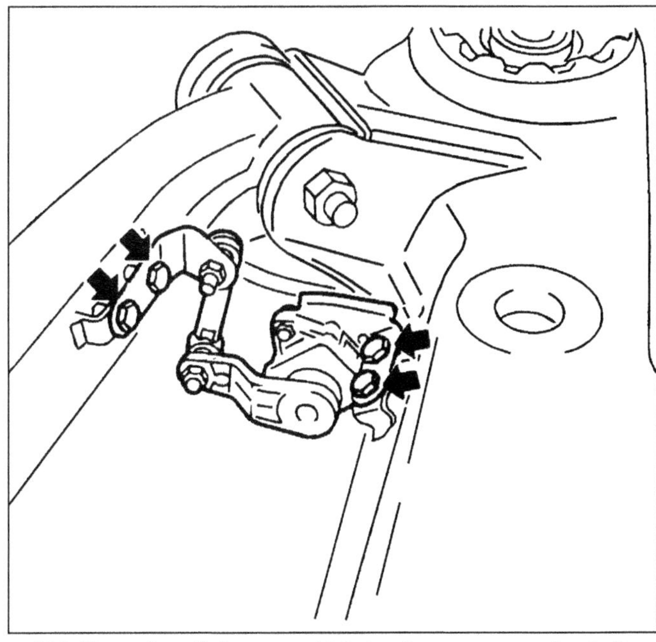

13.9 Xenon headlight rear vehicle level sensor mounting bolts (arrowed)

2 Remove the multi-function display unit as described in Section 11.

3 Carefully release the clips using a screwdriver, then release the front frame from the main housing.

4 Gauges within the instrument pack can be renewed, but it is recommended that this work is carried by an automotive electronics specialist, due the delicate nature of the components involved. Note that on models built from 1998 onwards, the instrument pack is supplied as a single assembly. On these models, although the illumination bulbs, tell-tale warning bulbs, front cover and multi-function display unit can be renewed separately from the instrument pack, it is not possible to renew individual gauges.

Refitting

5 Refitting is a reversal of removal.

11 Clock/ multi-function display unit - removal and refitting

Removal

1 Remove the instrument panel as described in Section 9.

2 Undo the screws then withdraw the multi-function display unit from the rear of the instrument panel.

Refitting

3 Refitting is a reversal of removal.

12 Cigarette lighter - removal and refitting

Removal

1 Open the ashtray, then depress the locking tab at the right hand side and detach the tray from its housing. Remove the securing screw and withdraw ashtray housing from the centre console.

2 Disconnect the wiring from the rear of the cigarette lighter.

3 Using a small screwdriver, release the retainer and illumination ring then remove the cigarette lighter from the ashtray housing.

Refitting

4 Refitting is a reversal of removal.

13 Xenon headlight beam levelling system - component removal and refitting

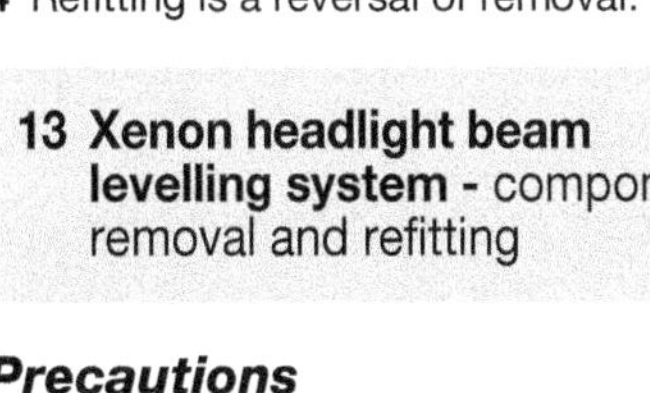

Precautions

1 Due to the intensity of the light emitted by Xenon discharge headlight bulbs, it is vitally important that the operation of the beam level control system is checked by a Vauxhall dealer, using dedicated electronic test equipment, following work on any of the components in the system. Failure to do so could result in other road uses being severely dazzled by your headlights. This applies equally to the main and dipped beam headlights.

Headlight bulbs

2 Refer to the information given in Section 5.

Vehicle front level sensor

Removal

3 Jack up the front of the vehicle and support it securely on axle stands.

4 Remove the left hand roadwheel.

5 Ensure that the ignition is switched off, then unplug the wiring from the level sensor body.

6 Unscrew the two securing bolt and detach the sensor body from the subframe.

7 Unscrew the securing bolt and detach the sensor link rod bracket from the front suspension **(see illustration)**.

Refitting

8 Refitting is a reversal of removal. On completion have the operation of the headlight beam level control system checked by a Vauxhall dealer.

Vehicle rear level sensor

9 The removal and refitting procedure is the same as that described for the front level sensor, noting that the sensor is mounted on the left hand side of the rear suspension subframe **(see illustration)**. Note also that there are two screws securing the sensor link rod bracket the rear suspension.

Electronic control unit

Removal

10 Jack up the front of the vehicle and support it securely on axle stands.

11 Remove the securing screws and detach the plastic liner(s) from the underside of the front right hand wheel arch.

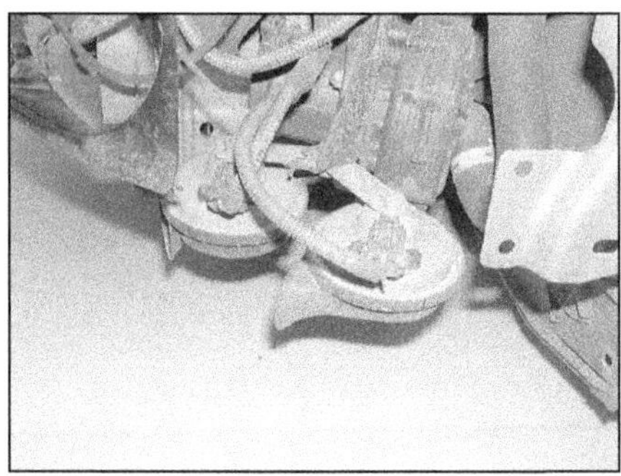
14.1 The horns are located behind the front bumper on the left-hand side of the vehicle

15.2 Prise the cover from the spindle end of the wiper arm

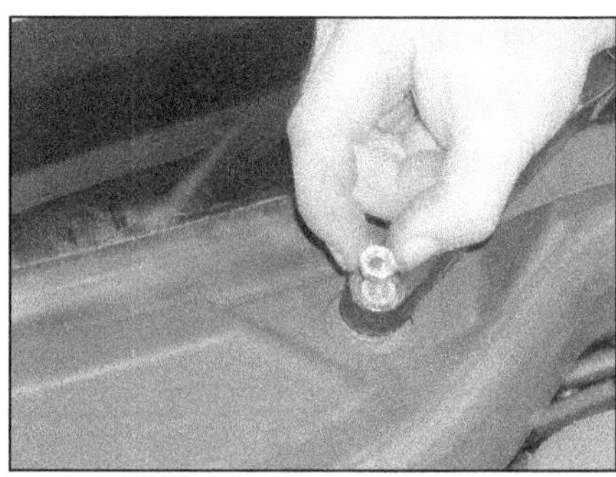
15.3a Unscrew the spindle nut . . .

12 The electronic control unit is located in front of the suspension strut upper mountings. Unclip the unit from its mounting bracket and unplug the wiring connector from it. To do this, slide the locking bar to one side and then pull the connector block squarely away from the control unit.

Refitting

13 Refitting is a reversal of removal.

Headlight levelling servo

Removal

14 Remove the headlight unit as described in Section 7.

15 Grasp the servo unit, rotate it through a quarter of a turn clockwise and withdraw it from the rear of the headlight unit.

Refitting

16 Refitting is a reversal of removal. Counterhold the reflector as the servo is refitted, to ensure that the pushrod engages correctly.

14 Horn(s) - removal and refitting

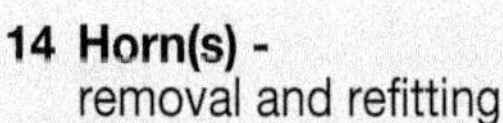

Removal

1 The horns are located behind the front bumper on the left-hand side of the vehicle **(see illustration)**. One or two horns are fitted according to model. First apply the handbrake, then jack up the front of the vehicle and support it on axle stands (see *Jacking and Vehicle Support*).

2 Where applicable, remove the securing screws and detach the undertray from the front lower edge of the bumper.

3 Disconnect the wiring from the horn.

4 Unscrew the mounting nut(s) and remove the horn together with its mounting bracket from the bodywork.

Refitting

5 Refitting is a reversal of removal.

15 Wiper arm - removal and refitting

Windscreen wiper arm

Removal

1 Operate the wiper motor, then switch it off so that the wiper arm returns to the at-rest position.

Stick a piece of masking tape on the windscreen, along the edge of the wiper blade, to use as an alignment aid on refitting.

2 Using a screwdriver prise the cover from the spindle end of the wiper arm **(see illustration)**.

3 Unscrew the spindle nut and recover the small washer **(see illustrations)**.

4 Lift the blade off the glass, and pull the wiper arm off its spindle. Note that the wiper arms may be very tight on the spindle splines - if necessary, lever the arm off the spindle, using a flat-bladed screwdriver (take care not to damage the scuttle cover panel). Alternatively use a proprietary puller to draw the arm from the shaft **(see illustrations)**.

5 If necessary, remove the blade from the arm with reference to *Weekly checks*.

Refitting

6 If removed, refit the wiper blade to the arm at this stage. This will prevent any damage to the windscreen from the upper end of the arm.

7 Ensure that the wiper arm and spindle splines are clean and dry, then refit the arm to the spindle and align the blade with the previously noted rest position. As a guide, the distance between the hinge which joins the wiper blade to the wiper arm and the sealing strip at the lower edge of the windscreen should be 55-65 mm for the left hand arm and 65-75 mm for the right hand arm.

8 Refit the washer and spindle nut, and tighten it securely. Refit the cover.

Tailgate wiper arm - Estate models

Removal

9 Operate the wiper motor, then switch it off so that the wiper arm returns to the at-rest position.

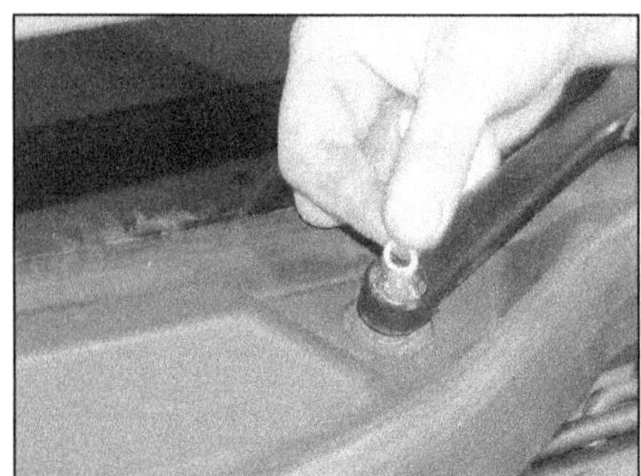
15.3b . . . and recover the small washer

15.4a Pull the wiper arm off its spindle

15.4b Using a proprietary puller to draw the wiper arm from its shaft

15.10a Lift the cover from the base of the wiper arm . . .

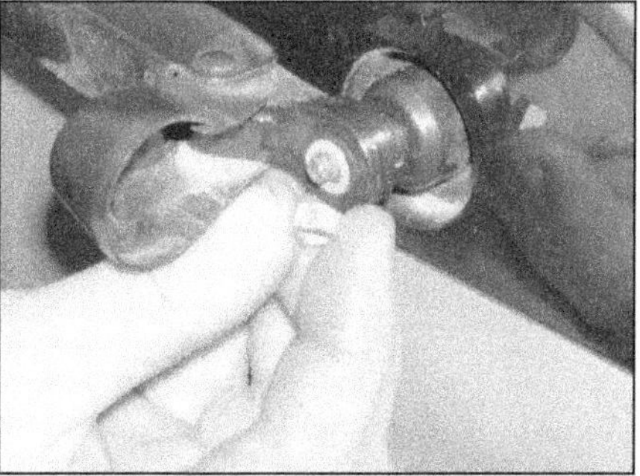
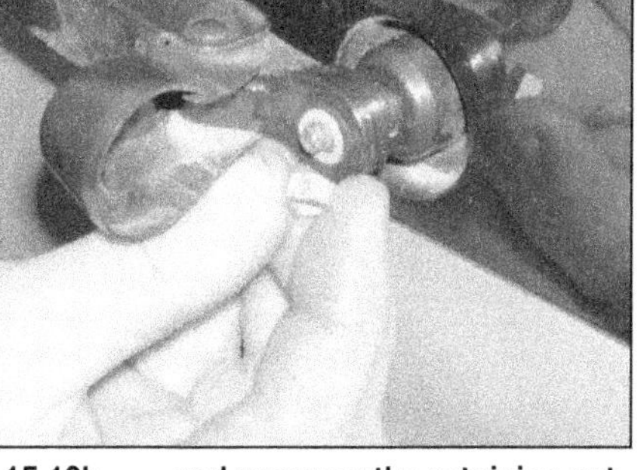

15.10b . . . and unscrew the retaining nut

15.11 Pull the wiper arm off its spindle

10 Lift the cover from the base of the wiper arm, unscrew the retaining nut and recover the washer **(see illustrations)**.

11 Lift the blade off the glass, and pull the wiper arm off its spindle **(see illustration)**.

12 If necessary, remove the blade from the arm with reference to *Weekly checks*.

Refitting

13 If removed, refit the wiper blade to the arm at this stage. This will prevent any damage to the rear window from the upper end of the arm.

14 Ensure that the wiper arm and spindle splines are clean and dry, then refit the arm to the spindle and align the blade with the previously noted rest position, parallel with strips of the heated rear screen elements.

15 Refit the spindle nut, and tighten it securely. Close the cover on the base of the arm.

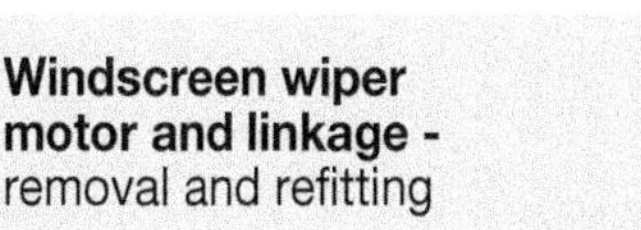

16 Windscreen wiper motor and linkage - removal and refitting

Removal

1 Remove both wiper arms as described in Section 15.

2 Release the rubber weatherstrip from the rear of the engine compartment bulkhead **(see illustration)**.

3 Slacken and withdraw the screws securing the ends of the water deflector panel to the bodywork **(see illustration)**.

4 Lift the lower edge of the windscreen sealing strip, then release the press stud clips securing the edge of the water deflector panel to the bodywork. Unclip and remove the panel **(see illustrations)**.

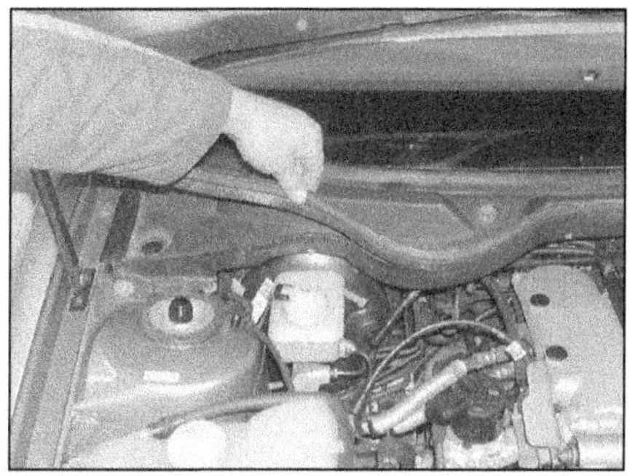

16.2 Release the rubber weatherstrip from the rear of the engine compartment bulkhead

5 Undo the screws and remove the hose support bracket **(see illustration)**.

6 Disconnect the wiring at the wiper motor **(see illustration)**.

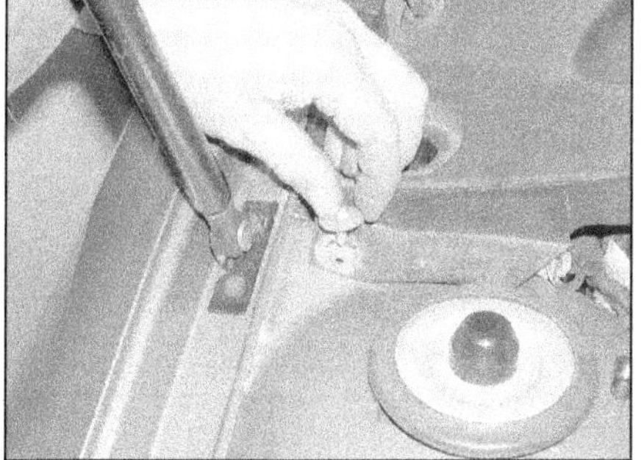

16.3 Slacken and withdraw the screws securing the ends of the water deflector panel to the bodywork

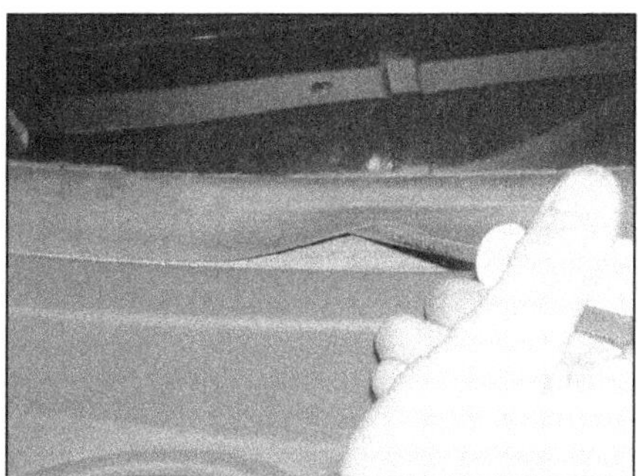

16.4a Lift the lower edge of the windscreen sealing strip . . .

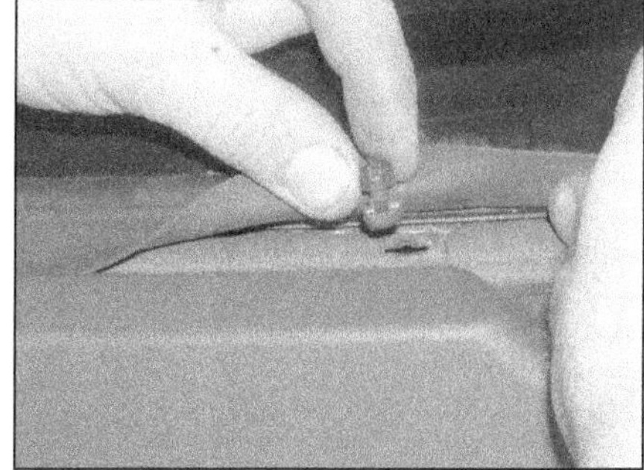

16.4b . . . then release the press stud clips securing the edge of the water deflector panel to the bodywork

16.4c Unclip and remove the water deflector panel

16.5 Remove the hose support bracket

16.6 Disconnect the wiring at the wiper motor

16.7a Unscrew the bolts securing the left hand end . . .

16.7b . . . right hand end . . .

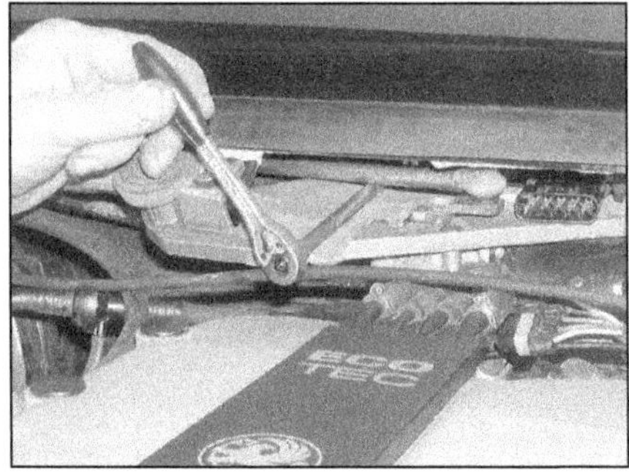

16.7c . . . and centre of the wiper motor assembly to the scuttle. Note that the centre securing bolt can only be accessed using an extension bar

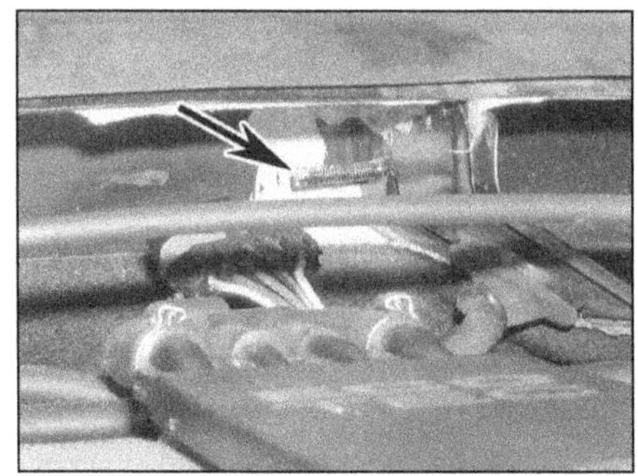
16.10 The grometed lug at the left hand end of the wiper assembly must engage with the corresponding peg (arrowed) on the bulkhead bracket

7 Unscrew the bolts securing the left hand end, right hand end and centre of the wiper motor assembly to the scuttle, and withdraw the assembly from the engine compartment **(see illustrations)**. Note that the centre securing bolt can only be accessed using an extension bar.

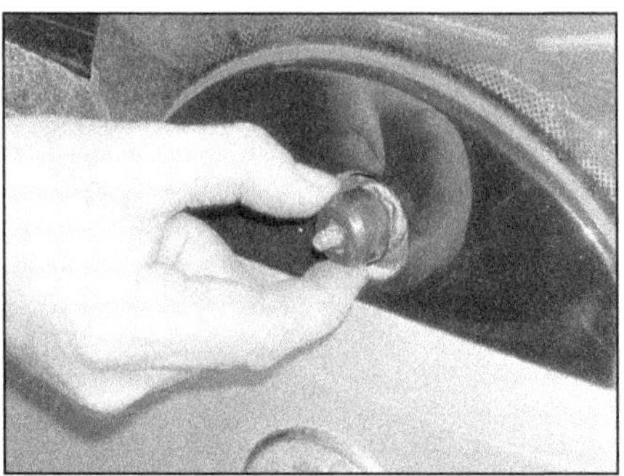
17.2 Remove the plastic cap and unscrew the wiper spindle nut

8 The motor can be removed from the linkage assembly by prising free the rod from the crank and unbolting the motor. The remaining linkage rods can also be dismantled if necessary.

9 Clean the assembly and examine the spindles and joints for wear and damage. Renew the components as required.

Refitting

10 Refitting is a reversal of removal, but lubricate the joints with a little grease before assembling them. Note that the grometed lug at the left hand end of the wiper assembly must engage with the corresponding peg on the bulkhead bracket **(see illustration)**. Refit the wiper arms with reference to Section 15.

17 Tailgate wiper motor - removal and refitting

Removal

1 Remove the wiper arm from the tailgate as described in Section 15.

2 Remove the plastic cap from the wiper spindle nut **(see illustration)**.

3 Unscrew the nut securing the spindle housing to the tailgate, and remove the washer and cover.

4 Open the tailgate, then work around the periphery of the tailgate trim panel and unscrew each of the securing screws. Lift the panel away from the tailgate **(see illustrations)**.

5 Disconnect the wiper motor wiring at the plug.

6 Unscrew the mounting bolts and withdraw the wiper motor while sliding the spindle housing through the rubber grommet **(see illustration)**.

7 If necessary remove the rubber grommet from the tailgate. Examine the grommet for wear and damage and renew it if necessary.

Refitting

8 Refitting is a reversal of removal; tighten the mounting nut to the specified torque. Refit the wiper arm with reference to Section 15.

18 Windscreen/tailgate/headlight washer system components - removal and refitting

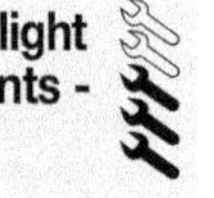

Washer fluid reservoir

Removal

1 Remove the front bumper as described in Chapter 11.

2 Undo the screws and remove the front section of the left-hand front wheel arch liner.

3 The reservoir is mounted behind the bumper inner section; position a container beneath the washer fluid pump and reservoir to collect the spilt fluid.

17.4a Unscrew each of the securing screws . . .

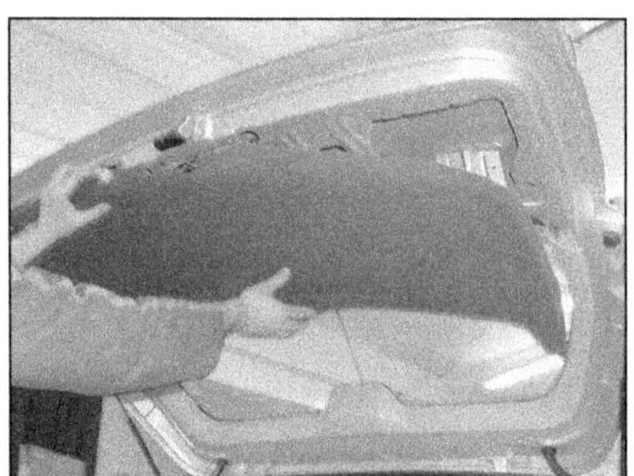
17.4b . . . and lift the trim panel away from the tailgate

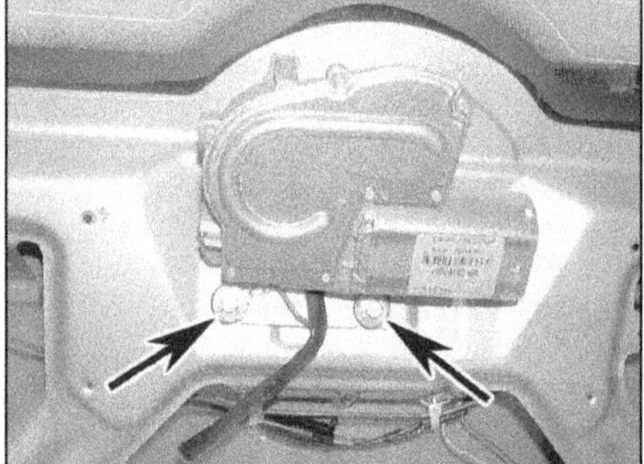
17.6 Unscrew the mounting bolts (arrowed) and withdraw the wiper motor

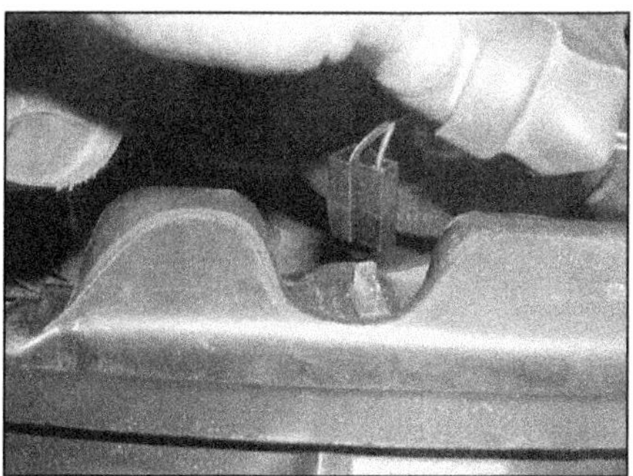

18.5 Disconnect the wiring from the top of the pump and position to one side

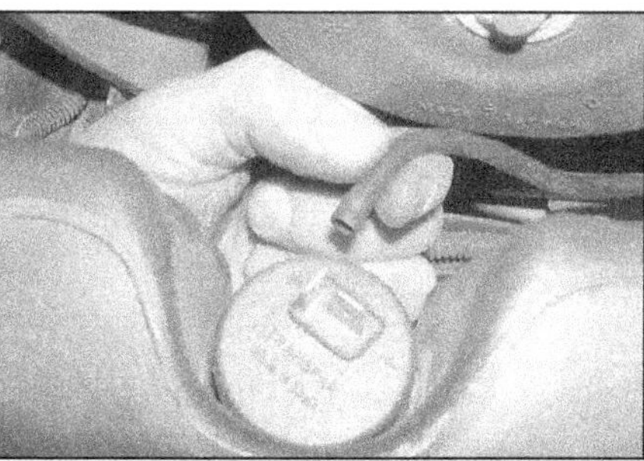

18.6 Disconnect the hose from the pump and allow the fluid to drain into the container

18.8 Disconnect the filler neck from the reservoir

4 Unbolt the bumper inner section and support it away from the front of the vehicle.
5 Disconnect the wiring from the top of the pump and position to one side **(see illustration)**. Where applicable, disconnect the wiring from the level sensor on the fluid reservoir.
6 Disconnect the hose from the pump and allow the fluid to drain into the container **(see illustration)**.
7 On models with a headlight washer system, disconnect the wiring and hose from the additional pump on the reservoir.
8 Disconnect the filler neck from the reservoir **(see illustration).**
9 Release the wiring from the clips on the bumper inner section, then withdraw the bumper inner section together with the reservoir from the front of the vehicle.
10 Unscrew the mounting bolts and withdraw the reservoir from the rear of the bumper inner section **(see illustration)**.

Refitting

11 Refitting is a reversal of removal. Fill the reservoir with washer fluid with reference to *Weekly checks*.

Washer fluid pump

Removal

12 Remove the front bumper as described in Chapter 11.
13 Position a suitable container beneath the washer fluid pump and reservoir to collect the fluid.
14 Disconnect the wiring from the top of the pump and position to one side.
15 Disconnect the hose from the pump and allow the fluid to drain into the container.
16 Incline the pump body back towards the engine compartment, then pull to extract it from the reservoir grommet **(see illustration)**.
17 If necessary, remove the grommet from the reservoir.

Refitting

18 Refitting is a reversal of removal. Fill the reservoir with washer fluid with reference to *Weekly checks*.

Windscreen washer nozzle

Removal

19 With the bonnet open, disconnect the wiring and supply hose from the bottom of the nozzle.
20 Depress the tabs at the rear of the nozzle, then release the nozzle body from the bonnet and remove it upwards.

Refitting

21 Refitting is a reversal of removal.

Tailgate washer nozzle - Estate models

Removal

22 Carefully insert a small screwdriver between the nozzle and the rubber seal. Depress the lugs and remove the nozzle from the tailgate.
23 Disconnect the nozzle from the hose.

Refitting

24 Refitting is a reversal of removal.

Headlight washer nozzle

Removal

25 Unclip the nozzle head from the high pressure tube.
26 Remove the headlight as described in Section 7.
27 Release the supply hose from the high pressure tube at the base of the headlight unit.
28 Undo the securing screws and detach the high pressure tube from the base of the headlight unit.

Refitting

30 Refitting is a reversal of removal.

19 Radio/cassette/CD player - removal and refitting

Note: *On models with a security-coded radio/cassette player, once the battery has been disconnected, the unit cannot be re-activated until the appropriate security code has been entered. Do not remove the unit unless the appropriate code is known. The following information applies to radio/cassette players having standard DIN fixings. Two DIN removal tools will be required for this operation.*

Radio/cassette/CD player

Removal

1 Using an Allen key, undo the grub screws from the four holes in each corner of the radio front face **(see illustration)**.

18.10 Unscrew the mounting bolts and withdraw the reservoir from the rear of the bumper inner section

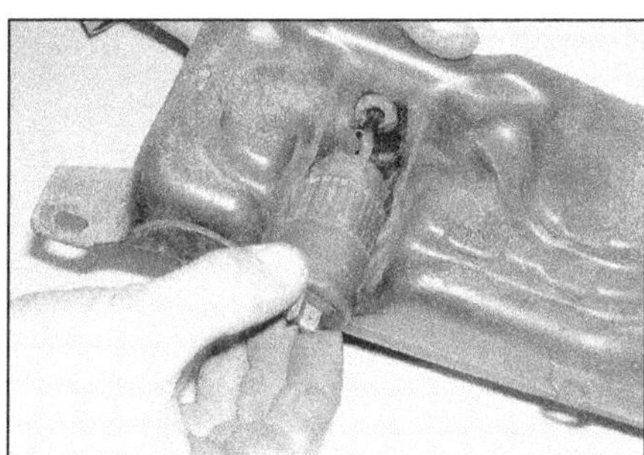

18.16 Pull the pump body to extract it from the reservoir grommet (shown with reservoir removed for clarity)

19.1 Using an Allen key, undo the grub screws from the four holes in each corner of the radio

19.3 Using the DIN removal tools carefully withdraw the radio/cassette/CD player from the facia

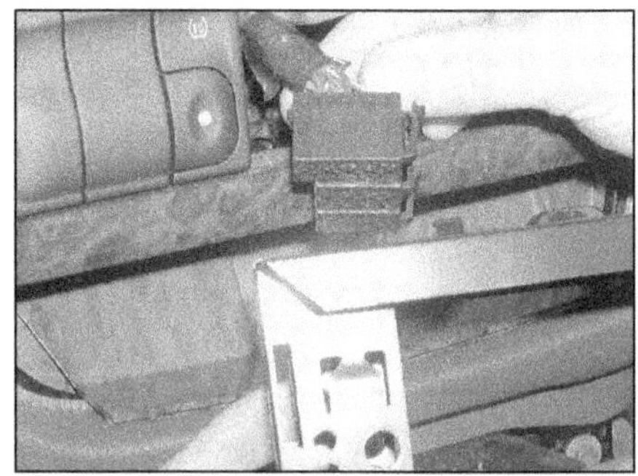
19.4a If required, bend back the securing tabs and release the mounting frame from the facia

19.4b Disconnect the wiring and aerial connectors from the rear of the radio mounting frame

2 Insert the two DIN removal tools into the holes on each side of the radio until they are felt to engage with the retaining strips.

3 Push the DIN removal tools outwards slightly then carefully withdraw the radio/cassette/CD player from the facia **(see illustration).** Note the electrical and coaxial connections are made via quick release connectors.

4 If required, bend back the securing tabs and release the mounting frame from the facia. Disconnect the wiring and aerial connectors from the rear of the radio mounting frame **(see illustrations)**.

5 Remove the removal tools and refit the grub screws.

Refitting

6 Refitting is a reversal of removal.

7 On completion, enter the security code as described in the audio unit handbook supplied with the vehicle.

CD autochanger

Removal

8 Open the bootlid/tailgate, and remove the first aid kit from its bracket. Open the right hand storage compartment by rotating the release knobs and pivoting the trim panel downwards.

9 Slide the CD autochanger unit from its mounting bracket until access to the wiring connectors can be gained.

10 Disconnect the wiring plugs and remove the CD autochanger unit from the vehicle.

11 If required, the mounting bracket can be unbolted from the bodywork and removed.

Refitting

12 Refitting is a reversal of removal.

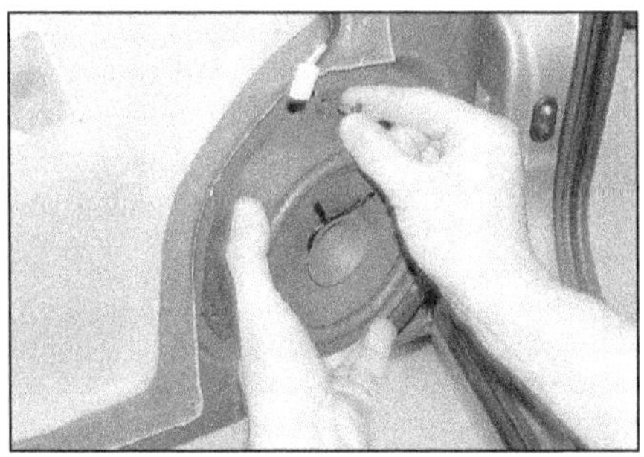
20.2 Undo the mounting screws and withdraw the loudspeaker from the door inner panel

20 Loudspeakers - removal and refitting

Front door-mounted low frequency loudspeakers

Removal

1 Remove the front door inner trim panel, as described in Chapter 11.

2 Undo the mounting screws and withdraw the loudspeaker from the door inner panel **(see illustration)**.

3 Disconnect the wiring from the loudspeaker **(see illustration)**.

Refitting

4 Refitting is a reversal of removal.

Front door-mounted high-frequency (tweeter) loudspeakers

Removal

5 With reference to Chapter 11, Section 23, carefully prise off the triangular plastic cover panel from the rear of the exterior door mirror mountings, then remove the foam padding beneath.

6 Disconnect the wiring, then release the loudspeaker from the plastic cover **(see illustration).**

Refitting

7 Refitting is a reversal of removal.

Rear door loudspeaker

Removal

8 Remove the rear door inner trim panel, as described in Chapter 11.

9 Undo the mounting screws and withdraw the loudspeaker from the door inner panel **(see illustration)**.

10 Disconnect the wiring from the loudspeaker **(see illustration)**.

Refitting

11 Refitting is a reversal of removal.

20.3 Disconnect the wiring from the loudspeaker

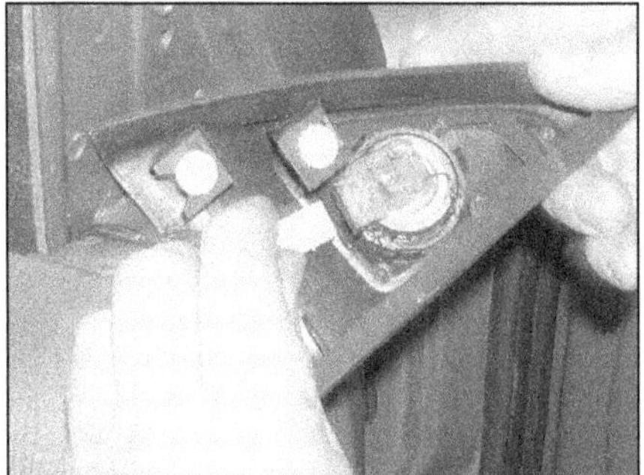
20.6 Unplug the wiring from the loudspeaker

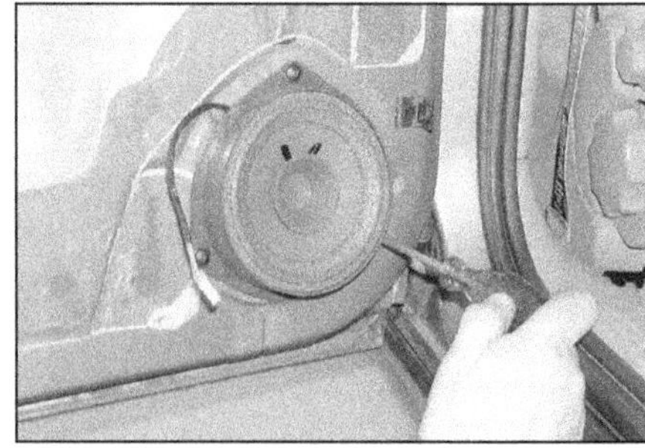
20.9 Undo the mounting screws and withdraw the loudspeaker from the door inner panel

20.10 Disconnect the wiring from the loudspeaker

Parcel shelf speakers - Saloon models

Removal

12 Remove the rear seat cushions and back rests as described in Chapter 11.

13 Where applicable unbolt and remove the centre three point seat belt with reference to Chapter 11.

14 Remove the rear headrests, then depress the locking tabs and remove the headrest guide sleeves from the seat frame.

15 Undo the securing screws and remove the centre arm rest.

16 Carefully prise out the press stud fasteners and remove the parcel shelf trim panel from the vehicle.

17 Unplug the wiring at the connector, then slacken and withdraw the screws and remove the speaker from the parcel shelf.

Refitting

18 Refitting is a reversal of removal.

21 Radio aerial - removal and refitting

Aerial - Saloon models

1 The aerial is integral with the rear heated screen element.

Aerial - Estate models

2 It is recommended that the removal of the aerial is carried by a Vauxhall dealer as the operation involves the partial removal of the load compartment headlining.

Aerial amplifier - Saloon models

Removal

3 Remove the rear seat cushions and back rests as described in Chapter 11.

4 Where applicable unbolt and remove the centre three point seat belt with reference to Chapter 11.

5 Remove the rear headrests, then depress the locking tabs and remove the headrest guide sleeves from the seat frame.

6 Undo the securing screws and remove the centre arm rest.

7 Carefully prise out the press stud fasteners and remove the parcel shelf trim panel from the vehicle.

8 Unscrew the coaxial cable connectors from the side of the amplifier unit, the unplug the power supply wiring connector from the front of the unit.

9 Slacken and withdraw the securing screws and remove the amplifier unit from the parcel shelf.

Refitting

10 Refitting is a reversal of removal.

Aerial amplifier - Estate models

Removal

11 Open the tailgate, then work around the periphery of the tailgate trim panel and unscrew each of the securing screws. Lift the panel away from the tailgate.

12 Unscrew the coaxial cable connectors from the side of the amplifier unit, the unplug the power supply wiring connector from the front of the unit.

13 Slacken and withdraw the securing screws and remove the amplifier unit from the tailgate.

Refitting

14 Refitting is a reversal of removal.

22 Anti-theft alarm system and engine immobiliser - general information

Note: *To avoid triggering the alarm when the battery removed or disconnected, ensure that the negative cable is disconnected not more than fifteen seconds after the ignition has been switched off. If the alarm has been activated, it will reset after 30 seconds, but can be deactivated during this time by reconnecting the battery and switching on the ignition.*

1 All models have an engine immobiliser which effectively prevents the engine from being started when the ignition key is in the OFF position or removed from the steering lock. The system is activated by the ignition key and an electronic sensor mounted on the steering lock. The driver's door lock barrel is freewheeling - if an attempt is made to forcefully turn the lock without the correct key, it will just turn within its housing.

2 The anti-theft alarm system monitors the doors, bootlid or tailgate, bonnet, radio, ignition, and on some models the passenger and luggage compartments. The control unit for the system is located behind the outer trim panel on the right-hand side of the right-hand footwell. On higher specification models an ultrasonic sensor is located at the top of each B-pillar. The anti-theft alarm system horn is located on the bulkhead in the engine compartment and the power sounder is located beneath the left-hand front wing. On Estate models, a glass breakage detector is fitted to the luggage compartment rear side windows.

3 To remove the ultrasonic sensor, carefully lever it out of its housing using a screwdriver then disconnect the wiring.

4 To remove the warning horn disconnect the wiring and unscrew the mounting nut.

5 To remove the bonnet contact, disconnect the wiring then detach the contact from the bulkhead.

6 To remove the power sounder, disconnect the battery negative lead, as described in Chapter 5A, within 15 seconds of switching off the ignition. Remove the wheel arch liner from under the left-hand front wing, then disconnect the wiring and unbolt the bracket and power sounder.

7 Refitting of the components is a reversal of the removal procedure.

8 Any faults with the system should be referred to a Vauxhall/Opel dealer.

23 Supplementary Restraint System - information, precautions and system de-activation

General information

1 A driver's side airbag is fitted as standard equipment on all models. The airbag is fitted to the steering wheel centre pad. Similarly, a passenger's side airbag is also fitted as standard equipment, or as an option, depending on model. On certain later models, side airbags, mounted in the sides of the front seats, and seat belt tensioners are also fitted.

2 The system is armed only when the ignition is switched on, however, a reserve power source maintains a power supply to the system in the event of a break in the main electrical supply. The system is activated by a combination of a g sensor (deceleration sensor), incorporated in the electronic control unit and air pressure sensors mounted inside the front doors. Note that the electronic control unit also controls the activation of the front seat belt tensioners.

3 The airbags are inflated by gas generators, which force the bags out from their locations in the steering wheel, and the passenger's side facia, where applicable.

4 On later models fitted with pyrotechical seat belt tensioners, actuation is by means of a gas generator. Some earlier models may be fitted with mechanical seat belt tensioners which must be deactivated individually.

5 In the event of a fault occurring in the airbag system (warning light illuminated on the instrument panel), seek the advice of a Vauxhall/Opel dealer.

Precautions

Warning: The following precautions must be observed when working on vehicles equipped with an airbag system, to prevent the possibility of personal injury.

General precautions

6 The following precautions **must** be

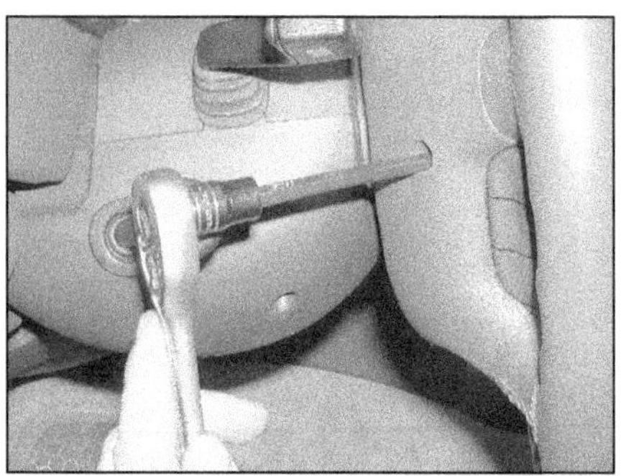
24.8a Unscrew and remove the two screws from the rear of the steering wheel . . .

24.8b . . . and carefully lift the airbag/horn-push from the steering wheel

observed when carrying out work on a vehicle equipped with an airbag.

a) *Do not disconnect the battery with the engine running.*
b) *Before carrying out any work in the vicinity of the airbag, removal of any of the airbag components, or any welding work on the vehicle, de-activate the system as described in the following sub-Section.*
c) *Do not attempt to test any of the airbag system circuits using test meters or any other test equipment.*
d) *If the airbag warning light comes on, or any fault in the system is suspected, consult a Vauxhall/Opel dealer without delay.* ***Do not*** *attempt to carry out fault diagnosis, or any dismantling of the components.*

Precautions to be taken when handling an airbag

a) *Transport the airbag by itself, bag upward.*
b) *Do not put your arms around the airbag.*
c) *Carry the airbag close to the body, bag outward.*
d) *Do not drop the airbag or expose it to impacts.*
e) *Do not attempt to dismantle the airbag unit.*
f) *Do not connect any form of electrical equipment to any part of the airbag circuit.*
g) *Do not allow any solvents or cleaning agents to contact the airbag assembly. The unit must be cleaned using only a damp cloth.*

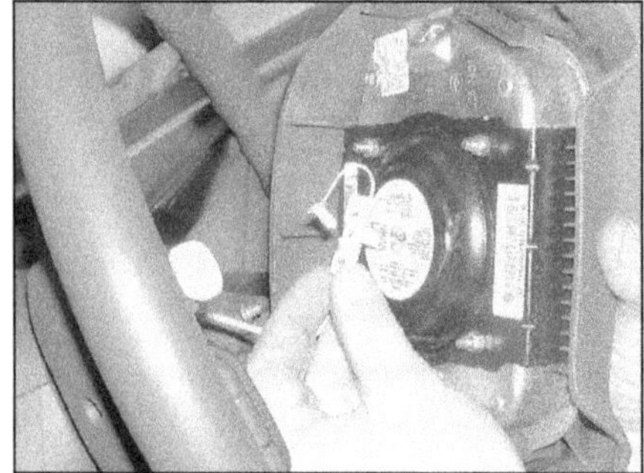
24.9 Disconnect the wiring from the airbag

Precautions to be taken when storing an airbag unit

a) *Store the unit in a cupboard with the airbag upward.*
b) *Do not expose the airbag to temperatures above 90°C.*
c) *Do not expose the airbag to flames.*
d) *Do not attempt to dispose of the airbag - consult a Vauxhall/Opel dealer.*
e) *Never refit an airbag which is known to be faulty or damaged.*

De-activation of the Supplementary Restraint System (SRS) airbag system

7 The system must be de-activated as follows, before carrying out any work on the airbag components or surrounding area.

a) *Switch off the ignition.*
b) *Remove the ignition key.*
c) *Switch off all electrical equipment.*
d) *Disconnect the battery negative lead (see Chapter 5A).*
e) *Insulate the battery negative terminal and the end of the battery negative lead to prevent any possibility of contact.*
f) *Wait for at least one minute before carrying out any further work. This will allow the system capacitor to discharge.*

Deactivation of mechanical seat belt tensioners

Note: *This section only applies to models fitted with mechanical seat belt tensioners. To deactivate the pyrotechnical seat belt tensioners fitted to later models, follow the SRS deactivation procedure detailed in the previous sub-section.*

8 Remove the seat runner trim panels as described at the beginning of Chapter 11, Section 27.

9 The seat belt tensioner unit is mounted adjacent to the seat runner. Remove the seat belt tensioner locking tool from its storage position and insert it fully into the groove provided at the end of the tensioner unit. This will prevent the tensioner mechanism from recoiling if it is accidentally activated.

10 On completion, remove the locking tool and refit the seat runner trim panels before bringing the vehicle back service.

24 Supplementary Restraint System (SRS) components - removal and refitting

Driver's side airbag unit

Warning: Refer to the precautions given in Section 23 before attempting to carry out work on the airbag components.

Removal - models up to 1996

1 The airbag unit is an integral part of the steering wheel centre pad.

2 De-activate the airbag system as described in Section 23.

3 Set the front wheels in the straight-ahead position, then turn the steering wheel one quarter turn to the right. Slacken and remove the left hand airbag securing screw.

4 Turn the steering wheel back to the straight ahead position, then turn it one quarter turn to the left. Slacken and remove the right hand airbag securing screw.

3 Return the steering wheel to the straight-ahead position, then lock the column in position after removing the ignition key.

4 Disconnect the wiring from the airbag. Position the airbag in a safe place where it cannot be tampered with, making sure that the padded side is facing upwards.

Removal - models from 1996 onwards

5 The airbag unit is an integral part of the steering wheel centre pad.

6 De-activate the airbag system as described in Section 23.

7 Set the front wheels in the straight-ahead position, then lock the column in position after removing the ignition key.

8 Unscrew and remove the two screws from the rear of the steering wheel and carefully lift the airbag/horn-push from the steering wheel **(see illustrations).**

9 Disconnect the wiring from the airbag **(see illustration)**. Observe the handling and storage precautions given in Section 23.

Refitting

10 Refitting is a reversal of removal, but make sure that the wiring connector is securely reconnected and tighten the retaining screws to the specified torque.

Passenger's side airbag unit

Warning: Refer to the precautions given in Section 23 before attempting to carry out work on the airbag components.

Removal

11 De-activate the airbag system as described in Section 23.

12 Remove the glovebox as described in Chapter 11.

13 Unclip the cover panel from the left hand facia end section.

14 Unclip the bulb holder from the rear of the air vent housing and position it to one side.

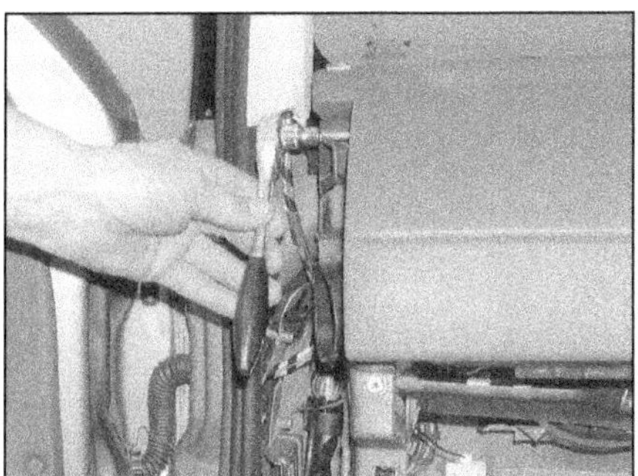
24.18a Using a long extension bar and a pair of long nosed pliers, slacken . . .

24.18b . . . and withdraw the airbag cover hinge bolt

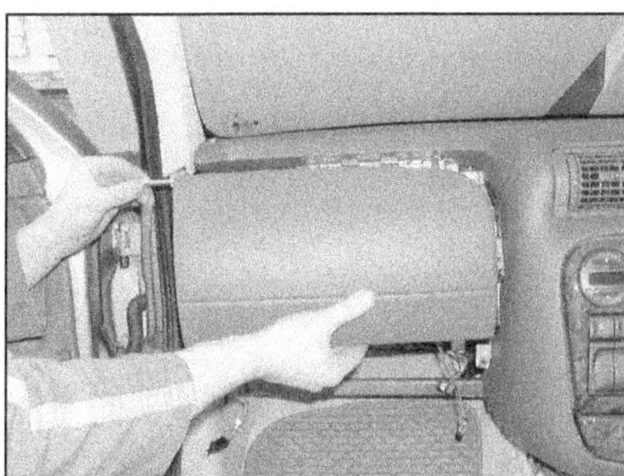
24.19 Remove the hinged cover to expose the airbag unit

15 Slacken and withdraw the securing screws then detach the nozzle from the left hand air vent housing.
16 Undo the securing screws and remove the left hand vent housing from the facia.
17 Unscrew the lower mounting screws and detach the lower edge of the hinged airbag cover from the facia.
18 Using a long extension bar and a pair of long nosed pliers, slacken and withdraw the airbag cover hinge bolt **(see illustrations).**
19 Remove the hinged cover to expose the airbag unit **(see illustration).**
20 Slacken and remove the airbag unit securing bolts, then withdraw the unit from its mounting bracket slightly **(see illustration).**
21 Unplug the wiring connector from the airbag, then remove the air bag unit from the vehicle **(see illustration).** Observe the handling and storage precautions given in Section 23.

Refitting

22 Refitting is a reversal of removal, but make sure that the wiring connector is securely reconnected. Use new airbag securing bolts and tighten them to the specified torque.

Side airbag unit

Warning: Refer to the precautions given in Section 23 before attempting to carry out work on the airbag components.

Removal

23 Removal of the side airbags involves partially dismantling the seat upholstery; it is therefore recommended that this work is carried out by a Vauxhall dealer.

Airbag contact unit (on steering column)

Removal

24 Remove the driver's airbag unit as described earlier in this Section.
25 Remove the steering wheel as described in Chapter 10.
26 Remove the steering column shrouds by unscrewing the tilt steering lever, then removing the screws from the end face and the lower shroud panel. Recover the ignition key position indicator from the ignition switch.
27 Using a small screwdriver release the locking plate, then disconnect the wiring plug **(see illustration).**
28 Release the four rear clips and remove the contact unit from the top of the column **(see illustrations)**. **Note:** *Make sure that the contact unit halves remain in their central position with the arrows aligned at the bottom. If necessary, apply tape to the halves to hold them. Note that on later models, as the unit is removed from the steering column, an integral locking catch engages, preventing unintentional rotation of the two halves of the contact unit.*

Refitting

29 Before refitting the contact unit, if the centre position has been lost or if a new unit is being fitted, determine the centre position as follows. Depress the detent on top of the unit and carefully turn the centre part of the unit anti-clockwise until resistance is felt. Now turn it 2.5 turns clockwise and align the arrows on the centre part and outer edge **(see illustration)**.
30 If a new unit is fitted, first remove the transport clip.
31 Locate the contact unit on the top of the steering column making sure that the guide

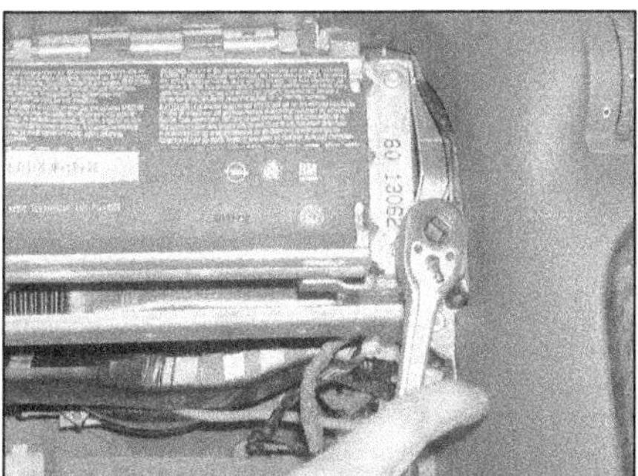
24.20 Slacken and remove the airbag unit securing bolts

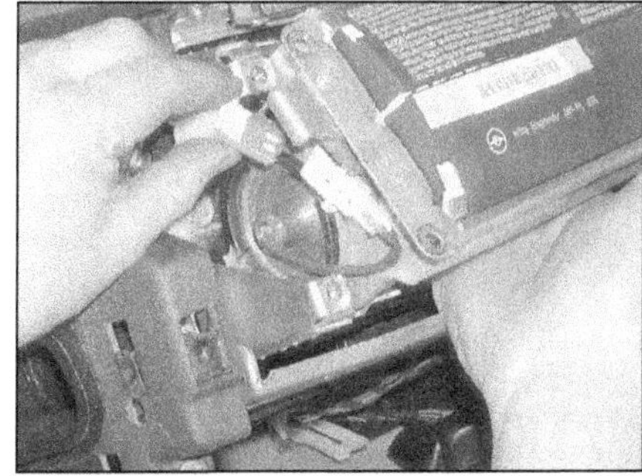
24.21 Unplug the wiring connector from the airbag

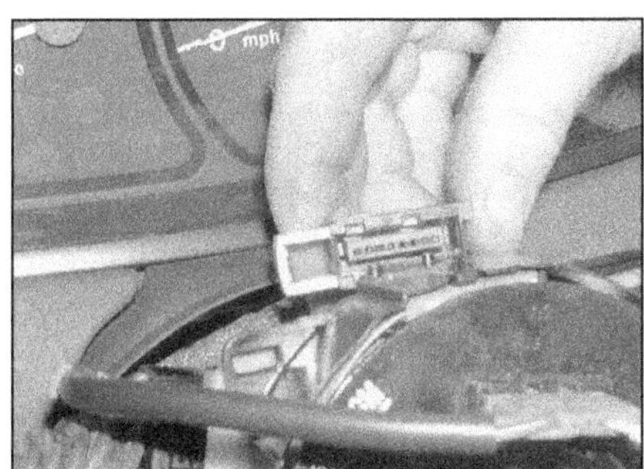
24.27 Release the locking plate, then disconnect the contact unit wiring plug

24.28a Release the rear clips . . .

24.28b . . . and remove the contact unit from the top of the column

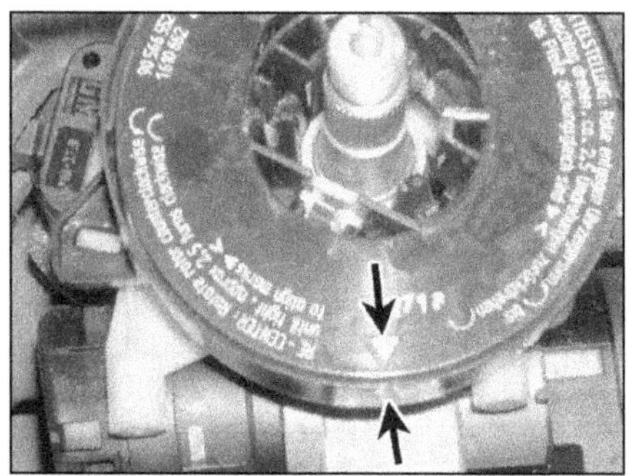
24.29 Airbag contact unit alignment markings (arrowed) - refer to text

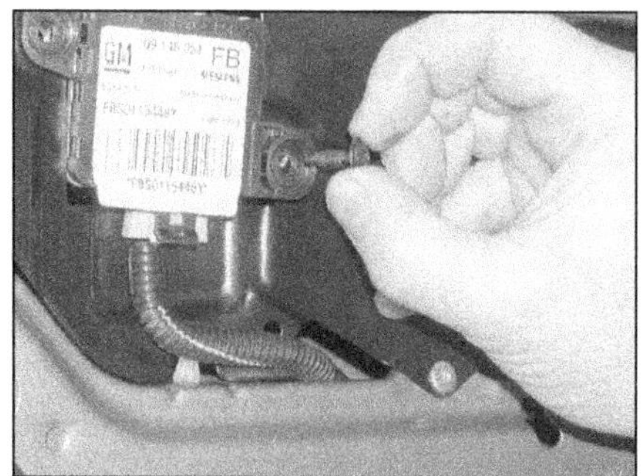
24.43a Unscrew the securing screws and remove the sensor from its mounting bracket

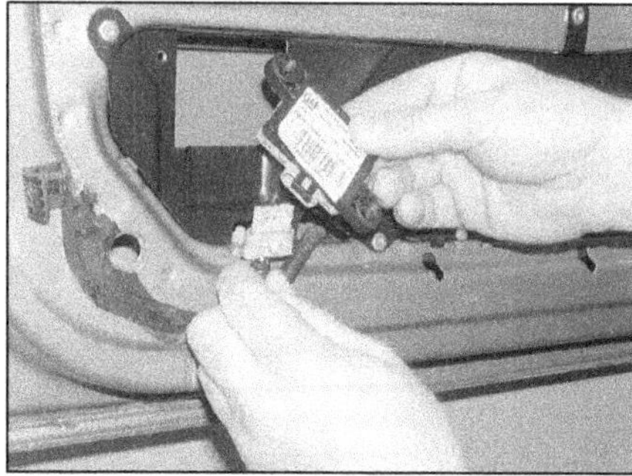
24.43b Unplug the wiring from the sensor at the connector

pins locate in the holes provided. Press the unit in until the clips engage. **Note:** *The clips must not be damaged in any way. If they are, the unit must be renewed.*

32 Reconnect the wiring while depressing the slider.

33 Refit the ignition key position indicator, then refit the steering column shrouds and tighten the securing screws. Refit and tighten the tilt steering lever.

34 Refit the steering wheel as described in Chapter 10.

35 Refit the driver's airbag unit as described earlier.

Electronic control unit

Removal

36 De-activate the airbag system as described in Section 23.

37 Remove the centre console as described in Chapter 11.

38 Disconnect the wiring from the control unit, then unscrew the mounting nuts and remove the unit from inside the vehicle.

Refitting

39 Refitting is a reversal of removal but tighten the mounting nuts to the specified torque.

Door-mounted side impact sensor

Removal

40 De-activate the airbag system as described in Section 23.

41 Remove the front door inner trim panel as described in Chapter 11.

42 Pull back the water membrane for access to the sensor.

Warning: The door side impact sensors are air pressure sensitive and will only operate correctly if the protective plastic door membrane is refitted correctly; bear this in mind when removing the membrane from the door.

43 Unscrew the securing screws and remove the sensor from its mounting bracket. Unplug the wiring from the sensor at the connector **(see illustrations).**

44 If required the sensor bracket can be removed by drilling out the securing rivets. New pop rivets will then be needed to secure the bracket tot he door on refitting.

Refitting

45 Refitting is a reversal of removal. Ensure that the plastic door membrane is securely refitted. The sealing strip around the edge of the membrane must adhere to the door without gaps, to form an airtight seal. If the membrane was cut or torn during its removal, ensure that the loose edges are stuck to the door using a suitable adhesive/sealant. If you are in doubt about the integrity of the seal, it's best to renew the membrane and sealing strip entirely.

25 Cruise control system components - removal and refitting

Actuator cable

Removal

1 Disconnect the accelerator cable from the throttle disc lever balljoint, with reference to Chapter 4A.

2 Remove the circlip, then disconnect the cruise control actuator cable from the throttle disc lever balljoint.

3 Depress the locking tabs and release the actuator cable guide tube from the mounting bracket.

4 At the actuator unit, turn the cable guide tube union through one quarter of a turn anticlockwise to release it. Unhook the cable nipple from the actuator and remove it from the vehicle.

Refitting

5 Refitting is a reversal of removal.

Actuator/control unit

Removal

6 The actuator/control unit is located on the right hand side of the engine compartment.

7 Disconnect the actuator cable from the unit as described in the previous sub-section.

8 Unplug the wiring from the unit at the multiway connector.

9 Unscrew the three nuts and remove the unit from the vehicle.

Refitting

10 Refitting is a reversal of removal.

Clutch pedal switch

Removal

11 Working in the drivers foot well, release the securing clips and remove the trim panel from the space above the foot pedals.

12 Remove the securing screws, detach the foot well vent moulded air ducting from the air distributor unit and remove it from the foot well.

13 Push the clutch pedal forwards, then pull out the actuator pin and locking sleeve from the switch body.

14 Depress the locking tabs and release the switch from its mounting bracket. Unplug the wiring at the connector and remove the switch from the vehicle.

Refitting

15 Pull the switch actuator pin out to its end stop. Similarly, pull the switch locking collar out to the end of its travel before fitting.

16 Depress the clutch pedal, the fit the switch into its mounting bracket until the locking tabs engage.

17 Press the locking collar fully into the switch body to lock the switch in position.

18 Ensure that the switch actuator is still pulled put to its end stop, then slowly release the clutch pedal until it contacts the switch actuator pin. The switch will self-adjust as the clutch pedal reaches its rest position.

19 Refit the remainder of the components removed for access.

Steering column control switches

20 The cruise control steering column switches are integral with the direction indicator switch assembly; refer to the information given in Section 4.

26 Wiring diagrams - general information

The wiring diagrams are of the current flow type, each circuit being shown in the simplest possible fashion. Note that since the diagrams were originally written in German (to the DIN standard), all wire colours and abbreviations used on the diagrams themselves are in German. Refer to the information given below for clarification.

The bottom line of the diagram represents the "earth" or negative connection; the numbers below this line are track numbers, enabling circuits and components to be located using the key.

The lines at the top of the diagram represent "live feed" or positive connection points. The line marked "30" is live at all times. The line marked "15" is live only when the ignition is switched on.

Numbers on the diagram that are framed in square boxes at the end of a wire show the track reference number in which that wire is continued. At the point indicated will be another framed number referring back to the circuit just left.

Explanations of abbreviations used in wiring diagrams

AB	Air bag
ABS	Anti-lock braking system
AC	Air conditioning
ASP	Outside mirror
AT	Automatic transmission
AZV	Trailer hitch
CC	Check control
CD	CD changer
CRC	Cruise control
D	Diesel
DS	Anti-theft device
DT	Turbodiesel
DTH	Turbodiesel X 20 DTH
DWA	Anti-theft warning system
DZM	Tachometer
ECC	Electronic Climate Control
EKP	Fuel pump
EMP	Radio
FH	Electric windows
FIN	Finland
GB	Great Britain
HS	Heated rear window
HSF	Glove compartment
HKL	Power steering
HRL	Luggage compartment light
HZG	Heating
ID	Info-Display (TID/MID)
IMO	Immobiliser
INS	Instrument panel
IRL	Courtesy lights
IRLT	Interior light
J	Japan
KAT	Catalytic converter
KBS	Wiring harness
KW	Estate
LED	Light-emitting diode
LHD	Left-hand drive
MID	Multi Info-Display
MT	Manual transmission
N	Norway
NB	Notchback
NS	Front foglights
NSL	Rear foglights
OEL	Oil level/pressure check system
PBSL	Park/brake lockout (automatic transmission)
P/N	Park/Neutral (automatic transmission)
RFS	Reversing lights
RHD	Right-hand drive
S	Sweden
SA	Saudi Arabia
SD	Sunroof
SH	Heated seats
SM	Engine control unit
SRA	Headlight washers and wipers
TC	Traction Control
TD	Turbodiesel
TEL	Telephone
TFL	Daytime driving lights
TID	Triple Info Display
TKS	Door contact switch
WEG	Odometer frequency/roadspeed sensor
WD	Washer nozzle
WS	Warning buzzer
ZIG	Cigarette lighter
ZV	Central locking

Colour codes

BL	Blue	RT	Red
HBL	Light blue	WS	White
BR	Brown	SW	Black
GE	Yellow	LI	Lilac
GR	Grey	VI	Violet
GN	Green		

Wiring identification

Example: GE WS 1.5
GE - Wire basic colour
WS - Wire tracer colour
1.5 - Wire cross-section in mm^2

Note: *Not all items shown are fitted to all models.*

Index of circuits 100 to 1199 - early models

Location of applicable circuits	Track	Location of applicable circuits	Track
Air conditioning	700	High beam	443
Airbag	528	Immobiliser	952
Alternator	115	Info display (MID/TID)	840
Anti-lock Braking System	122	Instrument	865
Anti-theft device	904	Interior light	483
Anti-theft warning system	928	Light switch	415
Automatic transmission	214	Licence plate light	419
Battery	101	Low beam	428
Brake light	461	Luggage compartment light	481
Car level control	542	Memory - driver's seat and mirrors	659
CD changer	1070	Outside mirror	600
Central locking	900	Parking lights	410
Check control	820	Power steering	200
Cigarette lighter	555	Radiator fan (with AC)	731
Coolant pump (S, N, FIN)	120	Radiator fan (without AC)	1111
Cruise control	588	Radio with sound processor	1034
Daytime driving light	400	Radio	1001
Door contact switch	485	Rear screen wiper	511
20SE engine - MOTRONIC 1.5.4	155	Rear door fan	960
X20SE engine - MOTRONIC 1.5.4	155	Rear fog lights	449
X20XEV engine - SIMTEC 56.1	353	Recirculating air	1154
X25XE engine - MOTRONIC 2.8.1	249	Reversing lights	538
X30XE engine - MOTRONIC 2.8.1	249	Seat heating	568
25DT engine - Turbodiesel	300	Seat adjustment	1179
Fanfare	523	Sliding roof	800
Front/rear door light	493	Sound processor	1034
Front fog lights	439	Starter	105
Front door light	966	Sunscreen	810
Fuel pump	197	Tail light	412
Glove compartment light	561	Telephone	1082
Hazard warning lights	466	Traction control	122
Headlight washer	519	Trailer socket	411
Headlight range control	429	Turn signal light	466
Heated rear screen	619	Vanity mirror	815
Heated washer nozzles	506	Warning buzzer/light switch	422
Heater nozzle lights	563	Window winders	967
Heating	1100	Windscreen wiper	500

Key to wiring diagrams for early models

No	Description	No	Description	No	Description
E1	Side light - left	E37	Left hand vanity mirror	H8	Headlight main beam warning light
E2	Tail light - left	E39	Rear foglight - right	H9	Brake light - left
E3	Number plate light	E40	Right hand vanity mirror	H10	Brake light - right
E4	Side light - right	E41	Courtesy light	H11	Direction indicator light - front left
E5	Tail light - right	E47	Left rear seat heater	H12	Direction indicator light - rear left
E7	Headlight main beam - left	E48	Right rear seat heater	H13	Direction indicator light - front right
E8	Headlight main beam - right	E50	Kerb light - left front door	H14	Direction indicator light - rear right
E9	Headlight dipped beam - left	E51	Kerb light - right front door	H15	Fuel level warning light
E10	Headlight dipped beam - right	E52	Kerb light - left rear door	H16	Glow plug warning light (Diesel models)
E11	Instrument illumination lights	E53	Kerb light - right rear door	H17	Trailer direction indicator warning light
E13	Luggage compartment light	E54	Cigarette lighter light, rear	H18	Horn
E15	Glovebox light	E55	Heating nozzle operating handle light	H22	Rear foglight warning light
E16	Cigarette lighter illumination light	E57	Heating nozzle light, left	H23	Airbag warning light
E17	Reversing light - left	E58	Heating nozzle light, right	H25	Door mirror heating warning light
E18	Reversing light - right	E59	Heating nozzle light, rear	H26	ABS warning light
E19	Heated rear window	F1 on	Fuses	H30	Engine fault warning light
E20	Front foglight - left	G1	Battery	H33	Direction indicator side repeater light - left
E21	Front foglight - right	G2	Alternator		
E24	Rear foglight - left	H1	Radio/cassette player	H34	Direction indicator side repeater light - right
E25	Driver's seat heater	H2	Horn		
E27	Courtesy light - rear left	H3	Direction indicator warning light	H36	Brake light - middle
E28	Courtesy light - rear right	H4	Oil pressure warning light	H37	Loudspeaker - left front door
E30	Passenger front seat heater	H5	Brake fluid level warning light	H38	Loudspeaker - right front door
E33	Ashtray light	H7	Alternator charge warning light	H39	Loudspeaker - left rear door

No	Description
H40	Loudspeaker - right rear door
H42	Automatic transmission warning light
H47	Anti-theft alarm horn
H48	Horn
H51	Traction control warning light
H52	Tweeter - left front door
H53	Tweeter - right front door
H54	Telephone
H55	Handset
H56	Microphone
H57	Tweeter - left rear door
H58	Tweeter - right rear door
H61	Sub-woofer - left rear
H62	Sub-woofer - right rear
H63	Immobiliser warning light
K3	Relay - starter motor (anti-theft alarm)
K6	Relay - air conditioning
K7	Relay - air conditioning blower
K8	Relay - intermittent windscreen wipe
K10	Relay - direction indicator/hazard warning flashers
K12	Relay - secondary air intake
K13	Relay - park/neutral signal (AT)
K14	Relay - cruise control
K16	Relay - reconveying pump
K17	Relay - polarity protection
K19	Relay - car level control
K21	Sensor - car level control
K22	Relay - air conditioning coolant pump
K25	Relay - glow plugs (Diesel models)
K26	Relay - blower
K28	Relay - blower
K30	Relay - intermittent rear wiper delay
K31	Airbag control unit
K35	Relay - time delay, heated mirror and rear window
K37	Central locking control unit
K41	Power steering control unit
K42	Relay - polary protection
K43	Relay - injectors
K44	Relay - fuel pump
K48	Relay - blower
K49	Relay - blower
K51	Relay - cooling fan
K52	Relay - blower
K59	Relay - daytime running lights
K60	Relay - air conditioning compressor
K61	Engine control unit (Motronic)
K63	Relay - horn
K64	Relay - air conditioning blower
K65	Relay - left rear seat heater
K66	Relay - right rear seat heater
K67	Relay - cooling fan
K69	Simtec 56 control unit
K70	Turbodiesel control unit
K73	Relay - headlight main beam relay
K80	Relay - fuel filter heater (Diesel models)
K85	Automatic transmission control unit
K87	Relay - auxiliary cooling fan
K88	Catalytic converter temp. control unit
K94	Anti-theft alarm control unit
K96	Relay - cooling fan
K97	Relay - headlight washer pump time delay
K101	Relay - electric mirror parking position
K102	Parking brake control unit (automatic transmission)

No	Description
K117	Immobiliser control unit
L2	Ignition coil
M1	Starter motor
M2	Windscreen wiper motor
M3	Heater blower motor
M4	Radiator cooling fan motor
M8	Rear window wiper motor
M10	Air conditioning blower motor
M11	Cooling fan motor
M18	Central locking motor - driver's door
M19	Central locking motor - left rear door
M20	Central locking motor - right rear door
M21	Fuel pump
M22	Compressor, car level control
M24	Headlight washer pump
M27	Secondary air intake pump
M28	Blower motor
M29	Interior mirror motor
M30	Door mirror assembly - driver's door
M30.1	Mirror adjustment motor
M30.2	Mirror heating
M30.4	Mirror memory potentiometer
M31	Door mirror assembly - passenger door
M31.1	Mirror adjustment motor
M31.2	Mirror heating
M31.4	Mirror memory potentiometer
M32	Central locking motor - passenger door
M33	Idle speed adjuster/idle air control stepper motor
M34	Sunvisor motor
M35	Cooling fan motor
M37	Central locking motor - boot lid/tailgate
M39	Headlight aim adjuster motor - left side
M40	Headlight aim adjuster motor - right side
M41	Central locking motor - fuel filler
M47	Electric window motor - front left
M48	Electric window motor - front right
M49	Electric window motor - rear left
M50	Electric window motor - rear right
M54	Coolant pump timing control
M55	Windscreen and rear window washer pump
M57	Coolant pump
M61	Sunroof assembly
M67	Blower motor - left rear door
M68	Blower motor - right rear door
M72	Seat adjustment assembly, driver
M72.1	Front seat height motor
M72.2	Rear seat height motor
M72.3	Forwards/backwards seat adjustment motor
M72.4	Seat backrest motor
M73	Seat adjustment assembly, driver
M73.1	Front seat height motor
M73.2	Rear seat height motor
M73.3	Forwards/backwards seat adjustment motor
M73.4	Seat backrest motor
M74	Seat adjustment assembly, passenger
M74.1	Front seat height motor
M74.2	Rear seat height motor
M74.3	Forwards/backwards seat adjustment motor

No	Description
M74.4	Seat backrest motor
P1	Fuel gauge
P2	Coolant temperature gauge
P4	Fuel level sender unit
P5	Coolant temperature gauge sender
P7	Tachometer
P13	Trip computer outside air temperature sensor
P17	ABS wheel sensor - front left
P18	ABS wheel sensor - front right
P19	ABS wheel sensor - rear left
P20	ABS wheel sensor - rear right
P25	Bulb failure sensor
P27	Brake pad wear sensor - front left
P28	Brake pad wear sensor - front right
P29	Air intake temperature sensor
P30	Coolant temperature sensor
P32	Oxygen sensor - heated
P34	Throttle position sensor/potentiometer
P35	Crankshaft speed/position sensor
P36	Oxygen sensor - heated
P37	Telephone aerial
P39	Trailer bulb failure sensor
P43	Electronic speedometer
P44	Air mass meter
P46	Knock sensor
P47	Camshaft sensor
P48	Automatic transmission output speed sensor
P50	Catalytic converter temperature sensor
P51	Crankshaft sensor
P53	Anti-theft alarm sensor - left side
P54	Anti-theft alarm sensor - right side
P56	Knock sensor
P58	Left rear window breakage sensor (Estate)
P59	Right rear window breakage sensor (Estate)
P63	Receiver, remote control
P64	Catalytic converter temperature sensor
P65	Load/pressure sensor
P66	Needle movement sensor
P67	Pedal position sensor
P68	Injection pump actuator
R3	Cigarette lighter
R5	Glow plugs (Diesel models)
R13	Heated windscreen washer nozzle - left
R14	Heated windscreen washer nozzle - right
R17	Cigarette lighter, rear
R19	Cooling fan motor resistor
S1	Ignition switch
S2	Lighting switch asssembly
S2.1	Lighting switch
S2.2	Courtesy light switch
S2.3	Instrument illumination light dimmer
S2.4	Warning buzzer
S2.5	Headlamp levelling
S2.6	Front fog lights switch
S2.7	Rear fog lights switch
S3	Heater blower switch
S4	Heated rear window and mirror switch
S5	Direction indicator switch assembly

Key to wiring diagrams for early models (continued)

No	Description
S5.2	Dipped beam switch
S5.3	Direction indicator switch
S5.4	Sidelight switch
S7	Reversing light switch
S8	Brake light switch
S9	Windscreen wiper switch assembly
S9.2	Windscreen wiper interval switch
S9.5	Rear window washer/wiper switch
S11	Brake fluid level warning sensor
S13	Handbrake-on warning switch
S15	Luggage compartment light switch
S17	Passenger door courtesy light switch
S18	Glove box light switch
S20	Pressure switch assembly
S20.1	Low pressure compressor switch
S20.2	High pressure compressor switch
S20.3	High pressure compressor switch
S24	Air conditioning blower motor switch
S29	Cooling fan switch
S30	Driver's seat heater switch
S31	Rear door courtesy light switch - left
S32	Rear door courtesy light switch - right
S33	Traction control switch
S37	Driver's door electric window switch assembly
S37.1	Electric window switch - front left
S37.2	Electric window switch - front right
S37.3	Electric window switch - rear left
S37.4	Electric window switch - rear right
S37.5	Electric window safety cut-out switch
S37.7	Electric window automatic control
S39	Electric window switch - rear left door
S40	Drivers seat adjustment assembly (with memory)
S41	Central locking switch - driver's door
S42	Central locking switch - passenger door
S43	Cruise control switch
S45	Cruise control clutch switch
S47	Driver's door courtesy light switch
S49	Sunvisor switch
S52	Hazard warning light switch
S55	Passenger seat heater switch
S56	Rear door blower switch
S58	Temperature switch - relay box
S59	Fog light switch, trailer socket
S63	Switch assembly - MID
S63.1	Trip computer function reset switch
S63.2	Trip computer clock hours adjustment switch
S64	Horn switch
S68	Door mirror switch assembly
S68.1	Door mirror adjustment switch
S68.3	Door mirror left/right selector switch
S68.4	Door mirror parking position switch
S82	Washer pump switch
S86	Passenger compartment switch (DWA)
S88	Cooling fan switch
S92	Boot lock switch (DWA)
S93	Coolant level sensor
S95	Oil level sensor
S96	Left rear seat heater switch
S97	Right rear seat heater switch
S101	Air conditioning compressor switch
S102	Air conditioning circulation switch
S104	Automatic transmission kickdown switch
S105	Automatic transmission "Winter" mode button
S106	Automatic transmission "Economy/Sport" mode button
S109	Revolution acceleration switch (Motronic)
S118	Automatic transmission switch
S119	Air conditioning refrigerant temperature switch
S120	Anti-theft alarm bonnet switch
S128	Air conditioning refrigerant temperature cooling switch
U4	ABS hydraulic modulator assembly
U4.1	ABS hydraulic pump relay
U4.2	ABS solenoid valves relay
U4.3	ABS hydraulic pump
U4.5	ABS solenoid valve - front left
U4.6	ABS solenoid valve - front right
U4.7	ABS solenoid valve - rear left
U4.8	ABS/TC control unit
U4.9	Solenoid valve plug
U6	LCD instruments
U10	Automatic transmission
U10.1	Solenoid - converter lock-up control
U10.2	Solenoid - main fluid pressure control
U12	Filter heating assembly (Diesel models)
U12.1	Temperature switch (Diesel models)
U12.2	Heating resistor (Diesel models)
U13	Automatic transmission
U13.1	Solenoid - 2/3 shift up
U13.2	Solenoid - 1/2 and 3/4 shift up
U13.3	Solenoid - converter lock-up control
U13.4	Solenoid - oil temperature sensor
U15	Display - TID
U16	Display - MID
U18	Aerial amplifier - heated rear window
U20	Airbag contact unit assembly
U21	Airbag unit assembly, driver
U21.1	Airbag unit squib
U22	Airbag unit assembly, passenger
U22.1	Airbag unit squib
U23	Sound processor
U24	CD-changer
V8	Air conditioning compressor diode
Y1	Air conditioning compressor clutch
Y5	Fuel solenoid valve (Diesel models)
Y7	Fuel injectors
Y9	Solenoid - car level control
Y14	Air conditioning coolant valve
Y15	Solenoid - secondary air intake
Y18	Solenoid - exhaust gas recirculation
Y19	Solenoid - inlet manifold
Y20	Solenoid - injection regulation
Y25	Power steering solenoid valve
Y34	Fuel tank vent valve
Y35	Air conditioning circulation solenoid valve
Y46	Solenoid - inlet manifold
Y47	Parking brake lock lifting magnet (automatic transmission)
X13	Diagnostic equipment connector
X15	Octane coding plug
X54	Ignition coding plug
X1-on	Wiring connectors

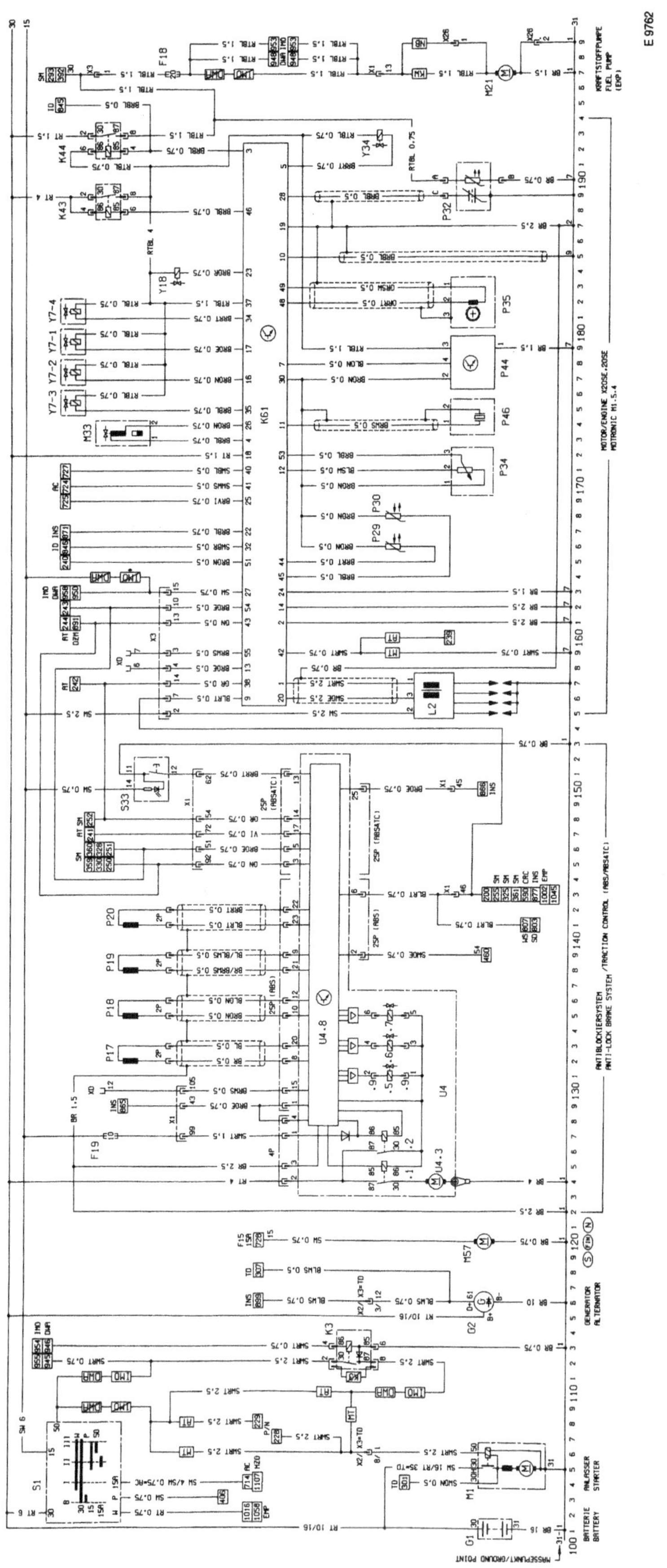

Current track 100 to 199 - Early models

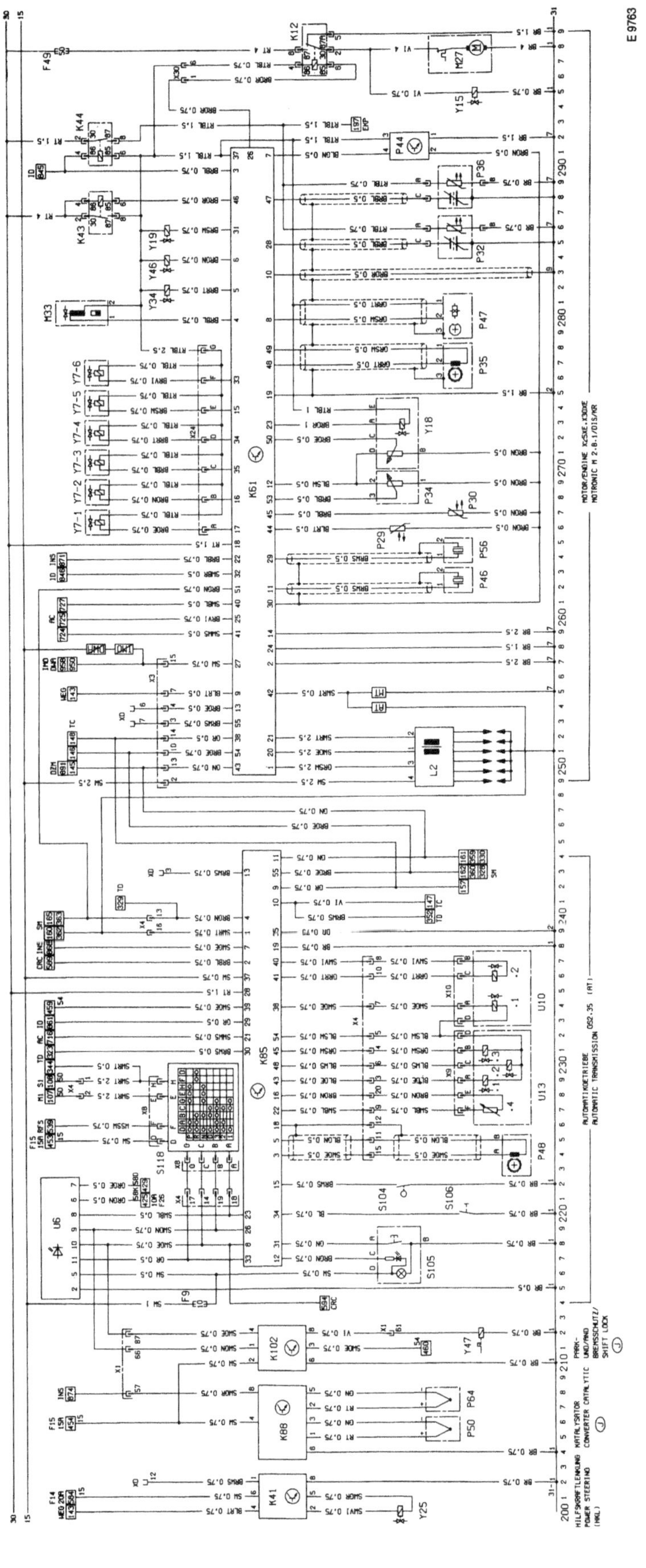

Current track 200 to 299 - Early models

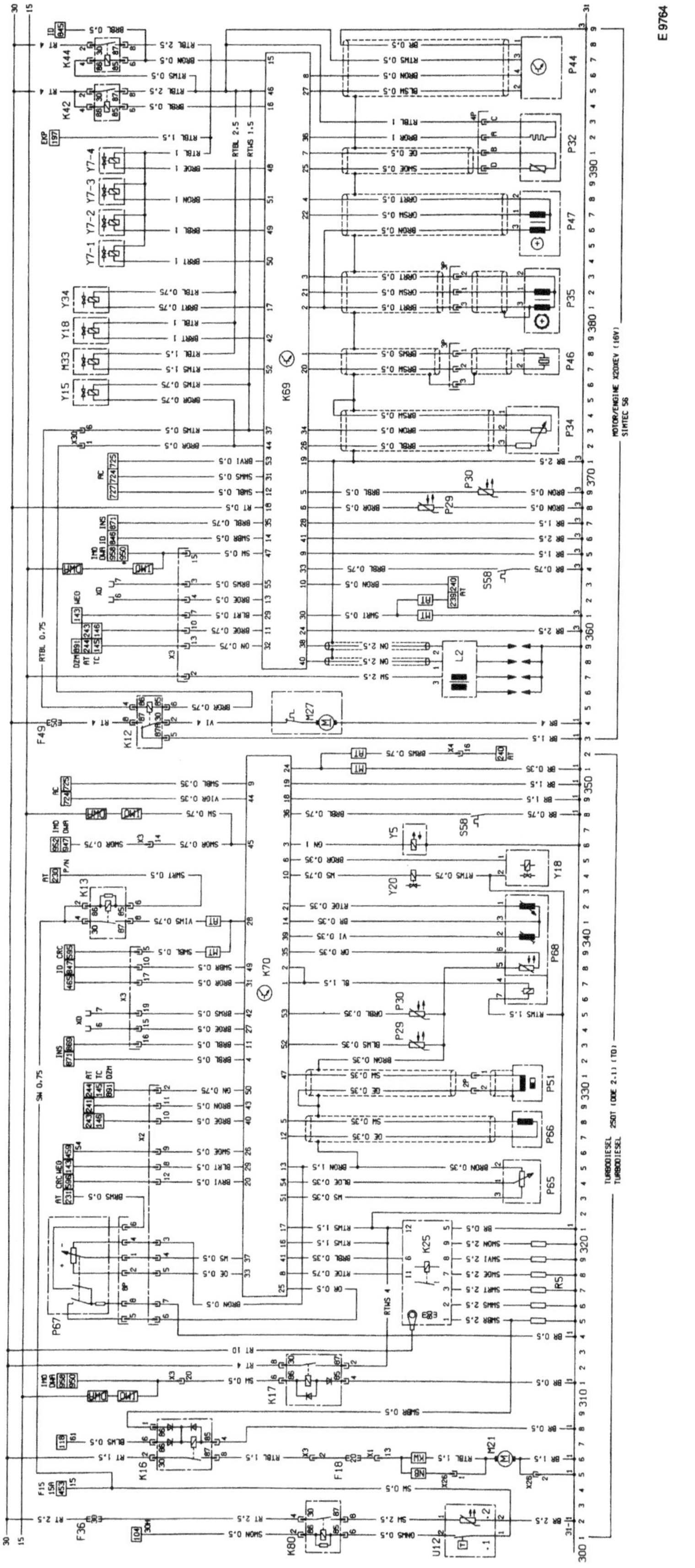

E 9764

Current track 300 to 399 - Early models

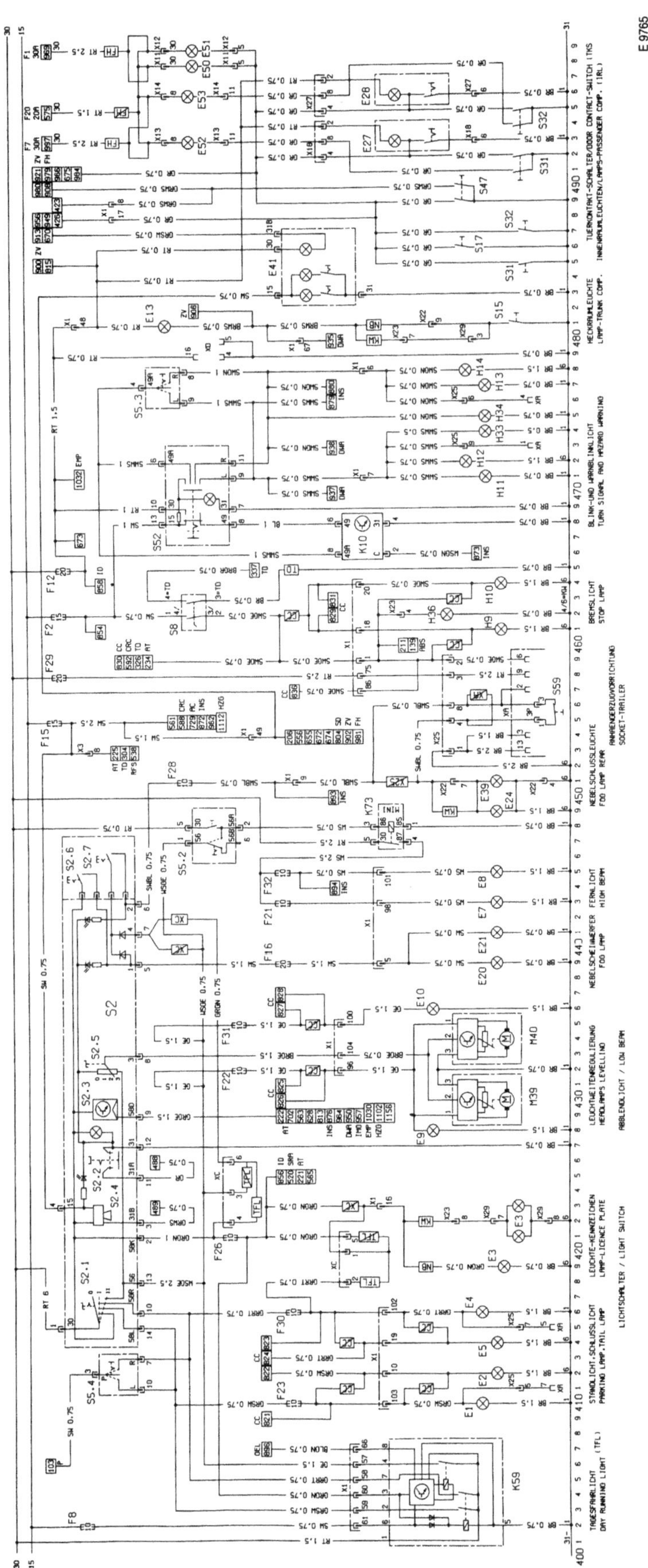

Current track 400 to 499 - Early models

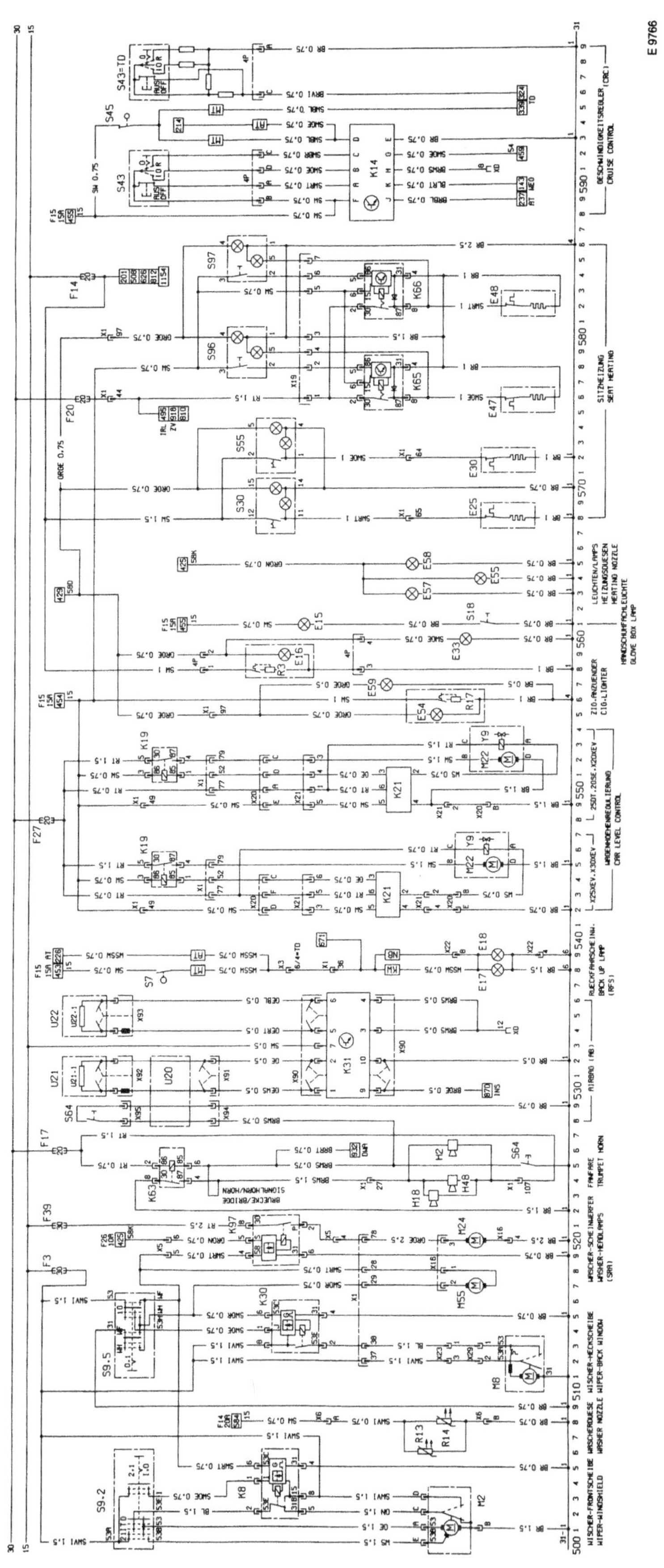

Current track 500 to 599 - Early models

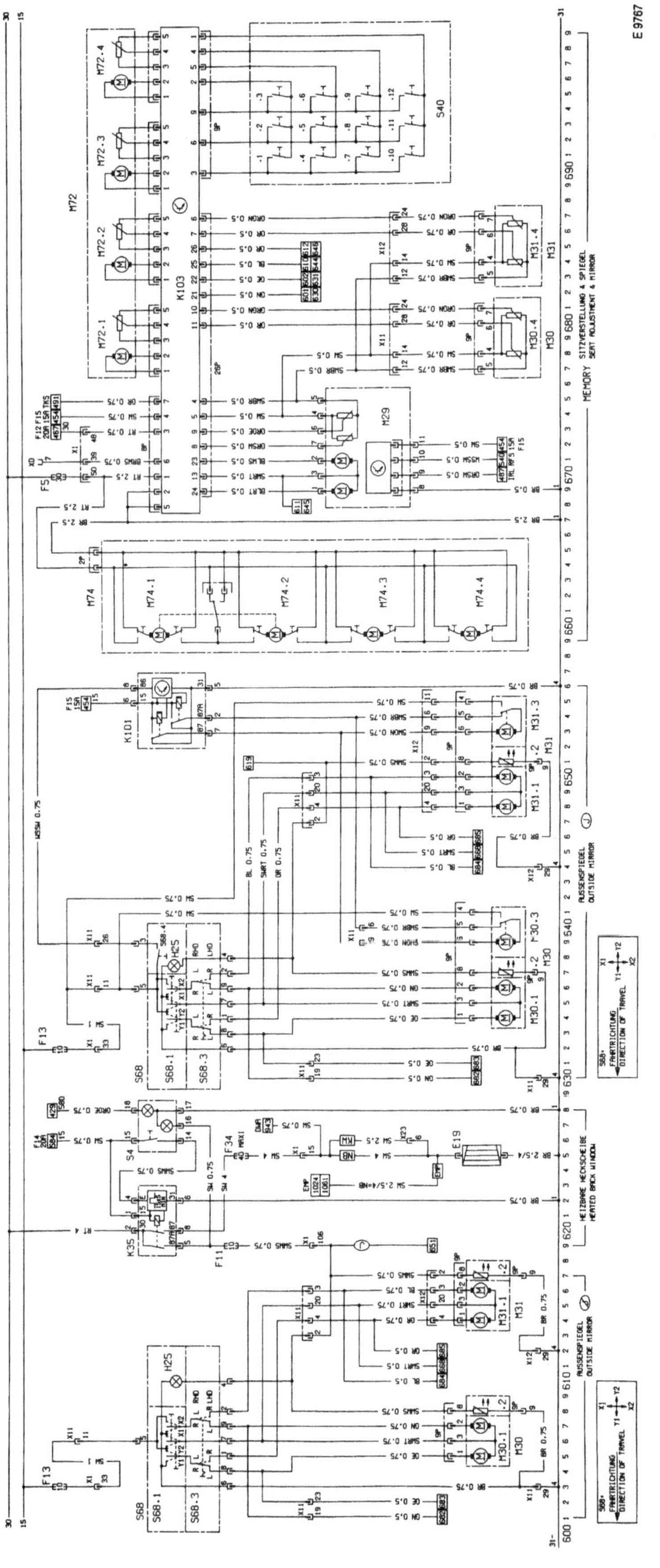

Current track 600 to 699 - Early models

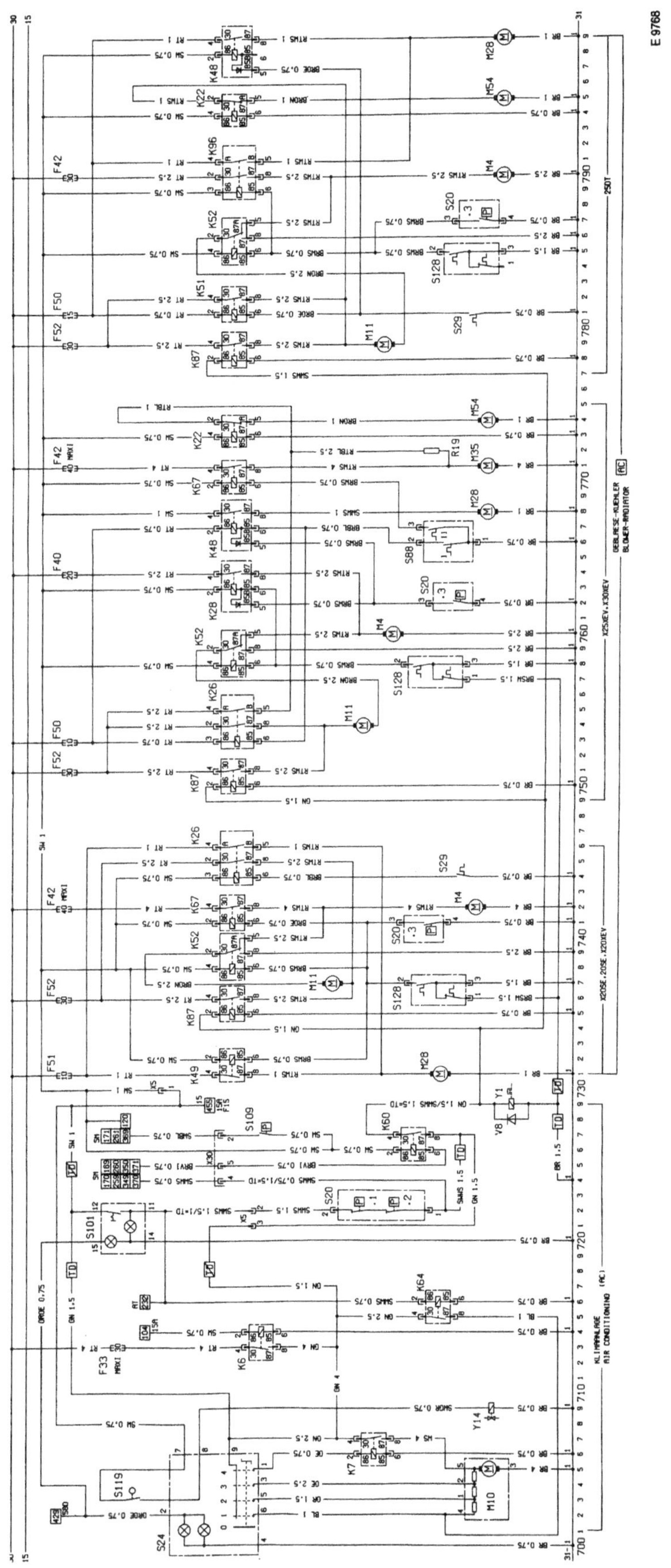

Current track 700 to 799 - Early models

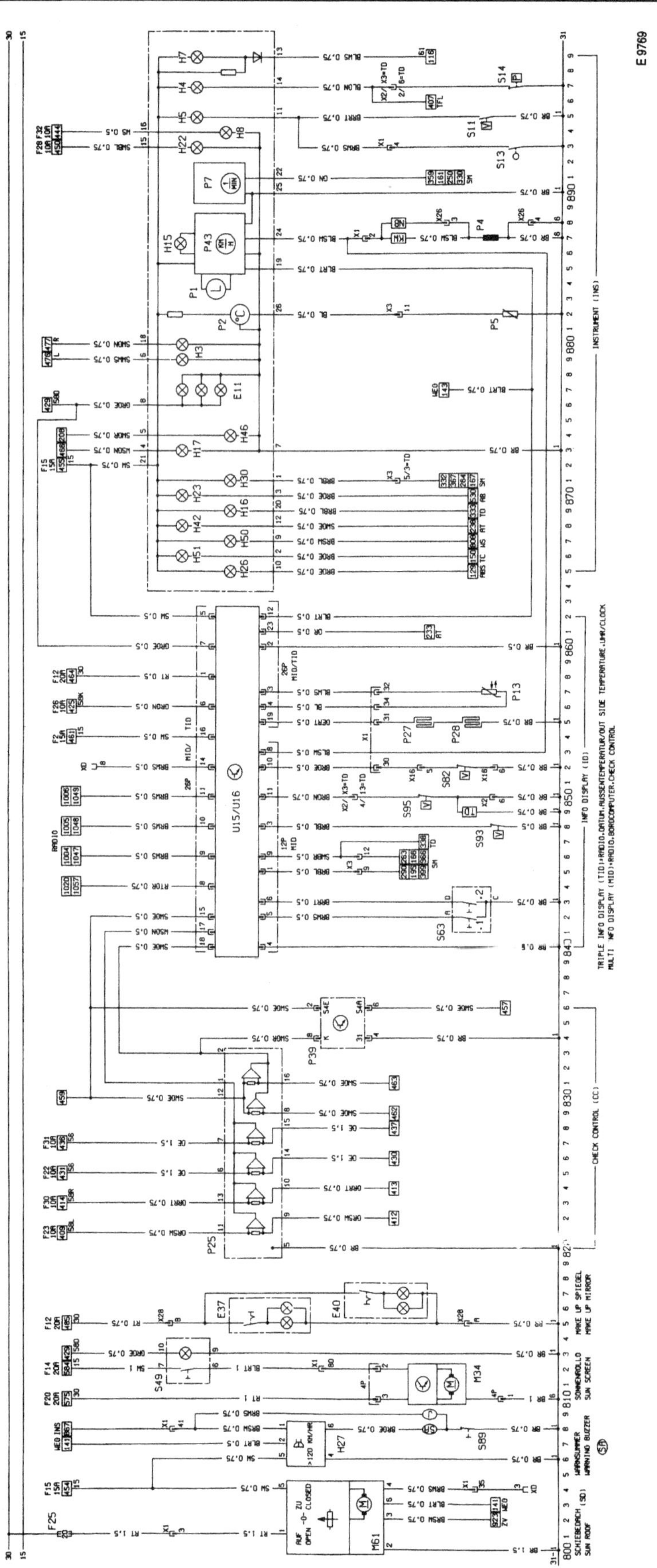

Current track 800 to 899 - Early models

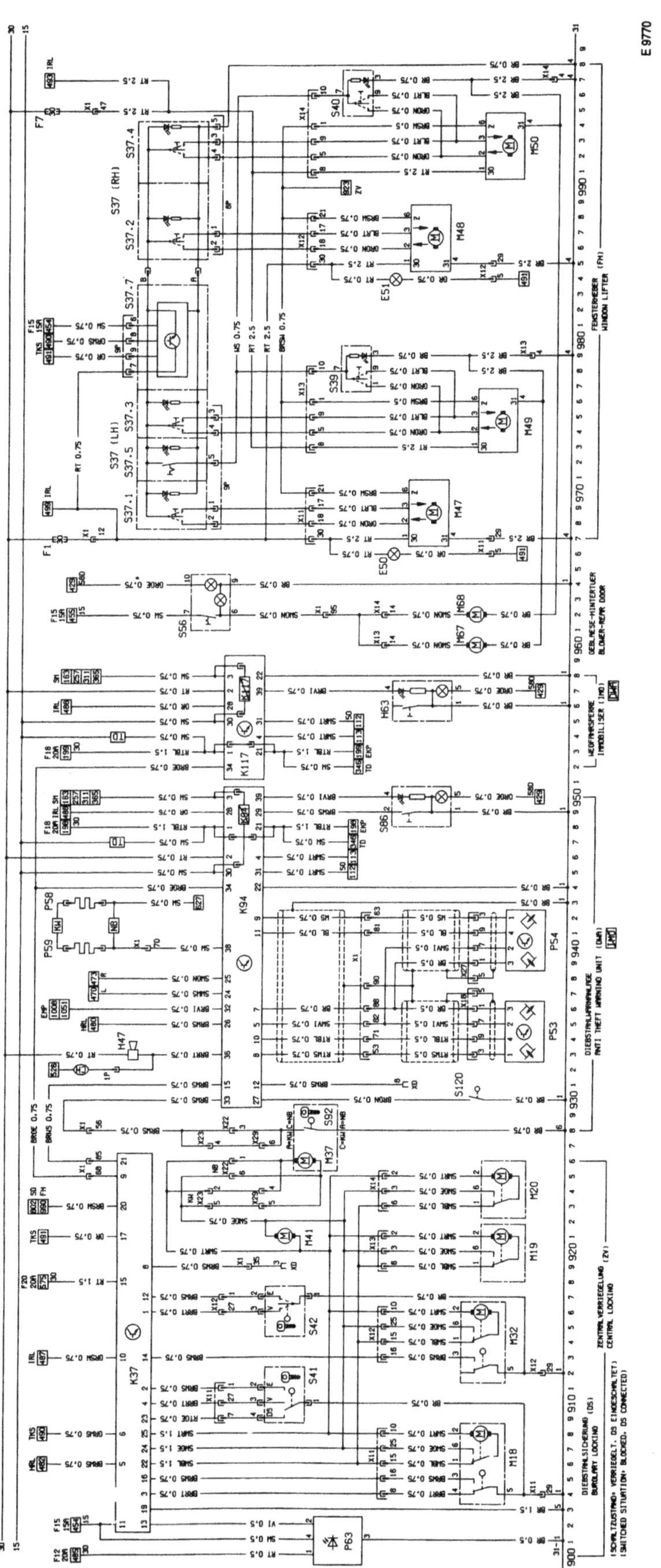

Current track 900 to 999 - Early models

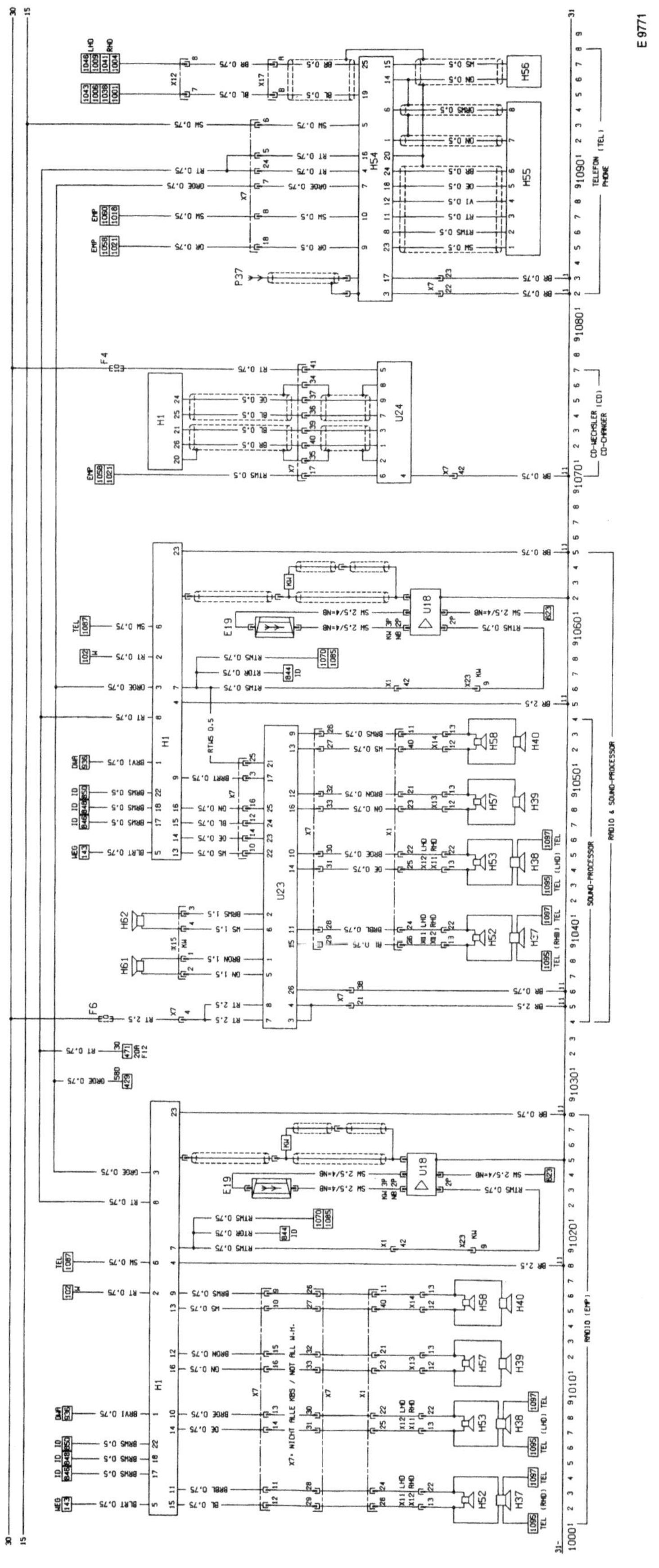

E 9771

Current track 1000 to 1099 - Early models

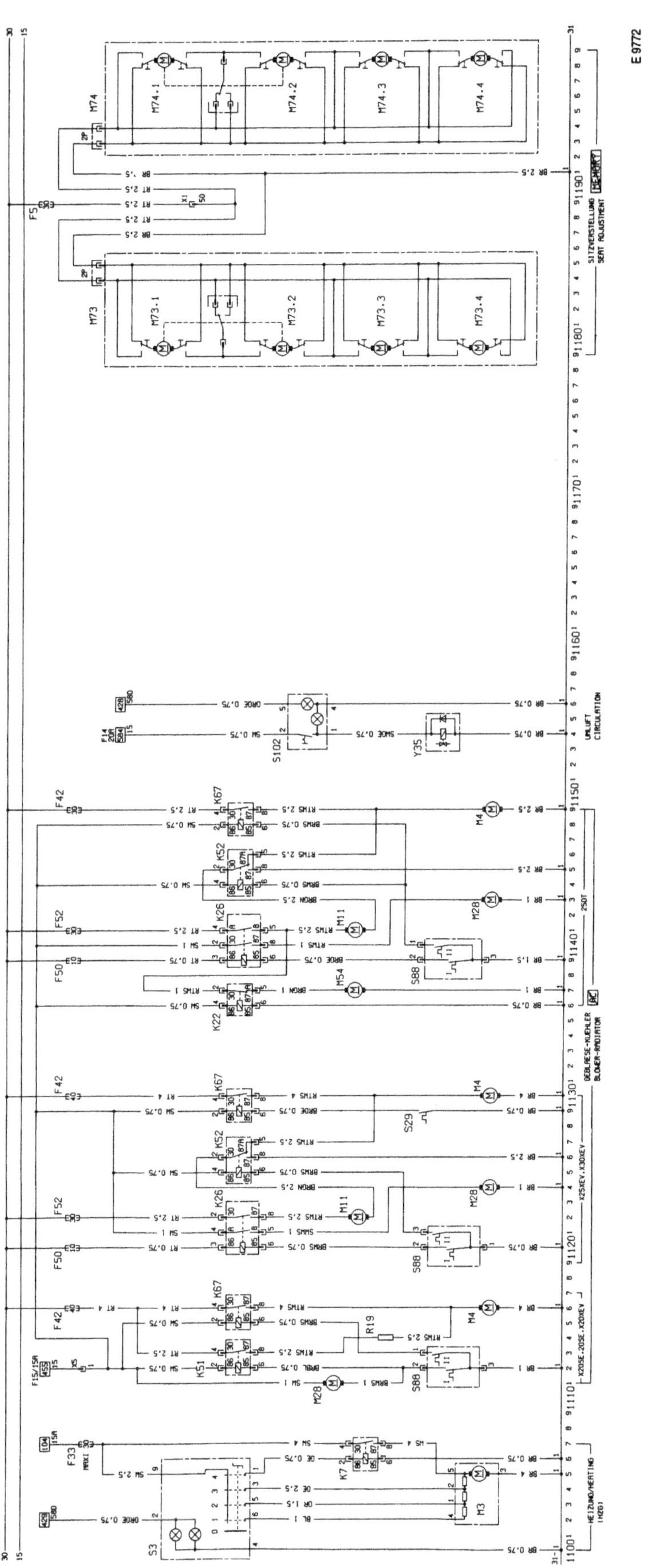

Current track 1100 to 1199 - Early models

Index of circuits 100 to 1699 - later models

Location of applicable circuits	Track
Air conditioning AC/ECC X 20 DTH	1264
Air conditioning, not X 20 DTH	700
Airbag	1313
Airbag, side airbag	1313
Alternator	112
Anti-lock Braking System	1406
Anti-theft device	900
Anti-theft warning system	900
Automatic transmission	208
Auxiliary heater	1651
Battery	101
Belt tensioner	1313
Brake light	411
Car level control	537
CD changer	1070
Central locking	900
Check control	820
Cigarette lighter	555
Coolant heating, auxiliary	1651
Coolant pump (S, N, FIN) without A/C	1109
Coolant pump (S, N, FIN) with A/C	748
Cruise control	524
Daytime driving light	1506
Door contact switch	460
Electronic climate control (ECC)	1200
Engine - 20 SE MOTRONIC	1455
Engine - X 20 DTH	1601
Engine - X 20 SE MOTRONIC	1455
Engine - X 20 XEV SIMTEC	353
Engine - X 25 DT Turbodiesel	301
Engine - X 25 XE MOTRONIC	243
Engine - X 30 XE MOTRONIC	243
Fanfare	1300
Front door light	467
Front fog light	1552
Fuel pump	1497
Fuses	102
Glove compartment light	563
Hazard warning lights	424
Headlight range control (xenon lights)	1578
Headlight range control	1535
Headlight washer	519
Heated rear screen	619
Heated washer nozzles	506
Heater nozzle lights	563
Heating	1100
Heating, coolant, auxiliary	1651
High beam	1556
Immobiliser	1159
Info display (MID/TID)	840
Instrument	865
Interior light	471
Light switch	1520
Licence plate light	1525
Low beam	1533
Low beam (LWR)	1533
Low beam (xenon)	1545
Luggage compartment light	447
Memory - driver's seat and mirrors	659
Outside mirror	601
Park/brake lockout	201
Parking light	1510
Power sounder	956
Power steering	1443
Pre-fuses	114
Radiator fan (AC/ECC)	731
Radiator fan (without AC)	1111
Radiator fan X 20 DTH	1673
Radiator fan X 20 DTH (AC)	1350
Radio	1001
Radio remote control	1338
Radio with sound processor	1034
Rear door fan	960
Rear door light	472
Rear fog light	1568
Rear screen wiper	511
Recirculating air	1154
Reversing lights	485
Seat adjustment & mirror with memory	659
Seat adjustment without memory	1179
Seat heating	568
Side airbag	1313
Sound processor	1034
Starter	105
Sun roller	810
Sun roof	800
Tail light	1513
Telephone	1082
Traction control	1406
Trailer socket	401/1573
Turn signal	424
Vanity mirror	815
Warning buzzer/light switch	1525
Warning buzzer, ignition key	587
Window winders	967
Windscreen wiper	500
Xenon lights	1544

Key to wiring diagrams for later models

No	Description
E1	Side light - left
E2	Tail light - left
E3	Number plate light
E4	Side light - right
E5	Tail light - right
E7	Headlight main beam - left
E8	Headlight main beam - right
E9	Headlight dipped beam - left
E10	Headlight dipped beam - right
E11	Instrument illumination lights
E13	Luggage compartment light
E15	Glovebox light
E16	Cigarette lighter illumination light
E17	Reversing light - left
E18	Reversing light - right
E19	Heated rear window
E20	Front foglight - left
E21	Front foglight - right
E24	Rear foglight - left
E25	Driver's seat heater
E27	Courtesy light - rear left
E28	Courtesy light - rear right
E30	Passenger front seat heater
E33	Ashtray light
E37	Left hand vanity mirror
E39	Rear foglight - right
E40	Right hand vanity mirror
E41	Courtesy light
E42.1	Add-on heater control unit
E42.2	Add-on heater blower motor
E42.3	Add-on heater glow plug
E42.4	Add-on heater flame and coolant sensor
E42.5	Add-on heater coolant sensor
E42.6	Add-on heater overheat sensor
E47	Left rear seat heater
E48	Right rear seat heater
E50	Kerb light - left front door
E51	Kerb light - right front door

No	Description
E52	Kerb light - left rear door
E53	Kerb light - right rear door
E54	Cigarette lighter light, rear
E55	Heating nozzle operating handle light
E57	Heating nozzle light, left
E58	Heating nozzle light, right
E59	Heating nozzle light, rear
F1 on	Fuses
G1	Battery
G2	Alternator
H1	Radio/cassette player
H2	Horn
H3	Direction indicator warning light
H4	Oil pressure warning light
H5	Brake fluid level warning light
H7	Alternator charge warning light
H8	Headlight main beam warning light
H9	Brake light - left
H10	Brake light - right
H11	Direction indicator light - front left
H12	Direction indicator light - rear left
H13	Direction indicator light - front right
H14	Direction indicator light - rear right
H15	Fuel level warning light
H16	Glow plug warning light (Diesel models)
H17	Trailer direction indicator warning light
H18	Horn
H22	Rear foglight warning light
H23	Airbag warning light
H24	Anti-theft warning horn
H26	ABS warning light
H30	Engine fault warning light
H33	Direction indicator side repeater light - left
H34	Direction indicator side repeater light - right
H36	Brake light - middle
H37	Loudspeaker - left front door
H38	Loudspeaker - right front door
H39	Loudspeaker - left rear door
H40	Loudspeaker - right rear door
H42	Automatic transmission warning light
H46	Catalytic converter temperature warning light
H47	Anti-theft alarm horn
H48	Horn
H50	Passive seatbelt system warning light
H51	Traction control warning light
H52	Tweeter - left front door
H53	Tweeter - right front door
H54	Telephone
H56	Microphone
H57	Tweeter - left rear door
H58	Tweeter - right rear door
H61	Sub-woofer - left rear
H62	Sub-woofer - right rear
H65	Fog light warning light
H72	Coolant temperature warning light
K7	Relay - air conditioning blower
K8	Relay - intermittent windscreen wipe
K10	Relay - direction indicator/hazard warning flashers
K12	Relay - secondary air intake
K13	Relay - park/neutral signal (AT)
K14	Relay - cruise control
K16	Relay - reconveying pump
K17	Relay - polarity protection
K19	Relay - car level control
K21	Sensor - car level control
K22	Relay - air conditioning coolant pump
K25	Relay - glow plugs (Diesel models)
K26	Relay - blower
K28	Relay - blower
K30	Relay - intermittent rear window wipe
K31	Airbag control unit
K34	Relay - radiator blower with time delay
K35	Relay - time delay, heated mirror and rear window
K37	Central locking control unit
K41	Power steering control unit
K43	Relay - injectors
K44	Relay - fuel pump
K46	Relay - indicators
K48	Relay - blower
K49	Relay - blower
K50	ABS control unit
K51	Relay - cooling fan
K52	Relay - blower
K53	Relay - blower
K59	Relay - daytime running lights
K60	Relay - air conditioning compressor
K61	Engine control unit (Motronic)
K63	Relay - horn
K64	Relay - air conditioning blower
K65	Relay - left rear seat heater
K66	Relay - right rear seat heater
K67	Relay - cooling fan
K69	Simtec control unit
K70	Turbodiesel control unit
K73	Relay - headlight main beam relay
K74	Relay - blower radiator
K76	Relay - glow plug timer
K80	Relay - fuel filter heater (Diesel models)
K85	Automatic transmission control unit
K87	Relay - auxiliary cooling fan
K88	Catalytic convertor temperature conrol unit
K94	Anti-theft alarm and central locking control unit
K95	ABS and traction control control unit
K96	Relay - cooling fan
K97	Relay - headlight washer pump time delay
K101	Relay - electric mirror parking position
K103	Seat and mirror memory control unit
K114	Main engine relay
K118	Immobiliser control unit
K127	Relay - charge cooler
K128	Injection pump control unit
K137	Low beam levelling control unit
K138	Left hand xenon light pre-switching
K139	Right hand xenon light pre-switching
K145	Relay - air recirculation
K146	Relay - delayed blower start
L2	Ignition coil
M1	Starter motor
M2	Windscreen wiper motor
M3	Heater blower motor
M4	Radiator cooling fan motor
M8	Rear window wiper motor
M10	Air conditioning blower motor
M11	Cooling fan motor
M12	Cooling fan motor
M18	Central locking motor - driver's door
M19	Central locking motor - left rear door
M20	Central locking motor - right rear door
M21	Fuel pump
M22	Compressor, car level control
M24	Headlight washer pump
M27	Secondary air intake pump
M28	Blower motor
M29	Interior mirror motor
M30	Door mirror assembly - driver's door
M30.1	Mirror adjustment motor
M30.2	Mirror heating
M30.4	Mirror memory potentiometer
M31	Door mirror assembly - passenger door
M31.1	Mirror adjustment motor
M31.2	Mirror heating
M31.4	Mirror memory potentiometer
M32	Central locking motor - passenger door
M34	Sunvisor motor
M37	Central locking motor - boot lid/tailgate
M39	Headlight aim adjuster motor - left side
M40	Headlight aim adjuster motor - right side
M41	Central locking motor - fuel filler
M47	Electric window motor - front left
M48	Electric window motor - front right
M49	Electric window motor - rear left
M50	Electric window motor - rear right
M54	Coolant pump timing control
M55	Windscreen and rear window washer pump
M57	Coolant pump
M61	Sunroof assembly
M66	Idle speed actuator
M67	Blower motor - left rear door
M68	Blower motor - right rear door
M69	Fuel metering pump
M72	Seat adjustment assembly, driver
M72.1	Front seat height motor
M72.2	Rear seat height motor
M72.3	Forwards/backwards seat adjustment motor
M72.4	Seat backrest motor
M73	Seat adjustment assembly, driver
M73.1	Front seat height motor
M73.2	Rear seat height motor
M73.3	Forwards/backwards seat adjustment motor
M73.4	Seat backrest motor
M74	Defrost stepmotor (ECC)
M75	Leg room stepmotor (ECC)
M76	Ventilation stepmotor (ECC)
M77	Left mixed air stepmotor (ECC)
M78	Right mixed air stepmotor (ECC)
M80	Charge cooler motor
P1	Fuel gauge
P2	Coolant temperature gauge
P4	Fuel level sender unit
P5	Coolant temperature gauge sender
P7	Tachometer
P13	Trip computer outside air temperature sensor
P16	Wiper interval potentiometer
P17	Wheel sensor - front left
P18	Wheel sensor - front right
P19	Wheel sensor - rear left
P20	Wheel sensor - rear right
P24	Engine oil temperature sensor
P25	Bulb failure sensor

No	Description
P27	Brake pad wear sensor - front left
P28	Brake pad wear sensor - front right
P29	Air intake temperature sensor
P30	Coolant temperature sensor
P32	Oxygen sensor - heated
P34	Throttle position sensor/potentiometer
P35	Crankshaft speed/position sensor
P36	Oxygen sensor - heated
P39	Trailer bulb failure sensor
P41	Outdoor temperature sensor, left
P42	Outdoor temperature sensor, right
P43	Electronic speedometer
P44	Air mass meter
P46	Knock sensor
P47	Camshaft sensor
P48	Automatic transmission output speed sensor
P50	Catalytic converter temp. sensor
P51	Sun sensor
P53	Anti-theft alarm sensor - left side
P54	Anti-theft alarm sensor - right side
P56	Knock sensor
P57	Aerial
P58	Left rear window breakage sensor
P59	Right rear window breakage sensor
P63	Receiver, remote control
P64	Catalytic converter temperature sensor
P65	Load/pressure sensor
P66	Needle movement sensor
P67	Pedal position sensor
P68	Injection pump actuator
P71	Driver's side airbag sensor
P72	Passenger side airbag sensor
P73	Front car level sensor
P74	Rear car level sensor
R3	Cigarette lighter
R5	Glow plugs (Diesel models)
R13	Heated windscreen washer nozzle - left
R14	Heated windscreen washer nozzle - right
R17	Cigarette lighter, rear
R19	Cooling fan motor resistor
S1	Ignition switch
S2	Lighting switch asssembly
S2.1	Lighting switch
S2.2	Courtesy light switch
S2.3	Instrument illumination light dimmer
S2.4	Warning buzzer
S2.5	Headlamp levelling
S2.6	Front fog lights switch
S2.7	Rear fog lights switch
S3	Heater blower switch
S4	Heated rear window and mirror switch
S5	Direction indicator switch assembly
S5.2	Dipped beam switch
S5.3	Direction indicator switch
S5.4	Sidelight switch
S7	Reversing light switch
S8	Brake light switch
S9	Windscreen wiper switch assembly
S9.2	Windscreen wiper interval switch
S9.5	Rear window washer/wiper switch
S11	Brake fluid level warning sensor
S13	Handbrake-on warning switch
S14	Oil pressure switch

No	Description
S15	Luggage compartment light switch
S17	Passenger door courtesy light switch
S18	Glove box light switch
S20	Pressure switch assembly
S20.1	Low pressure compressor switch
S20.2	High pressure compressor switch
S20.3	High pressure compressor switch
S24	Air conditioning blower motor switch
S29	Cooling fan switch
S30	Driver's seat heater switch
S31	Rear door courtesy light switch - left
S32	Rear door courtesy light switch - right
S33	Traction control switch
S37	Driver's door electric window switch assembly
S37.1	Electric window switch - front left
S37.2	Electric window switch - front right
S37.3	Electric window switch - rear left
S37.4	Electric window switch - rear right
S37.5	Electric window safety cut-out switch
S37.7	Electric window automatic control
S39	Electric window switch - rear left door
S40	Drivers seat adjustment assembly (with memory)
S41	Central locking switch - driver's door
S43	Cruise control switch
S45	Cruise control clutch switch
S47	Driver's door courtesy light switch
S49	Sunvisor switch
S52	Hazard warning light switch
S55	Passenger seat heater switch
S56	Rear door blower switch
S58	Temperature switch - relay box
S59	Fog light switch, trailer socket
S63	Switch assembly - MID
S63.1	Trip computer function reset switch
S63.2	Trip computer clock hours adjustment switch
S64	Horn switch
S65	Coolant pressure switch
S66	Coolant temperature switch
S67	Radio remote control switch
S68	Door mirror switch assembly
S68.1	Door mirror adjustment switch
S68.3	Door mirror left/right selector switch
S68.4	Door mirror parking position switch
S69	Air intake temperature switch
S80	Electric window switch - rear right door
S82	Washer pump switch
S84	Park/brake lockout selector switch
S85	Ignition key unlock switch
S86	Passenger compartment switch (DWA)
S88	Cooling fan switch
S92	Boot lock switch (DWA)
S93	Coolant level sensor
S95	Oil level sensor
S96	Left rear seat heater switch
S97	Right rear seat heater switch
S101	Air conditioning compressor switch
S102	Air conditioning circulation switch
S104	Automatic transmission kickdown switch
S105	Automatic transmission "Winter" mode button
S106	Automatic transmission "Economy/Sport" mode button
S109	Revolution acceleration switch (Motronic)

No	Description
S116	Stop light switch
S118	Automatic transmission switch
S119	Left temperature lever limit switch
S120	Anti-theft alarm bonnet switch
S121	Right temperature lever limit switch
S128	Air conditioning refrigerant temperature cooling switch
U6	Automatic transmission display
U10	Automatic transmission
U10.1	Solenoid - converter lock-up control
U10.2	Solenoid - main fluid pressure control
U12	Filter heating assembly (Diesel models)
U12.1	Temperature switch (Diesel models)
U12.2	Heating resistor (Diesel models)
U13	Automatic transmission
U13.1	Solenoid - 2/3 shift up
U13.2	Solenoid - 1/2 and 3/4 shift up
U13.3	Solenoid - converter lock-up control
U13.4	Solenoid - oil temperature sensor
U15	Display - TID
U16	Display - MID
U17	Aerial amplifier - roof
U18	Aerial amplifier - heated rear window
U20	Airbag contact unit assembly
U21	Airbag unit assembly, driver
U21.1	Airbag unit squib
U22	Airbag unit assembly, passenger
U22.1	Airbag unit squib
U23	Sound processor
U24	CD-changer
U26	Seatbelt pretensioner assembly, driver
U26.1	Squib pretensioner assembly, driver
U27	Seatbelt pretensioner assembly, passenger
U27.1	Squib pretensioner assembly, passenger
U29	AF transformer
U30	Side airbag assembly, driver
U30.1	Side airbag squib, driver
U31	Side airbag assembly, passenger
U31.1	Side airbag squib, passenger
V8	Air conditioning compressor diode
V21	Anti-theft warning diode
Y1	Air conditioning compressor clutch
Y5	Fuel solenoid valve (Diesel models)
Y7	Fuel injectors
Y9	Solenoid - car level control
Y14	Air conditioning coolant valve
Y15	Solenoid - secondary air intake
Y18	Solenoid - exhaust gas recirculation
Y19	Solenoid - inlet manifold
Y20	Solenoid - injection regulation
Y21	Ignition lock stroke magnet
Y25	Power steering solenoid valve
Y28	Solenoid - spin level regulation
Y29	Solenoid - boost pressure regulation
Y34	Fuel tank vent valve
Y35	Air conditioning circulation solenoid valve
Y46	Solenoid - inlet manifold
Y47	Parking brake lock lifting magnet (automatic transmission)
X13	Diagnostic equipment connector
X15	Octane coding plug
X54	Ignition coding plug
X1-on	Wiring connectors

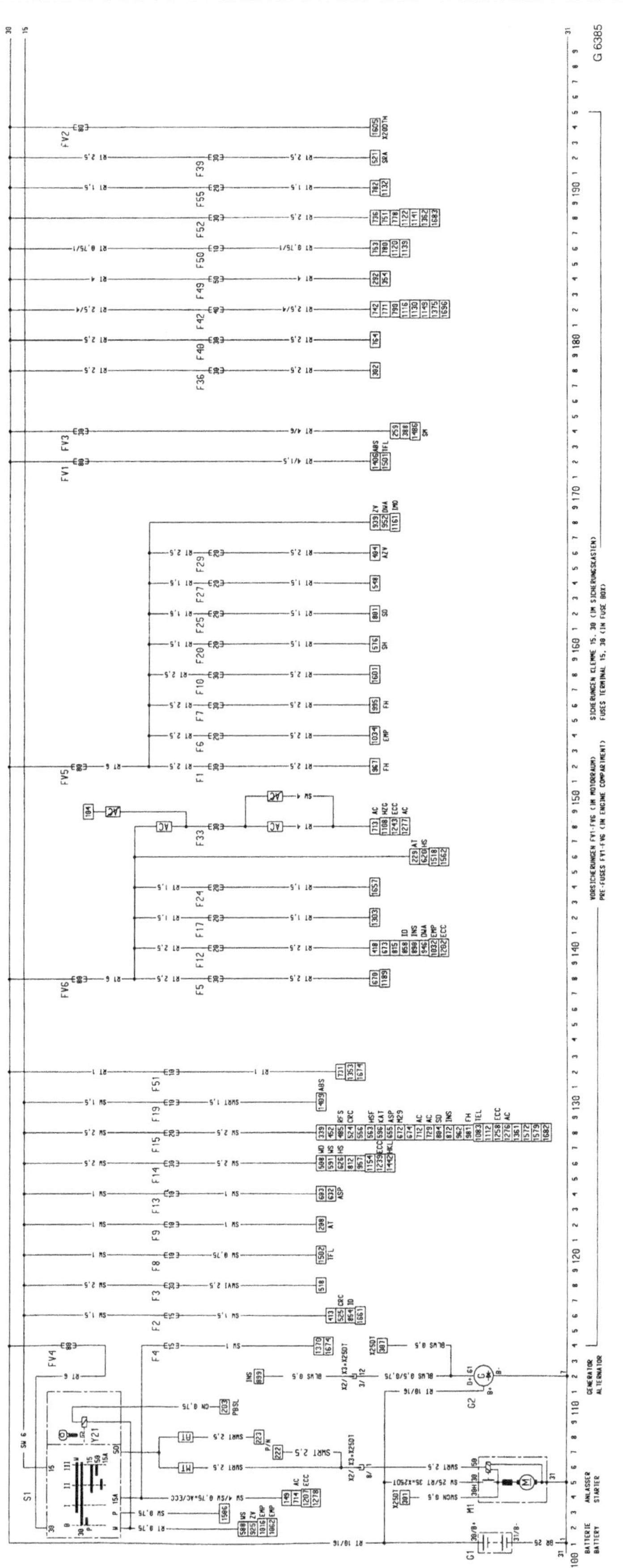

Current track 100 to 199 - Later models

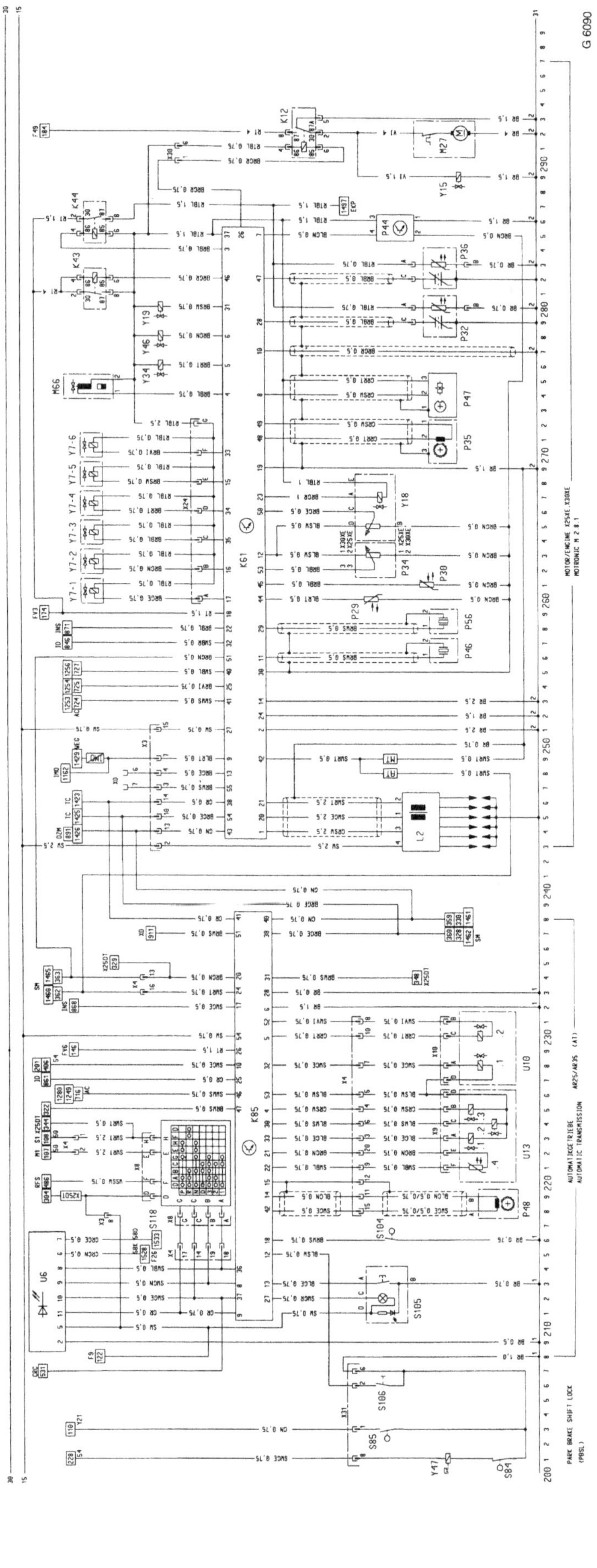

Current track 200 to 299 - Later models

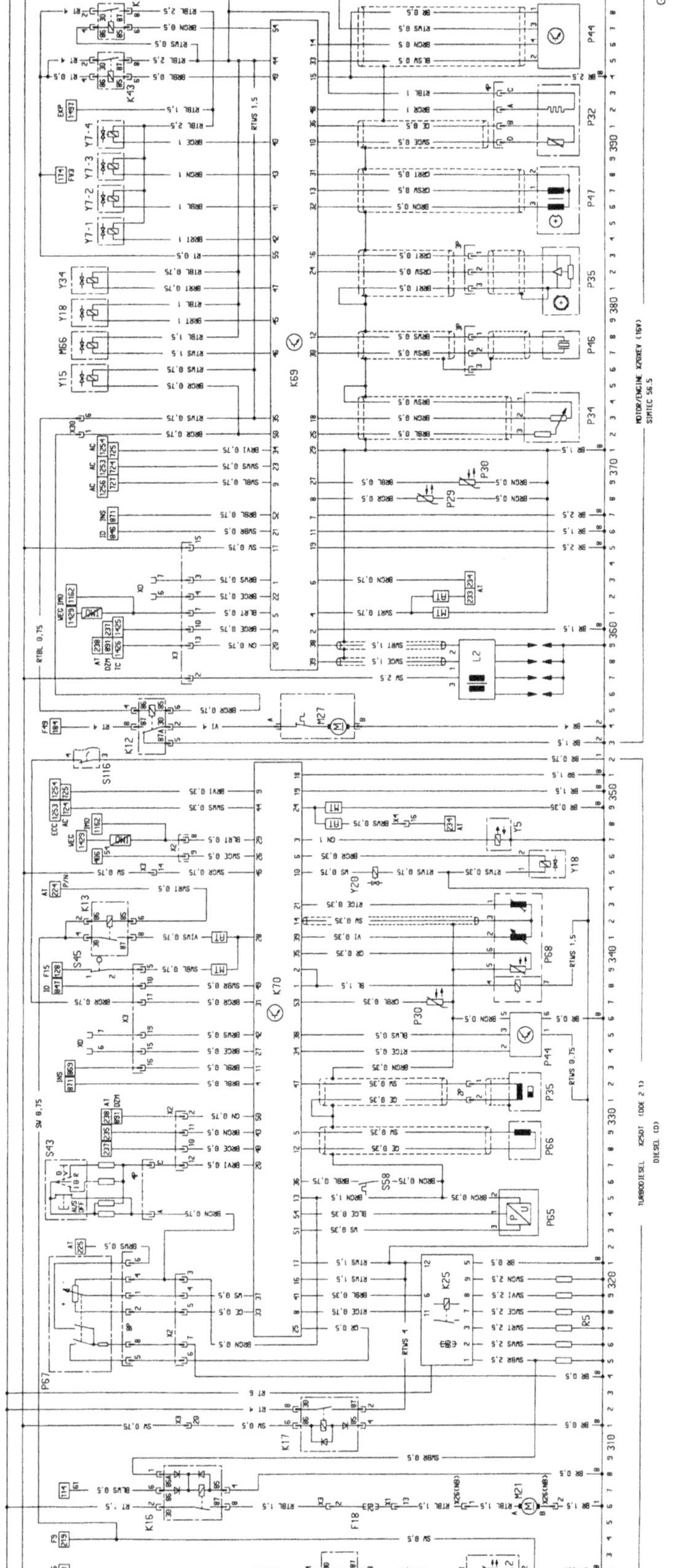

Current track 300 to 399 - Later models

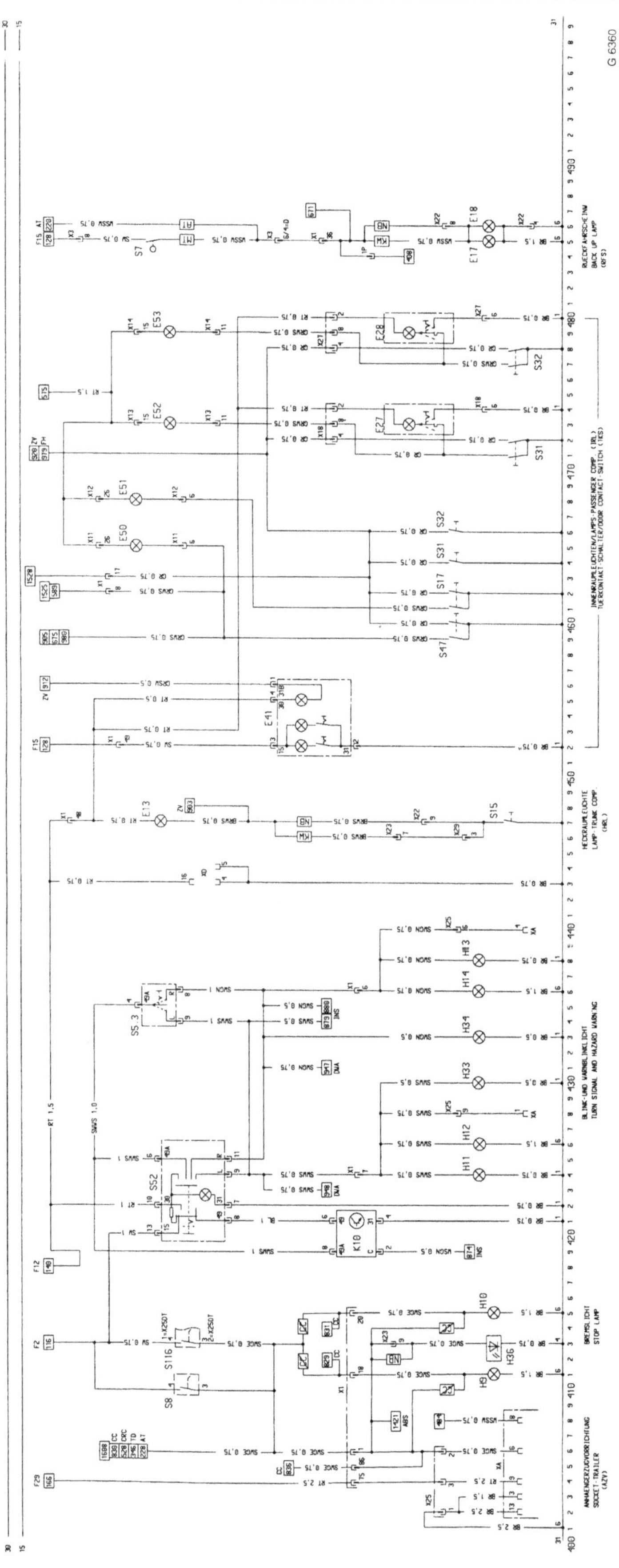

Current track 400 to 499 - Later models

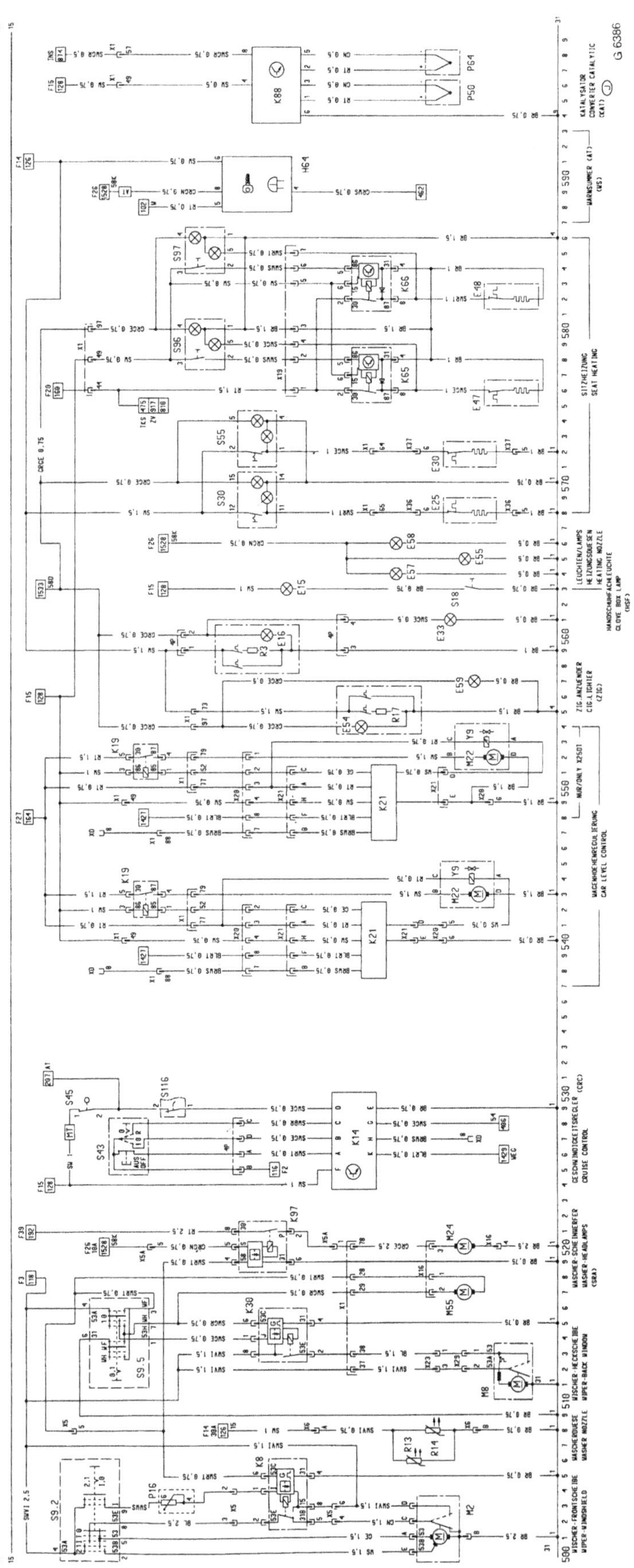

Current track 500 to 599 - Later models

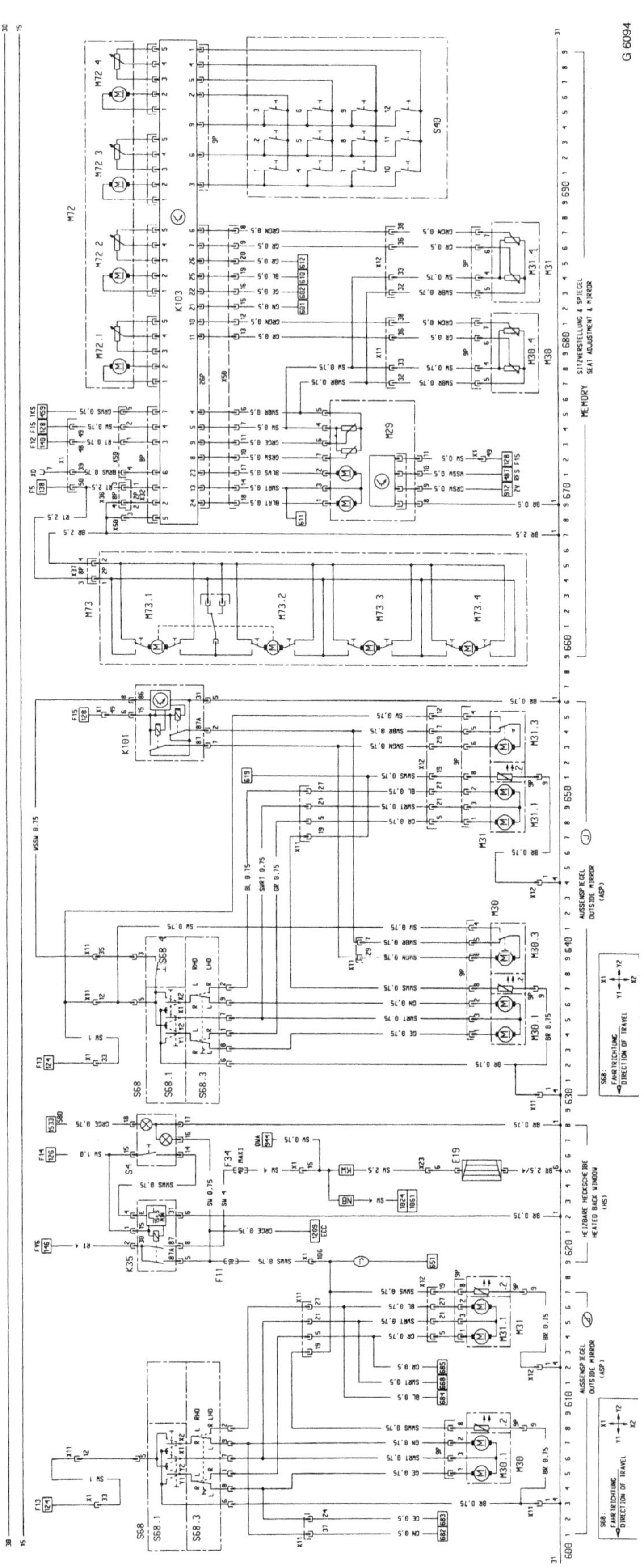

Current track 600 to 699 - Later models

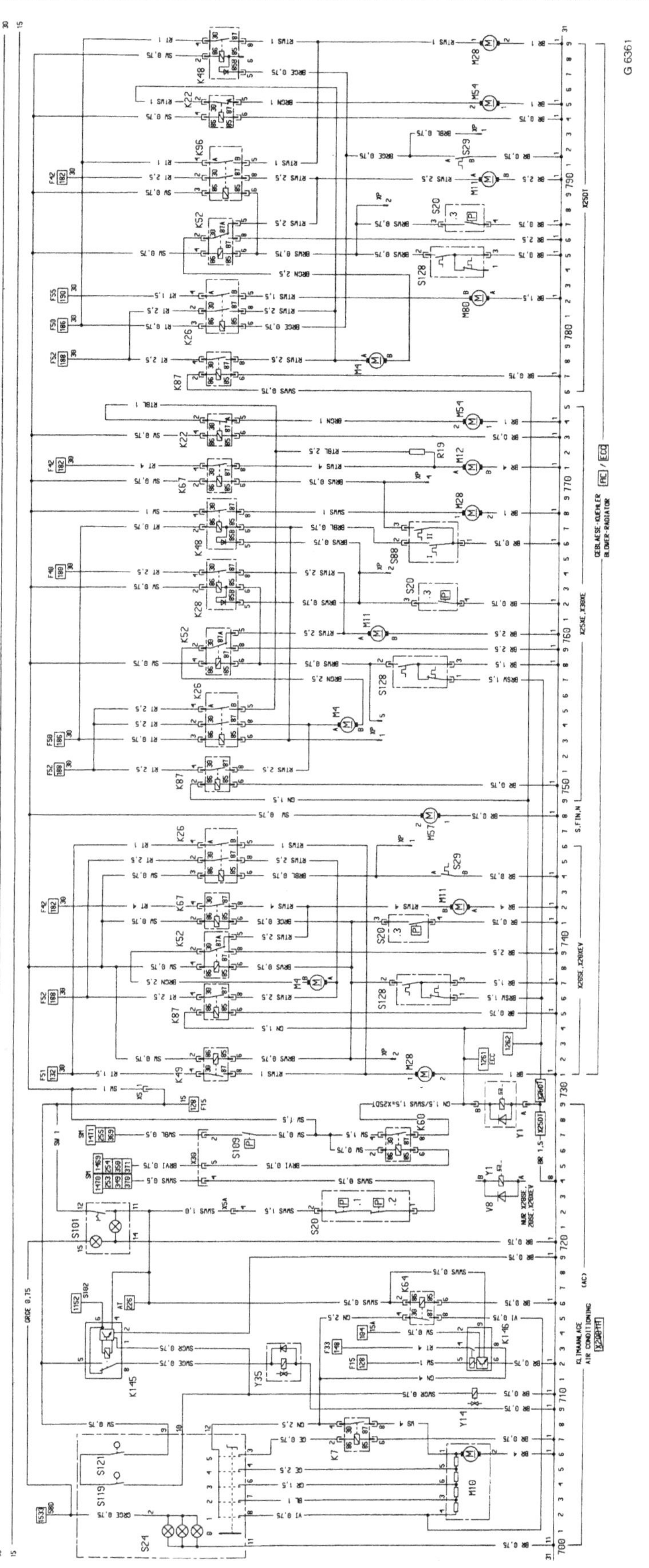

Current track 700 to 799 - Later models

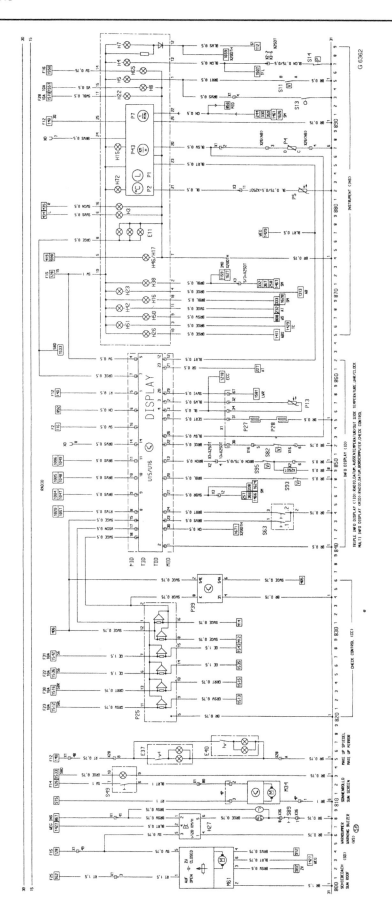

G 6362

Current track 800 to 899 - Later models

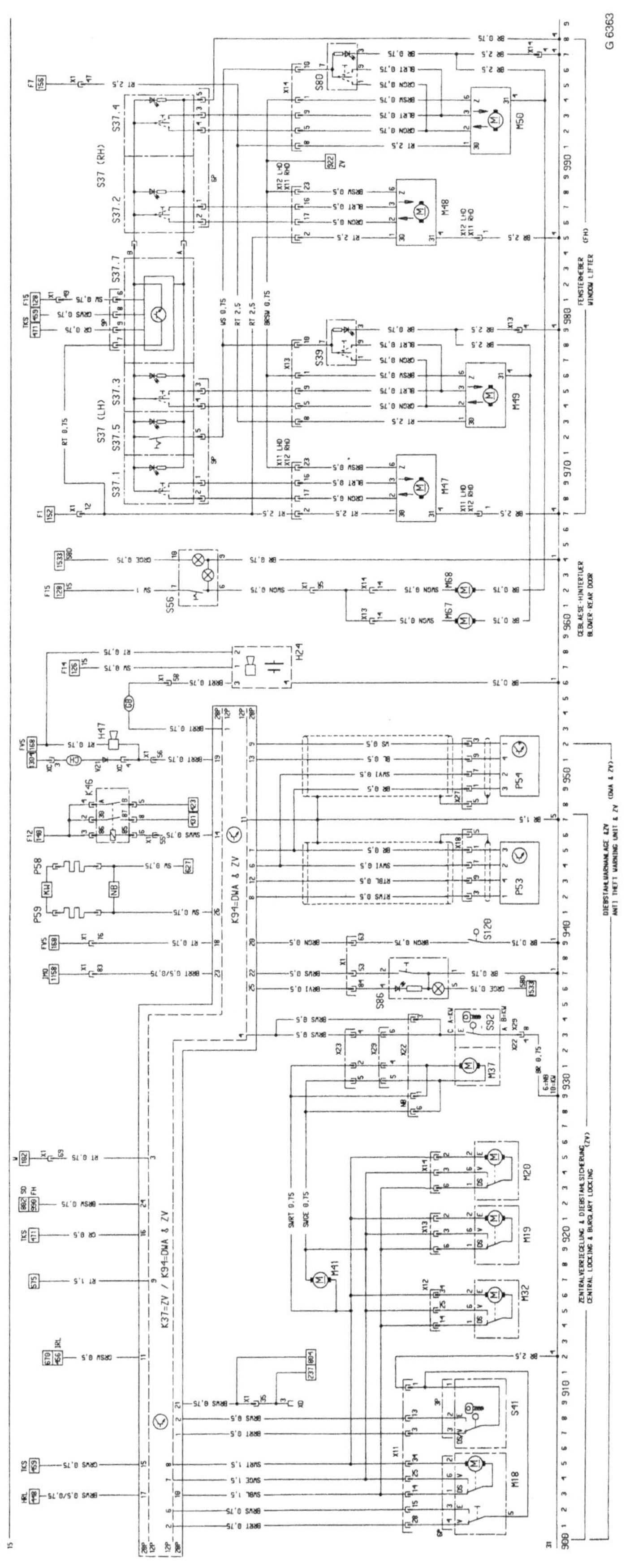

Current track 900 to 999 - Later models

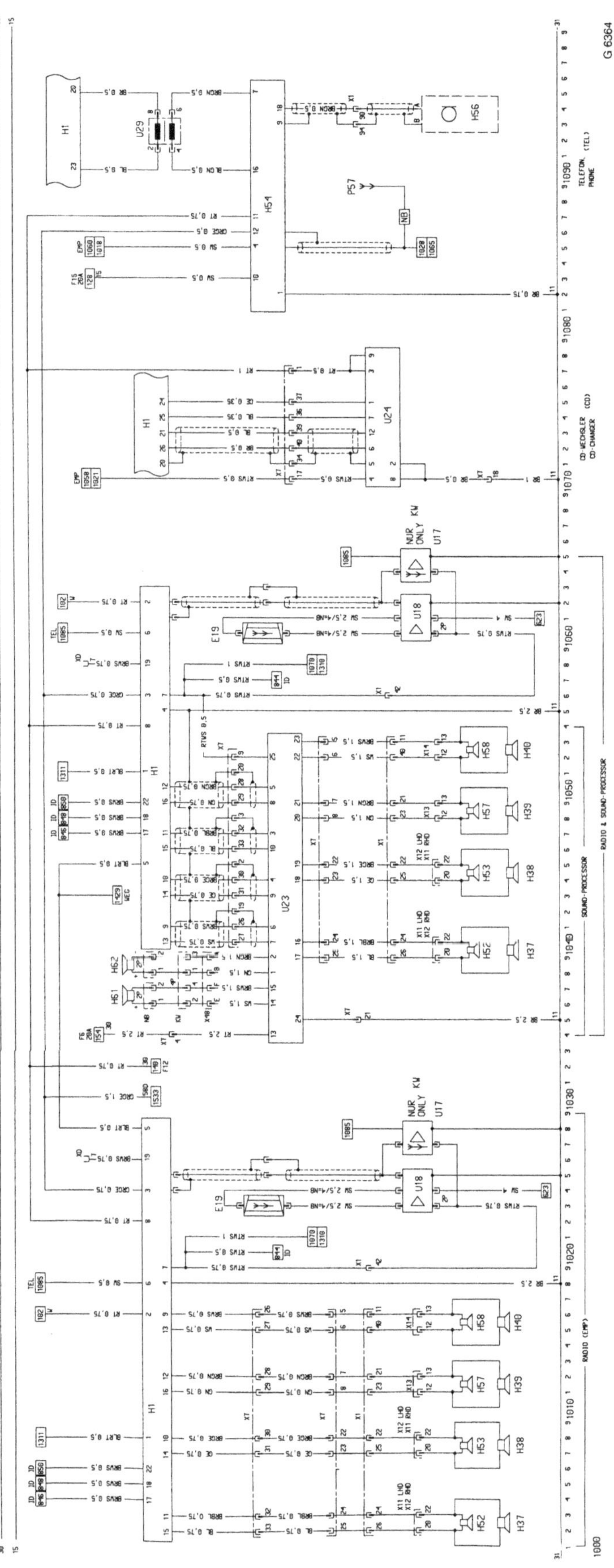

Current track 1000 to 1099 - Later models

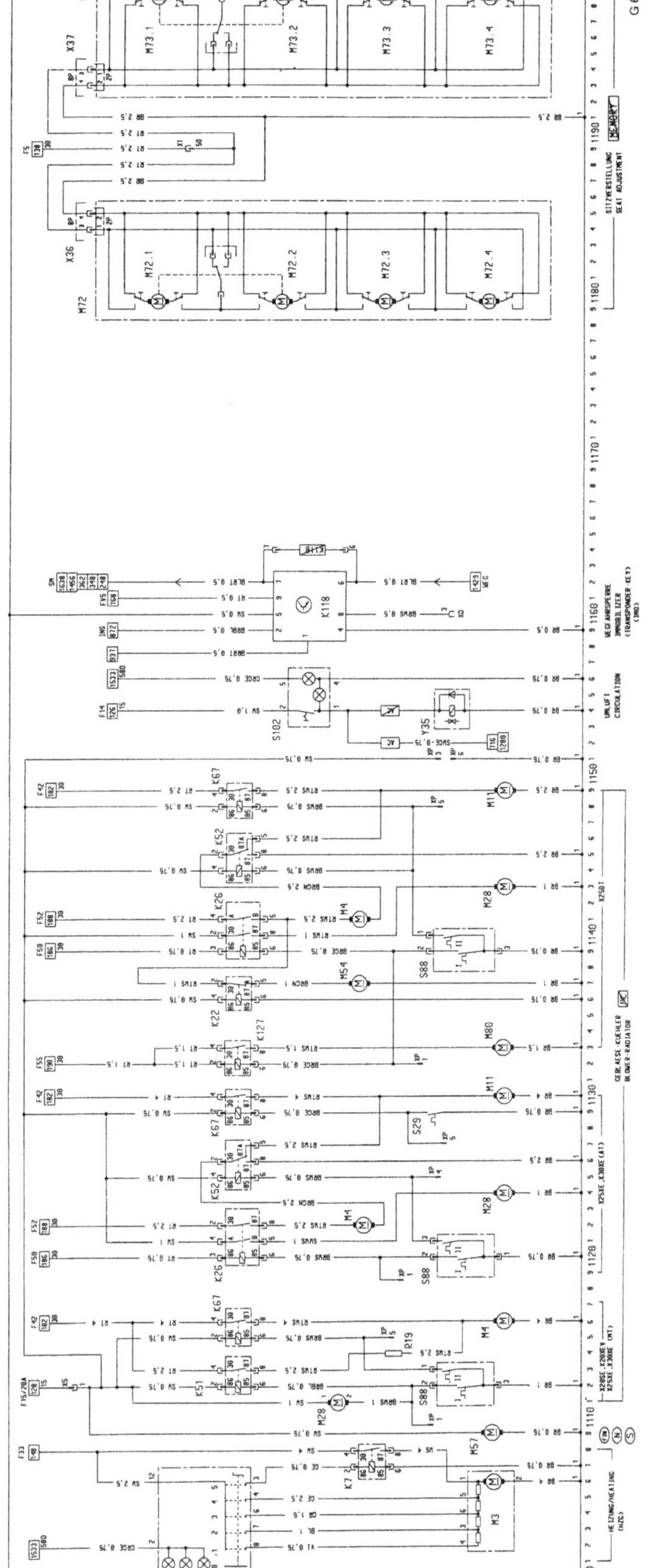

Current track 1100 to 1199 - Later models

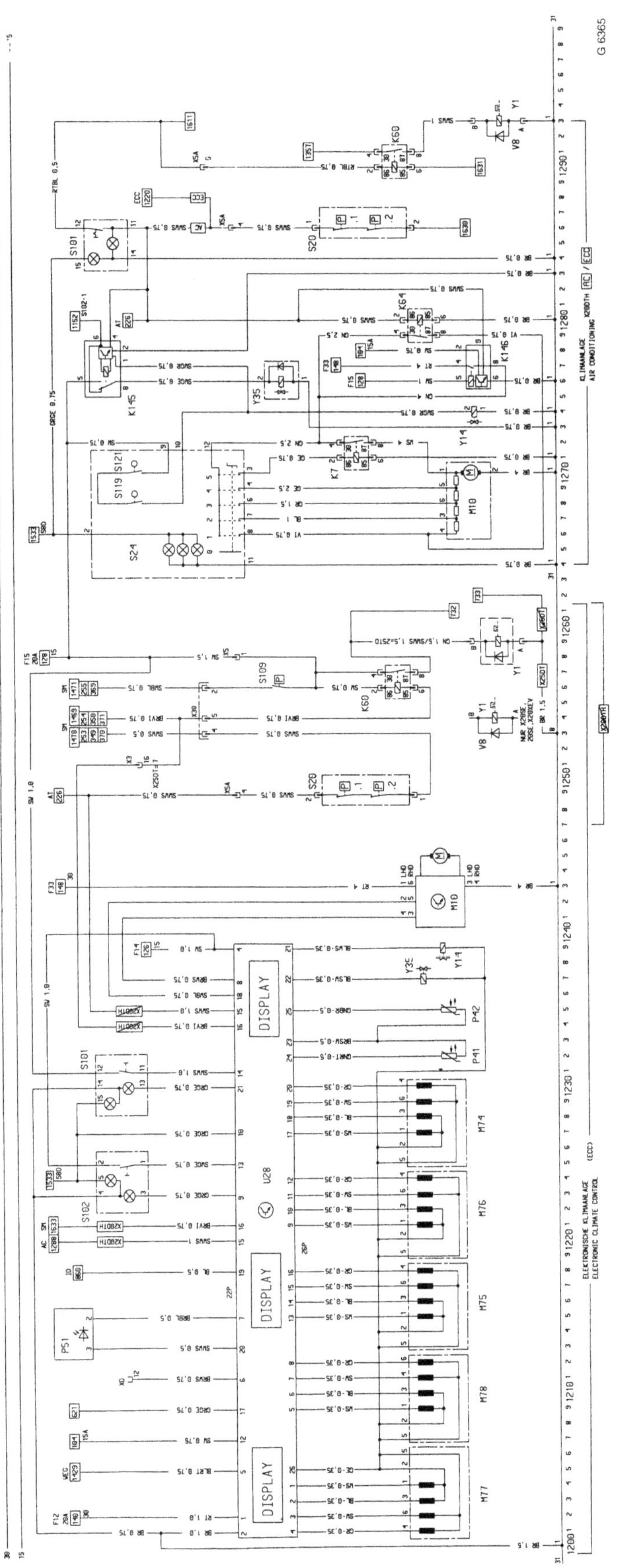

Current track 1200 to 1299 - Later models

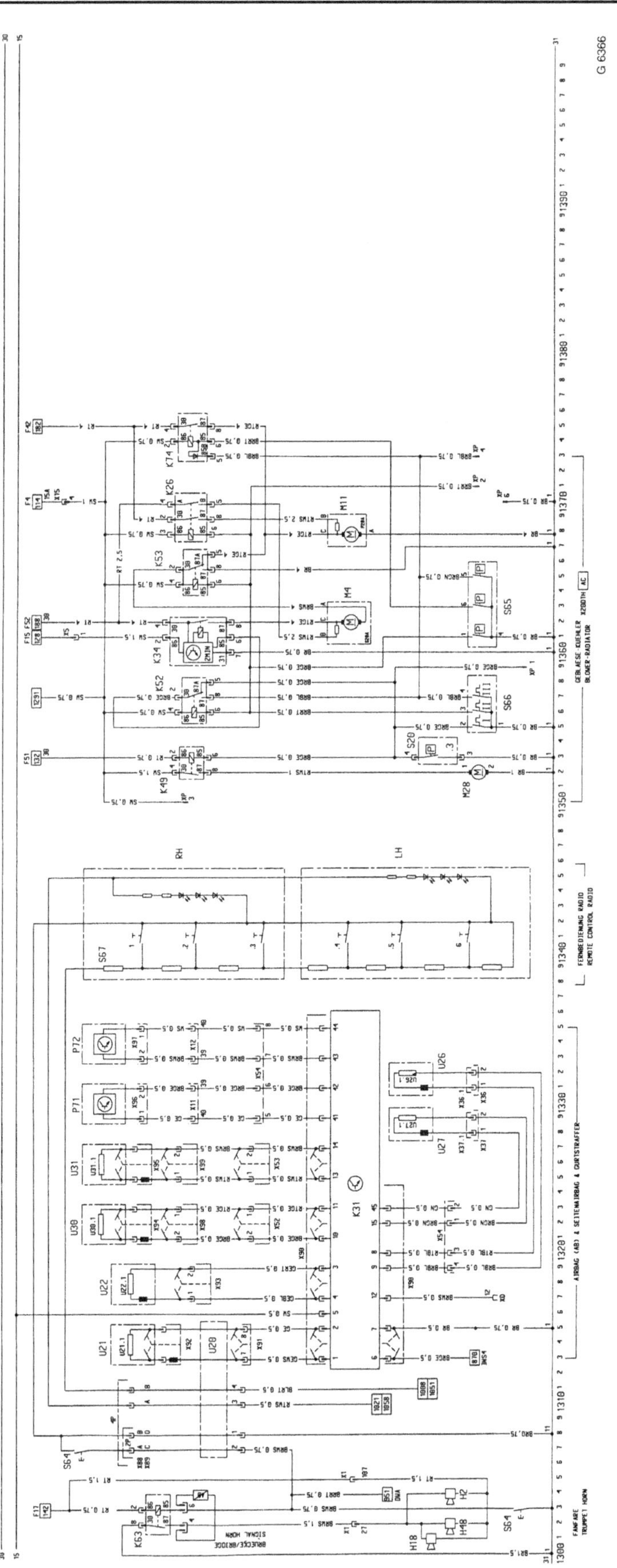

Current track 1300 to 1399 - Later models

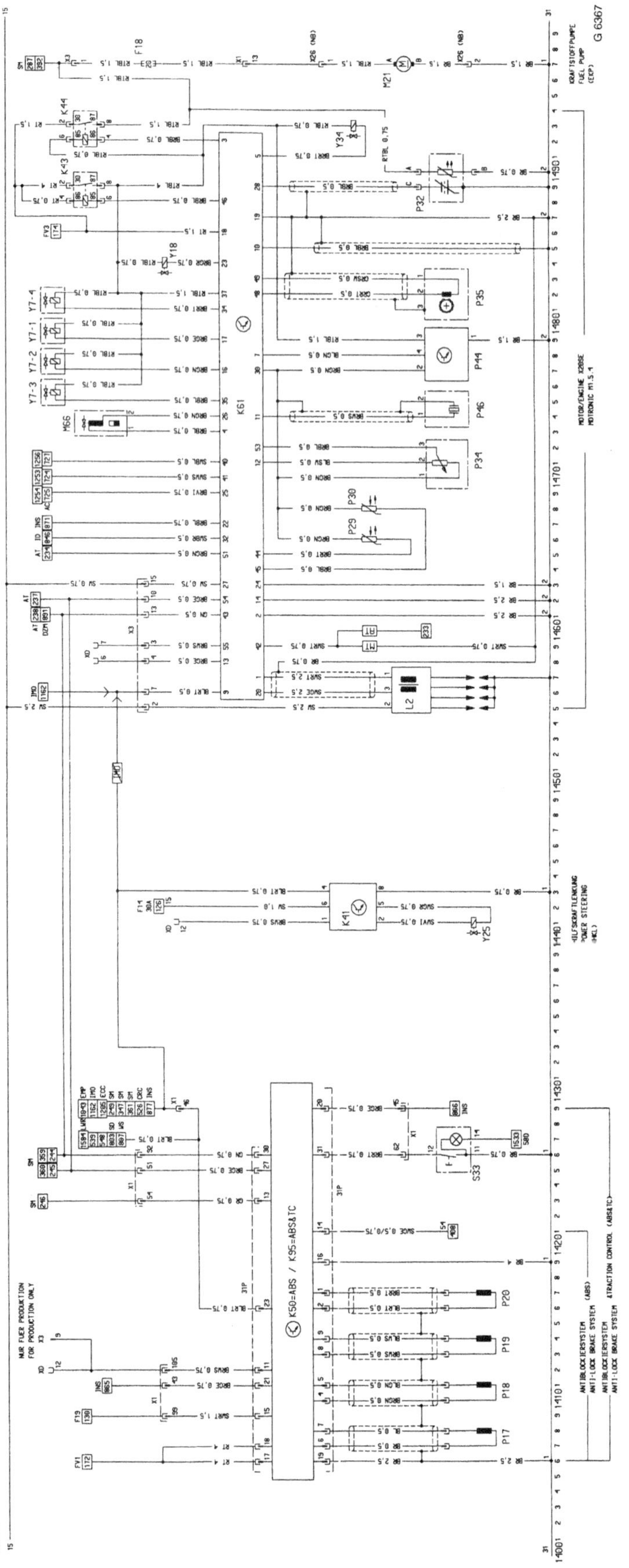

Current track 1400 to 1499 - Later models

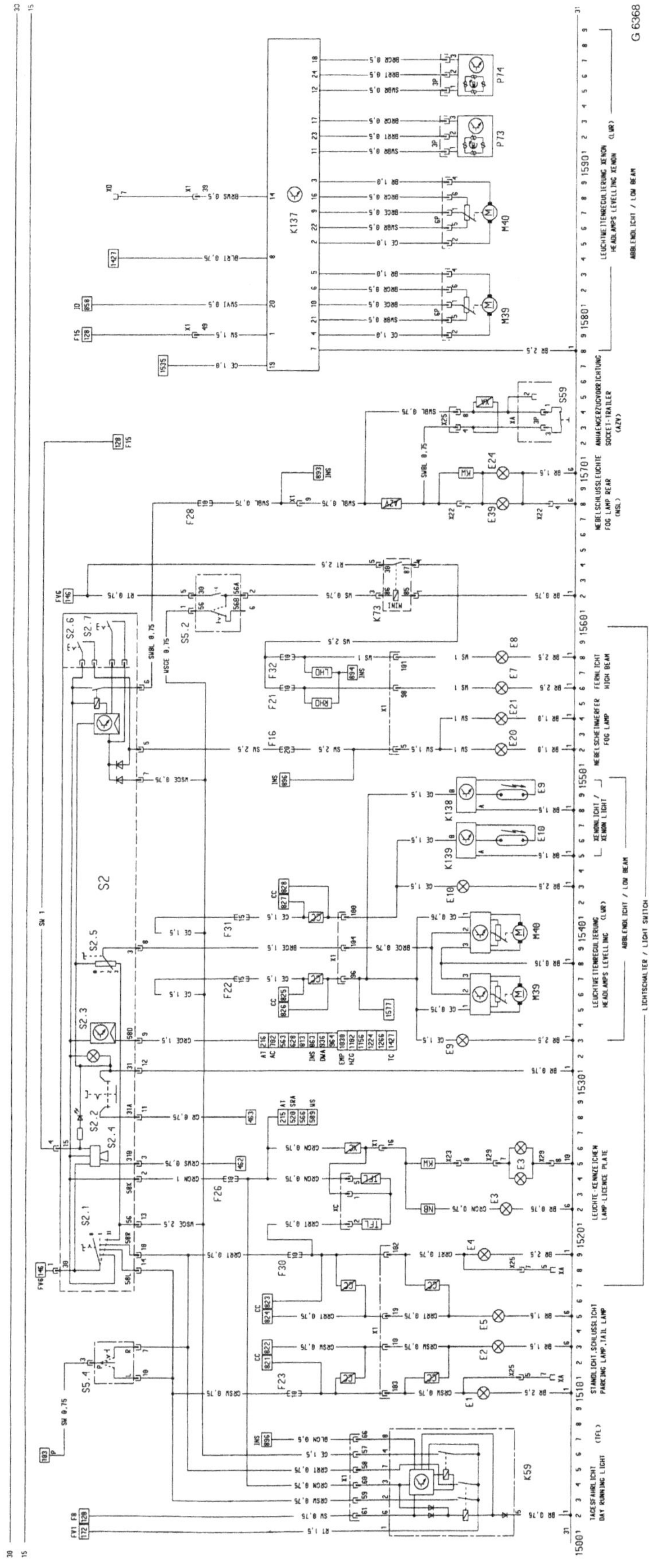

Current track 1500 to 1599 - Later models

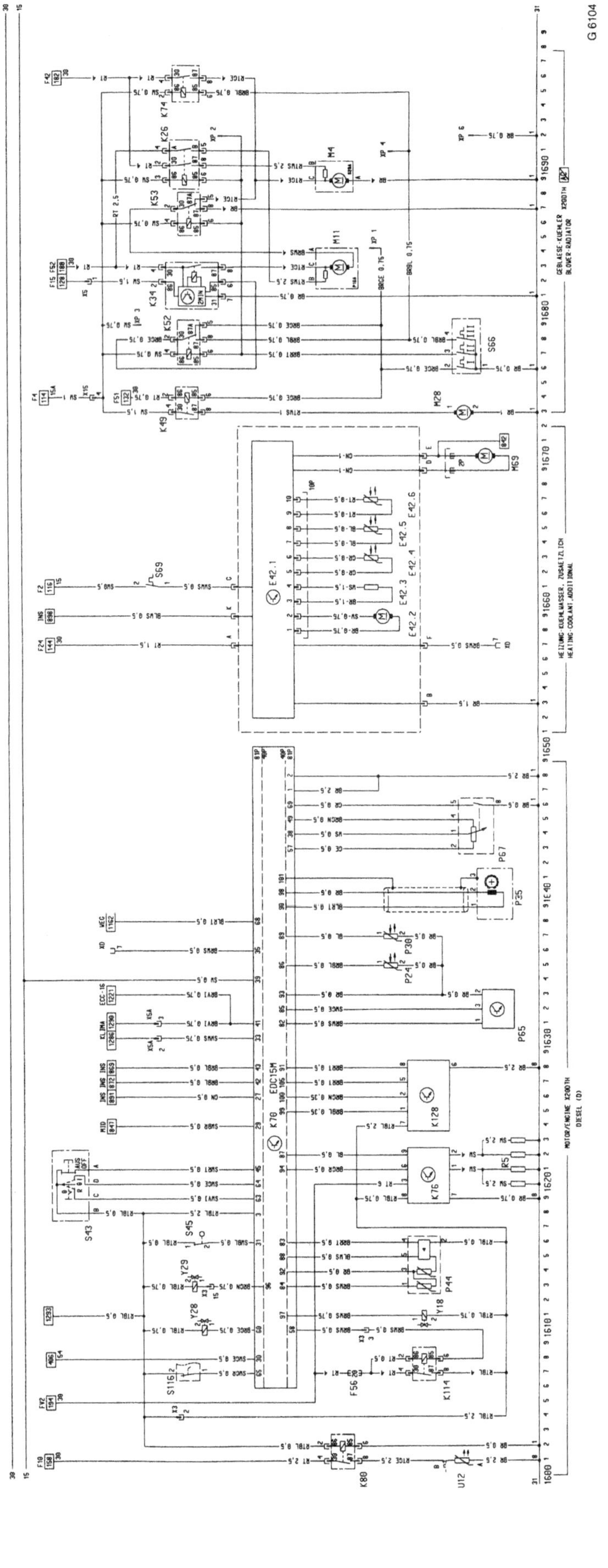

Current track 1600 to 1699 - Later models

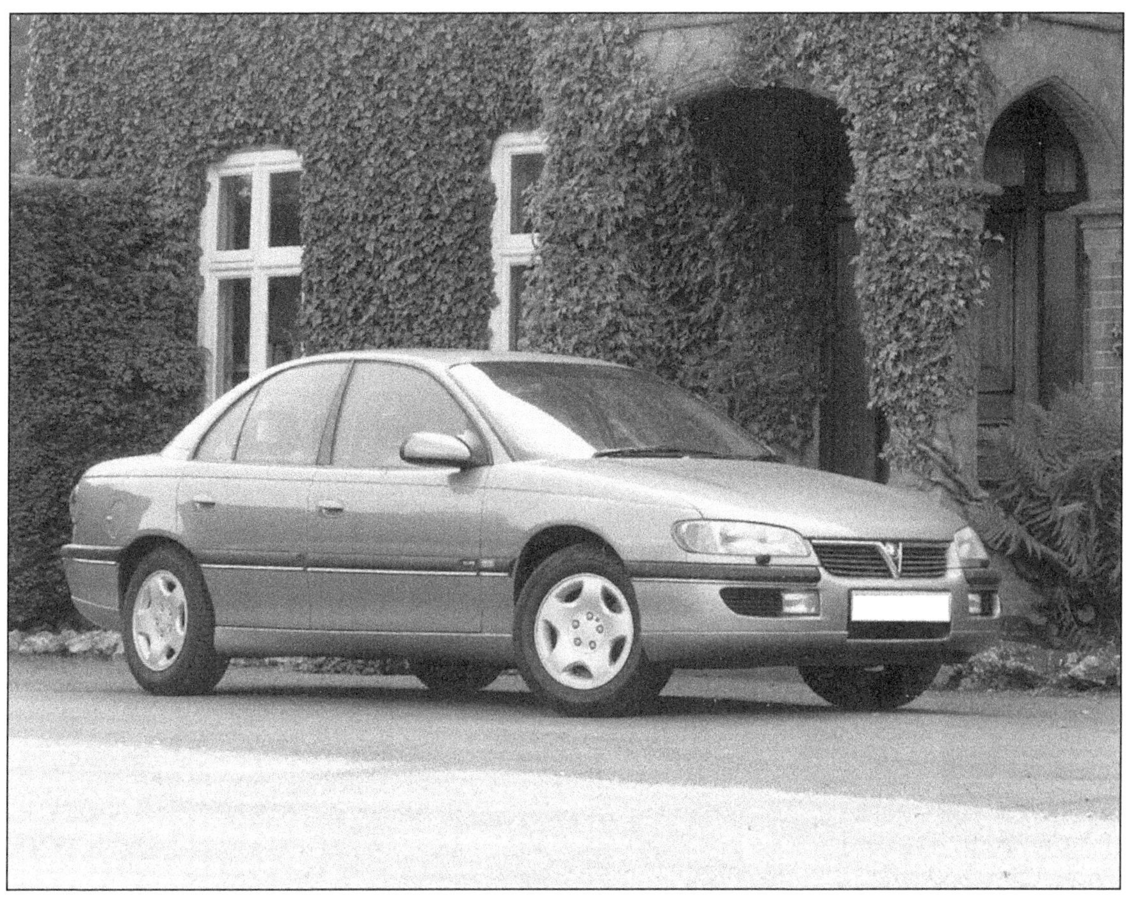

Dimensions and Weights

Note: *All figures are approximate, and may vary according to model depending on specification. Refer to manufacturer's data for exact figures.*

Dimensions	**Saloon model**	**Estate model**
Overall length	4787 mm	4819 mm
Overall width	1960 mm	1960 mm
Overall height (unladen)	1455 mm	1545 mm
Wheelbase	2730 mm	2730 mm
Ground clearance	135 mm	142 mm

Weights	**Saloon model**	**Estate model**
Kerb weight:*		
2.0 litre engine	1400 to 1475 kg	1460 to 1540 kg
2.5 litre engine	1510 to 1570 kg	1560 to 1623 kg
3.0 litre engine	1575 to 1625 kg	1625 to 1675 kg
Maximum gross vehicle weight:*		
2.0 litre engine	1955 to 1985 kg	2085 to 2165 kg
2.5 litre engine	2065 to 2095 kg	2195 to 2225 kg
3.0 litre engine	2095 to 2125 kg	2200 to 2250 kg
Maximum roof rack load	100 kg (including the weight of the roof rack)	
Maximum trailer nose weight	75 kg	

**Depending on specification - refer to manufacturer's vehicle handbook for exact amount*

Conversion factors

Length (distance)

Inches (in)	x 25.4	= Millimetres (mm)	x 0.0394	=	Inches (in)
Feet (ft)	x 0.305	= Metres (m)	x 3.281	=	Feet (ft)
Miles	x 1.609	= Kilometres (km)	x 0.621	=	Miles

Volume (capacity)

Cubic inches (cu in; in^3)	x 16.387	= Cubic centimetres (cc; cm^3)	x 0.061	=	Cubic inches (cu in; in^3)
Imperial pints (Imp pt)	x 0.568	= Litres (l)	x 1.76	=	Imperial pints (Imp pt)
Imperial quarts (Imp qt)	x 1.137	= Litres (l)	x 0.88	=	Imperial quarts (Imp qt)
Imperial quarts (Imp qt)	x 1.201	= US quarts (US qt)	x 0.833	=	Imperial quarts (Imp qt)
US quarts (US qt)	x 0.946	= Litres (l)	x 1.057	=	US quarts (US qt)
Imperial gallons (Imp gal)	x 4.546	= Litres (l)	x 0.22	=	Imperial gallons (Imp gal)
Imperial gallons (Imp gal)	x 1.201	= US gallons (US gal)	x 0.833	=	Imperial gallons (Imp gal)
US gallons (US gal)	x 3.785	= Litres (l)	x 0.264	=	US gallons (US gal)

Mass (weight)

Ounces (oz)	x 28.35	= Grams (g)	x 0.035	=	Ounces (oz)
Pounds (lb)	x 0.454	= Kilograms (kg)	x 2.205	=	Pounds (lb)

Force

Ounces-force (ozf; oz)	x 0.278	= Newtons (N)	x 3.6	=	Ounces-force (ozf; oz)
Pounds-force (lbf; lb)	x 4.448	= Newtons (N)	x 0.225	=	Pounds-force (lbf; lb)
Newtons (N)	x 0.1	= Kilograms-force (kgf; kg)	x 9.81	=	Newtons (N)

Pressure

Pounds-force per square inch (psi; lbf/in^2; lb/in^2)	x 0.070	= Kilograms-force per square centimetre (kgf/cm^2; kg/cm^2)	x 14.223	=	Pounds-force per square inch (psi; lbf/in^2; lb/in^2)
Pounds-force per square inch (psi; lbf/in^2; lb/in^2)	x 0.068	= Atmospheres (atm)	x 14.696	=	Pounds-force per square inch (psi; lbf/in^2; lb/in^2)
Pounds-force per square inch (psi; lbf/in^2; lb/in^2)	x 0.069	= Bars	x 14.5	=	Pounds-force per square inch (psi; lbf/in^2; lb/in^2)
Pounds-force per square inch (psi; lbf/in^2; lb/in^2)	x 6.895	= Kilopascals (kPa)	x 0.145	=	Pounds-force per square inch (psi; lbf/in^2; lb/in^2)
Kilopascals (kPa)	x 0.01	= Kilograms-force per square centimetre (kgf/cm^2; kg/cm^2)	x 98.1	=	Kilopascals (kPa)
Millibar (mbar)	x 100	= Pascals (Pa)	x 0.01	=	Millibar (mbar)
Millibar (mbar)	x 0.0145	= Pounds-force per square inch (psi; lbf/in^2; lb/in^2)	x 68.947	=	Millibar (mbar)
Millibar (mbar)	x 0.75	= Millimetres of mercury (mmHg)	x 1.333	=	Millibar (mbar)
Millibar (mbar)	x 0.401	= Inches of water (inH$_2$O)	x 2.491	=	Millibar (mbar)
Millimetres of mercury (mmHg)	x 0.535	= Inches of water (inH$_2$O)	x 1.868	=	Millimetres of mercury (mmHg)
Inches of water (inH$_2$O)	x 0.036	= Pounds-force per square inch (psi; lbf/in^2; lb/in^2)	x 27.68	=	Inches of water (inH$_2$O)

Torque (moment of force)

Pounds-force inches (lbf in; lb in)	x 1.152	= Kilograms-force centimetre (kgf cm; kg cm)	x 0.868	=	Pounds-force inches (lbf in; lb in)
Pounds-force inches (lbf in; lb in)	x 0.113	= Newton metres (Nm)	x 8.85	=	Pounds-force inches (lbf in; lb in)
Pounds-force inches (lbf in; lb in)	x 0.083	= Pounds-force feet (lbf ft; lb ft)	x 12	=	Pounds-force inches (lbf in; lb in)
Pounds-force feet (lbf ft; lb ft)	x 0.138	= Kilograms-force metres (kgf m; kg m)	x 7.233	=	Pounds-force feet (lbf ft; lb ft)
Pounds-force feet (lbf ft; lb ft)	x 1.356	= Newton metres (Nm)	x 0.738	=	Pounds-force feet (lbf ft; lb ft)
Newton metres (Nm)	x 0.102	= Kilograms-force metres (kgf m; kg m)	x 9.804	=	Newton metres (Nm)

Power

Horsepower (hp)	x 745.7	= Watts (W)	x 0.0013	=	Horsepower (hp)

Velocity (speed)

Miles per hour (miles/hr; mph)	x 1.609	= Kilometres per hour (km/hr; kph)	x 0.621	=	Miles per hour (miles/hr; mph)

Fuel consumption*

Miles per gallon, Imperial (mpg)	x 0.354	= Kilometres per litre (km/l)	x 2.825	=	Miles per gallon, Imperial (mpg)
Miles per gallon, US (mpg)	x 0.425	= Kilometres per litre (km/l)	x 2.352	=	Miles per gallon, US (mpg)

Temperature

Degrees Fahrenheit = (°C x 1.8) + 32

Degrees Celsius (Degrees Centigrade; °C) = (°F - 32) x 0.56

** It is common practice to convert from miles per gallon (mpg) to litres/100 kilometres (l/100km), where mpg x l/100 km = 282*

Buying spare parts

Spare parts are available from many sources, including maker's appointed garages, accessory shops, and motor factors. To be sure of obtaining the correct parts, it will sometimes be necessary to quote the vehicle identification number. If possible, it can also be useful to take the old parts along for positive identification. Items such as starter motors and alternators may be available under a service exchange scheme - any parts returned should be clean.

Our advice regarding spare parts is as follows.

Officially appointed garages

This is the best source of parts which are peculiar to your car, and which are not otherwise generally available (eg, badges, interior trim, certain body panels, etc). It is also the only place at which you should buy parts if the vehicle is still under warranty.

Accessory shops

These are very good places to buy materials and components needed for the maintenance of your car (oil, air and fuel filters, light bulbs, drivebelts, greases, brake pads, touch-up paint, etc). Components of this nature sold by a reputable shop are usually of the same standard as those used by the car manufacturer.

Besides components, these shops also sell tools and general accessories, usually have convenient opening hours, charge lower prices, and can often be found close to home. Some accessory shops have parts counters where components needed for almost any repair job can be purchased or ordered.

Motor factors

Good factors will stock all the more important components which wear out comparatively quickly, and can sometimes supply individual components needed for the overhaul of a larger assembly (eg, brake seals and hydraulic parts, bearing shells, pistons, valves). They may also handle work such as cylinder block reboring, crankshaft regrinding, etc.

Tyre and exhaust specialists

These outlets may be independent, or members of a local or national chain. They frequently offer competitive prices when compared with a main dealer or local garage, but it will pay to obtain several quotes before making a decision. When researching prices, also ask what extras may be added - for instance fitting a new valve and balancing the wheel are both commonly charged on top of the price of a new tyre.

Other sources

Beware of parts or materials obtained from market stalls, car boot sales or similar outlets. Such items are not invariably sub-standard, but there is little chance of compensation if they do prove unsatisfactory. in the case of safety-critical components such as brake pads, there is the risk not only of financial loss, but also of an accident causing injury or death.

Second-hand components or assemblies obtained from a car breaker can be a good buy in some circumstances, but this sort of purchase is best made by the experienced DIY mechanic.

Vehicle Identification

Modifications are a continuing and unpublicised process in vehicle manufacture, quite apart from major model changes. Spare parts manuals and lists are compiled upon a numerical basis, the individual vehicle identification numbers being essential to correct identification of the component concerned.

When ordering spare parts, always give as much information as possible. Quote the car model, year of manufacture and registration, chassis and engine numbers as appropriate.

The *Vehicle Identification Number (VIN)* plate is riveted to the bonnet lock crossmember, on the right-hand side of the lock, and is visible once the bonnet has been opened. The vehicle identification (chassis) number is also stamped onto the body floor panel between the driver's seat and sill panel; lift the flap in the trim panel to see it **(see illustrations)**.

The *engine number* can be found on the left-hand side of the cylinder block. The first five digits of the engine number form the engine identification code.

Note: *The vehicle is supplied with a Car Pass (similar to a credit card) which has all the vehicle identification data recorded on a magnetic strip. This card should be stored in a safe place away from the vehicle.*

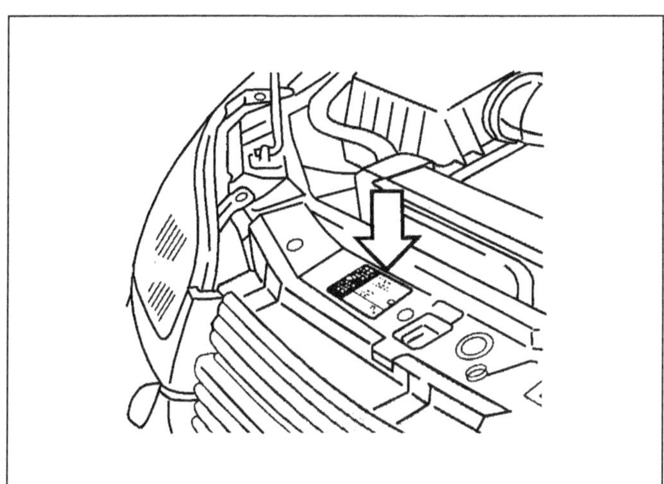

The VIN plate (arrowed) is riveted to the bonnet lock crossmember

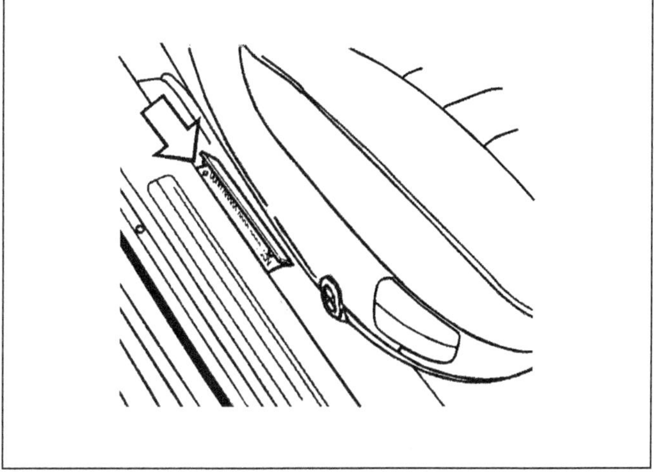

The VIN (chassis) number is also stamped on the floor between the driver's seat and sill panel. Open up the trim panel flap (arrowed) to see it

Whenever servicing, repair or overhaul work is carried out on the car or its components, observe the following procedures and instructions. This will assist in carrying out the operation efficiently and to a professional standard of workmanship.

Joint mating faces and gaskets

When separating components at their mating faces, never insert screwdrivers or similar implements into the joint between the faces in order to prise them apart. This can cause severe damage which results in oil leaks, coolant leaks, etc upon reassembly. Separation is usually achieved by tapping along the joint with a soft-faced hammer in order to break the seal. However, note that this method may not be suitable where dowels are used for component location.

Where a gasket is used between the mating faces of two components, a new one must be fitted on reassembly; fit it dry unless otherwise stated in the repair procedure. Make sure that the mating faces are clean and dry, with all traces of old gasket removed. When cleaning a joint face, use a tool which is unlikely to score or damage the face, and remove any burrs or nicks with an oilstone or fine file.

Make sure that tapped holes are cleaned with a pipe cleaner, and keep them free of jointing compound, if this is being used, unless specifically instructed otherwise.

Ensure that all orifices, channels or pipes are clear, and blow through them, preferably using compressed air.

Oil seals

Oil seals can be removed by levering them out with a wide flat-bladed screwdriver or similar implement. Alternatively, a number of self-tapping screws may be screwed into the seal, and these used as a purchase for pliers or some similar device in order to pull the seal free.

Whenever an oil seal is removed from its working location, either individually or as part of an assembly, it should be renewed.

The very fine sealing lip of the seal is easily damaged, and will not seal if the surface it contacts is not completely clean and free from scratches, nicks or grooves. If the original sealing surface of the component cannot be restored, and the manufacturer has not made provision for slight relocation of the seal relative to the sealing surface, the component should be renewed.

Protect the lips of the seal from any surface which may damage them in the course of fitting. Use tape or a conical sleeve where possible. Lubricate the seal lips with oil before fitting and, on dual-lipped seals, fill the space between the lips with grease.

Unless otherwise stated, oil seals must be fitted with their sealing lips toward the lubricant to be sealed.

Use a tubular drift or block of wood of the appropriate size to install the seal and, if the seal housing is shouldered, drive the seal down to the shoulder. If the seal housing is unshouldered, the seal should be fitted with its face flush with the housing top face (unless otherwise instructed).

Screw threads and fastenings

Seized nuts, bolts and screws are quite a common occurrence where corrosion has set in, and the use of penetrating oil or releasing fluid will often overcome this problem if the offending item is soaked for a while before attempting to release it. The use of an impact driver may also provide a means of releasing such stubborn fastening devices, when used in conjunction with the appropriate screwdriver bit or socket. If none of these methods works, it may be necessary to resort to the careful application of heat, or the use of a hacksaw or nut splitter device.

Studs are usually removed by locking two nuts together on the threaded part, and then using a spanner on the lower nut to unscrew the stud. Studs or bolts which have broken off below the surface of the component in which they are mounted can sometimes be removed using a stud extractor. Always ensure that a blind tapped hole is completely free from oil, grease, water or other fluid before installing the bolt or stud. Failure to do this could cause the housing to crack due to the hydraulic action of the bolt or stud as it is screwed in.

When tightening a castellated nut to accept a split pin, tighten the nut to the specified torque, where applicable, and then tighten further to the next split pin hole. Never slacken the nut to align the split pin hole, unless stated in the repair procedure.

When checking or retightening a nut or bolt to a specified torque setting, slacken the nut or bolt by a quarter of a turn, and then retighten to the specified setting. However, this should not be attempted where angular tightening has been used.

For some screw fastenings, notably cylinder head bolts or nuts, torque wrench settings are no longer specified for the latter stages of tightening, "angle-tightening" being called up instead. Typically, a fairly low torque wrench setting will be applied to the bolts/nuts in the correct sequence, followed by one or more stages of tightening through specified angles.

Locknuts, locktabs and washers

Any fastening which will rotate against a component or housing during tightening should always have a washer between it and the relevant component or housing.

Spring or split washers should always be renewed when they are used to lock a critical component such as a big-end bearing retaining bolt or nut. Locktabs which are folded over to retain a nut or bolt should always be renewed.

Self-locking nuts can be re-used in non-critical areas, providing resistance can be felt when the locking portion passes over the bolt or stud thread. However, it should be noted that self-locking stiffnuts tend to lose their effectiveness after long periods of use, and should then be renewed as a matter of course.

Split pins must always be replaced with new ones of the correct size for the hole.

When thread-locking compound is found on the threads of a fastener which is to be re-used, it should be cleaned off with a wire brush and solvent, and fresh compound applied on reassembly.

Special tools

Some repair procedures in this manual entail the use of special tools such as a press, two or three-legged pullers, spring compressors, etc. Wherever possible, suitable readily-available alternatives to the manufacturer's special tools are described, and are shown in use. In some instances, where no alternative is possible, it has been necessary to resort to the use of a manufacturer's tool, and this has been done for reasons of safety as well as the efficient completion of the repair operation. Unless you are highly-skilled and have a thorough understanding of the procedures described, never attempt to bypass the use of any special tool when the procedure described specifies its use. Not only is there a very great risk of personal injury, but expensive damage could be caused to the components involved.

Environmental considerations

When disposing of used engine oil, brake fluid, antifreeze, etc, give due consideration to any detrimental environmental effects. Do not, for instance, pour any of the above liquids down drains into the general sewage system, or onto the ground to soak away. Many local council refuse tips provide a facility for waste oil disposal, as do some garages. If none of these facilities are available, consult your local Environmental Health Department, or the National Rivers Authority, for further advice.

With the universal tightening-up of legislation regarding the emission of environmentally-harmful substances from motor vehicles, most vehicles have tamperproof devices fitted to the main adjustment points of the fuel system. These devices are primarily designed to prevent unqualified persons from adjusting the fuel/air mixture, with the chance of a consequent increase in toxic emissions. If such devices are found during servicing or overhaul, they should, wherever possible, be renewed or refitted in accordance with the manufacturer's requirements or current legislation.

Note: It is antisocial and illegal to dump oil down the drain. To find the location of your local oil recycling bank, call this number free.

The jack supplied with the vehicle tool kit should only be used for changing the roadwheels - see *Wheel changing* at the front of this manual. When carrying out any other kind of work, raise the vehicle using a hydraulic (or trolley) jack, and always supplement the jack with axle stands positioned under the vehicle jacking points.

To raise the front of the vehicle, position the jack head underneath the braced underbody section situated next to the vehicle jack location point. To raise the rear of the vehicle, position the jack head underneath the rear suspension subframe front mounting **(see illustration)**. Always position a block of wood between the jack head and underbody to prevent damage occurring.

With the vehicle raised to the correct height, unclip the plastic access cover from the sill trim panel and support the vehicle on an axle stand positioned directly underneath the vehicle jack location point. To protect the sill, position a block of wood with a groove cut into it on the jack head and locate the sill seam in the groove; this will spread the load on the sill over a wider area and prevent the sill seam being damaged.

The jack supplied with the vehicle should be located underneath the lifting points on the front and rear of the sills. Unclip the plastic covers from the sill trim panel to gain access to the lifting points. Ensure that the lug on the jack head is correctly located in the sill seam cutout before attempting to raise the vehicle.

Never work under, around, or near a raised vehicle, unless it is adequately supported in at least two places.

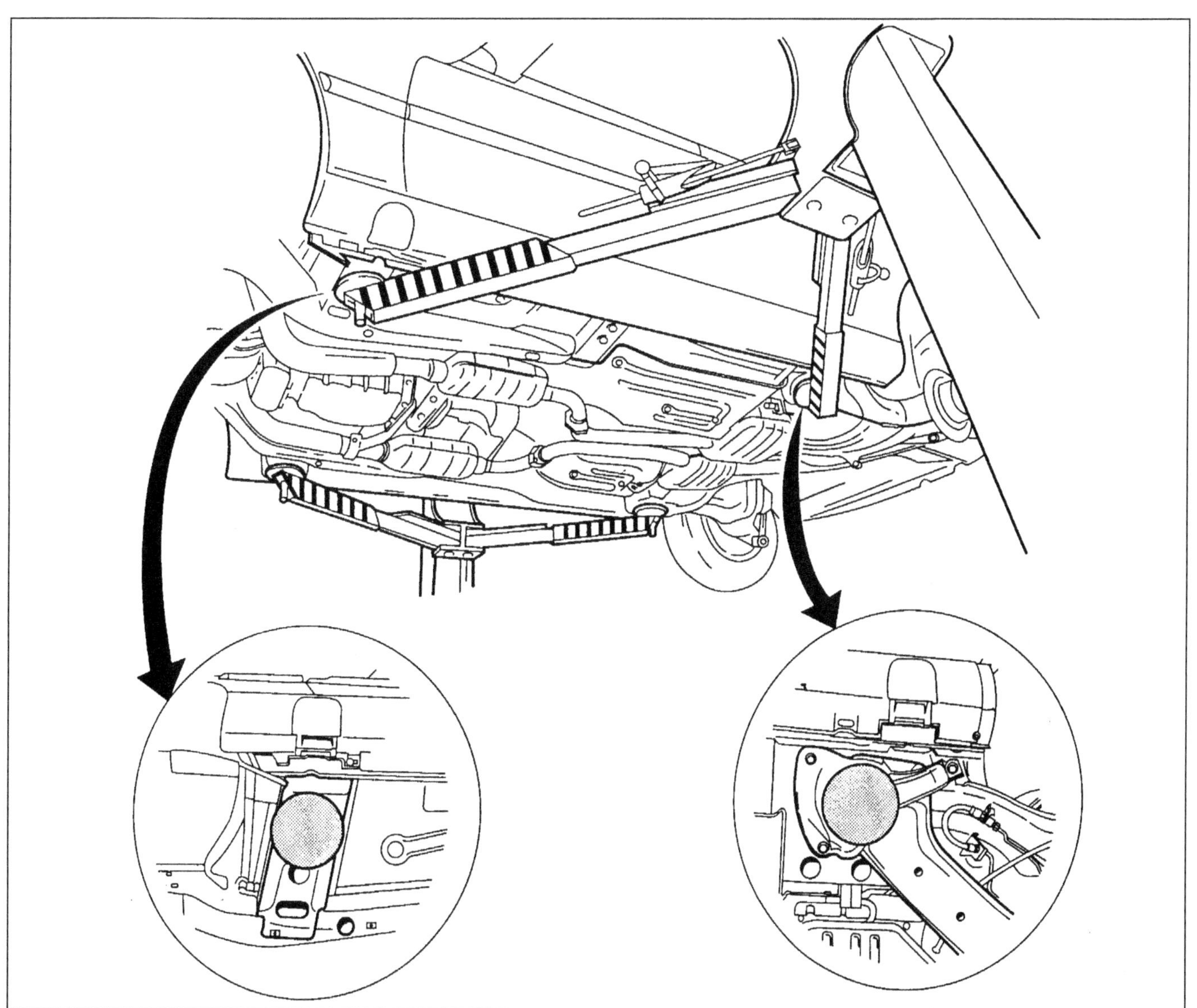

Vehicle lifting points for use with a hydraulic jack

Radio/cassette unit Anti-theft System precaution

The radio/cassette/CD player/autochanger unit fitted as standard equipment by Vauxhall is equipped with a built-in security code, to deter thieves. If the power source to the unit is cut, the anti-theft system will activate. Even if the power source is immediately reconnected, the radio/cassette unit will not function until the correct security code has been entered. Therefore if you do not know the correct security code for the unit, **do not** disconnect the battery negative lead, or remove the radio/cassette unit from the vehicle.

The procedure for reprogramming a unit that has been disconnected from its power supply varies from model to model - consult the handbook supplied with the unit for specific details or refer to your Vauxhall dealer.

Introduction

A selection of good tools is a fundamental requirement for anyone contemplating the maintenance and repair of a motor vehicle. For the owner who does not possess any, their purchase will prove a considerable expense, offsetting some of the savings made by doing-it-yourself. However, provided that the tools purchased meet the relevant national safety standards and are of good quality, they will last for many years and prove an extremely worthwhile investment.

To help the average owner to decide which tools are needed to carry out the various tasks detailed in this manual, we have compiled three lists of tools under the following headings: *Maintenance and minor repair*, *Repair and overhaul*, and *Special*. Newcomers to practical mechanics should start off with the *Maintenance and minor repair* tool kit, and confine themselves to the simpler jobs around the vehicle. Then, as confidence and experience grow, more difficult tasks can be undertaken, with extra tools being purchased as, and when, they are needed. In this way, a *Maintenance and minor repair* tool kit can be built up into a *Repair and overhaul* tool kit over a considerable period of time, without any major cash outlays. The experienced do-it-yourselfer will have a tool kit good enough for most repair and overhaul procedures, and will add tools from the *Special* category when it is felt that the expense is justified by the amount of use to which these tools will be put.

Maintenance and minor repair tool kit

The tools given in this list should be considered as a minimum requirement if routine maintenance, servicing and minor repair operations are to be undertaken. We recommend the purchase of combination spanners (ring one end, open-ended the other); although more expensive than open-ended ones, they do give the advantages of both types of spanner.

- ☐ *Combination spanners:*
  Metric - 8 to 19 mm inclusive
- ☐ *Adjustable spanner - 35 mm jaw (approx.)*
- ☐ *Spark plug spanner (with rubber insert) - petrol models*
- ☐ *Spark plug gap adjustment tool - petrol models*
- ☐ *Set of feeler gauges*
- ☐ *Brake bleed nipple spanner*
- ☐ *Screwdrivers:*
  Flat blade - 100 mm long x 6 mm dia
  Cross blade - 100 mm long x 6 mm dia
  Torx - various sizes (not all vehicles)
- ☐ *Combination pliers*
- ☐ *Hacksaw (junior)*
- ☐ *Tyre pump*
- ☐ *Tyre pressure gauge*
- ☐ *Oil can*
- ☐ *Oil filter removal tool*
- ☐ *Fine emery cloth*
- ☐ *Wire brush (small)*
- ☐ *Funnel (medium size)*
- ☐ *Sump drain plug key (not all vehicles)*

Repair and overhaul tool kit

These tools are virtually essential for anyone undertaking any major repairs to a motor vehicle, and are additional to those given in the *Maintenance and minor repair* list. Included in this list is a comprehensive set of sockets. Although these are expensive, they will be found invaluable as they are so versatile - particularly if various drives are included in the set. We recommend the half-inch square-drive type, as this can be used with most proprietary torque wrenches.

The tools in this list will sometimes need to be supplemented by tools from the *Special* list:

- ☐ *Sockets (or box spanners) to cover range in previous list (including Torx sockets)*
- ☐ *Reversible ratchet drive (for use with sockets)*
- ☐ *Extension piece, 250 mm (for use with sockets)*
- ☐ *Universal joint (for use with sockets)*
- ☐ *Flexible handle or sliding T "breaker bar" (for use with sockets)*
- ☐ *Torque wrench (for use with sockets)*
- ☐ *Self-locking grips*
- ☐ *Ball pein hammer*
- ☐ *Soft-faced mallet (plastic or rubber)*
- ☐ *Screwdrivers:*
  Flat blade - long & sturdy, short (chubby), and narrow (electrician's) types
  Cross blade – long & sturdy, and short (chubby) types
- ☐ *Pliers:*
  Long-nosed
  Side cutters (electrician's)
  Circlip (internal and external)
- ☐ *Cold chisel - 25 mm*
- ☐ *Scriber*
- ☐ *Scraper*
- ☐ *Centre-punch*
- ☐ *Pin punch*
- ☐ *Hacksaw*
- ☐ *Brake hose clamp*
- ☐ *Brake/clutch bleeding kit*
- ☐ *Selection of twist drills*
- ☐ *Steel rule/straight-edge*
- ☐ *Allen keys (inc. splined/Torx type)*
- ☐ *Selection of files*
- ☐ *Wire brush*
- ☐ *Axle stands*
- ☐ *Jack (strong trolley or hydraulic type)*
- ☐ *Light with extension lead*
- ☐ *Universal electrical multi-meter*

Sockets and reversible ratchet drive

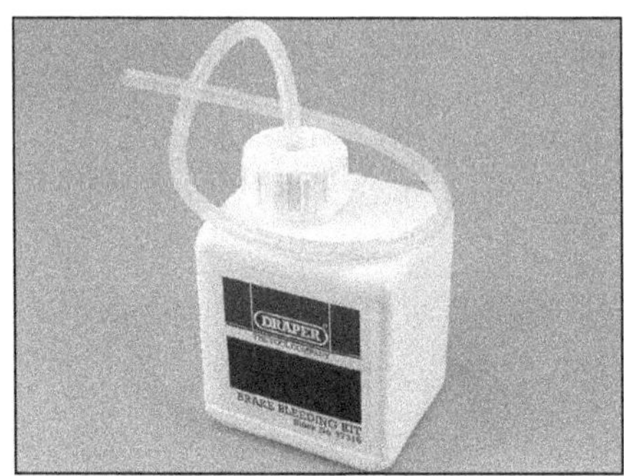

Brake bleeding kit

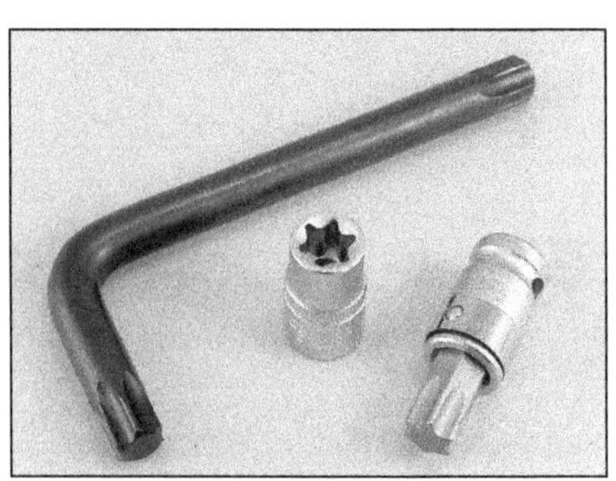
Torx key, socket and bit

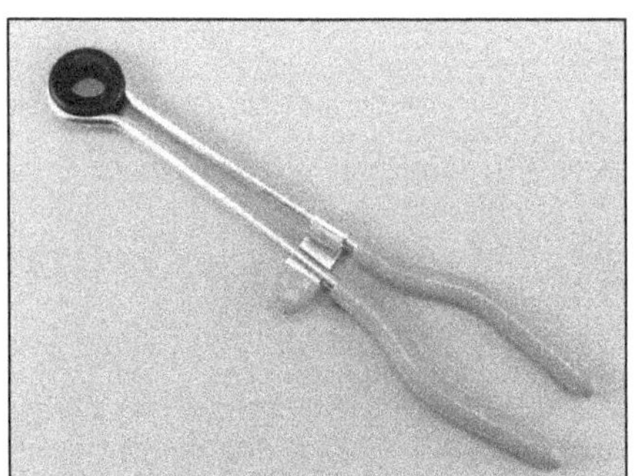
Hose clamp

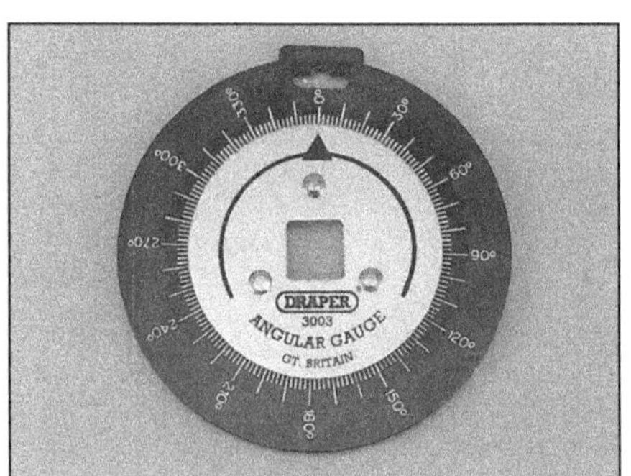

Angular-tightening gauge

Special tools

The tools in this list are those which are not used regularly, are expensive to buy, or which need to be used in accordance with their manufacturers' instructions. Unless relatively difficult mechanical jobs are undertaken frequently, it will not be economic to buy many of these tools. Where this is the case, you could consider clubbing together with friends (or joining a motorists' club) to make a joint purchase, or borrowing the tools against a deposit from a local garage or tool hire specialist. It is worth noting that many of the larger DIY superstores now carry a large range of special tools for hire at modest rates.

The following list contains only those tools and instruments freely available to the public, and not those special tools produced by the vehicle manufacturer specifically for its dealer network. You will find occasional references to these manufacturers' special tools in the text of this manual. Generally, an alternative method of doing the job without the vehicle manufacturers' special tool is given. However, sometimes there is no alternative to using them. Where this is the case and the relevant tool cannot be bought or borrowed, you will have to entrust the work to a dealer.

- ☐ *Angular-tightening gauge*
- ☐ *Valve spring compressor*
- ☐ *Valve grinding tool*
- ☐ *Piston ring compressor*
- ☐ *Piston ring removal/installation tool*
- ☐ *Cylinder bore hone*
- ☐ *Balljoint separator*
- ☐ *Coil spring compressors (where applicable)*
- ☐ *Two/three-legged hub and bearing puller*
- ☐ *Impact screwdriver*
- ☐ *Micrometer and/or vernier calipers*
- ☐ *Dial gauge*
- ☐ *Stroboscopic timing light*
- ☐ *Dwell angle meter/tachometer*
- ☐ *Fault code reader*
- ☐ *Cylinder compression gauge*
- ☐ *Hand-operated vacuum pump and gauge*
- ☐ *Clutch plate alignment set*
- ☐ *Brake shoe steady spring cup removal tool*
- ☐ *Bush and bearing removal/installation set*
- ☐ *Stud extractors*
- ☐ *Tap and die set*
- ☐ *Lifting tackle*
- ☐ *Trolley jack*

Buying tools

Reputable motor accessory shops and superstores often offer excellent quality tools at discount prices, so it pays to shop around.

Remember, you don't have to buy the most expensive items on the shelf, but it is always advisable to steer clear of the very cheap tools. Beware of 'bargains' offered on market stalls or at car boot sales. There are plenty of good tools around at reasonable prices, but always aim to purchase items which meet the relevant national safety standards. If in doubt, ask the proprietor or manager of the shop for advice before making a purchase.

Care and maintenance of tools

Having purchased a reasonable tool kit, it is necessary to keep the tools in a clean and serviceable condition. After use, always wipe off any dirt, grease and metal particles using a clean, dry cloth, before putting the tools away. Never leave them lying around after they have been used. A simple tool rack on the garage or workshop wall for items such as screwdrivers and pliers is a good idea. Store all normal spanners and sockets in a metal box. Any measuring instruments, gauges, meters, etc, must be carefully stored where they cannot be damaged or become rusty.

Take a little care when tools are used. Hammer heads inevitably become marked, and screwdrivers lose the keen edge on their blades from time to time. A little timely attention with emery cloth or a file will soon restore items like this to a good finish.

Working facilities

Not to be forgotten when discussing tools is the workshop itself. If anything more than routine maintenance is to be carried out, a suitable working area becomes essential.

It is appreciated that many an owner-mechanic is forced by circumstances to remove an engine or similar item without the benefit of a garage or workshop. Having done this, any repairs should always be done under the cover of a roof.

Wherever possible, any dismantling should be done on a clean, flat workbench or table at a suitable working height.

Any workbench needs a vice; one with a jaw opening of 100 mm is suitable for most jobs. As mentioned previously, some clean dry storage space is also required for tools, as well as for any lubricants, cleaning fluids, touch-up paints etc, which become necessary.

Another item which may be required, and which has a much more general usage, is an electric drill with a chuck capacity of at least 8 mm. This, together with a good range of twist drills, is virtually essential for fitting accessories.

Last, but not least, always keep a supply of old newspapers and clean, lint-free rags available, and try to keep any working area as clean as possible.

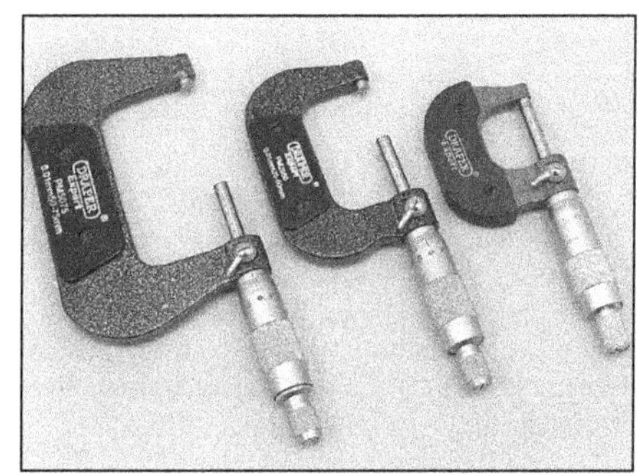

Micrometers

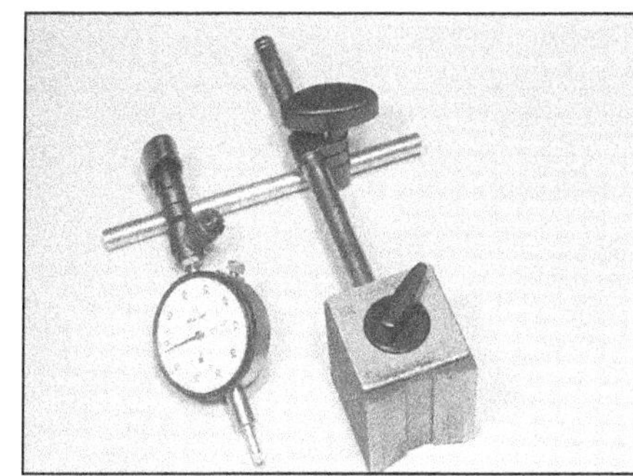

Dial test indicator ("dial gauge")

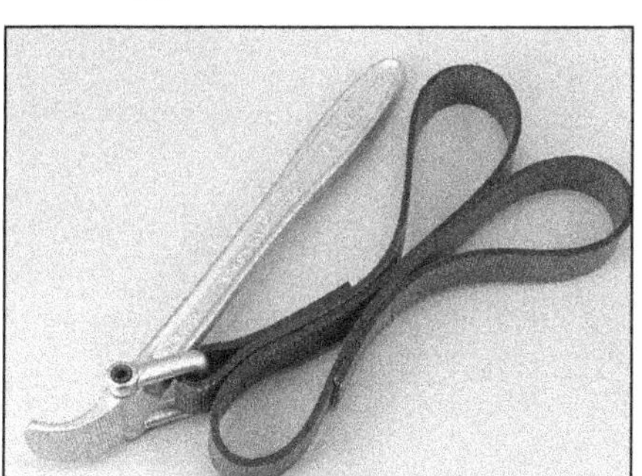

Strap wrench

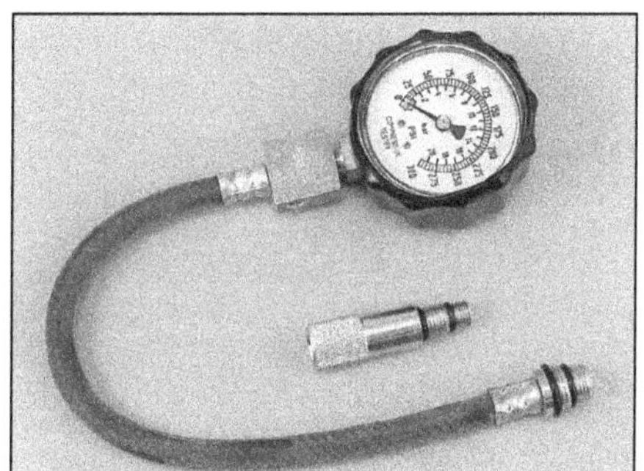

Compression tester

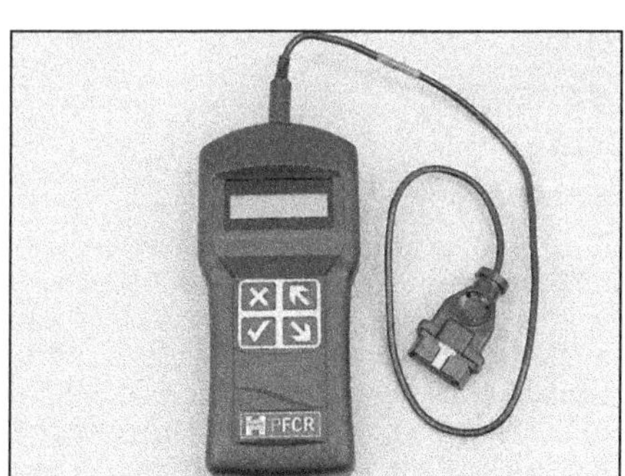

Fault code reader

This is a guide to getting your vehicle through the MOT test. Obviously it will not be possible to examine the vehicle to the same standard as the professional MOT tester. However, working through the following checks will enable you to identify any problem areas before submitting the vehicle for the test.

Where a testable component is in borderline condition, the tester has discretion in deciding whether to pass or fail it. The basis of such discretion is whether the tester would be happy for a close relative or friend to use the vehicle with the component in that condition. If the vehicle presented is clean and evidently well cared for, the tester may be more inclined to pass a borderline component than if the vehicle is scruffy and apparently neglected.

It has only been possible to summarise the test requirements here, based on the regulations in force at the time of printing. Test standards are becoming increasingly stringent, although there are some exemptions for older vehicles.

An assistant will be needed to help carry out some of these checks.

The checks have been sub-divided into four categories, as follows:

1 Checks carried out **FROM THE DRIVER'S SEAT**

2 Checks carried out **WITH THE VEHICLE ON THE GROUND**

3 Checks carried out **WITH THE VEHICLE RAISED AND THE WHEELS FREE TO TURN**

4 Checks carried out on **YOUR VEHICLE'S EXHAUST EMISSION SYSTEM**

1 Checks carried out FROM THE DRIVER'S SEAT

Handbrake

□ Test the operation of the handbrake. Excessive travel (too many clicks) indicates incorrect brake or cable adjustment.

□ Check that the handbrake cannot be released by tapping the lever sideways. Check the security of the lever mountings.

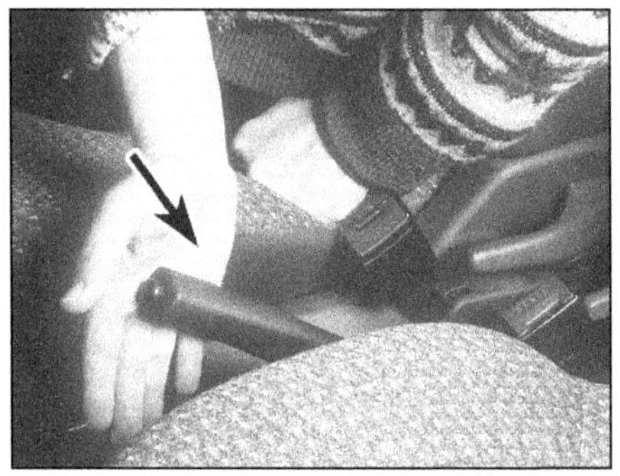

Footbrake

□ Depress the brake pedal and check that it does not creep down to the floor, indicating a master cylinder fault. Release the pedal, wait a few seconds, then depress it again. If the pedal travels nearly to the floor before firm resistance is felt, brake adjustment or repair is necessary. If the pedal feels spongy, there is air in the hydraulic system which must be removed by bleeding.

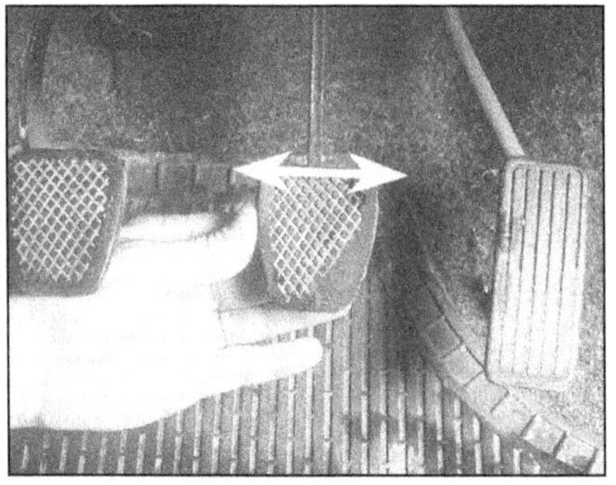

□ Check that the brake pedal is secure and in good condition. Check also for signs of fluid leaks on the pedal, floor or carpets, which would indicate failed seals in the brake master cylinder.

□ Check the servo unit (when applicable) by operating the brake pedal several times, then keeping the pedal depressed and starting the engine. As the engine starts, the pedal will move down slightly. If not, the vacuum hose or the servo itself may be faulty.

Steering wheel and column

□ Examine the steering wheel for fractures or looseness of the hub, spokes or rim.

□ Move the steering wheel from side to side and then up and down. Check that the steering wheel is not loose on the column, indicating wear or a loose retaining nut. Continue moving the steering wheel as before, but also turn it slightly from left to right.

□ Check that the steering wheel is not loose on the column, and that there is no abnormal

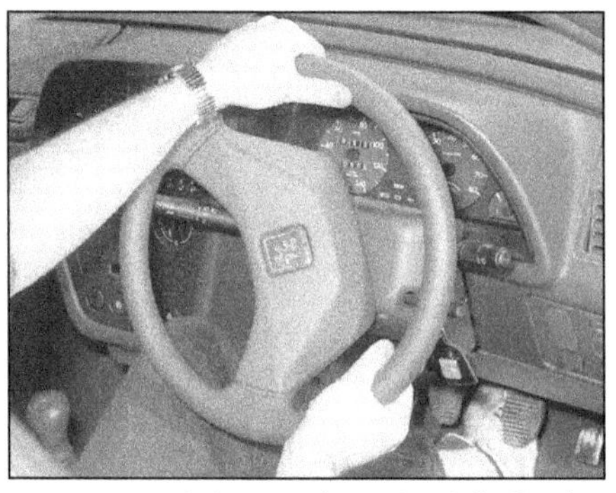

movement of the steering wheel, indicating wear in the column support bearings or couplings.

Windscreen, mirrors and sunvisor

□ The windscreen must be free of cracks or other significant damage within the driver's field of view. (Small stone chips are acceptable.) Rear view mirrors must be secure, intact, and capable of being adjusted.

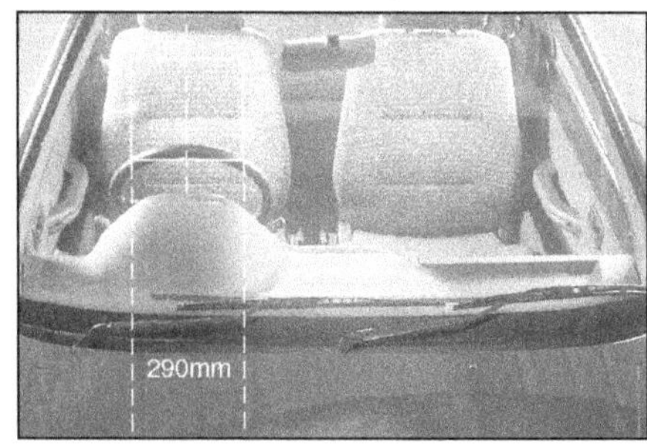

□ The driver's sunvisor must be capable of being stored in the "up" position.

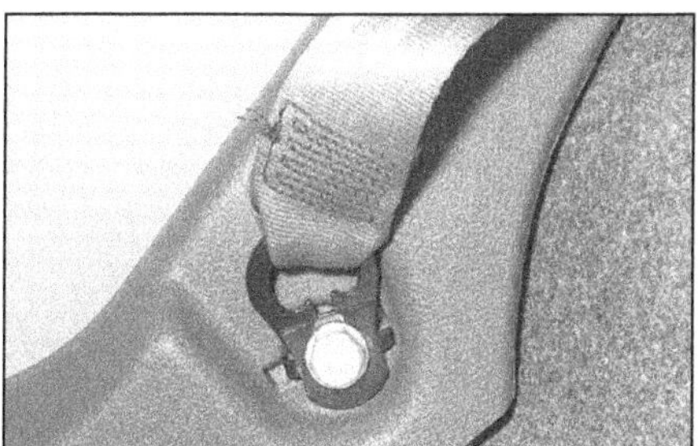

Seat belts and seats

Note: *The following checks are applicable to all seat belts, front and rear.*

☐ Examine the webbing of all the belts (including rear belts if fitted) for cuts, serious fraying or deterioration. Fasten and unfasten each belt to check the buckles. If applicable, check the retracting mechanism. Check the security of all seat belt mountings accessible from inside the vehicle.

☐ Seat belts with pre-tensioners, once activated, have a "flag" or similar showing on the seat belt stalk. This, in itself, is not a reason for test failure.

☐ The front seats themselves must be securely attached and the backrests must lock in the upright position.

Doors

☐ Both front doors must be able to be opened and closed from outside and inside, and must latch securely when closed.

2 Checks carried out WITH THE VEHICLE ON THE GROUND

Vehicle identification

☐ Number plates must be in good condition, secure and legible, with letters and numbers correctly spaced – spacing at (A) should be at least twice that at (B).

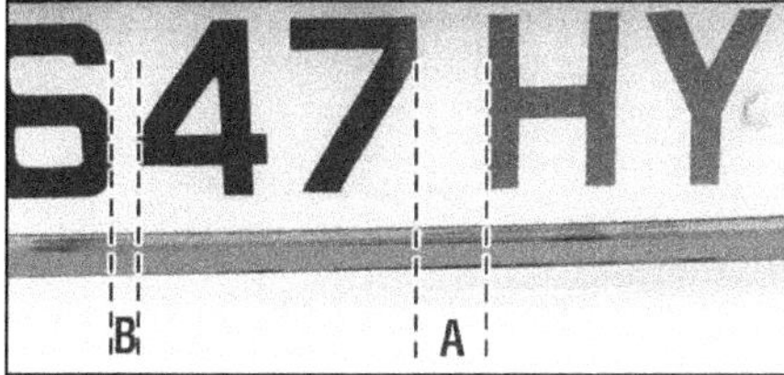

☐ The VIN plate and/or homologation plate must be legible.

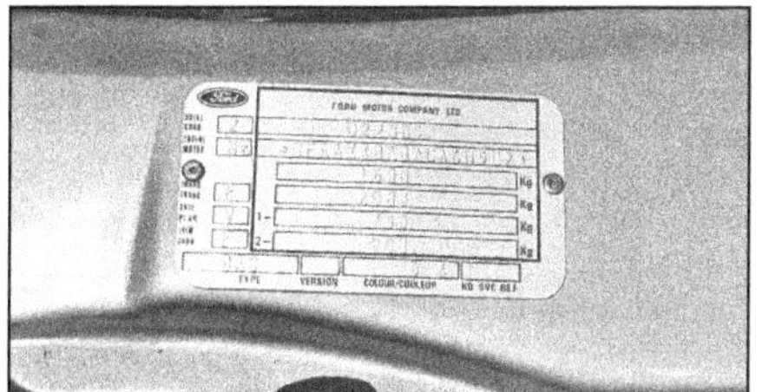

Electrical equipment

☐ Switch on the ignition and check the operation of the horn.

☐ Check the windscreen washers and wipers, examining the wiper blades; renew damaged or perished blades. Also check the operation of the stop-lights.

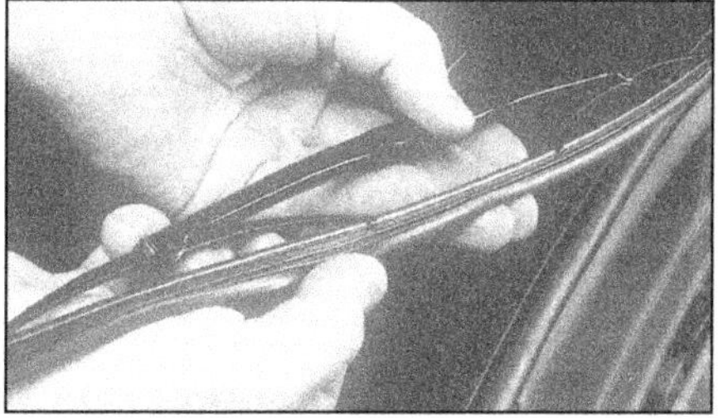

☐ Check the operation of the sidelights and number plate lights. The lenses and reflectors must be secure, clean and undamaged.

☐ Check the operation and alignment of the headlights. The headlight reflectors must not be tarnished and the lenses must be undamaged.

☐ Switch on the ignition and check the operation of the direction indicators (including the instrument panel tell-tale) and the hazard warning lights. Operation of the sidelights and stop-lights must not affect the indicators - if it does, the cause is usually a bad earth at the rear light cluster.

☐ Check the operation of the rear foglight(s), including the warning light on the instrument panel or in the switch.

☐ The ABS warning light must illuminate in accordance with the manufacturers' design. For most vehicles, the ABS warning light should illuminate when the ignition is switched on, and (if the system is operating properly) extinguish after a few seconds. Refer to the owner's handbook.

Footbrake

☐ Examine the master cylinder, brake pipes and servo unit for leaks, loose mountings, corrosion or other damage.

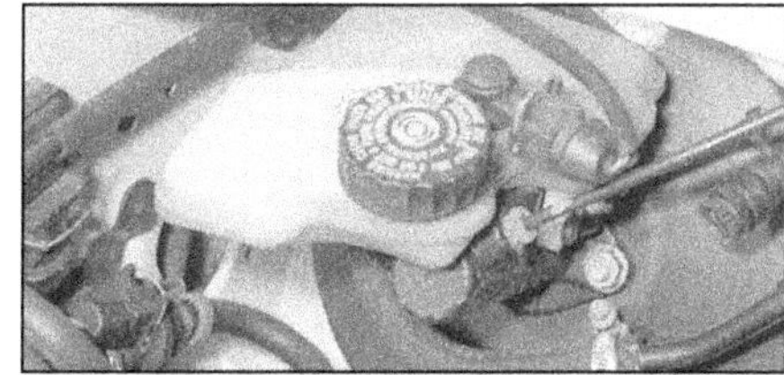

☐ The fluid reservoir must be secure and the fluid level must be between the upper (**A**) and lower (**B**) markings.

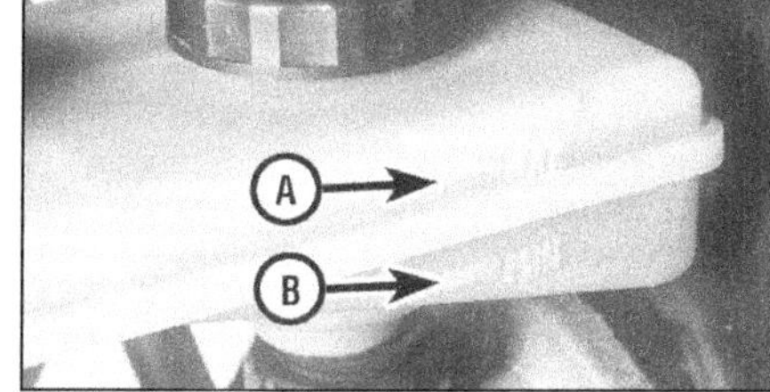

☐ Inspect both front brake flexible hoses for cracks or deterioration of the rubber. Turn the steering from lock to lock, and ensure that the hoses do not contact the wheel, tyre, or any part of the steering or suspension mechanism. With the brake pedal firmly depressed, check the hoses for bulges or leaks under pressure.

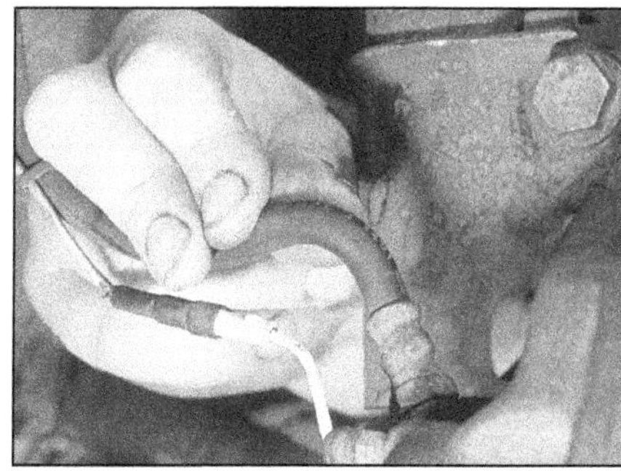

Steering and suspension

☐ Have your assistant turn the steering wheel from side to side slightly, up to the point where the steering gear just begins to transmit this movement to the roadwheels. Check for excessive free play between the steering wheel and the steering gear, indicating wear or insecurity of the steering column joints, the column-to-steering gear coupling, or the steering gear itself.

☐ Have your assistant turn the steering wheel more vigorously in each direction, so that the roadwheels just begin to turn. As this is done, examine all the steering joints, linkages, fittings and attachments. Renew any component that shows signs of wear or damage. On vehicles with power steering, check the security and condition of the steering pump, drivebelt and hoses.

☐ Check that the vehicle is standing level, and at approximately the correct ride height.

Shock absorbers

☐ Depress each corner of the vehicle in turn, then release it. The vehicle should rise and then settle in its normal position. If the vehicle continues to rise and fall, the shock absorber is defective. A shock absorber which has seized will also cause the vehicle to fail.

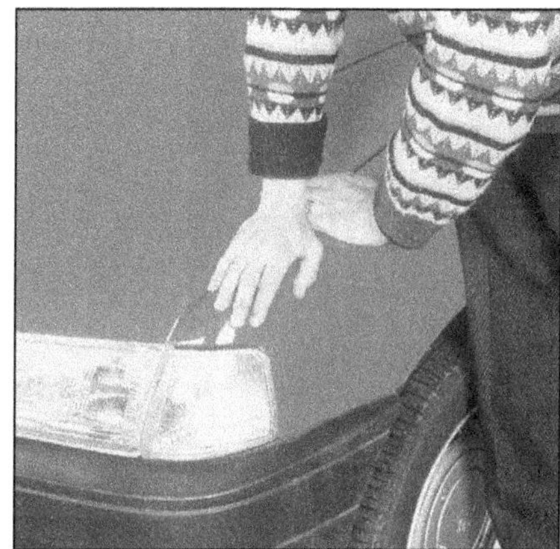

Exhaustive system

□ Start the engine. With your assistant holding a rag over the tailpipe, check the entire system for leaks. Repair or renew leaking sections.

3 Checks carried out WITH THE VEHICLE RAISED AND THE WHEELS FREE TO TURN

Jack up the front and rear of the vehicle, and securely support it on axle stands. Position the stands clear of the suspension assemblies. Ensure that the wheels are clear of the ground and that the steering can be turned from lock to lock.

Steering mechanism

□ Have your assistant turn the steering from lock to lock. Check that the steering turns smoothly, and that no part of the steering mechanism, including a wheel or tyre, fouls any brake hose or pipe or any part of the body structure.

□ Examine the steering rack rubber gaiters for damage or insecurity of the retaining clips. If power steering is fitted, check for signs of damage or leakage of the fluid hoses, pipes or connections. Also check for excessive stiffness or binding of the steering, a missing split pin or locking device, or severe corrosion of the body structure within 30 cm of any steering component attachment point.

Front and rear suspension and wheel bearings

□ Starting at the front right-hand side, grasp the roadwheel at the 3 o'clock and 9 o'clock positions and rock gently but firmly. Check for free play or insecurity at the wheel bearings, suspension balljoints, or suspension mountings, pivots and attachments.

□ Now grasp the wheel at the 12 o'clock and 6 o'clock positions and repeat the previous inspection. Spin the wheel, and check for roughness or tightness of the front wheel bearing.

□ If excess free play is suspected at a component pivot point, this can be confirmed by using a large screwdriver or similar tool and levering between the mounting and the component attachment. This will confirm whether the wear is in the pivot bush, its retaining bolt, or in the mounting itself (the bolt holes can often become elongated).

□ Carry out all the above checks at the other front wheel, and then at both rear wheels.

Springs and shock absorbers

□ Examine the suspension struts (when applicable) for serious fluid leakage, corrosion, or damage to the casing. Also check the security of the mounting points.

□ If coil springs are fitted, check that the spring ends locate in their seats, and that the spring is not corroded, cracked or broken.

□ If leaf springs are fitted, check that all leaves are intact, that the axle is securely attached to each spring, and that there is no deterioration of the spring eye mountings, bushes, and shackles.

□ The same general checks apply to vehicles fitted with other suspension types, such as torsion bars, hydraulic displacer units, etc. Ensure that all mountings and attachments are secure, that there are no signs of excessive wear, corrosion or damage, and (on hydraulic types) that there are no fluid leaks or damaged pipes.

□ Inspect the shock absorbers for signs of serious fluid leakage. Check for wear of the mounting bushes or attachments, or damage to the body of the unit.

Driveshafts (fwd vehicles only)

□ Rotate each front wheel in turn and inspect the constant velocity joint gaiters for splits or damage. Also check that each driveshaft is straight and undamaged.

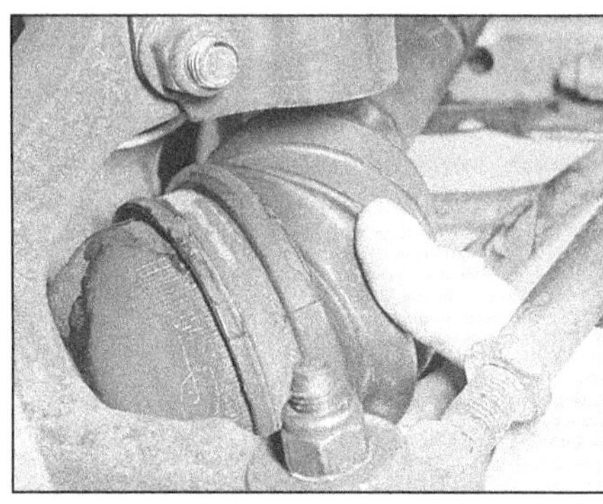

Braking system

□ If possible without dismantling, check brake pad wear and disc condition. Ensure that the friction lining material has not worn excessively, (A) and that the discs are not fractured, pitted, scored or badly worn (B).

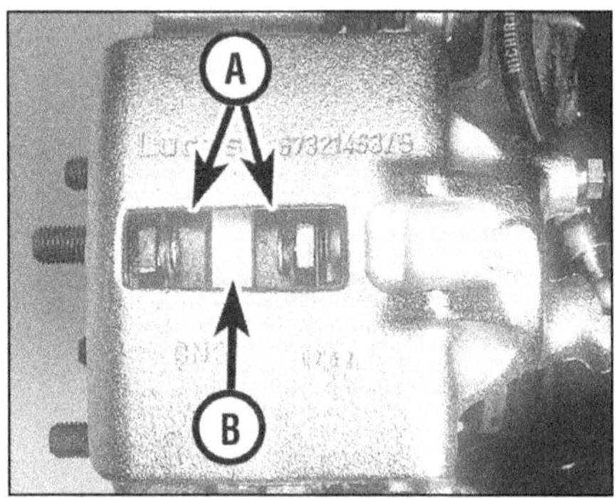

□ Examine all the rigid brake pipes underneath the vehicle, and the flexible hose(s) at the rear. Look for corrosion, chafing or insecurity of the pipes, and for signs of bulging under pressure, chafing, splits or deterioration of the flexible hoses.

□ Look for signs of fluid leaks at the brake calipers or on the brake backplates. Repair or renew leaking components.

□ Slowly spin each wheel, while your assistant depresses and releases the footbrake. Ensure that each brake is operating and does not bind when the pedal is released.

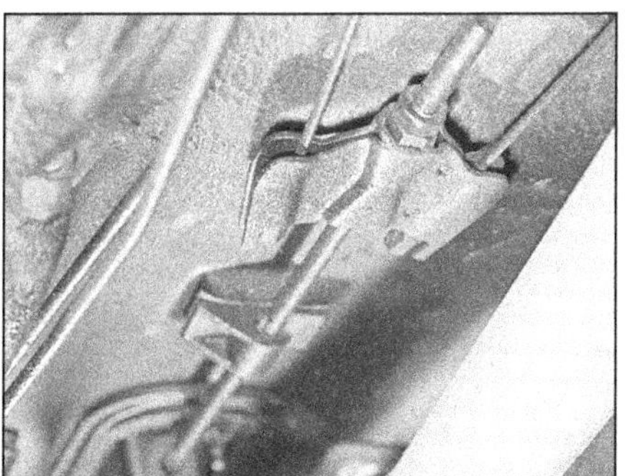

□ Examine the handbrake mechanism, checking for frayed or broken cables, excessive corrosion, or wear or insecurity of the linkage. Check that the mechanism works on each relevant wheel, and releases fully, without binding.

□ It is not possible to test brake efficiency without special equipment, but a road test can be carried out later to check that the vehicle pulls up in a straight line.

Fuel and exhaust systems

□ Inspect the fuel tank (including the filler cap), fuel pipes, hoses and unions. All components must be secure and free from leaks.

□ Examine the exhaust system over its entire length, checking for any damaged, broken or missing mountings, security of the retaining clamps and rust or corrosion.

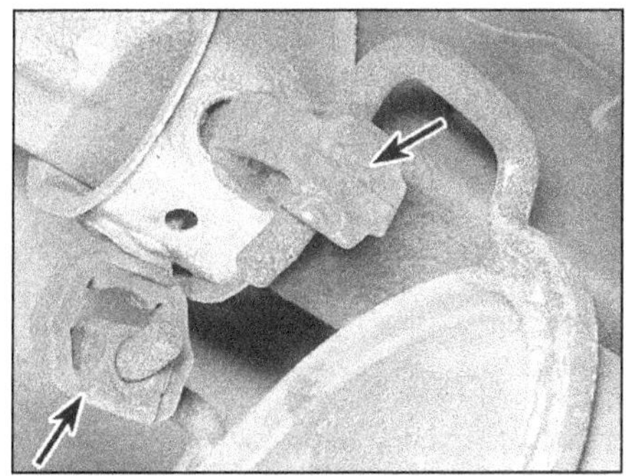

Wheels and tyres

□ Examine the sidewalls and tread area of each tyre in turn. Check for cuts, tears, lumps, bulges, separation of the tread, and exposure of the ply or cord due to wear or damage. Check that the tyre bead is correctly seated on the wheel rim, that the valve is sound and properly seated, and that the wheel is not distorted or damaged.

□ Check that the tyres are of the correct size for the vehicle, that they are of the same size and type on each axle, and that the pressures are correct.

□ Check the tyre tread depth. The legal minimum at the time of writing is 1.6 mm over at least three-quarters of the tread width. Abnormal tread wear may indicate incorrect front wheel alignment.

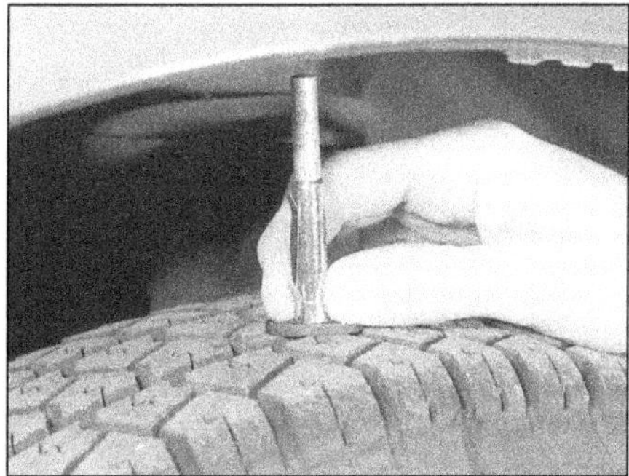

Body corrosion

□ Check the condition of the entire vehicle structure for signs of corrosion in load-bearing areas. (These include chassis box sections, side sills, cross-members, pillars, and all suspension, steering, braking system and seat belt mountings and anchorages.) Any corrosion which has seriously reduced the thickness of a load-bearing area is likely to cause the vehicle to fail. In this case professional repairs are likely to be needed.

□ Damage or corrosion which causes sharp or otherwise dangerous edges to be exposed will also cause the vehicle to fail.

4 Checks carried out on **YOUR VEHICLE'S EXHAUST EMISSION SYSTEM**

Petrol models

□ Have the engine at normal operating temperature, and make sure that it is in good tune (ignition system in good order, air filter element clean, etc).

□ Before any measurements are carried out, raise the engine speed to around 2500 rpm, and hold it at this speed for 20 seconds. Allow the engine speed to return to idle, and watch for smoke emissions from the exhaust tailpipe. If the idle speed is obviously much too high, or if dense blue or clearly-visible black smoke comes from the tailpipe for more than 5 seconds, the vehicle will fail. As a rule of thumb, blue smoke signifies oil being burnt (engine wear) while black smoke signifies unburnt fuel (dirty air cleaner element, or other carburettor or fuel system fault).

□ An exhaust gas analyser capable of measuring carbon monoxide (CO) and hydrocarbons (HC) is now needed. If such an instrument cannot be hired or borrowed, a local garage may agree to perform the check for a small fee.

CO emissions (mixture)

□ At the time of writing, for vehicles first used between 1st August 1975 and 31st July 1986 (P to C registration), the CO level must not exceed 4.5% by volume. For vehicles first used between 1st August 1986 and 31st July 1992 (D to J registration), the CO level must not exceed 3.5% by volume. Vehicles first used after 1st August 1992 (K registration) must conform to the manufacturer's specification. The MOT tester has access to a DOT database or emissions handbook, which lists the CO and HC limits for each make and model of vehicle. The CO level is measured with the engine at idle speed, and at "fast idle". The following limits are given as a general guide:

At idle speed -
CO level no more than 0.5%
At "fast idle" (2500 to 3000 rpm) -
CO level no more than 0.3%
(Minimum oil temperature 60°C)

□ If the CO level cannot be reduced far enough to pass the test (and the fuel and ignition systems are otherwise in good condition) then the carburettor is badly worn, or there is some problem in the fuel injection system or catalytic converter (as applicable).

HC emissions

□ With the CO within limits, HC emissions for vehicles first used between 1st August 1975 and 31st July 1992 (P to J registration) must not exceed 1200 ppm. Vehicles first used after 1st August 1992 (K registration) must conform to the manufacturer's specification. The MOT tester has access to a DOT database or emissions handbook, which lists the CO and HC limits for each make and model of vehicle. The HC level is measured with the engine at "fast idle". The following is given as a general guide:

At "fast idle" (2500 to 3000 rpm) -
HC level no more than 200 ppm
(Minimum oil temperature 60°C)

□ Excessive HC emissions are caused by incomplete combustion, the causes of which can include oil being burnt, mechanical wear and ignition/fuel system malfunction.

Diesel models

□ The only emission test applicable to Diesel engines is the measuring of exhaust smoke density. The test involves accelerating the engine several times to its maximum unloaded speed.

Note: *It is of the utmost importance that the engine timing belt is in good condition before the test is carried out.*

□ The limits for Diesel engine exhaust smoke, introduced in September 1995 are:

Vehicles first used before 1st August 1979:
Exempt from metered smoke testing, but must not emit "dense blue or clearly visible black smoke for a period of more than 5 seconds at idle" or "dense blue or clearly visible black smoke during acceleration which would obscure the view of other road users".

Non-turbocharged vehicles first used after 1st August 1979: $2.5m^{-1}$

Turbocharged vehicles first used after 1st August 1979: $3.0m^{-1}$

□ Excessive smoke can be caused by a dirty air cleaner element. Otherwise, professional advice may be needed to find the cause.

Engine

- ☐ Engine fails to rotate when attempting to start
- ☐ Engine rotates, but will not start
- ☐ Engine difficult to start when cold
- ☐ Engine difficult to start when hot
- ☐ Starter motor noisy or excessively-rough in engagement
- ☐ Engine starts, but stops immediately
- ☐ Engine idles erratically
- ☐ Engine misfires at idle speed
- ☐ Engine misfires throughout the driving speed range
- ☐ Engine hesitates on acceleration
- ☐ Engine stalls
- ☐ Engine lacks power
- ☐ Engine backfires
- ☐ Oil pressure warning light illuminated with engine running
- ☐ Engine runs-on after switching off
- ☐ Engine noises

Cooling system

- ☐ Overheating
- ☐ Overcooling
- ☐ External coolant leakage
- ☐ Internal coolant leakage
- ☐ Corrosion

Fuel and exhaust systems

- ☐ Excessive fuel consumption
- ☐ Fuel leakage and/or fuel odour
- ☐ Excessive noise or fumes from exhaust system

Clutch

- ☐ Pedal travels to floor - no pressure or very little resistance
- ☐ Clutch fails to disengage (unable to select gears).
- ☐ Clutch slips (engine speed increases, with no increase in vehicle speed).
- ☐ Judder as clutch is engaged
- ☐ Noise when depressing or releasing clutch pedal

Manual transmission

- ☐ Noisy in neutral with engine running
- ☐ Noisy in one particular gear
- ☐ Difficulty engaging gears
- ☐ Jumps out of gear
- ☐ Vibration
- ☐ Lubricant leaks

Automatic transmission

- ☐ Fluid leakage
- ☐ Transmission fluid brown, or has burned smell
- ☐ General gear selection problems
- ☐ Transmission will not downshift (kickdown) with accelerator pedal fully depressed
- ☐ Engine will not start in any gear, or starts in gears other than Park or Neutral
- ☐ Transmission slips, shifts roughly, is noisy, or has no drive in forward or reverse gears

Driveshafts

- ☐ Vibration when accelerating or decelerating
- ☐ Clicking or knocking noise on turns (at slow speed on full-lock)

Differential and propeller shaft

- ☐ Vibration when accelerating or decelerating
- ☐ Low pitched whining; increasing with road speed

Braking system

- ☐ Vehicle pulls to one side under braking
- ☐ Noise (grinding or high-pitched squeal) when brakes applied
- ☐ Excessive brake pedal travel
- ☐ Brake pedal feels spongy when depressed
- ☐ Excessive brake pedal effort required to stop vehicle
- ☐ Judder felt through brake pedal or steering wheel when braking
- ☐ Brakes binding
- ☐ Rear wheels locking under normal braking

Suspension and steering

- ☐ Vehicle pulls to one side
- ☐ Wheel wobble and vibration
- ☐ Excessive pitching and/or rolling around corners, or during braking
- ☐ Wandering or general instability
- ☐ Excessively-stiff steering
- ☐ Excessive play in steering
- ☐ Lack of power assistance
- ☐ Tyre wear excessive

Electrical system

- ☐ Battery will not hold a charge for more than a few days
- ☐ Ignition/no-charge warning light remains illuminated with engine running
- ☐ Ignition/no-charge warning light fails to come on
- ☐ Lights inoperative
- ☐ Instrument readings inaccurate or erratic
- ☐ Horn inoperative, or unsatisfactory in operation
- ☐ Windscreen wipers inoperative, or unsatisfactory in operation
- ☐ Windscreen washers inoperative, or unsatisfactory in operation
- ☐ Electric windows inoperative, or unsatisfactory in operation
- ☐ Central locking system inoperative, or unsatisfactory in operation

Introduction

The vehicle owner who does his or her own maintenance according to the recommended service schedules should not have to use this section of the manual very often. Modern component reliability is such that, provided those items subject to wear or deterioration are inspected or renewed at the specified intervals, sudden failure is comparatively rare. Faults do not usually just happen as a result of sudden failure, but develop over a period of time. Major mechanical failures in particular are usually preceded by characteristic symptoms over hundreds or even thousands of miles. Those components which do occasionally fail without warning are often small and easily carried in the vehicle.

With any fault-finding, the first step is to decide where to begin investigations. Sometimes this is obvious, but on other occasions, a little detective work will be necessary. The owner who makes half a dozen haphazard adjustments or replacements may be successful in curing a fault (or its symptoms), but will be none the wiser if the fault recurs, and ultimately may have spent more time and money than was necessary. A calm and logical approach will be found to be more satisfactory in the long run. Always take into account any warning signs or abnormalities that may have been noticed in the period preceding the fault - power loss, high or low gauge readings, unusual smells, etc - and remember that failure of components such as fuses or spark plugs may only be pointers to some underlying fault.

The pages which follow provide an easy-reference guide to the more common problems which may occur during the operation of the vehicle. These problems and their possible causes are grouped under headings denoting various components or systems, such as Engine, Cooling system, etc. The Chapter and/or Section which deals with the problem is also shown in brackets. Whatever the fault, certain basic principles apply. These are as follows:

Verify the fault. This is simply a matter of being sure that you know what the symptoms are before starting work. This is particularly important if you are investigating a fault for someone else, who may not have described it very accurately.

Don't overlook the obvious. For example, if the vehicle won't start, is there fuel in the tank? (Don't take anyone else's word on this particular point, and don't trust the fuel gauge either!) If an electrical fault is indicated, look for loose or broken wires before digging out the test gear.

Cure the disease, not the symptom. Substituting a flat battery with a fully-charged one will get you off the hard shoulder, but if the underlying cause is not attended to, the new battery will go the same way. Similarly, changing oil-fouled spark plugs for a new set will get you moving again, but remember that the reason for the fouling (if it wasn't simply an incorrect grade of plug) will have to be established and corrected.

Don't take anything for granted. Particularly, don't forget that a new component may itself be defective (especially if it's been rattling around in the boot for months), and don't leave components out of a fault diagnosis sequence just because they are new or recently-fitted. When you do finally diagnose a difficult fault, you'll probably realise that all the evidence was there from the start.

Engine

Engine fails to rotate when attempting to start

- ☐ Battery terminal connections loose or corroded (Weekly checks)
- ☐ Battery discharged or faulty (Chapter 5)
- ☐ Broken, loose or disconnected wiring in the starting circuit (Chapter 5)
- ☐ Defective starter solenoid or switch (Chapter 5)
- ☐ Defective starter motor (Chapter 5)
- ☐ Starter pinion or flywheel ring gear teeth loose or broken (Chapters 2 and 5)
- ☐ Engine earth strap broken or disconnected

Engine rotates, but will not start

- ☐ Fuel tank empty
- ☐ Battery discharged (engine rotates slowly) (Chapter 5)
- ☐ Battery terminal connections loose or corroded (Weekly checks)
- ☐ Ignition components damp or damaged (Chapters 1 and 5)
- ☐ Worn, faulty or incorrectly-gapped spark plugs (Chapter 1)
- ☐ Engine management system fault (Chapter 4)
- ☐ Major mechanical failure (eg camshaft drive) (Chapter 2)

Engine difficult to start when cold

- ☐ Battery discharged (Chapter 5)
- ☐ Battery terminal connections loose or corroded (Weekly checks)
- ☐ Worn, faulty or incorrectly-gapped spark plugs (Chapter 1)
- ☐ Engine management system fault (Chapter 4)
- ☐ Low cylinder compressions (Chapter 2)

Engine difficult to start when hot

- ☐ Air filter element dirty or clogged (Chapter 1)
- ☐ Engine management system fault (Chapter 4)
- ☐ Low cylinder compressions (Chapter 2)

Starter motor noisy or excessively-rough in engagement

- ☐ Starter pinion or flywheel ring gear teeth loose or broken (Chapters 2 and 5)
- ☐ Starter motor mounting bolts loose or missing (Chapter 5)
- ☐ Starter motor internal components worn or damaged (Chapter 5)

Engine starts, but stops immediately

- ☐ Vacuum leak at the throttle housing or inlet manifold (Chapter 4)
- ☐ Engine management system fault (Chapter 4)

Engine idles erratically

- ☐ Air filter element clogged (Chapter 1)
- ☐ Vacuum leak at the throttle housing, inlet manifold or associated hoses (Chapter 4)
- ☐ Worn, faulty or incorrectly-gapped spark plugs (Chapter 1)
- ☐ Uneven or low cylinder compressions (Chapter 2)
- ☐ Camshaft lobes worn (Chapter 2)
- ☐ Timing belt incorrectly fitted (Chapter 2)
- ☐ Engine management system fault (Chapter 4)

Engine misfires at idle speed

- ☐ Worn, faulty or incorrectly-gapped spark plugs (Chapter 1)
- ☐ Faulty spark plug HT leads (Chapter 5)
- ☐ Vacuum leak at the throttle housing, inlet manifold or associated hoses (Chapter 4)
- ☐ Engine management system fault (Chapter 4)
- ☐ Uneven or low cylinder compressions (Chapter 2)
- ☐ Disconnected, leaking, or perished emission control system hoses (Chapter 4)

Engine misfires throughout the driving speed range

- ☐ Fuel filter choked (Chapter 1)
- ☐ Fuel pump faulty, or delivery pressure low (Chapter 4)
- ☐ Fuel tank vent blocked, or fuel pipes restricted (Chapter 4)
- ☐ Vacuum leak at the throttle housing, inlet manifold or associated hoses (Chapter 4)
- ☐ Worn, faulty or incorrectly-gapped spark plugs (Chapter 1)
- ☐ Faulty spark plug HT leads (Chapter 5)
- ☐ Faulty DIS module (Chapter 5)
- ☐ Uneven or low cylinder compressions (Chapter 2)
- ☐ Engine management system fault (Chapter 4)

Engine hesitates on acceleration

- ☐ Worn, faulty or incorrectly-gapped spark plugs (Chapter 1)
- ☐ Vacuum leak at the throttle housing, inlet manifold or associated hoses (Chapter 4)
- ☐ Engine management system fault (Chapter 4)

Engine (continued)

Engine stalls

- ☐ Vacuum leak at the throttle housing, inlet manifold or associated hoses (Chapter 4)
- ☐ Fuel filter choked (Chapter 1)
- ☐ Fuel pump faulty, or delivery pressure low (Chapter 4)
- ☐ Fuel tank vent blocked, or fuel pipes restricted (Chapter 4)
- ☐ Engine management system fault (Chapter 4)

Engine lacks power

- ☐ Timing belt incorrectly fitted (Chapter 2)
- ☐ Fuel filter choked (Chapter 1)
- ☐ Fuel pump faulty, or delivery pressure low (Chapter 4)
- ☐ Uneven or low cylinder compressions (Chapter 2)
- ☐ Worn, faulty or incorrectly-gapped spark plugs (Chapter 1)
- ☐ Vacuum leak at the throttle housing, inlet manifold or associated hoses (Chapter 4)
- ☐ Engine management system fault (Chapter 4)
- ☐ Brakes binding (Chapters 1 and 9)
- ☐ Clutch slipping (Chapter 6)

Engine backfires

- ☐ Timing belt incorrectly fitted (Chapter 2)
- ☐ Vacuum leak at the throttle housing, inlet manifold or associated hoses (Chapter 4)
- ☐ Engine management system fault (Chapter 4)

Oil pressure warning light illuminated with engine running

- ☐ Low oil level, or incorrect oil grade (Weekly checks)
- ☐ Faulty oil pressure switch (Chapter 5)
- ☐ Worn engine bearings and/or oil pump (Chapter 2)
- ☐ High engine operating temperature (Chapter 3)
- ☐ Oil pressure relief valve defective (Chapter 2)
- ☐ Oil pick-up strainer clogged (Chapter 2)

Engine runs-on after switching off

- ☐ Excessive carbon build-up in engine (Chapter 2)
- ☐ High engine operating temperature (Chapter 3)
- ☐ Engine management system fault (Chapter 4)

Engine noises

Pre-ignition (pinking) or knocking during acceleration or under load

- ☐ Ignition timing incorrect/ignition system fault (Chapter 5)
- ☐ Incorrect grade of spark plug (Chapter 1)
- ☐ Incorrect grade of fuel (Chapter 4)
- ☐ Vacuum leak at the throttle housing, inlet manifold or associated hoses (Chapter 4)
- ☐ Excessive carbon build-up in engine (Chapter 2)
- ☐ Engine management system fault (Chapter 4)

Whistling or wheezing noises

- ☐ Leaking inlet manifold or throttle housing gasket (Chapter 4)
- ☐ Leaking exhaust manifold gasket or pipe-to-manifold joint (Chapter 4)
- ☐ Leaking vacuum hose (Chapters 4, 5 and 10)
- ☐ Blowing cylinder head gasket (Chapter 2)

Tapping or rattling noises

- ☐ Worn valve gear or camshaft (Chapter 2)
- ☐ Ancillary component fault (coolant pump, alternator, etc) (Chapters 3, 5, etc)

Knocking or thumping noises

- ☐ Worn big-end bearings (regular heavy knocking, perhaps less under load) (Chapter 2)
- ☐ Worn main bearings (rumbling and knocking, perhaps worsening under load) (Chapter 2)
- ☐ Piston slap (most noticeable when cold) (Chapter 2)
- ☐ Ancillary component fault (coolant pump, alternator, etc) (Chapters 3, 5, etc)

Cooling system

Overheating

- ☐ Insufficient coolant in system (Weekly checks)
- ☐ Thermostat faulty (Chapter 3)
- ☐ Radiator core blocked, or grille restricted (Chapter 3)
- ☐ Cooling fan faulty (Chapter 3)
- ☐ Inaccurate temperature gauge sender unit (Chapter 3)
- ☐ Airlock in cooling system (Chapter 3)
- ☐ Pressure cap faulty (Chapter 3)

Overcooling

- ☐ Thermostat faulty (Chapter 3)
- ☐ Inaccurate temperature gauge sender unit (Chapter 3)
- ☐ Cooling fan faulty (Chapter 3)

External coolant leakage

- ☐ Deteriorated or damaged hoses or hose clips (Chapter 1)
- ☐ Radiator core or heater matrix leaking (Chapter 3)
- ☐ Pressure cap faulty (Chapter 3)
- ☐ Coolant pump internal seal leaking (Chapter 3)
- ☐ Coolant pump-to-block seal leaking (Chapter 3)
- ☐ Boiling due to overheating (Chapter 3)
- ☐ Core plug leaking (Chapter 2)

Internal coolant leakage

- ☐ Leaking cylinder head gasket (Chapter 2)
- ☐ Cracked cylinder head or cylinder block (Chapter 2)

Corrosion

- ☐ Infrequent draining and flushing (Chapter 1)
- ☐ Incorrect coolant mixture or inappropriate coolant type (Chapter 1)

Fuel and exhaust systems

Excessive fuel consumption

- ☐ Air filter element dirty or clogged (Chapter 1)
- ☐ Engine management system fault (Chapter 4)

Fuel leakage and/or fuel odour

- ☐ Damaged or corroded fuel tank, pipes or connections (Chapter 4)

Excessive noise or fumes from exhaust system

- ☐ Leaking exhaust system or manifold joints (Chapters 1 and 4)
- ☐ Leaking, corroded or damaged silencers or pipe (Chapters 1 and 4)
- ☐ Broken mountings causing body or suspension contact (Chapter 1)

Clutch

Pedal travels to floor - no pressure or very little resistance

- ☐ Faulty hydraulic release system (Chapter 6)
- ☐ Broken diaphragm spring in clutch pressure plate (Chapter 6)

Clutch fails to disengage (unable to select gears).

- ☐ Faulty hydraulic release system (Chapter 6)
- ☐ Clutch disc sticking on transmission input shaft splines (Chapter 6)
- ☐ Clutch disc sticking to flywheel or pressure plate (Chapter 6)
- ☐ Faulty pressure plate assembly (Chapter 6)
- ☐ Clutch release mechanism worn or incorrectly assembled (Chapter 6)

Clutch slips (engine speed increases, with no increase in vehicle speed).

- ☐ Faulty hydraulic release system (Chapter 6)
- ☐ Clutch disc linings excessively worn (Chapter 6)
- ☐ Clutch disc linings contaminated with oil or grease (Chapter 6)
- ☐ Faulty pressure plate or weak diaphragm spring (Chapter 6)

Judder as clutch is engaged

- ☐ Clutch disc linings contaminated with oil or grease (Chapter 6)
- ☐ Clutch disc linings excessively worn (Chapter 6)
- ☐ Faulty or distorted pressure plate or diaphragm spring (Chapter 6).
- ☐ Worn or loose engine or transmission mountings (Chapter 2)
- ☐ Clutch disc hub or transmission input shaft splines worn (Chapter 6)

Noise when depressing or releasing clutch pedal

- ☐ Worn clutch release bearing (Chapter 6)
- ☐ Worn or dry clutch pedal bushes (Chapter 6)
- ☐ Faulty pressure plate assembly (Chapter 6)
- ☐ Pressure plate diaphragm spring broken (Chapter 6)
- ☐ Broken clutch disc cushioning springs (Chapter 6)

Manual transmission

Noisy in neutral with engine running

- ☐ Input shaft bearings worn (noise apparent with clutch pedal released, but not when depressed) (Chapter 7)*
- ☐ Clutch release bearing worn (noise apparent with clutch pedal depressed, possibly less when released) (Chapter 6)

Noisy in one particular gear

- ☐ Worn, damaged or chipped gear teeth (Chapter 7)*

Difficulty engaging gears

- ☐ Clutch fault (Chapter 6)
- ☐ Worn synchroniser units (Chapter 7)*

Jumps out of gear

- ☐ Worn synchroniser units (Chapter 7)*
- ☐ Worn selector forks (Chapter 7)*

Vibration

- ☐ Lack of oil (Chapter 7)
- ☐ Worn bearings (Chapter 7)*

Lubricant leaks

- ☐ Leaking output shaft oil seal (Chapter 7)
- ☐ Leaking housing joint (Chapter 7)*
- ☐ Leaking input shaft oil seal (Chapter 7)*

**Although the corrective action necessary to remedy the symptoms described is beyond the scope of the home mechanic, the above information should be helpful in isolating the cause of the condition, so that the owner can communicate clearly with a professional mechanic.*

Automatic transmission

Note: *Due to the complexity of the automatic transmission, it is difficult for the home mechanic to properly diagnose and service this unit. For problems other than the following, the vehicle should be taken to a dealer service department or automatic transmission specialist. Do not be too hasty in removing the transmission if a fault is suspected, as most of the testing is carried out with the unit still fitted.*

Fluid leakage

- ☐ Automatic transmission fluid is usually dark in colour. Fluid leaks should not be confused with engine oil, which can easily be blown onto the transmission by airflow.
- ☐ To determine the source of a leak, first remove all built-up dirt and grime from the transmission housing and surrounding areas using a degreasing agent, or by steam-cleaning. Drive the vehicle at low speed, so airflow will not blow the leak far from its source. Raise and support the vehicle, and determine where the leak is coming from. The following are common areas of leakage:
  - *a) Oil pan (Chapter 1 and 7)*
  - *b) Transmission-to-fluid cooler pipes/unions (Chapter 7)*

Transmission fluid brown, or has burned smell

- ☐ Transmission fluid level low, or fluid in need of renewal (Chapter 1)

General gear selection problems

- ☐ Chapter 7 deals with checking and adjusting the selector linkage on automatic transmissions. The following are common problems which may be caused by a poorly-adjusted cable:
  - *a) Engine starting in gears other than Park or Neutral.*
  - *b) Indicator panel indicating a gear other than the one actually being used.*
  - *c) Vehicle moves when in Park or Neutral.*
  - *d) Poor gear shift quality or erratic gear changes.*
- ☐ Refer to Chapter 7 for the selector cable adjustment procedure.

Transmission will not downshift (kickdown) with accelerator pedal fully depressed

- ☐ Low transmission fluid level (Chapter 1)
- ☐ Incorrect accelerator cable adjustment (Chapter 4)
- ☐ Incorrect selector cable adjustment (Chapter 7)

Engine will not start in any gear, or starts in gears other than Park or Neutral

- ☐ Incorrect selector lever position switch adjustment (Chapter 7)
- ☐ Incorrect selector cable adjustment (Chapter 7)

Transmission slips, shifts roughly, is noisy, or has no drive in forward or reverse gears

- ☐ There are many probable causes for the above problems, but the home mechanic should be concerned with only one possibility - fluid level. Before taking the vehicle to a dealer or transmission specialist, check the fluid level and condition of the fluid as described in Chapter 1. Correct the fluid level as necessary, or change the fluid and filter if needed. If the problem persists, professional help will be necessary.

Driveshafts

Vibration when accelerating or decelerating

- ☐ Worn constant velocity joint (Chapter 8)
- ☐ Bent or distorted driveshaft (Chapter 8)

Clicking or knocking noise

- ☐ Worn constant velocity joint (Chapter 8)
- ☐ Lack of constant velocity joint lubricant, possibly due to damaged gaiter (Chapter 8)

Differential and propeller shaft

Vibration when accelerating or decelerating

- ☐ Worn universal joint (Chapter 8)
- ☐ Bent, distorted or unbalanced propeller shaft (Chapter 8)

Low pitched whining; increasing with road speed

- ☐ Worn differential (Chapter 8)

Braking system

Note: *Before assuming that a brake problem exists, make sure that the tyres are in good condition and correctly inflated, that the front wheel alignment is correct, and that the vehicle is not loaded with weight in an unequal manner. Apart from checking the condition of all pipe and hose connections, any faults occurring on the anti-lock braking system should be referred to a Vauxhall dealer for diagnosis.*

Vehicle pulls to one side under braking

- ☐ Worn, defective, damaged or contaminated brake pads on one side (Chapter 9)
- ☐ Seized or partially-seized brake caliper piston (Chapter 9)
- ☐ A mixture of brake pad lining materials fitted between sides (Chapter 9)
- ☐ Brake caliper mounting bolts loose (Chapter 9)
- ☐ Worn or damaged steering or suspension components (Chapters 1 and 10)

Noise (grinding or high-pitched squeal) when brakes applied

- ☐ Brake pad friction lining material worn down to metal backing (Chapter 9)
- ☐ Excessive corrosion of brake disc (may be apparent after the vehicle has been standing for some time (Chapter 9)
- ☐ Foreign object (stone chipping, etc) trapped between brake disc and shield (Chapter 9)

Excessive brake pedal travel

- ☐ Faulty master cylinder (Chapter 9)
- ☐ Air in hydraulic system (Chapter 9)
- ☐ Faulty vacuum servo unit (Chapter 9)

Braking system (continued)

Brake pedal feels spongy when depressed

- ☐ Air in hydraulic system (Chapter 9)
- ☐ Deteriorated flexible rubber brake hoses (Chapter 9)
- ☐ Master cylinder mounting nuts loose (Chapter 9)
- ☐ Faulty master cylinder (Chapter 9)

Excessive brake pedal effort required to stop vehicle

- ☐ Faulty vacuum servo unit (Chapter 9)
- ☐ Disconnected, damaged or insecure brake servo vacuum hose (Chapter 9)
- ☐ Primary or secondary hydraulic circuit failure (Chapter 9)
- ☐ Seized brake caliper piston (Chapter 9)
- ☐ Brake pads incorrectly fitted (Chapter 9)
- ☐ Incorrect grade of brake pads fitted (Chapter 9)
- ☐ Brake pad linings contaminated (Chapter 9)

Judder felt through brake pedal or steering wheel when braking

- ☐ Excessive run-out or distortion of discs (Chapter 9)
- ☐ Brake pad linings worn (Chapter 9)
- ☐ Brake caliper mounting bolts loose (Chapter 9)
- ☐ Wear in suspension or steering components or mountings (Chapters 1 and 10)

Brakes binding

- ☐ Seized brake caliper piston (Chapter 9)
- ☐ Incorrectly-adjusted handbrake mechanism (Chapter 9)
- ☐ Faulty master cylinder (Chapter 9)

Rear wheels locking under normal braking

- ☐ Rear brake pad linings contaminated (Chapter 9)
- ☐ Rear brake discs warped (Chapter 9)

Suspension and steering

Note: *Before diagnosing suspension or steering faults, be sure that the trouble is not due to incorrect tyre pressures, mixtures of tyre types, or binding brakes.*

Vehicle pulls to one side

- ☐ Defective tyre (Weekly checks)
- ☐ Excessive wear in suspension or steering components (Chapters 1 and 10)
- ☐ Incorrect front wheel alignment (Chapter 10)
- ☐ Accident damage to steering or suspension components (Chapter 1)

Wheel wobble and vibration

- ☐ Front roadwheels out of balance (vibration felt mainly through the steering wheel) (Chapters 1 and 10)
- ☐ Rear roadwheels out of balance (vibration felt throughout the vehicle) (Chapters 1 and 10)
- ☐ Roadwheels damaged or distorted (Chapters 1 and 10)
- ☐ Faulty or damaged tyre (Weekly checks)
- ☐ Worn steering or suspension joints, bushes or components (Chapters 1 and 10)
- ☐ Wheel bolts loose (Chapters 1 and 10)

Excessive pitching and/or rolling around corners, or during braking

- ☐ Defective shock absorbers (Chapters 1 and 10)
- ☐ Broken or weak spring and/or suspension component (Chapters 1 and 10)
- ☐ Worn or damaged anti-roll bar or mountings (Chapter 10)

Wandering or general instability

- ☐ Incorrect front wheel alignment (Chapter 10)
- ☐ Worn steering or suspension joints, bushes or components (Chapters 1 and 10)
- ☐ Roadwheels out of balance (Chapters 1 and 10)
- ☐ Faulty or damaged tyre (Weekly checks)
- ☐ Wheel bolts loose (Chapters 1 and 10)
- ☐ Defective shock absorbers (Chapters 1 and 10)

Excessively-stiff steering

- ☐ Seized steering linkage balljoint or suspension balljoint (Chapters 1 and 10)
- ☐ Broken or incorrectly-adjusted auxiliary drivebelt (Chapter 1)
- ☐ Incorrect front wheel alignment (Chapter 10)
- ☐ Steering gear damaged (Chapter 10)

Excessive play in steering

- ☐ Worn steering column/intermediate shaft joints (Chapter 10)
- ☐ Worn track rod balljoints (Chapters 1 and 10)
- ☐ Worn steering box (Chapter 10)
- ☐ Worn steering or suspension joints, bushes or components (Chapters 1 and 10)

Lack of power assistance

- ☐ Broken or worn auxiliary drivebelt (Chapter 1)
- ☐ Incorrect power steering fluid level (Weekly checks)
- ☐ Restriction in power steering fluid hoses (Chapter 10)
- ☐ Faulty power steering pump (Chapter 10)
- ☐ Faulty steering box (Chapter 10)

Tyre wear excessive

Tyres worn on inside or outside edges

- ☐ Tyres under-inflated (wear on both edges) (Weekly checks)
- ☐ Incorrect camber or castor angles (wear on one edge only) (Chapter 10)
- ☐ Worn steering or suspension joints, bushes or components (Chapters 1 and 10)
- ☐ Excessively-hard cornering
- ☐ Accident damage

Tyre treads exhibit feathered edges

- ☐ Incorrect toe setting (Chapter 10)

Tyres worn in centre of tread

- ☐ Tyres over-inflated (Weekly checks)

Tyres worn on inside and outside edges

- ☐ Tyres under-inflated (Weekly checks)

Tyres worn unevenly

- ☐ Tyres/wheels out of balance (Chapter 1)
- ☐ Excessive wheel or tyre run-out (Chapter 1)
- ☐ Worn shock absorbers (Chapters 1 and 10)
- ☐ Faulty tyre (Weekly checks)

Electrical system

Note: *For problems associated with the starting system, refer to the faults listed under Engine earlier in this Section.*

Battery will not hold a charge for more than a few days

- ☐ Battery defective internally (Chapter 5)
- ☐ Battery terminal connections loose or corroded (Weekly checks)
- ☐ Auxiliary drivebelt broken or worn (Chapter 1)
- ☐ Alternator not charging at correct output (Chapter 5)
- ☐ Alternator or voltage regulator faulty (Chapter 5)
- ☐ Short-circuit causing continual battery drain (Chapters 5 and 12)

Ignition/no-charge warning light remains illuminated with engine running

- ☐ Auxiliary drivebelt broken or worn (Chapter 1)
- ☐ Alternator brushes worn, sticking, or dirty (Chapter 5)
- ☐ Alternator brush springs weak or broken (Chapter 5)
- ☐ Internal fault in alternator or voltage regulator (Chapter 5)
- ☐ Broken, disconnected, or loose wiring in charging circuit (Chapter 5)

Ignition/no-charge warning light fails to come on

- ☐ Warning light bulb blown (Chapter 12)
- ☐ Broken, disconnected, or loose wiring in warning light circuit (Chapter 12)
- ☐ Alternator faulty (Chapter 5)

Lights inoperative

- ☐ Bulb blown (Chapter 12)
- ☐ Corrosion of bulb or bulbholder contacts (Chapter 12)
- ☐ Blown fuse (Chapter 12)
- ☐ Faulty relay (Chapter 12)
- ☐ Broken, loose, or disconnected wiring (Chapter 12)
- ☐ Faulty switch (Chapter 12)

Instrument readings inaccurate or erratic

Instrument readings increase with engine speed

- ☐ Faulty voltage regulator (Chapter 12)

Fuel or temperature gauges give no reading

- ☐ Faulty gauge sender unit (Chapters 3 and 4)
- ☐ Wiring open-circuit (Chapter 12)
- ☐ Faulty gauge (Chapter 12)

Fuel or temperature gauges give continuous maximum reading

- ☐ Faulty gauge sender unit (Chapters 3 and 4)
- ☐ Wiring short-circuit (Chapter 12)
- ☐ Faulty gauge (Chapter 12)

Horn inoperative, or unsatisfactory in operation

Horn operates all the time

- ☐ Horn push either earthed or stuck down (Chapter 12)
- ☐ Horn cable-to-horn push earthed (Chapter 12)

Horn fails to operate

- ☐ Blown fuse (Chapter 12)
- ☐ Cable or cable connections loose, broken or disconnected (Chapter 12)
- ☐ Faulty horn (Chapter 12)

Horn emits intermittent or unsatisfactory sound

- ☐ Cable connections loose (Chapter 12)
- ☐ Horn mountings loose (Chapter 12)
- ☐ Faulty horn (Chapter 12)

Windscreen wipers inoperative, or unsatisfactory in operation

Wipers fail to operate, or operate very slowly

- ☐ Wiper blades stuck to screen, or linkage seized or binding (Weekly checks and Chapter 12)
- ☐ Blown fuse (Chapter 12)
- ☐ Cable or cable connections loose, broken or disconnected (Chapter 12)
- ☐ Faulty relay (Chapter 12)
- ☐ Faulty wiper motor (Chapter 12)

Wiper blades sweep over too large or too small an area of the glass

- ☐ Wiper arms incorrectly positioned on spindles (Chapter 12)
- ☐ Excessive wear of wiper linkage (Chapter 12)
- ☐ Wiper motor or linkage mountings loose or insecure (Chapter 12)

Wiper blades fail to clean the glass effectively

- ☐ Wiper blade rubbers worn or perished (Weekly checks)
- ☐ Wiper arm tension springs broken, or arm pivots seized (Chapter 12)
- ☐ Insufficient windscreen washer additive to adequately remove road film (Weekly checks)

Windscreen washers inoperative, or unsatisfactory in operation

One or more washer jets inoperative

- ☐ Blocked washer jet (Weekly checks)
- ☐ Disconnected, kinked or restricted fluid hose (Chapter 12)
- ☐ Insufficient fluid in washer reservoir (Weekly checks)

Washer pump fails to operate

- ☐ Broken or disconnected wiring or connections (Chapter 12)
- ☐ Blown fuse (Chapter 12)
- ☐ Faulty washer switch (Chapter 12)
- ☐ Faulty washer pump (Chapter 12)

Washer pump runs for some time before fluid is emitted from jets

- ☐ Faulty one-way valve in fluid supply hose (Chapter 12)

Electric windows inoperative, or unsatisfactory in operation

Window glass will only move in one direction

- ☐ Faulty switch (Chapter 12)

Window glass slow to move

- ☐ Regulator seized or damaged, or in need of lubrication (Chapter 11)
- ☐ Door internal components or trim fouling regulator (Chapter 11)
- ☐ Faulty motor (Chapter 11)

Window glass fails to move

- ☐ Blown fuse (Chapter 12)
- ☐ Faulty relay (Chapter 12)
- ☐ Broken or disconnected wiring or connections (Chapter 12)
- ☐ Faulty motor (Chapter 11)

Electrical system (continued)

Central locking system inoperative, or unsatisfactory in operation

Complete system failure

- ☐ Blown fuse (Chapter 12)
- ☐ Faulty relay (Chapter 12)
- ☐ Broken or disconnected wiring or connections (Chapter 12)
- ☐ Faulty motor (Chapter 11)

Latch locks but will not unlock, or unlocks but will not lock

- ☐ Faulty master switch (Chapter 11)
- ☐ Broken or disconnected latch operating rods or levers (Chapter 11)
- ☐ Faulty relay (Chapter 12)
- ☐ Faulty motor (Chapter 11)

One solenoid/motor fails to operate

- ☐ Broken or disconnected wiring or connections (Chapter 12)
- ☐ Faulty operating assembly (Chapter 11)
- ☐ Broken, binding or disconnected latch operating rods or levers (Chapter 11)
- ☐ Fault in door latch (Chapter 11)

A

ABS (Anti-lock brake system) A system, usually electronically controlled, that senses incipient wheel lockup during braking and relieves hydraulic pressure at wheels that are about to skid.
Air bag An inflatable bag hidden in the steering wheel (driver's side) or the dash or glovebox (passenger side). In a head-on collision, the bags inflate, preventing the driver and front passenger from being thrown forward into the steering wheel or windscreen.
Air cleaner A metal or plastic housing, containing a filter element, which removes dust and dirt from the air being drawn into the engine.
Air filter element The actual filter in an air cleaner system, usually manufactured from pleated paper and requiring renewal at regular intervals.

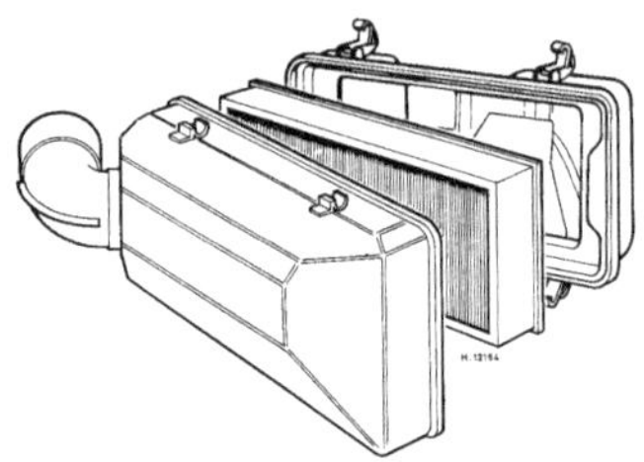

Air filter

Allen key A hexagonal wrench which fits into a recessed hexagonal hole.
Alligator clip A long-nosed spring-loaded metal clip with meshing teeth. Used to make temporary electrical connections.
Alternator A component in the electrical system which converts mechanical energy from a drivebelt into electrical energy to charge the battery and to operate the starting system, ignition system and electrical accessories.
Ampere (amp) A unit of measurement for the flow of electric current. One amp is the amount of current produced by one volt acting through a resistance of one ohm.
Anaerobic sealer A substance used to prevent bolts and screws from loosening. Anaerobic means that it does not require oxygen for activation. The Loctite brand is widely used.
Antifreeze A substance (usually ethylene glycol) mixed with water, and added to a vehicle's cooling system, to prevent freezing of the coolant in winter. Antifreeze also contains chemicals to inhibit corrosion and the formation of rust and other deposits that would tend to clog the radiator and coolant passages and reduce cooling efficiency.
Anti-seize compound A coating that reduces the risk of seizing on fasteners that are subjected to high temperatures, such as exhaust manifold bolts and nuts.
Asbestos A natural fibrous mineral with great heat resistance, commonly used in the composition of brake friction materials. Asbestos is a health hazard and the dust created by brake systems should never be inhaled or ingested.
Axle A shaft on which a wheel revolves, or which revolves with a wheel. Also, a solid beam that connects the two wheels at one end of the vehicle. An axle which also transmits power to the wheels is known as a live axle.
Axleshaft A single rotating shaft, on either side of the differential, which delivers power from the final drive assembly to the drive wheels. Also called a driveshaft or a halfshaft.

B

Ball bearing An anti-friction bearing consisting of a hardened inner and outer race with hardened steel balls between two races.
Bearing The curved surface on a shaft or in a bore, or the part assembled into either, that permits relative motion between them with minimum wear and friction.

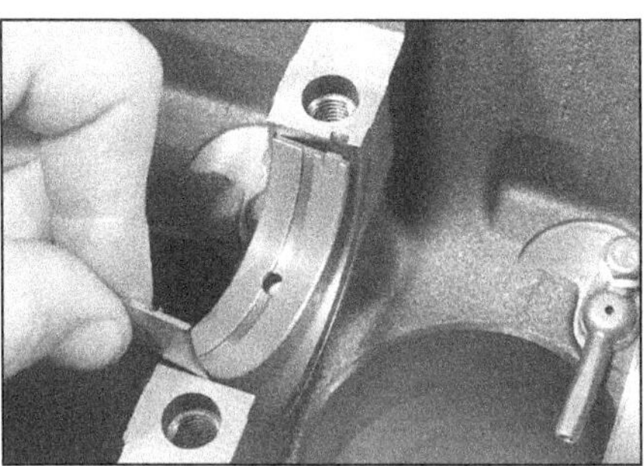

Bearing

Big-end bearing The bearing in the end of the connecting rod that's attached to the crankshaft.
Bleed nipple A valve on a brake wheel cylinder, caliper or other hydraulic component that is opened to purge the hydraulic system of air. Also called a bleed screw.
Brake bleeding Procedure for removing air from lines of a hydraulic brake system.

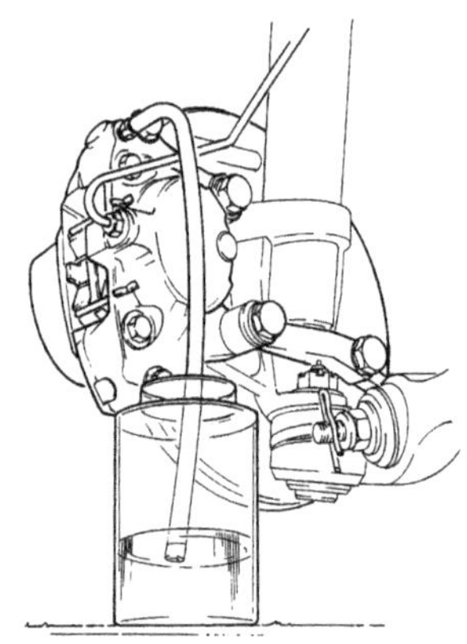

Brake bleeding

Brake disc The component of a disc brake that rotates with the wheels.
Brake drum The component of a drum brake that rotates with the wheels.
Brake linings The friction material which contacts the brake disc or drum to retard the vehicle's speed. The linings are bonded or riveted to the brake pads or shoes.
Brake pads The replaceable friction pads that pinch the brake disc when the brakes are applied. Brake pads consist of a friction material bonded or riveted to a rigid backing plate.
Brake shoe The crescent-shaped carrier to which the brake linings are mounted and which forces the lining against the rotating drum during braking.
Braking systems For more information on braking systems, consult the *Haynes Automotive Brake Manual*.
Breaker bar A long socket wrench handle providing greater leverage.
Bulkhead The insulated partition between the engine and the passenger compartment.

C

Caliper The non-rotating part of a disc-brake assembly that straddles the disc and carries the brake pads. The caliper also contains the hydraulic components that cause the pads to pinch the disc when the brakes are applied. A caliper is also a measuring tool that can be set to measure inside or outside dimensions of an object.
Camshaft A rotating shaft on which a series of cam lobes operate the valve mechanisms. The camshaft may be driven by gears, by sprockets and chain or by sprockets and a belt.
Canister A container in an evaporative emission control system; contains activated charcoal granules to trap vapours from the fuel system.

Canister

Carburettor A device which mixes fuel with air in the proper proportions to provide a desired power output from a spark ignition internal combustion engine.
Castellated Resembling the parapets along the top of a castle wall. For example, a castellated balljoint stud nut.
Castor In wheel alignment, the backward or forward tilt of the steering axis. Castor is positive when the steering axis is inclined rearward at the top.

Catalytic converter A silencer-like device in the exhaust system which converts certain pollutants in the exhaust gases into less harmful substances.

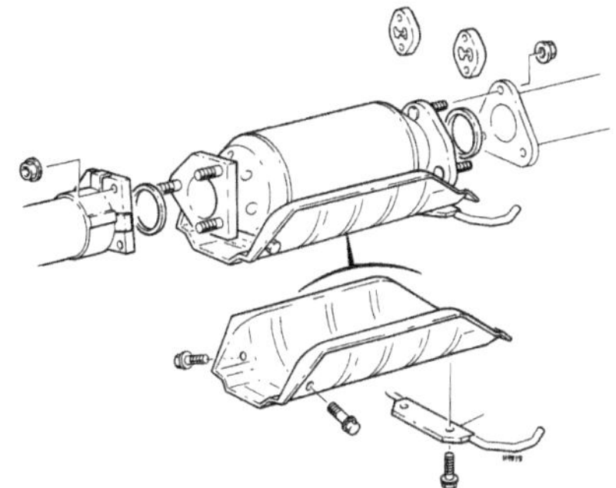

Catalytic converter

Circlip A ring-shaped clip used to prevent endwise movement of cylindrical parts and shafts. An internal circlip is installed in a groove in a housing; an external circlip fits into a groove on the outside of a cylindrical piece such as a shaft.

Clearance The amount of space between two parts. For example, between a piston and a cylinder, between a bearing and a journal, etc.

Coil spring A spiral of elastic steel found in various sizes throughout a vehicle, for example as a springing medium in the suspension and in the valve train.

Compression Reduction in volume, and increase in pressure and temperature, of a gas, caused by squeezing it into a smaller space.

Compression ratio The relationship between cylinder volume when the piston is at top dead centre and cylinder volume when the piston is at bottom dead centre.

Constant velocity (CV) joint A type of universal joint that cancels out vibrations caused by driving power being transmitted through an angle.

Core plug A disc or cup-shaped metal device inserted in a hole in a casting through which core was removed when the casting was formed. Also known as a freeze plug or expansion plug.

Crankcase The lower part of the engine block in which the crankshaft rotates.

Crankshaft The main rotating member, or shaft, running the length of the crankcase, with offset "throws" to which the connecting rods are attached.

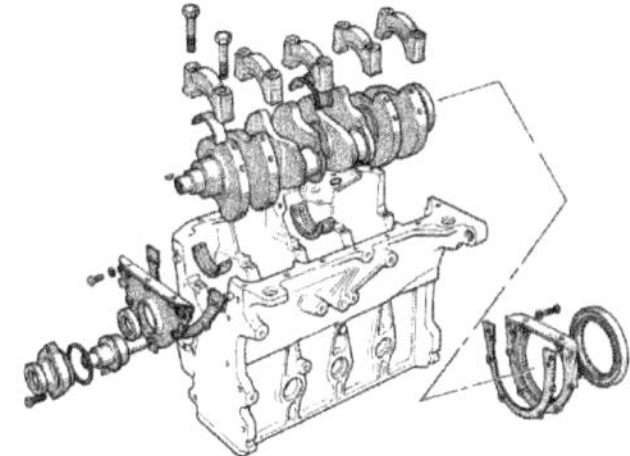

Crankshaft assembly

Crocodile clip See Alligator clip

D

Diagnostic code Code numbers obtained by accessing the diagnostic mode of an engine management computer. This code can be used to determine the area in the system where a malfunction may be located.

Disc brake A brake design incorporating a rotating disc onto which brake pads are squeezed. The resulting friction converts the energy of a moving vehicle into heat.

Double-overhead cam (DOHC) An engine that uses two overhead camshafts, usually one for the intake valves and one for the exhaust valves.

Drivebelt(s) The belt(s) used to drive accessories such as the alternator, water pump, power steering pump, air conditioning compressor, etc. off the crankshaft pulley.

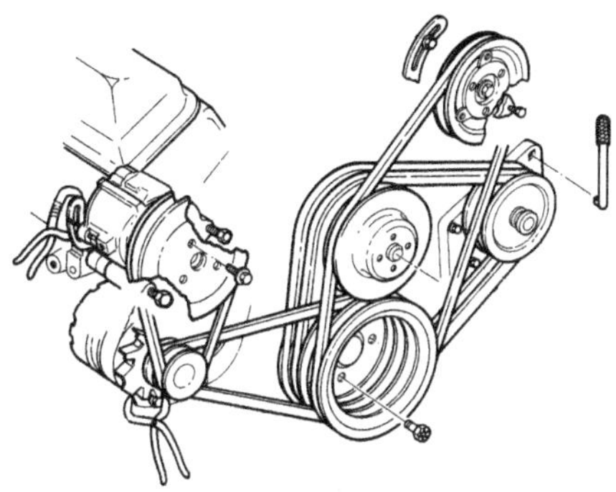

Accessory drivebelts

Driveshaft Any shaft used to transmit motion. Commonly used when referring to the axleshafts on a front wheel drive vehicle.

Drum brake A type of brake using a drum-shaped metal cylinder attached to the inner surface of the wheel. When the brake pedal is pressed, curved brake shoes with friction linings press against the inside of the drum to slow or stop the vehicle.

E

EGR valve A valve used to introduce exhaust gases into the intake air stream.

Electronic control unit (ECU) A computer which controls (for instance) ignition and fuel injection systems, or an anti-lock braking system. For more information refer to the *Haynes Automotive Electrical and Electronic Systems Manual.*

Electronic Fuel Injection (EFI) A computer controlled fuel system that distributes fuel through an injector located in each intake port of the engine.

Emergency brake A braking system, independent of the main hydraulic system, that can be used to slow or stop the vehicle if the primary brakes fail, or to hold the vehicle stationary even though the brake pedal isn't depressed. It usually consists of a hand lever that actuates either front or rear brakes mechanically through a series of cables and linkages. Also known as a handbrake or parking brake.

Endfloat The amount of lengthwise movement between two parts. As applied to a crankshaft, the distance that the crankshaft can move forward and back in the cylinder block.

Engine management system (EMS) A computer controlled system which manages the fuel injection and the ignition systems in an integrated fashion.

Exhaust manifold A part with several passages through which exhaust gases leave the engine combustion chambers and enter the exhaust pipe.

F

Fan clutch A viscous (fluid) drive coupling device which permits variable engine fan speeds in relation to engine speeds.

Feeler blade A thin strip or blade of hardened steel, ground to an exact thickness, used to check or measure clearances between parts.

Feeler blade

Firing order The order in which the engine cylinders fire, or deliver their power strokes, beginning with the number one cylinder.

Flywheel A heavy spinning wheel in which energy is absorbed and stored by means of momentum. On cars, the flywheel is attached to the crankshaft to smooth out firing impulses.

Free play The amount of travel before any action takes place. The "looseness" in a linkage, or an assembly of parts, between the initial application of force and actual movement. For example, the distance the brake pedal moves before the pistons in the master cylinder are actuated.

Fuse An electrical device which protects a circuit against accidental overload. The typical fuse contains a soft piece of metal which is calibrated to melt at a predetermined current flow (expressed as amps) and break the circuit.

Fusible link A circuit protection device consisting of a conductor surrounded by heat-resistant insulation. The conductor is smaller than the wire it protects, so it acts as the weakest link in the circuit. Unlike a blown fuse, a failed fusible link must frequently be cut from the wire for replacement.

G

Gap The distance the spark must travel in jumping from the centre electrode to the side electrode in a spark plug. Also refers to the spacing between the points in a contact breaker assembly in a conventional points-type ignition, or to the distance between the reluctor or rotor and the pickup coil in an electronic ignition.

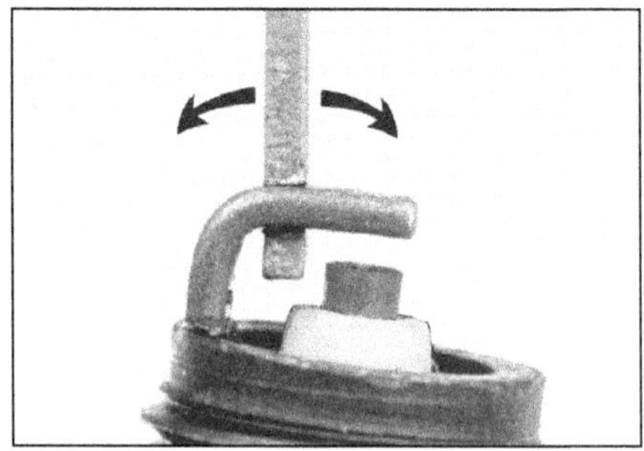

Adjusting spark plug gap

Gasket Any thin, soft material - usually cork, cardboard, asbestos or soft metal - installed between two metal surfaces to ensure a good seal. For instance, the cylinder head gasket seals the joint between the block and the cylinder head.

Gasket

Gauge An instrument panel display used to monitor engine conditions. A gauge with a movable pointer on a dial or a fixed scale is an analogue gauge. A gauge with a numerical readout is called a digital gauge.

H

Halfshaft A rotating shaft that transmits power from the final drive unit to a drive wheel, usually when referring to a live rear axle.

Harmonic balancer A device designed to reduce torsion or twisting vibration in the crankshaft. May be incorporated in the crankshaft pulley. Also known as a vibration damper.

Hone An abrasive tool for correcting small irregularities or differences in diameter in an engine cylinder, brake cylinder, etc.

Hydraulic tappet A tappet that utilises hydraulic pressure from the engine's lubrication system to maintain zero clearance (constant contact with both camshaft and valve stem). Automatically adjusts to variation in valve stem length. Hydraulic tappets also reduce valve noise.

I

Ignition timing The moment at which the spark plug fires, usually expressed in the number of crankshaft degrees before the piston reaches the top of its stroke.

Inlet manifold A tube or housing with passages through which flows the air-fuel mixture (carburettor vehicles and vehicles with throttle body injection) or air only (port fuel-injected vehicles) to the port openings in the cylinder head.

J

Jump start Starting the engine of a vehicle with a discharged or weak battery by attaching jump leads from the weak battery to a charged or helper battery.

L

Load Sensing Proportioning Valve (LSPV) A brake hydraulic system control valve that works like a proportioning valve, but also takes into consideration the amount of weight carried by the rear axle.

Locknut A nut used to lock an adjustment nut, or other threaded component, in place. For example, a locknut is employed to keep the adjusting nut on the rocker arm in position.

Lockwasher A form of washer designed to prevent an attaching nut from working loose.

M

MacPherson strut A type of front suspension system devised by Earle MacPherson at Ford of England. In its original form, a simple lateral link with the anti-roll bar creates the lower control arm. A long strut - an integral coil spring and shock absorber - is mounted between the body and the steering knuckle. Many modern so-called MacPherson strut systems use a conventional lower A-arm and don't rely on the anti-roll bar for location.

Multimeter An electrical test instrument with the capability to measure voltage, current and resistance.

N

NOx Oxides of Nitrogen. A common toxic pollutant emitted by petrol and diesel engines at higher temperatures.

O

Ohm The unit of electrical resistance. One volt applied to a resistance of one ohm will produce a current of one amp.

Ohmmeter An instrument for measuring electrical resistance.

O-ring A type of sealing ring made of a special rubber-like material; in use, the O-ring is compressed into a groove to provide the sealing action.

Overhead cam (ohc) engine An engine with the camshaft(s) located on top of the cylinder head(s).

Overhead valve (ohv) engine An engine with the valves located in the cylinder head, but with the camshaft located in the engine block.

Oxygen sensor A device installed in the engine exhaust manifold, which senses the oxygen content in the exhaust and converts this information into an electric current. Also called a Lambda sensor.

P

Phillips screw A type of screw head having a cross instead of a slot for a corresponding type of screwdriver.

Plastigage A thin strip of plastic thread, available in different sizes, used for measuring clearances. For example, a strip of Plastigage is laid across a bearing journal. The parts are assembled and dismantled; the width of the crushed strip indicates the clearance between journal and bearing.

Plastigage

Propeller shaft The long hollow tube with universal joints at both ends that carries power from the transmission to the differential on front-engined rear wheel drive vehicles.

Proportioning valve A hydraulic control valve which limits the amount of pressure to the rear brakes during panic stops to prevent wheel lock-up.

R

Rack-and-pinion steering A steering system with a pinion gear on the end of the steering shaft that mates with a rack (think of a geared wheel opened up and laid flat). When the steering wheel is turned, the pinion turns, moving the rack to the left or right. This movement is transmitted through the track rods to the steering arms at the wheels.

Radiator A liquid-to-air heat transfer device designed to reduce the temperature of the coolant in an internal combustion engine cooling system.

Refrigerant Any substance used as a heat transfer agent in an air-conditioning system. R-12 has been the principle refrigerant for many years; recently, however, manufacturers have begun using R-134a, a non-CFC substance that is considered less harmful to the ozone in the upper atmosphere.

Rocker arm A lever arm that rocks on a shaft or pivots on a stud. In an overhead valve engine, the rocker arm converts the upward movement of the pushrod into a downward movement to open a valve.

Rotor In a distributor, the rotating device inside the cap that connects the centre electrode and the outer terminals as it turns, distributing the high voltage from the coil secondary winding to the proper spark plug. Also, that part of an alternator which rotates inside the stator. Also, the rotating assembly of a turbocharger, including the compressor wheel, shaft and turbine wheel.
Runout The amount of wobble (in-and-out movement) of a gear or wheel as it's rotated. The amount a shaft rotates "out-of-true." The out-of-round condition of a rotating part.

S

Sealant A liquid or paste used to prevent leakage at a joint. Sometimes used in conjunction with a gasket.
Sealed beam lamp An older headlight design which integrates the reflector, lens and filaments into a hermetically-sealed one-piece unit. When a filament burns out or the lens cracks, the entire unit is simply replaced.
Serpentine drivebelt A single, long, wide accessory drivebelt that's used on some newer vehicles to drive all the accessories, instead of a series of smaller, shorter belts. Serpentine drivebelts are usually tensioned by an automatic tensioner.

Serpentine drivebelt

Shim Thin spacer, commonly used to adjust the clearance or relative positions between two parts. For example, shims inserted into or under bucket tappets control valve clearances. Clearance is adjusted by changing the thickness of the shim.
Slide hammer A special puller that screws into or hooks onto a component such as a shaft or bearing; a heavy sliding handle on the shaft bottoms against the end of the shaft to knock the component free.
Sprocket A tooth or projection on the periphery of a wheel, shaped to engage with a chain or drivebelt. Commonly used to refer to the sprocket wheel itself.
Starter inhibitor switch On vehicles with an automatic transmission, a switch that prevents starting if the vehicle is not in Neutral or Park.
Strut See MacPherson strut.

T

Tappet A cylindrical component which transmits motion from the cam to the valve stem, either directly or via a pushrod and rocker arm. Also called a cam follower.
Thermostat A heat-controlled valve that regulates the flow of coolant between the cylinder block and the radiator, so maintaining optimum engine operating temperature. A thermostat is also used in some air cleaners in which the temperature is regulated.
Thrust bearing The bearing in the clutch assembly that is moved in to the release levers by clutch pedal action to disengage the clutch. Also referred to as a release bearing.
Timing belt A toothed belt which drives the camshaft. Serious engine damage may result if it breaks in service.
Timing chain A chain which drives the camshaft.
Toe-in The amount the front wheels are closer together at the front than at the rear. On rear wheel drive vehicles, a slight amount of toe-in is usually specified to keep the front wheels running parallel on the road by offsetting other forces that tend to spread the wheels apart.
Toe-out The amount the front wheels are closer together at the rear than at the front. On front wheel drive vehicles, a slight amount of toe-out is usually specified.
Tools For full information on choosing and using tools, refer to the *Haynes Automotive Tools Manual.*
Tracer A stripe of a second colour applied to a wire insulator to distinguish that wire from another one with the same colour insulator.
Tune-up A process of accurate and careful adjustments and parts replacement to obtain the best possible engine performance.
Turbocharger A centrifugal device, driven by exhaust gases, that pressurises the intake air. Normally used to increase the power output from a given engine displacement, but can also be used primarily to reduce exhaust emissions (as on VW's "Umwelt" Diesel engine).

U

Universal joint or U-joint A double-pivoted connection for transmitting power from a driving to a driven shaft through an angle. A U-joint consists of two Y-shaped yokes and a cross-shaped member called the spider.

V

Valve A device through which the flow of liquid, gas, vacuum, or loose material in bulk may be started, stopped, or regulated by a movable part that opens, shuts, or partially obstructs one or more ports or passageways. A valve is also the movable part of such a device.
Valve clearance The clearance between the valve tip (the end of the valve stem) and the rocker arm or tappet. The valve clearance is measured when the valve is closed.
Vernier caliper A precision measuring instrument that measures inside and outside dimensions. Not quite as accurate as a micrometer, but more convenient.
Viscosity The thickness of a liquid or its resistance to flow.
Volt A unit for expressing electrical "pressure" in a circuit. One volt that will produce a current of one ampere through a resistance of one ohm.

W

Welding Various processes used to join metal items by heating the areas to be joined to a molten state and fusing them together. For more information refer to the *Haynes Automotive Welding Manual.*
Wiring diagram A drawing portraying the components and wires in a vehicle's electrical system, using standardised symbols. For more information refer to the *Haynes Automotive Electrical and Electronic Systems Manual.*

Note: *References throughout this index are in the form - "**Chapter number**" • "**Page number**"*

E

F

G

H

I

J

L

M

O

P

R

S

T

U

V